# Genesis to Deuteronomy

# Genesis to Deuteronomy

*Notes on the PENTATEUCH*

*by*

C. H. MACKINTOSH

LOIZEAUX BROTHERS
*Neptune, New Jersey*

Originally published in six volumes under the titles:

*Notes on Genesis* – 1880
*Notes on Exodus* – 1881
*Notes on Leviticus* – 1881
*Notes on Numbers* – 1882
*Notes on Deuteronomy I* – 1881
*Notes on Deuteronomy II* – 1882

First Edition in one volume - 1972
Second Printing - 1974



A Nonprofit Organization, Devoted to the Lord's Work
and to the Spread of His Truth

ISBN 0-87213-617-5
Library of Congress Catalog Card Number: 72-075082

PRINTED IN UNITED STATES OF AMERICA

## *PUBLISHER'S PREFACE*

After publishing C. H. Mackintosh's *Notes on the Pentateuch* in six volumes for nearly a century, Loizeaux Brothers now presents the complete work in a single volume under the title, *Genesis to Deuteronomy.* This new edition has been reset, word for word, from the original 1880 edition, which has been continuously in print and increasingly in demand. The binding in a single volume, instead of six, makes possible a substantially lower price, in spite of spiraling publishing costs.

Most gratifying are the reports of blessing from this work which we have received over the years, and are still receiving from around the world. It has already been a witness to the truths and teachings of Scripture, particularly the books of Moses, to four generations of Bible students. We believe the convenience and economy of this new one-volume edition will make it even more helpful to coming generations as well.

The preface to each of the five books is signed simply "A.M." as was frequently the custom a century ago. They are actually by Andrew Miller, a warm-hearted Scottish evangelist and contemporary of C. H. Mackintosh. An author in his own right, Andrew Miller wrote the valuable *Papers on Church History,* as well as several volumes of meditations. He encouraged "C.H.M." in the writing, wrote a preface, and largely helped to finance the initial publication of each of the volumes of *Notes on the Pentateuch,* "the most popular and extensively circulated of all the varied volumes connected with what is known as 'the Brethren movement.' "

LOIZEAUX BROTHERS, Inc.

Neptune, New Jersey
November 1972

*CONTENTS*

A Word Concerning the Author, by Wilbur M. Smith . . . . . . . . . . . . . . . . . 9

Notes on Genesis . . . . . . . . . . . . . . . . . . . . . . . . . . . . . . . . . . . . . . . . . . 13

Notes on Exodus . . . . . . . . . . . . . . . . . . . . . . . . . . . . . . . . . . . . . . . . . 135

Notes on Leviticus . . . . . . . . . . . . . . . . . . . . . . . . . . . . . . . . . . . . . . . 273

Notes on Numbers . . . . . . . . . . . . . . . . . . . . . . . . . . . . . . . . . . . . . . . 417

Notes on Deuteronomy . . . . . . . . . . . . . . . . . . . . . . . . . . . . . . . . . . . 589

## *A WORD CONCERNING THE AUTHOR*

Of all the groups of Christian believers that developed in the English-speaking world in the nineteenth century, the one which produced the greatest number of gifted writers was the Brethren. Of their founder himself, John Nelson Darby, over forty substantial volumes were published. But of all this notable group of writers, the one whose works have been most frequently printed is Charles Henry Mackintosh, generally known as C.H.M., which is all that appeared on the title pages of his major writings.

Charles H. Mackintosh was born in October 1820, at Glenmalure Barricks, County Wicklow, Ireland, the son of the captain of a Highland regiment. Mackintosh was converted at the age of eighteen through the letters of a devout sister, and the prayerful reading of J.N. Darby's *Operations of the Spirit.* When he was twenty-four years of age, he opened a private school at Westport, but it was not long before he concluded he must give himself entirely to the ministry of the Word of God, in writing and in public speaking. Soon thereafter he felt led to establish a periodical, which he continued to edit for twenty- one years, *Things New and Old.*

The opening pages of the first issue of *Things New and Old* outline its purpose:

> In presenting to the reader the first number of our periodical, we feel called upon to state our reasons for entering upon such a service, and also the objects which we hope, by the grace of God, to effect.
>
> We do not deem any apology necessary for adding another to the numerous publications already extant, having for their object the circulation of pure truth. We want them all, and thousands more, if we could get them. We cannot have too many agencies for the furtherance of that which is good, and the suppression of that which is evil.
>
> For, first of all, it is a lamentable fact that the enemy of souls has wrought, far more diligently, at the printing press, than the servants of the living God. Numerous as are the books, the pamphlets, the tracts, and the periodicals in which the words of eternal truth shine, for the instruction and comfort of souls, yet are they outnumbered, to an appalling amount, by publications of an infidel, immoral, and irreligious tendency.
>
> 2. We believe that the art of printing was designed, by a gracious Providence, as a powerful engine for the diffusion of scriptural knowledge; but we cannot shut our eyes to the startling fact that the enemy is making diligent use of that very art, for the purpose of corrupting, in all directions, the springs of thought and feeling. He is publishing, in the cheapest and most attractive form, gross evil, soul-destroying error, and perverted truth. And, we may safely say, if positive error has slain its thousands, perverted truth has slain its tens of thousands.
>
> 3. Now, we are fully assured that, notwithstanding all the enemy's efforts, the Lord is gathering out His own—that He is accomplishing His purposes, and hastening His everlasting kingdom. But should this be a reason for slackness, coldness, and indifference, on the part of the servants of Christ? The very reverse; yea, the assurance thereof is the basis of "stedfast" and "unmovable" service. It is because we know, on divine authority, that "our labour shall not be in vain in the Lord," that therefore we work. Thank God for such a solid foundation! It would be sad, indeed, if what our God has graciously given as a soul-stirring encouragement to *work* should be used as a plea for *inactivity* if the assurance of reaching God's end were to be a reason for neglecting God's means. This would be a grievous use to make of the goodness and faithfulness of God.
>
> 4. But, further, we undertake this service because we feel bound to serve and testify, while the time for service and testimony lasts. The day is rapidly approaching, in the which we shall not be called upon to render such fruits. When we get into the Master's presence, we shall admire and worship; but, now, in "the little while," in the night of His absence, it is our holy and happy privilege to be "always abounding in the work of the Lord" (1 Cor. 15:58). We are responsible to let the light shine forth, in every possible way—to circulate

> the truth of God, by all means, by word of mouth, by "paper and ink," in public and private, "in the morning and in the evening," "in season and out of season"; we should "sow beside all waters." In a word, whether we consider the importance of divine truth, the value of immortal souls, or the fearful progress of error and evil, we are imperatively called upon to be up and doing, in the name of the Lord, under the guidance of His word, and by the grace of His Spirit.

Mr. Mackintosh took a great interest in, and actively participated in, the great revival of 1859 and 1860. He died on November 2, 1896, and was buried in Cheltenham Cemetery, where, in what is known as the Plymouth Brethren plot, "the graves of Exclusive and Open Brethren lie side by side awaiting the resurrection morn."

Now that more than seventy years have passed since his death, it is difficult to come upon much factual detail concerning his own personal life. He was a man of a much milder spirit than Darby, and breathed an atmosphere of deep devotion, and a love not only for Christian believers but for lost souls. He had a gracious spirit, avoiding conflict as far as possible.

Mr. Mackintosh's fame rests primarily upon the work which is herewith being republished in a single volume, *Notes on the Pentateuch,* beginning with a volume of 334 pages on Genesis, and concluding with a two-volume work on Deuteronomy extending to over 800 pages. The chapters in these volumes are of different lengths, some discussed with considerable detail and some passed over briefly, e.g., some of the chapters in his commentary on Genesis vary from ten to thirty pages in length, while his comments on the last fifteen chapters are confined to only twenty pages. Now and then Mackintosh writes with eloquence, e.g., near the end of his commentary on Genesis:

> The close of Jacob's career stands in most pleasing contrast with all the previous scenes of his eventful history. It reminds one of a serene evening after a tempestuous day: the sun, which during the day had been hidden from view by clouds, mists, and fogs, sets in majesty and brightness, gilding with his beams the western sky, and holding out the cheering prospect of a bright tomorrow. Thus is it with our aged patriarch. The supplanting, the bargain-making, the cunning, the management, the shifting, the shuffling, the unbelieving selfish fears—all those dark clouds of nature and of earth seem to have passed away, and he comes forth, in all the calm elevation of faith, to bestow blessings, and impart dignities, in that holy skillfulness which communion with God can alone impart.

Probably Mr. Mackintosh's best work was on the book of Deuteronomy, and even here we notice how uneven were his discussions, e.g., the first volume embraces comments only on the first six chapters of the book of Deuteronomy, while the second volume, of equal size, discusses the remaining twenty-eight chapters. Even in volume one the amount of space given to each chapter varies, from twenty-five pages for chapter two to one hundred forty-two pages devoted to chapter four. As an illustration of his method of commenting, we might consider for a moment his manner of treatment of chapter five. He begins by quoting that great verse, "And Moses called unto all Israel, and said unto them, Hear, O Israel, the statutes and the ordinances which I speak in your ears this day, that ye may learn them, and observe to do them" (Deuteronomy 5:1). Here in the very verse itself one would conclude that we would be considering the fourfold exhortation of this sentence—*hear, learn, keep,* and *do*—but not so Mr. Mackintosh. He discusses only the first of these four, and out of this he develops a long discussion on the subject of obedience, extending to thirty-three pages, and then, to the surprise of the reader, almost at the beginning of his discussion, he gives extended consideration to the practice of a *false* obedience, such as that necessary in the lives of monks and nuns, so prevalent in monasteries and convents. In the middle of his discussion of chapter five is a very rich commentary on the fifteenth chapter of Acts, extending to sixteen pages, followed by a thirty-page treatment of the Sabbath day in contrast to the Lord's day celebrated by the Christian church, to which the divine author assigns three verses, 12-14. So we discover that even in this large book on the first six chapters of Deuteronomy, more verses are omitted from discussion than are commented upon. And yet, even though one does not find here a commentary, verse by verse, he will find rich truths unfolded, the gospel of the grace of God truthfully set forth, and many great principles of Christian living emphasized and elaborated upon. In other words, these volumes on the Pentateuch are so written that a Christian's mind is drawn into the area where Christ is honored and glorified, and where the great privileges of Christian believers are so effectively brought to the attention of the believer.

Incidentally, it may not be out of order to notice a prefatory note for the American edition written in 1879 and signed by Mr. Mackintosh.

> As several persons in America have, without any authority whatever from me, undertaken to publish my . . . volumes of *Notes,* I deem it my duty to inform the reader that I have given full permission to Messrs. Loizeaux Brothers to publish an edition of those books in such form as they shall consider most suitable.

Another series by Mr. Mackintosh also was frequently reprinted, under the general heading of *Miscellaneous Writings,* six volumes, totaling over 2500 pages, and most of it still definitely worth reading.

Let me especially call attention to Mr. Mackintosh's excellent comments on Evangelization, which seem to be remarkably up-to-date in this time when we are witnessing so much world-wide evangelization. In volume IV is a very thorough, illuminating, and sensible discussion of ninety pages on the Great Commission of Luke 24:44-49. His statements at the very beginning are refreshing to read:

> Our divine Master called upon sinners to repent and believe the gospel. Some would have us to believe that it is a mistake to call upon persons dead in trespasses and sins to do anything. "How," it is argued, "can those who are dead repent? They are incapable of any spiritual movement. They must first get the power ere they can either repent or believe."
>
> What is our reply to all this? A very simple one indeed—our Lord knows better than all the theologians in the world what ought to be preached. He knows all about man's condition—his guilt, his misery, his spiritual death, his utter helplessness, his total inability to think a single right thought, to utter a single right word, to do a single right act; and yet He called upon men to repent. This is quite enough for us. It is no part of our business to seek to reconcile seeming differences. It may seem to us difficult to reconcile man's utter powerlessness with his responsibility; but "God is His own interpreter, and He will make it plain." It is our happy privilege, and our bounden duty, to believe what He says, and do what He tells us. This is true wisdom, and it yields solid peace.
>
> Our Lord preached repentance, and He commanded His apostles to preach it; and they did so constantly.

Because many are teaching otherwise, one rejoices to see the author's emphasis on the need for genuine repentance.

In volume III there is a section of eighty-six pages with the general heading, "Papers on Evangelism," in the midst of which is a long and excellent commentary of Acts 16:8-31. I cannot help but quote a few lines from these rich pages:

> We increasingly feel the immense importance of an earnest, fervent gospel testimony everywhere; and we dread exceedingly any falling off therein. We are imperatively called to "do the work of an evangelist," and not to be moved from that work by any arguments or considerations whatsoever . . . . We observe, with deep concern, some who were once known amongst us as earnest and eminently successful evangelists, now almost wholly abandoning their work and becoming teachers and lecturers.
>
> This is most deplorable. *We really want evangelists.* A true evangelist is almost as great a rarity as a true pastor. Alas! alas! how rare are both! The two are closely connected . . . . We are perfectly aware of the fact that there is in some quarters a strong tendency to throw cold water upon the work of evangelization. There is a sad lack of sympathy with the preacher of the gospel; and, as a necessary consequence, of active co-operation with him in his work . . . . We have

> invariably found that those who think and speak slightingly of the work of the evangelist are persons of very little spirituality; and on the other hand, the most devoted, the most truehearted, the best taught saints of God, are always sure to take a profound interest in that work. . . . But I find in the Gospels, and in the Acts of the Apostles, that a quantity of most blessed evangelistic work was done by persons who were not specially gifted at all, but who had an earnest love for souls, and a deep sense of the preciousness of Christ and His salvation.

In the midst of these papers, our author discusses what I think is very rare in his writing, his own participation in the great revival in 1859 in Ulster.

Personally, I thought it would be appropriate, in the light of the famous Loizeaux Brothers firm publishing from time to time these twelve volumes of Mr. Mackintosh and so many other worthwhile books, that we might read again what our gifted author said nearly one hundred years ago about reaching the souls of men through Christian bookstores, what he calls tract depots:

> And how can we best reach the people, for whom the tracts and books are prepared? I believe by having the books and tracts exposed for sale in a shop window, where that is possible, so that people may see them as they pass, and step in and purchase what they want. Many a soul has been laid hold of in this way. Many, I doubt not, have been saved and blessed by means of tracts, seen for the first time in a shop window or arranged on a counter. . . . It seems to me that a grand point would be gained if the tract depot were placed on its proper footing, and viewed as an integral part of the evangelistic work, to be taken up in responsibility to the Lord, and carried on in the energy of faith in the living God. Every branch of gospel work—the depot, the preaching, the Sunday-school—must be carried on in this way.

WILBUR M. SMITH

# NOTES

*on the book of*

# GENESIS

*"Things New and Old"*

## *PREFACE*

To all who love and relish the simple gospel of the grace of God, I would earnestly recommend the following *Notes on the Book of Genesis.* They are characterized by a deep-toned evangelical spirit. Having had the privilege of reading them in ms., I can speak as one who has found profit therefrom. Man's complete ruin in sin, and God's perfect remedy in Christ, are fully, clearly, and often strikingly presented, especially in the earlier chapters.

To Christ's servants in the gospel, sound, forcible statements as to what *sin* is, and what *grace* is, are deeply valuable in the present time, when so much that is merely superficial is abroad.

The gospel of Christ, as perfectly meeting man's nature, condition and character, is comparatively little known, and less proclaimed. Hence, the numerous doubts, fears, and unsettled questions, which fill the hearts and perplex the consciences of many of God's dear children. Until the soul is led to see that the entire question of sin, and the claims of divine holiness, were *all and forever settled* on the cross, sweet, quiet rest of conscience will be but little known.

Nothing can meet the urgent cry of a troubled conscience but the one perfect sacrifice of Christ, offered *to* God, *for us,* on the cross—"For even Christ, *our* passover, is sacrificed *for us.*" There, and there alone, it will find a *perfect answer* to its every claim; because there it will find, through believing, all ground of doubt and fear removed, the whole question of sin eternally settled, every divine requirement fully met, and a solid foundation laid for present, settled peace in the presence of divine holiness. Christ, "delivered for our offences, and raised again for our justification," settles everything. The moment we believe the gospel, we *are* saved, and ought to be divinely happy. "He that believeth on the Son *hath* everlasting life" (Rom. 4—5; John 3).

We see the greatness of God's love to the sinner, in His judgment of sin, in the Person of His own dear Son, on the cross. There, God, in perfect grace to us, dealt with sin according to His infinite holiness and justice. He went down to the depths of our ruin, and all our sin, measured it, judged it, and put it forever away—*root* and *branch*—by shedding the precious blood of the spotless victim. "He condemned sin in the flesh"; that is, He there condemned the evil root of sin which is in our flesh—our carnal nature. But He also "made an end of sins"—of the actual sins of every believer. Thus, between God and Christ alone, the entire question of sin was gone into, and finally settled on the cross. "Simon Peter said unto Him, 'Lord, whither goest Thou?' Jesus answered Him, 'Whither I go, *thou canst not follow Me now.*'" Just as Abraham and Isaac were alone on the top of the mountain in the land of Moriah, so were God and Christ alone, amidst the solemnities and solitudes of Calvary. The only part we had in the cross was, that our *sins* were there. Jesus *alone* bore the full weight of their judgment. (Comp. Dan. 9:24; Rom. 8:3; 2 Cor. 5:21; Heb. 9:26,28.)

Whenever this blessed truth is learnt from God's own Word, and maintained in the soul by faith, through the power of the Holy Ghost, all is peace, joy and victory. It takes the believer completely away from himself, from his doubts, fears and questions; and his eye now gazes on *One,* who, by His finished work, has laid the foundation of divine and everlasting righteousness, and who is now at the right hand of the Majesty in the highest, as the perfect definition of every true believer. With Him—with Him alone—the believer's heart is now to be occupied.

Faith is fully assured, that when *God* puts away sin, it must be put away entirely—that, when Jesus exclaimed, *"It is finished,"* the work was done, God was glorified, the sinner saved, the whole power of Satan completely destroyed, and peace established on the most solid basis. Hence, we find, "The God of *peace* brought again from the dead our Lord Jesus, that great Shepherd of the sheep, through the blood of the everlasting covenant." He was the God of *judgment* at the cross; He is the God of *peace* at the opening grave. Every enemy has been vanquished, and eternal peace proclaimed, through the blood of His cross. "He was raised from the dead by the glory of the Father." He rose "in the power of an endless life," and associates every believer with Himself, in the power of that life in resurrection. Having been cleansed by His blood, they are accepted in His Person (see Eph. 1:6; Col. 2:10; 1 John 5:20).

Jesus, having thus fully accomplished the work that was given Him to do, and gone up on high, the Holy Ghost came down as a witness to us that redemption was finished, the believer "perfected forever," and Christ glorified in heaven.

The apostles then began to publish the glad tidings of salvation to the chief of sinners. The subject of their preaching was, *"Jesus and the resurrection";* and all who believed on Him as risen and glorified were immediately and eternally saved. "And this is the record, that God hath given to us eternal life, and this life is in His Son: he that hath the Son hath life, and he that hath not the Son of God hath not life" (1 John 5:11-12). There is no blessing outside of, or apart from, the *Person of Christ—the heavenly man;* "for in Him dwelleth all the fullness of the Godhead bodily." Ever since that time, God has been placing before the sinner, in connection with *His* gospel, a risen living Christ, as the *alone* object of faith, and "the end of the law for righteousness to *every one that believeth"* (Rom. 10).

When the eye is kept on this heavenly Christ, all is light, joy and peace; but if it be turned in on self, and occupied with what it *finds* there, and what it *feels,* or with anything whatever that may come between the heart and Christ, all will be darkness, uncertainty and unhappiness in the soul. Oh! how blessedly simple is the gospel of the grace of God.

The burden of its message to the *lost sinner* is, "Come, for all things are now ready"; the question of sin is not raised—*"Grace reigns* through righteousness unto eternal life by Jesus Christ our Lord." Christ having perfectly satisfied God about sin, the only question now, between God and your heart, is this: *Are you perfectly satisfied with His Christ as the alone portion of your soul?* This is the one grand question of the gospel. Christ has settled every other to the glory of God, and now the Father is going to "make a marriage for His Son," to honor, exalt and glorify Him. Is your heart in full harmony with God's on this point? Work is not required at your hands—strength is not needed—fruit is not demanded—God has provided everything, and prepared everything. It is all grace—the pure grace of God—"only believe." "Come, for all things are now ready"—the marriage supper, the wedding garment, royal honors, the Father's presence, fullness of joy, and pleasures for evermore—all are ready,—ready now—"ready to be revealed." Dear reader, are you ready? Oh! solemn question. Are you ready? Have you believed the message? Have you embraced the Son? Are you ready to "crown Him Lord of all"? The table is spread, the house is filling fast, "yet there is room." Already you have heard the midnight cry, "Behold the bridegroom cometh, go ye out to meet him," "and they that were *ready* went in *with him* to the marriage, *and the door was shut."* "Be ye therefore ready also; for the Son of man cometh at an hour when ye think not" (Matt. 22,25; Luke 12,14).

But I must now refer my reader to the *Notes* themselves, where he will find this most blessed subject fully, frequently and pointedly stated, and many other subjects of deep practical importance, such as the distinctive position and perfect unity of the Church of God, real saintship, practical discipleship, sonship, etc., etc.

With the exception of the four Gospels, I suppose there is no book in the Bible more deeply interesting than the book of Genesis. It comes to us with all the freshness of God's first book to His people. The contents are varied, highly instructive, and most precious to the student of God's entire book.

These *Notes* are again laid at the Master's feet, in earnest prayer that He would take them up and send them forth under the stamp of His own divine approval. Amen.

*London* *A. M.*

# NOTES

## on

# THE BOOK OF GENESIS

---

## CHAPTER 1

THERE is something peculiarly striking in the manner in which the Holy Ghost opens this sublime book. He introduces us at once to God, in the essential fullness of His Being, and the solitariness of His acting. All prefatory matter is omitted. It is to God we are brought. We hear Him, as it were, breaking earth's silence, and shining in upon earth's darkness, for the purpose of developing a sphere in which He might display His eternal power and Godhead.

There is nothing here on which idle curiosity may feed—nothing on which the poor, human mind may speculate. There is the sublimity and reality of *divine truth*, in its moral power to act on the heart and on the understanding. It could never come within the range of the Spirit of God to gratify idle curiosity, by the presentation of curious theories. Geologists may explore the bowels of the earth, and draw forth from thence materials from which to add to, and, in some instances, to contradict, the divine record. They may speculate upon fossil remains; but the disciple hangs, with sacred delight, over the page of inspiration. He reads, believes and worships. In this spirit may we pursue our study of the profound book which now lies open before us. May we know what it is to "inquire in the temple." May our investigations of the precious contents of holy Scripture be ever prosecuted in the true spirit of worship.

"In the beginning, God created the heavens and the earth." The first sentence in the divine canon sets us in the presence of Him who is the infinite source of all true blessedness. There is no elaborate argument in proof of the existence of God. The Holy Ghost could not enter upon anything of the kind. God reveals Himself. He makes Himself known by His works. "The heavens declare the glory of God, and the firmament showeth His handiwork." "All Thy works shall praise Thee, O Lord." "Great and marvelous are Thy works, Lord God Almighty." None but an infidel or an atheist would seek an argument in proof of the Being of One who, by the word of His mouth, called worlds into existence, and declared Himself the All-wise, the Almighty, and the everlasting God. Who but "God" could "create" anything? "Lift up your eyes on high, and behold who hath *created* these things, that bringeth out their host by number; He calleth them all by names, by the greatness of His might, for that He is strong in power; not one faileth" (Isa. 40:26). "The gods of the heathen are idols, but the Lord made the heavens." In the book of Job (chap. 38–41) we have an appeal of the very grandest description, on the part of Jehovah Himself, to the work of creation, as an unanswerable argument in proof of His infinite superiority; and this appeal, while it sets before the understanding the most vivid and convincing demonstration of God's omnipotence, touches the heart also by its amazing condescension. The majesty and the love, the power and the tenderness, are all divine.

"And the earth was without form, and void; and darkness was upon the face of the deep." Here was, in good truth, a scene in which God alone could act. Man, in the pride of his heart, has since proved himself but too ready to interfere with God in other and far higher spheres of action; but, in the scene before us, man had no place until, indeed, he became, like all the rest, the subject of creative power. God was alone in creation. He looked forth from His eternal dwelling-place of light upon the wild waste, and there beheld the sphere in which His wondrous plans and counsels were yet to be unfolded and brought out—where the Second Person of the Eternal Trinity was yet to live and labor and testify and bleed and die, in order to display, in the view of wondering worlds, the glorious perfections of the Godhead. All was darkness and chaos; but God is the God of light and order. "God is light, and in Him is no darkness at all." Darkness and confusion cannot live in His presence, whether we look at it in a physical, moral, intellectual, or spiritual point of view.

"The Spirit of God moved upon the face of the waters." He sat brooding over the scene of His future operations. A dark scene, truly; and one in which there was ample room for the God of light and life to act. He alone could enlighten the darkness, cause life to spring up, substitute order for chaos, open an expanse between the waters, where life might display itself without fear of death. These were operations worthy of God.

"God said, 'Let there be light': and there was light." How simple! and yet how God-like! "He spake, and it was done: He commanded, and it stood fast." Infidelity may ask, How? where? when? The answer is, "By faith we understand that the worlds were framed by the word of God, so that things which are seen were not made of things which do appear" (Heb. 11:3). This satisfies the teachable spirit. Philosophy may smile contemptuously at this, and pronounce it rude ignorance, or blind credulity, suitable enough for an age of semi-barbarism, but quite unworthy of men living in an enlightened age of the world's history, when the museum and the telescope have put us in possession of facts of which the inspired penman knew nothing. What wisdom! What learning! Yea, rather, what folly! What nonsense! What total inability to grasp the scope and design of sacred Scripture! It assuredly is not God's object to make us astronomers or geologists, or to occupy us with details which the microscope or the telescope lays before every school-boy. His object is to lead us into His presence, as worshipers, with hearts and understandings taught and duly governed by His holy word. But this would never do for the so-called philosopher, who, despising what he terms the vulgar and narrow-minded prejudices of the devout disciple of the Word, boldly seizes his telescope, and therewith scans the distant heavens, or travels into the deep recesses of earth in search of strata, formations and fossils—all of which, according to his account, greatly improve, if they do not flatly contradict, the inspired narrative.

With such "oppositions of science, falsely so called," we have nothing to do. We believe that all true discoveries, whether "in the heavens above, in the earth beneath, or in the waters under the earth," will harmonize with that which is written in the Word of God; and if they do not thus harmonize, they are perfectly contemptible in the judgment of every true lover of Scripture. This gives great rest to the heart in a day like the present, so productive of learned speculations and high-sounding theories, which, alas! in too many instances, savor of rationalism and positive infidelity. It is most needful to have the heart thoroughly established as to the fullness, the authority, the completeness, the majesty, the plenary inspiration of the sacred volume. This will be found to be the only effectual safeguard against the rationalism of Germany and the superstition of Rome. Accurate acquaintance with, and profound subjection to, the Word, are the great *desiderata* of the present moment. May the Lord, in His great grace, abundantly increase in our midst both the one and the other.

"And God saw the light, that it was good: and God divided the light from the darkness. And God called the light Day, and the darkness He called Night." Here we have the two great symbols so largely employed throughout the Word. The presence of light makes the day; the absence thereof makes the night. Thus it is in the history of souls. There are "the sons of light" and "the sons of darkness." This is a most marked and solemn distinction. All upon whom the light of Life has shone—all who have been effectually visited by "the dayspring from on high"—all who have received the light of the knowledge of the glory of God in the face of Jesus Christ—all such, whoever and wherever they may be, belong to the first class, are "the sons of light, and the sons of the day."

On the other hand, all who are still in nature's darkness, nature's blindness, nature's unbelief—all who have not yet received into their hearts, by faith, the cheering beams of the Sun of Righteousness,—all such are still wrapped in the shades of spiritual night, are "the sons of darkness," "the sons of the night."

Reader, pause and ask yourself, in the presence of the Searcher of hearts, to which of these two classes do you, at this moment, belong. That you belong to either the one or the other is beyond all question. You may be poor, despised, unlettered; but if, through grace, there is a link connecting you with the Son of God—"the light of the world," then you are, in very deed, a son of the day, and destined, ere long, to shine in that celestial sphere, that region of glory, of which "the slain Lamb" will be the central sun forever. This is not your own doing. It is the result of the counsel and operation of God Himself, who has given you light and life, joy and peace, in Jesus and His accomplished sacrifice. But if you are a total stranger to the hallowed action and influence of divine light, if your eyes have not been opened to behold any beauty in the Son of God, then, though you had all the learning of a Newton, though you were enriched with all the treasures of human philosophy, though you had drunk in with avidity all the streams of human science, though your name were adorned with all the learned titles which the schools and universities of this world could bestow, yet are you "a son of the night," "a son of darkness"; and, if you die in your present condition, you will be involved in the blackness and horror of an eternal night. Do not, therefore, read another page until you have fully satisfied yourself as to whether you belong to the "day" or the "night."

The next point on which I would dwell is the creation of lights. "And God said, 'Let there be lights in the firmament of the heaven, to divide the day from the night; and let them be for signs, and for seasons, and for days, and years. And let them be for lights in the firmament of the heaven, to give light upon the earth': and it was so. And God made two great lights: the greater light to rule the day, and the lesser light to rule the night: He made the stars also."

The sun is the great centre of light, and the centre of our system. Round him the lesser orbs revolve. From him, too, they derive their light. Hence he may very legitimately be viewed as an apt symbol of Him who is soon to arise, with healing in His wings, to gladden the hearts of those that fear the Lord. The aptness and beauty of the symbol would fully appear to one who, having spent the night in watching, beholds the rising sun gilding, with his bright beams, the eastern sky.

The mists and shades of night are all dispersed, and the whole creation seems to hail the returning orb of light. Thus will it be, by and by, when the Sun of Righteousness arises. The shadows of night shall flee away, and the whole creation shall be gladdened by the dawning of "a morning without clouds,"—the opening of a bright and never-ending day of glory.

The moon, being in herself opaque, derives all her light from the sun. She always reflects the sun's light, save when earth and its influences intervene.* No sooner has the sun sunk beneath our horizon than the moon presents herself to receive his beams and reflect them back upon a dark world; or should she be visible during the day, she always exhibits a pale light, the necessary result of appearing in the presence of superior brightness. True it is, as has been remarked, the world sometimes intervenes; dark clouds, thick mists, and chilling vapors too, arise from earth's surface, and hide from our view her silvery light.

Now, as the sun is a beautiful and an appropriate symbol of Christ, so the moon strikingly reminds us of the Church. The fountain of her light is hidden from view. The world seeth Him not, but she sees Him;

*It is an interesting fact that the moon, as viewed through a powerful telescope, presents the appearance of one vast ruin of nature.

and she is responsible to reflect His beams upon a benighted world. The world has no other way in which to learn anything of Christ but by the Church. "Ye," says the inspired apostle, "are our epistle, . . . known and read of all men." And again, "Forasmuch as ye are manifestly declared to be the epistle of Christ" (2 Cor. 3:2-3).

What a responsible place! How earnestly should she watch against everything that would hinder the reflection of the heavenly light of Christ, in all her ways! But how is she to reflect this light? By allowing it to shine upon her, in its undimmed brightness. If the Church only walked in the light of Christ, she would assuredly reflect His light; and this would ever keep her in her proper position. The light of the moon is not her own. So is it with the Church. She is not called to set herself before the world. She is a simple debtor to reflect the light which she herself receives. She is bound to study, with holy diligence, the path which He trod while down here, and, by the energy of the Holy Ghost, who dwells in her, to follow in that path. But, alas! earth, with its mists, its clouds and its vapors, intervenes, and hides the light and blots the epistle. The world can see but little of the traits of Christ's character in those who call themselves by His name; yea, in many instances they exhibit a humbling contrast rather than a resemblance. May we study Christ more prayerfully, that so we may copy Him more faithfully.

The stars are distant lights. They shine in other spheres, and have little connection with this system, save that their twinkling can be seen. "One star differeth from another star in glory." Thus will it be in the coming kingdom of the Son. He will shine forth in living and everlasting lustre. His body, the Church, will faithfully reflect His beams on all around, while the saints individually shall shine in those spheres which a righteous Judge shall allot to them, as a reward of faithful service during the dark night of His absence. This thought should animate us to a more ardent and vigorous pursuit after conformity to our absent Lord. (See Luke 19:12-19.)

The lower orders of creation are next introduced. The sea and the earth are made to teem with life. Some may feel warranted in regarding the operations of each successive day, as foreshadowing the various dispensations, and their great characteristic principles of action. I would only remark, as to this, that there is a great need, when handling the Word in this way, to watch, with holy jealousy, the working of imagination; and also to pay strict attention to the general analogy of Scripture, else we may make sad mistakes. I do not feel at liberty to enter upon such a line of interpretation; I shall therefore confine myself to what I believe to be the plain sense of the sacred text.

We shall now consider man's place, as set over the works of God's hands. All having been set in order, one was needed to take the headship. "And God said, 'Let us make man in our image, after our likeness; and let *them* have dominion over the fish of the sea, and over the fowl of the air, and over the cattle, and over all the earth, and over every creeping thing that creepeth upon the earth.' So God created man in His own image, in the image of God created He *him;* male and female created He *them.* And God blessed them, and God said unto them, 'Be fruitful and multiply, and replenish the earth, and subdue it; and have dominion over the fish of the sea, and over the fowl of the air, and over every living thing that moveth upon the earth.' " My reader will observe the change from "him" to "them." We are not presented with the actual fact of the formation of the woman until the next chapter; though here we find God blessing "them," and giving "them" jointly the place of universal government. All the inferior orders of creation were set under their joint dominion. Eve received all her blessings in Adam: in him, too, she got her dignity. Though not yet called into actual existence, she was, in the purpose of God, looked at as part of the man. "In Thy book were all my members written, which in continuance were fashioned, when as yet there was none of them."

Thus it is with the Church—the bride of the Second Man. She was viewed from all eternity in Christ, her Head and Lord; as we read in the first chapter of Ephesians, "According as He hath chosen us in Him, *before the foundation of the world,* that we should be holy and without blame before Him in love." Before a single member of the Church had yet breathed the breath of life, all were, in God's eternal mind, "predestinated to be conformed to the image of His Son." The counsels of God render the Church necessary to complete the mystic man. Hence the Church is called "the fullness [πληρωμα] of Him that filleth all in all." This is an amazing title, and it develops much of the dignity, importance and glory of the Church.

It is too common to view redemption as bearing merely upon the blessedness and security of individual souls. This is entirely too low a view to take of the matter. That all which pertains in any way to the individual is, in the fullest manner, secured, is, blessed be God, most true. This is the least part of redemption. But that Christ's glory is involved in, and connected with, the Church's existence, is a truth of far more dignity, depth and power. If I am entitled, on the authority of Holy Scripture, to regard myself as a constituent part of that which is actually needful to Christ, I can no longer entertain a doubt as to whether there is the fullest provision for all my personal necessities. And is not the Church thus needful to Christ? Yes, truly. "It is not good that *the* man should be alone; I will make him an helpmeet for him." And, again, "For the man is not of the woman; but the woman of the man. Neither was the man created for the woman; but the woman for the man. . . . Nevertheless, neither is the man without the woman, neither the woman without the man in the Lord. For as the woman is of the man, even so is the man also by the woman; but all things of God" (1 Cor. 11:8-12). Hence, it is no longer the mere question whether God can save a poor, helpless sinner—whether He can blot out his sins, and receive him in the power of divine righteousness. God has said, "It is not good that the man should be alone." He left not "the first man" without "an helpmeet"; neither would He leave the "Second." As, in the case of the former, there would have been a blank in the creation without Eve, so,—stupendous thought!—in the case of the latter, there would be a blank in the new creation without the Bride—the Church.

Let us now look at the manner in which Eve was brought into being, though, in so doing, we shall have to anticipate part of the contents of the next chapter. Throughout all the orders of creation there was not found a helpmeet for Adam. "A deep sleep" must fall on him, and a partner be formed, out of himself, to share his dominion and his blessedness. "And the Lord God caused a deep sleep to fall upon Adam, and he slept: and He took one of his ribs, and closed up the flesh instead thereof. And the rib, which the Lord God had taken from man, builded* He a woman, and brought her unto the man. And Adam said, 'This is now bone of my bones, and flesh of my flesh; she shall be called Woman, because she was taken out of man' " (chap. 2:21-23).

Looking at Adam and Eve as a type of Christ and the Church, as Scripture fully warrants us to do, we see how that the death of Christ needed to be an accomplished fact ere the Church could be set up; though, in the purpose of God, she was looked at and chosen in Christ before the foundation of the world. There is, however, a vast difference between the secret purpose of God and the revelation and accomplishment thereof. Before the divine purpose could be actualized in reference to the constituent parts of the Church, it was necessary that the Son should be rejected and crucified, that He should take His seat on high, that He should send down the Holy Ghost to baptize believers into one body. It is not that souls were not quickened and saved previous to the death of Christ. They assuredly were. Adam was saved, and thousands of others, from age to age, in virtue of the sacrifice of

*The Hebrew word which is rendered "builded" in the margin, is וַיִּבֶן which the LXX renders by *ωκοδομεσεν*. A reference to the original of Eph. 2:20,22 will show the reader that the words rendered "built" and "builded together" are inflections of the same verb.

Christ, though that sacrifice was not yet accomplished. But the salvation of individual souls is one thing, and the formation of the Church, as a distinctive thing, by the Holy Ghost, is quite another.

This distinction is not sufficiently attended to; and even where it is in theory maintained, it is accompanied with but little of those practical results which might naturally be expected to flow from a truth so stupendous. The Church's unique place—her special relationship to "the Second Man, the Lord from heaven"—her distinctive privileges and dignities—all these would, if entered into by the power of the Holy Ghost, produce the richest, the rarest and the most fragrant fruits. (See Eph. 5:23-32.)

When we look at the type before us, we may form some idea of the results which ought to follow from the understanding of the Church's position and relationship. What affection did not Eve owe to Adam! What nearness she enjoyed! What intimacy of communion. What full participation in all his thoughts! In all his dignity, and in all his glory, she was entirely one. He did not rule *over,* but *with* her. He was lord of the whole creation, and she was one with him. Yea, as has already been remarked, she was looked at and blessed *in* him. "The man" was the object; and as to "the woman," she was needful to him, and therefore she was brought into being. Nothing can be more profoundly interesting as a type. Man first set up, and the woman viewed in, and then formed out of, him,—all this forms a type of the most striking and instructive character. Not that a doctrine can ever be founded upon a type; but when we find the doctrine fully and clearly laid down in other parts of the Word, we are then prepared to understand, appreciate and admire the type.

The eighth psalm furnishes a fine view of man set over the work of God's hands: "When I consider Thy heavens, the work of Thy fingers; the moon and the stars which Thou hast ordained: what is man that Thou art mindful of him? and the son of man that Thou visitest him? For Thou hast made him a little lower than the angels, and hast crowned him with glory and honor. Thou madest him to have dominion over the works of Thy hands; Thou hast put all things under his feet,—all sheep and oxen, yea, and the beasts of the field, the fowl of the air, and the fish of the sea, and whatsoever passeth through the paths of the sea." Here, man is looked at without any distinctive mention of the woman; and this is quite in character, for the woman is looked at *in* the man.

There is no direct revelation of the mystery of the Church in any part of the Old Testament. The apostle expressly says, "In other ages it was not made known to the sons of men as it is *now* revealed unto His holy apostles and prophets (of the New Testament) by the Spirit" (Eph. 3:1-11). Hence, in the psalm just quoted, we have only "the man" presented to us; but we know that the man and the woman are looked at under one head. All this will find its full antitype in the ages to come. Then shall the True Man—the Lord from heaven—take His seat on the throne, and, in companionship with His bride—the Church—rule over a restored creation. This Church is quickened out of the grave of Christ, is part "of His body, of His flesh, and of His bones." He the Head and she the body, making one Man, as we read in the fourth chapter of Ephesians, "Till we all come, in the unity of the faith, and of the knowledge of the Son of God, unto a perfect man, unto the measure of the stature of the fullness of Christ." The Church, being thus part of Christ, will occupy a place in the glory quite unique. There was no other creature so near to Adam as Eve, because no other creature was part of himself. So in reference to the Church, she will hold the very nearest place to Christ in His coming glory.

Nor is it merely what the Church *will* be that commands our admiration, but what the Church *is.* She is now the body of which Christ is the Head; she is now the temple of which God is the Inhabitant. Oh! what manner of people ought we to be! If such is the present, such the future dignity of that of which we, through God's grace, form a part, surely a holy, a devoted, a separated, an elevated walk is what becomes us.

May the Holy Ghost unfold these things more fully and powerfully to our hearts, so that we may have a deeper sense of the conduct and character which are worthy of the high vocation wherewith we are called. "The eyes of your understanding being enlightened; that ye may know what is the hope of His calling, and what the riches of the glory of His inheritance in the saints, and what the exceeding greatness of His power to usward who believe, according to the working of His mighty power, which He wrought in Christ when He raised Him from the dead, and set Him at His own right hand in the heavenly places, far above all principality and power and might and dominion and every name that is named, not only in this world, but also in that which is to come; and hath put all things under His feet, and gave Him to be the Head over all things to the Church, which is His body, the fullness of Him that filleth all in all" (Eph. 1:18-23).

---

## *CHAPTER 2*

THIS chapter introduces to our notice two prominent subjects, namely, "the seventh day" and "the river." The first of these demands special attention.

There are few subjects on which so much misunderstanding and contradiction prevails as the doctrine of "the Sabbath." Not that there is the slightest foundation for either the one or the other; for the whole subject is laid down in the Word in the simplest possible manner. The distinct *commandment* to "keep holy the Sabbath day" will come before us, the Lord permitting, in our meditations on the book of Exodus. In the chapter now before us, there is no command given to man whatever, but simply the record that "God rested on the seventh day." "Thus the heavens and the earth were finished, and all the host of them. And on the seventh day God ended His work which He had made; and He rested on the seventh day from all His work which He had made. And God blessed the seventh day, and sanctified it; because that in it He had rested from all His work which God created and made." There is no commandment given to man here. We are simply told that God enjoyed His rest, because all was done, so far as the mere creation was concerned. There was nothing more to be done, and therefore the One who had, during six days, been working, ceased to work, and enjoyed His rest. All was complete; all was very good; all was just as He Himself had made it; and He rested in it. "The morning stars sang together, and all the sons of God shouted for joy." The work of creation was ended, and God was celebrating a Sabbath.

And, be it observed, this is the true character of a Sabbath. This is the only Sabbath which God ever celebrated, so far as the inspired record instructs us. After this, we read of God's commanding man to keep the Sabbath, and man utterly failing so to do; but we never read again the words, "God rested"; on the contrary, the word is, "My Father worketh hitherto, and I work" (John 5:17). The Sabbath, in the strict and proper sense of the term, could only be celebrated when there really was nothing to be done. It could only be celebrated amid an undefiled creation—a creation on which no spot of sin could be discerned. God can have no rest where there is sin; and one has only to look around him in order to learn the total impossibility of God's enjoying a rest in creation *now.* The thorn and the thistle, together with the ten thousand other melancholy and humiliating fruits of a groaning creation, rise before us, and declare that God must be at *work* and not at *rest.* Could God rest in the midst of thorns and briars? Could He rest amid the sighs and tears, the groans and sorrows, the sickness and death, the degradation and guilt of a ruined world! Could God sit down, as it were, and celebrate a Sabbath in the midst of such circumstances?

Whatever answer may be given to these questions, the Word of God teaches us that God has had no Sabbath as yet, save the one which the second of Genesis records. "The seventh day," and none other, was the Sabbath. It showed forth the completeness of creation work; but creation work is marred, and the seventh day rest interrupted; and thus, from the fall to the incarnation, God was working; from the incarnation to the cross, God the Son was working; and from Pentecost until now, God the Holy Ghost has been working.

Assuredly, Christ had no Sabbath when He was upon this earth. True, He finished His work—blessedly, gloriously finished it—but where did He spend the Sabbath day? *In the tomb!* Yes, the Lord Christ—God manifest in the flesh, the Lord of the Sabbath, the Maker and Sustainer of heaven and earth—spent the seventh day in the dark and silent tomb. Has this no voice for us? Does it convey no teaching? Could the Son of God lie in the grave on the seventh day if that day were to be spent in rest and peace, and in the full sense that nothing remained to be done? Impossible! We want no further proof of the impossibility of celebrating a Sabbath than that which is afforded at the grave of Jesus. We may stand beside that grave amazed to find it occupied by such an one on the seventh day; but, oh! the reason is obvious. Man is a fallen, ruined, guilty creature. His long career of guilt has ended in crucifying the Lord of glory; and not only crucifying Him, but placing a great stone at the mouth of the tomb, to prevent, if possible, His leaving it.

And what was the man doing while the Son of God was in the grave? He was observing the Sabbath day! What a thought! Christ in His grave to repair a broken Sabbath, and yet man attempting to keep the Sabbath as though it were not broken at all! It was *man's* Sabbath, and not God's. It was a Sabbath without Christ—an empty, powerless, worthless, because Christless and Godless, form.

But some will say, The day has been changed, while all the principles belonging to it remain the same. I do not believe that Scripture furnishes any foundation for such an idea. Where is the divine warrant for such a statement? Surely, if there is Scripture authority, nothing can be easier than to produce it. But the fact is, there is none; on the contrary, the distinction is most fully maintained in the New Testament. Take one remarkable passage, in proof,—"In the end of the Sabbath, as it began to dawn towards the first day of the week" (Matt. 28:1). There is, evidently, no mention here of the seventh day being changed to the first day; nor yet of any transfer of the Sabbath from the one to the other. The first day of the week is not the Sabbath changed, but altogether a new day. It is the first day of a new period, and not the last day of an old. The seventh day stands connected with earth and earthly rest; the first day of the week, on the contrary, introduces us to heaven and heavenly rest.

This makes a vast difference in the principle; and when we look at the matter in a practical point of view, the difference is most material. If I celebrate the seventh day, it marks me as an earthly man, inasmuch as that day is clearly the rest of earth—creation rest; but if I am taught by the Word and Spirit of God to understand the meaning of the first day of the week, I shall at once apprehend its immediate connection with that new and heavenly order of things, of which the death and resurrection of Christ form the everlasting foundation. The seventh day appertained to Israel and to earth: the first day of the week appertains to the Church and to heaven. Further, Israel was *commanded* to observe the Sabbath day: the Church is *privileged* to enjoy the first day of the week. The former was the *test* of Israel's moral condition; the latter is the significant *proof* of the Church's eternal acceptance. That made manifest what Israel *could do* for God: this perfectly declares what God *has done* for us.

It is quite impossible to over-estimate the value and importance of the Lord's day [*η κυριακη ημερα*], as the first day of the week is termed, in the first chapter of the Apocalypse. Being the day on which Christ rose from the dead, it sets forth, not the completion of creation, but the full and glorious triumph of redemption. Nor should we regard the celebration of the first day of the week as a matter of bondage, or as a yoke put on the neck of a Christian. It is his delight to celebrate that happy day. Hence we find that the first day of the week was pre-eminently the day on which the early Christians came together to break bread; and at that period of the Church's history, the distinction between the Sabbath and the first day of the week was fully maintained. The Jews celebrated the former by assembling in their synagogues to read "the law and the prophets"; the Christians celebrated the latter by assembling to break bread. There is not so much as a single passage of Scripture in which the first day of the week is called the Sabbath day, whereas there is the most abundant proof of their entire distinctness.

Why, therefore, contend for what which has no foundation in the Word? Love, honor and celebrate the Lord's day as much as possible; seek, like the apostle, to be "in the spirit" thereon; let your retirement from secular matters be as profound as ever you can make it; but, while you do all this, call it by its proper name; give it its proper place; understand its proper principles; attach to it its proper characteristics; and, above all, do not bind down the Christian, as with an iron rule, to observe the seventh day, when it is his high and holy privilege to observe the first. Do not bring him down from heaven, where he can rest, to a cursed and blood-stained earth, where he cannot. Do not ask him to keep a day which his Master spent in the tomb, instead of that blessed day on which He left it. (See, carefully, Matt. 28:1-6; Mark 16:1-2; Luke 24:1; John 20:1,19,26; Acts 20:7; 1 Cor. 16:2; Rev. 1:10; Acts 13:14; 17:2; Col. 2:16.)

But let it not be supposed that we lose sight of the important fact that the Sabbath will again be celebrated in the land of Israel, and over the whole creation. It assuredly will. "There remaineth a rest [σαβ βατισμος] for the people of God" (Heb. 4:9). When the Son of Abraham, Son of David, and Son of Man, shall assume His position of government over the whole earth, there will be a glorious Sabbath—a rest which sin shall never interrupt. But now, He is rejected, and all who know and love Him are called to take their place with Him in His rejection; they are called to "go forth to Him without the camp, bearing His reproach" (Heb. 13:13). If earth could keep a Sabbath, there would be no reproach; but the very fact of the professing church's seeking to make the first day of the week the Sabbath, reveals a deep principle. It is but the effort to get back to an earthly standing, and to an earthly code of morals.

Many may not see this. Many true Christians may, most conscientiously, observe the Sabbath day, as such; and we are bound to honor their consciences, though we are perfectly warranted in asking them to furnish a scriptural basis for their conscientious convictions. We would not stumble or wound their conscience, but we would seek to instruct it. However, we are not now occupied with conscience or its convictions, but only with the principle which lies at the root of what may be termed the Sabbath question; and I would only put the question to the Christian reader, which is more consonant with the entire scope and spirit of the New Testament—the celebration of the seventh day or Sabbath, or the celebration of the first day of the week or the Lord's day.*

---

*This subject will, if the Lord permit, come before us again in the twentieth chapter of Exodus; but I would here observe, that very much of the offence and misunderstanding connected with the important subject of the Sabbath, may be justly traced to the inconsiderate and injudicious conduct of some who, in their zeal for what they termed Christian liberty, in reference to the Sabbath, rather lose sight of the claims of honest consciences, and also of the place which the Lord's day occupies in the New Testament. Some have been known to enter upon their weekly avocations, simply to show their liberty, and thus they caused much needless offence. Such acting could never have been suggested by the Spirit of Christ. If I am ever so clear and free in my own mind, I should respect the consciences of my brethren; and, moreover, I do not believe that those who so carry themselves, really understand the true and precious privileges connected with the Lord's day. We should only be too thankful to be rid of all secular occupation and distraction, to think of having recourse to them for the purpose of showing our liberty. The good providence of our God has so arranged for His people throughout the British Empire, that they can, without pecuniary loss, enjoy the rest of the Lord's day, inasmuch as all are obliged to abstain from business. This must be regarded by every well-regulated mind, as a mercy; for, if it were not thus ordered, we know how man's covetous heart would, if possible, rob the Christian of the sweet privilege of attending the assembly on the Lord's day. And who can tell what would be the deadening effect of uninterrupted engagement with this world's traffic? Those Christians who, from Monday morning to Saturday night, breathe the dense atmosphere of the mart, the market and the manufactory, can form some idea of it.

It cannot be regarded as a good sign to find men introducing measures for the public profanation of the Lord's day. It assuredly marks the progress of infidelity and French influence.

We shall now consider the connection between the Sabbath and the river flowing out of Eden. There is much interest in this. It is the first notice we get of "the river of God," which is here introduced in connection with God's rest. When God was resting in His works, the whole world felt the blessing and refreshment thereof. It was impossible for God to keep a Sabbath, and earth not to feel its sacred influence. But, alas! the streams which flowed forth from Eden—the scene of earthly rest—were speedily interrupted, because the rest of creation was marred by sin.

Yet, blessed be God, sin did not put a stop to His activities, but only gave them a new sphere; and wherever He is seen acting, the river is seen flowing. Thus, when we find Him, with a strong hand and an outstretched arm, conducting His ransomed hosts across the sterile sand of the desert, there we see the stream flowing forth, not from Eden, but from the smitten Rock—apt and beautiful expression of the ground on which sovereign grace ministers to the need of sinners! This was redemption and not merely creation. "That rock was Christ," Christ smitten to meet His people's need. The smitten Rock was connected with Jehovah's place in the Tabernacle; and truly there was moral beauty in the connection. God dwelling in curtains, and Israel drinking from a smitten rock, had a voice for every opened ear, and a deep lesson for every circumcised heart (Exod. 17:6).

Passing onward, in the history of God's ways, we find the river flowing in another channel. "In the last day, that great day of the feast, Jesus stood and cried, saying, 'If any man thirst, let him come unto Me and drink. He that believeth on Me, as the Scripture hath said, out of his belly shall flow rivers of living water' " (John 7:37-38). Here, then, we find the river emanating from another source, and flowing through another channel; though, in one sense, the source of the river was ever the same, being God Himself; but then it was God known in a new relationship and upon a new principle. Thus, in the passage just quoted, the Lord Jesus was taking His place, in spirit, outside of the whole existing order of things, and presenting Himself as the Source of the river of living water, of which river the person of the believer was to be the channel. Eden of old was constituted a debtor to the whole earth to send forth the fertilizing streams; and in the desert, the rock, when smitten, became a debtor to Israel's thirsty hosts. Just so now, every one who believes in Jesus is a debtor to the scene around him to allow the streams of refreshment to flow forth from him.

The Christian should regard himself as the channel through which the manifold grace of Christ may flow out to a needy world; and the more freely he communicates, the more freely will he receive, "for there is that scattereth, and yet increaseth; and there is that withholdeth more than is meet, and it tendeth to poverty." This places the believer in a place of sweetest privilege, and, at the same time, of the most solemn responsibility. He is called to be the constant witness and exhibiter of the grace of Him on whom He believes.

Now, the more he enters into the privilege, the more will he answer the responsibility. If he is habitually feeding upon Christ, he cannot avoid exhibiting Him. The more the Holy Spirit keeps the Christian's eye fixed on Jesus, the more will his heart be occupied with His adorable Person, and his life and character bear unequivocal testimony to His grace. Faith is at once the power of ministry, the power of testimony, and the power of worship. If we are not living "by the faith of the Son of God, who loved us, and gave Himself for us," we shall neither be effectual servants, faithful witnesses, nor true worshipers. We may be doing a great deal, but it will not be service

But there are some who teach that the expression η κυριακη ημερα, which is rightly enough translated, "the Lord's day," refers to "the day of the Lord," and that the exiled apostle found himself carried forward, as it were, into the spirit of the day of the Lord. I do not believe the original would bear such an interpretation; and, besides, we have in 1 Thess. 5:2, and 2 Peter 3:10, the exact words, "the day of the Lord," the original of which is quite different from the expression above referred to, being, not η κυριακη ημερα, but η ημερα κυριου. This entirely settles the matter, so far as the mere criticism is concerned; and as to interpretation, it is plain that by far the greater portion of the Apocalypse is occupied, not with "the day of the Lord," but with events prior thereto.

to Christ: we may be saying a great deal, but it will not be testimony for Christ: we may exhibit a great deal of piety and devotion, but it will not be spiritual and true worship.

Finally, we have the river of God presented to us in the last chapter of the Apocalypse.* "And he showed me a pure river of water of life, clear as crystal, proceeding out of the throne of God and of the Lamb." "There is a river, the streams whereof shall make glad the city of God, the holy place of the tabernacles of the Most High." This is the last place in which we find the river. Its source can never again be touched, its channel never again interrupted. "The throne of God" is expressive of eternal stability, and the presence of the Lamb marks it as based upon the immediate ground of accomplished redemption. It is not God's throne in creation, nor in providence, but in redemption. When I see *the Lamb,* I know its connection with me as *a sinner.* "The throne of God," as such, would but deter me; but when God reveals Himself in the Person of the Lamb, the heart is attracted, and the conscience tranquilized.

The blood of the Lamb cleanses the conscience from every speck and stain of sin, and sets it, in perfect freedom, in the presence of a holiness which cannot tolerate sin. In the cross, all the claims of divine holiness were perfectly answered; so that the more I understand the latter, the more I appreciate the former. The higher our estimate of holiness, the higher will be our estimate of the work of the cross. "Grace reigns, through righteousness, unto eternal life, by Jesus Christ our Lord." Hence the Psalmist calls on the saints to give thanks at the remembrance of God's holiness. This is a precious fruit of a perfect redemption. Before ever a sinner can give thanks at the remembrance of God's holiness, he must look at it by faith, from the resurrection side of the cross.

Having thus traced the river, from Genesis to Revelation, we shall briefly look at Adam's position in Eden. We have seen him as a type of Christ; but he is not merely to be viewed typically, but personally—not merely as absolutely shadowing forth "the second Man, the Lord from heaven," but also as standing in the place of personal responsibility. In the midst of the fair scene of creation, the Lord God set up a testimony, and this testimony was also a test for the creature. It spoke of *death* in the midst of *life.* "In the day that thou eatest thereof, thou shalt surely die." Strange, solemn sound! Yet it was a needed sound. Adam's life was suspended upon his strict obedience. The link which connected him with the Lord God† was obedience, based on implicit confidence in the One who had set him in his position of dignity—confidence in His truth—confidence in His love. He could obey only while he confided. We shall see the truth and force of this more fully when we come to examine the next chapter.

I would here suggest the remarkable contrast between the testimony set up in Eden and that which is set up now. Then, when all around was *life,* God spoke of *death;* now, on the contrary, when all around is death, God speaks of life: then, the word was, "in the day thou eatest thou shalt *die";* now, the word is, "believe and *live.*" And, as in Eden the enemy sought to make void God's testimony as to the result of eating the fruit, so now he seeks to make void God's testimony as to the result of believing the gospel. God

*Compare, also, Ezekiel 47:1-12 and Zech. 14:8.

†My reader will observe the change in the second chapter from the expression "God" to "Lord God." There is much importance in the distinction. When God is seen acting in relation with man, He takes the title "Lord God"—(Jehovah Elohim); but until man appears on the scene, the word "Lord" is not used. I shall just point out three out of many passages in which the distinction is very strikingly presented. "And they that went in, went in male and female of all flesh, as *God* (Elohim) had commanded him; and the *Lord* (Jehovah) shut him in" (Gen. 7:16). Elohim was going to destroy the world which He had made, but Jehovah took care of the man with whom He stood in relation. Again—"That all the earth may know that there is a God (Elohim) in Israel. And all this assembly shall know that the Lord (Jehovah) saveth," etc. (1 Sam. 17:46-47). All the earth was to recognize the presence of Elohim; but Israel was called to recognize the actings of Jehovah, with whom they stood in relation. Lastly—"Jehoshaphat cried out, and *the Lord* (Jehovah) helped him; and *God* (Elohim) moved *them* to depart from him" (2 Chron. 18:31). Jehovah took care of His poor erring servant; but Elohim, though unknown, acted upon the hearts of the uncircumcised Syrians.

had said, "In the day that thou eatest thereof thou shalt surely *die*"; but the serpent said, "Ye shall not surely *die.*" And now, when God's Word plainly declares that "he that believeth on the Son *hath* everlasting *life*" (John 3:36), the same serpent seeks to persuade people that they have *not* everlasting *life,* nor should they presume to think of such a thing until they have first *done, felt* and *experienced* all manner of things.

My beloved reader, if you have not yet heartily believed the divine record, let me beseech you to allow "the voice of the Lord" to prevail above the hiss of the serpent. "He that heareth My word, and believeth on Him that sent Me, hath everlasting life, and shall not come into condemnation; but is passed from death unto life" (John 5:24).

---

## CHAPTER 3

THIS section of our book sets before us the breaking up of the whole scene on which we have been dwelling. It abounds in very weighty principles, and has very justly been, in all ages, resorted to as a most fruitful theme for those who desired to set forth the truth as to man's ruin and God's remedy. The serpent enters with a bold question as to divine revelation—terrible model and forerunner of all infidel questions since raised by those who have, alas! too faithfully served the serpent's cause in the world—questions which are only to be met by the supreme authority and divine majesty of Holy Scripture.

"Yea, hath God said, ye shall not eat of every tree of the garden?" This was Satan's crafty inquiry; and had the Word of God been dwelling richly in Eve's heart, her answer might have been direct, simple and conclusive. The true way in which to meet Satan's questions and suggestions, is to treat them as his, and repel them by the Word. To let them near the heart for a moment is to lose the only power by which to answer them. The devil did not openly present himself and say, I am the devil, the enemy of God, and I am come to traduce Him and ruin you. This would not be serpent-like; and yet he really did all this *by raising questions* in the mind of the creature. To admit the question, "Hath God said?" when I know that God has spoken, is positive infidelity; and the very fact of my admitting it, proves my total incapacity to meet it. Hence, in Eve's case, the form of her reply evidenced the fact that she had admitted to her heart the serpent's crafty inquiry. Instead of adhering strictly to the exact words of God, she, in her reply, actually adds thereto.

Now, either to add to or take from God's Word, proves very clearly that His Word is not dwelling in my heart or governing my conscience. If a man is finding his enjoyment in obedience, if it is his meat and his drink, if he is living by every word that proceedeth out of the mouth of Jehovah, he will assuredly be acquainted with, and fully alive to, His Word. He could not be indifferent to it. The Lord Jesus, in His conflict with Satan, accurately applied the Word, because He lived upon it, and esteemed it more than His necessary food. He could not misquote or misapply the Word, neither could He be indifferent about it. Not so Eve. She added to what God had said. His command was simple enough, "Thou shalt not eat of it." To this Eve adds her own words, "neither shall ye touch it." These were Eve's words and not God's. He had said nothing about touching; so that whether her misquotation proceeded from ignorance, or indifference, or a desire to represent God in an arbitrary light, or from all three together, it is plain that she was entirely off the true ground of simple confidence in, and subjection to, God's holy Word. "By the words of Thy mouth, I have kept me from the paths of the destroyer."

Nothing can possess more commanding interest than the way in which the Word is everywhere put forward throughout the sacred canon, together with the immense importance of strict obedience thereto. Obedience is due from us to God's Word, simply because it is His Word. To raise a question, when He has spoken, is blasphemy.

We are in the place of a creature. He is the Creator; He may, therefore, justly claim obedience from us. The infidel may call this "blind obedience," but the Christian calls this intelligent obedience, inasmuch as it is based upon the knowledge that it is God's Word to which he is obedient. If a man had not God's Word, he might well be said to be in blindness and darkness, for there is not so much as a single ray of divine light within or around us but what emanates from God's pure and eternal Word. All that we want to know is that God has spoken, and then obedience becomes the very highest order of intelligent acting. When the soul gets up to God, it has reached the very highest source of authority. No man, nor body of men, can claim obedience to their word, because it is theirs; and hence the claims of the Church of Rome are arrogant and impious. In her claiming obedience, she usurps the prerogative of God; and all who yield it, rob God of His right. She presumes to place herself between God and the conscience; and who can do this with impunity? When God speaks, man is bound to obey. Happy is he if he does so: woe be to him if he does not. Infidelity may question if God has spoken; superstition may place human authority between my conscience and what God has spoken; by both alike I am effectually robbed of the Word, and, as a consequence, of the deep blessedness of obedience.

There is blessing in every act of obedience; but the moment the soul hesitates, the enemy has the advantage, and he will assuredly use it to thrust the soul further and further from God. Thus, in the chapter before us, the question, "Hath God said?" was followed by, "Ye shall not surely die." That is to say, there was first the question raised as to whether God had spoken, and then followed the open contradiction of what God had said. This solemn fact is abundantly sufficient to show how dangerous it is to admit near the heart a question as to divine revelation in its fullness and integrity. A refined rationalism is very near akin to bold infidelity, and the infidelity that dares to judge God's Word is not far from the atheism that denies His existence. Eve would never have stood by to hear God contradicted if she had not previously fallen into looseness and indifference as to His Word. She, too, had her "phases of faith," or, to speak more correctly, her phases of infidelity: she suffered God to be contradicted by a creature, simply because His Word had lost its proper authority over her heart, her conscience and her understanding.

This furnishes a most solemn warning to all who are in danger of being ensnared by an unhallowed rationalism. There is no true security save in a profound faith in the plenary inspiration and supreme authority of *all Scripture."* The soul that is endowed with this has a triumphant answer to every objector, whether he issue from Rome or Germany. "There is nothing new under the sun." The self-same evil which is now corrupting the very springs of religious thought and feeling throughout the fairest portion of the continent of Europe, was that which laid Eve's heart in ruins in the garden of Eden. The first step in her downward course was her hearkening to the question, "Hath God said"; and then onward she went, from stage to stage, until at length she bowed before the serpent, and owned him as her god and the fountain of truth. Yes, my reader, the serpent displaced God, and the serpent's lie God's truth. Thus it was with fallen man, and thus it is with fallen man's posterity. God's Word has no place in the heart of the unregenerated man, but the lie of the serpent has. Let the formation of man's heart be examined, and it will be found that there is a place therein for Satan's lie, but none whatever for the truth of God. Hence the force of the word to Nicodemus—"Ye must be born again."

But it is important to observe the mode in which the serpent sought to shake Eve's confidence in God's truth, and thus bring her under the power of infidel *"reason."* It was by shaking her confidence in God's love. He sought to shake her confidence in what God had said by showing that the testimony was not founded in love. "For," said he, "God doth know that in the day ye eat thereof, then your eyes shall be opened, and ye shall be as gods, knowing good and evil" (ver. 5).

In other words, there is positive advantage connected with the eating of that fruit of which God is seeking to deprive you; why, therefore, should you believe God's testimony? You cannot place confidence in one who manifestly does not love you; for if He loved you, why should He prohibit your enjoying a positive privilege?

Eve's security against the influence of all this reasoning would have been simple repose in the infinite goodness of God. She should have said to the serpent, I have the fullest confidence in God's goodness, and therefore I deem it impossible that He could withhold any real good from me. If that fruit were good for me, I should surely have it; but the fact of its being forbidden by God proves that I would be no better, but much worse off by the eating of it. I am convinced of God's *love,* and I am convinced of God's *truth,* and I believe, too, that you are an evil one come to draw my heart away from the fountain of goodness and truth. Get thee behind me, Satan. This would have been a noble reply; but it was not given. Her confidence in truth and love gave way, and all was lost; and so we find that there is just as little place in the heart of fallen man for God's love as there is for God's truth. The heart of man is a stranger to both the one and the other until renewed by the power of the Holy Ghost.

Now, it is deeply interesting to turn from Satan's lie in reference to the truth and love of God, to the mission of the Lord Jesus Christ, who came from the bosom of the Father in order to reveal what He really is. "Grace and truth"—the very things which man lost in his fall—"came by Jesus Christ" (John 1:17). He was "the faithful witness" of what God was (Rev. 1:5). Truth reveals God as He is, but this truth is connected with the revelation of perfect grace; and thus the sinner finds, to his unspeakable joy, that the revelation of what God is, instead of being his destruction, becomes the basis of his eternal salvation. "This is life eternal, that they might know Thee, the only true God, and Jesus Christ whom Thou hast sent" (John 17:3). I cannot know God and not have life. The loss of the knowledge of God was death; but the knowledge of God is life. This necessarily makes life a thing entirely outside of ourselves, and dependent upon what God is. Let me arrive at what amount of self-knowledge I may, it is not said that this is life eternal, to know themselves; though, no doubt, the knowledge of God and the knowledge of self will go very much together; still, "eternal life" is connected with the former, and not with the latter. To know God as He is, is life; and "all who know not God" shall be "punished with everlasting destruction from His presence."

It is of the utmost importance to see that what really stamps man's character and condition is his ignorance or knowledge of God. This it is that marks his character here, and fixes his destiny hereafter. Is he evil in his thoughts, evil in his words, evil in his actions,—it is all the result of his being ignorant of God. On the other hand, is he pure in thought, holy in conversation, gracious in action,—it is but the practical result of his knowledge of God. So also as to the future. To know God, is the solid ground of endless bliss—everlasting glory: to know Him not, is "everlasting destruction." Thus the knowledge of God is everything. It quickens the soul, purifies the heart, tranquilizes the conscience, elevates the affections, sanctifies the entire character and conduct.

Need we wonder, therefore, that Satan's grand design was to rob the creature of the true knowledge of the only true God? He misrepresented the blessed God: he said He was not kind. This was the secret spring of all the mischief. It matters not what shape sin has since taken—it matters not through what channel it has flowed, under what head it has ranged itself, or in what garb it has clothed itself; it is all to be traced to this one thing, namely, ignorance of God. The most refined and cultivated moralist, the most devout religionist, the most benevolent philanthropist, if ignorant of God, is as far from life and true holiness as the publican and the harlot. The prodigal was just as much a sinner, and as positively away from the Father, when he had crossed the threshold as when he was feeding swine in the far country (Luke 15:13-15). So, in Eve's case, the moment she took herself out of the hands of God—out of the position of absolute dependence upon, and subjection to, His Word, she abandoned herself to the government of sense, as used of Satan for her entire overthrow.

The sixth verse presents three things; namely, "the lust of the flesh, the lust of the eye, and the pride of life"; which three, as the apostle states, comprehend "all that is in the world." These things necessarily took the lead when God was shut out. If I do not abide in the happy assurance of God's love and truth—His grace and faithfulness, I shall surrender myself to the government of some one or, it may be, all of the above principles; and this is only another name for the government of Satan. There is, strictly speaking, no such thing as man's free-will. If man be self-governed, he is really governed by Satan; and if not, he is governed by God.

Now, the three great agencies by which Satan works are "the lust of the flesh, the lust of the eye, and the pride of life." These were the things presented by Satan to the Lord Jesus in the temptation. He began by tempting the Second Man to take Himself out of the position of absolute dependence upon God. "Command these stones that they be made bread." He asked Him to do this, not, as in the case of the first man, to make Himself what He was not, but to prove what He was. Then followed the offer of the kingdoms of the world, with all their glory. And, finally, conducting Him to a pinnacle of the temple, he tempted Him to give Himself, suddenly and miraculously, to the admiration of the assembled people below. (Comp. Matt. 4:1-11 with Luke 4:1-13.) The plain design of each temptation was to induce the blessed One to step from the position of entire dependence upon God, and perfect subjection to His will; but all in vain. "*It is written*" was the unvarying reply of the only dependent, self-emptied, perfect man. Others might undertake to manage for themselves; none but God should manage for Him.

What an example for the faithful, under all their circumstances! Jesus kept close to Scripture, and thus conquered; without any other weapon, save the Sword of the Spirit, He stood in the conflict, and gained a glorious triumph. What a contrast with the first Adam! The One had everything to plead for God, the other had everything to plead against Him. The garden, with all its delights, in the one case; the wilderness, with all its privations, in the other: confidence in Satan, in the one case; confidence in God in the other: complete defeat in the one case; complete victory in the other. Blessed forever be the God of all grace, who has laid our help on One so mighty to conquer—mighty to save!

Let us now inquire how far Adam and Eve realized the serpent's promised advantage. This inquiry will lead us to a deeply important point in connection with the fall of man. The Lord God had so ordered it, that in and by the fall, man should get what previously he had not, and that was, *a conscience,* a knowledge of both good and evil. This, man evidently could not have had before. He could not have known aught about evil, inasmuch as evil was not there to be known. He was in a state of innocence, which is a state of ignorance of evil. Man got a conscience in and by the fall, and we find that the very first effect of conscience was to make him a coward. Satan had utterly deceived the woman. He had said, "your eyes shall be opened, and ye shall be as gods, knowing good and evil"; but he had left out a material part of the truth, namely, that they should know good without the power to do it, and that they should know evil without the power to avoid it. Their very attempt to elevate themselves in the scale of moral existence involved the loss of true elevation. They became degraded, powerless, Satan-enslaved, conscience-smitten, terrified creatures. "The eyes of them both were opened," no doubt; but, alas! to what a sight!—it was only to discover their own nakedness. They opened their eyes upon their own condition, which was "wretched and miserable and poor and blind and naked." "They knew that they were naked"—sad fruit of the tree of knowledge! It was not any fresh knowledge of divine excellency they had attained—no fresh beams of divine light from the pure and eternal fountain thereof—alas! no; the very earliest result of their disobedient effort after knowledge, was the discovery that they were naked.

Now, it is well to understand this; well, too, to know how conscience works,—to see that it can only make cowards of us, as being the consciousness of what we are. Many are astray as to this; they think that conscience will bring us to God. Did it operate thus in the case of Adam and Eve? Assuredly not. Nor will it in the case of any sinner. How could it? How could the sense of what *I am* ever bring me to God, if not accompanied by the faith of what *God is?* Impossible. It will produce shame, self-reproach, remorse, anguish. It may also give birth to certain efforts on my part to remedy the condition which it discloses; but these very efforts, so far from drawing us to God, rather act as a blind to hide Him from our view. Thus, in the case of Adam and Eve, the discovery of their nakedness was followed by an effort of their own to cover it, "they sewed fig-leaves together and made themselves aprons." This is the first record we have of man's attempt to remedy, by his own device, his condition, and the attentive consideration thereof will afford us not a little instruction as to the real character of human religiousness in all ages. In the first place, we see, not only in Adam's case, but in every case, that man's effort to remedy his condition is based upon the sense of his nakedness. He is confessedly naked, and all his works are the result of his being so. This can never avail. I must know that I am clothed, before I can do anything acceptable in the sight of God.

And this, be it observed, is the difference between true Christianity and human religiousness. The former is founded upon the fact of a man's being clothed; the latter, upon the fact of his being naked. The former has for its starting-post what the latter has for its goal. All that a true Christian does, is because he is clothed—perfectly clothed; all that a mere religionist does, is in order that he may be clothed. This makes a vast difference. The more we examine the genius of man's religion, in all its phases, the more we shall see its thorough insufficiency to remedy his state, or even to meet his own sense thereof. It may do very well for a time, it may avail so long as death, judgment and the wrath of God are looked at from a distance, if looked at at all; but when a man comes to look these terrible realities straight in the face, he will find, in good truth, that his religion is a bed too short for him to stretch himself upon, and a covering too narrow for him to wrap himself in.

The moment Adam heard the voice of the Lord God, in Eden, *"he was afraid,"* because, as he himself confessed, "I was naked." Yes, naked, although he had his apron on him. But it is plain that that covering did not even satisfy his own conscience. Had his conscience been divinely satisfied, he would not have been afraid. "If our heart condemn us not, then have we confidence toward God" (1 John 3:20-21). But if even the human conscience cannot find repose in man's religious efforts, how much less can the holiness of God. Adam's apron could not screen him from the eye of God, and he could not stand in His presence naked; therefore he fled to hide himself. This is what conscience will do at all times. It will cause man to hide himself from God; and, moreover, all that his own religiousness offers him is a hiding-place from God. This is a miserable provision, inasmuch as he must meet God some time or other, and if he has naught save the sad conscience of what he is, he must be afraid—yea, he must be wretched. Indeed, nothing is needed, save hell itself, to complete the misery of one who feels he has to meet God, and knows only his own unfitness to meet Him.

Had Adam known God's perfect love, he would not have been afraid. "There is no fear in love; but perfect love casteth out fear, because fear hath torment. He that feareth is not made perfect in love" (1 John 4:17-18). But Adam knew not this, because he had believed the serpent's lie. He thought that God was anything but love, and therefore the very last thought of his heart would have been to venture into His presence. He could not do it. Sin was there, and God and sin can never meet. So long as there is sin on the conscience, there must be the sense of distance from God. "He is of purer eyes than to behold evil, and cannot look upon iniquity" (Hab. 1:13). Holiness and sin cannot dwell together. Sin, wherever it is found, can only be met by the wrath of God.

But, blessed be God, there is something beside the *conscience of what I am.* There is *the revelation of what He is;* and this latter the fall of man really brought out. God had not revealed Himself fully in creation: He had shown "His eternal power and Godhead [θειοτης],*" but He had not told out all the deep secrets of His nature and character. Wherefore Satan made a grand mistake in coming to meddle with God's creation. He only proved to be the instrument of his own eternal defeat and confusion, and "his violent dealing" shall forever "come down upon his own pate." His *lie* only gave occasion for the display of the full *truth* in reference to God. Creation never could have brought out what God was. There was infinitely more in Him than power and wisdom: there was love, mercy, holiness, righteousness, goodness, tenderness, long-suffering. Where could these be displayed but in a world of sinners? God, at the first, came down to *create;* and then, when the serpent presumed to meddle with creation, God came down to *save.* This is brought out in the first words uttered by the Lord God after man's fall. "And the Lord God called unto Adam, and said unto him, 'Where art thou?' " This question proved two things,—it proved that man was lost, and that God had come to seek,—it proved man's sin and God's grace. "Where art thou?" Amazing faithfulness! Amazing grace! Faithfulness, to disclose, in the very question itself, the truth as to man's condition: grace, to bring out, in the very fact of God's asking such a question, the truth as to His character and attitude in reference to fallen man. Man was lost; but God had come down to look for him—to bring him out of his hiding-place behind the trees of the garden, in order that, in the happy confidence of faith, he might find a hiding-place in Himself. This was grace. To create man out of the dust of the ground was *power;* but to seek man in his lost estate was *grace.* But who can utter all that is wrapped up in the idea of God's being *a seeker?* God seeking a sinner! What could the blessed One have seen in man to lead Him to seek for him? Just what the shepherd saw in the lost sheep, or what the woman saw in the lost piece of silver, or what the father saw in the lost son. The sinner is valuable to God; but why he should be so, eternity alone will unfold.

How, then, did the sinner reply to the faithful and gracious inquiry of the blessed God? Alas! the reply only reveals the awful depth of evil into which he had fallen. "And he said, 'I heard Thy voice in the garden and I was afraid, because I was naked; and I hid myself.' And He said, 'Who told thee that thou wast naked? Hast thou eaten of the tree whereof I commanded thee that thou shouldest not eat?' And the man said, 'The woman whom *Thou gavest* to be with me, she gave me of the tree, and I did eat.' " Here we find him actually laying the blame of his shameful fall on the circumstances in which God had placed him, and thus, indirectly, upon God Himself. This has ever been the way with fallen man,—every one and everything is blamed but *self.* In the case of true conviction, the very reverse is exhibited. "Is it not *I* that have sinned?" is the inquiry of a truly humbled soul. Had Adam known himself, how different would have been his style! But he neither knew himself nor God, and, therefore, instead of throwing the blame entirely upon himself, he threw it upon God.

Here, then, was man's terrible position. He had lost all. His dominion, his dignity, his happiness, his innocence, his purity, his peace—all was gone from him; and, what was still worse, he accused God of being the cause of it.† There he stood, a lost, ruined, guilty,

*There is a profoundly interesting thought suggested by comparing the word θειοτης (Rom. 1:20) with the word θεοτης (Col. 2:9). They are both rendered "Godhead," but they present a very different thought. The heathen might have seen that there was something superhuman—something divine—in creation; but pure, essential, incomprehensible Deity dwelt in the adorable Person of the Son.

†Man not only accuses God of being the author of his fall, but also blames Him for his non-recovery. How often do we hear persons say that they cannot believe unless God gives them the power to believe; and, further, that unless they are the subjects of God's eternal decree, they cannot be saved.

and yet *self-vindicating,* and therefore *God-accusing* sinner.

But, just at this point, God began to reveal Himself and His purposes of redeeming love; and herein lay the true basis of man's peace and blessedness. When man has come to the end of himself, God can show what He is; but not until then. The scene must be entirely cleared of man and all his vain pretensions, empty boastings and blasphemous reasonings, ere God can or will reveal Himself. Thus it was when man was hidden behind the trees of the garden that God unfolded His wondrous plan of redemption through the instrumentality of the bruised seed of the woman. Here we are taught a valuable principle of truth as to what it is which alone will bring a man peacefully and confidingly into the presence of God.

It has been already remarked that conscience will never effect this. Conscience drove Adam behind the trees of the garden; revelation brought him forth into the presence of God. The consciousness of what he was terrified him; the revelation of what God was tranquilized him. This is truly consolatory for a poor sin-burdened heart. The reality of what I am is met by the reality of what God is; and this is salvation.

There is a point where God and man must meet, whether in grace or judgment, and that point is where both are revealed *as they are.* Happy are they who reach that point in grace! Woe be to them who will have to reach it in judgment! It is with what we are that God deals; and it is as He is that He deals with us. In the cross, I see God descending, in grace, to the lowest depths, not merely of my negative, but my positive condition as a sinner. This gives perfect peace. If God has met me in my actual condition, and Himself provided an adequate remedy, all is eternally settled. But all who do not thus by faith see God in the cross, will have to meet Him by and by in judgment, when He will have to deal, according to what He is, with what they are.

The moment a man is brought to know his real state, he can find no rest until he has found God in the cross, and then he rests in God Himself. He, blessed be His name, is the rest and hiding-place of the believing soul. This at once puts human works and human righteousness in their proper place. We can say, with truth, that those who rest in such things cannot possibly have arrived at the true knowledge of themselves. It is quite impossible that a divinely-quickened conscience can rest in aught save the perfect sacrifice of the Son of God. All effort to establish one's own righteousness must proceed from ignorance of the righteousness of God. Adam might learn, in the light of the divine testimony about "the seed of the woman," the worthlessness of his fig-leaf apron. The magnitude of that which had to be done, proved the sinner's total inability to do it. Sin had to be put away. Could man do that? Nay, it was by him it had come in. The serpent's head had to be bruised. Could man do that? Nay, he had become the serpent's slave. God's claims had to be met. Could man do that? Nay, he had already trampled them under foot. Death had to be abolished. Could man do that? Nay, he had, by sin, introduced it, and imparted to it its terrible sting.

Thus, in whatever way we view the

---

Now, it is perfectly true that no man can believe the gospel except by the power of the Holy Ghost, and it is also true that all who so believe the gospel are the happy subjects of God's eternal counsels; but does all this set aside man's responsibility to believe a plain testimony set before him in God's Word? It most certainly does no such thing. But it does reveal the sad evil of man's heart, which leads him to reject *God's testimony* which is plainly revealed, and to give as a reason for so doing, *God's decree,* which is a profound secret—known only to Himself. However, it will not avail, for we read in 1 Thess. 1:8-9, that those "who obey not the gospel of our Lord Jesus Christ, shall be punished with everlasting destruction."

Men are responsible to believe the gospel, and they will be punished for not believing it. They are not responsible to know anything about God's counsels, inasmuch as they are not revealed, and therefore there can be no guilt attached to ignorance concerning them. The apostle could say to the Thessalonians, "Knowing, brethren beloved, your election of God." How did he know it? Was it by having access to the page of God's secret and eternal decrees? By no means. How then? "Because [ὅτι] our gospel came not unto you in word only, but also in power" (1 Thess. 1:4-5). This is the way to know the election of any. When the gospel comes with power, it is a plain proof of God's election.

But, I doubt not, the people who draw a plea from the divine counsels for rejecting the divine testimony, only want some flimsy excuse to continue in sin. They really do not want God; and it would be far more honest in them to say so plainly, than to put forward a plea which is not merely flimsy, but positively blasphemous. Such a plea will not avail them much amid the terrors of the day of judgment, now fast approaching.

matter, we see the sinner's complete impotency, and, as a consequence, the presumptuous folly of all who attempt to assist God in the stupendous work of redemption, as all assuredly do who think to be saved in any other way but "by grace, through faith."

However, though Adam might, and, through grace, did, see and feel that he could never accomplish all that had to be done, yet God revealed Himself as about to achieve every jot and tittle thereof by the seed of the woman. In short, we see that He graciously took the entire matter into His own hands.

He made it altogether a question between Himself and the serpent; for although the man and the woman were called upon individually to reap, in various ways, the bitter fruits of their sin, yet it was to the serpent that the Lord God said, "Because thou hast done this." The serpent was the source of the ruin, and the seed of the woman was to be the source of the redemption. Adam heard all this and believed it, and, in the power of that belief, "he called his wife's name the mother of *all living.*"

This was a precious fruit of faith in God's revelation. Looking at the matter from nature's point of view, Eve might be called, the mother of all *dying;* but, in the judgment of faith, she was the mother of all *living.* "His mother called him Ben-oni (the son of my sorrow); but his father called him Benjamin (the son of my right hand)."

It was through the sustaining energy of faith that Adam was enabled to endure the terrible results of what he had done. It was God's wondrous mercy to allow him to hear what He said to the serpent, before he was called to listen to what He had to say to himself. Had it not been so, he must have been plunged in despair. It is despair to be called upon to look at myself without being able to look at God as revealed in the cross for my salvation. There is no child of fallen Adam who could bear to have his eyes opened to the reality of what he is and what he has done, without being plunged in despair, unless he could take refuge in the cross. Hence, in that place to which all who reject Christ must finally be consigned, hope cannot come. There, men's eyes will be opened to the reality of what they are and what they have done, but they will not be able to find relief and refuge in God. What God is, will *then* involve hopeless perdition, as truly as what God is doth *now* involve eternal salvation. The holiness of God will then be eternally against them, as it is now that in which all who believe are called to rejoice. The more I realize the holiness of God now, the more I know my security; but in the case of the lost, that very holiness will be but the ratification of their eternal doom. Solemn—unspeakably solemn—reflection!

We shall now briefly glance at the truth presented to us in God's providing coats for Adam and Eve. "Unto Adam, also, and to his wife, did the Lord God make coats of skins, and clothed them." We have here, in figure, the great doctrine of divine righteousness set forth. The robe which God provided was an effectual covering, because He provided it; just as the apron was an ineffectual covering, because man had provided it. Moreover, God's coat was founded upon blood-shedding; Adam's apron was not. So also now, God's righteousness is set forth in the cross; man's righteousness is set forth in the works—the sin-stained works—of his own hands. When Adam stood clothed in the coat of skin he could not say he was naked, nor had he any occasion to hide himself. The sinner may feel perfectly at rest when, by faith, he knows that God has clothed him; but to feel at rest till then, can only be the result of presumption or ignorance. To know that the dress I wear, and in which I appear before God, is of His own providing, must set my heart at perfect rest. There can be no true, permanent rest in aught else.

The closing verses of this chapter are full of instruction. Fallen man, in his fallen state, must not be allowed to eat of the fruit of the tree of life, for that would entail upon him endless wretchedness in this world. To take of the tree of life, and eat, and live forever in our present condition, would be unmingled misery. The tree of life can only be tasted in resurrection. To live forever in a frail tabernacle, in a body of sin and death, would be intolerable. Wherefore, the Lord God "drove out the man." He drove him out into a world which everywhere exhibited the lamentable results of his fall. The cherubim and the flaming sword, too, forbid fallen man to pluck the fruit of the tree of life; while God's revelation pointed him to the death and resurrection of the seed of the woman, as that wherein life was to be found beyond the power of death.

Thus Adam was a happier and a safer man outside the bounds of paradise than he had been within, for this reason: that within, his life depended upon himself; whereas outside, it depended upon another, even a promised Christ. And as he looked up and beheld "the cherubim and the flaming sword," he could bless the hand that had set them there, "to keep the way of the tree of life," inasmuch as the same hand had opened a better, a safer and a happier way to that tree. If the cherubim and flaming sword stopped up the way to paradise, the Lord Jesus Christ has opened "a new and living way" into the holiest of all. "I am the way, the truth and the life; no man cometh unto the Father, but by Me." (Compare John 14:6; Heb. 10:20.) In the knowledge of this, the believer now moves onward through a world which is under the curse—where the traces of sin are visible on all hands. He has found his way, by faith, to the bosom of the Father; and while he can secretly repose there, he is cheered by the blessed assurance that the One who has conducted him thither is gone to prepare a place in the many mansions of the Father's house, and that He will soon come again and receive him unto Himself, amid the glory of the Father's kingdom. Thus, in the bosom, the house and the kingdom of the Father, the believer finds his present portion, his future home and reward.

---

## *CHAPTERS 4—5*

As each section of the book of Genesis opens before us, we are furnished with fresh evidence of the fact that we are traveling over, what a recent writer has well termed, "the seed-plot of the whole Bible"; and not only so, but the seed-plot of man's entire history.

Thus, in the fourth chapter, we have, in the persons of Cain and Abel, the first examples of a religious man of the world and of a genuine man of faith. Born, as they were, outside of Eden, and being the sons of fallen Adam, they could have nothing, naturally, to distinguish them one from the other. They were both sinners,—both had a fallen nature,—neither was innocent. It is well to be clear in reference to this, in order that the reality of divine grace and the integrity of faith may be fully and distinctly seen. If the distinction between Cain and Abel were founded in nature, then it follows, as an inevitable conclusion, that they were not the partakers of the fallen nature of their father, nor the participators in the circumstances of his fall, and hence there could be no room for the display of grace and the exercise of faith.

Some would teach us that every man is born with qualities and capacities which, if rightly used, will enable him to work his way back to God. This is a plain denial of the fact so clearly set forth in the history now before us. Cain and Abel were born, not inside, but outside of paradise,—they were the sons, not of innocent, but of fallen Adam. They came into the world as the partakers of the nature of their father; and it mattered not in what phase that nature might display itself, it was nature still—fallen, ruined, irremediable nature. "That which is born of the flesh is [not merely fleshly, but] flesh, and that which is born of the Spirit is [not merely spiritual, but] spirit" (John 3).

If ever there was a fair opportunity for the distinctive qualities, capacities, resources and tendencies of nature to manifest themselves, the lifetime of Cain and Abel furnished it. If there were aught in nature whereby it could recover its lost innocence and establish itself again within the bounds of Eden, this was the moment for its display. But there was nothing of the kind. They were both *lost.* They were "flesh." They were not innocent. Adam lost his innocence and never regained it. He can only be looked at as the fallen head of a fallen race, who, by his "disobedience," were made "sinners" (Rom. 5:19). He became, so far as he was personally concerned, the corrupt source from whence have emanated the corrupt streams of ruined and guilty humanity—the dead trunk from which have shot forth the branches of a dead humanity, morally and spiritually dead.

True, as we have already remarked, he himself was made a subject of grace, and the possessor and exhibiter of a lively faith in a promised Saviour; but this was not anything natural, but something entirely divine. And, inasmuch as it was not natural, neither was it within the range of nature's capacity to communicate it. It was not, by any means, hereditary. Adam could not bequeath nor impart his faith to Cain or Abel. His possession thereof was simply the fruit of love divine. It was implanted in his soul by divine power, and he had not divine power to communicate it to another. Whatever was natural, Adam could, in the way of nature, communicate; but nothing more. And seeing that he, as a father, was in a condition of ruin, his son could only be in the same. As is the begetter, so are they also that are begotten of him. They must, of necessity, partake of the nature of him from whom they have sprung, "As is the earthy, such are they also that are earthy" (1 Cor. 15:48).

Nothing can be more important, in its way, than a correct understanding of the doctrine of federal headship. If my reader will turn, for a moment, to Rom. 5:12-21, he will find that the inspired apostle looks at the whole human race as comprehended under two heads. I do not attempt to dwell on the passage, but merely refer to it in connection with the subject in hand. The fifteenth chapter of first Corinthians will also furnish instruction of a similar character. In the first man, we have sin, disobedience and death: in the Second Man, we have righteousness, obedience and life. As we derive a nature from the former, so do we also from the latter. No doubt each nature will display, in each specific case its own peculiar energies; it will manifest, in each individual possessor thereof, its own peculiar powers. Still there is the absolute possession of a real, abstract, positive nature.

Now, as the mode in which we derive a nature from the first man is by birth, so the mode in which we derive a nature from the Second Man is by *new* birth. Being born, we partake of the nature of the former; being "born *again*," we partake of the nature of the latter. A newly born infant, though entirely incapable of performing the act which reduced Adam to the condition of a fallen being, is, nevertheless, a partaker of his nature; and so, also, a newly born child of God—a newly regenerated soul, though having nothing whatever to do with the working out of the perfect obedience of "the man Christ Jesus," is, nevertheless, a partaker of His nature. True it is, that attached to the former nature there is sin; and attached to the latter, there is righteousness—man's sin, in the former case; God's righteousness in the latter: yet, all the while, there is the actual, *bona fide* participation of a real nature, let the adjuncts be what they may. The child of Adam partakes of the human nature and its adjuncts; the child of God partakes of the divine nature and its adjuncts. The former nature is according to "the will of man" (John 1), the latter is according to "the will of God,"—as James, by the Holy Ghost, teaches us, "of His own will begat He us by the Word of Truth" (James 1:18).

From all that has been said, it follows, that Abel was not distinguished from his brother Cain by anything natural. The distinction between them was not grounded upon aught in their nature or circumstances, for, as to these, "there was no difference." What, therefore, made the vast difference? The answer is as simple as the gospel of the grace of God can make it. The difference was not in themselves, in their nature or their circumstances; it lay *entirely* in their *sacrifices.* This makes the matter most simple for any truly convicted sinner—for any one who truly feels that he not only partakes of a fallen nature, but is himself, also, a sinner. The history of Abel opens, to such an one, the only true ground of his approach to, his standing before, and his relationship with, God. It teaches him, distinctly, that he cannot come to God on the ground of anything in, of, or pertaining to, nature; and he must seek, *outside himself,* and in the person and work of another, the true and everlasting basis of his connection with the holy, the just and only true God. The eleventh chapter of Hebrews sets the whole subject before us in the most distinct and comprehensive way,—"By faith Abel offered unto God a more excellent sacrifice [πλειονα θυσιαν] than Cain, by which he obtained witness that he was righteous, God bearing witness [μαρτυρουντος] to his gifts; and by it he being dead yet speaketh." Here we are taught that it was in nowise a question as to the men, but only as to their "sacrifice"—it was not a question as to the offerer, but as to his offering. Here lay the grand distinction between Cain and Abel. My reader cannot be too simple in his apprehension of this point, for therein lies involved the truth as to any sinner's standing before God.

And now let us inquire what the offerings were. "And, in process of time, it came to pass that Cain brought, of the fruit of the ground, an offering unto Jehovah. And Abel, he also brought of the firstlings of his flock, and of the fat thereof. And the Lord had respect unto Abel and to his offering; but unto Cain and to his offering He had not respect" (Gen. 4:3-5). This passage sets the difference clearly before us. Cain offered to Jehovah the fruit of a cursed earth, and that, moreover, without any blood to remove the curse. He presented "an unbloody sacrifice," simply because he had no faith. Had he possessed that divine principle, it would have taught him, even at this early moment, that "without shedding of blood there is no remission" (Heb. 9). This is a great cardinal truth. The penalty of sin is death. Cain was a sinner, and, as such, death stood between him and Jehovah; but, in his offering, there was no recognition whatever of this fact,—there was no presentation of a sacrificed life, to meet the claims of divine holiness, or to answer to his own true condition as a sinner. He treated Jehovah as though He were altogether such an one as himself, who could accept the sin-stained fruit of a cursed earth.

All this, and much more, lay involved in Cain's "unbloody sacrifice." He displayed entire ignorance in reference to divine requirements, in reference to his own character and condition as a lost and guilty sinner, and in reference to the true state of that ground, the fruit of which he presumed to offer. No doubt reason might say, What more acceptable offering could a man present than that which he had produced by the labor of his hands and the sweat of his brow? Reason, and even man's religious mind, may think thus, but God thinks quite differently; and faith is always sure to agree with God's thoughts. God teaches, and faith believes, that there must be a sacrificed life, else there can be no approach to God.

Thus, when we look at the ministry of the Lord Jesus, we see, at once, that, had He not died upon the cross, all His services would have proved utterly unavailing as regards the establishment of our relationship with God. True, "He went about doing good" all His life; but it was His death that rent the vail (Matt. 27:51). Naught but His death could have done so. Had He continued to the present moment "going about doing good," the vail would have remained entire, to bar the worshiper's approach into "the holiest of all." Hence we can see the false ground on which Cain stood as an offerer and a worshiper. An unpardoned sinner coming into the presence of Jehovah to present "an unbloody sacrifice," could only be regarded as guilty of the highest degree of presumption. True, he had toiled to produce his offering; but what of that? Could a sinner's toil remove the curse and stain of sin? could it satisfy the claims of an infinitely holy God? could it furnish a proper ground of acceptance for a sinner? could it set aside the penalty which was due to sin? could it rob death of its sting, or the grave of its victory?—could it do any or all of these things? Impossible. "Without shedding of blood is no remission." Cain's "unbloody sacrifice," like every other unbloody sacrifice, was not only worthless, but actually abominable, in the divine estimation. It not only demonstrated his entire ignorance of his own condition, but also of the divine character. "God is not worshiped with men's hands, as though He needed anything"; and yet Cain thought He could be thus approached, and every mere religionist thinks the same. Cain has had many millions of followers, from age to age. Cain-worship had abounded all over the world. It is the worship of every unconverted soul, and is maintained by every false system of religion under the sun.

Man would fain make God a receiver instead of a giver; but this cannot be; for "it is more blessed to give than to receive"; and assuredly God must have the more blessed place. "Without all contradiction, the less is blessed of the better." "Who hath *first* given to Him?" God can accept the smallest gift from a heart which has learnt the deep truth contained in those words—"Of Thine own have we given Thee"; but the moment a man presumes to take the place of the "first" giver, God's reply is, "If I were hungry, I would not tell thee"; for "He is not worshiped with men's hands, as though He *needed anything,* seeing He *giveth* to *all* life and breath and *all* things." The great Giver of "all things" cannot possibly "need anything." Praise is all that we can offer to God; but this can only be offered in the full and clear intelligence that our sins are all put away; and this, again, can only be known by faith in the virtue of an accomplished atonement.

My reader may pause here, and read prayerfully the following Scriptures; namely, Psalm 1; Isaiah 1:11-18, and Acts 17:22-34, in all of which he will find distinctly laid down the truth as to man's true position before God, as also the proper ground of worship.

Let us now consider Abel's sacrifice. "And Abel, he also brought of the firstlings of his flock, and of the fat thereof." In other words, he entered, by faith, into the glorious truth, that God could be approached by sacrifice; that there was such a thing as a sinner's placing the death of another between himself and the consequence of sin; that the claims of God's nature and the attributes of His character could be met by the blood of a spotless victim—a victim offered to meet God's demands and the sinner's deep necessities. This is, in short, the doctrine of the cross, in which alone the conscience of a sinner can find repose, because therein God is fully glorified.

Every divinely convicted sinner must feel that death and judgment are before him, as "the due reward of his deeds"; nor can he, by aught that he can accomplish, alter that destiny. He may toil and labor; he may, by the sweat of his brow, produce an offering; he may make vows and resolutions; he may alter his way of life; he may reform his outward character; he may be temperate, moral, upright, and, in the human acceptation of the word, religious; he may, though entirely destitute of faith, read, pray, and hear sermons. In short, he may do anything or everything which lies within the range of human competency; but, notwithstanding all, "death" and "judgment" are before him. He has not been able to disperse those two heavy clouds which have gathered upon the horizon. There they stand; and, so far from being able to remove them by all his doings, he can only live in the gloomy anticipation of the moment when they shall burst upon his guilty head. It is impossible for a sinner, by his own works, to place himself in life and triumph at the other side of "death" and "judgment"—yea, his very works are only performed for the purpose of preparing him, if possible, for those dreaded realities.

Here, however, is exactly where the cross comes in. In that cross, the convicted sinner can behold a divine provision for all his guilt and all his need. There, too, he can see death and judgment entirely removed from the scene, and life and glory set in their stead. Christ has cleared the prospect of death and judgment, so far as the true believer is concerned, and filled it with life, righteousness and glory. "He hath abolished death, and brought life and incorruptibility to light through the gospel" (2 Tim. 1:10). He has glorified God in the putting away of that which would have separated us forever from His holy and blissful presence. "He has put away sin," and hence it is gone (Heb. 9:26). All this is, in type, set forth in Abel's "more excellent sacrifice." There was no attempt, on Abel's part, to set aside the truth as to his own condition and proper place as a guilty sinner—no attempt to turn aside the edge of the flaming sword, and force his way back to the tree of life—no presumptuous offering of an "unbloody sacrifice"—no presentation of the fruit of a cursed earth to Jehovah—he took the real ground of a sinner, and, as such, set the death of a victim between him and his sins, and between his sins and the holiness of a sin-hating God. This was most simple. Abel deserved death and judgment, but he found a substitute.

Thus is it with every poor, helpless, self-condemned, conscience-smitten sinner. Christ is his substitute, his ransom, his most excellent sacrifice, his *All.* Such an one will feel, like Abel, that the fruit of the ground could never avail for him; that were he to present to God the fairest fruits of earth, he would still have a sin-stained conscience, inasmuch as "without shedding of blood is no remission." The richest fruits and the most fragrant flowers, in the greatest profusion, could not remove a single stain from the conscience. Nothing but the perfect sacrifice of the Son of God can give ease to the heart and conscience. All who by faith lay hold of that divine reality, will enjoy a peace which the world can neither give nor take away. It is faith which puts the soul in present possession of this peace. "Being justified by faith, we have peace with God through our Lord Jesus Christ" (Rom. 5:1). "By faith Abel offered unto God a more excellent sacrifice than Cain."

It is not a question of feeling, as so many would make it: it is entirely a question of faith in an accomplished fact—faith wrought in the soul of a sinner, by the power of the Holy Ghost. This faith is something quite different from a mere feeling of the heart, or an assent of the intellect. Feeling is not faith: intellectual assent is not faith. Some would make faith to be the mere assent of the intellect to a certain proposition. This is fearfully false. It makes the question of faith human, whereas it is really divine,—it reduces it to the level of man, whereas it really comes from God. Faith is not a thing of to-day or to-morrow. It is an imperishable principle, emanating from an eternal source, even God Himself; it lays hold of God's truth, and sets the soul in God's presence.

Mere feeling and sentimentality can never rise above the source from whence they emanate, and that source is self; but faith has to do with God and His eternal Word, and is a living link, connecting the heart that possesses it with God who gives it. Human feelings, however intense; human sentiments, however refined, could not connect the soul with God. They are neither divine nor eternal, but are human and evanescent. They are like Jonah's gourd, which sprang up in a night and perished in a night. Not so faith. That precious principle partakes of all the value, all the power, and all the reality of the source from whence it emanates, and the object with which it has to do. It justifies the soul (Rom. 5:1); it purifies the heart (Acts 15:9); it works by love (Gal. 5:6); it overcomes the world (1 John 5:4). Feeling and sentiment never could accomplish such results; they belong to nature and to earth, faith belongs to God and to heaven; they are occupied with self, faith is occupied with Christ; they look inward and downward, faith looks outward and upward; they leave the soul in darkness and doubt, faith leads it into light and peace; they have to do with one's own fluctuating condition, faith has to do with God's immutable truth and Christ's eternally enduring sacrifice.

No doubt faith will produce feelings and sentiments—spiritual feelings and truthful sentiments—but the fruits of faith must never be confounded with faith itself. I am not justified by feelings, nor yet by faith *and* feelings, but simply by faith. And why? Because faith believes God when He speaks—it takes Him at His word; it apprehends Him as He has revealed Himself in the Person and work of the Lord Jesus Christ. This is life, righteousness and peace. To apprehend God as He is, is the sum of all present and eternal blessedness. When the soul finds out God, it has found out all it can possibly need, here or hereafter; but He can only be known by

His own revelation, and by the faith which He Himself imparts, and which, moreover, always seeks divine revelation as its proper object.

Thus, then, we can, in some measure, enter into the meaning and power of the statement, "By faith Abel offered unto God a more excellent sacrifice than Cain." Cain had no faith, and therefore he offered an unbloody sacrifice: Abel had faith, and therefore he offered both "blood" and "fat," which, in type, set forth the presentation of the life, and also the inherent excellency of the Person of Christ. "The blood" set forth the former; "the fat" shadowed forth the latter. Both blood and fat were forbidden to be eaten, under the Mosaic economy. The blood is the life; and man, under law, had no title to life. But, in the sixth of John, we are taught, that unless we eat blood, we have no life in us. Christ is *the* life. There is not a spark of life outside of Him. All out of Christ is death. "In Him was life," and in none else.

Now, He gave up His life on the cross; and to that life sin was, by imputation, attached, when the blessed One was nailed to the cursed tree. Hence, in giving up His life, He gave up also the sin attached thereto, so that it is effectually put away, having been left in His grave, from which He rose triumphant, in the power of a new life, to which righteousness as distinctly attaches itself as did sin to that life which He gave up on the cross. This will help us to an understanding of an expression used by our blessed Lord after His resurrection,—"A spirit hath not flesh and bones, as ye see Me have." He did not say, flesh and blood; because, in resurrection, He had not assumed into His sacred person the blood which He had shed out upon the cross as an atonement for sin. "The life of the flesh is in the blood, and I have given it to you upon the altar, to make an atonement for your souls: for it is the blood which maketh an atonement for the soul" (Lev. 17:11). Close attention to this point will have the effect of deepening in our souls the sense of the completeness of the putting away of sin by the death of Christ; and we know that whatever tends to deepen our sense of that glorious reality, must necessarily tend to the fuller establishment of our peace, and to the more effectual promotion of the glory of Christ, as connected with our testimony and service.

We have already referred to a point of much interest and value, in the history of Cain and Abel, and that is, the entire identification of each with the offering which he presented. My reader cannot possibly bestow too much attention upon this. The question, in each case, was not as to the person of the offerer, but entirely as to the character of his offering. Hence, of Abel we read that "God testified of his *gifts.*" He did not bear witness to Abel, but to Abel's sacrifice; and this fixes, distinctly, the proper ground of a believer's peace and acceptance before God.

There is a constant tendency in the heart to ground our peace and acceptance upon something in or about ourselves, even though we admit that that something is wrought by the Holy Ghost. Hence arises the constant looking *in,* when the Holy Ghost would ever have us looking *out.* The question for every believer is not, What am I? but, What is Christ? Having come to God "in the name of Jesus," he is wholly identified with Him, and accepted in His name, and, moreover, can no more be rejected than the One in whose name he has come. Before ever a question can be raised as to the feeblest believer, it must be raised as to Christ Himself. But this latter is clearly impossible, and thus the security of the believer is established upon a foundation which nothing can possibly move. Being in himself a poor worthless sinner, he has come in the name of Christ, he is identified with Christ, accepted in and as Christ, bound up in the same bundle of life with Christ. God testifies not of him, but of his gift, and his gift is Christ. All this is most tranquilizing and consolatory. It is our happy privilege to be able, in the confidence of faith, to refer every objection, and every objector, to Christ and His finished atonement. All our springs are in Him: in Him we boast all the day long. Our confidence is not in ourselves, but in Him who hath wrought everything for us. We hang on His name, trust in His work, gaze on His Person, and wait for His coming.

But the carnal mind at once displays its enmity against all this truth which so gladdens and satisfies the heart of a believer. Thus it was with Cain, "He was very wroth, and his countenance fell." That which filled Abel with peace, filled Cain with wrath. Cain, in unbelief, despised the only way in which a sinner could come to God. He refused to offer blood, without which there can be no remission; and then, because *he* was not received, *in his sins,* and because Abel was accepted, *in his gift,* "he was wroth, and his countenance fell." And yet, how else could it be? He should either be received with his sins or without them; but God could not receive him with them, and he would not bring the blood which alone maketh atonement, and therefore he was rejected, and being rejected, he manifests, in his ways, the fruits of corrupt religion. He persecutes and murders the true witness—the accepted, justified man—the man of faith; and, in so doing, he stands as the model and forerunner of all false religionists, in every age. At all times, and in all places, men have shown themselves more ready to persecute on religious grounds than on any other. This is Cain-like. Justification—full, perfect, unqualified justification, by faith only—makes God everything, and man nothing; and man does not like this—it causes his countenance to fall, and draws out his anger. Not that he can give any reason for his anger; for it is not, as we have seen, a question of man at all, but only of the ground on which he appears before God. Had Abel been accepted on the ground of aught in himself, then, indeed, Cain's wrath, and his fallen countenance, would have had some just foundation; but, inasmuch as he was accepted exclusively on the ground of his offering, and inasmuch as it was not to him, but to his gift, that Jehovah bore testimony, his wrath was entirely without any proper basis. This is brought out in Jehovah's word to Cain,—"If thou doest well, (or, as the LXX reads it, "if thou offer correctly [*ορθως προσενεγκης*]") shalt thou not be accepted?" The well-doing had reference to the offering. Abel did well by hiding himself behind an acceptable sacrifice: Cain did badly by bringing an offering without blood; and all his after-conduct was but the legitimate result of his false worship.

"And Cain talked with his brother Abel: and it came to pass, when they were in the field, that Cain rose up against Abel his brother, and slew him." Thus has it ever been,—the Cains have persecuted and murdered the Abels. At all times, man and his religion are the same, faith and its religion are the same; and wherever they have met there has been conflict.

However, it is well to see that Cain's act of murder was the true consequence—the proper fruit—of his false worship. His foundation was bad, and the superstructure erected thereon was also bad. Nor did he stop at the act of murder; but having heard the judgment of God thereon, despairing of forgiveness through ignorance of God, he went forth from His blessed presence and built a city, and had in his family the cultivators of the useful and ornamental sciences—agriculturists, musicians, and workers in metals. Through ignorance of the divine character, he pronounced his sin too great to be pardoned.* It was not that he really knew his sin, but that he knew not God. He fully exhibited the terrible fruit of the fall in the very thought of God to which he gave utterance. He did not want pardon, because he did not want God. He had no true sense of his own condition, no aspirations after God, no intelligence as to the ground of a sinner's approach to God. He was radically corrupt—fundamentally wrong; and all he wanted was to get out of the presence of God, and lose himself in the world and its pursuits. He thought he could live very well without God, and he therefore set about decorating the world as well as he could, for the purpose of making it a respectable place, and himself a respectable man therein, though in God's view it was

*The word used by Cain is מִנְּשׂרֹא which occurs in Psalm 32:1—"whose transgression is *forgiven.*" The LXX renders it by *αφεθηναι*—"to be remitted."

under the curse, and he was a fugitive and a vagabond.

Such was *"the way of Cain,"* in which way millions are, at this moment, rushing on. Such persons are not, by any means, divested of the religious element in their character. They would like to offer something to God—to do something for Him. They deem it right to present to Him the results of their own toil. They are ignorant of themselves, ignorant of God; but with all this there is the diligent effort to improve the world, to make life agreeable in various ways, to deck the scene with the fairest colors. God's remedy to *cleanse* is rejected, and man's effort to *improve* is put in its place. This is "the way of Cain" (Jude 11).

And you have only to look around you to see how this "way" prevails at the present moment. Though the world is stained with the blood of "a greater than" Abel, even with the blood of Christ, yet see what an agreeable place man seeks to make of it! As in Cain's day, the grateful sounds of "the harp and organ," no doubt, completely drowned, to man's ear, the cry of Abel's blood; so now, man's ear is filled with other sounds than those which issue from Calvary, and his eye filled with other objects than a crucified Christ. The resources of his genius, too, are put forth to render this world a hot-house, in which are produced, in their rarest form, all the fruit for which nature so eagerly longs. And not merely are the real wants of man, as a creature, supplied, but the inventive genius of the human mind has been set to work for the purpose of devising things which, the moment the eye sees, the heart desires, and not only desires, but imagines that life would be intolerable without them. Thus, for instance, some years ago, people were content to devote three or four days to the accomplishing of a journey of one hundred miles; but now they can accomplish it in three or four hours; and not only so, but they will complain sadly if they happen to be five or ten minutes late. In fact, man must be saved the trouble of living. He must travel without fatigue, he must hear news without having to exercise patience for it. He will lay iron rails across the earth, and electric wires beneath the sea, as if to anticipate, in his own way, that bright and blissful age, when "there will be no more sea."*

In addition to all this, there is abundance of religion, so called; but, alas! charity itself is compelled to harbor the apprehension that very much of what passes for religion is but a screw in the vast machine which has been constructed for man's convenience and man's exaltation. Man would not be without religion: it would not be respectable; and therefore he is content to devote one-seventh of his time to religion, or, as he thinks and professes, to his eternal interests, and then he has six-sevenths to devote to his temporal interests; but whether he works for time or eternity, it is for *himself,* in reality. Such is "the way of Cain." Let my reader see where this way begins, whither it tends, and where it terminates.

How different the way of the man of faith! Abel felt and owned the curse; he saw the stain of sin, and, in the holy energy of faith, offered that which met it, and met it thoroughly—met it divinely. He sought and found a refuge in God Himself; and instead of building a city on the earth, he found but a grave in its bosom. The earth, which on its surface displayed the genius and energy of Cain and his family, was stained underneath with the blood of a righteous man. Let the man of the world remember this; let the man of God remember it; let the worldly-minded Christian remember it. The earth which we tread upon is stained by the blood of the Son of God. The very blood which justifies the Church condemns the world. The dark shadow of the cross of Jesus may be seen by the eye of faith, looming over all the glitter and glare of this evanescent world. "The fashion of this world passeth away." It will soon all be over, so far as the present scene is concerned. "The way of Cain" will be followed by "the error of Balaam," in its consummated form; and then will come "the gainsaying of Core"; and what then? "The

*True, the Lord is using all those things for the furtherance of His own gracious ends; and the Lord's servant can freely use them also; but this does not hinder our seeing the spirit which originates and characterizes them.

pit" will open its mouth to receive the wicked, and close it again to shut them up in "blackness of darkness forever" (Jude 13).

In full confirmation of the foregoing lines, we may run the eye over the contents of chapter 5, and find therein the humiliating record of man's weakness, and subjection to the rule of death. He might live for hundreds of years, and "beget sons and daughters," but at last it must be recorded that *"he died."* "Death reigned from Adam to Moses." And again, "It is appointed unto men once to die." Man cannot get over this. He cannot, by steam, or electricity, or anything else within the range of his genius, disarm death of its terrible sting. He cannot, by his energy, set aside the sentence of *death,* although he may produce the comforts and luxuries of *life.*

But whence came this strange and dreaded thing—death? St. Paul gives us the answer,—"By one man sin entered into the world, and *death by sin"* (Rom. 5:12). Here we have the origin of death. It came by sin. Sin snapped asunder the link which bound the creature to the living God; and, that being done, he was handed over to the dominion of death, which dominion he had no power whatever to shake off. And this, be it observed, is one of the many proofs of the fact of man's total inability to meet God. There can be no fellowship between God and man, save in the power of life; but man is under the power of death; hence, on natural grounds, there can be no fellowship. Life can have no fellowship with death, no more than light with darkness, or holiness with sin. Man must meet God on an entirely new ground, and on a new principle, even faith; and this faith enables him to recognize his own position as "sold under sin," and therefore subject to death; while, at the same time, it enables him to apprehend God's character, as the dispenser of a new life—life beyond the power of death—a life which can never be touched by the enemy, nor forfeited by us.

This it is which marks the security of the believer's life. Christ is his life—a risen, glorified Christ—a Christ victorious over everything that could be against us. Adam's life was founded upon his own obedience; and, therefore, when he disobeyed, life was forfeited. But Christ, having life in Himself, came down into this world, and fully met all the circumstances of man's sin, in every possible form; and, by submitting to death, destroyed him who had the power thereof, and, in resurrection, becomes the life and righteousness of all who believe in His most excellent name.

Now, it is impossible that Satan can touch this life, either in its source, its channel, its power, its sphere, or its duration. God is its source; a risen Christ, its channel; the Holy Ghost, its power; heaven, its sphere; and eternity, its duration. Hence, therefore, as might be expected, to one possessing this wondrous life, the whole scene is changed; and while, in one sense, it must be said, "in the midst of life we are in death," yet, in another sense, it can be said, "in the midst of death we are in life." There is no death in the sphere into which a risen Christ introduces His people. How could there be? Has not He abolished it? It cannot be an abolished and an existing thing at the same time and to the same people; but God's Word tells us it is abolished. Christ emptied the scene of death, and filled it with life; and therefore it is not death, but glory that lies before the believer. Death is behind him, and behind him forever. As to the future, it is all glory—cloudless glory. True, it may be his lot to "fall asleep"—to "sleep in Jesus"—but that is not death, but "life in earnest." The mere matter of departing to be with Christ cannot alter the specific hope of the believer, which is, to meet Christ in the air, to be with Him and like Him forever.

Of this we have a very beautiful exemplification in Enoch, who forms the only exception to the rule of chapter 5. The rule is, "he died"; the exception is, "he should not see death." "By faith Enoch was translated that he should not see death; and was not found, because God had translated him; for before his translation he had this testimony, that he pleased God" (Heb. 11:5). Enoch was "the seventh from Adam"; and it is deeply interesting to find that death was not suffered to triumph over "the seventh"; but that, in his case, God interfered, and made him a trophy of His own glorious victory over all the power of death. The heart rejoices, after reading, six times, the sad record, "he died," to find that the seventh did not die; and when we ask, How was this? the answer is, "By faith." Enoch lived in the faith of his translation, and walked with God three hundred years. This separated him, practically, from all around. To walk with God must necessarily put one outside the sphere of this world's thoughts. Enoch realized this; for, in his day, the spirit of the world was manifested; and then, too, as now, it was opposed to all that was of God. The man of faith felt he had naught to do with the world, save to be a patient witness therein of the grace of God, and of coming judgment. The sons of Cain might spend their energies in the vain attempt to improve a cursed world, but Enoch found a better world, and lived in the power of it.* His faith was not given him to improve the world, but to walk with God.

And, oh! how much is involved in these three words—"walked with God"! What separation and self-denial! what holiness and moral purity! what grace and gentleness! what humility and tenderness! and yet what zeal and energy! What patience and long-suffering! and yet what faithfulness and uncompromising decision! To walk with God comprehends everything within the range of the divine life, whether active or passive. It involves the knowledge of God's character as He has revealed it. It involves, too, the intelligence of the relationship in which we stand to Him. It is not a mere living by rules and regulations; nor laying down plans of action; nor in resolutions to go hither and thither, to do this or that. To walk with God is far more than any or all of these things. Moreover, it will sometimes carry us right athwart the thoughts of men, and even of our brethren, if they are not themselves walking with God. It may sometimes bring against us the charge of doing too much; at other times, of doing too little; but the faith that enables one to "walk with God," enables him also to attach the proper value to the thoughts of man.

Thus we have, in Abel and Enoch, most valuable instruction as to the sacrifice on which faith rests, and as to the prospect which hope now anticipates; while, at the same time, the "walk with God" takes in all the details of actual life which lie between those two points. "The Lord will give grace and glory"; and between the grace that has been, and the glory that is to be, revealed, there is the happy assurance that "no good thing will He withhold from them that walk uprightly" (Psalm 84:11).

It has been remarked that "the cross and the coming of the Lord form the termini of the Church's existence," and these termini are prefigured in the sacrifice of Abel and the translation of Enoch. The Church knows her entire justification through the death and resurrection of Christ, and she waits for the day when He shall come and receive her to Himself. She, "through the Spirit, waits for the hope of righteousness by faith" (Gal. 5:5). She does not wait for righteousness, inasmuch as she, by grace, has that already; but she waits for the hope which properly belongs to the condition into which she has been introduced.

My reader should seek to be clear as to this. Some expositors of prophetic truth, from not seeing the Church's specific place, portion and hope, have made sad mistakes. They have, in effect, cast so many dark clouds and thick mists around "the bright and morning star," which is the proper hope of the Church, that many saints, at the present moment, seem unable to rise above the hope of the God-fearing remnant of Israel, which is, to see "the Sun of Righteousness arise with healing in His wings" (Mal. 4). Nor is this all. Very many have been deprived of the moral power of the hope of Christ's appearing, by being taught to look for various events and circumstances previous to the moment of His manifestation to the Church. The restoration of the Jews, the development of Nebuchadnezzar's image, the revelation of the man of sin,—all

*It is very evident that Enoch knew nothing whatever about the mode of "making the best of both worlds." To him there was but one world. Thus it should be with us.

these things, it is maintained, must take place ere Christ comes. That this is not true, might be proved from numerous passages of New Testament Scripture, were this the fitting place to adduce them.

The Church, like Enoch, will be taken away from the evil around and the evil to come. Enoch was not left to see the world's evil rise to a head, and the judgment of God poured forth upon it. He saw not "the fountains of the great deep broken up," nor "the windows of heaven opened." He was taken away before any of these things occurred; and he stands before the eye of faith as a beautiful figure of those "who shall not all sleep, but shall all be changed, in a moment, in the twinkling of an eye" (1 Cor. 15:51-52). Translation, not death, was the hope of Enoch; and as to the Church's hope, it is thus briefly expressed by the apostle: "To wait for His Son from heaven" (1 Thess. 1:10). This, the simplest and most unlettered Christian can understand and enjoy. Its power, too, he can, in some measure, experience and manifest. He may not be able to study prophecy very deeply, but he can, blessed be God, taste the blessedness, the reality, the comfort, the power, the elevating and separating virtue, of that celestial hope which properly belongs to him as a member of that heavenly body—the Church; which hope is not merely to see "the Sun of Righteousness," how blessed soever that may be in its place, but to see "the bright and morning star" (Rev. 2:28). And as, in the natural world, the morning star is seen, by those who watch for it, before the sun rises, so Christ, as the morning star, will be seen by the Church before the remnant of Israel can behold the beams of the Sun.

---

## *CHAPTERS 6–9*

WE have now arrived at a deeply-important and strongly-marked division of our book. Enoch has passed off the scene. His walk, as a stranger on earth, has terminated in his translation to heaven. He was taken away before human evil had risen to a head, and, therefore, before the divine judgment had been poured out. How little influence his course and translation had upon the world, is manifest from the first two verses of chapter 6. "And it came to pass, when men began to multiply on the face of the earth, and daughters were born unto them, that the sons of God saw the daughters of men that they were fair; and they took them wives of all which they chose."

The mingling of that which is of God with that which is of man, is a special form of evil, and a very effectual engine, in Satan's hand, for marring the testimony of Christ on the earth. This mingling may frequently wear the appearance of something very desirable; it may often look like a wider promulgation of that which is of God—a fuller and a more vigorous outgoing of a divine influence—a something to be rejoiced in rather than to be deplored; but our judgment as to this will depend entirely upon the point of view from which we contemplate it. If we look at it in the light of God's presence, we cannot possibly imagine that an advantage is gained when the people of God mingle themselves with the children of this world, or when the truth of God is corrupted by human admixture. Such is not the divine method of promulgating truth, or of advancing the interests of those who ought to occupy the place of witnesses for Him on the earth. Separation from all evil is God's principle; and this principle can never be infringed without serious damage to the truth.

In the narrative now before us, we see that the union of the sons of God with the daughters of men led to the most disastrous consequences. True, the fruit of that union seemed exceedingly fair, in man's judgment, as we read, "The same became mighty men, which were of old, men of renown"; yet God's judgment was quite different. He seeth not as man seeth. His thoughts are not as ours. "God saw that the wickedness of man was great in the earth, and that every imagination of the thoughts of his heart was only evil continually." Such was man's condition before God—"evil *only*"—"evil continually." So much for the mingling of the holy with the profane. Thus it must ever be. If the holy seed will not maintain its purity, all must be forfeited, as regards testimony on the earth. Satan's first effort was, to frustrate God's purpose, by putting the holy seed to death; and when that failed, he sought to gain his end by corrupting it.

Now, it is of the deepest moment that my reader should clearly understand the aim, the character, and the result of this union between "the sons of God" and "the daughters of men." There is great danger, at the present day, of compromising truth for the sake of union. This should be carefully guarded against. There can be no true union attained at the expense of truth. The true Christian's motto should ever be, "Maintain truth at all cost; if union can be promoted in this way, so much the better, but maintain the truth." The principle of expediency, on the contrary, may be thus enunciated: "Promote union at all cost; if truth can be maintained as well, so much the better, but promote union." This latter principle can only be carried out at the expense of all that is divine in the way of testimony.* There can, evidently, be no true testimony where truth is forfeited; and hence, in the case of the antediluvian world, we see that the unhallowed union between the holy and the profane—between that which was divine and that which was human, only had the effect of bringing the evil to a head, and then God's judgment was poured out.

"The Lord said, 'I will destroy man.' " Nothing less would do. There must be the entire destruction of that which had corrupted God's way on the earth. "The mighty men, and men of renown," must all be swept away, without distinction. "All flesh" must be set aside, as utterly unfit for God. "The end of *all* flesh is come before Me." It was not merely the end of *some* flesh; no, it was all corrupt in the sight of Jehovah—all irrecoverably bad. It had been tried, and found wanting; and the Lord announced His remedy to Noah in these words,—"Make thee an ark of gopher wood."

Thus was Noah put in possession of God's thoughts about the scene around him. The effect of the Word of God was to lay bare the roots of all that which man's eye might rest upon with complacency and pride. The human heart might swell with pride, and the bosom heave with emotion, as the eye ran down along the brilliant ranks of men of art, men of skill, "men of might," and "men of renown." The sound of the harp and the organ might send a thrill through the whole soul, while, at the same time, the ground was cultivated, and man's necessities were provided for in such a way as to contradict every thought in reference to approaching judgment. But oh, those solemn words, *"I will destroy"!* What a heavy gloom they would necessarily cast over the glittering scene! Could not man's genius invent some way of escape? Could not "the mighty man deliver himself by his much strength"? Alas! no. There was *one* way of escape, but it was revealed to faith, not to sight, not to reason, not to imagination.

"By faith Noah, being *warned of God* of things *not seen* as yet, moved with fear [ευλαβηθεις], prepared an ark to the saving of his house; by the which he condemned the world, and became heir of the righteousness which is by faith" (Heb. 11:7). The Word of God brings His light to shine upon all that by which man's heart is deceived. It removes, completely, the gilding with which the serpent covers a vain, deceitful, passing world, over which hangs the sword of divine judgment. But it is only "faith" that will be "warned of God," when the things of which He speaks are "not seen as yet." Nature is governed by what it sees,—it is governed by its senses. Faith is governed by the pure Word of God (inestimable treasure in this dark world!); this gives stability, let outward appearances be what they may. When God spoke to Noah of judgment impending, there was no sign of it,—it was "not seen as yet"; but the Word of God made it a present reality to the heart that was enabled to mix that Word with faith. Faith does not wait to

*We should ever bear in mind, that "the wisdom which is from above is *first pure* then peaceable" (James 3:17). The wisdom which is from beneath would put "peaceable" first, and therefore it can never be pure.

see a thing ere it believes, for "faith cometh by hearing, and hearing by the Word of God."

All that the man of faith needs, is to know that God has spoken; this imparts perfect certainty to his soul. "Thus saith the Lord," settles everything. A single line of sacred Scripture is an abundant answer to all the reasonings and all the imaginations of the human mind; and when one has the Word of God as the basis of his convictions, he may calmly stand against the full tide of human opinion and prejudice. It was the Word of God which sustained the heart of Noah during his long course of service; and the same Word has sustained the millions of God's saints from that day to this, in the face of the world's contradiction. Hence, we cannot set too high a value upon the Word of God. Without it, all is dark uncertainty; with it, all is light and peace. Where it shines, it marks out for the man of God a sure and blessed path; where it shines not, one is left to wander amid the bewildering mazes of human tradition. How could Noah have "preached righteousness," for one hundred and twenty years, if he had not had the Word of God as the ground of his preaching? How could he have withstood the scoffs and sneers of an infidel world? How could he have persevered in testifying of "judgment to come," when not a cloud appeared on the world's horizon? Impossible. The Word of God was the ground on which he stood, and "the Spirit of Christ" enabled him to occupy, with holy decision, that elevated and immovable ground.

And now, my beloved Christian reader, what else have we wherewith to stand, in service for Christ, in an evil day like the present? Surely, nothing; nor do we want aught else. The Word of God, and the Holy Ghost, by whom *alone* that Word can be understood, applied, or used, are all we want to equip us perfectly—to furnish us thoroughly "to all good works," under whatever head those works may range themselves (2 Tim. 3:16-17). What rest for the heart! What relief from all Satan's imagery, and man's imaginations! God's pure, incorruptible, eternal Word! May our hearts adore Him for the inestimable treasure! "Every imagination of the thoughts of man's heart was only evil continually"; but God's Word was the simple resting-place of Noah's heart.

"God said unto Noah, 'The end of all flesh is come before Me. . . . Make thee an ark of gopher wood.' " Here was man's ruin and God's remedy. Man had been allowed to pursue his career to the utmost limit, to bring his principles and his ways to maturity. The leaven had worked and filled the mass, the evil had reached its climax. "All flesh" had become so bad that it could not be worse; wherefore nothing remained but for God to destroy *it* totally; and, at the same time, to save all those who should be found, according to His eternal counsels, linked with "the eighth person"—the only righteous man then existing. This brings out the doctrine of the cross in a very vivid manner. There we find, at once, God's judgment of nature with all its evil; and, at the same time, the revelation of His saving grace, in all its fullness, and in all its perfect adaptation to those who have really reached the lowest point of their moral condition, as judged by Himself. "The day-spring from on high hath visited us" (Luke 1:78). Where? Just *where we are,* as sinners. God has come down to the very deepest depths of our ruin. There is not a point in all the sinner's state to which the light of that blessed day-spring has not penetrated; but if it has thus penetrated, it must, by virtue of what it is, reveal our true character. The light must judge everything contrary to itself; but, while it does so, it also "gives the knowledge of salvation through the remission of sins." The cross, while it reveals God's judgment upon "all flesh," reveals His salvation for the lost and guilty sinner. Sin is perfectly judged—the sinner perfectly saved—God perfectly revealed, and perfectly glorified, in the cross.

If my reader will turn, for a moment, to the first Epistle of Peter, he will find much light thrown upon this entire subject. At the third chapter, verse 18, we read, "For Christ also hath once suffered for sins, the just for the unjust, that He might bring us to God, being put to death in the flesh, but quickened by the Spirit: by which [Spirit] He went and preached [through Noah] to the spirits [now] in prison; which once were disobedient, when the long-suffering of God waited in the days of Noah, while the ark was being prepared, wherein few, that is, eight souls, were saved through water [*δι υδατος*]; to which the antitype [*αντιτυπον*]; baptism doth also now save us, not the putting away of the filth of the flesh, [as by water,]* but the answer of a good conscience toward God, by the resurrection of Jesus Christ, who, having gone into heaven, is at the right hand of God, angels and authorities and powers being made subject to Him."

This is a most important passage. It sets the doctrine of the ark and its connection with the death of Christ very distinctly before us. As in the deluge, so in the death of Christ, all the billows and waves of divine judgment passed over that which, in itself, was without sin. The creation was buried beneath the flood of Jehovah's righteous wrath; and the Spirit of Christ exclaims, "All Thy billows and Thy waves have gone over Me" (Psalm 42:7). Here is a profound truth for the heart and conscience of a believer. "*All* God's billows and waves" passed over the spotless Person of the Lord Jesus, when He hung upon the cross; and, as a most blessed consequence, not one of them remains to pass over the person of the believer. At Calvary, we see, in good truth, "the fountains of the great deep broken up, and the windows of heaven opened." "Deep calleth unto deep at the noise of Thy waterspouts." Christ drank the cup, and endured the wrath perfectly. He put Himself, judicially, under the full weight of all His people's liabilities, and gloriously discharged them. The belief of this gives settled peace to the soul. If the Lord Jesus has met all that could be against us, if He has removed out of the way every hindrance, if He has put away sin, if He has exhausted the cup of wrath and judgment on our behalf, if He has cleared the prospect of every cloud, should we not enjoy settled peace? Unquestionably. Peace is our unalienable portion. To us belong the deep and untold blessedness, and holy security, which redeeming love can bestow on the righteous ground of Christ's absolutely accomplished work.

Had Noah any anxiety about the billows of divine judgment? None whatever. How could he? He knew that "*all*" had been poured forth, while he himself was raised, by those very outpoured billows, into a region of cloudless peace. He floated in peace on that very water by which "all flesh" was judged. He was put beyond the reach of judgment; and put there, too, by God Himself. He might have said, in the triumphant language of Romans 8, "If God be for us, who can be against us?" He had been invited in by Jehovah Himself, as we read, in chapter 7:1, "Come thou and all thy house into the ark"; and when he had taken his place there, we read, "*the Lord shut him in.*" Here, assuredly, was full and perfect security for all within. Jehovah kept the door, and no one could go in or out without Him. There was both a window and a door to the ark. The Lord secured, with His own omnipotent hand, the door, and left Noah the window from which he might look upward to the place from whence all the judgment had emanated, and see that no judgment remained for him. The saved family could only look *upward,* because the window was "above" (chap. 6:16). They could not see the waters of judgment, nor the death and desolation which those waters

*It is impossible to over-estimate the wisdom of the Holy Ghost, as seen in the way in which He treats the ordinance of baptism, in the above remarkable passage. We know the evil use which has been made of baptism,—we know the false place it has gotten in the thoughts of many,—we know how that the efficacy, which belongs *only* to the blood of Christ, has been attributed to the water of baptism,—we know how the regenerating grace of the Holy Ghost has been transferred to water-baptism; and, with the knowledge of all this, we cannot but be struck with the way in which the Spirit of God guards the subject, by stating that it is not the mere washing away of the filth of the flesh, as by water, "but the answer of a good conscience toward God," which "answer" we get, not by baptism, how important soever it may be as an ordinance of the kingdom, but "by the resurrection of Jesus Christ," "who was delivered for our offences, and raised again for our justification."

Baptism, I need hardly say, as an ordinance of divine institution, and in its divinely-appointed place, is most important and deeply significant; but when we find men, in one way or another, putting the figure in place of the substance, we are bound to expose the work of Satan by the light of the Word of God.

had caused. God's salvation—the "gopher wood," stood between them and all these things. They had only to gaze upward into a cloudless heaven, the eternal dwelling-place of the One who had condemned the world, and saved them.

Nothing can more fully express the believer's perfect security in Christ than those words, "the Lord shut him in." Who could open what God had shut? None. The family of Noah were as safe as God could make them. There was no power—angelic, human, or diabolical—which could possibly burst open the door of the ark, and let the waters in. That door was shut by the self-same hand that had opened the windows of heaven, and broken up the fountains of the great deep. Thus Christ is spoken of as the One "that hath the key of David, He that openeth and no man shutteth, and shutteth and no man openeth" (Rev. 3:7). He also holds in His hand "the keys of hell and of death" (Rev. 1:18). None can enter the portals of the grave, nor go forth therefrom, without Him. He has "all power in heaven and on earth." He is "head over all things to the Church," and in Him the believer is perfectly secure (Matt. 28:18; Eph. 1:22). Who could touch Noah? What wave could penetrate that ark which was "pitched within and without with pitch"? Just so now, who can touch those who have, by faith, retreated into the shadow of the cross? Every enemy has been met and silenced—yes, silenced forever. The death of Christ has triumphantly answered every demur; while, at the same time, His resurrection is the satisfactory declaration of God's infinite complacency in that work which is, at once, the basis of His righteousness in receiving us, and of our confidence in drawing nigh unto Him.

Hence, therefore, the door of our Ark being secured, by the hand of God Himself, nothing remains for us but to enjoy the window; or, in other words, to walk in happy and holy communion with Him who has saved us from coming wrath, and made us heirs and expectants of coming glory. Peter speaks of those who "are blind, and cannot see afar off, and have forgotten that they were purged from their old sins" (2 Peter 1:9). This is a lamentable condition for any to be in, and it is the sure result of not cultivating diligent, prayerful communion with Him who has eternally shut us in in Christ.

Let us, now, ere we proceed further with Noah's history, glance, for a little, at the condition of those to whom he had so long preached righteousness. We have been looking at the *saved,* let us now look at the *lost;* we have been thinking of those *within* the ark, let us now look at those *without.* No doubt, many an anxious look would be cast after the vessel of mercy, as it rose with the water; but, alas! "the door was shut"—the day of grace was over—the time of testimony closed, and that forever, so far as they were concerned. The same hand which had shut Noah *in* had shut them *out,* and it was as impossible for those without to get in as it was for those within to get out. The former were irrecoverably lost; the latter, effectually saved. The long-suffering of God, and the testimony of His servant, had both been slighted. Present things had engrossed them. "They did eat, they drank, they married wives, and were given in marriage, *until* the day that Noah entered into the ark, and the flood came and destroyed them all" (Luke 17:26-27). There was nothing wrong in any of these things, abstractedly looked at. The wrong was not in the things done, but in the doers of them. Every one of them might be done in the fear of the Lord, and to the glory of His holy name, were they only done in faith. But, alas! they were not so done. The Word of God was rejected. He told of judgment, but they did not believe; He spoke of sin and ruin, but they were not convinced; He spoke of a remedy, but they would not give heed. They went on with their own plans and speculations, and had no room for God. They acted as if the earth belonged to them, by a lease, forever. They forgot that there was a clause of surrender. They thought not of that solemn *"until."* God was shut out. "Every imagination of the thoughts of their heart was only evil continually," and hence, they could do nothing right. They thought, spake and acted for themselves. They did their own pleasure, and forgot God.

And remember the words of the Lord Jesus Christ, how He said, *"As it was* in the days of Noah, *so shall it be* in the days of the Son of Man." Some would have us to believe, that ere the Son of Man appears in the clouds of heaven, this earth shall be covered, from pole to pole, with a fair mantle of righteousness. They would teach us to look for a reign of righteousness and peace, as the result of agencies now in operation; but the brief passage just quoted cuts up by the roots, in a moment, all such vain and delusive expectations. How was it in the days of Noah? Did righteousness cover the earth as the waters cover the sea?—was God's truth dominant?—was the earth filled with the knowledge of the Lord? Scripture replies, "The earth was filled with violence." —"All flesh had corrupted His way on the earth."—"The earth also was corrupt before God." Well then, *"so* shall it be in the days of the Son of Man." This is plain enough. "Righteousness" and "violence" are not very much like each other; neither is there any similarity between universal wickedness and universal peace. It only needs a heart subject to the Word, and freed from the influence of preconceived opinions, in order to understand the true character of the days immediately preceding "the coming of the Son of Man." Let not my reader be led astray. Let him reverently bow to Scripture. Let him look at the condition of the world "in the days before the flood"; and let him bear in mind that *"as"* it was then, *"so"* shall it be at the close of this present period. This is most simple—most conclusive. There was nothing like a state of universal righteousness and peace then, neither shall there be anything like it by and by.

No doubt, man displayed abundant energy in making the world a comfortable and an agreeable place for himself; but that was a very different thing from making it a suitable place for God. So, also, at this present time; man is as busy as he can be in clearing the stones off the pathway of human life, and making it as smooth as possible; but this is not "making straight in the desert a highway for our God"; nor is it making "the rough places smooth" that all flesh may see the salvation of Jehovah. Civilization prevails; but civilization is not righteousness. The sweeping and garnishing are going forward; but it is not in order to fit the house for Christ, but for Antichrist. The wisdom of man is put forth in order to cover, with the folds of his own drapery, the blots and blemishes of humanity; but, though covered, they are not removed!—they are underneath, and will, ere long, break out in more hideous deformity than ever. The painting of vermilion will soon be obliterated, and the carved cedar wood destroyed. The dams by which man sedulously seeks to stem the torrent of human wretchedness must soon give way before the overwhelming force thereof. All the efforts to confine the physical, the mental, and the moral degradation of Adam's posterity within those inclosures which human benevolence, if you please, has devised, must, in the sequel, prove abortive. The testimony has gone forth; "The end of *all* flesh has come before Me." It has not come before man, but it has come before God; and, albeit, the voice of the scoffers may be heard, saying, "Where is the promise of His coming? for since the fathers fell asleep, all things continue as they were from the beginning of creation"; yet the moment is rapidly hastening on, when those scoffers will get their answer. "The day of the Lord will come as a thief in the night, in the which the heavens shall pass away with a great noise, and the elements shall melt with fervent heat, the earth also, and the works that are therein, shall be burnt up" (2 Peter 3:4-10). This is the answer to the intellectual scoffs of the children of this world, but not to the spiritual affections and expectations of the children of God. These latter, thank God, have a totally different prospect, even to meet the Bridegroom in the air, before evil shall have reached its culminating point, and therefore before the divine judgment shall be poured forth thereon. The Church of God looks not for the burning up of the world, but for the arising of "the bright and morning Star."

Now, in whatever way we look at the future—from whatever point of view we contemplate it, whether the object which presents itself to the soul's vision be the Church in glory, or the world in flames—the coming of the Bridegroom, or the breaking in of the thief—the morning Star, or the scorching sun—the translation, or the deluge, we must feel the unspeakable importance of attending to God's present testimony in grace to lost sinners. "*Now* is the accepted time; behold, *now* is the day of salvation" (2 Cor. 6:2). "God was in Christ, reconciling the world unto Himself, not imputing their trespasses unto them" (2 Cor. 5:19). He is reconciling now; He will be judging by and by: it is all grace now; it will be all wrath then: He is pardoning sin now, through the cross; He will punish it then, in hell, and that forever. He is sending out a message of purest, richest, freest grace. He is telling sinners of an accomplished redemption through the precious sacrifice of Christ. He is declaring that all is done. He is waiting to be gracious. "The long-suffering of our Lord is salvation." "The Lord is not slack concerning His promise, as some men count slackness, but is long-suffering to usward, not willing that any should perish, but that all should come to repentance" (2 Peter 3). All this makes the present moment one of peculiar solemnity. Unmingled grace declared! unmingled wrath impending! How solemn!—how deeply solemn!

And, then, with what profound interest should we mark the unfolding of the divine purposes! Scripture sheds its light upon these things; and such a light too, that we need not, as another has said, "vacantly stare on passing events, as those who know not where they are and whither they are going." We should accurately know our bearings. We should fully understand the direct tendency of all the principles now at work. We should be well aware of the vortex toward which all the tributary streams are rapidly flowing on. Men dream of a golden age; they promise themselves a millennium of the arts and sciences; they feed upon the thought that "to-morrow shall be as this day, and more abundant." But, oh! how utterly vain are all those thoughts, dreams and promises. Faith can see the clouds gathering thickly around the world's horizon. Judgment is coming, the day of wrath is at hand. The door will soon be shut. The "strong delusion" will soon set in, with terrible intensity. How needful, then, it is to raise a warning voice—to seek, by faithful testimony, to counteract man's pitiable self-complacency. True, in so doing, we shall be exposed to the charge which Ahab brought against Micaiah, of always prophesying evil; but no matter for that. Let us prophesy what the Word of God prophesies, and let us do this simply for the purpose of "persuading men." The Word of God only removes from beneath our feet a hollow foundation, for the purpose of placing instead thereof a foundation which can never be moved. It only takes away from us a delusive hope, to give us, instead, "a hope which maketh not ashamed." It takes away "a broken reed," to give us "the rock of ages." It sets aside "a broken cistern, which can hold no water," to set in its place "the fountain of living waters." This is true love, it is God's love. He will not cry, "peace, peace, when there is no peace," nor "daub with untempered mortar." He would have the sinner's heart resting sweetly in His own eternal Ark of safety, enjoying present communion with Himself, and fondly cherishing the hope, that, when all the ruin, the desolation, and the judgment, have passed away, it shall rest with Him in a restored creation.

We shall now turn to Noah, and contemplate him in a new position. We have seen him building the ark, we have seen him in the ark, and we shall now view him going forth of the ark, and taking his place in the new world.*

*I would here mention, for my reader's prayerful consideration, a thought very familiar to the minds of those who have specially given themselves to the study of what is called "dispensational truth." It has reference to Enoch and Noah. The former was taken away, as we have seen, before the judgment came; whereas the latter was carried through the judgment. Now, it is thought that Enoch is a figure of the Church, who shall be taken away before human evil reaches its climax, and before the divine judgment falls thereon. Noah, on the other hand, is a figure of the remnant of Israel, who shall be brought through the deep waters of affliction, and through the fire of judgment, and led into the full enjoyment of millennial bliss, in virtue of God's everlasting covenant. I may add, that I quite receive this thought in reference to those two Old Testament fathers. I consider that it has the full support of the general scope and analogy of holy Scripture.

"And God remembered Noah." The strange work of judgment being over, the saved family, and all in association with them, come into remembrance. "God made a wind to pass over the earth; and the waters assuaged; the fountains also of the deep and the windows of heaven were stopped, and the rain from heaven was restrained." The beams of the sun now begin to act upon a world that had been baptized with a baptism of judgment. Judgment is God's "strange work." He delights not in, though He is glorified by, it. Blessed be His name, He is ever ready to leave the place of judgment, and enter that of mercy, because He delights in mercy.

"And it came to pass, at the end of forty days, that Noah opened the window of the ark which he had made: and he sent forth a raven, which went forth, to and fro, until the waters were dried up from off the earth." The unclean bird made its escape, and found, no doubt, a resting-place on some floating carcass. It sought not the ark again. Not so the dove; "She found no rest for the sole of her foot, and she returned unto him into the ark . . . and again he sent forth the dove out of the ark: and the dove came in to him in the evening; and, lo, in her mouth was an olive leaf, plucked off." Sweet emblem of the renewed mind, which, amid the surrounding desolation, seeks and finds its rest and portion in Christ; and not only so, but also lays hold of the earnest of the inheritance, and furnishes the blessed proof that judgment has passed away, and that a renewed earth is coming fully into view. The carnal mind, on the contrary, can rest in anything and everything but Christ. It can feed upon all uncleanness. "The olive leaf" has no attraction for it. It can find all it needs in a scene of death, and hence is not occupied with the thought of a new world and its glories; but the heart that is taught and exercised by the Spirit of God, can only rest and rejoice in that in which He rests and rejoices. It rests in the Ark of His salvation "until the times of the restitution of all things." May it be thus with you and me, may Jesus be the abiding rest and portion of our hearts, that so we may not seek them in a world which is under the judgment of God. The dove went back to Noah, and waited for his time of rest: and we should ever find our place with Christ, until the time of His exaltation and glory in the ages to come. "He that shall come will come, and will not tarry." All we want, as to this, is a little patience. May God direct our hearts into His love, and into "the patience of Christ."

"And God spake unto Noah, saying, 'Go forth of the ark.' " The same God that had said, "Make thee an ark," and "Come thou into the ark," now says, "Go forth of the ark." "And Noah went forth . . . and builded an altar unto the Lord." All is simple obedience. There is the obedience of faith and the worship of faith: both go together. The altar is erected where, just before, all had been a scene of death and judgment. The ark had borne Noah and his family safely over the waters of judgment. It had carried him from the old into the new world, where he now takes his place as a worshiper.* And, be it observed, it was "unto the Lord" he erected his altar. Superstition would have worshiped *the ark,* as being the means of salvation. It is ever the tendency of the heart to displace God by His ordinances. Now, the ark was a very marked and manifest ordinance; but Noah's faith passed beyond the ark to the God of the ark; and hence, when he stepped out of it, instead of casting back a lingering look at it, or regarding it as an object of worship or veneration, he built an altar unto the Lord, and worshiped Him; and the ark is never heard of again.

This teaches us a very simple, but, at the same time, a very seasonable lesson. The moment the heart lets slip the reality of God Himself, there is no placing a limit to its declension; it is on the highway to the grossest forms of idolatry. In the judgment of faith, an ordinance is only valuable as it conveys God, in living power, to the soul,—that is to say, so long as faith can enjoy Christ therein, accord-

*It is interesting to look at this entire subject of the ark and deluge, in connection with that most important and deeply significant ordinance of baptism. A truly baptized person, that is, one who, as the apostle says, "obeys from the heart that type of doctrine to which he is delivered," is one who has passed from the old world into the new, in spirit and principle, and by faith. The water rolls over his person, signifying that his old man is buried, that his place in nature is ignored—that his

ing to His own appointment. Beyond this, it is worth just nothing; and if it, in the smallest degree, comes between the heart and His precious work and His glorious Person, it ceases to be an ordinance of God, and becomes an instrument of the devil. In the judgment of superstition, the ordinance is everything, and God is shut out; and the name of God is only made use of to exalt the ordinance, and give it a deep hold of the human heart, and a mighty influence over the human mind. Thus it was that the children of Israel worshiped the brazen serpent. That which had once been a channel of blessing to them, because used of God, became, when their hearts had departed from the Lord, an object of superstitious veneration; and Hezekiah had to break it in pieces, and call it "a piece of brass." In itself, it was only a "Nehushtan," but when used of God, it was a means of rich blessing. Now, faith owned it to be what divine revelation said it was; but superstition, throwing, as it ever does, divine revelation overboard, lost the real purpose of God in the thing, and actually made a god of the thing itself. (See 2 Kings 18:4.)

And is there not a deep lesson in all this for the present age? I am convinced there is. We live in an age of ordinances. The atmosphere which enwraps the professing church, is impregnated with the elements of a traditionary religion, which robs the soul of Christ and His divinely full salvation. It is not that human traditions boldly deny that there is such a person as Christ, or such a thing as the cross of Christ: were they to do so, the eyes of many might be opened. However, it is not thus. The evil is of a far more insidious and dangerous character. Ordinances are added to Christ and the work of Christ. The sinner is not saved by Christ alone, but by Christ and ordinances. Thus he is robbed of Christ altogether; for it will assuredly be found that *Christ and ordinances* will prove, in the sequel, to be *ordinances and not Christ.* This is a solemn consideration for all who stand up for a religion of ordinances. "If ye be circumcised, Christ shall profit you nothing." It must be Christ wholly, or not at all. The devil persuades men that they are honoring Christ when they make much of His ordinances; whereas, all the while, he knows full well that they are, in reality, setting Christ entirely aside, and deifying the ordinance. I would only repeat here a remark which I have made elsewhere, namely, that superstition makes *everything* of the ordinance; infidelity, profanity, and mysticism make *nothing* of it; faith uses it according to divine appointment.

But I have already extended this section far beyond the limit which I had prescribed for it. I shall therefore close it with a hasty glance at the contents of chapter 9. In it we have the new covenant, under which creation was set, after the deluge, together with the token of that covenant. "And God blessed Noah and his sons, and said unto them, 'Be fruitful, and multiply, and replenish the earth.'" Observe, God's command to man, on his entrance into the restored earth, was to re-fill that earth,—not parts of the earth, but the earth. He desired to have men dispersed abroad, over the face of the world, and not relying upon their own concentrated energies. We shall see, in chapter 11, how man neglected all this.

The fear of man is now lodged in the heart of every other creature. Henceforth, the service rendered by the inferior orders of

---

old nature is entirely set aside—in short, that he is a dead man. When he is plunged beneath the water, expression is given to the fact that his name, place and existence in nature are put out of sight,—that the flesh, with all that pertained thereto—its sins, its iniquities, its liabilities—is buried in the grave of Christ, and never can come into God's sight again.

Again, when he rises up out of the water, expression is given to the truth, that he only comes up as the possessor of a new life, even the resurrection-life of Christ. If Christ had not been raised from the dead, the believer could not come up out of the water, but should remain buried beneath its surface, as the simple expression of the place which righteously belongs to nature. But, inasmuch as Christ rose from the dead, in the power of a new life, having entirely put away our sins, we also come up out of the water; and, in so doing, set forth the fact that we are put, by the grace of God, and through the death of Christ, in full possession of a new life, to which divine righteousness inseparably attaches. "We are buried with Him by baptism into death; that like as Christ was raised from the dead by the glory of the Father, even so we also should walk in newness of life." (See Rom. 6 and Col. 2, *passim.* Comp. also 1 Peter 3:18-22.) All this makes the institution of baptism one of immense importance, and pregnant with meaning.

creation to man, must be the constrained result of "fear and dread."

In life and in death, the lower animals were to be at the service of man. All creation is delivered, by God's everlasting covenant, from the fear of a second deluge. Judgment is never again to take that shape. "The world that then was, being overflowed with *water,* perished; but the heavens and the earth, which are now, by the same word are kept in store, reserved unto *fire* against the day of judgment and perdition of ungodly men." The earth was once purged with water; and it will be again purged by fire; and in this second purgation none will escape, save those who have fled for refuge to Him who has passed through the deep waters of death, and met the fire of divine judgment.

"And God said, 'This is the token of the covenant. . . . I do set My bow in the cloud . . . and I will remember My covenant.' " The whole creation rests, as to its exemption from a second deluge, on the eternal stability of God's covenant, of which the bow is the token; and it is happy to bear in mind, that when the bow appears, the eye of God rests upon it; and man is cast not upon his own imperfect and most uncertain memory, but upon God's. "I," says God, "will remember." How sweet to think of what God will, and what He will not, remember! He will remember His covenant, but He will not remember His people's sins. The cross, which ratifies the former, puts away the latter. The belief of this gives peace to the troubled heart and uneasy conscience.

"And it shall come to pass, when I bring a cloud over the earth, that *the bow shall be seen in the cloud.*" Beautiful and most expressive emblem! The beams of the sun, reflected from that which threatens judgment, tranquilize the heart, as telling of God's covenant, God's salvation, and God's remembrance. Precious, most precious sunbeams! deriving additional beauty from the very cloud which reflects them. How forcibly does this bow in the cloud remind us of Calvary. There we see a cloud indeed—a dark, thick, heavy cloud of judgment, discharging itself upon the sacred head of the Lamb of God—a cloud so dark, that even at midday "there was darkness over all the earth." But, blessed be God, faith discerns, in that heaviest cloud that ever gathered, the most brilliant and beauteous bow that ever appeared; for it sees the bright beams of God's eternal love darting through the awful gloom and reflected in the cloud. It hears, too, the words, "It is finished," issuing from amid the darkness; and in those words it recognizes the perfect ratification of God's everlasting covenant, not only with creation, but with the tribes of Israel and the Church of God.

The last paragraph of this chapter presents a humiliating spectacle. The lord of creation fails to govern himself: "And Noah began to be a husbandman, and he planted a vineyard; and he drank of the wine, and was drunken; and he was uncovered within his tent." What a condition for Noah, the only righteous man, the preacher of righteousness, to be found in! Alas! what is man? Look at him where you will, and you see only failure. In Eden, he fails; in the restored earth, he fails; in Canaan, he fails; in the Church, he fails; in the presence of millennial bliss and glory, he fails; he fails everywhere, and in all things: there is no good thing in him. Let his advantages be ever so great, his privileges ever so vast, his position ever so desirable, he can only exhibit failure and sin.

We must, however, look at Noah in two ways, namely, as *a type,* and as *a man;* and while the type is full of beauty and meaning, the man is full of sin and folly; yet the Holy Ghost has written these words: "Noah was a just man, and perfect in his generation; and Noah walked with God." Divine grace had covered all his sins, and clothed his person with a spotless robe of righteousness. Though Noah exposed his nakedness, God did not see it, for He looked not at him in the weakness of his own condition, but in the full power of divine and everlasting righteousness. Hence we may see how entirely astray—how totally alienated from God and His thoughts—Ham was, in the course he adopted; he evidently knew nothing of the blessedness of the man whose iniquity is forgiven, and his sin covered. On the contrary, Shem and Japheth exhibit, in their conduct, a fine specimen of the divine method of dealing with human nakedness; wherefore they inherit a blessing, whereas Ham inherits a curse.

---

## *CHAPTER 10*

THIS section of our book records the generations of Noah's three sons, noticing, especially, Nimrod, the founder of the kingdom of Babel, or Babylon, a name which occupies a very prominent place on the page of inspiration. Babylon is a well-known name—a well-known influence. From the tenth chapter of Genesis, down to the eighteenth chapter of Revelation, Babylon again and again appears before us, and always as something decidedly hostile to those who occupy, for the time being, the position of public testimony for God. Not that we are to look upon the Babylon of the Old Testament Scripture as identical with the Babylon of the Apocalypse. By no means. I believe the former is a city; the latter, a system; but both the city and the system exert a powerful influence against God's people. Hardly had Israel entered upon the wars of Canaan, when "a Babylonish garment" brought defilement and sorrow, defeat and confusion, into the host. This is the earliest record of Babylon's pernicious influence upon the people of God; but every student of Scripture is aware of the place which Babylon gets throughout the entire history of Israel.

This would not be the place to notice, in detail, the various passages in which this city is introduced. I would only remark here, that whenever God has a corporate witness on the earth, Satan has a Babylon to mar and corrupt that witness. When God connects His name with a city on the earth, then Babylon takes the form of a city; and when God connects His name with the Church, then Babylon takes the form of a corrupt religious system, called "the great whore," "the mother of abominations," etc. In a word, Satan's Babylon is always seen as the instrument moulded and fashioned by his hand, for the purpose of counteracting the divine operations, whether in Israel of old, or the Church now. Throughout the Old Testament, Israel and Babylon are seen, as it were, in opposite scales,—when Israel is up, Babylon is down; and when Babylon is up, Israel is down. Thus, when Israel had utterly failed as Jehovah's witness, "the king of Babylon broke his bones," and swallowed him up. The vessels of the house of God, which ought to have remained in the *city* of Jerusalem, were carried away to the *city* of Babylon. But Isaiah, in his sublime prophecy, leads us onward to the opposite of all this. He presents, in most magnificent strains, a picture, in which Israel's star is in the ascendant, and Babylon entirely sunk.—"And it shall come to pass in the day that the Lord shall give thee rest from thy sorrow, and from thy fear, and from the hard bondage wherein thou wast made to serve, that thou shalt take up this proverb against the king of Babylon, and say, How hath the oppressors ceased! the golden city ceased! . . . since *thou* art laid down, no feller is come up against *us*" (Isaiah 14:3-8).

Thus much as to the Babylon of the Old Testament. Then, as to the Babylon of Revelation, my reader has only to turn to the seventeenth and eighteenth chapters of that book to see her character and end. She is presented in marked contrast with the bride, the Lamb's wife; and as to her end, she is cast as a great millstone into the sea; after which we have the marriage of the Lamb, with all its accompanying bliss and glory.

However, I could not attempt to pursue this most interesting subject here: I have merely glanced at it in connection with the name of Nimrod. I feel assured that my reader will find himself amply repaid for any trouble he may take in the close examination of all those Scriptures in which the name of Babylon is introduced. We shall now return to our chapter.

And Cush begat Nimrod: he began to be *a mighty one in the earth.* He was a mighty hunter before the Lord: wherefore it is said, 'Even as Nimrod, the mighty hunter before the Lord.' And the beginning of his kingdom was Babel, and Erech, and Accad, and Calneh, *in the land of Shinar.*" Here, then, we have the character of the founder of Babylon. He was "a mighty one *in the earth*"— "a mighty hunter before the Lord." Such was the origin of Babylon; and its character, throughout the entire book of God, remarkably corresponds therewith. It is always seen as a mighty influence in the earth, acting in positive antagonism to everything which owes its origin to heaven; and it is not until this Babylon has been totally abolished that the cry is heard, amid the hosts above, "Alleluia! for the Lord God omnipotent reigneth." Then, all Babylon's mighty hunting will be over forever,—whether it be its hunting of wild beasts to subdue them, or its hunting of souls to destroy them. All its might and all its glory, all its pomp and pride, its wealth and luxury, its light and joy, its glitter and glare, its powerful attractions and wide-spread influence, shall have passed away forever. She shall be swept with the besom of destruction, and plunged in the darkness, the horror and desolation, of an everlasting night. "How long, O Lord?"

---

## *CHAPTER 11*

THIS is a chapter of very deep interest to the spiritual mind. It records two great facts, namely, the building of Babel, and the call of Abraham; or, in other words, man's effort to provide for himself, and God's provision made known to faith,—man's attempt to establish himself *in the earth,* and God's calling a man *out of* it, to find his portion and his home *in heaven.*

"And the whole earth was of one language and of one speech. And it came to pass, as they journeyed from the east, that they found a plain in the land of Shinar; and they dwelt there. . . . And they said, 'Go to, let us build us a city, and a tower whose top may reach unto heaven; and let us make us a name, lest we be scattered abroad upon the face of the whole earth.' " The human heart ever seeks a name, a portion, and a centre in the earth. It knows nothing of aspirations after heaven, heaven's God, or heaven's glory. Left to itself, it will ever find its objects in this lower world; it will ever "build beneath the skies." It needs God's call, God's revelation, and God's power, to lift the heart of man above this present world, for man is a groveling creature—alienated from heaven, and allied to earth. In the scene now before us, there is no acknowledgment of God, no looking up to, or waiting on, Him; nor was it the thought of the human heart to set up a place in which God might dwell—to gather materials for the purpose of building a habitation for Him—alas! no; His name is never once mentioned. To make a name for himself was man's object on the plain of Shinar; and such has been his object ever since. Whether we contemplate man on the plain of Shinar, or on the banks of the Tiber, we find him to be the same self-seeking, self-exalting, God-excluding creature throughout. There is a melancholy consistency in all his purposes, his principles and his ways,—he ever seeks to shut out God and exalt himself.

Now, in what light soever we view this Babel confederacy, it is most instructive to see in it the early display of man's genius and energies, regardless of God. In looking down along the stream of human history, we may easily perceive a marked tendency to confederacy, or association. Man seeks, for the most part, to compass his great ends in this way. Whether it be in the way of philanthropy, religion, or politics, nothing can be done without an association of men regularly organized. It is well to see this principle; well to mark its incipient working—to see the earliest model which the page of inspiration affords of a human association, as exhibited on the plain of Shinar, in its design, its object, its attempt, its overthrow. If we look around us at the present moment, we see the whole scene filled with associations. To name them were useless, for they are as numerous as are the purposes of the human heart. But it is important to mark, that the first of all these was the Shinar association, for the establishment of the human interests, and the exaltation of the human name,—objects which may well be set in competition with any that engage the attention of this enlightened and civilized age. But, in the judgment of faith, there is one grand defect, namely, God is shut out; and to attempt to exalt man without God, is to exalt him to a dizzy height, only that he may be dashed down into hopeless confusion and irretrievable ruin. The Christian should only know *one* association, and that is, the Church of the living God, incorporated by the Holy Ghost, who came down from heaven as the witness of Christ's glorification, to baptize believers into one body, and constitute them God's dwelling-place. Babylon is the very opposite of this, in every particular; and she becomes at the close, as we know, "the habitation of devils. (See Rev. 18.)

"And the Lord said, 'Behold, the people is one, and they have all one language; and this they begin to do: and now nothing will be restrained from them, which they have imagined to do. Go to, let us go down, and there confound their language, that they may not understand one another's speech.' So the Lord scattered them abroad from thence upon the face of all the earth; and they left off to build the city." Such was the end of man's first association. Thus it will be to the end. "Associate yourselves, O ye people, and ye shall be broken in pieces. . . . Gird yourselves, and ye shall be broken in pieces; gird yourselves, and ye shall be broken in pieces" (Isaiah 8:9). How different it is when God associates men! In the second chapter of Acts, we see the blessed One coming down, in infinite grace, to meet man, in the very circumstances in which his sin had set him. The Holy Ghost enabled the messengers of grace to deliver their message in the very tongue wherein each was born. Precious proof this, that God desired to reach man's heart with the sweet story of grace! The law from the fiery mount was not thus promulgated. When God was telling what man ought to be, He spoke in one tongue; but when He was telling what He Himself was, He spoke in many. Grace broke through the barrier which man's pride and folly had caused to be erected, in order that every man might hear and understand the glad tidings of salvation—"the wonderful works of God." And to what end was this? Just to associate men on God's ground, round God's centre, and on God's principles. It was to give them, in reality, one language, one centre, one object, one hope, one life. It was to gather them in such a way as that they never should be scattered or confounded again; to give them a name and a place which should endure forever; to build for them a tower and a city which should not only have their top reaching *to* heaven, but their imperishable foundation laid *in* heaven by the omnipotent hand of God Himself. It was to gather them around the glorious Person of a risen and highly exalted Christ, and unite them all in one grand design of magnifying and adoring Him.

If my reader will turn to the seventh chapter of Revelation, he will find, at the close thereof, "All nations, and kindreds, and people, and tongues," standing round the Lamb, and, with one voice, ascribing all praise to Him. Thus the three Scriptures may be read in most interesting and profitable connection. In Genesis 11, God gives various tongues as an expression of His *judgment;* in Acts 2, He gives various tongues as an expression of *grace;* and in Rev. 7, we see all those tongues gathered round the Lamb *in glory.* How much better it is, therefore, to find our place in God's association than in man's! The former ends in glory, the latter in confusion; the former is carried forward by the energy of the Holy Ghost, the latter by the unhallowed energy of fallen man; the former has for its object the exaltation of Christ, the latter has for its object the exaltation of man, in some way or other.

Finally, I would say, that all who sincerely desire to know the true character, object and issue of human associations, should read the opening verses of Genesis 11; and, on the other hand, all who desire to know the excellency, the beauty, the power, the enduring character of divine association, should look at that holy, living, heavenly corporation, which is called, in the New Testament, the Church of the living God—

the body of Christ—the bride of the Lamb.

May the Lord enable us to look at and apprehend all these things, in the power of faith; for only in this way can they profit our souls. Points of truth however interesting, scriptural knowledge however profound and extensive, Biblical criticism however accurate and valuable, may all leave the heart barren and the affections cold. We want to find Christ in the Word; and, having found Him, to feed on Him by faith. This would impart freshness, unction, power, vitality, energy and intensity, all of which we deeply stand in need of in this day of freezing formalism. What is the value of a chilling orthodoxy without a living Christ, known in all His powerful, personal attractions? No doubt, sound doctrine is immensely important,—every faithful servant of Christ will feel himself imperatively called upon to "hold fast the form of sound words";—but, after all, a living Christ is the very soul and life—the joints and marrow—the sinews and arteries—the essence and substance of sound doctrine. May we, by the power of the Holy Ghost, see more beauty and preciousness in Christ, and thus be weaned from the spirit and principles of Babylon.

We shall, God willing, consider the remainder of chapter 11 in the next section.

---

## *CHAPTER 12*

THE book of Genesis is, for the most part, taken up with the history of seven men, namely, Abel, Enoch, Noah, Abraham, Isaac, Jacob and Joseph. There is, I doubt not, a specific line of truth brought out in connection with each of those men. Thus, for example, in Abel we have the great foundation-truth of man's coming to God, in the way of atonement—atonement apprehended by faith. In Enoch, we have the proper portion and hope of the heavenly family; while Noah presents to us the destiny of the earthly family. Enoch was taken to heaven before the judgment came; Noah was carried through the judgment into a restored earth. Thus, in each, we have a distinct character of truth, and, as a consequence, a distinct phase of faith. My reader can pursue the subject fully in connection with the eleventh of Hebrews; and I feel assured he will find much interest and profit in so doing. We shall now proceed with our immediate theme, namely, the call of Abraham.

By comparing chapter 12:1, chapter 11:31, with Acts 7:2-4, we learn a truth of immense practical value to the soul. "The Lord *had* said unto Abram, 'Get thee out of thy country, and *from thy kindred,* and from thy father's house, unto a land that I will show thee' " (chap. 12:1). Such was the communication made to Abraham—a communication of the most definite character, designed of God to act upon Abraham's heart and conscience. "The God of glory appeared unto our father Abraham, when he was in Mesopotamia, before he dwelt in Charran, and said unto him, 'Get thee out of thy country, and from thy kindred, and come into a land that I shall show thee.' Then went he forth out of the land of the Chaldeans, and dwelt in Charran (or Haran); and from thence, *when his father was dead*, he removed him into this land wherein ye now dwell" (Acts 7:2-4). The result of this communication is given in chapter 11:31: "And Terah took Abram his son, and Lot the son of Haran, his son's son, and Sarai his daughter-in-law, his son Abram's wife; and they went forth with them from Ur of the Chaldees, *to go into the land of Canaan:* and they came *unto Haran, and dwelt there* . . . and Terah died in Haran."

From all these passages taken together, we learn that the ties of nature hindered the full response of Abraham's soul to the call of God. Though called to Canaan, he nevertheless tarried at Haran till nature's tie was snapped by death, and then, with unimpeded step, he made his way to the place to which "the God of glory" had called him. This is full of meaning. The influences of nature are ever hostile to the full realization and practical power of "the calling of God." We are sadly prone to take lower ground than that which the divine call would set before us. It needs great simplicity and integrity of faith to enable the soul to rise to the height of God's thoughts, and to make our own of that which He reveals.

The apostle's prayer (Eph. 1:15-22) demonstrates how fully he, by the Holy Ghost, entered into the difficulty with which the Church would ever have to contend, in seeking to apprehend "the hope of *God's calling*, and the riches of the glory of *His* inheritance in the saints;" because, evidently, if we fail to apprehend the calling, we cannot "walk worthy" thereof. I must know where I am called to go, before I can go thither. Had Abraham's soul been fully under the power of the truth that "God's calling" was to Canaan, and that there, too, lay "his inheritance," he could not have remained in Charran. And so with us. If we are led by the Holy Ghost into the understanding of the truth, that we are called with a heavenly calling, that our home, our portion, our hope, our inheritance, are all above, "where Christ sitteth at God's right hand," we could never be satisfied to maintain a standing, seek a name, or lay up an inheritance, on the earth. The two things are incompatible: this is the true way to look at the matter. The heavenly calling is not an empty dogma, a powerless theory, nor a crude speculation. It is either a divine reality, or it is absolutely nothing. Was Abraham's call to Canaan a speculation? Was it a mere theory about which he might talk or argue, while, at the same time, he continued in Charran? Assuredly not. It was a truth—a divine truth—a powerfully practical truth. He was called to Canaan, and God could not possibly sanction his stopping short thereof. Thus it was with Abraham, and thus it is with us. If we would enjoy the divine sanction and the divine presence, we must be seeking, by faith, to act upon the divine call. That is to say, we must seek to reach, in experience, in practice, and moral character, the point to which God has called us, and that point is, full fellowship with His own Son—fellowship with Him in His rejection below, fellowship with Him in His acceptance above.

But as, in Abraham's case, it was death that broke the link by which nature bound him to Charran, so, in our case, it is death which breaks the link by which nature ties us down to this present world. We must realize the truth that we have died in Christ, our Head and Representative,—that our place in nature, and in the world, is amongst the things that were,—that the cross of Christ is to us what the Red Sea was to Israel, namely, that which separates us forever from the land of death and judgment. Thus only shall we be able to walk, in any measure, "worthy of the calling wherewith we are called"—our high, our holy, our heavenly calling—our "calling of God in Christ Jesus."

And here I would dwell, for a little, on the cross of Christ, in its two grand, fundamental phases; or, in other words, the cross as the basis of our worship and our discipleship, our peace and our testimony, our relation with God and our relation with the world. If, as a convicted sinner, I look at the cross of the Lord Jesus Christ, I behold in it the everlasting foundation of my peace. I see my "sin" put away, as to the root or principle thereof, and I see my "sins" borne. I see God to be, in very deed, "for me," and that, moreover, in the very condition in which my convicted conscience tells me I am. The cross unfolds God as the *sinner's* Friend,—it reveals Him in that most wondrous character, as the Righteous Justifier of the most ungodly sinner. Creation never could do this: providence never could do this. Therein I may see God's power, His majesty, and His wisdom: but what if all these things should be ranged against me? Looked at in themselves, abstractedly, they would be so, for I am a sinner; and power, majesty, and wisdom, could not put away my sin, nor justify God in receiving me.

The introduction of the cross, however, changes the aspect of things entirely. There I find God dealing with sin in such a manner as to glorify Himself infinitely. There I see the magnificent display and perfect harmony of all the divine attributes. I see love, and such love as captivates and assures my heart, and weans it, in proportion as I realize it, from every other object. I see wisdom, and such wisdom as baffles devils and astonishes angels. I see power, and such power as bears down all opposition. I see holiness, and such holiness as repulses sin to the very furthest point of the moral universe, and gives the most intense expression of God's abhorrence thereof that could possibly be given. I see grace, and such grace as sets the sinner in the very presence of God—yea, puts him into His bosom. Where could I see all these things but in the cross? Nowhere else. Look where you please, and you cannot find aught that so blessedly combines those two great points, namely, "glory to God in the highest," and "on earth peace."

How precious, therefore, is the cross, in this its first phase, as the basis of the sinner's peace, the basis of his worship, and the basis of his eternal relationship with the God who is there so blessedly and so gloriously revealed? How precious to God, as furnishing Him with a righteous ground on which to go in the full display of all His matchless perfections, and in His most gracious dealings with the sinner! So precious is it to God, that, as a recent writer has well remarked, "All that He has said—all that He has done, from the very beginning, indicates that it was ever uppermost in His heart. And no wonder! His dear and well-beloved Son was to hang there, between heaven and earth, the object of all the shame and suffering that men and devils could heap upon Him, because He loved to do His Father's will, and redeem the children of His grace. It will be the grand centre of attraction, as the fullest expression of His love, throughout eternity."

Then, as the basis of our practical discipleship and testimony, the cross demands our most profound consideration. In this aspect of it, I need hardly say, it is as perfect as in the former. The same cross which connects me with God, has separated me from the world. A dead man is, evidently, done with the world; and hence, the believer, having died in Christ, is done with the world; and, having risen with Christ, is connected with God, in the power of a new life—a new nature. Being thus inseparably linked with Christ, he, of necessity, participates in His acceptance with God, and in His rejection by the world. The two things go together. The former makes him a worshiper and a citizen in heaven, the latter makes him a witness and a stranger on earth. That brings him inside the veil: this puts him outside the camp. The one is as perfect as the other. If the cross has come between me and my sins, it has just as really come between me and the world. In the former case, it puts me into the place of peace with God; in the latter, it puts me into the place of hostility with the world, *i.e.*, in a moral point of view; though, in another sense, it makes me the patient, humble witness of that precious, unfathomable, eternal grace which is set forth in the cross.

Now the believer should clearly understand, and rightly distinguish between, both the above phases of the cross of Christ. He should not profess to enjoy the one, while he refuses to enter into the other. If his ear is open to hear Christ's voice within the vail, it should be open also to hear His voice outside the camp; if he enters into the atonement which the cross has accomplished, he should also realize the rejection which it necessarily involves. The former flows out of the part which God had in the cross; the latter, out of the part which man had therein. It is our happy privilege not only to be done with our sins, but to be done with the world also. All this is involved in the doctrine of the cross. Well, therefore, might the apostle say, "God forbid that I should glory, save in the cross of our Lord Jesus Christ, by which the world is crucified unto me, and I unto the world." Paul looked upon the world as a thing which ought to be nailed to the cross; and the world, in having crucified Christ, had crucified all who belonged to Him. Hence there is a double crucifixion, as regards the believer and the world; and were this fully entered into, it would prove the utter impossibility of ever amalgamating the two. Let us deeply, honestly, and prayerfully ponder these things; and may the Holy Ghost give us the ability to enter into the full practical power of both the phases of the cross of Christ.

We shall now return to our theme.

We are not told how long Abraham tarried at Haran; yet God graciously waited on His servant until, freed from nature's clog, he could fully obey His command. There was, however, no accommodation of that command to the circumstances of nature. This would never do. God loves His servants too well to deprive them of the full blessedness of entire obedience. There was no fresh revelation to Abraham's soul during the time of his sojourn in Haran. It is well to see this. We must act up to the light already communicated, and then God will give us more. "To him that hath shall more be given,"—this is God's principle. Still, we must remember that God will never *drag* us along the path of true-hearted discipleship. This would greatly lack the moral excellency which characterizes all the ways of God. He does not *drag*, but *draw*, us along the path which leads to ineffable blessedness in Himself; and if we do not see that it is for our real advantage to break through all the barriers of nature, in order to respond to God's call, we forsake our own mercies. But, alas! our hearts little enter into this. We begin to calculate about the sacrifices, the hindrances, and the difficulties, instead of bounding along the path, in eagerness of soul, as knowing and loving the One whose call has sounded in our ears.

There is much true blessing to the soul in every step of obedience; for obedience is the fruit of faith, and faith puts us into living association and communion with God Himself. Looking at obedience in this light, we can easily see how distinctly it is marked off, in every feature of it, from legality. This latter sets a man, with the entire burden of his sins on him, to serve God by keeping the law; hence, the soul is kept in constant torture, and, so far from running in the path of obedience, it has not even taken the very first step. True obedience, on the contrary, is simply the manifestation or outflow of a new nature, communicated in grace. To this new nature God graciously imparts precepts for its guidance; and it is perfectly certain that the divine nature, guided by the divine precepts, can never, by any possibility, resolve itself into legality. What constitutes legality, is, the old nature taking up God's precepts and assaying to carry them out. To attempt to regulate man's fallen nature, by God's pure and holy law, is as useless and absurd as anything can be. How could fallen nature breathe an atmosphere so pure? Impossible. Both the atmosphere and the nature must be divine.

But not only does the blessed God impart a divine nature to the believer, and guide that nature by His heavenly precepts, He also sets before it suited hopes and expectations. Thus, in Abraham's case, "*the God of glory* appeared unto him." And for what purpose? To set before his soul's vision an attractive object—"a land that *I* will show thee." This was not compulsion, but attraction. God's land was, in the judgment of the new nature—the judgment of faith—far better than Ur, or Charran: and albeit, he had not *seen* the land, yet, inasmuch as it was God's land, faith judged it to be worth having, and not only worth having, but also fully worth the surrender of present things. Hence, we read, "by faith Abraham, when he was called to go out into a place which he should after receive as an inheritance, obeyed; and he went out, not knowing whither he went." That is to say, "he walked by faith, not by sight." Though he had not seen with his eyes, he believed with his heart, and faith became the great moving spring in his soul. Faith rests on a far more solid ground than the evidence of our senses, and that is, the Word of God. Our senses may deceive us, but God's Word never can.

Now, the entire truth of the divine nature, together with the precepts which guide, and the hopes which animate, it—the whole of the divine doctrine respecting these things, is completely thrown overboard by the system of legalism. The legalist teaches that we must surrender earth in order to get heaven. But how can fallen nature surrender that to which it is allied? How can it be attracted by that in which it sees no charms? Heaven has no charms for nature; yea, it is the very last place it would like to be found in. Nature has no taste for heaven, its occupations, or its occupants. Were it possible for nature to find itself there, it would be miserable. Thus, then, nature has no ability to surrender earth, and no desire to get heaven. True, it would be glad to escape hell and its ineffable torment, gloom and misery; but the desire to escape hell, and the desire to get heaven, spring from two very different sources. The former may exist in the old nature; the latter can only be found in the new. Were there no "lake of fire," and no "worm" in hell, nature would not so shrink from it. The same principle holds good in reference to all of nature's pursuits and desires. The legalist teaches that we must give up sin before we can get righteousness. But nature cannot give up sin; and as to righteousness, it absolutely hates it. True, it would like a certain amount of religion; but it is only with the idea that religion will preserve it from hell fire. It does not love religion because of its introducing the soul to the present enjoyment of God and His ways.

How different from all this miserable system of legalism, in every phase thereof, is "the gospel of the glory of the blessed God"! This gospel reveals God Himself coming down in perfect grace, and putting away sin by the sacrifice of the cross; putting it away, in the most absolute manner, on the ground of eternal righteousness, inasmuch as Christ suffered for it, having been made sin for us. And not only is God seen putting away sin, but also imparting a new life, even the risen life of His own risen, exalted, and glorified Son; which life every true believer possesses, in virtue of being linked, in God's eternal counsels, with Him who was nailed to the cross, but is now on the throne of the Majesty in the heavens. This nature, as we have remarked, He graciously guides by the precepts of His holy Word, applied in power by the Holy Ghost. He also animates it by the presentation of indestructible hopes. He reveals, in the distance, "the hope of glory"—"a city which hath foundations"—"a better country, that is, a heavenly"—the "many mansions" of the Father's house on high—"golden harps"—"green palms" and "white robes"—"a kingdom which cannot be moved"—everlasting association with Himself, in those regions of bliss and light, where sorrow and darkness can never enter—the unspeakable privilege of being led, throughout the countless ages of eternity, "beside the still waters, and through the green pastures" of redeeming love. How different is all this from the legalist's notion! Instead of calling upon me to educate and manage, by the dogmas of systematic religion, an irremediably corrupt nature, in order that thereby I may surrender an earth that I love, and attain to a heaven which I hate, He, in infinite grace, and on the ground of Christ's accomplished sacrifice, bestows upon me a nature which can enjoy heaven, and a heaven for that nature to enjoy; and not only a heaven, but Himself the unfailing spring of all heaven's joy.

Such is God's most excellent way. Thus He dealt with Abraham, thus He dealt with Saul of Tarsus, thus He deals with us. The God of glory showed Abraham a better country than Ur or Charran. He showed Saul of Tarsus a glory so bright, that it closed his eyes to all earth's brightest glories, and caused him to count them all "but dung," that He might win that blessed One who had appeared to him, and whose voice had spoken to his inmost soul. He saw a heavenly Christ in glory; and, throughout the remainder of his course, notwithstanding the weakness of the earthen vessel, that heavenly Christ and that heavenly glory engrossed his whole soul.

"And Abram passed through the land unto the place of Sichem, unto the plain of Moreh. And the Canaanite was then in the land." The presence of the Canaanite in God's land would necessarily prove a trial to Abraham. It would be a demand upon his faith and hope, an exercise of heart, a trial of patience. He had left Ur and Charran behind, and come into the country of which "the God of glory" had spoken to him, and there he finds "the Canaanite." But there, too, he finds the Lord,—"And the Lord appeared unto Abram, and said, 'Unto thy seed will I give this land.' " The connection between the two statements is beautiful and touching.

"The Canaanite was then in the land," and lest Abraham's eye should rest upon the

Canaanite, the present possessor of the land, Jehovah appears to him as the One who was going to give the land to him and to his seed forever. Thus Abraham was taken up with the Lord, and not with the Canaanite. This is full of instruction for us. The Canaanite in the land is the expression of the power of Satan; but, instead of being occupied with Satan's power to keep us out of the inheritance, we are called to apprehend Christ's power to bring us in. "We wrestle not with flesh and blood . . . but with spiritual wickedness in the heavenlies." The very sphere into which we are called is the sphere of our conflict. Should this terrify us? By no means. We have Christ there—a victorious Christ, in whom we are "more than conquerors." Hence, instead of indulging "a spirit of fear," we cultivate a spirit of worship. "And there builded he an *altar* unto the Lord, who appeared unto him." "And he removed from thence unto a mountain on the east of Bethel, and pitched his *tent.*" The altar and the tent give us the two great features of Abraham's character. A worshiper of God, a stranger in the world—most blessed characteristics! Having nothing on earth—having our all in God. Abraham had "not so much as to set his foot upon;" but he had God to enjoy, and that was enough.

However, faith has its trials, as well as its answers. It is not to be imagined that the man of faith, having pushed out from the shore of circumstances, finds it all smooth and easy sailing. By no means. Again and again, he is called to encounter rough seas and stormy skies; but it is all graciously designed to lead him into deeper and more matured experience of what God is to the heart that confides in Him. Were the sky always without a cloud, and the ocean without a ripple, the believer would not know so well the God with whom he has to do; for, alas! we know how prone the heart is to mistake the peace of circumstances for the peace of God. When everything is going on smoothly and pleasantly—our property safe, our business prosperous, our children and servants carrying themselves agreeably, our residence comfortable, our health excellent—everything, in short, just to our mind, how apt we are to mistake the peace which reposes upon such circumstances, for that peace which flows from the realized presence of Christ. The Lord knows this; and therefore He comes in, in one way or another, and stirs up the nest, that is, if we are found nestling in circumstances, instead of in Himself.

But, again, we are frequently led to judge of the rightness of a path by its exemption from trial, and *vice versa*. This is a great mistake. The path of obedience may often be found most trying to flesh and blood. Thus, in Abraham's case, he was not only called to encounter the Canaanite, in the place to which God had called him, but there was also "a famine in the land." Should he, therefore, have concluded that he was not in his right place? Assuredly not. That would have been to judge according to the sight of his eyes, the very thing which faith never does. No doubt it was a deep trial to the heart, an inexplicable puzzle to nature; but to faith it was all plain and easy. When Paul was called into Macedonia, almost the first thing he had to encounter was the prison at Philippi. This, to a heart out of communion, would have seemed a deathblow to the entire mission. But Paul never questioned the rightness of his position; he was enabled to "sing praises" in the midst of it all, assured that everything was just as it should be: and so it was; for in the prison of Philippi was one of God's vessels of mercy, who could not, humanly speaking, have heard the gospel, had not the preachers of it been thrust into the very place where he was. The devil was made, in spite of himself, the instrument of sending the gospel to the ears of one of God's elect.

Now, Abraham should have reasoned in the same way in reference to the famine. He was in the very place in which God had set him; and, evidently, he received no direction to leave it. True, the famine was there; and, moreover, Egypt was at hand, offering deliverance from pressure; still the path of God's servant was plain. *It is better to starve in Canaan, if it should be so, than live in luxury in Egypt*; it is better far to suffer in God's path, than be at ease in Satan's; it is better to be poor with Christ, than rich without Him. "Abraham had sheep, and oxen, and he-asses, and men-servants, and maid-servants, and she-asses, and camels." Substantial proofs, the natural heart would doubtless say, of the rightness of his step in going down to Egypt. But, ah! he had no altar—no communion. Egypt was not the place of God's presence. He lost more than he gained by going thither. This is ever the case. Nothing can ever make up for the loss of our communion with God. Exemption from temporary pressure, and the accession of the greatest wealth, are but poor equivalents for what one loses by diverging a hair's breadth from the straight path of obedience. How many of us can add our amen to this! How many, in order to avoid the trial and exercise connected with God's path, have slipped aside into the current of this present evil world, and thereby brought leanness and barrenness, heaviness and gloom, into their souls! It may be they have, to use the common expression, "made money," increased their store, obtained the world's favor, been "entreated well" by its Pharaohs, gotten a name and a position amongst men; but are these a proper equivalent for joy in God, communion, liberty of heart, a pure, uncondemning conscience, a thankful, worshiping spirit, vigorous testimony, and effectual service? Alas! for the man that can think so. And yet all the above incomparable blessings have been often sold for a little ease, a little influence, a little money.

Christian reader, let us watch against the tendency to slip aside from the narrow, yet safe, the *sometimes*-rough, yet *always*-pleasant, path of simple, whole-hearted obedience. Let us keep guard—jealous, careful guard—over "faith and a pure conscience," for which nothing can compensate. Should trial come, let us, instead of turning aside into Egypt, wait on God; and thus the trial, instead of proving an occasion of stumbling, will prove an opportunity for obedience. Let us, when tempted to slip into the course of the world, remember Him "who gave Himself for our sins, that He might deliver us from this present evil world, according to the will of God and our Father" (Gal. 1:4). If such was His love for us, and such His sense of the true character of this present world, that He gave Himself in order to deliver us from it, shall we deny Him by plunging again into that from which His cross has forever delivered us? May God Almighty forbid! May He keep us in the hollow of His hand, and under the shadow of His wings, until we see Jesus as He is, and be like Him, and with Him forever.

---

## *CHAPTER 13*

THE opening of this chapter presents to us a subject of immense interest to the heart, namely, the true character of divine restoration. When the child of God has, in any way, declined in his spiritual condition, and lost his communion, he is in great danger, when conscience begins to work, of failing in the apprehension of divine grace, and of stopping short of the proper mark of divine restoration. Now, we know that God does everything in a way entirely worthy of Himself. Whether He creates, redeems, converts, restores, or provides, He can only act like Himself. What is worthy of Himself is, ever and only, His standard of action. This is unspeakably happy for us, inasmuch as we would ever seek to "limit the Holy One of Israel;" and in nothing are we so prone to limit Him as in His restoring grace. In the case now before us, we see that Abraham was not only delivered out of Egypt, but brought back "unto the place where his tent had been *at the beginning* . . . unto the place of the altar which he had made there *at the first*: and there Abraham called on the name of the Lord." Nothing can satisfy God, in reference to a wanderer or backslider, but his being entirely restored. We, in the self-righteousness of our hearts, might imagine that such an one should take a lower place than that which he had formerly occupied; and so he should, were it a question of his merit or his character; but inasmuch as it is altogether a question of grace, it is God's prerogative to fix the standard of restoration; and His standard is set forth in the following passage: "If thou wilt return, O Israel, return *to Me.*" It is thus that God restores, and it would be unworthy of Himself to do anything else. He will either not restore at all, or else restore in such a way as to magnify and glorify the riches of His grace. Thus, when the leper was brought back, he was actually conducted "to the door of the tabernacle of the congregation;" when the prodigal returned, he was set down at the table with his father; when Peter was restored, he was able to stand before the men of Israel and say, "Ye denied the Holy One and the Just"—the very thing which he had done himself, under the most aggravated circumstances. In all these cases, and many more which might be adduced, we see the perfectness of God's restoration. He always brings the soul back to Himself, in the full power of grace, and the full confidence of faith. "If thou wilt return, return *to Me*." "Abraham came unto the place where his tent had been at *the beginning.*"

Then, as to the moral effect of divine restoration, it is most deeply practical. If legalism gets its answer in the *character* of the restoration, antinomianism gets its answer in the *effect* thereof. The restored soul will have a very deep and keen sense of the evil from which it has been delivered, and this will be evidenced by a jealous, prayerful, holy, and circumspect spirit. We are not restored in order that we may the more lightly go and sin again, but rather that we may "go and sin no more." The deeper my sense of the *grace* of divine restoration, the deeper will be my sense of the *holiness* of it also. This principle is taught and established throughout all Scripture, but especially in two well-known passages, namely, Psalm 23:3, and 1 John 1:9: "He restoreth my soul: *He leadeth me in the paths of righteousness* for His name's sake." And, again, "If we confess our sins, He is faithful and just to forgive us our sins, and to *cleanse us from all unrighteousness*." The proper path for a divinely-restored soul, is "the path of righteousness." In other words, having tasted divine grace, we walk in righteousness. To talk of grace while walking in unrighteousness, is, as the apostle says, to turn "the grace of our God into lasciviousness." If "grace reigns through righteousness unto eternal life," it also manifests itself in righteousness, in the outflow of that life. The grace that forgives us our sins, cleanses us from all unrighteousness. Those things must never be separated. When taken together, they furnish a triumphant answer to the legalism and antinomianism of the human heart.

But there was a deeper trial for Abraham's heart than even the famine, namely, that arising from the company of one who evidently was not walking in the energy of personal faith, nor in the realization of personal responsibility. It seems plain that Lot was, from the very beginning, borne onward rather by Abraham's influence and example, than by his own faith in God. This is a very common case. If we look down along the history of the people of God, we can easily see how that in every great movement produced by the Spirit of God, certain individuals have attached themselves thereto who were not personally participators of the power which had produced the movement. Such persons go on for a time, either as a dead weight upon the testimony, or an active hindrance to it. Thus, in Abraham's case, the Lord called him to leave his kindred; but he brought his kindred with him. Terah retarded him in his movement, until death took him out of the way: Lot followed him somewhat further, until "the lusts of other things" overpowered him, and he entirely broke down.

The same thing is observable in the great movement of Israel out of Egypt. "A mixed multitude" followed them, and caused much defilement, weakness and sorrow; for we read, in Numbers 11, "The mixed multitude that was among them fell a lusting: and the children of Israel *also* wept again, and said, 'Who shall give us flesh to eat.' " So, also, in the early days of the Church,—and not only so, but in every revival which has taken place therein down to the present day,—many have been acted upon by various influences, which, not being divine, proved evanescent; and the persons so acted upon, sooner or later gave way, and found their proper level. Nothing will endure but that which is of God. I must realize the link between me and the living God: I must know myself as one called of Him into the position which I occupy, else I shall have no stability, and exhibit no consistency therein. It will not do to follow in the track of other people merely because it is their track. God will graciously give each a path to walk in, a sphere to move in, and a responsibility to fulfill; and we are bound to know our calling and the functions thereof, that, by His grace ministered to our souls daily, we may work therein effectually, to His glory. It matters not what our measure may be, provided it be what God hath dealt to us. We may have "five talents," or we may have but "one;" still, if we use the "one," with our eye fixed on the Master, we shall just be as sure to hear from His gracious lips the words, "Well done," as if we had used the "five." This is encouraging. Paul, Peter, James, and John had each his peculiar measure—his specific ministry; and so with all: none needs to interfere with another. A carpenter has a saw and a plane, a hammer and a chisel, and he uses each as he needs it. Nothing can be more worthless than imitation. If, in the natural world, we look at the various orders of creation, we see no imitation. All have their proper sphere, their proper functions. And if it be thus in the natural world, how much more in the spiritual. The field is wide enough for all. In every house there are vessels of various sizes and various shapes: the master wants them all.

Let us, therefore, search and see whether we are walking under a divine or a human influence; whether our faith stands in the wisdom of man, or in the power of God; whether we are doing things because others have done them, or because the Lord has called us to do them; whether we are merely propped up by the example and influence of our fellow, or sustained by personal faith in God. These are serious inquiries. It is, no doubt, a happy privilege to enjoy the fellowship of our brethren; but if we are propped up by them, we shall soon make shipwreck. So also, if we go beyond our measure, our action will be strained and unsightly, uneasy and unnatural. It is very easy to see when a man is working in his place, and according to his measure. All affectation, assumption, and imitation is contemptible in the extreme. Hence, though we cannot be great, let us be honest; and though we cannot be brilliant, let us be genuine. If a person goes beyond his depth without knowing how to swim, he will surely flounder: if a vessel put out to sea without being sea-worthy and in trim, it will surely be beaten back into harbor, or lost. Lot left "Ur of the Chaldees," but he fell in the plains of Sodom. The call of God had not reached his heart, nor the inheritance of God filled his vision. Solemn thought! may we ponder it deeply! Blessed be God, there is a path for each of His servants, along which shines the light of His approving countenance, and to walk therein should be our chief joy. His approval is enough for the heart that knows Him. True, we may not always be able to command the approval and concurrence of our brethren; we may frequently be misunderstood; but we cannot help these things. "The day" will set all this to rights, and the loyal heart can contentedly wait for that day, knowing that then "every man shall have praise of God."

But it may be well to examine more particularly what it was that caused Lot to turn aside off the path of public testimony. There is a crisis in every man's history, at which it will assuredly be made manifest on what ground he is resting, by what motives he is actuated, and by what objects he is animated. Thus it was with Lot. He did not die at Charran, but he fell at Sodom. The *ostensible* cause of his fall was the strife between his herdmen and those of Abraham; but the fact is, when one is not really walking with a single eye and purified affections, he will easily find a stone to stumble over. If he does not find it at one time, he will at another,—if he does not find it here, he will find it there. In one sense, it makes little matter as to what may be the apparent cause of turning aside; the *real* cause lies underneath, far away, it may be, from common observation, in the hidden chambers of the heart's affections and desires, where *the world*, in some shape or form, has been sought after. The strife between the herdmen might have been easily settled without spiritual damage to either Abraham or Lot. To the former, indeed, it only afforded an occasion for exhibiting the beautiful power of faith, and the moral elevation—the heavenly vantage-ground—on which faith ever sets the possessor thereof. But to the latter, it was an occasion for exhibiting the thorough worldliness of his heart. The strife no more produced the worldliness in Lot than it produced the faith in Abraham; it only manifested, in the case of each, what was really there.

Thus it is always: controversies and divisions arise in the Church of God, and many are stumbled thereby, and driven back into the world in one way or another. They then lay the blame on the controversy and division, whereas the truth is, that these things were only the means of developing the real condition of the soul, and the bent of the heart. The world was in the heart, and *would be* reached by some *route* or another; nor is there much of moral excellency exhibited in blaming men and things, when the root of the matter lies within. It is not that controversy and division are not to be deeply deplored: assuredly they are. To see brethren contending, in the very presence of "the Canaanite and the Perizzite," is truly lamentable and humiliating. Our language should ever be, "Let there be no strife, I pray thee, between me and thee . . . for we are brethren." Still, why did not Abraham make choice of Sodom? Why did not the strife drive him into the world? Why was it not an occasion of stumbling to him? Because he looked at it from God's point of view. No doubt he had a heart that could be attracted by "well-watered plains" just as powerfully as Lot's heart, but then he did not allow his own heart to choose. He first let Lot take his choice, and then left God to choose for him. This was heavenly wisdom. This is what faith ever does: it allows God to fix its inheritance, as it also allows Him to make it good. It is always satisfied with the portion which God gives. It can say, "The lines are fallen to me in pleasant places; yea, I have a goodly heritage." It matters not where "the lines" fall; for, in the judgment of faith, they always fall "in pleasant places," just because God casts them there.

The man of faith can easily afford to allow the man of sight to take his choice. He can say, "If thou wilt take the left hand, then I will go to the right; or if thou depart to the right hand, then I will go to the left." What beautiful disinterestedness and moral elevation we have here! and yet what security! It is certain that, let nature range where it will, let it take its most comprehensive grasp—its boldest and highest flight, there is never the slightest danger of its laying its hand upon faith's treasure. It will seek its portion in quite an opposite direction. Faith lays up its treasure in a place which nature would never dream of examining; and as to its approaching thereto, it could not if it would, and it would not if it could. Hence, therefore, faith is perfectly safe, as well as beautifully disinterested, in allowing nature to take its choice.

What, then, did Lot choose, when he got his choice? He chose Sodom—the very place that was about to be judged. But how was this? Why select such a spot? Because he looked at the outward appearance, and not at the intrinsic character and future destiny. The intrinsic character was "*wicked*:" its future destiny was "*judgment*"—to be destroyed by "fire and brimstone out of heaven." But, it may be said, Lot knew nothing of all this. Perhaps not, nor Abraham either; but God did; and had Lot allowed God to "choose his inheritance for him," He certainly would not have chosen a spot that He Himself was about to destroy. He did not, however: he judged for himself. Sodom suited him, though it did not suit God. His eye rested on the "well-watered plains," and his heart was attracted by them. "He pitched his tent *toward* Sodom." Such is nature's choice! "Demas hath forsaken me, having loved this present world." Lot forsook Abraham for the same reason. He left the place of testimony, and got into the place of judgment.

"And the Lord said unto Abram, after that Lot was separated from him, 'Lift up thine eyes, and look from the place where thou art, northward, and southward, and eastward, and westward; for all the land which thou seest, to thee will I give it, and to thy seed forever.' " The "strife" and "separation," so far from damaging Abraham's spiritual condition, rather brought out, in full relief, his heavenly principles, and strengthened, in his soul, the life of faith. Moreover, it cleared the prospect for him, and delivered him from the company of one who could only prove a dead weight. Thus it worked for good, and yielded a harvest of blessing. It is, at once, most solemn, and yet most encouraging, to bear in mind that, in the long run, men find their proper level. Men who run unsent, break down, in one way or another, and find their way back to that which they profess to have left. On the other hand, those who are called of God, and lean on Him, are, by His grace, sustained. "Their path is as the shining light, which shineth more and more unto the perfect day." The thought of this should keep us humble, watchful, and prayerful. "Let him that thinketh he standeth take heed lest he fall," for, truly, "there are first that shall be last, and there are last that shall be first." "He that endureth to the end, the same shall be saved," is a principle which, whatever be its specific application, has a wide moral bearing. Many a vessel has sailed out of harbor in gallant style, with all its canvass spread, amid cheering and shouting, and with many fair promises of a first-rate passage; but, alas! storms, waves, shoals, rocks, and quicksands have changed the aspect of things; and the voyage that commenced with hope has ended in disaster. I am here only referring to the path of service and testimony, and by no means to the question of a man's eternal acceptance in Christ. This latter, blessed be God, does not, in any wise, rest with ourselves, but with Him who has said, "I give unto My sheep eternal life, and they shall never perish, neither shall any pluck them out of My hand." But do we not know that many Christians set out on some special course of service or testimony, under the impression that they are called of God thereto, and, after a time, they break down? Unquestionably. And, further, very many set out in the profession of some special principle of action, respecting which they have not been divinely taught, or the consequences of which they have not maturely considered in the presence of God, and, as a necessary result, they themselves have been found, after a time, in the open violation of those very principles. All this is deplorable, and should be carefully avoided. It tends to weaken the faith of God's elect, and causes the enemies of the truth to speak reproachfully. Each one should receive his call and his commission directly from the Master Himself. All whom Christ calls into any special service, He will infallibly maintain therein, for He never sent any one a warfare at his own charges. But if we run unsent, we shall not only be left to *learn* our folly, but to *exhibit* it.

Yet, it is not that any one should set himself up as the impersonation of any principle, or as an example of any special character of service or testimony. God forbid. This would be the most egregious folly, and empty conceit. It is a teacher's business to set forth God's Word, and it is a servant's business to set forth the Master's will; but while all this is fully understood and admitted, we must ever remember the deep need there is of counting the cost ere we undertake to build a tower or go forth to war. Were this most seriously attended to, there would be far less confusion and failure in our midst. Abraham was called of God from Ur to Canaan, and hence God led him forth on the way. When Abraham tarried at Charran, God waited for him; when he went down into Egypt, He restored him; when he needed guidance, He guided him; when there was a strife and a separation, He took care of him; so that Abraham had only to say, "Oh, how great is Thy goodness which *Thou hast laid up* for them that fear Thee, which Thou hast wrought for them that trust in Thee, before the sons of men!" He lost nothing by the strife. He had his tent and his altar before, and he had his tent and his altar afterwards. "Then Abram removed *his tent*, and came and dwelt in the plain of Mamre, which is in Hebron, and built there *an altar* unto the Lord." Lot might choose Sodom; but as for Abraham, he sought and found his all in God. There was no altar in Sodom. Alas! all who travel in that direction are in quest of something quite different from that. It is never the worship of God, but the love of the world, that leads them thither. And even though they should attain their object, what is it?—how does it end? Just thus: "He gave them their request, but sent leanness into their souls."

---

## *CHAPTER 14*

WE are here presented with a historic record of the revolt of five kings from under the hand of Chederlaomer, and a battle consequent thereon. The Spirit of God can occupy Himself with the movements of "kings and their armies," when such movements are in anywise connected with the people of God. In the present case, Abraham personally had nothing whatever to do with the revolt or its consequences. His "tent" and "altar" were not likely to furnish an occasion for the declaration of war, nor yet to be much affected by the outbreak or issue thereof. The proper portion of a heavenly man could never, by any possibility, tempt the cupidity nor excite the ambition of the kings and conquerors of this world.

However, although Abraham was not affected by the battle of "four kings with five," yet Lot was. His position was such as to involve him in the whole affair. So long as we are enabled, through grace, to pursue the path of simple faith, we shall be thrown completely outside the range of this world's circumstances; but if we abandon our high and holy position as those whose "citizenship is in heaven," and seek a name, a place, and a portion in the earth, we must expect to participate in earth's convulsions and vicissitudes. Lot had taken up his abode in the plains of Sodom, and was therefore deeply and sensibly affected by the wars of Sodom. It must ever be thus. It is a bitter and a painful thing for the child of God to mingle himself with the children of this world. He can never do so without serious damage to his own soul, as well as to the testimony with which he is intrusted. What testimony was Lot in Sodom? A very feeble one indeed, if one at all. The very fact of his settling himself there was the death-blow to his testimony. To have spoken a word against Sodom and its ways, would have been to condemn himself, for why was he there? But, in truth, it does not by any means appear that to testify for God formed any part of his object in "pitching his tent toward Sodom." Personal and family interests seem to have been the leading springs of action in his heart; and though, as Peter tells us, "his righteous soul was vexed with the filthy conversation of the wicked, from day to day," yet had he but little power to act against it, even if inclined so to do.

It is important, in a practical point of view, to see that we cannot be governed by two objects at the same time. For example, I cannot have before my mind, as objects, my worldly interests and the interests of the gospel of Christ. If I go to a town for the purpose of setting up in business, then, clearly, business is my object, and not the gospel. I may, no doubt, propose to myself both to attend to business and to preach the gospel as well; but, all the while, either one or the other must be my object. It is not that a servant of Christ may not most blessedly and effectually preach the gospel and attend to business also; he assuredly may; but, in such a case, the gospel will be his object, and not business. Paul preached the gospel and made tents; but the gospel was his object, and not tent-making. If I make business my object, the gospel-preaching will speedily prove to be formal and unprofitable work; yea, it will be well if it be not made use of to sanctify my covetousness. The heart is very treacherous; and it is often truly astonishing to see how it deceives us when we desire to gain some special point. It will furnish, in abundance, the most plausible reasons; while the eyes of our understanding are so blinded by self-interest, or unjudged willfulness, as to be incapable of detecting their plausibility. How frequently do we hear persons defending a continuance in a position which they admit to be wrong, on the plea that they thereby enjoy a wider sphere of usefulness. To all such reasoning, Samuel furnishes a pointed and powerful reply: "To obey is better than sacrifice, and to hearken than the fat of rams." Which was able to do the more good? Abraham, or Lot? Does not the history of those two men prove, beyond a question, that the most effectual way to serve the world is to be faithful to it by separating from, and testifying against, it?

But be it remembered, that genuine separation from the world can only be the result of communion with God. I may seclude myself from the world, and constitute myself the centre of my being, like a monk or a cynic; but separation to God is a totally different thing. The one chills and contracts, the other warms and expands. That drives us in upon ourselves; this draws us out in love and interest for others. That makes self and its interests our centre; this makes God and His glory our centre. Thus, in Abraham's case, we see that the very fact of his separation enabled him to render effectual service to one who had involved himself in trouble by his worldly ways. "When Abram heard that *his brother* was taken captive, he armed his trained servants, born in his own house, three hundred and eighteen, and pursued them unto Dan . . . and he brought back all the goods, and also brought again his brother Lot, and his goods, and the women also, and the people." Lot was Abraham's brother after all, and brotherly love must act. "A brother is born for adversity;" and it often happens that a season of adversity softens the heart, and renders it susceptible of kindness, even from one with whom we have had to part company; and it is remarkable that while in verse 12 we read, "They took Lot, *Abram's brother's son,*" yet in verse 14 we read, "When Abram heard that *his brother* was taken captive." The claims of a brother's trouble are answered by the affections of a brother's heart. This is divine. Genuine faith, while it always renders us independent, never renders us indifferent; it will never wrap itself up in its fleece while a brother shivers in the cold. There are three things which faith does: it "purifies the heart," it "works by love," and it "overcomes the world"; and all these results of faith are beautifully exhibited in Abraham on this occasion. His heart was purified from Sodom's pollutions; he manifested genuine love to Lot, his brother; and, finally, he was completely victorious over the kings. Such are the precious fruits of faith, that heavenly, Christ-honoring principle.

However, the man of faith is not exempt from the assaults of the enemy; and it frequently happens that immediately after a victory, one has to encounter a fresh temptation. Thus it was with Abraham. "The king of Sodom went out to meet him, after his return from the slaughter of Chederlaomer, and of the kings that were with him." There was evidently a very deep and insidious design of the enemy in this movement. "The king of Sodom" presents a very different thought, and exhibits a very different phase of the enemy's power, from what we have in "Chederlaomer and the kings that were with him." In the former, we have rather the hiss of the serpent; in the latter, the roar of the lion. But whether it were the serpent or the lion, the Lord's grace was amply sufficient; and most seasonably was this grace ministered to the Lord's servant, at the exact moment of need. "And Melchisedek, king of Salem, brought forth bread and wine, and he was the priest of the most high God. And he blessed him, and said, 'Blessed be Abram of the most high God, possessor of heaven and earth; and blessed be the most high God, which hath delivered thine enemies into thy hand.' " We have here to remark, first, the peculiar point at which Melchisedek enters the scene; and, secondly, the double effect of his ministry. He did not come forth when Abraham was in pursuit of Chederlaomer, but when the king of Sodom was in pursuit of Abraham. This makes a great moral difference. A deeper character of communion was needed to meet the deeper character of conflict.

And then, as to the ministry, the "bread and wine" refreshed Abraham's spirit, after his conflict with Chederlaomer; while the benediction prepared his heart for his conflict with the king of Sodom. Abraham was a conqueror, and yet he was about to be a combatant, and the royal priest refreshed the conqueror's spirit, and fortified the combatant's heart.

It is peculiarly sweet to observe the manner in which Melchisedek introduces God to the thoughts of Abraham. He calls Him "the most high God, possessor of heaven and earth;" and not only so, but pronounces Abraham "blessed" of that same God. This was effectually preparing him for the king of Sodom. A man who was "blessed" of God did not need to take aught from the enemy; and if "the possessor of heaven and earth" filled his vision, "the goods" of Sodom could have but little attraction. Hence, as might be expected, when the king of Sodom made his proposal—"Give me the persons, and take the goods to thyself," Abraham replies, "I have lift up my hand unto the Lord, the most high God, the possessor of heaven and earth, that I will not take from a thread even to a shoelatchet, and that I will not take anything that is thine, lest thou shouldest say, I have made Abram rich." Abraham refuses to be enriched by the king of Sodom. How could he think of delivering Lot from the power of the world if he himself were governed thereby? The only true way in which to deliver another is to be thoroughly delivered myself. So long as I am in the fire, it is quite impossible I can pluck another out of it. The path of separation is the path of power, as it is also the path of peace and blessedness.

The world, in all its various forms, is the great instrument of which Satan makes use in order to weaken the hands and alienate the affections of the servants of Christ. But, blessed be God, when the heart is true to Him, He always comes in to cheer, to strengthen, and to fortify at the right time. "The eyes of the Lord run to and fro, throughout the whole earth, to show Himself strong in the behalf of them whose heart is perfect toward Him" (2 Chron. 16:9). This is an encouraging truth for our poor, timid, doubting, faltering hearts. Christ will be our strength and shield. He will "cover our heads in the day of battle;" He will "teach our hands to war, and our fingers to fight;" and finally, "He will bruise Satan under our feet shortly." All this is unspeakably comforting to a heart sincerely desirous of making way against "the world, the flesh and the devil." May the Lord keep our hearts true to Himself, in the midst of the ensnaring scene around us.

---

## *CHAPTER 15*

AFTER these things, the word of the Lord came unto Abram in a vision, saying, 'Fear not, Abram. I am thy shield, and thy exceeding great reward.' " The Lord would not suffer His servant to be a loser, by rejecting the offers of the world. It was infinitely better for Abraham to find himself hidden behind Jehovah's shield than to take refuge beneath the patronage of the king of Sodom, and to be anticipating his "exceeding great reward" than to accept "the goods" of Sodom. The position into which Abraham is put, in the opening verse of our chapter, is beautifully expressive of the position into which every soul is introduced by the faith of Christ. Jehovah was his "shield," that he might rest in Him; Jehovah was his "reward," that he might wait for Him. So with the believer now: he finds his present rest, his present peace, his present security, all in Christ. No dart of the enemy can possibly penetrate the shield which covers the weakest believer in Jesus.

And then, as to the future, Christ fills it. Precious portion! Precious hope! A portion which can never be exhausted: a hope which will never make ashamed. Both are infallibly secured by the counsels of God and the accomplished atonement of Christ. The present enjoyment thereof is by the ministry of the Holy Ghost, who dwells in us. This being the case, it is manifest that if the believer is pursuing a worldly career, or indulging in worldly or carnal desires, he cannot be enjoying either the "shield" or the "reward." If the Holy Ghost is grieved, He will not minister the enjoyment of that which is our proper portion—our proper hope. Hence, in the section of Abraham's history now before us, we see that when he had returned from the slaughter of the kings, and rejected the offer of the king of Sodom, Jehovah rose before his soul in the double character, as his "shield" and his "exceeding great reward." Let the heart ponder this, for it contains a volume of deeply practical truth. We shall now examine the remainder of this chapter.

In it we have unfolded to us the two great principles of sonship and heirship. "And Abram said, 'Lord God, what wilt Thou give me, seeing I go *childless,* and the steward of my house is this Eliezer of Damascus?' And Abram said, 'Behold, to me Thou hast given no *seed:* and lo, one born in my house is mine *heir.*' " Abraham desired a son, for he knew, upon divine authority, that his "seed" should inherit the land (chap. 13:15). Sonship and heirship are inseparably connected in the thoughts of God: "He that shall come forth out of thine own bowels shall be thine heir." Sonship is the proper basis of everything; and, moreover, it is the result of God's sovereign counsel and operation, as we read in James, "Of His own will begat He us." Finally, it is founded upon God's eternal principle of resurrection. How else could it be? Abraham's body was "dead;" wherefore, in his case, as in every other, sonship must be in the power of resurrection. Nature is dead, and can neither beget nor conceive aught for God. There lay the inheritance stretching out before the patriarch's eye, in all its magnificent dimensions; but where was the heir? Abraham's body and Sarah's womb alike answered *"death."* But Jehovah is the God of resurrection, and therefore a "dead body" was the very thing for Him to act upon. Had nature not been dead, God should have put it to death ere He could fully show Himself. The most suitable theatre for the living God is that from which nature, with all its boasted powers and empty pretensions, has been totally expelled by the sentence of death. Wherefore, God's word to Abraham was, " 'Look now toward heaven, and tell the stars, if thou be able to number them;' and He said unto him, 'So shall thy seed be.' " When the God of resurrection fills the vision, there is no limit to the soul's blessing; for He who can quicken the dead, can do anything.

"And he believed in the Lord, and He counted it unto him for righteousness." The imputation of righteousness to Abraham is here founded upon his believing in the Lord as the Quickener of the dead. It is in this character that He reveals Himself in a world where death reigns; and when a soul believes in Him as such, it is counted righteous in His sight. This necessarily shuts man out, as regards his cooperation, for what can he do in the midst of a scene of death? Can he raise the dead? Can he open the gates of the grave? Can he deliver himself from the power of death, and walk forth, in life and liberty, beyond the limits of its dreary domain? Assuredly not. Well, then, if he cannot do so, he cannot work out righteousness, nor establish himself in the relation of sonship. "God is not the God of the dead, but of the living," and therefore, so long as a man is under the power of death, and under the dominion of sin, he can neither know the position of a son, nor the condition of righteousness. Thus, God alone can bestow the adoption of sons, and He alone can impute righteousness, and both are connected with faith in Him as the One who raised up Christ from the dead.

It is in this way that the apostle handles the question of Abraham's faith, in Romans 4, where he says, "It was not written for his sake alone, that it was imputed unto him; but for us also, to whom it shall be imputed, *if we believe on Him that raised up Jesus our Lord from the dead.*" Here, the God of resurrection is presented "to us also" as the object of faith, and our faith in Him as the alone ground of our righteousness. If Abraham had looked up into heaven's vault, spangled with innumerable stars, and then looked at "his own body now dead," how could he ever grasp the idea of a seed as numerous as those stars? Impossible. But he did not look at his own body, but at the resurrection-power of God; and inasmuch as that was the power which was to produce the seed, we can easily see that the stars of heaven and the sand on the sea-shore are but feeble figures indeed; for what natural object could possibly illustrate the effect of that power which can raise the dead?

So also, when a sinner hearkens to the glad tidings of the gospel, were he to look up to the unsullied light of the divine presence, and then look down into the unexplored depths of his own evil nature, he might well exclaim, How can I ever get thither?—how can I ever be fit to dwell in that light? Where is the answer? In himself? Nay, blessed be God, but in that blessed One who traveled from the bosom to the cross and the grave, and from thence to the throne, thus filling up, in His Person and work, all the space between those extreme points. There can be nothing higher than the bosom of God—the eternal dwelling-place of the Son, and there can be nothing lower than the cross and the grave; but, amazing truth! I find Christ in both. I find Him in the bosom, and I find Him in the grave. He went down into death in order that He might leave behind Him, in the dust thereof, the full weight of His people's sins and iniquities. Christ in the grave exhibits the end of everything human—the end of sin—the full limit of Satan's power. The grave of Jesus forms the grand terminus of all. But resurrection takes us beyond this terminus, and constitutes the imperishable basis on which God's glory and man's blessing repose forever. The moment the eye of faith rests on a risen Christ, there is a triumphant answer to every question as to sin, judgment, death, and the grave. The One who divinely met all these is alive from the dead, and has taken His seat at the right hand of the Majesty in the heavens; and not only so, but the Spirit of that risen and glorified One, in the believer, constitutes him a son. He is quickened out of the grave of Christ: as we read, "And you, being dead in your sins, and the uncircumcision of your flesh, hath He quickened together with Him, having forgiven you all trespasses" (Col. 2:13).

Hence, therefore, sonship, being founded on resurrection, stands connected with perfect justification—perfect righteousness—perfect freedom from everything which could in anywise be against us. God could not have us in His presence with sin upon us. He could not suffer a single speck or stain of sin upon His sons and daughters. The father could not have the prodigal at *his* table with the rags of the far country upon him. He could go forth to meet him in those rags, he could fall upon his neck and kiss him in those rags,—it was worthy and beautifully characteristic of his *grace* so to do; but then to seat him at his table in the rags would never do. The grace that brought the father out to the prodigal, reigns through the righteousness which brought the prodigal in to the father. It would not have been grace had the father waited for the son to deck himself in robes of his own providing, and it would not have been righteous to bring him in in his rags; but both grace and righteousness shone forth in all their respective brightness and beauty when the father went out and fell on the prodigal's neck, but yet did not give him a seat at his table until he was clad and decked in a manner suited to that elevated and happy position. God, in Christ, has stooped to the very lowest point of man's moral condition, that, by stooping, He might raise man to the very highest point of blessedness, in fellowship with Himself. From all this, it follows, that our sonship, with all its consequent dignities and privileges, is entirely independent of us. We have just as little to do with it as Abraham's dead body and Sarah's dead womb had to do with a seed as numerous as the stars which garnish the heavens, or as the sand on the sea-shore. It is all of God. God the Father drew the plan, God the Son laid the foundation, and God the Holy Ghost raises the superstructure; and on this superstructure appears the inscription, *"Through grace, by faith, without works of law."*

But then our chapter opens another most

important subject to our view, namely, *heirship.* The question of sonship and righteousness being fully settled—divinely and unconditionally settled, the Lord said unto Abraham, "I am the Lord that brought thee out of Ur of the Chaldees, to give thee this land to inherit it." Here comes out the great question of heirship, and the peculiar path along which the chosen heirs are to travel ere they reach the promised inheritance. "If children, then heirs, heirs of God, and joint-heirs with Christ; if so be that we *suffer* with Him, that we may be also glorified together." Our way to the kingdom lies through suffering, affliction and tribulation; but, thank God, we can, by faith, say, "the *sufferings* of this present time are not worthy to be compared with the glory which shall be revealed in us." And further, we know that "our *light affliction,* which is but for a moment, worketh out for us a far more exceeding and eternal weight of glory." Finally, "we glory in *tribulation;* knowing that tribulation worketh patience; and patience, experience; and experience, hope." It is a high honor and a real privilege to be allowed to drink of our blessed Master's cup, and be baptized with His baptism,—to travel in blest companionship with Him along the road which leads directly to the glorious inheritance. The Heir and the joint-heirs reach that inheritance by the pathway of suffering.

But let it be remembered that the suffering of which the joint-heirs participate has no penal element in it. It is not suffering from the hand of infinite justice, because of sin; all that was fully met on the cross, when the divine victim bowed His sacred head beneath the stroke. "Christ also hath *once* suffered for sins," and that "once" was on the tree, and *nowhere else.* He never suffered for sins before, and He never can suffer for sins again. *"Once,* in the end of the world (the end of all flesh), hath He appeared to put away sin by the sacrifice of Himself." "Christ was *once* offered."

There are two ways in which to view a suffering Christ; first, as bruised of Jehovah; secondly, as rejected of men. In the former, He stood alone; in the latter, we have the honor of being associated with Him. In the former, I say, He stood alone, for who could have stood with Him? He bore the wrath of God alone; He traveled in solitude down into "the rough valley that had neither been eared nor sown," and there He settled forever the question of our sins. *With* this we had nothing to do, though *to* this we are eternally indebted for everything. He fought the fight and gained the victory alone, but He divides the spoils with us. He was in solitude "in the horrible pit and miry clay;" but directly He planted His foot on the everlasting "rock" of resurrection, He associates us with Him. He uttered the *cry* alone; He sings the *"new song"* in company (Psalm 40:2-3).

Now the question is, shall we refuse to suffer from the hand of man *with Him* who suffered from the hand of God *for us?* That it is, in a certain sense, a question, is evident, from the Spirit's constant use of the word "if," in connection with it.—"If so be we suffer with Him."—"If we suffer, we shall reign." There is no such question as to sonship. We do not reach the high dignity of sons through suffering, but through the quickening power of the Holy Ghost, founded on the accomplished work of Christ, according to God's eternal counsel. This can never be touched. We do not reach the *family* through suffering. The apostle does not say, That ye may be counted worthy of the *family* of God for which ye also suffer. They were in the family already; but they were bound for the kingdom, and their road to that kingdom lay through suffering; and not only so, but the measure of suffering for the kingdom would be according to their devotedness and conformity to the King. The more like we are *to* Him, the more we shall suffer *with* Him; and the deeper our fellowship with Him in the suffering, the deeper will be our fellowship in the glory. There is a difference between the *house* of the Father and the kingdom of the Son: in the former, it will be a question of capacity; in the latter, a question of assigned position. All my children may be around my table, but their enjoyment of my company and conversation will entirely depend on their capacity. One may be seated on my knee, in the full enjoyment of his relationship, as a child, yet perfectly unable to comprehend a word I say; another may exhibit uncommon intelligence in conversation, yet not be a whit happier in his relationship than the infant on my knee. But when it becomes a question of service for me, or public identification with me, it is evidently quite another thing. This is but a feeble illustration of the idea of capacity in the Father's house, and assigned position in the kingdom of the Son.

But let it be remembered that our suffering with Christ is not a yoke of bondage, but a matter of privilege; not an iron rule, but a gracious gift; not constrained servitude, but voluntary devotedness. "Unto you *it is given,* in the behalf of Christ, not only to believe on Him, but also to suffer for His sake" (Phil. 1:29). Moreover, there can be little doubt but that the real secret of suffering for Christ is to have the heart's affections centred in Him. The more I love Jesus, the closer I shall walk with Him, and the closer I walk with Him, the more faithfully I shall imitate Him, and the more faithfully I imitate Him, the more I shall suffer with Him. Thus it all flows from love to Christ; and then it is a fundamental truth that "we love Him because He first loved us." In this, as in everything else, let us beware of a legal spirit; for it must not be imagined that a man with the yoke of legality round his neck is suffering for Christ; alas! it is much to be feared that such an one does not know Christ, does not know the blessedness of sonship, has not yet been established in grace, is rather seeking to reach the family by works of law than to reach the kingdom by the path of suffering.

On the other hand, let us see that we are not shrinking from our Master's cup and baptism. Let us not profess to enjoy the benefits which His cross secures, while we refuse the rejection which that cross involves. We may rest assured that the road to the kingdom is not enlightened by the sunshine of this world's favor, nor strewed with the roses of its prosperity. If a Christian is advancing in the world, he has much reason to apprehend that he is not walking in company with Christ. "If any man serve Me, let him follow Me: and where I am, there shall also My servant be." What was the goal of Christ's earthly career? Was it an elevated, influential position in this world? By no means. What then? He found His place on the cross, between two condemned malefactors. But, it will be said, God was in this. True; yet man was in it likewise; and this latter truth is what must inevitably secure our rejection by the world, if only we keep in company with Christ. The companionship of Christ, which lets me into heaven, casts me out of earth; and to talk of the former, while I am ignorant of the latter, proves there is something wrong. If Christ were on earth now, what would His path be? whither would it tend? where would it terminate? Would we like to walk with Him? Let us answer those inquiries under the edge of the Word, and under the eye of the Almighty; and may the Holy Ghost make us faithful to an absent, a rejected, a crucified Master. The man who walks in the Spirit will be filled with Christ; and, being filled with Him, he will not be occupied with suffering, but with Him for whom he suffers. If the eye is fixed on Christ, the suffering will be as nothing in comparison with the present joy and future glory.

The subject of heirship has led me much further than I intended; but I do not regret it, as it is of considerable importance. Let us now briefly glance at the deeply significant vision of Abraham as set forth in the closing verses of our chapter. "And *when the sun was going down,* a deep sleep fell upon Abram; and, lo, a horror of great darkness fell upon him. And He said unto Abram, 'Know of a surety, that thy seed shall be a stranger in a land that is not theirs, and shall serve them; and they shall afflict them four hundred years; and also that nation, whom they shall serve, will I judge: and afterward shall they come out with great substance. . . .' And it came to pass, that, *when the sun went down,* and it was dark, behold a smoking furnace, and a burning lamp that passed between those pieces."

The entire of Israel's history is summed

up in those two figures—the "furnace" and the "lamp." The former presents to us those periods of their history in which they were brought into suffering and trial; such, for example, as the long period of Egyptian bondage, their subjection to the kings of Canaan, the Babylonish captivity, their present dispersed and degraded condition. During all these periods they may be considered as passing through the smoking furnace. (See Deut. 4:20; 1 Kings 8:51; Isaiah 48:10.)

Then, in the burning lamp, we have those points in Israel's eventful history at which Jehovah graciously appeared for their relief, such as, their deliverance from Egypt by the hand of Moses, their deliverance from under the power of the kings of Canaan by the ministry of the various judges, their return from Babylon by the decree of Cyrus, and their final deliverance when Christ shall appear in His glory. The inheritance must be reached through the furnace: and the darker the smoke of the furnace, the brighter and more cheering will be the lamp of God's salvation.

Nor is this principle confined merely to the people of God as a whole, it applies just as fully to individuals. All who have ever reached a position of eminence as *servants,* have endured the furnace before they enjoyed the lamp. "A horror of great darkness" passed across the spirit of Abraham: Jacob had to endure twenty-one years of sore hardship in the house of Laban: Joseph found his furnace of affliction in the dungeons of Egypt: Moses spent forty years in the desert. Thus it must be with all God's *servants.* They must be "tried" first, that, being found "faithful," they may be "put into the ministry." God's principle, in reference to those who serve Him, is expressed in those words of St. Paul, "Not a novice, lest being lifted up with pride he fall into the condemnation of the devil" (1 Tim. 3:6).

It is one thing to be *a child of God;* it is quite another to be *a servant of Christ.* I may love my child very much, yet, if I set him to work in my garden, he may do more harm than good. Why? Is it because he is not a dear child? No; but because he is not a practiced servant. This makes all the difference. Relationship and office are distinct things. Not one of the Queen's children is at present capable of being her prime minister. It is not that all God's children have not something to do, something to suffer, something to learn. Undoubtedly they have; yet it ever holds good, that *public service* and *private discipline* are intimately connected in the ways of God. One who comes forward much in public will need that chastened spirit, that matured judgment, that subdued and mortified mind, that broken will, that mellow tone, which are the sure and beautiful result of God's secret discipline; and it will generally be found that those who take a prominent place without more or less of the above moral qualifications, will sooner or later break down.

Lord Jesus, keep Thy feeble servants very near unto Thine own most blessed Person, and in the hollow of Thine hand!

---

## *CHAPTER 16*

HERE we find unbelief casting its dark shadow across the spirit of Abraham, and again turning him aside, for a season, from the path of simple, happy confidence in God. "And Sarai said unto Abram, 'Behold the Lord hath restrained me from bearing.' " These words bespeak the usual impatience of unbelief; and Abraham should have treated them accordingly, and waited patiently on the Lord for the accomplishment of His gracious promise. The poor heart naturally prefers anything to the attitude of *waiting.* It will turn to any expedient, any scheme, any resource, rather than be kept in that posture. It is one thing to believe a promise at the first, and quite another thing to wait quietly for the accomplishment thereof. We can see this distinction constantly exemplified in a child. If I promise my child anything, he has no idea of doubting my word; but yet I can detect the greatest possible restlessness and impatience in reference to the time and manner of accomplishment. And cannot the wisest sage find a true mirror in which to see himself reflected, in the conduct of a child? Truly so. Abraham exhibits faith in chapter 15, and yet he fails in patience in chapter 16. Hence the force and beauty of the apostle's word in Hebrews 6: "Followers of them who through *faith and patience* inherit the promises." God makes a promise; faith believes it, hope anticipates it, patience *waits* quietly for it.

There is such a thing, in the commercial world, as "the present worth" of a bill or promissory note; for if men are called upon to wait for their money, they must be paid for waiting. Now, in faith's world there is such a thing as the *present* worth of God's promise; and the scale by which that worth is regulated, is the heart's experimental knowledge of God; for according to my estimate of God, will be my estimate of His promise; and, moreover, the subdued and patient spirit finds its rich and full reward in waiting upon Him for the accomplishment of all that He has promised.

However, as to Sarah, the real amount of her word to Abraham is this: The Lord has failed me; it may be, my Egyptian maid will prove a resource for me. Anything but God for a heart under the influence of unbelief. It is often truly marvelous to observe the trifles to which we will betake ourselves when once we have lost the sense of God's nearness, His infallible faithfulness and unfailing sufficiency. We lose that calm and well-balanced condition of soul so essential to the proper testimony of the man of faith, and, just like other people, betake ourselves to any or every expedient in order to reach the wished-for end, and call that "a laudable use of means."

But it is a bitter thing to take ourselves out of the place of absolute dependence upon God: the consequences must be disastrous. Had Sarah said, Nature has failed me, but God is my resource, how different it would have been! This would have been her proper ground, for nature really had failed her. But then it was nature in one shape, and therefore she wished to try nature in another. She had not learnt to look away from nature in every shape. In the judgment of God and of faith, nature in Hagar was no better than nature in Sarah. Nature whether old or young is alike to God, and, therefore, alike to faith; but, ah! we are only in the power of this truth when we are experimentally finding our living centre in God Himself. When the eye is taken off that glorious Being, we are ready for the meanest device of unbelief. It is only when we are consciously leaning on the only true, the only wise, the living God, that we are enabled to look away from every creature stream. It is not that we shall despise God's instrumentality. By no means. To do so would be recklessness and not faith. Faith values the instrument, not because of itself, but because of Him who uses it. Unbelief looks only at the instrument, and judges of the success of a matter by the apparent efficiency thereof, instead of by the sufficiency of Him who, in grace, uses it. Like Saul, who, when he looked at David and then looked at the Philistine, said, "Thou art not able to go against this Philistine to fight with him, for thou art but a youth." Yet the question in David's heart was not as to whether he was able, but whether Jehovah was able.

The path of faith is a very simple and a very narrow one. It neither deifies the means on the one hand, nor despises it on the other; it simply values it so far as it is evidently God's means, and no further. There is a vast difference between God's using the creature to minister to me, and my using it to shut Him out. This difference is not sufficiently attended to. God used the ravens to minister to Elijah, but Elijah did not use them to exclude God. If the heart be really trusting in God, it will not trouble itself about His means. It waits on Him, in the sweet assurance that by what means soever He pleases, He will bless, He will minister, He will provide.

Now, in the case before us in this chapter, it is evident that Hagar was not God's instrument for the accomplishment of His promise to Abraham. He had promised a son, no doubt, but He had not said that this son should be Hagar's; and, in point of fact, we find, from the narrative, that both Abraham and Sarah "multiplied their sorrow" by having recourse to Hagar; for "when she saw that she had conceived, her mistress was despised in her eyes." This was but the beginning of those multiplied sorrows, which flowed from hastening after nature's resources. Sarah's dignity was trampled down by an Egyptian bondwoman, and she found herself in the place of weakness and contempt. The only true place of dignity and power is the place of felt weakness and dependence. There is no one so entirely independent of all around as the man who is really walking by faith, and waiting only upon God; but the moment a child of God makes himself a debtor to nature or the world, he loses his dignity, and will speedily be made to feel his loss. It is no easy task to estimate the loss sustained by diverging, in the smallest measure, from the path of faith. No doubt, all those who walk in that path will find trial and exercise; but one thing is certain, that the blessings and joys which peculiarly belong to them are infinitely more than a counterpoise; whereas, when they turn aside, they have to encounter far deeper trial, and naught but that.

"And Sarai said, 'My wrong be *upon thee*.' " When we act wrong, we are ofttimes prone to lay the blame on some one else. Sarah was only reaping the fruit of her own proposal, and yet she says to Abraham, "My wrong be upon thee"; and then, with Abraham's permission, she seeks to get rid of the trial which her own impatience had brought upon her. "But Abram said unto Sarai, 'Behold thy maid is in thy hand; do to her as it pleaseth thee.' And when Sarai dealt hardly with her, she fled from her face." This will not do. "The bondwoman" cannot be got rid of by hard treatment. When we make mistakes, and find ourselves called upon to encounter the results thereof, we cannot counteract those results by carrying ourselves with a high hand. We frequently try this method, but we are sure to make matters worse thereby. If we have done wrong, we should humble ourselves and confess the wrong, and wait on God for deliverance. But there was nothing like this manifested in Sarah's case. Quite the reverse. There is no sense of having done wrong; and, so far from waiting on God for deliverance, she seeks to deliver herself in her own way. However, it will always be found that every effort which we make to rectify our errors, previous to the full confession thereof, only tends to render our path more difficult. Thus Hagar had to return, and give birth to her son, which son proved to be not the child of promise at all, but a very great trial to Abraham and his house, as we shall see in the sequel.

Now, we should view all this in a double aspect: first, as teaching us a direct practical principle of much value; and secondly, in a doctrinal point of view. And, first, as to the direct, practical teaching, we may learn that when, through the unbelief of our hearts, we make mistakes, it is not all in a moment, nor yet by our own devices, we can remedy them. Things must take their course. "Whatsoever a man soweth, that shall he also reap. For he that soweth to his flesh shall of the flesh reap corruption; but he that soweth to the Spirit shall of the Spirit reap life everlasting." This is an unalterable principle, meeting us again and again on the page of inspiration, and also on the page of our personal history. Grace forgives the sin and restores the soul, but that which is sown must be reaped. Abraham and Sarah had to endure the presence of the bondwoman and her son for a number of years, and then get rid of them in God's way. There is peculiar blessedness in leaving ourselves in God's hands. Had Abraham and Sarah done so, on the present occasion, they would never have been troubled with the presence of the bondwoman and her son; but, having made themselves debtors to nature, they had to endure the consequences. But, alas! we are often "like a bullock unaccustomed to the yoke," when it would be our exceeding comfort to "behave and quiet ourselves as a child that is weaned of his mother." No two figures can be more opposite than a stubborn bullock and a weaned child. The former represents a person senselessly struggling under the yoke of circumstances, and rendering his yoke all the more galling by his efforts to get rid of it; the latter represents one meekly bowing his head to everything, and rendering his portion all the sweeter by entire subjection of spirit.

And now as to the doctrinal view of this chapter. We are authorized to look at Hagar and her son as figures of the covenant of works, and all who are thereby brought into bondage. (See Gal. 4:22-25.) "The flesh" is, in this important passage, contrasted with "promise;" and thus we not only get the divine idea as to what the term "flesh" implies, but also as to Abraham's effort to obtain the seed by means of Hagar, instead of resting in God's "promise." The two covenants are allegorized by Hagar and Sarah, and are diametrically opposite the one to the other. The one gendering to bondage, inasmuch as it raised the question as to man's competency "to do" and "not to do," and made life entirely dependent upon that competency. "The man that doeth these things shall live in them." This was the Hagar-covenant. But the Sarah-covenant reveals God as the God of promise, which promise is entirely independent of man, and founded upon God's willingness and ability to fulfill it. When God makes a promise, there is no "if" attached thereto. He makes it unconditionally, and is resolved to fulfill it; and faith rests in Him, in perfect liberty of heart. It needs no effort of nature to reach the accomplishment of a divine promise. Here was precisely where Abraham and Sarah failed. They made an effort of nature to reach a certain end, which end was absolutely secured by a promise of God. This is the grand mistake of unbelief. By its restless activity, it raises a hazy mist around the soul, which hinders the beams of the divine glory from reaching it. "He could there do no mighty works, because of their unbelief." One great characteristic virtue of faith is, that it ever leaves the platform clear for God to show Himself; and truly, when He shows Himself, man must take the place of a happy worshiper.

The error into which the Galatians allowed themselves to be drawn, was the addition of something of nature to what Christ had already accomplished for them by the cross. The gospel which had been preached to them, and which they had received, was the simple presentation of God's absolute, unqualified and unconditional grace. "Jesus Christ had been evidently set forth crucified among them." This was not merely promise divinely made, but promise divinely and most gloriously accomplished. A crucified Christ settled everything, in reference both to God's claims and man's necessities. But the false teachers upset all this, or sought to upset it, by saying, "Except ye be circumcised after the manner of Moses, ye cannot be saved." This, as the apostle teaches them, was, in reality, "making Christ of none effect." Christ must either be a *whole* Saviour, or *no* Saviour at all. The moment a man says, Except *ye* be this or that, ye cannot be saved, he totally subverts Christianity; for in Christianity I find God coming down to me, *just as I am*—a lost, guilty, self-destroyed sinner; and coming, moreover, with a full remission of *all* my sins, and a full salvation from my lost estate, all perfectly wrought by Himself on the cross.

Hence, therefore, a man who tells me, You must be so and so, in order to be saved, robs the cross of all its glory, and robs me of all my peace. If salvation depends upon *our* being or doing aught, we shall inevitably be lost. Thank God, it does not; for the great fundamental principle of the gospel is, that God is *all*: man is *nothing*. It is not a mixture of God and man,—it is all of God. The peace of the gospel does not repose in part on Christ's work and in part on man's work; it reposes *wholly* on Christ's work, because that work is perfect—perfect forever; and it renders all who put their trust in it as perfect as itself.

Under the law, God, as it were, stood still to see what man could do; but in the gospel, God is seen acting, and as for man, he has but to "stand still and see the salvation of God." This being so, the inspired apostle hesitates not to say to the Galatians, "Christ is become of no effect unto you; whosoever of you are justified by law [*εν νομω*], ye are fallen from grace." If man has anything to do in the matter, God is shut out; and if God is shut out, there can be no salvation, for it is impossible that man can work out a salvation by that which proves him a lost creature; and then if it be a question of *grace*, it must be all grace. It cannot be half grace, half law. The two covenants are perfectly distinct. It cannot be half Sarah and half Hagar: it must be either the one or the other. If it be Hagar, God has nothing to do with it; and if it be Sarah, man has nothing to do with it. Thus it stands throughout. The law addresses man, tests him, sees what he is really worth, proves him a ruin, and puts him under the curse; and not only puts him under it, but keeps him there, so long as he is occupied with it—so long as he is alive. "The law hath dominion over a man so long as he liveth;" but when he is dead, its dominion necessarily ceases, so far as he is concerned, though it still remains in full force to curse every *living* man.

The gospel, on the contrary, assuming man to be lost, ruined, dead, reveals God as He is—the Saviour of the lost, the Pardoner of the guilty, the Quickener of the dead. It reveals Him, not as exacting aught from man, (for what could be expected from one who has died a bankrupt?) but as exhibiting His own independent grace in redemption. This makes a material difference, and will account for the extraordinary strength of the language employed in the Epistle to the Galatians: "I marvel,"—"Who hath bewitched you?"—"I am afraid of you,"—"I stand in doubt of you,"—"I would they were even cut off that trouble you." This is the language of the Holy Ghost, who knows the value of a full Christ and a full salvation, and who also knows how essential the knowledge of both is to a lost sinner. We have no such language as this in any other Epistle, not even in that to the Corinthians, although there were some of the grossest disorders to be corrected amongst them. All human failure and error can be corrected by bringing in God's grace; but the Galatians, like Abraham in this chapter, were going away from God and returning to the flesh. What remedy could be devised for this? How can you correct an error which consists in departing from that which alone can correct anything? To fall from grace is to get back under the law, from which nothing can ever be reaped but "*the curse*." May the Lord establish our hearts in His own most excellent grace!

---

## CHAPTER 17

HERE we have God's remedy for Abraham's failure set before us. "And when Abram was ninety years old and nine, the Lord appeared unto Abram, and said unto him, '*I am the Almighty God:* walk before *Me*, and be thou *perfect*.' "* This is a most comprehensive verse. It is very evident that Abraham had not been walking before the Almighty God when he adopted Sarah's expedient in reference to Hagar. It is faith alone that can enable a man to walk up and down before an Almighty One. Unbelief will ever be thrusting in something of self, something of circumstances, second causes, and the like, and thus the soul is robbed of the joy and peace, and calm elevation and holy independence, which flow from leaning

*I would here offer a remark as to the word "perfect." When Abraham was called upon to be "perfect," it did not mean perfect in himself; for this he never was, and never could be. It simply meant that he should be perfect as regards the object before his heart—that his hopes and expectations were to be perfectly and undividedly centred in the "Almighty God."

In looking through the New Testament, we find the word "perfect" used in at least four distinct senses. In Matt. 5:48 we read, "Be ye therefore *perfect*, even as your Father which is in heaven is perfect." Here we learn from the context that the word "perfect" refers to the principle of our walk. At verse 44 we read, "Love your enemies . . . that ye may be the sons of your Father which is in heaven; for He maketh the sun to rise upon the evil and the good, and sendeth rain upon the just and the unjust." Hence, to be "perfect" in the sense of Matt. 5:48 is to act on a principle of grace toward all, even toward those who are injurious and hostile. A Christian going to law, and asserting or contending for his rights, is not "perfect as his Father;" for his Father is dealing in *grace*, whereas he is dealing in *righteousness*.

The question here is not as to the right or wrong of going to law with worldly people (as to brethren, 1 Cor. 6 is conclusive). All I contend for is, that a Christian so doing is acting in a character the direct opposite to that of his Father; for assuredly He is not going to law with the world. He is not now on a judgment-seat, but on a mercy-seat—a throne of grace. He showers His blessings upon those who, were He to go to law with them, should be in hell. Wherefore it is plain that a Christian, when he brings a man before the judgment-seat, is not "perfect as his Father which is in heaven is perfect."

upon the arm of One who can do everything. I believe we deeply need to ponder this. God is not such an abiding reality to our souls as He ought to be, or as He would be, were we walking in more simple faith and dependence.

"Walk before *Me*." This is true power. To walk thus, implies our having nothing whatever before our hearts save God Himself. If I am founding my expectation upon men and things, I am not walking before God, but before men and things. It is of the utmost importance to ascertain who or what I have before me as an object. To what am I looking? On whom or what am I leaning, at this moment? Does God *entirely* fill my future? Have men or circumstances aught to do therein? Is there any space allotted to the creature? The only way in which to get above the world is to walk by faith, because faith so completely fills the scene with God that there is no room for the creature—no room for the world. If God fills up my entire range of vision, I can see nothing else; and then I am able to say, with the Psalmist, "My soul, wait thou *only* upon God; for my expectation is from Him. He *only* is my rock and my salvation: He is my defence, I shall not be moved" (Ps. 62:5-6). This word "only" is deeply searching. Nature cannot say this. Not that it will, save when under the direct influence of a daring and blasphemous scepticism, formally shut out God altogether; but it assuredly cannot say, "*He only.*"

Now, it is well to see that as in the matter of salvation, so in all the details of actual life from day to day, God will not share His glory with the creature. From first to last, it must be "He only," and this, too, in reality. It will not do to have the language of dependence upon God on our lips, while our hearts are really leaning on some creature resource. God will make all this fully manifest; He will test the heart; He will put faith into the furnace. "Walk before Me, and be thou perfect." Thus it is we reach the proper point. When the soul is enabled, by grace, to get rid of all its fondly-cherished creature expectations, then, and only then, it is prepared to let God act; and when He acts, all must be well. He will not leave anything undone. He will perfectly settle everything on behalf of those who simply put their trust in Him. When unerring wisdom, omnipotent power, and infinite love combine, the confiding heart may enjoy unruffled repose. Unless we can find some circumstance too big or too little for "the Almighty God," we have no proper base on which to

---

At the close of Matt. 18 we have a parable which teaches us that a man who asserts his rights is ignorant of the true character and proper effect of grace. The servant was not *unrighteous* in demanding what was due to him, but he was *ungracious.* He was totally unlike his master. He had been forgiven ten thousand talents, and yet he could seize his fellow by the throat for a paltry hundred pence. What was the consequence? He was delivered to the tormentors. He lost the happy sense of *grace,* and was left to reap the bitter fruits of having asserted his *rights,* while being himself a subject of *grace.* And, observe further, he was called a "*wicked* servant," not because of having owed "ten thousand talents," but because of not having forgiven the "hundred pence." *The master* had ample grace to settle the former, but *he* had not grace to settle the latter. This parable has a solemn voice for all Christians going to law; for although, in the application of it, it is said, "So shall My heavenly Father do to you, if you, from your heart, forgive not every one *his brother* their trespasses," yet is the principle of general application, that a man acting in righteousness will lose *the sense* of grace.

In Hebrews 9 we have another sense of the term "perfect." Here, too, the context settles the import of the word. It is "perfect, as pertaining to the conscience." This is a deeply important use of the term. The worshiper under the law never could have a perfect conscience, for the simplest reason possible, because he never had a perfect sacrifice. The blood of a bullock and a goat did well enough *for a time,* but it could not do *forever,* and therefore could not give a perfect conscience. Now, however, the weakest believer in Jesus is privileged to have a perfect conscience. Why? Is it because he is a *better man* than the worshiper under the law? Nay; but because he has gotten *a better sacrifice.* If Christ's sacrifice is perfect forever, the believer's conscience is perfect forever. The two things necessarily go together. For the Christian not to have a perfect conscience is a dishonor to the sacrifice of Christ. It is tantamount to saying that His sacrifice is only temporary, and not eternal, in its effect; and what is this but to bring it down to the level of the sacrifices under the Mosaic economy.

It is very needful to distinguish between perfection in the flesh and perfection as to conscience. To pretend to the former, is to exalt *self;* to refuse the latter, is to dishonor Christ. The babe in Christ should have a perfect conscience; whereas St. Paul had not, nor could have, perfect flesh. The flesh is not presented in the Word as a thing which is to be perfected, but as a thing which has been crucified. This makes a wide difference. The Christian has sin *in* him, but not *on* him. Why? Because Christ, who had no sin *in* Him ever, had sin *on* Him when He was nailed to the cross.

Finally, in Phil. 3 we have two other senses of the word "perfect." The apostle says, "Not as though I had already attained, either were already *perfect;*" and yet a little further on he says, "Let as many as be *perfect* be thus minded." The former refers to the apostle's full and everlasting conformity to Christ in glory: the latter refers to our having Christ as the all-engrossing object before the heart's affections.

found a single anxious thought. This is an amazing truth, and one eminently calculated to put all who believe it into the blessed position in which we find Abraham in this chapter. When God had, in effect, said to him, Leave *all* to Me, and I will settle it for you, beyond your utmost desires and expectations: the seed and the inheritance, and everything pertaining thereto, will be fully and everlastingly settled, according to the covenant of the Almighty God,—then "*Abram fell on his face*." Truly blessed attitude! the only proper one for a thoroughly empty, feeble, and unprofitable sinner to occupy in the presence of the living God—the Creator of heaven and earth—the Possessor of all things—"the Almighty God."

"And God talked with him." It is when man is in the dust that God can talk to him in grace. Abraham's posture here is the beautiful expression of entire prostration, in the presence of God, in the sense of utter weakness and nothingness. And this, be it observed, is the sure precursor of God's revelation of Himself. It is when the creature is laid low that God can show Himself in the unclouded effulgence of what He is. He will not give His glory to another. He can reveal Himself, and allow man to worship in view of that revelation; but until the sinner takes his proper place, there can be no unfolding of the divine character. How different is Abraham's attitude in this and the preceding chapter! There, he had nature before him; here, he has the Almighty God: there, he is an actor; here, he is a worshiper: there, he was betaking himself to his own and Sarah's contrivance; here, he leaves himself and his circumstances, his present and his future, in God's hands, and allows Him to act in him, for him and through him. Hence God can say, "I will make,"—"I will establish,"—"I will give,"—"I will bless." In a word, it is all God and His actings; and this is real rest for the poor heart that has learnt anything of itself.

The covenant of circumcision is now introduced. Every member of the household of faith must bear in his body the seal of that covenant. There must be no exception. "He that is born in thy house, and he that is bought with thy money, must needs be circumcised: and My covenant shall be in your flesh, for an everlasting covenant. And the uncircumcised man-child, whose flesh of his foreskin is not circumcised, that soul shall be cut off from his people, he hath broken My covenant." We are taught, in Romans 4, that circumcision was "a seal of the righteousness of faith." "Abraham believed God, and it was counted unto him for righteousness." Being thus counted righteous, God set His "seal" upon him.

The seal with which the believer is now sealed is not a mark in the flesh, but "that Holy Spirit of promise, whereby he is sealed unto the day of redemption." This is founded upon his everlasting connection with Christ, and his perfect identification with Him, in death and resurrection; as we read, in Colossians, "And ye are complete in Him, which is the head of all principality and power: in whom also ye are *circumcised* with the circumcision made without hands, in putting off the body of the sins of the flesh by the circumcision of Christ: buried with Him in baptism, wherein also ye are risen with Him through the faith of the operation of God, who hath raised Him from the dead. And you, being dead in your sins and the uncircumcision of your flesh, hath He quickened together with Him, having forgiven you all trespasses." This is a most glorious passage, unfolding to us the true idea of what circumcision was meant to typify. Every believer belongs to "the circumcision" in virtue of his living association with Him who, by His cross, has forever abolished everything that stood in the way of His Church's perfect justification. There was not a speck of sin on the conscience, nor a principle of sin in the nature of His people, for which Christ was not judged on the cross; and they are now looked upon as having died with Christ, lain in the grave with Christ, been raised with Christ, perfectly accepted in Him—their sins, their iniquities, their transgressions, their enmity, their uncircumcision, having been entirely put away by the cross. The sentence of death has been written on the flesh; but the believer is in possession of a new life, in union with his risen Head in glory.

The apostle, in the above passage, teaches that the Church was quickened out of the grave of Christ; and, moreover, that the forgiveness of all her trespasses is as complete, and as entirely the work of God, as was the raising of Christ from the dead; and this latter, we know, was the result of "God's mighty power," or, as it may be rendered, "according to the energy of the might of His power" (Eph. 1:19)—a truly wonderful expression, calculated to set forth the magnitude and glory of redemption, as well as the solid basis on which it rests.

What rest—perfect rest—for the heart and conscience is here! What full relief for the burdened spirit! *All* our sins buried in the grave of Christ,—not one—even the smallest—left out! God did this for us! All that His searching eye could detect in us, He laid on the head of Christ when He hung upon the cross! He judged Him there and then, instead of judging us in hell forever! Precious fruit, this, of the admirable, the profound, the eternal counsels of redeeming love! And we are "sealed," not with a certain mark cut in our flesh, but with the Holy Ghost. The entire household of faith is sealed thus. Such is the dignity, the value, the changeless efficacy of the blood of Christ, that the Holy Ghost—the Third Person of the eternal Trinity—can take up His abode in all those who have put their trust therein.

And now what remains for those who know these things, save to "be steadfast, unmovable, always abounding in the work of the Lord." Thus may it be, O Lord, through the grace of Thy Holy Spirit!

---

## *CHAPTER 18*

THIS chapter affords a beautiful exemplification of the results of an obedient, separated walk. "Behold, I stand at the door, and knock: if any man hear My voice, and open the door, I will come in to him, and will sup with him, and he with Me" (Rev. 3:20). Again, we read, "Jesus answered and said unto him, 'If a man love Me, he will keep My words; and My Father will love him, and We will come unto him, and make our abode with him' " (John 14:23). From these passages, taken in connection with our chapter, we learn that an obedient soul enjoys a character of communion entirely unknown to one who moves in a worldly atmosphere.

This does not touch, in the most remote manner, the question of forgiveness or justification. All believers are clothed in the same spotless robe of righteousness,—all stand in one common justification, under the eye of God. The one life flows down from the Head in heaven through all the members on earth. This is plain. The doctrine in reference to the above important points is fully established in the Word, and has been again and again unfolded through the foregoing pages of this volume. But we should remember that justification is one thing, and the fruit thereof quite another: to be a child is one thing, to be an obedient child is quite another. Now, a father loves an obedient child, and will make such a child more the depositary of his thoughts and plans. And is this not true in reference to our heavenly Father? Unquestionably. John 14:23 puts this quite beyond dispute; and, moreover, it proves that for one to speak of loving Christ, and not to "keep His words," is hypocrisy. "If a man love Me, he will keep My words." Hence, if we are not keeping Christ's words, it is a sure proof we are not walking in the love of His name. Love to Christ is proved by doing the things which He commands, and not by merely saying, "Lord, Lord." It is of very little avail to say, "I go, sir," while the heart has no idea of going.

However, in Abraham we see one who, however he may have failed in detail, was nevertheless characterized in the main by a close, simple and elevated walk with God; and in the interesting section of his history now before us, we find him in the enjoyment of three special privileges, namely, providing refreshment *for* the Lord, enjoying full communion *with* the Lord, and interceding for others *before* the Lord. These are high distinctions; and yet are they only such as ever result from an obedient, separated, holy walk. Obedience refreshes the Lord, as being the fruit of His own grace in our hearts. We see in the only perfect Man that ever lived, how He constantly refreshed and delighted the Father. Again and again God bore testimony to Him from heaven, as His "beloved Son," in whom He was "well pleased." The path of Christ furnished a continual feast to heaven. His ways were ever sending up a fragrant incense to the throne of God. From the manger to the cross, He did always the things which pleased His Father. There was no interruption, no variation, no salient point. He was the only perfect One.

There only can the Spirit trace
A perfect life below.

Here and there, as we look along the current of inspiration, we find one and another who occasionally refreshed the mind of heaven. Thus, in the chapter before us, we find the tent of the stranger at Mamre affording refreshment to the Lord Himself,—refreshment lovingly offered, and willingly accepted (ver. 1-8).

Then we find Abraham enjoying high communion *with* the Lord, first, in reference to his own personal interests (ver. 9-15), and secondly, in reference to the destinies of Sodom (ver. 16-21). What confirmation to Abraham's heart in the absolute promise—"*Sarah* shall have a son"! Yet this promise only elicited a laugh from Sarah, as it had elicited one from Abraham in the preceding chapter.

There are two kinds of laughter spoken of in Scripture. There is, first, the laughter with which the Lord fills our mouth, when, at some trying crisis, He appears in a signal manner for our relief. "When the Lord turned again the captivity of Zion, we were like them that dream. Then was our mouth filled with *laughter*, and our tongue with singing: then said they among the heathen, 'The Lord hath done great things for them;' the Lord hath done great things for us, whereof we are glad" (Psalm 126:1-2). Again, there is the laughter with which unbelief fills our mouths, when God's promises are too magnificent for our narrow hearts to take in, or the visible agency too small, in our judgment, for the accomplishment of His grand designs. The first of these we are never ashamed or afraid to avow.—Zion's sons are not ashamed to say, "Then was our mouth filled with laughter" (Psalm 126:2). When Jehovah makes us to laugh, we may laugh heartily. "But Sarah denied, saying, 'I laughed not;' for she was afraid." Unbelief makes us cowards and liars: faith makes us bold and truthful,—it enables us to "come boldly," and to "draw near with true hearts."

But further, Abraham is made the depositary of God's thoughts and counsels about Sodom. Though having nothing to do with it personally, yet he was so near the Lord that he was let into His mind in reference to it. The way to know the divine purposes about this present evil world, is not to be mixed up with it, in its schemes and speculations, but to be entirely separated from it. The more closely we walk with God, and the more subject we are to His Word, the more we shall know of His mind about everything. I do not need to study the newspaper in order to know what is going to happen in the world: God's Word reveals all I want to know. In its pure and sanctifying pages I learn all about the character, the course, and the destiny of the world; whereas, if I go to the men of the world for news, I may expect that the devil will use them to cast dust in my eyes.

Had Abraham visited Sodom in order to obtain information about its facts, had he applied to some of its leading intelligent men, to know what they thought of Sodom's present condition and future prospects, how would he have been answered? Doubtless, they would have called his attention to their agricultural and architectural schemes, the vast resources of the country; they would have placed before his eyes one vast, mingled scene of buying and selling, building and planting, eating and drinking, marrying and giving in marriage. Doubtless, too, they would never dream of judgment, and if any one had made mention thereof, their mouths would have been filled with infidel laughter. Hence, then, it is plain that Sodom was not the place in which to learn about Sodom's end. No; the place where "Abraham stood before the Lord," afforded the only proper point from whence to take in the whole prospect. There he could stand entirely above the fogs and mists which had gathered upon Sodom's horizon. There, in the clearness and calmness of the divine presence, he could understand it all. And what use did he make of his knowledge and his elevated position? how was he occupied in the Lord's presence? The answer to these inquiries leads us to the third special privilege enjoyed by our patriarch in this chapter, namely,—

Intercession for others *before* the Lord. He was enabled to plead for those who were mixed up in Sodom's defilement, and in danger of being involved in Sodom's judgment. This was a happy and a holy use to make of his place of nearness to God. Thus it is ever. The soul that can "draw near to God," in the assurance of faith, having the heart and conscience perfectly at rest, being able to repose in God as to the past, the present, and the future—that soul will be able and willing to intercede for others. The man who has on "the whole armor of God," will be able to pray "for all saints." And, oh! what a view this gives us of the intercession of our Great High Priest, who has passed into the heavens! What infinite repose He enjoys in all the divine counsels! With what conscious acceptance He sits enthroned amid the brightness of the Majesty in the heavens! and with what efficacy He pleads before that Majesty for those who are toiling along amid the defilement of this present scene! Happy—ineffably happy—they who are the subjects of such all-prevailing intercession! At once happy and secure. Would that we had hearts to enter into all this,—hearts enlarged, by personal communion with God, to take in more of the infinite fullness of His grace, and the suitability of His provision for all our need.

We see, in this Scripture, that how blessed soever Abraham's intercession might be, yet it was limited, because the intercessor was *but a man*. It did not reach the need. He said, "I will speak *yet but this once*," and there he stopped short, as if afraid of having presented too large a draft at the treasury of infinite grace, or forgetting that faith's check was never yet dishonored at God's bank. It was not that he was straitened in God. By no means. There was abundance of grace and patience in Him to have hearkened to His dear servant had he proceeded even to three or one; but the servant was limited. He was afraid of overdrawing his account: he ceased to ask, and God ceased to give. Not so our blessed Intercessor. Of Him it can be said, "He is able to save *to the uttermost*, . . . seeing He *ever* liveth to make intercession." May our hearts cling to Him, in all our need, our weakness, and our conflict.

Before closing this section, I would offer a remark, which, whether it may be regarded as properly flowing out of the truth contained therein, or not, is nevertheless worthy of consideration. It is of the utmost importance, in the study of Scripture, to distinguish between God's moral government of the world, and the specific hope of the Church. The entire body of Old Testament prophecy, and much of the New, treats of the former, and, in so doing, presents, I need hardly say, a subject of commanding interest to every Christian. It is interesting to know what God is doing, and will do, with all the nations of the earth,—interesting to read God's thoughts about Tyre, Babylon, Nineveh, and Jerusalem; about Egypt, Assyria, and the land of Israel. In short, the entire range of Old Testament prophecy demands the prayerful attention of every true believer. But, let it be remembered, we do not find therein contained the proper hope of the Church. How could we? If we have not therein the Church's existence directly revealed, how could we have the Church's hope? Impossible. It is not that the Church cannot find there a rich harvest of divine moral principles, which she may most happily and profitably use. She undoubtedly can; but this is quite another thing from finding there her proper existence and specific hope. And yet a large portion of the

Old Testament prophecies has been applied to the Church; and this application has involved the whole subject in such mist and confusion, that simple minds are scared away from the study, and in neglecting the study of prophecy, they have also neglected that which is quite distinct from prophecy, properly so called—even the hope of the Church; which hope, be it well remembered, is not anything which God is going to do with the nations of the earth, but to meet the Lord Jesus in the clouds of heaven, to be forever with Him and forever like Him.

Many may say, I have no *head* for prophecy. Perhaps not, but have you a *heart* for Christ? Surely, if you love Christ you will love His appearing, though you may have no capacity for prophetic investigation. An affectionate wife may not have a head to enter into her husband's affairs, but she has a heart for her husband's return;—she might not be able to understand his ledger and day-book, but she knows his footstep and recognizes his voice. The most unlettered saint, if only he has affection for the Person of the Lord Jesus, can entertain the most intense desire to see Him; and this is the Church's hope. The apostle could say to the Thessalonians, "Ye turned to God from idols, to serve the living and true God, and to *wait for His Son from heaven*" (1 Thess. 1:9-10). Now, evidently, those Thessalonian saints could, at the moment of their conversion, have known little, if anything, of prophecy, or the special subject thereof; and yet they were, at that very moment, put into the full possession and power of the specific hope of the Church—even the coming of the Son. Thus is it throughout the entire New Testament. There, no doubt, we have prophecy,—there, too, we have God's moral government; but, at the same time, numberless passages might be adduced in proof of the fact, that the common hope of Christians in apostolic times—the simple, unimpeded, and unencumbered hope—was, *the return of the Bridegroom*. May the Holy Ghost revive "that blessed hope" in the Church; may He gather in the number of the elect, and "make ready a people prepared for the Lord."

## *CHAPTER 19*

THERE are two methods which the Lord graciously adopts, in order to draw the heart away from this present world. The first is, by setting before it the attractiveness and stability of "things above:" the second is, by faithfully declaring the evanescent and shakable nature of "things on the earth." The close of Hebrews 12 furnishes a beautiful example of each of these methods. After stating the truth, that we are come unto mount Zion, with all its attendant joys and privileges, the apostle goes on to say, "See that ye refuse not Him that speaketh; for if they escaped not who refused him that spake on earth, much more shall not we escape if we turn away from Him that speaketh from heaven; whose voice then shook the earth, but now He hath promised, saying, 'Yet once I shake, not only the earth, but also heaven.' Now this 'once' signifieth the removal of the shakable things, as of things that are made, that the unshakable things may remain." Now it is much better to be *drawn* by the joys of heaven, than *driven* by the sorrows of earth. The believer should not wait to be shaken out of present things. He should not wait for the world to give him up, before he gives up the world: he should give it up in the power of communion with heavenly things. There is no difficulty in giving up the world when we have, by faith, laid hold of Christ: the difficulty would then be to hold it. If a scavenger were left an estate of ten thousand a year, he would not long continue to sweep the streets. Thus, if we are realizing our portion amid the unshakable realities of heaven, we shall find little difficulty in resigning the delusive joys of earth. Let us now look at the solemn section of inspired history here set before us.

In it we find Lot "sitting in the gate of Sodom," the place of authority. He has evidently made progress,—he has "got on in the world." Looked at from a worldly point of view, his course has been a successful one. He at first "pitched his tent *toward* Sodom;" then, no doubt, he found his way into it; and now we find him sitting in the gate—a prominent, influential post. How different is all this from the scene with which the preceding chapter opens! But, ah! the reason is obvious. "*By faith* Abraham sojourned in the land of promise, as in a *strange country*, dwelling in tabernacles." We have no such statement in reference to Lot.* It could not be said, By faith Lot sat in the gate of Sodom. Alas! no; he gets no place among the noble army of confessors—the great cloud of witnesses to the power of faith. The world was his snare, present things his bane. He did not "endure as seeing Him who is invisible." He looked at "the things which are seen, and temporal;" whereas Abraham looked at "the things which are unseen and eternal." There was a most material difference between those two men, who, though they started together on their course, reached a very different goal, so far as their public testimony was concerned. No doubt Lot was saved, yet it was "so as by fire," for, truly, "his work was burned up." On the other hand, Abraham had "an abundant entrance ministered unto him into the everlasting kingdom of our Lord and Saviour Jesus Christ."

Further, we do not find that Lot is permitted to enjoy any of the high distinctions and privileges with which Abraham was favored. Instead of refreshing the Lord, Lot gets his righteous soul vexed; instead of enjoying communion *with* the Lord, he is at a lamentable distance *from* the Lord; and, lastly, instead of interceding for others, he finds enough to do to intercede for himself. The Lord remained to commune with Abraham, and merely sent His angels to Sodom; and these angels could with difficulty be induced to enter into Lot's house, or partake of his hospitality: "they said, 'Nay, but *we will abide in the street all night*.' " What a rebuke! How different from the willing acceptance of Abraham's invitation, as expressed in the words, "So do as thou hast said."

There is a great deal involved in the act of partaking of any one's hospitality. It expresses, when intelligently looked at, full fellowship with him.—"I will come in unto him, and sup *with him*, and *he with Me*."—"If ye have judged me to be faithful to the Lord, come into my house and abide." If they had not so judged her, they would not have accepted her invitation.

Hence, the angels' word to Lot contains a most unqualified condemnation of his position in Sodom. They would rather abide in the street all night than enter under the roof of one in a wrong position. Indeed, their only object in coming to Sodom seems to have been to deliver Lot, and that, too, because of Abraham; as we read, "And it came to pass, when God destroyed the cities of the plain, that God *remembered Abraham*, and sent Lot out of the midst of the overthrow, when He overthrew the cities in which Lot dwelt." This is strongly marked. It was simply for Abraham's sake that Lot was suffered to escape. The Lord has no sympathy with a worldly mind; and such a mind it was that had led Lot to settle down amid the defilement of that guilty city. Faith never put him there; a spiritual mind never put him there; "his righteous soul" never put him there: it was simple love for this present evil world that led him first to "*choose*," then to "pitch his tent toward," and finally to "sit in the gate of Sodom." And, oh, what a portion he chose! Truly, it was a broken cistern which could hold no water,—a broken reed which pierced his hand. It is a bitter thing to seek, in any wise, to manage for ourselves: we are sure to make the most grievous mistakes. It is infinitely better to allow God to order all our ways for us; to commit them all, in the spirit of a little child, to Him who is so willing and so able to manage for us; to put the pen, as it were, into His blessed hand, and allow Him to sketch out our entire course, according to His own unerring wisdom and infinite love.

No doubt Lot thought he was doing well for himself and his family when he moved to Sodom, but the sequel shows how entirely he erred; and it also sounds in our ears a voice of deepest solemnity—a voice telling us to beware how we yield to the incipient

*It would furnish a very searching question for the heart, in reference to every undertaking, were we to ask, Am I doing this by faith? "Whatever is not of faith is sin"; and "without faith, it is impossible to please God."

workings of a worldly spirit. "Be content with such things as ye have." Why? Is it because you are so well off in the world?—because you have all that your poor rambling hearts would seek after?—because there is not so much as a single chink in your circumstances through which a vain desire might make its escape? Is this to be the ground of our contentment? By no means. What then? "For He hath said, 'I will never leave thee nor forsake thee.' " Blessed portion! Had Lot been content therewith, he never would have sought the well-watered plains of Sodom.

And then, if we need any further ground of inducement to the exercise of a contented spirit, truly we have it in this chapter. What did Lot gain in the way of happiness and contentment? Little indeed. The people of Sodom surround his house, and threaten to break into it; he seeks to appease them by a most humiliating proposition, but all in vain. If a man will mingle with the world, for the purpose of self-aggrandizement, he must make up his mind to endure the sad consequences. We cannot profit by the world, and, at the same time, bear effectual testimony against its wickedness. "This one fellow came in to sojourn, and he will needs be a judge." This will never do. The true way to judge is to stand apart, in the moral power of grace, not in the supercilious spirit of pharisaism. To attempt to reprove the world's ways, while we profit by association with it, is vanity; the world will attach very little weight to such reproof and such testimony. Thus it was, too, with Lot's testimony to his sons-in-law; " he seemed as one that mocked." It is vain to speak of approaching judgment while finding our place, our portion, and our enjoyment in the very scene which is to be judged.

Abraham was in a far better position to speak of judgment, inasmuch as he was entirely outside of the sphere thereof. The tent of the stranger at Mamre was in no danger, though Sodom were in flames. O, that our hearts longed more after the precious fruits of a realized strangership, so that instead of having, like poor Lot, to be dragged by main force out of the world, casting a lingering look behind, we might, with holy alacrity, bound forward, like a racer, towards the goal.

Lot evidently longed after the scene which he was forced, by angelic power, to abandon; for not only had the angels to lay hold of him, and hasten him away from the impending judgment, but even when exhorted to escape for *his life,* (which was all he could save from the wreck,) and flee to the mountain, he replies, "Oh, not so, my Lord: behold, now, thy servant hath found grace in thy sight, and thou hast magnified thy mercy which thou hast showed unto me in saving *my life;* and I cannot escape to the mountain, lest some evil take me and I die: behold, now, *this city* is near to flee unto, and it is a little one: oh! let me escape thither, (is it not a litte one?) and my soul shall live." What a picture! He seems like a drowning man, ready to catch even at a floating feather. Though commanded by the angel to flee to the mountain, he refuses, and still fondly clings to the idea of "a little city,"—some little shred of the world. He feared death in the place to which God was mercifully directing him,—yea, he feared all manner of evil, and could only hope for safety in some little city—some spot of his own devising. "Oh! let me escape *thither, and my soul shall live.*" How sad! There is no casting himself wholly upon God. Alas! he had too long walked at a distance from Him,—too long breathed the dense atmosphere of a "city," to be able to appreciate the pure air of the divine presence, or lean on the arm of the Almighty. His soul seemed completely unhinged; his worldly nest had been abruptly broken up, and he was not quite able to nestle himself, by faith, in the bosom of God. He had not been cultivating communion with the invisible world, and now the visible was passing away from beneath his feet with tremendous rapidity. The "fire and brimstone from heaven" were about to fall upon that in which all his hopes and all his affections were centred. The thief had broken in upon him, and he seems entirely divested of spiritual nerve and self-possession. He is at his wits' end; but the worldly element, being strong in his heart, prevails, and he seeks his only refuge in "a little city." Yet he is not at ease even there, for he leaves it and gets up to the mountain. He does through fear what he would not do at the command of God's messenger.

And then see his end!—His own children make him drunk, and in his drunkenness he becomes the instrument of bringing into existence the Ammonites and the Moabites—the determined enemies of the people of God. What a volume of solemn instruction is here! Oh, my reader, see here what the world is! see what a fatal thing it is to allow the heart to go out after it! What a commentary is Lot's history upon that brief but comprehensive admonition, "Love not the world"! This world's Sodoms and its Zoars are all alike. There is no security, no peace, no rest, no solid satisfaction for the heart therein. The judgment of God hangs over the whole scene; and He only holds back the sword in long-suffering mercy, not willing that any should perish, but that all should come to repentance.

Let us, then, seek to pursue a path of holy separation from the world. Let us, while standing outside its entire range, be found cherishing the hope of the Master's return. May its well-watered plains have no charms for our hearts. May its honors, its distinctions, and its riches be all surveyed by us in the light of the coming glory of Christ. May we be enabled, like the holy patriarch Abraham, to get up into the presence of the Lord, and, from that elevated ground, look forth upon the scene of widespread ruin and desolation—to see it all, by faith's anticipative glance, a smoking ruin. *Such it will be.* "The earth also, and the things that are therein, shall be burned up." All that about which the children of this world are so intensely anxious—after which they are so eagerly grasping—for which they are so fiercely contending, all—all will be burned up. And who can tell how soon? Where is Sodom? Where is Gomorrah? Where are the cities of the plain—those cities which were once all life and stir and bustle? Where are they now? All gone! swept away by the judgment of God! consumed by His fire and brimstone! Well, His judgments now hang over this guilty world. The day is at hand; and while judgments impend, the sweet story of grace is being told out to many an ear. Happy they who hear and believe that story! Happy they who flee to the strong mountain of God's salvation! who take refuge behind the cross of the Son of God, and therein find pardon and peace!

God grant that the reader of these lines may know what it is (with a conscience purged from sin, and his heart's affections purged from the defiling influence of the world) to wait for the Son from heaven.

---

## *CHAPTER 20*

We have two distinct points in this chapter: first, the moral degradation to which the child of God sometimes subjects himself, in the view of the world; and secondly, the moral dignity which *always* belongs to him in the view of God. Abraham again exhibits the dread of circumstances, which the heart can so easily understand. He sojourns in Gerar, and fears the men of that place. Judging that God was not there, he forgets that He is always with him. He seems to be more occupied with the men of Gerar than with the One who was stronger than they. Forgetting God's ability to protect his wife, he has recourse to the same stratagem which, years before, he had adopted in Egypt. This is very admonitory. The father of the faithful was carried away by taking his eye off God. He lost, for a little, his centre in God, and therefore gave way. How true it is, that we are only strong as we cling to God in the sense of our perfect weakness. So long as we are in the path of His appointment, nothing can harm us. Had Abraham simply leaned on God, the men of Gerar would not have meddled with him; and it was his privilege to have vindicated God's faithfulness in the midst of the most appalling difficulties. Thus, too, he would have maintained his own dignity as a man of faith.

It is often a source of sorrow to the heart

to mark how the children of God dishonor Him, and, as a consquence, lower themselves before the world by losing the sense of His sufficiency for every emergency. So long as we live in the realization of the truth that *all* our springs are in God, so long shall we be above the world in every shape and form. There is nothing so elevating to the whole moral being as faith: it carries one entirely beyond the reach of this world's thoughts; for how can the men of the world, or even worldly-minded Christians, understand the life of faith? Impossible. The springs on which it draws lie far away beyond their comprehension. They live on the surface of present things. So long as they can *see* what they deem a proper foundation for hope and confidence, so long they are hopeful and confident; but the idea of resting solely on the promise of an unseen God, they understand not. But the man of faith is calm in the midst of scenes in which nature can *see* nothing. Hence it is that faith ever seems, in the judgment of nature, such a reckless, improvident, visionary thing. None but those who know God can ever approve the actings of faith; for none but they really understand the solid and truly-reasonable ground of such actings.

In this chapter we find the man of God actually exposing himself to the rebuke and reproach of the men of the world, by reason of his actings when under the power of unbelief. Thus it must ever be. Nothing but faith can impart true elevation to a man's course and character. We may, it is true, see some who are naturally upright and honorable in their ways, yet nature's uprightness and honor cannot be trusted; they rest on a bad foundation, and are liable to give way at any moment. It is only faith which can impart a truly elevated moral tone, because it connects the soul in living power with God, the only source of true morality. And it is a remarkable fact, that in the case of all those whom God has graciously taken up, we see that, when off the path of faith, they sank even lower than other men. This will account for Abraham's conduct in this part of his history.

But there is another point of much interest and value brought out here. We find that Abraham had harbored an evil thing for a number of years;—he had, it seems, started upon his course with a certain reserve in his soul, which reserve was the result of his want of full, unqualified confidence in God. Had he been able fully to trust God in reference to Sarah, there would have been no need of any reserve or subterfuge whatever. God would have fenced her round about from every ill; and who can harm those who are the happy subjects of His unslumbering guardianship? However, through mercy, Abraham is enabled to bring out the root of the whole matter—to confess and judge it thoroughly, and get rid of it. This is the true way to act. There can be no real blessing and power till every particle of leaven is brought forth into the light and there trampled under foot. God's patience is exhaustless. He can wait,—He can bear with us; but He never will conduct a soul to the culminating point of blessing and power while leaven remains known and unjudged. Thus much as to Abimelech and Abraham. Let us now look at the moral dignity of the latter in the view of God.

In the history of God's people, whether we look at them as a whole, or as individuals, we are often struck with the amazing difference between what they are in God's view, and what they are in the view of the world. God sees His people in Christ. He looks at them through Christ; and hence He sees them "without spot or wrinkle or any such thing." They are as Christ is before God. They are perfected forever, as to their standing in Christ. "They are not in the flesh, but in the Spirit."

But in themselves, they are poor, feeble, imperfect, stumbling, inconsistent creatures; and, inasmuch as it is what they are in themselves, and that alone, that the world takes knowledge of, therefore it is that the difference seems so great between the divine and the human estimate.

Yet it is God's prerogative to set forth the beauty, the dignity, and the perfection of His people. It is His exclusive prerogative, inasmuch as it is He Himself who has bestowed those things. They are only comely through the comeliness which He has put upon them, and it is therefore due to Him to declare what that comeliness is; and, truly, He does it in a manner worthy of Himself, and never more blessedly than when the enemy comes forth to injure, to curse, or accuse. Thus, when Balak seeks to curse the seed of Abraham, Jehovah's word is, "I have not beheld iniquity in Jacob, neither have I seen perverseness in Israel." "How goodly are thy tents, O Jacob, and thy tabernacles, O Israel." Again, when Satan stands forth to resist Joshua, the word is, "The Lord rebuke thee, O Satan, . . . is not this a brand plucked out of the fire?" Thus He ever puts Himself between His people and every tongue that would accuse them. He does not answer the accusation by a reference to what His people are in themselves, or to what they are in the view of the men of this world, but to what He Himself has made them, and where He set them.

Thus, in Abraham's case, he might lower himself in the view of Abimelech, king of Gerar, and Abimelech might have to rebuke him, yet when God comes to deal with the case, He says to Abimelech, "Behold, thou art but a dead man;" and of Abraham He says, "He is a prophet, and he shall pray for thee." Yes, with all "the integrity of his heart and the innocency of his hands," the king of Gerar was "but a dead man;" and, moreover, he must be a debtor to the prayers of the erring and inconsistent stranger for the restoration of the health of his household. Such is the manner of God. He may have many a secret controversy with His child, on the ground of his practical ways, but directly the enemy enters a suit against him, Jehovah ever pleads His servant's cause.—"Touch not Mine anointed, and do My prophets no harm."—"He that toucheth you, toucheth the apple of Mine eye."—"It is God that justifieth, who is he that condemneth?" No dart of the enemy can ever penetrate the shield behind which the Lord has hidden the very feeblest lamb of His blood-bought flock. He hides His people in His pavilion, sets their feet upon the Rock of Ages, lifts their heads above their enemies round about, and fills their hearts with the everlasting joy of His salvation.

His name be praised for evermore!

---

## *CHAPTER 21*

"AND the Lord visited Sarah, as He had said, and He did unto Sarah as He had spoken." Here we have accomplished promise—the blessed fruit of patient waiting upon God. None ever waited in vain. The soul that takes hold of God's promise by faith, has gotten a stable reality which will never fail him. Thus was it with Abraham; thus was it with all the faithful from age to age; and thus will it be with all those who are enabled, in any measure, to trust in the living God. Oh! it is a wonderful blessing to have God Himself as our portion and resting-place, amid the unsatisfying shadows of this scene through which we are passing,—to have our anchor cast within the vail,—to have the word and oath of God—the two immutable things—to lean upon, for the comfort and tranquility of our souls.

When God's promise stood before the soul of Abraham as an accomplished fact, he might well have learnt the futility of his own effort to reach that accomplishment. Ishmael was of no use whatever, so far as God's promise was concerned. He might, and did, afford something for nature's affections to entwine themselves around, thus furnishing a more difficult task for Abraham to perform afterwards; but he was in no wise conducive to the development of the purpose of God, or to the establishment of Abraham's faith—quite the reverse. Nature can never do aught for God. The Lord must "visit," and the Lord must "do," and faith must wait, and nature must be still,—yea, must be entirely set aside as a dead, worthless thing, and then the divine glory can shine out, and faith find in that outshining all its rich and sweet reward. "Sarah conceived and bare Abraham a son in his old age, *at the set time* of which God had spoken to him." There is such a thing as God's "set time"—His "due season," and for this the faithful must be content to wait. The time may seem long, and hope deferred may make the heart sick; but the spiritual mind will ever find its relief in the assurance that all is for the ultimate display of God's glory. "For the vision is for an appointed time, but *at the end* it shall speak and not lie; though it tarry, wait for it; because it will assuredly come, it will not tarry . . . but the just shall live by his faith" (Hab. 2:3-4). This wondrous faith! It brings into our present all the power of God's future, and feeds upon God's promise as a present reality. By its power, the soul is kept hanging upon God when every outward thing seems to be against it, and, "at the set time," the mouth is filled with laughter. "Abraham was a hundred years old when his son Isaac was born unto him." Thus nature had nothing to glory in. "Man's extremity was God's opportunity;" and Sarah said, "*God* hath made me to laugh." All is triumph when God is allowed to show Himself.

Now, while the birth of Isaac filled Sarah's mouth with laughter, it introduced an entirely new element into Abraham's house. The son of the free-woman very speedily developed the true character of the son of the bondwoman. Indeed, Isaac proved, in principle, to be to the household of Abraham what the implantation of the new nature is in the soul of a sinner. It was not *Ishmael changed*, but it was *Isaac born*. The son of the bondwoman could never be anything else but that. He might become a great nation, he might dwell in the wilderness and become an archer, he might become the father of twelve princes, but he was the son of the bondwoman all the while. On the contrary, no matter how weak and despised Isaac might be, he was the son of the free-woman. His position and character, his standing and prospects, were all from the Lord. "That which is born of the flesh is flesh; and that which is born of the Spirit is spirit."

Regeneration is not a change of the old nature, but the introduction of a new; it is the implantation of the nature or life of the Second Adam, by the operation of the Holy Ghost, founded upon the accomplished redemption of Christ, and in full keeping with the sovereign will or counsel of God. The moment a sinner believes in his heart, and confesses with his mouth, the Lord Jesus, he becomes the possessor of a new life, and that life is Christ. He is born of God, is a child of God, is a son of the free-woman. (See Rom. 10:9; Col. 3:4; 1 John 3:1-2; Gal. 3:26; 4:31.)

Nor does the introduction of this new nature alter, in the slightest degree, the true, essential character of the old. This latter continues what it was, and is made in no respect better; yea, rather, there is the full display of its evil character in opposition to the new element. "The flesh lusteth against the Spirit, and the Spirit against the flesh; and these are contrary the one to the other." There they are in all their distinctness, and the one is only thrown into relief by the other.

I believe this doctrine of the two natures in the believer is not generally understood; and yet, so long as there is ignorance of it, the mind must be utterly at sea in reference to the true standing and privileges of the child of God. Some there are who think that regeneration is a certain change which the old nature undergoes; and, moreover, that this change is gradual in its operation, until, at length, the whole man becomes transformed. That this idea is unsound, can be proved by various quotations from the New Testament. For example, "The carnal mind is enmity against God." How can that which is thus spoken of ever undergo any improvement? The apostle goes on to say, "It is not subject to the law of God, *neither indeed can be*." If it *cannot be* subject to the law of God, how can it be improved? how can it undergo any change? Again, "That which is born of the flesh is flesh." Do what you will with flesh, and it is flesh all the while. As Solomon says, "Though thou shouldest bray a fool in a mortar, among wheat with a pestle, yet will not his foolishness depart from him" (Prov. 27:22). There is no use in seeking to make foolishness wise: you must introduce heavenly wisdom into the heart that has been heretofore only governed by folly. Again, "Ye have put off the old man" (Col. 3:9). He does not say, Ye have improved, or are seeking to improve, "the old man," but, Ye have put it off. This gives us a totally different idea. There is a very great difference between seeking to mend an old garment, and casting it aside altogether and putting on a new one. This is the idea of the last-quoted passage. It is a putting off the old, and a putting on of the new. Nothing can be more distinct or simple.

Passages might easily be multiplied to prove the unsoundness of the theory with respect to the gradual improvement of the old nature,—to prove that the old nature is dead in sins, and utterly unrenewable and unimprovable; and, moreover, that the only thing we can do with it is to keep it under our feet in the power of that new life which we have in union with our risen Head in the heavens.

The birth of Isaac did not improve Ishmael, but only brought out his real opposition to the child of promise. He might have gone on very quietly and orderly till Isaac made his appearance; but then he showed what he was, by persecuting and mocking at the child of resurrection. What then was the remedy? to make Ishmael better? By no means; but, "Cast out this bondwoman and her son; for the son of this bondwoman shall not be heir with my son, even with Isaac" (8-10). Here was the only remedy. "That which is crooked cannot be made straight;" therefore you have only to get rid of the crooked thing altogether, and occupy yourself with that which is divinely straight. It is labor lost to seek to make a crooked thing straight. Hence all efforts after the improvement of nature are utterly futile, so far as God is concerned. It may be all very well for men to cultivate and improve that which is of use to themselves; but God has given His children something infinitely better to do, even to cultivate that which is His own creation, the fruits of which, while they in no wise serve to exalt nature, are entirely to His praise and glory.

Now the error into which the Galatian churches fell, was the introduction of that which addressed itself to nature. "Except ye be circumcised after the manner of Moses, ye cannot be saved." Here salvation was made to depend upon something that man could be, or man could do, or man could keep. This was upsetting the whole glorious fabric of redemption, which, as the believer knows, rests exclusively upon what Christ is, and what He has done. To make salvation dependent, in the most remote manner, upon anything in, or done by, man, is to set it entirely aside. In other words, Ishmael must be entirely cast out, and all Abraham's hopes be made to depend upon what God had done and given in the person of Isaac. This, it is needless to say, leaves man nothing to glory in. If present or future blessedness were made to depend upon even a divine change wrought in nature, flesh might glory. Though my nature were improved, it would be something of *me*, and thus God would not have *all* the glory. But when I am introduced into a new creation, I find it is all of God,—designed, matured, developed by Himself alone. God is the actor, and I am a worshiper; He is the blesser, and I am the blessed; He is "the better," and I am "the less" (Heb. 7:7); He is the giver, and I am the receiver. This is what makes Christianity what it is; and, moreover, distinguishes it from every system of human religion under the sun, whether it be Romanism, Puseyism, or any other *ism* whatsoever. Human religion gives the creature a place, more or less; it keeps the bondwoman and her son in the house; it gives man something to glory in. On the contrary, Christianity excludes the creature from all interference in the work of salvation—casts out the bondwoman and her son, and gives *all* the glory to Him to whom alone it is due.

But let us inquire who this bondwoman and her son really are, and what they shadow forth. Galatians 4 furnishes ample teaching as to these two points. In a word, then, the bondwoman represents the covenant of the law; and her son represents all who are "of works of law," or on that principle [εξ εργων νομου]. This is very plain. The bondwoman only genders to bondage, and can never bring forth a free man. How can she? The law never could give liberty; for so long as a man was alive, it ruled him (Rom. 7:1). I can never be free so long as I am under the dominion of any one; but while I live, the law rules me, and nothing but death can give me deliverance from its dominion. This is the blessed doctrine of Rom. 7. "Wherefore, my brethren, ye also are become dead to the law by the body of Christ, that ye should be married to another, even to Him that is raised from the dead, that we should bring forth fruit unto God." This is freedom; for "if the Son shall make you free, ye shall be free indeed" (John 8:36). "So then, brethren, we are not children of the bondwoman, but of the free" (Gal. 4:31).

Now, it is in the power of this freedom that we are enabled to obey the command, "cast out this bondwoman and her son." If I am not consciously free, I shall be seeking to attain liberty in the strangest way possible, even by keeping the bondwoman in the house: in other words, I shall be seeking to get life by keeping the law; I shall be establishing my own righteousness. No doubt it will involve a struggle to cast out this element of bondage, for legalism is natural to our hearts. "The thing was very grievous in Abraham's sight, because of his son." Still, however grievous it may be, it is according to the divine mind that we should abidingly "stand fast in the liberty wherewith Christ hath made us free, and not be entangled again with the yoke of bondage" (Gal. 5:1). May we, beloved reader, so fully and experimentally enter into the blessedness of God's provision for us in Christ, that we may be done with all thoughts about the flesh, and all that it can be, do, or produce. There is a fullness in Christ which renders all appeal to nature utterly superfluous and vain.

---

## *CHAPTER 22*

ABRAHAM is now in a fit moral position to have his heart put to a most severe test. The long-cherished reserve being put forth from his heart, in chapter 20; the bondwoman and her son being put forth from his house, as in chapter 21; he now stands forth in the most honored position in which any soul can be placed, and that is a position of trial from the hand of God Himself. There are various kinds of trial; trial from the hand of Satan; trial from surrounding circumstances; but the highest character of trial is that which comes directly from the hand of God, when He puts His dear child into the furnace for the purpose of testing the reality of his faith. God will do this: He must have reality. It will not do to say, "Lord, Lord," or, "I go, sir." The heart must be probed to the very bottom, in order that no element of hypocrisy or false profession may be allowed to lodge there. "My son, give Me *thine heart*." He does not say, Give Me thine head, or thine intellect, or thy talents, or thy tongue, or thy money; but, "Give Me thine heart:" and in order to prove the sincerity of our response to this gracious command, He will lay His hand upon something very near our hearts. Thus he says to Abraham, "Take now thy son, thine only son Isaac, whom thou lovest, and get thee into the land of Moriah, and offer him there for a burnt-offering, upon one of the mountains which I will tell thee of." This was coming very close to Abraham's heart: it was passing him through a searching crucible indeed. God "requires truth in the inward parts." There may be much truth on the lips, and much in the intellect, but God looks for it in the heart. It is no ordinary proof that will satisfy God, as to the love of our hearts. He Himself did not rest satisfied with giving an ordinary proof. He gave His Son, and we should aim at giving very striking proofs of our love to Him who so loved us, even when we were dead in trespasses and sins.

However, it is well to see that God confers a signal honor upon us when He thus tests our hearts. We never read that the Lord did tempt Lot. No; Sodom tempted Lot. He never reached a sufficiently high elevation to warrant his being tried by the hand of Jehovah. It was too plainly manifest that there was plenty between his heart and the Lord, and it did not, therefore, require the furnace to bring that out. Sodom would have held out no temptation whatever to Abraham. This was made manifest in his interview with Sodom's king, in chapter 14. God knew well that Abraham loved Him far better than Sodom; but He would make it manifest that he loved Him better than any one or anything, by laying His hand upon the nearest and dearest object.—"Take now thy son, thine only son Isaac." Yes, Isaac, the child of promise,—Isaac, the object of long-deferred hope, the object of parental love, and the one in whom all the kindreds of the earth were to be blessed,—this Isaac must be offered as a burnt-offering. This, surely, was putting faith to the test, in order that, being more precious than gold that perisheth, though it be tried with fire, it might be found unto praise and honor and glory. Had Abraham's whole soul not been stayed simply on the Lord, he never could have yielded unhesitating obedience to such a searching command; but God Himself was the living and abiding support of his heart, and therefore he was prepared to give up all for Him.

The soul that has found *all* its springs in God, can, without any demur, retire from *all* creature streams. We can give up the creature just in proportion as we have found out, or become experimentally acquainted with, the Creator, and no further. To attempt to give up the visible things in any other way save in the energy of that faith which lays hold of the invisible, is the most fruitless labor possible. It cannot be done. I will hold fast my Isaac until I have found my all in God. It is when we are enabled, by faith, to say, "God is our refuge and strength, a very present help in trouble," that we can also add, "Therefore will we not fear, though the earth be removed, and though the mountains be carried into the midst of the sea" (Ps. 46:1-2).

"And Abraham rose up early in the morning." There is ready obedience. "I made haste and delayed not to keep Thy commandments." Faith never stops to look at circumstances, or ponder results; it only looks at God; it expresses itself thus: "But when it pleased God, who separated me from my mother's womb, and called me by His grace, to reveal His Son in me, that I might preach Him among the gentiles; immediately I conferred not with flesh and blood" (Gal. 1:15-16). The moment we confer with flesh and blood, our testimony and service are marred, for flesh and blood can never obey. We must rise early, and carry out, through grace, the divine command. Thus we are blessed, and God is glorified. Having God's own Word as the basis of our acting, will ever impart strength and stability to our acting. If we merely act from impulse, when the impulse subsides, the acting will subside also.

There are two things needful to a course of steady and consistent action, viz., the Holy Ghost as the power of action, and the Word to give proper direction. To use a familiar illustration,—on a railway, we should find steam of little use without the iron rails firmly laid down: the former is the power by which we move; and the latter, the direction. It is needless to add that the rails would be of little use without the steam. Now Abraham was blessed with both. He had the power of action conferred by God, and the command to act given by God also. His devotedness was of a most definite character; and this is deeply important. We frequently find much that looks like devotedness, but which, in reality, is but the desultory activity of a will not brought under the powerful action of the Word of God. All such apparent devotedness is worthless, and the spirit from which it proceeds will very speedily evaporate. We may lay down the following principle; viz., whenever devotedness passes beyond divinely-appointed bounds, it is suspicious; if it comes not up to these bounds, it is defective; if it flows without them, it is erratic. I quite admit that there are extraordinary operations and ways of the Spirit of God, in which He asserts His own sovereignty, and rises above ordinary bounds; but, in such cases, the evidence of divine activity will be sufficiently strong to carry home conviction to every spiritual mind; nor will they, in the slightest degree, interfere with the truth of the principle that true devotedness will ever be founded upon and governed by divine principle. To sacrifice a son might seem to be an act of most extraordinary devotedness, but be it remembered, that what gave that act all its value in God's sight was the simple fact of its being based upon God's command.

Then we have another thing connected with true devotedness, and that is, a spirit of worship.—"I and the lad will go yonder and *worship.*" The really-devoted servant will keep his eye not on his service, be it ever so great, but on the Master, and this will produce a spirit of worship. If I love my master according to the flesh, I shall not mind whether I am cleaning his shoes or driving his carriage; but if I am thinking more of myself than of him, I shall rather be a coachman than a shoeblack. So is it precisely in the service of the heavenly Master; if I am thinking only of Him, planting churches and making tents will be both alike to me. We may see the same thing in angelic ministry. It matters not to an angel whether he be sent to destroy an army or to protect the person of some heir of salvation; it is the Master who entirely fills his vision. As some one has remarked, "if two angels were sent from heaven, one to rule an empire, and the other to sweep the streets, they would not dispute about their respective work." This is most true, and so should it be with us. The servant should ever be combined with the worshiper, and the works of our hands perfumed with the ardent breathings of our spirits. In other words, we should go forth to our work in the spirit of those memorable words, "I and the lad will go yonder and worship." This would effectually preserve us from that merely mechanical service into which we are so prone to drop; doing things for doing's sake, and being more occupied with our work than with our Master. All must flow from simple faith in God, and obedience to His Word.

"By faith Abraham, when he was tried, offered up Isaac; and he that had received the promises offered up his only begotten" (Heb. 11:17). It is only as we are walking by faith that we can begin, continue, and end our works in God. Abraham not merely set out to offer his son, but he went on and reached the spot which God had appointed. "And Abraham took the wood of the burnt-offering, and laid it upon Isaac his son; and he took the fire in his hand, and a knife; and they went both of them together." And further on we read, "And Abraham built an altar there, and laid the wood in order, and bound Isaac his son, and laid him on the altar upon the wood. And Abraham stretched forth his hand, and took the knife to slay his son." This was real work, a "work of faith and labor of love" in the highest sense. It was no mere mockery—no drawing near with the lips, while the heart was far off,—no saying, " 'I go, sir,' and went not." It was all deep reality, just such as faith ever delights to produce, and which God delights to accept. It is easy to make a show of devotedness when there is no demand for it,—it is easy to say, "Though all shall be offended because of Thee, yet will I never be offended . . . though I should die with Thee, yet will I not deny Thee;" but the point is to stand the trial. When Peter was put to the test, he entirely broke down. Faith never talks of what it will do, but does what it can in the strength of the Lord. Nothing can be more thoroughly worthless than a spirit of empty pretension. It is just as worthless as the basis on which it rests. But faith acts "when it is tried;" till then it is content to be unseen and silent.

Now, it needs hardly to be remarked that God is glorified in those holy activities of faith; He is the immediate object of them, as He is the spring from whence they emanate. There was not a scene in Abraham's entire history in which God was so much glorified as the scene on Mount Moriah. There it was that he was enabled to bear testimony to the fact that he had found all his fresh springs in God—found them not merely previous to, but after, Isaac's birth. This is a most touching point. It is one thing to rest in God's blessings, and another thing to rest in Himself: it is one thing to trust God when I have before my eyes the channel through which the blessing is to flow, and quite another thing to trust Him when that channel is entirely stopped up. This was what proved the excellency of Abraham's faith. He showed that he could not merely trust God for an innumerable seed while Isaac stood before him in health and vigor, but just as fully if he were a smoking victim on the altar. This was a high order of confidence in God—it was unalloyed confidence; it was not a confidence propped up in part by the Creator and in part by the creature. No; it rested on one solid pedestal, viz., God Himself. "He accounted that God was able." He never accounted that Isaac was able. Isaac, without God, was nothing: God, without Isaac, was everything. This is a principle of the very last importance, and one eminently calculated to test the heart most keenly. Does it make any difference to me to see the apparent channel of all my blessings dried up? Am I dwelling sufficiently near the fountain-head to be able, with a worshiping spirit, to behold all the creature streams dried up? This I do feel to be a searching question. Have I such a simple view of God's sufficiency as to be able, as it were, to "stretch forth my hand and take the knife to slay my son"? Abraham was enabled to do this, because his eye rested on the God of resurrection,—"he accounted that God was able to raise him up even from the dead."

In a word, it was with God he had to do, and that was quite enough. He was not suffered to strike the blow. He had gone to the very utmost bounds; he had come up to the line beyond which God could not suffer him to go. The blessed One spared the father's heart the pang which He did not spare His own heart, even that of smiting His Son. He, blessed be His name, passed beyond the utmost bounds, for "He spared not His own Son, but delivered Him up for us all." "It pleased the Lord to bruise Him; He hath put Him to grief." There was no voice from heaven when, on Calvary, the Father offered up His only begotten Son. No; it was a perfectly-accomplished sacrifice, and in its accomplishment our everlasting peace is sealed.

However, Abraham's devotedness was fully proved and fully accepted. "For now I know that thou fearest God, seeing thou hast not withheld thy son, thine only son, from Me." Mark, it is "*now* I know." It had never been proved before. It was there, no doubt, and if there, God knew it; but the valuable point here is, that God founds His knowledge of it upon the palpable evidence afforded at the altar upon Mount Moriah. Faith is always proved by action, and the fear of God by the fruits which flow from it. "Was not Abraham our father justified by works when he had offered Isaac his son on the altar?" (James 2:21) Who could think of calling his faith in question? Take away faith, and Abraham appears on Moriah as a murderer and a madman: take faith into account, and he appears as a devoted worshiper—a God-fearing, justified man. But faith must be proved. "What doth it profit, my brethren, though a man *say* he hath faith, and have not works?" (James 2:14) Will either God or man be satisfied with a powerless and profitless profession? Surely not. God looks for reality, and honors it where He sees it; and as for man, he can understand naught save the living and intelligible utterance of a faith that shows itself in acts. We are surrounded by the profession of religion,—the phraseology of faith is on every lip; but faith itself is as rare a gem as ever—that faith which will enable a man to push out from the shore of present circumstances, and meet the waves and the winds, and not only meet them, but endure them, even though the Master should seem to be asleep on the pillow.

And here I would remark the beautiful harmony between St. James and St. Paul, on the subject of justification. The intelligent and spiritual reader, who bows to the important truth of the plenary inspiration of Holy Scripture, knows full well that on this question it is not with Paul or James we have to do, but with the Holy Ghost, who graciously used each of those honored men as the pen to write His thoughts, just as I might take up a quill pen or a steel pen to write my thoughts, in which case it would be quite preposterous to speak of a discrepancy between the two pens, inasmuch as the writer is one. Hence it is just as impossible that two divinely-inspired penmen could clash, as that two heavenly bodies, while moving in their divinely-appointed orbits, could come into collision.

But, in reality, as might be expected, there is the fullest and most perfect harmony between those two apostles; indeed, on the subject of justification, the one is the counterpart or exponent of the other. St. Paul gives us the inward principle; St. James, the outward development of that principle. The former presents the hidden life; the latter, the manifested life: the former looks at man in relation to God; the latter looks at him in his relation to man. Now we want both: the inward would not do without the outward, and the outward would be valueless and powerless without the inward. "Abraham was justified" when "he believed God," and "Abraham was justified" when "he offered Isaac his son." In the former case, we have his secret standing; in the latter, his public acknowledgment by heaven and earth. It is well to understand this distinction. There was no voice from heaven when "Abraham believed God," though in God's view he was there, then, and thus "counted righteous;" but "when he had offered his son upon the altar," God could say, "Now I know," and all the world had a powerful and unanswerable proof of the fact that Abraham was a justified man. Thus it will ever be. Where there is the inward principle, there will be the outward acting; but all the value of the latter springs from its connection with the former. Disconnect, for one moment, Abraham's acting, as set forth by St. James, from Abraham's faith, as set forth by St. Paul, and what justifying virtue did it possess? None whatever. All its value, all its efficacy, all its virtue, springs from the fact that it was the outward manifestation of that faith, by virtue of which he had been already counted righteous before God. Thus much as to the admirable harmony between St. Paul and St. James, or rather, as to the unity of the voice of the Holy Ghost, whether that voice be uttered by St. Paul or St. James.

We now return to our chapter. It is deeply interesting to mark here how Abraham's soul is led into a fresh discovery of God's character by the trial of his faith. When we are enabled to bear the testings of God's own hand, it is sure to lead us into some new experience with respect to His character, which makes us to know how valuable the testing is. If Abraham had not stretched out his hand to slay his son, he never would have known the rich and exquisite depths of that title which he here bestows upon God, viz., "Jehovah-jireh." It is only when we are really put to the test that we discover what God is. Without trial, we can be but theorists, and God would not have us such: He would have us entering into the living depths that are in Himself—the divine realities of personal communion with Him. With what different feelings and convictions must Abraham have retraced his steps from Moriah to Beer-sheba!—from the mount of the Lord to the well of the oath! What very different thoughts of God! What different thoughts of Isaac! What different thoughts of everything! Truly we may say, "Happy is the man that endureth trial." It is an honor put upon one by the Lord Himself, and the deep blessedness of the experience to which it leads cannot be easily estimated. It is when men are brought (to use the language of the one hundred and seventh Psalm,) "to their wit's end," that they discover what God is. Oh, for grace to endure trial, that God's workmanship may appear, and His name be glorified in us!

There is one point which, before closing my remarks on this chapter, I shall notice, and that is, the gracious way in which God gives Abraham credit for having done the act which he had showed himself so fully prepared to do. " 'By Myself have I sworn,' saith the Lord; 'for because *thou hast done this thing,* and hast not withheld thy son, thine only son, that in blessing, I will bless thee, and in multiplying, I will multiply thy seed as the stars of heaven, and as the sand which is upon the sea-shore; and thy seed shall possess the gate of *his enemies*; and in thy seed shall all the nations of the earth be blessed: because thou hast obeyed My voice.' " This beautifully corresponds with the Spirit's notice of Abraham's acting, as put before us in Hebrews 11, and also in James 2, in both of which Scriptures he is looked upon as having offered Isaac his son upon the altar. The grand principle conveyed in the whole matter is this: Abraham proved that he was prepared to have the scene entirely cleared of *all* but God; and, moreover, it was this same principle which both *constituted* and *proved* him a justified man. Faith can do without every one and everything but God. It has the full sense of His sufficiency, and can therefore let go all beside. Hence Abraham could rightly estimate the words, "*By Myself* have I sworn." Yes, this wondrous word, "Myself," was everything to the man of faith. "For when God made promise to Abraham, because He could swear by no greater, He sware by Himself. . . . For men verily swear by the greater, and an oath for confirmation is to them an end of all strife. Wherein God, willing more abundantly to show unto the heirs of promise the immutability of His counsel, confirmed it by an oath." The word and oath of the living God should put an end to all the strivings and workings of the human will, and form the immovable anchor of the soul amid all the tossing and tumult of this stormy world.

Now, we must condemn ourselves constantly, because of the little power which the promise of God has in our hearts. There it is, and we profess to believe it; but, ah! it is not that deep, abiding, influential reality which it ought ever to be; we do not draw from it that "strong consolation" which it is calculated to afford. How little prepared are we, in the power of faith in the promise of God, to slay our Isaac! We need to cry to God that He would be graciously pleased to endow us with a deeper insight into the blessed reality of a life of faith in Himself, that so we may understand better the import of that word of St. John—"This is the victory that overcometh the world, even our faith." We can only overcome the world by faith. Unbelief puts us under the power of present things; in other words, it gives the world the victory over us. A soul that has entered, by the teaching of the Holy Ghost, into the sense of God's sufficiency, is entirely independent of things here. Beloved reader, may we know this, for our peace and joy in God, and His glory in us.

---

## *CHAPTER 23*

THIS little section of inspiration furnishes much sweet and profitable instruction to the soul. In it the Holy Spirit sets before us a beautiful exhibition of the mode in which the man of faith should carry himself toward those that are without. While it is true—divinely true—that faith makes a man independent of the men of the world, it is no less true that faith will ever teach him to walk honestly toward them. We are told to "walk honestly toward them that are without" (1 Thess. 4:12), "to provide things honest in the sight of all" (2 Cor. 8:21), to "owe no man anything" (Rom. 13:8). These are weighty precepts; precepts which, even before their distinct enunciation, were duly observed in all ages by the faithful servants of Christ, but which in modern times, alas! have not been sufficiently attended to.

The twenty-third of Genesis, therefore, is worthy of special notice. It opens with the death of Sarah, and introduces Abraham in a new character, viz., that of a mourner: "Abraham came to mourn for Sarah, and to weep for her." The child of God must meet such things, but he must not meet them as others. The great fact of resurrection comes in to his relief, and imparts a character to his sorrow quite peculiar (1 Thess. 4:13-14). The man of faith can stand at the grave of a brother or sister in the happy consciousness that it shall not long hold its captive, "for if we believe that Jesus died and rose again, even so them also which sleep in Jesus will God bring with Him." The redemption of the soul secures the redemption of the body: the former, we have; the latter, we wait for (Rom. 8:23).

Now, I believe that in purchasing Machpelah for a burying-place, Abraham gave expression to his faith in resurrection. "*He stood up from* before his dead." Faith cannot long keep death in view; it has a higher object, blessed be the "living God" who has given it. Resurrection is that which ever fills the vision of faith, and, in the power thereof, it can rise up from before the dead. There is much conveyed in this action of Abraham. We want to understand its meaning much more fully, because we are much too prone to be occupied with death and its consequences. Death is the boundary of Satan's power; but where Satan ends, God begins. Abraham understood this when he rose up and purchased the cave of Machpelah as a sleeping-place for Sarah. This was the expression of Abraham's thought in reference to the future. He knew that in the ages to come God's promise about the land of Canaan would be fulfilled, and he was able to lay the body of Sarah in the tomb "in sure and certain hope of a glorious resurrection."

The sons of Heth knew nothing about this. The thoughts which were filling the patriarch's soul were entirely foreign to the uncircumcised children of Heth. To them it seemed a small matter where he buried his dead, but it was by no means a small matter to him. "I am a stranger and a sojourner with you: give me a possession of a burying-place with you, that I may bury my dead out of my sight." It might, and manifestly did, appear strange to them to make so much ado about a grave; but, "beloved, the world knoweth us not, even as it knew Him not." The finest traits and characteristics of faith are those which are the most incomprehensible to the natural man. The Canaanites had no idea of the expectations which were giving character to Abraham's actings on this occasion. They had no idea that he was looking forward to the possession of the land, while he was merely looking for a spot in which, as a dead man, he might wait for God's time and God's manner, viz., the *morning of resurrection*. He felt *he* had no controversy with the children of Heth, and hence he was quite prepared to lay his head in the grave, and allow God to act for him and with him and by him.

"These all died in [or according to] faith [κατα πιστιν], not having received the promises, but having seen them afar off, and were persuaded of them, and embraced them, and confessed that they were strangers and pilgrims on the earth" (Heb. 11:13). This is a truly-exquisite feature in the divine life. Those "witnesses" of whom the apostle is speaking in Hebrews 11 not merely lived by faith, but even when they arrived at the close of their career, they proved that the promises of God were as real and satisfying to their souls as when they first started. Now, I believe this purchase of a burying-place in the land was an exhibition of the power of faith, not only to live, but to die. Why was Abraham so particular about this purchase? Why was he so anxious to make good his claim to the field and cave of Ephron on righteous principles? Why so determined to weigh out the full price "current with the merchant"? *Faith* is the answer. He did it all by faith. He knew the land was his in prospect, and that in resurrection-glory his seed should yet possess it, and until then he would be no debtor to those who were yet to be dispossessed.

Thus we may view this beautiful chapter in a two-fold light; first, as setting before us a plain, practical principle, as to our dealings with the men of this world; and secondly, as presenting the blessed hope which should ever animate the man of faith. Putting both these points together, we have an example of what the child of God should ever be. The hope set before us in the gospel is a glorious immortality; and this, while it lifts the heart above every influence of nature and the world, furnishes a high and holy principle with which to govern all our intercourse with those who are without. "We know that when He shall appear, we shall be like Him, for we shall see Him as He is." This is our hope. What is the moral effect of this? "Every man that hath this hope in Him purifieth himself, even as He is pure" (1 John 3:2-3). If I am to be like Christ by and by, I shall seek to be as like Him now as I can; hence, the Christian should ever seek to walk in purity, integrity and moral grace, in the view of all around.

Thus it was with Abraham, in reference to

the sons of Heth. His whole deportment and conduct, as set forth in our chapter, would seem to have been marked with very pure elevation and disinterestedness. He was "a mighty prince among them," and they would fain have done him a favor; but Abraham had learnt to take his favors only from the God of resurrection, and while he would pay *them* for Machpelah, he would look to *Him* for Canaan. The sons of Heth knew well the value of "current money with the merchant," and Abraham knew the value of the cave of Machpelah. It was worth much more to him than it was to them. "The land was worth [to them,] four hundred shekels of silver," but to him it was priceless, as the earnest of an everlasting inheritance, which, because it was an everlasting inheritance, could only be possessed in the power of resurrection. Faith conducts the soul onward into God's future; it looks at things as He looks at them, and estimates them according to the judgment of the sanctuary. Therefore, in the intelligence of faith, Abraham stood up from before his dead, and purchased a burying-place, which significantly set forth his hope of resurrection, and an inheritance founded thereon.

---

## *CHAPTER 24*

THE connection of this chapter with the two which precede it is worthy of notice. In chapter 22, the son is offered up; in chapter 23, Sarah is laid aside; and in chapter 24, the servant is sent forth to procure a bride for him who had been, as it were, received from the dead in a figure. This connection, in a very striking manner, coincides with the order of events connected with the calling out of the Church. Whether this coincidence is to be regarded as of divine origin, will, it may be, raise a question in the minds of some; but it must at least be regarded as not a little remarkable.

When we turn to the New Testament, the grand events which meet our view are, first, the rejection and death of Christ; secondly, the setting aside of Israel after the flesh; and, lastly, the calling out of the Church to occupy the high position of the bride of the Lamb.

Now all this exactly corresponds with the contents of this and the two preceding chapters. The death of Christ needed to be an accomplished fact ere the Church, properly so called, could be called out. "The middle wall of partition" needed to be broken down ere the "*one new man*" could be developed.

It is well to understand this in order that we may know the place which the Church occupies in the ways of God. So long as the Jewish economy subsisted, there was the most strict separation maintained between Jew and Gentile; and hence the idea of both being united in one new man was far removed from the mind of a Jew. He was led to view himself in a position of entire superiority to that of a Gentile, and to view the latter as utterly unclean, to whom it was unlawful to come in (Acts 10:28).

If Israel had walked with God according to the truth of the relationship into which He had graciously brought them, they would have continued in their peculiar place of separation and superiority; but this they did not do; and therefore, when they had filled up the measure of their iniquity, by crucifying the Lord of life and glory, and rejecting the testimony of the Holy Ghost, we find St. Paul is raised up to be the minister of a new thing, which was held back in the counsels of God, while the testimony to Israel was going on. "For this cause I, Paul, the prisoner of Jesus Christ for you Gentiles, if ye have heard of the dispensation of the grace of God, which is given me to you-ward; how that by revelation He made known unto me the mystery . . . which in other ages was not made known unto the sons of men, *as it is now* revealed unto His holy apostles and prophets [i.e., New-Testament prophets,—*τοις ἁγιοις αποστολοις αυτου και προφηταις*,] by the Spirit; that the Gentiles should be fellow-heirs, and of the same body, and partakers of His promise in Christ by the gospel" (Eph. 3:1-6). This is conclusive. The mystery of the Church, composed of Jew and Gentile, baptized by one Spirit into one body, united to the glorious Head in the heavens, had never been revealed until Paul's day. Of this mystery the apostle goes on to say, "*I* was made a minister according to the gift of the grace of God given unto me by the effectual working of His power" (ver. 7). The apostles and prophets of the New Testament formed, as it were, the first layer of this glorious building. (See Eph. 2:20.) This being so, it follows, as a consequence, that the building could not have been begun before. If the building had been going on from the days of Abel downwards, the apostle would then have said, the foundation of the Old Testament saints. But he has not said so, and therefore we conclude that whatever be the position assigned to the Old Testament saints, they cannot possibly belong to a body which had no existence, save in the purpose of God, until the death and resurrection of Christ, and the consequent descent of the Holy Ghost. Saved they were, blessed be God; saved by the blood of Christ, and destined to enjoy heavenly glory with the Church; but they could not have formed a part of that which did not exist for hundreds of years after their time.

It were easy to enter upon a more elaborate demonstration of this most important truth were this the place for so doing; but I shall now go on with our chapter, having merely touched upon a question of commanding interest, because of its being suggested by the position of the twenty-fourth of Genesis.

There may be a question in some minds as to whether we are to view this deeply-interesting portion of Scripture as a *type* of the calling out of the Church by the Holy Ghost. For myself, I feel happier in merely handling it as *an illustration* of that glorious work. We cannot suppose that the Spirit of God would occupy an unusually long chapter with the mere detail of a family compact, were that compact not typical or illustrative of some great truth. "Whatsoever things were written aforetime, were written for our learning." This is emphatic. What therefore, are we to learn from the chapter before us? I believe it furnished us with a beautiful illustration or foreshadowing of the great mystery of the Church. It is important to see that while there is no direct revelation of this mystery in the Old Testament, there are, nevertheless, scenes and circumstances which, in a very remarkable manner, shadow it forth; as, for example, the chapter before us. As has been remarked, the son being, in a figure, offered up and received again from the dead, the original parent-stem, as it were, being laid aside, the messenger is sent forth by the father to procure a bride for the son.

Now, in order to the clear and full understanding of the contents of the entire chapter, we may consider the following points; viz., first, *the oath*; second, *the testimony*; third, *the result*. It is beautiful to observe that the call and exaltation of Rebekah were founded upon the oath between Abraham and his servant. She knew nothing of this, though she was, in the purpose of God, so entirely the subject of it all. So is it exactly with the Church of God as a whole and each constituent part.—"In Thy book were all my members written, which in continuance were fashioned, when as yet there were none of them" (Ps. 139:16). "Blessed be the God and Father of our Lord Jesus Christ, who hath blessed us with all spiritual blessings in the heavenlies in Christ; according as He hath chosen us in Him before the foundation of the world, that we should be holy and without blame before Him in love" (Eph. 1:3-4). "For whom He did foreknow, He also did predestinate to be conformed to the image of His Son, that He might be the firstborn among many brethren. Moreover, whom He did predestinate, them He also called; and whom He called, them He also justified; and whom He justified, them He also glorified" (Rom. 8:29-30). These Scriptures are all in beautiful harmony with the point immediately before us. The call, the justification, and the glory of the Church, are all founded on the eternal purpose of God—His word and oath, ratified by the death, resurrection and exaltation of the Son. Far back, beyond the bounds of time, in the deep recesses of God's eternal mind, lay this wondrous purpose respecting the Church, which cannot by any means be separated from the divine thought respecting the glory of the Son. The oath between Abraham and the servant had for its object the provision of a partner for the son. It was the father's desire with respect to the son that led to all Rebekah's after-dignity. It is happy to see this—happy to see how the Church's security and blessing stand inseparably connected with Christ and His glory. "For the man is not of the woman, but the woman of the man. Neither was the man created for the woman, but the woman for the man" (1 Cor. 11:8-9). So it is in the beautiful parable of the marriage-supper—"The kingdom of heaven is like unto a certain king which made a marriage for his son" (Matt. 22:2). *The Son* is the grand object of all the thoughts and counsels of God; and if any are brought into blessing or glory or dignity, it can only be in connection with Him. All title to these things, and even to life itself, was forfeited by sin; but Christ met all the penalty due to sin; He made Himself responsible for everything on behalf of His body the Church; He was nailed to the cross as her representative; He bore her sins in His own body on the tree, and went down into the grave under the full weight of them. Hence, nothing can be more complete than the Church's deliverance from all that was against her. She is quickened out of the grave of Christ, where all her trespasses were laid. The life which she has is a life taken up at the other side of death, after every possible demand had been met. Hence, this life is connected with, and founded upon, divine righteousness, inasmuch as Christ's title to life is founded upon His having entirely exhausted the power of death; and He is the Church's life. Thus the Church enjoys divine life; she stands in divine righteousness; and the hope that animates her is the hope of righteousness. (See, amongst many other Scriptures, John 3:16, 36; 5:39-40; 6:27, 40, 47, 68; 11:25; 17:2; Rom. 5:21; 6:23; 1 Tim. 1:16; 1 John 2:25; 5:20; Jude 21; Eph. 2:1-6, 14, 15; Col. 1:12-22; 2:10-15; Rom. 1:17; 3:21-26; 4:5, 23-25; 2 Cor. 5:21; Gal. 5:5.)

These Scriptures most fully establish the three points, viz., the life, the righteousness, and the hope of the Church, all of which flow from her being one with Him who was raised from the dead. Now, nothing can be so calculated to assure the heart as the conviction that the Church's existence is essential to the glory of Christ. "The woman is the glory of the man" (1 Cor. 11:7). And again, the Church is called "the fullness of Him that filleth all in all." (Eph. 1:23) This last is a remarkable expression. The word translated "fullness" means the complement—that which, being added to something else, makes up a whole. Thus it is that Christ the Head, and the Church the body, make up the "one new man" (Eph. 2:15). Looking at the matter in this point of view, it is no marvel that the Church should have been the object of God's eternal counsels. When we view her as the body, the bride, the companion, the counterpart, of His only begotten Son, we feel that there was, through grace, wondrous reason for her being so thought of before the foundation of the world. Rebekah was necessary to Isaac, and therefore she was the subject of secret counsel while yet in profound ignorance about her high destiny. All Abraham's thought was about Isaac. "I will make thee swear by the Lord, the God of heaven, and the God of the earth, that thou shalt not take *a wife unto my son* of the daughters of the Canaanites, among whom I dwell." Here we see that the all-important point was, "a wife unto my son." "It is not good that the man should be alone." This opens up a very deep and blessed view of the Church. In the counsels of God she is necessary to Christ; and, in the accomplished work of Christ, divine provision has been made for her being called into existence.

While occupied with such a character of truth as this, it is no longer a question as to whether God *can* save poor sinners; He actually wants to "make a marriage for His Son," and the Church is the destined bride—she is the object of the Father's purpose, the object of the Son's love, and of the testimony of the Holy Ghost. She is to be the sharer of all the Son's dignity and glory, as she is the sharer of all that love of which He has been the everlasting object. Hear His own words,—"And the glory which Thou gavest Me I have given them; that they may be one, even as We are one: I in them, and Thou in Me, that they may be made perfect in one; and that the world may know that Thou hast sent Me, and hast loved them as Thou hast loved Me" (John 17:22-23). This settles the whole question. The words just quoted give us the thoughts of Christ's heart in reference to the Church. She is to be as He is, and not only so, but she is so even now, as St. John tells us, "Herein is love perfected with us, that we may have boldness in the day of judgment; because as He is, *so are we* in this world" (1 John 4:17). This gives full confidence to the soul. "We are in Him that is true, in His Son Jesus Christ. This is the true God and eternal life" (1 John 5:20). There is here no ground for uncertainty. Everything is secured for the bride in the bridegroom. All that belonged to Isaac became Rebekah's because Isaac was hers; and so all that belongs to Christ is made available to the Church. "All things are yours; whether Paul, or Apollos, or Cephas, or the world, or life, or death, or things present, or things to come—all are yours, and ye are Christ's, and Christ is God's" (1 Cor. 3:21-23). Christ is "head over all things to the Church" (Eph. 1:22). It will be His joy throughout eternity to exhibit the Church in all the glory and beauty with which He has endowed her, for her glory and beauty will be but the reflection of His. Angels and principalities shall behold in the Church the marvelous display of the wisdom, power, and grace of God in Christ.

But we shall now look at the second point for consideration, viz., *the testimony*. Abraham's servant carried with him a very distinct testimony.—"And he said, 'I am Abraham's servant. And the Lord hath blessed my master greatly, and he is become great; and He hath given him flocks, and herds, and silver, and gold, and men-servants, and maid-servants, and camels, and asses. And Sarah, my master's wife, bare a son to my master when she was old; and unto him hath he given all that he hath' " (ver. 34-36). He reveals the father and the son. Such was his testimony. He speaks of the vast resources of the father, and of the son's being endowed with all these in virtue of his being "the only begotten," and the object of the father's love. With this testimony he seeks to obtain a bride for the son.

All this, I need hardly remark, is strikingly illustrative of the testimony with which the Holy Ghost was sent from heaven upon the day of Pentecost.—"When the Comforter is come, whom I will send unto you from the Father, even the Spirit of truth, which proceedeth from the Father, He shall testify of Me" (John 15:26). Again, "Howbeit when He, the Spirit of truth, is come, He will guide you into all truth; for He shall not speak of Himself; but whatsoever He shall hear, that shall He speak; and He will show you things to come. He shall glorify Me; for He shall receive of Mine and show it unto you. *All things that the Father hath are Mine*; therefore said I, that He shall take of Mine and shall show it unto you" (John 16:13-15). The coincidence of these words with the testimony of Abraham's servant is instructive and interesting. It was by telling of Isaac that he sought to attract the heart of Rebekah; and it is, as we know, by telling of Jesus, that the Holy Ghost seeks to draw poor sinners away from a world of sin and folly, into the blessed and holy unity of the body of Christ. "He shall take of Mine and show it unto you." The Spirit of God will never lead any one to look at Himself or His work, but only and always at Christ. Hence, the more really spiritual any one is, the more entirely will he be occupied with Christ.

Some there are who regard it as a great mark of spirituality to be ever looking in at their own hearts, and dwelling upon what they find there, even though that be the work of the Spirit. This is a great mistake. So far from its being a proof of spirituality, it is a proof of the very reverse; for it is expressly declared of the Holy Ghost that "He shall not speak of Himself," but that, on the contrary, "He shall take of Mine and show it unto you." Therefore, whenever one is looking inward, and building on the evidences of the Spirit's work there, he may be assured he is not led by the Spirit of God in so doing. It is by holding up Christ that the Spirit draws souls to God. This is very important. The knowledge of Christ is life eternal; and it is the Father's revelation of Christ, by the Holy Ghost, that constitutes the basis of the Church. When Peter confessed Christ to be the Son of the living God, Christ's answer was, "Blessed art thou, Simon Bar-jonah; for flesh and blood hath not revealed it unto thee, but My Father which is in heaven. And I say unto thee, that thou art Peter; and upon this rock *I will build* My Church; and the gates of hell shall not prevail against it" (Matt. 16:17-18). What rock? Peter? God forbid. "This rock" [ταυτη τη πετρα] simply means the Father's revelation of Christ, as the Son of the living God, which is the only means by which any one is introduced into the assembly of Christ. Now this opens to us very much the true character of the gospel. It is, pre-eminently and emphatically, a revelation—a revelation not merely of a doctrine, but of a Person—the Person of the Son. This revelation being received by faith, draws the heart to Christ, and becomes the spring of life and power—the ground of membership—the power of fellowship. "When it pleased God . . . to *reveal His Son* in me," etc. Here we have the true principle of "the rock," viz., God revealing His Son. It is thus the superstructure is reared up; and on this solid foundation it reposes, according to God's eternal purpose.

It is therefore peculiarly instructive to find in this twenty-fourth of Genesis such a marked and beautiful illustration of the mission and special testimony of the Holy Ghost. Abraham's servant, in seeking to procure a bride for Isaac, sets forth all the dignity and wealth with which he had been endowed by the father; the love of which he was the object; and, in short, all that was calculated to affect the heart, and draw it off from present things. He showed Rebekah an object in the distance, and set before her the blessedness and reality of being made one with that beloved and highly-favored object. All that belonged to Isaac would belong to Rebekah too when she became part of him. Such was his testimony. Such, also, is the testimony of the Holy Ghost. He speaks of Christ, the glory of Christ, the beauty of Christ, the fullness of Christ, the grace of Christ, "the unsearchable riches of Christ," the dignity of His Person, and the perfectness of His work.

Moreover, He sets forth the amazing blessedness of being one with such a Christ—"members of His body, of His flesh, and of His bones." Such is the Spirit's testimony always; and herein we have an excellent touchstone by which to try all sorts of teaching and preaching. The most spiritual teaching will ever be characterized by a full and constant presentation of Christ—He will ever form the burden of such teaching. The Spirit cannot dwell on aught but Jesus. Of Him He delights to speak; He delights in setting forth His attractions and excellencies. Hence, when a man is ministering by the power of the Spirit of God, there will always be more of Christ than anything else in his ministry. There will be little room in such ministry for human logic and reasoning. Such things may do very well where a man desires to set forth himself; but the Spirit's sole object—be it well remembered by all who minister—will ever be to set forth Christ.

Let us now look, in the last place, at *the result* of all this. Truth, and the practical application of truth, are two very different things. It is one thing to speak of the peculiar glories of the Church, and quite another thing to be practically influenced by those glories. In Rebekah's case, the effect was most marked and decisive. The testimony of Abraham's servant sank down into her ears and into her heart, and entirely detached her heart's affections from the scene of things around her. She was ready to leave all and follow after, in order that she might apprehend that for which she had been apprehended. It was morally impossible that she could believe herself to be the subject of such high destinies and yet continue amid the circumstances of nature. If the report concerning the future were true, attachment to the present was the worst of folly. If the hope of being Isaac's bride, joint-heir with him of all his dignity and glory—if this were a reality, then to continue to tend Laban's sheep would be practically to despise all that God had, in grace, set before her.

But no, the prospect was far too bright to be thus lightly given up. True, she had not yet seen Isaac, nor yet the inheritance, but she had believed the report—the testimony of *him,* and had received, as it were, the earnest of *it*, and these were enough for her heart; and hence she unhesitatingly arises and expresses her readiness to depart in the memorable words, "*I will go*." She was fully prepared to enter upon an unknown path in companionship with one who had told her of an object far away, and of a glory connected with him, to which she was about to be raised. "I will go," said she; and, "forgetting the things which were behind, and reaching forth toward the things which were before, she pressed toward the mark for the prize of her high calling." Most touching and beautiful illustration this of the Church, under the conduct of the Holy Ghost, going onward to meet her heavenly Bridegroom. This is what the Church should be; but, alas! there is sad failure here. There is little of that holy alacrity in laying aside every weight and every entanglement, in the power of communion with the Holy Guide and Companion of our way, whose office and delight it is to take of the things of Jesus and show them unto us; just as Abraham's servant took of the things of Isaac and showed them to Rebekah: and no doubt, too, he found his joy in pouring fresh testimonies concerning the son into her ear, as they moved onward toward the consummation of all her joy and glory. Thus it is, at least with our heavenly Guide and Companion. He delights to tell of Jesus, "He shall take of Mine and show it unto you;" and again, "He shall show you things to come." Now this is what we really want—this ministry of the Spirit of God, unfolding Christ to our souls, producing earnest longing to see Him as He is, and be made like Him forever. Naught but this will ever detach our hearts from earth and nature. What, save the hope of being associated with Isaac, would ever have led Rebekah to say, "I will go," when her "brother and her mother said, 'Let the damsel abide with us a few days, at least ten.' " And so with us: nothing but the hope of seeing Jesus as He is, and being like Him, will ever enable or lead us to purify ourselves, even as He is pure.

---

## *CHAPTER 25*

IN the opening of this chapter, Abraham's second marriage is set before us, an event not without its interest to the spiritual mind, when viewed in connection with what we have been considering in the preceding chapter. With the light furnished by the prophetic Scriptures of the New Testament, we understand that after the completion and taking up of the elect bride of Christ, the seed of Abraham will again come into notice. Thus, after the marriage of Isaac, the Holy Ghost takes up the history of Abraham's seed by a new marriage, together with other points in his history, and that of his seed, according to the flesh. I do not press any special interpretation of all this; I merely say that it is not without its interest.

We have already referred to the remark of some one on the book of Genesis, namely, that it is "full of the seeds of things;" and as we pass along its comprehensive pages, we shall find them teeming with all the fundamental principles of truth, which are more elaborately wrought out in the New Testament. True, in Genesis these principles are set forth illustratively, and in the New Testament didactically; still, the illustration is deeply interesting, and eminently calculated to bring home the truth with power to the soul.

At the close of this chapter, we are presented with some principles of a very solemn and practical nature. Jacob's character and actings will hereafter, if the Lord will, come more fully before us; but I would just notice, ere passing on, the conduct of Esau in reference to the birthright, and all which it involved. The natural heart places no value on the things of God. To it, God's promise is a vague, valueless, powerless thing, simply because God is not known. Hence it is that present things carry such weight and influence in man's estimation. Anything that man can *see,* he values, because he is governed by sight and not by faith. To him, the present is everything; the future is a mere uninfluential thing—a matter of the merest uncertainty. Thus it was with Esau. Hear his fallacious reasoning: "Behold, I am at the point to die; and what profit shall this birthright do to me?" What strange reasoning!—*The present* is slipping from beneath my feet, I will therefore despise and entirely let go the *future!*—Time is fading from my view, I will therefore abandon all interest in eternity! "Thus Esau despised his birthright:" thus Israel despised the pleasant land (Ps. 106:24); thus they despised Christ (Zech. 11:13): thus those who were bidden to the marriage despised the invitation (Matt. 22:5). Man has no heart for the things of God. The present is everything to him. A mess of pottage is better than a title to Canaan. Hence, the very reason why Esau made light of the birthright was the very reason why he ought to have grasped it with the greater intensity. The more clearly I see the vanity of man's present, the more I shall cleave to God's future. Thus it is in the judgment of faith, "Seeing, then, that *all these things shall be dissolved*, what manner of persons ought ye to be in all holy conversation and godliness, looking for and hasting unto the coming of the day of God, wherein the heavens being on fire shall be dissolved, and the elements shall melt with fervent heat? Nevertheless we, *according to His promise,* look for new heavens and a new earth, wherein dwelleth righteousness" (2 Pet. 3:11-13). These are the thoughts of God, and therefore the thoughts of faith. The things that are seen shall be dissolved. What! then, are we to despise the unseen? By no means. The present is rapidly passing away. What is our resource? "Looking for and hasting unto the coming of the day of God." This is the judgment of the renewed mind; and any other judgment is only that of "a profane person, as Esau, who for one morsel of meat sold his birthright" (Heb. 12:16). The Lord keep us judging of things as He judges. This can only be done by faith.

---

## *CHAPTER 26*

THE opening verse of this chapter connects itself with chapter 12. "There was a famine in the land, beside the first famine that was in the days of Abraham." The trials which meet God's people in their course are very much alike, and they ever tend to make manifest how far the heart has found its *all* in God. It is a difficult matter—a rare attainment—so to walk in sweet communion with God as to be rendered thereby entirely independent of things and people here. The Egypts and the Gerars which lie on our right hand and on our left present great temptations, either to turn aside out of the right way, or to stop short of our true position as servants of the true and living God.

"And Isaac went unto Abimelech, king of the Philistines, unto Gerar." There is a manifest difference between Egypt and Gerar. Egypt is the expression of the world in its natural resources and its independence of God. "My river is mine own," is the language of an Egyptian who knew not Jehovah, and thought not of looking to Him for aught. Egypt was, locally, further removed from Canaan than Gerar; and, morally, it expresses a condition of soul further from God. Gerar is thus referred to in chapter 10: "And the border of the Canaanites was from Sidon, as thou comest to Gerar, unto Gaza; as thou goest unto Sodom, and Gomorrah, and Admah, and Zeboim, even unto Lasha" (ver. 19). We are informed that "from Gerar to Jerusalem was three days' journey." It was, therefore, as compared with Egypt, an advanced position; but still it lay within the range of very dangerous influences. Abraham got into trouble there, and so does Isaac in this chapter, and that, too, in the very same way. Abraham denied his wife, and so does Isaac. This is peculiarly solemn. To see both the father and the son fall into the same evil, in the same place, tells us plainly that the influence of that place was not good.

Had Isaac not gone to Abimelech, king of Gerar, he would have no necessity for denying his wife; but the slightest divergence from the true line of conduct superinduces spiritual weakness. It was when Peter stood and warmed himself at the high-priest's fire that he denied his Master. Now, it is manifest that Isaac was not really happy in Gerar. True, the Lord says unto him, "Sojourn in this land;" but how often does the Lord give directions to His people morally suitable to the condition He knows them to be in, and calculated also to arouse them to a true sense of that condition? He directed Moses, in Numbers 13, to send men to search the land of Canaan; but had they not been in a low moral condition, such a step would not have been necessary. We know well that faith does not need *"to spy out"* when God's promise lies before us. Again, He directed Moses to choose out seventy elders to help him in the work; but had Moses fully entered into the dignity and blessedness of his position, he would not have needed such a direction. So, in reference to the setting up of a king, in 1 Samuel 8, they ought not to have needed a king. Hence, we must always take into consideration the condition of an individual or a people to whom a direction is given before we can form any correct judgment as to the direction.

But again it may be said, If Isaac's position in Gerar was wrong, how do we read, "Then Isaac sowed in that land, and received the same year a hundred fold; and the Lord blessed him" (ver. 12)? I reply, we can never judge that a person's condition is right because of prosperous circumstances. We have had already to remark that there is a great difference between the Lord's presence and His blessing. Many have the latter without the former; and, moreover, the heart is prone to mistake the one for the other—prone to put the blessing for the presence, or at least to argue that the one must ever accompany the other. This is a great mistake. How many do we see surrounded by God's blessings, who neither have nor wish for God's presence? It is important to see this. A man may "wax great, and go forward, and grow until he becomes very great, and have possession of flocks, and possession of herds, and great store of servants," and all the while not have the full unhindered joy of the Lord's presence with him. Flocks and herds are not the Lord. They are things on account of which the Philistines might envy Isaac, whereas they never would have envied him on account of the Lord's presence. He might have been enjoying the sweetest and richest communion with God, and the Philistines have thought nothing whatever about it, simply because they had no heart to understand or appreciate such a reality. Flocks, herds, servants, and wells of water they could appreciate; but the divine presence they could not appreciate.

However, Isaac at length makes his way from amongst the Philistines, and gets up to Beersheba. "And *the Lord appeared unto him* the same night, and said, 'I am the God of Abraham thy father; fear not, for *I am with thee,* and will bless thee' " (ver. 24). Mark, it was not the Lord's blessing merely, but the Lord Himself. And why? Because Isaac had left the Philistines, with all their envy and strife and contention, behind, and gone up to Beersheba. Here the Lord could show Himself to His servant. The blessings of His liberal hand might follow him during his sojourn in Gerar, but His presence could not there be enjoyed. To enjoy God's presence, we must be where He is, and He certainly is not to be found amid the strife and contention of an ungodly world; and hence, the sooner the child of God gets away from all such, the better. So Isaac found it. He had no rest in his own spirit; and he assuredly did not, in any wise, serve the Philistines by his sojourn amongst them. It is a very common error to imagine that we serve the men of this world by mixing ourselves up with them in their associations and ways. The true way to serve them is to stand apart from them in the power of communion with God, and thus show them the pattern of a more excellent way.

Mark the progress in Isaac's soul, and the moral effect of his course.—"He went up from thence," "the Lord appeared unto him," "he builded an altar," "he called on the name of the Lord," "he pitched his tent," "his servants digged a well." Here we have most blessed progress. The moment he took a step in the right direction, he went from strength to strength. He entered into the joy of God's presence—tasted the sweets of true worship, and exhibited the character of a stranger and pilgrim, and found peaceful refreshment—an undisputed well, which the Philistines could not stop because they were not there.

These were blessed results in reference to Isaac himself; and now observe the effect produced upon others.—"Then Abimelech went to him from Gerar, and Ahuzzath, one of his friends, and Phicol, the chief captain of his army. And Isaac said unto them, "Wherefore come ye to me, seeing ye hate me, and have sent me away from you?' And they said, 'We saw certainly that the Lord was with thee; and we said, Let there now be an oath betwixt us,' " etc. The true way to act on the hearts and consciences of the men of the world is to stand in decided separation from them, while dealing in perfect grace toward them. So long as Isaac continued in Gerar, there was nothing but strife and contention. He was reaping sorrow for himself, and producing no effect whatever upon those around him. On the contrary, the moment he went away from them, their hearts were touched, and they followed him and desired a covenant. This is very instructive. The principle unfolded here may be seen constantly exemplified in the history of the children of God. The first point with the heart should ever be, to see that in our position we are *right with God;* and not only right in position, but in the moral condition of the soul. When we are right with God, we may expect to act salutarily upon men. The moment Isaac got up to Beersheba, and took his place as a worshiper, his own soul was refreshed, and he was used of God to act upon others. So long as we continue in a low position, we are robbing ourselves of blessing, and failing totally in our testimony and service.

Now should we, when in a wrong position, stop to inquire, as we so often do, Where can I find anything better? God's order is, "Cease to do evil;" and when we have acted upon that holy precept, we are furnished with another, namely, "Learn to do well." If we expect to "learn" how "to do well" before we "cease to do evil," we are entirely mistaken. "Awake, thou that sleepest, and arise from among the dead [*εκ των νεκρων*]." And what then? "Christ shall give thee light" (Eph. 5:14).

My beloved reader, if you are doing what you know to be wrong, or if you are identified in any way with what you own to be contrary to Scripture, hearken to the word of the Lord: "Cease to do evil"; and, be assured, when you have yielded obedience to this word, you will not long be left in ignorance as to your path. It is sheer unbelief that leads us to say, I cannot cease to do evil, until I find something better. The Lord grant us a single eye and a docile spirit.

---

## *CHAPTERS 27–35*

THESE chapters present to us the history of Jacob—at least, the principal scenes in that history. The Spirit of God here sets before us the deepest instruction,—first, as to God's purpose of infinite grace; and secondly, as to the utter worthlessness and depravity of human nature.

There is a passage in chapter 25 which I purposely passed over, in order to take it up here, so that we might have the truth in reference to Jacob fully before us: "And Isaac entreated the Lord for his wife, because she was barren; and the Lord was entreated of him, and Rebekah his wife conceived. And the children struggled together within her; and she said, 'If it be so, why am I thus?' And she went to inquire of the Lord. And the Lord said unto her, 'Two nations are in thy womb, and two manner of people shall be separated from thy bowels; and the one people shall be stronger than the other people; and the elder shall serve the younger.' " This is referred to in Malachi, where we read, " 'I have loved you,' saith the Lord; 'yet ye say, Wherein hast Thou loved us? Was not Esau Jacob's brother?' saith the Lord; 'yet I have loved Jacob, and hated Esau.' " This is again referred to in Romans 9: "(For the children being not yet born, neither having done any good or evil, that the purpose of God according to election might stand, not of works, but of Him that calleth;) it was said unto her, 'The elder shall serve the younger.' As it is written, 'Jacob have I loved, but Esau have I hated.' "

Thus we have very distinctly before us, God's eternal purpose according to *the election of grace.* There is much involved in this expression. It banishes all human pretension from the scene, and asserts God's right to act as He will. This is of the very last importance. The creature can enjoy no real blessedness until he is brought to bow his head to sovereign grace. It becomes him so to do, inasmuch as he is a sinner, and, as such, utterly without claim to act or dictate. The great value of finding one's self on this ground is, that it is then no longer a question of what we deserve to get, but simply of what God is pleased to give. The prodigal might talk of being a servant, but he really did not deserve the place of a servant, if it were to be made a question of desert; and therefore he had only to take what the father was pleased to give, and that was, the very highest place, even the place of fellowship with himself. Thus it must ever be.—

Grace all the work shall crown,
Through everlasting days.

Happy for us that it is so. As we go on, day by day, making fresh discoveries of ourselves, we need to have beneath our feet the solid foundation of God's grace: nothing else could possibly sustain us in our growing self-knowledge. The ruin is hopeless, and therefore the grace must be infinite: and infinite it is, having its source in God Himself, its channel in Christ, and the power of application and enjoyment in the Holy Ghost. The Trinity is brought out in connection with the grace that saves a poor sinner. "Grace reigns through righteousness, unto eternal life, by Jesus Christ our Lord." It is only in redemption that this reign of grace could be seen. We may see in creation the reign of wisdom and power; we may see in providence the reign of goodness and long-suffering; but only in redemption do we see the reign of grace, and that, too, on the principle of righteousness.

Now, we have, in the person of Jacob, a most striking exhibition of the power of divine grace; and for this reason, that we have in him a striking exhibition of the power of human nature. In him we see nature in all its obliquity, and therefore we see grace in all its moral beauty and power. From the facts of his remarkable history, it would seem that before his birth, at his birth, and after his birth the extraordinary energy of nature was seen. Before his birth, we read, "the children struggled together within her;" at his birth, we read, "his hand took hold on Esau's heel;" and after his birth—yea, to the turning-point of his history, in chapter 32, without any exception—his course exhibits nothing but the most unamiable traits of nature; but all this only serves, like a dark back-ground, to throw into relief the grace of Him who condescends to call Himself by the peculiarly-touching name, "The God of Jacob"—a name most sweetly expressive of free grace.

Let us now examine the chapters consecutively. Chapter 27 exhibits a most humbling picture of sensuality, deceit and cunning; and when one thinks of such things in connection with the people of God, it is sad and painful to the very last degree. Yet how true and faithful is the Holy Ghost! He must tell all out: He cannot give us a partial picture. If He gives us a history of man, He must describe man as he is, and not as he is not.

So, if He unfolds to us the character and ways of God, He gives us God as He is. And this, we need hardly remark, is exactly what we need. We need the revelation of One perfect in holiness, yet perfect in grace and mercy; who could come down into all the depths of man's need, his misery and his degradation, and deal with him there, and raise him up out of it into full, unhindered fellowship with Himself in all the reality of what He is. This is what Scripture gives us.

God knew what we needed, and He has given it to us, blessed be His name!

And be it remembered, that in setting before us, in faithful love, all the traits of man's character, it is simply with a view to magnify the riches of divine grace, and to admonish our souls. It is not, by any means, in order to perpetuate the memory of sins, forever blotted out from His sight. The blots, the failures, and the errors of Abraham, Isaac, and Jacob have been perfectly washed away, and they have taken their place amid "the spirits of just men made perfect;" but their history remains, on the page of inspiration, for the display of God's grace, and for the warning of God's people in all ages; and, moreover, that we may distinctly see that the blessed God has not been dealing with perfect men and women, but with those of "like passions as we are,"—that He has been walking and bearing with the same failures, the same infirmities, the same errors, as those over which we mourn every day.

This is peculiarly comforting to the heart; and it may well stand in striking contrast with the way in which the great majority of human biographies are written, in which, for the most part, we find, not the history of men, but of beings devoid of error and infirmity. Such histories have rather the effect of discouraging than of edifying those who read them. They are rather histories of what ought to be, than of what they really are, and they are therefore useless to us—yea, not only useless, but mischievous.

Nothing can edify save the presentation of God dealing with man as he really is; and this is what the Word gives us. The chapter before us illustrates this very fully. Here we find the aged patriarch Isaac, standing, as it were, at the very portal of eternity, the earth and nature fast fading away from his view, yet occupied about "savory meat," and about to act in direct opposition to the divine counsel, by blessing the elder instead of the younger. Truly this was nature, and nature with its "eyes dim." If Esau had sold his birthright for a mess of pottage, Isaac was about to give away the blessing for a mess of venison. How very humiliating!

But God's purpose must stand, and He will do all His pleasure. Faith knows this, and, in the power of that knowledge, can wait for God's time. This, nature never can do, but must set about gaining its own ends, by its own inventions. These are the two grand points brought out in Jacob's history—God's purpose of grace, on the one hand; and on the other, nature plotting and scheming to reach what that purpose would have infallibly brought about, without any plot or scheme at all. This simplifies Jacob's history amazingly, and not only simplifies it, but heightens the soul's interest in it also. There is nothing, perhaps, in which we are so lamentably deficient, as in the grace of patient, self-renouncing dependence upon God. Nature will be working in some shape or form, and thus, so far as in it lies, hindering the outshining of divine grace and power. God did not need the aid of such elements as Rebekah's cunning and Jacob's gross deceit, in order to accomplish His purpose. He had said, "The elder shall serve the younger." This was enough—enough for faith, but not enough for nature, which must ever adopt its own ways, and know nothing of what it is to wait on God.

Now, nothing can be more truly blessed than the position of hanging in childlike dependence upon God, and being entirely content to wait for His time. True, it will involve trial; but the renewed mind learns some of its deepest lessons, and enjoys some of its sweetest experiences, while waiting on the Lord; and the more pressing the temptation to take ourselves out of His hands, the richer will be the blessing of leaving ourselves there. It is so exceedingly sweet to find ourselves wholly dependent upon one who finds infinite joy in blessing us. It is only those who have tasted, in any little measure, the reality of this wondrous position that can at all appreciate it. The only one who ever occupied it perfectly and uninterruptedly was the Lord Jesus Himself. He was ever dependent upon God, and utterly rejected every proposal of the enemy to be anything else. His language was, "In Thee do I put My trust;" and again, "I was cast upon Thee from the womb." Hence, when tempted by the devil to make an effort to satisfy His hunger, His reply was, "It is written, 'Man shall not live by bread alone, but by every word that proceedeth out of the mouth of God.' " When tempted to cast Himself from the pinnacle of the temple, His reply was, "It is written again, 'Thou shalt not tempt the Lord thy God.' " When tempted to take the kingdoms of the world from the hand of another than God, and by doing homage to another than Him, His reply was, "It is written, 'Thou shalt worship the Lord thy God, and Him only shalt thou serve.' " In a word, nothing could allure the perfect man from the place of absolute dependence upon God. True, it was God's purpose to sustain His Son; it was His purpose that He should suddenly come to His temple; it was His purpose to give Him the kingdoms of this world; but this was the very reason why the Lord Jesus would simply and uninterruptedly wait on God for the accomplishment of His purpose, in His own time and in His own way. He did not set about accomplishing His own ends: He left Himself thoroughly at God's disposal. He would only eat when God gave Him bread; He would only enter the temple when sent of God; He will ascend the throne when God appoints the time.—"Sit Thou at My right hand, *until I make* Thy foes Thy footstool" (Ps. 110).

This profound subjection of the Son to the Father is admirable beyond expression. Though entirely equal with God, He took, as a man, the place of dependence, rejoicing always in the will of the Father; giving thanks even when things seemed to be against Him; doing always the things which pleased the Father; making it His grand and unvarying object to glorify the Father; and finally, when all was accomplished, when He had perfectly finished the work which the Father had given, He breathed His spirit into the Father's hand, and His flesh rested in hope of the promised glory and exaltation. Well, therefore, may the inspired apostle say, "Let this mind be in you, which was also in Christ Jesus; who, being in the form of God, thought it not robbery to be equal with God; but made Himself of no reputation, and took upon Him the form of a servant, and was made in the likeness of men; and being found in fashion as a man, He humbled Himself, and became obedient unto death, even the death of the cross. Wherefore God also hath highly exalted Him, and given Him a name which is above every name: that at the name of Jesus every knee should bow, of things in heaven, and things in earth, and things under the earth; and that every tongue should confess that Jesus Christ is Lord, to the glory of God the Father" (Phil. 2:5-11).

How little Jacob knew, in the opening of his history, of this blessed mind! How little was he prepared to wait for God's time and God's way!—he much preferred Jacob's time and Jacob's way. He thought it much better to arrive at the blessing and the inheritance by all sorts of cunning and deception than by simple dependence upon and subjection to God, whose electing grace had promised, and whose almighty power and wisdom would assuredly accomplish all for him.

But, oh, how well one knows the opposition of the human heart to all this! Any attitude for it save that of patient waiting upon God. It is almost enough to drive nature to distraction to find itself bereft of all resource but God. This tells us, in language not to be misunderstood, the true character of human nature. In order to know what nature is, I need not travel into those scenes of vice and crime which justly shock all refined moral sense. No; all that is needful is just to try it for a moment in the place of dependence, and see how it will carry itself there. It really knows nothing of God, and therefore cannot trust Him; and herein lies the secret of all its misery and moral degradation. It is totally ignorant of the true God, and can therefore be naught else but a ruined and worthless thing. The knowledge of God is the source of life—yea, is itself life; and until a man has life, what is he? or what can he be?

Now, in Rebekah and Jacob, we see nature taking advantage of nature in Isaac and Esau. It was really this. There was no waiting upon God whatever. Isaac's eyes were dim, he could therefore be imposed upon, and they set about doing so, instead of looking to God, who would have entirely frustrated Isaac's purpose to bless the one whom God would not bless—a purpose founded in nature, and most unlovely nature, for "Isaac loved Esau," not because he was the first-born, but "because he did eat of his venison." How humiliating!

But we are sure to bring unmixed sorrow upon ourselves when we take ourselves, our circumstances, or our destinies out of the hands of God.* Thus it was with Jacob, as we shall see in the sequel. It has been observed by another, that "whoever observes Jacob's life, after he had surreptitiously obtained his father's blessing, will perceive that he enjoyed very little worldly felicity. His brother purposed to murder him, to avoid which he was forced to flee from his father's house; his uncle Laban deceived him, as he had deceived his father, and treated him with great rigor; after a servitude of twenty-one years, he was obliged to leave him in a clandestine manner, and not without danger of being brought back, or murdered by his enraged brother; no sooner were these fears over, than he experienced the baseness of his son Reuben, in defiling his bed; he had next to bewail the treachery and cruelty of Simeon and Levi towards the Shechemites; then he had to feel the loss of his beloved wife; he was next imposed upon by his own sons, and had to lament the supposed untimely end of Joseph; and, to complete all, he was forced by famine to go into Egypt, and there died in a strange land. So just, wonderful, and instructive are all the ways of providence."

This is a true picture, so far as Jacob was concerned; but it only gives us one side, and that the gloomy side. Blessed be God, there is a bright side likewise, for God had to do with Jacob; and, in every scene of his life, when Jacob was called to reap the fruits of his own plotting and crookedness, the God of Jacob brought good out of evil, and caused His grace to abound over all the sin and folly of His poor servant. This we shall see as we proceed with his history.

I shall just offer a remark here upon Isaac, Rebekah, and Esau. It is very interesting to observe how, notwithstanding the exhibition of nature's excessive weakness, in the opening of this twenty-seventh chapter, Isaac maintains, by faith, the dignity which God had conferred upon him. He blesses with all the consciousness of being endowed with power to bless. He says, "I have blessed him; yea, and he shall be blessed. . . . Behold, I have made him thy lord, and all his brethren have I given to him for servants; and with corn and wine have I sustained him; and what shall I do now unto thee, my son?" He speaks as one who, by faith, had at his disposal all the treasures of earth. There is no false humility, no taking a low ground by reason of the manifestation of nature. True, he was on the eve of making a grievous mistake—even of moving right athwart the counsel of God; still, he knew God, and took his place accordingly, dispensing blessings in all the dignity and power of faith. "I have blessed him; yea, and he shall be blessed. . . . With corn and wine have I sustained him." It is the proper province of faith to rise above all one's own failure and the consequences thereof, into the place where God's grace has set us.

As to Rebekah, she was called to feel all the sad results of her cunning actings. She no doubt imagined she was managing matters most skillfully; but, alas! she never saw Jacob again: so much for management! How different it would have been had she left the matter entirely in the hands of God! This is the way in which faith manages, and it is ever a gainer. "Which of you by taking thought can add to his stature one cubit?" We gain nothing by our anxiety and planning; we only shut out God, and that is no gain. It is a just judgment from the hand of God to be left to reap the fruits of our own devices; and I know of few things more sad than to see a child of God so entirely forgetting his proper place and privilege as to take the management of his affairs into his own hands. The birds of the air and the lilies of the field may well be our teachers when

*We should ever remember, in a place of trial, that what we want is not a change of circumstances, but victory over self.

we so far forget our position of unqualified dependence upon God.

Then, again, as to Esau, the apostle calls him "a profane person, who for one morsel of meat sold his birthright," and "afterwards, when he would have inherited the blessing, he was rejected; for he found no place of change of mind, though he sought it carefully with tears." Thus we learn what a profane person is, viz., one who would like to hold both worlds, one who would like to enjoy the present without forfeiting his title to the future. This is by no means an uncommon case. It expresses to us the merely worldly professor, whose conscience has never felt the action of divine truth, and whose heart has never felt the influence of divine grace.

---

## *CHAPTER 28*

WE are now called to trace Jacob in his movement from under his father's roof, to view him as a homeless and lonely wanderer on the earth. It is here that God's special dealings with him commence. Jacob now begins to realize, in some measure, the bitter fruit of his conduct in reference to Esau; while, at the same time, God is seen rising above all the weakness and folly of His servant, and displaying His own sovereign grace and profound wisdom in His dealings with him. God will accomplish His own purpose, no matter by what instrumentality; but if His child, in impatience of spirit and unbelief of heart, will take himself out of His hands, he must expect much sorrowful exercise and painful discipline. Thus it was with Jacob: he might not have had to flee to Haran had he allowed God to act for him. God would assuredly have dealt with Esau, and caused him to find his destined place and portion; and Jacob might have enjoyed that sweet peace which nothing can yield save entire subjection in all things to the hand and counsel of God.

But here is where the excessive feebleness of our hearts is constantly disclosed. We do not lie passive in God's hand, we will be acting; and, by our acting, we hinder the display of God's grace and power on our behalf. "*Be still* and know that I am God," is a precept which naught, save the power of divine grace, can enable one to obey. "Let your moderation be known unto all men. The Lord is at hand [εγγυς]. Be careful for nothing; but in everything by prayer and supplication with thanksgiving let your requests be made known unto God." What will be the result of thus acting? "The peace of God, which passeth all understanding, shall garrison [φρουρησει] your hearts and minds by Christ Jesus" (Phil. 4:5-7).

However, God graciously overrules our folly and weakness, and while we are called upon to reap the fruits of our unbelieving and impatient ways, He takes occasion from them to teach our hearts still deeper lessons of His own tender grace and perfect wisdom. This, while it assuredly affords no warrant whatever for unbelief and impatience, does most wonderfully exhibit the goodness of our God, and comfort the heart even while we may be passing through the painful circumstances consequent upon our failure. God is above all; and, moreover, it is His special prerogative to bring good out of evil, to make the eater yield meat, and the strong yield sweetness; and hence, while it is quite true that Jacob was compelled to be an exile from his father's roof in consequence of his own restless and deceitful acting, it is equally true that he never could have learnt the meaning of "Bethel" had he been quietly at home. Thus the two sides of the picture are strongly marked in every scene of Jacob's history. It was when he was driven, by his own folly, from Isaac's house, that he was led to taste, in some measure, the blessedness and solemnity of "God's house."

"And Jacob went out from Beersheba, and went toward Haran. And he lighted upon a certain place, and tarried there all night, because the sun was set; and he took of the stones of that place and put them for his pillows, and lay down in that place to sleep." Here we find the homeless wanderer just in the very position in which God could meet him, and in which He could unfold His purposes of grace and glory. Nothing could possibly be more expressive of helplessness and nothingness than Jacob's condition as here set before us. Beneath the open canopy of heaven, with a pillow of stone, in the helpless condition of sleep. Thus it was that the God of Bethel unfolded to Jacob His purposes respecting him and his seed. "And he dreamed, and behold a ladder set up on the earth, and the top of it reached to heaven: and behold the angels of God ascending and descending on it. And behold the Lord stood above it, and said, 'I am the Lord God of Abraham thy father, and the God of Isaac: the land whereon thou liest, to thee will I give it, and to thy seed. And thy seed shall be as the dust of the earth, and thou shalt spread abroad to the west, and to the east, and to the north, and to the south; and in thee and in thy seed shall all the families of the earth be blessed. And, behold, I am with thee, and will keep thee in all places whither thou goest, and will bring thee again into this land; for I will not leave thee until I have done that which I have spoken to thee of.' "

Here we have, indeed, "grace and glory." The ladder "set *on the earth*" naturally leads the heart to meditate on the display of God's grace, in the Person and work of His Son. On the earth it was that the wondrous work was accomplished which forms the basis—the strong and everlasting basis—of all the divine counsels in reference to Israel, the Church, and the world at large. On the earth it was that Jesus lived, labored and died; that, through His death, He might remove out of the way every obstacle to the accomplishment of the divine purpose of blessing to man.

But "the top of the ladder reached to heaven." It formed the medium of communication between heaven and earth; and "behold the angels of God ascending and descending upon it,"—striking and beautiful picture of Him by whom God has come down into all the depth of man's need, and by whom also He has brought man up and set him in His own presence forever, in the power of divine righteousness! God has made provision for the accomplishment of all His plans, despite of man's folly and sin; and it is for the everlasting joy of any soul to find itself, by the teaching of the Holy Ghost, within the limits of God's gracious purpose.

The prophet Hosea leads us on to the time when that which was foreshadowed by Jacob's ladder shall have its full accomplishment.—"And in that day I will make a covenant for them with the beasts of the field, and with the fowls of heaven, and with the creeping things of the ground; and I will break the bow and the sword and the battle out of the earth, and will make them to lie down safely. And I will betroth thee unto Me forever; yea, I will betroth thee unto Me in righteousness and in judgment and in loving-kindness and in mercies; I will even betroth thee unto Me in faithfulness, and thou shalt know the Lord. And it shall come to pass in that day, I will hear, saith the Lord, I will hear the heavens, and they shall hear the earth, and the earth shall hear the corn and the wine and the oil, and they shall hear Jezreel. And I will sow her unto Me in the earth; and I will have mercy upon her that had not obtained mercy; and I will say to them which were not My people, Thou art My people; and they shall say, Thou art my God" (Hosea 2:18-23). There is also an expression in the first chapter of John, bearing upon Jacob's remarkable vision; it is Christ's word to Nathanael—"Verily, verily, I say unto you, Hereafter ye shall see heaven open, and the angels of God ascending and descending upon the Son of Man" (ver. 51).

Now this vision of Jacob's is a very blessed disclosure of divine grace to Israel. We have been led to see something of Jacob's real character, something, too, of his real condition; both were evidently such as to show that it should either be divine grace for him, or nothing. By birth he had no claim; nor yet by character. Esau might put forward some claim on both these grounds (*i.e.,* provided God's prerogative were set aside), but Jacob had no claim whatsoever; and hence, while Esau could only stand upon the exclusion of God's prerogative, Jacob could only stand upon the introduction and establishment thereof. Jacob was such a sinner, and so utterly divested of all claim, both by birth and by practice, that he had nothing whatever to rest upon save God's purpose of pure, free, and sovereign grace. Hence, in the revelation which the Lord makes to His chosen servant in the passage just quoted, it is a simple record or prediction of what He Himself would yet do. "*I* am . . . *I* give . . . *I* will keep . . . *I* will bring . . . *I* will not leave thee until *I* have done that which *I* have spoken to thee of." It was all Himself. There is no condition whatever, no *if* or *but;* for when *grace* acts, there can be no such thing. Where there is an *if,* it cannot possibly be grace. Not that God cannot put man into a position of responsibility, in which He must needs address him with an "if." We know He can; but Jacob asleep on a pillow of stone was not in a position of responsibility, but of the deepest helplessness and need; and therefore he was in a position to receive a revelation of the fullest, richest, and most unconditional grace.

Now, we cannot but own the blessedness of being in such a condition that we have nothing to rest upon save God Himself; and, moreover, that it is in the most perfect establishment of God's own character and prerogative that we obtain all our true joy and blessing. According to this principle, it would be an irreparable loss to us to have any ground of our own to stand upon; for in that case, God should address us on the ground of responsibility, and failure would then be inevitable. Jacob was so bad, that none but God Himself could do for him.

And be it remarked, that it was his failure in the habitual recognition of this that led him into so much sorrow and pressure. God's revelation of Himself is one thing, and our resting in that revelation is quite another. God shows Himself to Jacob in infinite grace; but no sooner does Jacob awake out of sleep, than we find him developing his true character, and proving how little he knew, practically, of the blessed One who had just been revealing Himself so marvelously to him. "He was afraid, and said, 'How dreadful is this place! This is none other but the house of God, and this is the gate of heaven.' " His heart was not at home in the presence of God; nor can any heart be so until it has been thoroughly emptied and broken. God is at home, blessed be His name, with a broken heart, and a broken heart at home with Him. But Jacob's heart was not yet in this condition; nor had he yet learnt to repose, like a little child, in the perfect love of one who could say, "Jacob have I loved." "Perfect love casteth out fear;" but where such love is not known and fully realized, there will always be a measure of uneasiness and perturbation. God's house and God's presence are not dreadful to a soul who knows the love of God as expressed in the perfect sacrifice of Christ: such a soul is rather led to say, "Lord, I have loved the habitation of Thy house, and the place where Thine honor dwelleth" (Ps. 26:8). And again, "One thing have I desired of the Lord, that will I seek after; that I may dwell in the house of the Lord all the days of my life, to behold the beauty of the Lord, and to inquire in His temple" (Ps. 27:4). And again, "How amiable are Thy tabernacles, O Lord of hosts! My soul longeth, yea, even fainteth, for the courts of the Lord" (Ps. 84). When the heart is established in the knowledge of God, it will assuredly love His house, whatever the character of that house may be,—whether it be Bethel, or the temple at Jerusalem, or the Church now composed of all true believers, "builded together for a habitation of God through the Spirit." However, Jacob's knowledge both of God and His house was very shallow at that point in his history on which we are now dwelling.

We shall have occasion again to refer to some principles connected with Bethel, and shall now close our meditations upon this chapter with a brief notice of Jacob's bargain with God, so truly characteristic of him, and so demonstrative of the truth of the statement with respect to the shallowness of his knowledge of the divine character. "And Jacob vowed a vow, saying, 'If God will be with me, and will keep me in this way that I go, so that I come again to my father's house in peace, then shall the Lord be my God, and this stone which I have set for a pillar shall be God's house, and of all that Thou shalt give me I will surely give the tenth unto Thee.' " Observe, "*If* God will be with me." Now, the Lord had just said, emphatically, "I *am* with thee, and *will keep thee in all places* whither thou goest, and will bring thee again into this land," etc. And yet poor Jacob's heart cannot get beyond an *"if;"* nor, in its thoughts of God's goodness, can it rise higher than "bread to eat and raiment to put on." Such were the thoughts of one who had just seen the magnificent vision of the ladder reaching from earth to heaven, with the Lord standing above, and promising an innumerable seed and an everlasting possession. Jacob was evidently unable to enter into the reality and fullness of God's thoughts. He measured God by himself, and thus utterly failed to apprehend Him. In short, Jacob had not yet really got to the end of himself; and hence he had not really begun with God.

---

## *CHAPTERS 29–31*

"THEN Jacob went on his journey, and came into the land of the people of the east." As we have just seen, in chapter 28 Jacob utterly fails in the apprehension of God's real character, and meets all the rich grace of Bethel with an "if," and a miserable bargain about food and raiment. We now follow him into a scene of thorough bargain-making. "Whatsoever a man soweth, that shall he also reap." There is no possibility of escaping from this. Jacob had not yet found his true level in the presence of God, and therefore God uses circumstances to chasten and break him down.

This is the real secret of much, very much, of our sorrow and trial in the world. Our hearts have never been really broken before the Lord, we have never been self-judged and self-emptied; and hence, again and again, we, as it were, knock our heads against the wall. No one can really enjoy God until he has got to the bottom of self, and for this plain reason, that God has begun the display of Himself at the very point at which the end of flesh is seen. If, therefore, I have not reached the end of my flesh, in the deep and positive experience of my soul, it is morally impossible that I can have anything like a just apprehension of God's character. But I must, in some way or other, be conducted to the true measure of nature. To accomplish this end, the Lord makes use of various agencies, which, no matter what they are, are only effectual when used by Him for the purpose of disclosing, in our view, the true character of all that is in our hearts. How often do we find, as in Jacob's case, that even although the Lord may come near to us and speak in our ears, yet we do not understand His voice or take our true place in His presence. "The Lord is in this place, and I knew it not. . . . How dreadful is this place!" Jacob learnt nothing by all this, and it therefore needed twenty years of terrible schooling, and that, too, in a school marvelously adapted to his flesh; and even that, as we shall see, was not sufficient to break him down.

However, it is remarkable to see how he gets back into an atmosphere so entirely suited to his moral constitution. The bargain-making Jacob meets with the bargain-making Laban, and they are both seen, as it were, straining every nerve to outwit each other. Nor can we wonder at Laban, for he had never been at Bethel, he had seen no open heaven, with a ladder reaching from thence to earth, he had heard no magnificent promises from the lips of Jehovah, securing to him all the land of Canaan, with a countless seed: no marvel, therefore, that he should exhibit a grasping groveling spirit; he had no other resource. It is useless to expect from worldly men aught but a worldly spirit, and worldly principles and ways; they have gotten naught superior, and you cannot bring a clean thing out of an unclean. But to find Jacob, after all he had seen and heard at Bethel, struggling with a man of the world, and endeavoring, by such means, to accumulate property, is peculiarly humbling.

And yet, alas! it is no uncommon thing to find the children of God thus forgetting their high destinies and heavenly inheritance, and descending into the arena with the children of this world, to struggle there for the riches and honors of a perishing, sin-stricken earth. Indeed, to such an extent is this true in many instances, that it is often hard to trace a single evidence of that principle which St. John tells us "overcometh the world." Looking at Jacob and Laban, and judging of them upon natural principles, it would be hard to trace any difference. One should get behind the scenes, and enter into God's thoughts about both, in order to see how widely they differed. But it was God that had made them to differ, not Jacob; and so it is now. Difficult as it may be to trace any difference between the children of light and the children of darkness, there is, nevertheless, a very wide difference indeed, a difference founded on the solemn fact that the former are "the vessels of mercy, which God has afore prepared unto glory," while the latter are "the vessels of wrath, fitted [not by God, but by sin] to destruction"* (Rom. 9:22-23). This makes a very serious difference. The Jacobs and the Labans differ materially, and have differed, and will differ forever, though the former may so sadly fail in the realization and practical exhibition of their true character and dignity.

Now, in Jacob's case, as set forth in the three chapters now before us, all his toiling and working like his wretched bargain before, is the result of his ignorance of God's grace, and his inability to put implicit confidence in God's promise. The man that could say, after a most unqualified promise from God to give him the whole land of Canaan, "*If* God will give me food to eat and raiment to put on," could have had but a very faint apprehension of who God was, or what His promise was either; and because of this, we see him seeking to do the best he can for himself. This is always the way when grace is not understood: the principles of grace may be professed, but the real measure of our experience of the power of grace is quite another thing. One would have imagined that Jacob's vision had told him a tale of grace; but God's revelation at Bethel, and Jacob's actings at Haran, are two very different things; yet the latter tell out what was Jacob's sense of the former. Character and conduct prove the real measure of the soul's experience and conviction, whatever the profession may be. But Jacob had never yet been brought to measure himself in God's presence, and therefore he was ignorant of grace, and he proved his ignorance by measuring himself with Laban, and adopting his maxims and ways.

One cannot help remarking the fact that inasmuch as Jacob failed to learn and judge the inherent character of his flesh before God, therefore he was, in the providence of God, led into the very sphere in which that character was fully exhibited in its broadest lines. He was conducted to Haran, the country of Laban and Rebekah, the very school from whence those principles, in which he was such a remarkable adept, had emanated, and where they were taught, exhibited and maintained. If one wanted to learn what God was, he should go to Bethel; if to learn what man was, he should go to

*It is deeply interesting to the spiritual mind to mark how sedulously the Spirit of God, in Romans 9, and indeed throughout all Scripture, guards against the horrid inference which the human mind draws from the doctrine of God's election. When He speaks of "vessels of wrath," He simply says, "fitted to destruction;" He does not say that God "fitted" them. Whereas, on the other hand, when He refers to "the vessels of mercy," He says, "whom *He* had afore prepared unto glory." This is most marked.

If my reader will turn for a moment to Matthew 25:34-41, he will find another striking and beautiful instance of the same thing.

When the King addresses those on His right hand, He says, "Come, ye *blessed of My Father,* inherit the kingdom *prepared for you* from the foundation of the world" (verse 34). But when He addresses those on His left, He says, "Depart from Me, ye cursed." He does not say, Cursed of My Father. And further, He says, "Into everlasting fire, prepared [not for *you,* but] for the devil and his angels" (verse 41).

In a word, then, it is plain that God has "prepared" a kingdom of glory, and "vessels of mercy" to inherit that kingdom; but He has not prepared "everlasting fire" for men, but for "the devil and his angels;" nor has He fitted the "vessels of wrath," but they have fitted themselves.

The Word of God as clearly establishes *"election"* as it sedulously guards against *"reprobation."* Every one who finds himself in heaven will have to thank God for it, and every one that finds himself in hell will have to thank himself.

Haran. But Jacob had failed to take in God's revelation of Himself at Bethel, and he therefore went to Haran, and there showed what he was,—and oh, what scrambling and scraping! what shuffling and shifting! There is no holy and elevated confidence in God, no simply looking to and waiting on Him. True, God was with Jacob—for nothing can hinder the outshinings of divine grace. Moreover, Jacob in a measure owns God's presence and faithfulness; still nothing can be done without a scheme and a plan. Jacob cannot allow God to settle the question as to his wives and his wages, but seeks to settle all by his own cunning and management. In short, it is "the supplanter" throughout. Let the reader turn, for example, to chapter 30:37-42, and say where he can find a more masterly piece of cunning. It is verily a perfect picture of Jacob. In place of allowing God to multiply "the ringstraked, speckled, and spotted cattle," as He most assuredly would have done had He been trusted, he sets about securing their multiplication by a piece of policy which could only have found its origin in the mind of a Jacob. So in all his actings, during his twenty years' sojourn with Laban; and finally, he most characteristically "steals away," thus maintaining in everything his consistency with himself.

Now, it is in tracing out Jacob's real character, from stage to stage of his extraordinary history, that one gets a wondrous view of divine grace. None but God could have borne with such an one, as none but God would have taken such an one up. Grace begins at the very lowest point,—it takes up man as he is, and deals with him in the full intelligence of what he is. It is of the very last importance to understand this feature of grace at one's first starting; it enables us to bear, with steadiness of heart, the after-discoveries of personal vileness, which so frequently shake the confidence and disturb the peace of the children of God.

Many there are who, at first, fail in the full apprehension of the utter ruin of nature, as looked at in God's presence, though their hearts have been attracted by the grace of God, and their consciences tranquilized, in some degree, by the application of the blood of Christ. Hence, as they get on in their course, they begin to make deeper discoveries of the evil within, and, being deficient in their apprehensions of God's grace, and the extent and efficacy of the sacrifice of Christ, they immediately raise a question as to their being children of God at all. Thus they are taken off Christ and thrown on themselves, and then they either betake themselves to ordinances in order to keep up their tone of devotion, or else fall back into thorough worldliness and carnality. These are disastrous consequences, and all the result of not having "the heart established in grace."

It is this that renders the study of Jacob's history so profoundly interesting and eminently useful. No one can read the three chapters now before us and not be struck at the amazing grace that could take up such an one as Jacob, and not only take him up, but say, after the full discovery of all that was in him, "He hath not beheld iniquity in Jacob, neither hath He seen perverseness in Israel" (Num. 23:21). He does not say that iniquity and perverseness were not in him. This would never give the heart confidence—the very thing, above all others, which God desires to give. It could never assure a poor sinner's heart to be told that there was *no sin in* him; for, alas! he knows too well there is; but to be told there is no sin *on* him, and that, moreover, in God's sight, on the simple ground of Christ's perfect sacrifice, must infallibly set his heart and conscience at rest. Had God taken up Esau, we should not have had, by any means, such a blessed display of grace; for this reason, that he does not appear before us in the unamiable light in which we see Jacob. The more man sinks, the more God's grace rises. As my debt rises, in my estimation, from the fifty pence up to the five hundred, so my sense of grace rises also—my experience of that love which, when we "had *nothing* to pay," could "frankly forgive" us all (Luke 7:42). Well might the apostle say, "It is a good thing that the heart be established with grace; not with meats, which have not profited them that have been occupied therein" (Heb. 13:9).

## CHAPTER 32

"AND Jacob went on his way, and the angels of God met him." Still God's grace follows him, notwithstanding all. "Nothing changeth God's affection." Whom He loves, and how He loves, He loves to the end. His love is like Himself—"the same yesterday, to-day, and forever." But how little effect "God's host" had upon Jacob may be seen by his actings, as here set before us. "And Jacob sent messengers before him to Esau his brother, unto the land of Seir, the country of Edom." He evidently feels uneasy in reference to Esau, and not without reason. He had treated him badly, and his conscience was not at ease; but instead of casting himself unreservedly upon God, he betakes himself to his usual planning again, in order to avert Esau's wrath. He tries to *manage* Esau, instead of leaning on God.

"And he commanded them, saying, 'Thus shall ye speak unto *my lord* Esau: *Thy servant* Jacob saith thus: I have sojourned with Laban, and stayed there until now.' " All this bespeaks a soul very much off its centre in God. "My lord," and "thy servant," is not like the language of a brother, or of one in the conscious dignity of the presence of God; but it was the language of Jacob, and of Jacob, too, with a bad conscience.

"And the messengers returned to Jacob, saying, 'We came to thy brother Esau, and also he cometh to meet thee, and four hundred men with him.' Then Jacob was greatly afraid and distressed." But what does he first do? Does he at once cast himself upon God? No; he begins to manage. "He divided the people that was with him, and the flocks and herds and the camels, into two bands; and said, 'If Esau come to the one company and smite it, then the other company which is left shall escape.' " Jacob's first thought was always *a plan,* and in this we have a true picture of the poor human heart. True, he turns to God after he makes his plan, and cries to Him for deliverance; but no sooner does he cease praying than he resumes the planning. Now, praying and planning will never do together. If I plan, I am leaning more or less on my plan; but when I pray, I should lean exclusively upon God. Hence, the two things are perfectly incompatible,—they virtually destroy each other. When my eye is filled with my own management of things, I am not prepared to see God acting for me; and, in that case, prayer is not the utterance of my need, but the mere superstitious performance of something which I think ought to be done, or it may be, asking God to sanctify my plans. This will never do. It is not asking God to sanctify and bless my means, but it is asking Him to do it all Himself.*

Though Jacob asked God to deliver him from his brother Esau, he evidently was not satisfied with that, and therefore he tried to "appease him with a present." Thus his confidence was in the "present," and not entirely in God. "The heart is deceitful above all things, and desperately wicked." It is often hard to detect what is the real ground of the heart's confidence. We imagine, or would fain persuade ourselves, that we are leaning upon God, when we are, in reality, leaning upon some scheme of our own devising. Who, after hearkening to Jacob's prayer, wherein he says, "Deliver me, I pray Thee, from the hand of my brother—from the hand of Esau; for I fear him, lest he will come and smite me, and the mother with the children," could imagine him saying, "I will appease him with a present." Had he forgotten his prayer? was he making a god of his present? did he place more confidence in a few cattle than in Jehovah, to whom he had just been committing himself? These are questions which naturally arise out of Jacob's actings in reference to Esau, and we can readily answer them by looking into the glass of our own hearts. There we learn, as well as on the page of Jacob's history, how much more apt we are to lean on our own management than on God; but it will not do; we must be brought to see the end of our management, that it is perfect folly, and that the true path of wisdom is to repose in full confidence upon God.

*No doubt, when faith allows God to act, He will use His own agency; but this is a totally different thing from His owning and blessing the plans and arrangements of unbelief and impatience. This distinction is not sufficiently understood.

Nor will it do to make our prayers part of our management. We often feel very well satisfied with ourselves when we add prayer to our arrangement, or when we have used all lawful means, and called upon God to bless them. When this is the case, our prayers are worth about as much as our plans, inasmuch as we are leaning upon them instead of upon God. We must be really brought to the end of everything with which self has aught to do; for until then, God cannot show Himself. But we can never get to the end of our plans until we have been brought to the end of ourselves. We must see that "all flesh is grass, and all the goodliness thereof is as the flower of the field" (Isa. 40:6).

Thus it is in this interesting chapter: when Jacob had made all his prudent arrangements, we read, "And Jacob was left alone; and there wrestled a man with him until the breaking of the day." This is a turning-point in the history of this very remarkable man. To be left alone with God is the only true way of arriving at a just knowledge of ourselves and our ways. We can never get a true estimate of nature and all its actings until we have weighed them in the balance of the sanctuary, and there we ascertain their real worth. No matter what we may think about ourselves, nor yet what man may think about us; the great question is, What does God think about us? and the answer to this question can only be heard when we are "left alone." Away from the world; away from self; away from all the thoughts, reasonings, imaginations, and emotions of mere nature, and "alone" with God; thus, and thus alone, can we get a correct judgment about ourselves.

"Jacob was left alone; and there wrestled a man with him." Mark, it was not Jacob wrestling with a man, but a man wrestling with Jacob. This scene is very commonly referred to as an instance of Jacob's power in prayer. That it is not this is evident from the simple wording of the passage. My wrestling with a man, and a man wrestling with me, present two totally different ideas to the mind. In the former case, I want to gain some object from him; in the latter, he wants to gain some object from me. Now, in Jacob's case, the divine object was to bring him to see what a poor, feeble, worthless creature he was; and when Jacob so pertinaciously held out against the divine dealing with him, "He touched the hollow of his thigh; and the hollow of Jacob's thigh was out of joint as He wrestled with him." The sentence of death must be written on the flesh—the power of the cross must be entered into before we can steadily and happily walk with God. We have followed Jacob so far, amid all the windings and workings of his extraordinary character—we have seen him planning and managing during his twenty years' sojourn with Laban; but not until he "was left alone" did he get a true idea of what a perfectly helpless thing he was in himself. Then, the seat of his strength being touched, he learnt to say, "I will not let *Thee* go."

Other refuge have I none;
Clings my helpless soul to Thee.

This was a new era in the history of the supplanting, planning Jacob. Up to this point he had held fast by his own ways and means; but now he is brought to say, "I will not let *Thee* go." Now, let my reader remark, that Jacob did not express himself thus until "the hollow of his thigh was touched." This simple fact is quite sufficient to settle the true interpretation of the whole scene. God was wrestling with Jacob to bring him to this point. We have already seen that, as to Jacob's power in prayer, he had no sooner uttered a few words to God than he let out the real secret of his soul's dependence, by saying, "I will appease him (Esau) with a present." Would he have said this if he had really entered into the meaning of prayer, or true dependence upon God? Assuredly not. If he had been looking to God alone to appease Esau, could he have said, "I will appease him with a present"? Impossible. God and the creature must be kept distinct, and will be kept so in every soul that knows much of the sacred reality of a life of faith.

But, alas! here is where we fail (if one may speak for another). Under the plausible and apparently pious formula of using means, we really cloke the positive infidelity of our poor deceitful hearts; we think we are looking to God to bless our means, while, in reality, we are shutting Him out by leaning on the means instead of leaning on Him. Oh! may our hearts be taught the evil of thus acting. May we learn to cling more simply to God *alone,* that so our history may be more characterized by that holy elevation above the circumstances through which we are passing. It is not, by any means, an easy matter so to get to the end of the creature, in every shape and form, so as to be able to say, "I will not let Thee go except Thou bless me." To say this from the heart, and to abide in the power of it, is the secret of all true strength. Jacob said it when the hollow of his thigh was touched; but not till then. He struggled long, ere he gave way, because his confidence in the flesh was strong. But God can bring down to the dust the stoutest character. He knows how to touch the spring of nature's strength, and write the sentence of death thoroughly upon it; and until this is done, there can be no real "power with God or man." We must be "weak" ere we can be "strong." "The power of Christ" can only "rest on us" in connection with the knowledge of our infirmities. Christ cannot put the seal of His approval upon nature's strength, its wisdom, or its glory: all these must sink that He may rise. Nature can never form, in any one way, a pedestal on which to display the grace or power of Christ; for if it could, then might flesh glory in His presence; but this, we know, can never be.

And inasmuch as the display of God's glory and God's name or character is connected with the entire setting aside of nature, so, until this latter is set aside, the soul can never enjoy the disclosure of the former. Hence, though Jacob is called to tell out his name,—to own that his name is "Jacob," or a "supplanter," he yet receives no revelation of the name of Him who had been wrestling with him, and bringing him down into the dust. He received for himself the name of "Israel," or "prince," which was a great step in advance; but when he says, "Tell me, I pray Thee, Thy name," he received the reply, "Wherefore is it that thou dost ask after My name?" The Lord refuses to tell His name, though He had elicited from Jacob the truth as to himself, and He blesses him accordingly. How often is this the case in the annals of God's family! There is the disclosure of self in all its moral deformity; but we fail to get hold practically of what God is, though He has come so very close to us, and blessed us, too, in connection with the discovery of ourselves. Jacob received the new name of "Israel" when the hollow of his thigh had been touched;—he became a mighty "prince" when he had been brought to know himself as a weak man; but still the Lord had to say, "Wherefore is it that thou dost ask after My name?" There is no disclosure of the name of Him who, nevertheless, had brought out the real name and condition of Jacob.

From all this we learn that it is one thing to be blessed by the Lord, and quite another thing to have the revelation of His character, by the Spirit, to our hearts. "He blessed him there," but He did not tell His name. There is blessing in being brought, in any measure, to know ourselves; for therein we are led into a path in which we are able more clearly to discern what God is to us in detail. Thus it was with Jacob. When the hollow of his thigh was touched, he found himself in a condition in which it was either God or nothing. A poor halting man could do little, it therefore behoved him to cling to one who was almighty.

I would remark, ere leaving this chapter, that the book of Job is, in a certain sense, a detailed commentary on this scene in Jacob's history. Throughout the first thirty-one chapters, Job grapples with his friends, and maintains his point against all their arguments; but in chapter 32, God, by the instrumentality of Elihu, begins to wrestle with him; and in chapter 38, He comes down upon him directly with all the majesty of His power, overwhelms him by the display of His greatness and glory, and elicits from him the well-known words, "I have heard of Thee by the hearing of the ear; but now mine eye seeth Thee. Wherefore I abhor myself, and repent in dust and ashes" (chap.

42:5-6). This was really touching the hollow of his thigh. And mark the expression, "Mine eye seeth *Thee.*" He does not say, "I see myself" merely; no; but "Thee." Nothing but a view of what God is can really lead to repentance and self-loathing. Thus it will be with the people of Israel, whose history is very analagous with that of Job. When they shall look upon Him whom they have pierced, they will mourn, and then there will be full restoration and blessing. Their latter end, like Job's, will be better than their beginning. They will learn the full meaning of that word, "O Israel, thou hast destroyed thyself; but in Me is thine help" (Hosea 13:9).

---

## *CHAPTERS 33–34*

We may here see how groundless were all Jacob's fears, and how useless all his plans. Notwithstanding the wrestling, the touching the hollow of the thigh, and the halting, we find Jacob still planning.—"And Jacob lifted up his eyes and looked, and behold Esau came, and with him four hundred men. And he divided the children unto Leah, and unto Rachel, and unto the two handmaids. And he put the handmaids and their children foremost, and Leah and her children after, and Rachel and Joseph hindermost." This arrangement proved the continuance of his fears. He still anticipated vengeance from the hand of Esau, and he exposed those about whom he cared least to the first stroke of that vengeance. How wondrous are the depths of the human heart! How slow it is to trust God! Had Jacob been really leaning upon God, he never could have anticipated destruction for himself and his family; but, alas! the heart knows something of the difficulty of simply reposing, in calm confidence, upon an ever-present, all-powerful, and infinitely-gracious God.

But mark, now, the thorough vanity of the heart's anxiety. "And Esau ran to meet him, and embraced him, and fell on his neck and kissed him; and they wept." The present was quite unnecessary—the plan, useless. God "appeased" Esau, as He had already appeased Laban. Thus it is He ever delights to rebuke our poor, coward, unbelieving hearts, and put to flight all our fears. Instead of the dreaded sword of Esau, Jacob meets his embrace and kiss; instead of strife and conflict, they mingle their tears. Such are God's ways. Who would not trust Him?—who would not honor Him with the heart's fullest confidence? Why is it that, notwithstanding all the sweet evidences of His faithfulness to those who put their trust in Him, we are so ready, on every fresh occasion, to doubt and hesitate? The answer is simple,—We are not sufficiently acquainted with God. "Acquaint now thyself with Him, and be at peace" (Job 22:21). This is true, whether in reference to the unconverted sinner or to the child of God. The true knowledge of God—real acquaintance with Him, is life and peace. "This is life eternal, that they might know Thee, the only true God, and Jesus Christ whom Thou hast sent" (John 17:3). The more intimate our acquaintance with God, the more solid will be our peace, and the more will our souls be lifted above every creature dependence. "God is a rock," and we only need to lean our whole weight upon Him, to know how ready and how able He is to sustain us.

After all this manifestation of God's goodness, we find Jacob settling down in Succoth, and, contrary to the spirit and principles of a pilgrim life, building a house, as if it were his home. Now, Succoth was evidently not his divinely-appointed destination. The Lord had not said to him, I am the God of Succoth; no; but, "I am the God of Bethel." Bethel, therefore, and not Succoth, should have been Jacob's grand object. But, alas! the heart is always prone to rest satisfied with a position and portion short of what God would graciously assign.

Jacob then moves on to Shechem, and purchases ground, still falling short of the divine mark, and the name by which he calls his altar is indicative of the moral condition of his soul. He calls it "El-elohe-Israel," or, "God, the God of Israel." This was taking a very contracted view of God. True, it is our privilege to know God as our God; but it is a higher thing to know Him as the God of His own house, and to view ourselves as part of that house. It is the believer's privilege to know Christ as *his* Head; but it is a higher thing to know Him as the Head of His body the Church, and to know ourselves as members of that body.

We shall see, when we come to chapter 35, that Jacob is led to take a higher and a wider view of God; but at Shechem he was manifestly on low ground, and he was made to smart for it, as is always the case when we stop short of God's own ground. The two tribes and a half took up their position on this side of the Jordan, and they were the first to fall into the enemy's hand. So it was with Jacob. We see, in chapter 34, the bitter fruits of his sojourn at Shechem. There is a blot cast upon his family, which Simeon and Levi attempt to wipe out, in the mere energy and violence of nature, which only led to still deeper sorrow; and that, too, which touched Jacob still more keenly than the insult offered to his daughter.—"And Jacob said to Simeon and Levi, 'Ye have troubled *me,* to make *me* to stink among the inhabitants of the land, among the Canaanites and the Perizzites; and *I* being few in number, they shall gather themselves together against *me,* and slay *me;* and *I* shall be destroyed, *I* and my house." Thus, it was the consequences in reference to himself that affected Jacob most. He seems to have walked in constant apprehension of danger to himself or his family, and in the manifestation of an anxious, a cautious, timid, calculating spirit, utterly incompatible with a life of genuine faith in God.

It is not that Jacob was not, in the main, a man of faith; he assuredly was, and as such, gets a place amongst the "cloud of witnesses" in Hebrews 11: but then he exhibited sad failure from not walking in the habitual exercise of that divine principle. Could faith have led him to say, "I shall be destroyed, I and my house"? Surely not. God's promise in chapter 28:14-15, should have banished every fear from his poor timid spirit.—"I will keep thee. . . . I will not leave thee." This should have tranquilized his heart. But the fact is, his mind was more occupied with his danger among the Shechemites than with his security in the hand of God. He ought to have known that not a hair of his head could be touched, and therefore, instead of looking at Simeon and Levi, or the consequences of their rash acting, he should have judged himself for being in such a position at all. If he had not settled at Shechem, Dinah would not have been dishonored, and the violence of his sons would not have been exhibited. We constantly see Christians getting into deep sorrow and trouble through their own unfaithfulness; and then, instead of judging themselves, they begin to look at circumstances, and to cast upon them the blame.

How often do we see Christian parents, for instance, in keen anguish of soul about the wildness, unsubduedness, and worldliness of their children; and, all the while, they have mainly to blame themselves for not walking faithfully before God in reference to their family. Thus was it with Jacob. He was on low moral ground at Shechem; and, inasmuch as he lacked that refined sensibility which would have led him to detect the low ground, God, in very faithfulness, used his circumstances to chastise him. "God is not mocked; for whatsoever a man soweth, that shall he also reap." This is a principle flowing out of God's moral government—a principle, from the application of which none can possibly escape; and it is a positive mercy to the children of God that they are obliged to reap the fruits of their errors. It is a mercy to be taught, in any way, the bitterness of departing from, or stopping short of, the living God. We must learn that this is not our rest; for, blessed be God, He would not give us a polluted rest. He would ever have us resting *in* and *with* Himself. Such is His perfect grace; and when our hearts wander or fall short, His word is, "If thou wilt return, return *unto Me.*" False humility, which is simply the fruit of unbelief, would lead the wanderer or backslider to take lower ground, not knowing the principle or measure of God's restoration. The prodigal would seek to be made a servant, not knowing that, so far as he was concerned, he had no more title to the place of a servant than to that of a son; and, moreover, that it would be utterly unworthy of the father's character to put him in such a position. We must come to God on a principle and in a manner worthy of Himself, or not at all.

---

## *CHAPTER 35*

"AND God said unto Jacob, 'Arise, go up to Bethel and dwell there.' " This confirms the principle on which we have been dwelling. When there is failure or declension, the Lord calls the soul back to Himself. "Remember, therefore, *from whence thou art fallen;* and repent, and do *the first works*" (Rev. 2:5). This is the divine principle of restoration. The soul must be recalled to the very highest point,—it must be brought back to the divine standard. The Lord does not say, Remember where you are; no; but, "Remember the lofty position from whence you have fallen." Thus only can one learn how far he has declined, and how he is to retrace his steps.

Now, it is when thus recalled to God's high and holy standard, that one is really led to see the sad evil of one's fallen condition. What a fearful amount of moral evil had gathered round Jacob's family, unjudged by him, until his soul was roused by the call to "go up to Bethel." Shechem was not the place in which to detect all this evil. The atmosphere of that place was too much impregnated with impure elements to admit of the soul's discerning, with any degree of clearness and precision, the true character of evil. But the moment the call to Bethel fell on Jacob's ear, "then Jacob said unto his household, and to all that were with him, 'Put away the strange gods that are among you, and be clean and change your garments, and let us arise and go up to Bethel; and I will make there an altar unto God, who answered me in the day of my distress, and was with me in the way which I went.' " The very mention of "the house of God" struck a chord in the soul of the patriarch; it carried him, in the twinkling of an eye, over the history of twenty eventful years. It was at Bethel he had learnt what God was, and not at Shechem; hence he must get back to Bethel again, and erect an altar upon a totally different base, and under a totally different name, from his altar at Shechem. This latter was connected with a mass of uncleanness and idolatry.

Jacob could speak of "El-elohe-Israel" while surrounded by a quantity of things utterly incompatible with the holiness of the house of God. It is important to be clear in reference to this point. Nothing can keep the soul in a path of consistent, intelligent separation from evil save the sense of what "the house of God" is, and what becomes that house. If I merely look at God in reference to myself, I shall not have a clear, full, divine sense of all that flows out of a due recognition of God's relation to His house. Some there are who deem it a matter of no importance how they are mixed up with impure materials in the worship of God, provided they themselves are true and upright in heart. In other words, they think they can worship God at Shechem, and that an altar named "El-elohe-Israel" is just as elevated—just as much according to God—as an altar named "El-Bethel." This is evidently a mistake. The spiritually-minded reader will at once detect the vast moral difference between Jacob's condition at Shechem, and his condition at Bethel; and the same difference is observable between the two altars. Our ideas in reference to the worship of God must, of necessity, be affected by our spiritual condition; and the worship which we present will be low and contracted, or elevated and comprehensive, just in proportion as we enter into the apprehension of His character and relationship.

Now, the name of our altar and the character of our worship express the same idea. El-Bethel worship is higher than El-elohe-Israel worship, for this simple reason, that it conveys a higher idea of God. It gives me a more elevated thought of God to speak of Him as the God of His house than as the God of a solitary individual. True, there is beautiful grace expressed in the title, "God, the God of Israel," and the soul must ever feel happy in looking at the character of God as graciously connecting Himself with every separate stone of His house and every separate member of the body. Each stone in the building of God is a "lively stone," as connected with the "living stone," having communion with the "living God," by the power of "the Spirit of life." But while all this is blessedly true, God is the God of His house; and when we are enabled, by an enlarged spiritual intelligence, to view Him as such, we enjoy a higher character of worship than that which flows from merely apprehending what He is to ourselves individually.

But there is another thing to be remarked in Jacob's recall to Bethel. He is told to make an altar "unto God, that appeared unto thee when thou fleddest from the face of Esau thy brother." He is thus reminded of "the day of his distress." It is often well to have our minds led in this way to the point in our history in which we found ourselves brought down to the lowest step of the ladder. Thus Saul is brought back to the time when he was "little in his own eyes." This is the true starting-point with all of us. "When thou wast little in thine own eyes," is a point of which we often need to be reminded. It is then that the heart really leans on God. Afterwards we begin to fancy ourselves to be something, and the Lord is obliged to teach us afresh our own nothingness. When first one enters upon a path of service or testimony, what a sense there is of personal weakness and incapacity! and, as a consequence, what leaning upon God! what earnest, fervent appeals to Him for help and strength! Afterwards we begin to think that, from being so long at the work, we can get on by ourselves,—at least, there is not the same sense of weakness, or the same simple dependence upon God; and then our ministry becomes a poor, meagre, flippant, wordy thing, without unction or power—a thing flowing, not from the exhaustless tide of the Spirit, but from our own wretched minds.

From verse 9 to 15, God renews His promise to Jacob, and confirms the new name of "prince," instead of "supplanter;" and Jacob again calls the name of the place "Bethel." At verse 18 we have an interesting example of the difference between the judgment of faith and the judgment of nature. The latter looks at things through the hazy mist with which it is surrounded; the former looks at them in the light of the presence and counsels of God.—"And it came to pass, as her soul was in departing, (for she died,) that she called his name Ben-oni; but his father called him Benjamin." Nature called him "The son of my sorrow;" but faith called him "The son of the right hand." Thus is it ever. The difference between the thoughts of nature and those of faith must ever be wide indeed; and we should earnestly desire that our souls should be governed only by the latter, and not by the former.

---

## *CHAPTER 36*

THIS chapter furnishes a catalogue of Esau's sons, with their various titles and localities. We shall not dwell on this, but pass on to one of the most fruitful and interesting sections in the entire canon of inspiration.

## *CHAPTERS 37—50*

THERE is not in Scripture a more perfect and beautiful type of Christ than Joseph. Whether we view Christ as the object of the Father's love, the object of the envy of "His own,"—in His humiliation, sufferings, death, exaltation and glory—in all, we have Him strikingly typified by Joseph.

In chapter 37 we have Joseph's dreams, the statement of which draws out the enmity of his brethren. He was the object of his father's love, and the subject of very high destinies, and, inasmuch as the hearts of his brethren were not in communion with these things, they hated him. They had no fellowship in the father's love, and they would not yield to the thought of Joseph's exaltation. In all this they represent the Jews in Christ's day. "He came to His own, and His own received Him not." He had "no form nor comeliness" in their eyes. They would neither own Him as the Son of God, nor King of Israel. Their eyes were not open to behold "His glory, the glory as of the only begotten of the Father, full of grace and truth." They would not have Him—yea, they hated Him.

Now, in Joseph's case, we see that he in no wise relaxed his testimony in consequence of his brethren's refusal of his first dream. "And Joseph dreamed a dream, and he told it to his brethren; and they hated him yet the more. . . . And he dreamed yet another dream, and told it to his brethren." This was simple testimony founded upon divine revelation; but it was testimony which brought Joseph down to the pit. Had he kept back his testimony, or taken off aught of its edge and power, he might have spared himself; but no; he told them the truth, and therefore they hated him.

Thus was it with Joseph's great Antitype. He bore witness to the truth--He witnessed a good confession—He kept back nothing—He could only speak the truth because He was *the* truth, and His testimony to the truth was answered, on man's part, by the cross, the vinegar, the soldier's spear. The testimony of Christ, too, was connected with the deepest, fullest, richest grace. He not only came as "the truth," but also as the perfect expression of all the love of the Father's heart: "grace and truth came by Jesus Christ." He was the full disclosure to man of what God was; hence man was left entirely without excuse. He came and showed God to man, and man hated God with a perfect hatred. The fullest exhibition of divine love was answered by the fullest exhibition of human hatred. This is seen in the cross; and we have it touchingly foreshadowed at the pit into which Joseph was cast by his brethren.

"And when they saw him afar off, even before he came near unto them, they conspired against him to slay him. And they said one to another, 'Behold, this dreamer cometh; come now, therefore, and let us slay him, and cast him into some pit; and we will say, some evil beast hath devoured him; and we shall see what will become of his dreams.' " These words forcibly remind us of the parable in Matthew 21: "But last of all he sent unto them his son, saying, 'They will reverence my son.' But when the husbandmen saw the son, they said among themselves, 'This is the heir; come, let us kill him, and let us seize on his inheritance.' And they caught him, and cast him out of the vineyard, and slew him." God sent His Son into the world with this thought, "They will reverence My Son;" but, alas! man's heart had no reverence for the "well-beloved" of the Father;—they cast Him out. Earth and heaven were at issue in reference to Christ, and they are at issue still. *Man* crucified Him; but *God* raised Him from the dead. Man placed Him on a cross between two thieves; God set Him at His own right hand in the heavens. Man have Him the very lowest place on earth; God gave Him the very highest place in heaven, in brightest majesty.

All this is shown out in Joseph's history. "Joseph is a fruitful bough, even a fruitful bough by a well, whose branches run over the wall. The archers have sorely grieved him, and shot at him, and hated him; but his bow abode in strength, and the arms of his hands were made strong by the hands of the mighty God of Jacob; (from thence is the Shepherd, the Stone of Israel;) even by the God of thy father, who shall help thee; and by the Almighty, who shall bless thee with blessings of heaven above, blessings of the deep that lieth under, blessings of the breasts and of the womb: the blessings of thy father have prevailed above the blessings of my progenitors, unto the utmost bound of the everlasting hills; they shall be upon the head of Joseph, and on the crown of the head of him that was separate from his brethren" (Gen. 49:22-26).

These verses beautifully exhibit to our view "the sufferings of Christ, and the glory that should follow." "The archers" have done their work; but God was stronger than they. The true Joseph has been shot at and grievously wounded in the house of his friends; but "the arms of his hands have been made strong" in the power of resurrection, and faith now knows Him as the basis of all God's purposes of blessing and glory in reference to the Church, Israel, and the whole creation. When we look at Joseph in the pit and in the prison, and look at him afterwards as ruler over all the land of Egypt, we see the difference between the thoughts of God and the thoughts of men; and so when we look at the cross, and at "the throne of the Majesty in the heavens," we see the same thing.

Nothing ever brought out the real state of man's heart toward God but the coming of Christ. "If I had not come and spoken unto them, they had not had sin" (John 15:22). It is not that they would not have been sinners. No; but "they had not had sin." So He says, in another place, "If ye were blind, ye should have no sin" (John 9:41). God came near to man in the Person of His Son, and man was able to say, "This is the heir;" but yet he said, "Come, let us kill Him." Hence, "they have no cloak for their sin." Those who say they see, have no excuse. *Confessed blindness* is not at all the difficulty, but *professed sight.* This is a truly-solemn principle for a professing age like the present. The permanence of sin is connected with the mere profession to see. A man who is blind, and knows it, can have his eyes opened; but what can be done for one who thinks he sees, when he really does not?

---

## *CHAPTER 38*

HERE is one of those remarkable circumstances in which divine grace is seen gloriously triumphing over man's sin. "It is evident that our Lord sprang out of Juda" (Heb. 7:14). But how? "Judas begat Phares and Zara of *Thamar*" (Matt. 1:3). This is peculiarly striking. God, in His great grace, rising above the sin and folly of man, in order to bring about His own purposes of love and mercy. Thus, a little further on in Matthew, we read: "David the king begat Solomon, of her that had been the wife of Urias." It is worthy of God thus to act. The Spirit of God is conducting us along the line through which, according to the flesh, Christ came; and, in doing so, He gives us, as links in the genealogical chain, Tamar and Bathsheba! How evident it is that there is nothing of man in this! How plain it is that when we reach the close of the first chapter of Matthew, it is "God manifest in the flesh" we find, and that, too, from the pen of the Holy Ghost! Man could never have devised such a genealogy. It is entirely divine; and no spiritual person can read it without seeing in it a blessed exhibition of divine grace, in the first place, and of the divine inspiration of Matthew's Gospel, in the second place, at least of his account of Christ's genealogy according to the flesh. I believe a comparison of 2 Samuel 11 and Genesis 38 with Matthew 1 will furnish the thoughtful Christian with matter for a very sweet and edifying meditation.

---

## *CHAPTERS 39–45*

IN perusing these interesting sections of inspiration, we perceive a remarkable chain of providential actings, all tending to one grand point, namely, the *exaltation of the man who had been in the pit;* and, at the same time, bringing out, by the way, a number of subordinate objects. "The thoughts of many hearts" were to be "revealed;" but Joseph was to be exalted. "He called for a famine upon the land: He brake the whole staff of bread. He sent a man before them, even Joseph, who was sold for a servant; whose feet they hurt with fetters; he was laid in iron; until the time that His word came; the word of the Lord tried him. The king sent and loosed him; even the ruler of the people, and let him go free. He made him lord of his house, and ruler of all his substance; to bind his princes at his pleasure, and teach his senators wisdom" (Psalm 105:16-22).

It is well to see that the leading object was to exalt the one whom men had rejected, and then to produce in those same men a sense of their sin in rejecting. And how admirably all this is effected! The most trivial and the most important, the most likely and the most unlikely, circumstances are made to minister to the development of God's purposes. In chapter 39, Satan uses Potiphar's wife; and in chapter 40, he uses Pharaoh's chief butler. The former he used to put Joseph into the dungeon; and the latter he used to keep him there, through his ungrateful negligence; but all in vain. God was behind the scenes. His finger was guiding all the springs of the vast machine of circumstances; and when the due time was come, He brought forth the man of His purpose, and set his feet in a large room. Now this is ever God's prerogative. He is above all, and can use all for the accomplishment of His grand and unsearchable designs. It is sweet to be able thus to trace our Father's hand and counsel in everything; sweet to know that all sorts of agents are at His sovereign disposal: angels, men and devils—all are under His omnipotent hand, and all are made to carry out His purposes.

In the Scripture now before us, all this is seen in a most remarkable manner. God visits the domestic circle of a heathen captain, the household of a heathen king,—yea, and his bedside, and makes the very visions of his head upon his bed contribute to the development of His counsels. Nor is it merely individuals and their circumstances that we see thus taken up and used for the furtherance of God's ends; but Egypt and all the surrounding countries are brought into the scene; in short, the whole earth was prepared by the hand of God to be a theatre on which to display the glory and greatness of the one "who was separate from his brethren." Such are God's ways; and it is one of the happiest and most elevating exercises for the soul of a saint to trace thus the admirable actings of his heavenly Father. How forcibly is God's providence brought out in this profoundly interesting history of Joseph! Look, for a moment, into the dungeon of the captain of the guard. See there a man "laid in iron," charged with a most abominable crime, the outcast and offscouring of society; and yet see him, almost in a moment, raised to the very highest eminence; and who can deny that God is in it all?

"And Pharaoh said unto Joseph, 'Forasmuch as God hath showed thee all this, there is none so discreet and wise as thou art; thou shalt be over my house, and according unto thy word shall all my people be ruled; only in the throne will I be greater than thou.' And Pharaoh said unto Joseph, 'See, I have set thee over all the land of Egypt.' And Pharaoh took off his ring from his hand, and put it upon Joseph's hand, and arrayed him in vestures of fine linen, and put a gold chain about his neck. And he made him to ride in the second chariot that he had; and they cried before him, 'Bow the knee'; and he made him ruler over all the land of Egypt. And Pharaoh said unto Joseph, 'I am Pharaoh, and without thee shall no man lift up his hand or foot in all the land of Egypt' " (chap. 41:39-44).

Here, then, was exaltation of no ordinary kind. Contrast this with the pit and the dungeon; and mark the chain of events by which it was all brought about, and you have, at once, a marked exhibition of the hand of God, and a striking type of the sufferings and glory of the Lord Jesus Christ. Joseph was taken from the pit and the dungeon, into which he had been brought by the envy of his brethren, and the false judgment of the Gentile, to be ruler over the whole land of Egypt; and not only so, but to be the channel of blessing and the sustainer of life to Israel and the whole earth. This is all typical of Christ; indeed, a type could hardly be more perfect. We see a man laid, to all intents and purposes, in the place of death, by the hand of man, and then raised up by the hand of God, and set in dignity and glory. "Ye men of Israel, hear these words: Jesus of Nazareth, a Man approved of God among you by miracles and wonders and signs, which God did by Him in the midst of you, as ye yourselves also know;

Him, being delivered by the determinate counsel and foreknowledge of God, ye have taken, and by wicked hands have crucified and slain; whom God hath raised up, having loosed the pains of death; because it was not possible that He should be holden of it" (Acts 2:22-24).

But there are two points in Joseph's history which, together with what has been noticed, render the type remarkably perfect; I allude to his marriage with a stranger, in chapter 41, and his interview with his brethren, in chapter 45. The following is the order of events: Joseph presents himself to his brethren as one sent by the father; they reject him, and, so far as lies in them, put him in the place of death; God takes him up from thence, and raises him to a position of highest dignity: thus exalted, he gets a bride; and when his brethren according to the flesh are thoroughly broken and prostrate before him, he makes himself known to them, tranquilizes their hearts, and brings them into blessing; he then becomes the channel of blessing to them and to the whole world.

I shall just make a few remarks on Joseph's marriage and the restoration of his brethren. The strange wife shadows forth the Church. Christ presented Himself to the Jews, and being rejected, took His seat on high, and sent down the Holy Ghost to gather out an elect Church, composed of Jew and Gentile, to be united with Him in heavenly glory. The doctrine of the Church has already been dwelt upon, in our remarks on chapter 24, but one or two points remain to be noticed here. And, first, we may observe, that Joseph's Egyptian bride was intimately associated with him in his glory.* She, as being part of himself, shared in all that was his. Moreover, she occupied a place of nearness and intimacy known only to herself. Thus it is with the Church, the bride of the Lamb. She is gathered to Christ to be the sharer, at once, of His rejection and His glory. It is Christ's position which gives character to the position of the Church, and her position should ever give character to her walk. If we are gathered to Christ, it is as exalted in glory, and not as humbled down here. "Henceforth know we no man after the flesh; yea, though we have known Christ after the flesh, yet now henceforth know we Him no more" (2 Cor. 5:16). The Church's gathering-point is Christ in glory.—"I, if I be lifted up from the earth, will draw all unto Me" (John 12:32).

There is far more of practical value in the clear apprehension of this principle than might, at first sight, appear. It is ever the aim of Satan, as it is the tendency of our hearts, to lead us to stop short of God's mark in everything, and especially in the centre of our unity as Christians. It is a popular sentiment, that "the blood of the Lamb is the union of saints," *i.e.,* it is the blood which forms their centre of unity. Now, that it is the infinitely precious blood of Christ which sets us individually as worshipers in the presence of God, is blessedly true. The blood, therefore, forms the divine basis of our fellowship with God. But when we come to speak of the centre of our unity as a church, we must see that the Holy Ghost gathers us to the Person of a risen and glorified Christ; and this grand truth gives character—high and holy character—to our association as Christians. If we take lower ground than this, we must inevitably form a sect or an *ism.* If we gather round an ordinance however important, or round a truth however indisputable, we make something less than Christ our centre.

Hence, it is more important to ponder the practical consequences which flow out of the truth of our being gathered to a risen and glorified Head in the heavens. If Christ were on earth, we should be gathered to Him here; but inasmuch as He is hidden in the heavens, the Church takes her character from His position there. Hence, Christ could say, "They are not of the world, even as I am not of the world;" and again, "For their sakes I sanctify Myself, that they also might be sanctified through the truth" (John 17:16,19). So also, in 1 Peter, we read, "To whom coming, as unto a living Stone, disallowed indeed of men, but chosen of God

*Joseph's wife sets forth the Church as united to Christ in His glory: Moses' wife presents the Church as united to Christ in His rejection.

and precious; ye also, as lively stones, are built up a spiritual house, a holy priesthood, to offer up spiritual sacrifices, acceptable to God by Jesus Christ" (chap. 2:4-5). If we are gathered to Christ, we must be gathered to Him *as* He is and *where* He is; and the more the Spirit of God leads our souls into the understanding of this, the more clearly we shall see the character of walk that becomes us. Joseph's bride was united to him, not in the pit or the dungeon, but in the dignity and glory of his position in Egypt; and, in her case, we can have no difficulty in perceiving the vast difference between the two positions.

But further, we read, "And unto Joseph were born two sons, *before the years of famine came.*" There was a time of trouble coming; but previous thereto, the fruit of his union appeared. The children whom God had given him were called into existence previous to this time of trial. So will it be in reference to the Church. All the members thereof will be called out, the whole body will be completed and gathered to the Head in heaven, previous to "the great tribulation" which shall come upon all the earth.

We shall now turn, for a little, to Joseph's interview with his brethren, in which we shall find some points of resemblance to Israel's history in the latter day. During the period that Joseph was hidden from the view of his brethren, these latter were called to pass through deep and searching trial—through intensely painful exercises of conscience. One of these exercises is poured out in the following words: "And they said one to another, *'We are verily guilty* concerning our brother, in that we saw the anguish of his soul, and when he besought us, and *we would not hear;* therefore *is this distress come upon us.'* And Reuben answered them, saying, 'Spake I not unto you, saying, Do not sin against the child; and ye would not hear? therefore, behold, also, *his blood is required'* " (chap. 42:21-22).

Again in chapter 44, we read, "And Judah said, 'What shall we say unto my lord? What shall we speak? or how shall we clear ourselves? God hath found out the iniquity of thy servants.' " None can teach like God. He alone can produce in the conscience the true sense of sin, and bring the soul down into the profound depths of its own condition in His presence. This is all His own work. Men run on in their career of guilt, heedless of everything, until the arrow of the Almighty pierces their conscience, and then they are led into those searchings of heart and intensive exercises of soul which can only find relief in the rich resources of redeeming love. Joseph's brethren had no conception of all that was to flow to them from their actings toward him. "They took him and cast him into a pit . . . and they sat down to eat bread." "Woe to them . . . that drink wine in bowls, and anoint themselves with the chief ointments; but they are not grieved for the affliction of Joseph" (Amos 6:6).

However, God produced grief of heart, and exercises of conscience, and that in a most wonderful way. Years rolled on, and these brethren might have vainly imagined that all was right; but, then, "seven years of plenty, and seven years of scarcity"! What did they mean? Who sent them? And for what were they designed? Admirable providence! Unsearchable wisdom! The famine reaches to Canaan, and the calls of hunger actually bring the guilty brethren to the feet of the injured Joseph! How marked is the display of God's own hand in all this! There they stand, with the arrow of conviction thrust through and through their consciences, in the presence of the man whom they had "with wicked hands," cast into the pit. Surely their sin had found them out; but it was in the presence of Joseph. Blessed place!

"Then Joseph could not refrain himself before all them that stood by him; and he cried, 'Cause every man to go out from me.' And there stood no man with him, while Joseph made himself known unto his brethren" (chap. 45:1). No stranger was allowed to witness this sacred scene. What stranger could understand or appreciate it? We are here called to witness, as it were, divinely-wrought conviction in the presence of divine grace; and, we may say, when these two come together, there is an easy settlement of every question.

"And Joseph said unto his brethren, '*Come near to me,* I pray you.' And they came near. And he said, 'I am Joseph your brother, whom ye sold into Egypt. Now, therefore, be not grieved, nor angry with yourselves, that ye sold me hither; for God did send me before you, to preserve life. . . . And God sent me before you to preserve you a posterity in the earth, and to save your lives by a great deliverance. So now it was not you sent me hither, but God.' " This is grace indeed, setting the convicted conscience perfectly at rest. The brethren had already most thoroughly condemned themselves, and hence Joseph had only to pour in the blessed balm into their broken hearts. This is all sweetly typical of God's dealings with Israel in the latter day, when "they shall look upon Him whom they have pierced, and mourn." Then they shall prove the reality of divine grace, and the cleansing efficacy of that "fountain which shall be opened to the house of David, and to the inhabitants of Jerusalem, for sin and for uncleanness" (Zech. 13:1).

In the third chapter of Acts, we find the Spirit of God in Peter seeking to produce this divine conviction in the consciences of the Jews.—"The God of Abraham, and of Isaac, and of Jacob, the God of our fathers, hath glorified His Son Jesus; whom ye delivered up, and denied Him in the presence of Pilate, when he was determined to let Him go. But ye denied the Holy One and the just, and desired a murderer to be granted unto you; and killed the Prince of Life, whom God hath raised from the dead, whereof we are witnesses." These statements were designed to elicit from the hearts and lips of the hearers the confession made by Joseph's brethren—"We are verily guilty." Then follows the grace. "And now, brethren, I wot that through ignorance ye did it, as did also your rulers. But those things, which God before had showed by the mouth of all His prophets, that Christ should suffer, He hath so fulfilled. Repent ye, therefore, and be converted, that your sins may be blotted out, when the times of refreshing shall come from the presence of the Lord." We here see, that although the Jews really carried out the enmity of their hearts in the death of Christ, as did also Joseph's brethren in their treatment of him, yet the grace of God to each is seen in this, that all is shown to be decreed and foreshown of God for their blessing. This is perfect grace, surpassing all human thought; and all that is needed, in order to the enjoyment thereof, is a conscience truly convicted by the truth of God. Those who could say, "We are verily guilty," could rightly understand the words of precious grace, "It was not you, but God." Thus it must ever be. The soul that has thoroughly pronounced its own condemnation, is prepared to understand and appreciate God's pardon.

The remaining chapters of this book are taken up with the removal of Jacob and his family into Egypt, and their settlement there; Joseph's actings during the remaining years of famine; Jacob's blessing the twelve patriarchs; his death and burial. We shall not dwell in detail upon these things, though the spiritual mind may find much to feed upon therein.* Jacob's groundless fears dissipated by the sight of his son alive, and exalted, the peculiar grace of God seen in its overruling power, yet evidently mingled with judgment, inasmuch as Jacob's sons have to go down into the very place whither they had sent their brother. Again, Joseph's remarkable grace throughout: though exalted by Pharaoh, he hides himself, as it were, and binds the people in abiding obligation to the king. Pharaoh says, "Go to Joseph," and Joseph, in effect, says, "All you have and all you are belong to Pharaoh." This is sweetly

*The close of Jacob's career stands in most pleasing contrast with all the previous scenes of his eventful history. It reminds one of a serene evening after a tempestuous day: the sun, which during the day had been hidden from view by clouds, mists and fogs, sets in majesty and brightness, gilding with his beams the western sky, and holding out the cheering prospect of a bright tomorrow. Thus is it with our aged patriarch. The supplanting, the bargain-making, the cunning, the management, the shifting, the shuffling, the unbelieving selfish fears,—all those dark clouds of nature and of earth seem to have passed away, and he comes forth, in all the calm elevation of faith, to bestow blessings, and impart dignities, in that holy skillfulness which communion with God can alone impart.

interesting, and leads the soul on to that glorious time when the Son of Man shall take the reins of government into His own hand, by divine appointment, and rule over the whole redeemed creation; His Church—the bride of the Lamb—occupying the nearest and most intimate place, according to the eternal counsels. The house of Israel, fully restored, shall be nourished and sustained by His gracious hand; and all the earth shall know the deep blessedness of being under His sceptre. Finally, having brought everything into subjection, He shall hand back the reins of government into the hands of God, that "He may be all in all." From all this we may form some idea of the richness and copiousness of Joseph's history. In short, it sets before us, distinctly, in type, the mission of the Son to the house of Israel, His humiliation and rejection, the deep exercises and final repentance and restoration of Israel, the union of the Church with Christ, His exaltation and universal government, and, finally, it points us forward to the time when "God shall be all in all." It is quite needless to remark that all these things are largely taught, and fully established, throughout the entire canon of inspiration; we do not, therefore, build their truth upon Joseph's history; still it is edifying to find such early foreshadowings of these precious truths; it proves to us the divine unity which pervades Holy Scripture. Whether we turn to Genesis or to Ephesians—to the prophets of the Old or those of the New Testament—we learn the same truths. *"All Scripture is given by inspiration of God."*

---

Though nature's eyes are dim, faith's vision is sharp. He is not to be deceived as to the relative positions assigned to Ephraim and Manasseh in the counsels of God. He has not, like his father Isaac, in chapter 27, to "tremble very exceedingly" in view of an almost fatal mistake. Quite the reverse. His intelligent reply to his less-instructed son is, "I know it, my son, I know it." The power of sense has not, as in Isaac's case, dimmed his spiritual vision. He has been taught, in the school of experience, the importance of keeping close to the divine purpose, and nature's influence cannot move him from thence.

In chapter 48:11, we have a very beautiful example of the mode in which our God ever rises above all our thoughts, and proves Himself better than all our fears. "And Israel said unto Joseph, 'I had not thought to see thy face; and, lo, God hath showed me also thy seed.' " To nature's view, Joseph was dead; whereas, in God's view, he was alive, and seated in the highest place of authority, next the throne. "Eye hath not seen, nor ear heard, neither have entered into the heart of man, the things which God hath prepared for them that love Him" (1 Cor. 2:9). Would that our souls could rise higher in their apprehension of God and His ways.

It is interesting to notice the way in which the titles "Jacob" and "Israel" are introduced in the close of the book of Genesis; as, for example, "One told *Jacob,* and said, 'Behold, thy son Joseph cometh unto thee'; and *Israel* strengthened himself, and sat upon the bed." Then, it is immediately added, "And *Jacob* said unto Joseph, 'God Almighty appeared unto me at Luz.' " Now, we know, there is nothing in Scripture without its specific meaning, and hence this interchange of names contains some instruction. In general, it may be remarked that "Jacob" sets forth the depth to which God had descended; "Israel," the height to which Jacob was raised.

# NOTES

*on the book of*

# EXODUS

*"He led them forth by the right way"*

## *PREFACE*

IN manuscript and proof-sheets, we have been traveling over a deeply instructive and most interesting portion of the Word of God—*the book of Exodus.*

Redemption by blood occupies a prominent place therein—it characterizes the book. God's many mercies to His redeemed, in the display of His power, the patience of His love, and the riches of His grace, flow from it. The great question of Israel's relationship to God is settled by the blood of the lamb. It changes their condition entirely. Israel within the blood-sprinkled door-posts was God's redeemed, blood-bought people.

God being holy, and Israel guilty, no happy relationship could exist between them till judgment had been accomplished. Sin must be judged. A happy friendship once existed between God and man, on the ground of innocence; but sin having entered and snapped the link asunder, there can be no reconciliation but through the full expression of the moral judgment of God against sin. We can only have "life through death." God is the God of holiness, and He must judge sin. In saving the sinner, He condemns his sin. The cross is the full and perfect expression of this.

Typically, this was the great question, on "the evening of the fourteenth day of the first month; namely, *How can God exempt from judgment, and receive into His favor, those whom His holiness condemns?* To this most solemn question, there was but one answer that would satisfy the demands of the God of holiness, and that was *the blood of the Lamb of His own providing.* "When I see the blood, I will pass over you." This settled the all-important question. It was one of life or death, of deliverance or judgment. The blood-sprinkled door-post was a perfect answer to all the claims of holiness, and to all the need of the congregation. All was settled now. God was glorified, sin judged and put away, and Israel saved through the blood of the lamb.

Blessed truth! Israel was now at peace with God, a sheltered, saved, and happy people, though still in Egypt—the land of death and judgment. God was now *pledged* to deliver Israel,—precious type of the perfect security of all who are trusting to the blood of Christ! They were securely and peacefully feeding on the roasted lamb, when, "at midnight, the Lord smote all the first-born in the land of Egypt, from the first-born of Pharaoh that sat on his throne, unto the first-born of the captive that was in the dungeon, and all the first-born of cattle. And Pharaoh rose up in the night, he and all his servants, and all the Egyptians; and there was a great cry in Egypt; for there was not a house where there was not one dead" (12:29-30). "But against any of the children of Israel shall not a dog move his tongue, against man or beast; that ye may know how the Lord doth put a difference between the Egyptians and Israel" (11:7).

But why, some may ask, put this difference? The Israelites were sinners as well as the Egyptians. True, on this ground there was "no difference;" but, in type, the judgment of God against sin had been expressed in the death of the unblemished lamb. The blood "on the lintel and the two side-posts" was the proof of this. It proclaimed, with a loud voice, that the lamb was slain, the ransom paid, the captive freed, justice satisfied, and the hour of Israel's deliverance fully come. *It was the blood that made the difference, and nothing else;* "for all have sinned and come short of the glory of God" (Rom. 3:23).

But oh, what a difference! The one, divinely shielded from the sword of judgment; the other, defenceless and slain by it: the one, feasting on the rich provisions of grace; the other, compelled to taste the bitterness of the cup of wrath. The destroying angel entered every house, throughout all the land of Egypt, that was not sprinkled with the blood. The first-born of Pharaoh on the throne, and the first-born of the captive in the dungeon, fell together.

No rank, age, or character escaped. The day of God's long-suffering was ended, and the hour of His judgment was come. One thing alone guided the angel of death on that dark and dreadful night, and that was, *where there is no blood, there is no salvation.*

This is as true now as it was then! Where there is no blood, there is no salvation—"without shedding of blood is no remission." Can any question be of such importance to you as this one: Am I shielded by the blood of Jesus? Oh! have you fled for refuge to the blood that was shed on Calvary? There, "Christ, our passover, was sacrificed for us." His blood is represented as being sprinkled on "the mercy-seat above." There, God's eye ever sees the blood of our true paschal Lamb. Have you faith in that precious blood? Though deeply sensible of your guilt, can you say in truth, This is my only hiding-place: I do depend upon the blood? Then rest assured that you are perfectly safe—that you are eternally saved. You have God's own word for it—"When I see the blood, I will pass over you."—"We have redemption *through His blood,* the forgiveness of sins, according to the riches of His grace."—"But now, in Christ Jesus, ye who sometimes were far off, are made nigh *by the blood of Christ.*"—"Whom God hath set forth to be a propitiation *through faith in His blood*" (Eph. 1:7; 2:13; Rom. 3:25).

> Happy they who trust in Jesus,
> Sweet their portion is and sure.

But, on the other hand, if the blood of Jesus is neglected or despised, there can be no security, no peace, and no salvation. "How shall we escape if we neglect so great salvation?" (Heb. 2:3) Unless the destroying angel sees the blood, he enters as the judge of sin. Every sin must be punished, either in the person of the sinner, or the sinner's substitute. This is a deeply solemn truth; but how blessed to know that "Christ hath once suffered for sins, the just for the unjust, that He might bring us to God." "For He hath made Him to be sin for us, who knew no sin, that we might be made the righteousness of God in Him" (1 Peter 3:18; 2 Cor. 5:21). To neglect this divine Substitute, and the shelter which He has provided, is to expose the soul to the unrelenting judgment of God. No sin, however small, can escape judgment, either on the cross of Christ, or in the lake of fire. Oh, the priceless value of that blood which "cleanseth us from *all* sin"!—which makes us clean enough for heaven!

Redemption being now accomplished, and Israel divinely prepared, they commence their journey. But observe, in passing, *how* they start. Before taking one step, every question between the conscience and God is divinely settled. They are forgiven, justified, and accepted, in His sight. Hence it is written, "When Israel was a child, then I loved him, and called my son out of Egypt" (Hosea 11:1). Blessed type of the real condition in which every true believer begins his Christian course! He may not see this blessed truth, or he may have a very feeble apprehension of it, as Israel had, but that does not alter the fact. God acts according to His own knowledge of the relationship, and the affections which belong to it. We see this in the glorious deliverance of His beloved people at the Red Sea, in the manna from heaven, the water from the flinty rock, and in the pillar of His presence, which accompanied them in all their wanderings. He ever acts according to the purposes of His love, and the value of the blood of Jesus.

Once more, allow me to ask, Are you sure that you are under the safe shelter, the secure refuge, the blessed hiding-place, of the Redeemer's blood?

But I must now leave my reader, earnestly recommending him to pursue the journey across the wilderness in company with God and His redeemed. He will find the *Notes* most useful. They convey truth, agreeably and intelligently to the heart, the conscience, and the understanding. May many find them to be a real oasis in the desert. The journey will prove a most profitable one if we thereby learn more of the natural unbelief of our own heart and the abiding faithfulness of God's. He never changes, blessed be His name; and the blood of the slain Lamb never loses its efficacy.

> Blest Lamb of God! Thy precious blood
> Shall never lose its power,
> Till every ransomed saint of God
> Be saved to sin no more.

May the Lord graciously own and use the following *Notes* for His own glory and the blessing of many souls.

*London* *A. M.*

# *NOTES*

# *ON*

# *THE BOOK OF EXODUS*

---

## *CHAPTER 1*

WE now approach, by the mercy of God, the study of the book of Exodus, of which the great prominent theme is redemption. The first five verses recall to the mind the closing scenes of the preceding book. The favored objects of God's electing love are brought before us; and we find ourselves very speedily conducted, by the inspired penman, into the action of the book.

In our meditations on the book of Genesis, we were led to see that the conduct of Joseph's brethren toward him was that which led to their being brought down into Egypt. This fact is to be looked at in two ways. In the first place, we can read therein a deeply solemn lesson, as taught in Israel's actings toward God; and, secondly, we have therein unfolded an encouraging lesson, as taught in God's actings toward Israel.

First, as to Israel's actings toward God, what can be more deeply solemn than to follow out the results of their treatment of him who stands before the spiritual mind as the marked type of the Lord Jesus Christ? They, utterly regardless of the anguish of his soul, consigned Joseph into the hands of the uncircumcised. And what was the issue, as regards them? They were carried down into Egypt, there to experience the deep and painful exercises of heart which are so graphically and touchingly presented in the closing chapters of Genesis. Nor was this all. A long and dreary season awaited their offspring in that very land in which Joseph had found a dungeon.

But then God was in all this, as well as man; and it is His prerogative to bring good out of evil. Joseph's brethren might sell him to the Ishmaelites, and the Ishmaelites might sell him to Potiphar, and Potiphar might cast him into prison; but Jehovah was above all, and He was accomplishing His own mighty ends. "The wrath of man shall praise Him." The time had not arrived in which the heirs were ready for the inheritance and the inheritance for the heirs. The brick-kilns of Egypt were to furnish a rigid school for the seed of Abraham, while as yet "the iniquity of the Amorites" was rising to a head amid the "hills and valleys" of the promised land.

All this is deeply interesting and instructive. There are "wheels within wheels" in the government of God. He makes use of an endless variety of agencies in the accomplishment of His unsearchable designs. Potiphar's wife, Pharaoh's butler, Pharaoh's dreams, Pharaoh himself, the dungeon, the throne, the fetter, the royal signet, the famine—all are at His sovereign disposal, and all are made instrumental in the development of His stupendous counsels. The spiritual mind delights to dwell upon this, it delights to range through the wide domain of creation and providence, and to recognize, in all, the machinery which an All-wise and an Almighty God is using for the purpose of unfolding His counsels of redeeming love. True, we may see many traces of the serpent, many deep and well-defined footprints of the enemy of God and man, many things which we cannot explain nor even comprehend; suffering innocence and successful wickedness may furnish an apparent basis for the infidel reasoning of the sceptic mind; but the true believer can piously repose in the assurance that "the Judge of all the earth shall do right." He knows right well that—

> Blind unbelief is sure to err,
> And scan His ways in vain;
> God is His own interpreter,
> And He will make it plain.

Blessed be God for the consolation and

encouragement flowing out of such reflections as these. We need them every hour while passing through an evil world, in which the enemy has wrought such appalling mischief, in which the lusts and passions of men produce such bitter fruits, and in which the path of the true disciple presents roughnesses which mere nature could never endure. Faith knows, of a surety, that there is One behind the scenes whom the world sees not nor regards; and, in the consciousness of this, it can calmly say, "It is well," and, "It shall be well."

The above train of thought is distinctly suggested by the opening lines of our book. "God's counsel shall stand, and He will do all His pleasure." The enemy may oppose, but God will ever prove Himself to be above him; and all we need is a spirit of simple, childlike confidence and repose in the divine purpose. Unbelief will rather look at the enemy's efforts to countervail than at God's power to accomplish. It is on the latter that faith fixes its eye. Thus it obtains victory and enjoys abiding peace. It has to do with God and His infallible faithfulness. It rests not upon the ever-shifting sands of human affairs and earthly influences, but upon the immovable rock of God's eternal Word. That is faith's holy and solid resting-place. Come what may, it abides in that sanctuary of strength. "Joseph died, and all his brethren, and all that generation." What then? Could death affect the counsels of the living God? Surely not. He only waited for the appointed moment—the due time, and then the most hostile influences were made instrumental in the development of His purposes.

"Now there arose up a new king over Egypt, which knew not Joseph. And he said unto his people, 'Behold the people of the children of Israel are more and mightier than we: come on, let us deal *wisely* with them, lest they multiply, and it come to pass that when there falleth out any war they join also unto our enemies and fight against us, and so get them up out of the land" (ver. 8-10). All this is the reasoning of a heart that had never learnt to take God into its calculations. The unrenewed heart never can do so; and hence, the moment you introduce God, all its reasonings fall to the ground. Apart from, or independent of, Him, they may seem very wise; but only bring Him in, and they are proved to be perfect folly.

But why should we allow our minds to be, in any wise, influenced by reasonings and calculations which depend, for their *apparent* truth, upon the total exclusion of God? To do so is, in principle, and according to its measure, practical atheism. In Pharaoh's case, we see that he could accurately recount the various contingencies of human affairs—the multiplying of the people, the falling out of war, their joining with the enemy, their escape out of the land. All these circumstances he could, with uncommon sagacity, put into the scale; but it never once occurred to him that God could have anything whatever to do in the matter. Had he only thought of this, it would have upset his entire reasoning, and have written folly upon all his schemes.

Now, it is well to see that it is ever thus with the reasonings of man's sceptic mind. God is entirely shut out; yea, the truth and consistency thereof depend upon His being kept out. The death-blow to all scepticism and infidelity is the introduction of God into the scene. Till He is seen, they may strut up and down upon the stage with an amazing show of wisdom and cleverness; but the moment the eye catches even the faintest glimpse of that blessed One, they are stripped of their cloak, and disclosed in all their nakedness and deformity.

In reference to the king of Egypt, it may assuredly be said, he did "greatly err," not knowing God or His changeless counsels. He knew not that, hundreds of years back, before even he had breathed the breath of mortal life, God's word and oath—"two immutable things"—had infallibly secured the full and glorious deliverance of that very people whom he was going, in his wisdom, to crush. All this was unknown to him, and therefore all his thoughts and plans were founded upon ignorance of that grand foundation-truth of all truths, namely, that *God is*. He vainly imagined that he, by his management, could prevent the increase of those concerning whom God had said, "They shall be as the stars of heaven, and as the sand which is upon the sea-shore." His wise dealing, therefore, was simply madness and folly.

The wildest mistake which a man can possibly fall into is to act without taking God into his account. Sooner or later, the thought of God will force itself upon him, and then comes the awful crash of all his schemes and calculations. At best, everything that is undertaken independently of God, can last but for the present time. It cannot, by any possibility, stretch itself into eternity. All that is merely human, however solid, however brilliant, or however attractive, must fall into the cold grasp of death, and moulder in the dark, silent tomb. The clod of the valley must cover man's highest excellencies and brightest glories; mortality is engraved upon his brow, and all his schemes are evanescent. On the contrary, that which is connected with, and based upon, God, shall endure forever. "His name shall endure forever, and His memorial to all generations."

What a sad mistake, therefore, for a feeble mortal to set himself up against the eternal God,—to "rush upon the thick bosses of the shield of the Almighty"! As well might the monarch of Egypt have sought to stem, with his puny hand, the ocean's tide, as to prevent the increase of those who were the subjects of Jehovah's everlasting purpose. Hence, although "they did set over them taskmasters to afflict them with their burdens," yet, "the more they afflicted them, the more they multiplied and grew." Thus it must ever be. "He that sitteth in the heavens shall laugh; the Lord shall have them in derision." (Ps. 2:4) Eternal confusion shall be inscribed upon all the opposition of men and devils. This gives sweet rest to the heart in the midst of a scene where all is apparently so contrary to God and so contrary to faith. Were it not for the settled assurance that "the wrath of man shall praise" the Lord, the spirit would often be cast down while contemplating the circumstances and influences which surround one in the world. Thank God, "we look not at the things which are seen, but at the things which are not seen: for the things which are seen are temporal; but the things which are not seen are eternal" (2 Cor. 4:18). In the power of this, we may well say, "*Rest* in the Lord, and *wait patiently for Him:* fret not thyself because of him who prospereth in his way, because of the man who bringeth wicked devices to pass" (Ps. 37:7). How fully might the truth of this be seen in the case of both the oppressed and the oppressor, as set before us in our chapter! Had Israel "looked at the things that are seen," what were they? Pharaoh's wrath, stern taskmasters, afflictive burdens, rigorous service, hard bondage, mortar and brick. But, then, "the things which are not seen," what were they? God's eternal purpose, His unfailing promise, the approaching dawn of a day of salvation, the "burning lamp" of Jehovah's deliverance. Wondrous contrast! Faith alone could enter into it. Naught save that precious principle could enable any poor, oppressed Israelite to look from out the smoking furnace of Egypt, to the green fields and vine-clad mountains of the land of Canaan. Faith alone could recognize in those oppressed slaves, toiling in the brick-kilns of Egypt, the heirs of salvation, and the objects of Heaven's peculiar interest and favor.

Thus it was then, and thus it is now. "We walk by faith, not by sight" (2 Cor. 5:7). "It doth not yet appear what we shall be" (1 John 3:2). We are "here in the body pent," "absent from the Lord." As to fact, we are in Egypt, yet, in spirit, we are in the heavenly Canaan. Faith brings the heart into the power of divine and unseen things, and thus enables it to mount above everything down here, in this place "where death and darkness reign." O, for that simple childlike faith that sits beside the pure and eternal fountain of truth, there to drink those deep and refreshing draughts which lift up the fainting spirit and impart energy to the new man, in its upward and onward course!

The closing verses of this section of our book present an edifying lesson in the conduct of those God-fearing women, Shiprah and Puah. They would not carry out the king's cruel scheme, but braved his wrath, and hence God made them houses. "Them that honor Me I will honor, and they that despise Me shall be lightly esteemed" (1 Sam. 2:30). May we ever remember this, and act for God, under all circumstances!

---

### *CHAPTER 2:1-10*

THIS section of our book abounds in the weightiest principles of divine truth—principles which range themselves under the three following heads, namely, the power of Satan, the power of God, and the power of faith.

In the last verse of the previous chapter, we read, "And Pharaoh charged all his people, saying, 'Every son that is born ye shall cast into the river.' " This was Satan's power. The river was the place of death; and, by death, the enemy sought to frustrate the purpose of God. It has ever been thus. The serpent has at all times watched with malignant eye those instruments which God was about to use for His own gracious ends. Look at the case of Abel, in Genesis 4. What was that but the serpent watching God's vessel and seeking to put it out of the way by death? Look at the case of Joseph, in Genesis 37. There you have the enemy seeking to put the man of God's purpose in the place of death. Look at the case of "the seed royal," in 2 Chronicles 22; the act of Herod, in Matthew 2; the death of Christ, in Matthew 27. In all these cases, you find the enemy seeking, by death, to interrupt the current of divine action.

But, blessed be God, there is something beyond death. The entire sphere of divine action, as connected with redemption, lies beyond the limits of death's domain. When Satan has exhausted his power, then God begins to show Himself. The grave is the limit of Satan's activity; but there it is that divine activity begins. This is a glorious truth. Satan has the power of death; but God is the God of the living, and He gives life beyond the reach and power of death—a life which Satan cannot touch. The heart finds sweet relief in such a truth as this, in the midst of a scene where death reigns. Faith can stand and look on at Satan putting forth the plenitude of his power. It can stay itself upon God's mighty instrumentality of resurrection. It can take its stand at the grave which has closed over a beloved object, and drink in, from the lips of Him who is "the resurrection and the life," the elevating assurance of a glorious immortality. It knows that God is stronger than Satan, and it can therefore quietly wait for the full manifestation of that superior strength, and, in thus waiting, find its victory and its settled peace. We have a noble example of this power of faith in the opening verses of our chapter.

"And there went a man of the house of Levi, and took to wife a daughter of Levi. And the woman conceived and bare a son; and when she saw him that he was a goodly child, she hid him three months. And when she could no longer hide him, she took for him an ark of bulrushes and daubed it with slime and with pitch, and put the child therein; and she laid it in the flags by the river's brink. And his sister stood afar off, to wit what would be done to him" (chap. 2:1-4). Here we have a scene of touching interest, in whatever way we contemplate it. In point of fact, it was simply faith triumphing over the influences of nature and death, and leaving room for the God of resurrection to act in His own proper sphere and character. True, the enemy's power is apparent, in the circumstance that the child had to be placed in such position—a position of death, in principle. And, moreover, a sword was piercing through the mother's heart in thus beholding her precious offspring laid, as it were, in death. Satan might act, and nature might weep; but the Quickener of the dead was behind the dark cloud, and faith beheld Him there, gilding heaven's side of that cloud with His bright and life-giving beams. "By faith Moses, when he was born, was hid three months of his parents, because they saw he was a proper child; and they were not afraid of the king's commandment" (Heb. 11:23).

Thus this honored daughter of Levi teaches us a holy lesson. Her *"ark* of bulrushes, daubed with slime and *pitch,"* declares her confidence in the truth that there was a something which could keep out the waters of death, in the case of this "proper child," as well as in the case of Noah, "the preacher of righteousness." Are we to suppose, for a moment, that this "ark" was the invention of mere nature? Was it nature's forethought that devised it? or nature's ingenuity that constructed it? Was the babe placed in the ark at the suggestion of a mother's heart, cherishing the fond but visionary hope of thereby saving her treasure from the ruthless hand of death? Were we to reply to the above inquiries in the affirmative, we should, I believe, lose the beauteous teaching of this entire scene. How could we ever support that the *"ark"* was devised by one who saw no other portion or destiny for her child but death by *drowning?* Impossible. We can only look upon that significant structure as faith's draft handed in at the treasury of the God of resurrection. It was devised by the hand of faith, as a vessel of mercy, to carry "a proper child" safely over death's dark waters, into the place assigned him by the immutable purpose of the living God. When we behold this daughter of Levi bending over that "ark of bulrushes," which her faith had constructed, and depositing therein her babe, we see her "walking in the steps of that faith of her father Abraham, which he had," when "he rose up from before his dead," and purchased the cave of Machpelah from the sons of Heth (Gen. 23). We do not recognize in her the energy of mere nature, hanging over the object of its affections, about to fall into the iron grasp of the king of terrors. No; but we trace in her the energy of a faith which enabled her to stand, as a conqueror, at the margin of death's cold flood, and behold the chosen servant of Jehovah in safety at the other side.

Yes, faith can take those bold and lofty flights into regions far removed from this land of death and wide-spread desolation. Its eagle gaze can pierce the gloomy clouds which gather around the tomb, and behold the God of resurrection displaying the results of His everlasting counsels, in the midst of a sphere which no arrow of death can reach. It can take its stand upon the top of the Rock of Ages, and listen, in holy triumph, while the surges of death are lashing its base.

And what was "the king's commandment" to one who was in possession of this heavenborn principle? What weight had that commandment with one who could calmly stand beside her "ark of bulrushes" and look death straight in the face? The Holy Ghost replies, "They were not afraid of the king's commandment." The spirit that knows aught of communion with Him who quickens the dead, is not afraid of anything. Such an one can take up the triumphant language of 1 Cor. 15, and say, "O death, where is thy sting? O grave, where is thy victory? The sting of death is sin, and the strength of sin is the law. But thanks be to God, which giveth us the victory through our Lord Jesus Christ." He can give forth these words of triumph over a martyred Abel; over Joseph in the pit; over Moses in the ark of bulrushes; in the midst of "the seed royal," slain by the hand of Athaliah; amid the babes of Bethlehem, murdered by the hand of the cruel Herod; and far above all, he can utter them at the tomb of the Captain of our salvation.

Now, it may be there are some who cannot trace the activities of faith, in the matter of the ark of bulrushes. Many may not be able to travel beyond the measure of Moses' sister, when "she stood afar off, to wit what would be done to him." It is very evident that "his sister" was not up to "the measure of faith" possessed by "his mother." No doubt she possessed deep interest and true affection, such as we may trace in "Mary Magdalene and the other Mary sitting over against the sepulchre" (Matt. 27:61); but there was something far beyond either interest or affection in the maker of the "ark." True, she did not "stand afar off, to wit what would be done to" her child, and hence, what frequently happens, the dignity of faith might seem like indifference, on her part. It was not, however, indifference, but true elevation—the elevation of faith. If natural affection did not cause her to linger near the scene of death, it was only because the power of faith was furnishing her with nobler work in the presence of the God of resurrection. Her faith had cleared the stage for Him, and most gloriously did He show Himself thereon.

"And the daughter of Pharaoh came down to wash herself at the river; and her maidens walked along by the river's side: and when she saw the ark among the flags, she sent her maid to fetch it. And when she had opened it, she saw the child; and, behold, the babe wept. And she had compassion on him, and said, 'This is one of the Hebrews' children.' " Here, then, the divine response begins to break, in sweetest accents, on the ear of faith. God was in all this. Rationalism, or scepticism, or infidelity, or atheism, may laugh at such an idea. And faith can laugh also; but the two kinds of laughter are very different. The former laughs, in cold contempt, at the thought of divine interference in the trifling affair of a royal maiden's walk by the river's side: the latter laughs, with real heartfelt gladness, at the thought that God is in everything. And, assuredly, if ever God was in anything, He was in this walk of Pharaoh's daughter, though she knew it not.

The renewed mind enjoys one of its sweetest exercises while tracing the divine footsteps in circumstances and events in which a thoughtless spirit sees only blind chance or rigid fate. The most trifling matter may, at times, turn out to be a most important link in a chain of events by which the Almighty God is helping forward the development of His grand designs. Look, for instance, at Esther 6:1, and what do you see? A heathen monarch spending a restless night. No uncommon circumstance, we may suppose; and yet, this very circumstance was a link in a great chain of providences at the end of which you find the marvelous deliverance of the oppressed seed of Israel.

Thus was it with the daughter of Pharaoh, in her walk by the river's side. Little did she think that she was helping forward the purpose of "the Lord God of the Hebrews." How little idea had she that the weeping babe in that ark of bulrushes was yet to be Jehovah's instrument in shaking the land of Egypt to its very centre! Yet so it was. The Lord can make the wrath of man to praise Him, and restrain the remainder. How plainly the truth of this appears in the following passage!—

"Then said his sister to Pharaoh's daughter, 'Shall I go and call to thee a nurse of the Hebrew women, that she may nurse the child for thee?' And Pharaoh's daughter said unto her, 'Go.' And the maid went and called the child's mother. And Pharaoh's daughter said unto her, 'Take this child away and nurse it for me, and I will give thee thy wages.' And the woman took the child and nursed it. And the child grew, and she brought him unto Pharaoh's daughter, and he became her son. And she called his name Moses; and she said, 'Because I drew him out of the water' " (chap. 2:7-10). The beautiful faith of Moses' mother here meets its full reward; Satan is confounded; and the marvelous wisdom of God is displayed. Who would have thought that the one who had said, "If it be a son, then ye shall kill him," and, again, "Every son that is born ye shall cast into the river," should have in his court one of those very sons, and *such* "a son." The devil was foiled by his own weapon, inasmuch as Pharaoh, whom he was using to frustrate the purpose of God, is used of God to nourish and bring up Moses, who was to be His instrument in confounding the power of Satan. Remarkable providence! Admirable wisdom! Truly, Jehovah is "wonderful in counsel and excellent in working." May we learn to trust Him with more artless simplicity, and thus our path shall be more brilliant, and our testimony more effective.

---

## *CHAPTER 2:11-25*

IN considering the history of Moses, we must look at him in two ways, namely, personally and typically.

First, in his personal character, there is much, very much, for us to learn. God had not only to raise him up, but also to train him, in one way or another, for the lengthened period of eighty years, first in the house of Pharaoh's daughter, and then at "the backside of the desert." This, to our shallow thoughts, would seem an immense space of time to devote to the education of a minister of God. But then God's thoughts are not as our thoughts. He knew the need of those forty years twice told, in the preparation of His chosen vessel. When God educates, He educates in a manner worthy of Himself and His most holy service. He will not have a novice to do His work. The servant of Christ has to learn many a lesson, to undergo many an exercise, to pass through many a conflict, in secret, ere he is really qualified to act in public. Nature does not like this. It would rather figure in public than learn in private,—it would rather be gazed upon and admired by the eye of man than be disciplined by the hand of God. But it will not do. We must take God's way. Nature may rush into the scene of operation; but God does not want it there. It must be withered, crushed, set aside. The place of death is the place for nature. If it *will* be active, God will so order matters, in His infallible faithfulness and perfect wisdom, that the results of its activity will prove its utter defeat and confusion. He knows what to do with nature, where to put it, and where to keep it. O, that we may all be in deeper communion with the mind of God, in reference to self and all that pertains thereto! Then shall we make fewer mistakes; then shall our path be steady and elevated, our spirit tranquil, and our service effective.

"And it came to pass in those days, when Moses was grown, that he went out unto his brethren, and looked on their burdens; and he spied an Egyptian smiting a Hebrew, one of his brethren. And he looked this way and that way, and when he saw there was no man, he slew the Egyptian, and hid him in the sand." This was zeal for his brethren; but it was "not according to knowledge." God's time was not yet come for judging Egypt and delivering Israel; and the intelligent servant will ever wait for God's time. "Moses was grown," and "he was learned in all the wisdom of the Egyptians;" and, moreover, "he supposed his brethren would have understood how that God by his hand would deliver them." All this was true; yet he evidently ran before the time, and when one does this, failure must be the issue.*

And not only is there failure in the end, but also manifest uncertainty, and lack of calm elevation and holy independence in the progress of a work begun before God's time. Moses *"looked this way and that way."* There is no need of this when a man is acting with and for God, and in the full intelligence of His mind, as to the detail of his work. If God's time had really come, and if Moses was conscious of being divinely commissioned to execute judgment upon the Egyptian, and if he felt assured of the divine presence with him, he would not have "looked this way and that way."

This action teaches a deep practical lesson to all the servants of God. There are two things by which it is superinduced, namely, the fear of man's wrath, and the hope of man's favor. The servant of the living God should neither regard the one nor the other. What avails the wrath or favor of a poor mortal to one who holds the divine commission and enjoys the divine presence? It is, in the judgment of such an one, less than the

*In Stephen's address to the council at Jerusalem, there is an allusion to Moses' acting, to which it may be well to advert. "And when he was full forty years old, it came into his heart to visit his brethren the children of Israel. And seeing one of them suffer wrong, he defended him, and avenged him that was oppressed, and smote the Egyptian; for he supposed his brethren would have understood how that God by his hand would deliver them; but they understood not" (Acts 7:23-25). It is evident that Stephen's object, in his entire address, was to bring the history of the nation to bear upon the consciences of those whom he had before him; and it would have been quite foreign to this object, and at variance with the Spirit's rule in the New Testament, to raise a question as to whether Moses had not acted before the divinely appointed time.

Moreover, he merely says, "It came into his heart to visit his brethren." He does not say that God sent him, *at that time.* Nor does this, in the least, touch the question of the moral condition of those who rejected him. "They understood not." This was the fact as to them, whatever Moses might have personally to learn in the matter. The spiritual mind can have no difficulty in apprehending this.

Looking at Moses typically, we can see the mission of Christ to Israel, and their rejection of Him, and refusal to have Him to reign over them. On the other hand, looking at Moses personally, we find that he, like others, made mistakes and displayed infirmities,—sometimes went too fast and sometimes too slow. All this is easily understood, and only tends to magnify the infinite grace and exhaustless patience of God.

small dust of the balance. *"Have not I commanded thee?* Be strong and of a good courage; be not afraid, neither be thou dismayed: for *the Lord thy God is with thee* whithersoever thou goest" (Joshua 1:9). "Thou, therefore, gird up thy loins, and arise, and speak unto them *all that I command thee:* be not dismayed at their faces, lest I confound thee before them. For, behold, I have made thee this day a defenced city, and an iron pillar, and brazen walls against the whole land, against the kings of Judah, against the princes thereof, against the priests thereof, and against the people of the land. And they shall fight against thee, but they shall not prevail against thee; for *I am with thee,* saith the Lord, to deliver thee" (Jer. 1:17-19).

When the servant of Christ stands upon the elevated ground set forth in the above quotations, he will not "look this way and that way"; he will act on wisdom's heavenly counsel—"Let thine eyes look straight on, and thine eyelids look straight before thee." Divine intelligence will ever lead us to look upward and onward. Whenever we look around to shun a mortal's frown or catch his smile, we may rest assured there is something wrong; we are off the proper ground of divine service. We lack the assurance of holding the divine commission and of enjoying the divine presence, both of which are absolutely essential.

True, there are many who through profound ignorance, or excessive self-confidence, stand forward in a sphere of service for which God never intended them, and for which He therefore never qualified them. And not only do they thus stand forward, but they exhibit an amount of coolness and self-possession perfectly amazing to those who are capable of forming an impartial judgment about their gifts and merits. But all this will very speedily find its level; nor does it in the least interfere with the integrity of the principle that nothing can effectually deliver a man from the tendency to "look this way and that way" save the consciousness of the divine commission and the divine presence. When these are possessed, there is entire deliverance from human influence, and consequent independence. No man is in a position to serve others who is not wholly independent of them; but a man who knows his proper place can stoop and wash his brethren's feet.

When we turn away our eyes from man, and fix them upon the only true and perfect Servant, we do not find Him looking this way and that way, for this simple reason, that He never had His eye upon men, but always upon God. He feared not the wrath of man, nor sought his favor. He never opened His lips to elicit human applause, nor kept them closed to avoid human censure. This gave holy stability and elevation to all He said and did. Of Him alone could it be truly said, "His leaf shall not wither, and *whatsoever* he doeth shall prosper." Everything He did turned to profitable account, because everything was done to God. Every action, every word, every movement, every look, every thought, was like a beauteous cluster of fruit, sent up to refresh the heart of God. He was never afraid of the results of His work, because He always acted with and for God, and in the full intelligence of His mind. His own will, though divinely perfect, never once mingled itself in aught that He did, as a man, on the earth. He could say, "I came down from heaven, not to do Mine own will, but the will of Him that sent Me." Hence, He brought forth fruit *"in its season."* He did *"always* those things which pleased the Father," and therefore never had any occasion to "fear," to "repent," or to "look this way and that way."

Now in this, as in everything else, the blessed Master stands in marked contrast with His most honored and eminent servants. Even a Moses "feared," and a Paul "repented"; but the Lord Jesus never did either. He never had to retrace a step, to recall a word, or correct a thought. All was absolutely perfect: all was "fruit in season." The current of His holy and heavenly life flowed onward without a ripple and without a curve. His will was divinely subject. The best and most devoted men make mistakes; but it is perfectly certain that the more we are enabled, through grace, to mortify our own will, the fewer our mistakes will be. Truly happy it is when, in the main, our path is really a path of faith and single-eyed devotedness to Christ.

Thus it was with Moses. He was a man of faith—a man who drank deeply into the spirit of his Master, and walked with marvelous steadiness in His footprints. True, he anticipated, as has been remarked, by forty years, the Lord's time of judgment on Egypt and deliverance for Israel; yet, when we turn to the inspired commentary, in Hebrews 11, we find nothing about this; we there find only the divine principle upon which, in the main, his course was founded. "By faith Moses, *when he was come to years,* refused to be called the son of Pharaoh's daughter, choosing rather to suffer affliction with the people of God than to enjoy the pleasures of sin for a season; esteeming the reproach of Christ greater riches than the treasures in Egypt; for he had respect unto the recompense of the reward. By faith he forsook Egypt, not fearing the wrath of the king; for he endured as seeing Him who is invisible" (ver. 24-27).

This quotation furnishes a most gracious view of the actings of Moses. It is ever thus the Holy Ghost deals with the history of Old Testament saints. When He *writes* a man's history, He presents him to us as he is, and faithfully sets forth all his failures and imperfections. But when, in the New Testament, He *comments* upon such history, He merely gives the real principle and main result of a man's life. Hence, though we read, in Exodus, that "Moses looked this way and that way"—that "he feared and said, 'Surely this thing is known,' " and, finally, "Moses fled from the face of Pharaoh;" yet we are taught, in Hebrews, that what he did, he did "by faith"—that he did not fear "the wrath of the king"—that "he endured as seeing Him who is invisible."

Thus will it be, by and by, "when the Lord comes, who both will bring to light the hidden things of darkness, and will make manifest *the counsels of the hearts:* and then shall every man have praise of God" (1 Cor. 4:5). This is a precious and consolatory truth for every upright mind and every loyal heart. Many a "counsel" the *"heart"* may form, which, from various causes, the *hand* may not be able to execute. All such "counsels" will be made "manifest" when "the Lord comes." Blessed be the grace that has told us so! The affectionate counsels of the heart are far more precious to Christ than the most elaborate works of the hand. The latter may shine before the eye of man; the former are designed *only* for the heart of Jesus. The latter may be spoken of amongst men; the former will be made manifest before God and His holy angels. May all the servants of Christ have their hearts undividedly occupied with His person, and their eyes steadily fixed upon His advent.

In contemplating the path of Moses, we observe how that faith led him entirely athwart the ordinary course of nature. It led him to despise all the pleasures, the attractions, and the honors of Pharaoh's court. And not only that, but also to relinquish an apparently wide sphere of usefulness. Human expediency would have conducted him along quite an opposite path. It would have led him to use his influence on behalf of the people of God—to act *for* them instead of suffering *with* them. According to man's judgment, providence would seem to have opened for Moses a wide and most important sphere of labor; and surely, if ever the hand of God was manifest in placing a man in a distinct position, it was in his case. By a most marvelous interposition—by a most unaccountable chain of circumstances, every link of which displayed the finger of the Almighty—by an order of events which no human foresight could have arranged, had the daughter of Pharaoh been made the instrument of drawing Moses out of the water, and of nourishing and educating him until he was "full forty years old." With all these circumstances in his view, to abandon his high, honorable, and influential position, could only be regarded as the result of a misguided zeal which no sound judgment could approve.

Thus might poor blind nature reason. But faith thought differently; for nature and faith are always at issue. They cannot agree upon a single point. Nor is there anything, perhaps, in reference to which they differ so widely as what are commonly called "openings of providence." Nature will constantly regard such openings as warrants for self-indulgence; whereas faith will find in them opportunities for self-denial. Jonah might have deemed it a very remarkable opening of providence to find a ship going to Tarshish; but, in truth, it was an opening through which he slipped off the path of obedience.

No doubt it is the Christian's privilege to see his Father's hand, and hear His voice, in everything; but he is not to be guided by circumstances. A Christian so guided is like a vessel at sea without rudder or compass; she is at the mercy of the waves and the winds. God's promise to His child is, "I will guide thee with Mine eye" (Ps. 32:8). His warning is, "Be not as the horse or as the mule, which have no understanding; whose mouth must be held in with bit and bridle, lest they come near unto thee." It is much better to be guided by our Father's eye than by the bit and bridle of circumstances; and we know that, in the ordinary acceptation of the term, "providence" is only another word for the impulse of circumstances.

Now, the power of faith may constantly be seen in refusing and forsaking the apparent openings of providence. It was so in the case of Moses. "By faith he refused to be called the son of Pharaoh's daughter," and "by faith he forsook Egypt." Had he judged according to the sight of his eyes, he would have grasped at the proffered dignity, as the manifest gift of a kind providence, and he would have remained in the court of Pharaoh as in a sphere of usefulness plainly thrown open to him by the hand of God. But, then, he walked by faith, and not by the sight of his eyes; and hence he forsook all. Noble example! May we have grace to follow it!

Observe what it was that Moses "esteemed greater riches than the treasures in Egypt"; it was the "reproach of Christ." It was not merely reproach *for* Christ. "The reproaches of them that reproached Thee have fallen upon Me." The Lord Jesus, in perfect grace, identified Himself with His people. He came down from heaven, leaving His Father's bosom, and laying aside all His glory, He took His people's place, confessed their sins, and bore their judgment on the cursed tree. Such was His voluntary devotedness; He not merely acted *for* us, but made Himself one *with* us, thus perfectly delivering us from all that was or could be against us.

Hence we see how much in sympathy Moses was with the spirit and mind of Christ in reference to the people of God. He was in the midst of all the ease, the pomp, and dignity of Pharaoh's house, where "the pleasures of sin," and "the treasures of Egypt," lay scattered around him in richest profusion. All these things he might have enjoyed if he would. He could have lived and died in the midst of wealth and splendor; his entire path, from first to last, might, if he had chosen, have been enlightened by the sunshine of royal favor: but that would not have been "faith"; it would not have been Christlike. From his elevated position, he saw his brethren bowed down beneath their heavy burden, and faith led him to see that his place was to be *with* them. Yes; with them, in all their reproach, their bondage, their degradation, and their sorrow. Had he been actuated by mere benevolence, philanthropy, or patriotism, he might have used his personal influence on behalf of his brethren. He might have succeeded in inducing Pharaoh to lighten their burden, and render their path somewhat smoother, by royal grants in their favor; but this would never do, never satisfy a heart that had a single pulsation in common with the heart of Christ. Such a heart Moses, by the grace of God, carried in his bosom; and, therefore, with all the energies and all the affections of that heart, he threw himself, body, soul, and spirit, into the very midst of his oppressed brethren. He "chose rather to suffer affliction *with* the people of God." And, moreover, he did this by "faith."

Let us ponder this deeply. We must not be satisfied with wishing well to, doing service for, or speaking kindly on behalf of, the people of God. We ought to be fully identified *with* them, no matter how despised or reproached they may be. It is, in a measure, an agreeable thing to be a benevolent and generous spirit, to patronize Christianity; but it is a wholly different thing to be identified with Christians, or to suffer with Christ. A *patron* is one thing, a *martyr* is quite another. This distinction is apparent throughout the entire book of God. Obadiah took care of God's witnesses, but Elijah was a witness for God. Darius was so attached to Daniel that he lost a night's rest on his account, but Daniel spent that self-same night in the lion's den, as a witness for the truth of God. Nicodemus ventured to speak a word *for* Christ, but a more matured discipleship would have led him to identify himself *with* Christ.

These considerations are eminently practical. The Lord Jesus does not want patronage; He wants fellowship. The truth concerning Him is declared to us, not that we might patronize His cause on earth, but have fellowship with His Person in heaven. He identified Himself with us, at the heavy cost of all that love could give. He might have avoided this. He might have continued to enjoy His eternal place "in the bosom of the Father." But how, then, could that mighty tide of love, which was pent up in His heart, flow down to us guilty and hell-deserving sinners? Between Him and us there could be no oneness, save on conditions which involved the surrender of everything on His part. But, blessed, throughout the everlasting ages, be His adorable name, that surrender was voluntarily made. "He gave Himself for us, that He might redeem us from all iniquity, and purify *unto Himself* a peculiar people, zealous of good works" (Titus 2:14). He would not enjoy His glory alone. His loving heart would gratify itself by associating "many sons" with Him in that glory. "Father," He says, "I will that they also, whom Thou hast given Me, be *with Me* where I am; that they may behold My glory, which Thou hast given Me: for Thou lovedst Me before the foundation of the world" (John 17:24). Such were the thoughts of Christ in reference to His people; and we can easily see how much in sympathy with these precious thoughts was the heart of Moses. He unquestionably partook largely of his Master's spirit; and he manifested that excellent spirit in freely sacrificing every personal consideration, and associating himself, unreservedly, with the people of God.

The personal character and actings of this honored servant of God will come before us again in the next section of our book. We shall here briefly consider him as a type of the Lord Jesus Christ. That he was a type of Him is evident from the following passage,—"The Lord thy God will raise up unto thee a Prophet from the midst of thee, of thy brethren, like unto me; unto Him ye shall hearken" (Deut. 18:15). We are not, therefore, trafficking in human imagination in viewing Moses as a type; it is the plain teaching of Scripture, and in the closing verses of Exodus 2 we see this type in a double way: first, in the matter of his rejection by Israel; and secondly, in his union with a stranger in the land of Midian.

These points have already been, in some measure, developed in the history of Joseph, who, being cast out by his brethren according to the flesh, forms an alliance with an Egyptian bride. Here, as in the case of Moses, we see shadowed forth Christ's rejection by Israel, and His union with the Church, but in a different phase. In Joseph's case, we have the exhibition of positive enmity against his *person:* in Moses, it is the rejection of his *mission.* In Joseph's case, we read, "They hated *him,* and could not speak peaceably unto *him*" (Gen. 37:4). In the case of Moses, the word is, *"Who made thee a prince and a judge over us?"* In short, the former was personally hated; the latter, officially refused.

So also in the mode in which the great mystery of the Church is exemplified in the history of those two Old Testament saints. "Asenath" presents quite a different phase of the Church from that which we have in the person of "Zipporah." The former was united to Joseph in the time of his exaltation; the latter was the companion of Moses in the obscurity of his desert life (comp. Gen. 41:41-45 with Exod. 2:15; 3:1). True, both Joseph and Moses were, at the time of their union with a stranger, rejected by their brethren; yet the former was "governor over all the land of Egypt," whereas the latter tended a few sheep at "the backside of the desert."

Whether, therefore, we contemplate Christ as manifested in glory, or as hidden from the world's gaze, the Church is intimately associated with Him. And now, inasmuch as the world seeth Him not, neither can it take knowledge of that body which is wholly one with Him. "The world knoweth us not, because it knew Him not" (1 John 3:1). By and by, Christ will appear in His glory, and the Church *with* Him. "When Christ our life shall appear, then shall ye also appear *with* Him in glory" (Col. 3:4). And again, "The glory which Thou gavest Me I have given them; that they may be one, even as We are one: I in them, and Thou in Me, that they may be made perfect in one; and that the world may know that Thou hast sent Me, and hast loved them as Thou hast loved Me" (John 17:22-23).*

Such, then, is the Church's high and holy position. She is one with Him who is cast out by this world, but who occupies the throne of the Majesty in the heavens. The Lord Jesus made Himself responsible for her on the cross, in order that she might share with Him His present rejection and His future glory. Would that all who form a part of such a highly privileged body were more impressed with a sense of what becomes them as to course and character down here! Assuredly, there should be a fuller and clearer response, on the part of all the children of God, to that love wherewith He has loved them, to that salvation wherewith He has saved them, and to that dignity wherewith He has invested them. The walk of the Christian should ever be the natural result of realized privilege, and not the constrained result of legal vows and resolutions,—the proper fruit of a position known and enjoyed by faith, and not the fruit of one's own efforts to reach a position "by works of law." All true believers *are* a part of the bride of Christ; hence, they owe Him those affections which become that relation. The relationship is not obtained because of the affections, but the affections flow out of the relationship.

So let it be, O Lord, with all Thy beloved and blood-bought people!

---

## *CHAPTER 3*

WE shall now resume the personal history of Moses, and contemplate him during that deeply interesting period of his career which he spent in retirement—a period including, as we should say, forty of his very best years—the prime of life. This is full of meaning. The Lord had graciously, wisely, and faithfully led His dear servant apart from the eyes and thoughts of men, in order that He might train him under His own immediate hand. Moses needed this. True, he had spent forty years in the house of Pharaoh; and, while his sojourn there was not without its influence and value, yet was it as nothing when compared with his sojourn in the desert. The former might be valuable; but the latter was indispensable.

Nothing can possibly make up for the lack of secret communion with God, or the training and discipline of His school. "All the wisdom of the Egyptians" would not have qualified Moses for his future path. He might have pursued a most brilliant course through the schools and colleges of Egypt. He might have come forth laden with literary honors—his intellect stored with learning, and his heart full of pride and self-sufficiency. He might have taken out his degree in the school of man, and yet have to learn his alphabet in the school of God. Mere human wisdom and learning, how valuable soever in themselves, can never constitute any one a servant of God, nor equip him for any department of divine service. Such things may qualify unrenewed nature to figure before the world; but the man whom God will use must be endowed with widely-different qualifications—such qualifications as can alone

*There are two distinct unities spoken of in John 17:21,23. The first is that unity which the Church is responsible to have maintained, but in which she has utterly failed. The second is that unity which God will infallibly accomplish, and which He will manifest in glory. If the reader will turn to the passage, he will at once see the difference, both as to character and result of the two.

be found in the deep and hallowed retirement of the Lord's presence.

All God's servants have been made to know and experience the truth of these statements. Moses at Horeb, Elijah at Cherith, Ezekiel at Chebar, Paul in Arabia, and John at Patmos, are all striking examples of the immense practical importance of being alone with God. When we look at the Divine Servant, we find that the time He spent in private was nearly ten times as long as that which He spent in public. He, though perfect in understanding and in will, spent nearly thirty years in the obscurity of a carpenter's house at Nazareth ere He made His appearance in public. And even when He had entered upon His public career, how oft did He retreat from the gaze of men, to enjoy the sweet and sacred retirement of the divine presence!

Now we may feel disposed to ask, How could the urgent demand for workmen ever be met if all need such protracted training, in secret, ere they come forth to their work? This is the Master's care—not ours. He can provide the workmen, and He can train them also. This is not man's work. God alone can provide and prepare a true minister. Nor is it a question with Him as to the length of time needful for the education of such an one. We know He could educate him in a moment, if it were His will to do so. One thing is evident, namely, that God has had all His servants very much alone with Himself, both before and after their entrance upon their public work; nor will any one ever get on without this. The absence of secret training and discipline will necessarily leave us barren, superficial, and theoretic. A man who ventures forth upon a public career ere he has duly weighed himself in the balances of the sanctuary, or measured himself in the presence of God, is like a ship putting out to sea without proper ballast: he will doubtless overset with the first stiff breeze. On the contrary, there is a depth, a solidity, and a steadiness flowing from our having passed from form to form in the school of God, which are essential elements in the formation of the character of a true and effective servant of God.

Hence, therefore, when we find Moses, at the age of forty years, taken apart from all the dignity and splendor of a court, for the purpose of spending forty years in the obscurity of a desert, we are led to expect a remarkable course of service; nor are we disappointed. The man whom God educates is educated, and none other. It lies not within the range of man to prepare an instrument for the service of God. The hand of man could never mould "a vessel meet for the Master's use." The One who is to use the vessel can alone prepare it; and we have before us a singularly beautiful sample of His mode of preparation.

"Now, Moses kept the flock of Jethro, his father-in-law, the priest of Midian; and he led the flock to the backside of the desert, and came to the mountain of God, even to Horeb" (Exod. 3:1). Here, then, we have a marvelous change of circumstances. In Genesis, chapter 46:31, we read, "Every shepherd is an abomination to the Egyptians"; and yet Moses, who was "learned in all the wisdom of the Egyptians," is transferred from the Egyptian court to the back of a mountain to tend a flock of sheep, and to be educated for the service of God. Assuredly, this is not "the manner of man." This is not nature's line of things. Flesh and blood could not understand this. We should have thought that Moses' education was finished when he had become master of all Egypt's wisdom, and that, moreover, in immediate connection with the rare advantages which a court life affords. We should have expected to find in one so highly favored, not only a solid and varied education, but also such an exquisite polish as would fit him for any sphere of action to which he might be called. But then, to find such a man with such attainments, called away from such a position to mind sheep at the back of a mountain, is something entirely beyond the utmost stretch of human thought and feeling. It lays prostrate in the dust all man's pride and glory. It declares plainly that this world's appliances are of little value in the divine estimation; yea, not only in the eyes of the Lord, but also in the eyes of all those who have been taught in His school.

There is a very wide difference between human and divine education. The former has for its end the refinement and exaltation of nature; the latter begins with withering it up and setting it aside. "The natural man receiveth not the things of the Spirit of God; for they are foolishness unto him; neither can he know them, because they are spiritually discerned" (1 Cor. 2:14). Educate the "natural man" as much as you please, and you cannot make him a "spiritual man." "That which is born of the flesh is flesh; and that which is born of the Spirit is spirit" (John 3:6). If ever an educated "natural man" might look for success in the service of God, Moses might have counted upon it; he was "grown," he was "learned," he was "mighty in word and deed," and yet he had to learn something at "the backside of the desert" which Egypt's schools could never have taught him. Paul learnt more in Arabia than ever he had learnt at the feet of Gamaliel.* None can teach like God; and all who will learn *of* Him must be alone *with* Him.

In the desert God will teach thee.

There it was that Moses learnt his sweetest, deepest, most influential and enduring lessons. Thither, too, must all repair who mean to be educated for the ministry.

Beloved reader, may you prove, in your own deep experience, the real meaning of "the backside of the desert"—that sacred spot where nature is laid in the dust, and God alone exalted. There it is that men and things, the world and self, present circumstances and their influences, are all valued at what they are really worth. There it is, and there alone, that you will find a divinely-adjusted balance in which to weigh all within and all around. There are no false colors, no borrowed plumes, no empty pretentions there. The enemy of your soul cannot gild the sand of that place. All is reality there. The heart that has found itself in the presence of God, at "the backside of the desert," has right thoughts about everything. It is raised far above the exciting influence of this world's schemes. The din and noise, the bustle and confusion of Egypt do not fall upon the ear in that distant place. The crash in the monetary and commercial world is not heard there; the sigh of ambition is not heaved there; this world's fading laurels do not tempt there; the thirst for gold is not felt there; the eye is never dimmed with lust, nor the heart swollen with pride there; human applause does not elate, nor human censure depress there. In a word, everything is set aside save the stillness and light of the divine presence. God's voice alone is heard, His light enjoyed, His thoughts received. This is the place to which all must go to be educated for the ministry; and there all must remain if they would succeed in the ministry.

Would that all who come forward to serve in public knew more of what it is to breathe the atmosphere of this place. We should then have far less vapid attempts at ministry, but far more effective Christ-honoring service.

Let us now inquire what Moses saw and what he heard at "the backside of the desert." We shall find him learning lessons which lay far beyond the reach of Egypt's most gifted masters. It might appear, in the eyes of human reason, a strange loss of time for a man like Moses to spend forty years doing nothing save to keep a few sheep in the wilderness. But he was there with God, and the time that is thus spent is never lost. It is salutary for us to remember that there is something more than mere *doing* necessary on the part of a true servant. A man who is always doing will be apt to do too much. Such an one would need to ponder over the deeply-practical words of the perfect Servant, "He wakeneth morning by morning,

*Let not my reader suppose for a moment that the design of the above remarks is to detract from the value of really useful information, or the proper culture of the mental powers. By no means. If, for example, he is a parent, let him store his child's mind with useful knowledge; let him teach him everything which may, hereafter, turn to account in the Master's service: let him not burden him with aught which he would have to "lay aside" in running his Christian course, nor conduct him, for educational purposes, through a region from which it is well-nigh impossible to come forth with an unsoiled mind. You might just as well shut him up for ten years in a coal mine in order to qualify him for discussing the properties of light and shade, as cause him to wade through the mire of a heathen mythology in order to fit him for the interpretation of the oracles of God, or prepare him for feeding the flock of Christ.

He wakeneth Mine ear *to hear* as the learned" (Isa. 1:4). This is an indispensable part of the servant's business. The servant must frequently stand in his master's presence, in order that he may know what he has to do. The "ear" and the "tongue" are intimately connected, in more ways than one; but, in a spiritual or moral point of view, if my ear be closed and my tongue loose, I shall be sure to talk a great deal of folly. "Wherefore, my beloved brethren, let every man be swift *to hear,* slow *to speak*" (James 1:19). This seasonable admonition is based upon two facts, namely, that everything good comes from above, and that the heart is brimful of naughtiness, ready to flow over. Hence the need of keeping the ear open and the tongue quiet—rare and admirable attainments!—attainments in which Moses made great proficiency at "the backside of the desert," and which all can acquire if only they are disposed to learn in that school.

"And the angel of the Lord appeared unto him in a flame of fire, out of the midst of a bush: and he looked, and behold the bush burned with fire, and the bush was not consumed. And Moses said, 'I will now turn aside, and see this great sight, why the bush is not burnt' " (chap. 3:2-3). This was truly "a great sight"—a bush burning, yet not burnt. The palace of Pharaoh could never have afforded such a sight. But it was a gracious sight as well as a great sight, for therein was strikingly exhibited the condition of God's elect. They were in the furnace of Egypt; and Jehovah reveals Himself in a burning bush. But as the bush was not consumed, so neither were they, for God was there. "The Lord of hosts is with us, the God of Jacob is our refuge" (Psalm 46). Here is strength and security—victory and peace. God *with* us, God *in* us, and God *for* us. This is ample provision for every exigence.

Nothing can be more interesting or instructive than the mode in which Jehovah was pleased to reveal Himself to Moses, as presented in the above quotation. He was about to furnish him with his commission to lead forth His people out of Egypt, that they might be His assembly—His dwelling-place, in the wilderness and in the land of Canaan; and the place from which He speaks is a burning bush. Apt, solemn, and beautiful symbol of Jehovah dwelling in the midst of His elect and redeemed congregation! "Our God is a consuming fire," not to consume *us,* but to consume all in us and about us which is contrary to His holiness, and, as such, subversive of our true and permanent happiness. "Thy testimonies are very sure; holiness becometh Thy house, O Lord, forever."

There are various instances, both in the Old and New Testaments, in which we find God displaying Himself as "a consuming fire." Look, for example, at the case of Nadab and Abihu, in Leviticus 10. This was a deeply solemn occasion. God was dwelling in the midst of His people, and He would keep them in a condition worthy of Himself. He could not do otherwise. It would neither be for His glory nor for their profit were He to tolerate aught in them inconsistent with the purity of His presence. God's dwelling-place must be holy.

So, also, in Joshua 7 we have another striking proof, in the case of Achan, that Jehovah could not possibly sanction, by His presence, evil, in any shape or form, how covert soever that evil might be. He was "a consuming fire," and as such He should act, in reference to any attempt to defile that assembly in the midst of which He dwelt. To seek to connect God's presence with evil unjudged is the very highest character of wickedness.

Again, in Acts 5, Ananias and Sapphira teach us the same solemn lesson. God the Holy Ghost was dwelling in the midst of the Church, not merely as an influence, but as a divine Person, in such a way as that one could lie to Him. The Church was, and is still, His dwelling-place; and He must rule and judge in the midst thereof. Men may walk in company with deceit, covetousness, and hypocrisy; but God cannot. If God is going to walk with us, we must judge our ways, or He will judge them for us (see also 1 Cor. 11:29-32).

In all these cases, and many more which might be adduced, we see the force of that solemn word, "Holiness becometh Thy house, O Lord, forever." The moral effect of this will ever be similar to that produced in the case of Moses, as recorded in our chapter. "Draw not nigh hither: put off thy shoes from off thy feet, for *the place whereon thou standest is holy ground*" (verse 5). The place of God's presence is holy, and can only be trodden with unshod feet. God, dwelling in the midst of His people, imparts a character of holiness to their assembly, which is the basis of every holy affection and every holy activity. The character of the dwelling-place takes its stamp from the character of the Occupant.

The application of this to the Church, which is now the habitation of God, through the Spirit, is of the very utmost practical importance. While it is blessedly true that God, by His Spirit, inhabits each individual member of the Church, thereby imparting a character of holiness to the individual; it is equally true that He dwells in the assembly, and hence the assembly must be holy. The centre round which the members are gathered is nothing less than the Person of a living, victorious, and glorified Christ. The energy by which they are gathered is nothing less than God the Holy Ghost; and the Lord God Almighty dwells in them and walks in them (see Matt. 18:20; 1 Cor. 6:19; 3:16,17; Eph. 2:21-22). Such being the holy elevation belonging to God's dwelling-place, it is evident that nothing which is unholy, either in principle or practice, must be tolerated. Each one connected therewith should feel the weight and solemnity of that word, "The place whereon thou standest is holy ground." "If any man defile the temple of God, him shall God destroy" (1 Cor. 3:17). Most weighty words these, for every member of God's assembly—for every stone in His holy temple! May we all learn to tread Jehovah's courts with unshod feet!

However, the visions of Horeb bear witness to the grace of the God of Israel as well as to His holiness. If God's holiness is infinite, His grace is infinite also; and while the manner in which He revealed Himself to Moses declared the former, the very fact of His revealing Himself at all evidenced the latter. He came down because He was gracious; but when come down, He should reveal Himself as holy. "Moreover He said, 'I am the God of thy father, the God of Abraham, the God of Isaac, and the God of Jacob.' And Moses hid his face; for he was afraid to look upon God" (verse 6). The effect of the divine presence must ever be to make nature hide itself; and when we stand before God with unshod feet and covered head—*i.e.,* in the attitude of soul which those acts so aptly and beautifully express, we are prepared to hearken to the sweet accents of grace. When man takes his suited place, God can speak in the language of unmingled mercy.

"And the Lord said, 'I have surely seen the affliction of My people which are in Egypt, and have heard their cry by reason of their taskmasters; for I know their sorrows; and I am come down to deliver them out of the hand of the Egyptians, and to bring them up out of that land unto a good land and a large, unto a land flowing with milk and honey. . . . Now, therefore, behold, the cry of the children of Israel is come unto Me; and I have also seen the oppression wherewith the Egyptians oppress them' " (ver. 7-9). Here the absolute, free, unconditional grace of the God of Abraham, and the God of Abraham's seed, shines forth in all its native brightness, unhindered by the "ifs" and "buts," the vows, resolutions, and conditions of man's legal spirit. God had come down to display Himself, in sovereign grace, to do the whole work of salvation, to accomplish His promise made to Abraham, and repeated to Isaac and Jacob. He had not come down to see if, indeed, the subjects of His promise were in such a condition as to *merit* His salvation: it was sufficient for Him that they *needed* it. Their oppressed state, their sorrows, their tears, their sighs, their heavy bondage, had all come in review before Him; for, blessed be His name, He counts His people's sighs, and puts their tears into His bottle. He was not attracted by their excellencies or their virtues. It was not on the ground of aught that was good in them, either seen or foreseen, that He was about to visit them, for He knew what was in them. In one word, we have the true ground of His gracious acting set before us in the words, "I am the God of Abraham," and "I have seen the affliction of My people."

These words reveal a great fundamental principle in the ways of God. It is on the ground of what He is that He ever acts. "*I am*," secures all for "*My people.*" Assuredly, He was not going to leave *His* people amid the brick-kilns of Egypt, and under the lash of Pharaoh's taskmasters. They were His people, and He would act toward them in a manner worthy of Himself. To be His people,—to be the favored objects of Jehovah's electing love—the subjects of His unconditional promise, settled everything. Nothing should hinder the public display of His relationship with those for whom His eternal purpose had secured the land of Canaan. He had come down to deliver them; and the combined power of earth and hell could not hold them in captivity one hour beyond His appointed time. He might and did use Egypt as a school, and Pharaoh as a schoolmaster; but when the needed work was accomplished, both the school and the schoolmaster were set aside, and His people were brought forth with a high hand and an outstretched arm.

Such, then, was the double character of the revelation made to Moses at Mount Horeb. What he saw and what he heard combined the two elements of holiness and grace,—elements which, as we know, enter into and distinctly characterize all the ways and all the relationships of the blessed God, and which should also mark the ways of all those who in any wise act for, or have fellowship with, Him. Every true servant is sent forth from the immediate presence of God, with all its holiness and all its grace; and he is called to be holy and gracious—he is called to be the reflection of the grace and holiness of the divine character; and, in order that he may be so, he should not only start from the immediate presence of God at the first, but abide there, in spirit, habitually. This is the true secret of effectual service.

Childlike, attend what Thou wilt say,
Go forth and do it, while 'tis day,
Yet never leave my sweet retreat.

The spiritual man alone can understand the meaning of the two things, "go forth and do," and, "yet never leave." In order to act *for* God outside, I should be *with* Him inside. I must be in the secret sanctuary of His presence, else I shall utterly fail.

Very many break down on this point. There is the greatest possible danger of getting out of the solemnity and calmness of the divine presence, amid the bustle of intercourse with men, and the excitement of active service. This is to be carefully guarded against. If we lose that hallowed tone of spirit which is expressed in "the unshod foot," our service will very speedily become vapid and unprofitable. If I allow my work to get between my heart and the Master, it will be little worth. We can only effectually serve Christ as we are enjoying Him. It is while the heart dwells upon His powerful attractions that the hands perform the most acceptable service to His name; nor is there any one who can minister Christ with unction, freshness, and power to others, if he be not feeding upon Christ, in the secret of his own soul. True, he may preach a sermon; deliver a lecture, utter prayers, write a book, and go through the entire routine of outward service, and yet not minister Christ. The man who will present Christ to others must be occupied with Christ for himself.

Happy is the man who ministers thus, whatever be the success or reception of his ministry. For should his ministry fail to attract attention, to command influence, or to produce apparent results, he has his sweet retreat and his unfailing portion in Christ, of which nothing can deprive him. Whereas, the man who is merely feeding upon the fruits of his ministry, who delights in the gratification which it affords, or the attention and interest which it commands, is like a mere pipe, conveying water to others, and retaining only rust itself. This is a most deplorable condition to be in; and yet is it the actual condition of every servant who is more occupied with his work and its results, than with the Master and His glory.

This is a matter which calls for the most rigid self-judgment. The heart is deceitful, and the enemy is crafty; and hence there is great need to hearken to the word of exhortation, "Be sober, be vigilant." It is when the soul is awakened to a sense of the varied and manifold dangers which beset the servant's path, that it is, in any measure, able to understand the need there is for being much alone with God: it is there one is secure and happy. It is when we begin, continue, and end our work at the Master's feet, that our service will be of the right kind.

From all that has been said, it must be evident to my reader that every servant of Christ will find the air of "the backside of the desert" most salutary. Horeb is really the starting-post for all whom God sends forth to act for Him. It was at Horeb that Moses learnt to put off his shoes and hide his face. Forty years before, he had gone to work; but his movement was premature. It was amid the flesh-subduing solitudes of the mount of God, and forth from the burning bush, that the divine commission fell on the servant's ear, "Come now, therefore, and I will send thee unto Pharaoh, that thou mayest bring forth My people, the children of Israel, out of Egypt" (ver. 10). Here was real authority. There is a vast difference between God sending a man, and a man running unsent. But it is very manifest that Moses was not ripe for service when first he set about acting. If forty years of secret training were needful for him, how could he have got on without it? Impossible! He had to be divinely educated and divinely commissioned; and so must all who go forth upon a path of service or testimony for Christ. O, that these holy lessons may be deeply graven on all our hearts, that so our every work may wear upon it the stamp of the Master's authority and the Master's approval.

However, we have something further to learn at the foot of Mount Horeb. The soul finds it seasonable to linger in this place. "It is good to be here." The presence of God is ever a deeply practical place; the heart is sure to be laid open there. The light that shines in that holy place makes everything manifest; and this is what is so much needed in the midst of the hollow pretension around us, and the pride and self-complacency within.

We might be disposed to think that the very moment the divine commission was given to Moses, his reply would be, Here am I, or, Lord, what wilt Thou have me to do? But no; he had yet to be brought to this. Doubtless, he was affected by the remembrance of his former failure. If a man acts in anything without God, he is sure to be discouraged, even when God is sending him. "And Moses said unto God, 'Who am I that I should go unto Pharaoh, and that I should bring forth the children of Israel out of Egypt?' " (ver. 11) This is very unlike the man who, forty years before, "supposed that his brethren would have understood how that God by his hand would deliver them." Such is man!—at one time too hasty; at another time too slow. Moses had learnt a great deal since the day in which he smote the Egyptian. He had grown in the knowledge of himself, and this produced diffidence and timidity. But then he manifestly lacked confidence in God. If I am merely looking at myself, I shall do "nothing;" but if I am looking at Christ, "I can do all things." Thus, when diffidence and timidity led Moses to say, "Who am I?" God's answer was, "Certainly *I* will be with thee" (ver. 12). This ought to have been sufficient. If God be with me, it makes very little matter who I am, or what I am. When God says, "I will send thee," and "I will be with thee," the servant is amply furnished with divine authority and divine power; and he ought, therefore, to be perfectly satisfied to go forth.

But Moses puts another question; for the human heart is full of questions. "And Moses said unto God, 'Behold, when I come unto the children of Israel and shall say unto them, The God of your fathers hath sent me unto you; and they shall say to me, What is His name? what shall I say unto them?' " It is marvelous to see how the human heart reasons and questions, when unhesitating obedience is that which is due to God; and still more marvelous is the grace that bears with all the reasonings and answers all the questions. Each question seems but to elicit some new feature of divine grace.

"And God said unto Moses, 'I AM THAT

I AM'; and He said, 'Thus shalt thou say unto the children of Israel, I AM hath sent me unto you' " (ver. 14). The title which God here gives Himself is one of wondrous significancy. In tracing through Scripture the various names which God takes, we find them intimately connected with the varied need of those with whom He was in relation. "Jehovah-jireh" (the Lord will provide), "Jehovah-nissi" (the Lord my banner), "Jehovah-shalom" (the Lord send peace), "Jehovah-tsidkenu" (the Lord our righteousness),—all these His gracious titles are unfolded to meet the necessities of His people; and when He calls Himself "I AM," it comprehends them all. Jehovah, in taking this title, was furnishing His people with a blank check, to be filled up to any amount. He calls Himself "I AM," and faith has but to write over against that ineffably precious name whatever we want. God is the only significant figure, and human need may add the ciphers. If we want life, Christ says, "I AM the life;" if we want righteousness, He is "THE LORD OUR RIGHTEOUSNESS"; if we want peace, "He is our peace"; if we want "wisdom, sanctification, and redemption," He "is made" all these "unto us." In a word, we may travel through the wide range of human necessity, in order to have a just conception of the amazing depth and fullness of this profound and adorable name, "I AM."

What a mercy to be called to walk in companionship with One who bears such a name as this! We are in the wilderness, and there we have to meet with trial, sorrow, and difficulty; but, so long as we have the happy privilege of betaking ourselves, at all times and under all circumstances, to One who reveals Himself in His manifold grace, in connection with our every necessity and weakness, we need not fear the wilderness. God was about to bring His people across the sandy desert, when He disclosed this precious and comprehensive name; and although the believer now, as being endowed with the Spirit of adoption, can cry, "Abba, Father," yet is he not deprived of the privilege of enjoying communion with God in each and every one of those manifestations which He has been pleased to make of Himself. For example, the title "God" reveals Him as acting in the solitariness of His own being, displaying His eternal power and Godhead in the works of creation. "The Lord God" is the title which He takes in connection with man. Then, as "the Almighty God," He rises before the view of His servant Abraham, in order to assure his heart in reference to the accomplishment of His promise touching the seed. As "Jehovah," He made Himself known to Israel, in delivering them out of the land of Egypt, and bringing them into the land of Canaan.

Such were the various measures and various modes in which "God spake in times past unto the fathers, by the prophets" (Heb. 1:1); and the believer, under this dispensation or economy, as possessing the Spirit of sonship, can say, It was my Father who thus revealed Himself, thus spoke, thus acted.

Nothing can be more interesting or practically important in its way than to follow out those great dispensational titles of God. These titles are always used in strict moral consistency with the circumstances under which they are disclosed; but there is, in the name "I AM," a height, a depth, a length, a breadth, which truly pass beyond the utmost stretch of human conception.

> When God would teach mankind His name,
> He calls Himself the great 'I AM,'
> And leaves a blank—believers may
> Supply those things for which they pray.

Be it observed, it is only in connection with His own people that He takes this name. He did not address Pharaoh in this name. When speaking to him, He calls Himself by that commanding and majestic title, "The Lord God of the Hebrews;" *i.e.*, God, in connection with the very people whom he was seeking to crush. This ought to have been sufficient to show Pharaoh his awful position with respect to God. "I AM" would have conveyed no intelligible sound to an uncircumcised ear—no divine reality to an unbelieving heart. When God manifest in the flesh declared to the unbelieving Jews of His day those words, "Before Abraham was, I *am,*" they took up stones to cast at Him. It is only the true believer who can feel, in any measure, the power, or enjoy the sweetness, of that ineffable name, "I AM." Such an one can rejoice to hear from the lips of the blessed Lord Jesus such declarations as these:—"*I am* that bread of life," "*I am* the light of the world," "*I am* the good Shepherd," "*I am* the resurrection and the life," "*I am* the way, the truth, and the life," "*I am* the true vine," "*I am* Alpha and Omega," "*I am* the bright and morning star." In a word, he can take every name of divine excellence and beauty, and, having placed it after "I AM," find JESUS therein, and admire, adore, and worship.

Thus, there is a sweetness, as well as a comprehensiveness, in the name "I AM," which is beyond all power of expression. Each believer can find therein that which exactly suits his own spiritual need, whatever it be. There is not a single winding in all the Christian's wilderness journey, not a single phase of his soul's experience, not a single point in his condition, which is not divinely met by this title, for the simplest of all reasons, that whatever he wants, he has but to place it, by faith, over against "I AM" and find it all in Jesus. To the believer, therefore, however feeble and faltering, there is unmingled blessedness in this name.

But although it was to the elect of God that Moses was commanded to say, "I AM hath sent me unto you," yet is there deep solemnity and reality in that name when looked at with reference to the unbeliever. If one who is yet in his sins contemplates, for a moment, this amazing title, he cannot, surely, avoid asking himself the question, How do I stand as to this Being who calls Himself, "I AM THAT I AM"? If, indeed, it be true that *He is,* then what *is* He to *me?* What am *I* to write over against this solemn name, "I AM"? I shall not rob this question of its characteristic weight and power by any words of my own; but I pray that God the Holy Ghost may make it searching to the conscience of any reader who really needs to be searched thereby.

I cannot close this section without calling the attention of the Christian reader to the deeply interesting declaration contained in the fifteenth verse: "And God said, moreover, unto Moses, 'Thus shalt thou say unto the children of Israel, The Lord God of your fathers, the God of Abraham, the God of Isaac, and the God of Jacob, hath sent me unto you: *this is My name forever, and this is My memorial to all generations.*'" This statement contains a very important truth—a truth which many professing Christians seem to forget, namely, that God's relationship with Israel is an eternal one. He is just as much Israel's God now as when He visited them in the land of Egypt. Only, because of rejecting their Messiah, they are, in His governmental dealings, set aside for a time. But His word is clear and emphatic: "This is My name forever." He does not say, This is My name for a time, so long as they continue what they ought to be. No; "This is My name *forever,* and this is My memorial unto *all generations.*" Let my reader ponder this. "God hath not cast away His people which He foreknew" (Rom. 11:2). They are His people still, whether obedient or disobedient, united together or scattered abroad, manifested to the nations or hidden from their view. They are His people, and He is their God. Exodus 3:15 is unanswerable. The professing church has no warrant whatever for ignoring a relationship which God says is to endure "forever." Let us beware how we tamper with this weighty word, "forever." If we say it does not mean forever when applied to Israel, what proof have we that it means forever when applied to us? God means what He says; and He will, ere long, make manifest to all the nations of the earth that His connection with Israel is one which shall outlive all the revolutions of time. "The gifts and calling of God are without repentance." When He said, "This is My name forever," He spoke absolutely. "I AM" declared Himself to be Israel's God forever; and all the Gentiles shall be made to bow to this; and to know, moreover, that all God's providential dealings with them, and all their destinies, are connected, in some way or other, with that favored and honored, though now judged and scattered, people. "When the Most High divided to the nations their inheritance, when He separated the sons of Adam, He set the bounds of the people according to the number of the children of Israel. For the Lord's portion is His people; Jacob is the lot of His inheritance" (Deut. 32:8-9).

Has this ceased to be true? Has Jehovah given up His "portion," and surrendered "the lot of His inheritance"? Does His eye of tender love no longer rest on Israel's scattered tribes, long lost to man's vision? Are the walls of Jerusalem no longer before Him? or has her dust ceased to be precious in His sight? To reply to these inquiries would be to quote a large portion of the Old Testament, and not a little of the New; but this would not be the place to enter elaborately upon such a subject. I would only say, in closing this section, let not christendom "be ignorant of this mystery, that blindness *in part* is happened to Israel, until the fullness of the Gentiles be come in. And so *all Israel shall be saved*" (Rom. 11:25-26).

---

## *CHAPTER 4*

WE are still called to linger at the foot of Mount Horeb, at "the backside of the desert;" and truly, the air of this place is most healthful for the spiritual constitution. Man's unbelief and God's boundless grace are here made manifest in a striking way.

"And Moses answered and said, 'But, behold, they will not believe me, nor hearken unto my voice; for they will say, The Lord hath not appeared unto thee.' " How hard it is to overcome the unbelief of the human heart! How difficult man ever finds it to trust God! How slow he is to venture upon the naked promise of Jehovah! Anything, for nature, but that. The most slender reed that the human eye can *see* is counted more substantial, by far, as a basis for nature's confidence, than the unseen "Rock of ages." Nature will rush with avidity to any creature stream or broken cistern, rather than abide by the unseen "Fountain of living waters."

We might suppose that Moses had seen and heard enough to set his fears entirely aside. The consuming fire in the unconsumed bush, the condescending grace, the precious, endearing, and comprehensive titles, the divine commission, the assurance of the divine presence,—all these might have quelled every anxious thought, and have imparted a settled assurance to the heart. Still, however, Moses raises questions, and still God answers them; and, as we have remarked, each successive question brings out fresh grace. "And the Lord said unto him, 'What is that in thine hand?' And he said, 'A rod.' " The Lord would just take him as he was, and use what he had in his hand. The rod with which he had tended Jethro's sheep was about to be used to deliver the Israel of God, to chastise the land of Egypt, to make a way through the deep, for the ransomed of the Lord to pass over, and to bring forth water from the flinty rock to refresh Israel's thirsty hosts in the desert. God takes up the weakest instruments to accomplish His mightiest ends. "A rod," "a ram's horn," "a cake of barley meal," "an earthen pitcher," "a shepherd's sling,"—anything, in short, when used of God, will do the appointed work. Men imagine that splendid ends can only be reached by splendid means; but such is not God's way. He can use a crawling worm as well as a scorching sun, a gourd as well as a vehement east wind (see Jonah).

But Moses had to learn a deep lesson, both as to the rod and the hand that was to use it. He had to learn, and the people had to be convinced. "And He said, 'Cast it on the ground.' And he cast it on the ground, and it became a serpent; and Moses fled from before it. And the Lord said unto Moses, 'Put forth thine hand and take it by the tail.' And he put forth his hand and caught it, and it became a rod in his hand; 'that they may believe that the Lord God of their fathers, the God of Abraham, the God of Isaac, and the God of Jacob, hath appeared unto thee.' " This is a deeply significant sign. The rod became a serpent, so that Moses fled from it; but, being commissioned by Jehovah, he took the serpent by the tail, and it became a rod. Nothing could more aptly express the idea of Satan's power being turned against himself. This is largely exemplified in the ways of God. Moses himself was a striking example. The serpent is entirely under the hand of Christ; and when he has reached the highest point in his mad career, he shall be hurled into the lake of fire, there to reap the fruits of his work throughout eternity's countless ages. "That old serpent, the accuser, and the adversary," shall be eternally crushed beneath the rod of God's Anointed.

Then the end—beneath His rod,
Man's last enemy shall fall;
Hallelujah! Christ in God,
God in Christ, is all in all.

"And the Lord said furthermore unto him, 'Put now thine hand into thy bosom.' And he put his hand into his bosom; and when he took it out, behold his hand was leprous as snow. And He said, 'Put thine hand into thy bosom again.' And he put his hand into his bosom again, and plucked it out of his bosom; and, behold, it was turned again as his other flesh." The leprous hand and the cleansing thereof present to us the moral effect of sin, as also the way in which sin has been met in the perfect work of Christ. The clean hand, placed in the bosom, becomes leprous; and the leprous hand, placed there, becomes clean. Leprosy is the well-known type of sin; and sin came in by the first man and was put away by the second. "By man came death, by man came also the resurrection of the dead" (1 Cor. 15:21). Man brought in ruin, man brought in redemption; man brought in guilt, man brought in pardon; man brought in sin, man brought in righteousness; man filled the scene with death, man abolished death and filled the scene with life, righteousness, and glory. Thus, not only shall the serpent himself be eternally defeated and confounded, but every trace of his abominable work shall be eradicated and wiped away by the atoning sacrifice of Him "who was manifested that He might destroy the works of the devil."

"And it shall come to pass, if they will not believe also these two signs, neither hearken unto thy voice, that thou shalt take of the water of the river, and pour it upon the dry land; and the water which thou takest out of the river shall become blood upon the dry land." This was a solemn and most expressive figure of the consequence of refusing to bow to the divine testimony. This sign was only to be wrought in the event of their refusing the other two. It was first to be a sign to Israel, and afterwards a plague upon Egypt (comp. chapter 7:17).

All this, however, fails to satisfy the heart of Moses. "And Moses said unto the Lord, 'O my Lord, I am not eloquent, neither heretofore nor since Thou hast spoken unto Thy servant; but I am slow of speech, and of a slow tongue.' " Terrible backwardness! Naught save Jehovah's infinite patience could have endured it. Surely, when God Himself had said, "I will be with thee," it was an infallible security, in reference to everything which could possibly be needed. If an eloquent tongue were necessary, what had Moses to do but to set it over against "I AM"? Eloquence, wisdom, might, energy,—everything was contained in that exhaustless treasury. "And the Lord said unto him, 'Who hath made man's mouth? or who maketh the dumb, or deaf, or the seeing, or the blind? have not *I the Lord?* Now, therefore, go, and I will be with thy mouth, and teach thee what thou shalt say.' " Profound, adorable, matchless grace! worthy of God! There is none like unto the Lord our God, whose patient grace surmounts all our difficulties, and proves itself amply sufficient for our manifold need and weakness. "I THE LORD" ought to silence forever the reasonings of our carnal hearts. But, alas! these reasonings are hard to be put down. Again and again they rise to the surface, to the disturbance of our peace, and the dishonor of that blessed One, who sets Himself before our souls, in all His own essential fullness, to be used according to our need.

It is well to bear in mind that when we have the Lord with us, our very deficiencies and infirmities become an occasion for the display of His all-sufficient grace and perfect patience. Had Moses remembered this, his want of eloquence need not have troubled him. The apostle Paul learnt to say, "Most gladly, therefore, *will I rather glory* in my infirmities, that the power of Christ may rest upon me. Therefore *I take pleasure* in infirmities, in reproaches, in necessities, in persecutions, in distresses for Christ's sake; for when I am weak, then am I strong" (2 Cor. 12:9-10). This is, assuredly, the utterance of one who had reached an advanced form in the school of Christ. It is the experience of one who would not have been much troubled because of not possessing an eloquent tongue, inasmuch as he had found an answer to every description of need in the precious grace of the Lord Jesus Christ.

The knowledge of this truth ought to have delivered Moses from his diffidence and inordinate timidity. When the Lord had so graciously assured him that He would be with his mouth, it should have set his mind at rest as to the question of eloquence. The Maker of man's mouth could fill that mouth with the most commanding eloquence, if such were needed. This, in the judgment of faith, is most simple; but, alas! the poor doubting heart would place far more confidence in an eloquent toungue than in the One who created it. This would seem most unaccountable, did we not know the materials of which the natural heart is composed. That heart cannot trust God; and hence it is that even the people of God, when they suffer themselves to be in any measure governed by nature, exhibit such a humiliating lack of confidence in the living God.

Thus, in the scene before us, we find Moses still demurring. "And he said, 'O my Lord, send, I pray Thee, by the hand of him whom Thou wilt send.' " This was, in reality, casting from him the high honor of being Jehovah's sole messenger to Egypt and to Israel.

It were needless to say that divinely-wrought humility is an inestimable grace. To "be clothed with humility" is a divine precept; and humility is unquestionably the most becoming dress in which a worthless sinner can appear. But it cannot be called humility to refuse to take the place which God assigns, or to tread the path which His hand marks out for us. That it was not true humility in Moses is obvious from the fact that "the anger of the Lord was kindled against him." So far from its being humility, it had actually passed the limit of mere weakness. So long as it wore the aspect of an excessive timidity, however reprehensible, God's boundless grace bore with it, and met it with renewed assurances; but when it assumed the character of unbelief and slowness of heart, it drew down Jehovah's just displeasure; and Moses, instead of being the sole, is made a joint, instrument in the work of testimony and deliverance.

Nothing is more dishonoring to God, or more dangerous for us, than a mock humility. When we refuse to occupy a position which the grace of God assigns us, because of our not possessing certain virtues and qualifications, this is not humility, inasmuch as if we could but satisfy our own consciences in reference to such virtues and qualifications, we should then deem ourselves entitled to assume the position. If, for instance, Moses had possessed such a measure of eloquence as he deemed needful, we may suppose he would have been ready to go. Now the question is, How much eloquence would he have needed to furnish him for his mission? The answer is, Without God, no amount of human eloquence would have availed; but with God, the merest stammerer would have proved an efficient minister.

This is a great practical truth. Unbelief is not humility, but thorough pride. It refuses to believe God because it does not find in *self* a reason for believing. This is the very height of presumption. If, when God speaks, I refuse to believe, on the ground of something in myself, I make Him a liar (1 John 5:10). When God declares His love, and I refuse to believe because I do not deem myself a sufficiently worthy object, I make Him a liar, and exhibit the inherent pride of my heart. The bare supposition that I could ever be worthy of aught save the lowest pit of hell, can only be regarded as the most profound ignorance of my own condition and of God's requirements. And the refusal to take the place which the redeeming love of God assigns me, on the ground of the finished atonement of Christ, is to make God a liar, and cast gross dishonor upon the sacrifice of the cross. God's love flows forth spontaneously. It is not drawn forth by my deserts, but by my misery. Nor is it a question as to the place which I deserve, but which Christ deserves. Christ took the sinner's place on the cross, that the sinner might take His place in the glory. Christ got what the sinner deserved, that the sinner might get what Christ deserves. Thus *self* is totally set aside, and this is true humility. No one can be truly humble until he has reached heaven's side of the cross; but there he finds divine life, divine righteousness, and divine favor. He is done with himself forever, as regards any expectation of goodness or righteousness, and he feeds upon the princely wealth of another. He is morally prepared to join in that cry which shall echo through the spacious vault of heaven, throughout the everlasting ages, "Not unto us, O Lord, not unto us, but unto Thy name give glory" (Psalm 115:1).

It would ill become us to dwell upon the mistakes or infirmities of so honored a servant as Moses, of whom we read that he "was verily faithful in all his house, as a servant, for a testimony of those things which were to be spoken after" (Heb. 3:5). But, though we should not dwell upon them in a spirit of self-complacency, as if we would have acted differently in his circumstances, we should nevertheless learn from such things those holy and seasonable lessons which they are manifestly designed to teach. We should learn to judge ourselves and to place more implicit confidence in God, to set self aside, that He might act in us, through us, and for us. This is the true secret of power.

We have remarked that Moses forfeited the dignity of being Jehovah's sole instrument in that glorious work which He was about to accomplish. But this was not all. "The anger of the Lord was kindled against Moses; and He said, 'Is not Aaron the Levite thy brother? I know that he can speak well: and also, behold, he cometh forth to meet thee; and when he seeth thee, he will be glad in his heart. And *thou shalt speak unto him, and put words in his mouth:* and I will be with thy mouth, and with his mouth, and will teach you what ye shall do. And he shall be thy spokesman unto the people: and he shall be, even he shall be to thee instead of a mouth, and thou shalt be to him instead of God. And thou shalt take this rod in thine hand, wherewith thou shalt do signs' " (chap. 4:14-17). This passage contains a mine of most precious practical instruction. We have noted the timidity and hesitation of Moses, notwithstanding the varied promises and assurances with which divine grace had furnished him. And now, although there was nothing gained in the way of real power, although there was no more virtue or efficacy in one mouth than in another, although it was Moses after all who was to speak unto Aaron; yet was Moses quite ready to go when assured of the presence and co-operation of a poor feeble mortal like himself; whereas he could not go when assured, again and again, that Jehovah would be with him.

Oh! my reader, does not all this hold up before us a faithful mirror in which you and I can see our hearts reflected? Truly it does. We are more ready to trust anything than the living God. We move along with bold decision when we possess the countenance and support of a poor frail mortal like ourselves; but we falter, hesitate, and demur when we have the light of the Master's countenance to cheer us, and the strength of His omnipotent arm to support us. This should humble us deeply before the Lord, and lead us to seek a fuller acquaintance with Him, so that we might trust Him with a more unmixed confidence, and walk on with a firmer step, as having Him *alone* for our resource and portion.

No doubt the fellowship of a brother is most valuable,—"Two are better than one," —whether in labor, rest, or conflict. The Lord Jesus, in sending forth His disciples, "sent them two by two,"—for unity is ever better than isolation;—still, if our personal acquaintance with God, and our experience of His presence, be not such as to enable us, if needful, to walk alone, we shall find the presence of a brother of very little use. It is not a little remarkable that Aaron, whose companionship seemed to satisfy Moses, was the man who afterwards made the golden calf (Exod. 32:21). Thus it frequently happens, that the very person whose presence we deem essential to our progress and success, afterwards proves a source of deepest sorrow to our hearts. May we ever remember this!

However, Moses at length consents to go; but ere he is fully equipped for his work, he must pass through another deep exercise,—yea, he must have the sentence of death inscribed by the hand of God upon his very nature. He had learnt deep lessons at "the backside of the desert;" he is called to learn something deeper still, "by the way in the inn." It is no light matter to be the Lord's servant. No ordinary education will qualify a man for such a position. Nature must be put in the place of death, and kept there. "We had the sentence of death in ourselves, that we should not trust in ourselves, but in God which raiseth the dead" (2 Cor. 1:9). Every successful servant will need to know something of this. Moses was called to enter into it, in his own experience, ere he was morally qualified. He was about to sound in the ears of Pharaoh the following deeply solemn message: "Thus saith the Lord, 'Israel is My son, even My first-born: and I say unto thee, Let My son go, that he may serve Me: and if thou refuse to let him go, behold I will slay thy son, even thy first-born.' " Such was to be his message to Pharaoh,—a message of death, a message of judgment; and, at the same time, his message to Israel was a message of life and salvation. But, be it remembered, that the man who will speak, on God's behalf, of death and judgment, life and salvation, must, ere he does so, enter into the practical power of these things in his own soul. Thus it was with Moses. We have seen him, at the very outset, in the place of death, typically; but this was a different thing from entering into the experience of death in his own person. Hence we read, "And it came to pass, by the way in the inn, that the Lord met him, and sought to kill him. Then Zipporah took a sharp stone, and cut off the foreskin of her son, and cast it at his feet, and said, 'Surely, a bloody husband art thou to me.' So He let him go: then she said, 'A bloody husband thou art, because of the circumcision.' " This passage lets us into a deep secret in the personal and domestic history of Moses. It is very evident that Zipporah's heart had, up to this point, shrunk from the application of *the knife* to that around which the affections of nature were entwined. She had avoided that mark which had to be set in the flesh of every member of the Israel of God. She was not aware that her relationship with Moses was one involving death to nature. She recoiled from the cross. This was natural. But Moses had yielded to her in the matter; and this explains to us the mysterious scene "in the inn." If Zipporah refuses to circumcise her *son*, Jehovah will lay His hand upon her *husband;* and if Moses spares the feelings of his wife, Jehovah will "seek to kill him." The sentence of death must be written on nature; and if we seek to avoid it in one way, we shall have to encounter it in another.

It has been already remarked that Zipporah furnishes an instructive and interesting type of the Church. She was united to Moses during the period of his rejection; and from the passage just quoted, we learn that the Church is called to know Christ as the One related to her "by blood." It is her privilege to drink of His cup, and be baptized with His baptism. Being crucified with Him, she is to be conformed to His death—to mortify her members which are on the earth—to take up the cross daily, and follow Him. Her relationship with Christ is founded upon blood, and the manifestation of the power of that relationship will necessarily involve death to nature. "And ye are complete in Him, which is the head of all principality and power; in whom also ye are circumcised with the circumcision made without hands, in putting off the body of the sins of the flesh by the circumcision of Christ: buried with Him in baptism, wherein also ye are risen with Him through the faith of the operation of God, who hath raised Him from the dead" (Col. 2:10-12).

Such is the doctrine as to the Church's place with Christ,—a doctrine replete with the richest privileges for the Church, and each member thereof. Everything, in short, is involved:—the perfect remission of sin, divine righteousness, complete acceptance, everlasting security, full fellowship with Christ in all His glory. "Ye are *complete* in Him." This, surely, comprehends everything. What could be added to one who is "complete"? Could "philosophy," "the tradition of men," "the rudiments of the world," "meats, drinks, holy days, new moons, or Sabbaths"? "Touch not" this, "taste not" that, "handle not" the other, "the commandments and doctrines of men," "days, and months, and times, and years"—could any of these things, or all of them put together, add a single jot or tittle to one whom God has pronounced "complete"? We might just as well inquire if man could have gone forth upon the fair creation of God, at the close of the six days' work, to give the finishing touch to that which God had pronounced "very good."

Nor is this completeness to be, by any means, viewed as a matter of attainment,—some point which we have not yet reached, but after which we must diligently strive, and of the possession of which we cannot be sure until we lie upon a bed of death, or stand before a throne of judgment. It is the portion of the feeblest, the most inexperienced, the most unlettered child of God. The very weakest saint is included in the apostolic *"ye."* All the people of God *"are* complete in Christ." The apostle does not say, Ye *will* be, Ye *may* be, *Hope* that ye may be, *Pray* that ye may be: no; he, by the Holy Ghost, states, in the most absolute and unqualified manner, that "ye *are* complete." This is the true Christian starting-post; and for man to make a goal of what God makes a starting-post, is to upset everything.

But, then, some will ask, Have we no sin, no failure, no imperfection? Assuredly we have. "If we say that we have no sin, we deceive ourselves, and the truth is not in us" (1 John 1:8). We have sin *in* us, but no sin *on* us. Moreover, our standing is not in *self,* but in Christ. It is *"in Him"* we "are complete." God sees the believer in Christ, with Christ, and as Christ. This is his changeless condition—his everlasting standing. "The body of the sins of the flesh" is "put off by the circumcision of Christ." The believer is not in the flesh, though the flesh is in him. He is united to Christ in the power of a new and an endless life, and that life is inseparably connected with divine righteousness in which the believer stands before God. The Lord Jesus has put away everything that was against the believer, and He has brought him nigh to God, in the selfsame favor as that which He Himself enjoys. In a word, Christ is his righteousness. This settles every question, answers every objection, silences every doubt. "Both He that sanctifieth and they who are sanctified are all of one" (Heb. 2:11).

The foregoing line of truth has flowed out of the deeply interesting type presented to us in the relationship between Moses and Zipporah. We must now hasten to close this section, and take our leave, for the present, of "the backside of the desert," though not of its deep lessons and holy impressions, so essential to every servant of Christ, and every messenger of the living God. All who would serve effectually, either in the important work of evangelization, or in the varied ministries of the house of God—which is the Church—will need to imbibe the precious instructions which Moses received at the foot of Mount Horeb, and "by the way in the inn."

Were these things properly attended to, we should not have so many running unsent—so many rushing into spheres of ministry for which they were never designed. Let each one who stands up to preach, or teach, or exhort, or serve in any way, seriously inquire if, indeed, he be fitted and taught and sent of God. If not, his work will neither be owned of God nor blessed to men, and the sooner he ceases, the better for himself and for those upon whom he has been imposing the heavy burden of hearkening to him. Neither a humanly-appointed nor a self-appointed ministry will ever suit within the hallowed precincts of the Church of God. All must be divinely gifted, divinely taught, and divinely sent.

"And the Lord said to Aaron, 'Go into the wilderness to meet Moses.' And he went and met him in the mount of God, and kissed him. And Moses told Aaron all the words of the Lord who had sent him, and all the signs which He had commanded him." This was a fair and beauteous scene—a scene of sweet brotherly love and union—a scene which stands in marked contrast with many of those scenes which were afterwards enacted in the wilderness-career of these two men. Forty years of wilderness life are sure to make great changes in men and things. Yet it is sweet to dwell upon those early days of one's Christian course, before the stern realities of desert life had, in any measure, checked the gush of warm and generous affections,—before deceit and corruption and hypocrisy had well-nigh dried up the springs of the heart's confidence, and placed the whole moral being beneath the chilling influences of a suspicious disposition.

That such results have been produced, in many cases, by years of experience, is, alas, too true. Happy is he who, though his eyes have been opened to see nature in a clearer light than that which this world supplies, can nevertheless serve his generation by the energy of that grace which flows forth from the bosom of God. Who ever knew the depths and windings of the human heart as Jesus knew them? "He knew *all,* and needed not that any should testify of man; for He knew what was in man" (John 2:24-25). So well did He know man, that He could not commit Himself unto him. He could not accredit man's professions, or endorse his pretensions. And yet, who so gracious as He? Who so loving, so tender, so compassionate, so sympathizing? With a heart that understood all, He could feel for all. He did not suffer His perfect knowledge of human worthlessness to keep Him aloof from human need. "He went about doing good." Why? Was it because He imagined that all those who flocked around Him were real? No; but "because God was with Him" (Acts 10:38). This is our example. Let us follow it, though, in doing so, we shall have to trample on *self* and all its interests, at every step of the way.

Who would desire that wisdom, that knowledge of nature, that experience, which only lead men to ensconce themselves within the inclosures of a hard-hearted selfishness, from which they look forth with an eye of dark suspicion upon everybody? Surely, such a result could never follow from aught of a heavenly or excellent nature. God gives wisdom; but it is not a wisdom which locks the heart against all the appeals of human need and misery. He gives a knowledge of nature; but it is not a knowledge which causes us to grasp with selfish eagerness that which we, falsely, call "our own." He gives experience; but it is not an experience which results in suspecting everybody except myself. If I am walking in the footprints of Jesus, if I am imbibing, and therefore manifesting, His excellent spirit, if, in short, I can say, "To me to live is Christ;" then, while I walk through the world, with a knowledge of what the world is; while I come in contact with man, with a knowledge of what I am to expect from him; I am able, through grace, to manifest Christ in the midst of it all. The springs which move me, and the objects which animate me, are all *above,* where He is, who is "the same yesterday, and today, and forever" (Heb. 13:8). It was this which sustained the heart of that beloved and honored servant, whose history, even so far, has furnished us with such deep and solid instruction. It was this which carried him through the trying and varied scenes of his wilderness course. And we may safely assert that, at the close of all, notwithstanding the trial and exercise of forty years, Moses could embrace his brother when he stood on Mount Hor, with the same warmth as he had when first he met him "in the mount of God." True, the two occasions were very different. At "the mount of God" they met and embraced, and started together on their divinely-appointed mission. Upon "Mount Hor" they met by the commandment of Jehovah, in order that Moses might strip his brother of his priestly robes, and see him gathered to his fathers, because of an error in which he himself had participated. (How solemn! How touching!) Circumstances vary: men turn away from one; but with God "is no variableness, neither shadow of turning" (James 1:17).

"And Moses and Aaron went and gathered together all the elders of the children of Israel; and Aaron spake all the words which the Lord had spoken unto Moses, and did the signs in the sight of the people. And the people believed; and when they heard that the Lord had visited the children of Israel, and that He had looked upon their affliction, then they bowed their heads and worshiped" (ver. 29-31). When God works, every barrier must give way. Moses had said, "The people will not believe me." But the question was not as to whether they would believe him, but whether they would believe God. When a man is enabled to view himself simply as the messenger of God, he may feel quite at ease as to the reception of his message. It does not detract, in the smallest degree, from his tender and affectionate solicitude in reference to those whom he addresses. Quite the contrary; but it preserves him from that inordinate anxiety of spirit which can only tend to unfit him for calm, elevated, steady testimony. The messenger of God should ever remember whose message he bears. When Zacharias said to the angel, "Whereby shall I know this?" was the latter perturbed by the question? Not in the least. His calm, dignified reply was, "I am Gabriel, that stand in the presence of God, and am sent to speak unto thee, and to show thee these glad tidings" (Luke 1:18-19). The angel rises before the doubting mortal, with a keen and exquisite sense of the dignity of his message. It is as if he would say, How can you doubt, when a messenger has actually been dispatched from the very presence-chamber of the Majesty of heaven? Thus should every messenger of God, in his measure, go forth, and, in this spirit, deliver his message.

---

## *CHAPTERS 5–6*

THE effect of the first appeal to Pharaoh seemed aught but encouraging. The thought of losing Israel made him clutch them with greater eagerness and watch them with greater vigilance. Whenever Satan's power becomes narrowed to a point, his rage increases. Thus it is here. The furnace is about to be quenched by the hand of redeeming love; but ere it is, it blazes forth with greater fierceness and intensity. The devil does not like to let go any one whom he has had in his terrible grasp. He is "a strong man armed," and while he "keepeth his palace, his goods are in peace." But, blessed be God, there is "a stronger than he," who has taken from him "his armor wherein he trusted," and divided the spoils among the favored objects of His everlasting love.

"And afterward, Moses and Aaron went in, and told Pharaoh, 'Thus saith the Lord God of Israel, Let My people go, that they may hold a feast unto Me in the wilderness' " (chap. 5:1). Such was Jehovah's message to Pharaoh. He claimed full deliverance for the people on the ground of their being His, and in order that they might hold a feast unto Him in the wilderness. Nothing can ever satisfy God in reference to His elect, but their entire emancipation from the yoke of bondage. "Loose him and let him go" is really the grand motto in God's gracious dealings with those who, though held in bondage by Satan, are nevertheless the objects of His eternal love.

When we contemplate Israel amid the brick-kilns of Egypt, we behold a graphic figure of the condition of every child of Adam by nature. There they were, crushed beneath the enemy's galling yoke, and having no power to deliver themselves. The mere mention of the word *liberty* only caused the oppressor to bind his captives with a stronger fetter, and to lade them with a still more grievous burden. It was absolutely necessary that deliverance should come from without. But from whence was it to come! Where were the resources to pay their ransom? or where was the power to break their chains? And even were there both the one and the other, where was the *will?* Who would take the trouble of delivering them? Alas! there was no hope, either within or around. They had only to look up. Their refuge was in God. He had both the power and the will. He could accomplish a redemption both by price and by power. In Jehovah, and in Him alone, was there salvation for ruined and oppressed Israel.

Thus it is in every case. "Neither is there salvation in any other; for there is none other name under heaven, given among men, whereby we must be saved" (Acts 4:12). The sinner is in the hands of one who rules him with despotic power. He is "sold under sin"—"led captive by Satan at his will," fast bound in the fetters of lust, passion, and temper,—"without strength," "without hope," "without God." Such is the sinner's condition. How, then, can he help himself? What can he do? He is the slave of another, and everything he does is done in the capacity of a slave. His thoughts, his words, his acts, are the thoughts, words, and acts of a slave. Yea, though he should weep and sigh for emancipation, his very tears and sighs are the melancholy proofs of his slavery. He may struggle for freedom; but his very struggle, though it evinces a desire for liberty, is the positive declaration of his bondage.

Nor is it merely a question of the sinner's *condition;* his very *nature* is radically corrupt—wholly under the power of Satan. Hence he not only needs to be introduced into a new condition, but also to be endowed with a new nature. The nature and the condition go together. If it were possible for the sinner to better his condition, what would it avail so long as his nature was irrecoverably bad? A nobleman might take a beggar off the streets and adopt him; he might endow him with a noble's wealth and set him in a noble's position; but he could not impart to him nobility of nature; and thus the nature of a beggarman would never be at home in the condition of a nobleman. There must be a nature to suit the condition; and there must be a condition to suit the capacity, the desires, the affections, and the tendencies of the nature.

Now, in the gospel of the grace of God, we are taught that the believer is introduced into an entirely new condition; that he is no longer viewed as in his former state of guilt and condemnation, but as in a state of perfect and everlasting justification; that the condition in which God now sees him is not only one of full pardon, but it is such that infinite holiness cannot find so much as a single stain. He has been taken out of his former condition of guilt, and placed absolutely and eternally in a new condition of unspotted righteousness. It is not, by any means, that his old condition is improved. This is utterly impossible. "That which is crooked cannot be made straight." "Can the Ethiopian change his skin, or the leopard his spots?" Nothing can be more opposed to the fundamental truth of the gospel than the theory of a gradual improvement in the sinner's condition. He is born in a certain condition, and until he is "born again" he cannot be in any other. He may try to improve, he may resolve to be better for the future—to "turn over a new leaf"—to live a different sort of life; but, all the while, he has not moved a single hair's breadth out of his real condition as a sinner. He may become "religious," as it is called; he may try to pray, he may diligently attend to ordinances, and exhibit an appearance of moral reform; but none of these things can, in the smallest degree, affect his positive condition before God.

The case is precisely similar as to the question of *nature.* How can a man alter his nature? He may make it undergo a process, he may try to subdue it—to place it under discipline; but it is nature still. "That which is born of the flesh is flesh." There must be a new nature as well as a new condition. And how is this to be had? By believing God's testimony concerning His Son. "As many as received Him, to them gave He power to become the sons of God, even *to them that believe on His name:* which were born, not of blood, nor of the will of the flesh, nor of the will of man, but of God" (John 1:12-13). Here we learn that those who believe on the name of the only begotten Son of God, have the right or privilege of being sons of God. They are made partakers of a new nature: they have gotten eternal life. "He that believeth on the Son *hath* everlasting life" (John 3:36). "Verily, verily, I say unto you, He that *heareth* My word, and *believeth* on Him that sent Me, *hath* everlasting life, and shall not come into condemnation; but *is* passed from death unto life" (John 5:24). "And this *is* life eternal, that they might know Thee, the only true God, and Jesus Christ, whom Thou hast sent" (John 17:3). "And this is the record, that God hath given to us eternal life, and this life is in His Son. He that hath the Son *hath* life" (1 John 5:11-12).

Such is the plain doctrine of the Word in reference to the momentous questions of condition and nature. But on what is all this founded? How is the believer introduced into a condition of divine righteousness and made partaker of the divine nature? It all rests on the great truth that *"Jesus died and rose again."* That blessed One left the bosom of eternal love, the throne of glory, the mansions of unfading light; came down into this world of guilt and woe; took upon Him the likeness of sinful flesh; and, having perfectly exhibited and perfectly glorified God in all the movements of His blessed life here below, He died upon the cross, under the full weight of His people's transgressions. By so doing, He divinely met all that was or could be against us. He magnified the law and made it honorable; and, having done so, He became a curse by hanging on the tree. Every claim was met, every enemy silenced, every obstacle removed. "Mercy and truth are met together; righteousness and peace have kissed each other." Infinite justice was satisfied, and infinite love can flow, in all its soothing and refreshing virtues, into the broken heart of the sinner; while, at the same time, the cleansing and atoning stream that flowed from the pierced side of a crucified Christ, perfectly meets all the cravings of a guilty and convicted conscience. The Lord Jesus, on the cross, stood in our place. He was our representative. He died, "the just for the unjust." "He was made sin for us" (2 Cor. 5:21; 1 Peter 3:18). He died the sinner's death, was buried, and rose again, having accomplished all. Hence, there is absolutely nothing against the believer. He is linked with Christ, and stands in the same condition of righteousness. "As He is, so are we in this world" (1 John 4:17).

This gives settled peace to the conscience. If I am no longer in a condition of guilt, but in a condition of justification—if God only sees me *in* Christ and as Christ, then, clearly, my portion is perfect peace. "Being justified by faith, we *have* peace with God through our Lord Jesus Christ" (Rom. 5:1). The blood of the Lamb has canceled all the believer's guilt,—blotted out his heavy debt, and given him a perfectly blank page, in the presence of that holiness which "cannot look upon sin."

But the believer has not merely found peace with God; he is made a child of God, so that he can taste the sweetness of communion with the Father and the Son, through the power of the Holy Ghost. The cross is to be viewed in two ways: first, as satisfying God's claims; secondly, as expressing God's affections. If I look at my sins in connection with the claims of God as a Judge, I find, in the cross, a perfect settlement of those claims. God, as a Judge, has been divinely satisfied—yea, glorified, in the cross. But there is more than this. God had affections as well as claims; and, in the cross of the Lord Jesus Christ, all those affections are sweetly and touchingly told out into the sinner's ear; while, at the same time, he is made partaker of a new nature which is capable of enjoying those affections and having fellowship with the heart from which they flow. "For Christ also hath once suffered for sins, the just for the unjust, that He might bring us to God" (1 Peter 3:18). Thus, we are not only brought into *a condition,* but unto *a Person,* even God Himself, and we are endowed with *a nature* which can delight in Him. *"We also joy in God,* through our Lord Jesus Christ, by whom we have now received the reconciliation [margin]" (Rom. 5:11).

What force and beauty, therefore, can we see in those emancipating words, "Let My people go, that they may hold a feast unto Me in the wilderness." "The Spirit of the Lord is upon Me, because He hath anointed Me to preach the gospel; He hath sent Me to heal the broken-hearted, to preach deliverance to the captives, and recovering of sight to the blind, to set at liberty them that are bruised" (Luke 4:18). The glad tidings of the gospel announce full deliverance from every yoke of bondage. Peace and liberty are the boons which that gospel bestows on all who believe it, as God has declared it.

And mark, it is "that they may hold a feast to *Me.*" If they were to get done with Pharaoh, it was that they might begin with God. This was a great change. Instead of toiling under Pharaoh's taskmasters, they were to feast in company with Jehovah; and, although they were to pass from Egypt into the wilderness, still the divine presence was to accompany them; and if the wilderness was rough and dreary, it was the way to the land of Canaan. The divine purpose was, that they should hold a feast unto the Lord in the wilderness, and in order to do this, they should be *"let go"* out of Egypt.

However, Pharaoh was in no wise disposed to yield obedience to the divine mandate. "Who is the Lord," said he, "that I should obey His voice to let Israel go? I know not the Lord, neither will I let Israel go" (chap. 5:2). Pharaoh most truly expressed, in these words, his real condition. His condition was one of ignorance and consequent disobedience. Both go together. If God be not known, He cannot be obeyed; for obedience is ever founded upon knowledge. When the soul is blessed with the knowledge of God, it finds this knowledge to be life (John 17:3), and life is power; and when I get power, I can act. It is obvious that one cannot act without life; and therefore it is most unintelligent to set people upon doing certain things in order to get that by which alone they can do anything.

But Pharaoh was as ignorant of himself as he was of the Lord. He did not know that he was a poor, vile worm of the earth, and that he had been raised up for the express purpose of making known the glory of the very One whom he said he knew not (Exod. 9:16; Rom. 9:17). "And they said, 'The God of the Hebrews has met with us: let us go, we pray thee, three days' journey into the desert, and sacrifice unto the Lord our God; lest He fall upon us with pestilence or with the sword.' And the king of Egypt said unto them, 'Wherefore do ye, Moses and Aaron, let the people from their work? Get you unto your burdens . . . let there more work be laid upon the men, that they may labor therein; and let them not regard *vain words*' " (ver. 3-9).

What a development of the secret springs of the human heart we have here! What complete incompetency to enter into the things of God! All the divine titles and the divine revelations were, in Pharaoh's estimation, "vain words." What did he know or care about "three days' journey into the wilderness," or "a feast to Jehovah"? How could he understand the need of such a journey, or the nature or object of such a feast? Impossible. He could understand burden-bearing and brick-making; these things had an air of reality about them, in his judgment; but as to aught of God, His service, or His worship, he could only regard it in the light of an idle chimera, devised by those who only wanted an excuse to make their escape from the stern realities of actual life.

Thus has it too often been with the wise and great of this world. They have ever been the most forward to write folly and vanity upon the divine testimonies. Hearken, for example, to the estimate which the "most noble Festus" formed of the grand question at issue between Paul and the Jews:—"They had certain questions against him of their own superstition, and *of one Jesus, which was dead, whom Paul affirmed to be alive*" (Acts 25:19). Alas! how little he knew what he was saying! How little he knew what was involved in the question, as to whether "Jesus" was "dead" or "alive"! He thought not of the solemn bearing of that momentous question upon himself and his friends, Agrippa and Bernice; but that did not alter the matter; he and they know somewhat more about it now, though in their passing moment of earthly glory they regarded it as a superstitious question, wholly beneath the notice of men of common sense, and only fit to occupy the disordered brain of visionary enthusiasts. Yes; the stupendous question which fixes the destiny of every child of Adam—on which is founded the present and everlasting condition of the Church and the world—which stands connected with all the divine counsels,—this question was, in the judgment of Festus, a vain superstition.

Thus was it in Pharaoh's case. He knew nothing of "the Lord God of the Hebrews"—

the great "I AM," and hence he regarded all that Moses and Aaron had said to him, in reference to doing sacrifice to God, as "vain words." The things of God must ever seem vain, profitless, and unmeaning to the unsanctified mind of man. His name may be made use of as part of the flippant phraseology of a cold and formal religiousness; but He Himself is not known. His precious name, which, to a believer's heart, has wrapped up in it all that he can possibly need or desire, has no significancy, no power, nor virtue for an unbeliever. All, therefore, connected with God—His words, His counsels, His thoughts, His ways—everything, in short, that treats of or refers to Him, is regarded as "vain words."

However, the time is rapidly approaching when it will not be thus. The judgment-seat of Christ, the terrors of the world to come, the surges of the lake of fire, will not be "vain words." Assuredly not; and it should be the great aim of all who, through grace, believe them now to be realities, to press them upon the consciences of those who, like Pharaoh, regard the making of bricks as the only thing worth thinking about—the only thing that can be called real and solid.

Alas! that even Christians should so frequently be found living in the region of sight—the region of earth—the region of nature—as to lose the deep, abiding, influential sense of the reality of divine and heavenly things. We want to live more in the region of faith—the region of heaven—the region of the "new creation." Then we should see things as God sees them, think about them as He thinks; and our whole course and character would be more elevated, more disinterested, more thoroughly separated from earth and earthly things.

But Moses' sorest trial did not arise from Pharaoh's judgment about his mission. The true and whole-hearted servant of Christ must ever expect to be looked on, by the men of this world, as a mere visionary enthusiast. The point of view from which they contemplate him is such as to lead us to look for this judgment and none other. The more faithful he is to his heavenly Master, the more he walks in His footsteps, the more conformed he is to His image, the more likely he is to be considered, by the sons of earth, as one "beside himself." This, therefore, should neither disappoint nor discourage him. But then it is a far more painful thing when his service and testimony are misunderstood, unheeded, or rejected by those who are themselves the specific objects thereof. When such is the case, he needs to be much with God, much in the secret of His mind, much in the power of communion, to have his spirit sustained in the abiding reality of his path and service. Under such trying circumstances, if one be not fully persuaded of the divine commission, and conscious of the divine presence, he will be almost sure to break down.

Had not Moses been thus upheld, his heart must have utterly failed him when the augmented pressure of Pharaoh's power elicited from the officers of the children of Israel such desponding and depressing words as these: "The Lord look upon you, and judge; because ye have made our savor to be abhorred in the eyes of Pharaoh, and in the eyes of his servants, to put a sword in their hand to slay us." This was gloomy enough; and Moses felt it so, for "he returned unto the Lord, and said, 'Lord, wherefore hast Thou so evil entreated this people? Why is it that Thou hast sent me? For since I came unto Pharaoh to speak in Thy name, he hath done evil to this people; neither hast Thou delivered Thy people at all.' " The aspect of things had become most discouraging, at the very moment when deliverance seemed at hand; just as, in nature, the darkest hour of the night is often that which immediately precedes the dawn of the morning. Thus will it assuredly be in Israel's history in the latter day. The moment of most profound darkness and depressing gloom will precede the bursting of "the Sun of Righteousness" from behind the cloud, with healing in His wings to heal eternally "the hurt of the daughter of His people."

We may well question how far genuine faith, or a mortified will, dictated the "*wherefore?*" and the "*why?*" of Moses, in the above quotation. Still, the Lord does not rebuke a remonstrance drawn forth by the intense pressure of the moment. He most graciously replies, "Now shalt thou see what I will do to Pharaoh: for with a strong hand shall he let them go, and with a strong hand shall he drive them out of his land" (chap. 6:1). This reply breathes peculiar grace. Instead of reproving the petulance which could presume to call in question the unsearchable ways of the great I AM, that ever-gracious One seeks to relieve the harassed spirit of His servant by unfolding to him what He was about to do. This was worthy of the blessed God—the unupbraiding Giver of every good and every perfect gift. "He knoweth our frame; He remembereth that we are dust" (Ps. 103:14).

Nor is it merely in His actings that He would cause the heart to find its solace, but in Himself—in His very name and character. This is full, divine, and everlasting blessedness. When the heart can find its sweet relief in God Himself—when it can retreat into the strong tower which His name affords—when it can find, in His character, a perfect answer to all its need, then, truly, it is raised far above the region of the creature, it can turn away from earth's fair promises, it can place the proper value on man's lofty pretensions. The heart which is endowed with an experimental knowledge of God can not only look forth upon earth, and say, "All is vanity;" but it can also look straight up to Him, and say, "All my springs are in Thee."

"And God spake unto Moses, and said unto him, 'I am the Lord: and I appeared unto Abraham, unto Isaac, and unto Jacob, by the name of God Almighty; but by My name *Jehovah* was I not known to them. And I have also established My covenant with them to give them the land of Canaan, the land of their pilgrimage, wherein they were strangers. And I have also heard the groaning of the children of Israel, whom the Egyptians keep in bondage; and I have remembered My covenant.' " *"Jehovah"* is the title which He takes as the Deliverer of His people, on the ground of His covenant of pure and sovereign grace. He reveals Himself as the great self-existing Source of redeeming love, establishing His counsels, fulfilling His promises, delivering His elect people from every enemy and every evil. It was Israel's privilege ever to abide under the safe covert of that significant title—a title which displays God acting for His own glory, and taking up His oppressed people in order to show forth in them that glory.

"Wherefore say unto the children of Israel, 'I am the Lord, and I will bring you out from under the burdens of the Egyptians, I will rid you out of their bondage, and I will redeem you with a stretched-out arm, and with great judgments; and I will take you to Me for a people, and I will be to you a God; and ye shall know that I am the Lord your God, which bringeth you out from under the burdens of the Egyptians. And I will bring you in unto the land concerning the which I did swear to give it unto Abraham, to Isaac, and to Jacob; and I will give it to you for a heritage: I am the Lord' " (ver. 6-8). All this speaks the purest, freest, richest grace. Jehovah presents Himself to the hearts of His people as the One who was to act *in* them, *for* them, and *with* them, for the display of His own glory. Ruined and helpless as they were, He had come down to show forth His glory, to exhibit His grace, and to furnish a sample of His power, in their full deliverance. His glory and their salvation were inseparably connected. They were afterwards reminded of all this, as we read in the book of Deuteronomy, "The Lord did not set His love upon you, nor choose you, because ye were more in number than any people; for ye were the fewest of all people: but because the Lord loved you, and because He would keep the oath which He had sworn unto your fathers, hath the Lord brought you out with a mighty hand, and redeemed you out of the house of bondmen, from the hand of Pharaoh, king of Egypt" (chap. 7:7-8).

Nothing is more calculated to assure and establish the doubting, trembling heart than the knowledge that God has taken us up *just as we are,* and in the full intelligence of what we are; and, moreover, that He can never make any fresh discovery to cause an alteration in the character and measure of His love. "Having loved His own which were in the world, He loved them unto the end" (John 13). *Whom* He loves and *as* He loves,

He loves unto the end. This is an unspeakable comfort. God knew all about us—He knew the very worst of us, when He manifested His love to us in the gift of His Son. He knew what was needed, and He provided it; He knew what was due, and He paid it; He knew what was to be wrought, and He wrought it; His own requirements had to be met, and He met them. It is all His own work. Hence, we find Him saying to Israel, as in the above passage, "I will bring you out," "I will bring you in," "I will take you to Me," "I will give you the land," "I am Jehovah." It was all what *He would do,* as founded upon what *He was.* Until this great truth is fully laid hold of, until it enters into the soul, in the power of the Holy Ghost, there cannot be settled peace. The heart can never be happy, or the conscience at rest, until one knows and believes that all divine requirements have been divinely answered.

The remainder of our section is taken up with a record of "the heads of their fathers' houses," and is very interesting, as showing us Jehovah coming in and numbering those that belonged to Himself, though they were still in the possession of the enemy. Israel was God's people, and He here counts up those on whom He had a sovereign claim. Amazing grace! To find an object in those who were in the midst of all the degradation of Egyptian bondage! This was worthy of God. The One who had made the worlds, who was surrounded by hosts of unfallen angels, ever ready to "do His pleasure," should come down for the purpose of taking up a number of bond-slaves with whom He condescended to connect His name. He came down and stood amid the brick-kilns of Egypt, and there beheld a people groaning beneath the lash of the taskmasters, and He uttered those memorable accents, "Let *My* people go;" and, having so said, He proceeded to count them up, as much as to say, These are Mine; let Me see how many I have, that not one may be left behind. "He taketh up the beggar from the dunghill, to set him amongst the princes of His people, and to make him inherit the throne of glory" (1 Sam. 2).

## *CHAPTERS 7–11*

THESE five chapters form one distinct section, the contents of which may be distributed into the three following divisions, namely, the ten judgments from the hand of Jehovah, the resistance of "Jannes and Jambres," and the four objections of Pharaoh.

The whole land of Egypt was made to tremble beneath the successive strokes of the rod of God. All, from the monarch on His throne to the menial at the mill, were made to feel the terrible weight of that rod. "He sent Moses His servant, and Aaron whom He had chosen. They showed His signs among them, and wonders in the land of Ham. He sent darkness and made it dark; and they rebelled not against His word. He turned their waters into blood, and slew their fish. Their land brought forth frogs in abundance, in the chambers of their kings. He spake, and there came divers sorts of flies and lice in all their coasts. He gave them hail for rain, and flaming fire in their land. He smote their vines also, and their fig-trees; and brake the trees of their coasts. He spake, and their locusts came, and the caterpillars, and that without number, and did eat up all the herbs in their land, and devoured the fruit of their ground. He smote also all the firstborn in their land, the chief of all their strength" (Ps. 105:26-36).

Here the inspired Psalmist has given a condensed view of those appalling inflictions which the hardness of Pharaoh's heart brought upon his land and upon his people. This haughty monarch had set himself to resist the sovereign will and course of the Most High God; and, as a just consequence, he was given over to judicial blindness and hardness of heart. "And the Lord hardened the heart of Pharaoh, and he hearkened not unto them, as the Lord had spoken unto Moses. And the Lord said unto Moses, 'Rise up early in the morning, and stand before Pharaoh, and say unto him, Thus saith the Lord God of the Hebrews, Let My people go, that they may serve Me. For I will at this time send all My plagues upon thine heart, and upon thy servants, and upon thy people; that thou mayest know that there is none like Me in all the earth. For now I will stretch out My hand that I may smite thee and thy people with pestilence; and thou shalt be cut off from the earth. And in very deed for this cause have I raised thee up, for to show in thee My power, and that My name may be declared throughout all the earth' " (Exod. 9:12-16).

In contemplating Pharaoh and his actings, the mind is carried forward to the stirring scenes of the book of Revelation, in which we find the last proud oppressor of the people of God bringing down upon his kingdom and upon himself the seven vials of the wrath of the Almighty. It is God's purpose that Israel shall be pre-eminent in the earth; and, therefore, every one who presumes to stand in the way of that pre-eminence must be set aside. Divine grace must find its object; and every one who would act as a barrier in the way of that grace, must be taken out of the way, whether it be Egypt, Babylon, or "the beast that was, is not, and yet is," it matters not. Divine power will clear the channel for divine grace to flow, and eternal woe be to all who stand in the way. They shall taste, throughout the everlasting course of ages, the bitter fruit of having exalted themselves against "the Lord God of the Hebrews."

He has said to His people, "No weapon that is formed against thee shall prosper," and His infallible faithfulness will assuredly make good what His infinite grace hath promised.

Thus, in Pharaoh's case, when he persisted in holding, with an iron grasp, the Israel of God, the vials of divine wrath were poured forth upon him; and the land of Egypt was covered, throughout its entire length and breadth, with darkness, disease, and desolation. So will it be by and by, when the last great oppressor shall emerge from the bottomless pit, armed with satanic power, to crush beneath his "foot of pride" the favored objects of Jehovah's choice. His throne shall be overturned, his kingdom devastated by the seven last plagues, and, finally, he himself plunged, not in the Red Sea, but "in the lake that burneth with fire and brimstone" (comp. Rev. 17:8; 20:10).

Not one jot or one tittle of what God had promised to Abraham, Isaac, and Jacob shall fail. He will accomplish all. Notwithstanding all that has been said and done to the contrary, God remembers His promises, and He will fulfill them. They are all "yea and amen in Christ." Dynasties have risen and acted on the stage of this world; thrones have been erected on the apparent ruins of Jerusalem's ancient glory; empires have flourished for a time, and then fallen to decay; ambitious potentates have contended for the possession of "the land of promise"—all these things have taken place; but Jehovah has said concerning Palestine, "The land shall not be sold forever: for the land is Mine" (Lev. 25:23). No one, therefore, shall ever finally possess that land but Jehovah Himself, and He will inherit it through the seed of Abraham. One plain passage of Scripture is quite sufficient to establish the mind in reference to this or any other subject. The land of Canaan is for the seed of Abraham, and the seed of Abraham for the land of Canaan; nor can any power of earth or hell ever reverse this divine order. The eternal God has pledged His word, and the blood of the everlasting covenant has flowed to ratify that word. Who, then, shall make it void? "Heaven and earth shall pass away, but that word shall never pass away." Truly, "there is none like unto the God of Jeshurun, who rideth upon the heaven in thy help, and in His excellency on the sky. The eternal God is thy refuge, and underneath are the everlasting arms; and He shall thrust out the enemy from before thee; and shall say, Destroy them. Israel then shall dwell in safety alone: the fountain of Jacob shall be upon a land of corn and wine; also his heavens shall drop down dew. Happy art thou, O Israel, who is like unto thee, O people saved by the Lord, the shield of thy help, and who is the sword of thy excellency! and thy enemies shall be found liars unto thee; and thou shalt tread upon their high places" (Deut. 33:26-29).

We shall now consider, in the second place, the opposition of "Jannes and Jambres," the magicians of Egypt. We should not have known the names of these ancient opposers of the truth of God, had they not been recorded by the Holy Ghost, in connection with "the perilous times" of which the apostle Paul warns his son Timothy. It is important that the Christian reader should clearly understand the real nature of the opposition given to Moses by those magicians, and in order that he may have the subject fully before him, I shall quote the entire passage from St. Paul's Epistle to Timothy. It is one of deep and awful solemnity.

"This know also, that in the last days perilous times shall come. For men shall be lovers of their own selves, covetous, boasters, proud, blasphemers, disobedient to parents, unthankful, unholy, without natural affection, truce-breakers, false accusers, incontinent, fierce, despisers of those that are good, traitors, heady, high-minded, lovers of pleasures rather than lovers of God; having a form of godliness, but denying the power thereof: from such turn away. For of this sort are they which creep into houses, and lead captive silly women laden with sins, led away with divers lusts, ever learning, and never able to come to the knowledge of the truth. Now as Jannes and Jambres withstood Moses, so do these also resist the truth: men of corrupt minds, reprobate concerning the faith. But they shall proceed no further; for their folly shall be manifest unto all, as theirs also was" (2 Tim. 3:1-9).

Now, it is peculiarly solemn to mark the nature of this resistance to the truth. The mode in which "Jannes and Jambres withstood Moses" was simply by imitating, as far as they were able, whatever he did. We do not find that they attributed his actings to a false or evil energy, but rather that they sought to neutralize their power upon the conscience, by doing the same things. What Moses did they could do, so that after all there was no great difference. One was as good as the other. A miracle is a miracle. If Moses wrought miracles to get the people out of Egypt, they could work miracles to keep them in; so where was the difference?

From all this we learn the solemn truth that the most satanic resistance to God's testimony in the world is offered by those who, though they imitate the effects of the truth, have but "the form of godliness," and "deny the power thereof." Persons of this class can do the same things, adopt the same habits and forms, use the same phraseology, profess the same opinions as others. If the true Christian, constrained by the love of Christ, feeds the hungry, clothes the naked, visits the sick, circulates the Scriptures, distributes tracts, supports the gospel, engages in prayer, sings praise, preaches the gospel, the formalist can do every one of these things; and this, be it observed, is the special character of the resistance offered to the truth "in the last days"—this is the spirit of "Jannes and Jambres." How needful to understand this! How important to remember that, "*as* Jannes and Jambres withstood Moses, *so* do" those self-loving, world-seeking, pleasure-hunting professors "resist the truth." They would not be without "a form of godliness;" but, while adopting "the form," because it is customary, they hate "the power," because it involves self-denial. "The power" of godliness involves the recognition of God's claims, the implanting of His kingdom in the heart, and the consequent exhibition thereof in the whole life and character; but the formalist knows nothing of this. "The power" of godliness could never comport with any one of those hideous features set forth in the foregoing quotation; but "the form," while it covers them over, leaves them wholly unsubdued; and this the formalist likes. He does not want his lusts subdued, his pleasures interfered with, his passions curbed, his affections governed, his heart purified. He wants just as much religion as will enable him "to make the best of both worlds." He knows nothing of giving up the world that is, because of having found "the world to come."

In marking the forms of Satan's opposition to the truth of God, we find that his method has ever been, first, to oppose it by violence; and then, if that did not succeed, to corrupt it by producing a counterfeit. Hence, he first sought to slay Moses (chap.

2:15), and having failed to accomplish his purpose, he sought to imitate his works.

Thus, too, has it been in reference to the truth committed to the Church of God. Satan's early efforts showed themselves in connection with the wrath of the chief priests and elders, the judgment-seat, the prison, and the sword. But in the passage just quoted from 2 Timothy, we find no reference to any such agency. Open violence has made way for the far more wily and dangerous instrumentality of a powerless form, an empty profession, a human counterfeit. The enemy, instead of appearing with the sword of persecution in his hand, walks about with the cloak of profession on his shoulders. He professes and imitates that which he once opposed and persecuted; and, by so doing, gains most appalling advantages for the time being. The fearful forms of moral evil which, from age to age, have stained the page of human history, instead of being found only where we might naturally look for them, amid the dens and caves of human darkness, are to be found carefully arranged beneath the drapery of a cold, powerless, uninfluential profession; and this is one of Satan's grand masterpieces.

That man, as a fallen, corrupt creature, should love himself, be covetous, boastful, proud, and the like, is natural; but that he should be all these beneath the fair covering of "a form of godliness," marks the special energy of Satan in his resistance to the truth in "the last days." That man should stand forth in the bold exhibition of those hideous vices, lusts, and passions which are the necessary results of departure from the source of infinite holiness and purity, is only what might be expected, for man will be what he is to the end of the chapter. But on the other hand, when we find the holy name of the Lord Jesus Christ connected with man's wickedness and deadly evil, when we find holy principles connected with unholy practices, when we find all the characteristics of Gentile corruption, referred to in the first chapter of Romans, associated with "a form of godliness," then, truly, we may say, these are the terrible features of "the last days"—this is the resistance of "Jannes and Jambres."

However, there were only three things in which the magicians of Egypt were able to imitate the servants of the true and living God, namely, in turning their rods into serpents (chap. 7:12), turning the water into blood (chap. 7:22), and bringing up the frogs (chap. 8:7); but in the fourth, which involved the exhibition of life, in connection with the display of nature's humiliation, they were totally confounded, and obliged to own, "This is the finger of God" (chap. 8:16-19). Thus it is also with the latter-day resisters of the truth. All that they do is by the direct energy of Satan, and lies within the range of his power. Moreover, its specific object is to "resist the truth."

The three things which "Jannes and Jambres" were able to accomplish were characterized by satanic energy, death, and uncleanness; that is to say, the serpents, the blood, and the frogs. Thus it was they "withstood Moses;" and "so do these also resist the truth," and hinder its moral weight and action upon the conscience. There is nothing which so tends to deaden the power of the truth as the fact that persons who are not under its influences at all, do the self-same things as those who are. This is Satan's agency just now. He seeks to have all regarded as Christians. He would fain make us believe ourselves surrounded by "a Christian world;" but it is counterfeit Christianity, which, so far from being a testimony to the truth, is designed by the enemy of the truth, to withstand its purifying and elevating influence.

In short, the servant of Christ and the witness for the truth is surrounded, on all sides, by the spirit of "Jannes and Jambres;" and it is well for him to remember this—to know thoroughly the evil with which he has to grapple—to bear in mind that it is Satan's imitation of God's reality, produced, not by the wand of an openly-wicked magician, but by the actings of false professors, who have "a form of godliness, but deny the power thereof," who do things apparently right and good, but who have neither the life of Christ in their souls, the love of God in their hearts, nor the power of the Word in their consciences.

"But," adds the inspired apostle, "they shall proceed no further, for their folly shall be manifested unto all, as theirs also was." Truly the "folly" of "Jannes and Jambres" was manifest unto all, when they not only failed to imitate the further actings of Moses and Aaron, but actually became involved in the judgments of God. This is a solemn point. The folly of all who are merely possessed of the form will, in like manner, be made manifest. They will not only be quite unable to imitate the full and proper effects of divine life and power, but they themselves become the subjects of those judgments which will result from the rejection of that truth which they have resisted.

Will any one say that all this has no voice for a day of powerless profession? Assuredly it has. It should speak to each conscience in living power; it should tell on each heart, in accents of impressive solemnity. It should lead each one to inquire seriously whether he is testifying for the truth, by walking in the power of godliness, or hindering it, and neutralizing its action, by having only the form. The effect of the power of godliness will be seen by our "continuing in the things which we have learned." None will continue, save those who are taught of God; those, by the power of the Spirit of God, have drunk in divine principle, at the pure fountain of inspiration.

Blessed be God, there are many such throughout the various sections of the professing Church. There are many, here and there, whose consciences have been bathed in the atoning blood of "the Lamb of God," whose hearts beat high with genuine attachment to His Person, and whose spirits are cheered by "that blessed hope" of seeing Him as He is, and of being eternally conformed to His image. It is encouraging to think of such. It is an unspeakable mercy to have fellowship with those who can give a reason of the hope that is in them, and for the position which they occupy. May the Lord add to their number daily. May the power of godliness spread far and wide in these last days, so that a bright and well-sustained testimony may be raised to the name of Him who is worthy.

The third point in our section yet remains to be considered, namely, Pharaoh's four subtle objections to the full deliverance and complete separation of God's people from the land of Egypt. The first of these we have in chapter 8:25: "And Pharaoh called for Moses and Aaron, and said, 'Go ye, *sacrifice to your God in the land.*' " It is needless to remark here, that whether the magicians withstood, or Pharaoh objected, it was, in reality, Satan that stood behind the scenes; and his manifest object, in this proposal of Pharaoh, was to hinder the testimony to the Lord's name—a testimony connected with the thorough separation of His people from Egypt. There could evidently be no such testimony had they remained in Egypt, even though they were to sacrifice to Him. They would have taken common ground with the uncircumcised Egyptians, and put Jehovah on a level with the gods of Egypt. In this case, an Egyptian could have said to an Israelite, I see no difference between us; you have your worship, we have ours; it is all alike.

As a matter of course, men think it quite right for every one to have a religion, let it be what it may. Provided we are sincere, and do not interfere with our neighbor's creed, it does not matter what shape our religion may happen to wear. Such are the thoughts of men in reference to what they call religion; but it is very obvious that the glory of the name of Jesus finds no place in all this. The demand for separation is that which the enemy will ever oppose, and which the heart of man cannot understand. The heart may crave religiousness, because conscience testifies that all is not right; but it craves the world as well. It would like to "sacrifice to God in the land;" and Satan's object is gained when people accept of a worldly religion, and refuse to "come out and be separate" (2 Cor. 6). His unvarying purpose from the beginning has been to hinder the testimony to God's name on the earth. Such was the dark tendency of the proposal, "Go ye, sacrifice to your God in the land." What a complete damper to the testimony, had this proposal been acceded to! God's people in

Egypt and God Himself linked with the idols of Egypt! Terrible blasphemy!

Reader, we should deeply ponder this. The effort to induce Israel to worship God in Egypt reveals a far deeper principle than we might, at first sight, imagine. The enemy would rejoice, at any time, by any means, or under any circumstances, to get even the semblance of divine sanction for the world's religion. He has no objections to such religion. He gains his end as effectually by what is termed "the religious world" as by any other agency; and hence, when he can succeed in getting a true Christian to accredit the religion of the day, he gains a grand point. As a matter of actual fact, one knows that nothing elicits such intense indignation as the divine principle of separation from this present evil world. You may hold the same opinions, preach the same doctrines, do the same work; but if you only attempt, in ever so feeble a manner, to act upon the divine commands, "From such turn away" (2 Tim. 3:5), and "Come out from among them" (2 Cor. 6:17), you may reckon assuredly upon the most vigorous opposition. Now how is this to be accounted for? Mainly by the fact that Christians, in separation from this world's hollow religiousness, bear a testimony for Christ which they never can bear while connected with it.

There is a very wide difference between human religion and Christ. A poor, benighted Hindoo might talk to you of his religion, but he knows nothing of Christ. The apostle does not say, If there be any consolation in religion; though, doubtless, the votaries of each kind of religion find what they deem consolation therein. Paul, on the other hand, found his consolation in Christ, having fully proved the worthlessness of religion, and that, too, in its fairest and most imposing form (comp. Gal. 1:13-14; Phil. 3:4-11).

True, the Spirit of God speaks to us of "pure religion and undefiled;" but the unregenerate man cannot, by any means, participate therein; for how could he possibly take part in aught that is "pure and undefiled"? This religion is from heaven, the source of all that is pure and lovely; it is exclusively before the eye of "God and the Father;" it is for the exercise of the functions of that new nature with which all are endowed who believe on the name of the Son of God (John 1:12-13; James 1:18; 1 Peter 1:23; 1 John 5:1). Finally, it ranges itself under the two comprehensive heads of active benevolence and personal holiness—"To visit the fatherless and widows in their affliction, and to keep himself unspotted from the world" (James 1:27).

Now, if you go through the entire catalogue of the genuine fruits of Christianity, you will find them all classed under these two heads; and it is deeply interesting to observe that, whether we turn to the eighth of Exodus or the first of James, we find separation from the world put forward as an indispensable quality in the true service of God. Nothing could be acceptable before God—nothing could receive from His hand the stamp of "pure and undefiled," which was polluted by contact with an "evil world." " 'Come out from among them, and be ye separate,' saith the Lord, 'and touch not the unclean thing; and I will receive you, and will be a Father unto you, and ye shall be My sons and daughters,' saith the Lord Almighty" (2 Cor. 6:17-18).

There was no meeting-place for Jehovah and His redeemed in Egypt; yea, with them, redemption and separation from Egypt were one and the same thing. God had said, "I am come down to deliver them," and nothing short of this could either satisfy or glorify Him. A salvation which would have left them still in Egypt could not possibly be God's salvation. Moreover, we must bear in mind that Jehovah's purpose in the salvation of Israel, as well as in the destruction of Pharaoh, was, that "His name might be declared throughout all the earth;" and what declaration could there be of that name or character were His people to attempt to worship Him in Egypt? Either none whatever or an utterly false one. Wherefore it was essentially necessary, in order to the full and faithful declaration of God's character, that His people should be wholly delivered and completely separated from Egypt; and it is as essentially necessary now, in order to a clear and unequivocal testimony for the Son of God, that all who are really His should be separated from this present world. Such is the will of God; and for this end Christ gave Himself. "Grace unto you and peace from God the Father, and our Lord Jesus Christ, who gave Himself for our sins, that He might deliver us from this present evil world, according to the will of God and our Father; to whom be glory forever and ever. Amen" (Gal. 1:3-5).

The Galatians were beginning to accredit a carnal and worldly religion—a religion of ordinances—a religion of "days, and months, and times, and years;" and the apostle commences his Epistle by telling them that the Lord Jesus Christ gave Himself for the purpose of delivering His people from that very thing. God's people must be separate, not, by any means, on the grounds of their superior personal sanctity, but because they are His people, and in order that they may rightly and intelligently answer His gracious end in taking them into connection with Himself, and attaching His name to them. A people still amid the defilements and abominations of Egypt could not have been a witness for the Holy One; nor can any one now, while mixed up with the defilements of a corrupt worldly religion, possibly be a bright and steady witness for a crucified and risen Christ.

The answer given by Moses to Pharaoh's first objection was a truly memorable one. "And Moses said, 'It is not meet so to do; for we shall sacrifice the abomination of the Egyptians to the Lord our God; lo, shall we sacrifice the abomination of the Egyptians before their eyes, and will they not stone us? We will go three days' journey into the wilderness, and sacrifice to the Lord our God, as He shall command us' " (chap. 8:26-27). Here is true separation from Egypt—"three days' journey." Nothing less than this could satisfy faith. The Israel of God must be separated from the land of death and darkness, in the power of resurrection. The waters of the Red Sea must roll between God's redeemed and Egypt ere they can properly sacrifice to Jehovah. Had they remained in Egypt, they would have to sacrifice to the Lord the very objects of Egypt's abominable worship.* This would never do. There could be no tabernacle, no temple, no altar, in Egypt. It had no site, throughout its entire limits, for aught of that kind. In point of fact, as we shall see further on, Israel never presented so much as a single note of praise until the whole congregation stood, in the full power of an accomplished redemption, on Canaan's side of the Red Sea. Exactly so is it now. The believer must know where the death and resurrection of the Lord Jesus Christ have forever set him, ere he can be an intelligent worshiper, an acceptable servant, or an effectual witness.

It is not a question of being a child of God, and, as such, a saved person. Many of the children of God are very far from knowing the full results, as regards themselves, of the death and resurrection of Christ. They do not apprehend the precious truth, that the death of Christ has made an end of their sins forever, and that they are the happy partakers of His resurrection life, with which sin can have nothing whatever to do. Christ became a curse for us, not, as some would teach us, by being born under the curse of a broken law, but by hanging on a tree. (Compare, attentively, Deut. 21:23; Gal. 3:13.) We were under the curse because we had not kept the law; but Christ, the perfect Man, having magnified the law and made it honorable, by the very fact of His obeying it perfectly, became a curse for us by hanging on the tree. Thus, in His life He magnified God's law, and in His death He bore our curse. There is therefore now no guilt, no curse, no wrath, no condemnation for the believer; and, albeit, he must be manifested before the judgment-seat of Christ; but even there the question of *sin* is not raised. The cross of Christ has settled that forever; so that it is written of those that believe, *"And their sins and iniquities will I remember no more"* (Heb. 10:17). The Christian's whole course must indeed be manifested before the judgment-seat of Christ; but the Judge Him-

*The word "abomination" has reference to that which the Egyptians worshiped.

self has put away all his sins, and is his righteousness, so that the judgment-seat cannot but be friendly to him. He surely will not condemn His own work. The righteousness that was required, God Himself has provided it. He surely will not find any flaw therein. The light of the judgment-seat will be bright enough to disperse every mist and cloud which might tend to obscure the matchless glories and eternal virtues which belong to the cross, and to show that the believer is "clean every whit" (John 13:10; 15:3; Eph. 5:27).

It is because these foundation-truths are not laid hold of in the simplicity of faith that many of the children of God complain of their lack of settled peace—the constant variation in their spiritual condition—the continual ups and downs in their experience. Every doubt in the heart of a Christian is a dishonor done to the Word of God and the sacrifice of Christ. It is because he does not, even now, bask in the light which shines from the cross of Christ, that he is ever afflicted with a doubt or a fear. And yet those things which so many have to deplore —those fluctuations and waverings—are but trifling consequences, comparatively, inasmuch as they merely affect their experience. The effect produced upon their worship, their service, and their testimony, is far more serious, inasmuch as the Lord's honor is concerned. But, alas! this latter is but little thought of, generally speaking, simply because the personal salvation is the grand object—the aim and end—with the majority of professing Christians. We are prone to look upon everything that affects ourselves as *essential;* whereas, all that merely affects the glory of Christ in and by us is counted *non-essential.*

However, it is well to see with distinctness, that the same truth which gives the soul settled peace, puts it also into the position of intelligent worship, acceptable service, and effectual testimony. In the fifteenth chapter of 1 Corinthians, the apostle sets forth the death and resurrection of Christ as the grand foundation of everything. "Moreover, brethren, I declare unto you the gospel which I preached unto you, which also ye have received, and wherein ye stand; by which also ye are saved, if ye keep in memory what I preached unto you, unless ye have believed in vain. For I delivered unto you first of all that which I also received, how that Christ died for our sins according to the Scriptures, and that He was buried, and that He rose again the third day according to the Scriptures" (ver. 1-4). Here is the gospel in one brief and comprehensive statement. A dead and risen Christ is the groundwork of salvation. "He was delivered for our offences, and raised again for our justification" (Rom. 4:25). To see Jesus, by the eye of faith, nailed to the cross, and seated on the throne, must give solid peace to the conscience and perfect liberty to the heart. We can look into the tomb, and see it empty; we can look up to the throne, and see it occupied, and go on our way rejoicing. The Lord Jesus settled everything on the cross on behalf of His people; and the proof of this settlement is that He is now at the right hand of God. A risen Christ is the eternal proof of an accomplished redemption; and if redemption is an accomplished fact, the believer's peace is a settled reality. We did not make peace, and never could make it; indeed, any effort on our part to make peace could only tend more fully to manifest us as *peace-breakers.* But Christ, having made peace by the blood of His cross, has taken His seat on high, triumphant over every enemy. By Him, God preaches peace. The word of the gospel conveys this peace; and the soul that believes the gospel, has peace—settled peace before God, for Christ is his peace (see Acts 10:36; Rom. 5:1; Eph. 2:14; Col. 1:20). In this way, God has not only satisfied His own claims, but, in doing so, He has found out a divinely righteous vent through which His boundless affections may flow down to the guiltiest of Adam's guilty progeny.

Then, as to the practical result of all this. The cross of Christ has not only put away the believer's sins, but also dissolved forever his connection with the world; and, on the ground of this, he is privileged to regard the world as a crucified *thing,* and to be regarded by it as a crucified one. Thus it stands with the believer and the world—it is crucified to him and he to it. This is the real, dignified position of every true Christian. The world's judgment about Christ was expressed in the position in which it deliberately placed Him. It got its choice as to whether it would have a murderer or Christ. It allowed the murderer to go free, but nailed Christ to the cross, between two thieves. Now, if the believer walks in the footprints of Christ—if he drinks into and manifests His spirit, he will occupy the very same place in the world's estimation; and, in this way, he will not merely know that, as to standing before God, he is crucified with Christ, but be led to realize it in his walk and experience every day.

But while the cross has thus effectually cut the connection between the believer and the world, the resurrection has brought him into the power of new ties and associations. If in the cross we see the world's judgment about Christ, in resurrection we see God's judgment. The world crucified Him, but "God hath highly exalted Him." Man gave Him the very lowest, God the very highest, place; and, inasmuch as the believer is called into full fellowship with God in His thoughts about Christ, he is enabled to turn the tables upon the world, and look upon it as a crucified thing. If, therefore, the believer is on one cross and the world on another, the moral distance between the two is vast indeed. And if it is vast in principle, so should it be in practice. The world and the Christian should have absolutely nothing in common; nor will they, except so far as he denies his Lord and Master. The believer proves himself false to Christ to the very same degree that he has fellowship with the world.

All this is plain enough; but where does it put us as regards this world? Truly, it puts us outside, and that completely. We are dead to the world and alive with Christ. We are at once partakers of His rejection by earth and His acceptance in heaven; and the joy of the latter makes us count as nothing the trial connected with the former. To be cast out of earth, without knowing that I have a place and a portion on high, would be intolerable; but when the glories of heaven fill the soul's vision, a little of earth goes a great way.

But some may feel led to ask, What is the world? It would be difficult to find a term more inaccurately defined than "world," or "worldliness;" for we are generally disposed to make worldliness begin a point or two above where we are ourselves. The Word of God, however, has, with perfect precision, defined what "the world" is, when it marks it as that which is "not of the Father." Hence, the deeper my fellowship with the Father, the keener will be my sense of what is worldly. This is the divine way of teaching. The more you delight in the Father's love, the more you reject the world. But who reveals the Father? The Son. How? By the power of the Holy Ghost. Wherefore, the more I am enabled, in the power of an ungrieved Spirit, to drink in the Son's revelation of the Father, the more accurate does my judgment become as to what is of the world. It is as the limits of God's kingdom expand in the heart, that the judgment as to worldliness becomes refined. You can hardly attempt to define worldliness. It is, as some one has said, "shaded off gradually from white to jet black." This is most true. You cannot place a bound and say, Here is where worldliness begins; but the keen and exquisite sensibilities of the divine nature recoil from it; and all we need is, to walk in the power of that nature, in order to keep aloof from every form of worldliness. "Walk in the Spirit, and ye shall not fulfill the lusts of the flesh." Walk with God, and ye shall not walk with the world. Cold distinctions and rigid rules will avail nothing. The power of the divine life is what we want. We want to understand the meaning and spiritual application of the "three days' journey into the wilderness," whereby we are separated forever, not only from Egypt's brick-kilns and taskmasters, but also from its temples and altars.

Pharaoh's second objection partook very much of the character and tendency of the first. "And Pharaoh said, 'I will let you go, that ye may sacrifice unto the Lord your God in the wilderness; *only ye shall not go very far away*'" (chap. 8:28). If he could not keep them *in* Egypt, he would at least seek to keep them *near* it, so that he might act upon them by its varied influences. In this way, they might be brought back again, and the testimony more effectually quashed than if they had never left Egypt at all. There is always much more serious damage done to the cause of Christ by persons seeming to give up the world and returning to it again, than if they had remained entirely of it; for they virtually confess that, having tried heavenly things, they have discovered that earthly things are better and more satisfying.

Nor is this all. The moral effect of truth upon the conscience of unconverted people is sadly interfered with, by the example of professors going back again into those things which they seemed to have left. Not that such cases afford the slightest warrant to any one for the rejection of God's truth, inasmuch as each one is personally responsible and will have to give account of himself to God. Still, however, the effect in this, as well as in everything else, is bad. "For if after they have escaped the pollutions of the world, through the knowledge of the Lord and Saviour Jesus Christ, they are again entangled therein and overcome, the latter end is worse with them than the beginning. For it would have been better for them not to have known the way of righteousness than, after they have known it, to turn from the holy commandment delivered unto them" (2 Peter 2:20-21).

Wherefore, if people do not "go very far away," they had better not go at all. The enemy knew this well; and hence his second objection. The maintenance of a border position suits his purpose amazingly. Those who occupy this ground are neither one thing nor the other; and, in point of fact, whatever influence they possess, tells entirely in the wrong direction.

It is deeply important to see that Satan's design, in all these objections, was to hinder that testimony to the name of the God of Israel, which could only be rendered by a "three days' journey into the wilderness." This was, in good truth, going "very far away." It was much farther than Pharaoh could form any idea of, or than he could follow them. And oh! how happy it would be if all who profess to set out from Egypt would really, in the spirit of their minds and in the tone of their character, go thus far away from it; if they would intelligently recognize the cross and grave of Christ as forming the boundary between them and the world! No man, in the mere energy of nature, can take this ground. The Psalmist could say, "Enter not into judgment with Thy servant, for in Thy sight shall no man living be justified" (Ps. 143:2). So also is it with regard to true and effectual separation from the world. *"No man living"* can enter into it. It is only as *"dead* with Christ," and "risen again with Him, through faith of the operation of God," that any one can either be "justified" before God, or separated from the world. This is what we may call going "very far away." May all who profess and call themselves Christians go thus far. Then will their lamp yield a steady light. Then would their trumpet give a certain sound. Their path would be elevated; their experience deep and rich; their peace would flow as a river; their affections would be heavenly and their garments unspotted. And, far above all, the name of the Lord Jesus Christ would be magnified in them, by the power of the Holy Ghost, according to the will of God their Father.

The third objection demands our most special attention. "And Moses and Aaron were brought again unto Pharaoh: and he said unto them, 'Go, serve the Lord your God; but who are they that shall go?' And Moses said, 'We will go with our young and with our old, with our sons and with our daughters, with our flocks and with our herds will we go; for we must hold a feast unto the Lord.' And he said unto them, 'Let the Lord be so with you, as I will let you go, and your little ones: look to it; for evil is before you. Not so; go now ye that are men, and serve the Lord; for that ye did desire.' And they were driven out from Pharaoh's presence" (chap. 10:8-11). Here, again, we have the enemy aiming a deadly blow at the testimony to the name of the God of Israel. Parents in the wilderness and their children in Egypt! Terrible anomaly! This would only have been a half deliverance, at once useless to Israel and dishonoring to Israel's God. This could not be. If the children remained in Egypt, the parents could not possibly be said to have left it, inasmuch as their children were part of themselves. The most that could be said in such a case was, that in part they were serving Jehovah, and in part Pharaoh. But Jehovah could have no part with Pharaoh. He should either have all or nothing. This is a weighty principle for Christian parents. May we lay it deeply to heart! It is our happy privilege to count on God for our children, and to "bring them up in the nurture and admonition of the Lord" (Eph. 6). We should not be satisfied with any other portion for "our little ones" than that which we ourselves enjoy.

Pharaoh's fourth and last objection had reference to the flocks and herds. "And Pharaoh called unto Moses, and said, 'Go ye, serve the Lord; only let your flocks and herds be stayed: let your little ones also go with you' " (chap. 10:24). With what perseverance did Satan dispute every inch of Israel's way out of the land of Egypt! He first sought to keep them *in* the land, then to keep them *near* the land, next to keep part of themselves in the land, and finally, when he could not succeed in any of these three, he sought to send them forth without any ability to serve the Lord. If he could not keep the servants, he would seek to keep their ability to serve, which would answer much the same end. If he could not induce them to sacrifice in the land, he would send them out of the land without sacrifices.

In Moses' reply to this last objection, we are furnished with a fine statement of the Lord's paramount claim upon His people and all pertaining to them. "And Moses said, 'Thou must give us also sacrifices and burnt offerings, that we may sacrifice unto the Lord our God. Our cattle also shall go with us; *there shall not a hoof be left behind:* for thereof must we take to serve the Lord our God; and we know not with what we must serve the Lord until we come thither' " (ver. 25-26). It is only when the people of God take their stand, in simple childlike faith, upon that elevated ground on which death and resurrection set them, that they can have anything like an adequate sense of His claims upon them. "We know not with what we must serve the Lord until we come thither." That is, they had no knowledge of the divine claim, or their responsibility, until they had gone "three days' journey." These things could not be known amid the dense and polluted atmosphere of Egypt. Redemption must be known as an accomplished fact, ere there can be any just or full perception of responsibility. All this is perfect and beautiful. "If any man will do His will, he shall know of the doctrine." I must be up out of Egypt, in the power of death and resurrection, and then, but not until then, shall I know what the Lord's service really is. It is when we take our stand, by faith, in that "large room," that wealthy place into which the precious blood of Christ introduces us,—when we look around us and survey the rich, rare, and manifold results of redeeming love, —when we gaze upon the Person of Him who has brought us into this place, and endowed us with these riches, then we are constrained to say, in the language of one of our own poets,—

> Were the whole realm of nature mine,
> That were an offering far too small;
> Love so amazing, so divine,
> Demands my heart, my life, my all.

"There shall not a hoof be left behind." Noble words! Egypt is not the place for aught that pertains to God's redeemed. He is worthy of all—"body, soul, and spirit;" all we are and all we have belongs to Him. "We are not our own, we are bought with a price;" and it is our happy privilege to consecrate ourselves and all that we possess to Him whose we are, and Him whom we are called to serve. There is naught of a legal spirit in this. The words, "until we come thither," furnish a divine guard against this horrible evil. We have traveled the "three days' journey," ere a word concerning sacrifice can be heard or understood. We are put in full and undisputed possession of resurrection life and eternal righteousness. We have left that land of death and darkness; we have been brought to God Himself, so that we may enjoy Him, in the energy of that life with which we are endowed, and in the sphere of righteousness in which we are placed: thus it is our joy to serve. There is not an affection in the heart of which He is not worthy; there is not a sacrifice in all the flock too costly for His altar. The more closely we walk with Him, the more we shall esteem it to be our meat and drink to do His blessed will. The believer counts it his highest privilege to serve the Lord. He delights in every exercise and every manifestation of the divine nature. He does not move up and down with a grievous yoke upon his neck, or an intolerable weight upon his shoulder. The yoke is broken "because of the anointing," the burden has been forever removed by the blood of the cross, while he himself walks abroad, "redeemed, regenerated, and disenthralled," in pursuance of those soul-stirring words, *"Let My people go."*

---

## *CHAPTER 11*

WE shall consider the contents of chapter 11 in connection with the security of Israel, under the shelter of the blood of the paschal lamb.

---

## *CHAPTER 12*

"AND the Lord said unto Moses, 'Yet will I bring one plague more upon Pharaoh, and upon Egypt; afterwards he will let you go hence: when he shall let you go, he shall surely thrust you out hence altogether' " (chap. 11:1). One more heavy blow must fall upon this hard-hearted monarch and his land ere he will be compelled to let go the favored objects of Jehovah's sovereign grace.

How utterly vain it is for man to harden and exalt himself against God; for, truly, He can grind to powder the hardest heart, and bring down to the dust the haughtiest spirit. "Those that walk in pride He is able to abase" (Dan. 4:37). Man may fancy himself to be something; he may lift up his head, in pomp and vainglory, as though he were his own master. Vain man! how little he knows of his real condition and character! He is but the tool of Satan, taken up and used by him, in his malignant efforts to counteract the purposes of God. The most splendid intellect, the most commanding genius, the most indomitable energy, if not under the direct control of the Spirit of God, are but so many instruments in Satan's hand to carry forward his dark designs. No man is his own master; he is either governed by Christ or governed by Satan. The king of Egypt might fancy himself to be a free agent, yet he was but a tool in the hands of another. Satan was behind the throne; and, as the result of Pharaoh's having set himself to resist the purposes of God, he was judicially handed over to the blinding and hardening influence of his self-chosen master.

This will explain to us an expression occurring very frequently throughout the earlier chapters of this book, "The Lord hardened Pharaoh's heart." There is no need whatever for any one to seek to avoid the full, plain sense of this most solemn statement. If man resists the light of divine testimony, he is shut up to judicial blindness and hardness of heart. God leaves him to himself, and then Satan comes in and carries him headlong to perdition. There was abundant light for Pharaoh, to show him the extravagant folly of his course in seeking to detain those whom God had commanded him to let go. But the real disposition of his heart was to act against God, and therefore God left him to himself, and made him a monument for the display of His glory "through all the earth." There is no difficulty in this to any, save those whose desire is to argue against God—"to rush upon the thick bosses of the shield of the Almighty"—to ruin their own immortal souls.

God gives people, at times, according to the real bent of their hearts' desire; ". . . because of this, God shall send them strong delusion, that they should believe a lie; that they all might be damned who believed not the truth, but *had pleasure in unrighteousness*" (2 Thess. 2:11-12). If men will not have the truth when it is put before them, they shall assuredly have a lie. If they will not have Christ, they shall have Satan; if they will not have heaven, they shall have hell.* Will the infidel mind find fault with this? Ere it does so, let it prove that all who are thus judicially dealt with have fully answered their responsibilities. Let it, for instance, prove, in Pharaoh's case, that he acted, in any measure, up to the light he possessed. The same is to be proved in every case. Unquestionably, the task of proving rests on those who are disposed to quarrel with God's mode of dealing with the rejecters of His truth. The simple-hearted child of God will justify Him, in view of the most inscrutable dispensations; and even if he cannot meet and satisfactorily solve the difficult questions of a sceptical mind, he can rest perfectly satisfied with this word, "Shall not the Judge of all the earth do right?" There is far more wisdom in this method of settling an apparent difficulty, than in the most elaborate argument; for it is perfectly certain that the heart which is in a condition to "reply against God," will not be convinced by the arguments of man.

However, it is God's prerogative to answer all the proud reasonings, and bring down the lofty imaginations of the human mind. He can write the sentence of death upon nature, in its fairest forms. "It is appointed unto men once to die." This cannot be avoided. Man may seek to hide his humiliation in various ways—to cover his retreat through the valley of death in the most heroic manner possible, to call the last humiliating stage of his career by the most honorable titles he can devise; to gild the bed of death with a false light; to adorn the funeral procession and the grave with the appearance of pomp, pageantry, and glory; to raise above the mouldering ashes a splendid monument, on which are engraven the records of human shame; all these things he may do; but death is death after all, and he cannot keep it off for a moment, or make it aught else than what it is, namely, "the wages of sin."

The foregoing thoughts are suggested by the opening verse of chapter 11—"One plague more!" Solemn word! It signed the death-warrant of Egypt's first-born—"the chief of all their strength." "And Moses said, 'Thus saith the Lord, About midnight will I go out into the midst of Egypt; and all the first-born in the land of Egypt shall die, from the first-born of Pharaoh that sitteth upon his throne, even unto the first-born of the maid-servant that is behind the mill; and all the first-born of beasts. And there shall be a great cry throughout all the land of Egypt, such as there was none like it, nor shall it be like it any more' " (chap. 11:4-6). This was to be the final plague—death in every house. "But against any of the children of Israel shall not a dog move his tongue, against man or beast; that ye may know how that the Lord doth put a difference between the Egyptians and Israel." It is the Lord alone who can "put a difference" between those who are His and those who are not. It is not our province to say to any one, "Stand by thyself; I am holier than thou:" this is the language of a Pharisee. "But when God puts a difference," we are bound to inquire what that difference is; and, in the case before us, we see it to be a simple question of *life or death.* This is God's grand "difference." He draws a line of demarkation, and on one side of this line is "life," on the other "death." Many of Egypt's first-born might have been as fair and attractive as those of Israel, and much more so; but Israel had life and light, founded upon God's counsels of redeeming love, established, as we shall see presently, by the blood of the lamb. This was Israel's happy position; while, on the other hand,

*There is a vast difference between the divine method of dealing with the heathen (Rom. 1) and with the rejecters of the gospel (2 Thess. 1:11). In reference to the former, we read, "And even as they did not like to retain God in their knowledge, God gave them over to a reprobate mind:" but with respect to the latter, the word is, "Because they received not the love of *the truth* that they might *be saved* . . . God shall send them strong delusion, that they should believe *a lie;* that they all might *be damned.*" The heathen refuse the testimony of creation, and are therefore left to themselves. The rejecters of the gospel refuse the full blaze of light which shines from the cross, and therefore "a strong delusion" will, ere long, be sent from God upon them. This is deeply solemn for an age like this, in the which there is so much light and so much profession.

throughout the length and breadth of the land of Egypt, from the monarch on the throne to the menial behind the mill, nothing was to be seen but death; nothing to be heard but the cry of bitter anguish, elicited by the heavy stroke of Jehovah's rod. God can bring down the haughty spirit of man. He can make the wrath of man to praise Him, and restrain the remainder. "And all these thy servants shall come down unto me, and bow down themselves unto me, saying, Get thee out, and all the people that follow thee: and after that I will go out." God will accomplish His own ends. His schemes of mercy must be carried out at all cost, and confusion of face must be the portion of all who stand in the way. "O, give thanks unto the Lord; for He is good: for His mercy endureth forever. . . . To Him that smote Egypt in their first-born; for His mercy endureth forever: and brought out Israel from among them; for His mercy endureth forever: with a strong hand and with a stretched-out arm; for His mercy endureth forever" (Ps. 136).

"And the Lord spake unto Moses and Aaron in the land of Egypt, saying, 'This month shall be unto you the beginning of months: it shall be the first month of the year to you' " (chap. 12:1-2). There is here a very interesting change in the order of time. The common or civil year was rolling on in its ordinary course, when Jehovah interrupted it in reference to His people, and thus, in principle, taught them that they were to begin a new era in company with Him; their previous history was henceforth to be regarded as a blank. Redemption was to constitute the first step in *real life.*

This teaches a plain truth. A man's life is really of no account until he begins to walk with God, in the knowledge of full salvation and settled peace, through the precious blood of the Lamb. Previous to this, he is, in the judgment of God, and in the language of Scripture, "dead in trespasses and sins;" "alienated from the life of God." His whole history is a complete blank, even though, in man's account, it may have been one uninterrupted scene of bustling activity. All that which engages the attention of the man of this world—the honors, the riches, the pleasures, the attractions of life, so called—all, when examined in the light of the judgment of God, when weighed in the balances of the sanctuary, must be accounted as a dismal blank, a worthless void, utterly unworthy of a place in the records of the Holy Ghost. "He that believeth not the Son shall not see life" (John 3:36). Men speak of "seeing life" when they launch forth into society, travel hither and thither, and see all that is to be seen; but they forget that the only true, the only real, the only divine way to "see life," is to "believe on the Son of God."

How little do men think of this! They imagine that "real life" is at an end when a man becomes a Christian, in truth and reality, not merely in name and outward profession; whereas God's Word teaches us that it is only then we can see life and taste true happiness. "He that hath the Son, hath life" (1 John 5:12). And, again, "Happy is he whose transgression is forgiven, whose sin is covered" (Ps. 32:1). We can get life and happiness *only* in Christ. Apart from Him, all is death and misery, in Heaven's judgment, whatever the outward appearance may be. It is when the thick vail of unbelief is removed from the heart, and we are enabled to behold, with the eye of faith, the bleeding Lamb, bearing our heavy burden of guilt upon the cursed tree, that we enter upon the path of life, and partake of the cup of divine happiness, a life which begins at the cross, and flows onward into an eternity of glory, a happiness which, each day, becomes deeper and purer, more connected with God and founded on Christ, until we reach its proper sphere, in the presence of God and the Lamb. To seek life and happiness in any other way is vainer work by far than seeking to make bricks without straw.

True, the enemy of souls spreads a gilding over this passing scene, in order that men may imagine it to be all gold. He sets up many a puppet-show to elicit the hollow laugh from a thoughtless multitude, who will not remember that it is Satan who is in the box, and that his object is to keep them from Christ, and drag them down into eternal perdition. There is nothing real, nothing solid, nothing satisfying, but in Christ. Outside of Him, "all is vanity and vexation of spirit." In Him alone true and eternal joys are to be found; and we only begin to live when we begin to live *in,* live *on,* live *with,* and live *for* Him. "This month shall be unto you the beginning of months: it shall be the first month of the year to you." The time spent in the brick-kilns and by the flesh-pots must be ignored. It is henceforth to be of no account, save that the remembrance thereof should ever and anon serve to quicken and deepen their sense of what divine grace had accomplished on their behalf.

"Speak ye unto all the congregation of Israel, saying, In the tenth day of this month they shall take to them every man a lamb according to the house of their fathers, a lamb for a house. . . . Your lamb shall be without blemish, a male of the first year; ye shall take it out from the sheep or from the goats: and ye shall keep it up until the fourteenth day of the same month; and the whole assembly of the congregation of Israel shall kill it in the evening." Here we have the redemption of the people founded upon the blood of the lamb, in pursuance of God's eternal purpose. This imparts to it all its divine stability. Redemption was no afterthought with God. Before the world was, or Satan, or sin—before ever the voice of God was heard breaking the silence of eternity, and calling worlds into existence, He had His deep counsels of love; and these counsels could never find a sufficiently solid basis in creation. All the blessings, the privileges, and the dignities of creation were founded upon a creature's obedience, and the moment that failed, all was gone. But then, Satan's attempt to mar creation only opened the way for the manifestation of God's deeper purposes of redemption.

This beautiful truth is typically presented to us in the circumstance of the lamb's being "kept up" from the "tenth" to "the fourteenth day." That this lamb pointed to Christ is unquestionable. 1 Cor. 5:7 settles the application of this interesting type beyond all question,—"For even Christ our passover is sacrificed for us." We have, in the first Epistle of Peter, an allusion to the keeping up of the lamb,—"Forasmuch as ye know that ye were not redeemed with corruptible things, as silver and gold, from your vain conversation, received by tradition from your fathers; but with the precious blood of Christ, as of a lamb without blemish and without spot: who verily was *foreordained before the foundation of the world,* but was *manifest in these last times for you*" (chap. 1:18-20).

All God's purposes from everlasting had reference to Christ, and no effort of the enemy could possibly interfere with those counsels; yea, his efforts only tended to the display of the unfathomable wisdom and immovable stability thereof. If the "Lamb without blemish and without spot" was "foreordained before the foundation of the world," then, assuredly, redemption must have been in the mind of God before the foundation of the world. The blessed One had not to pause in order to devise some plan to remedy the terrible evil which the enemy had introduced into His fair creation. No; He had only to bring forth, from the unexplored treasury of His precious counsels, the truth concerning the spotless Lamb, who was foreordained from everlasting, and to be "manifest in these last times for us."

There was no need for the blood of the Lamb in creation as it came fresh from the hand of the Creator, exhibiting, in every stage and every department of it, the beauteous impress of His hand—"the infallible proofs" of "His eternal power and Godhead" (Rom. 1); but when, "by one man," sin was introduced into the world, then came out the higher, richer, fuller, deeper thought of redemption by the blood of the Lamb. This glorious truth first broke through the thick clouds which surrounded our first parents, as they retreated from the garden of Eden; its glimmerings appear in the types and shadows of the Mosaic economy; it burst upon the world in full brightness when "the dayspring from on high" appeared in the Person of "God manifest in the flesh;" and its rich and rare results will be realized when the white-robed, palm-bearing multitude shall cluster round the throne of God and the Lamb, and the whole creation shall rest beneath the peaceful sceptre of the Son of David.

Now, the lamb taken on the tenth day, and kept up until the fourteenth day, shows us Christ foreordained of God from eternity, but manifest for us in time. God's eternal purpose in Christ becomes the foundation of the believer's peace. Nothing short of this would do. We are carried back far beyond creation, beyond the bounds of time, beyond the entrance in of sin and everything that could possibly affect the ground-work of our peace. The expression, "foreordained before the foundation of the world," conducts us back into the unfathomed depths of eternity, and shows us God forming His own counsels of redeeming love, and basing them all upon the atoning blood of His own precious, spotless Lamb. Christ was ever the primary thought in the divine mind; and hence, the moment He began to speak or act, He took occasion to shadow forth that One who occupied the highest place in His counsels and affections; and, as we pass along the current of inspiration, we find that every ceremony, every rite, every ordinance, and every sacrifice pointed forward to "the Lamb of God that taketh away the sin of the world," and not one more strikingly than the passover. The paschal lamb, with all the attendant circumstances, forms one of the most profoundly interesting and deeply instructive types of Scripture.

In the interpretation of Exodus 12, we have to do with *one* assembly and *one* sacrifice.—"The whole assembly of the congregation of Israel shall kill *it* in the evening" (ver. 6). It is not so much a number of families with several lambs—a thing quite true in itself—as one assembly and one lamb. Each house was but the local expression of the whole assembly gathered round the lamb. The antitype of this we have in the whole Church of God, gathered by the Holy Ghost, in the name of Jesus, of which each separate assembly, wherever convened, should be the local expression.

"And they shall take of the blood, and strike it on the two side-posts and on the upper door-post of the houses, wherein they shall eat it. And they shall eat the flesh in that night, roast with fire, and unleavened bread; and with bitter herbs they shall eat it. Eat not of it raw, nor sodden at all with water, but roast with fire; his head with his legs, and with the purtenance thereof" (ver. 7-9). We have to contemplate the paschal lamb in two aspects, namely, as the ground of peace, and the centre of unity. The blood on the lintel secured Israel's peace.—"When I see the blood, I will pass over you" (ver. 13). There was nothing more required in order to enjoy settled peace, in reference to the destroying angel, than the application of the blood of sprinkling. Death had to do its work in every house throughout the land of Egypt. "It is appointed unto men once to die." But God, in His great mercy, found an unblemished substitute for Israel, on which the sentence of death was executed. Thus God's claims and Israel's need were met by one and the same thing, namely, the blood of the lamb. That blood outside proved that *all* was perfectly, because divinely, settled; and therefore perfect peace reigned within. A shade of doubt in the bosom of an Israelite would have been a dishonor offered to the divinely appointed ground of peace—the blood of atonement.

True it is that each one within the blood-sprinkled door would necessarily feel that were he to receive his due reward, the sword of the destroyer should most assuredly find its object in him; but then the lamb was treated in his stead. This was the solid foundation of his peace. The judgment that was due to him fell upon a divinely appointed victim; and believing this, he could feed in peace within. A single doubt would have made Jehovah a liar; for He had said, "When I see the *blood,* I will pass over you." This was enough. It was no question of personal worthiness. Self had nothing whatever to do in the matter. All under the cover of the blood were safe. They were not merely in a salvable state, they were *saved.* They were not hoping or praying to be saved; they knew it as an assured fact, on the authority of that Word which shall endure throughout all generations. Moreover, they were not partly saved and partly exposed to judgment; they were wholly saved. The blood of the lamb and the word of the Lord formed the foundation of Israel's peace on that terrible night in which Egypt's first-born were laid low. If a hair of an Israelite's head could be touched, it would have proved Jehovah's word void, and the blood of the lamb valueless.

It is most needful to be simple and clear as to what constitutes the ground of a sinner's peace in the presence of God. So many things are mixed up with the finished work of Christ, that souls are plunged into darkness and uncertainty as to their acceptance. They do not see the absolutely settled character of redemption through the blood of Christ, in its application to themselves. They seem not to be aware that full forgiveness of sin rests upon the simple fact that a full atonement has been offered,—a fact attested, in the view of all created intelligence, by the resurrection of the sinner's Surety from the dead. They know that there is no other way of being saved but by the blood of the cross (but the devils know this, yet it avails them naught). What is so much needed is to know that *we are saved.* The Israelite not merely knew that there was safety in the blood; he knew that *he* was *safe.* And why safe? Was it because of anything that he had done, or felt, or thought? By no means; but because God had said, "When I see the blood, I will pass over you." He rested upon God's testimony: he believed what God said, because God said it: "He set to his seal that God was true."

And, observe, my reader, it was not by his own thoughts, feelings, or experiences, respecting the blood, that the Israelite rested. This would have been a poor, sandy foundation to rest upon. His thoughts and feelings might be deep or they might be shallow; but, deep or shallow, they had nothing to do with the ground of his peace. It was not said, When *you* see the blood, and value it as you ought, I will pass over you. This would have been sufficient to plunge him in dark despair about himself, inasmuch as it was quite impossible that the human mind could ever sufficiently appreciate the precious blood of the lamb. What gave peace was the fact that Jehovah's eye rested upon the blood, and that He knew its worth. This tranquilized the heart. The blood was outside, and the Israelite inside, so that he could not possibly see it; but God saw it, and that was quite enough.

The application of this to the question of a sinner's peace is very plain. The Lord Jesus Christ having shed His precious blood, as a perfect atonement for sin, has taken it into the presence of God, and sprinkled it there; and God's testimony assures the believing sinner that everything is settled on his behalf—settled not by his estimate of the blood, but by the blood itself, which God estimates so highly, that because of it, without a single jot or tittle added thereto, He can righteously forgive all sin, and accept the sinner as perfectly righteous in Christ. How can any one ever enjoy settled peace if his peace depends upon his estimate of the blood? Impossible! The loftiest estimate which the human mind can form of the blood must fall infinitely short of its divine preciousness; and therefore, if our peace were to depend upon our valuing it as we ought, we could no more enjoy settled peace than if we were seeking it by "works of law." There must either be a sufficient ground of peace in the blood *alone,* or we can never have peace. To mix up our estimate with it, is to upset the entire fabric of Christianity, just as effectually as if we were to conduct the sinner to the foot of mount Sinai, and put him under a covenant of works. Either Christ's atoning sacrifice is sufficient or it is not. If it is sufficient, why those doubts and fears? The words of our *lips* profess that the work is finished; but the doubts and fears of the *heart* declare that it is not. Every one who doubts his full and everlasting forgiveness, denies, so far as he is concerned, the completeness of the sacrifice of Christ.

But there are very many who would shrink from the idea of deliberately and avowedly calling in question the efficacy of the blood of Christ, who, nevertheless, have not settled peace. Such persons profess to be quite assured of the sufficiency of the blood, *if* only *they* were sure of an interest therein —*if only* they had the right kind of faith.

There are many precious souls in this unhappy condition. They are occupied with their interest and their faith, instead of with Christ's blood and God's word. In other words, they are looking in at self, instead of out at Christ. This is not faith; and, as a consequence, they have not peace. An Israelite within the blood-stained lintel could teach such souls a most seasonable lesson. He was not saved by his interest in, or his thoughts about, the blood, but simply by the blood. No doubt he had a blessed interest in it, and he would have his thoughts likewise; but then God did not say, When I see your interest in the blood, I will pass over you. Oh, no! *The Blood,* in all its solitary dignity and divine efficacy, was set before Israel; and had they attempted to place even a morsel of unleavened bread beside the blood, as a ground of security, they would have made Jehovah a liar, and denied the sufficiency of His remedy.

We are ever prone to look at something in or connected with ourselves as necessary, in order to make up, with the blood of Christ, the ground-work of our peace. There is a sad lack of clearness and soundness on this vital point, as is evident from the doubts and fears with which so many of the people of God are afflicted. We are apt to regard the fruits of the Spirit *in* us, rather than the work of Christ *for* us, as the foundation of peace. We shall see, presently, the place which the work of the Holy Spirit occupies in Christianity; but it is never set forth in Scripture as being that on which our peace reposes. The Holy Ghost did not make peace, but Christ did. The Holy Ghost is not said to be our peace, but Christ is. God did not send preaching peace by the Holy Ghost, but by Jesus Christ (comp. Acts 10:36; Eph. 2:14,17; Col. 1:20). My reader cannot be too simple in his apprehension of this important distinction. It is the blood of Christ which gives peace, imparts perfect justification—divine righteousness, purges the conscience, brings us into the holiest of all, justifies God in receiving the believing sinner, and constitutes our title to all the joys, the dignities, and the glories of heaven. (See Rom. 3:24-26; 5:9; Eph. 2:13-18; Col. 1:20-22; Heb. 9:14; 10:19; 1 Peter 1:19; 2:24; 1 John 1:7; Rev. 7:14-17.)

It will not be supposed that, in seeking to put "the precious blood of Christ" in its divinely appointed place, I would write a single line which might seem to detract from the value of the Spirit's operations. God forbid. The Holy Ghost reveals Christ; makes us to know, enjoy, and feed upon Christ; He bears witness to Christ; He takes of the things of Christ and shows them unto us. He is the power of communion, the seal, the witness, the earnest, the unction. In short, His blessed operations are absolutely essential. Without Him, we can neither see, hear, know, feel, experience, enjoy, nor exhibit aught of Christ. This is plain. The doctrine of the Spirit's operations is clearly laid down in the Word, and is understood and admitted by every true and rightly-instructed Christian.

Yet, notwithstanding all this, the work of the Spirit is not the ground of peace; for, if it were, we could not have settled peace until Christ's coming, inasmuch as the work of the Spirit, in the Church, will not, properly speaking, be complete till then. He still carries on His work in the believer. "He maketh intercession with groanings which cannot be uttered" (Rom. 8). He labors to bring us up to the predestinated standard, namely, perfect conformity, in all things, to the image of "the Son." He is the sole Author of every right desire, every holy aspiration, every pure affection, every divine experience, every sound conviction; but, clearly, His work *in* us will not be complete until we have left this present scene and taken our place with Christ in the glory. Just as, in the case of Abraham's servant, his work was not complete, in the matter of Rebecca, until he had presented her to Isaac.

Not so the work of Christ *for* us. That is absolutely and eternally complete. He could say, "I have finished the work which Thou gavest Me to do" (John 17:4). And, again, "It is finished" (John 19:30). The Holy Ghost cannot yet say He has finished His work. As the true Vicar of Christ upon earth, He still labors amid the varied hostile influences which surround the sphere of His operations. He works in the hearts of the people of God to bring them up, practically and experimentally, to the divinely appointed standard; but He never teaches a soul to lean on His work for peace in the presence of God. His office is to speak of Jesus. He does not speak of Himself. "He," says Christ, "shall receive of Mine and shall show it unto you" (John 16:13-14). If, then, it is only by the Spirit's teaching that any one can understand the true ground of peace, and if the Spirit never speaks of Himself, it is obvious that He can only present Christ's work as the foundation on which the soul must rest forever; yea, it is in virtue of that work that He takes up His abode and carries on His marvelous operations in the believer. He is not our title, though He reveals that title and enables us to understand and enjoy it.

Hence, therefore, the paschal lamb, as the ground of Israel's peace, is a marked and beautiful type of Christ as the ground of the believer's peace. There was nothing to be added to the blood on the lintel; neither is there anything to be added to the blood on the mercy-seat. The "unleavened bread" and "bitter herbs" were necessary, but not as forming, either in whole or in part, the ground of peace. They were for the inside of the house, and formed the characteristics of the communion there; but *the blood of the lamb was the foundation of everything.* It saved them from death, and introduced them into a scene of life, light, and peace. It formed the link between God and His redeemed people. As a people linked with God, on the ground of accomplished redemption, it was their high privilege to meet certain responsibilities; but these responsibilities did not form the link, but merely flowed out of it.

And I would further remind my reader that the obedient *life* of Christ is not set forth in Scripture as the procuring cause of our forgiveness. It was His death upon the cross that opened those everlasting floodgates of love which else should have remained pent up forever. If He had remained to this very hour, going through the cities of Israel, "doing good," the vail of the temple would continue unrent, to bar the worshiper's approach to God. It was His death that rent that mysterious curtain "from top to bottom." It is "by *His stripes,*" not by His obedient life, that "we are healed;" and those "stripes" He endured *on the cross,* and no where else. His own words, during the progress of His blessed life, are quite sufficient to settle this point.—"I have a baptism to be baptized with; and how am I straitened till it be accomplished" (Luke 12:50). To what does this refer but to His death upon the cross, which was the accomplishment of His baptism and the opening up of a righteous vent through which His love might freely flow out to the guilty sons of Adam? Again, He says, "Except a corn of wheat fall into the ground and die, it abideth alone" (John 12:24). He was that precious "corn of wheat;" and He should have remained forever "alone," even though incarnate, had He not, by His death upon the accursed tree, removed out of the way everything that could have hindered the union of His people with Him in resurrection. "If it die, it bringeth forth much fruit."

My reader cannot too carefully ponder this subject. It is one of immense weight and importance. He has to remember two points in reference to this entire question, namely, that there could be no union with Christ, save in resurrection; and that Christ *only* suffered for sins on the cross. We are not to suppose that incarnation was, by any means, Christ taking us into union with Himself. This could not be. How could sinful flesh be thus united? The body of sin had to be destroyed by death. Sin had to be put away according to the divine requirement; all the power of the enemy had to be abolished. How was all this to be done? Only by the precious, spotless Lamb of God submitting to the death of the cross. "It became Him, for whom are all things, and by whom are all things, in bringing many sons unto glory, to make the Captain of their salvation perfect *through sufferings*" (Heb. 2:10). "Behold, I cast out devils, and I do cures to-day and to-morrow, and *the third day I shall be perfected*" (Luke 13:32). The expressions "perfect" and "perfected" in the above passages, do not refer to Christ in His own Person abstractedly, for He was perfect from all eternity, as Son of God; and as to His humanity, He was absolutely perfect likewise. But then, as "the Captain of salvation"—as "bringing many sons unto glory"—as "bringing forth much fruit"—as associating a redeemed people *with* Himself—He had to reach "the third day" in order to be "perfected." He went down *alone* into the "horrible pit, and miry clay"; but directly He plants His "foot on the rock" of resurrection, He associates with Himself the "many sons" (Psalm 40:1-3). He fought the fight alone; but, as the mighty Conqueror, He scatters around Him, in rich profusion, the spoils of victory, that we might gather them up and enjoy them forever.

Moreover, we are not to regard the cross of Christ as a mere circumstance in the life of sin-bearing. It was *the* grand and only scene of sin-bearing. "His own self bare our sins in His own body on the tree" (1 Peter 2:24). He did not bear them any where else. He did not bear them in the manger, nor in the wilderness, nor in the garden; but *only "on the tree."* He never had aught to say to sin, save on the cross; and there He bowed His head, and yielded up His precious life, under the accumulated weight of His people's sins. Neither did He ever suffer at the hand of God, save on the cross; and there Jehovah hid His face from Him because He was "made sin" (2 Cor. 5).

The above train of thought, and the various passages of Scripture referred to, may perhaps enable my reader to enter more fully into the divine power of the words, *"When I see the blood,* I will pass over you." The lamb needed to be without blemish, no doubt, for what else could meet the holy eye of Jehovah? But had the blood not been shed, there could have been no passing over, for "without shedding of blood is no remission" (Heb. 9:22). This subject will, the Lord permitting, come more fully and appropriately before us in the types of Leviticus. It demands the prayerful attention of every one who loves our Lord Jesus Christ in sincerity.

We shall now consider the second aspect of the passover, as the centre round which the assembly was gathered, in peaceful, holy, happy fellowship. Israel saved by the blood was one thing, and Israel feeding on the lamb was quite another. They were saved *only* by the blood; but the object round which they were gathered was, manifestly, the roasted lamb. This is not, by any means, a distinction without a difference. The blood of the lamb forms the foundation both of our connection with God, and our connection with one another. It is as those who are washed in that blood, that we are introduced to God and to one another. Apart from the perfect atonement of Christ, there could obviously be no fellowship either with God or His assembly. Still we must remember that it is to a living Christ in heaven that believers are gathered by the Holy Ghost. It is with a living Head we are connected—to "a living stone" we have come. He is our centre. Having found peace through His blood, we own Him as our grand gathering-point and connecting link.—"Where two or three are gathered together in My name, there am I in the midst of them" (Matt. 18:20). The Holy Ghost is the only Gatherer; Christ Himself is the only object to which we are gathered; and our assembly, when thus convened, is to be characterized by holiness, so that the Lord our God may dwell among us. The Holy Ghost can only gather to Christ. He cannot gather to a system, a name, a doctrine, or an ordinance. He gathers to a Person, and that Person is a glorified Christ in heaven. This must stamp a peculiar character on God's assembly. Men may associate on any ground, round any centre, or for any object they please; but when the Holy Ghost associates, it is on the ground of accomplished redemption, around the Person of Christ, in order to form a holy dwelling-place for God (1 Cor. 3:16-17; 6:19; Eph. 2:21-22; 1 Pet. 2:4-5).

We shall now look in detail at the principles brought before us in the paschal feast. The assembly of Israel, as under the cover of the blood, was to be ordered by Jehovah in a manner worthy of Himself. In the matter of safety from judgment, as we have already seen, nothing was needed but the blood; but in the fellowship which flowed out of this safety, other things were needed which could not be neglected with impunity.

And first, then, we read, "They shall eat the flesh in that night, roast with fire, and unleavened bread; and with bitter herbs they shall eat it. Eat not of it raw, nor sodden at all with water, but roast with fire; his head with his legs, and with the purtenance thereof" (ver. 8-9). The lamb round which the congregation was assembled, and on which it feasted, was a roasted lamb—a lamb which had undergone the action of fire. In this we see "Christ our passover" presenting Himself to the action of the fire of divine holiness and judgment which found in Him a perfect material. He could say, "Thou hast proved mine heart; thou hast visited me in the night; thou hast tried me and shalt find nothing: I am purposed that my mouth shall not transgress" (Psalm 17:3). All in Him was perfect. The fire tried Him, and there was no dross. "His head with his legs and with the purtenance thereof." That is to say, the seat of His understanding, His outward walk, with all that pertained thereto—all was submitted to the action of the fire, and all was entirely perfect. The process of roasting was therefore deeply significant, as is every circumstance in the ordinances of God. Nothing should be passed over, because all is pregnant with meaning.

"Eat not of it raw, nor sodden at all with water." Had it been eaten thus, there would have been no expression of the great truth which it was the divine purpose to shadow forth; namely, that our paschal Lamb was to endure, on the cross, the fire of Jehovah's righteous wrath,—a truth of infinite preciousness to the soul. We are not merely under the shelter of the blood of the Lamb, but we feed, by faith, upon the Person of the Lamb. Many of us come short here. We are apt to rest satisfied with being saved by what Christ has done for us, without cultivating holy communion with Himself. His loving heart could never be satisfied with this. He has brought us nigh to Himself, that we might enjoy Him, that we might feed on Him, and delight in Him. He presents Himself to us as the One who has endured, to the uttermost, the intense fire of the wrath of God, that He may, in this wondrous character, be the food of our ransomed souls.

But how was this lamb to be eaten? "With unleavened bread and bitter herbs." Leaven is invariably used, throughout Scripture, as emblematical of evil. Neither in the Old nor in the New Testament is it ever used to set forth anything pure, holy, or good. Thus, in this chapter, "the feast of unleavened bread" is the type of that practical separation from evil which is the proper result of being washed from our sins in the blood of the Lamb, and the proper accompaniment of communion with His sufferings. Naught but unleavened bread could at all comport with a roasted lamb. A single particle of that which was the marked type of evil, would have destroyed the moral character of the entire ordinance. How could we connect any species of evil with our fellowship with a suffering Christ? Impossible. All who enter, by the power of the Holy Ghost, into the meaning of the cross will assuredly, by the same power, put away leaven from all their borders. "For even Christ our passover is sacrificed for us: *therefore* let us keep the feast, not with old leaven, neither with the leaven of malice and wickedness; but with the unleavened bread of sincerity and truth" (1 Cor. 5:7-8). The feast spoken of in this passage is that which, in the life and conduct of the Church, corresponds with the feast of unleavened bread. This latter lasted "seven days"; and the Church collectively, and the believer individually, are called to walk in practical holiness, during the seven days, or entire period, of their course here below; and this, moreover, as the direct result of being washed in the blood, and having communion with the sufferings of Christ.

The Israelite did not put away leaven in order to be saved, but because he was saved; and if he failed to put away leaven, it did not raise the question of security through the blood, but simply of fellowship with the assembly. "Seven days shall there be no leaven found in your houses: for whosoever eateth that which is leavened, even that soul shall be cut off from the congregation of Israel, whether he be a stranger, or born in the land" (ver. 19). The cutting off of an Israelite from the congregation answers precisely to the suspension of a Christian's fellowship, if he be indulging in that which is contrary to the holiness of the divine presence. God cannot tolerate evil. A single unholy thought will interrupt the soul's communion; and until the soil contracted by any such thought is got rid of by confession, founded on the advocacy of Christ, the communion cannot possibly be restored (see 1 John 1:5-10). The true-hearted Christian rejoices in this. He can ever "give thanks at the remembrance of God's holiness." He would not, if he could, lower the standard a single hair's breadth. It is his exceeding joy to walk in company with One who will not go on, for a moment, with a single jot or tittle of "leaven."

Blessed be God, we know that nothing can ever snap asunder the link which binds the true believer to Him. We are "saved in the Lord," not with a temporary or conditional, but "with an everlasting salvation." But then salvation and communion are not the same thing. Many are saved who do not know it; and many, also, who do not enjoy it. It is quite impossible that I can enjoy a blood-stained lintel if I have leavened borders. This is an axiom in the divine life. May it be written on our hearts! Practical holiness, though not the basis of our *salvation,* is intimately connected with our *enjoyment* thereof. An Israelite was not saved by unleavened bread, but by the blood; and yet leaven would have cut him off from communion. And as to the Christian, he is not saved by his practical holiness, but by the blood; but if he indulges in evil, in thought, word, or deed, he will have no true enjoyment of salvation, and no true communion with the Person of the Lamb.

This, I cannot doubt, is the secret of much of the spiritual barrenness and lack of settled peace which one finds amongst the children of God. They are not cultivating holiness; they are not keeping "the feast of unleavened bread." The blood is on the lintel, but the leaven within their borders keeps them from enjoying the security which the blood provides. The allowance of evil destroys our fellowship, though it does not break the link which binds our souls eternally to God. Those who belong to God's assembly must be holy. They have not only been delivered from the guilt and consequences of sin, but also from the practice of it, the power of it, and the love of it. The very fact of being delivered by the blood of the paschal lamb, rendered Israel responsible to put away leaven from all their quarters. They could not say, in the frightful language of the antinomian, Now that we are delivered, we may conduct ourselves as we please. By no means. If they were saved *by grace,* they were saved *to holiness.* The soul that can take occasion, from the freedom of divine grace and the completeness of the redemption which is in Christ Jesus, to "continue in sin," proves very distinctly that he understands neither the one nor the other.

Grace not only saves the soul with an everlasting salvation, but also imparts a nature which delights in everything that belongs to God, because it is divine. We are made partakers of the divine nature, which cannot sin, because it is born of God. To walk in the energy of this nature is, in reality, to "keep" the feast of unleavened bread. There is no "old leaven" nor "leaven of malice and wickedness" in the new nature, because it is of God, and God is holy, and "God is love." Hence it is evident that we do not put away evil from us in order to better our old nature, which is irremediable; nor yet to obtain the new nature, but because we have it. We have life, and, in the power of that life, we put away evil. It is only when we are delivered from the guilt of sin that we can understand or exhibit the true power of holiness. To attempt it in any other way is hopeless labor. The feast of unleavened bread can only be kept beneath the perfect shelter of the blood.

We may perceive equal significancy and moral propriety in that which was to accompany the unleavened bread, namely, the "bitter herbs." We cannot enjoy communion with the sufferings of Christ without remembering what it was which rendered those sufferings needful, and this remembrance must necessarily produce a chastened and subdued tone of spirit, which is aptly expressed by the bitter herbs in the paschal feast. If the roasted lamb expressed Christ's endurance of the wrath of God in His own Person, on the cross, the bitter herbs express the believer's recognition of the truth that He "suffered *for us.*" "The chastisement of our peace was upon Him, and with His stripes we are healed" (Isaiah 53:5). It is well, owing to the excessive levity of our hearts, to understand the deep meaning of the bitter herbs. Who can read such psalms as the sixth, twenty-second, thirty-eighth, sixty-ninth, eighty-eighth, and one hundred and ninth, and not enter, in some measure, into the meaning of the unleavened bread with bitter herbs? Practical holiness of life, with deep subduedness of soul, must flow from real communion with Christ's sufferings; for it is quite impossible that moral evil and levity of spirit can exist in view of those sufferings.

But, it may be asked, is there not a deep joy for the soul in the consciousness that Christ has borne our sins; that He has fully drained, on our behalf, the cup of God's righteous wrath? Unquestionably. This is the solid foundation of all our joy. But can we ever forget that it was for *"our sins"* He suffered? Can we ever lose sight of the soul-subduing truth that the blessed Lamb of God bowed His head beneath the weight of our transgressions? Surely not. We must eat our lamb with bitter herbs, which, be it remembered, do not set forth the tears of a worthless and shallow sentimentality, but the deep and real experiences of a soul that enters, with spiritual intelligence and power, into the meaning and into the practical effect of the cross.

In contemplating the cross, we find in it that which cancels all our guilt. This imparts sweet peace and joy. But we find in it also the complete setting aside of nature—the crucifixion of "the flesh"—the death of "the old man." (See Rom. 6:6; Gal. 2:20; 6:14; Col. 2:11.) This, in its practical results, will involve much that is "bitter" to nature. It will call for self-denial—the mortification of our members which are on the earth (Col. 3:5)—the reckoning of self to be dead indeed unto sin (Rom. 6). All these things may seem terrible to look at; but when one gets inside the blood-stained door-post, he thinks quite differently. The very herbs which to an Egyptian's taste would no doubt have seemed so bitter, formed an integral part of Israel's redemption *feast.* Those who are redeemed by the blood of the Lamb, who know the joy of fellowship with Him, esteem it a "feast" to put away evil and to keep nature in the place of death.

"And ye shall let nothing of it remain until the morning; and that which remaineth of it until the morning ye shall burn with fire" (ver. 10). In this command, we are taught that the communion of the congregation was in no wise to be separated from the sacrifice on which that communion was founded. The heart must ever cherish the vivid remembrance that all true fellowship is inseparably connected with accomplished redemption. To think of having communion *with God* on any other ground is to imagine that He could have fellowship with our evil, and to think of fellowship *with man* on any other ground is but to form an unholy club, from which nothing could issue but confusion and iniquity. In a word, all must be founded upon, and inseparably linked with, the blood. This is the simple meaning of eating the paschal lamb the same night on which the blood was shed. The fellowship must not be separated from its foundation.

What a beauteous picture, then, we have in the blood-sheltered assembly of Israel, feeding peacefully on the roasted lamb, with unleavened bread and bitter herbs! No fear of judgment, no fear of the wrath of Jehovah, no fear of the terrible hurricane of righteous vengeance which was sweeping vehemently over the land of Egypt, at the midnight hour. All was profound peace within the blood-stained lintel. They had no need to fear anything from without; and nothing within could trouble them, save leaven, which would have proved a death-blow to all their peace and blessedness. What a picture for the Church! What a picture for the Christian! May we gaze upon it with an enlightened eye and a teachable spirit!

However, we are not yet done with this

most instructive ordinance. We have been looking at Israel's *position,* and Israel's *food,* let us now look at Israel's *habit.*

"And thus shall ye eat it: with your loins girded, your shoes on your feet, and your staff in your hand; and ye shall eat it in haste; it is the Lord's passover" (ver. 11). They were to eat it as a people prepared to leave behind them the land of death and darkness, wrath and judgment, to move onward toward the land of promise—their destined inheritance. The blood which had preserved them from the fate of Egypt's firstborn was also the foundation of their deliverance from Egypt's bondage; and they were now to set out and walk with God toward the land that flowed with milk and honey. True, they had not yet crossed the Red Sea,—they had not yet gone the "three days' journey;" still they were, in principle, a redeemed people, a separated people, a pilgrim people, an expectant people, a dependent people; and their entire habit was to be in keeping with their present position and future destiny. The girded loins bespoke intense separation from all around them, together with a readiness to serve. The shod feet declared their preparedness to leave that scene; while the staff was the expressive emblem of a pilgrim people, in the attitude of leaning on something outside themselves. Precious characteristics! Would that they were more exhibited by every member of God's redeemed family.

Let us "meditate on these things." We have tasted, through grace, the cleansing efficacy of the blood of Jesus; as such, it is our privilege to feed upon His adorable Person and delight ourselves in His "unsearchable riches;" to have fellowship in His sufferings, and be made conformable to His death. Oh! let us, therefore, be seen with the unleavened bread and bitter herbs, the girded loins, the shoes and staff. In a word, let us be marked as a holy people, a crucified people, a watchful and diligent people,—a people manifestly "on our way to God"—on our way to glory—"bound for the kingdom." May God grant us to enter into the depth and power of all these things, so that they may not be mere theories in our intellects—mere principles of scriptural knowledge and interpretation, but living, divine realities, known by experience, and exhibited in the life, to the glory of God.

We shall close this section by glancing, for a moment, at verses 43-49. Here we are taught that while it was the place and privilege of every true Israelite to eat the passover, yet no uncircumcised stranger should participate therein. "There shall no stranger eat thereof . . . all the congregation of Israel shall keep it." Circumcision was necessary ere the passover could be eaten. In other words, the sentence of death must be written upon nature ere we can intelligently feed upon Christ, either as the ground of peace or the centre of unity. Circumcision has its antitype in the cross. The male alone was circumcised; the female was represented in the male. So, in the cross, Christ represented His Church, and hence the Church is crucified with Christ; nevertheless she lives by the life of Christ, known and exhibited on earth, through the power of the Holy Ghost. "And when a stranger shall sojourn with thee, and will keep the passover unto the Lord, let all his males be circumcised, and then let him come near and keep it; and he shall be as one that is born in the land: for no uncircumcised person shall eat thereof." "They that are in the flesh cannot please God" (Rom. 8:8).

The ordinance of circumcision formed the grand boundary line between the Israel of God and all the nations that were upon the face of the earth; and the cross of the Lord Jesus Christ forms the boundary between the Church and the world. It matters not, in the smallest degree, what advantages of person or position a man possessed, he could have no part with Israel until he submitted to that flesh-cutting operation. A circumcised beggar was nearer to God than an uncircumcised king. So, also, now, there can be no participation in the joys of God's redeemed, save by the cross of our Lord Jesus Christ; and that cross sweeps away all pretensions, levels all distinctions, and unites all in one holy congregation of blood-washed worshipers. The cross forms a boundary so lofty, and a defense so impenetrable, that not a single atom of earth or of nature can cross over or pass through to mingle itself with "the new creation." "*All* things are of God, who hath reconciled us to Himself" (2 Cor. 5:18).

But not only was Israel's *separation* from all strangers strictly maintained, in the institution of the passover; Israel's *unity* was also as clearly enforced. "*In one house* shall it be eaten: thou shalt not carry forth aught of the flesh abroad out of the house: neither shall ye break a bone thereof" (ver. 46). Here is as fair and beauteous a type as we could have of the "one body and one Spirit." The Church of God is *one*. God sees it as such, maintains it as such, and will manifest it as such, in the view of angels, men, and devils, notwithstanding all that has been done to interfere with that hallowed unity. Blessed be God, the unity of His Church is as much in His keeping as is her justification, acceptance, and eternal security. "He keepeth all his bones; not one of them is broken" (Ps. 34:20). And again, "A bone of Him shall not be broken" (John 19:36). Despite the rudeness and hard-heartedness of Rome's soldiery, and despite all the hostile influences which have been set to work, from age to age, the body of Christ is *one* and its divine unity can never be broken. "*There is one body and one spirit,*" and that, moreover, down here on this very earth. Happy are they who have got faith to recognize this precious truth, and faithfulness to carry it out, in these last days, notwithstanding the almost insuperable difficulties which attend upon their profession and their practice. I believe God will own and honor such.

The Lord deliver us from that spirit of unbelief which would lead us to judge by the sight of our eyes, instead of by the light of His changeless Word.

---

## *CHAPTER 13*

In the opening verses of this chapter we are taught, clearly and distinctly, that personal devotedness and personal holiness are fruits which redeeming love produces in those who are the happy subjects thereof. The dedication of the first-born and the feast of unleavened bread are here set forth in their immediate connection with the deliverance of the people out of the land of Egypt. " 'Sanctify unto Me all the first-born, whatsoever openeth the womb among the children of Israel, both of man and of beast: it is Mine.' And Moses said unto the people, 'Remember this day, in which ye came out from Egypt, out of the house of bondage; for by strength of hand the Lord brought you out from this place: there shall no leavened bread be eaten.' " And again, "Seven days thou shalt eat unleavened bread, and in the seventh day shall be a feast unto the Lord. Unleavened bread shall be eaten seven days; and there shall no leavened bread be seen with thee; neither shall there be leaven seen with thee in all thy quarters."

Then we have the reason of both these significant observances laid down.—"And thou shalt show thy son in that day, saying, This is done *because of that* which the Lord did unto me when I came forth out of Egypt." And again, "It shall be, when thy son asketh thee in time to come, saying, What is this? that thou shalt say unto him, By strength of hand the Lord brought us out from Egypt, from the house of bondage. And it came to pass, when Pharaoh would hardly let us go, that the Lord slew all the first-born in the land of Egypt, both the first-born of man and the first-born of beast; *therefore* I sacrifice to the Lord all that openeth the matrix, being males; but all the first-born of my children I redeem."

The more fully we enter, by the power of the Spirit of God, into the redemption which is in Christ Jesus, the more decided will be our separation, and the more wholehearted will be our devotedness. The effort to produce either the one or the other, until redemption is known, will prove the most hopeless labor possible. All our doings must be "because of that which the Lord hath done," and not in order to get anything from Him. Efforts after life and peace prove that we are, as yet, strangers to the power of the blood; whereas the pure fruits of an experienced redemption are to the praise of Him who has redeemed us. "For by grace are ye saved through faith; and that not of yourselves: it is the gift of God: not of works, lest any man should boast. For we are His workmanship, created in Christ Jesus unto good works, which God hath before prepared that we should walk in them" (Eph. 2:8-10). God has already prepared a path of good works for us to walk in; and He, by grace, prepares us to walk therein. It is only as saved that we can walk in such a path. Were it otherwise, we might boast; but seeing that we ourselves are as much God's workmanship as the path in which we walk, there is no room whatever for boasting.

True Christianity is but the manifestation of the life of Christ, implanted in us by the operation of the Holy Ghost, in pursuance of God's eternal counsels of sovereign grace; and all our doings previous to the implantation of this life are but "dead works," from which we need to have our consciences purged just as much as from "wicked works" (Heb. 9:14). The term "dead works" comprehends all works which men do with the direct object of getting life. If a man is seeking for life, it is very evident that he has not yet gotten it. He may be very sincere in seeking it, but his very sincerity only makes it the more obvious that, as yet, he has not consciously reached it. Hence, therefore, everything done in order to get life is a dead work, inasmuch as it is done without life—the life of Christ, the only true life, the only source from whence good works can flow. And, observe, it is not a question of "wicked works;" no one would think of getting life by such. No; you will find, on the contrary, that persons continually have recourse to "dead works," in order to ease their consciences, under the sense of "wicked works," whereas divine revelation teaches us that the conscience needs to be purged from the one as well as the other.

Again, as to righteousness, we read that "all our righteousnesses are as filthy rags." It is not said that all our wickednesses, merely, are as filthy rags. This would at once be admitted. But the fact is, that the very best fruit which we can produce, in the shape of religiousness and righteousness, is represented, on the page of eternal truth, as "dead works," and "filthy rags." Our very efforts after life do but prove us to be dead, and our very efforts after righteousness do but prove us to be enwrapped in filthy rags. It is only as the actual possessors of eternal life and divine righteousness that we can walk in the divinely prepared path of good works. Dead works and filthy rags could never be suffered to appear in such a path. None but "the redeemed of the Lord" can walk therein. It was as a redeemed people that Israel kept the feast of unleavened bread, and dedicated their first-born to Jehovah. The former of these observances we have already considered; as to the latter, it contains a rich mine of instruction.

The destroying angel passed through the land of Egypt to destroy all the first-born; but Israel's first-born escaped through the death of a divinely provided substitute. Accordingly, these latter appear before us, in this chapter, as a living people, dedicated to God. Saved by the blood of the lamb, they are privileged to consecrate their ransomed life to Him who had ransomed it. Thus it was only as redeemed that they possessed life. The grace of God alone had made them to differ, and had given them the place of living men in His presence. In their case, assuredly, there was no room for boasting; for, as to any personal merit or worthiness, we learn from this chapter that they were put on a level with an unclean and worthless thing.—"Every firstling of an ass thou shalt redeem with a lamb; and if thou wilt not redeem it, then thou shalt break his neck; and all the first-born of man among thy children shalt thou redeem" (ver. 13). There were two classes—the clean and the unclean, and man was classed with the latter. The lamb was to answer for the unclean; and if the ass were not redeemed, his neck was to be broken; so that an unredeemed man was put upon a level with an unclean animal, and that, moreover, in a condition than which nothing could be more worthless and unsightly. What a humiliating picture of man in his natural condition! O, that our poor proud hearts could enter more into it! Then should we rejoice more unfeignedly in the happy privilege of being washed from our guilt in the blood of the Lamb, and having all our personal vileness left behind forever, in the tomb where our Surety lay buried.

Christ was the Lamb—the clean, the spotless Lamb: we were unclean; but (forever adored be His matchless name!) He took our position, and, *on the cross,* was made sin, and treated as such. That which we should have endured throughout the countless ages of eternity, He endured for us on the tree. He bore *all* that was due to us, there and then, in order that we might enjoy what is due to Him, forever. He got our deserts that we might get His. The clean took, for a time, the place of the unclean, in order that the unclean might take forever the place of the clean. Thus, whereas by nature we are represented by the loathsome figure of an ass with his neck broken, by grace we are represented by a risen and glorified Christ in heaven. Amazing contrast! It lays man's glory in the dust, and magnifies the riches of redeeming love. It silences man's empty boastings, and puts into his mouth a hymn of praise to God and the Lamb, which shall swell throughout the courts of heaven during the everlasting ages.*

How forcibly is one here reminded of the apostle's memorable and weighty words to the Romans, "Now if we be dead with Christ, we believe that we shall also live with Him: knowing that Christ being raised from the dead dieth no more; death hath no more dominion over Him. For in that He died, He died unto sin once; but in that He liveth, He liveth unto God. Likewise reckon ye also yourselves to be dead indeed unto sin, but alive unto God through Jesus Christ our Lord. Let not sin therefore reign in your mortal body, that ye should obey it in the lusts thereof. Neither yield ye your members as instruments of unrighteousness unto sin; but yield yourselves unto God, as those that are alive from the dead, and your members as instruments of righteousness unto God. For sin shall not have dominion over you; for ye are not under the law, but under grace" (Rom. 6:8-14). We are not only ransomed from the power of death and the grave, but also united to Him who has ransomed us at the heavy cost of His own precious life, that we might, in the energy of the Holy Ghost, dedicate our new life, with all its powers, to His service, so that His worthy name may be glorified in us according to the will of God and our Father.

We are furnished, in the last few verses of Exodus 13, with a touching and beautiful example of the Lord's tender consideration of His people's need. "He knoweth our frame; He remembereth that we are dust" (Psalm 103:14). When He redeemed Israel and took them into relationship with Himself, He, in His unfathomed and infinite grace, charged Himself with all their need and weakness. It mattered not what they were or what they needed when I AM was with them, in all the exhaustless treasures of that name. He had to conduct them from Egypt to Canaan, and we here find Him occupying Himself in selecting a suitable path for them. "And it came to pass, when Pharaoh had let the people go, that God led them not through the way of the land of the Philistines, although that was near; for God said, 'Lest peradventure the people repent when they see war, and they return to Egypt;' but God led the people about through the way of the wilderness of the Red Sea" (ver. 17-18).

The Lord, in His condescending grace, so orders for His people that they do not, at their first setting out, encounter heavy trials, which might have the effect of discouraging their hearts and driving them back. "The

*It is interesting to see that by nature we are ranked with an unclean animal; by grace we are associated with Christ the spotless Lamb. There can be nothing lower than the place which belongs to us by nature: nothing higher than that which belongs to us by grace. Look, for example, at an ass with his neck broken; there is what an unredeemed man is worth. Look at "the precious blood of Christ;" there is what a redeemed man is worth. "Unto you that believe is the preciousness." That is, all who are washed in the blood partake of Christ's preciousness. As He is "a living stone," they are "living stones;" as He is "a precious stone," they are "precious stones." They get life and preciousness all from Him and in Him. They are as He is. Every stone in the edifice is precious, because purchased at no less a price than "the blood of the Lamb." May the people of God know more fully their place and privileges in Christ!

way of the wilderness" was a much more protracted route; but God had deep and varied lessons to teach His people, which could only be learnt in the desert. They were afterwards reminded of this fact, in the following passage: "And thou shalt remember all the way which the Lord thy God led thee these forty years in the wilderness, to humble thee, and to prove thee, to know what was in thine heart, whether thou wouldest keep His commandments or no. And He humbled thee, and suffered thee to hunger, and fed thee with manna, which thou knewest not, neither did thy fathers know; that He might make thee know that man doth not live by bread only, but by every word that proceedeth out of the mouth of the Lord doth man live. Thy raiment waxed not old upon thee, neither did thy foot swell, these forty years" (Deut. 8:2-4). Such precious lessons as these could never have been learnt in "the way of the land of the Philistines." In that way, they might have learnt what *war* was, at an early stage of their career; but "in the way of the wilderness," they learnt what *flesh* was, in all its crookedness, unbelief, and rebellion. But I AM was there, in all His patient grace, unerring wisdom, and infinite power. None but Himself could have met the demand; none but He could endure the opening up of the depths of a human heart. To have my heart unlocked any where, save in the presence of infinite grace, would plunge me in hopeless despair. The heart of man is but a little hell. What boundless mercy, then, to be delivered from its terrible depths!

Oh, to grace how great a debtor
  Daily I'm constrained to be!
Let that grace, Lord, like a fetter,
  Bind my wandering heart to Thee!

"And they took their journey from Succoth, and encamped in Etham, in the edge of the wilderness. And the Lord went before them by day in a pillar of a cloud, to lead them the way; and by night in a pillar of fire, to give them light; to go by day and night; He took not away the pillar of the cloud by day, nor the pillar of fire by night, from before the people." Jehovah not only selected a path for His people, but He also came down to talk with them therein, and make Himself known to them according to their need. He not only conducted them safely outside the bounds of Egypt, but He also came down, as it were, in His traveling chariot, to be their Companion through all the vicissitudes of their wilderness journey. This was divine grace. They were not merely delivered out of the furnace of Egypt and then allowed to make the best of their way to Canaan—such was not God's manner toward them. He knew that they had a toilsome and perilous journey before them, through serpents and scorpions, snares and difficulties, drought and barrenness; and He, blessed be His name forever, would not suffer them to go alone. He would be the Companion of all their toils and dangers; yea, "He went before them." He was "a guide, a glory, a defense, to save from every fear." Alas! that they should ever have grieved that blessed One by their hardness of heart. Had they only walked humbly, contentedly, and confidingly with Him, their march would have been a triumphant one from first to last. With Jehovah in their forefront, no power could have interrupted their onward progress from Egypt to Canaan. He would have carried them through and planted them in the mountain of His inheritance, according to His promise, and by the power of His right hand; nor should as much as a single Canaanite have been allowed to remain therein to be a thorn in their side. Thus will it be by and by, when Jehovah shall set His hand a second time to deliver His people from under the power of all their oppressors. May the Lord hasten the time!

## *CHAPTER 14*

"THEY that go down to the sea in ships, that do business in great waters; these see the works of the Lord, and His wonders in the deep" (Ps. 107:23-24). How true is this! and yet our coward hearts do so shrink from those "great waters." We prefer carrying on our traffic in the shallows, and, as a result, we fail to see "the works" and "wonders" of our God; for these can only be seen and known "in the deep."

It is in the day of trial and difficulty that the soul experiences something of the deep and untold blessedness of being able to count on God. Were all to go on smoothly, this would not be so. It is not in gliding along the surface of a tranquil lake that the reality of the Master's presence is felt; but actually when the tempest roars, and the waves roll over the ship. The Lord does not hold out to us the prospect of exemption from trial and tribulation; quite the opposite: He tells us we shall have to meet both the one and the other; but He promises to be with us in them, and this is infinitely better. God's presence *in* the trial is much better than exemption *from* the trial. The sympathy of His heart *with us* is sweeter far than the power of His hand *for us.* The Master's presence with His faithful servants while passing through the furnace was better far than the display of His power to keep them out of it (Dan. 3). We would frequently desire to be allowed to pass on our way without trial, but this would involve serious loss. The Lord's presence is never so sweet as in moments of appalling difficulty.

Thus it was in Israel's case, as recorded in this chapter. They are brought into an overwhelming difficulty: they are called to "do business in great waters:" "they are at their wit's end." Pharaoh, repenting himself of having let them go out of his land, determines to make one desperate effort to recover them. "And he made ready his chariot, and took his people with him; and he took six hundred chosen chariots, and all the chariots of Egypt, and captains over every one of them. . . . And when Pharaoh drew nigh, the children of Israel lifted up their eyes, and, behold, the Egyptians marched after them; and they were sore afraid: and the children of Israel cried out unto the Lord." Here was a deeply trying scene—one in which human effort could avail nothing. As well might they have attempted to put back with a straw the ocean's mighty tide, as seek to extricate themselves by aught that they could do. The sea was before them, Pharaoh's hosts behind them, and the mountains around them. And all this, be it observed, permitted and ordered of God. He had marked out their position before "Pihahiroth, between Migdol and the sea, over against Baal-zephon." Moreover, He permitted Pharaoh to come upon them. And why? Just to display Himself in the salvation of His people, and the total overthrow of their enemies. "To Him that divided the Red Sea into parts: for His mercy endureth forever: and made Israel to pass through the midst of it: for His mercy endureth forever: but overthrew Pharaoh and his host in the Red Sea: for His mercy endureth forever" (Ps. 136).

There is not so much as a single position in all the desert-wanderings of God's redeemed, the boundaries of which are not marked off, with studious accuracy, by the hand of unerring wisdom and infinite love. The special bearings and peculiar influences of each position are carefully arranged. The Pihahiroths and the Migdols are all ordered with immediate reference to the moral condition of those whom God is conducting through the windings and labyrinths of the wilderness, and also to the display of His own character. Unbelief may ofttimes suggest the inquiry, Why is it thus? God knows why; and He will, without doubt, reveal the why whenever the revelation would promote His glory and His people's good. How often do we feel disposed to question as to the why and the wherefore of our being placed in such and such circumstances! How often do we perplex ourselves as to the reason of our being exposed to such and such trials! How much better to bow our heads in meek subjection, and say, "It is well," and "it shall be well"! When God fixes our position for us, we may rest assured it is a wise and salutary one; and even when we foolishly and willfully choose a position for ourselves, He most graciously overrules our folly, and causes the influences of our self-chosen circumstances to work for our spiritual benefit.

It is when the people of God are brought into the greatest straits and difficulties, that they are favored with the finest displays of God's character and actings; and for this reason He ofttimes leads them into a trying position, in order that He may the more markedly show Himself. He could have conducted Israel through the Red Sea, and far beyond the reach of Pharaoh's hosts, before ever the latter had started from Egypt; but that would not have so fully glorified His own name, or so entirely confounded the enemy, upon whom He designed to "get Him honor." We too frequently lose sight of this great truth, and the consequence is that our hearts give way in the time of trial. If we could only look upon a difficult crisis as an occasion of bringing out, on our behalf, the sufficiency of divine grace, it would enable us to preserve the balance of our souls, and to glorify God, even in the deepest waters.

We feel disposed, it may be, to marvel at Israel's language on the occasion now before us. We may feel at a loss to account for it; but the more we know of our own evil hearts of unbelief, the more we shall see how marvelously like them we are. They would seem to have forgotten the recent display of divine power on their behalf. They had seen the gods of Egypt judged, and the power of Egypt laid prostrate beneath the stroke of Jehovah's omnipotent hand; they had seen the iron chain of Egyptian bondage riven, and the furnace quenched by the same hand; —all these things they had seen, and yet the moment a dark cloud appeared upon their horizon, their confidence gave way, their hearts failed, and they gave utterance to their unbelieving murmurings in the following language: "Because there were no graves in Egypt, hast thou taken us away to die in the wilderness? Wherefore hast thou dealt thus with us, to carry us forth out of Egypt? . . . It had been better for us to serve the Egyptians than that we should die in the wilderness" (ver. 11-12). Thus is "blind unbelief" ever "sure to err, and scan God's ways in vain." This unbelief is the same in all ages. It led David, in an evil hour, to say, "I shall one day perish by the hand of Saul; there is nothing better for me than that I should speedily escape into the land of the Philistines" (1 Sam. 27:1). And how did it turn out? Saul fell on Mount Gilboa, and David's throne was established forever. Again, it led Elijah the Tishbite, in a moment of deep depression, to flee for his life from the wrathful threatenings of Jezebel. How did it turn out? Jezebel was dashed to pieces on the pavement, and Elijah was taken in a chariot of fire to heaven.

So it was with Israel in their very first moment of trial. They really thought that the Lord had taken such pains to deliver them out of Egypt merely to let them die in the wilderness. They imagined that they had been preserved by the blood of the paschal lamb in order that they might be buried in the wilderness. Thus it is that unbelief ever reasons. It leads us to interpret God in the presence of the difficulty, instead of interpreting the difficulty in the presence of God. Faith gets behind the difficulty, and there finds God, in all His faithfulness, love, and power. It is the believer's privilege ever to be in the presence of God. He has been introduced thither by the blood of the Lord Jesus Christ, and nothing should be suffered to take him thence. The place itself he never can lose, inasmuch as his Head and Representative, Christ, occupies it on his behalf. But although he cannot lose the thing itself, he can very easily lose the enjoyment of it—the experience and power of it. Whenever his difficulties come between his heart and the Lord, he is evidently not enjoying the Lord's presence, but suffering in the presence of his difficulties. Just as when a cloud comes between us and the sun, it robs us, for the time, of the enjoyment of his beams. It does not prevent him from shining, it merely hinders our enjoyment of him. Exactly so is it when we allow trials and sorrows, difficulties and perplexities, to hide from our souls the bright beams of our Father's countenance, which ever shine, with changeless lustre, in the face of Jesus Christ. There is no difficulty too great for our God; yea, the greater the difficulty, the more room there is for Him to act in His proper character, as the God of all power and grace. No doubt Israel's position, in the opening of our chapter, was a deeply trying one,—to flesh and blood, perfectly overwhelming; but then the Maker of heaven and earth was there, and they had but to use Him.

Yet, alas! how speedily we fail when trial arises! These sentiments sound very nicely on the ear, and look very well upon paper (and, blessed be God, they are divinely true); but then the thing is to practice them when opportunity offers. It is in the practice of them that their power and blessedness are really proved. "If any man will *do* His will, he shall *know* of the doctrine, whether it be of God" (John 7:17).

"And Moses said unto the people, 'Fear ye not, stand still, and see the salvation of the Lord, which He will show to you to-day; for the Egyptians whom ye have seen to-day ye shall see them again no more forever. The Lord shall fight for you, and ye shall hold your peace' " (ver. 13-14). Here is the first attitude which faith takes in the presence of a trial. *"Stand still."* This is impossible to flesh and blood. All who know, in any measure, the restlessness of the human heart under anticipated trial and difficulty, will be able to form some conception of what is involved in standing still. Nature must be *doing* something. It will rush hither and thither. It would fain have some hand in the matter. And although it may attempt to justify and sanctify its worthless doings, by bestowing upon them the imposing and popular title of "a legitimate use of means," yet are they the plain and positive fruits of unbelief, which always shuts out God, and sees naught save the dark cloud of its own creation. Unbelief creates or magnifies difficulties, and then sets us about removing them by our own bustling and fruitless activities, which, in reality, do but raise a dust around us which prevents our seeing God's salvation.

Faith, on the contrary, raises the soul above the difficulty, straight to God Himself, and enables one to "stand still." We gain nothing by our restless and anxious efforts. "We cannot make one hair white or black," or "add one cubit to our stature." What could Israel do at the Red Sea? Could they dry it up? Could they level the mountains? Could they annihilate the hosts of Egypt? Impossible! There they were, inclosed within an impenetrable wall of difficulties, in view of which nature could but tremble and feel its own perfect impotency. But this was just the time for God to act. When unbelief is driven from the scene, then God can enter; and, in order to get a proper view of His actings, we must "stand still." Every movement of nature is, so far as it goes, a positive hindrance to our perception and enjoyment of divine interference on our behalf.

This is true of us in every single stage of our history. It is true of us as sinners when, under the uneasy sense of sin upon the conscience, we are tempted to resort to our own doings in order to obtain relief. Then, truly, we must "stand still" in order to "see the salvation of God." For what could we do in the matter of making an atonement for sin? Could we have stood with the Son of God upon the cross? Could we have accompanied Him down into the "horrible pit and the miry clay"? Could we have forced our passage upward to that eternal rock on which, in resurrection, He has taken His stand? Every right mind will at once pronounce the thought to be a daring blasphemy. God is alone in redemption; and as for us, we have but to "stand still, and see the salvation of God." The very fact of its being God's salvation proves that man has naught to do in it.

The same is true of us, from the moment we have entered upon our Christian career. In every fresh difficulty, be it great or small, our wisdom is to stand still—to cease from our own works, and find our sweet repose in God's salvation. Nor can we make any distinction as to difficulties. We cannot say that there are some trifling difficulties which we ourselves can compass, while there are others in which naught save the hand of God can avail. No; all are alike beyond us. We are as little able to change the color of a hair as to remove a mountain,—to form a blade of grass as to create a world. All are alike to us, and all are alike to God. We have only, therefore, in confiding faith, to cast ourselves on Him who "humbleth Himself [alike] to behold the things that are in heaven and on earth." We sometimes find ourselves carried triumphantly through the heaviest trials, while at other times we quail, falter, and break down under the most ordinary dispensations. Why is this? Because, in the former, we are constrained to roll our burden over on the Lord; whereas, in the latter, we foolishly attempt to carry it ourselves. The Christian is, in himself, if he only realized it, like an exhausted receiver, in which a guinea and a feather have equal momenta.

"The Lord shall fight for you, and ye shall hold your peace." Precious assurance! How eminently calculated to tranquilize the spirit in view of the most appalling difficulties and dangers! The Lord not only places Himself between us and our sins, but also between us and our circumstances. By doing the former, He gives us peace of conscience; by doing the latter, He gives us peace of heart. That the two things are perfectly distinct, every experienced Christian knows. Very many have peace of conscience, who have not peace of heart. They have, through grace and by faith, found Christ, in the divine efficacy of His blood, between them and all their sins; but they are not able, in the same simple way, to realize Him as standing, in His divine wisdom, love, and power, between them and their circumstances. This makes a material difference in the practical condition of the soul, as well as in the character of one's testimony. Nothing tends more to glorify the name of Jesus than that quiet repose of spirit which results from having Him between us and everything that could be a matter of anxiety to our hearts. "Thou wilt keep him in perfect peace whose mind is stayed on Thee, because he trusteth in Thee."

But some feel disposed to ask the question, "Are we not to do anything?" This may be answered by asking another, namely, What can we do? All who really know themselves must answer, Nothing. If, therefore, we can do nothing, had we not better "stand still"? If the Lord is acting for us, had we not better stand back? Shall we run before Him? Shall we busily intrude ourselves upon His sphere of action? Shall we come in His way? There can be no possible use in two acting, when one is so perfectly competent to do all. No one would think of bringing a lighted candle to add brightness to the sun at midday: and yet the man who would do so might well be accounted wise, in comparison with him who attempts to assist God by his bustling officiousness.

However, when God, in His great mercy, opens the way, faith can walk therein. It only ceases from man's way in order to walk in God's. "And the Lord said unto Moses, 'Wherefore criest thou unto Me? Speak unto the children of Israel that they go forward.' " It is only when we have learnt to "stand still" that we are able effectually to go forward. To attempt the latter until we have learnt the former is sure to issue in the exposure of our folly and weakness. It is therefore true wisdom, in all times of difficulty and perplexity, to "stand still"—to wait only upon God, and He will assuredly open a way for us; and then we can peacefully and happily "go forward." There is no uncertainty when God makes a way for us; but every self-devised path must prove a path of doubt and hesitation. The unregenerate man may move along with great apparent firmness and decision in his own ways; but one of the most distinct elements in the new creation is self-distrust, and the element which answers thereto is confidence in God. It is when our eyes have seen God's salvation that we can walk therein; but this can never be distinctly seen until we have been brought to the end of our own poor doings.

There is peculiar force and beauty in the expression, "*See* the salvation of God." The very fact of our being called to "see" God's salvation, proves that the salvation is a complete one. It teaches that salvation is a thing wrought out and revealed by God, to be seen and enjoyed by us. It is not a thing made up partly of God's doing and partly of man's. Were it so, it could not be called *God's* salvation. In order to be His, it must be wholly divested of everything pertaining to man. The only possible effect of human efforts is to raise a dust which obscures the view of God's salvation.

"Speak to the children of Israel that they go forward." Moses himself seems to have been brought to a stand, as it appears from the Lord's question—"Wherefore criest thou to Me?" Moses could tell the people to "stand still, and see the salvation of God," while his own spirit was giving forth its exercises in an earnest cry to God. However, there is no use in crying when we ought to be acting; just as there is no use in acting when we ought to be waiting. Yet such is ever our way. We attempt to move forward when we ought to stand still, and we stand still when we ought to move forward. In Israel's case, the question might spring up in the heart, Whither are we to go? To all appearance, there lay an insurmountable barrier in the way of any movement forward. How were they to go through the sea? This was the point. Nature could never solve this question. But we may rest assured that God never gives a command without, at the same time, communicating the power to obey. The real condition of the heart may be tested by the command; but the soul that is, by grace, disposed to obey, receives power from above to do so. When Christ commanded the man with the withered hand to stretch it forth, the man might naturally have said, How can I stretch forth an arm which hangs dead by my side? But he did not raise any question whatever, for with the command, and from the same source, came the power to obey.

Thus, too, in Israel's case, we see that with the command to go forward came the provision of grace. "But lift thou up thy rod, and stretch out thy hand over the sea, and divide it; and the children of Israel shall go on dry ground through the midst of the sea." Here was the path of faith. The hand of God opens the way for us to take the first step, and this is all that faith ever asks. God never gives guidance for two steps at a time. I must take one step, and then I get light for the next. This keeps the heart in abiding dependence upon God. "By faith they passed through the Red Sea as by dry land." It is evident that the sea was not divided throughout at once. Had it been so, it would have been "sight" and not "faith." It does not require faith to begin a journey when I can see all the way through; but to begin when I can merely see the first step, this is faith. The sea opened as Israel moved forward, so that for every fresh step they needed to be cast upon God. Such was the path along which the redeemed of the Lord moved, under His own conducting hand. They passed through the dark waters of death, and found these very waters to be "a wall unto them, on their right hand and on their left."

The Egyptians could not move in such a path as this. They moved on because they saw the way open before them: with them it was sight, and not faith,—"Which the Egyptians assaying to do were drowned." When people *assay* to do what faith alone can accomplish, they only encounter defeat and confusion. The path along which God calls His people to walk is one which nature can never tread. "Flesh and blood cannot inherit the kingdom of God" (1 Cor. 15:50), neither can it walk in the ways of God. Faith is the great characteristic principle of God's kingdom, and faith alone can enable us to walk in God's ways. "Without faith it is impossible to please God" (Heb. 11). It glorifies God exceedingly when we move on with Him, as it were, blindfold. It proves that we have more confidence in His eyesight than in our own. If I know that God is looking out for me, I may well close my eyes, and move on in holy calmness and stability. In human affairs, we know that when there is a sentinel or watchman at his post, others can sleep quietly. How much more may we rest in perfect security when we know that He who neither slumbers nor sleeps has His eye upon us, and His everlasting arms around us!

"And the angel of God which went before the camp of Israel, removed and went behind them; and the pillar of the cloud went from before their face, and stood behind them. And it came between the camp of the Egyptians and the camp of Israel; and it was a cloud and darkness to them, but it gave light by night to these; so that the one came not near the other all the night" (ver. 19-20). Jehovah placed Himself right between Israel and the enemy: this was protection indeed. Before ever Pharaoh could touch a hair of Israel's head, he should make his way through the very pavilion of the Almighty—yea, through the Almighty Himself. Thus it is that God ever places Himself between His people and every enemy, so that "no weapon formed against them can prosper." He has placed Himself between us and our sins; and it is our happy privilege to find Him between us and every one and every thing that could be against us. This is the true way in which to find both peace of heart and peace of conscience. The believer may institute a diligent and anxious search for his sins, but he cannot find them. Why? Because God is between him and them. He has cast all our sins behind His back, while, at the same time, He sheds forth upon us the light of His reconciled countenance.

In the same manner, the believer may look for his difficulties, and not find them, because God is between him and them. If, therefore, the eye, instead of resting on our sins and sorrows, could rest only upon Christ, it would sweeten many a bitter cup, and enlighten many a gloomy hour. But one finds constantly that nine-tenths of our trials and sorrows are made up of anticipated or imaginary evils, which only exist in our own disordered, because unbelieving, minds. May my reader know the solid peace, both of heart and conscience, which results from having Christ, in all His fullness, between him and *all* his sins and *all* his sorrows.

It is at once most solemn and interesting to note the double aspect of the "pillar" in this chapter. "It was a cloud and darkness" to the Egyptians, but "it gave light by night" to Israel. How like the cross of our Lord Jesus Christ! Truly, that cross has a double aspect likewise. It forms the foundation of the believer's peace, and, at the same time, seals the condemnation of a guilty world. The self-same blood which purges the believer's conscience and gives him perfect peace, stains this earth and consummates its guilt. The very mission of the Son of God which strips the world of its cloak, and leaves it wholly without excuse, clothes the Church with a fair mantle of righteousness, and fills her mouth with ceaseless praise. The very same Lamb who will terrify, by His unmitigated wrath, all tribes and classes of earth, will lead, by His gentle hand, His blood-bought flock through the green pastures and beside the still waters forever! (Compare Rev. 6:15-17 with 7:13-17.)

The close of our chapter shows us Israel triumphant on the shore of the Red Sea, and Pharaoh's hosts submerged beneath its waves. The fears of the former and the boastings of the latter had both alike been proved utterly groundless: Jehovah's glorious work had annihilated both the one and the other. The same waters which formed a wall for God's redeemed, formed a grave for Pharaoh. Thus it is ever: those who walk by faith find a path to walk in, while all who assay to do so find a grave. This is a solemn truth, which is not in any wise weakened by the fact that Pharaoh was acting in avowed and positive hostility to God when he "assayed" to pass through the Red Sea. It will ever be found true that all who attempt to imitate faith's actings will be confounded. Happy are they who are enabled, however feebly, to walk by faith. They are moving along a path of unspeakable blessedness,—a path which, though it may be marked by failure and infirmity, is nevertheless "begun, continued, and ended in God." O, that we may all enter more fully into the divine reality, the calm elevation, and the holy independence of this path!

We ought not to turn from this fruitful section of our book without a reference to 1 Cor. 10 in which we have an allusion to "the cloud and the sea."—"Moreover, brethren, I would not that ye should be ignorant, how that all our fathers were *under the cloud,* and all passed *through the sea;* and were all baptized unto Moses in the cloud and in the sea" (ver. 1-2). There is much deep and precious instruction for the Christian in this passage. The apostle goes on to say, "Now these things were our types," thus furnishing us with a divine warrant for interpreting Israel's baptism "in the cloud and in the sea" in a typical way; and, assuredly, nothing could be more deeply significant or practical. It was as a people thus baptized that they entered upon their wilderness journey, for which provision was made in "the spiritual meat" and "spiritual drink" provided by the hand of love. In other words, they were typically a people dead to Egypt and all pertaining thereto. The cloud and the sea were to them what the cross and grave of

Christ are to us. The cloud secured them from their enemies; the sea separated them from Egypt: the cross, in like manner, shields us from all that could be against us, and we stand at heaven's side of the empty tomb of Jesus. Here we commence our wilderness journey,—here we begin to taste the heavenly Manna, and to drink of the streams which emanate from "that spiritual Rock," while, as a pilgrim people, we make our way onward to that land of rest of the which God has spoken to us.

I would further add here, that my reader should seek to understand the difference between the Red Sea and Jordan. They both have their antitype in the death of Christ; but in the former we see separation from Egypt; in the latter, introduction into the land of Canaan. The believer is not merely separated from this present evil world by the cross of Christ, but he is quickened out of the grave of Christ, raised up together, and made to sit together in Christ, in the heavenlies (Eph. 2:5-6). Hence, though surrounded by the things of Egypt, he is, as to his actual experience, in the wilderness; while, at the same time, he is borne upward, by the energy of faith, to that place where Jesus sits, at the right hand of God. Thus, the believer is not merely "forgiven all trespasses," but actually associated *with* a risen Christ in heaven;—he is not merely saved *by* Christ, but linked *with* Him forever. Nothing short of this could either satisfy God's affections or actualize His purposes in reference to the Church.

Reader, do we understand these things? do we believe them? are we realizing them? do we manifest the power of them? Blessed be the grace that has made them unalterably true with respect to every member of the body of Christ, whether it be an eye or an eye-lash, a hand or a foot. Their truth, therefore, does not depend upon our manifestation, our realization, or our understanding, but upon *"the precious blood of Christ,"* which has canceled all our guilt and laid the foundation of all God's counsels respecting us. Here is true rest for every broken heart and every burdened conscience.

## *CHAPTER 15*

THIS chapter opens with Israel's magnificent song of triumph on the shore of the Red Sea, when they had seen "that great work which the Lord did upon the Egyptians." They had seen God's salvation, and they therefore sing His praise and recount His mighty acts. "*Then* sang Moses and the children of Israel this song unto the Lord." Up to this moment, we have not heard so much as a single note of praise. We have heard their cry of deep sorrow as they toiled amid the brick-kilns of Egypt, we have hearkened to their cry of unbelief when surrounded by what they deemed insuperable difficulties, but, until now, we have heard no song of praise. It was not until, as a saved people, they found themselves surrounded by the fruits of God's salvation, that the triumphal hymn burst forth from the whole redeemed assembly. It was when they emerged from their significant baptism "in the cloud and in the sea," and were able to gaze upon the rich spoils of victory which lay scattered around them, that six hundred thousand voices were heard chanting the song of victory. The waters of the Red Sea rolled between them and Egypt, and they stood on the shore as a fully delivered people, and therefore they were able to praise Jehovah.

In this, as in everything else, they were our types. We, too, must know ourselves as saved, in the power of death and resurrection, before ever we can present clear and intelligent worship. There will always be reserve and hesitancy in the soul, proceeding, no doubt, from positive inability to enter into the accomplished redemption which is in Christ Jesus. There may be the acknowledgment of the fact that there is salvation in Christ, and in none other; but this is a very different thing from apprehending, by faith, the true character and ground of that salvation, and realizing it as *ours.* The Spirit of God reveals, with unmistakable clearness, in the Word, that the Church is united to Christ in death and resurrection; and, moreover, that a risen Christ, at God's right hand, is the measure and pledge of the Church's acceptance. When this is believed, it conducts the soul entirely beyond the region of doubt and uncertainty. How can the Christian doubt when he knows that he is continually represented before the throne of God by an Advocate, even "Jesus Christ the righteous"? It is the privilege of the very feeblest member of the Church of God to know that he was represented by Christ on the cross, that *all* his sins were confessed, borne, judged, and atoned for there. This is a divine reality, and, when laid hold of by faith, must give peace; but nothing short of it ever can give peace. There may be earnest, anxious, and most sincere desires after God,—there may be the most pious and devout attendance upon all the ordinances, offices, and forms of religion; but there is no other possible way in which to get the sense of sin entirely removed from the conscience, but seeing it judged in the Person of Christ, as a sin-offering, on the cursed tree. If it was judged there once for all, it is now by the believer to be regarded as a divinely, and therefore eternally, settled question; and that it was so judged is proved by the resurrection of the Surety. "I know that whatsoever God doeth it shall be forever: nothing can be put to it nor anything taken from it: and God doeth it that men should fear before Him" (Eccles. 3:14).

However, while it is generally admitted that all this is true in reference to the Church collectively, many find considerable difficulty in making a personal application thereof. They are ready to say, with the Psalmist, "Truly, God is good to Israel, even to such as are of a clean heart. *But as for me . . .*" (Ps. 73:1-2). They are looking at themselves instead of at Christ in death and Christ in resurrection; they are occupied rather with their appropriation of Christ than with Christ Himself; they are thinking of their capacity rather than their title. Thus they are kept in a state of the most distressing uncertainty, and, as a consequence, they are never able to take the place of happy, intelligent worshipers. They are praying for salvation instead of rejoicing in the conscious possession of it; they are looking at their imperfect fruits instead of Christ's perfect atonement.

Now in looking through the various notes of this song in Exodus 15, we do not find a single note about *self,* its doings, its sayings, its feelings, or its fruits; it is all about Jehovah, from beginning to end. It begins with, "I will sing unto the Lord, for *He* hath triumphed gloriously: the horse and his rider hath *He* thrown into the Sea." This is a specimen of the entire song. It is a simple record of the attributes and actings of Jehovah. In chapter 14, the hearts of the people had, as it were, been pent up by the excessive pressure of their circumstances; but in chapter 15, the pressure is removed, and their hearts find full vent in a sweet song of praise. Self is forgotten; circumstances are lost sight of; one object, and but one, fills their vision, and that object is the Lord Himself, in His character and ways. They were able to say, "Thou, Lord, hast made me glad through Thy work; I will triumph in the works of Thy hands" (Ps. 92:4). This is true worship. It is when poor, worthless self, with all its belongings, is lost sight of, and Christ alone fills the heart, that we present proper worship. There is no need for the efforts of a fleshly pietism to awaken in the soul feelings of devotion; nor is there any demand whatever for the adventitious appliances of religion, so called, to kindle in the soul the flame of acceptable worship. Oh, no! Let but the heart be occupied with the Person of Christ, and "songs of praise" will be the natural result. It is impossible for the eye to rest on Him and the spirit not be bowed in holy worship. If we contemplate the worship of the hosts which surround the throne of God and the Lamb, we shall find that it is ever evoked by the presentation of some special feature of divine excellence or divine acting. Thus should it be with the Church on earth; and when it is not so, it is because we allow things to intrude upon us which have no place in the regions of unclouded light and unalloyed blessedness. In all true worship, God Himself is at once the object, subject, and power of worship.

Hence Exodus 15 is a fine specimen of a song of praise. It is the language of a redeemed people celebrating the worthy praise of Him who had redeemed them. "The Lord is my strength and song, and He is become my salvation: He is my God, and I will prepare Him a habitation; my father's God, and I will exalt Him. The Lord is a man of war: the Lord is His name. . . . Thy right hand, O Lord, is become glorious in power: Thy right hand, O Lord, hath dashed in pieces the enemy. . . . Who is like unto Thee, O Lord, among the gods? who is like Thee, glorious in holiness, fearful in praises, doing wonders? . . . Thou in Thy mercy hast led forth the people which Thou hast redeemed: Thou hast guided them in Thy strength unto Thy holy habitation. . . . The Lord shall reign forever and ever." How comprehensive is the range of this song! It begins with redemption and ends with the glory. It begins with the cross and ends with the kingdom. It is like a beauteous rainbow, of which one end dips in "the sufferings," and the other in "the glory that should follow." It is all about Jehovah. It is an outpouring of soul produced by a view of God and His gracious and glorious actings.

Moreover, it does not stop short of the actual accomplishment of the divine purpose, as we read, "Thou *hast guided* them in Thy strength unto Thy holy habitation." The people were able to say this, though they had but just planted their foot on the margin of the desert. It was not the expression of a vague hope,—it was not feeding upon poor, blind chance. Oh, no! When the soul is wholly occupied with God, it is enabled to launch out into all the fullness of His grace, to bask in the sunshine of His countenance, and delight itself in the rich abundance of His mercy and loving-kindness. There is not a cloud upon the prospect when the believing soul, taking its stand upon the eternal rock on which redeeming love has set it in association with a risen Christ, looks up into the spacious vault of God's infinite plans and purposes, and dwells upon the effulgence of that glory which God has prepared for all those who have washed their robes and made them white in the blood of the Lamb.

This will account for the peculiarly brilliant, elevated, and unqualified character of all those bursts of praise which we find throughout sacred Scripture. The creature is set aside: God is the object. He fills the entire sphere of the soul's vision. There is nothing of man, his feelings, or his experiences, and therefore the stream of praise flows copiously and uninterruptedly forth. How different is this from some of the hymns we so often hear sung in Christian assemblies, so full of our failings, our feebleness, our shortcomings. The fact is, we can never sing with real, spiritual intelligence and power when we are looking at ourselves. We shall ever be discovering something within which will act as a drawback to our worship. Indeed, with many, it seems to be accounted a Christian grace to be in a continual state of doubt and hesitation; and, as a consequence, their hymns are quite in character with their condition. Such persons, however sincere and pious, have never yet, in the actual experience of their souls, entered upon the proper ground of worship. They have not yet got done with themselves; they have not passed through the sea, and, as a spiritually baptized people, taken their stand on the shore, in the power of resurrection. They are still, in some way or another, occupied with self: they do not regard self as a crucified thing, with which God is forever done.

May the Holy Ghost lead all God's people into fuller, clearer, and worthier apprehensions of their place and privilege as those who, being washed from their sins in the blood of Christ, are presented before God in all that infinite and unclouded acceptance in which He stands, as the risen and glorified Head of His Church. Doubts and fears do not become them, for their divine Surety has not left a shadow of a foundation on which to build a doubt or a fear. Their place is within the vail. They "have boldness to enter into the holiest by the blood of Jesus" (Heb. 10:19). Are there any doubts or fears in the holiest? Is it not evident that a doubting spirit virtually calls in question the perfectness of Christ's work—a work which has been attested, in the view of all created intelligence, by the resurrection of Christ from the dead? That blessed One could not have left the tomb unless all ground of doubting and fearing had been perfectly removed on behalf of His people. Wherefore it is the Christian's sweet privilege ever to triumph in a full salvation. The Lord Himself has become his salvation; and he has only to enjoy the fruits of that which God has wrought for him, and to walk to His praise while waiting for that time when "Jehovah shall reign forever and ever."

But there is one note in this song to which I shall just invite my reader's attention: "He is my God, and I will prepare Him a habitation." It is worthy of note that when the heart was full to overflowing with the joy of redemption, it gives expression to its devoted purpose in reference to "a habitation for God." Let the Christian reader ponder this. God dwelling with man is a grand thought pervading Scripture from Exodus 15 to Revelation. Hearken to the following utterance of a devoted heart: "Surely I will not come into the tabernacle of my house, nor go up into my bed; I will not give sleep to mine eyes, nor slumber to mine eyelids, until I find out a place for the Lord, *a habitation* for the mighty God of Jacob" (Ps. 132:3-5). Again, "For the zeal of Thine house hath eaten me up" (Ps. 69:9; John 2:17). I do not attempt to pursue this subject here; but I would fain awaken such an interest concerning it in the breast of my reader as shall lead him to pursue it, prayerfully, for himself, from the very earliest notice of it in the Word until he arrives at that soul-stirring announcement, "Behold, the tabernacle of God is with men, and He will dwell with them, and they shall be His people, and God Himself shall be with them, and be their God. And God shall wipe away all tears from their eyes" (Rev. 21:3-4).

"So Moses brought Israel from the Red Sea; and they went out into the wilderness of Shur: and they went three days into the wilderness and found no water" (ver. 22). It is when we get into wilderness experience that we are put to the test as to the real measure of our acquaintance with God and with our own hearts. There is a freshness and an exuberance of joy connected with the opening of our Christian career, which very soon receives a check from the keen blast of the desert; and then, unless there is a deep sense of what God is to us, above and beyond everything else, we are apt to break down, and, "in our hearts, turn back again into Egypt." The discipline of the wilderness is needful, not to furnish us with a title to Canaan, but to make us acquainted with God and with our own hearts; to enable us to enter into the power of our relationship, and to enlarge our capacity for the enjoyment of Canaan when we actually get there (see Deut. 8:2-5).

The greenness, freshness, and luxuriance of spring have peculiar charms, which all pass away before the scorching heat of summer; but then, with proper care, that very heat which removes the fair traces of spring, produces the mellowed and matured fruits of autumn. Thus it is also in the Christian life; for there is, as we know, a striking and deeply instructive analogy between the principles which obtain in the kingdom of nature and those which characterize the kingdom of grace, seeing it is the same God whose handiwork meets our view in both.

There are three distinct positions in which we may contemplate Israel, namely, in Egypt, in the wilderness, and in the land of Canaan. In all these, they are "our types;" but we are in all three together. This may seem paradoxical, but it is true. As a matter of actual fact, we are in Egypt, surrounded by natural things, which are entirely adapted to the natural heart. But, inasmuch as we have been called by God's grace into fellowship with His Son Jesus Christ, we, according to the affections and desires of the new nature, necessarily find our place outside of all that which belongs to Egypt* (*i.e.*, the

*There is a wide moral difference between Egypt and Babylon, which it is important to understand. Egypt was that out of which Israel came; Babylon was that into which they were afterwards carried. (Comp. Amos 5:25-27 with Acts 7:42-43.) Egypt expresses what man has made of the world; Babylon expresses what Satan has made, is making, or will make, of the professing church. Hence, we are not only surrounded with the *circumstances* of Egypt, but also by the moral *principles* of Babylon.

*(Footnote continued on next page)*

world in its natural state), and this causes us to taste of wilderness experience, or, in other words, it places us, as a matter of experience, in the wilderness. The divine nature earnestly breathes after a different order of things—after a purer atmosphere than that with which we find ourselves surrounded, and thus it causes us to feel Egypt to be a moral desert.

But then, inasmuch as we are, in God's view, eternally associated with Him who has passed right through into the heavenlies, and taken His seat there in triumph and majesty, it is our happy privilege to know ourselves, by faith, as "sitting together in Him" there (Eph. 2). So that although we are, as to our bodies, in Egypt, we are, as to our experience, in the wilderness, while, at the same time, faith conducts us, in spirit, into Canaan, and enables us to feed upon "the old corn of the land," *i.e.,* upon Christ, not as One come down to earth merely, but as One gone back to heaven and seated there in glory.

The concluding verses of this fifteenth chapter show us Israel in the wilderness. Up to this point, it seemed to them to be all fair sailing. Heavy judgments poured upon Egypt, but Israel perfectly exempt—the army of Egypt dead upon the sea shore, but Israel in triumph. All this was well enough; but, alas! the aspect of things speedily changed. The notes of praise were soon exchanged for the accents of discontent. "When they came to Marah, they could not drink of the waters of Marah, for they were bitter; therefore the name of it was called Marah. And the people murmured against Moses, saying, 'What shall we drink?' " Again, "The whole congregation of the children of Israel murmured against Moses and Aaron in the wilderness; and the children of Israel said unto them, 'Would to God we had died by the hand of the Lord in the land of Egypt, when we sat by the flesh-pots, and when we did eat bread to the full! for ye have brought us forth into this wilderness to kill this whole assembly with hunger.' "

Here were the trials of the wilderness: "What shall we eat?" and "What shall we drink?" The waters of Marah tested the heart of Israel and developed their murmuring spirit; but the Lord showed them that there was no bitterness which He could not sweeten with the provision of His own grace. "And the Lord showed him a tree, which when he had cast into the waters, the waters were made sweet; there he made for them a

---

This renders our "days" what the Holy Ghost has termed "perilous" (χαλεποι—"difficult"). It demands a special energy of the Spirit of God, and complete subjection to the authority of the Word, to enable one to meet the combined influence of the realities of Egypt and the spirit and principles of Babylon. The former meet the natural desires of the heart; while the latter connect themselves with, and address themselves to, the *religiousness* of nature, which gives them a peculiar hold upon the heart. Man is a religious being, and peculiarly susceptible of the influences which arise from music, sculpture, painting, and pompous rites and ceremonies. When these things stand connected with the full supply of all his natural wants—yea, with all the ease and luxury of life, nothing but the mighty power of God's Word and Spirit can keep one true to Christ.

We should also remark that there is a vast difference between the destinies of Egypt and those of Babylon. The nineteenth of Isaiah sets before us the blessings that are in store for Egypt. It concludes thus: "And the Lord shall smite Egypt; He shall smite and heal it; and they shall return even to the Lord, and He shall be entreated of them, and shall heal them. . . . In that day shall Israel be the third with Egypt and with Assyria, even a blessing in the midst of the land; whom the Lord of Hosts shall bless, saying, Blessed be Egypt My people, and Assyria the work of My hands, and Israel Mine inheritance" (ver. 22-25).

Very different is the close of Babylon's history, whether viewed as a literal city or a spiritual system.—"I will also make it a possession for the bittern, and pools of water; and I will sweep it with the besom of destruction, saith the Lord of Hosts" (Isaiah 14:23). "It shall never be inhabited, neither shall it be dwelt in from generation to generation" (Isaiah 13:20). So much for Babylon literally; and looking at it from a mystic or spiritual point of view, we read its destiny in Rev. 18. The entire chapter is a description of Babylon, and it concludes thus: "A strong angel took up a stone, like a great millstone, and cast it into the sea, saying, 'Thus, with violence shall that great city Babylon be thrown down, and shall be found no more at all' " (ver. 21).

With what immense solemnity should those words fall upon the ears of all who are in any wise connected with Babylon—that is to say, with the false, professing church,—"Come out of her, My people, that ye be not partakers of her sins, and that ye receive not of her plagues!" (Rev. 18:5) The "power" of the Holy Ghost will necessarily produce, or express itself in, a certain "form," and the enemy's aim has ever been to rob the professing church of the power, while he leads her to cling to and perpetuate the form—to stereotype the form when all the spirit and life has passed away. Thus he builds the spiritual Babylon. The stones of which this city is built are lifeless professors; and the slime or mortar which binds these stones together is "a form of godliness without the power."

Oh! let us see to it that we fully, clearly, and influentially understand these things.

statute and an ordinance, and there he proved them." Beauteous figure this of Him who was, in infinite grace, cast into the bitter waters of death, in order that those waters might yield naught but sweetness to us forever! We can truly say, "The bitterness of death is past," and nothing remains for us but the eternal sweets of resurrection.

Verse 26 sets before us the momentous character of this first stage of God's redeemed in the wilderness. We are in great danger, at this point, of falling into a fretful, impatient, murmuring spirit. The only remedy for this is to keep the eye steadily fixed on Jesus—"looking unto Jesus." He, blessed be His name, ever unfolds Himself according to the need of His people; and they, instead of complaining of their circumstances, should only make their circumstances an occasion of drawing afresh upon Him. Thus it is that the wilderness ministers to our experience of what God is. It is a school, in which we learn His patient grace and ample resources. "Forty years suffered He their manners in the wilderness" (Acts 13:18). The spiritual mind will ever own that it is worth having bitter waters for God to sweeten. "We glory in tribulations also: knowing that tribulation worketh patience; and patience, experience; and experience, hope; and hope maketh not ashamed; because the love of God is shed abroad in our hearts by the Holy Ghost which is given unto us" (Rom. 5:3-5).

However, the wilderness has its Elims as well as its Marahs,—its wells and palm trees, as well as its bitter waters. "And they came to Elim, where were twelve wells of water, and threescore and ten palm trees; and they encamped there by the waters" (ver. 27). The Lord graciously and tenderly provides green spots in the desert for His journeying people; and though they are, at best, but oases, yet are they refreshing to the spirit and encouraging to the heart. The sojourn at Elim was eminently calculated to soothe the hearts of the people, and hush their murmurings. The grateful shade of its palm trees, and the refreshing of its wells, came in sweetly and seasonably after the trial of Marah, and significantly set forth, in our view, the precious virtues of that spiritual ministry which God provides for His people down here. "The twelve" and "the seventy" are numbers intimately associated with ministry.

But Elim was not Canaan. Its wells and palm trees were but foretastes of that happy land which lay beyond the bounds of the sterile desert on which the redeemed had just entered. It furnished refreshment, no doubt, but it was wilderness refreshment. It was but for a passing moment, designed, in grace, to encourage their depressed spirits, and nerve them for their onward march to Canaan. Thus it is, as we know, with ministry in the Church. It is a gracious provision for our need, designed to refresh, strengthen, and encourage our hearts, "until we all come to the fullness of the measure of the stature of Christ" (Eph. 4).

---

## *CHAPTER 16*

"AND they took their journey from Elim, and all the congregation of the children of Israel came unto the wilderness of Sin, which is between Elim and Sinai, on the fifteenth day of the second month after their departure out of the land of Egypt" (chap. 16:1). Here we find Israel in a very marked and interesting position. It is still the wilderness, no doubt, but it is a most important and significant stage thereof, namely, "between Elim and Sinai." The former was the place where they had so recently experienced the refreshing springs of divine ministry; the latter was the place where they entirely got off the ground of free and sovereign grace, and placed themselves under a covenant of works. These facts render "the wilderness of Sin" a singularly interesting portion of Israel's journey. Its features and influences are as strongly marked as those of any point in their whole career. They are here seen as the subjects of the same grace which had brought them up out of the land of Egypt, and therefore all their murmurings are instantly met by divine supplies. When

God acts in the display of His grace, there is no hindrance. The streams of blessing which emanate from Him, flow onward without interruption. It is only when man puts himself under law that he forfeits everything; for then God must allow him to prove how much he can claim on the ground of his own works.

When God visited and redeemed His people, and brought them forth out of the land of Egypt, it assuredly was not for the purpose of suffering them to die of hunger and thirst in the wilderness. They should have known this. They ought to have trusted Him, and walked in the confidence of that love which had so gloriously delivered them from the horrors of Egyptian bondage. They should have remembered that it was infinitely better to be in the desert with God than in the brick-kilns with Pharaoh. But no; the human heart finds it immensely difficult to give God credit for pure and perfect love. It has far more confidence in Satan than God. Look, for a moment, at all the sorrow and suffering, the misery and degradation, which man has endured by reason of his having hearkened to the voice of Satan; and yet he never gives utterance to a word of complaint of his service, or of desire to escape from under his hand. He is not discontented with Satan, or weary of serving him. Again and again he reaps bitter fruits in those fields which Satan has thrown open to him, and yet again and again he may be seen sowing the self-same seed, and undergoing the self-same labors.

How different it is in reference to God! When we have set out to walk in His ways, we are ready, at the earliest appearance of pressure or trial, to murmur and rebel. Indeed, there is nothing in which we so signally fail as in the cultivation of a confiding and thankful spirit. Ten thousand mercies are forgotten in the presence of a single trifling privation. We have been frankly forgiven all our sins, "accepted in the Beloved," made heirs of God and joint-heirs with Christ, the expectants of eternal glory, and, in addition to all, our path through the desert is strewed with countless mercies; and yet let but a cloud the size of a man's hand appear on the horizon, and we at once forget the rich mercies of the past in view of this single cloud, which, after all, may only "break in blessings on our head." The thought of this should humble us deeply in the presence of God. How unlike we are in this, as in every other respect, to our blessed Exemplar! Look at Him—the true Israel in the wilderness—surrounded by wild beasts, and fasting forty days. How did He carry Himself? Did He murmur? did He complain of His lot? did He wish Himself in other circumstances? Ah, no. God was the portion of His cup and the lot of His inheritance (Ps. 16); and, therefore, when the tempter approached and offered Him the necessaries, the glories, the distinctions, and the honors of this life, He refused them all, and tenaciously held fast the position of absolute dependence upon God and implicit obedience to His word. He would only take bread from God, and glory from Him likewise.

Very different was it with Israel after the flesh! No sooner did they feel the pressure of hunger than "they murmured against Moses and Aaron in the wilderness." They seemed to have actually lost the sense of having been delivered by the hand of Jehovah, for they said, "*Ye* have brought us forth into this wilderness." And again, in chapter 17, "the people murmured against Moses, and said, 'Wherefore is this that *thou* hast brought us up out of Egypt to kill us and our children and our cattle with thirst?' " Thus did they, on every occasion, evince a fretful, murmuring spirit, and prove how little they realized the presence and the hand of their almighty and infinitely gracious Deliverer.

Now, nothing is more dishonoring to God than the manifestation of a complaining spirit on the part of those that belong to Him. The apostle gives it as a special mark of Gentile corruption that, "when they knew God, they glorified Him not as God, *neither were thankful.*" Then follows the practical result of this unthankful spirit,—"They became vain in their imaginations, and their foolish heart was darkened" (Rom. 1:21). The heart that ceases to retain a thankful sense of God's goodness will speedily become "dark." Thus Israel lost the sense of being in God's hands; and this led, as might be expected, to still thicker darkness, for we find them, further on in their history, saying, "Wherefore hath the Lord brought us into this land, *to fall by the sword,* that our wives and our children shall be a prey?" (Num. 14:3) Such is the line along which a soul out of communion will travel. It first loses the sense of being in God's hands for good, and finally begins to deem itself in His hands for evil. Melancholy progress this!

However, the people, being so far the subjects of grace, are provided for; and our chapter furnishes the marvelous account of this provision: "Then said the Lord unto Moses, 'Behold, I will rain bread from heaven for you.' " They, when enveloped in the chilling cloud of their unbelief, had said, "Would to God we had died by the hand of the Lord in the land of Egypt, when we sat by the flesh-pots, and when we did eat bread to the full." But now the word is, "Bread from heaven." Blessed contrast! How amazing the difference between the flesh pots, the leeks, onions, and garlic of Egypt, and this heavenly manna—"angels' food"! The former belonged to earth, the latter to heaven.

But then this heavenly food was, of necessity, a test of Israel's condition, as we read, "That I may prove them, whether they will walk in My law or no." It needed a heart weaned from Egypt's influences, to be satisfied with or enjoy "bread from heaven." In point of fact, we know that the people were not satisfied with it, but despised it, pronounced it "light food," and lusted for flesh. Thus they proved how little their hearts were delivered from Egypt, or disposed to walk in God's law. "In their hearts they turned back again into Egypt" (Acts 7:39). But instead of getting back thither, they were ultimately carried away beyond Babylon (Acts 7:43). This is a solemn and salutary lesson for Christians. If those who are redeemed from this present evil world do not walk with God in thankfulness of heart, satisfied with His provision for the redeemed in the wilderness, they are in danger of falling into the snare of Babylonish influences. This is a serious consideration. It demands a heavenly taste to feed on bread from heaven. Nature cannot relish such food; it will ever yearn after Egypt, and therefore it must be kept down. It is our privilege, as those who have been baptized unto Christ's death, and "risen again through the faith of the operation of God," to feed upon Christ as "the bread of life which came down from heaven." This is our wilderness food—Christ as ministered by the Holy Ghost, through the written Word; while, for our spiritual refreshment, the Holy Ghost has come down as the precious fruit of the smitten Rock—Christ, as smitten for us. Such is our rare portion in this desert world.

Now, it is obvious that, in order to enjoy such a portion as this, our hearts must be weaned from everything in this present evil world—from all that would address itself to us as natural men—as men alive in the flesh. A worldly heart—a carnal mind, would neither find Christ in the Word, nor enjoy Him if found. The manna was so pure and delicate that it could not bear contact with earth. It fell upon the dew (see Num. 11:9), and had to be gathered ere the sun was up. Each one, therefore, had to rise early and seek his daily portion. So it is with the people of God now. The heavenly Manna must be gathered fresh every morning. Yesterday's Manna will not do for to-day, nor to-day's for tomorrow. We must feed upon Christ every day, with fresh energy of the Spirit, else we shall cease to grow. Moreover, we must make Christ our primary object. We must seek Him, *"early,"* before "other things" have had time to take possession of our poor susceptible hearts. Many of us, alas! fail in this. We give Christ a secondary place, and the consequence is, we are left feeble and barren. The enemy, ever watchful, takes advantage of our excessive spiritual indolence to rob us of the blessedness and strength which flow from feeding upon Christ. The new life in the believer can *only* be nourished and sustained by Christ. "As the living Father hath sent Me, and I live by the Father; so he that eateth Me, even he shall live by Me" (John 6:57).

The grace of the Lord Jesus Christ, as the

One who came down from heaven to be His people's food, is ineffably precious to the renewed soul; but, in order to enjoy Him thus, we need to realize ourselves as in the wilderness, separated to God in the power of accomplished redemption. If I am walking with God through the desert, I shall be satisfied with the food He provides, and that is, Christ as come down from heaven. "The old corn of the land of Canaan" has its antitype in *Christ ascended up* on high, and seated in the glory. As such, He is the proper food of those who, by faith, know themselves as raised up together, and seated together in Him in the heavenlies. But the Manna, that is, *Christ as come down* from heaven, is for the people of God in their wilderness life and experience. As a people journeying down here, we need a Christ who also journeyed down here; as a people seated in spirit up there, we have a Christ who is seated up there. This may help to explain the difference between the manna and the old corn of the land. It is not a question of redemption; that we have in the blood of the cross, and there alone. It is simply the provision which God has made for His people, according to their varied attitudes, whether as actually toiling in the desert, or in spirit taking possession of the heavenly inheritance.

What a striking picture is presented by Israel in the wilderness! Egypt was behind them, Canaan before them, and the sand of the desert around them; while they themselves were called to look up to heaven for their daily supply. The wilderness afforded not one blade of grass nor one drop of water for the Israel of God. In Jehovah alone was their portion. Most touching illustration of God's pilgrim people in this wilderness world! They have nothing here. Their life, being heavenly, can only be sustained by heavenly things. Though *in* the world, they are not *of* it, for Christ has chosen them out of it. As a heaven-born people, they are on their way to their birth-place, and sustained by food sent from thence. Theirs is an upward and onward course. The glory leads *only* thus. It is utterly vain to cast the eye backward in the direction of Egypt; not a ray of the glory can there be discerned. "They looked *toward the wilderness,* and behold the glory of the Lord appeared in the cloud." "Jehovah's chariot was in the wilderness, and all who desired companionship with Him should be there likewise; and if there, the heavenly manna should be their food, and that alone.

True, this manna was strange sustenance, such as an Egyptian could never understand, appreciate, or live upon; but those who had been "baptized in the cloud and in the sea" could, if walking in consistency with that significant baptism, enjoy and be nourished by it. Thus is it now in the case of the true believer. The worldling cannot understand how he lives. Both his life and that which sustains it lie entirely beyond the range of nature's keenest vision. Christ is his life, and on Christ he lives. He feeds, by faith, upon the powerful attractions of One who, though being "God over all, blessed forever," "took upon Him the form of a servant, and was made in the likeness of men" (Phil. 2:7). He traces Him from the bosom of the Father to the cross, and from the cross to the throne, and finds Him, in every stage of His journey, and in every attitude of His life, to be most precious food for his new man. All around, though, in fact, Egypt, is morally a waste howling wilderness, affording nothing for the renewed mind; and just in proportion as the Christian finds any material to feed upon must his spiritual man be hindered in his progress. The only provision which God has made is the heavenly Manna, and on this the true believer should ever feed.

It is truly deplorable to find Christians seeking after the things of this world. It proves, very distinctly, that they are "loathing" the heavenly Manna, and esteeming it "light food;" they are ministering to that which they ought to mortify. The activities of the new life will ever show themselves in connection with the subjugation of "the old man with his deeds;" and the more that is accomplished, the more will we desire to feed upon the "Bread which strengthens man's heart." As in nature, the more we exercise, the better the appetite, so in grace, the more our renewed faculties are called into play, the more we feel the need of feeding, each day, upon Christ. It is one thing to know that we have life in Christ, together with full forgiveness and acceptance before God, and it is quite another to be in habitual communion with Him—feeding upon Him by faith—making Him the exclusive food of our souls. Very many profess to have found pardon and peace in Jesus, who, in reality, are feeding upon a variety of things which have no connection with Him. They feed their minds with the newspapers and the varied frivolous and vapid literature of the day. Will they find Christ there? Is it by such instrumentality that the Holy Ghost ministers Christ to the soul? Are these the pure dew-drops on which the heavenly Manna descends for the sustenance of God's redeemed in the desert? Alas, no; they are the gross materials in which the carnal mind delights. How, then, can a true Christian live upon such? We know, by the teaching of God's Word, that he carries about with him two natures; and it may be asked, Which of the two is it that feeds upon the world's news and the world's literature?—Is it the old, or the new? There can be but one reply. Well, then, which of the two am I desirous of cherishing? Assuredly my conduct will afford the truest answer to this inquiry. If I sincerely desire to grow in the divine life—if my one grand object is to be assimilated and devoted to Christ—if I am earnestly breathing after an extension of God's kingdom *within,* I shall, without doubt, seek continually that character of nourishment which is designed of God to promote my spiritual growth. This is plain. A man's acts are always the truest index of his desires and purposes. Hence, if I find a professing Christian neglecting his Bible, yet finding abundance of time—yea, some of his choicest hours—for the newspaper, I can be at no loss to decide as to the true condition of his soul. I am sure he cannot be spiritual—cannot be feeding upon, living for, or witnessing to, Christ.

If an Israelite neglected to gather, in the freshness of the morning hour, his daily portion of the divinely appointed food, he would speedily have become lacking in strength for his journey. Thus is it with us. We must make Christ the paramount object of our soul's pursuit, else our spiritual life will inevitably decline. We cannot even feed upon feelings and experiences connected with Christ, for they, inasmuch as they are fluctuating, cannot form our spiritual nourishment. It was Christ yesterday, and it must be Christ to-day, and Christ forever. Moreover, it will not do to feed partly on Christ and partly on other things. As in the matter of *life* it is Christ *alone,* so in the matter of *living* it must be Christ *alone.* As we cannot mingle any thing with that which *imparts* life, so neither can we mingle any thing with that which *sustains* it.

It is quite true that, in spirit, and by faith, we can even now feed upon a risen and glorified Christ, ascended up to heaven in virtue of accomplished redemption, as prefigured by "the old corn of the land" (see Joshua 5). And not only so, but we know that when God's redeemed shall have entered upon those fields of glory, rest, and immortality which lie beyond the Jordan, they shall, in actual fact, be done with wilderness food; but they will not be done with Christ, nor with the remembrance of that which constitutes the specific nourishment of their desert life.

Israel were never to forget, amid the milk and honey of the land of Canaan, that which had sustained them during their forty years' sojourn in the wilderness. "This is the thing which the Lord commandeth: 'Fill an omer of it to be kept for your generations; that they may see the bread wherewith I have fed you in the wilderness, when I brought you forth from the land of Egypt' . . . . As the Lord commanded Moses, so Aaron laid it up before the testimony, to be kept" (ver. 32-34). Most precious memorial of the faithfulness of God! He did not suffer them to die of hunger, as their foolish hearts had unbelievingly anticipated. He rained bread from heaven for them, fed them with angels' food, watched over them with all the tenderness of a nurse, bore with them, carried them on eagles' wings, and, had they only continued on the proper ground of grace, He would have put them in eternal possession of all the promises made to their fathers. The pot of manna, therefore, containing, as it did, a man's daily portion, and laid up before the Lord, furnishes a volume of truth. There was no worm therein, nor aught of taint. It was the record of Jehovah's faithfulness in providing for those whom He had redeemed out of the hand of the enemy.

Not so, however, when man hoarded it up for himself. Then the symptoms of corruptibility soon made their appearance. We cannot, if entering into the truth and reality of our position, hoard up. It is our privilege, day by day, to enter into the preciousness of Christ, as the One who came down from heaven to give life unto the world. But if any, in forgetfulness of this, should be found hoarding up for to-morrow, that is, laying up truth beyond his present need, instead of turning it to profit in the way of renewing strength, it will surely become corrupt. This is a salutary lesson for us. It is a deeply solemn thing to learn truth; for there is not a principle which we profess to have learnt which we shall not have to prove practically. God will not have us theorists. One often trembles to hear persons make high professions and use expressions of intense devotedness, whether in prayer or otherwise, lest, when the hour of trial comes, there may not be the needed spiritual power to carry out what the lips have uttered.

There is a great danger of the intellect's outstripping the conscience and the affections. Hence it is that so many seem, at first, to make such rapid progress up to a certain point; but there they stop short and appear to retrograde. Like an Israelite gathering up more manna than he required for one day's food. He might appear to be accumulating the heavenly food far more diligently than others; yet every particle beyond the day's supply was not only useless, but far worse than useless, inasmuch as it "bred worms." Thus is it with the Christian. He must *use* what he gets; he must feed upon Christ as a matter of actual need, and the need is brought out in actual service. The character and ways of God, the preciousness and beauty of Christ, and the living depths of the Word, are only unfolded to faith and need. It is as we use what we receive that more will be given. The path of the believer is to be a practical one; and here it is that so many of us come short. It will often be found that those who get on most rapidly in theory are the slowest in the practical and experimental elements, because it is more a work of intellect than of heart and conscience. We should ever remember that Christianity is not a set of opinions, a system of dogmas, or a number of views; it is pre-eminently a living reality—a personal, practical, powerful thing, telling itself out in all the scenes and circumstances of daily life, shedding its hallowed influence over the entire character and course, and imparting its heavenly tone to every relationship which one may be called of God to fill. In a word, it is that which flows from being associated and occupied with Christ. This is Christianity. There may be clear views, correct notions, sound principles, without any fellowship with Jesus; but an orthodox creed without Christ will prove a cold, barren, dead thing.

Christian reader, see carefully to it that you are not only saved by Christ, but also living on Him. Make Him the daily portion of your soul. Seek Him *"early,"* seek him *"only."* When any thing solicits your attention, ask the question, Will this bring Christ to my heart? Will it unfold Him to my affections, or draw me near to His Person? If not, reject it at once: yes, reject it, though it present itself under the most specious appearance and with the most commanding authority. If your honest purpose be to get on in the divine life, to progress in spirituality, to cultivate personal acquaintance with Christ, then challenge your heart solemnly and faithfully as to this. Make Christ your habitual food. Go, gather the Manna that falls on the dew-drops, and feed upon it with an appetite sharpened by a diligent walk with God through the desert. May the rich grace of God the Holy Ghost abundantly strengthen you in all this! *

*My reader will find it profitable to turn to the sixth of John, and prayerfully meditate upon it, in connection with the subject of the manna. The passover being near, Jesus feeds the multitude, and then takes His departure to a mountain, there to be alone. From thence He comes to the relief of His distressed people tossed upon the troubled waters. After this, He

There is one point more in our chapter which we shall notice, namely, the institution of the Sabbath, in its connection with the manna and Israel's position as here set forth. From the second chapter of Genesis down to the chapter now before us, we find no mention made of this institution. This is remarkable. Abel's sacrifice, Enoch's walk with God, Noah's preaching, Abraham's call, together with the detailed history of Isaac, Jacob, and Joseph, are all presented; but there is no allusion to the Sabbath until we find Israel recognized as a people in relationship and consequent responsibility to Jehovah. The Sabbath was interrupted in Eden; and here we find it again instituted for Israel in the wilderness. But, alas! man has no heart for God's rest. And it came to pass that "there went out some of the people on the seventh day for to gather, and they found none. And the Lord said unto Moses, 'How long refuse ye to keep My commandments and My laws? See, for that the Lord hath given you the Sabbath, therefore He giveth you on the sixth day the bread of two days: abide ye every man in his place; let no man go out of his place on the seventh day' " (ver. 27-29). God would have His people enjoying sweet repose with Himself. He would give them rest, food, and refreshment, even in the wilderness. But man's heart is not disposed to rest with God. The people could remember and speak of the time when they "*sat* by the flesh pots" in Egypt, but they could not appreciate the blessedness of sitting in their tents, enjoying with God "the rest of the holy Sabbath," feeding upon the heavenly manna.

And, be it remarked, that the Sabbath is here presented as a matter of gift. "The Lord hath *given* you the Sabbath. Further on in this book we shall find it put in the form of a law, with a curse and a judgment attached to it in the case of disobedience. But whether fallen man gets a privilege or a law, a blessing or a curse, it is all alike. His *nature* is bad. He can neither rest with nor work for God. If God works and makes a rest for him, he will not keep it; and if God tells him to work, he will not do it. Such is man. He has no heart for God. He can make use of the name of the Sabbath as a something to exalt himself, or as the badge of his own religiousness; but when we turn to Exodus 16, we find that he cannot prize *God's* Sabbath as *a gift,* and when we turn to Numbers 15:32-36, we find he cannot keep it as *a law.*

Now, we know that the Sabbath, as well as the manna, was a type. In itself, it was a real blessing—a sweet mercy from the hand of a loving and gracious God who would relieve the toil and travail of a sin-stricken earth by the refreshment of one day of rest out of the seven. Whatever way we look at the institution of the Sabbath, we must see it to be pregnant with richest mercy; whether we view it in reference to man or to the animal creation. And, albeit, that Christians observe the first day of the week—the Lord's day—and attach to it its proper principles, yet is the gracious providence equally observable, nor would any mind at all governed by right feelings, seek, for a moment, to interfere with such a signal mercy. "The Sabbath was made for man;" and although man never has kept it, according to the divine thought about it, that does not detract from the grace which shines in the appointment of it, nor divest it of its deep significancy as a type of that eternal rest which remains for the people of God, or as a shadow of that substance which faith now enjoys in the Person and work of a risen Christ.

Let not the reader therefore suppose that in any thing which has been or may be stated in these pages the object is to touch, in the slightest degree, the merciful provision of one day's rest for man and the animal creation, much less to interfere with the distinct place which the Lord's day occupies in the New Testament. Nothing is further from the writer's thoughts. As a man he values the former, and as a Christian he

---

unfolds the doctrine of His Person and work, and declares how He was to give His flesh for the life of the world, and that none could have life save by eating His flesh and drinking His blood. Finally, He speaks of Himself as ascending up where He was before and of the quickening power of the Holy Ghost. It is, indeed, a rich and copious chapter, in which the spiritual reader will find a vast fund of truth for the comfort and edification of his soul.

rejoices in the latter, far too deeply to admit of his penning or uttering a single syllable which would interfere with either the one or the other. He would only ask the reader to weigh, with a dispassionate mind, in the balance of Holy Scripture, every line and every statement, and not form any harsh judgment beforehand.

This subject will come before us again, in our further meditations, if the Lord will. May we learn to value more the rest which our God has provided for us in Christ, and while enjoying Him as our rest, may we feed upon Him as the "hidden Manna," laid up, in the power of resurrection, in the inner sanctuary—the record of what God has accomplished, on our behalf, by coming down into this world, in His infinite grace, in order that we might be before Him according to the perfectness of Christ, and feed on His unsearchable riches forever.

---

## *CHAPTER 17*

"AND all the congregation of the children of Israel journeyed from the wilderness of Sin, after their journeys, according to the commandment of the Lord, and pitched in Rephidim: and there was no water for the people to drink. Wherefore the people did chide with Moses, and said, 'Give us water that we may drink.' And Moses said unto them, 'Why chide ye with me? Wherefore do ye tempt the Lord?' " (chap. 17:1-2) Did we not know something of the humiliating evil of our own hearts, we should be quite at a loss to account for Israel's marvelous insensibility to all the Lord's goodness, faithfulness, and mighty acts. They had just seen bread descending from heaven to feed six hundred thousand people in the wilderness; and now they are "ready to stone" Moses for bringing them out into the wilderness to kill them with thirst. Nothing can exceed the desperate unbelief and wickedness of the human heart save the superabounding grace of God. In that grace alone can any one find relief under the growing sense of his evil nature which circumstances tend to make manifest. Had Israel been transported directly from Egypt to Canaan, they would not have made such sad exhibitions of what the human heart is, and, as a consequence, they would not have proved such admirable ensamples or types for us; but their forty years' wandering in the desert furnishes us with a volume of warning, admonition, and instruction, fruitful beyond conception. From it we learn, amongst many other things, the unvarying tendency of the heart to distrust God. Any thing, in short, for it but God. It would rather lean upon a cobweb of human resources than upon the arm of an omnipotent, all-wise, and infinitely gracious God; and the smallest cloud is more than sufficient to hide from its view the light of His blessed countenance. Well, therefore, may it be termed "an evil heart of unbelief," which will ever show itself ready to "depart from the living God."

It is interesting to note the two great questions raised by unbelief in this and the preceding chapter. They are precisely similar to those which spring up within and around us every day, namely, "What shall we eat?" and "What shall we drink?" We do not find the people raising the third question in the category—"Wherewithal shall we be clothed?" But here are the questions of the wilderness —*"What?" "Where?" "How?"* Faith has a brief but comprehensive answer to all three, namely, *God!* Precious, perfect answer! O that the writer and the reader were more thoroughly acquainted with its force and fullness! We assuredly need to remember, when placed in a position of trial, that "there hath no temptation taken us but such as is common to man: but God is faithful, who will not suffer you to be tempted above that ye are able; but will with the temptation also make a way to escape [or, an "issue"—*εκβασιν*], that ye may be able to bear it" (1 Cor. 10:13). Whenever we get into trial, we may feel confident that with the trial there is an issue, and all we need is a broken will and a single eye to see it.

"And Moses cried unto the Lord, saying, 'What shall I do unto this people? they be almost ready to stone me.' And the Lord said unto Moses, 'Go on before the people, and take with thee of the elders of Israel; and thy rod, wherewith thou smotest the river, take in thine hand, and go. Behold, I will stand before thee there upon the rock in Horeb, and thou shalt smite the rock, and there shall come water out of it, that the people may drink.' And Moses did so in the sight of the elders of Israel" (ver. 4-6). Thus all is met by the most perfect grace. Every murmur brings out a fresh display. Here we have the refreshing stream gushing from the smitten rock—beauteous type of the Spirit given as the fruit of Christ's accomplished sacrifice. In chapter 16, we have a type of Christ coming down from heaven to give life to the world. In chapter 17, we have a type of the Holy Ghost, "shed forth" in virtue of Christ's finished work. "They drank of that spiritual Rock that followed them, and that Rock was Christ" (1 Cor. 10:4). But who could drink till the Rock was smitten? Israel might have gazed on that rock and died of thirst while gazing; but until smitten by the rod of God, it could yield no refreshment. This is plain enough. The Lord Jesus Christ was the centre and foundation of all God's counsels of love and mercy. Through Him all blessing was to flow to man. The streams of grace were designed to gush forth from "the Lamb of God;" but then it was needful that the Lamb should be slain—that the work of the cross should be an accomplished fact—ere any of these things could be actualized. It was when the Rock of Ages was cleft by the hand of Jehovah that the flood-gates of eternal love were thrown wide open, and perishing sinners invited, by the testimony of the Holy Ghost, to "drink abundantly," drink deeply, drink freely. "The gift of the Holy Ghost" is the result of the Son's accomplished work upon the cross. "The promise of the Father" could not be fulfilled until Christ had taken His seat at the right hand of the Majesty in the heavens, having wrought out perfect righteousness, answered all the claims of holiness, magnified the law and made it honorable, borne the unmitigated wrath of God against sin, exhausted the power of death, and deprived the grave of its victory. He, having done all this, "ascended up on high, led captivity captive, and gave gifts unto men. Now that He ascended, what is it but that He also descended first into the lower parts of the earth? He that descended is the same also that ascended up far above all heavens, that He might fill all things" (Eph. 4:8-10).

This is the true foundation of the Church's peace, blessedness, and glory forever. Until the rock was smitten, the stream was pent up, and man could do nothing. What human hand could bring forth water from a flinty rock? And so we may ask, What human righteousness could afford a warrant for opening the flood-gates of divine love? This is the true way in which to test man's competency. He could not, by his doings, his sayings, or his feelings, furnish a ground for the mission of the Holy Ghost. Let him be or do what he may, he could not do this. But thank God, it is done; Christ has finished the work; the true Rock has been smitten, and the refreshing stream has issued forth, so that thirsty souls may drink. "The water that I shall give him," says Christ, "shall be in him a well of water, springing up into everlasting life" (John 4:14). Again: "In the last day, that great day of the feast, Jesus stood and cried, saying, 'If any man thirst, let him come unto Me and drink. He that believeth on Me, as the Scripture hath said, out of his belly shall flow rivers of living water.' (But this spake He of the Spirit, which they that believe on Him should receive; for the Holy Ghost was not yet given, because that Jesus was not yet glorified)" (John 7:37-39; compare also, Acts 19:2).

Thus, as in the manna we have a type of Christ, so in the stream gushing from the rock we have a type of the Holy Ghost. "If thou knewest the gift of God [*i.e.,* Christ] . . . thou wouldest have asked of Him, and He would have given thee living water [*i.e.,* the Spirit]."

Such, then, is the teaching conveyed to the spiritual mind by the smitten rock; but the name of the place in which this significant type was presented is a standing memorial of man's unbelief.—"He called the name of the place Massah [*i.e.,* temptation], and Meribah [*i.e.,* chiding], because of the chiding of the children of Israel, and because they tempted the Lord, saying, 'Is the Lord among us, or not?' " (ver. 7) After such repeated assurances and evidences of Jehovah's presence, to raise such an inquiry proves the deep-seated unbelief of the human heart. It was, in point of fact, tempting Him. Thus did the Jews, in the day of Christ's presence amongst them, seek of Him a sign from heaven, tempting Him. Faith never acts thus; it believes in and enjoys the divine presence, not by a sign, but by the knowledge of Himself. It knows He is there to be enjoyed, and it enjoys Him. Lord, grant us a more artless spirit of confidence!

The next point suggested by our chapter is one of special interest to us. "Then came Amalek and fought with Israel in Rephidim. And Moses said unto Joshua, 'Choose us out men, and go out, fight with Amalek: to-morrow I will stand on the top of the hill with the rod of God in mine hand' " (ver. 8-9). The gift of the Holy Ghost leads to conflict. The light rebukes and conflicts with the darkness. Where all is dark there is no struggle; but the very feeblest struggle bespeaks the presence of light. "The flesh lusteth against the Spirit, and the Spirit against the flesh; and these are contrary the one to the other, so that ye should not do the things that ye would" (Gal. 5:17). Thus it is in the chapter before us; we have the rock smitten and the water flowing forth, and immediately we read, "Then came Amalek and fought with Israel."

This is the first time that Israel are seen in conflict with an external foe. Up to this point, the Lord had fought for them, as we read in chapter 14, "The Lord shall fight for you, and ye shall hold your peace." But now the word is, "Choose us out *men.*" True, God must now fight *in* Israel, as, before, He had fought *for* them. This marks the difference, as to the type; and as to the antitype, we know that there is an immense difference between Christ's battles *for* us, and the Holy Ghost's battles *in* us. The former, blessed be God, are all over, the victory gained, and a glorious and an everlasting peace secured: the latter, on the contrary, are still going on.

Pharaoh and Amalek represent two different powers or influences. Pharaoh represents the hindrance to Israel's deliverance from Egypt: Amalek represents the hindrance to their walk with God through the wilderness. Pharaoh used the things of Egypt to keep Israel from serving the Lord; he therefore prefigures Satan, who uses "this present evil world" against the people of God: Amalek, on the other hand, stands before us as the type of the flesh. He was the grandson of Esau, who preferred a mess of pottage to the birthright (see Gen. 36:12). He was the first who opposed Israel after their baptism "in the cloud and in the sea." These facts serve to fix his character with great distinctness; and, in addition to these, we know that Saul was set aside from the kingdom of Israel in consequence of his failing to destroy Amalek (1 Sam. 15). And further, we find that Haman is the last of the Amalekites of whom we find any notice in Scripture. He was hanged on a gallows in consequence of his wicked attempt against the seed of Israel (see Esther). No Amalekite could obtain entrance into the congregation of the Lord. Finally, in the chapter now before us, the Lord declares perpetual war with Amalek.

All these circumstances may be regarded as furnishing conclusive evidence of the fact that Amalek is a type of the flesh. The connection between his conflict with Israel and the water flowing out of the rock is most marked and instructive, and in full keeping with the believer's conflict with his evil nature, which conflict is, as we know, consequent upon his having the new nature, and the Holy Ghost dwelling therein. Israel's conflict began when they stood in the full power of redemption, and had tasted "that spiritual meat, and drunk of that spiritual Rock." Until they met Amalek, they had nothing to do. They did not cope with Pharaoh; they did not break the power of Egypt, nor snap asunder the chains of its thraldom; they did not divide the sea, nor submerge Pharaoh's hosts beneath its waves; they did not bring down bread from heaven, nor draw forth water out of the flinty rock;—they neither had done, nor could they do, any of these things; but now they are called to fight with Amalek. All the previous conflict had been between Jehovah and the enemy. They had but to "stand still" and gaze upon the mighty triumphs of Jehovah's outstretched arm, and enjoy the fruits of victory. The Lord had fought *for* them; but now He fights *in* or *by* them.

Thus is it also with the Church of God. The victories on which her eternal peace and blessedness are founded were gained, single-handed, by Christ *for* her. He was alone on the cross, alone in the tomb. The Church had to stand aside, for how could she be there?—how could she vanquish Satan, endure the wrath of God, or rob death of its sting? Impossible. These things lay far beyond the reach of sinners, but not beyond the reach of Him who came to save them, and who alone was able to bear upon His shoulder the ponderous weight of all their sins, and roll the burden away forever, by His infinite sacrifice, so that God the Holy Ghost, proceeding from God the Father, in virtue of the perfect atonement of God the Son, can take up His abode in the Church collectively, and in each member thereof individually.

Now it is when the Holy Ghost thus takes up His abode in us, consequent upon Christ's death and resurrection, that our conflict begins. Christ has fought *for* us; the Holy Ghost fights *in* us. The very fact of our enjoying this first rich spoil of victory, puts us into direct conflict with the foe; but the comfort is that we are victors ere we enter upon the field of conflict at all. The believer approaches to the battle singing, "Thanks be to God which giveth us the victory through our Lord Jesus Christ" (1 Cor. 15:57). We do not, therefore, fight uncertainly, or as those that beat the air, while we seek to keep under the body and bring it into subjection (1 Cor. 9:26-27). "We are more than conquerors through Him that loved us" (Rom. 8:37). The grace in which we stand renders the flesh utterly void of power to lord it over us (see Rom. 6, *passim*). If the law is "the strength of sin," grace is the weakness thereof. The former gives sin power over us; the latter gives us power over sin.

"And Moses said unto Joshua, 'Choose us out men, and go out, fight with Amalek: to-morrow I will stand on the top of the hill with the rod of God in mine hand.' So Joshua did as Moses had said unto him, and fought with Amalek; and Moses, Aaron, and Hur went up to the top of the hill. And it came to pass, when Moses held up his hand, that Israel prevailed; and when he let down his hand, Amalek prevailed. But Moses' hands were heavy; and they took a stone and put it under him, and he sat thereon; and Aaron and Hur stayed up his hands, the one on the one side and the other on the other side; and his hands were steady until the going down of the sun. And Joshua discomfited Amalek and his people with the edge of the sword" (verses 9-13).

We have here two distinct things, namely, conflict and intercession. Christ is on high *for* us, while the Holy Ghost carries on the mighty struggle *in* us. The two things go together. It is as we enter by faith into the prevalency of Christ's intercession on our behalf that we make head against our evil nature.

Some there are who seek to overlook the fact of the Christian's conflict with the flesh. They look upon regeneration as a total change or renewal of the old nature. Upon this principle it would necessarily follow that the believer has nothing to struggle with. If my nature is renewed, what have I to contend with? Nothing. There is nothing within, inasmuch as my old nature is made new; and nothing without can affect me, inasmuch as there is no response from within. The world has no charms for one whose flesh is entirely changed, and Satan has nothing by or on which to act. To all who maintain such a theory, it may be said that they seem to forget the place which Amalek occupies in the history of the people of God. Had Israel conceived the idea that when Pharaoh's hosts were gone their conflict was at an end, they would have been sadly put about when Amalek came upon them. The fact is, *theirs* only then began. Thus it is with the believer, for "all these things happened unto Israel for ensamples, and they are written for our admonition" (1 Cor. 10:11). But there could be no "type," no "ensample," no "admonition," in "these things" for one whose old nature is made new. Indeed, such an one can have but little need of any of those gracious provisions which God has made in His kingdom for those who are the subjects thereof.

We are distinctly taught in the Word that the believer carries about with him that which answers to Amalek, that is, "the flesh"—"the old man"—"the carnal mind" (Rom. 6:6; 8:7; Gal. 5:17). Now, if the Christian, upon perceiving the stirrings of his evil nature, begins to doubt his being a Christian, he will not only render himself exceedingly unhappy, but also deprive himself of his vantage-ground against the enemy. The flesh exists in the believer and will be there to the end of the chapter. The Holy Ghost fully recognizes it as existing, as we may easily see, from various parts of the New Testament. In Romans 6, we read, "Let not sin therefore *reign* in your mortal bodies." Such a precept would be entirely uncalled for if the flesh were not existing in the believer. It would be out of character to tell us not to let sin reign, if it were not actually dwelling in us. There is a great difference between dwelling and reigning. It dwells in a believer, but it reigns in an unbeliever.

However, though it dwells in us, we have, thank God, a principle of power over it. "Sin shall not have dominion over you; for ye are not under the law, but under grace." The grace which, by the blood of the cross, has put away sin, insures us the victory, and gives us present power over its indwelling principle.

We have died to sin, and hence it has no claim over us. "He that has died is justified from sin." "Knowing this, that our old man has been crucified with Him, that the body of sin might be destroyed, that henceforth we should not serve sin" (Rom. 6:6). "And Joshua discomfited Amalek and his people with the edge of the sword." All was victory; and Jehovah's banner floated over the triumphant host, bearing the sweet and heart-sustaining inscription, "Jehovah-nissi" (the Lord my banner). The assurance of victory should be as complete as the sense of forgiveness, seeing both alike are founded upon the great fact that Jesus died and rose again. It is in the power of this that the believer enjoys a purged conscience and subdues indwelling sin. The death of Christ having answered all the claims of God in reference to our sins, His resurrection becomes the spring of power in all the details of conflict afterwards. He died *for* us, and now He lives *in* us. The former gives us peace, the latter gives us power.

It is edifying to remark the contrast between Moses on the hill and Christ on the throne. The hands of our great Intercessor can never hang down. His intercession never fluctuates. "He *ever* liveth to make intercession for us" (Heb. 7). His intercession is never-ceasing and all-prevailing. Having taken His place on high, in the power of divine righteousness, He acts for us according to what He is, and according to the infinite perfectness of what He has done. His hands can never hang down, nor can He need any one to hold them up. His perfect advocacy is founded upon His perfect sacrifice. He presents us before God, clothed in His own perfections, so that though we may ever have to keep our faces in the dust, in the sense of what we are, yet the Spirit can only testify to us of what He is before God for us, and of what we are in Him. "We are not in the flesh, but in the Spirit" (Rom. 8). We are in *the body,* as to the fact of our condition; but we are not in *the flesh,* as to the principle of our standing. Moreover, the flesh is in us, though we are dead to it; but we are not in the flesh, because we are alive with Christ.

We may further remark, on this chapter, that Moses had the rod of God with him on the hill—the rod with which he had smitten the rock. This rod was the expression or symbol of the power of God, which is seen alike in atonement and intercession. When the work of atonement was accomplished, Christ took His seat in heaven, and sent down the Holy Ghost to take up His abode in the Church; so that there is an inseparable connection between the work of Christ and the work of the Spirit. There is the application of the power of God in each.

---

## *CHAPTER 18*

We here arrive at the close of a very marked division of the book of Exodus. We have seen God, in the exercise of His perfect grace, visiting and redeeming His people, bringing them forth out of the land of Egypt, delivering them first from the hand of Pharaoh and then from the hand of Amalek. Furthermore, we have seen, in the manna, a type of Christ come down from heaven; in the rock, a type of Christ smitten for His people; and in the gushing stream, a type of the Spirit given. Then follows, in striking and beautiful order, a picture of the future glory, divided into its three grand departments, namely, "the Jew, the Gentile, and the Church of God."

During the period of Moses' rejection by his brethren, he was taken apart and presented with a bride—the companion of his rejection. We were led to see, at the opening of this book, the character of Moses' relationship with this bride. He was "a husband by blood" to her. This is precisely what Christ is to the Church. Her connection with Him is founded upon death and resurrection; and she is called to fellowship with His sufferings. It is, as we know, during the period of Israel's unbelief and of Christ's rejection that the Church is called out; and when the Church is complete, according to the divine counsels—when the "fullness of the Gentiles is come in"—Israel shall again be brought into notice.

Thus it was with Zipporah and Israel of old. Moses had sent her back during the period of his mission to Israel; and when the latter were brought forth as a fully delivered people, we read that "Jethro, Moses' father-in-law, took Zipporah, Moses' wife, after he had sent her back, and her two sons, of which the name of the one was Gershom; 'For,' he said, 'I have been an alien in a strange land;' and the name of the other was Eliezer; 'For the God of my fathers,' said he, 'was mine help, and delivered me from the sword of Pharaoh.' And Jethro, Moses' father-in-law, came with his sons and his wife unto Moses into the wilderness, where he encamped at the mount of God. And he said unto Moses, 'I, thy father-in-law, Jethro, am come unto thee, and thy wife and her two sons with her.' And Moses went out to meet his father-in-law, and did obeisance, and kissed him; and they asked each other of their welfare; and they came into the tent. And Moses told his father-in-law all that the Lord had done unto Pharaoh and to the Egyptians for Israel's sake, and all the travail that had come upon them by the way, and how the Lord delivered them. And Jethro rejoiced for all the goodness which the Lord had done to Israel, whom He had delivered from the hand of the Egyptians. And Jethro said, 'Blessed be the Lord, who hath delivered you out of the hand of the Egyptians, and out of the hand of Pharaoh; who hath delivered the people from under the hand of the Egyptians. Now I know that the Lord is greater than all gods; for in the thing wherein they dealt proudly He was above them.' And Jethro, Moses' father-in-law, took a burnt-offering and sacrifices for God; and Aaron came, and all the elders of Israel, to eat bread with Moses' father-in-law before God" (chap. 18:2-12).

This is a deeply interesting scene. The whole congregation assembled in triumph before the Lord, the Gentile presenting sacrifice, and in addition, to complete the picture, the bride of the deliverer, together with the children whom God had given him, are all introduced. It is, in short, a singularly striking foreshadowing of the coming kingdom. "The Lord will give grace and glory." We have already seen, in what we have traveled over of this book, very much of the actings of "grace;" and here we have, from the pencil of the Holy Ghost, a beauteous picture of "glory,"—a picture which must be regarded as peculiarly important, as exhibiting the varied fields in which that glory shall be manifested.

"The Jew, the Gentile, and the Church of

God" are scriptural distinctions which can never be overlooked without marring that perfect range of truth which God has revealed in His holy Word. They have existed ever since the mystery of the Church was fully developed by the ministry of the apostle Paul, and they shall exist throughout the millennial age. Hence, every spiritual student of Scripture will give them their due place in his mind.

The apostle expressly teaches us, in his Epistle to the Ephesians, that the mystery of the Church had not been made known, in other ages, to the sons of men, as it was revealed to him. But though not directly revealed, it had been shadowed forth in one way or another; as, for example, in Joseph's marriage with an Egyptian, and in Moses' marriage with an Ethiopian. The type or shadow of a truth is a very different thing from a direct and positive revelation of it. The great mystery of the Church was not revealed until Christ, in heavenly glory, revealed it to Saul of Tarsus. Hence, all who look for the full unfolding of this mystery in the law, the prophets, or the psalms, will find themselves engaged in unintelligent labor. When, however, they find it distinctly revealed in the Epistle to the Ephesians, they will be able, with interest and profit, to trace its foreshadowing in Old Testament Scripture.

Thus we have, in the opening of our chapter, a millennial scene. All the fields of glory lie open in vision before us. *"The Jew"* stands forth as the great earthly witness of Jehovah's faithfulness, His mercy, and His power. This is what the Jew has been in bygone ages, it is what he is now, and what he will be, world without end. "The Gentile" reads, in the book of God's dealings with the Jew, his deepest lessons. He traces the marvelous history of that peculiar and elect people—"a people terrible from their beginning hitherto;" he sees thrones and empires overturned, nations shaken to their centre, every one and every thing compelled to give way, in order to establish the supremacy of that people on whom Jehovah has set His love. "Now I know," he says, "that the Lord is greater than all gods; for in the thing wherein they dealt proudly He was above them" (ver. 11). Such is the confession of "the Gentile" when the wondrous page of Jewish history lies open before him.

Lastly, *"the Church of God"* collectively, as prefigured by Zipporah, and the members thereof individually, as seen in Zipporah's sons, are presented as occupying the most intimate relationship with the deliverer. All this is perfect in its way. We may be asked for our proofs. The answer is, "I speak as unto wise men: judge ye what I say." We can never build a doctrine upon a type; but when a doctrine is revealed, a type thereof may be discerned with accuracy and studied with profit. In every case, a spiritual mind is essentially necessary, either to understand the doctrine or discern the type. "The natural man receiveth not the things of the Spirit of God; for they are foolishness unto him; neither can he know them, because they are spiritually discerned" (1 Cor. 2:14).

From verse 13 to the end of our chapter, we have the appointment of rulers, who were to assist Moses in the management of the affairs of the congregation. This was the suggestion of Jethro, who feared that Moses would "wear away" in consequence of his labors. In connection with this, it may be profitable to look at the appointment of the seventy elders in Numbers 11. Here we find the spirit of Moses crushed beneath the ponderous responsibility which devolved upon him, and he gives utterance to the anguish of his heart in the following accents: "And Moses said unto the Lord, 'Wherefore hast Thou afflicted Thy servant? And wherefore have I not found favor in Thy sight, that Thou layest the burden of all this people upon me? Have I conceived all this people? have I begotten them, that Thou shouldest say unto me, Carry them in thy bosom, as a nursing father beareth the suckling child, unto the land which Thou swarest unto their fathers? . . . I am not able to bear all this people alone, because it is too heavy for me. And if Thou deal thus with me, kill me, I pray Thee, out of hand, if I have found favor in Thy sight; and let me not see my wretchedness" (Num. 11:11-15).

In all this we see Moses evidently retiring

from a post of honor. If God were pleased to make him the sole instrument in managing the assembly, it was only so much the more dignity and privilege conferred upon him. True, the responsibility was immense; but faith would own that God was amply sufficient for that. Here, however, the heart of Moses failed him (blessed servant as he was), and he says, "I am not able to bear this people *alone,* because it is too heavy for *me.*" But he was not asked to bear them alone, for God was with him. They were not too heavy for God. It was He that was bearing them; Moses was but the instrument. He might just as well have spoken of his rod as bearing the people; for what was he but a mere instrument in God's hand, as the rod was in his? It is here the servants of Christ constantly fail; and the failure is all the more dangerous because it wears the appearance of humility. It seems like distrust of one's self, and deep lowliness of spirit, to shrink from heavy responsibility; but all we need to inquire is, Has God imposed that responsibility? If so, He will assuredly be with me in sustaining it; and having Him with me, I can sustain any thing. With Him, the weight of a mountain is nothing; without Him, the weight of a feather is overwhelming. It is a totally different thing if a man, in the vanity of his mind, thrust himself forward and take a burden upon his shoulder which God never intended him to bear, and therefore never fitted him to bear it; we may then surely expect to see him crushed beneath the weight: but if God lays it upon him, He will qualify and strengthen him to carry it.

It is never the fruit of humility to depart from a divinely-appointed post. On the contrary, the deepest humility will express itself by remaining there in simple dependence upon God. It is a sure evidence of being occupied about *self* when we shrink from service on the ground of inability. God does not call us unto service on the ground of our ability, but of His own; hence, unless I am filled with thoughts about myself, or with positive distrust of Him, I need not relinquish any position of service or testimony because of the heavy responsibilities attaching thereto. All power belongs to God, and it is quite the same whether that power acts through one agent or through seventy—the power is still the same; but if one agent refuse the dignity, it is only so much the worse for him. God will not force people to abide in a place of honor if they cannot trust Him to sustain them there. The way lies always open to them to step down from their dignity, and sink into place where base unbelief is sure to put us.

Thus it was with Moses. He complained of the burden, and the burden was speedily removed; but with it the high honor of being allowed to carry it. "And the Lord said unto Moses, 'Gather unto Me seventy men of the elders of Israel whom thou knowest to be the elders of the people, and officers over them; and bring them unto the tabernacle of the congregation, that they may stand there with thee. And I will come down and talk with thee there: and I will take of the spirit which is upon thee, and will put it upon them; and they shall bear the burden of the people with thee, that thou bear it not thyself alone" (Num. 11:16-17). There was no fresh power introduced. It was the same spirit, whether in one or in seventy. There was no more value or virtue in the flesh of seventy men than in the flesh of one man. "It is the spirit that quickeneth; the flesh profiteth nothing" (John 6:63). There was nothing in the way of power gained, but a great deal in the way of dignity lost, by this movement on the part of Moses.

In the after-part of Numbers 11, we find Moses giving utterance to accents of unbelief, which called forth from the Lord a sharp rebuke.—"Is the Lord's hand waxed short? Thou shalt see now whether My word shall come to pass unto thee, or not." If my reader will compare verses 11-15 with verses 21-22, he will see a marked and solemn connection. The man who shrinks from responsibility, on the ground of his own feebleness, is in great danger of calling in question the fullness and sufficiency of God's resources. This entire scene teaches a most valuable lesson to every servant of Christ who may be tempted to feel himself alone or overburdened in his work. Let such an one bear in mind that, where the Holy

Ghost is working, one instrument is as good and as efficient as seventy; and where He is not working, seventy are of no more value than one. It all depends upon the energy of the Holy Ghost. With Him, one man can do all, endure all, sustain all; without Him, seventy men can do nothing. Let the lonely servant remember, for the comfort and encouragement of his sinking heart, that, provided he has the presence and power of the Holy Ghost with him, he need not complain of his burden nor sigh for a division of labor. If God honor a man by giving him a great deal of work to do, let him rejoice therein and not murmur; for if he murmur, he can very speedily lose his honor. God is at no loss for instruments. He could from the stones raise up children unto Abraham, and He can raise up from the same the needed agents to carry on His glorious work.

O for a heart to serve Him!—a patient, humble, self-emptied, devoted heart,—a heart ready to serve in company, ready to serve alone,—a heart so filled with love to Christ that it will find its joy, its chief joy, in serving Him, let the sphere or character of service be what it may! This assuredly is the special need of the day in which our lot is cast. May the Holy Ghost stir up our hearts to a deeper sense of the exceeding preciousness of the name of Jesus, and enable us to yield a fuller, clearer, more unequivocal response to the changeless love of His heart!

---

## *CHAPTER 19*

WE have now arrived at a most momentous point in Israel's history. We are called to behold them standing at the foot of "the mount that might be touched, and that burned with fire." The fair millennial scene which opened before us in the preceding chapter has passed away. It was but a brief moment of sunshine in which a very vivid picture of the kingdom was afforded; but the sunshine was speedily followed by the heavy clouds which gathered around that "palpable mount," where Israel, in a spirit of dark and senseless legality, abandoned Jehovah's covenant of pure grace for man's covenant of works. Disastrous movement! A movement fraught with the most dismal results. Hitherto, as we have seen, no enemy could stand before Israel,—no obstacle was suffered to interrupt their onward and victorious march. Pharaoh's hosts were overthrown, Amalek and his people were discomfited with the edge of the sword: all was victory, because God was acting on behalf of His people, in pursuance of His promise to Abraham, Isaac, and Jacob.

In the opening verses of the chapter now before us, the Lord recapitulates His actings toward Israel in the following touching and beautiful language: "Thus shalt thou say to the house of Jacob, and tell the children of Israel: Ye have seen what I did unto the Egyptians, and how I bare you on eagles' wings, and brought you unto Myself. Now, therefore, if ye will obey My voice indeed, and keep My covenant, then ye shall be a peculiar treasure unto Me above all people; for all the earth is Mine. And ye shall be unto Me a kingdom of priests and a holy nation" (ver. 3-6). Observe, it is *"My voice"* and *"My covenant."* What was the utterance of that "voice"? and what did that "covenant" involve? Had Jehovah's voice made itself heard for the purpose of laying down the rules and regulations of a severe and unbending lawgiver? By no means. It had spoken to demand freedom for the captive, to provide a refuge from the sword of the destroyer, to make a way for the ransomed to pass over, to bring down bread from heaven, to draw forth water out of the flinty rock;—such had been the gracious and intelligible utterances of Jehovah's "voice" up to the moment at which "Israel camped before the mount."

And as to His "covenant," it was one of unmingled grace. It proposed no condition, it made no demands, it put no yoke on the neck, no burden on the shoulder. When "the God of glory appeared unto Abraham," in Ur of the Chaldees, He certainly did not address him in such words as, Thou shalt do this, and Thou shalt not do that. Ah, no;

such language was not according to the heart of God. It suits Him far better to place "a fair mitre" upon a sinner's head than to "put a yoke upon his neck." His word to Abraham was, *"I will give."* The land of Canaan was not to be purchased by man's doings, but to be given by God's grace. Thus it stood; and in the opening of the book of Exodus, we see God coming down in grace to make good His promise to Abraham's seed. The condition in which He found that seed made no difference, inasmuch as the blood of the lamb furnished Him with a perfectly righteous ground on which to make good His promise. He evidently had not promised the land of Canaan to Abraham's seed on the ground of aught that He foresaw in them, for this would have totally destroyed the real nature of a promise,—it would have made it a compact and not a promise; "but God gave it to Abraham by promise," and not by compact (read Gal. 3).

Hence, in the opening of this nineteenth chapter, the people are reminded of the grace in which Jehovah had hitherto dealt with them; and they are also assured of what they should yet be, provided they continued to hearken to Mercy's heavenly "voice," and to abide in the "covenant" of free and absolute grace. "Ye shall be a peculiar treasure unto Me above all people." How could they be this? Was it by stumbling up the ladder of self-righteousness and legalism? Would they be "a peculiar treasure" when blasted by the curses of a broken law—a law which they had broken before ever they received it? Surely not. How, then, were they to be this "peculiar treasure"? By standing in that position in which Jehovah surveyed them when he compelled the covetous prophet to exclaim, "How goodly are thy tents, O Jacob, and thy tabernacles, O Israel! As the valleys are they spread forth, as gardens by the river's side, as the trees of lign aloes which the Lord hath planted, and as cedar trees beside the waters. He shall pour the water out of his buckets, and his seed shall be in many waters, and his king shall be higher than Agag, and his kingdom shall be exalted. God brought him forth out of Egypt; he hath, as it were, the strength of an unicorn" (Num. 24:5-8).

However, Israel was not disposed to occupy this blessed position. Instead of rejoicing in God's "holy promise," they undertook to make the most presumptuous vow that moral lips could utter. "All the people answered together, and said, *'All that the Lord hath spoken, we will do'* " (chap. 19:8). This was bold language. They did not even say, We hope to do, or We will endeavor to do. This would have expressed a measure of self-distrust. But no; they took the most absolute ground—"We will do." Nor was this the language of a few vain self-confident spirits who presumed to single themselves out from the whole congregation. No; *"all* the people answered *together."* They were unanimous in the abandonment of the "holy promise"—the "holy covenant."

And now, observe the result. The moment Israel uttered their "singular vow," the moment they undertook to "do," there was a total alteration in the aspect of things. "And the Lord said unto Moses, 'Lo, I come unto thee *in a thick cloud*. . . . And thou shalt set bounds unto the people, round about, saying, Take heed to yourselves, that ye go not up into the mount, or touch the border of it: whosoever toucheth the mount shall be surely put to death.' " This was a very marked change. The One who had just said, "I bare you on eagles' wings, and brought you unto Myself," now envelopes Himself "in a thick cloud," and says, "Set bounds unto the people, round about." The sweet accents of grace and mercy are exchanged for the "thunderings and lightnings" of the fiery mount. Man had presumed to talk of his miserable doings in the presence of God's magnificent grace. Israel had said, "We will do," and they must be put at a distance in order that it may be fully seen what they are able to do. God takes the place of moral distance; and the people are but too well disposed to have it so, for they are filled with fear and trembling; and no marvel, for the sight was "terrible,"—"so terrible, that Moses said, 'I exceedingly fear and quake.' " Who could endure the sight of that "devouring fire," which was the apt expression of divine holiness? "The Lord came from Sinai, and rose up from Seir unto them; He shined forth from Paran, and He came with ten thousand of His saints; from His right hand went a fiery law for them" (Deut. 33:2). The term "fiery," as applied to the law, is expressive of its holiness,—"Our God is a consuming fire"—perfectly intolerant of evil, in thought, word, and deed.

Thus, then, Israel made a fatal mistake in saying, "We will do." It was taking upon themselves a vow which they were not able, even were they willing, to pay; and we know who has said, "Better that thou shouldest not vow, than that thou shouldest vow and not pay." It is of the very essence of a vow that it assumes the competency to fulfill; and where is man's competency? As well might a bankrupt draw a check on the bank, as a helpless sinner make a vow. A man who makes a vow denies the truth as to his nature and condition. He is ruined, what can he do? He is utterly without strength, and can neither will nor do any thing good. Did Israel keep their vow? Did they do "all that the Lord commanded"? Witness the golden calf, the broken tables, the desecrated Sabbath, the despised and neglected ordinances, the stoned messengers, the rejected and crucified Christ, the resisted Spirit. Such are the overwhelming evidences of man's dishonored vows. Thus must it ever be when fallen humanity undertakes to vow.

Christian reader, do you not rejoice in the fact that your eternal salvation rests not on your poor shadowy vows and resolutions, but on "the one offering of Jesus Christ once"? Oh, yes, "this is our joy, which ne'er can fail." Christ has taken all our vows upon Himself, and gloriously discharged them forever. His resurrection-life flows through His members and produces in them results which legal vows and legal claims never could effect. He is our life, and He is our righteousness. May His name be precious to our hearts. May His cause ever command our energies. May it be our meat and our drink to spend and be spent in His dear service.

I cannot close this chapter without noticing, in connection, a passage in the book of Deuteronomy which may present a difficulty to some minds. It has direct reference to the subject on which we have been dwelling. "And the Lord heard the voice of your words, when ye spake unto me; and the Lord said unto me, 'I have heard the voice of the words of this people, which they have spoken unto thee: *they have well said all that they have spoken'* " (Deut. 5:28). From this passage it might seem as though the Lord approved of their making a vow; but if my reader will take the trouble of reading the entire context, from verse twenty-four to twenty-seven, he will see at once that it has nothing whatever to say to the vow, but that it contains the expression of their terror at the consequences of their vow. They were not able to endure that which was commanded. "If" said they, "we hear the voice of the Lord our God any more, then we shall die. For who is there of all flesh that hath heard the voice of the living God speaking out of the midst of the fire, as we have, and lived? Go thou near, and hear all that the Lord our God shall say; and speak thou unto us all that the Lord our God shall speak unto thee, and we will hear it and do it." It was the confession of their own inability to encounter Jehovah in that awful aspect which their proud legality had led Him to assume. It is impossible that the Lord could ever commend an abandonment of free and changeless grace for a sandy foundation of "works of law."

---

## *CHAPTER 20*

IT is of the utmost importance to understand the true character and object of the moral law, as set forth in this chapter. There is a tendency in the mind to confound the principles of law and grace, so that neither the one nor the other can be rightly understood. Law is shorn of its stern and unbending majesty, and grace is robbed of all its divine attractions. God's holy claims remain unanswered, and the sinner's deep and manifold necessities remain unreached, by the anomalous system framed by those who attempt to mingle law and grace. In point of fact, they can never be made to coalesce, for they are as distinct as any two things can be. Law sets forth what man ought to be, grace exhibits what God is. How can these ever be wrought up into one system? How can the sinner ever be saved by a system made up of half law, half grace? Impossible. It must be either the one or the other.

The law has sometimes been termed "the transcript of the mind of God." This definition is entirely defective. Were we to term it a transcript of the mind of God as to what man ought to be, we should be nearer the truth. If I am to regard the ten commandments as the transcript of the mind of God, then, I ask, is there nothing in the mind of God save "Thou shalt" and "Thou shalt not"? Is there no grace? no mercy? no loving-kindness? Is God not to manifest what He is? Is He not to tell out the deep secrets of that love which dwells in His bosom? Is there naught in the divine character but stern requirement and prohibition? Were this so, we should have to say, God is law, instead of "God is love." But, blessed be His name, there is more in His heart than could ever be wrapped up in the "ten words" uttered on the fiery mount. If I want to see what God is, I must look at Christ; "for in Him dwelleth all the fullness of the Godhead bodily" (Col. 2:9). "The law was given by Moses, but grace and truth came by Jesus Christ" (John 1:17). Assuredly there was a measure of truth in the law; it contained the truth as to what man ought to be. Like everything else emanating from God, it was perfect so far as it went—perfect for the object for which it was administered; but that object was not, by any means, to unfold, in the view of guilty sinners, the nature and character of God. There was no grace, no mercy. "He that despised Moses' law died without mercy" (Heb. 10:28). "The man that doeth these things shall live by them" (Lev. 18:5; Rom. 10:5). "Cursed is every one that continueth not in all things that are written in the book of the law to do them" (Deut. 27:26; Gal. 3:10). This was not grace. Indeed, Mount Sinai was not the place to look for any such thing. There Jehovah revealed Himself in awful majesty, amid blackness, darkness, tempest, thunderings, and lightnings. These were not the attendant circumstances of an economy of grace and mercy; but they were well suited to one of truth and righteousness, and the law was that and nothing else.

In the law, God sets forth what a man ought to be, and pronounces a curse upon him if he is not that. But then a man finds, when he looks at himself in the light of the law, that he actually *is* the very thing which the law condemns. How then is he to get life by it? It proposes life and righteousness as the ends to be attained by keeping it; but it proves, at the very outset, that we are in a state of death and unrighteousness. We want the very things at the beginning which the law proposed to be gained at the end. How, therefore, are we to gain them? In order to *do* what the law requires, I must have life; and in order to *be* what the law requires, I must have righteousness; and if I have not both the one and the other, I am "cursed." But the fact is, I have neither. What am I to do? This is the question. Let those who "desire to be teachers of the law" furnish an answer. Let them furnish a satisfactory reply to an upright conscience, bowed down under the double sense of the spirituality and inflexibility of the law and its own hopeless carnality.

The truth is, as the apostle teaches us, "the law entered that the offense might abound" (Rom. 5:20). This shows us very distinctly the real object of the law. It came in by the way in order to set forth the exceeding sinfulness of sin (Rom. 7:13). It was, in a certain sense, like a perfect mirror let down from heaven to reveal to man his moral derangement. If I present myself with deranged habit before a mirror, it shows me the derangement, but does not set it right. If I measure a crooked wall with a perfect plumb-line, it reveals the crookedness, but does not remove it. If I take out a lamp on a dark night, it reveals to me all the hindrances and disagreeables in the way, but it does not remove them. Moreover, the mirror, the plumb-line and the lamp do not *create* the evils which they severally point out; they neither *create* nor *remove,* but simply *reveal.* Thus it is with the law; it does not create the evil in man's heart, neither does it remove it; but, with unerring accuracy, it reveals it.

"What shall we say then? Is the law sin? God forbid. Nay, I had not known sin, but by the law; for I had not known lust, except the law had said, 'Thou shalt not covet' " (Rom. 7:7). He does not say that he would not have had "lust." No; but merely that he "had not known" it. The "lust" was there; but he was in the dark about it until the law, as "the candle of the Almighty," shone in upon the dark chambers of his heart and revealed the evil that was there. Like a man in a dark room, who may be surrounded with dust and confusion, but he cannot see aught thereof by reason of the darkness. Let the beams of the sun dart in upon him, and he quickly perceives all. Do the sunbeams create the dust? Surely not. The dust is there, and they only detect and reveal it. This is a simple illustration of the effect of the law. It judges man's character and condition; it proves him to be a sinner, and shuts him up under the curse; it comes to judge what he is, and curses him if he is not what it tells him he ought to be.

It is therefore a manifest impossibility that any one can get life and righteousness by that which can only curse him; and unless the condition of the sinner, and the character of the law are totally changed, it can do naught else but curse him. It makes no allowance for infirmities, and knows nothing of sincere, though imperfect, obedience. Were it to do so, it would not be what it is—"holy, just, and good." It is just because the law is what it is that the sinner cannot get life by it. If he could get life by it, it would not be perfect, or else he would not be a sinner. It is impossible that a sinner can get life by a perfect law, for inasmuch as it is perfect, it must needs condemn him. Its absolute perfectness makes manifest and seals man's absolute ruin and condemnation. "Therefore, by deeds of law shall no flesh living be justified in His sight; for by the law is the knowledge of sin" (Rom. 3:20). He does not say, By the law is sin, but only "the knowledge of sin." "For until the law, sin was in the world; but sin is not imputed when there is no law" (Rom. 5:13). Sin was there, and it only needed law to develop it in the form of "transgression." It is as if I say to my child, You must not touch that knife. My very prohibition reveals the tendency in his heart to do his own will. It does not create the tendency, but only reveals it.

The apostle John says that "sin is lawlessness" (1 John 3:4). The word "transgression" does not develop the true idea of the Spirit in this passage. In order to have "transgression," I must have a definite rule or line laid down. Transgression means a passing across a prohibited line; such a line I have in the law. I take any one of its prohibitions, such as, "Thou shalt not kill," "Thou shalt not commit adultery," "Thou shalt not steal." Here I have a rule or line set before me; but I find I have within me the very principles against which these prohibitions are expressly directed. Yea, the very fact of my being told not to commit murder shows that I have murder in my nature. There would be no necessity to tell me not to do a thing which I had not tendency to do; but the exhibition of God's will as to what I ought to be makes manifest the tendency of my will to be what I ought not. This is plain enough, and is in full keeping with the whole of the apostolic reasoning on the point.

Many, however, will admit that we cannot get life by the law; but they maintain, at the same time, that the law is our rule of life. Now, the apostle declares that "as many as are of works of law are under the curse" (Gal. 3:10). It matters not who they are, if they occupy the ground of law, they are, of necessity, under the curse. A man may say, I am regenerate, and therefore not exposed to the curse. This will not do. If regeneration does not take one off the ground of law, it cannot take him beyond the range of the curse of the law. If the Christian be under the former, he is, of necessity, exposed to the latter. But what has the law to do with regeneration? where do we find any thing about it in Exodus 20?

The law has but one question to put to a man, a brief, solemn, pointed question, namely, Are you what you ought to be? If he answer in the negative, it can but hurl its terrible anathema at him and slay him. And who will so readily and emphatically admit that, in himself, he is any thing but what he ought to be, as the really regenerate man? Wherefore, if he is under the law, he must inevitably be under the curse. The law cannot possibly lower its standard, nor yet amalgamate with grace. Men do constantly seek to lower its standard; they feel that they cannot get up to it, and they therefore seek to bring it down to them; but the effort is in vain: it stands forth in all its purity, majesty, and stern inflexibility, and will not accept a single hair's breadth short of perfect obedience; and where is the man, regenerate or unregenerate, that can undertake to produce that? It will be said, We have perfection in Christ. True; but that is not by the law, but by grace; and we cannot possibly confound the two economies. Scripture largely and distinctly teaches that we are not justified by the law; nor is the law our rule of life. That which can only curse can never justify, and that which can only kill can never be a rule of life. As well might a man attempt to make a fortune by a deed of bankruptcy filed against him.

If my reader will turn to the fifteenth of Acts, he will see how the attempt to put Gentile believers under the law as a rule of life was met by the Holy Ghost. "There rose up certain of the sect of the Pharisees which believed, saying, that it was needful to circumcise them, and to command them to keep the law of Moses." This was nothing else than the hiss of the old serpent, making itself heard in the dark and depressing suggestion of those early legalists. But let us see how it was met by the mighty energy of the Holy Ghost, and the unanimous voice of the twelve apostles and the whole Church. "And when there had been much disputing, Peter rose up, and said unto them, 'Men and brethren, ye know how that a good while ago God made choice among us, that the Gentiles by my mouth should hear' "—what? Was it the requirements and the curses of *the law* of Moses? No. Blessed be God, these are not what He would have falling on the ears of helpless sinners. Hear what, then? "*Should hear the Word of the gospel, and believe.*" This was what suited the nature and character of God. He never would have troubled men with the dismal accents of requirement and prohibition. These Pharisees were not His messengers; far from it. They were not the bearers of glad tidings, nor the publishers of peace, and therefore their "feet" were aught but "beautiful" in the eyes of One who only delights in mercy.

"Now, therefore," continues the apostle, "why tempt ye God, to put a yoke upon the neck of the disciples, which neither our fathers nor we were able to bear?" This was strong, earnest language. God did not want "to put a yoke upon the neck" of those whose hearts had been set free by the gospel of peace. He would rather exhort them to stand fast in the liberty of Christ, and not be "entangled again with the yoke of bondage." He would not send those whom He had received to His bosom of love to be terrified by the "blackness and darkness and tempest" of "the mount that might be touched." How could we ever admit the thought that those whom God had received in grace He would rule by law? Impossible. "We believe," says Peter, "that through the *grace of the Lord Jesus Christ* we shall be saved, even as they." Both the Jews, who had received the law, and the Gentiles, who never had, were now to be "*saved* through *grace.*" And not only were they to be "saved" by grace, but they were to "stand" in grace (Rom. 5:2) and to "grow in grace" (2 Pet. 3:18). To teach any thing else was to "tempt God." Those Pharisees were subverting the very foundations of the Christian faith; and so are all those who seek to put believers under the law. There is no evil or error more abominable in the sight of the Lord than legalism. Hearken to the strong language—the accents of righteous indignation—which fell from the Holy Ghost in reference to those teachers of the law—"I would they were even cut off which trouble you" (Gal. 5:12).

Are the thoughts of the Holy Ghost

changed in reference to this question? Has it ceased to be a tempting of God to place the yoke of legality upon a sinner's neck? Is it now in accordance with His gracious will that the law should be read out in the ears of sinners? Let my reader reply to these inquiries in the light of the fifteenth of Acts and the Epistle to the Galatians. These Scriptures, were there no other, are amply sufficient to prove that God never intended that the "Gentiles should hear the word" of the law. Had He so intended, He would assuredly have "made choice" of some one to proclaim it in their ears. But no; when He sent forth His "fiery law," He spoke only in *one* tongue; but when He proclaimed the glad tidings of salvation through the blood of the Lamb, He spoke in the language *"of every nation under heaven."* He spoke in such a way as that *"every man in his own tongue, wherein he was born,"* might hear the sweet story of grace (Acts 2:1-11).

Further, when He was giving forth, from Mount Sinai, the stern requirements of the covenant of works, He addressed Himself exclusively to *one* people. His voice was only heard within the narrow inclosures of the Jewish nation; but when, on the plains of Bethlehem, "the angel of the Lord" declared "good tidings of great joy," He added those characteristic words, "which shall be *to all people."* And again, when the risen Christ was sending forth His heralds of salvation, His commission ran thus: "Go ye into *all the world* and preach the gospel to *every creature"* (Mark 16:15; Luke 2:10). The mighty tide of grace, which had its source in the bosom of God, and its channel in the blood of the Lamb, was designed to rise, in the resistless energy of the Holy Ghost, far above the narrow inclosures of Israel, and roll through the length and breadth of a sin-stained world. "Every creature" must hear, "in his own tongue," the message of peace—the word of the gospel—the record of salvation through the blood of the cross.

Finally, that nothing might be lacking to prove to our poor legal hearts that Mount Sinai was not, by any means, the spot where the deep secrets of the bosom of God were told out, the Holy Ghost has said, both by the mouth of a prophet and an apostle, "How beautiful are the feet of them that preach the gospel of peace, and bring glad tidings of good things!" (Isa. 3:7; Rom. 10:15) But of those who sought to be teachers of the law, the same Holy Ghost has said, "I would they were even cut off which trouble you."

Thus, then, it is obvious that the law is neither the ground of life to the sinner nor the rule of life to the Christian: Christ is both the one and the other,—He is our life and He is our rule of life. The law can only curse and slay. Christ is our life and righteousness. He became a curse for us by hanging on a tree. He went down into the place where the sinner lay—into the place of death and judgment; and having, by His death, entirely discharged all that was or could be against us, He became, in resurrection, the source of life and the ground of righteousness to all who believe in His name. Having thus life and righteousness in Him, we are called to walk not merely as the law directs, but to "walk even as He walked." It will hardly be deemed needful to assert that it is directly contrary to Christian ethics to kill, commit adultery, or steal. But were a Christian to shape his way according to these commands, or according to the entire decalogue, would he yield the rare and delicate fruits which the Epistle to the Ephesians sets forth? Would the ten commandments ever cause a thief to give up stealing, and go to work that he might have to give?—would they ever transform a thief into a laborious and liberal man? Assuredly not. The law says, "Thou shalt not steal;" but does it say, Go and give to him that needeth,—Go, feed, clothe, and bless your enemy,—Go, gladden by your benevolent feelings and your beneficent acts the heart of him who only and always seeks your hurt? By no means; and yet, were I under the law, as a rule, it could only curse me and slay me. How is this, when the standard in the New Testament is so much higher? Because I am weak, and the law gives me no strength and shows me no mercy. The law *demands* strength from one that has none, and *curses* him if he cannot display it. The gospel *gives* strength to one that has none, and *blesses* him in the exhibition of it. The law proposes life as the end of obedience, the gospel gives life as the only proper *ground* of obedience.

But that I may not weary the reader with arguments, let me ask, If the law be indeed the rule of a believer's life, where are we to find it so presented in the New Testament? The inspired apostle evidently had no thought of its being the rule when he penned the following words: "For in Christ Jesus neither circumcision availeth any thing nor uncircumcision, but a new creation. And as many as walk according to *this rule,* peace be on them, and mercy, and on the Israel of God" (Gal. 6:15-16). What "rule"? The law? No; but the "new creation." Where shall we find this in Exodus 20? It speaks not a word about "new creation." On the contrary, it addresses itself to man as he is—in his natural or old-creation state—and puts him to the test as to what he is really able to do. Now if the law were the rule by which believers are to walk, why does the apostle pronounce his benediction on those who walk by another rule altogether? Why does he not say, As many as walk according to the rule of the ten commandments? Is it not evident, from this one passage, that the Church of God has a higher rule by which to walk? Unquestionably. The ten commandments, though forming, as all true Christians admit, a part of the canon of inspiration, could never be the rule of life to one who has, through infinite grace, been introduced into the new creation—one who has received new life in Christ.

But some may ask, Is not the law perfect? and if perfect, what more would you have? The law is divinely perfect. Yea, it is the very perfection of the law which causes it to curse and slay those who are not perfect if they attempt to stand before it. "The law is spiritual, but I am carnal." It is utterly impossible to form an adequate idea of the infinite perfectness and spirituality of the law. But then this perfect law coming in contact with fallen humanity—this spiritual law coming in contact with "the carnal mind," could only "work wrath" and "enmity" (Rom. 4:15; 8:7). Why? Is it because the law is not perfect? No, but because it is, and man is a sinner. If man were perfect, he would carry out the law in all its spiritual perfectness; and even in the case of true believers, though they still carry about with them an evil nature, the apostle teaches us "that the righteousness of the law is fulfilled in us, who walk not after the flesh, but after the Spirit" (Rom. 8:4). "He that loveth another hath fulfilled the law.... Love worketh no ill to his neighbor; therefore love is the fulfilling of the law" (Rom. 13:8-10). If I love a man, I shall not steal his property—nay, I shall seek to do him all the good I can. All this is plain, and easily understood by the spiritual mind; but it leaves entirely untouched the question of the law, whether as the ground of life to a sinner or the rule of life to the believer.

If we look at the law, in its two grand divisions, it tells a man to love God with all his heart, and with all his soul, and with all his mind; and to love his neighbor as himself. This is the sum of the law: this, and not a tittle less, is what the law demands. But where has this demand ever been responded to by any member of Adam's fallen posterity? Where is the man who could say he loves God after such a fashion? "The carnal mind [*i.e.,* the mind which we have by nature] is enmity against God." Man hates God and His ways. God came, in the Person of Christ, and showed Himself to man—showed Himself, not in the overwhelming brightness of His majesty, but in all the charm and sweetness of perfect grace and condescension. What was the result? Man hated God.—"Now have they both seen and hated both Me and My Father" (John 15:24). But, it may be said, man ought to love God. No doubt, and he deserves death and eternal perdition if he does not; but can the law produce this love in man's heart? was that its design? By no means, "for the law worketh wrath." The law finds man in a state of enmity against God; and without ever altering that state (for that was not its province), it commands him to love God with all his heart, and curses him if he does not. It was not the province of the law to alter or improve man's nature; nor yet could it impart any power to carry out its righteous demands. It said, "This do, and thou shalt live." It commanded man to love God. It did not reveal what God was to man, even in his guilt and ruin; but it told man what he ought to be toward God. This was dismal work. It was not the unfolding of the powerful attractions of the divine character, producing in man true repentance toward God, melting his icy heart, and elevating his soul in genuine affection and worship. No: it was an inflexible command to love God; and, instead of producing love, it "worked wrath;" not because God ought not to be loved, but because man was a sinner.

Again, "Thou shalt love thy neighbor as thyself." Can "the natural man" do this? Does he love his neighbor as himself? Is this the principle which obtains in the chambers of commerce, the exchanges, the banks, the marts, the fairs, and the markets of this world? Alas! no. Man does not love his neighbor as he loves himself. No doubt he ought; and if he were right, he would; but then he is all wrong—totally wrong—and unless he is "born again" of the Word and the Spirit of God, he cannot "see nor enter the kingdom of God." The law cannot produce this new birth. It kills "the old man," but does not, and cannot, create "the new." As an actual fact, we know that the Lord Jesus Christ embodied, in His glorious Person, both God and our neighbor, inasmuch as He was, according to the foundation-truth of the Christian religion, "God manifest in the flesh." How did man treat Him? Did he love Him with all his heart, or as himself? The very reverse. He crucified Him between two thieves, having previously preferred a murderer and a robber to that blessed One who had gone about doing good—who had come forth from the eternal dwelling-place of light and love—Himself the very living personification of that light and love—whose bosom had ever heaved with purest sympathy with human need—whose hand had ever been ready to dry the sinner's tears and alleviate his sorrows. Thus we stand and gaze upon the cross of Christ, and behold in it an unanswerable demonstration of the fact that it is not within the range of man's nature or capacity to keep the law.*

It is peculiarly interesting to the spiritual mind, after all that has passed before us, to observe the relative position of God and the sinner at the close of this memorable chapter. "And the Lord said unto Moses, 'Thus thou shalt say unto the children of Israel. . . . An altar of earth thou shalt make unto Me, and shalt sacrifice thereon thy burnt-offerings and thy peace-offerings, thy sheep and thine oxen: in all places where I record My name *I will come unto thee, and I will bless thee.* And if thou wilt make Me an altar of stone, thou shalt not build it of hewn stone; for if thou lift up thy tool upon it, thou hast polluted it. Neither shalt thou go up by steps unto Mine altar, that thy nakedness be not discovered thereon' " (ver. 22-26).

Here we find man not in the position of *a doer,* but of *a worshiper;* and this, too, at the close of Exodus 20. How plainly this teaches us that the atmosphere of Mount Sinai is not that which God would have the sinner breathing,—that it is not the proper meeting-place between God and man! "In all places where I record *My name I will come unto thee, and I will bless thee."* How unlike the terrors of the fiery mount is that spot where Jehovah records *His name,* whither He "comes" to "bless" His worshiping people!

But further, God will meet the sinner at an altar without a hewn stone or a step—a place of worship which requires no human workmanship to erect, or human effort to approach. The former could only pollute, and the latter could only display human "nakedness." Admirable type of the meeting-place where God meets the sinner now, even the Person and work of His Son, Jesus Christ, where all the claims of law, of justice, and of conscience are perfectly answered! Man has, in every age and in every clime, been prone, in one way or another, to "lift up his tool" in the erection of his altar, or to

*For further exposition of the law, and also of the doctrine of the Sabbath, the reader is referred to a tract entitled "A Scriptural Inquiry into the True Nature of the Sabbath, the Law, and the Christian Ministry," in the author's *Miscellaneous Writings, vol. 3.*

approach thereto by steps of his own making; but the issue of all such attempts has been "pollution" and "nakedness." "We all do fade as a leaf, and all our righteousnesses are as filthy rags." Who will presume to approach God clad in a garment of "filthy rags"? or who will stand to worship with a revealed "nakedness"? What can be more preposterous than to think of approaching God in a way which necessarily involves either pollution or nakedness? And yet thus it is in every case in which human effort is put forth to open the sinner's way to God. Not only is there no need of such effort, but defilement and nakedness are stamped upon it. God has come down so very near to the sinner, even in the very depths of his ruin, that there is no need for his lifting up the tool of legality, or ascending the steps of self-righteousness,—yea, to do so, is but to expose his uncleanness and his nakedness.

Such are the principles with which the Holy Ghost closes this most remarkable section of our inspiration. May they be indelibly written upon our hearts, that so we may more clearly and fully understand the essential difference between *law* and *grace.*

---

## *CHAPTERS 21–23*

THE study of this section of our book is eminently calculated to impress the heart with a sense of God's unsearchable wisdom and infinite goodness. It enables one to form some idea of the character of a kingdom governed by laws of divine appointment. Here, too, we may see the amazing condescension of Him who, though He is the great God of heaven and earth, can, nevertheless, stoop to adjudicate between man and man in reference to the death of an ox, the loan of a garment, or the loss of a servant's tooth. "Who is like unto the Lord our God, who humbleth Himself to behold the things that are in heaven and on earth?" He governs the universe, and yet He can occupy Himself with the provision of a covering for one of His creatures. He guides the angel's flight and takes notice of a crawling worm. He humbles Himself to regulate the movements of those countless orbs that roll through infinite space, and to record the fall of a sparrow.

As to the character of the judgment set forth in the chapter before us, we may learn a double lesson. These judgments and ordinances bear a twofold witness: they convey to the ear a twofold message, and present to the eye two sides of a picture. They tell of God and they tell of man.

In the first place, on God's part, we find Him enacting laws which exhibit strict, even-handed, perfect justice. "Eye for eye, tooth for tooth, hand for hand, foot for foot, burning for burning, wound for wound, stripe for stripe." Such was the character of the laws, the statutes, and the judgments by which God governed His earthly kingdom of Israel. Everything was provided for, every interest was maintained, and every claim was met. There was no partiality—no distinction made between the rich and the poor. The balance in which each man's claim was weighed was adjusted with divine accuracy, so that no one could justly complain of a decision. The pure robe of justice was not to be tarnished with the foul stains of bribery, corruption, and partiality. The eye and the hand of a divine Legislator provided for everything, and a divine Executive inflexibly dealt with every defaulter. The stroke of justice fell only on the head of the guilty, while every obedient soul was protected in the enjoyment of all his rights and privileges.

Then, as regards man, it is impossible to read over these laws and not be struck with the disclosure which they indirectly, but really, make of his desperate depravity. The fact of Jehovah's having to enact laws against certain crimes, proves the capability on man's part of committing those crimes. Were the capability and the tendency not there, there would be no need of the enactments. Now there are many who, if the gross abominations forbidden in these chapters were named to them, might feel disposed to adopt the language of Hazael, and say, "Is thy servant a dog that he should do this thing?" Such persons have not yet traveled down into the deep abyss of their own hearts. For albeit there are crimes here forbidden which would seem to place man, as regards his habits and tendencies, below the level of a "dog," yet do those very statutes prove, beyond all question, that the most refined and cultivated member of the human family carries about in his bosom the seeds of the very darkest and most horrifying abominations. For whom were those statutes enacted? For man. Were they needful? Unquestionably. But they would have been quite superfluous if man were incapable of committing the sins referred to. But man *is* capable; and hence we see that man is sunk to the very lowest possible level—that his nature is wholly corrupt—that from the crown of his head to the sole of his foot there is not so much as a speck of moral soundness.

How can such a being ever stand, without an emotion of fear, in the full blaze of the throne of God? how can he stand within the holiest? how can he stand on the sea of glass? how can he enter in by the pearly gates and tread the golden streets? The reply to these inquiries unfolds the amazing depths of redeeming love and the eternal efficacy of the blood of the Lamb. Deep as is man's ruin, the love of God is deeper still: black as is his guilt, the blood of Jesus can wash it all away: wide as is the chasm separating man from God, the cross has bridged it. God has come down to the very lowest point of the sinner's condition, in order that He might lift him up into a position of infinite favor, in eternal association with His own Son. Well may we exclaim, "Behold, what manner of love the Father hath bestowed upon us, that we should be called the sons of God" (1 John 3:1). Nothing could fathom man's ruin but God's love, and nothing could equal man's guilt but the blood of Christ. But now the very depth of the ruin only magnifies the love that has fathomed it, and the intensity of the guilt only celebrates the efficacy of the blood that can cleanse it. The very vilest sinner who believes in Jesus can rejoice in the assurance that God sees him and pronounces him *"clean every whit."*

Such, then, is the double character of instruction to be gleaned from the laws and ordinances in this section, looked at as a whole; and the more minutely we look at them in detail, the more impressed we shall be with a sense of their fullness and beauty. Take, for instance, the very first ordinance that presents itself, namely, that of the Hebrew servant.

"Now these are the judgments which thou shalt set before them: If thou buy a Hebrew servant, six years he shall serve, and in the seventh he shall go out free for nothing. If he came in by himself, he shall go out by himself: if he were married, then his wife shall go out with him. If his master have given him a wife, and she have borne him sons or daughters, the wife and her children shall be her master's, and he shall go out by himself. And if the servant shall plainly say, I love my master, my wife, and my children; I will not go out free; then his master shall bring him unto the judges: he shall also bring him to the door, or unto the door-post; and his master shall bore his ear through with an awl; and he shall serve him forever" (chap. 21:1-6). The servant was perfectly free to go out, so far as he was personally concerned. He had discharged every claim, and could therefore walk abroad in unquestioned freedom; but because of his love to his master, his wife, and his children, he voluntarily bound himself to perpetual servitude; and not only so, but he was also willing to bear, in his own person, the marks of that servitude.

The application of this to the Lord Jesus Christ will be obvious to the intelligent reader. In Him we behold the One who dwelt in the bosom of the Father before all worlds—the object of His eternal delight—who might have occupied, throughout eternity, this His personal and entirely peculiar place, inasmuch as there lay upon Him no obligation (save that which ineffable love created and ineffable love incurred) to abandon that place. Such, however, was His love to the Father, whose counsels were involved, and for the Church collectively and each individual member thereof, whose salvation was involved, that He voluntarily came down to earth, emptied Himself, and made Himself of no reputation, took upon Him the form of a servant and the marks of perpetual service. To these marks we probably have a striking allusion in the Psalms. "Mine ears hast Thou digged" (Ps. 40:6, marg.). This psalm is the expression of Christ's devotedness to God. "Then said I, 'Lo, I come: in the volume of the book it is written of Me, I delight to do Thy will, O My God; yea, Thy law is within My heart.' " He came to do the will of God, whatever that will might be. He never once did His own will, not even in the reception and salvation of sinners, though surely His loving heart, with all its affections, was most fully in that glorious work. Still He receives and saves only as the servant of the Father's counsels. "All that the Father giveth Me shall come to Me; and him that cometh to Me I will in no wise cast out. For I came down from heaven, not to do Mine own will, but the will of Him that sent Me. And this is the Father's will which hath sent Me, that of all which He hath given Me I should lose nothing, but should raise it up again at the last day" (John 6:37-39).

Here we have a most interesting view of the servant-character of the Lord Jesus Christ. He, in perfect grace, holds Himself responsible to receive all who come within the range of the divine counsels; and not only to receive them, but to preserve them through all the difficulties and trials of their devious path down here,—yea, in the article of death itself, should it come, and to raise them all up in the last day. Oh, how secure is the very feeblest member of the Church of God! He is the subject of God's eternal counsels, which counsels the Lord Jesus Christ is pledged to carry out. Jesus loves the Father, and in proportion to the intensity of that love is the security of each member of the redeemed family. The salvation of the sinner who believes on the name of the Son of God is, in one aspect of it, but the expression of Christ's love to the Father. If one such could perish, through any cause whatsoever, it would argue that the Lord Jesus Christ was unable to carry out the will of God, which were nothing short of positive blasphemy against His sacred name, to whom be all honor and majesty throughout the everlasting ages.

Thus we have, in the Hebrew servant, a type of Christ in His pure devotedness to the Father. But there is more than this. "I love my wife and my children." "Christ loved the Church, and gave Himself for it; that He might sanctify and cleanse it with the washing of water by the Word, that He might present it to Himself a glorious Church, not having spot, or wrinkle, or any such thing; but that it should be holy and without blemish" (Eph. 5:25-27). There are various other passages of Scripture presenting Christ as the antitype of the Hebrew servant, both in His love for the Church as a body, and for all believers personally. In Matthew 13, John 10 and 13, and Hebrews 2, is special teaching on the point.

The apprehension of this love of the heart of Jesus cannot fail to produce a spirit of fervent devotedness to the One who could exhibit such pure, such perfect, such disinterested love. How could the wife and children of the Hebrew servant fail to love one who had voluntarily surrendered his liberty in order that he and they might be together? And what is the love presented in the type, when compared with that which shines in the antitype? It is as nothing. "The love of Christ passeth knowledge." It led Him to think of us before all worlds—to visit us in the fullness of time—to walk deliberately to the door-post—to suffer for us on the cross, in order that He might raise us to companionship with Himself in His everlasting kingdom and glory.

Were I to enter into a full exposition of the remaining statutes and judgments of this portion of the book of Exodus, it would carry me much further than I feel, at present, led to go.* I will merely observe, in conclusion, that it is impossible to read the

*I would here observe, once for all, that the feasts referred to in chapter 23:14-19, and the offerings in chapter 29, being brought out, in all their fullness and detail, in the book of Leviticus, I shall reserve them until we come to dwell upon the contents of that singularly rich and interesting book.

section and not have the heart drawn out in adoration of the profound wisdom, well-balanced justice, and yet tender considerateness which breathe throughout the whole. We rise up from the study of it with this conviction deeply wrought into the soul, that the One who speaks here is "the only true," "the only wise," and the infinitely gracious God.

May all our meditations on His eternal Word have the effect of prostrating our souls in worship before Him whose perfect ways and glorious attributes shine there, in all their blessedness and brightness, for the refreshment, the delight, and the edification of His blood-bought people.

---

## *CHAPTER 24*

THIS chapter opens with an expression remarkably characteristic of the entire Mosaic economy. "And He said unto Moses, 'Come up unto the Lord, thou, and Aaron, Nadab, and Abihu, and seventy of the elders of Israel; and worship ye *afar off . . . they shall not come nigh,* neither shall the people *go up* with him." We may search from end to end of the legal ritual, and not find those two precious words, *"draw nigh."* Ah, no; such words could never be heard from the top of Sinai, nor from amid the shadows of the law. They could only be uttered at heaven's side of the empty tomb of Jesus, where the blood of the cross has opened a perfectly cloudless prospect to the vision of faith. The words, "afar off," are as characteristic of the law as "draw nigh" are of the gospel. Under the law, the work was never done which could entitle a sinner to draw nigh. Man had not fulfilled his promised obedience; and the "blood of calves and goats" could not atone for the failure, or give his guilty conscience peace. Hence, therefore, he had to stand "afar off." Man's vows were broken and his sin unpurged; how, then, could he draw nigh? The blood of ten thousand bullocks could not wipe away one stain from the conscience, or give the peaceful sense of nearness as being reconciled to God.

However, the "first covenant" is here dedicated with blood. An altar is erected at the foot of the hill, with "twelve pillars, according to the twelve tribes of Israel." "And he sent young men of the children of Israel, which offered burnt-offerings, and sacrificed peace-offerings of oxen unto the Lord. And Moses took half of the blood, and put it in basins; and half of the blood he sprinkled on the altar. . . . And Moses took the blood, and sprinkled it on the people, and said, 'Behold the blood of the covenant, which the Lord hath made with you concerning all these words.' " Although, as the apostle teaches us, it was "impossible that the blood of bulls and goats could take away sin," yet did it "sanctify to the purifying of the flesh," and, as "a shadow of good things to come," it availed to maintain the people in relationship with Jehovah.

"Then went up Moses, and Aaron, Nadab, and Abihu, and seventy of the elders of Israel; and they saw the God of Israel: and there was under His feet as it were a paved work of a sapphire stone, and as it were the body of heaven in clearness. And upon the nobles of the children of Israel He laid not His hand: also they saw God and did eat and drink." This was the manifestation of "the God of Israel," in light and purity, majesty and holiness. It was not the unfolding of the affections of a Father's bosom, or the sweet accents of a Father's voice, breathing peace and inspiring confidence into the heart. No; the "paved work of a sapphire stone" told out that unapproachable purity and light which could only tell a sinner to keep off. Still, "they saw God and did eat and drink." Touching proof of divine forbearance and mercy, as also of the power of the blood!

Looking at this entire scene as a mere illustration, there is much to interest the heart. There is the defiled camp *below* and the sapphire pavement *above;* but the altar, at the foot of the hill, tells us of that way by which the sinner can make his escape from the defilement of his own condition, and mount up to the presence of God, there to feast and worship in perfect peace. The blood which flowed around the altar furnished man's only title to stand in the presence of that glory which "was like a devouring fire on the top of the mount in the eyes of the children of Israel."

"And Moses went into the midst of the cloud, and gat him up into the mount; and Moses was in the mount forty days and forty nights." This was truly a high and holy position for Moses. He was called away from earth and earthly things. Abstracted from natural influences, he is shut in with God, to hear from His mouth the deep mysteries of the Person and work of Christ; for such, in point of fact, we have unfolded in the tabernacle and all its significant furniture—"the patterns of things in the heavens." The blessed One knew full well what was about to be the end of man's covenant of works; but He unfolds to Moses, in types and shadows, His own precious thoughts of love and counsels of grace, manifested in, and secured by, Christ.

Blessed for evermore be the grace which has not left us under a covenant of works. Blessed be He who has "hushed the law's loud thunders and quenched mount Sinai's flame" by "the blood of the everlasting covenant," and given us a peace which no power of earth or hell can shake. "Unto Him that loved us, and washed us from our sins in His blood, and hath made us kings and priests unto God and His Father; to Him be glory and dominion forever and ever. Amen."

---

## *CHAPTER 25*

THIS chapter forms the commencement of one of the richest veins in Inspiration's exhaustless mine—a vein in which every stroke of the mattock brings to light untold wealth. We know the mattock with which alone we can work in such a mine, namely, the distinct ministry of the Holy Ghost. Nature can do nothing here. Reason is blind, imagination utterly vain; the most gigantic intellect, instead of being able to interpret the sacred symbols, appears like a bat in the sunshine, blindly dashing itself against the objects which it is utterly unable to discern. We must compel reason and imagination to stand without, while, with a chastened heart, a single eye, and a spiritual mind, we enter the hallowed precincts and gaze upon the deeply significant furniture. God the Holy Ghost is the only One who can conduct us through the courts of the Lord's house, and expound to our souls the true meaning of all that there meets our view. To attempt the exposition by the aid of intellect's unsanctified powers, would be infinitely more absurd than to set about the repairs of a watch with a blacksmith's tongs and hammer. "The pattern of things in the heavens" cannot be interpreted by the natural mind, in its most cultivated form. They must all be read in the light of heaven: earth has no light which could at all develop their beauties. The One who furnished the patterns can alone explain what the patterns mean,—the One who furnished the beauteous symbols can alone interpret them.

To the human eye there would seem to be a desultoriness in the mode in which the Holy Ghost has presented the furniture of the tabernacle; but in reality, as might be expected, there is the most perfect order, the most remarkable precision, the most studious accuracy. From chapter 25 to chapter 30, inclusive, we have a distinct section of the book of Exodus. This section is divided into two parts, the first terminating at chapter 27:19, and the second at the close of chapter 30. The former begins with the ark of the covenant, inside the vail, and ends with the brazen altar and the court in which that altar stood. That is, it gives us, in the first place, Jehovah's throne of judgment, whereon He sat as Lord of all the earth; and it conducts us to that place where He met the sinner, in the credit and virtue of accomplished atonement. Then, in the latter, we have the mode of man's approach to God—the privileges, dignities, and responsibilities of those who, as priests, were permitted to draw nigh to the Divine Presence and enjoy worship and communion there. Thus the arrangement is perfect and beautiful. How could it be otherwise, seeing that it is divine? The ark and the brazen altar present, as it were, two extremes. The former was the throne of God established in "justice and judgment" (Ps. 89:14); the latter was the place of approach for the sinner where "mercy and truth" went before Jehovah's face. Man, in himself, dared not to approach the ark to meet God, for "the way into the holiest of all was not yet made manifest" (Heb. 9:8); but God could approach the altar of brass, to meet man as a sinner. "Justice and judgment" could not admit the sinner in, but "mercy and truth" could bring God out; not, indeed, in that overwhelming brightness and majesty in which He was wont to shine forth from between those mystic supporters of His throne—"the cherubim of glory," but in that gracious ministry which is symbolically presented to us in the furniture and ordinances of the tabernacle.

All this may well remind us of the path trodden by that blessed One who is the antitype of all these types—the substance of all these shadows. He traveled from the eternal throne of God in heaven, down to the depth's of Calvary's cross. He came from all the glory of the former, down into all the shame of the latter, in order that He might conduct His redeemed, forgiven, and accepted people back with Himself, and present them faultless before that very throne which He had left on their account. The Lord Jesus fills up, in His own Person and work, every point between the throne of God and the dust of death, and every point between the dust of death and the throne of God. In Him, God has come down, in perfect grace, to the sinner; in Him, the sinner is brought up, in perfect righteousness, to God. All the way from the ark to the brazen altar was marked with the footprints of love, and all the way from the brazen altar to the ark of God was sprinkled with the blood of atonement; and as the ransomed worshiper passes along that wondrous path, he beholds the name of Jesus stamped on all that meets his view. May that name be dearer to our hearts! Let us now examine the chapters consecutively.

It is most interesting to note here that the first thing which the Lord communicates to Moses is His gracious purpose to have a sanctuary, or holy dwelling-place, in the midst of His people—a sanctuary composed of materials which directly point to Christ, His Person, His work, and the precious fruit of that work, as seen in the light, the power, and the varied graces of the Holy Ghost. Moreover, these materials were the fragrant fruit of the grace of God—the voluntary offerings of devoted hearts. Jehovah, whose majesty "the heaven of heavens could not contain," was graciously pleased to dwell in a boarded and curtained tent erected for Him by those who cherished the fond desire to hail His presence amongst them. This tabernacle may be viewed in two ways: first, as furnishing "a pattern of things in the heavens," and secondly, as presenting a deeply significant type of the body of Christ. The various materials of which the tabernacle was composed will come before us as we pass along; we shall therefore consider the three comprehensive subjects put before us in this chapter, namely, the ark, the table, and the candlestick.

The ark of the convenant occupies the leading place in the divine communications to Moses. Its position, too, in the tabernacle was most marked. Shut in within the vail, in the holiest of all, it formed the base of Jehovah's throne. Its very name conveys to the mind its import. An ark, so far as the Word instructs us, is designed to preserve *intact* whatever is put therein. An ark carried Noah and his family, together with all the orders of creation, in safety over the billows of judgment which covered the earth: an ark, at the opening of this book, was faith's vessel for preserving "a proper child" from the waters of death. When, therefore, we read of "the ark of the covenant," we are led to believe that it was designed of God to preserve His covenant unbroken in the midst of an erring people. In it, as we know, the second set of tables were deposited. As to the first set, they were broken in pieces beneath the mount, showing that man's covenant was wholly abolished—that his work could never, by any possibility, form the basis of Jehovah's throne of government. "Justice and judgment are the habitation of that throne," whether in its earthly or heavenly aspect. The ark could not contain within its hallowed inclosure broken tables. Man might fail to fulfill his self-chosen vow, but God's law must be preserved in its divine integrity and perfectness. If God was to set up His throne in the midst of His people, He could only do so in a way worthy of Himself. His standard of judgment and government must be perfect.

"And thou shalt make staves of shittim wood, and overlay them with gold. And thou shalt put the staves into the rings by the sides of the ark, that the ark may be borne with them." The ark of the covenant was to accompany the people in all their wanderings. It never rested while they were a traveling or a conflicting host; it moved from place to place in the wilderness; it went before them into the midst of Jordan; it was their grand rallying-point in all the wars of Canaan; it was the sure and certain earnest of power wherever it went. No power of the enemy could stand before that which was the well-known expression of the divine presence and power. The ark was to be Israel's companion-in-travel in the desert, and "the staves" and "the rings" were the apt expression of its traveling character.

However, it was not always to be a traveler. "The afflictions of David," as well as the wars of Israel, were to have an end. The prayer was yet to be breathed and answered, "Arise, O Lord, into *Thy rest:* Thou and *the ark of Thy strength*" (Ps. 132:8). This most sublime petition had its partial accomplishment in the palmy days of Solomon, when "the priests brought in the ark of the covenant of the Lord unto his place, into the oracle of the house, to the most holy place, even under the wings of the cherubim. For the cherubim spread forth their two wings over the place of the ark, and the cherubim covered the ark and the staves thereof above. And *they drew out the staves,* that the ends of the staves were seen out in the holy place before the oracle, and they were not seen without: and there they are unto this day" (1 Kings 8:6-8). The sand of the desert was to be exchanged for the golden floor of the temple (1 Kings 6:30). The wanderings of the ark were to have an end: there was "neither enemy nor evil occurrent," and therefore "the staves were drawn out."

Nor was this the only difference between the ark in the tabernacle and in the temple. The apostle, speaking of the ark in its wilderness habitation, describes it as "the ark of the covenant, overlaid round about with gold, wherein was the golden pot that had manna, and Aaron's rod that budded, and the tables of the covenant" (Heb. 9:4). Such were the contents of the ark in its wilderness journeyings—the pot of manna, the record of Jehovah's faithfulness in providing for His redeemed in the desert, and Aaron's rod, "a token against the rebels," to "take away their murmurings." (Compare Exod. 16:32-34, and Num. 17:10.) But when the moment arrived in which "the staves" were to be "drawn out," when the wanderings and wars of Israel were over, when the "exceeding magnifical" house was completed, when the sun of Israel's glory had reached, in type, its meridian, as marked by the wealth and splendor of Solomon's reign, then the records of wilderness need and wilderness failure were unnoticed, and nothing remained save that which constituted the eternal foundation of the throne of the God of Israel, and of all the earth. "*There was nothing in the ark save the two tables of stone*, which Moses put there at Horeb" (1 Kings 8:9).

But all this brightness was soon to be overcast by the heavy clouds of human failure and divine displeasure. The rude foot of the uncircumcised was yet to walk across the ruins of that beautiful house, and its faded light and departed glory was yet to elicit the contemptuous "hiss" of the stranger. This would not be the place to follow out these things in detail; I shall only refer my reader to the last notice which the Word of God affords us of "the ark of the covenant,"—a notice which carries us forward to a time when human folly and sin shall no more disturb the resting-place of that ark, and when neither a curtained tent nor yet a temple made with hands shall contain it. "And the seventh angel sounded; and there were great voices in heaven, saying, 'The kingdoms of this world are become the kingdoms of our Lord, and of His Christ; and He shall reign forever and ever.' And the four and twenty elders, which sat before God on their seats, fell upon their faces, and worshiped God, saying, 'We give Thee thanks, O Lord God Almighty, which art, and wast, and art to come; because Thou hast taken to Thee Thy great power, and hast reigned. And the nations were angry, and Thy wrath is come, and the time of the dead, that they should be judged, and that Thou shouldest give reward unto Thy servants the prophets, and to the saints, and them that fear Thy name, small and great; and shouldest destroy them which destroy the earth.' And the temple of God was open in heaven, and there was seen in His temple *the ark of His covenant:* and there were lightnings, and voices, and thunderings, and an earthquake, and great hail" (Rev. 11:15-19).

The mercy-seat comes next in order.—"And thou shalt make a mercy-seat of pure gold; two cubits and a half shall be the length thereof, and a cubit and a half the breadth thereof. And thou shalt make two cherubim of gold, of beaten work shalt thou make them, in the two ends of the mercy-seat. And make one cherub on the one end, and the other cherub on the other end; even of the mercy-seat shall ye make the cherubim on the two ends thereof. And the cherubim shall stretch forth their wings on high, covering the mercy-seat with their wings, and their faces shall look one to another; toward the mercy-seat shall the faces of the cherubim be. And thou shalt put the mercy-seat above upon the ark; and in the ark shalt thou put the testimony that I shall give thee. There I will meet with thee, and I will commune with thee from above the mercy-seat, from between the two cherubim which are upon the ark of the testimony, of all things which I will give thee in commandment unto the children of Israel."

Here Jehovah gives utterance to His gracious intention of coming down from the fiery mount to take His place upon the mercy-seat. This He could do, inasmuch as the tables of testimony were preserved unbroken beneath, and the symbols of His power, whether in creation or providence, rose on the right hand and on the left—the inseparable adjuncts of that throne on which Jehovah had seated Himself—a throne of grace founded upon divine righteousness and supported by justice and judgment. Here the glory of the God of Israel shone forth. From hence He issued His commands, softened and sweetened by the gracious source from whence they emanated, and the medium through which they came—like the beams of the mid-day sun, passing through a cloud, we can enjoy their genial and enlivening influence without being dazzled by their brightness. "His commandments are not grievous," when received from off the mercy-seat, because they come in connection with grace, which gives the ears to hear and the power to obey.

Looking at the ark and mercy-seat together, we may see in them a striking figure of Christ in His Person and work. He having, in His life, magnified the law and made it honorable, became, through death, a propitiation (or mercy-seat) for every one that believeth. God's mercy could only repose on a pedestal of perfect righteousness. "Grace reigns through righteousness unto eternal life by Jesus Christ our Lord" (Rom. 5:21). The only proper meeting-place between God and man is the point where grace and righteousness meet and perfectly harmonize. Nothing but perfect righteousness could suit God, and nothing but perfect grace could suit the sinner. But where could these attributes meet in one point? Only in the cross. There it is that "mercy and truth are met together; righteousness and peace have kissed each other" (Ps. 85:10). Thus it is that the soul of the believing sinner finds peace. He sees that God's righteousness and his justification rest upon precisely the same basis, namely, Christ's accomplished work. When man, under the powerful action of *the truth* of God, takes his place as a sinner, God can, in the exercise of *grace,* take His place as a Saviour, and then every question is settled, for the cross having answered all the claims of divine justice, mercy's copious streams can flow unhindered. When a righteous God and a ruined sinner meet on a blood-sprinkled platform, all is settled forever—settled in such a way as perfectly glorifies God, and eternally saves the sinner. God must be true, though every man be proved a liar; and when man is so thoroughly brought down to the lowest point of his own moral condition before God as to be willing to take the place which God's truth assigns him, he then learns that God has revealed Himself as the righteous Justifier of such an one. This must give settled peace to the conscience; and not only so, but impart a capacity to commune with God, and hearken to His holy precepts, in the intelligence of that relationship into which divine grace has introduced us.

Hence, therefore, "the holiest of all" unfolds a truly wondrous scene—the ark, the mercy-seat, the cherubim, the glory! What a sight for the high-priest of Israel to behold as, once a year, he went in within the vail! May the Spirit of God open the eyes of our understanding, that we may understand more fully the deep meaning of those precious types.

Moses is next instructed about "the table of show-bread," or bread of presentation. On this table stood the food of the priests of God. For seven days those twelve loaves of "fine flour with frankincense" were presented before the Lord, after which, being replaced by others, they became the food of the priests, who fed upon them in the holy place (see Lev. 24:5-9). It is needless to say that those twelve loaves typify "the Man Christ Jesus." The "fine flour," of which they were composed, marks His perfect manhood, while the "frankincense" points out the entire devotion of that manhood to God. If God has His priests ministering in the holy place, He will assuredly have a table for them, and a well-furnished table too. Christ is the table, and Christ is the bread thereon. The pure table and the twelve loaves shadow forth Christ as presented before God unceasingly in all the excellency of His spotless humanity, and administered as food to the priestly family. The "seven days" set forth the perfection of the divine enjoyment of Christ, and the "twelve loaves" the administration of that enjoyment in and by man. There is also, I should venture to suggest, the idea of Christ's connection with the twelve tribes of Israel, and the twelve apostles of the Lamb.

The candlestick of pure gold comes next in order, for God's priests need *light* as well as *food;* and they have both the one and the other in Christ. In this candlestick there is no mention of any thing but pure gold.—"All of it shall be one *beaten* work of pure gold." "The seven lamps" which "gave light over against the candlestick" express the perfection of the light and energy of the Spirit, founded upon and connected with the perfect efficacy of the work of Christ. The work of the Holy Ghost can never be separated from the work of Christ. This is set forth in a double way in this beautiful figure of the golden candlestick. "The seven lamps" being connected with "the shaft" of "beaten gold," points us to Christ's finished work as the sole basis of the manifestation of the Spirit in the Church. The Holy Ghost was not given until Jesus was glorified (comp. John 7:39 with Acts 19:2-6). In the third chapter of Revelation, Christ is presented to the Church in Sardis as "having the seven Spirits." It was as "exalted to the right hand of God" that the Lord Jesus "shed forth" the Holy Ghost upon His Church, in order that she might shine, according to the power and perfection of her position, in the holy place, her proper sphere of being, of action, and of worship.

Then, again, we find it was one of Aaron's specific functions to light and trim those seven lamps. "And the Lord spake unto Moses, saying, 'Command the children of Israel that they bring unto thee pure oil olive beaten for the light, to cause the lamps to burn continually. Without the vail of the testimony, in the tabernacle of the congregation, shall Aaron order it from the evening unto the morning before the Lord continually: it shall be a statute forever in your generations. He shall order the lamps upon the pure candlestick before the Lord continually" (Lev. 24:1-4). Thus we may see how the work of the Holy Ghost in the Church is linked with Christ's work on earth and His work in heaven. "The seven lamps" were there, no doubt; but priestly energy and diligence were needed in order to keep them trimmed and lighted. The priest would continually need "the tongs and snuff-dishes" for the purpose of removing aught that would not be a fit vehicle for the "pure beaten oil." Those tongs and snuff-dishes were of "beaten gold" likewise, for the whole matter was the direct result of divine operation. If the Church shine, it is only by the energy of the Spirit, and that energy is founded upon Christ, who, in pursuance of God's eternal counsel, became, in His sacrifice and priesthood, the spring and power of every thing to His Church. All is of God. Whether we look within that mysterious vail, and behold the ark with its cover, and the two significant figures attached thereto; or if we gaze on that which lay without the vail—the pure table and the pure candlestick, with their distinctive vessels and instruments—all speak to us of God, whether as revealed to us in connection with the Son or the Holy Ghost.

Christian reader, your high calling places you in the very midst of all these precious realities. Your place is not merely amid "the patterns of things in the heavens," but amid "the heavenly things themselves." You have "boldness to enter into the holiest by the blood of Jesus;" you are a priest unto God; "the showbread" is yours; your place is at "the pure table," to feed on the priestly food, in the light of the Holy Ghost. Nothing can ever deprive you of those divine privileges,—they are yours forever. Let it be your care to watch against every thing that might rob you of the *enjoyment* of them. Beware of all unhallowed tempers, lusts, feelings, and imaginations. Keep nature down; keep the world out; keep Satan off. May the Holy Ghost fill your whole soul with Christ. Then you will be practically holy and abidingly happy;—you will bear fruit, and the Father will be glorified, and your joy shall be full.

---

## *CHAPTER 26*

THE section of our book which now opens before us contains the instructive description of the curtains and coverings of the tabernacle, wherein the spiritual eye discerns the shadows of the various features and phases of Christ's manifested character. "Moreover, thou shalt make the tabernacle with ten curtains of fine twined linen, and blue, and purple, and scarlet: with cherubim of cunning work shalt thou make them." Here we have the different aspects of "the Man Christ Jesus." The "fine twined linen" prefigures the spotless purity of His walk and character; while the "blue, the purple, and the scarlet" present Him to us as "the Lord from *heaven,*" who is to *reign* according to the divine counsels, but whose royalty is to be the result of His *sufferings.* Thus we have a spotless Man, a heavenly Man, a royal Man, a suffering Man. These materials were not confined to the "curtains" of the tabernacle, but were also used in making "the vail" (ver. 31), "the hanging for the door of the tent" (ver. 36), "the hanging for the gate of the court" (chap. 27:16), "the cloths of service and the holy garments of Aaron" (chap. 39:1). In a word, it was Christ every where, Christ in all, Christ alone.*

The "fine twined linen," as expressive of Christ's spotless manhood, opens a most precious and copious spring of thought to the spiritual mind; it furnishes a theme on which we cannot meditate too profoundly. The truth respecting Christ's humanity must be received with scriptural accuracy, held with spiritual energy, guarded with holy jealousy, and confessed with heavenly power. If we are wrong as to this, we cannot

*The expression, "*white* and *clean,*" gives peculiar force and beauty to the type which the Holy Ghost has presented in the "fine twined linen." Indeed, there could not be a more appropriate emblem of spotless manhood.

be right as to any thing. It is a grand, vital fundamental truth; and if it be not received, held, guarded, and confessed as God has revealed it in His holy Word, the entire superstructure must be unsound. Nothing can be more deplorable than the looseness of thought and expression which seems to prevail in reference to this all-important doctrine. Were there more reverence for the Word of God, there would be more accurate acquaintance with it; and, in this way, we should happily avoid all those erroneous and unguarded statements which surely must grieve the Holy Spirit of God, whose province it is to testify of Jesus.

When the angel had announced to Mary the glad tidings of the Saviour's birth, she said to him, "How shall this be, seeing I know not a man?" Her feeble mind was utterly incompetent to enter into, much less to fathom, the stupendous mystery of "God manifest in the flesh." But mark carefully the angelic reply—a reply, not to a sceptic mind, but to a pious, though ignorant, heart.—"The Holy Ghost shall come upon thee, and the power of the Highest shall overshadow thee; wherefore, also, that holy thing which shall be born of thee shall be called the Son of God" (Luke 1:34-35). Mary, doubtless, imagined that this birth was to be according to the principles of ordinary generation; but the angel corrects her mistake, and, in correcting it, enunciates one of the grandest truths of revelation. He declares to her that divine power was about to form *a real man*—"the second Man—the Lord from heaven"—One whose nature was divinely pure, utterly incapable of receiving or communicating any taint. This holy One was made *"in the likeness* of sinful flesh," without sin in the flesh. He partook of real *bona fide* flesh and blood without a particle or shadow of the evil thereto attaching.

This is a cardinal truth which cannot be too accurately laid hold of or too tenaciously held. The incarnation of the Son, the second Person in the eternal Trinity—His mysterious entrance into pure and spotless flesh, formed, by the power of the Highest, in the virgin's womb, is the foundation of the "great mystery of godliness," of which the topstone is a glorified God-man in heaven, the Head, Representative, and Model of the redeemed Church of God. The essential purity of His manhood perfectly met the claims of God; the reality thereof met the necessities of man. He was a Man, for none else would do to meet man's ruin. But He was such a Man as could satisfy all the claims of the throne of God. He was a spotless, real Man, in whom God could perfectly delight, and on whom man could unreservedly lean.

I need not remind the enlightened reader that all this, if taken apart from death and resurrection, is perfectly unavailable to us. We need not only an incarnate, but a crucified and risen, Christ. True, He should be incarnate to be crucified; but it is death and resurrection which render incarnation available to us. It is nothing short of a deadly error to suppose that in incarnation Christ was taking man into union with Himself. This could not be. He Himself expressly teaches the contrary.—"Verily, verily, I say unto you, Except a corn of wheat fall into the ground and *die,* it abideth *alone;* but if it die, it bringeth forth much fruit" (John 12:24). There could be no union between sinful and holy flesh, pure and impure, corruptible and incorruptible, mortal and immortal. Accomplished death is the only base of a unity between Christ and His elect members. It is in beautiful connection with the words, "Rise, let us go hence," that He says, "I am the vine, ye are the branches." "We have been planted together in the likeness of His death." "Our old man is crucified with Him, that the body of sin might be destroyed." "In whom also ye are circumcised with the circumcision made without hands, in putting off the body of the sins of the flesh by the circumcision of Christ: buried with Him in baptism, wherein also ye are risen with Him through the faith of the operation of God, who hath raised Him from the dead." I would refer my reader to Romans 6, and Colossians 2, as a full and comprehensive statement of the truth on this important subject. It was only as dead and risen that Christ and His people could become one. The true corn of wheat had to fall into the ground and die ere a full ear could spring up and be gathered into the heavenly garner.

But while this is a plainly revealed truth of Scripture, it is equally plain that incarnation formed, as it were, the first layer of the glorious superstructure; and the curtains of "fine twined linen" prefigure the moral purity of "the Man Christ Jesus." We have already seen the manner of His conception; and, as we pass along the current of His life here below, we meet with instance after instance of the same spotless purity. He was forty days in the wilderness, tempted of the devil, but there was no response in His pure nature to the tempter's foul suggestions. He could touch the leper and receive no taint; He could touch the bier and not contract the smell of death; He could pass unscathed through the most polluted atmosphere. He was, as to His manhood, like a sunbeam emanating from the fountain of light, which can pass without a soil through the most defiling medium. He was perfectly unique in nature, constitution, and character. None but He could say, "Thou wilt not suffer Thine holy One to see corruption." This was in reference to His humanity, which, as being perfectly holy and perfectly pure, was capable of being a sin-bearer. "His own self bare our sins in His own body on the tree." Not *to* the tree, as some would teach us; but *"on* the tree." It was on the cross that Christ was our sin-bearer, and only there. "He hath made Him to be sin for us who knew no sin, that we might be made the righteousness of God in Him" (2 Cor. 5:21).

*"Blue"* is the ethereal color, and marks the heavenly character of Christ, who, though He had come down into all the circumstances of actual and true humanity (sin excepted), yet was He "the Lord from heaven." Though He was "very man," yet He ever walked in the uninterrupted consciousness of His proper dignity, as a heavenly stranger. He never once forgot whence He had come, where He was, or whither He was going. The spring of all His joys was on high. Earth could neither make Him richer nor poorer. He found this world to be "a dry and thirsty land, where no water is," and hence His spirit could only find its refreshment above. It was entirely heavenly.—"No man hath ascended up to heaven, but He that came down from heaven, even the Son of Man *who is in heaven"* (John 3:13).

*"Purple"* denotes royalty, and points us to Him who "was born King of the Jews;" who offered Himself as such to the Jewish nation, and was rejected; who before Pontius Pilate witnessed a good confession, avowing Himself a king, when, to mortal vision, there was not so much as a single trace of royalty.—"Thou sayest that I am a king." And "hereafter ye shall see the Son of Man sitting at the right hand of power, and coming in the clouds of heaven." And, finally, the inscription upon His cross, "in letters of Hebrew, and Greek, and Latin"—the language of religion, of science, and of government—declared Him, to the whole known world, to be "Jesus of Nazareth, the King of the Jews." Earth disowned His claims (so much the worse for it), but not so heaven; there His claim was fully recognized. He was received as a conqueror into the eternal mansions of light, crowned with glory and honor, and seated, amid the acclamations of angelic hosts, on the throne of the Majesty in the heavens, there to wait until His enemies be made His footstool. "Why do the heathen rage, and the people imagine a vain thing? The kings of the earth set themselves, and the rulers take counsel together, against the Lord, and against His anointed, saying, 'Let us break their bands asunder, and cast away their cords from us.' He that sitteth in the heavens shall laugh; the Lord shall have them in derision. Then shall He speak unto them in His wrath, and vex them in His sore displeasure. Yet have I set *My King* upon My holy hill of Zion. I will declare the decree: the Lord hath said unto Me, 'Thou art My Son; this day have I begotten Thee. Ask of Me, and I shall give Thee the heathen for Thine inheritance, and the uttermost parts of the earth for Thy possession. Thou shalt break them with a rod of iron; Thou shalt dash them in pieces like a potter's vessel.' Be wise now therefore, O ye kings; be instructed, ye judges of the

earth. Serve the Lord with fear, and rejoice with trembling. Kiss the Son, lest He be angry, and ye perish from the way, when His wrath is kindled but a little. *Blessed are all they that put their trust in Him*" (Ps. 2).

*"Scarlet,"* when genuine, is produced by death; and this makes its application to a suffering Christ safe and appropriate. "Christ hath suffered for us in the flesh." Without death, all would have been unavailing. We can admire "the blue" and "the purple," but without "the scarlet" the tabernacle would have lacked an all-important feature. It was by death that Christ destroyed him that had the power of death. The Holy Ghost, in setting before us a striking figure of Christ—the true tabernacle—could not possibly omit that phase of His character which constitutes the ground-work of His connection with His body the Church, of His claim to the throne of David, and the headship of all creation. In a word, He not only unfolds the Lord Jesus to our view, in these significant curtains, as a spotless Man, a royal Man, but also a suffering Man,—One who, *by death,* should make good His claims to all that to which, as man, He was entitled, in the divine counsels.

But we have much more in the curtains of the tabernacle than the varied and perfect phases of the character of Christ,—we have also the unity and consistency of that character. Each phase is displayed in its own proper perfectness; and one never interferes with, or mars the exquisite beauty of, another. All was in perfect harmony beneath the eye of God, and was so displayed in "the pattern which was showed to Moses on the mount," and in the copy which was exhibited below. "Every one of the curtains shall have one measure. The five curtains shall be coupled together one to another; and other five curtains shall be coupled one to another." Such was the fair proportion and consistency in all the ways of Christ, as a perfect Man, walking on the earth, in whatever aspect or relationship we view Him. When acting in one character, we never find aught that is, in the very least degree, inconsistent with the divine integrity of another. He was, at all times, in all places, under all circumstances, the perfect Man. There was nothing out of that fair and lovely proportion which belonged to Him, in all His ways. "Every one of the curtains shall have one measure."

The two sets of five curtains each may symbolize the two grand aspects of Christ's character, as acting toward God and toward man. We have the same two aspects in the law, namely, what was due to God, and what was due to man; so that as to Christ, if we look in, we find "Thy law is within My heart;" and if we look at His outward character and walk, we see those two elements adjusted with perfect accuracy, and not only adjusted, but inseparably linked together by the heavenly grace and divine energy which dwelt in His most glorious Person.

"And thou shalt make *loops of blue* upon the edge of the one curtain, from the selvedge in the coupling; and likewise shalt thou make in the uttermost edge of another curtain, in the coupling of the second. . . . And thou shalt make fifty *taches of gold,* and couple the curtains together with the taches; and *it shall be one tabernacle.*" We have here displayed to us, in the "loops of *blue,*" and "taches of *gold,*" that *heavenly* grace and *divine* energy in Christ which enabled Him to combine and perfectly adjust the claims of God and man; so that in responding to both the one and the other, He never, for a moment, marred the unity of His character. When crafty and hypocritical men tempted Him with the inquiry, "Is it lawful to give tribute to Caesar, or not?" His wise reply was, "Render to Caesar the things that are Caesar's, and to God the things that are God's."

Nor was it merely Caesar, but man in every relation that had all his claims perfectly met in Christ. As He united in His perfect Person the nature of God and man, so He met in His perfect ways the claims of God and man. Most interesting would it be to trace, through the gospel narrative, the exemplification of the principle suggested by the "loops of blue," and "taches of gold;" but I must leave my reader to pursue this study under the immediate guidance of the Holy Ghost, who delights to expatiate upon every feature and every phase of that perfect One whom it is His unvarying purpose and undivided object to exalt.

The curtains on which we have been dwelling were covered with other "curtains of goats' hair" (ver. 7-14). Their beauty was hidden from those without by that which bespoke roughness and severity. This latter did not meet the view of those within. To all who were privileged to enter the hallowed inclosure, nothing was visible save "the blue, the purple, the scarlet, and fine twined linen," the varied yet combined exhibition of the virtues and excellencies of that divine Tabernacle in which God dwelt within the vail—that is, of Christ, through whose flesh, the antitype of all these, the beams of the divine nature shone so delicately that the sinner could behold without being overwhelmed by their dazzling brightness.

As the Lord Jesus passed along this earth, how few really knew Him! How few had eyes anointed with heavenly eye-salve to penetrate and appreciate the deep mystery of His character! How few saw "the blue, the purple, the scarlet, and fine twined linen"! It was only when faith brought man into His presence that He ever allowed the brightness of what He was to shine forth—ever allowed the glory to break through the cloud. To nature's eye there would seem to have been a reserve and a severity about Him which were aptly prefigured by the "covering of goats' hair." All this was the result of His profound separation and estrangement, not from sinners personally, but from the thoughts and maxims of men. He had nothing in common with man as such, nor was it within the compass of mere nature to comprehend or enjoy Him. "No man," said He, "can come to Me, except the Father which hath sent Me draw him;" and when one of those "drawn" ones confessed His name, He declared that "flesh and blood hath not revealed it unto thee, but My Father which is in heaven" (comp. John 6:44; Matt. 16:17). He was "a root out of a dry ground," having neither "form nor comeliness" to attract the eye or gratify the heart of man. The popular current could never flow in the direction of One who, as He passed rapidly across the stage of this vain world, wrapped Himself up in a "covering of goats' hair." Jesus was not popular. The multitude might follow Him for a moment, because His ministry stood connected, in their judgment, with "the loaves and fishes" which met their need; but they were just as ready to cry, "Away with Him!" as "Hosanna to the Son of David!" Oh, let Christians remember this! Let the servants of Christ remember it! Let all preachers of the gospel remember it! Let one and all of us ever seek to bear in mind the *"covering of goats' hair"!*

But if the goats' skins expressed the severity of Christ's separation from earth, "the rams' skins *dyed red*" exhibit His intense consecration and devotedness to God, which was carried out even unto *death.* He was the only perfect Servant that ever stood in God's vineyard. He had one object, which He pursued with an undeviating course from the manger to the cross, and that was, to glorify the Father, and finish His work. "Wist ye not that I must be about My Father's business?" was the language of His youth, and the accomplishment of that "business" was the design of His life. "His meat was to do the will of Him that sent Him, and to finish His work." "The rams' skins dyed red" formed as distinct a part of His ordinary habit as the "goats' hair." His perfect devotion to God separated Him from the habits of men.

"The badgers' skins" may exhibit to us the holy vigilance with which the Lord Jesus guarded against the approach of every thing hostile to the purpose which engrossed His whole soul. He took up His position for God, and held it with a tenacity which no influence of men or devils, earth or hell, could overcome. The covering of badger's skins was "above" (ver. 14), teaching us that the most prominent feature in the character of "the Man Christ Jesus" was an invincible determination to stand as a witness of God on the earth. He was the true Naboth, who gave up His life rather than surrender the truth of God, or give up that for which He had taken His place in this world.

The goat, the ram, and the badger must be

regarded as exhibiting certain natural features, and also as symbolizing certain moral qualities; and we must take both into account in our application of these figures to the character of Christ. The human eye could only discern the former. It could see none of the moral grace, beauty, and dignity which lay beneath the outward form of the despised and humble Jesus of Nazareth. When the treasures of heavenly wisdom flowed from His lips, the inquiry was, "Is not this the carpenter?" or, "How knoweth this Man letters, having never learned?" When He asserted His eternal Sonship and Godhead, the word was, "Thou art not yet fifty years old," or, "They took up stones to cast at Him." In short, the acknowledgment of the Pharisees in John 9 was true in reference to men in general. "As for this fellow, we know not from whence He is."

It would be utterly impossible, in the compass of a volume like this, to trace the unfoldings of those precious features of Christ's character through the Gospel narratives. Sufficient has been said to open up springs of spiritual thought to my reader, and to furnish some faint idea of the rich treasures which are wrapped up in the curtains and coverings of the tabernacle. Christ's hidden being, secret springs, and inherent excellencies—His outward and unattractive form—what He was in Himself, what He was Godward, and what He was manward—what He was in the judgment of faith, and what in the judgment of nature—all is sweetly and impressively told out, to the circumcised ear, in the "curtains of blue, purple, scarlet, and fine twined linen," and the "coverings of skins."

"The boards for the tabernacle" were made of the same wood as was used in constructing "the ark of the covenant." Moreover, they were upheld by the sockets of silver formed out of the atonement; their hooks and chapiters being of the same. (Compare attentively chap. 30:11-16, with chap. 38:25-28.) The whole frame-work of the tent of the tabernacle was based on that which spoke of atonement or ransom, while the "hooks and chapiters" at the top set forth the same. The sockets were buried in the sand, and the hooks and chapiters were above. It matters not how deep you penetrate, or how high you rise, that glorious and eternal truth is emblazoned before you, *I have found a ransom.*" Blessed be God, "we are not redeemed with corruptible things, as silver and gold . . . but with the precious blood of Christ, as of a lamb without blemish and without spot."

The tabernacle was divided into three distinct parts, namely, "the holy of holies," "the holy place," and "the court of the tabernacle." The entrance into each of these was of the same materials—"blue, purple, scarlet, and fine twined linen." (Compare chapter 26:31,36; 27:16.) The interpretation of which is simply this: Christ forms the only doorway into the varied fields of glory which are yet to be displayed, whether on earth, in heaven, or in the heaven of heavens. "Every family, in heaven and earth," will be ranged under His headship, as all will be brought into everlasting felicity and glory on the ground of His accomplished atonement. This is plain enough, and needs no stretch of the imagination to grasp it. We know it to be true; and when we know the truth which is shadowed forth, the shadow is easily understood. If only our hearts be filled with Christ, we shall not go far astray in our interpretations of the tabernacle and its furniture. It is not a head full of learned criticism that will avail us much here, but a heart full of affection for Jesus, and a conscience at rest in the blood of His cross.

May the Spirit of God enable us to study these things with more interest and intelligence. May He "open our eyes that we may behold wondrous things out of His law."

---

## *CHAPTER 27*

We have now arrived at the brazen altar, which stood at the door of the tabernacle; and I would call my reader's most particular attention to the order of the Holy Ghost in this portion of our book. We have already remarked that from chapter 25 to the nineteenth verse of chapter 27 forms a distinct division, in which we are furnished with a description of the ark and mercy-seat, the table and candlestick, the curtains and the vail; and, lastly, the brazen altar and the court in which that altar stood. If my reader will turn to chapter 35:15; chapter 37:25; and chapter 40:26, he will remark that the golden altar of incense is noticed, in each of the three instances, between the candlestick and the brazen altar; whereas, when Jehovah is giving directions to Moses, the brazen altar is introduced immediately after the candlestick and the curtains of the tabernacle. Now, inasmuch as there must be a divine reason for this difference, it is the privilege of every diligent and intelligent student of the Word to inquire what that reason is.

Why, then, does the Lord, when giving directions about the furniture of the "holy place," omit the altar of incense, and pass out to the brazen altar which stood at the door of the tabernacle? The reason, I believe, is simply this: He first describes the mode in which He would manifest Himself to man, and then He describes the mode of man's approach to Him. He took His seat upon the throne, as "the Lord of all the earth." The beams of His glory were hidden behind the vail—type of Christ's flesh (Heb. 10:20); but there was the manifestation of Himself in connection with man, as in "the pure table," and by the light and power of the Holy Ghost, as in the candlestick. Then we have the manifested character of Christ as a man down here on this earth, as seen in the curtains and coverings of the tabernacle. And, finally, we have the brazen altar as the grand exhibition of the meeting-place between a holy God and a sinner. This conducts us, as it were, to the extreme point, from which we return, in company with Aaron and his sons, back to the holy place, the ordinary priestly position, where stood the golden altar of incense. Thus the order is strikingly beautiful. The golden altar is not spoken of until there is a priest to burn incense thereon, for Jehovah showed Moses the patterns of things in the heavens according to the order in which these things are to be apprehended by faith. On the other hand, when Moses gives directions to the congregation (chap. 35), when he records the labors of "Bezaleel and Aholiab" (chap. 37 and 38), and when he sets up the tabernacle (chap. 40), he follows the simple order in which the furniture was placed.

The prayerful investigation of this interesting subject, and a comparison of the passages above referred to, will amply repay my reader. We shall now examine the brazen altar.

This altar was the place where the sinner approached God, in the power and efficacy of the blood of atonement. It stood "at the door of the tabernacle of the tent of the congregation," and on it all the blood was shed. It was composed of "shittim wood and brass." The wood was the same as that of the golden altar of incense; but the metal was different, and the reason of this difference is obvious. The altar of brass was the place where sin was dealt with according to the divine judgment concerning it. The altar of gold was the place from whence the precious fragrance of Christ's acceptableness ascended to the throne of God. The "shittim wood" as the figure of Christ's humanity, must be the same in each case; but in the brazen altar we see Christ meeting the fire of divine justice; in the golden altar we behold Him feeding the divine affections. At the former, the fire of divine wrath was quenched; at the latter, the fire of priestly worship is kindled. The soul delights to find Christ in both; but the altar of brass is what meets the need of a guilty conscience,—it is the very first thing for a poor, helpless, needy, convicted sinner. There cannot be settled peace, in reference to the question of sin, until the eye of faith rests on Christ as the antitype of the brazen altar. I must see my sin reduced to ashes in the pan of that altar ere I can enjoy rest of conscience in the presence of God. It is when I know, by faith in the record of God, that He Himself has dealt with my sin in the Person of Christ, at the brazen altar—that He has satisfied all His own righteous claims—that He has put away my sin out of His holy presence, so that it can never come back again—it is then, but not until then, that I can enjoy divine and everlasting peace.

I would here offer a remark as to the real meaning of the "gold" and "brass" in the furniture of the tabernacle. "Gold" is the symbol of divine righteousness, or the divine nature in "the Man Christ Jesus." "Brass" is the symbol of righteousness, demanding judgment of sin, as in the brazen altar; or the judgment of uncleanness, as in the brazen laver. This will account for the fact that *inside* the tent of the tabernacle all was gold,—the ark, the mercy-seat, the table, the candlestick, the altar of incense. All these were the symbols of the divine nature—the inherent personal excellence of the Lord Jesus Christ. On the other hand, *outside* the tent of the tabernacle all was brass,—the brazen altar and its vessels, the laver and its foot.

The claims of righteousness, as to sin and uncleanness, must be divinely met ere there can be any enjoyment of the precious mysteries of Christ's Person, as unfolded in the inner sanctuary of God. It is when I see all sin and all uncleanness perfectly judged and washed away that I can, as a priest, draw nigh and worship in the holy place, and enjoy the full display of all the beauty and excellency of the God-man, Christ Jesus.

The reader can, with much profit, follow out the application of this thought in detail, not merely in the study of the tabernacle and the temple, but also in various passages of the Word; for example, in the first chapter of Revelation, Christ is seen "girt about the paps with a *golden* girdle," and having "His feet like unto fine *brass,* as if they burned in a furnace." The "golden girdle" is the symbol of His intrinsic righteousness. The "feet like unto fine brass" express the unmitigated judgment of evil (He cannot tolerate evil, but must crush it beneath His feet).

Such is the Christ with whom we have to do. He judges sin, but He saves the sinner. Faith sees sin reduced to ashes at the brazen altar; it sees all uncleanness washed away at the brazen laver; and, finally, it enjoys Christ as He is unfolded, in the secret of the divine presence, by the light and power of the Holy Ghost. It finds Him at the golden altar, in all the value of His intercession; it feeds on Him at the pure table; it recognizes Him in the ark and mercy-seat, as the One who answers all the claims of justice, and, at the same time, meets all human need; it beholds Him in the vail, with all its mystic figures; it reads His precious name on every thing. O, for a heart to prize and praise this matchless, glorious Christ!

Nothing can be of more vital importance than a clear understanding of the doctrine of the brazen altar; that is to say, of the doctrine taught there. It is from the want of clearness as to this that so many souls go mourning all their days. They have never had a clean, thorough settlement of the whole matter of their guilt at the brazen altar; they have never really beheld, by faith, God Himself settling, on the cross, the entire question of their sins; they are seeking peace for their uneasy consciences in regeneration and its evidences,—the fruits of the Spirit, frames, feelings, experiences,—things quite right and most valuable in themselves, but they are not the ground of peace. What fills the soul with perfect peace is the knowledge of what God hath wrought at the brazen altar. The ashes in yonder pan tell me the peace-giving story that *all is done.* The believer's sins were all put away by God's own hand of redeeming love. "He hath made Christ to be sin for us, who knew no sin, that we might be made the righteousness of God in Him" (2 Cor. 5). All sin must be judged: but the believer's sins have been already judged in the cross; hence, he is perfectly justified. To suppose that there could be any thing against the very feeblest believer, is to deny the entire work of the cross. His sins and iniquities have been *all* put away by God Himself, and therefore they must needs be perfectly put away. They all went with the outpoured life of the Lamb of God.

Dear Christian reader, see that your heart is thoroughly established in the peace which Jesus has made "by the blood of His cross."

## CHAPTERS 28–29

THESE chapters unfold to us the priesthood, in all its value and efficacy. They are full of deep interest. The very word "priesthood" awakens in the heart feelings of the most profound thankfulness for the grace which has not only provided a way for us to get into the divine presence, but also the means of keeping us there, according to the character and claims of that high and holy position.

The Aaronic priesthood was God's provision for a people who were, in themselves, at a distance, and needed one to appear for them in His presence continually. We are taught in Hebrews 7 that this order of priesthood belonged to the law—that it was made "after the law of a carnal commandment"—that it "could not continue by reason of death"—that the priests belonging to it had infirmity. It could not, therefore, impart perfection, and hence we have to bless God that it was instituted "without an oath." The oath of God could only stand connected with that which was to endure forever, even the perfect, immortal, untransferable priesthood of our great and glorious Melchisedek, who imparts both to His sacrifice and His priesthood all the value, the dignity, and the glory of His own peerless Person. The thought of having such a Sacrifice and such a Priest as He causes the bosom to heave with emotions of the liveliest gratitude.

But we must proceed to the examination of the chapters which lie before us.

In chapter 28 we have the robes, and in chapter 29 we have the sacrifices. The former have more especial reference to the need of the people; the latter, on the other hand, to the claims of God. The robes express the varied functions and qualities of the priestly office. "The ephod" was the great priestly robe. It was inseparably connected with the shoulder-pieces and the breastplate, teaching us, very distinctly, that the *strength* of the priest's shoulder, and the *affection* of the priest's heart, were wholly devoted to the interests of those whom he represented, and on whose behalf he wore the ephod—that special priestly robe. This, which was typified in Aaron, is actualized in Christ. His omnipotent strength and infinite love are ours—ours eternally—ours unquestionably. The shoulder which sustains the universe upholds the feeblest and most obscure member of the blood-bought congregation. The heart of Jesus beats with an undying affection—with an everlasting and an all-enduring love for the most neglected member of the redeemed assembly.

The names of the twelve tribes, engraven on precious stones, were borne both on the shoulders and on the breast of the high-priest (see verses 9-12,15-29). The peculiar excellence of a precious stone is seen in this, that the more intense the light which is brought to bear upon it, the more brightly it shines. Light can never make a precious stone look dim; it only increases and develops its lustre. The twelve tribes—one as well as another, the smallest as well as the greatest—were borne continually upon the breast and shoulders of Aaron before the Lord. They were each and every one maintained in the divine presence in all that undimmed lustre and unalterable beauty which belonged to the position in which the perfect grace of the God of Israel had set them. The people were represented before God by the high-priest. Whatever might be their infirmities, their errors, or their failures, yet their names glittered on the breastplate with unfading brilliancy. Jehovah had set them there, and who could pluck them thence? Jehovah had put them thus, and who could put them otherwise? Who could penetrate into the holy place to snatch from Aaron's breast the name of one of Israel's tribes? Who could sully the lustre which gathered round those names, in the position which Jehovah had placed them? Not one. They lay beyond the reach of every enemy—beyond the influence of every evil.

How encouraging and consolatory it is for the tried, tempted, buffeted, and self-abased children of God to remember that God only sees them on the heart of Jesus! In His view, they ever shine in all the effulgence of Christ—they are arrayed in divine comeliness. The world cannot see them thus; but God does, and this makes all the difference. Men, in looking at the people of God, see only their blots and blemishes. They have no ability whatever to see further, and as a consequence, their judgment is always wrong—always one-sided. They cannot see the sparkling jewels, bearing the names of God's redeemed, engraven by the hand of changeless love. True it is that Christians should be most careful not to furnish the men of the world with any just occasion to speak reproachfully. They should seek, "by patient continuance in well-doing, to put to silence the ignorance of foolish men." If only they entered, by the power of the Holy Ghost, into the comeliness in which they ever shine, in God's vision, it would assuredly lead to a walk of practical holiness, moral purity, and elevation before the eyes of men. The more clearly we enter, by faith, into objective truth, or what is true of us in Christ, the deeper, more experimental and practical will be the subjective work in us, and the more complete will be the exhibition of the moral effect in our life and character.

But, thank God, our judgment is not with men, but with Himself; and He graciously shows us our great High-Priest, "bearing our judgment on His heart before the Lord continually." This imparts deep and settled peace—a peace which nothing can shake. We may have to confess and mourn over our constant failures and short-comings,—the eye may, at times, be so dimmed with the tears of a genuine contrition as to be but little able to catch the lustre of the precious stones on which our names are engraven, yet there they are all the while. God sees them, and that is enough. He is glorified by their brightness—a brightness not of our attaining, but of His imparting. We had naught save darkness, dullness, and deformity. He has imparted brightness, lustre, and beauty.

"The girdle" is the well-known symbol of service; and Christ is the perfect Servant—the Servant of the divine counsels and affections, and of the deep and manifold need of His people. With an earnest spirit of devotedness, which nothing could damp, He girded Himself for His work; and when faith sees the Son of God thus girded, it judges, assuredly, that no occasion can be too great for Him. We find, from the type before us, that all the virtues, the dignities, and the glories of Christ, in His divine and human nature, enter fully into His servant-character. —"The curious girdle of the ephod, which is upon it, shall be of the same, according to the work thereof; even of gold, of blue, and purple, and scarlet, and fine twined linen" (verse 8). The faith of this must meet every necessity of the soul, and satisfy the most ardent longings of the heart. We not only see Christ as the slain Victim at the brazen altar, but also as the girded High-Priest over the house of God. Well, therefore, may the inspired apostle say, *"Let us draw near," "Let us hold fast," "Let us consider one another"* (Heb. 10:19-24).

"And thou shalt put in the breastplate of judgment the Urim and the Thummim ['lights and perfections'] ; and they shall be upon Aaron's heart, when he goeth in before the Lord: and Aaron shall bear the judgment of the children of Israel upon his heart before the Lord continually." We learn, from various passages of the Word, that the "Urim" stood connected with the communication of the mind of God in reference to the various questions which arose in the details of Israel's history. Thus, for example, in the appointment of Joshua, we read, "And he shall stand before Eleazar the priest, who shall ask counsel for him, *after the judgment of Urim before the Lord"* (Num. 27:21). "And of Levi he said, 'Let thy Thummim and thy Urim [thy perfections and thy lights] be with thy holy one. . . . They shall teach Jacob thy judgments, and Israel thy law' " (Deut. 33:8-10). "And when Saul inquired of the Lord, the Lord answered him not, neither by dreams, *nor by Urim,* nor by prophets" (1 Sam. 28:6). "And Tirshatha said unto them that they should not eat of the most holy things till there stood up a priest with Urim and with

Thummim" (Ezra 2:63). Thus we learn that the high-priest not only bore the judgment of the congregation before the Lord, but also communicated the judgment of the Lord to the congregation. Solemn, weighty, and most precious functions! All this we have, in divine perfectness, in our "great High-Priest, who has passed into the heavens." He bears the judgment of His people on His heart continually; and He, by the Holy Ghost, communicates to us the counsel of God, in reference to the most minute circumstances of our daily course. We do not want dreams or visions; if only we walk in the Spirit, we shall enjoy all the certainty which the perfect "Urim," on the breast of our High-Priest, can afford.

"And thou shalt make the robe of the ephod all of blue. . . . And beneath, upon the hem of it, thou shalt make pomegranates of blue, and of purple, and of scarlet, round about the hem thereof; and bells of gold between them round about: a golden bell and a pomegranate, a golden bell and a pomegranate, upon the hem of the robe round about. And it shall be upon Aaron to minister; and his sound shall be heard when he goeth in unto the holy place before the Lord, and when he cometh out, that he die not" (ver. 31-35). The blue robe of the ephod is expressive of the entirely heavenly character of our High-Priest. He is gone into heaven, He is beyond the range of mortal vision; but, by the power of the Holy Ghost, there is divine testimony to the truth of His being alive, in the presence of God; and not only testimony, but fruit likewise. "A golden bell and a pomegranate, a golden bell and a pomegranate,"—such is the beauteous order. True testimony to the great truth that Jesus ever liveth to make intercession for us will be inseparably connected with fruitfulness in His service. O, for a deeper understanding of these precious and holy mysteries!*

"And thou shalt make a plate of pure gold, and grave upon it, like the engravings of a signet, HOLINESS TO THE LORD. And thou shall put it on a blue lace, that it may be upon the mitre, upon the forefront of the mitre it shall be. And it shall be upon Aaron's forehead, that Aaron may bear the iniquity of the holy things, which the children of Israel shall hallow in all their holy gifts; and it shall be always upon *his* forehead, that *they* may be accepted before the Lord" (ver. 36-38). Here is a weighty truth for the soul. The golden plate on Aaron's forehead was the type of the essential holiness of the Lord Jesus Christ. "It shall be *always* upon *his* forehead, that *they* may be accepted before the Lord." What rest for the heart amid all the fluctuations of one's experience! Our High-Priest is "always" in the presence of God for us. We are represented by, and accepted in, Him. His holiness is ours. The more deeply we become acquainted with our own personal vileness and infirmity, the more we enter into the humiliating truth that in us dwelleth no good thing, the more fervently shall we bless the God of all grace for the soul-sustaining truth contained in these words, "It shall be always upon *his* forehead, that *they* may be accepted before the Lord."

If my reader should happen to be one who is frequently tempted and harassed with doubts and fears, ups and downs in his spiritual condition, with a constant tendency to look inward upon his poor, cold, wandering, wayward heart,—if he be tried with an excessive vagueness and want of holy reality, oh, let him stay his whole soul upon the precious truth that this great High-Priest represents him before the throne of God. Let him fix his eye upon the golden plate, and read in the inscription thereon the measure of his eternal acceptance with God. May the Holy Ghost enable him to taste the peculiar sweetness and sustaining power of this divine and heavenly doctrine.

"And for Aaron's sons thou shalt make coats, and thou shalt make for them girdles, and bonnets shalt thou make for them, for glory and for beauty. . . . And thou shalt make them linen breeches to cover their

*It is needless to remark that there is divine appropriateness, as well as significancy, in all the figures presented to us in the Word. Thus, the "pomegranate," when opened, is found to consist of a number of seeds, contained in a *red* fluid. Surely this has a voice. Let spirituality, not imagination, judge.

nakedness . . . and they shall be upon Aaron, and upon his sons, when they come in unto the tabernacle of the congregation, or when they come near unto the altar to minister in the holy place; that they bear not iniquity and die." Here we have Aaron and his sons, typifying Christ and the Church, standing in the power of one divine and everlasting righteousness. Aaron's priestly robes express those inherent, essential, personal, and eternal qualities in Christ; while the "coats" and "bonnets" of Aaron's sons represent those graces with which the Church is endowed, in virtue of its association with the great Head of the priestly family.

Thus, in all that has passed before us in this chapter, we may see with what gracious care Jehovah made provision for the need of His people, in that He allowed them to see the one who was about to act on their behalf, and to represent them in His presence, clothed with all those robes which directly met their actual condition, as known to Him. Nothing was left out which the heart could possibly need or desire. They might survey him from head to foot and see that all was complete. From the holy mitre that wreathed his brow, to the bells and pomegranates on the hem of the garment, all was as it should be, because all was according to the pattern shown in the mount—all was according to Jehovah's estimate of the people's need and of His own requirements.

But there is yet one point connected with Aaron's robes which demands the reader's special attention, and that is the mode in which the gold was introduced in the making of them. This is presented to us in chapter 39, but the interpretation comes in suitably enough in this place. "And they did beat the gold into thin plates, and cut it into wires, to work it in the blue, and in the purple, and in the scarlet, and in the fine linen, with cunning work" (ver. 3). We have already remarked that "the blue, the purple, the scarlet, and fine twined linen" exhibit the various phases of Christ's manhood, and the gold represents His divine nature. The wire of gold was curiously insinuated into all the other materials, so as to be inseparably connected with, and yet perfectly distinct from, them.

The application of this striking figure to the character of the Lord Jesus is full of interest. In various scenes throughout the Gospel narrative, we can easily discern this rare and beauteous union of manhood and Godhead, and, at the same time, their mysterious distinctness.

Look, for example, at Christ on the sea of Galilee. In the midst of the storm "He was asleep on a pillow" (precious exhibition of His perfect manhood!); but in a moment He rises from the attitude of real humanity into all the dignity and majesty of Godhead, and, as the supreme Governor of the universe, He hushes the storm and calms the sea. There is no effort, no haste, no girding Himself up for an occasion. With perfect ease, He rises from the condition of positive humanity into the sphere of essential deity. The repose of the former is not more natural than the activity of the latter. He is as perfectly at home in the one as in the other.

Again, see Him in the case of the collectors of tribute, at the close of Matthew 17. As the "Most High God, possessor of heaven and earth," He lays His hand upon the treasures of the ocean, and says, "They are Mine;" and, having declared that "the sea is His, and He made it," He turns round and, in the exhibition of perfect humanity, He links Himself with His poor servant by those touching words, "That take, and give unto them *for Me and thee.*" Gracious words!—peculiarly gracious, when taken in connection with the miracle so entirely expressive of the Godhead of the One who was thus linking Himself, in infinite condescension, with a poor, feeble worm.

Once more, see Him at the grave of Lazarus (John 11). He groans and weeps, and those groans and tears issue from the profound depths of a perfect manhood—from that perfect human heart which felt, as no other heart could feel, what it was to stand in the midst of a scene in which sin had produced such terrible fruits. But then, as the Resurrection and the Life, as the One who held in His omnipotent grasp "the keys of hell and of death," He cries, "Lazarus, come forth!" and death and the grave, responsive to His authoritative voice, throw open their massy doors and let go their captive.

My reader's mind will easily recur to other scenes, in the Gospels, illustrative of the beautiful combination of the wire of gold with "the blue, the purple, the scarlet, and the fine-twined linen;" that is to say, the union of the Godhead with the manhood, in the mysterious Person of the Son of God. There is nothing new in the thought; it has often been noticed by those who have studied, with any amount of care, the Scriptures of the Old Testament.

It is, however, always edifying to have the blessed Lord Jesus introduced to our thoughts as "very God and very man." The Holy Ghost has, with "cunning workmanship," wrought the two together and presented them to the renewed mind of the believer to be enjoyed and admired. May we have hearts to appreciate such teaching!

Let us now look at chapter 29.

It has been already remarked that Aaron and his sons represent Christ and the Church, but in the opening verses of this chapter Aaron gets the precedency. "And Aaron and his sons thou shalt bring unto the door of the tabernacle of the congregation, and shalt wash them with water." The washing of water rendered Aaron typically what Christ is intrinsically—holy. The Church is holy in virtue of her being linked with Christ in resurrection life. He is the perfect definition of what she is before God. The ceremonial act of washing with water expresses the action of the Word of God (see Eph. 5:26).

"Then shalt thou take the anointing oil, and pour it upon *his* head, and anoint *him*" (ver. 7). Here we have the Spirit; but let it be noted that Aaron was anointed *before the blood was shed,* because he stands before us as the type of Christ, who, in virtue of what He was in His own Person, was anointed with the Holy Ghost, long before the work of the cross was accomplished. The sons of Aaron, on the other hand, were not anointed until after the blood was shed. "Then shalt thou kill the ram, and take of his blood, and put it upon the tip of the right ear of Aaron, and upon the tip of the right ear of his sons, and upon the thumb of their right hand, and upon the great toe of their right foot, and sprinkle the blood upon the altar round about.* And thou shalt take of the blood that is upon the altar, and of *the anointing oil,* and sprinkle it upon Aaron, and upon his garments, and upon his sons, and upon the garments of his sons with him" (ver. 20-21). As regards the Church, the blood of the cross lies at the foundation of every thing. She could not be anointed with the Holy Ghost until her risen Head had gone into heaven, and laid upon the throne of the divine Majesty the record of His accomplished sacrifice. "This Jesus hath God raised up, whereof we all are witnesses. Therefore being by the right hand of God exalted, and having received of the Father the promise of the Holy Ghost, He hath shed forth this which ye now see and hear" (Acts 2:32-33; comp. also John 7:39; Acts 19:1-6). From the days of Abel downward, souls had been regenerated, influenced, acted upon, and qualified for office by the Holy Ghost; but the Church could not be anointed with the Holy Ghost until her victorious Lord had entered heaven and received, on her behalf, the promise of the Father. The truth of this doctrine is taught, in the most direct and absolute manner, throughout the New Testament; and its strict integrity is maintained, in the type before us, by the obvious fact that though Aaron was anointed before the blood was shed (ver. 7), yet his sons were not, and could not be, anointed till after.

But we learn more from the order of anointing in our chapter than the important truth with respect to the work of the Spirit and the position of the Church; we have also set before us the personal pre-eminence of the Son.—"Thou hast loved righteousness, and hated iniquity; therefore God, even Thy God, hath anointed Thee with the oil of

*The ear, the hand, and the foot, are all consecrated to God in the power of accomplished atonement, and by the energy of the Holy Ghost.

gladness *above* Thy fellows" (Ps. 45:7; Heb. 1:9). This must ever be held fast in the convictions and experience of the people of God. True, the infinite grace of God is set forth in the marvelous fact that guilty, hell-deserving sinners should ever be spoken of in such terms—should ever be styled the *"fellows"* of the Son of God; but let us never for a moment forget the work *"above."* No matter how close the union (and it is as close as God's eternal counsels of redeeming love could make it), yet "in all things" Christ must "have the pre-eminence." It could not be otherwise. He is Head over all—Head of the Church, Head of creation, Head of angels, Lord of the universe. There is not a single orb that rolls along the heavens that does not belong to Him, and move under His control; there is not a single worm that crawls along the earth which is not under His sleepless eye. He is "high over all," "the first-begotten from the dead," and "of all creation," "the beginning of the creation of God." "Every family in heaven and earth" must range itself, in the divine category, under Christ. All this will ever be thankfully owned by every spiritual mind; yea, the very enunciation of it sends a thrill through the Christian's heart. All who are led of the Spirit will rejoice in every unfolding of the personal glories of the Son; nor can they tolerate, for a single instant, any thing derogatory thereto. Let the Church be raised to the loftiest heights of glory, it will be her joy to bow at the feet of Him who stooped to raise her, by virtue of His completed sacrifice, into union with Himself; who, having satisfied, in the fullest way, all the claims of divine justice, can gratify all the divine affections by making her inseparably one with Himself, in all His infinite acceptableness with the Father, and in His eternal glory. "He is not *ashamed* to call them brethren."

NOTE—I purposely forbear entering upon the subject of the offerings in chapter 29, inasmuch as we shall have the various classes of offerings, in all their minute detail, fully before us in the book of Leviticus, if the Lord will.

## *CHAPTER 30*

THE priesthood being instituted, as in the two preceding chapters, we are here introduced to the position of true priestly worship and communion. The order is marked and instructive, and, moreover, precisely corresponds with the order of the believer's experience. At the brazen altar, he sees the ashes of his sins; he then sees himself linked with One who, though personally pure and spotless, so that He could be anointed without blood, has, nevertheless, associated us with Himself in life, righteousness, and favor; and, finally, he beholds, in the golden altar, the preciousness of Christ, as the material on which the divine affections feed.

Thus it is ever; there must be a brazen altar and a priest before there can be a golden altar and incense. Very many of the children of God have never passed the brazen altar; they have never yet, in spirit, entered into the power and reality of true priestly worship. They do not rejoice in a full, clear, divine sense of pardon and righteousness,—they have never reached the golden altar. They hope to reach it when they die; but it is their privilege to be at it *now.* The work of the cross has removed out of the way every thing which would act as a barrier to their free and intelligent worship. The present position of all true believers is at the golden altar of incense.

This altar typifies a position of wondrous blessedness. There we enjoy the reality and efficacy of Christ's intercession. Forever done with self and all pertaining thereto, so far as any expectation of good is concerned, we are to be occupied with what He is before God. We shall find nothing in self but defilement. Every exhibition of it is defiling; it has been condemned and set aside in the judgment of God, and not a shred or particle thereof is to be found in the pure incense and pure fire, on the altar of pure gold: it could not be. We have been introduced, "by the blood of Jesus," into the sanctuary—a sanctuary of priestly service and worship, in which there is not so much as a trace of sin. We see the pure table, the pure candlestick, and the pure altar; but there is nothing to remind us of self and its wretchedness. Were it possible for aught of that to meet our view, it could but prove the death-knell of our worship, mar our priestly food, and dim our light. Nature can have no place in the sanctuary of God. It, together with all its belongings, has been consumed to ashes; and we are now to have before our souls the fragrant odor of Christ, ascending in grateful incense to God: this is what God delights in. Every thing that presents Christ in His own proper excellence is sweet and acceptable to God. Even the feeblest expression or exhibition of Him, in the life or worship of a saint, is an odor of a sweet smell in which God is well pleased.

Too often, alas! we have to be occupied with our failures and infirmities. If ever the workings of indwelling sin be suffered to rise to the surface, we must deal with our God about them, for He cannot go on with sin. He can forgive it, and cleanse us from it; He can restore our souls by the gracious ministry of our great High-Priest; but He cannot go on in company with a single sinful thought. A light or foolish thought, as well as an unclean or covetous one, is amply sufficient to mar a Christian's communion, and interrupt his worship. Should any such thought spring up, it must be judged and confessed, ere the elevated joys of the sanctuary can be known afresh. A heart in which lust is working is not enjoying the proper occupations of the sanctuary. When we are in our proper priestly condition, nature is as though it had no existence; then we can feed upon Christ: we can taste the divine luxury of being wholly at leisure from ourselves, and wholly engrossed with Christ.

All this can only be produced by the power of the Spirit. There is no need of seeking to work up nature's devotional feelings, by the various appliances of systematic religion; there must be pure fire as well as pure incense. (Comp. Lev. 10:1, with 16:12.) All efforts at worshiping God by the unhallowed powers of nature come under the head of "strange fire." God is the object of worship; Christ the ground and the material of worship; and the Holy Ghost the power of worship.

Properly speaking, then, as in the brazen altar we have Christ in the value of His sacrifice, so in the golden altar we have Christ in the value of His intercession. This will furnish my reader with a still clearer sense of the reason why the priestly office is introduced between the two altars. There is, as might be expected, an intimate connection between the two, for Christ's intercession is founded upon His sacrifice. "And Aaron shall make an atonement upon the horns of it once in a year with the blood of the sin-offering of atonements: once in the year shall he make atonement upon it throughout your generations: it is most holy unto the Lord" All rests upon the immovable foundation of *shed blood.* "Almost all things are by the law purged with blood; and without shedding of blood is no remission. It was therefore necessary that the patterns of things in the heavens should be purified with these; but the heavenly things themselves with better sacrifices than these. For Christ is not entered into the holy places made with hands, which are the figures of the true; but into heaven itself, now to appear in the presence of God for us" (Heb. 9:22-24).

From verses 11-16 we have the atonement money for the congregation. All were to pay alike: "The rich shall not give more, and the poor shall not give less, than half a shekel, when they give an offering unto the Lord, to make an atonement for your souls." In the matter of atonement, all must stand on one common platform. There may be a vast difference in knowledge, in experience, in capacity, in attainment, in zeal, in devotedness, but the ground of atonement is alike to all. The great apostle of the Gentiles and the feeblest lamb in all the flock of Christ stand on the same level as regards atonement. This is a very simple and a very blessed truth. All may not be alike devoted and fruitful; but "the precious blood of Christ," and not devotedness or fruitfulness, is the solid and everlasting ground of the believer's rest. The more we enter into the truth and power of this, the more fruitful shall we be.

In the last chapter of Leviticus we find another kind of valuation. When any one made "a singular vow," Moses valued him according to his age. In other words, when any one ventured to assume the ground of capacity, Moses, as the representative of *the claims* of God, estimated him, "after the shekel of the sanctuary." If he were "poorer" than Moses' estimation, then he was to "present himself before the priest," the representative of *the grace* of God, who was to value him "according to his ability that vowed."

Blessed be God, we know that all His claims have been answered, and all our vows discharged, by One who was at once the Representative of His claims and the Exponent of His grace, who finished the work of atonement upon the cross, and is now at the right hand of God. Here is sweet rest for the heart and conscience. Atonement is the first thing to get hold of, and we shall never lose sight of it. Let our range of intelligence be ever so wide, our fund of experience ever so rich, our tone of devotion ever so elevated, we shall always have to fall back upon the one simple, divine, unalterable, soul-sustaining doctrine of *the blood.* Thus it has ever been in the history of God's people, thus it is, and thus it ever will be. The most deeply-taught and gifted servants of Christ have always rejoiced to come back to "that one well-spring of delight," at which their thirsty spirits drank when first they knew the Lord; and the eternal song of the Church in glory will be, "Unto Him that loved us, and washed us from our sins in His own blood." The courts of heaven will ever resound with the glorious doctrine of the blood.

From verses 17-21 we are presented with "the brazen laver and its foot"—the vessel of washing and the basis thereof. These two are always presented together (see chap. 30:28; 38:8; 40:11). In this laver the priests washed their hands and feet, and thus maintained that purity which was essential to the proper discharge of their priestly functions. It was not, by any means, a question of a fresh presentation of blood; but simply that action by which they were preserved in fitness for priestly service and worship. "When they go into the tabernacle of the congregation, they shall wash with water, that they die not; or when they come near to the altar to minister, to burn offering made by fire unto the Lord: so they shall wash their hands and their feet, that they die not."

There can be no true communion with God, save as personal holiness is diligently maintained. "If we say that we have fellowship with Him, and walk in darkness, we lie, and do not the truth" (1 John 1:6). This personal holiness can only flow from the action of the Word of God on our works and ways. "By the words of Thy lips I have kept me from the paths of the destroyer." Our constant failure in priestly ministry may be accounted for by our neglecting the due use of the laver. If our ways are not submitted to the purgative action of the Word—if we continue in the pursuit or practice of that which, according to the testimony of our own consciences, the Word distinctly condemns, the energy of our priestly character will assuredly be lacking. Deliberate continuance in evil and true priestly worship are wholly incompatible. "Sanctify them through Thy truth: Thy Word is truth." If we have any uncleanness upon us, we cannot enjoy the presence of God. The effect of His presence would then be to convict us by its holy light. But when we are enabled, through grace, to cleanse our way, by taking heed thereto according to God's Word, we are then morally capacitated for the enjoyment of His presence.

My reader will at once perceive what a vast field of practical truth is here laid open to him, and also how largely the doctrine of the brazen laver is brought out in the New Testament. Oh that all those who are privileged to tread the courts of the sanctuary, in priestly robes, and to approach the altar of God, in priestly worship, may keep their hands and feet clean by the use of the true laver.

It may be interesting to note that the laver, with its foot, was made "of the looking-glasses of the women assembling, which assembled at the door of the tabernacle of the congregation" (see chap. 38:8). This fact is full of meaning. We are ever prone to be "like a man beholding his natural face in a glass; for he beholdeth himself and goeth away, and straightway forgetteth what manner of man he was." Nature's looking-glass can never furnish a clear and permanent view of our true condition. "But whoso looketh into the perfect law of liberty, and continueth therein, he being not a forgetful hearer, but a doer of the work, this man shall be blessed in his deed" (James 1:23-25). The man who has constant recourse to the Word of God, and who allows that Word to tell upon his heart and conscience, will be maintained in the holy activities of the divine life.

Intimately connected with the searching and cleansing action of the Word is the efficacy of the priestly ministry of Christ. "For the Word of God is quick and powerful [*i.e., living* and *energetic*], and sharper than any two-edged sword, piercing even to the dividing asunder of soul and spirit, and of the joints and marrow, and is a discerner of the thoughts and intents of the heart; neither is there any creature that is not manifest in His sight; but all things are naked and opened unto the eyes of Him with whom we have to do." Then the inspired apostle immediately adds, "Seeing then that we have a great High-Priest, that is passed into the heavens, Jesus the Son of God, let us hold fast our profession. For we have not a high-priest which cannot be touched with the feeling of our infirmities; but was in all points tempted like as we are, yet without sin.* Let us therefore come boldly unto the throne of grace, that we may obtain mercy, and find grace to help in time of need" (Heb. 4:12-16).

The more keenly we feel the edge of the Word, the more we shall prize the merciful and gracious ministry of our High-Priest. The two things go together. They are the inseparable companions of the Christian's path. Hence, it is only as I am making use of the laver that I can approach the altar. Worship must ever be presented in the power of holiness. We must lose sight of nature, as reflected in a looking-glass, and be wholly occupied with Christ, as presented in the Word. In this way only shall the "hands and feet"—the works and ways—be cleansed, according to the purification of the sanctuary.

From verses 22-23 we have the "holy anointing oil," with which the priests, together with all the furniture of the tabernacle, were anointed. In this we discern a type of the varied graces of the Holy Ghost, which were found, in all their divine fullness, in Christ. "All thy garments smell of myrrh, and aloes, and cassia, out of the ivory palaces, whereby they have made thee glad" (Ps. 45:8). "God anointed Jesus of Nazareth with the Holy Ghost and with power" (Acts 10:38). All the graces of the Spirit, in their perfect fragrance, centred in Christ; and it is from Him alone they can flow. He, as to His humanity, was conceived of the Holy Ghost; and, ere He entered upon His public ministry, He was anointed with the Holy Ghost; and finally, when He had taken His seat on high, in token of an accomplished redemption, He shed forth upon His body, the Church, the precious gifts of the Holy Ghost (see Matt. 1:20; 3:16-17; Luke 4:18-19; Acts 2:33; 10:45-46; Eph. 4:8-13).

It is as those who are associated with this ever-blessed and highly-exalted Christ that believers are partakers of the gifts and graces of the Holy Ghost; and, moreover, it is as they walk in habitual nearness to Him that they either enjoy or emit the fragrance thereof. The unrenewed man knows nothing of this. "Upon man's flesh it shall not be poured." The graces of the Spirit can never be connected with man's flesh, for the Holy Ghost cannot own nature. Not one of the fruits of the Spirit was ever yet produced "in nature's barren soil." We "must be born again." It is only as connected with the new man, as being part of "the new creation," that we can know any thing of the fruits of the Holy Ghost. It is of no possible value to

*Literally, "sin excepted" (χωρις ἁμαρτιας); *i.e.,* He was tempted—tested and tried—in every way from without, sin excepted, for sin was not in Him.

seek to imitate those fruits and graces. The fairest fruits that ever grew in nature's fields, in their highest state of cultivation—the most amiable traits which nature can exhibit—must be utterly disowned in the sanctuary of God. "Upon man's flesh shall it not be poured; neither shall ye make any other like it, after the composition of it: it is holy, and it shall be holy unto you. Whosoever compoundeth any like it, or whosoever putteth any of it upon a stranger, shall even be cut off from his people." There must be no counterfeit of the Spirit's work; all must be of the Spirit—wholly, really of the Spirit. Moreover, that which is of the Spirit must not be attributed to man. "The natural man receiveth not the things of the Spirit of God; for they are foolishness unto him: neither can he know them, because they are spiritually discerned" (1 Cor. 2:14).

There is a very beautiful allusion to this "holy anointing oil" in one of the "songs of degrees."—"Behold," says the Psalmist, "how good and how pleasant it is for brethren to dwell together in unity! It is like the precious ointment upon the head, that ran down upon the beard, even Aaron's beard; that went down to the skirts of his garments" (Psalms 133:1-2). The head of the priestly house being anointed with the holy oil, the very "skirts of his garments" must exhibit the precious effects. May my reader experience the power of this anointing! May he know the value of having "an unction from the Holy One," and of being "sealed with that Holy Spirit of promise"! Nothing is of any value in the divine estimation save that which connects itself immediately with Christ, and whatever is so connected can receive the holy anointing.

In the concluding paragraph of this most comprehensive chapter, we have the "sweet spices tempered together, pure and holy." This surpassingly precious perfume presents to us the unmeasured and unmeasurable perfections of Christ. There was no special quantity of each ingredient prescribed, because the graces that dwell in Christ, the beauties and excellencies that are concentrated in His adorable Person, are without limit. Naught save the infinite mind of Deity could scan the infinite perfections of Him in whom all the fullness of Deity dwelleth; and as eternity rolls along its course of everlasting ages, those glorious perfections will ever be unfolding themselves in the view of worshiping saints and angels. Ever and anon, as some fresh beams of light shall burst forth from that central Sun of divine glory, the courts of heaven above, and the wide fields of creation beneath, shall resound with thrilling Alleluiahs to Him who was, who is, and who ever shall be the object of praise to all the ranks of created intelligence.

But not only was there no prescribed quantity of the ingredients; we also read, "Of each there shall be a like weight." Every feature of moral excellence found its due place and proper proportions in Christ. No one quality ever displaced or interfered with another; all was "tempered together, pure and holy," and emitted an odor so fragrant that none but God could appreciate it.

"And thou shalt beat some of it *very small,* and put of it before the testimony in the tabernacle of the congregation, where I will meet with thee: it shall be unto you most holy." There is uncommon depth and power in the expression "very small." It teaches us that every little movement in the life of Christ, every minute circumstance, every act, every word, every look, every feature, every trait, every lineament, emits an odor produced by an equal proportion—"a like weight" of all the divine graces that compose His character. The smaller the perfume was beaten, the more its rare and exquisite temper was manifested.

"And as for the perfume which thou shalt make, ye shall not make to yourselves according to the composition thereof; it shall be unto thee holy for the Lord. Whosoever shall make like unto that, to smell thereto, shall even be cut off from his people." This fragrant perfume was designed exclusively for Jehovah. Its place was "before the testimony." There is that in Jesus which only God could appreciate. True, every believing heart can draw nigh to His matchless Person, and more than satisfy its deepest and most intense longings; still, after all God's redeemed have drunk to the utmost of their capacity, after angels have gazed on the peerless glories of the Man Christ Jesus as earnestly as their vision is capable of,—after all, there will be that in Him which God alone can fathom and enjoy. No human or angelic eye could duly trace the exquisitely minute parts of that holy perfume "beaten very small," nor could earth afford a proper sphere in which to emit its divine and heavenly odor.

Thus, then, we have, in our rapid sketch, reached the close of a clearly marked division of our book. We began at "the ark of the covenant," and traveled out to "the altar of brass;" we returned from "the altar of brass," and have come to the "holy perfume;" and, oh, what a journey is this, if only it be traveled, not in company with the false and flickering light of human imagination, but by the infallible lamp of the Holy Ghost! What a journey, if only it be traveled, not amid the shadows of a by-gone dispensation, but amid the personal glories and powerful attractions of the Son which are there portrayed! If my reader has so traveled it, he will find his affections more drawn to Christ than ever; he will have a loftier conception of His glory, His beauty, His preciousness, His excellency, His ability to heal a wounded conscience and satisfy a longing heart; he will have his eyes more thoroughly closed to all earth's attractions, and his ears closed to all earth's pretensions and promises;—in one word, he will be prepared to utter a deeper and more fervent Amen to the words of the inspired apostle when he says, *"If any man love not the Lord Jesus Christ, let him be Anathema Maran-atha"** (1 Cor. 16:22).

---

## CHAPTER 31

THE opening of this brief chapter records the divine call and the divine qualification of "Bezaleel and Aholiab" to do the work of the tabernacle of the congregation. "And the Lord spake unto Moses, saying, 'See, *I have called* by name Bezaleel, the son of Uri, the son of Hur, of the tribe of Judah; and *I have filled* him with the spirit of God, in wisdom, and in understanding, and in knowledge, and in all manner of workmanship. . . . And I, behold, *I have given* with him Aholiab, the son of Ahisamach, of the tribe of Dan; and in the hearts of all that are wise-hearted *I have put* wisdom, that they may make all that *I have commanded."* Whether for "the work of the tabernacle" of old, or "the work of the ministry" now, there should be the divine selection, the divine call, the divine qualification, the divine appointment, and all must be done according to the divine commandment. Man could not select, call, qualify, or appoint to do the work of the tabernacle; neither can he to do the work of the ministry. Furthermore, no man could presume to appoint himself to do the work of the tabernacle; neither can he to do the work of the ministry. It was, it is, it must be, wholly and absolutely divine. Men may run as sent of their fellow, or men may run of themselves; but let it be remembered that all who run without being sent of God shall one day or other be covered with shame and confusion of face. Such is the plain and wholesome doctrine suggested by the words, "I have called," "I have filled," "I have given," "I have put," "I have commanded." The words of the Baptist must ever hold good—"A man can receive nothing except it be given him from heaven" (John 3:27). He can therefore have but little room to boast of himself, and just as little to be jealous of his fellow.

There is a profitable lesson to be learnt from a comparison of this chapter with Genesis 4; "Tubal-cain was an instructor of every artificer in brass and iron." The descendants of Cain were endowed with unhallowed skill to make a cursed and groaning earth a delectable spot, without the presence of God: "Bezaleel and Aholiab,"

*It is interesting to note the position of this most solemn and startling denunciation. It occurs at the close of a long Epistle in the progress of which the apostle had to rebuke some of the grossest practical evils and doctrinal errors. How solemn, therefore, how full of meaning the fact, that when he comes to pronounce his anathema, it is not hurled at those on the contrary, were endowed with divine skill to beautify a sanctuary which was to be hallowed and blessed by the presence and glory of the God of Israel.

Let me ask you just to pause and put this solemn question to your conscience: Whether I am devoting whatever of skill or energy I possess to the interests of the Church which is God's dwelling-place, or to beautify an ungodly, Christless world? Say not in thine heart, I am not divinely called or divinely qualified for the work of the ministry. Remember that though all Israel were not Bezaleels or Aholiabs, yet all could serve the interests of the sanctuary. There was an open door for all to communicate. Thus it is now. Each one has *a* place to occupy, a ministry to fulfill, a responsibility to discharge; and you and I are at this moment either promoting the interests of the house of God—the body of Christ—the Church, or helping on the Godless schemes of a world yet stained with the blood of Christ and the blood of all His martyred saints. Oh, let us deeply ponder this, as in the presence of the great Searcher of hearts, whom none can deceive—to whom all are known.

Our chapter closes with a special reference to the institution of the Sabbath. It was referred to in chapter 16, in connection with the manna; it was distinctly enjoined in chapter 20, when the people were formally put under law; and here we have it again, in connection with the setting up of the tabernacle. Whenever the nation of Israel is presented in some special position, or recognized as a people in special responsibility, then the Sabbath is introduced. Carefully note both the day and the mode in which it was to be observed, and also the object for which it was instituted in Israel: "Ye shall keep the Sabbath, therefore, for it is holy unto you: *every one that defileth it shall surely be put to death;* for whosoever doeth *any work* therein, that soul shall be *cut off* from among his people. Six days may work be done; but *in the seventh* is the Sabbath of rest, holy to the Lord: whosoever doeth *any work* in the Sabbath day, *he shall surely be put to death.*" This is as explicit and absolute as any thing can be. It fixes "the seventh day" and none other; and it positively forbids, on pain of death, all manner of work. There can be no avoiding the plain sense of this. And be it remembered that there is not so much as a single line of Scripture to prove that the Sabbath has been changed, or the strict principles of its observance in the smallest degree relaxed. If there be any Scripture proof, let my reader look it out for his own satisfaction.

Now, let us inquire if indeed professing Christians do keep God's Sabbath on the day and after the manner which He commanded. It were idle to lose time in proving that they do not. Well, what are the consequences of a single breach of the Sabbath? *"Cut off"*—*"put to death."*

But, it will be said, we "are not under law, but under grace." Blessed be God for the sweet assurance! Were we under the law, there is not one throughout the wide range of christendom who should not long since have fallen beneath the stone of judgment, even upon the one solitary point of the Sabbath. But, if we are under grace, what is the day which belongs to us? Assuredly, "the first day of the week"—"the Lord's day." This is the Church's day—the resurrection day of Jesus, who, having spent the Sabbath in the tomb, rose triumphant over all the powers of darkness; thus leading His people out of the old creation, and all that pertains thereto, into the new creation, of which He is the Head, and of which the first day of the week is the apt expression.

This distinction is worthy of the serious attention of the reader. Let him examine it prayerfully in the light of Scripture. There may be nothing and there may be a great deal in a mere name. In the present instance, there is a great deal more involved in the distinction between "the Sabbath" and "the

who had introduced those errors and evils, but at the man who loves not the Lord Jesus Christ! Why is this? Is it because the Spirit of God makes little of errors and evils? Surely not: the entire Epistle unfolds His thoughts as to these. But the truth is, when the heart is filled with love to the Lord Jesus Christ, there is an effectual safeguard against all manner of false doctrine and evil practice. If a man does not love Christ, there is no accounting for the notions he may adopt, or the course he may pursue. Hence the form and the position of the apostolic anathema.

Lord's day" than many Christians seem to be aware of. It is very evident that the first day of the week gets a place in the Word of God which no other day gets. No other day is ever called by that majestic and elevated title, "The Lord's day." Some, I am aware, deny that Rev. 1:10 refers to the first day of the week; but I feel most fully assured that sound criticism and sound exegesis do both warrant—yea, demand the application of that passage, not to the day of Christ's advent in glory, but to the day of His resurrection from the dead.

But, most assuredly, the Lord's day is never once called the Sabbath. So far from this, the two days are again and again spoken of in their proper distinctness. Hence, therefore, my reader will have to keep clear of two extremes. In the first place, he will have to avoid the legalism which one finds so much linked with the term "Sabbath;" and, in the second place, he will need to bear a very decided testimony against every attempt to dishonor the Lord's day, or lower it to the level of an ordinary day. The believer is delivered, most completely, from the observance of "days, and months, and times, and years." Association with a risen Christ has taken him clean out of all such superstitious observances. But, while this is most blessedly true, we see that "the first day of the week" has a place assigned to it in the New Testament which no other has. Let the Christian give it that place. It is a sweet and happy privilege, not a grievous yoke.

Space forbids my further entrance upon this interesting subject. It has been gone into elsewhere, as already intimated, in the earlier pages of this volume. I shall close these remarks by pointing out, in one or two particulars, the contrast between "the Sabbath" and "the Lord's day."

1. The Sabbath was the *seventh* day; the Lord's day is the *first.*

2. The Sabbath was a *test* of Israel's condition; the Lord's day is the *proof* of the Church's acceptance, on wholly unconditional grounds.

3. The Sabbath belonged to the old creation; the Lord's day belongs to the new.

4. The Sabbath was a day of *bodily* rest for the Jew; the Lord's day is a day of *spiritual* rest for the Christian.

5. If the Jew worked on the Sabbath, he was to be put to *death:* if the Christian does not work on the Lord's day, he gives little proof of *life;* that is to say, if he does not work for the benefit of the souls of men, the extension of Christ's glory, and the spread of His truth. In point of fact, the devoted Christian who possesses any gift is generally more fatigued on the evening of the Lord's day than on any other in the week, for how can he *rest* while souls are perishing around him?

6. The Jew was *commanded* by the *law* to abide in his tent; the Christian is *led* by the spirit of the *gospel* to go forth, whether it be to attend the public assembly or to minister to the souls of perishing sinners.

The Lord enable us, beloved reader, to rest more artlessly *in,* and labor more vigorously *for,* the name of the Lord Jesus Christ! We should *rest* in the spirit of a *child,* and *labor* with the energy of a *man.*

---

## *CHAPTER 32*

WE have now to contemplate something very different from that which has hitherto engaged our attention. "The patterns of things in the heavens" has been before us—Christ in His glorious Person, gracious offices, and perfect work, as set forth in the tabernacle and all its mystic furniture. We have been, in spirit, on the mount, hearkening to God's own words—the sweet utterances of Heaven's thoughts, affections, and counsels of which Jesus is "the Alpha and Omega—the beginning and the ending—the first and the last."

Now, however, we are called down to earth, to behold the melancholy wreck which man makes of every thing to which he puts his hand. "And when the people saw that Moses delayed to come down out of the mount, the people gathered themselves together unto Aaron, and said unto him, 'Up, make us gods, which shall go before us;

for as for this Moses, the man that brought us up out of the land of Egypt, we wot not what is become of him.' " What degradation is here! *Make us gods!* They were abandoning Jehovah, and placing themselves under the conduct of manufactured gods—gods of man's making. Dark clouds and heavy mists had gathered round the mount. They grew weary of waiting for the absent one, and of hanging on an unseen but real arm. They imagined that a god formed by "graving tool" was better than Jehovah,—that a calf which they could *see* was better than the invisible, yet every-where-present, God,—a visible counterfeit, than an invisible reality.

Alas! it has ever been thus in man's history. The human heart loves something that can be seen; it loves that which meets and gratifies the senses. It is only faith that can "endure as seeing Him who is invisible." Hence, in every age, men have been forward to set up and lean upon human imitations of divine realities. Thus it is we see the counterfeits of corrupt religion multiplied before our eyes. Those things which we know, upon the authority of God's Word, to be divine and heavenly realities, the professing church has transformed into human and earthly imitations. Having become weary of hanging upon an invisible arm, of trusting in an invisible sacrifice, of having recourse to an invisible Priest, of committing herself to the guidance of an invisible Head, she has set about "making" these things; and thus, from age to age, she has been busily at work, with "graving tool" in hand, graving and fashioning one thing after another, until we can at length recognize as little similarity between much that we *see* around us and what we *read* in the Word, as between "a molten calf" and the God of Israel.

*"Make us gods!"* What a thought! Man called upon to make gods, and people willing to put their trust in such! My reader, let us look within, and look around, and see if we cannot detect something of all this. We read, in 1 Cor. 10, in reference to Israel's history, that "all these things happened unto them for ensamples [or types]; and they are written *for our admonition,* upon whom the ends of the world are come" (ver. 11). Let us, then, seek to profit by the "admonition." Let us remember that although we may not just form and bow down before "a molten calf," yet that Israel's sin is a "type" of something into which we are in danger of falling. Whenever we turn away in heart from leaning exclusively upon God Himself, whether in the matter of salvation or the necessities of the path, we are, in principle, saying, "Up, make us gods." It is needless to say we are not, in ourselves, a whit better than Aaron or the children of Israel; and if they acknowledge a calf instead of Jehovah, we are in danger of acting on the same principle, and manifesting the same spirit. Our only safeguard is to be much in the presence of God. Moses knew that the "molten calf" was not Jehovah, and therefore he did not acknowledge it. But when we get out of the divine presence, there is no accounting for the gross errors and evils into which we may be betrayed.

We are called to live by faith; we can see nothing with the eye of sense. Jesus is gone up on high, and we are told to wait patiently for His appearing. God's Word, carried home to the heart in the energy of the Holy Ghost, is the ground of confidence in all things—temporal and spiritual, present and future. He tells us of Christ's completed sacrifice; we, by grace, believe, and commit our souls to the efficacy thereof, and know we shall never be confounded. He tells us of a great High-Priest, passed into the heavens—Jesus, the Son of God, whose intercession is all-prevailing; we, by grace, believe, and confidingly lean upon His ability, and know we shall be saved to the uttermost. He tells us of the living Head to whom we are linked, in the power of resurrection life, and from whom we can never be severed by any influence, angelic, human, or diabolical; we, by grace, believe, and cling to that blessed Head in simple faith, and know we shall never perish. He tells us of the glorious appearing of the Son from heaven; we, through grace, believe, and seek to prove the purifying and elevating power of "that blessed hope," and know we shall not be disappointed. He tells us of "an inheritance, incorruptible, undefiled, and that fadeth not away, reserved in heaven for us, who are kept by the power of God," for entrance thereinto in due time; we, through grace, believe, and know we shall never be confounded. He tells us the hairs of our head are all numbered, and that we shall never want any good thing; we, through grace, believe, and enjoy a sweetly tranquilized heart.

Thus it is, or, at least, thus our God would have it. But then the enemy is ever active in seeking to make us cast away these divine realities, take up the "graving tool" of unbelief, and "make gods" for ourselves. Let us watch against him, pray against him, believe against him, testify against him, act against him: thus he shall be confounded, God glorified, and we ourselves abundantly blessed.

As to Israel, in the chapter before us, their rejection of God was most complete. "And Aaron said unto them, 'Break off the golden earrings, which are in the ears of your wives, of your sons, and of your daughters, and bring them unto me.' . . . And he received them at their hand, and fashioned it with a graving tool, after he had made it a molten calf; and they said, *'These be thy gods,* O Israel, which brought thee up out of the land of Egypt.' And when Aaron saw it, he built an altar before it; and Aaron made proclamation, and said, 'To-morrow is *a feast unto the Lord.'* " This was entirely setting aside God, and putting a calf in His stead. When they could say that a calf had brought them up out of Egypt, they had evidently abandoned all idea of the presence and character of the true God. How *"quickly"* they must "have turned aside out of the way," to have made such a gross and terrible mistake! And Aaron, the brother and yoke-fellow of Moses, led them on in this; and, with a calf before him, he could say, "To-morrow is a feast unto Jehovah"! How sad! How deeply humbling! God was displaced by an idol. A thing "graven by art and man's device" was set in the place of "the Lord of all the earth."

All this involved, on Israel's part, a deliberate abandonment of their connection with Jehovah. They had given Him up; and, accordingly, we find Him, as it were, taking them on their own ground. "And the Lord said unto Moses, 'Go, get thee down; for thy people, which thou broughtest out of the land of Egypt, have corrupted themselves: they have turned aside quickly out of the way which I commanded them. . . . I have seen this people, it is a stiff-necked people: now therefore let Me alone, that My wrath may wax hot against them, and that I may consume them: and I will make of *thee* a great nation.' " Here was an open door for Moses; and here he displays uncommon grace, and similarity of spirit to that Prophet whom the Lord was to raise up like unto him. He refuses to be or to have any thing without the people. He pleads with God on the ground of His own glory, and puts the people back upon Him in these touching words, "Lord, why doth Thy wrath wax hot against *Thy people,* which *Thou* hast brought up out of the land of Egypt with great power and a mighty hand? Wherefore should the Egyptians speak and say, For mischief did He bring them out, to slay them in the mountains, and to consume them from the face of the earth? Turn from Thy fierce wrath, and repent of this evil against *Thy* people. Remember Abraham, Isaac, and Israel, Thy servants, to whom Thou swarest by Thine own self, and saidst unto them, 'I will multiply your seed as the stars of heaven, and all this land that I have spoken of will I give unto your seed, and they shall inherit it forever.' " This was powerful pleading. The glory of God, the vindication of His holy name, the accomplishment of His oath—these are the grounds on which Moses entreats the Lord to turn from His fierce wrath. He could not find in Israel's conduct or character any plea or ground to go upon; he found it all in God Himself.

The Lord hath said unto Moses, *"Thy* people which *thou* broughtest up;" but Moses replies to the Lord, *"Thy* people which *Thou* hast brought up." They were the Lord's people notwithstanding all; and His name, His glory, His oath, were all involved in their destiny. The moment the Lord links Himself with a people, His character is involved, and faith will ever look at Him upon this solid ground. Moses loses sight of himself entirely. His whole soul is engrossed with thoughts of the Lord's glory and the Lord's people. Blessed servant! How few like him! And yet when we contemplate him in all this scene, we perceive how infinitely he is below the blessed Master. He came down from the mount, and when he saw the calf and the dancing, his "anger waxed hot, and he cast the tables out of his hands, and break them beneath the mount." The covenant was broken, and the memorials thereof shattered to pieces; and then, having executed judgment in righteous indignation, he "said unto the people, 'Ye have sinned a great sin: and now I will go up unto the Lord; *peradventure* I shall make an atonement for your sin.' "

How different is this from what we see in Christ! He came down from the bosom of the Father, not with the tables in His hands, but with the law in His heart. He came down, not to be made acquainted with the condition of the people, but with a perfect knowledge of what that condition was. Moreover, instead of destroying the memorials of the covenant and executing judgment, He magnified the law and made it honorable, and bore the judgment of His people, in His own blessed Person, on the cross; and, having done all, He went back to heaven, not with a "*peradventure* I shall make an atonement for your sin;" but to lay upon the throne of the Majesty in the highest the imperishable memorials of an atonement already accomplished. This makes a vast and truly glorious difference. Thank God, we need not anxiously gaze after our Mediator, to know if haply He shall accomplish redemption for us, and reconcile offended Justice. No; He has done it all. His presence on high declares that the whole work is finished. He could stand upon the confines of this world, ready to take His departure, and, in all the calmness of a conscious Victor (though He had yet to encounter the darkest scene of all), say, "I have glorified Thee on the earth: I have finished the work which Thou gavest Me to do" (John 17). Blessed Saviour! we may well adore Thee, and well exult in the place of dignity and glory in which eternal justice has set Thee. The highest place in heaven belongs to Thee; and Thy saints only wait for the time when "every knee shall bow, and every tongue confess that Jesus Christ is Lord, to the glory of God the Father." May that time speedily arrive!

At the close of this chapter, Jehovah asserts His rights, in moral government, in the following words: "Whosoever hath sinned against Me, him will I blot out of My book. Therefore now go, lead the people unto the place of which I have spoken unto thee: behold, Mine Angel shall go before thee: nevertheless, in the day when I visit I will visit their sin upon them." This is God *in government,* not God *in the gospel.* Here He speaks of blotting out *the sinner;* in the gospel He is seen blotting out *sin.* A wide difference!

The people are to be sent forward, under the mediatorship of Moses, by the hand of an angel. This was very unlike the condition of things which obtained from Egypt to Sinai. They had forfeited all claim on the ground of law, and hence it only remained for God to fall back upon His own sovereignty and say, "I will be gracious to whom I will be gracious, and will show mercy on whom I will show mercy."

---

## *CHAPTERS 33–34*

JEHOVAH refuses to accompany Israel to the land of promise. "I will not go up in the midst of thee, (for thou art a stiff-necked people,) lest I consume thee in the way." At the opening of this book, when the people were in the furnace of Egypt, the Lord could say, "I have surely seen the affliction of My people which are in Egypt, and have heard their cry by reason of their taskmasters; for I know their sorrows." But now He has to say, "I have seen this people, and, behold, it is a stiff-necked people." An afflicted people is an object of grace; but a stiff-necked people must be humbled. The cry of oppressed Israel had been answered by the exhibition of grace; but the song of idolatrous Israel must be answered by the voice of stern rebuke.

"Ye are a stiff-necked people: I will come up into the midst of thee in a moment, and consume thee: therefore now put off thy ornaments from thee, that I may know what to do unto thee." It is only when we are really stripped of all nature's ornaments that God can deal with us. A naked sinner can be clothed; but a sinner decked with ornaments must be stripped. This is always true. We must be stripped of all that pertains to self ere we can be clothed with that which pertains to God.

"And the children of Israel stripped themselves of their ornaments by the mount Horeb." There they stood, beneath that memorable mount, their feasting and singing changed into bitter lamentations, their ornaments gone, the tables of testimony in fragments. Such was their condition, and Moses at once proceeds to act according to it. He could no longer own the people in their corporate character. The assembly had become entirely defiled, having set up an idol of their own making in the place of God—a calf instead of Jehovah. "And Moses took the tabernacle, and pitched it *without the camp,* afar off from the camp, and called it 'The tabernacle of the congregation.' " Thus the camp was disowned as the place of the divine presence. God was not, could not, be there. He had been displaced by a human invention. A new gathering-point was therefore set up. "And it came to pass, that every one which sought the Lord went out unto the tabernacle of the congregation, which was without the camp."

There is here a fine principle of truth, which the spiritual mind will readily apprehend. The place which Christ now occupies is "without the camp," and we are called upon to "go forth unto Him." It demands much subjection to the Word to be able, with accuracy, to know what "the camp" really is, and much spiritual power to be able to go forth from it: and still more to be able, while "far off from it," to act towards those in it in the combined power of holiness and grace;—holiness, which separates from the defilement of the camp; grace, which enables us to act toward those who are involved therein.

"And the Lord spake unto Moses face to face, as a man speaketh unto his friend. And he turned again into the camp; but his servant Joshua, the son of Nun, a young man, departed not out of the tabernacle." Moses exhibits a higher degree of spiritual energy than his servant Joshua. It is much easier to assume a position of separation from the camp than to act aright towards those within.

"And Moses said unto the Lord, 'See, Thou sayest unto me, Bring up this people; and Thou hast not let me know whom Thou wilt send with me; yet Thou hast said, I know thee by name, and thou hast also found grace in My sight.' " Moses entreats the accompanying presence of Jehovah, as a proof of their having found *grace* in His sight. Were it a question of mere *justice,* He could only consume them by coming in their midst, because they were "a stiff-necked people;" but directly He speaks of grace, in connection with the mediator, the very stiff-neckedness of the people is made a plea for demanding His presence. "If now I have found grace in Thy sight, O Lord, let my Lord, I pray Thee, go among us; *for it is a stiff-necked people;* and pardon our iniquity and our sin, and take us for Thine inheritance." This is touchingly beautiful. A "stiff-necked people" demanded the boundless grace and exhaustless patience of God. None but He could bear with them.

"And He said, 'My presence shall go with thee, and I will give thee rest.' " Precious portion! Precious hope! The presence of God with us, all the desert through, and everlasting rest at the end! Grace to meet our present need, and glory as our future portion! Well may our satisfied hearts exclaim, "It is enough, my precious Lord."

In chapter 34, the second set of tables is given, not to be broken, like the first, but to be hidden in the ark, above which, as already noticed, Jehovah was to take His place, as Lord of all the earth, in moral government. "And he hewed two tables of stone like unto the first; and Moses rose up early in the morning, and went up unto Mount Sinai, as the Lord had commanded him, and took in his hand the two tables of stone. And the Lord descended in the cloud, and stood with him there, and proclaimed the name of the Lord. And the Lord passed by before him, and proclaimed, "The Lord, The Lord God, merciful and gracious, long-suffering, and abundant in goodness and truth, keeping mercy for thousands, forgiving iniquity and transgression and sin, and that will by no means clear the guilty; visiting the iniquity of the fathers upon the children, and upon the children's children, unto the third and to the fourth generation.' " This, be it remembered, is God as seen in His moral government of the world, and not as He is seen in the cross—not as He shines in the face of Jesus Christ—not as He is proclaimed in the gospel of His grace. The following is an exhibition of God in the gospel: "And all things are of God, *who hath reconciled us to Himself by Jesus Christ,* and hath given to us the ministry of reconciliation; to wit, that God was in Christ, *reconciling the world unto Himself, not imputing* their trespasses unto them; and hath committed unto us *the word of reconciliation*" (2 Cor. 5:18-19). "Not clearing" and "not imputing" present two totally different ideas of God. "Visiting iniquities" and canceling them are not the same thing. The former is God in government, the latter is God in the gospel. In 2 Cor. 3 the apostle contrasts the "ministration" recorded in Exodus 34 with "the ministration" of the gospel. My reader would do well to study that chapter with care. From it he will learn that any one who regards the view of God's character given to Moses on Mount Horeb as unfolding the gospel, must have a very defective apprehension indeed of what the gospel is. Neither in creation nor yet in moral government do I or can I read the deep secrets of the Father's bosom. Could the prodigal have found his place in the arms of the One revealed on Mount Sinai? Could John have leaned his head on the bosom of that One? Surely not. But God has revealed Himself in the face of Jesus Christ. He has told out, in divine harmony, all His attributes in the work of the cross. There "Mercy and Truth have met together, Righteousness and Peace have kissed each other." Sin is perfectly put away, and the believing sinner perfectly justified, *"by the blood of the cross."* When we get a view of God as thus unfolded, we have only, like Moses, to "bow our head toward the earth and worship"—suited attitude for a pardoned and accepted sinner in the presence of God!

---

## *CHAPTERS 35–40*

THESE chapters contain a recapitulation of the various parts of the tabernacle and its furniture; and inasmuch as I have already given what I believe to be the import of the more prominent parts, I will not add more. There are, however, two things in this section from which we may deduce most profitable instruction, and these are (first), *the voluntary devotedness* and (secondly), *the implicit obedience* of the people with respect to the work of the tabernacle of the congregation.

First, as to their voluntary devotedness, we read, "And all the congregation of the children of Israel departed from the presence of Moses. And they came, every one *whose heart stirred him up,* and every one whom *his spirit made willing,* and they brought *the Lord's offering* to the work of the tabernacle of the congregation, and for all His service, and for the holy garments. And they came, both men and women, *as many as were willing-hearted,* and brought bracelets, and earrings, and rings, and tablets, all jewels of gold: and every man that offered offered an offering of gold unto the Lord. And every man with whom was found blue, and purple, and scarlet, and fine linen, and goats' hair, and red skins of rams, and badgers' skins, brought them. Every one that did offer an offering of silver and brass, brought the Lord's offering: and every man with whom was found shittim wood, for any work of the service, brought it. And all the women that were wise-hearted did spin with their hands, and brought that which they had spun, both of blue, and of purple, and of scarlet, and of fine linen. And all the women *whose heart stirred them up* in wisdom spun goats' hair. And the rulers brought onyx stones, and stones to be set, for the ephod, and for the breastplate; and spice, and oil for the light, and for the anointing oil, and for the sweet incense. The children of Israel brought *a willing offering* unto *the Lord*, every man and woman, *whose heart made them willing* to bring, for all manner of work which the Lord had commanded to be made by the hand of Moses" (chap. 35:20-29). And, again, we read, "And all the wise men that wrought all the work of the sanctuary, came every man from his work which they made; and they spake unto Moses, saying, 'The people bring *much more than enough* for the service of the work, which the Lord commanded to make. . . .' For the stuff they had was sufficient for all the work to make it, and too much" (ver. 4-7).

A lovely picture this of devotedness to the work of the sanctuary! It needed no effort to move the hearts of the people to give, no earnest appeals, no impressive arguments. Oh, no! their *"hearts* stirred them up." This was the true way. The streams of voluntary devotedness flowed from within. "Rulers," "men," "women"—all felt it to be their sweet privilege to give to the Lord, not with a narrow heart or niggard hand, but after such a princely fashion that they had *"enough, and too much."*

Then, as to *their implicit obedience*, we read, *"According to all that the Lord commanded Moses*, so the children of Israel made all the work. And Moses did look upon all the work, and, behold, *they had done it as the Lord had commanded, even so had they done it:* and Moses blessed them" (chap. 39:42-43). The Lord had given the most minute instructions concerning the entire work of the tabernacle. Every pin, every socket, every loop, every tach, was accurately set forth. There was no room left for man's expediency, his reason, or his common sense. Jehovah did not give a great outline and leave man to fill it up. He left no margin whatever in which man might enter his regulations. By no means. " 'See,' saith He, 'that thou make *all things according to the pattern showed to thee in the mount*' " (Exod. 25:40; 26:30; Heb. 8:5). This left no room for human device. If man had been allowed to make a single pin, that pin would most assuredly have been out of place in the judgment of God. We can see what man's "graving tool" produces in chapter 32. Thank God, it had no place in the tabernacle. They did, in this matter, just what they were told – nothing more, nothing less. Salutary lesson this for the professing church! There are many things in the history of Israel which we should earnestly seek to avoid—their impatient murmurings, their legal vows, and their idolatry; but in those two things may we imitate them. May our devotedness be more whole-hearted, and our obedience more implicit! We may safely assert that if all had not been done "according to the pattern showed in the mount," we should not have to read, "then a cloud covered the tent of the congregation, and the glory of the Lord filled the tabernacle. And Moses was not able to enter into the tent of the congregation, because the cloud abode thereon, and the glory of the Lord filled the tabernacle" (chap. 40:34-35). The tabernacle was in all respects according to *the divine pattern*, and therefore it could be filled with *the divine glory.*

There is a volume of instruction in this. We are too prone to regard the Word of God as insufficient for the most minute details connected with His worship and service. This is a great mistake—a mistake which has proved the fruitful source of evils and errors in the professing church. The Word of God is amply sufficient for every thing, whether as regards personal salvation and walk, or the order and rule of the assembly. "All scripture is given by inspiration of God, and is profitable for doctrine, for reproof, for correction, for instruction in righteousness, that the man of God may be *perfect, thoroughly furnished* unto *all good works"* (2 Tim. 3:16-17). This settles the question. If the Word of God furnishes a man *thoroughly* unto *"all* good works," it follows, as a necessary consequence, that whatever I find not in its pages cannot possibly be a good work. And, further, be it remembered, that the divine glory cannot connect itself with aught that is not according to the divine pattern.

---

We have now traveled together through this most precious book. We have, I fondly hope, reaped some profit from our study. I trust we have gathered up some refreshing thoughts of Jesus and His sacrifice as we passed along. Feeble, indeed, must be our most vigorous thoughts, and shallow our deepest apprehensions, as to the mind of God in all that this book contains. It is happy to remember that, through grace, we are on our way to that glory where we shall know even as we are known, and where we shall bask in the sunshine of His countenance who is the beginning and ending of the ways of God, whether in creation, in providence, or redemption. To Him I do most affectionately commend you, in body, soul, and spirit. May you know the deep blessedness of having your portion in Christ, and be kept in patient waiting for His glorious advent. Amen.

*C.H.M.*

# NOTES

*on the book of*

# LEVITICUS

*"All Scripture is given by inspiration of God"*

## *PREFACE*

IN the Person and work of the Lord Jesus Christ there is an infinite fullness, which meets every necessity of man, both as a sinner and as a worshiper. The infinite dignity of His Person gives eternal value to His work. In the book of Genesis we have seen "God's remedy for man's ruin" in the promised seed—the Ark of Salvation, and in the rich unfoldings of divine grace to fallen and sinful man. There we have the *Bud,* the full-blown glories and fragrance of which shall yet fill the heavens and the earth with joy and gladness.

In the book of Exodus we have seen "God's answer to man's question." There, man is not only outside of Eden, but he has fallen into the hands of a cruel and powerful enemy,—he is the bond-slave of the world. How is he to be delivered from Pharaoh's thraldom—from Egypt's furnace? How can he be redeemed, justified, and brought into the promised land? God only could answer such questions, and this He did in the blood of the slain Lamb. In the redemption-power of that blood, every question is settled. It meets Heaven's highest claims, and man's deepest necessities. Through its amazing efficacy, God is glorified, man is redeemed, saved, justified, and brought to God's holy habitation; while the enemy is completely overthrown, and his power destroyed.

And now, in our meditations on the book of Leviticus, we find most fully unfolded what we may call, "God's provision for man's need;" or, a Sacrifice, a Priest, and a Place of Worship. These are essentially necessary in drawing near unto God, as this book most abundantly proves. But every thing therewith connected was appointed by God, and established by His law. Nothing was left to be supplied by man's fertile imagination, or his prudential arrangement.—"So Aaron and his sons did *all things which the Lord commanded* by the hand of Moses" (chap. 8:36; 9:6-7). Without the word of the Lord, neither priest nor people could take a single step in the right direction. *It is so still.* There is not a single ray of light in this dark world but that which is shed from holy Scripture. —"Thy Word is a lamp unto my feet, and a light unto my path" (Ps. 119:105). It is truly happy when the children of God so honor His Word as to be guided by it in all things. We need *now,* as much as the Jew did *then,* divine direction and divine guidance for acceptable worship. "But the hour cometh, and now is, when the *true worshipers* shall worship the Father in spirit and in truth; for the Father seeketh such to worship Him" (John 4:23-24). More than sincerity or devoutness of feeling is required in the children's worship: it must be in the unction of the Spirit, and according to the truth of God. But we have all (blessed be His name!) in the Person and work of our blessed Lord Jesus. He is both our Sacrifice and Priest, and our right of entrance into the holiest of all. O, to be kept near to His wounded side, and in the abiding sense that He is the ground, the material, and the sweet incense of all our worship!

Let us now briefly notice the three points already mentioned.

I. In the first place, we would observe that *sacrifice is the basis of worship.* Acceptable worship to God must be based on a sacrifice acceptable to Him. Man being in himself guilty and unclean, he needs a sacrifice to remove his guilt, cleanse him from his defilements, and fit him for the holy presence of God. "Without shedding of blood is no remission;" and without remission, and the *knowledge* of remission, there can be no happy worship,—no real, hearty praise, adoration, and thanksgiving. Going to what is called "a place of worship," and worshiping God, are widely different things. God is holy, and man must approach Him in His own way, and according to what He is. As Moses said unto Aaron on the solemn occasion of the sin of Nadab and Abihu, "This is it that the Lord spake, saying, *'I will be sanctified in them that come nigh Me,* and before all the people I will be glorified.' " The Lord alone could give directions as to how the people were to draw nigh unto

Him: this is the great subject of the book of Leviticus. The *Notes* on the first seven and the sixteenth chapters will give the reader a very full and interesting view of the ordinance of sacrifice, and the character of Jewish worship.

It was on the ground of offered and accepted sacrifice that the children of Israel were constituted the worshiping people of God. It is on the same ground, namely, offered and accepted sacrifice, that believers in Jesus are constituted the worshiping people of God now. (Read carefully Lev. 16; Heb. 9–10.) They have taken Israel's place, but after a much higher order, whether we look at the sacrifice, the priest, or the place of worship. The contrast between them is great, and strongly marked in Scripture, especially in the Epistle to the Hebrews. The Jewish sacrifices never reached the *conscience* of the offerer, and the Jewish priest never could pronounce him "clean every whit." The gifts and sacrifices which were offered under the law, as the apostle tells us, "could not make him that did the service perfect, as pertaining to the conscience." The conscience, observe, always being the *reflection* of the sacrifice, it could not be perfect, seeing the sacrifice was not perfect; "for it is not possible that the blood of bulls and of goats should take away sins." Hence, Jewish worship was connected with inefficient sacrifices, a burdensome ritual, and an unpurged conscience, which gendered in the worshiper a spirit of bondage and fear.

But, now, mark the contrast to all this in the once-offered and accepted sacrifice of Christ. He "put away sin by the sacrifice of Himself." All is done. Having "by Himself purged our sins, He sat down on the right hand of the Majesty on high." When the worshiper comes before God on the ground of this Sacrifice, he finds that he has nothing to do save, as a priest, to show forth the praises of Him "who hath called us out of darkness into His marvelous light." Even Christ has nothing more to do as regards our justification and acceptance, "for by one offering He hath perfected forever them that are sanctified." The Jew, by his sacrifice, was merely *ceremonially* clean, and that only for a moment, as it were; but the Christian, through the sacrifice of Christ, is *really* so, and that forever. Oh, that sweet word, *"forever"!* It is the common privilege of all believers to be perfected as worshipers before God, "through the offering of the body of Jesus Christ once for all." On this deeply important point the testimony of Scripture is most full and explicit. For the worshipers once purged should have *"no more conscience of sins."*—"The blood of Jesus Christ His son cleanseth us from all sin."—"And their sins and inquities will I remember no more" (1 John 4:7; Heb. 10). By the work of Christ *for us,* our sins were all put away; and now, by faith in God's Word, we know that they are all forgiven and forgotten. Hence, we can draw near to God, and stand in His holy presence, in the happy assurance that there is neither sin nor stain upon us. Our Great High-Priest has pronounced us "clean every whit" (John 13). Believing this, the sense of guilt is taken away, we have *"no more conscience of sins."*

This deeply precious truth, observe, does not mean that there is no more *consciousness* of sins. Far from it. Or that we may not get a bad conscience through failure; or that we need not be exercised "to have a conscience void of offense toward God and toward man." Not at all. It simply means that Christ, by the one, perfect, finished sacrifice of Himself, has forever put away all our sins—root and branch. And having been led to know and believe this, how can there be sins on the conscience? Christ has put them all away. The precious blood of our once-offered and accepted Sacrifice has cleansed us from every spot and stain of sin. There may be the deepest sense of indwelling sin, and of many sins and shortcomings in our every-day life, and the painful confession of them all to God; still there is the full assurance that Christ died for our sins, put them all away, and that not one of them can ever be laid to our charge. This is indeed a most wonderful truth; but it is the great, the needed truth for a worshiper. How could we stand in God's presence, where all is perfection, if we were not as clean as He would have us to be? We must be clean enough for the eye of Infinite Holiness. But, blessed be God, all who believe in Jesus, and rest on His finished sacrifice, are forgiven and justified; they have eternal life, righteousness, and peace. The first cry for mercy of the guilty sinner is answered by the blood of the Sacrifice. It penetrates to the deepest depths of his need; it raises him to the highest heights of heaven, and fits him to be there, a happy worshiper, in the immediate presence of the throne of God.—"For Christ also hath once suffered for sins, the just for the unjust, that He might bring us to God."—"For if the blood of bulls and of goats, and the ashes of a heifer sprinkling the unclean, sanctifieth to the purifying of the flesh; how much more shall the blood of Christ, who through the Eternal Spirit offered Himself without spot to God, purge your conscience from dead works to serve the living God!" (1 Peter 3:18; Heb. 9:13-14)

II. In the second place, we have in the rich provisions of God's grace, *the Lord Jesus Christ as our Great High-Priest in the presence of God for us.* He ministers there for us.—"We have such a High-Priest, who is set on the right hand of the throne of the Majesty in the heavens; a Minister of the sanctuary, and of the true tabernacle, which the Lord pitched, and not man" (Heb. 8:1-2). His work of sacrifice having been fully completed, He sat down. Aaron is represented as being always in a standing position. His work was never finished. He stood "daily ministering, and offering oftentimes the same sacrifices, which can never take away sins; but this Man, after He had offered one sacrifice for sins, forever sat down on the right hand of God." Immediately after the law of the Lord had been given as to sacrifice, the priesthood was established. The saints have both in Christ. He is our Sacrifice and our Priest. He appeared once on the cross *for us:* He now appears in heaven *for us:* ere long He will appear in glory *with us.* To know what He accomplished on the cross, and what He is doing in the sanctuary above, will nourish in our hearts the hope of His coming, and lead us to long for His appearing in glory.

In the New Testament we only read of two orders of priests, namely, Christ as the Great High-Priest in heaven, and the common priesthood of all believers on the earth. "Ye also, as lively stones, are built up a spiritual house, a holy priesthood, to offer up spiritual sacrifices, acceptable to God by Jesus Christ" (1 Peter 2:5). And again, "Unto Him that loved us, and washed us from our sins in His own blood, and hath made us kings and priests unto God and His Father" (Rev. 1:5-6). These passages clearly prove the common standing of all believers as priests unto God. There is no mention in the New Testament of any peculiar class or order of Christians who hold the office of priests, as distinct from other Christians. Christ is the *Great* High-Priest over the house of God, and all His people are, in virtue of their connection with Him, priests, and privileged to enter, as once-purged worshipers, into the holiest of all. Even the apostles never took the place of priests, as distinct from or superior to the humblest child of God. They might know their privileges better than many, and enjoy them more. Their gifts and callings as to the ministry of the Word were distinct and special, but as worshipers, they stood on the same ground as all others, and, together with them, worshiped God through Jesus Christ, the Great High-Priest of all His people.

In the priestly ministry of our blessed Lord, there are many points of special interest; we only notice the two following:

1. As our Great High-Priest, He *represents* us in the sanctuary above. And, oh, what a Representative!—God's beloved Son, the glorified Man, whose name is above every name!—"For Christ is not entered into the holy places made with hands, which are the figures of the true; but into heaven itself, now to appear in the presence of God *for us*" (Heb. 9:24). Oh, what dignity! what nearness to God is ours! Oh that our hearts appreciated it more! When Aaron appeared before the Lord in his garments of glory and beauty, he represented the children of Israel. Their names were engraven in precious stones in the beautiful breastplate. Blessed

type of our real and everlasting place in the heart of Christ, who appears, not *annually,* like Aaron of old, but *continually* in the presence of God *for us.* The name of each believer is kept continually before the eye of God, in all the glory and beauty of Christ, His well-beloved Son. He is our righteousness, we possess His life, enjoy His peace, are filled with His joy, and radiate His glory. Although without right, title, or privilege in ourselves, we have all in Him. He is there *for us* and *as us.* His name be forever praised.

He stands in heaven their Great High-Priest,
And bears their names upon His breast.

It is by His continual intercession in heaven that saints on earth are succored and sustained in their wilderness journey, and, at the same time, upheld as worshipers within the vail, in all the sweet fragrance of His own divine excellencies; and neither their ignorance nor their lack of enjoyment of these things alters or affects their blessed, glorious, and eternal reality, "seeing He ever liveth to make intercession for them" (Heb. 7:25).

2. As our Great High-Priest, He presents to God the gifts and sacrifices of His worshiping people. Under the law, the worshiper brought his offering to the priest, and by him it was presented to the Lord, on His own altar. Every thing was arranged by the priest, according to the word of the Lord. How perfectly all this is done for the worshiper now by his High-Priest in heaven! Our prayers, praises, and thanksgiving, all pass through His hands before they reach the throne of God. What a wonderful mercy this is, when we think of our confused and mixed services! So much that is of the flesh mingles with that which is of the Spirit. But the blessed Lord knows how to divide and separate between them. That which is of the flesh must be rejected, and consumed as wood, hay, and stubble, while that which is of the Spirit is precious, preserved, and presented to God in the value and sweet savor of His own perfect sacrifice. "*By Him* therefore let us offer the sacrifice of praise to God continually, that is, the fruit of our lips giving thanks unto His name" (Heb. 13:15). The kindness of the Philippians to Paul was "an odor of a sweet smell, a sacrifice acceptable, well-pleasing to God." Hence the importance of the exhortation, "Whatsoever ye do in word or deed, do all in the name of the Lord Jesus, giving thanks to God and the Father by Him" (Col. 3:17).

III. In the third place, we observe that *the Christian's only place of worship is inside the vail,* "whither the forerunner is for us entered." Outside the camp is his place as a witness; inside the vail is his place as a worshiper. In both positions Christ is surely with him. "Let us go forth therefore unto Him without the camp, bearing His reproach." "Having therefore, brethren, *boldness to enter into the holiest* by the blood of Jesus" (Heb. 13:13; 10:19). To know these two positions in communion with Christ Himself, through the teaching of the Spirit, is unspeakable blessedness. The Church has no divinely consecrated place of worship on earth. Our place is in heaven, in virtue of the sacrifice and of the priestly ministry of Christ there for us. Whatever may be the character of the building in which Christians are gathered together in the name of the Lord Jesus, their true and only sphere of worship is the heavenly sanctuary. Through faith in God's Word, and by the power of His Holy Spirit, they worship Him in "the true tabernacle, which the Lord pitched, and not man."

Israel had "a worldly sanctuary," and accordingly the character of their worship was worldly; "the way into the holiest of all was not yet made manifest, while as the first tabernacle was yet standing." But the way has been opened up by the blood of Jesus. The same stroke that slew the Lamb rent the vail from top to bottom. The way into the holiest of all was then laid open, and Christ, with all His blood-washed ones, entered into the immediate presence of God, without a vail. There is no *outer*-court-worship now for the people, and *temple*-worship for the priest, as under the law. These distinctions are unknown in the Church of the living God. It is all priestly worship and temple worship now. All are equally near, all have equal liberty, all are equally acceptable, through the presence and intervention of the Great High-Priest of His people. The same precious blood that cleansed us from all sin, has brought us near to God as children, and as worshiping priests. And if we really know the wondrous efficacy and power of that blood in the heavenly places, we shall be at home and happy there in all the liberty and dignity of sonship, and in all the official nearness and standing of once-purged worshipers, in the most holy place.

Oh that our hearts may be kept in the sweet remembrance, knowledge, and power of the rich provisions of God's grace for all our need! Oh that we may never lose sight of the blood on the mercy-seat, the Minister of the sanctuary, and of our holy, heavenly, and eternal place of worship!

We must now leave the dear reader, earnestly commending to his most prayerful and diligent study this precious book of Leviticus. The light which it sheds on the Person and work of Christ—the ground and character of our communion with God, is deeply blessed to the heart that desires to live in the enjoyment of these eternal realities. He will find the *Notes* most helpful in unfolding the text, and in giving an interesting and practical view to many of the ceremonies which we are prone to pass over as uninteresting and uninstructive to us. See, for example, the eleventh chapter.

And now, may the Lord graciously own, use, and bless this little volume, for the glory of His own name, and for the comfort and blessing of many precious souls.

*London, May 1860.* A.M.

# *NOTES*

## *on*

# *THE BOOK OF LEVITICUS*

---

## *CHAPTER 1*

ERE entering upon the details of the chapter before us, there are two things which demand our careful consideration; namely, first, Jehovah's position; and secondly, the order in which the offerings are presented.

"And the Lord called unto Moses, and spake unto him out of the tabernacle of the congregation." Such was the position from which Jehovah made the communications contained in this book. He had been speaking from Mount Sinai, and His position there gave marked character to the communication. From the fiery mount "went a fiery law;" but here, He speaks "out of the tabernacle of the congregation." This was an entirely different position. We have seen this tabernacle set up, at the close of the preceding book.—"And he reared up the court round about the tabernacle and the altar, and set up the hanging of the court gate. So Moses finished the work. Then a cloud covered the tent of the congregation, and the glory of the Lord filled the tabernacle. . . . For the cloud of the Lord was upon the tabernacle by day, and fire was on it by night, in the sight of all the house of Israel, throughout all their journeys" (Exod. 40:33-38).

Now, the tabernacle was God's dwelling-place in grace. He could take up His abode there, because He was surrounded on all sides by that which vividly set forth the ground of His relationship with the people. Had He come into their midst in the full display of the character revealed upon Mount Sinai, it could only have been to "consume them in a moment," as "a stiff-necked people;" but He retired within the vail—type of Christ's flesh (Heb. 10:20), and took His place on the mercy-seat, where the blood of atonement, and not the "stiff-neckedness" of Israel, was that which met His view and satisfied the claims of His nature. The blood which was brought into the sanctuary by the high-priest was the type of that precious blood which cleanses from all sin; and although Israel after the flesh saw nothing of this, it nevertheless justified God in abiding amongst them—it "sanctified to the purifying of the flesh" (Heb. 9:13).

Thus much as to Jehovah's position in this book, which must be taken into account in order to a proper understanding of the communications made therein. In them we shall find inflexible holiness united with the purest grace. God is holy, no matter from whence He speaks. He was holy on Mount Sinai, and holy above the mercy-seat; but in the former case, His holiness stood connected with "a devouring fire," in the latter, it was connected with patient grace. Now the connection of perfect holiness with perfect grace is that which characterizes the redemption which is in Christ Jesus, which redemption is, in various ways, shadowed forth in the book of Leviticus. God must be holy, even though it should be in the eternal condemnation of impenitent sinners; but the full display of His holiness in the salvation of sinners calls forth Heaven's loudest and loftiest note of praise.—"Glory to God in the highest, and on earth peace, good-will toward men" (Luke 2:14). This doxology could not have been sung in connection with "the fiery law." No doubt there was "glory to God in the highest," but there was no "peace on earth" nor "good pleasure in men," inasmuch as it was the declaration of what men ought to be ere God could take pleasure in them. But when "the Son" took His place as a man on the earth, the mind of Heaven could express its entire delight in Him as the One whose Person and work could combine, in the most perfect manner, divine glory with human blessedness.

And now, one word as to the order of the offerings, in the opening chapters of the book of Leviticus. The Lord begins with the burnt-offering, and ends with the trespass-offering. That is to say, He leaves off where we begin. This order is marked and most instructive. When first the arrow of conviction enters the soul, there are deep searchings of conscience in reference to sins actually committed. Memory casts back its enlightened eye over the page of one's past life, and sees it stained with numberless trespasses against God and man. At this point of the soul's history, it is not so much occupied with the question of the root from whence those trespasses have sprung, as with the stern and palpable fact that such and such things have actually been committed; and hence it needs to know that God has provided a Sacrifice through which "all trespasses" can be "frankly forgiven." This is presented to us in the trespass-offering.

But, as one advances in the divine life, he becomes conscious that those *sins* which he has committed are but branches from a root, streams from a fountain; and, moreover, that *sin* in his nature is that fountain—that root. This leads to far deeper exercise, which can only be met by a deeper insight into the work of the cross. In a word, the cross will need to be apprehended as that in which God Himself has "condemned *sin in the flesh*" (Rom. 8:3). My reader will observe, it does not say, "*sins* in the *life,*" but the root from whence these have sprung, namely, "*sin* in the *flesh.*" This is a truth of immense importance. Christ not merely "died for our *sins,* according to the Scriptures," but He was "made *sin* for us" (2 Cor. 5:21). This is the doctrine of the sin-offering.

Now, it is when the heart and conscience are set at rest, through the knowledge of Christ's work, that we can feed upon Himself as the ground of our peace and joy in the presence of God. The trespass-offering and the sin-offering must be known ere the peace-offering, joy-offering, or thanksgiving-offering can be appreciated. Hence, therefore, the order in which the peace-offering stands corresponds with the order of our spiritual apprehension of Christ.

The same perfect order is observable in reference to the meat-offering. When the soul is led to taste the sweetness of spiritual communion with Christ—to feed upon Him, in peace and thankfulness, in the divine presence, it is drawn out in earnest desire to know more of the wondrous mysteries of His Person; and this desire is most blessedly met in the meat-offering, which is the type of Christ's perfect manhood.

Then, in the burnt-offering, we are conducted to a point beyond which it is impossible to go, and that is, the work of the cross, as accomplished under the immediate eye of God, and as the expression of the unswerving devotion of the heart of Christ. All these things will come before us, in beauteous detail, as we pass along; we are here only looking at the order of the offerings, which is truly marvelous, whichever way we travel, whether *outward* from God to us, or *inward* from us to God. In either case, we begin with the cross and end with the cross. If we begin with the burnt-offering, we see Christ, on the cross, doing the will of God—making atonement according to the measure of His perfect surrender of Himself to God. If we begin with the trespass-offering, we see Christ, on the cross, bearing our sins, and putting them away according to the perfection of His atoning sacrifice; while in each and all we behold the excellency, the beauty, and the perfection of His divine and adorable Person. Surely, all this is sufficient to awaken in our hearts the deepest interest in the study of those precious types which we shall now proceed to consider in detail. May God the Holy Ghost, who penned the book of Leviticus, expound its contents in living power to our hearts, so that, when we have reached the close, we may have abundant cause to bless His name for many thrilling and soul-stirring views of the Person and work of our blessed Lord and Saviour Jesus Christ, to whom be glory, now, henceforth and for evermore. Amen.

---

In the burnt-offering, with which our book opens, we have a type of Christ "offering

Himself without spot to God." Hence the position which the Holy Ghost assigns to it. If the Lord Jesus Christ came forth to accomplish the glorious work of atonement, His highest and most fondly cherished object in so doing was the glory of God. "Lo, I come to do Thy will, O God," was the grand motto in every scene and circumstance of His life, and in none more markedly than in the work of the cross. Let the will of God be what it might, He came to do it. Blessed be God, we know what our portion is in the accomplishment of this "will;" for by it "we are sanctified, through the offering of the body of Jesus Christ once" (Heb. 10:10). Still, the primary aspect of Christ's work was Godward. It was an ineffable delight to Him to accomplish the will of God on this earth. No one had ever done this before. Some had, through grace, done "that which was right in the sight of the Lord;" but no one had ever perfectly, invariably, from first to last, without hesitation, and without divergence, done the will of God. But this was exactly what the Lord Jesus did. He was "obedient unto death, even the death of the cross" (Phil. 2:8). "He steadfastly set His face to go to Jerusalem." And as He walked from the garden of Gethsemane to the cross of Calvary, the intense devotion of His heart told itself forth in these accents: "The cup which My Father hath given Me, shall I not drink it?"

Now, in all this self-emptied devotedness to God there was truly a sweet savor. A perfect Man on the earth accomplishing the will of God, even in death, was an object of amazing interest to the mind of Heaven. Who could fathom the profound depths of that devoted heart which displayed itself, under the eye of God, on the cross? Surely, none but God; for in this, as in every thing else, it holds good that "no man knoweth the Son, but the Father," and no one can know aught about Him save as the Father reveals Him. The mind of man can, in some measure, grasp any subject of knowledge "under the sun"—human science can be laid hold of by the human intellect; but no man knoweth the Son save as the Father reveals Him, by the power of the Holy Ghost, through the written Word. The Holy Ghost delights to reveal the Son—to take of the things of Jesus and show them unto us. These things we have, in all their fullness and beauty, in the Word. There can be no new revelation, inasmuch as the Spirit brought "*all* things" to the apostles' memory, and led them into "*all* truth." There can be nothing beyond "all truth;" and hence, all pretension to a new revelation and the development of new truth (meaning thereby truth not contained in the sacred canon of inspiration) is an effort on man's part to add to what God calls "all truth." No doubt the Spirit may unfold and apply, with new and extraordinary power, truth contained in the Word; but this is obviously a very different thing from our traveling outside the range of divine revelation for the purpose of finding principles, ideas, or dogmas which shall command the conscience. This latter can only be regarded in the light of impious presumption.

In the gospel narrative, we have Christ presented to us in the varied phases of His character, His Person, and His work. To those precious documents the people of God in all ages have rejoiced to betake themselves, and drink in their heavenly revelations of the object of their love and confidence—the One to whom they owed every thing, for time and eternity. But very few, comparatively, have ever been led to regard the rites and ceremonies of the Levitical economy as fraught with the most minute instruction in reference to the same commanding theme. The offerings of Leviticus, for example, have been too much regarded as so many antiquated records of Jewish customs, conveying no intelligible voice to our ears—no spiritual light to our understandings. However, it must be admitted that the apparently abstruse records of Leviticus, as well as the sublime strains of Isaiah, take their place amongst the "things which were written aforetime," and they are, therefore, "for our learning." True, we shall need to study those records, as indeed all Scripture, with a humble, self-emptied spirit; with reverent dependence upon the teaching of Him who graciously penned them for us; with sedulous attention to the general scope, bearing, and analogy of the entire body of divine revelation; with an effectual curb on the imagination, that it may not take unhallowed flights; but if thus, through grace, we enter upon the study of the types of Leviticus, we shall find in them a vein of the richest and finest ore.

We shall now proceed to examine the burnt-offering, which, as we have remarked, presents Christ offering Himself without spot to God.

"If his offering be a burnt sacrifice of the herd, let him offer a male, without blemish." The essential glory and dignity of Christ's Person form the basis of Christianity. He imparts that dignity and glory to every thing He does, and to every office He sustains. No office could possibly add glory to Him who is "God over all, blessed forever"—"God manifest in the flesh"—the glorious "Immanuel"—"God with us"—the Eternal Word—the Creator and Sustainer of the universe. What office could add to the dignity of such an One? In point of fact, we know that all His offices are connected with His humanity; and in assuming that humanity, He stooped from the glory which He had with the Father before the world was. He thus stooped in order to glorify God perfectly in the very midst of a scene where all was hostile to Him. He came to be "eaten up" by a holy, unquenchable zeal for the glory of God, and the effectual carrying out of His eternal counsels.

The unblemished male of the first year was a type of the Lord Jesus Christ offering Himself for the perfect accomplishment of the will of God. There should be nothing expressive either of weakness or imperfection. "A male of the first year" was required. We shall see, when we come to examine the other offerings, that "a female" was in some cases permitted; but that was only expressive of the imperfection which attached to the worshiper's apprehension, and in no wise of any defect in the offering, inasmuch as it was "unblemished" in the one case as well as in the other. Here, however, it was an offering of the very highest order, because it was Christ offering Himself to God. Christ, in the burnt-offering, was exclusively for the eye and heart of God. This point should be distinctly apprehended. God alone could duly estimate the Person and work of Christ; He alone could fully appreciate the cross as the expression of Christ's perfect devotedness. The cross, as foreshadowed by the burnt-offering, had an element in it which only the divine mind could apprehend; it had depths so profound, that neither mortal nor angel could fathom them. There was a voice in it which was intended exclusively for, and went directly to, the ear of the Father. There were communications between the cross of Calvary and the throne of God which lay far beyond the highest range of created intelligence.

"He shall offer it of his own voluntary will at the door of the tabernacle of the congregation before the Lord." The use of the word *"voluntary"* here brings out with great clearness the grand idea in the burnt-offering. It leads us to contemplate the cross in an aspect which is not sufficiently apprehended. We are too apt to look upon the cross merely as the place where the great question of sin was gone into and settled between eternal Justice and the spotless Victim—as the place where our guilt was atoned for, and where Satan was gloriously vanquished. Eternal and universal praise to redeeming love! the cross was all this; but it was more than this,—it was the place where Christ's love to the Father was told out in language which only the Father could hear and understand. It is in the latter aspect that we have it typified in the burnt-offering, and therefore it is that the word "voluntary" occurs. Were it merely a question of the imputation of sin, and of enduring the wrath of God on account of sin, such an expression would not be in moral order. The blessed Lord Jesus could not, with strict propriety, be represented as *willing* to be "made sin"—*willing* to endure the wrath of God and the hiding of His countenance; and in this one fact we learn, in the clearest manner, that the *burnt-offering does not foreshadow Christ on the cross bearing sin,* but Christ on the cross accomplishing the will of God. That Christ Himself contemplated the cross in these two aspects of it is evident from His own words. When He looked at the cross as the place of sin-bearing—when He anticipated the horrors with which, in this point of view, it stood invested, He exclaimed, "Father, if Thou be willing, remove this cup from Me" (Luke 23:42). He shrank from that which His work, as a sin-bearer, involved. His pure and holy mind shrank from the thought of contact with sin, and His loving heart shrank from the thought of losing, for a moment, the light of God's countenance.

But then, the cross had another aspect. It stood before the eye of Christ as a scene in which He could fully tell out all the deep secrets of His love to the Father—a place in which He could, "of His own voluntary will," take the cup which the Father had given Him, and drain it to the very dregs. True it is that the whole life of Christ emitted a fragrant odor, which ever ascended to the Father's throne—He did always those things which pleased the Father—He ever did the will of God; but the burnt-offering does not typify Him in His life—precious, beyond all thought, as was every act of that life—but in His death, and in that, not as one "made a curse for us," but as one presenting to the heart of the Father an odor of incomparable fragrance.

This truth invests the cross with peculiar charms for the spiritual mind. It imparts to the sufferings of our blessed Lord an interest of the most intense character. The guilty sinner, no doubt, finds in the cross a divine answer to the deepest and most earnest cravings of heart and conscience: the true believer finds in the cross that which captivates every affection of his heart, and transfixes his whole moral being: the angels find in the cross a theme for ceaseless admiration. All this is true; but there is that in the cross which passes far beyond the loftiest conceptions of saints or angels, namely, the deep-toned devotion of the heart of the Son presented to and appreciated by the heart of the Father. This is the elevated aspect of the cross which is so strikingly shadowed in the burnt-offering.

And here let me remark that the distinctive beauty of the burnt-offering must be entirely sacrificed if we admit the idea that Christ was a sin-bearer all His life. There would then be no force, no value, no meaning in the word "voluntary." There could be no room for voluntary action in the case of one who was compelled, by the very necessity of his position, to yield up his life. If Christ were a sin-bearer in His life, then, assuredly, His death must have been a *necessary,* not a voluntary, act. Indeed, it may be safely asserted that there is not one of the offerings the beauty of which would not be marred, and its strict integrity sacrificed, by the theory of *a life* of sin-bearing. In the burnt-offering, this is especially the case, inasmuch as it is not, in it, a question of sin-bearing, or enduring the wrath of God, but entirely one of voluntary devotedness, manifested in the death of the cross. In the burnt-offering, we recognize a type of God the Son accomplishing, by God the Spirit, the will of God the Father. This He did "of His own voluntary will." "Therefore doth My Father love Me, because I lay down My life, that I might take it again" (John 10:17). Here we have the burnt-offering aspect of the death of Christ. On the other hand, the prophet, contemplating Him as the sin-offering, says, "His life *is taken* from the earth" (Acts 8:33), (which is the LXX version of Isaiah 53:8). Again, Christ says, "No one [*ου δεις*] taketh it from Me, but I lay it down of Myself." Was He a sin-bearer when He said this? Observe, it is "No one"—man, angel, devil, or else. It was His own voluntary act, to lay down His life that He might take it again. "I delight to do Thy will, O My God." Such was the language of the divine burnt-offering—of Him who found His unutterable joy in offering Himself without spot to God.

Now, it is of the last importance to apprehend with distinctness the primary object of the heart of Christ in the work of redemption. It tends to consolidate the believer's peace. The accomplishment of God's will, the establishment of God's counsels, and the display of God's glory, occupied the fullest, deepest, and largest place in that devoted heart which viewed and estimated every thing in reference to God. The Lord Jesus never once stopped to inquire how any act or circumstance would affect Himself. "He humbled Himself"—"He made Himself of no reputation"—He surrendered all. And hence, when He arrived at the close of His career, He could look back upon it all, and say, with His eyes lifted up to heaven, "I have glorified Thee on the earth; I have finished the work which Thou gavest Me to do" (John 17:4). It is impossible to contemplate the work of Christ, in this aspect of it, without having the heart filled with the sweetest affections toward His Person. It does not detract, in the smallest degree, from our sense of His love to us, to know that He made God His primary object in the work of the cross. Quite the opposite. His love to us, and our salvation in Him, could only be founded upon God's established glory. That glory must form the solid basis of every thing. "As truly as I live, all the earth shall be filled with the glory of the Lord" (Num. 14:21). But we know that God's eternal glory and the creature's eternal blessedness are, in the divine counsels, inseparably linked together, so that if the former be secured, the latter must needs be so likewise.

"And he shall put his hand upon the head of the burnt-offering; and it shall be accepted for him, to make atonement for him." The act of laying on of hands was expressive of full identification. By that significant act, the offerer and the offering became one; and this oneness, in the case of the burnt-offering, secured for the offerer all the acceptableness of his offering. The application of this to Christ and the believer sets forth a truth of the most precious nature, and one largely developed in the New Testament, namely, the believer's everlasting identification with, and acceptance in, Christ. "As He is, so are we in this world." "We are in Him that is true" (1 John 4:17; 5:20). Nothing, in any measure, short of this could avail. The man who is not in Christ is in his sins. There is no middle ground: you must be either in Christ or out of Him. There is no such thing as being *partly* in Christ. If there is a single hair's breadth between you and Christ, you are in an actual state of wrath and condemnation; but, on the other hand, if you are in Him, then are you "as He is" before God, and so accounted in the presence of infinite holiness. Such is the plain teaching of the Word of God. "Ye are complete in Him"—"accepted in the Beloved"—"members of His body, of His flesh, and of His bones." "He that is joined unto the Lord is one spirit" (1 Cor. 6:17; Eph. 1:6; 5:30; Col. 2:10). Now, it is not possible that the Head can be in one degree of acceptance and the members in another. No; the head and the members are one. God counts them one, and therefore they are one. This truth is at once the ground of the loftiest confidence, and of the most profound humility. It imparts the fullest assurance of "boldness in the day of judgment," inasmuch as it is not possible that aught can be laid to the charge of Him with whom we are united: it imparts the deep sense of our own nothingness, inasmuch as our union with Christ is founded upon the death of nature and the utter abolition of all its claims and pretensions.

Since, therefore, the Head and the members are viewed in the same position of infinite favor and acceptance before God, it is perfectly evident that all the members stand in one acceptance, in one salvation, in one life, in one righteousness. There are no degrees in justification. The babe in Christ stands in the same justification as the saint of fifty years' experience. The one is in Christ, and so is the other; and this, as it is the only ground of life, so it is the only ground of justification. There are not two kinds of life, neither are there two kinds of justification. No doubt there are various measures of enjoyment of this justification—various degrees in the knowledge of its fullness and extent—various degrees in the ability to exhibit its power upon the heart and life; these things are frequently confounded with the justification itself, which, as being divine, is necessarily eternal, absolute, unvarying, entirely unaffected by fluctuations of human feeling and experience.

But further, there is no such thing as progress in justification. The believer is not more justified to-day than he was yesterday; nor will he be more justified to-morrow than he is to-day; yea, a soul who is "in Christ Jesus" is as completely justified as if he were before the throne. He is "*complete* in Christ; he is *"as"* Christ. He is, on Christ's own authority, "clean every whit" (John 13:10). What more could he be at this side of the glory? He may [and if he walks in the Spirit, will] make progress in the sense and enjoyment of this glorious reality; but, as to the thing itself, the moment he, by the power of the Holy Ghost, believed the gospel, he passed from a positive state of unrighteousness and condemnation into a positive state of righteousness and acceptance. All this is based upon the divine perfectness of Christ's work; just as, in the case of the burnt-offering, the worshiper's acceptance was based upon the acceptableness of his offering. It was not a question of what he was, but simply of what the sacrifice was.—"*It* shall be accepted *for him,* to make atonement for him."

"And he shall kill the bullock before the Lord; and the priests, Aaron's sons, shall bring the blood, and sprinkle the blood round about upon the altar that is by the door of the tabernacle of the congregation." It is most needful, in studying the doctrine of the burnt-offering, to bear in mind that the grand point set forth therein is not the meeting of the sinner's need, but the presentation to God of that which was infinitely acceptable to Him. Christ as foreshadowed by the burnt-offering is not for the sinner's conscience, but for the heart of God. Further, the cross in the burnt-offering is not the exhibition of the exceeding hatefulness of sin, but of Christ's unshaken and unshakable devotedness to the Father; neither is it the scene of God's outpoured wrath on Christ the sin-bearer, but of the Father's unmingled complacency in Christ the voluntary and most fragrant Sacrifice. Finally, "atonement" as seen in the burnt-offering is not merely commensurate with the claims of man's conscience, but with the intense desire of the heart of Christ to carry out the will and establish the counsels of God—a desire which stopped not short of surrendering up His spotless, precious life, as "a voluntary offering" of "sweet savor" to God.

From the carrying out of this desire, no power of earth or hell, men or devils, could shake Him. When Peter ignorantly sought to dissuade Him, by words of false tenderness, from encountering the shame and degradation of the cross—"Pity Thyself, Lord: this shall not be unto Thee"—what was the reply? "Get thee behind Me, Satan: Thou art an offense unto Me; for thou savorest not the things that be of God, but those that be of men" (Matt. 16:22-23). So, also, on another occasion, He says to His disciples, "Hereafter I will not talk much with you; for the prince of this world cometh, and hath nothing in Me. But that the world may know that *I love the Father,* and as the Father gave Me commandment, even so I do" (John 14:30). These and numerous other kindred Scriptures bring out the burnt-offering phase of Christ's work, in which, it is evident, the primary thought is His "offering Himself without spot to God."

In full keeping with all that has been stated in reference to the special point in the burnt-offering, is the place which Aaron's sons get, and the functions assigned them therein. They "sprinkle the blood;" they "put the fire upon the altar;" they "lay the wood in order upon the fire;" they "lay the parts, the head and the fat, in order upon the wood that is on the fire which is upon the altar." These are very prominent actions, and they form a marked feature of the burnt-offering, as contrasted with the sin-offering, in which Aaron's sons are not mentioned at all. "The sons of Aaron" represent the Church, not as "one body," but as a priestly house. This is easily apprehended. If Aaron was a type of Christ, then Aaron's house was a type of Christ's house, as we read, in Heb. 3, "But Christ as a Son over His own house; whose house are we." And again, "Behold I and the children whom God hath given Me." Now, it is the privilege of the Church, as led and taught by the Holy Ghost, to gaze upon and delight in that aspect of Christ which is presented in this opening type of Leviticus. "Our fellowship is with the Father," who graciously calls us to participate with Him in His thoughts about Christ. True, we can never rise to the height of those thoughts, but we can have fellowship therein, by the Holy Ghost, who dwells in us. It is not here a question of having the conscience tranquilized by the blood of Christ as the sin-bearer, but of communion with God in the matter of Christ's perfect surrender of Himself on the cross.

"*The priests,* Aaron's sons, shall bring the blood, and sprinkle the blood round about upon the altar that is by the door of the tabernacle of the congregation." Here we have a type of the Church bringing the memorial of an accomplished sacrifice, and presenting it in the place of individual approach to God. But we must remember, it is the blood of the burnt-offering, and not of the sin-offering;—it is the Church, in the power of the Holy Ghost, entering into the stupendous thought of Christ's accomplished devotedness to God, and not a convicted sinner entering into the value of the blood of the sin-bearer. I need hardly say that the Church is composed of sinners, and convicted sinners, too; but "Aaron's sons" do not represent convicted sinners, but worshiping saints—it is as "*priests*" they have to do with the burnt-offering. Many err as to this. They imagine that because one takes the place of a worshiper (being invited by the grace of God, and fitted by the blood of Christ so to do), he thereby refuses to acknowledge himself a poor worthless sinner. This is a great mistake. The believer is, in himself, "nothing at all"; but in Christ, he is a purged worshiper. He does not stand in the sanctuary as a guilty sinner, but as a worshiping priest, clothed in "garments of glory and beauty." To be occupied with my guilt in the presence of God is not humility as regards myself, but unbelief as regards the Sacrifice.

However, it must be very evident that the idea of sin-bearing—the imputation of sin—the wrath of God—does not appear in the burnt-offering. True, we read, "It shall be accepted for him, *to make atonement* for him"; but then, it is "atonement," not according to the depths and enormity of human guilt, but according to the perfection of Christ's surrender of Himself to God, and the intensity of God's delight in Christ. This gives us the very loftiest idea of atonement. If I contemplate Christ as the sin-offering, I see atonement made according to the claims of divine justice with respect to sin; but when I see atonement in the burnt-offering, it is according to the measure of Christ's willingness and ability to accomplish the will of God, and according to the measure of God's complacency in Christ and His work. What a perfect atonement must that be which is the fruit of Christ's devotion to God! Could there be any thing beyond this? Assuredly not. The burnt-offering aspect of atonement is that about which the priestly household may well be occupied in the courts of the Lord's house forever.

"And he shall flay the burnt-offering, and cut it into his pieces." The ceremonial act of "flaying" was peculiarly expressive. It was simply the removing of the outward covering, in order that what was *within* might be fully revealed. It was not sufficient that the offering should be outwardly "without blemish," "the hidden parts" should be all disclosed, in order that every sinew and every joint might be seen. It was only in the case of the burnt-offering that this action was specially named. This is quite in character, and tends to set forth the depth of Christ's devotedness to the Father. It was no mere surface-work with Him. The more the secrets of His inner life were disclosed—the more the depths of His being were explored, the more clearly was it made manifest that pure devotion to the will of His Father, and earnest desire for His glory, were the springs of action in the great Antitype of the burnt-offering. He was, most assuredly, a whole burnt-offering.

"And cut it into his pieces." This action presents a somewhat similar truth to that taught in the "sweet incense *beaten small*" (Lev. 16). The Holy Ghost delights to dwell upon the sweetness and fragrance of the sacrifice of Christ, not only as a whole, but also in all its minute details. Look at the burnt-offering as a whole, and you see it without blemish: look at it in all its parts, and you see it to be the same. Such was Christ; and as such He is shadowed forth in this important type.

"And the sons of Aaron the priest shall put fire upon the altar, and lay the wood in order upon the fire. And the priests, Aaron's sons, shall lay the parts, the head, and the fat, in order upon the wood that is on the fire which is upon the altar." This was a high position for the priestly family. The burnt-offering was wholly offered to God,—it was all burnt upon the altar.* Man did not partake of it; but the sons of Aaron the priest (themselves being likewise priests) are here seen standing round the altar of God, to behold the flame of an acceptable sacrifice ascending to Him—an odor of sweet smell. This was a high position—high communion—a high order of priestly service—a striking type of the Church having fellowship with God, in reference to the perfect accomplishment of His will in the death of Christ. As convicted sinners, we gaze on the cross of our Lord Jesus Christ, and behold therein that which meets all our need. The cross, in this aspect of it, gives perfect peace to the conscience. But then, as priests, as purged worshipers, as members of the priestly family, we can look at the cross in another light—even as the grand consummation of Christ's holy purpose to carry out, even unto death, the will of the Father. As convicted sinners, we stand at the brazen altar, and find peace through the blood of atonement; but as priests, we stand there to behold and admire the completeness of that burnt-offering—the perfect surrender and presentation of the spotless One to God.

We should have a very defective apprehension of the mystery of the cross were we only to see in it that which meets man's need as a sinner. There were depths in that mystery which only the mind of God could fathom. It is therefore important to see that when the Holy Ghost would furnish us with foreshadowings of the cross, He gives us, in the very first place, one which sets it forth in its aspect Godward. This alone would be sufficient to teach us that there are heights and depths in the doctrine of the cross which man never could reach. He may approach to "that one well-spring of delight," and drink forever—he may satisfy the utmost longings of his spirit—he may explore it with all the powers of the renewed nature; but, after all, there is that in the cross which only God could know and appreciate. Hence it is that the burnt-offering gets the first place. It typifies Christ's death as viewed and valued by God alone. And surely, we may say, we could not have done without such a type as this; for not only does it give us the highest possible aspect of the death of Christ, but it also gives us a most precious thought in reference to God's peculiar interest in that death. The very fact of His

---

*It may be well, at this point, to inform the reader that the Hebrew word which is rendered "burn" in the case of the burnt-offering is wholly different from that which is used in the sin-offering. I shall, because of the peculiar interest of the subject, refer to a few of the passages in which each word occurs. The word used in the burnt-offering signifies "incense," or to "burn incense," and occurs in the following passages, in some one or other of its various inflections: Lev. 6:15—"And all the *frankincense,* . . . and shall *burn* it upon the altar;" Deut. 33:10—"They shall put *incense* before Thee, and whole *burnt*-sacrifice upon Thine altar;" Exod. 30:1—"And thou shalt make an altar to *burn incense* upon;" Ps. 66:15—"With the *incense* of rams;" Jer. 44:21—"The *incense* that ye *burned* in the cities of Judah;" Cant. 3:16—"Perfumed with myrrh and *frankincense.*" Passages might be multiplied, but the above will suffice to show the use of the word which occurs in the burnt-offering.

The Hebrew word which is rendered "burn" in connection with the sin-offering, signifies to burn in general, and occurs in the following passages: Gen. 40:3—"Let us make brick, and *burn* them thoroughly." Lev. 10:16—"And Moses diligently sought the goat of the *sin*-offering, and, behold, it was *burnt.*" 2 Chron. 16:14—"And they made a very great *burning* for him.

Thus, not only was the sin-offering burnt in a different place, but a different word is adopted by the Holy Ghost to express the burning of it. Now, we cannot imagine, for a moment, that this distinction is a mere interchange of words, the use of which is indifferent. I believe the wisdom of the Holy Ghost is as manifest in the use of the two words as it is in any other point of difference in the two offerings. The spiritual reader will attach the proper value to the above most interesting distinction.

instituting a type of Christ's death which was to be exclusively for Himself, contains a volume of instruction for the spiritual mind.

But though neither man nor angel can ever fully sound the amazing depths of the mystery of Christ's death, we can, at least, see some features of it which would needs make it precious, beyond all thought, to the heart of God. From the cross, He reaps His richest harvest of glory. In no other way could He have been so glorified as by the death of Christ. In Christ's voluntary surrender of Himself to death, the divine glory shines out in its fullest brightness; in it, too, the solid foundation of all the divine counsels was laid. This is a most comforting truth. Creation never could have furnished such a basis. Moreover, the cross furnishes a righteous channel through which divine love can flow. And, finally, by the cross Satan is eternally confounded, and "principalities and powers made a show of openly." These are glorious fruits produced by the cross; and, when we think of them, we can see just reason why there should have been a type of the cross exclusively for God Himself, and also a reason why that type should occupy the leading place—should stand at the very top of the list. Again let me say, there would have been a grievous blank among the types had the burnt-offering been lacking, and there would be a grievous blank in the page of inspiration had the record of that type been withheld.

"But his inwards and his legs shall he wash in water; and the priest shall burn all on the altar, to be a burnt-sacrifice, an offering made by fire, of a sweet savor unto the Lord." This action rendered the sacrifice typically what Christ was essentially—pure—both inwardly and outwardly pure. There was the most perfect correspondence between Christ's inward motives and His outward conduct. The latter was the index of the former. All tended to the one point, namely, the glory of God. The members of His body perfectly obeyed and carried out the counsels of His devoted heart—that heart which only beat for God, and for His glory, in the salvation of men. Well, therefore, might the priest "burn *all* on the altar." It was all typically pure, and all designed only as food for the altar of God. Of some sacrifices the priest partook; of some, the offerer; but the burnt-offering was "all" consumed on the altar. It was exclusively for God. The priests might arrange the wood and the fire, and see the flame ascend (and a high and holy privilege it was so to do); but they did not eat of the sacrifice: God alone was the object of Christ in the burnt-offering aspect of His death. We cannot be too simple in our apprehension of this. From the moment that the unblemished male was voluntarily presented at the door of the tabernacle of the congregation, until it was reduced to ashes by the action of the fire, we discern in it Christ offering Himself, by the Eternal Spirit, without spot to God.

This makes the burnt-offering unspeakably precious to the soul. It gives us the most exalted view of Christ's work. In that work, God had His own peculiar joy—a joy into which no created intelligence could enter. This must never be lost sight of. It is unfolded in the burnt-offering, and confirmed by "the law of the burnt-offering," to which we shall just refer.

"And the Lord spake unto Moses, saying, 'Command Aaron and his sons, saying, This is the law of the burnt-offering: It is the burnt-offering, because of the burning upon the altar all night unto the morning, and the fire of the altar shall be burning in it. And the priest shall put on his linen garment, and his linen breeches shall he put upon his flesh, and take up the ashes which the fire hath consumed with the burnt-offering on the altar, and he shall put them beside the altar. And he shall put off his garments, and put on other garments, and carry forth the ashes without the camp unto a clean place. And the fire upon the altar shall be burning in it; it shall not be put out: and the priest shall burn wood on it every morning, and lay the burnt-offering in order upon it; and he shall burn thereon the fat of the peace-offerings. The fire shall ever be burning upon the altar; it shall never go out' " (Lev. 6:8-13). The fire on the altar consumed the burnt-offering and the fat of the peace-offering. It was the apt expression of divine holiness, which found in Christ and His perfect sacrifice a proper material on which to feed. That fire was never to go out. There was to be the perpetual maintenance of that which set forth the action of divine holiness. Through the dark and silent watches of the night, the fire blazed on the altar of God.

"And the priest shall put on his linen garment," etc. Here, the priest takes, in type, the place of Christ, whose personal righteousness is set forth by the white linen garment. He having given Himself up to the death of the cross in order to accomplish the will of God, has entered, in His own eternal righteousness, into heaven, bearing with Him the memorials of His finished work. The ashes declared the completion of the sacrifice, and God's acceptance thereof. Those ashes placed beside the altar indicated that the fire had consumed the sacrifice—that it was not only a completed, but also an accepted, sacrifice. The ashes of the burnt-offering declared the acceptance of the sacrifice: the ashes of the sin-offering declared the judgment of the sin.

Many of the points on which we have been dwelling will, with the divine blessing, come before us with increasing clearness, fullness, precision, and power as we proceed with the offerings. Each offering is, as it were, thrown into relief by being viewed in contrast with all the rest. All the offerings taken together give us a full view of Christ. They are like so many mirrors, arranged in such a manner as to reflect in various ways the figure of that true and only-perfect Sacrifice. No one type could fully present Him. We needed to have Him reflected in life and in death—as a Man and as a Victim, Godward and usward; and we have Him thus in the offerings of Leviticus. God has graciously met our need; and may He give us an enlarged capacity to enter into and enjoy His provision.

---

## *CHAPTER 2*

WE now come to consider the meat-offering, which presents, in a very distinct manner, "the Man Christ Jesus." As the burnt-offering typifies Christ in *death,* the meat-offering typifies Him in *life.* In neither the one nor the other is there a question of sin-bearing. In the burnt-offering, we see atonement, but no sin-bearing*—no imputation of sin—no outpoured wrath on account of sin. How can we know this? Because it was all consumed on the altar. Had there been aught of sin-bearing, it would have been consumed outside the camp (comp. Lev. 4:11,12, with Heb. 13:11).

But in the meat-offering, there was not even a question of bloodshedding. We simply find in it a beauteous type of Christ as He lived and walked and served down here on this earth. This one fact is, of itself, sufficient to draw the spiritual mind to the close and prayerful consideration of this offering. The pure and perfect manhood of our blessed Lord is a theme which must command the attention of every true Christian. It is to be feared that great looseness of thought prevails in reference to this holy mystery. The expressions which one sometimes hears and reads are sufficient to prove that the fundamental doctrine of incarnation is not laid hold of as the Word presents it. Such expressions may very probably proceed from misapprehension as to the real nature of His relations, and as to the true character of His sufferings; but, from what cause soever they arise, they should be judged in the light of holy Scripture, and rejected. Doubtless, many who make use of those expressions would recoil, with just horror and indignation, from the real doctrine contained in them were it put before them in its broad and true characters; and, for this reason, one should be sorry to attribute unsoundness as to fundamental truth, where it may merely be inaccuracy of statement.

There is, however, one consideration which should weigh heavily in the estimation of every Christian, and that is, the vital nature of the doctrine of Christ's humanity. It lies at the very foundation of Christianity; and, for this reason, Satan has diligently

*That is to say, sin-bearing is not prominent. Of course, where there is atonement, sin must be in question.

sought, from the beginning, to lead people astray in reference to it. Almost all the leading errors which have found their way into the professing church disclose the satanic purpose to undermine the truth as to the Person of Christ. Even when earnest, godly men have sought to combat those errors, they have, in many cases, plunged into errors on the opposite side. Hence, therefore, the need of close adherence to the veritable words which the Holy Ghost has made use of in unfolding this profound and most sacred mystery. Indeed, I believe that, in every case, subjection to the authority of holy Scripture, and the energy of that divine life in the soul, will prove effectual safeguards against every complexion of error. It does not require high theological attainments to enable a soul to keep clear of error with respect to the doctrine of Christ. If only the word of Christ be dwelling richly, and "the Spirit of Christ" be in energy, in the soul, there will be no room for Satan to thrust in his dark and horrible suggestions. If the heart be delighting in the Christ which Scripture unfolds, it will assuredly shrink from the false Christs which Satan would introduce. If we are feeding upon God's reality, we shall unhesitatingly reject Satan's counterfeit. This is the best possible way in which to escape the entanglements of error, in every shape and character. "The sheep *hear His voice,* and . . . follow Him; for they *know His voice.* And a stranger will they not follow, but will flee from him; for *they know not the voice of strangers"* (John 10:3-5). It is not, by any means, needful to be acquainted with the voice of a stranger in order to turn away from it: all we require is to know the voice of "the good Shepherd." This will secure us against the ensnaring influence of every strange sound. While, therefore, I feel called upon to warn the reader against strange sounds in reference to the divine mystery of Christ's humanity, I do not deem it needful to discuss such sounds, but would rather seek, through grace, to arm him against them by unfolding the doctrine of Scripture on the subject.

There are few things in which we exhibit more failure than in maintaining vigorous communion with the perfect manhood of the Lord Jesus Christ. Hence it is that we suffer so much from vacancy, barrenness, restlessness, and wandering. Did we but enter with a more artless faith into the truth that there is a real Man at the right hand of the Majesty in the heavens—One whose sympathy is perfect, whose love is fathomless, whose power is omnipotent, whose wisdom is infinite, whose resources are exhaustless, whose riches are unsearchable, whose ear is open to our every breathing, whose hand is open to our every need, whose heart is full of unspeakable love and tenderness towards us—how much more happy and elevated we should be, and how much more independent of creature streams, through what channel soever they may flow! There is nothing the heart can crave which we have not in Jesus. Does it long for genuine sympathy? Where can it find it, save in Him who could mingle His tears with those of the bereaved sisters of Bethany? Does it desire the enjoyment of sincere affection? It can only find it in that heart which told forth its love in drops of blood. Does it seek the protection of real power? It has but to look to Him who made the world. Does it feel the need of unerring wisdom to guide? Let it betake itself to Him who is wisdom personified, and "who of God is made unto us wisdom." In one word, we have all in Christ. The divine mind and the divine affections have found a perfect object in "the Man Christ Jesus"; and surely, if there is that in the Person of Christ which can perfectly satisfy God, there is that which ought to satisfy us, and which will satisfy us in proportion as, by the grace of the Holy Ghost, we walk in communion with God.

The Lord Jesus Christ was the only perfect Man that ever trod this earth. He was all perfect—perfect in thought, perfect in word, perfect in action. In Him every moral quality met in divine and therefore perfect proportion. No one feature preponderated. In Him were exquisitely blended a majesty which overawed, and a gentleness which gave perfect ease in His presence. The scribes and the Pharisees met His withering rebuke, while the poor Samaritan and "the woman that was a sinner" found themselves unaccountably, yet irresistibly, attracted to Him. No one feature displaced another, for all was in fair and comely proportion. This may be traced in every scene of His perfect life. He could say, in reference to five thousand hungry people, "Give ye them to eat"; and when they were filled, He could say, "Gather up the fragments that remain, that nothing be lost." The benevolence and the economy are both perfect, and neither interferes with the other: each shines in its own proper sphere. He could not send unsatisfied hunger away; neither could He suffer a single fragment of God's creatures to be wasted. He would meet, with a full and liberal hand, the need of the human family, and when that was done, He would carefully treasure up every atom. The self-same hand that was widely open to every form of human need was firmly closed against all prodigality. There was nothing niggardly nor yet extravagant in the character of the perfect—the heavenly Man.

What a lesson for us! How often, with us, does benevolence resolve itself into an unwarrantable profusion! and, on the other hand, how often is our economy marred by the exhibition of a miserly spirit! At times, too, our niggard hearts refuse to open themselves to the full extent of the need which presents itself before us; while, at other times, we squander, through a wanton extravagance, that which might satisfy many a needy fellow-creature. Let us carefully study the divine picture set before us in the life of "the Man Christ Jesus." How refreshing and strengthening to "the inward man" to be occupied with Him who was perfect in all His ways, and who "in all things must have the pre-eminence"!

See Him in the garden of Gethsemane. There, He kneels in the profound depths of a humility which none but Himself could exhibit; but yet before the traitor's band He exhibits a self-possession and majesty which cause them to go backward and fall to the ground. His deportment before God is prostration; before His judges and accusers, unbending dignity. All is perfect. The self-emptiness and the self-possession, the prostration and the dignity, are all divine.

So also, when we contemplate the beauteous combination of His divine and human relations, the same perfectness is observable. He could say, "How was it that ye sought Me? Wist ye not that I must be about My Father's business?" And, at the same time, He could go down to Nazareth, and there set an example of perfect subjection to parental authority (see Luke 2:49-51). He could say to His mother, "Woman, what have I to do with thee?" Yet, when passing through the unutterable agony of the cross, He could tenderly commit that mother to the care of the beloved disciple. In the former case, He separated Himself, in the spirit of perfect Nazariteship, to accomplish His Father's will; while in the latter, He gave expression to the tender feelings of the perfect human heart. The devotion of the Nazarite and the affection of the Man were both perfect. Neither was permitted to interfere with the other: each shone with undimmed lustre in its proper sphere.

Now, the shadow of this perfect Man passes before us in the "fine flour" which formed the basis of the meat-offering. There was not so much as a single coarse grain. There was nothing uneven—nothing unequal—nothing rough to the touch. No matter what pressure came from without, there was always an even surface. He was never ruffled by any circumstance or set of circumstances. He never had to retrace a step or recall a word. Come what might, He always met it in that perfect evenness which is so strikingly typified by the "fine flour."

In all these things, it is needless to say, He stands in marked contrast with His most honored and devoted servants. For example, Moses, though "the meekest man in all the earth," yet "spoke unadvisedly with his lips." In Peter, we find a zeal and an energy which at times proved too much for the occasion; and, again, a cowardice which shrank from the place of testimony and reproach. There was the assertion of a devotedness which, when the time for action arrived, was not forthcoming. John, who breathed so much of the atmosphere of the immediate presence of Christ, exhibited, at times, a sectarian and an intolerant spirit. In Paul, the most devoted of servants, we observe considerable unevenness. He uttered words to the high-priest which he had to recall: he sent a letter to the Corinthians of which at first he repented and afterwards repented not. In all, we find some flaw, save in Him who is "the fairest among ten thousand, and altogether lovely."

In the examination of the meat-offering, it will give clearness and simplicity to our thoughts to consider, first, the materials of which it was composed; secondly, the various forms in which it was presented; and, thirdly, the persons who partook of it.

1. As to the materials, the "fine flour" may be regarded as the basis of the offering; and in it we have a type of Christ's humanity, wherein every perfection met. Every virtue was there, and ready for effectual action in due season. The Holy Ghost delights to unfold the glories of Christ's Person, to set Him forth in all His peerless excellence, to place Him before us in contrast with all beside. He contrasts Him with Adam, even in his very best and highest state; as we read, "The first man is of the earth, earthy: the second Man is the Lord from heaven" (1 Cor. 15:47). The first Adam, even in his unfallen condition, was "of the earth;" but the second Man was "the Lord from heaven."

The "oil," in the meat-offering, is a type of the Holy Ghost. But inasmuch as the oil is applied in a twofold way, so we have the Holy Ghost presented in a double aspect, in *connection* with the *incarnation* of the Son. The fine flour was *"mingled"* with oil, and there was oil *"poured"* upon it. Such was the type; and in the Antitype, we see the blessed Lord Jesus Christ first *"conceived,"* and then *"anointed,"* by the Holy Ghost (comp. Matt. 1:18-23 with chap. 3:16). This is divine! The accuracy, which is here so apparent, draws forth the soul's admiration. It is one and the same Spirit which records the ingredients of the type, and gives us the facts in the Antitype. The One who has detailed for us, with such amazing precision, the types and shadows of the book of Leviticus, has also given us the glorious subject thereof in the gospel narratives. The same Spirit breathes through the pages of the Old and those of the New Testament, and enables us to see how exactly the one corresponds with the other.

The conception of Christ's humanity by the Holy Ghost, in the womb of the virgin, unfolds one of the most profound mysteries which can possibly engage the attention of the renewed mind. It is most fully set forth in Luke's Gospel; and this is entirely characteristic, inasmuch as, throughout that Gospel, it would seem to be the special object of the Holy Ghost to unfold, in His own divinely touching manner, "the Man Christ Jesus." In Matthew, we have "the Son of Abraham—the Son of David"; in Mark, we have the divine Servant—the heavenly Workman; in John, we have "the Son of God"—the Eternal Word—the Life—the Light, by whom all things were made; but the great theme of the Holy Ghost in Luke is "the Son of Man."

When the angel Gabriel had announced to Mary the dignity which was about to be conferred upon her, in connection with the great work in incarnation, she, not in a spirit of scepticism, but of honest ignorance, inquired, "How shall this be, seeing I know not a man?" It manifestly seemed to her that the birth of this glorious Person who was about to appear should be according to the ordinary principles of generation; and this her thought is made the occasion, in the exceeding goodness of God, of developing much valuable light in reference to the cardinal truth of incarnation. The angel's reply to the virgin's question is unspeakably interesting, and cannot be too closely considered. "And the angel answered and said unto her, 'The Holy Ghost shall come upon thee, and the power of the Highest shall overshadow thee; *therefore* also that *holy Thing* which shall be born of thee shall be called the Son of God" (Luke 1:35).

From this magnificent passage, we learn that the human body into which the Eternal Son entered was formed by "the power of the Highest." "A body hast *Thou* prepared Me" (comp. Ps. 40:6 with Heb. 10:5). It was a real human body—real "flesh and blood."

There is no possible foundation here on which gnosticism or mysticism can base its vapid and worthless theories, no warrant for the cold abstractions of the former, or the misty fancies of the latter. All is deep, solid, and divine reality: the very thing which our hearts needed—the very thing which God has given. The early promise had declared that "the seed of the woman shall bruise the serpent's head," and none but a real man could accomplish this prediction—one whose nature was as real as it was pure and incorruptible. "Thou shalt conceive in thy womb," said the angelic messenger, "and bring forth a Son."* Then, lest there should be any room for an error in reference to the mode of this conception, he adds such words as prove, unanswerably, that the "flesh and blood" of which the Eternal Son "took part," while absolutely real, was absolutely incapable of receiving, or retaining, or of communicating a single taint. The humanity of the Lord Jesus was emphatically *"that holy Thing."* And inasmuch as it was wholly without taint, it was wholly without a seed of mortality. We cannot think of mortality, save in connection with sin; and Christ's humanity had naught to do with sin, either personally or relatively. Sin was imputed to Him on the cross, where He was "made sin for us." But the meat-offering is not the type of Christ as a sin-bearer. It foreshadows Him in His perfect life here below—a life in which He suffered, no doubt, but not as a sin-bearer—not as a substitute—not at the hand of God. Let this be distinctly noted. Neither in the burnt-offering nor in the meat-offering have we Christ as a sin-bearer. In the latter, we see Him *living;* and in the former, we see Him *dying;* but in neither is there a question of the imputation of sin, nor of enduring the wrath of God on account of sin. In short, to present Christ as the sinner's substitute any where else save on the cross, is to rob His life of all its divine beauty and excellency, and to displace the cross altogether. Moreover, it would involve the types of Leviticus in hopeless confusion.

I would, at this point, solemnly admonish my reader that he cannot be too jealous in reference to the vital truth of the Person and the relations of the Lord Jesus Christ. If there be error as to this, there is no security as to any thing. God cannot give the sanction of His presence to aught that has not this truth for its foundation. The Person of Christ is the living, divine centre round which the Holy Ghost carries on all His operations. Let slip the truth as to Him, and you are like a vessel broken from its moorings, and carried, without rudder or compass, over the wild watery waste, and in imminent danger of being dashed to fragments upon the rocks of Arianism, infidelity, or atheism. Question the eternal Sonship of Christ, question His deity, question His unspotted humanity, and you have opened the floodgate for a desolating tide of deadly error to rush in. Let no one imagine, for a moment, that this is a mere matter to be discussed by learned theologians—a curious question—a recondite mystery—a point about which we may lawfully differ. No; it is a vital, fundamental truth, to be held in the power of the Holy Ghost, and maintained at the expense of all beside—yea, to be confessed under all circumstances, whatever may be the consequences.

What we want, is, simply to receive into our hearts, by the grace of the Holy Spirit, the Father's revelation of the Son, and then our souls shall be effectually preserved from the snares of the enemy, let them take what shape they may. He may speciously cover the trap of Arianism or Socinianism with the grass and leaves of a most plausible and attractive system of interpretation; but directly the devoted heart discovers what this system attempts to make of the blessed One to whom it owes every thing, and where it attempts to put Him, it finds but little difficulty in sending it back to where it manifestly came from. We can well afford to do without human theories; but we can

---

*"But when the fullness of the time was come, God sent forth His Son, made of a woman, made under the law." (*γενομενον εκ γυναικος, γενομενον ὑπο νομον.*) This is a most important passage, inasmuch as it sets forth our blessed Lord as Son of God and Son of Man. "God sent forth *His* Son, made *of a woman.*" Precious testimony!

never do without Christ—the Christ of God—the Christ of God's affections—the Christ of God's counsels—the Christ of God's Word.

The Lord Jesus Christ, God's eternal Son—a distinct Person in the glorious Trinity—God manifest in the flesh—God over all, blessed forever, assumed a body which was inherently and divinely pure, holy, and without the possibility of taint—absolutely free from every seed or principle of sin and mortality. Such was the humanity of Christ, that He could at any moment, so far as He was personally concerned, have returned to heaven, from whence He had come and to which He belonged. I speak not here of the eternal counsels of redeeming love, or of the unswerving love of the heart of Jesus—His love to God—His love to God's elect, or of the work that was needful to ratify God's everlasting covenant with the seed of Abraham and with the whole creation. Christ's own words teach us that "it behoved Him to suffer, and to rise from the dead the third day" (Luke 24:46). It was necessary that He should suffer, in order to the full manifestation and perfect accomplishment of the great mystery of redemption. It was His gracious purpose to "bring many sons unto glory." He would not "abide alone," and therefore He, as the "corn of wheat," should "fall into the ground and die." The more fully we enter into the *truth* of His Person, the more fully do we apprehend the *grace* of His work.

When the apostle speaks of Christ's being "made perfect through suffering," it is as "the Captain of our salvation" that he contemplates Him, and not as the Eternal Son, who, as regards His own abstract Person and nature, was divinely perfect, and could not possibly have aught added to Him. So, also, when He Himself, says, "Behold, I cast out devils, and I do cures to-day and to-morrow, and the third day I shall be perfected" (Luke 13:32), He refers to His being perfected, in the power of resurrection, as the Accomplisher of the entire work of redemption. So far as He was personally concerned, He could say, even on His way forth from the garden of Gethsemane, "Thinkest thou that I cannot now pray to My Father, and He shall presently give Me more than twelve legions of angels? But how then shall the Scriptures be fulfilled, that thus it must be?" (Matt. 26:53-54)

It is well that the soul be clear as to this—well to have a divine sense of the harmony which exists between those Scriptures which present Christ in the essential dignity of His Person and the divine purity of His nature, and those which present Him in His relation with His people and as accomplishing the great work of redemption. At times we find both these things combined in the same passage, as in Heb. 5:8-9, "Though *He were a Son,* yet learned He obedience by the things which He suffered; and being made perfect, He became the author of eternal salvation to all them that obey Him." We must, however, bear in mind that not one of those relations into which Christ voluntarily entered—whether as the expression of divine love to a lost world, or the Servant of the divine counsels—not one of these could possibly interfere with the essential purity, excellency, and glory of His Person. "The Holy Ghost came upon" the virgin, and "the power of the Highest overshadowed her"; and "therefore that holy Thing which was born of her was called the Son of God." Most magnificent unfolding, this, of the deep secret of Christ's pure and perfect humanity—the great Antitype of the *"fine flour mingled with oil"!*

Here let me observe, that between humanity as seen in the Lord Jesus Christ and humanity as seen in us there could be no union. That which is pure could never coalesce with that which is impure. That which is incorruptible could never unite with that which is corruptible. The spiritual and the carnal—the heavenly and the earthly—could never combine. Hence, therefore, it follows that incarnation was not, as some have attempted to teach, Christ's taking our fallen nature into union with Himself. If He could have done this, there would have been no need of the death of the cross. He needed not, in that case, to feel "straitened" until the baptism was accomplished—the corn of wheat did not need to "fall into the ground and die." This is a point of grave moment. Let the spiritual mind ponder it deeply. Christ could not possibly take sinful humanity into union with Himself. Hear what the angel saith to Joseph, in the first chapter of Matthew's Gospel: "Joseph, thou son of David, fear not to take unto thee Mary thy wife; for *that which is conceived in her is of the Holy Ghost.*" See how Joseph's natural sensibilities, as well as Mary's pious ignorance, are made the occasion of a fuller unfolding of the holy mystery of Christ's humanity; and also of guarding that humanity against all the blasphemous attacks of the enemy.

How, then, is it that believers are united to Christ? Is it in incarnation, or resurrection? In resurrection, assuredly. How is this proved? "Except a corn of wheat fall into the ground and die, it abideth *alone*" (John 12:24). At this side of death, there could be no union between Christ and His people. It is in the power of a new life that believers are united to Christ. They were dead *in sin,* and He, in perfect grace, came down and (though Himself pure and sinless) was "made sin," "died *unto sin,*" put it away, rose triumphant over it and all pertaining to it, and, in resurrection, became the Head of a new race. Adam was the head of the old creation, which fell with him. Christ, by dying, put Himself under the full weight of His people's condition, and having perfectly met all that was against them, rose victorious over all, and carried them with Him into the new creation, of which He is the glorious Head and Centre. Hence, we read, "He that is joined unto the Lord is one spirit" (1 Cor. 6:17). "But God, who is rich in mercy, for His great love wherewith He loved us, even when we were *dead in sins,* hath quickened us *together with Christ,* (by grace ye are saved;) and hath raised us up together, and made us sit together in heavenly places in Christ Jesus" (Eph. 2:4-6). "For we are members of His body, of His flesh, and of His bones" (Eph. 5:30). "And you, being *dead in your sins* and the uncircumcision of your flesh, *hath He quickened together with Him,* having forgiven you all trespasses" (Col. 2:13).

Passages might be multiplied, but the above are amply sufficient to prove that it was not in incarnation, but in death, that Christ took a position in which His people could be "quickened together with Him." Does this seem unimportant to the reader? Let him examine it in the light of Scripture. Let him weigh all the consequences. Let him view it in its bearing upon Christ's Person, upon His life, upon His death, upon our condition by nature in the old creation, and our place through mercy in the new. Let him consider it thus, and I feel persuaded he will no longer regard it as a light matter. Of one thing, at least, he may rest assured, that the writer of these pages would not pen a single line to prove this point did he not consider it to be fraught with the most momentous results. The whole of divine revelation so hangs together—is so adjusted by the hand of the Holy Ghost—is so consistent in all its parts, that if one truth be disturbed, the entire arch is injured. This consideration should suffice to produce, in the mind of every Christian, a holy caution, lest, by some rude touch, he mar the beauteous superstructure. Every stone must be left in its divinely appointed place; and, unquestionably, the truth as to Christ's Person is the key-stone of the arch.

Having thus endeavored to unfold the truth typified by the "fine flour *mingled* with oil," we may remark another point of much interest in the expression, "He shall *pour* oil upon it." In this we have a type of the anointing of the Lord Jesus Christ by the Holy Ghost. The body of the Lord Jesus was not merely formed mysteriously by the Holy Ghost, but that pure and holy vessel was also anointed for service by the same power. "And it came to pass when all the people were baptized, and Jesus also being baptized, and praying, the heaven was opened, and the Holy Ghost descended in a bodily shape as a dove upon Him, and there was a voice from heaven, saying, 'Thou art My beloved Son; in Thee I am well pleased' " (Luke 3:21-22).

The anointing of the Lord Jesus by the Holy Ghost previous to His entrance upon His public ministry is of immense practical importance to every one who really desires to be a true and an effectual servant of God. Though conceived, as to His manhood, by the Holy Ghost; though, in His own proper Person, "God manifest in the flesh;" though embodying in Himself all the fullness of the Godhead; yet, be it well observed, when coming forth as man to do the will of God on the earth, whatever that will might be—whether preaching the gospel, teaching in the synagogues, healing the sick, cleansing the leper, casting out devils, feeding the hungry, or raising the dead—He did all by the Holy Ghost. That holy and heavenly vessel in which God the Son was pleased to appear in this world was formed, filled, anointed, and led by the Holy Ghost.

What a deep and holy lesson for us! A most needful and salutary lesson! How prone are we to run unsent! How prone to act in the mere energy of the flesh! How much of that which looks like ministry is only the restless and unhallowed activity of a nature which has never been measured and judged in the divine presence! Truly, we need to contemplate more closely our divine "meat-offering"—to understand more fully the meaning of the "fine flour anointed with oil." We need to meditate more deeply upon Christ Himself, who, though possessing, in His own Person, divine power, nevertheless, did all His work, wrought all His miracles, and, finally, "offered Himself, without spot to God, by the eternal Spirit." He could say, "I by the Spirit of God cast out devils."

Nothing is of any value save that which is wrought by the power of the Holy Ghost. A man may write; but if his pen be not guided and used by the Holy Ghost, his lines will produce no permanent results. A man may speak; but if his lips be not anointed by the Holy Ghost, his word will not take permanent root. This is a solemn consideration, and if properly weighed, would lead to much watchfulness over ourselves, and much earnest dependence upon the Holy Ghost. What we need is thorough self-emptiness, so that there may be room left for the Spirit to act by us. It is impossible that a man full of himself can be the vessel of the Holy Ghost. Such an one must first be emptied of himself, and then the Spirit can use him. When we contemplate the Person and ministry of the Lord Jesus, we see how that in every scene and circumstance He acted by the direct power of the Holy Ghost. Having taken His place as man down here, He showed that man should not only live by the Word, but act by the Spirit of God. Even though, as man, His will was perfect—His thoughts, His words, His acts, all perfect—yet He would not act save by the direct authority of the Word, and by the direct power of the Holy Ghost. Oh that in this, as in every thing else, we could more closely, more faithfully, follow in His steps! Then, indeed, would our ministry be more effective, our testimony more fruitful, our whole course more entirely to the glory of God.

The next ingredient in the meat-offering demanding our consideration is "the frankincense." As has been remarked, the "fine flour" was the basis of the offering. The "oil" and "frankincense" were the two leading adjuncts; and, truly, the connection between these two latter is most instructive. The "oil" typifies the *power* of Christ's ministry; the "frankincense" typifies the *object* thereof. The former teaches us that He did every thing by the Spirit of God; the latter, that He did every thing to the glory of God. The frankincense presents that in the life of Christ which was exclusively for God. This is evident from the second verse—"And he shall bring it [the meat-offering] to Aaron's sons, the priests: and he shall take thereout his handful of flour thereof, and of the oil thereof, and *all the frankincense* thereof; and the priest shall burn the memorial of it upon the altar, to be an offering made by fire, of a sweet savor unto the Lord." Thus was it in the true meat-offering—the Man Christ Jesus. There was that in His blessed life which was exclusively for God. Every thought, every word, every look, every act of His emitted a fragrance which went up immediately to God. And as, in the type, it was the "fire of the altar" that drew forth the sweet odor of the frankincense; so, in the Antitype, the more He was "tried," in all the scenes and circumstances of His blessed life, the more fully was it manifested that, in His manhood, there was nothing that could not ascend as an odor of a sweet smell to the throne of God. If in the burnt-offering we behold Christ "offering Himself without spot to God," in the meat-offering we behold Him presenting all the intrinsic excellence and perfect actings of His human nature to God. A perfect, a self-emptied, an obedient Man on the earth doing the will of God, acting by the authority of the Word, and by the power of the Spirit, had a sweet odor which could only be for divine acceptance. The fact that "all the frankincense" was consumed on the altar, fixes its import in the simplest manner.

It now only remains for us to consider an ingredient which was an inseparable adjunct of the meat-offering, namely, *"salt."*—"And every oblation of thy meat-offering shalt thou season with salt; neither shalt thou suffer the salt of the covenant of thy God to be lacking from thy meat-offering: with all thine offerings thou shalt offer salt." The expression, "salt of the covenant," sets forth the enduring character of that covenant. God Himself has so ordained it, in all things, that naught can ever alter it—no influence can ever corrupt it. In a spiritual and practical point of view, it is impossible to overestimate the value of such an ingredient. "Let your conversation be always with grace, seasoned with *salt.*" The whole conversation of the Perfect Man exhibited the power of this principle. His words were not merely words of grace, but words of pungent power—words divinely adapted to preserve from all taint and corrupting influence. He never uttered a word which was not redolent with "frankincense," and "seasoned with salt." The former was most acceptable to God; the latter, most profitable for man.

Sometimes, alas! man's corrupt heart and vitiated taste could not tolerate the pungency of the divinely-salted meat-offering. Witness, for example, the scene in the synagogue of Nazareth (Luke 4:16-29). The people could "bear Him witness, and wonder at the *gracious* words which proceeded out of His mouth;" but when He proceeded to season those words with *salt,* which was so needful in order to preserve them from the corrupting influence of their national pride, they would fain have cast Him over the brow of the hill whereon their city was built.

So, also, in Luke 14, when His words of "grace" had drawn "great multitudes" after Him, He instantly throws in the "salt," by setting forth, in words of holy faithfulness, the sure results of following Him. "Come, for all things are now ready"—here was the "grace"; but then, "Whosoever forsaketh not all that he hath, cannot be My disciple"—here was the "salt." Grace is attractive; but "salt is good." Gracious discourse may be popular; but salted discourse never will. The pure gospel of the grace of God may, at certain times, and under certain circumstances, be run after by "the multitude" for awhile; but when the "salt" of a fervid and faithful application is introduced, it will soon thin the benches of all save such as are brought under the power of the Word.

Having thus considered the ingredients which composed the meat-offering, we shall now refer to those which were excluded from it.

The first of these was "leaven." "No meat-offering, which ye shall bring unto the Lord, shall be made with leaven." This ingredient is used throughout the inspired volume, without so much as a single exception, as the symbol of *evil.* In chap. 23 of our book, which will be noticed in due course, we find leaven admitted in the two loaves which were offered on the day of Pentecost; but from the meat-offering leaven was most sedulously excluded. There was to be nothing sour—nothing that would puff up—nothing expressive of evil in that which typified "the Man Christ Jesus." In Him, there could be nothing savoring of nature's sourness, nothing turgid—nothing inflated: all was pure, solid, and genuine. His word might, at times, cut to the quick; but it was never sour. His style never rose above the occasion. His deportment ever exhibited the deep reality of one walking in the immediate presence of God.

In those who bear the name of Jesus, we know, too well, alas! how leaven shows itself in all its properties and effects. There has been but one untainted sheaf of human fruit—but one perfectly unleavened meat-offering; and, blessed be God, that one is ours—ours to feed upon in the sanctuary of the divine presence, in fellowship with God. No exercise can be more truly edifying and refreshing for the renewed mind than to dwell upon the unleavened perfectness of Christ's humanity—to contemplate the life and ministry of One who was absolutely and essentially unleavened. In all His springs of thought, affection, desire, and imagination, there was not so much as a particle of leaven. He was the sinless, spotless, perfect Man. And the more we are enabled, by the power of the Spirit, to enter into all this, the deeper will be our experience of the grace which led this perfect One to place Himself under the full consequences of His people's sins, as He did when He hung upon the cross. This thought, however, belongs entirely to the sin-offering aspect of our blessed Lord. In the meat-offering, sin is not in question. It is not the type of a sin-bearer, but of a real, perfect, unblemished Man, conceived and anointed by the Holy Ghost, possessing an unleavened nature, and living an unleavened life down here, emitting ever Godward the fragrance of His own personal excellency, and maintaining amongst men a deportment characterized by "grace seasoned with salt."

But there was another ingredient, as positively excluded from the meat-offering as "leaven," and that was "honey." "For ye shall burn no leaven, *nor any honey,* in any offering of the Lord made by fire" (ver. 11). Now, as "leaven" is the expression of that which is positively and palpably *evil* in nature, we may regard "honey" as the significant symbol of that which is apparently *sweet* and attractive. Both are disallowed of God, both were carefully excluded from the meat-offering, both were unfit for the altar. Men may undertake, like Saul, to distinguish between what is "vile and refuse" and what is not; but the judgment of God ranks the delicate Agag with the vilest of the sons of Amalek. No doubt, there are some good moral qualities in man, which must be taken for what they are worth. "Hast thou found *honey,* eat so much as is convenient"; but be it remembered, it found no place in the meat-offering, nor in its Antitype. There was the fullness of the Holy Ghost, there was the fragrant odor of the frankincense, there was the preservative virtue of "the salt of the covenant"—all these things accompanied the "fine flour" in the Person of the true "Meat-offering," but "no honey."

What a lesson for the heart is here! yea, what a volume of wholesome instruction! The blessed Lord Jesus knew how to give nature and its relationships their proper place: He knew how much "honey" was "convenient." He could say to His mother, "Wist ye not that I must be about My Father's business?" and yet He could say, again, to the beloved disciple, "Behold thy mother." In other words, nature's claims were never allowed to interfere with the presentation to God of all the energies of Christ's perfect manhood. Mary, and others too, might have thought that her human relation to the blessed One gave her some peculiar claim or influence, on merely natural grounds. "There came, then, His brethren ["after the flesh"] and His mother, and standing without, sent unto Him, calling Him. And the multitude sat about Him; and they said unto Him, 'Behold, Thy mother and Thy brethren without seek for Thee.'" What was the reply of the true Meat-offering? Did He at once abandon His work, in order to respond to nature's call? By no means. Had He done so, it would have been to mingle "honey" with the meat-offering, which could not be. The honey was faithfully excluded on this as on every occasion when God's claims were to be attended to, and instead thereof, the power of the Spirit, the odor of the "frankincense," and the virtues of the "salt" were blessedly exhibited. "And He answered them, saying, 'Who is My mother, or My brethren?' And He looked round about on them which sat about Him, and said, 'Behold My mother and My brethren! For whosoever shall do the will of God, the same is My brother, and My sister, and mother'"*

*How important to see, in the above beautiful passage, that doing God's will brings the soul into a relationship with

(Mark 3:31-35).

There are few things which the servant of Christ finds more difficult than to adjust, with spiritual accuracy, the claims of natural relationship, so as not to suffer them to interfere with the claims of the Master. In the case of our blessed Lord, as we know, the adjustment was divine. In our case, it often happens that divinely recognized duties are openly neglected for what we imagine to be the service of Christ—the doctrine of God is constantly sacrificed to the apparent work of the gospel. Now, it is well to remember that true devotedness always starts from a point within which all godly claims are fully secured. If I hold a situation which demands my services from ten till four every day, I have no right to go out to visit or preach during those hours. If I am in business, I am bound to maintain the integrity of that business in a godly manner. I have no right to run hither and thither preaching while my business at home lies "in sixes and sevens," bringing great reproach on the holy doctrine of God. A man may say, I feel myself called to preach the gospel, and I find my situation, or my business, a clog. Well, *if you are divinely called and fitted* for the work of the gospel, and that you cannot combine the two things, then resign your situation, or wind up your business, in a godly manner, and go forth in the name of the Lord. But, clearly, so long as I hold a situation, or carry on a business, my work in the gospel must begin from a point within which the godly claims of such business or situation are fully responded to. This is devotedness: aught else is confusion, however well intended. Blessed be God, we have a perfect example before us in the life of the Lord Jesus, and ample guidance for the new man in the Word of God; so that we need not make any mistakes in the varied relationships which we may be called, in the providence of God, to fill, or as to the various claims which God's moral government has set up in connection with such relationships.

2. The second point in our theme is the mode in which the meat-offering was prepared. This was, as we read, by the action of fire—it was "baken in an oven," "baken in a pan," or "baken in a frying-pan." The process of baking suggests the idea of suffering. But inasmuch as the meat-offering is called "a sweet savor" (a term which is never applied to the sin-offering or trespass-offering), it is evident that there is no thought of suffering for sin—no thought of suffering the wrath of God on account of sin—no thought of suffering at the hand of Infinite Justice, as the sinner's substitute. The two ideas of "sweet savor" and suffering for sin are wholly incompatible according to the Levitical economy. It would completely destroy the type of the meat-offering were we to introduce into it the idea of suffering for sin.

In contemplating the *life* of the Lord Jesus, which, as we have already remarked, is the special subject foreshadowed in the meat-offering, we may notice three distinct kinds of suffering, namely, suffering for righteousness, suffering by the power of sympathy, and suffering in anticipation.

As the righteous Servant of God, He suffered in the midst of a scene in which all was contrary to Him; but this was the very

Christ of which His brethren according to the flesh knew nothing, on merely natural grounds! It was as true with respect to those brethren as any one else that "except a man be born again, he cannot see the kingdom of God." Mary would not have been saved by the mere fact of her being the mother of Jesus. She needed personal faith in Christ as much as any other member of Adam's fallen family: she needed to pass, by being born again, out of the old creation into the new. It was by treasuring up Christ's words in her heart that this blessed woman was saved. No doubt she was "highly favored" in being chosen as a vessel to such a holy office; but then, as a lost sinner, she needed to "rejoice in God her Saviour," like any one else. She stands on the same platform, is washed in the same blood, clothed in the same righteousness, and will sing the same song as all the rest of God's redeemed.

This simple fact will give additional force and clearness to a point already stated, namely, that incarnation was not Christ's taking our nature into union with Himself. This truth should be carefully pondered. It is fully brought out in 2 Cor. 5—"For the love of Christ constraineth us; because we thus judge, that if one died for all, then were all dead: and that He died for all, that they which live should not henceforth live unto themselves, but unto Him which died for them, and rose again. Wherefore henceforth know we no man after the flesh; yea, *though we have known Christ after the flesh, yet now henceforth know we Him no more.* Therefore if any man be *in Christ,* he is a new creation: old things are passed away; behold, all things are become new" (ver. 14-17).

opposite of suffering for sin. It is of the utmost importance to distinguish between these two kinds of suffering. The confounding of them must lead to serious error. Suffering as a righteous One standing amongst men on God's behalf is one thing, and suffering instead of man under the hand of God is quite another. The Lord Jesus suffered for righteousness during His *life:* He suffered for sin in His *death.* During His life, man and Satan did their utmost; and even at the cross they put forth all their powers; but when all that they could do was done—when they had traveled, in their deadly enmity, to the utmost limit of human and diabolical opposition, there lay, far beyond, a region of impenetrable gloom and horror into which the Sin-bearer had to travel, in the accomplishment of His work. During His life, He ever walked in the unclouded light of the divine countenance; but on the cursed tree, the dark shadow of sin intervened and shut out that light, and drew forth that mysterious cry, "My God, My God, why hast Thou forsaken Me?" This was a moment which stands absolutely alone in the annals of eternity. From time to time during the life of Christ down here, heaven had opened to give forth the expression of divine complacency in Him; but on the cross, God forsook Him, because He was making His soul an offering for sin. If Christ had been a sin-bearer all His life, then what was the difference between the cross and any other period? Why was He not forsaken of God during His entire course? What was the difference between Christ on the cross, and Christ on the holy mount of transfiguration? Was He forsaken of God on the mount? was He a sin-bearer there? These are very simple questions, which should be answered by those who maintain the idea of a life of sin-bearing.

The plain fact is this: there was nothing either in Christ's humanity or in the nature of His associations which could possibly connect Him with sin, or wrath, or death. He was "made sin" on the cross; and there He endured the wrath of God, and there He gave up His life, as an all-sufficient atonement for sin; but nothing of this finds a place in the meat-offering. True, we have the process of baking—the action of fire; but this is not the wrath of God. The meat-offering was not a a sin-offering, but a "sweet savor" offering. Thus, its import is definitely fixed; and, moreover, the intelligent interpretation of it must ever guard, with holy jealousy, the precious truth of Christ's spotless humanity, and the true nature of His associations. To make Him, by the necessity of His birth, a sin-bearer, or to place Him thereby under the curse of the law and the wrath of God, is to contradict the entire truth of God as to incarnation—truth announced by the angel, and repeated again and again by the inspired apostle. Moreover, it destroys the entire character and object of Christ's life, and robs the cross of its distinctive glory. It lowers the sense of what sin is, and of what atonement is. In one word, it removes the key-stone of the arch of revelation, and lays all in hopeless ruin and confusion around us.

But, again, the Lord Jesus suffered by the power of sympathy; and this character of suffering unfolds to us the deep secrets of His tender heart. Human sorrow and human misery ever touched a chord in that bosom of love. It was impossible that a perfect human heart could avoid feeling, according to its own divine sensibilities, the miseries which sin had entailed upon the human family. Though personally free both from the cause and the effect—though belonging to heaven, and living a perfect heavenly life on the earth, yet did He descend, by the power of an intense sympathy, into the deepest depths of human sorrow; yea, He felt the sorrow more keenly, by far, than those who were the direct subjects thereof, inasmuch as His humanity was perfect. Further, He was able to contemplate both the sorrow and its cause according to their just measure and character in the presence of God. He felt as none else could feel. His feelings, His affections, His sensibilities, His whole moral and mental constitution, were perfect; and hence none can tell what such an One must have suffered in passing through such a world as this. He beheld the human family struggling beneath the ponderous weight of guilt and wretchedness; He beheld the whole creation groaning under the yoke; the cry of the prisoner fell upon His ear; the tear of the widow met His view; bereavement and poverty touched His sensitive heart; sickness and death made Him "groan in the spirit"; His sympathetic sufferings were beyond all human conception.

I shall quote a passage illustrative of that character of suffering to which we are now referring: "When the even was come, they brought unto Him many that were possessed with devils; and He cast out the spirits with His word, and healed all that were sick; that it might be fulfilled which was spoken by Esaias the prophet, saying, *'Himself took our infirmities and bare our sicknesses'* " (Matt. 8:16-17). This was entirely sympathetic—the power of fellow-feeling, which in Him was perfect. He had no sicknesses or infirmities of His own. Those things which are sometimes spoken of as "sinless infirmities," were, in His case, but the evidences of a veritable, a real, a perfect manhood. But by sympathy—by perfect fellow-feeling, "He *took* our infirmities, and *bare* our sicknesses." None but a perfect man could have done this. We may feel for and with each other, but only Jesus could make human infirmity and sickness His own.

Now, had He been bearing all these things by the necessity of His birth, or of His relations with Israel and the human family, we should have lost all the beauty and preciousness of His voluntary sympathy. There could be no room for voluntary action when absolute necessity was laid upon Him. But, on the other hand, when we see His entire freedom, both personally and relatively, from human misery and that which produced it, we can enter into that perfect grace and compassion which led Him to "take our infirmities, and bear our sicknesses," in the power of true sympathy. There is, therefore, a very manifest difference between Christ's suffering as a voluntary sympathizer with human misery, and His sufferings as the sinner's substitute. The former are apparent throughout His entire *life;* the latter are confined to His *death.*

Finally, we have to consider Christ's sufferings by anticipation. We find the dark shadow of the cross casting itself athwart His path, and producing a very keen order of suffering, which, however, must be as clearly distinguished from His atoning suffering as either His suffering for righteousness or His suffering by sympathy. Let us take a passage in proof—"And He came out, and went, as He was wont, to the mount of Olives; and His disciples also followed Him. And when He was at the place, He said unto them, 'Pray that ye enter not into temptation.' And He was withdrawn from them about a stone's cast, and kneeled down, and prayed, saying, 'Father, if Thou be willing, remove this cup from Me: nevertheless not My will, but Thine, but done.' And there appeared an angel unto Him from heaven, strengthening Him. And being in an agony, He prayed more earnestly: and His sweat was as it were great drops of blood falling down to the ground" (Luke 22:39-44). Again, we read, "And He took with Him Peter and the two sons of Zebedee, and began to be sorrowful and very heavy. Then saith He unto them, 'My soul is exceeding sorrowful, even unto death: tarry ye here, and watch with Me.' . . . He went away again the second time, and prayed, saying, 'O My Father, if this cup may not pass from Me, except I drink it, Thy will be done' " (Matt. 26:37-42).

From these verses, it is evident there was a something in prospect which the blessed Lord had never encountered before—there was a "cup" being filled out for Him of which He had not yet drunk. If He had been a sin-bearer all His life, then why this intense "agony" at the thought of coming in contact with sin and enduring the wrath of God on account of sin? What was the difference between Christ in Gethsemane and Christ at Calvary if He were a sin-bearer all His life? There was a material difference; but it is because He was not a sin-bearer all His life. What is the difference? In Gethsemane, He was *anticipating* the cross; at Calvary, He was actually *enduring* it. In Gethsemane, "there appeared an angel unto Him from heaven, strengthening Him"; at Calvary, He was forsaken of all. There was no angelic ministry there. In Gethsemane, He addresses God as *"Father,"* thus enjoying the full communion of that ineffable relationship; but at Calvary, He cries, "My *God,* My *God,* why hast Thou forsaken Me?" Here the Sin-bearer looks up and beholds the throne of Eternal Justice enveloped in dark clouds, and the countenance of Inflexible Holiness averted from Him, because He was being "made sin for us."

The reader will, I trust, find no difficulty in examining this subject for himself. He will be able to trace, in detail, the three characters of the *life*-sufferings of our blessed Lord, and to distinguish between them and His *death*-sufferings—His sufferings for sin. He will see how that when man and Satan had done their utmost, there yet remained a character of suffering which was perfectly unique, namely, suffering at the hand of God on account of sin—suffering as the sinner's substitute. Until He came to the cross, He could ever look up and bask in the clear light of His Father's countenance; in the darkest hour, He found a sure resource above. His path down here was a rough one. How could it be otherwise, in a world where all was directly contrary to His pure and holy nature? He had to "endure the contradiction of sinners against Himself;" He had to endure "the reproach of them that reproached God." What had He not to endure? He was misunderstood, misinterpreted, abused, maligned, accused of being mad, and of having a devil. He was betrayed, denied, deserted, mocked, buffeted, spit upon, crowned with thorns, cast out, condemned, and nailed between two malefactors. All these things He endured at the hand of man, together with all the unutterable terrors which Satan brought to bear upon His spirit; but, let it be once more emphatically repeated, when man and Satan had exhausted their power and enmity, our blessed Lord and Saviour had to endure a something compared with which all the rest was as nothing, and that was the hiding of God's countenance—the three hours of darkness and awful gloom, during which He suffered what none but God could know.

Now, when Scripture speaks of our having fellowship with Christ's sufferings, it refers simply to His sufferings for righteousness—His sufferings at the hand of man. Christ suffered for sin that we might not have to suffer for it; He endured the wrath of God that we might not have to endure it (this is the ground of our peace); but as regards suffering from man, we shall always find that the more faithfully we follow in the footsteps of Christ, the more we shall suffer in this respect; but this is a matter of gift, a matter of privilege, a favor, a dignity (see Phil. 1:29-30). To walk in the footsteps of Christ—to enjoy companionship with Him—to be thrown into a place of sympathy with Him, are privileges of the very highest order. Would that we all entered more fully into them! But, alas! we are too well content to do without them—too well satisified, like Peter, to "follow afar off"—to keep aloof from a despised and suffering Christ. All this is, undoubtedly, our heavy loss. Had we only more fellowship with His sufferings, the crown would glisten far more brightly in our soul's vision. When we shrink from fellowship with Christ's sufferings, we rob ourselves of the deep joy of His present companionship, and also of the moral power of the hope of His future glory.

3. Having considered the ingredients which composed the meat-offering, and the various forms in which it was presented, it only remains for us to refer to the persons who partook of it. These were the head and members of the priestly house. "And that which is left of the meat-offering shall be Aaron's and his sons': It is a thing most holy of the offerings of the Lord made by fire" (ver. 10). As in the burnt-offering we observed the sons of Aaron introduced as types of all true believers, not as convicted sinners, but as worshiping priests; so in the meat-offering we find them feeding upon the remnant of that which had been laid, as it were, on the table of the God of Israel. This was a high and holy privilege. None but priests could enjoy it. This is set forth with great distinctness in "the law of the meat-offering," which I shall here quote at length. "And this is the law of the meat-offering: The sons of Aaron shall offer

it before the Lord, before the altar. And he shall take of it his handful, of the flour of the meat-offering, and of the oil thereof, and *all the frankincense* which is upon the meat-offering, and shall burn it upon the altar for a sweet savor, even the memorial of it, unto the Lord. And the remainder thereof shall Aaron and his sons eat: *with unleavened bread* shall it be eaten *in the holy place;* in the court of the tabernacle of the congregation they shall eat it. It shall not be baken with leaven. I have given it unto them for their portion of My offerings made by fire; it is most holy, as is the sin-offering, and as the trespass-offering. *All the males* among the children of Aaron shall eat of it. It shall be a statute forever in your generations concerning the offerings of the Lord made by fire: *every one that toucheth them shall be holy*" (Lev. 6:14-18).

Here, then, we are furnished with a beauteous figure of the Church feeding "in the holy place," in the power of practical holiness, upon the perfections of "the Man Christ Jesus." This is our portion, through the grace of God; but, we must remember, it is to be eaten "with unleavened bread." We cannot feed upon Christ if we are indulging in any thing evil. "Every one that toucheth them shall be holy." Moreover, it must be "in the holy place." Our position, our practice, our persons, our associations, must be holy ere we can feed upon the meat-offering. Finally, it is "all the males among the children of Aaron shall eat of it." That is to say, real priestly energy, according to the divine idea of it, is required in order to enjoy this holy portion. Aaron's *"sons"* set forth the idea of *energy* in priestly action: his *"daughters," feebleness* therein (compare Num. 18:8-13). There were some things which the sons could eat which the daughters could not. Our hearts should earnestly desire the highest measure of priestly energy, so that we may discharge the highest priestly functions, and partake of the highest order of priestly food.

In conclusion, let me add, that inasmuch as we are made, through grace, "partakers of the divine nature," we can, if living in the energy of that nature, walk in the footsteps of Him who is foreshadowed in the meat-offering. If only we are self-emptied, our every act may emit a sweet odor to God. The smallest as well as the greatest services may, by the power of the Holy Ghost, present the fragrance of Christ. The paying of a visit, the writing of a letter, the public ministry of the Word, giving a cup of cold water to a disciple, giving a penny to a pauper, yea, the commonplace acts of eating and drinking—all may emit the sweet perfume of the name and grace of Jesus.

So also, if only nature be kept in the place of death, there may be in us the exhibition of that which is not corruptible, even a conversation seasoned with the "salt" of abiding communion with God. But in all these things we fail and come short; we grieve the Holy Spirit of God in our ways. We are prone to self-seeking or men-pleasing in our very best services, and we fail to "season" our conversation. Hence our constant deficiency in the "oil," the "frankincense," and the "salt"; while, at the same time, there is the tendency to suffer the "leaven" or the "honey" of nature to make its appearance. There has been but one perfect "meat-offering"; and, blessed be God, we are accepted in Him. We are the "sons" of the true Aaron; our place is in the sanctuary, where we can feed upon the holy portion. Happy place! Happy portion! May we enjoy them more than ever we have done! May our retirement of heart from all but Christ be more profound! May our gaze at Him be so intense that we shall have no heart for the attractions of the scene around us, nor yet for the ten thousand petty circumstances in our path which would fret the heart and perplex the mind! May we rejoice in Christ in the sunshine and in the darkness; when the gentle breezes of summer play around us, and when the storms of winter rage fiercely abroad; when passing over the surface of a placid lake, or tossed on the bosom of a stormy ocean. Thank God, "we have found Him" who is to be our satisfying portion forever! We shall spend eternity dwelling upon the divine perfections of the Lord Jesus. Our eyes shall never be averted from Him when once we have seen

Him as He is.

May the Spirit of God work mightily in us, to strengthen us "in the inner man"! May He enable us to feed upon that perfect Meat-offering, the memorial of which has been fed upon by God Himself! This is our holy and happy privilege. May we realize it yet more fully!

---

## *CHAPTER 3*

THE more closely we contemplate the offerings, the more fully do we see how that no one offering furnishes a complete view of Christ. It is only by putting all together that any thing like a just idea can be formed. Each offering, as might be expected, has features peculiar to itself. The peace-offering differs from the burnt-offering in many points, and a clear understanding of the points in which any one type differs from the others will be found to help much in the apprehension of its special import.

Thus, in comparing the peace-offering with the burnt-offering, we find that the threefold action of "flaying," "cutting it into its pieces," and "washing the inwards and legs" is entirely omitted; and this is quite in character. In the burnt-offering, as we have seen, we find Christ offering Himself to and accepted by God; and hence the completeness of His self-surrender, and also the searching process to which He submitted Himself, had to be typified. In the peace-offering, the leading thought is the communion of the worshiper. It is not Christ as enjoyed exclusively by God, but as enjoyed by the worshiper in communion with God; therefore it is that the whole line of action is less intense. No heart, be its love ever so elevated, could possibly rise to the height of Christ's devotedness to God, or of God's acceptance of Christ. None but God Himself could duly note the pulsations of that heart which throbbed in the bosom of Jesus; and therefore a type was needed to set forth that one feature of Christ's death, namely, His perfect devotedness therein to God. This type we have in the burnt-offering, in which alone we observe the threefold action above referred to.

So also in reference to the character of the sacrifice. In the burnt-offering, it should be "a male without blemish"; whereas in the peace-offering, it might be "a male or female," though equally "without blemish." The nature of Christ, whether we view Him as enjoyed exclusively by God, or by the worshiper in fellowship with God, must ever be one and the same; there can be no alteration in that. The only reason why "a female" was permitted in the peace-offering, was because it was a question of the worshiper's capacity to enjoy that blessed One, who, in Himself, is "the same yesterday, to-day, and forever" (Heb. 13).

Again, in the burnt-offering, we read, "The priest shall burn *all*"; whereas in the peace-offering, *a part* only was burnt, that is, "the fat, the kidneys, and the caul." This makes it exceedingly simple. The most excellent portion of the sacrifice was laid on God's altar. The inward parts—the hidden energies—the tender sensibilities of the blessed Jesus, were devoted to God, as the only One who could perfectly enjoy them. Aaron and his sons fed upon "the wave breast" and "the heave shoulder"* (see, carefully, Lev. 7:28-36). All the members of the priestly family, in communion with their head, had their proper portion of the peace-offering; and now, all true believers constituted, by grace, priests unto God, can feed upon the *affections* and the *strength* of the true Peace-offering,—can enjoy the happy assurance of having His loving heart and powerful shoulder to comfort and sustain them continually.** "This is the portion of the anointing of Aaron, and of the anointing of his sons, out of the

*The "breast" and the "shoulder" are emblematical of love and power—strength and affection.

**There is much force and beauty in verse 31—"The breast shall be Aaron's and his sons'." It is the privilege of all true believers to feed upon the affections of Christ—the changeless love of that heart which beats with a deathless and changeless love for them.

offerings of the Lord made by fire, in the day when he presented them to minister unto the Lord in the priest's office; which the Lord commanded to be given them of the children of Israel, in the day that He anointed them by a statute forever throughout their generations" (chap. 7:35-36).

All these are important points of difference between the burnt-offering and the peace-offering, and when taken together, they set the two offerings with great clearness before the mind. There is something more in the peace-offering than the abstract devotedness of Christ to the will of God. The worshiper is introduced; and that not merely as a spectator, but as a participator—not merely to gaze, but to feed. This gives very marked character to this offering. When I look at the Lord Jesus in the burnt-offering, I see Him as One whose heart was devoted to the one object of glorifying God and accomplishing His will; but when I see Him in the peace-offering, I find One who has a place in His loving heart and on His powerful shoulder for a worthless, helpless sinner. In the burnt-offering, the breast and shoulder, legs and inwards, head and fat, were all burnt on the altar—all went up as a sweet savor to God; but in the peace-offering, the very portion that suits me is left for me. Nor am I left to feed in solitude on that which meets my individual need. By no means. I feed in communion—in communion with God, and in communion with my fellow-priests. I feed in the full and happy intelligence that the self-same sacrifice which feeds my soul has already refreshed the heart of God; and, moreover, that the same portion which feeds me feeds all my fellow-worshipers. Communion is the order here—communion with God—the communion of saints. There was no such thing as isolation in the peace-offering. God had His portion, and so had the priestly family.

Thus it is in connection with the Antitype of the peace-offering. The very same Jesus who is the object of Heaven's delight, is the spring of joy, of strength, and of comfort to every believing heart; and not only to every heart in particular, but also to the whole Church of God in fellowship. God, in His exceeding grace, has given His people the very same object that He has Himself. "Truly our fellowship is with the Father, and with His Son Jesus Christ" (1 John 1). True, our thoughts of Jesus can never rise to the height of God's thoughts. Our estimation of such an object must ever fall far short of His; and hence, in the type, the house of Aaron could not partake of the fat. But though we can never rise to the standard of the divine estimation of Christ's Person and sacrifice, it is nevertheless the same object we are occupied with, and therefore the house of Aaron had "the wave breast and the heave shoulder." All this is replete with comfort and joy to the heart. The Lord Jesus Christ, the One "who was dead, but is alive for evermore," is now the exclusive object before the eye and thoughts of God; and, in perfect grace, He has given unto us a portion in the same blessed and all-glorious Person. Christ is our object too—the object of our hearts and the theme of our song. "Having made peace by the blood of His cross," He ascended into heaven, and sent down the Holy Ghost, that "other Comforter," by whose powerful ministrations we feed upon "the breast and shoulder" of our divine "Peace-offering." He is indeed our peace; and it is our exceeding joy to know that such is God's delight in the establishment of our peace, that the sweet odor of our Peace-offering has refreshed His heart. This imparts a peculiar charm to this type. Christ as the Burnt-offering commands the admiration of the heart; Christ as the Peace-offering establishes the peace of the conscience, and meets the deep and manifold necessities of the soul. The sons of Aaron might stand around the altar of burnt-offering; they might behold the flame of that offering ascending to the God of Israel; they might see the sacrifice reduced to ashes; they might, in view of all this, bow their heads and worship; but they carried naught away for themselves. Not so in the peace-offering. In it, they not only beheld that which was capable of emitting a sweet odor to God, but also of yielding a most substantial portion for themselves, on which they could feed in happy and holy fellowship.

Assuredly it heightens the enjoyment of every true priest to know that God (to use the language of our type) has had His portion ere he gets the breast and the shoulder. The thought of this gives tone and energy, unction and elevation, to the worship and communion; it unfolds the amazing grace of Him who has given us the same object, the same theme, the same joy with Himself. Nothing lower—nothing less than this could satisfy Him. The Father will have the prodigal feeding upon the fatted calf, in fellowship with Himself. He will not assign him a lower place than at His own table, nor any other portion than that on which He feeds Himself. The language of the peace-offering is, "It is meet that *we* should make merry and be glad"—"Let *us* eat and be merry." Such is the precious grace of God! No doubt we have reason to be glad, as being the partakers of such grace; but when we can hear the blessed God saying, "Let *us* eat and be merry," it should call forth from our hearts a continual stream of praise and thanksgiving. God's joy in the salvation of sinners, and His joy in the communion of saints, may well elicit the admiration of men and angels throughout eternity.

Having thus compared the peace-offering with the burnt-offering, we may now briefly glance at it in connection with the meat-offering. The leading point of difference here is, that in the peace-offering there was blood-shedding, and in the meat-offering there was not. They were both "sweet savor" offerings; and, as we learn from chap. 7:12, the two offerings were very intimately associated. Now, both the connection and the contrast are full of meaning and instruction.

It is only in communion with God that the soul can delight itself in contemplating the perfect humanity of the Lord Jesus Christ. God the Holy Ghost must *impart,* as He must also *direct,* by the Word, the vision by which we can gaze on "the Man Christ Jesus." He might have been revealed "in the likeness of sinful flesh"—He might have lived and labored on this earth—He might have shone amid the darkness of this world in all the heavenly lustre and beauty which belonged to His Person—He might have passed rapidly, like a brilliant luminary, across this world's horizon—and all the while have been beyond the range of the sinner's vision.

Man could not enter into the deep joy of communion with all this, simply because there would be no basis laid down on which this communion might rest. In the peace-offering, this necessary basis is fully and clearly established. "He shall lay his hand upon the head of his offering, and kill it at the door of the tabernacle of the congregation: and Aaron's sons, the priests, shall sprinkle the blood upon the altar round about" (chap. 3:2). Here, we have that which the meat-offering does not supply, namely, a solid foundation for the worshiper's communion with all the fullness, the preciousness, and the beauty of Christ, so far as he, by the gracious energy of the Holy Ghost, is enabled to enter thereinto. Standing on the platform which "the precious blood of Christ" provides, we can range, with tranquilized hearts and worshiping spirits, throughout all the wondrous scenes of the manhood of the Lord Jesus Christ. Had we naught save the meat-offering aspect of Christ, we should lack the title by which, and the ground on which, we can contemplate and enjoy Him therein. If there were no blood-shedding, there could be no title—no standing-place for the sinner. But Leviticus 7:12 links the meat-offering with the peace-offering, and, by so doing, teaches us, that, when our souls have found peace, we can delight in the One who has "made peace," and who is "our peace."

But let it be distinctly understood that while in the peace-offering we have the shedding and sprinkling of blood, yet sin-bearing is not the thought. When we view Christ in the peace-offering, He does not stand before us as the bearer of our sins, as in the sin and trespass offerings, but (having borne them) as the ground of our peaceful and happy fellowship with God. If sin-bearing were in question, it could not be said, "It is an offering made by fire, of a sweet savor unto the Lord" (chap. 3:5, comp. with chap. 4:10-12). Still, though sin-bearing is not the thought, there is full provision for one who knows himself to be a sinner, else he could not have any portion therein. To have fellowship with God, we must be "in the light"; and how can we be there? Only on the ground of that precious statement—"The blood of Jesus Christ His Son cleanseth us from *all* sin" (1 John 1). The more we abide in the light, the deeper will be our sense of every thing which is contrary to that light; and the deeper, also, our sense of the value of that blood which entitles us to be there. The more closely we walk with God, the more we shall know of "the unsearchable riches of Christ."

It is most needful to be established in the truth that we are in the presence of God only as the partakers of divine life, and as standing in divine righteousness. The father could only have the prodigal at his table clothed in "the best robe," and in all the integrity of that relationship in which he viewed him. Had the prodigal been left in his rags, or placed "as a hired servant" in the house, we never should have heard those glorious words, "Let us eat and be merry: for this *my son* was dead, and is alive again; he was lost, and is found." Thus it is with all true believers. Their old nature is not recognized as existing before God. He counts it dead, and so should they. It is dead to God, dead to faith. It must be kept in the place of death. It is not by improving our old nature that we get into the divine presence, but as the possessors of a new nature. It was not by repairing the rags of his former condition that the prodigal got a place at the father's table, but by being clothed in a robe which he had never seen or thought of before. He did not bring this robe with him from the "far country," neither did he provide it as he came along; but the father had it for him in the house. The prodigal did not make it, or help to make it; but the father provided it for him, and rejoiced to see it on him. Thus it was they sat down together, to feed in happy fellowship upon "the fatted calf."

I shall now proceed to quote at length "the law of the sacrifice of peace-offering," in which we shall find some additional points of much interest—points which belong peculiarly to itself. "And this is the law of the sacrifice of peace-offerings, which he shall offer unto the Lord: If he offer it for a thanksgiving, then he shall offer with the sacrifice of thanksgiving unleavened cakes mingled with oil, and unleavened wafers anointed with oil, and cakes mingled with oil, of fine flour, fried. Besides the cakes, he shall offer for his offering leavened bread with the sacrifice of thanksgiving of his peace-offerings. And of it he shall offer one out of the whole oblation for a heave-offering unto the Lord, and it shall be the priest's that sprinkleth the blood of the peace-offerings. And the flesh of the sacrifice of his peace-offerings for thanksgiving shall be eaten the same day that it is offered; he shall not leave any of it until the morning. But if the sacrifice of his offering be a vow, or a voluntary offering, it shall be eaten the same day that he offereth his sacrifice; and on the morrow also the remainder of it shall be eaten; but the remainder of the flesh of the sacrifice on the third day shall be burnt with fire. And if any of the flesh of the sacrifice of his peace-offerings be eaten at all on the third day, it shall not be accepted, neither shall it be imputed unto him that offereth it: it shall be an abomination, and the soul that eateth of it shall bear his iniquity. And the flesh that toucheth any unclean thing shall not be eaten; it shall be burnt with fire: and as for the flesh, all that be clean shall eat thereof. But the soul that eateth of the flesh of the sacrifice of peace-offerings, that pertain unto the Lord, having his uncleanness upon him, even that soul shall be cut off from his people. Moreover the soul that shall touch any unclean thing, as the uncleanness of man, or any unclean beast, or any abominable unclean thing, and eat of the flesh of the sacrifice of peace-offerings, which pertain unto the Lord, even that soul shall be cut off from his people" (Lev. 7:11-21).

It is of the utmost importance that we accurately distinguish between sin *in the flesh* and sin *on the conscience.* If we confound these two, our souls must necessarily be unhinged, and our worship marred. An attentive consideration of 1 John 1:8-10 will throw much light upon this subject, the understanding of which is so essential to a due appreciation of the entire doctrine of the peace-offering, and more especially of that point therein at which we have now arrived. There is no one who will be so conscious of indwelling sin as the man who walks in the light. "If we say that we have *no sin,* we deceive ourselves, and the truth is not in us." In the verse immediately preceding, we read, "The blood of Jesus Christ His Son cleanseth us from *all sin.*" Here, the distinction between sin *in* us and sin *on* us is fully brought out and established. To say that there is sin on the believer, in the presence of God, is to call in question the purging efficacy of the blood of Jesus, and to deny the truth of the divine record. If the blood of Jesus can perfectly purge, then the believer's conscience is perfectly purged. The Word of God thus puts the matter; and we must ever remember that it is from God Himself we are to learn what the true condition of the believer is in His sight. We are more disposed to be occupied in telling God what we are in ourselves, than to allow Him to tell us what we are in Christ. In other words, we are more taken up with our own self-consciousness than with God's revelation of Himself. God speaks to us on the ground of what He is in Himself, and of what He has accomplished in Christ. Such is the nature and character of His revelation, of which faith takes hold, and thus fills the soul with perfect peace. God's revelation is one thing; my consciousness is quite another.

But the same Word which tells us we have no sin *on* us, tells us, with equal force and clearness, that we have sin *in* us. "If we say that we have no sin, we deceive ourselves, and the truth is not in us." Every one who has "truth" in him, will know that he has "*sin*" in him likewise; for truth reveals every thing as it is. What, then, are we to do? It is our privilege so to walk in the power of the new nature, that the "*sin*" which dwells in us may not manifest itself in the form of "*sins.*" The Christian's position is one of victory and liberty. He is not only delivered from the guilt of sin, but also from sin as a ruling principle in his life. "Knowing this, that our old man is crucified with Him, that the body of sin might be destroyed, that henceforth we should not serve sin. For he that is dead is freed from sin. . . . Let not sin therefore *reign* in your mortal body, that ye should *obey it* in the lusts thereof. . . . For sin shall not have dominion over you; for ye are not under the law, but under grace" (Rom. 6:6-14). Sin is there in all its native vileness; but the believer is "dead to it." How? He died in Christ. By nature, he was dead *in* sin: by grace, he is dead *to* it. What claim can any thing or any one have upon a dead man? None whatever. Christ "died unto sin once," and the believer died in Him. "Now if we be dead with Christ, we believe that we shall also live with Him: knowing that Christ being raised from the dead dieth no more; death hath no more dominion over Him. For in that He died, He died unto sin once; but in that He liveth, He liveth unto God." What is the result of this in reference to believers? "*Likewise* reckon ye also yourselves to be *dead indeed unto sin,* but alive unto God through Jesus Christ our Lord." Such is the believer's unalterable position before God! so that it is his holy privilege to enjoy freedom from sin as a *ruler* over him, though it be a *dweller* in him.

But then, "if any man sin," what is to be done? The inspired apostle furnishes a full and most blessed answer: "If we confess our sins, He is faithful and just to forgive us our sins, and to cleanse us from all unrighteousness" (1 John 1:9). Confession is the mode in which the conscience is to be kept free. The apostle does not say, If we pray for pardon, He is gracious and merciful to forgive us. No doubt it is ever happy for a child to breathe the sense of need into his father's ear—to tell him of feebleness, to confess folly, infirmity, and failure. All this is most true: moreover, it is equally true that our Father is most gracious and merciful to meet His children in all their weakness and ignorance; but, while all this is true, the Holy Ghost declares, by the apostle, that "if we *confess,*" God is *"faithful* and *just* to forgive." Confession, therefore, is the divine mode. A Christian, having erred, in thought, word, or deed, might pray for pardon for days and months together, and not have any assurance, from 1 John 1:9, that he was forgiven; whereas the moment he truly confesses his sin before God, it is a simple matter of faith to know that he is perfectly forgiven and perfectly cleansed.

There is an immense moral difference between praying for forgiveness and confessing our sins, whether we look at it in reference to the character of God, the sacrifice of Christ, or the condition of the soul. It is quite possible that a person's prayer may involve the confession of his sin, whatever it may happen to be, and thus come to the same thing; but then it is always well to keep close to Scripture in what we think and say and do. It must be evident that when the Holy Ghost speaks of *confession,* He does not mean *praying;* and it is equally evident that He knows there are moral elements in, and practical results flowing out of, confession, which do not belong to prayer. In point of fact, one has often found that a habit of importuning God for the forgiveness of sins displayed ignorance as to the way in which God has revealed Himself in the Person and work of Christ, as to the relation in which the sacrifice of Christ has set the believer, and as to the divine mode of getting the conscience relieved from the burden and purified from the soil of sin.

God has been perfectly satisfied as to all the believer's sins in the cross of Christ. On that cross, a full atonement was presented for every jot and tittle of sin in the believer's nature and on his conscience. Hence, therefore, God does not need any further propitiation. He does not need aught to draw His heart toward the believer. We do not require to supplicate Him to be "faithful and just," when His faithfulness and justice have been so gloriously displayed, vindicated, and answered in the death of Christ. Our sins can never come into God's presence, inasmuch as Christ, who bore them all and put them away, is there instead. But if we sin, conscience will feel it—must feel it; yea, the Holy Ghost will make us feel it. He cannot allow so much as a single light thought to pass unjudged. What then? Has our sin made its way into the presence of God? Has it found its place in the unsullied light of the inner sanctuary? God forbid! The "Advocate" is there—"Jesus Christ the righteous," to maintain, in unbroken integrity, the relationship in which we stand. But though sin cannot affect God's thoughts in reference to us, it can and does affect our thoughts in reference to Him;* though it cannot make its way into His presence, it can make its way into ours, in a most distressing and humiliating manner; though it cannot hide the Advocate from God's view, it can hide Him from ours. It gathers, like a thick, dark cloud, on our spiritual horizon, so that our souls cannot bask in the blessed beams of our Father's countenance. It cannot affect our relationship with God, but it can very seriously affect our enjoyment thereof. What, therefore, are we to do? The Word answers, "If we confess our sins, He is faithful and just to forgive us our sins, and to cleanse us from all unrighteousness." By confession, we get our conscience cleared, the sweet sense of relationship restored, the dark cloud dispersed, the chilling, withering influence removed, our thoughts of God set straight. Such is the divine method; and we may truly say that the heart that knows what it is to have ever been in the place of confession, will feel the divine power of the apostle's words—"My little children, these things write I unto you, *that ye sin not*" (1 John 2:1).

Then, again, there is a style of praying for forgiveness which involves a losing sight of the perfect ground of forgiveness which has been laid in the sacrifice of the cross. If God forgives sins, He must be "faithful and just"

*The reader will bear in mind that the subject treated of in the text leaves wholly untouched the important and most practical truth taught in John 14:21-23, namely, the peculiar love of the Father for an obedient child, and the special communion of such a child with the Father and the Son. May this truth be written on all our hearts, by the pen of God the Holy Ghost!

in so doing; but it is quite clear that our prayers, be they ever so sincere and earnest, could not form the basis of God's faithfulness and justice in forgiving us our sins. Naught save the work of the cross could do this. There, the faithfulness and justice of God have had their fullest establishment, and that, too, in immediate reference to our actual sins, as well as to the root thereof in our nature. God has already judged our sins in the Person of our Substitute "on the tree"; and, in the act of confession, we judge ourselves. This is essential to divine forgiveness and restoration. The very smallest unconfessed, unjudged sin on the conscience will entirely mar our communion with God. Sin *in* us need not do this; but if we suffer sin to remain *on* us, we cannot have fellowship with God. He has put away our sins in such manner as that He can have us in His presence; and so long as we abide in His presence, sin does not trouble us; but if we get out of His presence, and commit sin, even in thought, our communion must, of necessity, be suspended, until, by confession, we have got rid of the sin. All this, I need hardly add, is founded exclusively upon the perfect sacrifice and righteous advocacy of the Lord Jesus Christ.

Finally, as to the difference between prayer and confession, as respects the condition of the heart before God, and its moral sense of the hatefulness of sin, it cannot possibly be over-estimated. It is a much easier thing to ask, in a general way, for the forgiveness of our sins than to confess those sins. Confession involves *self-judgment;* asking for forgiveness may not, and, in itself, does not. This alone would be sufficient to point out the difference. Self-judgment is one of the most valuable and healthful exercises of the Christian life, and therefore any thing which produces it must be highly esteemed by every earnest Christian.

The difference between asking for pardon and confessing the sin is continually exemplified in dealing with children. If a child has done any thing wrong, he finds much less difficulty in asking his father to forgive him than in openly and unreservedly confessing the wrong. In asking for forgiveness, the child may have in his mind a number of things which tend to lessen the sense of the evil,—he may be secretly thinking that he was not so much to blame after all, though, to be sure, it is only proper to ask his father to forgive him; whereas, in confessing the wrong, there is just the one thing, and that is, self-judgment. Further, in asking for forgiveness, the child may be influenced mainly by a desire to escape the consequences of his wrong; whereas, a judicious parent will seek to produce a just sense of its moral evil, which can only exist in connection with the full confession of the fault—in connection with self-judgment.

Thus it is, in reference to God's dealings with His children when they do wrong. He must have the whole thing brought out and thoroughly judged. He will make us not only dread the consequences of sin (which are unutterable), but hate the thing itself, because of its hatefulness in His sight. Were it possible for us, when we commit sin, to be forgiven merely for the asking, our sense of sin and our shrinking from it would not be nearly so intense, and, as a consequence, our estimate of the fellowship with which we are blessed would not be nearly so high. The moral effect of all this upon the general tone of our spiritual constitution, and also upon our whole character and practical career, must be obvious to every experienced Christian.*

This entire train of thought is intimately connected with, and fully borne out by, two leading principles laid down in "the law of the peace-offering."

In verse 13 of the seventh of Leviticus we

*The case of Simon Magus, in Acts 8, may present a difficulty to the reader. But of him it is sufficient to say that one "in the gall of bitterness and in the bond of iniquity" could never be set forth as a model for God's dear children. His case in no wise interferes with the doctrine of 1 John 1:9. He was not in the relationship of a child, and, as a consequence, was not a subject of the advocacy. I would further add, that the subject of the Lord's prayer is by no means involved in what is stated above. I wish to confine myself to the immediate passage under consideration. We must ever avoid laying down iron rules. A soul may cry to God under any circumstances, and ask for what it needs: He is ever ready to hear and answer.

read, "He shall offer for his offering *leavened* bread"; and yet at verse 20 we read, "But the soul that eateth of the flesh of the sacrifice of peace-offerings, that pertain unto the Lord, having his uncleanness *upon* him, even that soul shall be cut off from his people." Here, we have the two things clearly set before us, namely, sin *in* us and sin *on* us. "Leaven" was permitted, because there was sin in the worshiper's nature; "uncleanness" was forbidden, because there should be no sin on the worshiper's conscience. If sin be in question, communion must be out of the question. God has met and provided for the sin, which He knows to be in us, by the blood of atonement; and hence, of the leavened bread in the peace-offering, we read, "Of it he shall offer one out of the whole oblation for a heave offering unto the Lord, and it shall be *the priest's that sprinkleth the blood of the peace-offerings*" (ver. 14). In other words, the "leaven" in the worshiper's nature was perfectly met by the "blood" of the sacrifice. The priest who gets the leavened bread must be the sprinkler of the blood. God has put our sin out of His sight forever. Though it be in us, it is not the object on which His eye rests. He sees only the blood, and therefore He can go on with us, and allow us the most unhindered fellowship with Him. But if we allow the *"sin"* which is in us to develop itself in the shape of *"sins,"* there must be confession, forgiveness, and cleansing ere we can again eat of the flesh of the Peace-offering. The cutting off of the worshiper because of ceremonial uncleanness, answers to the suspension of the believer's communion now because of unconfessed sin. To attempt to have fellowship with God in our sins would involve the blasphemous insinuation that He could walk in companionship with sin. "If we say that we have fellowship with Him, and walk in darkness, we lie, and do not the truth" (1 John 1:6).

In the light of the foregoing line of truth, we may easily see how much we err when we imagine it to be a mark of spirituality to be occupied with our sins. Could sin or sins ever be the ground or material of our communion with God? Assuredly not. We have just seen that, so long as sin is the object before us, communion must be interrupted. Fellowship can only be "in the light;" and, undoubtedly, there is no sin in the light. There is naught to be seen there save the blood which has put our sins away and brought us nigh, and the Advocate which keeps us nigh. Sin has been forever obliterated from that platform on which God and the worshiper stand in hallowed fellowship. What was it which constituted the material of communion between the father and the prodigal? Was it the rags of the latter? Was it the husks of "the far country"? By no means. It was not any thing that the prodigal brought with him: it was the rich provision of the father's love—"the fatted calf." Thus it is with God and every true worshiper. They feed together, in holy and elevated communion, upon Him whose precious blood has brought them into everlasting association, in that light to which no sin can ever approach.

Nor need we, for an instant, suppose that true humility is either evidenced or promoted by looking at or dwelling upon our sins. An unhallowed and melancholy mopishness may thus be superinduced; but the deepest humility springs from a totally different source. Whether was the prodigal a humbler man "when he came to himself" in the far country, or when he came to the father's bosom and the father's house? Is it not evident that the grace which elevates us to the loftiest heights of fellowship with God is that alone which leads us into the most profound depths of a genuine humility? Unquestionably. The humility which springs from the removal of our sins must ever be deeper than that which springs from the discovery of them. The former connects us with God: the latter has to do with self. The way to be truly humble is to walk with God in the intelligence and power of the relationship in which He has set us. He has made us His children; and if only we walk as such, we shall be humble.

Ere leaving this part of our subject, I would offer a remark as to the Lord's Supper, which, as being a prominent act of the Church's communion, may, with strict propriety, be looked at in connection with the doctrine of the peace-offering. The intelligent celebration of the Lord's Supper must ever depend upon the recognition of its purely eucharistic or thanksgiving character. It is very especially a feast of thanksgiving—thanksgiving for an accomplished redemption. "The cup of blessing which we bless, is it not the communion of the blood of Christ? The bread which we break, is it not the communion of the body of Christ?" (1 Cor. 10:16) Hence, a soul bowed down under the heavy burden of sin cannot, with spiritual intelligence, eat the Lord's Supper, inasmuch as that feast is expressive of the complete removal of sin by the death of Christ. "Ye do show the Lord's death till He come" (1 Cor. 11). In the death of Christ, faith sees the end of every thing that pertained to our old-creation standing; and seeing that the Lord's Supper "shows forth" that death, it is to be viewed as the memento of the glorious fact that the believer's burden of sin was borne by One who put it away forever. It declares that the chain of our sins, which once tied and bound us, has been eternally snapped by the death of Christ, and can never tie and bind us again. We gather round the Lord's table in all the joy of conquerors. We look back to the cross, where the battle was fought and won; and we look forward to the glory, where we shall enter into the full and eternal results of the victory.

True, we have "leaven" *in* us; but we have no "uncleanness" *on* us. We are not to gaze upon our sins, but upon Him who bore them on the cross and put them away forever. We are not to "deceive ourselves" by the vain notion "that we have no sin" in us; nor are we to deny the truth of God's Word, and the efficacy of Christ's blood, by refusing to rejoice in the precious truth that we have no sin on us, for "the blood of Jesus Christ His Son cleanseth us from all sin." It is truly deplorable to observe the heavy cloud that gathers round the Supper of the Lord, in the judgment of so many professing Christians. It tends, as much as any thing else, to reveal the immense amount of misapprehension which obtains in reference to the very elementary truths of the gospel. In fact, we know that when the Lord's Supper is resorted to on any ground save that of known salvation—enjoyed forgiveness—conscious deliverance, the soul becomes wrapped up in thicker and darker mists than ever. That which is only a memorial of Christ is used to displace Him; that which celebrates an accomplished redemption is used as a stepping-stone thereto. It is thus that the ordinances are abused, and souls plunged in darkness, confusion, and error.

How different from this is the beautiful ordinance of the peace-offering! In this latter, looked at in its typical import, we see that the moment the blood was shed, God and the worshiper could feed in happy, peaceful fellowship. Nothing more was needed. Peace was established by the blood, and on that ground the communion proceeded. A single question as to the establishment of peace must be the death-blow to communion. If we are to be occupied with the vain attempt to make peace with God, we must be total strangers to either communion or worship. If the blood of the peace-offering has not been shed, it is impossible that we can feed upon "the wave breast" or "the heave shoulder." But if, on the other hand, the blood has been shed, then peace is made already. God Himself has made it, and this is enough for faith; and therefore, by faith, we have fellowship with God, in the intelligence and joy of accomplished redemption. We taste the freshness of God's own joy in that which He has wrought. We feed upon Christ in all the fullness and blessedness of God's presence.

This latter point is connected with and based upon another leading truth laid down in "the law of the peace-offering." "And the flesh of the sacrifice of his peace-offerings for thanksgiving shall be eaten the same day that it is offered: he shall not leave any of it until the morning." That is to say, the communion of the worshiper must never be separated from the sacrifice on which that communion is founded. So long as one has spiritual energy to maintain the connection, the worship and communion are also maintained, in freshness and acceptableness;

but no longer. *We must keep close to the Sacrifice,* in the spirit of our minds, the affections of our hearts, and the experience of our souls. This will impart power and permanency to our worship. We may commence some act or expression of worship with our hearts in immediate occupation with Christ, and ere we reach the close we may become occupied with what we are doing or saying, or with the persons who are listening to us, and, in this way, fall into what may be termed "iniquity in our holy things." This is deeply solemn, and should make us very watchful. We may begin our worship in the Spirit and end in the flesh. Our care should ever be, not to suffer ourselves to proceed for a single moment beyond the energy of the Spirit, at the time; for the Spirit will always keep us occupied directly with Christ. If the Holy Ghost produces "five words" of worship or thanksgiving, let us utter the five and have done. If we proceed further, we are eating the flesh of our sacrifice beyond the time; and, so far from its being "accepted," it is really "an abomination." Let us remember this, and be watchful. It need not alarm us. God would have us led by the Spirit, and so filled with Christ in all our worship. He can only accept of that which is divine, and therefore He would have us presenting that only which is divine.

"But if the sacrifice of his offering be a vow or a voluntary-offering, it shall be eaten the same day that he offereth his sacrifice: and *on the morrow also the remainder of it shall be eaten*" (chap. 7:16). When the soul goes forth to God in a voluntary act of worship, such worship will be the result of a larger measure of spiritual energy than where it merely springs from some special mercy experienced at the time. If one had been visited with some marked favor from the Lord's own hand, the soul at once ascends in thanksgiving. In this case, the worship is awakened by and connected with that favor or mercy, whatever it may happen to be, and there it ends; but where the heart is led forth by the Holy Ghost in some voluntary or deliberate expression of praise, it will be of a more enduring character. But spiritual worship will always connect itself with the precious sacrifice of Christ.

"The remainder of the flesh of the sacrifice, on the third day, shall be burnt with fire. And if any of the flesh of the sacrifice of his peace-offerings be eaten at all on the third day, it shall not be accepted, neither shall it be imputed unto him that offereth it: it shall be an abomination, and the soul that eateth of it shall bear his iniquity." Nothing is of any value, in the judgment of God, which is not immediately connected with Christ. There may be a great deal of what looks like worship, which is, after all, the mere excitement and outgoing of natural feeling; there may be much apparent devotion, which is merely fleshly pietism. Nature may be acted upon, in a religious way, by a variety of things, such as pomp, ceremony, and parade, tones and attitudes, robes and vestments, an eloquent liturgy, all the varied attractions of a splendid ritualism, while there may be a total absence of spiritual worship. Yea, it not unfrequently happens that the very same tastes and tendencies which are called forth and gratified by the splendid appliances of so-called religious worship, would find most suited aliment at the opera or in the concert-room.

All this has to be watched against by those who desire to remember that "God is a spirit, and they that worship Him must worship Him in spirit and in truth" (John 4). Religion, so called, is, at this moment, decking herself with her most powerful charms. Casting off the grossness of the middle ages, she is calling to her aid all the resources of refined taste, and of a cultivated and enlightened age. Sculpture, music, and painting are pouring their rich treasures into her lap, in order that she may therewith prepare a powerful opiate to lull the thoughtless multitude into a slumber, which shall only be broken in upon by the unutterable horrors of death, judgment, and the lake of fire. She, too, can say, "I have *peace-offerings* with me; this day have I paid my *vows. . . .* I have decked my bed with coverings of tapestry, with carved works, with fine linen of Egypt. I have perfumed my bed with myrrh, aloes, and cinnamon" (Prov. 7). Thus does corrupt religion allure, by her powerful influence, those who will not hearken to Wisdom's heavenly voice.

Beware of all this. See that your worship stands inseparably connected with the work of the cross. See that Christ is the ground, Christ the material, and the Holy Ghost the power of your worship. Take care that your outward act of worship does not stretch itself beyond the inward power. It demands much watchfulness to keep clear of this evil. Its incipient workings are most difficult to be detected and counteracted. We may commence a hymn in the true spirit of worship, and, through lack of spiritual power, we may, ere we reach the close, fall into the evil which answers to the ceremonial act of eating the flesh of the peace-offering on the third day. Our only security is in keeping close to Jesus. If we lift up our hearts in "thanksgiving" for some special mercy, let us do so in the power of the name and sacrifice of Christ. If our souls go forth in "voluntary" worship, let it be in the energy of the Holy Ghost. In this way shall our worship exhibit that freshness, that fragrance, that depth of tone, that moral elevation, which must result from having the Father as the object, the Son as the ground, and the Holy Ghost as the power of our worship.*

Thus may it be, O Lord, with all Thy worshiping people, until we find ourselves—body, soul, and spirit—in the security of Thine own eternal presence, beyond the reach of all the unhallowed influences of false worship and corrupt religion, and also beyond the reach of the various hindrances which arise from these bodies of sin and death which we carry about with us!

---

*Note.*—It is interesting to observe that although the peace-offering itself stands third in order, yet "the law" thereof is given us last of all. This circumstance is not without its import. There is none of the offerings in which the communion of the worshiper is so fully unfolded as in the peace-offering. In the burnt-offering, it is Christ offering Himself to God. In the meat-offering, we have Christ's perfect humanity. Then, passing on to the sin-offering, we learn that *sin,* in its root, is fully met. In the trespass-offering, there is a full answer to the actual *sins,* in the life. But in none is the doctrine of the communion of the worshiper unfolded. This latter belongs to "the peace-offering;" and hence, I believe, the position which the law of that offering occupies. It comes in at the close of all, thereby teaching us that, when it becomes a question of the soul's feeding upon Christ, it must be a full Christ—looked at in every possible phase of His life, His character, His Person, His work, His offices; and, furthermore, that, when we shall have done forever with sin and sins, we shall delight in Christ, and feed upon Him, throughout the everlasting ages. It would, I believe, be a serious defect in our study of the offerings were we to pass over a circumstance so worthy of notice as the above. If "the law of the peace-offering" were given in the order in which the offering itself occurs, it would come in immediately after the law of the

*The statement in the text affords no warrant for the idea that our Lord Jesus Christ is not, equally with the Father, the object of worship. We utterly abhor and reject such a blasphemy.

Let the reader turn to John 5:23—"That all men should honor the Son, even as they honor the Father. He that honoreth not the Son honoreth not the Father which hath sent Him." How can any one, in the face of such a passage as this, attempt to teach that it is wrong to present worship to the Lord Jesus? Woe be to the man who so teaches! He is plainly at issue with God.

Again, look at Rev. 5:12—"Worthy is the Lamb that was slain to receive power, and riches, and wisdom, and strength, and honor, and glory, and blessing." What mean these words if our Lord Jesus Christ is not to be addressed in prayer or worship?

Was the martyr, Stephen, wrong when he said, "Lord Jesus, receive my spirit"? Was Paul mistaken when he besought the Lord to remove the thorn?

But it is needless to multiply passages: the teaching of the inspired volume, from cover to cover, establishes, beyond all question, the rightness of presenting prayer and worship to our Lord Jesus Christ; and therefore all who teach otherwise are in direct opposition to the Word of God.

meat-offering; but instead of that, "the law of the sin-offering" and "the law of the trespass-offering" are given, and then "the law of the peace-offering" closes the entire.

---

## *CHAPTERS 4—5:13*

HAVING considered the "sweet savor" offerings, we now approach the "sacrifices for sin." These were divided into two classes, namely, sin-offerings and trespass-offerings. Of the former, there were three grades; first, the offering for "the priest that is anointed," and for "the whole congregation." These two were the same in their rites and ceremonies (compare ver. 3-12 with ver. 13-21). It was the same in result, whether it were the representative of the assembly or the assembly itself that sinned. In either case there were three things involved: God's dwelling-place in the assembly, the worship of the assembly, and individual conscience. Now, inasmuch as all three depended upon the blood, we find, in the first grade of sin-offering, there were three things done with the blood. It was sprinkled "seven times before the Lord, *before the vail of the sanctuary.*" This secured Jehovah's relationship with the people, and His dwelling in their midst. Again, we read, "The priest shall put some of the blood upon the horns of the altar of sweet incense before the Lord, which is in the tabernacle of the congregation." This secured the worship of the assembly. By putting the blood upon "the golden altar," the true basis of worship was preserved; so that the flame of the incense and the fragrance thereof might continually ascend. Finally, "He shall pour all the blood of the bullock at the bottom of the altar of the burnt-offering, which is at the door of the tabernacle of the congregation." Here, we have the claims of individual conscience fully answered; for the brazen altar was the place of individual approach—it was the place where God met the sinner.

In the two remaining grades, for "a ruler" or "one of the common people," it was merely a question of individual conscience, and therefore there was only one thing done with the blood—it was all poured "at the bottom of the altar of burnt-offering" (comp. ver. 7 with ver. 25,30). There is divine precision in all this, which demands the close attention of my reader, if only he desires to enter into the marvelous detail of this type.*

The effect of individual sin could not extend beyond individual conscience. The sin of "a ruler," or of "one of the common people," could not, in its influence, reach "the altar of incense"—the place of priestly worship; neither could it reach to "the vail of the sanctuary"—the sacred boundary of God's dwelling-place in the midst of His people. It is well to ponder this. We must never raise a question of personal sin or failure in the place of priestly worship or in the assembly; it must be settled in the place of personal approach. Many err as to this.

*There is this difference between the offering for "a ruler" and for "one of the common people:" in the former, it was "a *male* without blemish;" in the latter, "a *female* without blemish." The sin of a ruler would necessarily exert a wider influence than that of a common person, and therefore a more powerful application of the value of the blood was needed. In chapter 5:13, we find cases demanding a still lower application of the sin-offering—cases of swearing, and of touching any uncleanness, in which "the tenth part of an ephah of fine flour" was admitted as a sin-offering (see chap. 5:11-13). What a contrast between the view of atonement presented by a ruler's bullock and a poor man's handful of flour! And yet, in the latter, just as truly as in the former, we read, "It shall be forgiven him."

The reader will observe that chapter 5:1-13 forms a part of chapter 4. Both are comprehended under one head, and present the doctrine of the sin-offering in all its applications, from the bullock to the handful of flour. Each class of offering is introduced by the words, "And the Lord spake unto Moses." Thus, for example, the sweet savor offerings (chap. 1—3) are introduced by the words, "The Lord called unto Moses." These words are not repeated until chapter 4:1, where they introduce the sin-offering. They occur again at chapter 5:14, where they introduce the trespass-offering for wrongs done "in the holy things of the Lord;" and again at chapter 6:1, where they introduce the trespass-offering for wrongs done to one's neighbor.

This classification is beautifully simple, and will help the reader to understand the different classes of offering. As to the different grades in each class, whether "a bullock," "a ram," "a female," "a bird," or "a handful of flour," they would seem to be so many varied applications of the same grand truth.

They come into the assembly, or into the ostensible place of priestly worship, with their conscience defiled, and thus drag down the whole assembly and mar its worship. This should be closely looked into, and carefully guarded against. We need to walk more watchfully, in order that our conscience may ever be in the light. And when we fail (as, alas! we do in many things), let us have to do with God in secret about our failure, in order that true worship and the true position of the assembly may always be kept with fullness and clearness before the soul.

Having said thus much as to the three grades of sin-offering, we shall proceed to examine, in detail, the principles unfolded in the first of these. In so doing, we shall be able to form, in some measure, a just conception of the principles of all. Before, however, entering upon the direct comparison already proposed, I would call my reader's attention to a very prominent point set forth in the second verse of this fourth chapter; it is contained in the expression, "If a soul shall sin through *ignorance.*" This presents a truth of the deepest blessedness, in connection with the atonement of the Lord Jesus Christ. In contemplating that atonement, we see infinitely more than the mere satisfaction of the claims of conscience, even though that conscience had reached the highest point of refined sensibility. It is our privilege to see therein that which has fully satisfied all the claims of divine holiness, divine justice, and divine majesty. The holiness of God's dwelling-place, and the ground of His association with His people, could never be regulated by the standard of man's conscience, no matter how high the standard might be. There are many things which man's conscience would pass over—many things which might escape man's cognizance—many things which his heart might deem all right, which God could not tolerate; and which, as a consequence, would interfere with man's approach to, his worship of, and his relationship with God. Wherefore, if the atonement of Christ merely made provision for such sins as come within the compass of man's apprehension, we should find ourselves very far short of the true ground of peace. We need to understand that sin has been atoned for, according to God's measurement thereof—that the claims of His throne have been perfectly answered—that sin, as seen in the light of His inflexible holiness, has been divinely judged. This is what gives settled peace to the soul. A full atonement has been made for the believer's sins of ignorance, as well as for his known sins. The sacrifice of Christ lays the foundation of his relationship and fellowship with God, according to the divine estimate of the claims thereof.

A clear sense of this is of unspeakable value. Unless this feature of the atonement be laid hold of, there cannot be settled peace; nor will there be any just moral sense of the extent and fullness of the work of Christ, or of the true nature of the relationship founded thereon. God knew what was needed in order that man might be in His presence without a single misgiving, and He has made ample provision for it in the cross. Fellowship between God and man were utterly impossible if sin had not been disposed of according to God's thoughts about it; for, albeit man's conscience were satisfied, the question would ever be suggesting itself, Has God been satisfied? If this question could not be answered in the affirmative, fellowship could never subsist.* The thought would be continually intruding itself upon the heart, that things were manifesting themselves in the details of life which divine holiness could not tolerate. True, we might be doing such things "through ignorance," but this could not alter the matter before God, inasmuch as all is known to Him. Hence, there would be continual apprehension, doubt, and misgiving. All these things are divinely met by the fact that sin has been atoned for, not

*I would desire it to be particularly remembered that the point before us in the text is simply atonement. The Christian reader is fully aware, I doubt not, that the possession of "the divine nature" is essential to fellowship with God. I not only need a *title* to approach God, but a *nature* to enjoy Him. The soul that "believes in the name of the only begotten Son of God" has both the one and the other. (See John 1:12-13, 3:36; 5:24; 20:31; 1 John 5:11-13.)

according to our "ignorance," but according to God's knowledge. The assurance of this gives great rest to the heart and conscience. All God's claims have been answered by His own work. He Himself has made the provision; and therefore the more refined the believer's conscience becomes, under the combined action of the Word and Spirit of God—the more he grows in a divinely-adjusted sense of all that morally befits the sanctuary—the more keenly alive he becomes to every thing which is unsuited to the divine presence, the fuller, clearer, deeper, and more vigorous will be his apprehension of the infinite value of that Sin-offering which has not only traveled beyond the utmost bounds of human conscience, but also met, in absolute perfection, all the requirements of divine holiness.

Nothing can more forcibly express man's incompetency to deal with sin than the fact of there being such a thing as a "sin of ignorance." How could he deal with that which he knows not? How could he dispose of that which has never even come within the range of his conscience? Impossible. Man's ignorance of sin proves his total inability to put it away. If he does not know of it, what can he do about it? Nothing. He is as powerless as he is ignorant. Nor is this all. The fact of a "sin of ignorance" demonstrates most clearly the uncertainty which must attend upon every settlement of the question of sin, in which no higher claims have been responded to than those put forth by the most refined human conscience. There can never be settled peace upon this ground. There will always be the painful apprehension that there is something wrong underneath. If the heart be not led into settled repose by the Scripture testimony that the inflexible claims of divine Justice have been answered, there must, of necessity, be a sensation of uneasiness, and every such sensation presents a barrier to our worship, our communion, and our testimony. If I am uneasy in reference to the settlement of the question of sin, I cannot worship, I cannot enjoy communion either with God or His people, nor can I be an intelligent or effective witness for Christ. The heart must be at rest before God as to the perfect remission of sin ere we can "worship Him in spirit and in truth." If there be guilt on the conscience, there must be terror in the heart; and, assuredly, a heart filled with terror cannot be a happy or a worshiping heart. It is only from a heart filled with that sweet and sacred repose which the blood of Christ imparts, that true and acceptable worship can ascend to the Father. The same principle holds good with respect to our fellowship with the people of God and our service and testimony amongst men,—all must rest upon the foundation of settled peace, and this peace rests upon the foundation of a perfectly purged conscience, and this purged conscience rests upon the foundation of the perfect remission of all our sins, whether they be sins of knowledge or sins of ignorance.

We shall now proceed to compare the sin-offering with the burnt-offering, in doing which we shall find the two very different aspects of Christ. But although the aspects are different, it is one and the same Christ; and hence the sacrifice in each case was "without blemish." This is easily understood. It matters not in what aspect we contemplate the Lord Jesus Christ, He must ever be seen as the same pure, spotless, holy, perfect One. True, He did, in His abounding grace, stoop to be the Sin-bearer of His people; but it was a perfect, spotless Christ who did so; and it would be nothing short of diabolical wickedness to take occasion from the depth of His humiliation to tarnish the personal glory of the humbled One. The intrinsic excellence, the unsullied purity, and the divine glory of our blessed Lord appear in the sin-offering as fully as in the burnt-offering. It matters not in what relationship He stands, what office He fills, what work He performs, what position He occupies, His personal glories shine out in all their divine effulgence.

This truth of one and the same Christ, whether in the burnt-offering or in the sin-offering, is seen not only in the fact that in each case the offering was "without blemish," but also in "the law of the sin-offering," where we read, "This is the law of the sin-offering: In the place where the burnt-offering is killed shall the sin-offering be killed before the Lord: it is most holy" (Lev. 6:25). Both types point to one and the same great Antitype, though they present Him in such contrasted aspects of His work. In the burnt-offering, Christ is seen meeting the divine affections; in the sin-offering, He is seen meeting the depths of human need. That presents Him to us as the Accomplisher of the will of God; this, as the Bearer of the sin of man. In the former, we are taught the preciousness of the Sacrifice; in the latter, the hatefulness of sin. Thus much as to the two offerings, in the main. The most minute examination of the details will only tend to establish the mind in the truth of this general statement.

In the first place, when considering the burnt-offering, we observed that it was a voluntary offering. "He shall offer it of his own voluntary will."* Now, the word "voluntary" does not occur in the sin-offering. This is precisely what we might expect. It is in full keeping with the specific object of the Holy Ghost, in the burnt-offering, to set it forth as a free will offering. It was Christ's meat and drink to do the will of God, whatever that will might be. He never thought of inquiring what ingredients were in the cup which the Father was putting into His hand. It was quite sufficient for Him that the Father had mingled it. Thus it was with the Lord Jesus as foreshadowed by the burnt-offering. But in the sin-offering, we have quite a different line of truth unfolded. This type introduces Christ to our thoughts, not as the "voluntary" Accomplisher of the will of God, but as the Bearer of that terrible thing called "sin," and the Endurer of all its appalling consequences, of which the most appalling to Him was the hiding of God's countenance. Hence, the word "voluntary" would not harmonize with the object of the Spirit in the sin-offering. It would be as completely out of place in that type as it is divinely in place in the burnt-offering. Its presence and its absence are alike divine; and both alike exhibit the perfect, the divine precision of the types of Leviticus.

Now, the point of contrast which we have been considering, explains, or rather harmonizes, two expressions used by our Lord. He says, on one occasion, "The cup which My Father hath given Me, shall I not drink it?" And again, "Father, if it be possible, let this cup pass from Me." The former of these expressions was the full carrying out of the words with which He entered upon His course, namely, "Lo, I come to do Thy will, O God"; and, moreover, it is the utterance of Christ as the Burnt-offering. The latter, on the other hand, is the utterance of Christ when contemplating the place which He was about to occupy as the Sin-offering. What that place was, and what was involved to Him in taking it, we shall see as we proceed; but it is interesting and instructive to find the entire doctrine of the two offerings involved, as it were, in the fact that a single word introduced in the one is omitted in the other. If in the burnt-offering we find the perfect readiness of heart with which Christ offered Himself for the accomplishment of the will of God, then in the sin-offering we find how perfectly He entered into all the consequences of man's sin, and how He traveled into the most remote distance of man's position as regards God. He delighted to do the will of God; He shrank from losing, for a moment, the light of His blessed countenance. No one offering could have foreshadowed Him in both these phases. We needed a type to present Him to us as One delighting to do the will of God, and we needed a type to present Him to us as One whose holy nature shrank from the consequences of imputed sin. Blessed be God, we have both. The burnt-offering furnishes the one; the sin-offering, the other. Wherefore, the more fully we enter into the devotion of Christ's heart to God, the more fully we shall apprehend His abhorrence of sin; and *vice versa.* Each throws the other into relief; the word "voluntary" in the one and not in the other, fixes the leading import of each.

*Some may find difficulty in the fact that the word "voluntary" has reference to the worshiper and not to the sacrifice; but this can in no wise affect the doctrine put forward in the text, which is founded upon the fact that a special word used in the burnt-offering is omitted in the sin-offering. The contrast holds good whether we think of the offerer or the offering.

But it may be said, Was it not the will of God that Christ should offer Himself as an atonement for sin? If so, how could there be aught of shrinking from the accomplishment of that will? Assuredly, it was "the determinate counsel" of God that Christ should suffer, and, moreover, it was Christ's joy to do the will of God; but how are we to understand the expression, "If it be possible, let this cup pass from Me"? Is it not the utterance of Christ? And is there no express type of the Utterer thereof? Unquestionably. There would be a serious blank among the types of the Mosaic economy were there not one to reflect the Lord Jesus in the exact attitude in which the above expression presents Him. But the burnt-offering does not thus reflect Him. There is not a single circumstance connected with that offering which would correspond with such language. The sin-offering alone furnishes the fitting type of the Lord Jesus as the One who poured forth those accents of intense agony; for in it alone do we find the circumstances which evoked such accents from the depths of His spotless soul. The awful shadow of the cross, with its shame, its curse, and its exclusion from the light of God's countenance, was passing across His spirit, and He could not even contemplate it without an "If it be possible, let this cup pass from Me." But no sooner had He uttered these words than His profound subjection manifests itself in "Thy will be done." What a bitter "cup" it must have been to elicit from a perfectly subject heart the words, "Let it pass from Me"! What perfect subjection there must have been, when, in the presence of so bitter a cup, the heart could breathe forth, "Thy will be done"!

We shall now consider the typical act of "laying on of hands." This act was common both to the burnt-offering and the sin-offering; but in the case of the former, it identified the offerer with an unblemished offering; in the case of the latter, it involved the transfer of the sin of the offerer to the head of the offering. Thus it was in the type; and when we look at the Antitype, we learn a truth of the most comforting and edifying nature—a truth which, were it more clearly understood and fully experienced, would impart a far more settled peace than is ordinarily possessed.

What, then, is the doctrine set forth in the laying on of hands? It is this: Christ was "made sin for us, that we might be made the righteousness of God in Him" (2 Cor. 5). He took our position with all its consequences, in order that we might get His position with all its consequences. He was treated as sin upon the cross, that we might be treated as righteousness in the presence of Infinite Holiness. He was cast out of God's presence because He had sin on Him by imputation, that we might be received into God's house and into His bosom because we have a perfect righteousness by imputation. He had to endure the hiding of God's countenance, that we might bask in the light of that countenance. He had to pass through three hours' darkness, that we might walk in everlasting light. He was forsaken of God for a time, that we might enjoy His presence forever. All that was due to us as ruined sinners was laid upon Him, in order that all that was due to Him as the Accomplisher of redemption might be ours. There was every thing against Him when He hung upon the cursed tree, in order that there might be nothing against us. He was identified with us in the reality of death and judgment, in order that we might be identified with Him in the reality of life and righteousness. He drank the cup of wrath—the cup of trembling, that we might drink the cup of salvation—the cup of infinite favor. He was treated according to our deserts, that we might be treated according to His.

Such is the wondrous truth illustrated by the ceremonial act of imposition of hands. When the worshiper had laid his hand upon the head of the burnt-offering, it ceased to be a question as to what he was or what He deserved, and became entirely a question of what the offering was in the judgment of Jehovah. If the offering was without blemish, so was the offerer; if the offering was accepted, so was the offerer. They were perfectly identified. The act of laying on of hands constituted them one in God's view.

He looked at the offerer through the medium of the offering. Thus it was in the case of the burnt-offering. But in the sin-offering, when the offerer had laid his hand upon the head of the offering, it became a question of what the offerer was, and what he deserved: the offering was treated according to the deserts of the offerer. They were perfectly identified. The act of laying on of hands constituted them one in the judgment of God. The sin of the offerer was dealt with in the sin-offering; the person of the offerer was accepted in the burnt-offering. This made a vast difference. Hence, though the act of laying on of hands was common to both types, and, moreover, though it was expressive, in the case of each, of identification, yet were the consequences as different as possible. The just treated as the unjust; the unjust accepted in the just. "Christ hath once suffered for sins, the just for the unjust, that He might bring us to God." This is the doctrine. Our sins brought Christ to the cross, but He brings us to God. And if He brings us to God, it is in His own acceptableness, as risen from the dead, having put away our sins, according to the perfectness of His own work. He bore away our sins far from the sanctuary of God, in order that He might bring us nigh, even into the holiest of all, in full confidence of heart, having the conscience purged by His precious blood from every stain of sin.

Now, the more minutely we compare all the details of the burnt-offering and the sin-offering, the more clearly shall we apprehend the truth of what has been above stated in reference to the laying on of hands and the results thereof in each case.

In the first chapter of this volume, we noticed the fact that "the sons of Aaron" are introduced in the burnt-offering, but not in the sin-offering. As priests, they were privileged to stand around the altar and behold the flame of an acceptable sacrifice ascending to the Lord. But in the sin-offering, in its primary aspect, it was a question of the solemn judgment of sin, and not of priestly worship or admiration, and therefore the sons of Aaron do not appear. It is as convicted sinners that we have to do with Christ as the Antitype of the sin-offering: it is as worshiping priests, clothed in garments of salvation, that we contemplate Christ as the Antitype of the burnt-offering.

But, further, observe that the burnt-offering was "flayed," the sin-offering was not; the burnt-offering was "cut into his pieces," the sin-offering was not; "the inwards and the legs" of the burnt-offering were "washed in water," which act was entirely omitted in the sin-offering. Lastly, the burnt-offering was burnt upon the altar, the sin-offering was burnt without the camp. These are weighty points of difference, arising simply out of the distinctive character of the offerings. We know there is nothing in the Word of God without its own specific meaning; and every intelligent and careful student of Scripture will notice the above points of difference, and when he notices them, he will naturally seek to ascertain their real import. *Ignorance* of this import there may be, but *indifference* to it there should not. In any section of inspiration, but especially one so rich as that which lies before us, to pass over a single point would be to offer dishonor to the divine Author, and to deprive our own souls of much profit. We should hang over the most minute details, either to adore God's wisdom in them, or to confess our own ignorance of them. To pass them by, in a spirit of indifference, is to imply that the Holy Ghost has taken the trouble to write what we do not deem worthy of the desire to understand. This is what no right-minded Christian would presume to think. If the Spirit, in writing upon the ordinance of the sin-offering, has omitted the various rites above alluded to—rites which get a prominent place in the ordinance of the burnt-offering, there must assuredly be some good reason for, and some important meaning in, His doing so. These we should seek to apprehend, and no doubt they arise out of the special design of the divine mind in each offering. The sin-offering sets forth that aspect of Christ's work in which He is seen taking judicially the place which belonged to us morally. For this reason we could not look for that intense expression of what He was in all His secret springs of action, as unfolded in the typical act of "flaying." Neither could there be that enlarged exhibition of what he was, not merely as a whole, but in the most minute features of his character, as seen in the act of "cutting it into his pieces." Nor yet could there be that manifestation of what He was personally, practically, and intrinsically, as set forth in the significant act of "washing the inwards and legs in water."

All these things belonged to the burnt-offering phase of our blessed Lord, and to that alone, because in it we see Him offering Himself to the eye, to the heart, and to the altar of Jehovah, without any question of imputed sin, of wrath, or of judgment. In the sin-offering, on the contrary, instead of having, as the great prominent idea, what Christ is, we have what sin is; instead of the preciousness of Jesus, we have the odiousness of sin. In the burnt-offering, inasmuch as it is Christ Himself offered to and accepted by God, we have every thing done that could possibly make manifest what He was in every respect. In the sin-offering, because it is sin as judged by God, the very reverse is the case. All this is so plain as to need no effort of the mind to understand it. It naturally flows out of the distinctive character of the type.

However, although the leading object in the sin-offering is to shadow forth what Christ became for us, and not what He was in Himself, there is nevertheless one rite connected with this type which most fully expresses His personal acceptableness to Jehovah. This rite is laid down in the following words: "And he shall take off from it all the fat of the bullock for the sin-offering; the fat that covereth the inwards, and all the fat that is upon the inwards, and the two kidneys, and the fat that is upon them, which is by the flanks, and the caul above the liver, with the kidneys, it shall he take away, as it was taken off from the bullock of the sacrifice of peace-offering; and the priest shall burn them upon the altar of the burnt-offering" (chap. 4:8-10). Thus the intrinsic excellency of Christ is not omitted even in the sin-offering. The fat burnt upon the altar is the apt expression of the divine appreciation of the preciousness of Christ's Person, no matter what place He might, in perfect grace, take on our behalf or in our stead. He was made sin for us, and the sin-offering is the divinely appointed shadow of Him in this respect; but inasmuch as it was the Lord Jesus Christ—God's Elect, His Holy One—His pure, His spotless, His eternal Son that was made sin, therefore the fat of the sin-offering was burnt upon the altar, as a proper material for that fire which was the impressive exhibition of divine holiness.

But even in this very point we see what a contrast there is between the sin-offering and the burnt-offering. In the case of the latter, it was not merely the fat, but the whole sacrifice that was burnt upon the altar, because it was Christ, without any question of sin-bearing whatever. In the case of the former, there was nothing but the fat to be burnt upon the altar, because it was a question of sin-bearing, though Christ was the Sin-bearer. The divine glories of Christ's Person shine out even from amid the darkest shades of that cursed tree to which He consented to be nailed as a curse for us. The hatefulness of that with which, in the exercise of divine love, He connected His blessed Person on the cross, could not prevent the sweet odor of His preciousness from ascending to the throne of God. Thus have we unfolded to us the profound mystery of God's face hidden from that which Christ *became,* and God's heart refreshed by what Christ *was*. This imparts a peculiar charm to the sin-offering. The bright beams of Christ's Personal glory shining out from amid the awful gloom of Calvary—His Personal worth set forth in the very deepest depths of His humiliation—God's delight in the One from whom He had, in vindication of His inflexible justice and holiness, to hide His face—all this is set forth in the fact that the fat of the sin-offering was burnt upon the altar.

Having thus endeavored to point out, in the first place, what was done with "the blood," and, in the second place, what was done with "the fat," we have now to consider what was done with "the flesh." "And the skin of the bullock, and *all his flesh* . . . even *the whole bullock* shall he carry forth without the camp unto a clean place, where the ashes are poured out, and burn him on the wood with fire: where the ashes are poured out shall he be burnt" (ver. 11-12). In this act, we have the main feature of the sin-offering—that which distinguished it both from the burnt-offering and the peace-offering. Its flesh was not burnt upon the altar as in the burnt-offering, neither was it eaten by the priest or the worshiper as in the peace-offering; it was wholly burnt without the camp.* "No sin-offering, whereof any of the blood is brought into the tabernacle of the congregation to reconcile withal in the holy place, shall be eaten: it shall be burnt in the fire" (Lev. 6:30). "For the bodies of those beasts, whose blood is brought into the sanctuary by the high-priest for sin, are burned without the camp. Wherefore Jesus also, that He might sanctify the people with His own blood, suffered without the gate" (Heb. 13:11-12).

Now, in comparing what was done with the "blood" with what was done with the "flesh," or "body," of the sacrifice, two great branches of truth present themselves to our view, namely, worship and discipleship. The blood brought into the sanctuary is the foundation of the former; the body burnt outside the camp is the foundation of the latter. Before ever we can worship in peace of conscience and liberty of heart, we must know, on the authority of the Word, and by the power of the Spirit, that the entire question of *sin* has been forever settled by the blood of the divine Sin-offering—that His blood has been sprinkled perfectly before the Lord—that all God's claims, and all our necessities as ruined and guilty sinners, have been forever answered. This gives perfect peace; and, in the enjoyment of this peace, we worship God. When an Israelite of old had offered his sin-offering, his conscience was set at rest, insofar as the offering was capable of imparting rest. True, it was but a temporary rest, being the fruit of a temporary sacrifice; but, clearly, whatever kind of rest the offering was fitted to impart, that the offerer might enjoy. Hence, therefore, our Sacrifice being divine and eternal, our rest is divine and eternal also. As is the sacrifice, such is the rest which is founded thereon. A Jew never had an eternally purged conscience, simply because he had not an eternally efficacious sacrifice. He might, in a certain way, have his conscience purged for a day, a month, or a year; but he could not have it purged forever. "But Christ being come a High-Priest of good things to come, by a greater and more perfect tabernacle, not made with hands, that is to say, not of this building; neither by the blood of goats and calves, but by His own blood He entered in once into the holy place, having obtained *eternal* redemption. For if the blood of bulls and of goats, and the ashes of a heifer sprinkling the unclean, sanctifieth to the purifying of the flesh; how much more shall the blood of Christ, who through the eternal Spirit offered Himself without spot to God, purge your conscience from dead works to serve the living God?" (Heb. 9:11-14)

Here, we have the full, explicit statement of the doctrine. The blood of goats and calves procured a temporary redemption: the blood of Christ procures eternal redemption. The former purified outwardly; the latter, inwardly. That purged the flesh for a time; this, the conscience forever. The whole question hinges, not upon the character or condition of the offerer, but upon the value of the offering. The question is not, by any means, whether a Christian is a better man than a Jew, but whether the blood of Christ is better than the blood of a bullock. Assuredly, it is better. How much better? Infinitely better. The Son of God imparts all the dignity of His own divine Person to the sacrifice which He offered; and if the blood of a bullock purified the flesh for a year, "how much more" shall the blood of the Son of God purge the conscience forever? If that took away *some* sin, how much more shall this take away "*all*"?

*The statement in the text refers only to the sin-offerings of which the blood was brought into the holy place. There were sin-offerings of which Aaron and his *sons* partook. (See Lev. 6:26,29; Num. 18:9-10.)

Now, why was the mind of a Jew set at rest, for the time being, when he had offered his sin-offering? How did he know that the special sin for which he had brought his sacrifice was forgiven? Because God had said, "It shall be forgiven him." His peace of heart, in reference to that particular sin, rested upon the testimony of the God of Israel and the blood of the victim. So now, the peace of the believer, in reference to *"all sin,"* rests upon the authority of God's Word and "the precious blood of Christ." If a Jew had sinned, and neglected to bring his sin-offering, he should have been "cut off from among his people;" but when he took his place as a sinner—when he laid his hand upon the head of a sin-offering, then the offering was "cut off" instead of him, and he was free, so far. The offering was treated as the offerer deserved; and hence, for him not to know that his sin was forgiven him, would have been to make God a liar, and to treat the blood of the divinely appointed sin-offering as nothing.

And if this were true in reference to one who had only the blood of a goat to rest upon, "how much more" powerfully does it apply to one who has the precious blood of Christ to rest upon? The believer sees in Christ One who has been judged for all his sin—One who, when He hung upon the cross, sustained the entire burden of his sin—One who, having made Himself responsible for that sin, could not be where He now is if the whole question of sin had not been settled according to all the claims of Infinite Justice. So absolutely did Christ take the believer's place on the cross—so entirely was he identified with Him—so completely was all the believer's sin imputed to Him, there and then, that all question of the believer's liability—all thought of his guilt—all idea of his exposure to judgment and wrath, is eternally set aside.* It was all settled on the cursed tree, between Divine Justice and the spotless Victim. And now the believer is as absolutely identified with Christ on the throne, as Christ was identified with him on the cross. Justice has no charge to bring against the believer, because it has no charge to bring against Christ. Thus it stands forever. If a charge could be preferred against the believer, it would be calling in question the reality of Christ's identification with him on the cross, and the perfectness of Christ's work on his behalf. If, when the worshiper of old was on his way back, after having offered his sin-offering, any one had charged him with that special sin for which his sacrifice had bled, what would have been his reply? Just this: The sin has been rolled away by the blood of the victim, and Jehovah has pronounced the words, "It shall be forgiven him." The victim had died instead of him, and he lived instead of the victim.

Such was the type. And as to the Antitype, when the eye of faith rests on Christ as the Sin-offering, it beholds Him as One who having assumed a perfect human life, gave up that life on the cross, because sin was there and then attached to it by imputation. But it beholds Him also as One who having in Himself the power of divine and eternal life, rose from the tomb therein, and who now imparts this His risen, His divine, His eternal life to all who believe in His name. The sin is gone, because the life to which it was attached is gone. And now, instead of the life to which sin was attached, all true believers possess the life to which righteousness attaches. The question of sin can never once be raised, in reference to the risen and victorious life of Christ; but this is the life which believers possess. There is no other life. All beside is death, because all beside is under the power of sin. "He that hath the Son hath life," and he that hath life hath righteousness also. The two things are inseparable, because Christ is both the one and the other. If the judgment and death of Christ upon the cross were realities, then the life and righteousness of the believer are realities; if imputed sin was a reality to Christ, imputed righteousness is a reality to the believer. The one is as real as the other;

*We have a singularly beautiful example of the divine accuracy of Scripture in 2 Cor. 5:21: "He hath *made* Him to be sin [αμαρτιαν εποιηδεν] for us, that we might *become* [γιωωμεθα] the righteousness of God in Him." The English reader might suppose that the word which is rendered "made" is the same in each clause of the passage. This is not the case.

for if not, Christ would have died in vain. The true and irrefragable ground of peace is this,—that the claims of God's nature have been perfectly met as to sin. The death of Jesus has satisfied them all—satisfied them forever. What is it that proves this to the satisfaction of the awakened conscience? The great fact of resurrection. A risen Christ declares the full deliverance of the believer—his perfect discharge from every possible demand. "He was delivered for our offenses, and raised again for our justification" (Rom. 4:25). For a Christian not to know that his sin is gone, and gone forever, is to cast a slight upon the blood of his divine Sin-offering; it is to deny that there has been the perfect presentation—the sevenfold sprinkling of the blood before the Lord.

And now, ere turning from this fundamental point which has been occupying us, I would desire to make an earnest and a most solemn appeal to my reader's heart and conscience. Have you been led to repose on this holy and happy foundation? Do you know that the question of your sin has been forever disposed of? Have you laid your hand, by faith, on the head of the Sin-offering? Have you seen the atoning blood of Jesus rolling away all your guilt, and carrying it into the mighty waters of God's forgetfulness? Has Divine Justice any thing against you? Are you free from the unutterable horrors of a guilty conscience? Do not, I pray you, rest satisfied until you can give a joyous answer to these inquiries. It is the happy privilege of the feeblest babe in Christ to rejoice in a full and everlasting remission of sins, on the ground of a finished atonement; and hence, for any to teach otherwise, is to lower the sacrifice of Christ to the level of "goats and calves." If we cannot know that our sins are forgiven, then where are the glad tidings of the gospel? Is a Christian in no wise better off, in the matter of a sin-offering, than a Jew? The latter was privileged to know that his matters were set straight for a year, by the blood of an animal sacrifice. Can the former not have any certainty at all? Unquestionably. Well, then, if there is any certainty, it must be eternal, inasmuch as it rests on an eternal sacrifice.

This, and this alone, is the basis of worship. The full assurance of sin put away ministers, not to a spirit of self-confidence, but to a spirit of praise, thankfulness, and worship. It produces, not a spirit of self-complacency, but of Christ-complacency, which, blessed be God, is the spirit which shall characterize the redeemed throughout eternity. It does not lead one to think little of sin, but to think much of the grace which has perfectly pardoned it, and of the blood which has perfectly canceled it. It is impossible that any one can gaze on the cross—can see the place which Christ took—can meditate upon the sufferings which He endured—can ponder on those three terrible hours of darkness, and at the same time think lightly of sin. When all these things are entered into, in the power of the Holy Ghost, there are two results which must follow, namely, an abhorrence of sin in all its forms, and a genuine love to Christ, His people, and His cause.

Let us now consider what was done with the "flesh," or "body," of the sacrifice, in which, as has been stated, we have the true ground of discipleship. "The whole bullock shall he carry forth, *without the camp,* unto a clean place, where the ashes are poured out, and burn him on the wood with fire" (chap. 4:12). This act is to be viewed in a double way; first, as expressing the place which the Lord Jesus took for us as bearing sin; secondly, as expressing the place into which He was cast by a world which had rejected Him. It is to this latter point that I would here call my reader's attention.

The use which the apostle, in Heb. 13, makes of Christ's having "suffered without the gate," is deeply practical. "Let us go forth therefore *unto Him* without the camp, *bearing His reproach.*" If the sufferings of Christ have secured us an entrance into heaven, the place where He suffered expresses our rejection from earth. His death has procured us a city on high; the place where He died divests us of a city below.*

*The Epistle to the Ephesians furnishes the most elevated view of the Church's place above, and gives it to us, not merely as to the title, but also as to the mode. The title is assuredly the blood; but the mode is thus stated: "But God, who is rich in

"He suffered without the gate," and, in so doing, He set aside Jerusalem as the present centre of divine operation. There is no such thing now as a consecrated spot on the earth. Christ has taken His place, as a suffering One, outside the range of this world's religion, its politics, and all that pertains to it. The world hated Him and cast Him out. Wherefore, the word is, *"Go forth."* This is the motto as regards every thing that men would set up here in the form of a "camp," no matter what that camp may be. If men set up "a holy city," you must look for a rejected Christ "without the gate." If men set up a religious camp, call it by what name you please, you must "go forth" out of it, in order to find a rejected Christ. It is not that blind superstition will not grope amid the ruins of Jerusalem in search of relics of Christ. It assuredly will do so, and has done so. It will affect to find out and do honor to the site of His cross and to His sepulchre. Nature's covetousness, too, taking advantage of nature's superstition, has carried on for ages a lucrative traffic, under the crafty plea of doing honor to the so-called sacred localities of antiquity. But a single ray of light from Revelation's heavenly lamp is sufficient to enable us to say that you must "go forth" of all these things, in order to find and enjoy communion with a rejected Christ.

However, there is far more involved in the soul-stirring call to "go forth" than a mere escape from the gross absurdities of an ignorant superstition, or the designs of a crafty covetousness. There are many who can powerfully and eloquently expose all such things, who are very far indeed from any thought of responding to the apostolic summons. When men set up a "camp," and rally round a standard on which is emblazoned some important dogma of truth, or some valuable institution—when they can appeal to an orthodox creed—an advanced and enlightened scheme of doctrine—a splendid ritual, capable of satisfying the most ardent aspirations of man's devotional nature—when any or all of these things exist, it demands much spiritual intelligence to discern the real force and proper application of the words, "Let us go forth," and much spiritual energy and decision to act upon them. They should, however, be discerned and acted upon, for it is perfectly certain that the atmosphere of a camp, let its ground or standard be what it may, is destructive of personal communion with a rejected Christ; and no so-called religious advantage can ever make up for the loss of that communion. It is the tendency of our hearts to drop into cold stereotyped forms. This has ever been the case in the professing church. These forms may have originated in real power; they may have resulted from positive visitations of the Spirit of God. The temptation is to stereotype the form when the spirit and power have all departed. This is, in principle, to set up a camp. The Jewish system could boast a divine origin. A Jew could triumphantly point to the temple, with its splendid system of worship, its priesthood, its sacrifices, its entire furniture, and show that it had all been handed down from the God of Israel. He could give chapter and verse, as we say, for every thing connected with the system to which he was attached. Where is the system, ancient, medieval, or modern, that could put forth such lofty and powerful pretensions, or come down upon the heart with such an overwhelming weight of authority? And yet, the command was to *"go forth."*

This is a deeply solemn matter. It concerns us all, because we are all prone to slip away from communion with a living Christ and sink into dead routine. Hence the practical power of the words, "Go forth therefore unto *Him.*" It is not, Go forth from one system to another—from one set of opinions to another—from one company of people to another. No; but, Go forth from every thing that merits the appellation of a camp, *"to Him"* who "suffered without the gate." The Lord Jesus is as thoroughly outside the gate now as He was when He

---

mercy, for His great love wherewith He loved us, even when we were dead in sins, hath quickened us together with Christ, (by grace ye are saved;) and hath raised us up together, and made us sit together in heavenly places in Christ Jesus" (Eph. 2:4-6).

suffered there eighteen centuries ago. What was it that put Him outside? "The religious world" of that day; and the religious world of that day is, in spirit and principle, the religious world of the present moment. The world is the world still. "There is nothing new under the sun." Christ and the world are not one. The world has covered itself with the cloak of Christianity; but it is only in order that its hatred to Christ may work itself up into more deadly forms underneath. Let us not deceive ourselves. If we will walk with a rejected Christ, we must be a rejected people. If our Master "suffered *without* the gate," we cannot expect to reign *within* the gate. If we walk in His footsteps, whither will they lead us? Surely, not to the high places of this Godless, Christless world.

His path, uncheered by earthly smiles,
Led only to the cross.

He is a despised Christ—a rejected Christ—a Christ outside the camp. Oh, then, dear Christian reader, let us go forth to Him, bearing His reproach. Let us not bask in the sunshine of this world's favor, seeing it crucified, and still hates with an unmitigated hatred, the beloved One to whom we owe our present and eternal all, and who loves us with a love which many waters cannot quench. Let us not, directly or indirectly, accredit that thing which calls itself by His sacred name, but, in reality, hates His Person, hates His ways, hates His truth, hates the bare mention of His advent. Let us be faithful to an absent Lord. Let us live for Him who died for us. While our consciences repose in His blood, let our heart's affections entwine themselves around His Person; so that our separation from "this present evil world" may not be merely a matter of cold principle, but an affectionate separation, because the object of our affections is not here. May the Lord deliver us from the influence of that consecrated, prudential selfishness so common at the present time, which would not be without religiousness, but is the enemy of the cross of Christ. What we want, in order to make a successful stand against this terrible form of evil, is not peculiar views, or special principles, or curious theories, or cold intellectual accuracy: we want a deep-toned devotedness to the Person of the Son of God, a whole-hearted consecration of ourselves—body, soul, and spirit—to His service, an earnest longing for His glorious advent. These are the special wants of the times in which you and I live. Will you not, then, join in uttering, from the very depths of your heart, the cry, "O Lord, revive Thy work!" "Accomplish the number of Thine elect!" "Hasten Thy kingdom!" "Come, Lord Jesus, come!"

---

## *CHAPTERS 5:14—6:7*

THESE verses contain the doctrine of the trespass-offering, of which there were two distinct kinds, namely, trespass against *God,* and trespass against *man*. "If a soul commit a trespass, and sin *through ignorance,* in the holy things of the Lord, then shall he bring for his trespass unto the Lord a ram without blemish out of the flocks, with thy estimation by shekels of silver, after the shekel of the sanctuary, for a trespass-offering." Here we have a case in which a positive wrong was done, in the holy things which pertained unto the Lord; and, albeit this was done "through ignorance," yet could it not be passed over. God can forgive all manner of trespass, but He cannot pass over a single jot or tittle. His grace is perfect, and therefore He can forgive *all:* His holiness is perfect, and therefore He cannot pass over any thing. He cannot sanction iniquity, but He can blot it out; and that, moreover, according to the perfection of His grace, and according to the perfect claims of His holiness.

It is a very grave error to suppose that, provided a man acts up to the dictates of his conscience, he is all right and safe. The peace which rests upon such a foundation as this will be eternally destroyed when the light of the judgment-seat shines in upon the conscience. God could never lower His claim to such a level. The balances of the sanctuary are regulated by a very different scale from that afforded by the most sensitive conscience. We have had occasion to dwell upon this point before, in the notes on the sin-offering. It cannot be too strongly insisted upon. There are two things involved in it: first, a just perception of what the holiness of God really is; and secondly, a clear sense of the ground of a believer's peace in the divine presence.

Whether it be a question of my condition or my conduct—my nature or my acts—God alone can be the Judge of what suits Himself, and of what befits His holy presence. Can human ignorance furnish a plea when divine requirements are in question? God forbid. A wrong has been done "in the holy things of the Lord," but man's conscience has not taken cognizance of it. What then? Is there to be nothing more about it? Are the claims of God to be thus lightly disposed of? Assuredly not. This would be subversive of every thing like divine relationship. The righteous are called to give thanks at the remembrance of God's holiness (Ps. 97:12). How can they do this? Because their peace has been secured on the ground of the full vindication and perfect establishment of that holiness. Hence, the higher their sense of what that holiness is, the deeper and more settled must be their peace. This is a truth of the most precious nature. The unregenerate man could never rejoice in the divine holiness. His aim would be to lower that holiness, if he could not ignore it altogether. Such an one will console himself with the thought that God is good, God is gracious, God is merciful; but you will never find him rejoicing in the thought that God is holy. He has unholy thoughts respecting God's goodness, His grace, and His mercy. He would fain find in those blessed attributes an excuse for his continuing in sin.

On the contrary, the renewed man exults in the holiness of God. He sees the full expression thereof in the cross of the Lord Jesus Christ. It is that holiness which has laid the foundation of his peace; and not only so, but he is made a partaker of it, and he delights in it, while he hates sin with a perfect hatred. The instincts of the divine nature shrink from it, and long after holiness. It would be impossible to enjoy true peace and liberty of heart if one did not know that all the claims connected with "the holy things of the Lord" had been perfectly met by our divine Trespass-offering. There would ever be springing up in the heart the painful sense that those claims had been slighted, through our manifold infirmities and shortcomings. Our very best services, our holiest seasons, our most hallowed exercises, may present something of trespass "in the holy things of the Lord"—"something that ought not to be done." How often are our seasons of public worship and private devotion infringed upon and marred by barrenness and distraction! Hence it is that we need the assurance that our trespasses have all been divinely met by the precious blood of Christ. Thus, in the ever-blessed Lord Jesus, we find One who has come down to the full measure of our necessities as sinners by nature, and trespassers in act. We find in Him the perfect answer to all the cravings of a guilty conscience, and to all the claims of Infinite Holiness, in reference to *all* our sins and *all* our trespasses; so that the believer can stand, with an uncondemning conscience and emancipated heart, in the full light of that holiness which is too pure to behold iniquity or look upon sin.

"And he shall make amends for the harm that he hath done in the holy thing, and shall add the fifth part thereto, and give it unto the priest; and the priest shall make an atonement for him with the ram of the trespass-offering, and it shall be forgiven him" (chap. 5:16). In the addition of "the fifth part," as here set forth, we have a feature of the true Trespass-offering which, it is to be feared, is but little appreciated. When we think of all the wrong and all the trespass which we have done against the Lord, and, further, when we remember how God has been wronged of His rights in this wicked world, with what interest can we contemplate the work of the cross as that wherein God has not merely received back what was lost, but whereby He is an actual gainer. He has gained more by redemption than ever He lost by the fall. He reaps a richer harvest of glory, honor, and praise in the fields of redemption than ever He could have reaped from those of creation. "The sons of God" could raise a loftier song of praise around the empty tomb of Jesus than ever they raised in view of the Creator's accomplished work. The wrong has not only been perfectly atoned for, but an eternal advantage has been gained by the work of the cross. This is a stupendous truth. God is a gainer by the work of Calvary. Who could have conceived this? When we behold man, and the creation of which he was lord, laid in ruins at the feet of the enemy, how could we conceive that, from amid those ruins, God should gather richer and nobler spoils than any which our unfallen world could have yielded? Blessed be the name of Jesus for all this! It is to Him we owe it all. It is by His precious cross that ever a truth so amazing, so divine, could be enunciated. Assuredly, that cross involves a mysterious wisdom "which none of the princes of this world knew; for had they known it, they would not have crucified the Lord of glory" (1 Cor. 2:8). No marvel, therefore, that around that cross, and around Him who was crucified thereon, the affections of patriarchs, prophets, apostles, martyrs, and saints have ever entwined themselves. No marvel that the Holy Ghost should have given forth that solemn, but just, decree, "If any man love not the Lord Jesus Christ, let him be Anathema Maran-atha" (1 Cor. 16:22). Heaven and earth shall echo forth a loud and an eternal amen to this anathema. No marvel that it should be the fixed and immutable purpose of the divine mind, that "at the name of Jesus every knee should bow, of things in heaven, and things in earth, and things under the earth; and that every tongue should confess that Jesus Christ is Lord, to the glory of God the Father" (Phil. 2:10-11).

The same law in reference to "the fifth part" obtained in the case of a trespass committed against a man, as we read, "If a soul sin, and commit a trespass *against the Lord,** and lie unto his neighbor in that which was delivered him to keep, or in fellowship, or in a thing taken away by violence, or hath deceived his neighbor; or have found that which was lost, and lieth concerning it, and sweareth falsely; in any of all these that a man doeth, sinning therein: then it shall be, because he hath sinned, and is guilty, that he shall restore that which he took violently away, or the thing which he hath deceitfully gotten, or that which was delivered him to keep, or the lost thing which he found, or all that about which he hath sworn falsely; he shall even restore it in the principal, *and shall add the fifth part more thereto,* and give it unto him to whom it appertaineth, in the day of his trespass-offering" (chap. 6:2-5).

Man, as well as God, is a positive gainer by the cross. The believer can say, as he gazes upon that cross, Well, it matters not how I have been wronged—how I have been trespassed against—how I have been deceived—what ills have been done to me, I am a gainer by the cross. I have not merely received back all that was lost, but much more beside.

Thus, whether we think of the injured or the injurer, in any given case, we are equally struck with the glorious triumphs of redemption, and the mighty practical results which flow from that gospel which fills the soul with the happy assurance that "all trespasses" are "forgiven," and that the root from whence those trespasses have sprung has been judged. "The gospel of the glory of the blessed God" is that which alone can send forth a man into the midst of a scene which has been the witness of his sins, his trespasses, and his injurious ways—can send him back to all who in any wise have been sufferers by his evil doings, furnished with grace, not only to repair the wrongs, but far more, to allow the full tide of practical

*There is a fine principle involved in the expression, "against the Lord." Although the matter in question was a wrong done to one's neighbor, yet the Lord looked upon it as a trespass against Himself. Every thing must be viewed in reference to the Lord. It matters not who may be affected, Jehovah must get the first place. Thus, when David's conscience was pierced by the arrow of conviction, in reference to his treatment of Uriah, he exclaims, "I have sinned *against the Lord*" (2 Sam 12:13). This principle does not in the least interfere with the injured man's claim.

benevolence to flow forth in all his ways—yea, to love his enemies, to do good to them that hate him, and to pray for them that despitefully use him and persecute him. Such is the precious grace of God that acts in connection with our great Trespass-offering! such are its rich, rare, and refreshing fruits!

What a triumphant answer to the caviler who could say, "Shall we continue in sin, that grace may abound?" Grace not merely cuts up sin by the roots, but transforms the sinner from a curse, into a blessing—from a moral plague, into a channel of divine mercy—from an emissary of Satan, into a messenger of God—from a child of darkness, into a son of the light—from a self-indulgent pleasure-hunter, into a self-denying lover of God—from a slave of vile, selfish lusts, into a willing-hearted servant of Christ—from a cold, narrow-hearted miser, into a benevolent minister to the need of his fellow-man. Away, then, with the oft-repeated taunts, "Are we to do nothing?" "That is a marvelously easy way to be saved." "According to this gospel, we may live as we list." Let all who utter such language behold yonder thief transformed into a liberal donor, and let them be silent forever (see Eph. 4:28). They know not what grace means; they have never felt its sanctifying and elevating influences. They forget that, while the blood of the trespass-offering cleanses the conscience, the law of that offering sends the trespasser back to the one whom he has wronged, with "the principal" and "the fifth" in his hand. Noble testimony this, both to the grace and righteousness of the God of Israel! Beauteous exhibition of the results of that marvelous scheme of redemption, whereby the injurer is forgiven, and the injured becomes an actual gainer! If the conscience has been set to rights, by the blood of the cross, in reference to the claims of God, the conduct must be set to rights, by the holiness of the cross, in reference to the claims of practical righteousness. These things must never be separated; God has joined them together, and let not man put them asunder. The hallowed union will never be dissolved by any mind which is governed by pure gospel morality. Alas! it is easy to profess the principles of grace, while the practice and power thereof are completely denied,—it is easy to talk of resting in the blood of the Trespass-offering, while "the principal" and "the fifth" are not forthcoming. This is vain, and worse than vain. "He that doeth not righteousness is not of God" (1 John 3:10).

Nothing can be more dishonoring to the pure grace of the gospel than the supposition that a man may belong to God while his conduct and character exhibit not the fair traces of practical holiness. "Known unto God are all His works," no doubt; but He has given us, in His holy Word, those evidences by which we can discern those that belong to Him. "The foundation of God standeth sure, having this seal, 'The Lord knoweth them that are His.' And, 'Let every one that nameth the name of Christ depart from iniquity' " (2 Tim. 2:19). We have no right to suppose that an evil-doer belongs to God. The holy instincts of the divine nature are shocked by the mention of such a thing. People sometimes express much difficulty in accounting for such and such evil practices on the part of those whom they cannot help regarding in the light of Christians. The Word of God settles the matter so clearly and so authoritatively, as to leave no possible ground for any such difficulty. "In this the children of God are manifest, and the children of the devil: whosoever doeth not righteousness is not of God, neither he that loveth not his brother." It is well to remember this, in this day of laxity and self-indulgence. There is a fearful amount of easy, uninfluential profession abroad, against which the genuine Christian is called upon to make a firm stand, and bear a severe testimony—a testimony resulting from the steady exhibition of "the fruits of righteousness which are by Jesus Christ unto the glory and praise of God." It is most deplorable to see so many going along the beaten path—the well-trodden highway of religious profession, and yet manifesting not a trace of love or holiness in their conduct. Christian reader, let us be faithful; let us rebuke, by a life of self-denial and genuine benevolence, the self-indulgence and culpable inactivity of evangelical, yet worldly, profession. May God grant unto all His true-hearted people abundant grace for these things!

Let us now proceed to compare the two classes of trespass-offering; namely, the offering on account of trespass "in the holy things of the Lord," and that which had reference to a trespass committed in the common transactions and relations of human life. In so doing, we shall find one or two points which demand our attentive consideration.

First, the expression, "if a soul sin through ignorance," which occurs in the former, is omitted in the latter. The reason of this is obvious. The claims which stand connected with the holy things of the Lord must pass infinitely beyond the reach of the most elevated human sensibility. Those claims may be continually interfered with—continually trespassed upon, and the trespasser not be aware of the fact. Man's consciousness can never be the regulator in the sanctuary of God. This is an unspeakable mercy. God's holiness alone must fix the standard when God's rights are in question.

On the other hand, the human conscience can readily grasp the full amount of a human claim, and can readily take cognizance of any interference with such claim. How often may we have wronged God, in His holy things, without ever taking a note of it in the tablet of conscience—yea, without having the competency to detect it (see Mal. 3:8). Not so, however, when man's rights are in question. The wrong which the human eye can see, and the human heart feel, the human conscience can take notice of. A man, "through ignorance" of the laws which governed the sanctuary of old, might commit a trespass against those laws without being aware of it, until a higher light had shone in upon his conscience; but a man could not "through ignorance" tell a lie, swear falsely, commit an act of violence, deceive his neighbor, or find a lost thing and deny it. These were all plain and palpable acts, lying within the range of the most sluggish sensibility. Hence it is that the expression, "through ignorance" is introduced in reference to "the holy things of the Lord," and omitted in reference to the common affairs of men. How blessed it is to know that the precious blood of Christ has settled all questions, whether with respect to God or man—our sins of ignorance or our known sins! Here lies the deep and settled foundation of the believer's peace. The cross has divinely met *all.*

Again, when it was a question of trespass "in the holy things of the Lord," the unblemished sacrifice was first introduced; and afterward, "the principal" and "the fifth." This order was reversed when it was a question of the common affairs of life (comp. chap. 5:15-16 with chap. 6:4-7). The reason of this is equally obvious. When the divine rights were infringed, the blood of atonement was made the great prominent matter; whereas when human rights were interfered with, restitution would naturally assume the leading place in the mind. But inasmuch as the latter involved the question of the soul's relation with God as well as the former, therefore the sacrifice is introduced, though it be last in order. If I wrong my fellow-man, that wrong will undoubtedly interfere with my communion with God; and that communion can only be restored on the ground of atonement. Mere restitution would not avail; it might satisfy the injured man, but it could not form the basis of restored communion with God. I might restore "the principal" and add "the fifth" ten thousand times over, and yet my sin remain, for "without shedding of blood is no remission" (Heb. 9:22). Still, if it be a question of injury done to my neighbor, then restitution must first be made.—"If thou bring thy gift to the altar, and there rememberest that thy brother hath aught against thee, leave there thy gift before the altar, and go thy way; first be reconciled to thy brother, and then come and offer thy gift" (Matt. 5:23-24).*

There is far more involved in the divine

*From a comparison of Matt. 5:23-24 with Matt. 18:21-22, we may learn a fine principle as to the way in which wrongs and injuries are to be settled between two brothers. The injurer is sent back from the altar, in order to have his matters set order prescribed in the trespass-offering than might at first sight appear. The claims which arise out of our human relations must not be disregarded; they must ever get their proper place in the heart. This is distinctly taught in the trespass-offering. When an Israelite had, by an act of trespass, deranged his relation with Jehovah, the order was, sacrifice and restitution: when he had, by an act of trespass, deranged his relation with his neighbor, the order was, restitution and sacrifice. Will any one undertake to say this is a distinction without a difference? Does the change of the order not convey its own appropriate, because divinely appointed, lesson? Unquestionably. Every point is pregnant with meaning, if we will but allow the Holy Ghost to convey that meaning to our hearts, and not seek to grasp it by the aid of our poor vain imaginings. Each offering conveys its own characteristic view of the Lord Jesus and His work, and each is presented in its own characteristic order; and, we may safely say, it is at once the business and the delight of the spiritual mind to apprehend both the one and the other. The very same character of mind which would seek to make nothing of the peculiar order of each offering, would also set aside the idea of a peculiar phase of Christ in each. It would deny the existence of any difference between the burnt-offering and the sin-offering, and between the sin-offering and the trespass-offering, and between any or all of these and the meat-offering or the peace-offering. Hence, it would follow that the first seven chapters of the book of Leviticus are all a vain repetition, each successive chapter going over the same thing. Who could cede aught so monstrous as this? What Christian mind could suffer such an insult to be offered to the sacred page? A German rationalist or neologian may put forth such vain and detestable notions, but those who have been divinely taught that "all scripture is given by inspiration of God," will be led to regard the various types, in their specific order, as so many variously-shaped caskets, in which the Holy Ghost has treasured up, for the people of God, "the unsearchable riches of Christ." There is no tedious repetition, no redundancy. All is rich, divine, heavenly variety; and all we need is to be personally acquainted with the great Antitype, in order to enter into the beauties and seize the delicate touches of each type. Directly the heart lays hold of the fact that it is Christ we have in each type, it can hang with spiritual interest over the most minute details, it sees meaning and beauty in every thing, it finds Christ in all. As in the kingdom of nature, the telescope and the microscope present to the eye their own special wonders, so with the Word of God; whether we look at it as a whole, or scrutinize each clause, we find that which elicits the worship and thanksgiving of our hearts.

May the name of the Lord Jesus ever be more precious to our hearts! Then shall we value every thing that speaks of Him—every thing that sets Him forth—every thing affording a fresh insight into His peculiar excellency and matchless beauty.

---

*Note.*—The remainder of chapter 6, together with the whole of chapter 7, is occupied with the law of the various offerings, to which reference has already been made. There are, however, some points presented in the law of the sin-offering and the trespass-offering which may be noticed ere we leave this copious section of our book.

In none of the offerings is Christ's personal holiness more strikingly presented than in the sin-offering. "Speak unto Aaron and to his sons, saying, This is the law of the sin-offering: In the place where the burnt-offering is killed shall the sin-offering be

straight with the injured one; for there can be no communion with the Father so long as my brother "hath aught against me." But then, mark the beauteous way in which the injured one is taught to receive the injurer. "Lord, how oft shall my brother sin against me, and I forgive him? till seven times?' Jesus saith unto him, 'I say not unto thee, Until seven times; but, *Until seventy times seven.*' " Such is the divine mode of settling all questions between brethren. "Forbearing one another, and forgiving one another, if any man have a quarrel against any; even as Christ forgave you, so also do ye" (Col. 3:13).

killed before the Lord: *it is most holy*. . . . Whatsoever shall touch the flesh thereof *shall be holy*. . . . All the males among the priests shall eat thereof: *it is most holy"* (chap. 6:25-29). So also in speaking of the meat-offering, "It is most holy, *as is the sin-offering,* and as the trespass-offering." This is most marked and striking. The Holy Ghost did not need to guard with such jealousy the personal holiness of Christ in the burnt-offering; but lest the soul should, by any means, lose sight of that holiness while contemplating the place which the blessed One took in the sin-offering, we are again and again reminded of it by the words, "It is most holy." Truly edifying and refreshing it is to behold the divine and essential holiness of the Person of Christ shining forth in the midst of Calvary's profound and awful gloom. The same point is observable "in the law of the trespass-offering" (see chap. 7:1,6). Never was the Lord Jesus more fully seen to be "the Holy One of God" than when He was "made sin" upon the cursed tree. The vileness and blackness of that with which He stood identified on the cross, only served to show out more clearly that He was "most holy." Though a sin-bearer, He was sinless; though enduring the wrath of *God,* He was the *Father's* delight; though deprived of the light of *God's* countenance, He dwelt in the *Father's* bosom. Precious mystery! Who can sound its mighty depths? How wonderful to find it so accurately shadowed forth in "the law of the sin-offering"!

Again, my reader should seek to apprehend the meaning of the expression, "All the *males* among the priests shall eat thereof." The ceremonial act of eating the sin-offering or the trespass-offering was expressive of full identification; but to eat the sin-offering—to make another's sin one's own, demanded a higher degree of priestly energy, such as was expressed in "the *males* among the priests." "And the Lord spake unto Aaron, 'Behold, I also have given thee the charge of Mine heave-offerings of all the hallowed things of the children of Israel; unto thee have I given them by reason of the anointing, and *to thy sons,* by an ordinance forever. This shall be thine of the most holy things, reserved from the fire: every oblation of theirs, every meat-offering of theirs, and every sin-offering of theirs, and every trespass-offering of theirs, which they shall render unto Me, shall be most holy for thee and for *thy sons.* In the most holy place shalt thou eat it; *every male* shall eat it: I shall be holy unto thee. And this is thine; the heave-offering of their gift, with all the wave-offerings of the children of Israel: I have given them unto thee, and to thy sons and to *thy daughters* with thee, by a statute forever: *every one that is clean* in thy house shall eat of it" (Num. 18:8-11).

It demanded a larger measure of priestly energy to eat of the sin or trespass-offering than merely to partake of the heave and wave-offerings of gift. The "daughters" of Aaron could eat of the latter: none but the "sons" could eat of the former. In general, "the male" expresses a thing according to the divine idea; "the female," according to human development. The former gives you the thing in full energy; the latter, in its imperfections. How few of us have sufficient priestly energy to enable us to make another's sin or trespass our own! The blessed Lord Jesus did this perfectly. He made His people's sins His own, and bore the judgment thereof, on the cross. He fully identified Himself with us, so that we may know, in full and blessed certainty, that the whole question of sin and trespass has been divinely settled. If Christ's identification was perfect, then the settlement was perfect likewise; and that it was perfect, the scene enacted at Calvary declares. All is accomplished. The sin, the trespasses, the claims of God, the claims of man—all have been eternally settled; and now, perfect peace is the portion of all who, by grace, accept as true the record of God. It is as simple as God could make it, and the soul that believes it is made happy. The peace and happiness of the believer depend wholly upon the perfection of Christ's sacrifice. It is not a question of his mode of receiving it, his thoughts about it, or his feelings respecting it; it is simply a question of his crediting, by faith, the testimony of God as to the value of the sacrifice. The Lord be praised for His own simple and perfect way of peace! May many troubled souls be led by the Holy Spirit into an understanding thereof!

We shall here close our meditations upon one of the richest sections in the whole canon of inspiration. It is but little we have been enabled to glean from it. We have hardly penetrated below the surface of an exhaustless mine. If, however, the reader has, for the first time, been led to view the offerings as so many varied exhibitions of the great Sacrifice, and if he is led to cast himself at the feet of the great Teacher, to learn more of the living depths of these things, I cannot but feel that an end has been gained for which we may well feel deeply thankful.

## *CHAPTERS 8—9*

HAVING considered the doctrine of sacrifice, as unfolded in the first seven chapters of this book, we now approach the subject of priesthood. The two subjects are intimately connected. The sinner needs a *sacrifice;* the believer needs a *priest.* We have both the one and the other in Christ, who, having offered Himself without spot to God, entered upon the sphere of His priestly ministry in the sanctuary above. We need no other sacrifice, no other priest: Jesus is divinely sufficient. He imparts the dignity and worth of His own Person to every office He sustains, and to every work He performs. When we see Him as a sacrifice, we know that we have in Him all that a perfect sacrifice could be; and when we see Him as a priest, we know that every function of the priesthood is perfectly discharged by Him. As a sacrifice, He introduces His people into a settled relationship with God; and as a priest, He maintains them therein, according to the perfectness of what He is. Priesthood is designed for those who already stand in a certain relationship with God. As sinners, by nature and by practice, we are "brought nigh to God by the blood of the cross;" we are brought into an established relationship with Him; we stand before Him as the fruit of His own work. He has put away our sins in such a manner as suits Himself, so that we might be before Him to the praise of His name, as the exhibition of what He can accomplish through the power of death and resurrection.

But though so fully delivered from every thing that could be against us—though so perfectly accepted in the Beloved—though so complete in Christ—though so highly exalted, yet are we, in ourselves, while down here, poor feeble creatures, ever prone to wander, ready to stumble, exposed to manifold temptations, trials, and snares. As such, we need the ceaseless ministry of our "great High-Priest," whose very presence in the sanctuary above maintains us in the full integrity of that place and relationship in which, through grace, we stand. "He ever liveth to make intercession for us" (Heb. 7:25). We could not stand for a moment down here if He were not living for us up there. "Because I live, ye shall live also" (John 14:19). "For if, when we were enemies, we were reconciled to God by the death of His Son, much more, being reconciled, we shall be saved by His life" (Rom. 5:10). The "death" and the "life" are inseparably connected in the economy of grace. But, be it observed, the life comes after the death. It is Christ's life as risen from the dead, and not His life down here, that the apostle refers to in the last-quoted passage. This distinction is eminently worthy of my reader's attention. The life of our blessed Lord Jesus while down here was, I need hardly remark, infinitely precious; but He did not enter upon His sphere of priestly service until He had accomplished the work of redemption. Nor could He have done so, inasmuch as "it is evident that our Lord sprang out of Juda, of which tribe Moses spake nothing concerning priesthood" (Heb. 7:14). "For every high-priest is ordained to offer gifts and sacrifices: wherefore it is of necessity that this Man have somewhat also to offer. For if He were on earth, He should not be a priest, seeing that there are priests that offer gifts according to the law" (Heb. 8:3-4). "But Christ being come a high-priest of good things to come, by a greater and more perfect tabernacle, not made with hands, that is to say, not of this building; neither by the blood of goats and calves, but by His own blood He entered in once into the holy place, having obtained eternal redemption. . . . For Christ is not entered into the holy places made with hands, which are the figures of the true; but into heaven itself, now to appear in the presence of God for us" (Heb. 9:11-12,24).

Heaven, not earth, is the sphere of Christ's priestly ministry; and on that sphere He entered when He had offered Himself without spot to God. He never appeared as a priest in the temple below. He ofttimes went up to the temple to teach, but never to sacrifice or burn incense. There never was any one ordained of God to discharge the functions of the priestly office on earth save Aaron and his sons. "If He were on earth, He should not be a priest." This is a point of much interest and value in connection with the doctrine of priesthood. Heaven is the sphere, and accomplished redemption the basis, of Christ's priesthood. Save in the sense that all believers are priests (1 Pet. 2:5), there is no such thing as a priest upon earth. Unless a man can show his descent from Aaron—unless he can trace his pedigree up to that ancient source, he has no right to exercise the priestly office. Apostolic succession itself, could it be proved, would be of no possible value here, inasmuch as the apostles themselves were not priests, save in the sense above referred to. The feeblest member of the household of faith is as much a priest as the apostle Peter himself. He is a spiritual priest, he worships in a spiritual temple, he stands at a spiritual altar, he offers a spiritual sacrifice, he is clad in spiritual vestments. "Ye also, as lively stones, are built up a spiritual house, a holy priesthood, to offer up spiritual sacrifices, acceptable to God by Jesus Christ" (1 Pet. 2:5). "By Him, therefore, let us offer the sacrifice of praise to God continually, that is, the fruit of our lips, giving thanks to His name. But to do good and to communicate forget not, for with such sacrifices God is well pleased" (Heb. 13:15-16).

If one of the direct descendants of the house of Aaron were converted to Christ, he would enter upon an entirely new character and ground of priestly service. And be it observed, that the passages just quoted present the two great classes of spiritual sacrifice which the spiritual priest is privileged to offer. There is the sacrifice of praise to God, and the sacrifice of benevolence to man. There is a double stream continually going forth from the believer who is living in the realization of his priestly place—a stream of grateful praise ascending to the throne of God, and a stream of active benevolence flowing forth to a needy world. The spiritual priest stands with one hand lifted up to God in the presentation of the incense of grateful praise, and the other opened wide to minister, in genuine beneficence, to every form of human need. Were these things more distinctly apprehended, what hallowed elevation and what moral grace would they not impart to the Christian character! Elevation, inasmuch as the heart would ever be lifted up to the infinite Source of all that is capable of elevating; moral grace, inasmuch as the heart would ever be kept open to all demands upon its sympathies. The two things are inseparable. Immediate occupation of heart with God must, of necessity, elevate and enlarge; but, on the other hand, if one walks at a distance from God, the heart will become groveling and contracted. Intimacy of communion with God—the habitual realization of our priestly dignity, is the only effectual remedy for the downward and selfish tendencies of the old nature.

Having said thus much on the subject of priesthood in general, both as to its primary and secondary aspects, we shall proceed to examine the contexts of the eighth and ninth chapters of the book of Leviticus.

"And the Lord spake unto Moses, saying, 'Take Aaron and his sons with him, and the garments, and the anointing oil, and a bullock for the sin-offering, and two rams, and a basket of unleavened bread; and gather thou all the congregation together unto the door of the tabernacle of the congregation.'

And Moses did as the Lord commanded him; and the assembly was gathered together unto the door of the tabernacle of the congregation." There is special grace unfolded here. The whole assembly is convened at the door of the tabernacle of the congregation, in order that all might have the privilege of beholding the one who was about to be intrusted with the charge of their most important interests. In the twenty-eighth and twenty-ninth of Exodus we are taught the same general truth with respect to the vestments and sacrifices connected with the priestly office; but in Leviticus, the congregation is introduced, and allowed to look on at every movement in the solemn and impressive service of consecration. The humblest member of the assembly had his own place. Each one—the lowest as well as the highest—was permitted to gaze upon the person of the high-priest, upon the sacrifice which he offered, and upon the robes which he wore. Each one had his own peculiar need, and the God of Israel would have each to see and know that his need was fully provided for by the varied qualifications of the high-priest who stood before him. Of these qualifications the priestly robes were the apt typical expression. Each portion of the dress was designed and adapted to set forth some special qualification in which the assembly as a whole, and each individual member, would, of necessity, be deeply interested. The coat, the girdle, the robe, the ephod, the breastplate, the Urim and the Thummim, the mitre, the holy crown—all told out the varied virtues, qualifications, and functions of the one who was to represent the congregation and maintain the interests thereof in the divine presence.

Thus it is the believer can, with the eye of faith, behold his great High-Priest in the heavens, and see in Him the divine realities of which the Aaronic vestments were but the shadows. The Lord Jesus Christ is the holy One, the anointed One, the mitred One, the girded One. He is all these, not in virtue of outward garments to be put on or off, but in virtue of the divine and eternal graces of His Person, the changeless efficacy of His work, and the imperishable virtue of His sacred offices. This is the special value of studying the types of the Mosaic economy. The enlightened eye sees Christ in all. The blood of the sacrifice and the robe of the high-priest both point to Him—both were designed of God to set Him forth. If it be a question of conscience, the blood of the sacrifice meets it, according to the just claims of the sanctuary. Grace has met the demand of holiness. And then, if it be a question of the need connected with the believer's position down here, he can see it all divinely answered in the official robes of the high-priest.

There are two ways in which to contemplate the believer's position—two ways in which that position is presented in the Word, which must be taken into account ere the true idea of priesthood can be intelligently laid hold of. The believer is represented as being part of a body of which Christ is the Head. This body, with Christ its Head, is spoken of as forming one man, complete in every respect. It was quickened with Christ, raised with Christ, and in Christ seated in the heavens. It is one with Him, complete in Him, accepted in Him, possessing His life, and standing in His favor before God. All trespasses are blotted out. There is no spot. All is fair and lovely beneath the eye of God. (See 1 Cor. 12:12-13; Eph. 2:5-10; Col. 2:6-15; 1 John 4:17.)

Then, again, the believer is contemplated as in the place of need, weakness, and dependence down here in this world. He is ever exposed to temptation, prone to wander, liable to stumble and fall. As such, he continually stands in need of the perfect sympathy and powerful ministrations of the High-Priest, who ever appears in the presence of God in the full value of His Person and work, and who represents the believer and maintains his cause before the throne.

Now, my reader should ponder both these aspects of the believer, in order that he may see, not only what a highly exalted and privileged place he occupies with Christ on high, but also what ample provision there is for him in reference to his every need and weakness here below. This distinction might further be developed in this way: The believer is represented as being *of the Church,* and *in the kingdom.* As the former, heaven is his place, his home, his portion, the seat of his affections: as the latter, he is on earth, in the place of trial, responsibility, and conflict. Hence, therefore, priesthood is a divine provision for those who though being of the Church, and belonging to heaven, are nevertheless in the kingdom, and walking on the earth. This distinction is a very simple one, and, when apprehended, explains a vast number of passages of Scripture in which many minds encounter considerable difficulty.*

In looking into the contents of the chapters which lie open before us, we may remark three things put prominently forward, namely, the authority of the Word, the value of the blood, the power of the Spirit. These are weighty matters—matters of unspeakable importance—matters which must be regarded by every Christian as unquestionably vital and fundamental.

And, first, as to the authority of the Word, it is of the deepest interest to see that in the consecration of the priests, as well as in the entire range of the sacrifices, we are brought immediately under the authority of the Word of God. "And Moses said unto the congregation, '*This is the thing which the Lord* commanded to be done' " (chap. 8:5). And again, "Moses said, '*This is the thing which the Lord commanded* that ye should do: *and the glory of the Lord shall appear unto you'* " (chap. 9:6). Let these words sink down into our ears; let them be carefully and prayerfully pondered: they are priceless words. "*This* is *the* thing which *the Lord* commanded." He did not say, This is the thing which is expedient, agreeable, or suitable; neither did he say, This is the thing which has been arranged by the voice of the fathers, the decree of the elders, or the opinion of the doctors. Moses knew nothing of such sources of authority. To him there was one holy, elevated, paramount source of authority, and that was, the Word of Jehovah, and he would bring every member of the assembly into direct contact with that blessed source. This gave assurance to the heart, and fixedness to all the thoughts. There was no room left for tradition, with its uncertain sound, or for man, with his doubtful disputations. All was clear, conclusive, and authoritative. Jehovah had spoken; and all that was needed was to hear what He had said, and obey. Neither tradition nor expediency has any place in the heart that has learnt to prize, to reverence, and to obey the Word of God.

And what was to be the result of this strict adherence to the Word of God? A truly blessed result indeed. "The glory of the Lord shall appear unto you." Had the Word been disregarded, the glory would not have appeared. The two things were intimately connected. The slightest deviation from "Thus saith Jehovah" would have prevented the beams of the divine glory from appearing to the congregation of Israel. Had there been the introduction of a single rite or ceremony not enjoined by the Word, or had there been the omission of aught which that Word commanded, Jehovah would not have manifested His glory. He could not sanction by the glory of His presence the neglect or rejection of His Word. He can bear with ignorance and infirmity, but He cannot sanction neglect or disobedience.

Oh that all this were more solemnly considered, in this day of tradition and expediency! I would, in earnest affection, and in the deep sense of personal responsibility to my reader, exhort him to give diligent heed to the importance of close—I had almost said severe—adherence and reverent subjection to the Word of God. Let him try every thing by that standard, and reject all that comes not up to it,—let him weigh every thing in that balance, and cast aside all that is not full weight,—let him measure every thing by that rule, and refuse all deviation. If I could only be the means of awakening one soul to a proper sense of the place which belongs to the Word of God, I

*A comparison of the Epistle to the Ephesians with the first Epistle of Peter will furnish the reader with much valuable instruction in reference to the double aspect of the believer's position. The former shows him as seated in heaven; the latter, as a pilgrim and a sufferer on earth.

should feel I had not written my book for naught or in vain.

Pause and, in the presence of the Searcher of hearts, ask yourself this plain, pointed question: Am I sanctioning by my presence, or adopting in my practice, any departure from, or neglect of, the Word of God? Make this a solemn, personal matter before the Lord. Be assured of it, it is of the very deepest moment—the very last importance. If you find that you have been in any wise connected with, or involved in, aught that wears not the distinct stamp of divine sanction, reject it at once and forever. Yes, reject it, though arrayed in the imposing vestments of antiquity, accredited by the voice of tradition, and putting forward the almost irresistible plea of expediency. If you cannot say, in reference to every thing with which you stand connected, "This is the thing which the Lord hath commanded," then away with it unhesitatingly, away with it forever. Remember these words, "*As* He hath done this day, *so* the Lord hath commanded to do." Yes, remember the "as" and the "so"; see that you are connecting them in your ways and associations, and let them never be separated.

"So Aaron and his sons did *all* things *which the Lord commanded* by the hand of Moses" (chap. 8:36). "And Moses and Aaron went into the tabernacle of the congregation, and came out, and blessed the people: and the glory of the Lord appeared unto all the people. And there came a fire out from before the Lord, and consumed upon the altar the burnt-offering and the fat; which, when all the people saw, they shouted and fell on their faces" (chap. 9:23-24). Here we have an "eighth day" scene—a scene of resurrection-glory. Aaron, having offered the sacrifice, lifted up his hands in priestly benediction upon the people; and then Moses and Aaron retire into the tabernacle, and disappear, while the whole assembly is seen in waiting outside. Finally, Moses and Aaron, representing Christ in His double character as Priest and King, come forth, and bless the people; the glory appears in all its splendor, the fire consumes the sacrifice, and the entire congregation falls prostrate in worship before the presence of the Lord.

Now, all this was literally enacted at the consecration of Aaron and his sons; and, moreover, all this was the result of strict adherence to the Word of Jehovah. But ere I turn from this branch of the subject, let me remind the reader that all that these chapters contain is but "a shadow of good things to come." This, indeed, holds good in reference to the entire Mosaic economy (Heb. 10:1). Aaron and his sons together represent Christ and His priestly house; Aaron alone represents Christ in His sacrificial and intercessory functions; Moses and Aaron together represent Christ as King and Priest; "the eighth day" represents the day of resurrection-glory, when the congregation of Israel shall see the Messiah, seated as a Royal Priest upon His throne, and when the glory of Jehovah shall fill the whole earth, as the waters cover the sea. These sublime truths are largely unfolded in the Word, they glitter like gems of celestial brilliancy all along the inspired page; but lest they should, to any reader, wear the suspicious aspect of novelty, I shall refer him to the following direct Scripture proofs; viz., Num. 14:21; Isa. 9:6-7; 11; 25:6-12; 32:1-2; 35; 37:31-32; 40:1-5; 54; 59:16-21; 60—66; *passim*, Jer. 23:5-8; 30:10-24; 33:6-22; Ezek. 48:35; Dan. 7:13-14; Hos. 14:4-9; Zeph. 3:14-20; Zech. 3:8-10; 6:12-13; 14.

Let us now consider the second point presented in our section, namely, the efficacy of the blood. This is unfolded with great fullness, and put forward in great prominence. Whether we contemplate the doctrine of sacrifice or the doctrine of priesthood, we find the shedding of blood gets the same important place. "And he brought the bullock for the sin-offering; and Aaron and his sons laid their hands upon the head of the bullock for the sin-offering. And he slew it; and Moses took the blood, and put it upon the horns of the altar round about with his finger, and purified the altar, and poured the blood at the bottom of the altar, and sanctified it, to make reconciliation upon it" (chap. 8:14-15). "And he brought the ram for the burnt-offering; and Aaron and his sons laid their hands upon the head of the ram. And he killed it; and Moses sprinkled the blood upon the altar round about" (ver. 18-19). "And he brought the other ram, the ram of consecration; and Aaron and his sons laid their hands upon the head of the ram. And he slew it; and Moses took of the blood of it, and put it upon the tip of Aaron's right ear, and upon the thumb of his right hand, and upon the great toe of his right foot. And he brought Aaron's sons, and Moses put of the blood upon the tip of their right ear, and upon the thumbs of their right hands, and upon the great toes of their right feet; and Moses sprinkled the blood upon the altar round about" (ver. 22-24).

The import of the various sacrifices has been, in some degree, developed in the opening chapters of this volume; but the passages just quoted serve to show the prominent place which the blood occupies in the consecration of the priests. A blood-stained *ear* was needed to hearken to the divine communications, a blood-stained *hand* was needed to execute the services of the sanctuary, and a blood-stained *foot* was needed to tread the courts of the Lord's house. All this is perfect in its way. The shedding of blood was the grand foundation of all sacrifice for sin, and it stood connected with all the vessels of the ministry and with all the functions of the priesthood. Throughout the entire range of Levitical service, we observe the value, the efficacy, the power, and the wide application of the blood. "Almost all things are by the law purged with blood" (Heb. 9:22). Christ has entered, by His own blood, into heaven itself. He appears on the throne of the Majesty in the heavens in the value of all that He has accomplished on the cross. His presence on the throne attests the worth and acceptableness of His atoning blood. He is there *for us.* Blessed assurance! He ever liveth. He never changeth; and we are in Him, and as He is. He presents us to the Father in His own eternal perfectness; and the Father delights in us as thus presented, even as He delights in the One who presents us. This identification is typically set forth in "Aaron and his sons" laying their hands upon the head of each of the sacrifices. They all stood before God in the value of the same sacrifice. Whether it were the "bullock for the sin-offering," "the ram for the burnt-offering," or "the ram of consecration," they jointly laid their hands on all. True, Aaron alone was anointed before the blood was shed, he was clad in his robes of office and anointed with the holy oil before ever his sons were clothed or anointed. The reason of this is obvious. Aaron, when spoken of by himself, typifies Christ in His own peerless excellency and dignity; and, as we know, Christ appeared in all His own personal worth and was anointed by the Holy Ghost previous to the accomplishment of His atoning work. In all things He has the pre-eminence (Col. 1). Still, there is the fullest identification afterwards between Aaron and his sons, as there is the fullest identification between Christ and His people. "The Sanctifier and the sanctified are all of one" (Heb. 2). The personal distinctness enhances the value of the mystic oneness.

This truth of the distinctness and yet oneness of the Head and members leads us naturally to our third and last point, namely, the power of the Spirit. We may remark how much takes place between the anointing of Aaron and the anointing of his sons with him. The blood is shed, the fat consumed on the altar, and the breast waved before the Lord. In other words, the Sacrifice is perfected, the sweet odor thereof ascends to God, and the One who offered it ascends in the power of resurrection, and takes His place on high. All this comes in between the anointing of the Head and the anointing of the members. Let us quote and compare the passages. First, as to Aaron alone, we read, "And he put upon him the coat, and girded him with the girdle, and clothed him with the robe, and put the ephod upon him, and he girded him with the curious girdle of the ephod, and bound it unto him therewith. And he put the breastplate upon him; also he put in the breastplate the Urim and the Thummim. And he put the mitre upon his head; and upon the mitre, even upon his forefront, did he put the golden plate, the holy crown; as the Lord commanded Moses. And Moses took the anointing oil, and anointed the tabernacle and all that was therein, and sanctified them. And he sprinkled thereof upon the altar seven times, and anointed the altar and all his vessels, both the laver and his foot, to sanctify them. And he poured of the anointing oil upon Aaron's head, and anointed him, to sanctify him" (chap. 8:7-12).

Here we have Aaron presented alone. The anointing oil is poured upon his head, and that, too, in immediate connection with the anointing of all the vessels of the tabernacle. The whole assembly was permitted to behold the high-priest clothed in his official robes, mitred and anointed; and not only so, but as each garment was put on—as each act was performed—as each ceremony was enacted, it was seen to be immediately founded upon the authority of the Word. There was nothing vague, nothing arbitrary, nothing imaginative: all was divinely stable. The need of the congregation was fully met, and met in such a way as that it could be said, "This is the thing which Jehovah commanded to be done."

Now, in Aaron anointed alone, previous to the shedding of the blood, we have a type of Christ, who, until He offered Himself upon the cross, stood entirely alone. There could be no union between Him and His people save on the ground of death and resurrection. This all-important truth has already been referred to, and, in some measure, developed in connection with the subject of sacrifice; but it adds force and interest to it to see it so distinctly presented in connection with the question of priesthood. Without shedding of blood there was no remission—the sacrifice was not completed. So, also, without shedding of blood Aaron and his sons could not be anointed together. Let the reader note this fact; let him be assured of it, it is worthy of his deepest attention. We must ever beware of passing lightly over any circumstances in the Levitical economy. Every thing has its own specific voice and meaning; and the One who designed and developed the order can expound to the heart and understanding what that order means.

"And Moses took of the anointing *oil,* and of the *blood* which was upon the altar, and sprinkled it upon Aaron, and upon his garments, and upon his sons, and upon his sons' garments *with him;* and sanctified Aaron, and his garments, and his sons, and his sons' garments *with him*" (chap. 8:30). Why were not Aaron's sons anointed with him at verse 12? Simply because the blood had not been shed. When "the blood" and "the oil" could be connected together, then Aaron and his sons could be "anointed" and "sanctified" together, but not until then. "And for their sakes I sanctify Myself, that they also might be sanctified through the truth" (John 17:19). The reader who could lightly pass over so marked a circumstance, or say it meant nothing, has yet to learn to value aright the types of the Old Testament Scriptures—"the shadows of good things to come;" and, on the other hand, the one who admits that it does mean something, but yet refuses to inquire and understand what that something is, is doing serious damage to his own soul, and manifesting but little interest in the precious oracles of God.

"And Moses said unto Aaron and to his sons, 'Boil the flesh at the door of the tabernacle of the congregation; and there eat it with the bread that is in the basket of consecrations, as I commanded, saying, Aaron and his sons shall eat it. And that which remaineth of the flesh and of the bread shall ye burn with fire. And ye shall not go out of the door of the tabernacle of the congregation in seven days, until the days of your consecration be at an end; for seven days shall He consecrate you. As He hath done this day, so the Lord hath commanded to do, to make an atonement for you. Therefore shall ye abide at the door of the tabernacle of the congregation day and night seven days, and keep the charge of the Lord, that ye die not; for so I am commanded' " (ver. 31-35). These verses furnish a fine type of Christ and His people feeding together upon the results of accomplished atonement. Aaron and his sons, having been anointed together on the ground of the shed blood, are here presented to our view as shut in within the precincts of the tabernacle during "seven days." A striking figure of the present position of Christ and His members during the entire of this dispensation—shut in with God, and waiting for the manifestation of the glory. Blessed position! Blessed portion! Blessed hope! To be associated with Christ, shut in with God, waiting for the day of glory, and, while waiting for the glory, feeding upon the riches of divine grace, in the power of holiness, are blessings of the most precious nature—privileges of the very highest order. Oh, for a capacity to take them in, a heart to enjoy them, a deeper sense of their magnitude! May our hearts be withdrawn from all that pertains to this present evil world, so that we may feed upon the contents of "the basket of consecrations," which is our proper food as priests in the sanctuary of God.

"And it came to pass *on the eighth day,* that Moses called Aaron, and his sons, and *the elders of Israel.* And he said unto Aaron, 'Take thee a young calf for a sin-offering, and a ram for a burnt-offering, without blemish, and offer them before the Lord. And unto *the children of Israel* thou shalt speak, saying, Take ye a kid of the goats for a sin-offering; and a calf and a lamb, both of the first year, without blemish, for a burnt-offering; also a bullock and a ram for peace-offerings, to sacrifice before the Lord; and a meat-offering mingled with oil; for *to-day the Lord will appear unto you'* " (chap. 9:1-4).

The "seven days" being over, during which Aaron and his sons were shut in in the retirement of the tabernacle, the whole congregation is now introduced, and the glory of Jehovah unfolds itself. This gives great completeness to the whole scene. The shadows of good things to come are here passing before us, in their divine order. "The "eighth day" is a shadow of that bright millennial morning which is about to dawn upon this earth, when the congregation of Israel shall behold the true Priest coming forth from the sanctuary, where He is now hidden from the eyes of men, and with Him a company of priests—the companions of His retirement, and the happy participators of His manifested glory. In short, nothing, as a type or shadow, could be more complete. In the first place, Aaron and his sons washed with water—a type of Christ and His people, as viewed in God's eternal decree, sanctified together in purpose (chap. 8:6). Then we have the mode and order in which this purpose was to be carried out. Aaron, in solitude, is robed and anointed—a type of Christ as sanctified and sent into the world, and anointed by the Holy Ghost (ver. 7-12; comp. Luke 3:21-22; John 10:36; 12:24). Then we have the presentation and acceptance of the sacrifice, in virtue of which Aaron and his sons were anointed and sanctified *together* (ver. 14-29)—a type of the cross, in its application to those who now constitute Christ's priestly household, who are united to Him, anointed with Him, hidden with Him, and expecting with Him "the eighth day," when He with them shall be manifested in all the brightness of that glory which belongs to Him in the eternal purpose of God (John 14:19; Acts 2:33; 19:1-7; Col. 3:1-4). Finally, we have Israel brought into the full enjoyment of the results of accomplished atonement. They are gathered before the Lord; "and Aaron lifted up his hand toward the people, and blessed them, and came down from offering of the sin-offering, and the burnt-offering, and peace-offerings" (see chap. 9:1-22).

What, now, we may legitimately inquire, remains to be done? Simply that the top-stone should be brought forth with shoutings of victory and hymns of praise. "And Moses and Aaron went into the tabernacle of the congregation, and came out, and blessed the people: and *the glory of the Lord appeared unto all the people.* And there came a fire out from before the Lord, and consumed upon the altar the burnt-offering and the fat: which when all the people saw, *they shouted, and fell on their faces*" (ver. 23-24). This was the shout of victory—the prostration of worship. All was complete. The sacrifice, the robed and mitred priest, the priestly family associated with their head, the priestly benediction, the appearance of the king and priest; in short, nothing was lacking, and therefore the divine glory appeared, and the whole assembly fell prostrate in adoring worship. It is altogether a truly magnificent scene—a marvelously beautiful shadow of good things to come. And be it remembered, that all which is here shadowed forth will ere long be fully actualized. Our great High-Priest has passed into the heavens, in the full value and power of accomplished atonement. He is hidden there now, and with Him all the members of His priestly family; but when the "seven days" have run their course, and "the eighth day" casts its beams upon the earth, then shall the remnant of Israel—a repentant and an expectant people—hail, with a shout of victory, the manifested presence of the Royal Priest; and in immediate association with Him shall be seen a company of worshipers, occupying the most exalted position. These are "the good things to come"—things, surely, well worth waiting for—things worthy of God to give—things in which He shall be eternally glorified, and His people eternally blessed.

---

## *CHAPTER 10*

THE page of human history has ever been a sadly blotted one. It is a record of failure from first to last. Amid all the delights of Eden, man hearkened to the tempter's lie (Gen. 3); when preserved from judgment by the hand of electing love, and introduced into a restored earth, he was guilty of the sin of intemperance (Gen. 9); when conducted, by Jehovah's outstretched arm, into the land of Canaan, he "forsook the Lord, and served Baal and Ashtaroth" (Judges 2:13); when placed at the very summit of earthly power and glory, with untold wealth at his feet, and all the resources of the world at his command, he gave his heart to the uncircumcised stranger (1 Kings 11). No sooner had the blessings of the gospel been promulgated than it became needful for the Holy Ghost to prophesy concerning "grievous wolves," "apostacy," and all manner of failure (Acts 20:29; 1 Tim. 4:1-3; 2 Tim. 3:1-5; 2 Pet. 2; Jude). And, to crown all, we have the prophetic record of human apostacy from amid all the splendors of millennial glory (Rev. 20:7-10).

Thus, man spoils every thing. Place him in a position of highest dignity, and he will degrade himself; endow him with the most ample privileges, and he will abuse them; scatter blessings around him in richest profusion, and he will prove ungrateful, place him in the midst of the most impressive institutions, and he will corrupt them. Such is man! Such is nature in its fairest forms and under the most favorable circumstances!

Hence, therefore, we are in a measure prepared for the words with which our chapter opens—"And Nadab and Abihu, the sons of Aaron, took either of them his censer, and put fire therein, and put incense thereon, and offered strange fire before the Lord, which He commanded them not." What a contrast to the scene with which our last section closed! There, all was done "as the Lord commanded," and the result was, manifested glory; here, something is done "which the Lord commanded them not," and the result is, judgment. Hardly had the echo of the shout of victory died away ere the elements of a spurious worship were prepared,—hardly had the divine position been assumed ere it was deliberately abandoned, through neglect of the divine commandment. No sooner were those priests inaugurated than they grievously failed in the discharge of their priestly functions.

In what did their failure consist? Were they spurious priests? Were they mere pretenders? By no means. They were genuine sons of Aaron—true members of the priestly family—duly appointed priests. Their vessels of ministry, and their priestly garments too, would seem to have been all right. What, then, was their sin? Did they stain the curtains of the tabernacle with human blood? or pollute the sacred precincts with some crime which shocks the moral sense? We have no proof of their having done so. Their sin was this: "They offered strange fire before the Lord, which He commanded them not." Here was their sin. They departed in their worship from the plain word of Jehovah, who had fully and plainly instructed them as to the mode of their worship. We have already alluded to the divine fullness and sufficiency of the word of the Lord, in reference to every branch of priestly service. There was no room left for man to introduce what he might deem desirable or expedient. "This is the thing which the Lord hath commanded" was quite sufficient. It made all very plain and very simple. Nothing was needed on man's part save a spirit of implicit obedience to the divine command. But herein they failed. Man has always proved himself ill-disposed to walk in the narrow path of strict adherence to the plain Word of God. The bypath has ever seemed to present resistless charms to the poor human heart. "Stolen waters are sweet, and bread eaten in secret is pleasant" (Prov. 9:17). Such is the enemy's language; but the lowly, obedient heart knows full well that the path of subjection to the Word of God is the only one that leads to "waters" that are really "sweet," or to "bread" that can be rightly called "pleasant." Nadab and Abihu might have deemed one kind of "fire" as good as another, but it was not their province to decide as to that. They should have acted according to the word of the Lord; but instead of this, they took their own way and reaped the awful fruits thereof. "He knoweth not that the dead are there; and that her guests are in the depths of hell."

"And there went out fire from the Lord, and devoured them, and they died before the Lord." How deeply solemn! Jehovah was dwelling in the midst of His people, to govern, to judge, and to act, according to the claims of His nature. At the close of chapter 9, we read, "And there came a fire out from before the Lord, and consumed upon the altar the burnt-offering and the fat." This was Jehovah's acceptance of a true sacrifice; but in chapter 10, it is His judgment upon erring priests. It is a double action of the same fire. The burnt-offering went up as a sweet odor: the "strange fire" was rejected as an abomination. The Lord was glorified in the former; but it would have been a dishonor to accept the latter. Divine grace accepted and delighted in that which was a type of Christ's most precious sacrifice: divine holiness rejected that which was the fruit of man's corrupt will—a will never more hideous and abominable than when active in the things of God.

"Then Moses said unto Aaron, 'This is it that the Lord spake, saying, I will be sanctified in them that come nigh Me, and before all the people I will be glorified.' " The dignity and glory of the entire economy depended upon the strict maintenance of Jehovah's righteous claims. If these were to be trifled with, all was forfeited. If man were permitted to defile the sanctuary of the divine presence by "strange fire," there was an end to every thing. Nothing could be permitted to ascend from the priestly censer but the pure fire, kindled from off the altar of God, and fed by the "pure incense beaten small." Beauteous type of true saintly worship, of which the Father is the object, Christ the material, and the Holy Ghost the power. Man must not be allowed to introduce his devices into the worship of God. All his efforts can only issue in the presentation of "strange fire"—unhallowed incense—false worship. His very best attempts are an absolute abomination in the sight of God.

I speak not here of the honest struggles of earnest spirits searching after peace with God—of the sincere efforts of upright, though unenlightened, consciences to attain to a knowledge of the forgiveness of sins by works of law or the ordinances of systematic religion; all such will doubtless issue, through the exceeding goodness of God, in the clear light of a known and an enjoyed salvation. They prove very clearly that peace is earnestly sought; though, at the same time, they prove just as clearly that peace has not yet been found. There never yet was one who honestly followed the faintest glimmerings of light which fell upon his understanding who did not, in due time, receive more. "To him that hath shall more be given." And again, "The path of the just is as the shining light, which shineth more and more unto the perfect day."

All this is as plain as it is encouraging; but

it leaves wholly untouched the question of the human will, and its impious workings in connection with the service and worship of God. All such workings must inevitably call down, sooner or later, the solemn judgment of a righteous God, who cannot suffer His claims to be trifled with. "I will be sanctified in them that come nigh Me, and before all the people I will be glorified." Men will be dealt with according to their profession. If men are honestly seeking, they will assuredly find; but when men approach as worshipers, they are no longer to be regarded as seekers, but as those who profess to have found; and then, if their priestly censer smokes with unhallowed fire—if they offer unto God the elements of a spurious worship—if they profess to tread His courts, unwashed, unsanctified, unsubdued—if they place on His altar the workings of their own corrupt will, what must be the result? Judgment! Yes, sooner or later, judgment must come. It may linger, but it will come. It could not be otherwise. And not only must judgment come at last, but there is, in every case, the immediate rejection on the part of Heaven of all worship which has not the Father for its object, Christ for its material, and the Holy Ghost for its power. God's holiness is as quick to reject all "strange fire" as His grace is ready to accept the faintest, feeblest breathings of a true heart. He must pour out His righteous judgment upon all false worship, though He will never "quench the smoking flax nor break the bruised reed." The thought of this is most solemnizing, when one calls to mind the thousands of censers smoking with strange fire throughout the wide domain of christendom. May the Lord, in His rich grace, add to the number of true worshipers, who worship the Father in spirit and in truth (John 4). It is infinitely happier to think of the true worship ascending from honest hearts to the throne of God, than to contemplate, even for a moment, the spurious worship on which the divine judgments must ere long be poured out. Every one who knows, through grace, the pardon of his sins through the atoning blood of Jesus, can worship the Father in spirit and in truth. He knows the proper ground, the proper object, the proper title, the proper capacity of worship. These things can only be known in a divine way. They do not belong to nature or to earth. They are spiritual and heavenly. Very much of that which passes among men for the worship of God is but "strange fire" after all. There is neither the pure fire nor the pure incense, and therefore Heaven accepts it not; and albeit the divine judgment is not seen to fall upon those who present such worship as it fell upon Nadab and Abihu of old, this is only because "God is in Christ reconciling the world unto Himself, not imputing their trespasses unto them." It is not because the worship is acceptable to God, but because God is gracious. The time, however, is rapidly approaching when the strange fire will be quenched forever—when the throne of God shall no longer be insulted by clouds of impure incense ascending from unpurged worshipers—when all that is spurious shall be abolished, and the whole universe shall be as one vast and magnificent temple, in which the one true God—Father, Son, and Holy Ghost—shall be worshiped throughout the everlasting ages.

Grateful incense this, ascending
  Ever to the Father's throne;
Every knee to Jesus bending,
  All the mind in heaven is one.

All the Father's counsels claiming
  Equal honors to the Son,
All the Son's effulgence beaming
  Makes the Father's glory known.

By the Spirit all pervading,
  Hosts unnumbered round the Lamb,
Crowned with light and joy unfading,
  Hail Him as the great "I AM."

For this the redeemed are waiting; and, blessed be God, it is but a little while when all their longing desires shall be fully met, and met forever—yea, met after such a fashion as to elicit from each and all the touching confession of Sheba's queen that "the half was not told me." May the Lord hasten the happy time!

We must now return to our solemn chapter, and, lingering a little longer over it, endeavor to gather up and bear away with us some of its salutary teaching; for truly salutary it is, in an age like the present, when there is so much "strange fire" abroad.

There is something unusually arresting and impressive in the way in which Aaron received the heavy stroke of divine judgment. *"Aaron held his peace."* It was a solemn scene. His two sons struck dead at his side—smitten down by the fire of divine judgment.* He had but just seen them clothed in their garments of glory and beauty—washed, robed, and anointed. They had stood with him before the Lord to be inaugurated into the priestly office; they had offered, in company with him, the appointed sacrifices; they had seen the beams of the divine glory darting from the shekinah; they had seen the fire of Jehovah fall upon the sacrifice and consume it; they had heard the shout of triumph issuing from an assembly of adoring worshipers; all this had but recently passed before him; and now, alas! his two sons lie at his side in the grasp of death. The fire of the Lord, which so recently fed upon an acceptable sacrifice, had now fallen in judgment upon them, and what could he say? Nothing. "Aaron held his peace." "I was dumb and opened not my mouth, because Thou didst it." It was the hand of God; and although it might, in the judgment of flesh and blood, seem to be a very heavy hand, yet he had only to bow his head in silent awe and reverent acquiescence. "*I* was dumb . . . because *Thou* didst it." This was the suited attitude in the presence of the divine visitation. Aaron doubtless felt that the very pillars of his house were shaken by the thunder of divine judgment, and he could only stand in silent amazement in the midst of the soul-subduing scene. A father bereaved of his two sons, and in such a manner, and under such circumstances, was no ordinary case. It furnished a deeply impressive commentary upon the words of the Psalmist, "God is greatly to be feared in the assembly of the saints, and to be had in reverence of all them that are about Him" (Psalm 89). "Who would not fear Thee, O Lord, and glorify Thy name?" May we learn to walk softly in the divine presence—to tread Jehovah's courts with unshod foot and reverent spirit. May our priestly censer ever bear upon it the one material—the beaten incense of Christ's manifold perfections, and may the power of the Spirit kindle up the hallowed flame. All else is not only worthless, but vile. Every thing that springs from nature's energy, every thing produced by the actings of the human will—the most fragrant incense of man's devising—the most intense ardor of natural devotion, will all issue in "strange fire," and evoke the solemn judgment of the Lord God Almighty. Oh for a thoroughly truthful heart and worshiping spirit, in the presence of our God and Father, continually!

But let not any upright, though timid, heart be discouraged or alarmed. It is too often the case that those who really ought to be alarmed take no heed, while those for whom the Spirit of grace would only design a word of comfort and encouragement apply to themselves in a wrong way the startling warnings of holy Scripture. No doubt, the meek and contrite heart that trembles at the word of the Lord is in a safe condition; but then we should remember that a father warns his child, not because he does not regard him as his child, but because he does,

*Lest any reader should be troubled with a difficulty in reference to the souls of Nadab and Abihu, I would say that no such question ought ever to be raised. In such cases as Nadab and Abihu in Leviticus 10, Korah and his company in Numbers 16, the whole congregation, Joshua and Caleb excepted, whose carcases fell in the wilderness (Num. 14 and Heb. 3), Achan and his family (Josh. 7), Ananias and Sapphira (Acts 5), those who were judged for abuses at the Lord's table (1 Cor. 11)—in all such cases, the question of the soul's salvation is never raised. We are simply called to see in them the solemn actings of God in government in the midst of His people. This relieves the mind from all difficulty. Jehovah dwelt, of old, between the cherubim, to judge His people in every thing; and God the Holy Ghost dwells now in the Church, to order and govern according to the perfection of His presence. He was so really and personally present that Ananias and Sapphira could lie to Him, and He could execute judgment upon them. It was as positive and as immediate an exhibition of His actings in government as we have in the matter of Nadab and Abihu, or Achan, or any other.

This is a great truth to get hold of. God is not only *for* His people, but *with* them, and *in* them. He is to be counted upon for every thing, whether it be great or small. He is present to comfort and help. He is there to chasten and judge; He is there "for exigence of every hour." He is sufficient. Let faith count upon Him. "Where two or three are gathered together in My name, there am I" (Matt. 18:20). And, assuredly, where He is, we want no more.

and one of the happiest proofs of the relationship is the disposition to receive and profit by the warning. The parental voice, even though its tone be that of solemn admonition, will reach the child's heart, but certainly not to raise in that heart a question as to its relationship with the one who speaks. If a son were to question his sonship whenever his father warns, it would be a poor affair indeed. The judgment which had just fallen upon Aaron's house did not make him doubt that he was really a priest; it merely had the effect of teaching him how to conduct himself in that high and holy position.

"And Moses said unto Aaron, and unto Eleazar and unto Ithamar, his sons, 'Uncover not your heads, neither rend your clothes; lest ye die, and lest wrath come upon all the people: but let your brethren, the whole house of Israel, bewail the burning which the Lord hath kindled. And ye shall not go out from the door of the tabernacle of the congregation, lest ye die; for the anointing oil of the Lord is upon you.' And they did according to the word of Moses."

Aaron, Eleazar, and Ithamar were to remain unmoved in their elevated place—their holy dignity—their position of priestly sanctity. Neither the failure nor yet the judgment consequent thereon was to be allowed to interfere with those who wore the priestly robes and were anointed with "the oil of the Lord." That holy oil had placed them in a sacred inclosure, where the influences of sin, of death, and of judgment could not reach them. Those who were outside, who were at a distance from the sanctuary, who were not in the position of priests, they might "bewail the burning;" but as for Aaron and his sons, they were to go on in the discharge of their hallowed functions as though nothing had happened. Priests in the sanctuary were not to bewail, but to worship—they were not to weep, as in the presence of death, but to bow their anointed heads in the presence of the divine visitation. "The fire of the Lord" might act, and do its solemn work of judgment; but to a priest it mattered not what that "fire" had come to do—whether to express the divine approval by consuming a sacrifice, or the divine displeasure by consuming the offerers of "strange fire"—he had but to worship. That "fire" was a well-known manifestation of the divine presence in Israel of old, and whether it acted in "mercy or in judgment," the business of all true priests was to worship. "I will sing of mercy and of judgment; unto Thee, O Lord, will I sing."

There is a deep and holy lesson for the soul in all this. Those who are brought nigh to God, in the power of the blood, and by the anointing of the Holy Ghost, must move in a sphere beyond the range of nature's influences. Priestly nearness to God gives the soul such an insight into all His ways, such a sense of the rightness of all His dispensations, that one is enabled to worship in His presence, even though the stroke of His hand has removed from us the object of tender affection. It may be asked, Are we to be Stoics? I ask, were Aaron and his sons Stoics? Nay, they were priests. Did they not feel as men? Yes; but they worshiped as priests. This is profound. It opens up a region of thought, feeling, and experience in which nature can never move—a region of which, with all its boasted refinement and sentimentality, nature knows absolutely nothing. We must tread the sanctuary of God in true priestly energy, in order to enter into the depth, meaning, and power of such holy mysteries.

The prophet Ezekiel was called, in his day, to sit down to this difficult lesson. "Also the word of the Lord came unto me, saying, 'Son of man, behold, I take away from thee the desire of thine eyes with a stroke: yet neither shalt thou mourn nor weep, neither shall thy tears run down. Forbear to cry, make no mourning for the dead, bind the tire of thine head upon thee, and put on thy shoes upon thy feet, and cover not thy lips, and eat not the bread of *men.'* . . . And I did in the morning as I was commanded" (Ezek. 24:16-18). It will be said that all this was as "a sign" to Israel. True; but it proves that in prophetic testimony, as well as in priestly worship, we must rise superior to all the claims and influences of nature and of earth. Aaron's sons and

Ezekiel's wife were cut down with a stroke, and yet neither the priest nor the prophet was to uncover his head or shed a tear.

How far have you and I progressed in this profound lesson? No doubt both reader and writer have to make the same humiliating confession. Too often, alas! we "walk as men" and "eat the bread of men"—too often are we robbed of our high priestly privileges by the workings of nature and the influences of earth. These things must be watched against. Nothing save realized priestly nearness to God can ever preserve the heart from the power of evil or maintain its spiritual tone. All believers are priests unto God, and nothing can possibly deprive them of their position as such; but though they cannot lose their position, they may grievously fail in the discharge of their functions. These things are not sufficiently distinguished. Some there are who, while looking at the precious truth of the believer's security, forget the possibility of his failing in the discharge of his priestly functions: others, on the contrary, looking at the failure, venture to call in question the security.

Now, I desire that my reader should keep clear of both the above errors. He should be fully established in the divine doctrine of the eternal security of every member of the true priestly house; but he should also bear in mind the possibility of failure, and the constant need of watchfulness and prayer, lest he should fail. May all those who have been brought to know the hallowed elevation of priests unto God be preserved, by His heavenly grace, from every species of failure, whether it be personal defilement or the presentation of any of the varied forms of "strange fire," which abound so in the professing church.

"And the Lord spake unto Aaron, saying, 'Do not drink wine nor strong drink, thou, nor thy sons with thee, when ye go into the tabernacle of the congregation, lest ye die: it shall be a statute forever throughout your generations: and that ye may put difference between holy and unholy, and between unclean and clean; and that ye may teach the children of Israel all the statutes which the Lord hath spoken unto them by the hand of Moses' " (ver. 8-11).

The effect of wine is to excite nature, and all natural excitement hinders that calm, well-balanced condition of soul which is essential to the proper discharge of the priestly office. So far from using any means to excite nature, we should treat it as a thing having no existence. Thus only shall we be in a moral condition to serve in the sanctuary, to form a dispassionate judgment between clean and unclean, and to expound and communicate the mind of God. It devolves upon each one to judge for himself what, in his special case, would act as "wine or strong drink."* The things which excite mere nature are manifold indeed—wealth, ambition, politics, the varied objects of emulation around us in the world. All these things act with exciting power upon nature, and entirely unfit us for every department of priestly service. If the heart be swollen with feelings of pride, covetousness, or emulation, it is utterly impossible that the pure air of the sanctuary can be enjoyed, or the sacred functions of priestly ministry discharged. Men speak of the versatility of genius, or a capacity to turn quickly from one thing to another; but the most versatile genius that was ever possessed could not enable a man to pass from an unhallowed arena of literary, commercial, or political competition, into the holy retirement of the sanctuary of the divine presence; nor could it ever adjust the

---

*Some have thought that, owing to the special place which this direction about wine occupies, Nadab and Abihu must have been under the influence of strong drink when they offered the "strange fire." But be this as it may, we have to be thankful for a most valuable principle in reference to our conduct as spiritual priests. We are to refrain from every thing which would produce the same effect upon our spiritual man as strong drink produces upon the physical man.

It needs hardly to be remarked that the Christian should be *most jealous* over himself as to the use of wine or strong drink. Timothy, as we know, needed an apostolic recommendation to induce him even to touch it for his health's sake (1 Tim. 5). A beauteous proof of Timothy's habitual self-denial, and of the thoughtful love of the Spirit in the apostle. I must confess that one's moral sense is offended by seeing Christians making use of strong drink in cases where it is very manifestly not medicinal. I rarely, ever, see a spiritual person indulge in such a thing. One trembles to see a Christian the mere slave of a habit, whatever that habit may be. It proves that he is not keeping his body in subjection.

eye that had become dimmed by the influence of such scenes, so as to enable it to discern, with priestly accuracy, the difference "between holy and unholy, and between unclean and clean." No, God's priests must keep themselves apart from "wine and strong drink." Theirs is a path of holy separation and abstraction. They are to be raised far above the influence of earthly joy as well as earthly sorrow. If they have aught to do with "strong wine," it is only that it may "be poured unto the Lord for a drink-offering, in the holy place" (Num. 28:7). In other words, the joy of God's priests is not the joy of earth, but the joy of heaven—the joy of the sanctuary. "The joy of the Lord is their strength."

Would that all this holy instruction were more deeply pondered by us! We surely stand much in need of it. If our priestly responsibilities are not duly attended to, all must be deranged. When we contemplate the camp of Israel, we may observe three circles, and the innermost of these circles had its centre in the sanctuary. There was first the circle of men of war (Num. 1—2); then the circle of Levites round about the tabernacle (Num. 3—4); and lastly, the innermost circle of priests, ministering in the holy place. Now, let it be remembered that the believer is called to move in all those circles. He enters into conflict as a man of war (Eph. 6:11-17; 1 Tim. 1:18; 6:12; 2 Tim. 4:7); he serves, as a Levite, in the midst of his brethren, according to his measure and sphere (Matt. 15:14-15; Luke 19:12-13); finally, he sacrifices and worships, as a priest, in the holy place (Heb. 13:15-16; 1 Pet. 2:5,9). The last of these shall endure forever. And, moreover, it is as we are enabled now to move aright in that holy circle that all other relations and responsibilities are rightly discharged. Hence, every thing that incapacitates us for our priestly functions—every thing that draws us off from the centre of that innermost circle, in which it is our privilege to move—every thing, in short, that tends to derange our priestly relation, or dim our priestly vision, must, of necessity, unfit us for the service which we are called to render, and for the warfare which we are called to wage.

These are weighty considerations. Let us dwell upon them. The heart must be kept right, the conscience pure, the eye single, the spiritual vision undimmed. The soul's business in the holy place must be faithfully and diligently attended to, else we shall go all wrong. Private communion with God must be kept up, else we shall be fruitless as servants, and defeated as men of war. It is vain for us to bustle about, and run hither and thither in what we call service, or indulge in vapid words about Christian armor and Christian warfare. If we are not keeping our priestly garments unspotted, and if we are not keeping ourselves free from all that would excite nature, we shall assuredly break down. The *priest* must keep his heart with all diligence, else the *Levite* will fail, and the *warrior* will be defeated.

It is, let me repeat it, the business of each one to be fully aware of what it is that to him proves to be "wine and strong drink"—what it is that produces excitement—that blunts his spiritual perception, or dims his priestly vision. It may be an auction-mart, a cattle-show, a newspaper,—it may be the merest trifle. But no matter what it is, if it tends to excite, it will disqualify us for priestly ministry; and if we are disqualified as priests, we are unfit for every thing, inasmuch as our success in every department and in every sphere must depend upon our cultivating a spirit of worship.

Let us, then, exercise a spirit of self-judgment—a spirit of watchfulness over our habits, our ways, and our associations; and when we, by grace, discover aught that tends, in the smallest degree to unfit us for the elevated exercises of the sanctuary, let us put it away from us, cost what it may. Let us not suffer ourselves to be the slaves of a habit. Communion with God should be dearer to our hearts than all beside; and just in proportion as we prize that communion, shall we watch and pray against any thing that would rob us of it—every thing that would excite, ruffle, or unhinge.*

"And Moses spake unto Aaron, and unto

*Some, perhaps, may think that the wording of Leviticus 10:9 affords a warrant for *occasional* indulgence in those

Eleazar, and unto Ithamar, his sons that were left, 'Take the meat-offering that remaineth of the offerings of the Lord made by fire, and eat it without leaven beside the altar; for it is most holy: and ye shall eat it in the holy place, because it is thy due, and thy sons' due, of the sacrifices of the Lord made by fire; for so I am commanded' " (ver. 12-13).

There are few things in which we are more prone to fail than in the maintenance of the divine standard when human failure has set in. Like David, when the Lord made a breach upon Uzzah because of his failure in putting his hand to the ark, "he was afraid of God that day, saying, 'How shall I bring the ark of God home to me?' " (1 Chron. 13:12) It is exceedingly difficult to bow to the divine judgment and, at the same time, to hold fast the divine ground. The temptation is to lower the standard—to come down from the lofty elevation—to take human ground. We must ever carefully guard against this evil, which is all the more dangerous as wearing the garb of modesty, self-distrust, and humility. Aaron and his sons, notwithstanding all that had occurred, were to eat the meat-offering in the holy place. They were to do so, not because all had gone on in perfect order, but "because it is thy due," and "so I am commanded." Though there had been failure, yet their place was in the tabernacle; and those who were there had certain "dues" founded upon the divine commandment. Though man had failed ten thousand times over, the word of the Lord could not fail; and that word had secured certain privileges for all true priests, which it was their place to enjoy. Were God's priests to have nothing to eat—no priestly food, because failure had set in? Were those that were left to be allowed to starve, because Nadab and Abihu had offered "strange fire"? This would never do. God is faithful, and He can never allow any one to be empty in His blessed presence. The prodigal may wander and squander and come to poverty, but it must ever hold good that "in my Father's house is bread enough and to spare."

"And the wave breast and the heave shoulder shall ye eat in a clean place; thou, and thy sons, and thy daughters with thee: for they be thy due, and thy sons' due, which are *given* out of the sacrifices of peace-offerings of the children of Israel . . . by *a statute forever, as the Lord hath commanded*" (ver. 14-15). What strength and stability we have here! All the members of the priestly family, "daughters" as well as "sons"—all, whatever be the measure of energy or capacity, are to feed upon "the breast" and "the shoulder"—the affections and the strength of the true Peace-offering, as raised from the dead, and presented, in resurrection, before God. This precious privilege is theirs as "given by a statute forever, as the Lord hath commanded." This makes all "sure and steadfast," come what may. Men may fail and come short, strange fire may be offered, but God's priestly family must never be deprived of the rich and gracious portion which divine love has provided and divine faithfulness secured "by a statute forever."

However, we must distinguish between those privileges which belonged to all the members of Aaron's family, "daughters" as well as "sons," and those which could only be enjoyed by the male portion of the family. This point has already been referred to in the notes on the offerings. There are certain blessings which are the common portion of all believers, simply as such; and there are those which demand a higher measure of spiritual attainment and priestly energy to apprehend and enjoy. Now, it is worse than vain, yea, it is impious, to set up

---

things which tend to excite the natural mind, inasmuch as it is said, "Do not drink wine nor strong drink . . . *when* ye go into the tabernacle of the congregation." To this we may reply that the sanctuary is not a place which the Christian is *occasionally* to visit, but a place in which he is *habitually* to serve and worship. It is the sphere in which he should "live, and move, and have his being." The more we live in the presence of God, the less can we bear to be out of it; and no one who knows the deep joy of being there could lightly indulge in aught that would take or keep him thence. There is not that object within the compass of earth which would, in the judgment of a spiritual mind, be an equivalent for one hour's fellowship with God.

for the enjoyment of this higher measure when we really have it not. It is one thing to hold fast the privileges which are "given" of God, and can never be taken away, and quite another to assume a measure of spiritual capacity to which we have never attained. No doubt, we ought to desire earnestly the very highest measure of priestly communion —the most elevated order of priestly privilege; but then desiring a thing, and assuming to have it, are very different.

This thought will throw light upon the closing paragraph of our chapter. "And Moses diligently sought the goat of the sin-offering, and, behold, it was burnt: and he was angry with Eleazar and Ithamar, the sons of Aaron which were left, saying, 'Wherefore have ye not eaten the sin-offering in the holy place, seeing it is most holy, and God hath given it to you to bear the iniquity of the congregation, to make atonement for them before the Lord? Behold, the blood of it was not brought in within the holy place: ye should indeed have eaten it in the holy place, as I commanded.' And Aaron said unto Moses, 'Behold, this day have they offered their sin-offering and their burnt-offering before the Lord; and such things have befallen me: and if I had eaten the sin-offering to-day, should it have been accepted in the sight of the Lord?' And when Moses heard that, he was content."

The "daughters" of Aaron were not permitted to eat of "the sin-offering." This high privilege belonged only to the "sons," and it was a type of the most elevated form of priestly service. To eat of the sin-offering was the expression of full identification with the offerer, and this demanded an amount of priestly capacity and energy which found its type in "the sons of Aaron." On the occasion before us, however, it is very evident that Aaron and his sons were not in a condition to rise to this high and holy ground. They ought to have been, but they were not. "Such things have befallen me," said Aaron. This, no doubt, was to be deplored; but yet, "when Moses heard that, he was content." It is far better to be real in the confession of our failure and shortcoming, than to put forth pretensions to spiritual power which are wholly without foundation.

Thus, then, the tenth chapter of the book of Leviticus opens with positive sin and closes with negative failure. Nadab and Abihu offered "strange fire," and Eleazar and Ithamar were unable to eat the sin-offering. The former was met by divine judgment; the latter, by divine forbearance. There could be no allowance for "strange fire." It was positively flying in the face of God's plain commandment. There is obviously a wide difference between a deliberate rejection of a plain command and mere inability to rise to the height of a divine privilege. The former is open dishonor done to God; the latter is a forfeiture of one's own blessing. There should be neither the one nor the other, but the difference between the two is easily traced.

May the Lord, in His infinite grace, ever keep us abiding in the secret retirement of His holy presence, abiding in His love, and feeding upon His truth. Thus shall we be preserved from "strange fire" and "strong drink"—from false worship of every kind and fleshly excitement in all its forms. Thus, too, shall we be enabled to carry ourselves aright in every department of priestly ministration, and to enjoy all the privileges of our priestly position. The communion of a Christian is like a sensitive plant. It is easily hurt by the rude influences of an evil world. It will expand beneath the genial action of the air of heaven, but must firmly shut itself up from the chilling breath of time and sense. Let us remember these things, and ever seek to keep close within the sacred precincts of the divine presence. There, all is pure, safe, and happy.

Far from a world of grief and sin,
With God eternally shut in.

---

## *CHAPTER 11*

THE book of Leviticus may be termed "The Priest's Guide-book." This is very much its character. It is full of principles for the guidance of such as desire to live in the enjoyment of priestly nearness to God. Had Israel gone on with Jehovah according to the grace in which He had brought them up out of the land of Egypt, they should have been to Him "a kingdom of priests and a holy nation" (Exod. 19:6). This, however, they failed to do. They put themselves at a distance; they got under law and failed to keep it. Hence, Jehovah had to take up a certain tribe, and from that tribe a certain family, and from that family a certain man, and to him and to his house was granted the high privilege of drawing nigh as priests unto God.

Now, the privileges of such a position were immense; but it had its heavy responsibilities likewise. There would be the ever-recurring demand for the exercise of a discerning mind. "The priest's lips should keep knowledge, and they should seek the law at his mouth; for he is the messenger of the Lord of hosts" (Mal. 2:7). The priest was not only to bear the judgment of the congregation before the Lord, but also to expound the ordinances of the Lord to the congregation. He was to be the ever-ready medium of communication between Jehovah and the assembly. He was not merely to know the mind of God for himself, but be able also to interpret that mind to the people. All this would demand, of necessity, constant watching, constant waiting, constant hanging over the page of inspiration, that he might drink in, to his very soul, all the precepts, the judgments, the statutes, the laws, the commandments, and the ordinances of the God of Israel, so as to be able to instruct the congregation in reference to "those things which ought to be done."

There was no room left for the play of fancy, the working of imagination, the introduction of man's plausible inferences, or the cunning devices of human expediency. Every thing was laid down with the divine precision and commanding authority of a "Thus saith the Lord." Minute and elaborate as was the detail of sacrifices, rites, and ceremonies, nothing was left for man's brain to originate. He was not even permitted to decide upon the kind of sacrifice to be offered upon any given occasion, nor yet as to the mode in which such sacrifice was to be presented. Jehovah took care of every thing. Neither the congregation nor the priest had any authority whatsoever to decree, enact, or suggest so much as a single item throughout all the vast array of ordinances in the Mosaic economy. *The work of the Lord settled all:* man had *only to obey.*

This, to an obedient heart, was nothing short of an unspeakable mercy. It is quite impossible to overestimate the privilege of being permitted to betake one's self to the oracles of God, and there find the most ample guidance as to all the details of one's faith and service day by day. All that we need is a broken will, a mortified mind, a single eye. The divine guide-book is as full as we can possibly desire: we want no more. To imagine for a moment that aught is left for man's wisdom to supply, must be regarded as a flagrant insult offered to the sacred canon. No one can read the book of Leviticus and not be struck with the extraordinary painstaking on the part of Israel's God to furnish His people with the most minute instruction upon every point connected with His service and worship. The most cursory reader of the book might at least bear away with him this touching and interesting lesson.

And truly, if ever there was a time when this self-same lesson needed to be read out in the ears of the professing church, this is the time. On all hands, the divine sufficiency of holy Scripture is called in question. In some cases, this is openly and deliberately done; in others, it is with less frankness hinted, insinuated, implied, and inferred. The Christian mariner is told, directly or indirectly, that the divine chart is insufficient for all the intricate details of his voyage—that such changes have taken place in the ocean of life since that chart was made that in many cases it is entirely deficient for the purposes of modern navigation. He is told that the currents, tides, coasts, strands, and shores of that ocean are quite different now from what they were some centuries ago, and that, as a necessary consequence, he must have recourse to the aids which modern navigation supplies, in order to make up for the deficiencies in the old chart, which is, as a matter of course, admitted to have been perfect at the time it was made.

Now, I earnestly desire that the Christian reader should be able, with clearness and decision, to meet this grievous dishonor done to the precious volume of inspiration, every line of which comes to him fresh from his Father's bosom, through the pen of God the Holy Ghost. I desire that he should meet it whether it comes before him in the shape of a bold and blasphemous statement or a learned and plausible inference. Whatever garb it wears, it owes its origin to the enemy of Christ, the enemy of the Bible, the enemy of the soul. If, indeed, the Word of God be not sufficient, then where are we? or whither shall we turn? To whom shall we betake ourselves for aid if our Father's book be in any respect defective? God says that His book can "furnish us *thoroughly* to *all* good works" (2 Tim. 3:17). Man says, No; there are many things about which the Bible is silent, which, nevertheless, we need to know. Whom am I to believe? God, or man? Our reply to any one who questions the divine sufficiency of Scripture is just this: Either you are not a "man of God," or else that for which you want a warrant is not "a good work." This is plain. No one can possibly think otherwise with his eye resting on 2 Timothy 3:17.

Oh for a deeper sense of the fullness, majesty, and authority of the Word of God! We very much need to be braced up on this point. We want such a deep, bold, vigorous, influential, and abiding sense of the supreme authority of the divine canon, and of its absolute completeness for every age, every clime, every position, every department—personal, social, and ecclesiastical, as shall enable us to withstand every attempt of the enemy to depreciate the value of that inestimable treasure. May our hearts enter more into the spirit of those words of the Psalmist—"Thy Word is true *from the beginning;* and every one of thy righteous judgments *endureth forever*" (Psalm 119:160).

The foregoing train of thought is awakened by the perusal of the eleventh chapter of the book of Leviticus. Therein we find Jehovah entering, in most marvelous detail, into a description of beasts, birds, fishes, and reptiles, and furnishing His people with various marks by which they were to know what was clean and what was unclean. We have the summing up of the entire contents of this remarkable chapter in the two closing verses. "This is the law of the beasts, and of the fowl, and of every living creature that moveth in the waters, and of every creature that creepeth upon the earth; *to make a difference* between the unclean and the clean, and between the beast that may be eaten and the beast that may not be eaten."

With regard to beasts, two things were essential to render them clean—they should chew the cud and divide the hoof. "Whatsoever parteth the hoof, and is cloven-footed, and cheweth the cud among the beasts, that shall ye eat." Either of these marks would, of itself, have been wholly insufficient to constitute ceremonial cleanness: the two should go together. Now, while these two marks were quite sufficient for the guidance of an Israelite as to the cleanness or uncleanness of an animal, without any reference as to why or wherefore such marks were given or what they meant, yet is the Christian permitted to inquire into the spiritual truth wrapped up in these ceremonial enactments.

What, then, are we to learn from those two features in a clean animal? The chewing of the cud expresses the natural process of "inwardly digesting" that which one eats, while the divided hoof sets forth the character of one's outward walk. There is, as we know, an intimate connection between the two in the Christian life. The one who feeds upon the green pastures of the Word of God, and inwardly digests what he takes in—the one who is enabled to combine calm meditation with prayerful study, will, without doubt, manifest that character of outward walk which is to the praise of Him who has graciously given us His Word to form our habits and govern our ways.

It is to be feared that many who *read the Bible* do not *digest the Word.* The two things are widely different. One may read chapter after chapter, book after book, and not digest so much as a single line. We may read the Bible as part of a dull and profitless routine, but, through lack of the ruminating powers—the digestive organs, we derive no profit whatsoever. This should be carefully looked into. The cattle that browse on the green may teach us a wholesome lesson. They first diligently gather up the refreshing pasture, and then calmly lie down to chew the cud. Striking and beautiful picture of a Christian feeding upon and inwardly digesting the precious contents of the volume of inspiration! Would that there were more of this amongst us! Were we more accustomed to betake ourselves to the Word as the necessary pasture of our souls, we should assuredly be in a more vigorous and healthy condition. Let us beware of reading the Bible as a dead form—a cold duty—a piece of religious routine.

The same caution is needful in reference to the public exposition of the Word. Let those who expound Scripture to their fellows first feed and digest for themselves, —let them read and ruminate in private, not merely for others, but for themselves. It is a poor thing for a man to be continually occupied in procuring food for other people, and he himself dying of starvation. Then, again, let those who attend upon the public ministry of the Word see that they are not doing so mechanically, as by the force of mere religious habit, but with an earnest desire to "read, mark, learn, and inwardly digest" what they hear. Then will both teachers and taught be well-conditioned, the spiritual life nourished and sustained, and the true character of outward walk exhibited.

But be it remembered that the chewing of the cud must never be separated from the divided hoof. If one but partially acquainted with the priest's guidebook—unpracticed in the divine ceremonial happened to see an animal chewing the cud, he might hastily pronounce him clean. This would have been a serious error. A more careful reference to the divine directory would at once show that he must mark the animal's *walk*—that he must note the impression made by each movement—that he must look for the result of the divided hoof. "Nevertheless these shall ye not eat of them that chew the cud, or of them that divide the hoof; as the camel, because he cheweth the cud, but divideth not the hoof, he is unclean unto you" etc., (ver. 4-6).

In like manner the divided hoof was insufficient if not accompanied by the chewing of the cud.—"The swine, though he divide the hoof and be cloven-footed, yet he cheweth not the cud; he is unclean to you" (ver. 7). In a word, then, the two things were inseparable in the case of every clean animal; and as to the spiritual application, it is of the very last importance, in a practical point of view. The inward life and the outward walk must go together. A man may profess to love and feed upon—to study and ruminate over the Word of God—the pasture of the soul; but if his footprints along the pathway of life are not such as the Word requires, he is not clean. And on the other hand, a man may seem to walk with pharisaic blamelessness; but if his walk be not the result of the hidden life, it is worse than worthless. There must be the divine principle within, which feeds upon and digests the rich pasture of God's Word, else the impression of the footstep will be of no avail. The value of each depends upon its inseparable connection with the other.

We are here forcibly reminded of a solemn passage in the first Epistle of John, in which the apostle furnishes us with the two marks whereby we may know those that are of God. "In this the children of God are manifest, and the children of the devil: whosoever *doeth not righteousness* is not of God, neither he that *loveth not his brother*" (1 John 3:10). Here we have the two grand characteristics of the eternal life of which all true believers are possessed, namely, "righteousness" and "love"—the outward and the inward. Both must be combined. Some professing Christians are all for love, so called, and some for righteousness. Neither can exist, in a divine way, without the other. If that which is called love exist without practical righteousness, it will, in reality, be but a lax, soft, easy-going habit of mind, which will tolerate all manner of error and evil; and if that which is called righteousness exist without love, it will be a stern, proud, pharisaic, self-sufficient temper of soul, resting upon the miserable basis of personal reputation. But where the divine life is in energy, there will ever be the inward charity combined with genuine practical righteousness. The two elements are essential in the formation of true Christian character. There must be the love that will express itself in reference to the very feeblest development of that which is of God, and, at the same time, the holiness that shrinks, with intense abhorrence, from all that is of Satan.

We shall now pass on to the consideration of that which the Levitical ceremonial taught with respect to "all that are in the waters." Here, again, we find the double mark. "These shall ye eat of all that are in the waters: whatsoever hath fins and scales in the waters, in the seas, and in the rivers, them shall ye eat. And all that have not fins and scales in the seas, and in the rivers, of all that move in the waters, and of any living thing which is in the waters, they shall be an abomination unto you" (ver. 9-10). Two things were necessary to render a fish ceremonially clean, namely, "fins and scales," which obviously set forth a certain fitness for the sphere and element in which the creature had to move.

But doubtless there was more than this. I believe it is our privilege to discern, in the natural properties with which God has endowed those creatures which move in the waters, certain spiritual qualities which belong to the Christian life. If a fish needs a "fin" to enable him to move through the water, and "scales" to resist the action thereof, so does the believer need that spiritual capacity which enables him to move onward through the scene with which he is surrounded, and, at the same time, to resist its influence—to prevent its penetrating—to keep it out. These are precious qualities. The fin and the scale are pregnant with meaning—full of practical instruction to the Christian. They exhibit to us, in ceremonial garb, two things which we specially need, namely, spiritual energy to move onward through the element which surrounds us, and the power to preserve us from its action. The one will not avail without the other. It is of no use to possess a capacity to get on through the world if we are not proof against the world's influence; and though we may seem to be able to keep the world out, yet if we have not the motive-power, we are defective. The "fins" would not do without the "scales," nor the "scales" without the "fins." Both were required, to render a fish ceremonially clean; and we, in order to be properly equipped, require to be incased against the penetrating influence of an evil world, and, at the same time, to be furnished with a capacity to pass rapidly on.

The whole deportment of a Christian should declare him a pilgrim and a stranger here. *"Onward"* must be his motto—ever and only onward. Let his locality and his circumstances be what they may, he is to have his eye fixed on a home beyond this perishing, passing world. He is furnished, by grace, with spiritual ability to go forward—to penetrate energetically through all, and carry out the earnest aspirations of his heaven-born spirit. And while thus vigorously pushing his way onward—while "forcing his passage to the skies," he is to keep his inward man fenced round about and fast closed up against all external influences.

Oh, for more of the onward bent—the upward tendency! for more holy fixedness of soul and profound retirement from this vain world! We shall have reason to bless the Lord for our meditations amid the ceremonial shadows of the book of Leviticus if we are led thereby to long more intensely after those graces which though so dimly portrayed there are nevertheless so manifestly needful for us.

From verse 13 to verse 24 of our chapter, we have the law with respect to birds. All of the carnivorous kind, that is, all that fed on flesh, were unclean; the omnivorous, or those who could eat any thing, were unclean; all those which though furnished with power to soar into the heavens would nevertheless grovel upon the earth were unclean. As to the latter class, there were some exceptional cases (ver. 21-22); but the general rule, the fixed principle, the standing ordinance, was as distinct as possible—"All fowls that creep, going upon all fours, shall be an abomination unto you" (ver. 20). All this is very simple in its instruction to us. Those fowls that could feed upon flesh, those that could swallow any thing or every thing, and all groveling fowls, were to be unclean to the Israel of God, because so pronounced by the God of Israel; nor can the spiritual mind have any difficulty in discerning the fitness of such an ordinance. We can not only trace in the habits of the above three classes of fowl the just ground of their being pronounced unclean, but we can also see in them the striking exhibition of that in nature which is to be strenuously guarded against by every true Christian. Such an one is called to refuse every thing of a carnal nature. Moreover, he cannot feed promiscuously upon every thing that comes before him. He must "try the things that differ;" he must "take heed what he hears;" he must exercise a discerning mind, a spiritual judgment, a heavenly taste. Finally, he must use his wings; he must rise on the pinions of faith, and find his place in the celestial sphere to which he belongs. In short, there must be nothing groveling, nothing promiscuous, nothing unclean, for the Christian.

As to "creeping things," the following was the general rule: "And every creeping thing that creepeth upon the earth shall be an abomination; it shall not be eaten" (ver. 41). How wonderful to think of the condescending grace of Jehovah! He could stoop to give directions about a crawling reptile. He would not leave His people at a loss as to the most trivial affair. The priest's guide-book contained the most ample instructions as to every thing. He desired to keep His people free from the defilement consequent upon touching, tasting, or handling aught that was unclean. They were not their own, and hence they were not to do as they pleased. They belonged to Jehovah; His name was called upon them; they were identified with Him. His Word was to be their grand regulating standard in every case. From it they were to learn the ceremonial *status* of beasts, birds, fishes, and creeping things. They were not to think their own thoughts, to exercise their own reasoning powers, or be guided by their own imaginations in such matters. *God's Word was to be their sole directory.* Other nations might eat what they pleased, but Israel enjoyed the high privilege of eating that only which was pleasing to Jehovah.

Nor was it as to the mere matter of *eating* aught that was unclean that the people of God were so jealously guarded. Bare *contact* was forbidden (see ver. 8,24,26-28,31-41). It was impossible for a member of the Israel of God to touch that which was unclean without contracting defilement. This is a principle largely unfolded both in the law and the prophets. "Thus saith the Lord of hosts, 'Ask ye now the priests concerning the law, saying, If one bear holy flesh in the skirt of his garment, and with his skirt do touch bread, or pottage, or wine, or oil, or any meat, shall it be holy?' And the priests answered and said, 'No.' Then said Haggai, 'If one that is unclean by a dead body *touch* any of these, shall it be unclean?' And the priests answered and said, 'It shall be unclean' " (Hag. 2:11-13). Jehovah would have His people holy in all things. They were neither to eat nor touch aught that was unclean.—"Ye shall not make yourselves abominable with any creeping thing that creepeth, neither shall ye make yourselves unclean with them, that ye should be defiled thereby." Then follows the powerful reason for all this careful separation. *"For I am the Lord your God:* ye shall therefore sanctify yourselves, and ye shall be holy; *for I am holy:* neither shall ye defile yourselves with any manner of creeping thing that creepeth upon the earth. For I am the Lord that bringeth you up out of the land of Egypt, to be *your God:* ye shall therefore be holy, *for I am holy"* (ver. 43-45).

It is well to see that the personal holiness of God's people—their entire separation from all manner of uncleanness, flows out of their relationship to Him. It is not upon the principle of "Stand by thyself: I am holier than thou;" but simply this: "God is holy," and therefore all who are brought into association with Him must be holy likewise. It is in every way worthy of God that *His* people should be holy. "Thy testimonies are very sure: holiness becometh Thy house, O Lord, forever." What else save holiness could become the house of such an One as Jehovah? If any one had asked an Israelite of old, Why do you shrink so from that reptile which crawls along the path? He would have replied, Jehovah is holy, and I belong to Him. He has said, "Touch not." So also now, if a Christian be asked why he walks apart from the ten thousand things in which the men of this world participate, his answer is simply to be, *My Father is holy.* This is the true foundation of personal holiness. The more we contemplate the divine character, and enter into the power of our relationship to God, in Christ, by the energy of the Holy Ghost, the holier we must, of necessity, be.

There can be no progress in the condition of holiness into which the believer is introduced, but there is and ought to be progress in the apprehension, experience, and practical exhibition of that holiness. These things should never be confounded. All believers are in the same condition of holiness or sanctification, but their practical measure may vary to any conceivable degree. This is easily understood. The condition arises out of our *being brought* nigh to God by the blood of the cross; the practical measure will depend upon our *keeping* nigh by the power of the Spirit. It is not a man setting up for something superior in himself—for a greater degree of personal sanctity than is ordinarily possessed—for being in any wise better than his neighbors. All such pretensions are utterly contemptible in the judgment of every right-thinking person. But then, if God, in His exceeding grace, stoop down to our low estate and lift us into the holy elevation of His blessed presence, in association with Christ, has He not a right to prescribe what our character is to be as thus brought nigh? Who could think of calling in question a truth so obvious? And further, are we not bound to aim at the maintenance of that character which He prescribes? Are we to be accused of presumption for so doing? Was it presumption in an Israelite to refuse to touch "a creeping thing"? Nay, it would have been presumption of the most daring and dangerous character to have done so. True, he might not have been able to make an uncircumcised stranger understand or appreciate the reason of his conduct; but this was not his province. Jehovah had said, "Touch not," not because an Israelite was holier in himself than a stranger, but because Jehovah was holy, and Israel belonged to Him. It needed the eye and the heart of a circumcised disciple of the law of God, in order to discern what was clean and what was not. An alien knew no difference. Thus it must ever be. It is only Wisdom's children that can justify her and approve her heavenly ways.

Ere turning from the eleventh chapter of Leviticus, my reader might, with much spiritual profit, compare it with the tenth chapter of Acts, ver. 11-16. How strange it must have appeared to one who had, from his earliest days, been taught the principles of the Mosaic ritual, to see a vessel descending from heaven, "wherein were *all manner* of four-footed beasts of the earth, and wild beasts, and *creeping things,* and fowls of the air;" and not only to see such a vessel so filled, but also to hear a voice, saying, "Rise, Peter; kill and eat." How wonderful! No examination of hoofs or habits! There was no need of this. The vessel and its contents had come from heaven. This was enough. The Jew might ensconce himself behind the narrow inclosures of the Jewish ritual, and exclaim, "Not so, Lord; for I have never eaten any thing that is common or unclean;" but then the tide of divine grace was rising majestically above all such inclosures, in order to embrace, in its mighty compass, "all manner" of objects, and bear them upward to heaven, in the power and on the authority of those precious words, "What God hath cleansed, that call not thou common." It mattered not what was in the vessel if God had cleansed it. The Author of the book of Leviticus was about to raise the thoughts of His servant above the barriers which that book had erected, into all the magnificence of Heaven's grace. He would teach him that true cleanness—the cleanness which Heaven demanded—was no longer to consist in chewing the cud, dividing the hoof, or any such ceremonial marks, but in being washed in the blood of the Lamb, which cleanseth from all sin, and renders the believer clean enough to tread the sapphire pavement of the heavenly courts.

This was a noble lesson for a Jew to learn; it was a divine lesson, before the light of which the shadows of the old economy must pass away. The hand of sovereign grace has thrown open the door of the kingdom, but not to admit aught that is unclean. This could not be. Nothing unclean can enter heaven. But then, a cloven hoof was no longer to be the criterion, but *"what God hath cleansed."* When God cleanses a man, he must needs be clean. Peter was about to be sent to open the kingdom to the Gentiles, as he had already opened it to the Jews, and his Jewish heart needed to be enlarged. He needed to get above the dark shadows of a by-gone age, into the meridian light that was shining from an open heaven, in virtue of a completed sacrifice. He needed to get out of the narrow current of Jewish prejudices, and be borne upon the bosom of that mighty tide of grace which was about to roll through the length and breadth of a lost world. He had to learn, too, that the standard by which true cleanness must be regulated was no longer carnal, ceremonial, and earthly, but spiritual, moral, and heavenly. Assuredly, we may say, these were noble lessons for the apostle of the circumcision to learn upon the housetop of Simon the tanner. They were eminently calculated to soften, to expand, and elevate a mind which had been trained amid the contracting influences of the Jewish system. We bless the Lord for these precious lessons. We bless Him for the large and wealthy place in which He has set us, by the blood of the cross. We bless Him that we are no longer hemmed round about by "Touch not this; taste not that; handle not the other thing;" but that His Word assures us that "every creature of God is good, and nothing to be refused, if it be received with thanksgiving; for it is sanctified by the Word of God and prayer" (1 Tim 4:4-5).

---

## *CHAPTER 12*

THIS brief section reads out to us, after its own peculiar fashion, the double lesson of "man's ruin and God's remedy." But though the fashion is peculiar, the lesson is most distinct and impressive. It is, at once, deeply humbling and divinely comforting. The effect of all Scripture, when interpreted to one's own soul directly by the power of the Holy Ghost, is to lead us out of self to Christ. Wherever we see our fallen nature, at whatever stage of its history we contemplate it—whether in its conception, at its birth, or at any point along its whole career, from the womb to the coffin, it wears the double stamp of infirmity and defilement. This is sometimes forgotten amid the glitter and glare, the pomp and fashion, the wealth and splendor, of human life. The mind of man is fruitful in devices to cover his humiliation. In various ways he seeks to ornament and gild, and put on an appearance of strength and glory, but it is all vain. He has only to be seen as he enters this world, a poor helpless creature, or as he passes away from it, to take his place with the clod of the valley, in order to have a most convincing proof of the hollowness of all his pride, the vanity of all his glory. Those whose path through this world has been brightened by what man calls glory, have entered in nakedness and helplessness, and retreated amid disease and death.

Nor is this all. It is not merely helplessness that belongs to man—that characterizes him as he enters this life: there is defilement also. "Behold," says the Psalmist, "I was shapen in iniquity, and in sin did my mother conceive me" (Ps. 51:5). "How can he be clean that is born of a woman?" (Job 25:4) In the chapter before us, we are taught that the conception and birth of "a man-child" involved "seven days" of ceremonial defilement to the mother, together with thirty-three days of separation from the sanctuary; and these periods were doubled in the case of "a maid-child." Has this no voice? Can we not read herein a humbling lesson? Does it not declare to us, in language not to be misunderstood, that man is "an unclean thing," and that he needs the blood of atonement to cleanse him? Truly so. Man may imagine that he can work out a righteousness of his own, he may vainly boast of the dignity of human nature, he may put on a lofty air and assume a haughty bearing as he moves across the stage of life; but if he would just retire for a few moments and ponder over the short section of our book which now lies open before us, his pride, pomp, dignity, and righteousness would speedily vanish, and instead thereof, he might find the solid basis of all true dignity, as well as the ground of divine righteousness, in the cross of our Lord Jesus Christ.

The shadow of this cross passes before us in a double way in our chapter; first, in the circumcision of the "man-child," whereby he became enrolled as a member of the Israel of God; and secondly, in the burnt-offering and sin-offering, whereby the mother was restored from every defiling influence, rendered fit once more to approach the sanctuary and to come in contact with holy things. "And when the days of her purifying are fulfilled, for a son or for a daughter, she shall bring a lamb of the first year for a burnt-offering, and a young pigeon or a turtle-dove for a sin-offering, unto the door of the tabernacle of the congregation, unto the priest; who shall offer it before the Lord, and make an atonement for her; and she shall be cleansed from the issue of her blood. This is the law for her that hath born a male or a female" (ver. 6-7). The death of Christ in its two grand aspects is here introduced to our thoughts as the only thing which could possibly meet and perfectly remove the defilement connected with man's natural birth. The burnt-offering presents the death of Christ according to the divine estimate thereof; the sin-offering, on the other hand, presents the death of Christ as bearing upon the sinner's need.

"And if she be not able to bring a lamb, then she shall bring two turtles, or two young pigeons; the one for a burnt-offering and the other for a sin-offering; and the priest shall make an atonement for her, and she shall be clean." Nothing but blood-shedding could impart cleanness. The cross is the only remedy for man's infirmity and man's defilement. Wherever that glorious work is apprehended, by faith, there is perfect cleanness enjoyed. Now, the apprehension may be feeble, the faith may be but wavering, the experience may be shallow; but let the reader remember, for his soul's joy and comfort, that it is not the depth of his experience, the stability of his faith, or the strength of his apprehension, but the divine value, the changeless efficacy, of the blood of Jesus. This gives great rest to the heart. The sacrifice of the cross is the same to every member of the Israel of God whatever be his *status* in the assembly. The tender considerateness of our ever-gracious God is seen in the fact that the blood of a turtle-dove was as efficacious for the poor as the blood of a bullock for the rich. The full value of the atoning work was alike maintained and exhibited in each. Had it not been so, the humble Israelite, if involved in ceremonial defilement, might, as she gazed upon the well-stocked pastures of some wealthy neighbor, exclaim, Alas! what shall I do? how shall I be cleansed? how shall I get back to my place and privilege in the assembly? I have neither flock nor herd: I am poor and needy. But, blessed be God, the case of such an one was fully met. A pigeon or turtle-dove was quite sufficient. The same perfect and beautiful grace shines forth in the case of the leper in chapter 14 of our book—"And *if he be poor and cannot get so much,* then he shall take. . . . And he shall offer the one of the turtle-doves, or of the young pigeons, *such as he can get; even such as he is able to get. . . .* This is the law of him in whom is the plague of leprosy, *whose hand is not able to get* that which pertaineth to his cleansing" (ver. 21,30-32).

Grace meets the needy one just where he is and as he is. The atoning blood is brought within the reach of the very lowest, the very poorest, the very feeblest. All who need it can have it. "If he be poor"—what then? Let him be cast aside? Ah, no; Israel's God could never so deal with the poor and needy. There is ample provision for all such in the gracious expression, "Such as he can get; even such as he is able to get." Most exquisite grace! "To the poor the gospel is preached." None can say, The blood of Jesus was beyond me. Each can be challenged with the inquiry, How near would you have it brought to you? "I bring *near* My righteousness." How "near"? So near, that it is "to him that worketh not, but believeth on Him that justifieth the ungodly" (Rom. 4:5). Again, "The Word is *nigh* thee." How "nigh"? So nigh, "that if thou shalt confess with thy mouth the Lord Jesus, and shalt believe in thine heart that God hath raised Him from the head, thou shalt be saved" (Rom. 10:9). So also that most touching and beautiful invitation, "Ho, every one that thirsteth, come ye to the waters, and *he that hath no money*" (Isa. 55:1).

What matchless grace shines in the expressions, "To him that *worketh not,*" and, "He that hath *no money*"*!* They are as like God as they are unlike man. Salvation is as free as the air we breathe. Did we create the air? did we mingle its component parts? No; but we enjoy it, and, by enjoying it, get power to live and act for Him who made it. So is it in the matter of salvation. We get it without a fraction, without an effort. We feed upon the wealth of another, we rest in the work finished by another; and, moreover, it is by so feeding and resting that we are enabled to work for Him on whose wealth we feed and in whose work we rest. This is a grand gospel paradox, perfectly inexplicable to legality, but beautifully plain to faith. Divine grace delights in making provision for those who are "not able" to make provision for themselves.

There is another invaluable lesson furnished by this twelfth chapter of Leviticus. We not only read herein the grace of God to the poor, but, by comparing its closing verse with Luke 2:24, we learn the amazing depth to which God stooped in order to manifest that grace. The Lord Jesus Christ—God manifest in the flesh—the pure and spotless Lamb—the Holy One, who knew no sin, was "made of a woman," and that woman (wondrous mystery!), having borne in her womb, and brought forth, that pure and perfect, that holy and spotless, human body, had to undergo the usual ceremonial, and accomplish the days of her purification, according to the law of Moses. Not only do we read divine grace in the fact of her having thus to purify herself, but also the mode in which this was accomplished. "And to offer a sacrifice according to that which is said in the law of the Lord, *a pair of turtle-doves or two young pigeons.*" From this simple circumstance we learn that the reputed parents of our blessed Lord Jesus were so poor as to be obliged to take advantage of the gracious provision made for those whose means did not afford "a lamb for a burnt-offering." What a thought! The Lord of glory, the most high God, Possessor of heaven and earth, the One to whom pertained "the cattle upon a thousand hills"—yea, the wealth of the universe, appeared in the world which His hands had made, in the narrow circumstances of humble life. The Levitical economy had made provision for the poor, and the mother of Jesus availed herself thereof. Truly there is a profound lesson in this for the human heart. The Lord Jesus did not make His appearance in this world in connection with the great or the noble. He was pre-eminently a poor man. He took His place with the poor. "For ye know the grace of our Lord Jesus Christ, that though He was rich, yet for your sakes He became poor, that ye through His poverty might be rich" (2 Cor. 8:9).

May it ever be our joy to feed upon this precious grace of our Lord Jesus Christ, by which we have been made rich for time and for eternity. He emptied Himself of all that love could give, that we might be filled; He stripped Himself that we might be clothed; He died that we might live. He, in the greatness of His grace, traveled down from the height of divine wealth into the depth of human poverty, in order that we might be raised from the dunghill of nature's ruin, to take our place amid the princes of His people forever. Oh that the sense of this grace, wrought in our hearts by the power of the Holy Ghost, may constrain us to a more unreserved surrender of ourselves to Him, to whom we owe our present and everlasting felicity, our riches, our life, our all!

---

## *CHAPTERS 13–14*

OF all the functions which, according to the Mosaic ritual, the priest had to discharge, none demanded more patient attention or more strict adherence to the divine guide-book than the discernment and proper treatment of leprosy. This fact must be obvious to every one who studies, with any measure of care, the very extensive and important section of our book at which we have now arrived.

There were two things which claimed the priest's vigilant care, namely, the purity of the assembly, and the grace which could not admit of the exclusion of any member save on the most clearly established grounds. Holiness could not permit any one to remain in who ought to be out; and on the other hand, grace would not have any one out who ought to be in. Hence, therefore, there was the most urgent need, on the part of the priest, of watchfulness, calmness, wisdom, patience, tenderness, and enlarged experience. Things might seem trifling which in reality were serious, and things might look like leprosy which were not it at all. The greatest care and coolness were needed. A judgment rashly formed, a conclusion hastily arrived at, might involve the most serious consequences, either as regards the assembly or some individual member thereof.

This will account for the frequent occurrence of such expressions as the following; namely, "The priest shall look"—"The priest shall shut up him that hath the plague *seven days*"—"And the priest shall look on him the seventh day"—"Then the priest shall shut him up *seven days more*"—"And the priest shall *look on him again* the seventh day"—"And the priest shall *see him*"—"Then the priest shall *consider.*" No case was to be hastily judged or rashly decided. No opinion was to be formed from mere hearsay. Personal observation, priestly discernment, calm reflection, strict adherence to the written Word—the holy, infallible guide-book—all these things were imperatively demanded of the priest if he would form a sound judgment of each case. He was not to be guided by his own thoughts, his own feelings, his own wisdom, in any thing. He had ample guidance in the Word, if only he was subject thereto. Every point, every feature, every movement, every variation, every shade and character, every peculiar symptom and affection—all was provided for, with divine fullness and forethought, so that the priest only needed to be acquainted with and subject to the Word in all things, in order to be preserved from ten thousand mistakes.

Thus much as to the priest and his holy responsibilities.

We shall now consider the disease of leprosy, as developed in a person, in a garment, or in a house.

Looking at this disease in a physical point of view, nothing can possibly be more loathsome; and being, so far as man is concerned, totally incurable, it furnishes a most vivid and appalling picture of sin—sin in one's nature, sin in his circumstances, sin in an assembly. What a lesson for the soul in the fact that such a vile and humiliating disease should be used as a type of moral evil, whether in a member of God's assembly, in the circumstances of any member, or in the assembly itself!

1. And first, then, as to leprosy in a person; or in other words, the working of moral evil, or of that which might seem to be evil, in any member of the assembly. This is a matter of grave and solemn import—a matter demanding the utmost vigilance and care on the part of all who are concerned in the good of souls and in the glory of God, as involved in the well-being and purity of His assembly as a whole or of each individual member thereof.

It is important to see that while the broad

principles of leprosy and its cleansing apply in a secondary sense to any sinner, yet in the Scripture now before us, the matter is presented in connection with those who were God's recognized people. The person who is here seen as the subject of priestly examination is a member of the assembly of God. It is well to apprehend this. God's assembly must be kept pure, because it is His dwelling-place. No leper can be allowed to remain within the hallowed precincts of Jehovah's habitation.

But then, mark the care, the vigilance, the perfect patience, inculcated upon the priest, lest aught that was not leprosy might be treated as such, or lest aught that really was leprosy might be suffered to escape. Many things might appear "in the skin"—the place of manifestation—"like the plague of leprosy," which, upon patient, priestly investigation, would be found to be merely superficial. This was to be carefully attended to. Some blemish might make its appearance upon the surface, which, though demanding the jealous care of the one who had to act for God, was not, in reality, defiling. And yet, that which seemed but a superficial blemish might prove to be something deeper than the skin, something below the surface, something affecting the hidden springs of the constitution. All this claimed the most intense care on the part of the priest (see ver. 2-11). Some slight neglect, some trifling oversight, might lead to disastrous consequences. It might lead to the defilement of the assembly, by the presence of a confirmed leper, or to the expulsion, for some superficial blemish, of a genuine member of the Israel of God.

Now, there is a rich fund of instruction in all this for the people of God. There is a difference between personal infirmity and the positive energy of evil—between mere defects and blemishes in the outward character, and the activity of sin in the members. No doubt it is important to watch against our infirmities; for, if not watched, judged, and guarded against, they may become the source of positive evil (see ver. 14-28). Every thing of nature must be judged and kept down. We must not make any allowance for personal infirmity *in ourselves*, though we should make ample allowance for it *in others.* Take for example, the matter of an irritable temper. I should judge it in myself; I should make allowance for it in another. It may, like "the burning boil" in the case of an Israelite (ver. 19-20), prove the source of real defilement—the ground of exclusion from the assembly. Every form of weakness must be watched, lest it become an occasion of sin. "A bald forehead" was not leprosy, but it was that in which leprosy might appear, and hence it had to be watched. There may be a hundred things which are not in themselves sinful, but which may become the occasion of sin if not diligently looked after. Nor is it merely a question of what, in our estimation, may be termed blots, blemishes, and personal infirmities, but even of what our hearts might feel disposed to boast of. Wit, humor, vivacity of spirit and temper—all these may become the source and centre of defilement. Each one has something to guard against—something to keep him ever upon the watch-tower. How happy it is that we have a Father's heart to come to and count on with respect to all such things! We have the precious privilege of coming, at all times, into the presence of unrebuking, unupbraiding love, there to tell out all, and obtain grace to help in all, and full victory over all. We need not be discouraged so long as we see such a motto inscribed on the door of our Father's treasury—"He giveth more grace." Precious motto! It has no limit: it is bottomless and boundless.

We shall now proceed to inquire what was done in every case in which the plague of leprosy was unquestionably and unmistakably defined. The God of Israel could bear with infirmity, blemish, and failure; but the moment it became a case of defilement, whether in the head, the beard, the forehead, or any other part, it could not be tolerated in the holy assembly. "The leper in whom the plague is, his clothes shall be rent, and his head bare, and he shall put a covering upon his upper lip, and shall cry, Unclean, unclean. All the days wherein the plague shall be in him he shall be defiled; he is unclean: he shall dwell alone; without the camp shall his habitation be" (ver. 45-46). Here was the leper's condition, the leper's occupation, the leper's place. With rent garments, bare head, and covered lip; crying, "Unclean, unclean"; and dwelling outside, in the dreary solitude—the dismal desert waste. What could be more humiliating, what more depressing, than this? "He shall dwell alone." He was unfit for communion or companionship. He was excluded from the only spot in all the world in which Jehovah's presence was known or enjoyed.

Behold, in the poor, solitary leper, a vivid type of one in whom sin is working. This is really what it means. It is not, as we shall see presently, a helpless, ruined, guilty, convicted sinner, whose guilt and misery have come thoroughly out, and who is, therefore, a fit subject for the love of God and the blood of Christ. No; we see in the excluded leper one in whom sin is actually working—one in whom there is the positive energy of evil. This is what defiles and shuts out from the enjoyment of the divine presence and the communion of saints. So long as sin is working, there can be no fellowship with God or with His people. "He shall dwell alone; without the camp shall his habitation be." How long? "All the days wherein *the plague* shall be *in* him." This is a great practical truth. The energy of evil is the death-blow to communion. There may be the outward appearance—the mere form—the hollow profession, but communion there can be none so long as the energy of evil is there. It matters not what the character or amount of the evil may be—if it were but the weight of a feather—if it were but some foolish thought, so long as it continues to work, it must hinder communion—it must cause a suspension of fellowship. It is when it rises to a head—when it comes to the surface—when it is brought thoroughly out that it can be perfectly met and put away by the grace of God and by the blood of the Lamb.

This leads us to a deeply interesting point in connection with the leper—a point which must prove a complete paradox to all save those who understand God's mode of dealing with sinners. "And if a leprosy break out abroad in the skin, and the leprosy cover all the skin of him that hath the plague, from his head even to his foot, wheresoever the priest looketh; then the priest shall consider; and, behold, if the leprosy have covered all his flesh, he shall pronounce him clean that hath the plague: it is all turned white: he is clean" (chap. 13:12-13). The moment a sinner is in his true place before God, the whole question is settled: directly his real character is fully brought out, there is no further difficulty. He may have to pass through much painful exercise ere he reaches this point—exercise consequent upon his refusal to take his true place—to bring out "all the truth" with respect to what he is; but the moment he is brought to say, from his heart, *"just as I am,"* the free grace of God flows down to him. "When I kept silence, my bones waxed old through my roaring all the day long. For day and night Thy hand was heavy upon me: my moisture is turned into the drought of summer" (Ps. 32:3-4). How long did this painful exercise continue? Until the whole truth was brought out—until all that which was working inwardly came fully to the surface. "I acknowledged my sin unto Thee, and mine iniquity have I not hid. I said, 'I will confess my transgressions unto the Lord,' and Thou forgavest the iniquity of my sin" (ver. 5).

It is deeply interesting to mark the progress of the Lord's dealing with the leprous man, from the moment that the suspicion is raised, by certain features in the place of manifestation, until the disease covers the whole man, "from the crown of the head unto the sole of the foot." There was no haste and no indifference. God ever enters the place of judgment with a slow and measured pace; but when He does enter, He must act according to the claims of His nature. He can patiently investigate. He can wait for "seven days;" and should there be the slightest variation in the symptoms, He can wait "seven days more;" but the moment it is found to be the positive working of leprosy, there can be no toleration. "Without the camp shall his habitation be." How long? Until the disease comes fully to the surface. "If the leprosy have covered *all* his flesh, he shall pronounce him clean." This is a most precious and interesting point. The very smallest speck of leprosy was intolerable to God; and yet when the whole man was covered, from head to foot, he was pronounced clean—that is, he was a proper subject for the grace of God and the blood of atonement.

Thus is it, in every case, with the sinner. God is "of purer eyes than to behold evil, and cannot look upon iniquity" (Hab. 1:13); and yet the moment a sinner takes his true place, as one thoroughly lost, guilty, and undone—as one in whom there is not so much as a single point on which the eye of Infinite Holiness can rest with complacency —as one who is so bad that he cannot possibly be worse, there is an immediate, a perfect, a divine settlement of the entire matter. The grace of God deals with sinners, and when I know myself to be a sinner, I know myself to be one whom Christ came to save. The more clearly any one can prove me to be a sinner, the more clearly he establishes my title to the love of God and the work of Christ. "For Christ also hath once suffered for sins, the just for the unjust, that He might bring us to God" (1 Pet. 3:18). Now, if I am "unjust," I am one of those very people for whom Christ died, and I am entitled to all the benefits of His death. "There is not a just man upon earth;" and inasmuch as I am "upon earth," it is plain that I am "unjust," and it is equally plain that Christ died for me—that He suffered for my sins. Since, therefore, Christ died for me, it is my happy privilege to enter into the immediate enjoyment of the fruits of His sacrifice. This is as plain as plainness itself. It demands no effort whatsoever. I am not called to be any thing but just what I am. I am not called to feel, to experience, to realize any thing. The Word of God assures me that Christ died for me just as I am; and if He died for me, I am as safe as He is Himself. There is nothing against me: Christ met all. He not only suffered for my *"sins,"* but He "made an end of *sin."* He abolished the entire system in which, as a child of the first Adam, I stood, and He has introduced me into a new position, in association with Himself, and there I stand before God, free from all charge of sin and all fear of judgment.

> Just as I am—without one plea,
> But that Thy blood was shed for me,
> And that Thou bid'st me come to Thee,
> O Lamb of God, I come!

How do I know that His blood was shed for me? By the Scriptures. Blessed, solid, eternal ground of knowledge! Christ suffered for sins: I have gotten sins. Christ died, "the just for the unjust:" I am unjust. Wherefore the death of Christ appropriates itself to me as fully, as immediately, and as divinely as though I were the only sinner upon earth. It is not a question of my appropriation, realization, or experience. Many souls harass themselves about this. How often has one heard such language as the following: "Oh, I believe that Christ died for sinners, but I cannot *realize* that my sins are forgiven. I cannot apply, I cannot appropriate, I do not experience the benefit of Christ's death"! All this is self, and not Christ; it is feeling, and not Scripture. If we search from cover to cover of the blessed volume, we shall not find a syllable about being saved by realization, experience, or appropriation. The gospel applies itself to all who are on the ground of being lost. Christ died for sinners. That is just what I am; wherefore He died for me. How do I know this? is it because I feel it? By no means. How then? By the Word of God. "Christ died for our sins according to the Scriptures; He was buried, and rose again the third day according to the Scriptures" (1 Cor. 15:3-4). Thus it is all "according to the Scriptures." If it were according to our feelings, we should be in a deplorable way, for our feelings are hardly the same for the length of a day, but the Scriptures are ever the same. "Forever, O Lord, Thy Word is settled in heaven." "Thou hast magnified Thy Word above all Thy name."

No doubt it is a very happy thing to realize, to feel, and to experience; but if we put these things in the place of Christ, we shall neither have them nor the Christ that yields them. If I am occupied with Christ, I shall realize; but if I put my realization in place of Christ, I shall have neither the one nor the other. This is the sad condition of thousands. Instead of resting on the stable authority of "the Scriptures," they are ever looking into their own hearts, and hence they are always uncertain and, as a consequence, always unhappy. A condition of doubt is a condition of torture; but how can I get rid of my doubt? Simply by relying on the divine authority of "the Scriptures." Of what do the Scriptures testify? Of Christ (John 5). They declare that Christ died for our sins, and that He was raised again for our justification (Rom. 4). This settles every thing. The self-same authority that tells me I am unjust tells me also that Christ died for me. Nothing can be plainer than this. If I were aught else than unjust, the death of Christ would not be for me at all; but being unjust, it is divinely fitted, divinely intended, and divinely applied to me. If I am occupied with any thing in, of, or about myself, it is plain I have not entered into the full spiritual application of Leviticus 13:12-13—I have not come to the Lamb of God *"just as I am."* It is when the leper is covered from head to foot that he is on the true ground. It is there and there alone that grace can meet him. "Then the priest shall consider; and, behold, if the leprosy have covered all his flesh, he shall pronounce him clean that hath the plague: it is all turned white: he is clean." Precious truth! "Where sin abounded, grace did much more abound." So long as I think there is a single spot which is not covered with the direful disease, I have not come to the end of myself. It is when my true condition is fully disclosed to my view that I really understand the meaning of salvation by grace.

The force of all this will be more fully apprehended when we come to consider the ordinances connected with the cleansing of the leper, in chapter 14 of our book. We shall now briefly enter upon the question of leprosy in a garment, as presented in chapter 13:47-59.

2. The garment or skin suggests to the mind the idea of a man's circumstances or habits. This is a deeply practical point. We are to watch against the working of evil in our ways just as carefully as against evil in ourselves. The same patient investigation is observable with respect to a garment as in the case of a person. There is no haste, neither is there any indifference. "The priest shall look upon the plague, and shut up it that hath the plague seven days." There must be no indifference, no indolence, no carelessness. Evil may creep into our habits and circumstances in numberless ways, and hence the moment we perceive aught of a suspicious nature, it must be submitted to a calm, patient process of priestly investigation. It must be "shut up seven days," in order that it may have full time to develop itself perfectly.

"And he shall look on the plague on the seventh day: if the plague be spread in the garment, either in the warp, or in the woof, or in a skin, or in any work that is made of skin, the plague is a fretting leprosy; it is unclean. He shall therefore burn that garment." The wrong habit must be given up the moment I discover it. If I find myself in a thoroughly wrong position, I must abandon it. The burning of the garment expresses the act of judgment upon evil, whether in a man's habits or circumstances. There must be no trifling with evil. In certain cases the garment was to be "washed," which expresses the action of the Word of God upon a man's habits. "Then the priest shall command that they wash the thing wherein the plague is, and he shall shut it up *seven days more.*" There is to be patient waiting, in order to ascertain the effect of the Word. "And the priest shall look on the plague, after that it is washed; and, behold, if the plague have not changed . . . thou shalt burn it in the fire." When there is any thing radically and irremediably bad in one's position or habits, the whole thing is to be given up. "And if the priest look, and, behold, the plague be somewhat dark after the washing of it; then he shall rend it out of the garment." The Word may produce such an effect as that the wrong features in a man's character, or the wrong points in his position, shall be given up, and the evil be got rid of; but if the evil continue, the whole thing must be condemned and set aside.

There is a rich mine of practical instruction in all this. We must look well to the position which we occupy, the circumstances in which we stand, the habits we adopt, the character we wear. There is special need of watchfulness. Every suspicious symptom and trait must be sedulously guarded, lest it should prove, in the sequel, to be "a fretting" or "spreading leprosy," whereby we ourselves and many others may be defiled. We may be placed in a position attached to which there are certain wrong things which can be given up without entirely abandoning the position; and on the other hand, we may find ourselves in a situation in which it is impossible to "abide with God." Where the eye is single, the path will be plain. Where the one desire of the heart is to enjoy the divine presence, we shall easily discover those things which tend to deprive us of that unspeakable blessing.

May our hearts be tender and sensitive; may we cultivate a deeper, closer walk with God; and may we carefully guard against every form of defilement, whether in person, in habit, or in association.

We shall now proceed to consider the beauteous and significant ordinances connected with the cleansing of the leper, in which we shall find some of the most precious truths of the gospel presented to us.

"And the Lord spake unto Moses, saying, 'This shall be the law of the leper in the day of his cleansing: he shall be brought unto the priest: and the priest shall go forth out of the camp" (chap. 14:1-3). We have already seen the place which the leper occupied. He was outside the camp, in the place of moral distance from God—from His sanctuary and His assembly. Moreover, he dwelt in dreary solitude, in a condition of uncleanness. He was beyond the reach of human aid, and as for himself, he could only communicate defilement to every one and every thing he touched. It was therefore obviously impossible that he could do aught to cleanse himself. If, indeed, he could *only* defile by his very touch, how could he possibly cleanse himself? how could he contribute towards, or co-operate in, his cleansing? Impossible. As an unclean leper, he could not do so much as a single thing for himself; *all* had to be done *for* him. He could not make his way to God, but God could make His way to him. He was shut up to God. There was no help for him either in himself or in his fellowman. It is clear that one leper could not cleanse another; and it is equally clear that if a leper touched a clean person, he rendered him unclean. His *only* resource was in God. He was to be a debtor to grace for every thing.

Hence, we read, "The priest shall go forth out of the camp." It is not said, The leper shall go. This was wholly out of the question. It was of no use talking to the leper about going or doing. He was consigned to dreary solitude; whither could he go? He was involved in helpless defilement; what could he do? He might long for fellowship and long to be clean, but his longings were those of a lonely helpless leper. He might make efforts after cleansing, but his efforts could but prove him unclean, and tend to spread defilement. Before ever he could be pronounced "clean," a work had to be wrought for him—a work which he could neither do nor help to do—a work which had to be wholly accomplished by another. The leper was called to "stand still" and behold the priest doing a work in virtue of which the leprosy could be perfectly cleansed. The priest accomplished *all:* the leper did *nothing.*

"Then shall the priest command to take for him that is to be cleansed, two birds, alive and clean, and cedar-wood, and scarlet, and hyssop. And the priest shall command that one of the birds be killed in an earthen vessel over running water." In the priest going forth from the camp—forth from God's dwelling-place—we behold the blessed Lord Jesus coming down from the bosom of the Father, His eternal dwelling-place, into this polluted world of ours, where He beheld us sunk in the polluting leprosy of sin. He, like the good Samaritan, "came where we were." He did not come half-way merely; He did not come nine-tenths of the way; He came all the way. This was indispensable. He could not consistently with the holy claims of the throne of God have bidden our leprosy to depart had He remained in the bosom. He could call worlds into existence by the word of His mouth, but when leprous sinners had to be cleansed, something more was needed. "God so loved the world, that He gave His only begotten Son." When worlds were to be framed, God had but to speak; when sinners had to be saved, He had to give His Son. "In this was manifested the love of God towards us, because that God sent His only begotten Son into the world, that we might live through Him. Herein is love, not that we loved God, but that He loved us, and sent His Son to be the propitiation for our sins" (1 John 4:9-10).

But there was far more to be accomplished than the mission and incarnation of the Son. It would have availed the leper but little indeed had the priest merely gone forth from the camp and looked upon his low and forlorn condition. Blood-shedding was essentially necessary ere leprosy could be removed. The death of a spotless victim was needed. "Without shedding of blood is no remission" (Heb. 9:22). And be it observed that the shedding of blood was the real basis of the leper's cleansing. It was not a mere circumstance, which, in conjunction with others, contributed to the leper's cleansing. By no means. The giving up of the life was the grand and all-important fact. When this was accomplished, the way was open, every barrier was removed, God could deal in perfect grace with the leper. This point should be distinctly laid hold of if my reader would fully enter into the glorious doctrine of the blood.

"And the priest shall command that one of the birds be killed in an earthen vessel over running water." Here we have the acknowledged type of the death of Christ, "who through the eternal Spirit offered Himself without spot to God." "He was crucified in weakness" (Heb. 9; 2 Cor. 13). The greatest, the mightiest, the most glorious, the most momentous work that ever was accomplished, throughout the wide universe of God, was wrought "in weakness." Oh, my reader, how terrible a thing must sin be in the judgment of God when His own beloved Son had to come down from heaven and hang upon yonder cursed tree, a spectacle to men, to angels, and to devils, in order that you and I might be forgiven! And what a type of sin have we in leprosy! Who would have thought that that little "bright spot" appearing on the person of some member of the congregation was a matter of such grave consequence? But, ah! that little "bright spot" was nothing less than the energy of evil in the place of manifestation. It was the index of the dreadful working of sin in the nature; and ere that person could be fitted for a place in the assembly, or for the enjoyment of communion with a holy God, the Son of God had to leave those bright heavens and descend into the lowest parts of the earth, in order to make a full atonement for that which exhibited itself merely in the form of a little "bright spot." Let us remember this. Sin is a dreadful thing in the estimation of God. He cannot tolerate so much as a single sinful thought. Before one such thought could be forgiven, Christ had to die upon the cross. The most trifling sin (if any sin can be called trifling,) demanded nothing less than God's eternal and co-equal Son. But, eternal praise be to God, what sin demanded, redeeming love freely gave; and now God is infinitely more glorified in the forgiveness of sins than He could have been had Adam maintained his original innocency. God is more glorified in the salvation, the pardon, the justification, the preservation, and final glorification of guilty man than He could have been in maintaining an innocent man in the enjoyment of creation-blessings. Such is the precious mystery of redemption. May our hearts enter, by the power of the Holy Ghost, into the living and profound depths of this wondrous mystery.

"As for the living bird, he shall take it, and the cedar-wood, and the scarlet, and the hyssop, and shall dip them and the living bird in the blood of the bird that was killed over the running water. And he shall sprinkle upon him that is to be cleansed from the leprosy seven times, and shall pronounce him clean, and shall let the living bird loose into the open field." The blood being shed, the priest can enter directly and fully upon his work. Up to this, we read, "The priest shall command"; but now he acts immediately himself. The death of Christ is the basis of His priestly ministration. Having entered with His own blood into the holy place, He acts as our great High-Priest, applying to our souls all the precious results of His atoning work, and maintaining us in the full and divine integrity of the position into which His sacrifice has introduced us. "For every high-priest is ordained to offer gifts and sacrifices: wherefore it is of necessity that this Man have somewhat also to offer. For if He were on earth, He should not be a priest" (Heb. 8:3-4).

We could hardly have a more perfect type of the resurrection of Christ than that presented in "the living bird let loose into the open field." It was not let go until after the death of its companion; for the two birds typify one Christ in two stages of His blessed work, namely, death and resurrection. Ten thousand birds let loose would not have availed for the leper. It was that living bird, mounting upward into the open heavens, bearing upon his wing the significant token of accomplished atonement—it was that which told out the great fact that the work was done, the ground cleared, the foundation laid. Thus is it in reference to our blessed Lord Jesus Christ. His resurrection declares the glorious triumph of redemption. "He rose again the third day according to the Scriptures." "He was raised again for our justification." It is this that sets the burdened heart free and liberates the struggling conscience. The Scriptures assure me that Jesus was nailed to the cross under the weight of my sins; but the same Scriptures assure me that He rose from the grave without one of those sins upon Him. Nor is this all. The same Scriptures assure me that all who put their trust in Jesus are as free from all charge of guilt as He is; that there is no more wrath or condemnation for them than for Him; that they are in Him, one with Him, accepted in Him, co-quickened, co-raised, co-seated, with Him. Such is the peace-giving testimony of the Scriptures of truth—such the record of God who cannot lie (see Rom. 6:6-11; 8:1-4; 2 Cor. 5:21; Eph. 2:5-6; Col. 2:10-15; 1 John 4:17).

But we have another most important truth set before us in verse 6 of our chapter. We not only see our full deliverance from guilt and condemnation, as beautifully exhibited in the living bird let loose, but we see also our entire deliverance from all the attractions of earth and all the influences of nature. "The scarlet" would be the apt expression of the former, while "the cedar-wood and hyssop" would set forth the latter. The cross is the end of all this world's glory. God presents it as such, and the believer recognizes it as such. "God forbid that I should glory, save in the cross of our Lord Jesus Christ, whereby the world is crucified unto me, and I unto the world" (Gal. 6:14).

Then, as to the "cedar-wood and hyssop," they present to us, as it were, the two extremes of nature's wide range. Solomon "spake of trees, from the cedar-tree that is in Lebanon even unto the hyssop that springeth out of the wall" (1 Kings 4:33). From the lofty cedar which crowns the sides of Lebanon, down to the lowly hyssop—the wide extremes and all that lies between—nature in all its departments is brought under the power of the cross; so that the believer sees in the death of Christ the end of all his guilt, and end of all earth's glory, and the end of the whole system of nature—the entire old creation. And with what is he to be occupied? With Him who is the Antitype of that living bird, with blood-stained feathers, ascending into the open heavens. Precious, glorious, soul-satisfying object! A risen, ascended, triumphant, glorified Christ, who has passed into the heavens, bearing in His sacred Person the marks of an accomplished atonement. It is with Him we have to do: we are shut up to Him. He is God's exclusive object; He is the centre of heaven's joy, the theme of angels' song. We want none of earth's glory, none of nature's attractions. We can behold them all, together with our sin and guilt, forever set aside by the death of Christ. We can well afford to dispense with earth and nature, inasmuch as we have gotten, instead thereof, the "unsearchable riches of Christ."

"And he shall sprinkle upon him that is to be cleansed from the leprosy seven times, and shall pronounce him clean, and shall let the bird loose into the open field." The more deeply we ponder over the contents of chapter 13, the more clearly we shall see how utterly impossible it was for the leper to do aught towards his own cleansing. All he could do was to "put a covering upon his upper lip;" and all he could say was, "Unclean, unclean." It belonged to God, and to Him alone, to devise and accomplish a work whereby the leprosy could be perfectly cleansed; and further, it belonged to God, and to Him alone, to pronounce the leper "clean." Hence it is written, "The priest shall sprinkle," and "he shall pronounce him clean." It is not said, The leper shall sprinkle and pronounce or imagine himself clean. This would never do. God was the Judge—God was the Healer—God was the Cleanser. He alone knew what leprosy was, how it could be put away, and when to pronounce the leper clean. The leper might have gone on all his days covered with leprosy, and yet be wholly ignorant of what was wrong with him. It was the Word of God—the Scriptures of truth—the divine Record that declared the full truth as to leprosy; and nothing short of the self-same authority could pronounce the leper clean, and that, moreover, only on the solid and indisputable ground of death and resurrection. There is the most precious connection between the three things in verse 7: the blood is sprinkled, the leper pronounced clean, and the living bird let loose. There is not so much as a single syllable about what the leper was to do, to say, to think, or to feel. It was enough that he was a leper—a fully revealed, a thoroughly judged leper, covered from head to foot. This sufficed for him; all the rest pertained to God.

It is of all importance for the anxious inquirer after peace to enter into the truth unfolded in this branch of our subject. So many are tried by the question of *feeling, realizing,* and *appropriating,* instead of seeing, as in the leper's case, that the sprinkling of the blood was as independent and as divine as the shedding of it. It is not said, The leper shall apply, appropriate, or realize, and then he shall be clean. By no means. The plan of deliverance was divine; the provision of the sacrifice was divine; the shedding of the blood was divine; the sprinkling of the blood was divine; the record as to the result was divine: in short, it was all divine.

It is not that we should undervalue realization, or, to speak more correctly, communion, through the Holy Ghost, with all the precious results of Christ's work for us. Far from it: we shall see presently the place assigned thereto in the divine economy. But then we are no more saved by realization than the leper was cleansed by it. The gospel, by which we are saved, is that "Christ died for our sins according to the Scriptures; and that He was buried, and that He rose again the third day according to the Scriptures." There is nothing about realization here. No doubt it is happy to realize. It is a very happy thing for one who was just on the point of being drowned to realize himself in a life-boat; but clearly he is saved by the boat and not by his realization. So it is with the sinner that believes on the Lord Jesus Christ. He is saved by death and resurrection. Is it because he realizes it? No; but because God says it. It is *"according to the Scriptures."* Christ died and rose again; on that ground God pronounces him clean.

No condemnation, O my soul!
*'Tis God that speaks the word.*

This gives immense peace to the soul. I have to do with God's plain record, which nothing can ever shake. That record has reference to God's own work. It is He Himself who has wrought all that was needful in order to my being pronounced clean in His sight. My pardon no more depends upon my realization than upon any "works of righteousness that I have done"; and it no more depends upon my works of righteousness than it does upon my crimes. In a word, it depends exclusively upon the death and resurrection of Christ. How do I know it? God tells me. It is "according to the Scriptures.

There are perhaps few things which disclose the deep-seated legality of our hearts more strikingly than this oft-raised question of realization. We *will* have in something of self, and thus so sadly mar our peace and liberty in Christ. It is mainly because of this that I dwell at such length upon the beautiful ordinance of the cleansing of the leper, and especially on the truth unfolded in chapter 14:7. It was the priest that sprinkled the blood, and it was the priest that pronounced the leper clean. Thus it is in the case of the sinner. The moment he is on his true ground, the blood of Christ and the Word of God apply themselves without any further question or difficulty whatever; but the moment this harassing question of realization is raised, the peace is disturbed, the heart depressed, and the mind bewildered. The more thoroughly I get done with self, and become occupied with Christ, as presented in "the Scriptures," the more settled my peace will be. If the leper had looked at himself when the priest pronounced him clean, would he have found any basis for the declaration? Surely not. The sprinkled blood was the basis of the divine record, and not any thing in or connected with the leper. The leper was not asked how he felt or what he thought; he was not questioned as to whether he had a deep sense of the vileness of his disease. He was an acknowledged leper; that was enough. It was for such an one the blood was shed, and that blood made him clean. How did he know this? was it because he felt it? No; but because the priest, on God's behalf and by His authority, told him so. The leper was pronounced clean on the very same ground that the living bird was let loose. The same blood which stained the feathers of that living bird was sprinkled upon the leper. This was a perfect settlement of the whole affair, and that, too, in a manner entirely independent of the leper, the leper's thoughts, his feelings, and his realization. Such is the type. And when we look from the type to the Antitype, we see that our blessed Lord Jesus Christ entered heaven and laid on the throne of God the eternal record of an accomplished work, in virtue of which the believer enters also. This is a most glorious truth, divinely calculated to dispel from the heart of the anxious inquirer every doubt, every fear, every bewildering thought, and every harassing question. A risen Christ is God's exclusive object, and He sees every believer in Him. May every awakened soul find abiding repose in this emancipating truth.

"And he that is to be cleansed shall wash his clothes, and shave off all his hair, and wash himself in water, that he may be clean; and after that he shall come into the camp, and shall tarry abroad out of his tent seven days" (ver.8). The leper, being pronounced clean, can begin to do what he could not even have attempted to do before, namely, to cleanse himself, cleanse his habits, shave off all his hair; and, having done so, he is privileged to take his place in the camp—the place of ostensible, recognized, public relationship with the God of Israel, whose presence in that camp it was which rendered the expulsion of the leper needful. The blood having been applied in its expiating virtue, there is the washing of water, which expresses the action of the Word on the character, the habits, the ways, so as to render the person, not only in God's view, but also in the view of the congregation, morally and practically fit for a place in the public assembly.

But, be it observed, the man, though sprinkled with blood and washed with water, and thus entitled to a position in the public assembly, was not permitted to enter his own tent. He was not permitted to enter upon the full enjoyment of those private, personal privileges which belonged to his own peculiar place in the camp. In other words, though knowing redemption through the shed and sprinkled blood, and owning the Word as the rule according to which his person and all his habits should be cleansed and regulated, he had yet to be brought, in the power of the Spirit, into full, intelligent communion with his own special place, portion, and privileges in Christ.

I speak according to the doctrine of the type; and I feel it to be of importance to apprehend the truth unfolded therein. It is too often overlooked. There are many who own the blood of Christ as the alone ground of pardon, and the Word of God as that whereby alone their habits, ways, and associations are to be cleansed and ordered, who nevertheless are far from entering, by the power of the Holy Ghost, into communion with the preciousness and excellency of that One whose blood has put away their sins and whose Word is to cleanse their practical habits. They are in the place of ostensible and actual relationship, but not in the power of personal communion. It is perfectly true that all believers are in Christ, and, as such, entitled to communion with the very highest truths; moreover, they have the Holy Ghost as the power of communion —all this is divinely true; but then there is not that entire setting aside of all that pertains to nature, which is really essential to the power of communion with Christ in all the aspects of His character and work. In point of fact, this latter will not be fully known to any until "the eighth day"—the day of resurrection-glory, when we shall know even as we are known. Then, indeed, each one for himself, and all together, shall enter into the full, unhindered power of communion with Christ, in all the precious phases of His Person and features of His character unfolded from verse 10 to 20 of our chapter. Such is the hope set before us; but even now, in proportion as we enter, by faith, through the mighty energy of the indwelling Spirit, into the death of nature and all pertaining thereto, we can feed upon and rejoice in Christ as the portion of our souls, in the place of individual communion.

"But it shall be on the seventh day, that he shall shave all his hair off his head and his beard and his eyebrows, even all his hair he shall shave off; and he shall wash his clothes, also he shall wash his flesh in water, and he shall be clean" (ver. 9). Now, it is clear that the leper was just as clean, in God's judgment, on the first day, when the blood was sprinkled upon him in its sevenfold or perfect efficacy, as he was on the seventh day. Wherein, then, was the difference? Not in his actual standing and condition, but in his personal intelligence and communion. On the seventh day he was called to enter into the full and complete abolition of all that pertained to nature. He was called to apprehend that not merely was nature's leprosy to be put away, but nature's ornaments—yea, all that was natural—all that belonged to the old condition.

It is one thing to know, as a doctrine, that God sees my nature to be dead, and it is quite another thing for me to "reckon" myself as dead—to put off, practically, the old man and his deeds—to mortify my members which are on the earth. This, probably, is what many godly persons mean when they speak of progressive sanctification. They mean a right thing, though they do not put it exactly as the Scriptures do. The leper was pronounced clean the moment the blood was sprinkled upon him, and yet he had to cleanse himself. How was this? In the former case, he was clean in the judgment of God; in the latter, he was to be clean practically, in his own personal intelligence, and in his manifested character. Thus it is with the believer. He is, as one with Christ, "washed, sanctified, and justified"—"accepted"—"complete" (1 Cor. 6:11; Eph. 1:6; Col. 2:10). Such is his unalterable standing and condition before God. He is as perfectly sanctified as he is justified, for Christ is the measure of both the one and the other, according to God's judgment and view of the case. But then the believer's apprehension of all this in his own soul, and his exhibition thereof in his habits and ways, open up quite another line of things. Hence it is we read, "Having therefore these promises, dearly beloved, let us *cleanse ourselves* from all filthiness of the flesh and spirit, perfecting holiness in the fear of God" (2 Cor. 7:1). It is because Christ has cleansed us by His precious blood that therefore we are called to "cleanse ourselves" by the application of the Word, through the Spirit. "This is He that came by water and blood, Jesus Christ; not by water only, but by water and blood. And it is the Spirit that beareth witness, because the Spirit is truth. For there are three that bear record, the Spirit, and the water, and the blood; and these three agree in one" (1 John 5:6,8). Here we have atonement by the blood, cleansing by the Word, and power by the Spirit—all founded upon the death of Christ, and all vividly foreshadowed in the ordinances connected with the cleansing of the leper.

"And on the eighth day he shall take two he lambs without blemish, and one ewe lamb of the first year without blemish, and three tenth deals of fine flour for a meat-offering, mingled with oil, and one log of oil. And the priest that maketh him clean shall present the man that is to be made clean, and those things, before the Lord, at the door of the tabernacle of the congregation. And the priest shall take one he lamb, and offer him for a trespass-offering, and the log of oil, and wave them for a wave-offering before the Lord" (ver. 10-12). The entire range of offerings is here introduced; but it is the trespass-offering which is first killed, inasmuch as the leper is viewed as an actual trespasser. This is true in every case. As those who have trespassed against God, we need Christ as the One who atoned, on the cross, for those trespasses. "Himself bare our *sins* in His own body on the tree." The first view which the sinner gets of Christ is as the Antitype of the trespass-offering.

"And the priest shall take some of the blood of the trespass-offering, and the priest shall put it upon the tip of the right ear of him that is to be cleansed, and upon the thumb of his right hand, and upon the great toe of his right foot. "The ear,"—that guilty member which had so frequently proved a channel of communication for vanity, folly, and even uncleanness—that ear must be cleansed by the blood of the trespass-offering. Thus all the guilt which I have ever contracted by that member is forgiven according to God's estimate of the blood of Christ. *"The right hand,"* which had so frequently been stretched forth for the execution of deeds of vanity, folly, and even uncleanness, must be cleansed by the blood of the trespass-offering. Thus all the guilt which I have ever contracted by that member is forgiven according to God's estimate of the blood of Christ. *"The foot,* which had so often run in the way of vanity, folly, and even uncleanness, must now be cleansed by the blood of the trespass-offering, so that all the guilt which I have ever contracted by that member is forgiven according to God's estimate of the blood of Christ. Yes; *all, all, all* is forgiven—all is canceled—all forgotten—all sunk as lead in the mighty waters of eternal oblivion. Who shall bring it up again? Shall angel, man, or devil be able to plunge into those unfathomed and unfathomable waters, to bring up from thence those trespasses of "foot," "hand," or "ear," which redeeming love has cast thereinto? Oh, no; blessed be God, they are gone, and gone forever! I am better off, by far, than if Adam had never sinned. Precious truth! To be washed in the blood is better far than to be clothed in innocency.

But God could not rest satisfied with the mere blotting out of trespasses by the atoning blood of Jesus. This in itself is a great thing, but there is something greater still.

"And the priest shall take some of the log of oil, and pour it into the palm of his own left hand: and the priest shall dip his right finger in the oil that is in his left hand, and shall sprinkle of the oil with his finger seven times before the Lord. And of the rest of the oil that is in his hand shall the priest put upon the tip of the right ear of him that is to be cleansed, and upon the thumb of his right hand, and upon the great toe of his right foot, upon the blood of the trespass-offering; and the remnant of the oil that is in the priest's hand he shall pour upon the head of him that is to be cleansed; and the priest shall make an atonement for him before the Lord" (ver. 15-18). Thus, not only are our members cleansed by the blood of Christ, but also consecrated to God in the power of the Spirit. God's work is not only negative, but positive. The ear is no longer to be the vehicle for communicating defilement, but to be "swift to hear" the voice of the Good Shepherd; the hand is no longer to be used as the instrument of unrighteousness, but to be stretched forth in acts of righteousness, grace, and true holiness; the foot is no longer to tread in folly's paths, but to run in the way of God's holy commandments: and, finally, the whole man is to be dedicated to God in the energy of the Holy Ghost.

It is deeply interesting to see that "the oil" was put "upon the blood of the trespass-offering." The blood of Christ is the divine basis of the operations of the Holy Ghost. The blood and the oil go together. As sinners, we could know nothing of the latter save on the ground of the former. The oil could not have been put upon the leper until the blood of the trespass-offering had first been applied. "In whom also, after that ye believed, ye were sealed with that Holy Spirit of promise." The divine accuracy of the type evokes the admiration of the renewed mind. The more closely we scrutinize it—the more of the light of Scripture we concentrate upon it, the more its beauty, force, and precision are perceived and enjoyed. All, as might justly be expected, is in the most lovely harmony with the entire analogy of the Word of God. There is no need for any effort of the mind. Take Christ as the key to unlock the rich treasury of the types; explore the precious contents by the light of Inspiration's heavenly lamp; let the Holy Ghost be your Interpreter; and you cannot fail to be edified, enlightened, and blessed.

"And the priest shall offer the sin-offering, and make an atonement for him that is to be cleansed from his uncleanness." Here we have a type of Christ, not only as the Bearer of our trespasses, but also as the One who made an end of *sin,* root and branch; the One who destroyed the entire system of sin—"the Lamb of God, who taketh away the sin of the world"—"the propitiation for the whole world." As the Trespass-offering, Christ put away all my trespasses; as the Sin-offering, He met the great root from whence those trespasses emanated. He met all; but it is as the Trespass-offering I first know Him, because it is as such I first need Him. It is the "conscience of sins" that first troubles me. This is divinely met by my precious Trespass-offering. Then, as I get on, I find that all these sins had a root, a parent stem, and that root or stem I find within me. This, likewise, is divinely met by my precious Sin-offering. The order, as presented in the leper's case, is perfect. It is precisely the order which we can trace in the actual experience of every soul. The trespass-offering comes first, and then the sin-offering.

"And afterward he shall kill the burnt-offering." This offering presents the highest possible aspect of the death of Christ. It is Christ offering Himself without spot to God, without special reference to either trespasses or sin: it is Christ, in voluntary devotedness, walking to the cross, and there offering Himself as a sweet savor to God.

"And the priest shall offer the burnt-offering and the meat-offering upon the altar; and the priest shall make an atonement for him, and he shall be clean" (ver. 20). The meat-offering typifies "the Man Christ Jesus" in His perfect human life. It is intimately associated, in the case of the cleansed leper, with the burnt-offering; and so it is in the experience of every saved sinner. It is when we know our *trespasses* are forgiven, and the root or principle of *sin* judged, that we can, according to our measure, by the power of the Spirit, enjoy communion with God about that blessed One who lived a perfect human life down here and then offered Himself without spot to God on the cross. Thus the four classes of offerings are brought before us in their divine order in the cleansing of the leper, namely, the trespass-offering, the sin-offering, the burnt-offering, and the meat-offering, each exhibiting its own specific aspect of our blessed Lord Jesus Christ.

Here closes the record of the Lord's dealings with the leprous man; and, oh, what a marvelous record it is! what an unfolding of the exceeding hatefulness of sin, the grace and holiness of God, the preciousness of Christ's Person, and the efficacy of His work! Nothing can be more interesting than to mark the footprints of divine grace forth from the hallowed precincts of the sanctuary to the defiled place where the leper stood, with bare head, covered lip, and rent garments. God visited the leper where he was, but He did not leave him there. He went forth prepared to accomplish a work in virtue of which He could bring the leper into a higher place and higher communion than ever he had known before. On the ground of this work, the leper was conducted from his place of defilement and loneliness to the very door of the tabernacle of the congregation, the priestly place, to enjoy priestly privileges (comp. Exod. 29:20-21,32). How could he ever have climbed to such an elevation? Impossible! For aught he could do, he might have languished and died in his leprosy had not the sovereign grace of the God of Israel stooped to lift him from the dunghill, to set him among the princes of his people. If ever there was a case in which the question of human effort, human merit, and human righteousness could be fully tried and perfectly settled, the leper is unquestionably that case. Indeed it were a sad loss of time to discuss such a question in the presence of such a case. It must be obvious to the most cursory reader that naught but free grace reigning through righteousness could meet the leper's condition and the leper's need. And how gloriously and triumphantly did that grace act! It traveled down into the deepest depths, that it might raise the leper to the loftiest heights. See what the leper lost, and see what he gained! He lost all that pertained to nature, and he gained the blood of atonement and the grace of the Spirit. I mean typically. Truly he was a gainer, to an incalculable amount. He was infinitely better off than if he had never been thrust forth from the camp. Such is the grace of God! such the power and value, the virtue and efficacy, of the blood of Jesus!

How forcibly does all this remind us of the prodigal in Luke 15! In him, too, leprosy had wrought and risen to a head. He had been afar off, in the defiled place, where his own sins and the intense selfishness of the far country had created a solitude around him; but, blessed forever be a father's deep and tender love, we know how it ended. The prodigal found a higher place and tasted higher communion than ever he had known before; "the fatted calf" had never been slain for him before; "the best robe" had never been on him before. And how was this? was it a question of the prodigal's merit? Oh, no; it was simply a question of the father's love.

Can you ponder over the record of God's dealings with the leper in Leviticus 14, or the father's dealings with the prodigal in Luke 15, and not have an enlarged sense of the love that dwells in the bosom of God, that flows through the Person and work of Christ, that is recorded in the Scriptures of truth, and brought home to the heart by the Holy Ghost? Lord grant us a deeper and more abiding fellowship with Himself!

From verse 21 to 32 we have "the law of him in whom is the plague of leprosy, whose hand is not able to get that which pertaineth to his cleansing." This refers to the sacrifices of "the eighth day," and not to the "two birds alive and clean." These latter could not be dispensed with in any case, because they set forth the death and resurrection of Christ as the alone ground on which God can receive a sinner back to Himself. On the other hand, the sacrifices of "the eighth day" being connected with the soul's communion, must, in some degree, be affected by the measure of the soul's apprehension; but whatever that measure may be, the grace of God can meet it with those peculiarly touching words, *"such as he is able to get."* And not only so, but the "two turtle-doves" conferred the same privileges on the "poor" as the two lambs conferred upon the rich, inasmuch as both the one and the other pointed to "the precious blood of Christ," which is of infinite, changeless, and eternal efficacy in the judgment of God. All stand before God on the ground of death and resurrection. All are brought into the same place of nearness, but all do not enjoy the same measure of communion—all have not the same measure of apprehension of the preciousness of Christ in all the aspects of His work. They might, if they would; but they allow themselves to be hindered in various ways. Earth and nature, with their respective influences, act prejudicially: the Spirit is grieved, and Christ is not enjoyed as He might be. It is utterly vain to expect that if we are living in the region of nature, we can be feeding upon Christ. No; there must be self-emptiness, self-denial, self-judgment, if we would habitually feed upon Christ. It is not a question of salvation; it is not a question of the leper introduced into the camp—the place of recognized relationship. By no means. It is only a question of the soul's communion, of its enjoyment of Christ. As to this, the largest measure lies open to us. We may have communion with the very highest truths; but if our measure be small, the unupbraiding grace of our Father's heart breathes in the sweet words, *"such as he is able to get."* The title of all is the same, however our capacity may vary; and, blessed be God, when we get into His presence, all the desires of the new nature, in their utmost intensity, are satisfied; all the powers of the new nature, in their fullest range, are occupied. May we prove these things in our soul's happy experience day by day.

We shall close this section with a brief reference to the subject of leprosy in a house.

3. The reader will observe that a case of leprosy in a person, or in a garment, might occur in the wilderness; but in the matter of a house, it was of necessity confined to the land of Canaan.

"When ye be come into the land of Canaan, which I give to you for a possession, and I put the plague of leprosy in a house of the land of your possession . . . then the priest shall command that they empty the house, before the priest go into it to see the plague, that all that is in the house be not made unclean; and afterward the priest shall go in to see the house: and he shall look on the plague, and, behold, if the plague be in the walls of the house with hollow strakes, greenish or reddish, which in sight are lower than the wall; then the priest shall go out of the house to the door of the house, and shut up the house seven days."

Looking at the house as the type of an assembly, we have some weighty principles presented to us as to the divine method of dealing with moral evil, or suspicion of evil, in a congregation. We observe the same holy calmness and perfect patience with respect to the house as we have already seen in reference to the person or the garment. There was no haste and no indifference, either as regards the house, the garment, or the individual. The man who had an interest in the house was not to treat with indifference any suspicious symptoms appearing in the wall thereof; neither was he to pronounce judgment himself upon such symptoms: it belonged to the priest to investigate and to judge. The moment that aught of a questionable nature made its appearance, the priest assumed a judicial attitude with respect to the house. The house was under judgment, though not condemned. The perfect period was to be allowed to run its course ere any decision could be arrived at. The symptoms might prove to be merely superficial, in which case there would be no demand for any action whatever.

"And the priest shall *come again the seventh day,* and shall *look:* and, behold, if the plague be spread in the walls of the house, then the priest shall command that they take away the stones in which the plague is, and they shall cast them into an unclean place without the city." The whole house was not to be condemned: the removal of the leprous stones was first to be tried.

"And if the plague come again, and break out in the house, after that he hath taken away the stones, and after that he hath scraped the house, and after that it is plastered; then the priest shall come and look, and, behold, if the plague be spread in the house, it is a fretting leprosy in the house: it is unclean. And he shall break down the house, the stones of it, and the timber thereof, and all the mortar of the house; and he shall carry them forth out of the city into an unclean place." The case was hopeless, the evil irremediable, the whole building was annihilated.

"Moreover, he that goeth into the house all the while that it is shut up shall be unclean until the even. And he that lieth in the house shall wash his clothes; and he that eateth in the house shall wash his clothes." This is a solemn truth. *Contact defiles!* Let us remember this. It was a principle largely inculcated under the Levitical economy, and surely it is not less applicable now.

"And if the priest shall come in, and look upon it, and, behold, the plague hath not spread in the house, after the house was plastered; then the priest shall pronounce the house clean, because the plague is healed." The removal of the defiled stones, etc., had arrested the progress of the evil, and rendered all further judgment needless. The house was no longer to be viewed as in a judicial place; but being cleansed by the application of the blood, it was again fit for occupation.

And now as to the moral of all this. It is at once interesting, solemn, and practical. Look, for example, at the church at Corinth. It was a spiritual house, composed of spiritual stones; but, alas! the eagle eye of the apostle discerned upon its walls certain symptoms of a most suspicious nature. Was he indifferent? Surely not. He had imbibed far too much of the spirit of the Master of the house to admit, for one moment, of any such thing. But he was no more hasty than indifferent. He commanded the leprous stone to be removed, and gave the house a thorough scraping. Having acted thus faithfully, he patiently awaited the result. And what was that result? All that the heart could desire. "Nevertheless God, that comforteth those that are cast down, comforted us by the coming of Titus; and not by his coming only, but by the consolation wherewith he was comforted in you, when he told us your earnest desire, your mourning, your fervent mind toward me; so that I rejoiced the more. . . . *In all things ye have approved yourselves to be clear in this matter*" (comp. 1 Cor. 5 with 2 Cor. 7:11). This is a lovely instance. The zealous care of the apostle was amply rewarded; the plague was stayed, and the assembly delivered from the defiling influence of unjudged moral evil.

Take another solemn example. "And to the angel of the church in Pergamos write: 'These things saith He that hath the sharp sword with two edges; I know thy works, and where thou dwellest, even where Satan's seat is; and thou holdest fast My name, and hast not denied My faith, even in those days wherein Antipas was My faithful martyr, who was slain among you, where Satan dwelleth. But I have a few things against thee, because thou hast there them that hold the doctrine of Balaam, who taught Balak to cast a stumbling-block before the children of Israel, to eat things sacrificed unto idols, and to commit fornication. So hast thou also them that hold the doctrine of the Nicolaitanes, which thing I hate. Repent; or else I will come unto thee quickly, and will fight against them with the sword of My mouth" (Rev. 2:12-16). Here the divine Priest stands in a judicial attitude with respect to His house at Pergamos. He could not be indifferent to symptoms so alarming, but He patiently and graciously gives time to repent. If reproof, warning, and discipline prove unavailing, judgment must take its course.

These things are full of practical teaching as to the doctrine of the assembly. The seven churches of Asia afford various striking illustrations of the house under priestly judgment. We should ponder them deeply and prayerfully; they are of immense value. We should never sit down at ease so long as aught of a suspicious nature is making its appearance in the assembly. We may be tempted to say, "It is none of my business;" but it is the business of every one who loves the Master of the house to have a jealous, godly care for the purity of that house; and if we shrink from the due exercise of this care, it will not be for our honor or profit in the day of the Lord.

I shall not pursue this subject any further in these pages; and shall merely remark, in closing this section, that I do not doubt in the least that this whole subject of leprosy has a great dispensational bearing, not only upon the house of Israel, but also upon the professing church.

---

## *CHAPTER 15*

THIS chapter treats of a variety of ceremonial uncleannesses of a much less serious nature than leprosy. This latter would seem to be presented as the expression of the deep-seated energy of nature's evil; whereas chapter 15 details a number of things which are merely unavoidable infirmities, but which, as being in any measure the outflow of nature, were defiling, and needed the provisions of divine grace. The divine presence in the assembly demanded a high order of holiness and moral purity. Every movement of nature had to be counteracted. Even things which, so far as man was concerned, might seem to be unavoidable weaknesses, had a defiling influence, and required cleansing, because Jehovah was in the camp. Nothing offensive, nothing unsightly, nothing in any way uncomely, should be suffered within the pure, unsullied, and sacred precincts of the presence of the God of Israel. The uncircumcised nations around would have understood nothing of such holy ordinances; but Jehovah would have Israel holy, because He was Israel's God. If they were to be privileged and distinguished by having the presence of a holy God, they would need to be a holy people.

Nothing can be more calculated to elicit the soul's admiration than the jealous care of Jehovah over all the habits and practices of His people. At home and abroad, asleep and awake, by day and by night, He guarded them. He attended to their food, He attended to their clothing, He attended to their most minute and private concerns. If some trifling spot appeared upon the person, it had to be instantly and carefully looked into. In a word, nothing was overlooked which could in any wise affect the well-being or purity of those with whom Jehovah had associated Himself, and in whose midst He dwelt. He took an interest in their most trivial affairs. He carefully attended to every thing connected with them, whether publicly, socially, or privately.

This, to an uncircumcised person, would have proved an intolerable burden. For such an one to have a God of infinite holiness about his path by day and about his bed by night, would have involved an amount of restraint beyond all power of endurance; but to a true lover of holiness—a lover of God, nothing could be more delightful. Such an one rejoices in the sweet assurance that God is always near, and he delights in the holiness which is at once demanded and secured by the presence of God.

Is it thus with you? Do you love the divine presence and the holiness which that presence demands? Are you indulging in any thing incompatible with the holiness of God's presence? Are your habits of thought, feeling, and action such as comport with the purity and elevation of the sanctuary? Remember, when you read this fifteenth chapter of Leviticus, that it was written for your learning. You are to read it in the Spirit, for to you it has a spiritual application. To read it in any other way is to wrest it to your own destruction, or, to use a ceremonial phrase, "to seethe a kid in its mother's milk."

Do you ask, What am I to learn from such a section of Scripture? what is its application to me? In the first place, let me ask, do you not admit that it was written for your learning? This, I imagine, you will not question, seeing the inspired apostle so expressly declares that "*whatsoever* things were written aforetime were written for our learning" (Rom. 15:4). Many seem to forget this important statement, at least insofar as the book of Leviticus is concerned. They cannot conceive it possible that they are to learn aught from the rites and ceremonies of a by-gone age, and particularly from such rites and ceremonies as the fifteenth of Leviticus records; but when we remember that God the Holy Ghost has written this very chapter—that every paragraph, every verse, every line of it "is given by inspiration of God, and is profitable," it should lead us to inquire what it means. Surely, what God has written His child should read. No doubt there is need of spiritual power to know *how,* and spiritual wisdom to know *when,* to read such a chapter; but the same holds good with respect to any chapter. One thing is certain, if we were sufficiently spiritual, sufficiently heavenly, sufficiently abstracted from nature and elevated above earth, we should deduce naught but purely spiritual principles and ideas from this and kindred chapters. If an angel from heaven were to read such sections, how should he regard them? Only in a spiritual and heavenly light, only as the depositories of the purest and highest morality. And why should not we do the same? I believe we are not aware of what positive contempt we pour upon the sacred Volume by suffering any portion of it to be so grossly neglected as the book of Leviticus has been. If this book ought not to be read, surely it ought not to have been written. If it be not "profitable," surely it ought not to have had a place assigned it in the canon of divine inspiration; but inasmuch as it hath pleased "the only wise God" to write this book, it surely ought to please His children to read it.

No doubt, spiritual wisdom, holy discernment, and that refined moral sense which only communion with God can impart—all these things would be needed in order to form a judgment as to when such Scripture ought to be read. We should feel strongly disposed to question the sound judgment and refined taste of a man who could stand up and read the fifteenth of Leviticus in the midst of an ordinary congregation. But why? Is it because it is not "divinely inspired," and as such, "profitable"? By no means; but because the generality of persons are not sufficiently spiritual to enter into its pure and holy lessons.

What, then, are we to learn from the chapter before us? In the first place, we learn to watch, with holy jealousy, every thing that emanates from nature. Every movement of, and every emanation from nature is defiling. Fallen human nature is an impure fountain, and all its streams are polluting. It cannot send forth aught that is pure, holy, or good. This is a lesson frequently inculcated in the book of Leviticus, and it is impressively taught in this chapter.

But blessed be the grace that has made such ample provision for nature's defilement! This provision is presented under two distinct forms throughout the entire of the book of God, and throughout this section of it in particular, namely, "water and blood." Both these are founded upon the death of Christ. The blood that expiates and the water that cleanses flowed from the pierced side of a crucified Christ (comp. John 19:34 with 1 John 5:6.). "The blood of Jesus Christ His Son cleanseth us from all sin" (1 John 1:7). And the Word of God cleanseth our practical habits and ways (Ps. 119:9; Eph. 5:26). Thus we are maintained in fitness for communion and worship, though passing through a scene where all is defiling, and carrying with us a nature every movement of which leaves a soil behind.

It has been already remarked that our chapter treats of a class of ceremonial defilements less serious than leprosy. This will account for the fact that atonement is here foreshadowed, not by a bullock or a lamb, but by the lowest order of sacrifice, namely, "two turtle-doves." But on the other hand, the cleansing virtue of the Word is continually introduced in the ceremonial actions of "washing," "bathing," and "rinsing." "Wherewithal shall a young man *cleanse* his way? By taking heed thereto according to Thy *Word.*" "Husbands, love your wives, even as Christ also loved the Church, and gave Himself for it; that He might *sanctify and cleanse it with the washing of water by the Word.*" Water held a most important place in the Levitical system of purification, and as a type of the Word, nothing can be more interesting or instructive.

Thus we can gather up the most valuable points from this fifteenth chapter of Leviticus. We learn, in a very striking manner, the intense holiness of the divine presence. Not a soil, not a stain, not a speck, can be tolerated for a moment in that thrice-hallowed region. "Thus shall ye separate the children of Israel from their uncleanness, that they die not in their uncleanness, when they defile My tabernacle that is among them" (ver. 31).

Again, we learn that human nature is the everflowing fountain of uncleanness. It is hopelessly defiled; and not only defiled, but defiling. Awake or asleep, sitting, standing, or lying, nature is defiled and defiling: its very touch conveys pollution. This is a deeply humbling lesson for proud humanity; but thus it is. The book of Leviticus holds up a faithful mirror to nature: it leaves "flesh" nothing to glory in. Men may boast of their refinement, their moral sense, their dignity: let them study the third book of Moses, and there they will see what it is all really worth in God's estimation.

Finally, we learn afresh the expiatory value of the blood of Christ, and the cleansing, purifying, sanctifying virtues of the precious Word of God. When we think of the unsullied purity of the sanctuary, and then reflect upon nature's irremediable defilement, and ask the question, However can *we* enter and dwell *there?* the answer is found in "the blood and water" which flowed from the side of a crucified Christ—a Christ who gave up His life unto death for us, that we might live by Him. "There are three that bear record in earth, the Spirit and the water and the blood; and," blessed be God, "these three agree in one." The Spirit does not convey to our ears a message diverse from that which we find in the Word, and both the Word and the Spirit declare to us the preciousness and efficacy of the blood.

Can we not therefore say that the fifteenth chapter of Leviticus was "written for our learning"? Has it not its own distinct place in the divine canon? Assuredly. There would be a blank were it omitted. We learn in it what we could not learn in the same way any where else. True, all Scripture teaches us the holiness of God, the vileness of nature, the efficacy of the blood, the value of the Word; but the chapter upon which we have been pondering, presents these great truths to our notice, and presses them upon our hearts, in a manner quite peculiar to itself.

May *every section* of our Father's Volume be precious to our hearts. May *every one* of His testimonies be sweeter to us than honey and the honeycomb, and may "*every one* of His righteous judgments" have its due place in our souls.

## *CHAPTER 16*

THIS chapter unfolds some of the weightiest principles of truth which can possibly engage the renewed mind. It presents the doctrine of atonement with uncommon fullness and power. In short, we must rank the sixteenth chapter of Leviticus amongst the most precious and important sections of inspiration, if indeed it be allowable to make comparisons where all is divine.

Looking at this chapter historically, it furnishes a record of the transactions of the great day of atonement in Israel, whereby Jehovah's relationship with the assembly was established and maintained, and all the sins, failures, and infirmities of the people fully atoned for, so that the Lord God might dwell among them. The blood which was shed upon this solemn day formed the basis of Jehovah's throne in the midst of the congregation. In virtue of it, a holy God could take up His abode in the midst of the people, notwithstanding all their uncleanness. "The tenth day of the seventh month" was a unique day in Israel: there was no other day in the year like it. The sacrifices of this one day formed the ground of God's dealing in grace, mercy, patience, and forbearance.

Furthermore, we learn from this portion of inspired history, "that the way into the holiest of all was not yet made manifest." God was hidden behind a vail, and man was at a distance. "And the Lord spake unto Moses after the death of the two sons of Aaron, when they offered before the Lord, and died; and the Lord said unto Moses, 'Speak unto Aaron thy brother, that he come not at all times unto the holy place within the vail before the mercy-seat, which is upon the ark, that he die not; for I will appear in the cloud upon the mercy-seat.' "

The way was not open for man to approach at all times into the divine presence, nor was there any provision, in the entire range of the Mosaic ritual, for his abiding there continually. God was shut in from man, and man was shut out from God; nor could "the blood of bulls and goats" open a permanent meeting-place; "a sacrifice of nobler name and richer blood" was needed to accomplish this. "For the law having a shadow of good things to come, and not the very image of the things, can never with those sacrifices which they offered year by year continually make the comers thereunto perfect. For then would they not have ceased to be offered? because that the worshipers once purged should have had no more conscience of sins. But in those sacrifices there is a remembrance again made of sins every year. For it is not possible that the blood of bulls and of goats should take away sins" (Heb. 10:1-4). Neither the Levitical priesthood nor the Levitical sacrifices could yield perfection. Insufficiency was stamped on the latter, infirmity on the former, imperfection on both. An imperfect man could not be a perfect priest; nor could an imperfect sacrifice give a perfect conscience. Aaron was not competent or entitled to take his seat within the vail, nor could the sacrifices which he offered rend that vail.

Thus much as to our chapter historically: let us now look at it typically.

"Thus shall Aaron come into the holy place: with a young bullock for a *sin*-offering, and a ram for a *burnt*-offering" (ver. 3). Here we have the two grand aspects of Christ's atoning work—as that which perfectly maintains the divine glory, and perfectly meets man's deepest need. There is no mention, throughout all the services of this unique and solemn day, of a *meat*-offering or a *peace*-offering. The perfect human life of our blessed Lord is not foreshadowed here, nor is the communion of the soul with God, consequent upon His accomplished work, unfolded. In a word, the one grand subject is "atonement," and that in a double way, namely, first, as meeting all the claims of God—the claims of His nature, the claims of His character, the claims of His throne; and secondly, as perfectly meeting all man's guilt and all his necessities. We must bear these two points in mind if we would have a clear understanding of the truth presented in this chapter, or of the doctrine of the great day of atonement. "Thus shall Aaron come into the holy place," with atonement, as securing the glory of God in every possible way, whether as respects His counsels of redeeming love toward the Church, toward Israel, and toward the whole creation, or in reference to all the claims of His moral administration; and with atonement as fully meeting man's guilty and needy condition. These two aspects of the atonement will continually present themselves to our view as we ponder the precious contents of our chapter. Their importance cannot possibly be over-estimated.

"He shall put on the holy linen coat, and he shall have the linen breeches upon his flesh, and he shall be girded with a linen girdle, and with the linen mitre shall he be attired: these are holy garments; therefore shall he wash his flesh in water, and so put them on" (ver. 4). Aaron's person, washed in pure water, and robed in the white linen garments, furnishes a lovely and impressive type of Christ entering upon the work of atonement. He is seen to be *personally* and *characteristically* pure and spotless. "For their sakes I sanctify Myself, that they also might be sanctified through the truth" (John 17:19). It is peculiarly precious to be called, as it were, to gaze upon the Person of our divine Priest, in all His essential holiness. The Holy Ghost delights in every thing that unfolds Christ to the view of His people; and wherever we behold Him, we see him to be the same spotless, perfect, glorious, precious, peerless Jesus, "the fairest among ten thousand, yea, altogether lovely." He did not need to *do* or to *wear* any thing in order to be pure and spotless; He needed no pure water, no fine linen; He was, intrinsically and practically, "the holy One of God." What Aaron *did,* and what he *wore*—the washing and the robing, are but the faint shadows of what Christ *is*. The law had only a "shadow," and "not the very image of good things to come." Blessed be God, we have not merely the shadow, but the eternal and divine reality—Christ Himself.

"And he shall take of the congregation of

the children of Israel two kids of the goats for a sin-offering, and one ram for a burnt-offering. And Aaron shall offer his bullock of the sin-offering, which is for himself, and make atonement for himself and for his house" (ver. 5-6). Aaron and his house represent the Church, not indeed as the "one body," but as a priestly house. It is not the Church as we find it developed in Ephesians and Colossians, but rather as we find it in the first Epistle of Peter, in the following well-known passage: "Ye also, as lively stones, are built up a *spiritual house,* a holy priesthood, to offer up spiritual sacrifices, acceptable to God by Jesus Christ" (chap. 2:5). So also in Hebrews—"But Christ as a Son over His own house; *whose house are we,* if we hold fast the confidence and the rejoicing of the hope firm unto the end" (chap. 3:6). We must ever remember that there is no revelation of the mystery of the Church in the Old Testament. Types and shadows there are, but no revelation. That wondrous mystery of Jew and Gentile forming "one body," "one new man," and united to a glorified Christ in heaven, could not, as is obvious, be revealed until Christ had taken His place above. Of this mystery Paul was pre-eminently made a steward and a minister, as he tells us in Ephesians 3:1-12, a passage which I would commend to the prayerful attention of the Christian reader.

"And he shall take the two goats, and present them before the Lord at the door of the tabernacle of the congregation. And Aaron shall cast lots upon the two goats; one lot for the Lord, and the other lot for the scape-goat. And Aaron shall bring the goat upon which the Lord's lot fell, and offer him for a sin-offering. But the goat on which the lot fell to be the scape-goat, shall be presented alive before the Lord, to make an atonement with him, and to let him go for a scape-goat into the wilderness" (ver. 7-10). In these two goats, we have the two aspects of atonement already referred to; "the Lord's lot" fell upon one, and the people's lot fell upon the other. In the case of the former, it was not a question of the persons or the sins which were to be forgiven, nor of God's counsels of grace toward His elect. These things, I need hardly say, are of infinite moment; but they are not involved in the case of "the goat on which the Lord's lot fell." This latter typifies the death of Christ as that wherein God has been perfectly glorified with respect to sin in general. This great truth is fully set forth in the remarkable expression, "the Lord's lot." God has a peculiar portion in the death of Christ—a portion quite distinct—a portion which would hold eternally good even though no sinner were ever to be saved. In order to see the force of this, it is needful to bear in mind how God has been dishonored in this world. His truth has been despised; His authority has been condemned; His majesty has been slighted; His law has been broken; His claims have been disregarded; His name has been blasphemed; His character has been traduced.

Now, the death of Christ has made provision for all this. It has perfectly glorified God in the very place where all these things have been done; it has perfectly vindicated the majesty, the truth, the holiness, the character of God; it has divinely met all the claims of His throne; it has atoned for *sin*; it has furnished a divine remedy for all the mischief which sin introduced into the universe; it affords a ground on which the blessed God can act in grace, mercy, and forbearance toward all; it furnishes a warrant for the eternal expulsion and perdition of the prince of this world; it forms the imperishable foundation of God's moral government. In virtue of the cross, God can act according to His own sovereignty; He can display the matchless glories of His character and the adorable attributes of His nature. He might, in the exercise of inflexible justice, have consigned the human family to the lake of fire, together with the devil and his angels; but in that case, where would be His love, His grace, His mercy, His kindness, His long-suffering, His compassion, His patience, His perfect goodness?

Then on the other hand, had these precious attributes been exercised in the absence of atonement, where were the justice, the truth, the majesty, the holiness, the righteousness, the governmental claims, yea, the entire moral glory of God? How could "mercy and truth meet together"? or "righteousness and peace kiss each other"? How could "truth spring out of the earth"? or "righteousness look down from heaven"? Impossible. Naught save the atonement of our Lord Jesus Christ could have fully glorified God; but that has glorified Him. It has reflected the full glory of the divine character as it never could have been reflected amid the brightest splendors of an unfallen creation. By means of that atonement, in prospect and retrospect, God has been exercising forbearance toward this world for well-nigh six thousand years. In virtue of that atonement, the most wicked, daring, and blasphemous of the sons of men "live, move, and have their being;" eat, drink, and sleep. The very morsel which yonder open blaspheming infidel puts into his mouth, he owes to the atonement, which he knows not, but impiously ridicules; the sunbeams and showers which fertilize the fields of the atheist, reach him in virtue of the atonement of Christ; yea, the very breath which the infidel and the atheist spend in blaspheming God's revelation, or denying His existence, they owe to the atonement of Christ. Were it not for that precious atonement, instead of blaspheming upon earth, they would be weltering in hell.

I speak not here of the forgiveness or salvation of persons. This is quite another thing, and stands connected, as every true Christian knows, with the confession of the name of Jesus and the hearty belief that God raised Him from the dead (Rom. 10). This is plain enough, and fully understood; but it is in no wise involved in that aspect of the atonement which we are at present contemplating, and which is so strikingly foreshadowed by "the goat on which the Lord's lot fell." God's pardoning and accepting a sinner is one thing; His bearing with that man, and showering temporal blessings upon him, is quite another. Both are in virtue of the cross, but in a totally different aspect and application thereof.

Nor is this distinction by any means unimportant. Quite the opposite. Indeed, so important is it that where it is overlooked, there must be confusion as to the full doctrine of atonement. Nor is this all. A clear understanding of God's ways in government, whether in the past, the present, or the future, will be found involved in this profoundly interesting point. And finally, in it will be found the key wherewith to expound a number of texts in which many Christians find considerable difficulty. I shall just adduce two or three of these passages as examples.

"Behold the Lamb of God, which taketh away the *sin* of the world" (John 1:29). With this we may connect a kindred passage in John's first Epistle, in which the Lord Jesus Christ is spoken of as "the propitiation for the whole world"* (chap. 2:2). In both these passages the Lord Jesus is referred to as the One who has perfectly glorified God with respect to *"sin"* and *"the world,"* in their broadest acceptation. He is here seen as the great Antitype of "the goat on which the Lord's lot fell." This gives us a most precious view of the atonement of Christ, and one which is too much overlooked, or not clearly apprehended. Whenever the question of *persons* and the forgiveness of *sins* is raised in connection with these and kindred passages of Scripture, the mind is sure to get involved in insuperable difficulties.

So, also, with respect to all those passages in which God's grace to the world at large is presented. They are founded upon that special aspect of the atonement with which we are more immediately occupied. "Go ye into *all the world* and preach the gospel *to every creature*" (Mark 16). "God so loved *the world,* that He gave His only begotten

*The reader will observe, in the above passage, that the words "the sins of" are introduced by the translators, and are not inspired. The divine accuracy of the passage is completely lost by retaining those uninspired words. The doctrine laid down is simply this: In the first clause of the verse, Christ is set forth as the propitiation for His people's actual *sins;* but in the last clause, it is not a question of *sins* or of *persons* at all, but of *sin* and the *world* in general. In fact, the whole verse presents Christ as the Antitype of the two goats, as the One who has borne His people's sins; and also as the One who has perfectly glorified God with respect to sin in general, and made provision for dealing in grace with the world at large, and for the final deliverance and blessing of the whole creation.

Son, that whosoever believeth in Him might not perish, but have everlasting life. For God sent not His Son into the world to condemn *the world,* but that the world through Him might be saved" (John 3:16-17). "I exhort, therefore, that first of all, supplications, prayers, intercessions, and giving of thanks, be made for *all men;* for kings, and for all that are in authority; that we may lead a quiet and peaceable life in all godliness and honesty. For this is good and acceptable in the sight of God our Saviour; who will have *all men* to be saved, and to come unto the knowledge of the truth. For there is one God, and one Mediator between God and men, the Man Christ Jesus; who gave Himself *a ransom for all,* to be testified in due time" (1 Tim. 2:1-6). "For *the grace of God* that bringeth salvation hath appeared to *all men*" (Titus 2:11). "But we see Jesus, who was made a little lower than the angels, for the suffering of death, crowned with glory and honor; that He by *the grace of God* should taste death *for every man*" (Heb. 2:9). "The Lord is not slack concerning His promise, as some men count slackness; but is long-suffering to usward, not willing that *any* should perish, but that *all* should come to repentance" (2 Peter 3:9).

There is no need whatsoever for seeking to avoid the plain sense of the above and similar passages. They bear a clear and unequivocal testimony to divine grace toward all, without the slightest reference to man's responsibility on the one hand, or to God's eternal counsels on the other. These things are just as clearly, just as fully, just as unequivocally, taught in the Word. Man is responsible and God is sovereign. All who bow to Scripture admit these things. But, at the same time, it is of the very last importance to recognize the wide aspect of the grace of God and of the cross of Christ. It glorifies God, and leaves man *wholly* without excuse. Men argue about God's decrees and man's incompetency to believe without divine influence. Their arguments prove that they do not want God; for did they only want Him, He is near enough to be found of them. The grace of God and the atonement of Christ are as wide as they could desire. *"Any," "every," "whosoever,"* and *"all"* are God's own words; and I should like to know who is shut out. If God sends a message of salvation to a man, He surely intends it for him; and what can be more wicked and impious than to reject God's grace, and make Him a liar, and then give His secret decrees as a reason for so doing? It would be, in a certain sense, honest for a man to say at once, The fact is, I do not believe God's Word, and I do not want His grace or His salvation. One could understand this; but for men to cover their hatred of God and His truth with the drapery of a false, because one-sided, theology, is the very highest character of wickedness. It is such as to make us feel, of a truth, that the devil is never more diabolical than when he appears with the Bible in his hand.

If it be true that men are prevented by God's secret decrees and counsels from receiving the gospel, which He has commanded to be preached to them, then on what principle of righteousness will they be "punished with everlasting destruction" for not obeying that gospel? (2 Thess. 1:6-10) Is there a single soul throughout all the gloomy regions of the lost who blames God's counsels for his being there? Not one. Oh, no; God has made such ample provision in the atonement of Christ, not only for the salvation of those that believe, but also for the aspect of His grace toward those that reject the gospel, that there is no excuse. It is not because a man *cannot,* but because he *will not* believe that he "shall be punished with everlasting destruction." Never was there a more fatal mistake than for a man to ensconce himself behind God's decrees, while deliberately and intelligently refusing God's grace; and this is all the more dangerous because supported by the dogmas of a one-sided theology. God's grace is free to all; and if we ask, How is this? the answer is, "Jehovah's lot" fell upon the true Victim, in order that He might be perfectly glorified as to sin, in its widest aspect, and be free to act in grace toward all, and "preach the gospel to every creature." This grace and this preaching must have a solid basis, and that basis is found in the atonement; and though man should reject, God is glorified in the exercise of grace and in the offer of salvation, because of the basis on which both the one and the other repose. He *is* glorified, and He *shall be* glorified throughout eternity's countless ages.—"Now is My soul troubled: and what shall I say? Father, save Me from this hour: but for this cause came I unto this hour. Father, glorify Thy name. Then came there a voice from heaven, saying, 'I have both glorified it, and will glorify it again.' . . . Now is the judgment of this world: now shall the prince of this world be cast out. And I, if I be lifted up from the earth, will draw all unto Me" (John 12:27-32).

Thus far we have been occupied only with one special point, namely, "the goat on which the Lord's lot fell"; and a cursory reader might suppose that the next thing in order would be the scape-goat, which gives us the other great aspect of the death of Christ, or its application to the sins of the people. But no: ere we come to that, we have the fullest confirmation of that precious line of truth which has been before us, in the fact that the blood of the slain goat, together with the blood of the bullock, was sprinkled upon and before Jehovah's throne, in order to show that all the claims of that throne were answered in the blood of atonement, and full provision made for all the demands of God's moral administration.

"And Aaron shall bring the bullock of the sin-offering which is for himself, and shall make an atonement for himself, and for his house, and shall kill the bullock of the sin-offering which is for himself. And he shall take a censer full of burning coals of fire from off the altar before the Lord, and his hands full of sweet incense beaten small, and bring it within the vail. And he shall put the incense upon the fire before the Lord, that the cloud of the incense may cover the mercy-seat that is upon the testimony, that he die not." Here we have a most vivid and striking presentation indeed. The blood of atonement is carried in within the vail, into the holiest of all, and there sprinkled upon the throne of the God of Israel. The cloud of the divine presence was there; and in order that Aaron might appear in the immediate presence of the glory and not die, "the cloud of incense" ascends and "covers the mercy-seat," on which the blood of atonement was to be sprinkled "seven times." The *"sweet* incense beaten *small"* expresses the fragrance of Christ's Person—the sweet odor of His most precious sacrifice.

"And he shall take of the blood of the bullock, and sprinkle it with his finger upon the mercy-seat eastward; and before the mercy-seat shall he sprinkle of the blood with his finger seven times. Then shall he kill the goat of the sin-offering that is for the people, and bring his blood within the vail, and do with that blood as he did with the blood of the bullock, and sprinkle it upon the mercy-seat, and before the mercy-seat" (ver. 14-15). "Seven" is the perfect number; and in the sprinkling of the blood seven times before the mercy-seat, we learn that whatever be the application of the atonement of Christ, whether as to things, to places, or to persons, it is perfectly estimated in the divine presence. The blood which secures the salvation of the Church—the "house" of the true Aaron; the blood which secures the salvation of the "congregation" of Israel; the blood which secures the final restoration and blessedness of the whole creation—that blood has been presented before God, sprinkled and accepted according to all the perfectness, fragrance, and preciousness of Christ. In the power of that blood God can accomplish all His eternal counsels of grace. He can save the Church, and raise it into the very loftiest heights of glory and dignity, despite of all the power of sin and Satan; He can restore Israel's scattered tribes; He can unite Judah and Ephraim; He can accomplish all the promises made to Abraham, Isaac, and Jacob; He can save and bless untold millions of the Gentiles; He can restore and bless the wide creation; He can allow the beams of His glory to lighten up the universe forever; He can display, in the view of angels, men, and devils, His own eternal glory—the glory of His character, the glory of His nature, the glory of His works, the glory of His government; all this He can do, and will do;

but the one solitary pedestal upon which the stupendous fabric of glory shall rest forever, is the blood of the cross—that precious blood which has spoken peace—divine and everlasting peace—to your heart and conscience, in the presence of Infinite Holiness. The blood which is sprinkled upon the believer's conscience has been sprinkled "seven times" before the throne of God. The nearer we get to God, the more importance and value we find attached to the blood of Jesus. If we look at the brazen altar, we find the blood there; if we look at the brazen laver, we find the blood there; if we look at the golden altar, we find the blood there; if we look at the vail of the tabernacle, we find the blood there: but in no place do we find so much about the blood as within the vail, before Jehovah's throne, in the immediate presence of the divine glory.

In heaven His blood forever speaks,
In God the Father's ears.

"And he shall make an atonement for the holy place, because of the uncleanness of the children of Israel, and because of their transgressions in all their sins: and so shall he do for the tabernacle of the congregation, that remaineth among them in the midst of their uncleanness." The same truth meets us all along. The claims of the sanctuary must be provided for. Jehovah's courts, as well as His throne, must bear witness to the value of the blood. The tabernacle, in the midst of Israel's uncleanness, must be fenced round about by the divine provisions of atonement. Jehovah provided, in all things, for His own glory. The priests and their priestly service, the place of worship and all therein, must stand in the power of the blood. The Holy One could not have remained for a moment in the midst of the congregation were it not for the power of the blood. It was that which left Him free to dwell and act and rule in the midst of an erring people.

"And there shall be no man in the tabernacle of the congregation when he goeth in to make an atonement in the holy place, until he come out, and have made an atonement for himself, and for his household, and for all the congregation of Israel" (ver. 17). Aaron needed to offer up sacrifice for his own sins, as well as for the sins of the people. He could only enter into the sanctuary in the power of the blood. We have, in verse 17, a type of the atonement of Christ in its application both to the Church and to the congregation of Israel. The Church now enters into the holiest by the blood of Jesus (Heb. 10). As to Israel, the vail is still on their hearts (2 Cor. 3). They are still at a distance, although full provision has been made in the cross for their forgiveness and restoration when they shall turn to the Lord. This entire period is, properly speaking, the day of atonement. The true Aaron is gone in, with His own blood, into heaven itself, now to appear in the presence of God for us. By and by He will come forth to lead the congregation of Israel into the full results of His accomplished work. Meanwhile, His house—that is to say, all true believers—is associated with Him, having boldness to enter into the holiest, being brought nigh by the blood of Jesus.

"And he shall go out unto the altar that is before the Lord, and make an atonement for it; and shall take of the blood of the bullock, and of the blood of the goat, and put it upon the horns of the altar round about. And he shall sprinkle of the blood upon it with his finger seven times, and cleanse it, and hallow it from the uncleanness of the children of Israel" (ver. 18-19). Thus the atoning blood was sprinkled every where, from the throne of God within the vail, to the altar which stood in the court of the tabernacle of the congregation. "It was therefore necessary that the patterns of things in the heavens should be purified with these, but the heavenly things themselves with better sacrifices than these. For Christ is not entered into the holy places made with hands, which are the figures of the true; but into heaven itself, now to appear in the presence of God for us: nor yet that He should offer Himself often, as the high-priest entereth into the holy place every year with blood of others; for then must He often have suffered since the foundation of the world; but now *once* in the end of the world [at the end of every thing earthly, every thing human] hath He appeared to put away sin by the sacrifice of Himself. And as it is appointed unto men once to die, but after this the judgment; so Christ was once offered to bear the sins of many; and unto them that look for Him shall He appear the second time without sin unto salvation" (Heb. 9:23-28).

There is but one way into the holiest of all, and that is a blood-sprinkled way. It is vain to strive to enter by any other. Men may attempt to work themselves in, to pray themselves in, to buy themselves in, to get in by a pathway or ordinances, or it may be, of half ordinances, half Christ; but it is of no use. God speaks of *one* way, and but one, and that way has been thrown open through the rent vail of the Saviour's flesh. Along that way have the millions of the saved passed, from age to age; patriarchs, prophets, apostles, martyrs, saints in every age, from Abel downwards, have trod that blessed way, and found thereby sure and undisputed access. The *one* sacrifice of the cross is divinely sufficient for all. God asks no more, and He can take no less. To add aught thereto is to cast dishonor upon that with which God has declared Himself well pleased, yea, in which He is infinitely glorified: to diminish aught therefrom is to deny man's guilt and ruin, and offer an indignity to the justice and majesty of the eternal Trinity.

"And when he hath made an end of reconciling the holy place, and the tabernacle of the congregation, and the altar, he shall bring the live goat. And Aaron shall lay both his hands upon the head of the live goat, and confess over him *all* the iniquities of the children of Israel, and *all* their transgressions in *all* their sins, putting them upon the head of the goat, and shall send him away by the hand of a fit man into the wilderness. And the goat shall bear upon him *all* their iniquities unto a land not inhabited; and he shall let go the goat in the wilderness."

Here, then, we have the other grand idea attached to the death of Christ, namely, the full and final forgiveness of the people. If the death of Christ forms the foundation of the glory of God, it also forms the foundation of the perfect forgiveness of sins to all who put their trust in it. This latter, blessed be God, is but a secondary—an inferior application of the atonement, though our foolish hearts would fain regard it as the very highest possible view of the cross to see in it that which puts away all our sins. This is a mistake. God's glory is the first thing, our salvation is the second. To maintain God's glory was the chief—the darling object of the heart of Christ. This object He pursued from first to last, with an undeviating purpose and unflinching fidelity. "Therefore doth My Father love Me, because I lay down My life, that I might take it again" (John 10:17). "Now is the Son of Man glorified, and God is glorified in Him. If God be glorified in Him, God shall also glorify Him in Himself, and shall straightway glorify Him" (John 13:31-32). "Listen, O isles, unto Me; and hearken, ye people from far: the Lord hath called Me from the womb; from the bowels of My mother hath He made mention of My name. And He hath made My mouth like a sharp sword; in the shadow of His hand hath He hid Me, and made Me a polished shaft: in His quiver hath He hid Me; and said unto Me, 'Thou art My servant, O Israel, in whom *I will be glorified*" (Isaiah 49:1-3).

Thus the glory of God was the paramount object of the Lord Jesus Christ, in life and in death. He lived and died to glorify His Father's name. Does the Church lose aught by this? Nay. Does Israel? Nay. Do the Gentiles? Nay. In no way could their salvation and blessedness be so perfectly provided for as by being made subsidiary to the glory of God. Hearken to the divine response to Christ the true Israel, in the sublime passage just quoted. "It is a light thing that Thou shouldest be My Servant to raise up the tribes of Jacob, and to restore the preserved of Israel: I will also give Thee for a light to the Gentiles, that Thou mayest be My salvation to the ends of the earth."

And is it not a blessed thing to know that God is glorified in the putting away of our sins? We may ask, Where are our sins? Put away. By what? By that act of Christ upon the cross, in which God has been eternally glorified. Thus it is. The two goats, on the day of atonement, give the double aspect of the one act. In the one, we see God's glory maintained; in the other, sins put away. The one is as perfect as the other. We are as perfectly forgiven as God is perfectly glorified, by the death of Christ. Was there one single point in which God was not glorified in the cross? Not one. Neither is there one single point in which we are not perfectly forgiven. I say "we;" for albeit the congregation of Israel is the primary object contemplated in the beautiful and impressive ordinance of the scape-goat, yet does it hold good, in the fullest way, with respect to every soul that believes on the Lord Jesus Christ, that he is as perfectly forgiven as God is perfectly glorified, by the atonement of the cross. How many of the sins of Israel did the scape-goat bear away? *"All."* Precious word! Not one left behind. And whither did he bear them? "Into a land not inhabited"—a land where they could never be found, because there was no one there to look for them. Could any type be more perfect? could we possibly have a more graphic picture of Christ's accomplished sacrifice, in its primary and secondary aspects? Impossible. We can hang with intense admiration over such a picture, and as we gaze, exclaim, Of a truth, the pencil of the Master is here!

Do *you* know that *all* your sins are forgiven, according to the perfection of Christ's sacrifice? If you simply *believe* on His name, they are so,—they are all gone, and gone forever. Say not, as so many anxious souls do, "I fear I do not *realize.*" There is no such word as "realize" in the entire gospel. We are not saved by realization, but by Christ; and the way to get Christ in all His fullness and preciousness is to believe—*"only believe!"* And what will be the result? "The worshipers once purged should have no more conscience of sins." Observe this,—"No more conscience of sins." This must be the result, inasmuch as Christ's sacrifice is perfect—so perfect, that God is glorified therein. Now, it must be obvious to you that Christ's work does not need your realization to be added to it to make it perfect. This could not be. We might as well say that the work of creation was not complete until Adam realized it in the garden of Eden. True, he did realize; but what did he realize? A perfect work. Thus let it be with your precious soul this moment, if it has never been so before. May you now and evermore repose, in artless simplicity, upon the One who has, by one offering, perfected forever them that are sanctified. And how are they sanctified? Is it by realization? By no means. How then? By the perfect work of Christ.

Having sought (alas! most feebly) to unfold the doctrine of this marvelous chapter, so far as God has given me light upon it, there is just one point further to which I shall merely call my reader's attention ere I close this section. It is contained in the following quotation: "And this shall be a statute forever unto you, that in the seventh month, on the tenth day of the month, ye shall afflict your souls, and do no work at all, whether it be one of your own country or a stranger that sojourneth among you. For on that day shall the priest make an atonement for you, to cleanse you, that ye may be clean from *all* your sins *before the Lord.* It shall be *a Sabbath of rest,* and ye shall *afflict your souls,* by a statute forever" (ver. 29-31).

This shall have its full accomplishment in the saved remnant of Israel by and by, as foretold by the prophet Zechariah—"And I will pour upon the house of David, and upon the inhabitants of Jerusalem, the spirit of grace and of supplications; and they shall look upon Me whom they have pierced, and they shall mourn for Him, as one mourneth for his only son, and shall be in bitterness for Him, as one that is in bitterness for his first-born. *In that day* shall there be *a great mourning* in Jerusalem, as the mourning of Hadadrimmon in the valley of Megiddon. . . . *In that day* shall there be *a fountain opened* to the house of David, and to the inhabitants of Jerusalem, for sin and for uncleanness. . . . And it shall come to pass *in that day* that the light shall not be clear [in one place] and dark [in another] ; but it shall be one day, [the true and long-expected Sabbath,] which shall be known to the Lord, not day nor night; but it shall come to pass that at evening time it shall be light.

And it shall be *in that day* that living waters shall go out from Jerusalem; half of them toward the former sea, and half of them toward the hinder sea: in summer and in winter shall it be. And *The Lord shall be King over all the earth: in that day* shall there be one Lord, and His name one. . . . *In that day* shall there be upon the bells of the horses, HOLINESS UNTO THE LORD. . . . And *in that day* there shall be no more the Canaanite in the house of the Lord of hosts" (Zech. 12–14).

What a day that will be! No marvel that it should be so frequently and so emphatically introduced in the above glowing passage. It will be a bright and blessed "Sabbath of rest" when the mourning remnant shall gather, in the spirit of true penitence, around the open fountain, and enter into the full and final results of the great day of atonement. They shall "afflict their souls," no doubt; for how could they do otherwise, while fixing their repentant gaze "upon Him whom they have pierced"? But, oh, what a Sabbath they will have! Jerusalem will have a brimming cup of salvation, after her long and dreary night of sorrow. Her former desolations shall be forgotten, and her children, restored to their long-lost dwellings, shall take down their harps from the willows, and sing once more the sweet songs of Zion, beneath the peaceful shade of the vine and fig-tree.

Blessed be God, the time is at hand. Every setting sun brings us nearer to that blissful Sabbath. The word is, "Surely, I come quickly;" and all around seems to tell us that "the days are at hand, and the effect of every vision." May we be "sober, and watch unto prayer." May we keep ourselves unspotted from the world; and thus, in the spirit of our minds, the affections of our hearts, and the experience of our souls, be ready to meet the heavenly Bridegroom. Our place for the present is outside the camp. Thank God that it is so! It would be an unspeakable loss to be inside. The same cross which has brought us inside the vail has cast us outside the camp. Christ was cast out thither, and we are with Him there; but He has been received up into heaven, and we are with Him there. Is it not a mercy to be outside of all that which has rejected our blessed Lord and Master? Truly so; and the more we know of Jesus, and the more we know of this present evil world, the more thankful we shall be to find our place outside of it all *with Him.*

---

## *CHAPTER 17*

IN this chapter are two special points, namely, first, that life belongs to Jehovah; and secondly, that the power of atonement is in the blood. The Lord attached peculiar importance to both these things. He would have them impressed upon every member of the congregation.

"And the Lord spake unto Moses, saying, 'Speak unto Aaron, and unto his sons, and unto all the children of Israel, and say unto them, This is the thing which the Lord hath commanded, saying, What man soever there be of the house of Israel, that killeth an ox, or lamb, or goat, in the camp, or that killeth it out of the camp, and bringeth it not unto the door of the tabernacle of the congregation, to offer an offering unto the Lord, before the tabernacle of the Lord; blood shall be imputed unto that man; he hath shed blood; and that man shall be cut off from among his people." This was a most solemn matter; and we may ask what was involved in offering a sacrifice otherwise than in the manner here prescribed. It was nothing less than robbing Jehovah of His rights, and presenting to Satan that which was due to God. A man might say, Can I not offer a sacrifice in one place as well as another? The answer is, Life belongs to God, and His claim thereto must be recognized in the place which He has appointed—before the tabernacle of the Lord. That was the only meeting-place between God and man. To offer elsewhere proved that the heart did not want God.

The moral of this is plain. There is one place where God has appointed to meet the sinner, and that is the cross—the antitype of the brazen altar. There and there alone has God's claims upon the life been duly recognized. To reject this meeting-place is to bring down judgment upon one's self—it is to trample under foot the just claims of God, and to arrogate to one's self a right to life which all have forfeited. It is important to see this.

"And the priest shall sprinkle the blood upon the altar of the Lord, at the door of the tabernacle of the congregation, and burn the fat for a sweet savor unto the Lord." The blood and the fat belonged to God. The blessed Jesus fully recognized this. He surrendered His life to God, and all His hidden energies were devoted to Him likewise. He voluntarily walked to the altar and there gave up His precious life; and the fragrant odor of His intrinsic excellency ascended to the throne of God. Blessed Jesus! it is sweet, at every step of our way, to be reminded of Thee.

The second point above referred to is clearly stated in verse 11. "For the life of the flesh is in the blood; and I have given it to you upon the altar, to make an atonement for your souls, for *it is the blood that maketh an atonement for the soul.*" The connection between the two points is deeply interesting. When man duly takes his place as one possessing no title whatsoever to life—when he fully recognizes God's claims upon him, then the divine record is, "I have given you the life to make an atonement for your soul." Yes; atonement is God's gift to man; and be it carefully noted that this atonement is in the blood, and *only* in the blood. "It is *the blood* that maketh an atonement for the soul." It is not the blood *and* something else. The word is most explicit. It attributes atonement exclusively to *the blood.* "Without shedding of *blood* is no remission" (Heb. 9:22). It was the *death* of Christ that rent the vail. It is "by *the blood* of Jesus" we have "boldness to enter into the holiest." "We have redemption through His *blood*, the forgiveness of sins" (Eph. 1:7; Col. 1:14). "Having made peace by *the blood* of His cross." "Ye who were afar off are made nigh by *the blood* of His cross." "*The blood* of Jesus Christ His Son cleanseth us from all sin" (1 John 1:7). "They washed their robes and made them white in *the blood* of the Lamb" (Rev. 7). "They overcame him by *the blood* of the Lamb" (Rev. 12).

I would desire to call attention to the precious and vital doctrine of the blood. I am anxious that we should see its true place. The blood of Christ is the foundation of every thing. It is the ground of God's righteousness in justifying an ungodly sinner that believes on the name of the Son of God; and it is the ground of the sinner's confidence in drawing nigh to a holy God, who is of purer eyes than to behold evil. God would be just in the condemnation of the sinner; but through the death of Christ, He can be just and the justifier of him that believeth—a just God and a Saviour. The righteousness of God is His consistency with Himself—His acting in harmony with His revealed character. Hence, were it not for the cross, His consistency with Himself would, of necessity, demand the death and judgment of the sinner; but in the cross, that death and judgment were borne by the sinner's Surety, so that the same divine consistency is perfectly maintained, while a holy God justifies an ungodly sinner through faith. *It is all through the blood of Jesus*—nothing less, nothing more, nothing different. "It is the blood that maketh an atonement for the soul." This is conclusive. This is God's simple plan of justification. Man's plan is much more cumbrous, much more roundabout. And not only is it cumbrous and roundabout, but it attributes righteousness to something quite different from what I find in the Word. If I look from the third chapter of Genesis down to the close of Revelation, I find the blood of Christ put forward as the alone ground of righteousness. We get pardon, peace, life, righteousness—all by the blood, and nothing but the blood. The entire book of Leviticus, and particularly the chapter upon which we have just been meditating, is a commentary upon the doctrine of the blood. It seems strange to have to insist upon a fact so obvious to every dispassionate, teachable student of holy Scripture; yet so it is. Our minds are prone to slip away from the plain testimony of the Word. We are ready to adopt opinions without ever calmly investigating them in the light of the divine testimonies. In this way we get into confusion, darkness, and error.

May we learn to give the blood of Christ its due place. It is so precious in God's sight that He will not suffer aught else to be added to or mingled with it. "The life of the flesh is in the blood, and I have given it to you upon the altar, to make an atonement for your souls: for *it is the blood that maketh an atonement for the soul.*"

---

## *CHAPTERS 18–20*

THIS section sets before us, in a very remarkable manner, the personal sanctity and moral propriety which Jehovah looked for on the part of those whom He had graciously introduced into relationship with Himself; and, at the same time, it presents a most humiliating picture of the enormities of which human nature is capable.

"And the Lord spake unto Moses, saying, 'Speak unto the children of Israel, and say unto them, *I am the Lord your God.*' " Here we have the foundation of the entire superstructure of moral conduct which these chapters present. Israel's actings were to take their character from the fact that Jehovah was *their* God. They were called to comport themselves in a manner worthy of so high and holy a position. It was God's prerogative to set forth the special character and line of conduct becoming a people with whom He was pleased to associate His name. Hence the frequency of the expressions, "I am the Lord," "I am the Lord your God," "I the Lord your God am holy." Jehovah was their God, and He was holy; hence, therefore, they were called to be holy likewise. His name was involved in their character and acting.

This is the true principle of holiness for the people of God in all ages. They are to be governed and characterized by the revelation which He has made of Himself. Their conduct is to be founded upon what He is, not upon what they are in themselves. This entirely sets aside the principle expressed in the words, "Stand by thyself, I am holier than thou;" a principle so justly repudiated by every sensitive mind. It is not a comparison of one man with another, but a simple statement of the line of conduct which God looks for in those who belong to Him. "After the doings of the land of Egypt, wherein ye dwelt, shall ye not do; and after the doings of the land of Canaan, whither I bring you, shall ye not do; neither shall ye walk in their ordinances." The Egyptians and the Canaanites were all wrong. How was Israel to know this? Who told them? How came they to be right and all besides wrong? These are interesting inquiries; and the answer is as simple as the questions are interesting. Jehovah's Word was the standard by which all questions of right and wrong were to be definitely settled in the judgment of every member of the Israel of God. It was not, by any means, the judgment of an Israelite in opposition to the judgment of an Egyptian or of a Canaanite; but it was the judgment of God above *all.* Egypt might have her practices and her opinions, and so might Canaan; but Israel were to have the opinions and practices laid down in the Word of God. "Ye shall do My judgments, and keep Mine ordinances, to walk therein: I am the Lord your God. Ye shall therefore keep My statutes and My judgments; which, if a man do, he shall live in them: I am the Lord."

It will be well to get a clear, deep, full, practical sense of this truth. The Word of God must settle every question and govern every conscience: there must be no appeal from its solemn and weighty decision. When God speaks, every heart must bow. Men may form and hold their opinions; they may adopt and defend their practices; but one of the finest traits in the character of "the Israel of God" is, profound reverence for, and implicit subjection to, "every word that proceedeth out of the mouth of the Lord." The exhibition of this valuable feature may perhaps lay them open to the charge of dogmatism, superciliousness, and self-sufficiency, on the part of those who have never duly weighed the matter; but, in truth, nothing can be more unlike dogmatism than simple subjection to the plain truth of God; nothing more unlike superciliousness than reverence for the statements of inspiration; nothing more unlike self-sufficiency than subjection to the divine authority of holy Scripture.

True, there will ever be the need of carefulness as to the tone and manner in which we set forth the authority for our convictions and our conduct. It must be made manifest, so far as it may be, that we are wholly governed, not by our own opinions, but by the Word of God. There is great danger of attaching an importance to an opinion merely because *we* have adopted it. This must be carefully guarded against. *Self* may creep in and display its deformity in the defense of our opinions as much as in any thing else; but we must disallow it in every shape and form, and be governed in all things by "Thus saith the Lord."

But then we are not to expect that every one will be ready to admit the full force of the divine statutes and judgments. It is as persons walk in the integrity and energy of the divine nature that the Word of God will be owned, appreciated, and reverenced. An Egyptian or a Canaanite would have been wholly unable to enter into the meaning or estimate the value of these statutes and judgments, which were to govern the conduct of the circumcised people of God; but that did not in any wise affect the question of Israel's obedience. They were brought into a certain relationship with Jehovah, and that relationship had its distinctive privileges and responsibilities. "I am the Lord *your* God." This was to be the ground of their conduct. They were to act in a way worthy of the One who had become *their* God, and made them *His* people. It was not that they were a whit better than other people. By no means. The Egyptians or Canaanites might have considered that the Israelites were setting themselves up as something superior in refusing to adopt the habits of either nation. But no; the foundation of their peculiar line of conduct and tone of morality was laid in these words; *"I am the Lord your God."*

In this great and practically important fact, Jehovah set before His people a ground of conduct which was immovable, and a standard of morality which was as elevated and as enduring as the eternal throne itself. The moment He entered into a relationship with a people, their ethics were to assume a character and tone worthy of Him. It was no longer a question as to what they were, either in themselves or in comparison with others; but of what God was in comparison with all. This makes a material difference. To make *self* the ground of action or the standard of ethics is not only presumptuous folly, but it is sure to set one upon a descending scale of action. If self be my object, I must, of necessity, sink lower and lower every day; but if, on the other hand, I set the Lord before me, I shall rise higher and higher as, by the power of the Holy Ghost, I grow in conformity to that perfect model which is unfolded to the gaze of faith in the sacred pages of inspiration. I shall undoubtedly have to prostrate myself in the dust, under a sense of how infinitely short I come of the mark set before me; but then I can never consent to the setting up of a lower standard, nor can I ever be satisfied until I am conformed in all things to Him who was my substitute on the cross, and is my model in the glory.

Having said thus much on the main principle of the section before us—a principle of unspeakable importance to Christians, in a practical point of view, I feel it needless to enter into any thing like a detailed exposition of the statutes which speak for themselves in most obvious terms. I would merely remark that those statutes range themselves under two distinct heads, namely, first, those which set forth the shameful enormities which the human heart is capable of devising; and secondly, those which exhibit the exquisite tenderness and considerate care of the God of Israel.

As to the first, it is manifest that the Spirit of God could never enact laws for the purpose of preventing evils that have no existence. He does not construct a dam where there is no flood to be resisted: He does not deal with abstract ideas, but with positive realities. Man is, in very deed, capable of perpetrating each and every one of the shameful crimes referred to in this most faithful section of the book of Leviticus. If he were not, why should he be told not to do so. Such a code would be wholly unsuitable for angels, inasmuch as they are incapable of committing the sins referred to; but it suits man, because he has gotten the seeds of those sins in his nature. This is deeply humbling. It is a fresh declaration of the truth that man is a total wreck. From the crown of his head to the sole of his foot, there is not so much as a single speck of moral soundness, as looked at in the light of the divine presence. The being for whom Jehovah thought it needful to write Leviticus 18—20 must be a vile sinner; but that being is *man*—the writer and reader of these lines. How plain it is, therefore, that "they that are in the flesh *cannot* please God" (Rom. 8). Thank God, the believer is "not in the flesh, but in the Spirit." He has been taken completely out of his old-creation standing, and introduced into the new creation, in which the moral evils aimed at in this our section can have no existence. True, he has gotten the old nature; but it is his happy privilege to "reckon" it as a dead thing, and to walk in the abiding power of the new creation, wherein "all things are of God." This is Christian liberty, even liberty to walk up and down in that fair creation where no trace of evil can ever be found,—hallowed liberty to walk in holiness and purity before God and man,—liberty to tread those lofty walks of personal sanctity whereon the beams of the divine countenance ever pour themselves in living lustre. Reader, this is Christian liberty. It is liberty, not to commit sin, but to taste the celestial sweets of a life of true holiness and moral elevation. May we prize more highly than we have ever done this precious boon of heaven—Christian liberty.

And now, one word as to the second class of statutes contained in our section, namely, those which so touchingly bring out divine tenderness and care. Take the following: "And when ye reap the harvest of your land, thou shalt not wholly reap the corners of thy field, neither shalt thou gather the gleanings of thy harvest. And thou shalt not glean thy vineyard, neither shalt thou gather every grape of thy vineyard; *thou shalt leave them for the poor and stranger:* I am the Lord your God" (chap. 19:9-10). This ordinance will meet us again in chapter 23, but there we shall see it in its dispensational bearing. Here, we contemplate it morally, as unfolding the precious grace of Israel's God. He would think of "the poor and stranger," and He would have His people think of them likewise. When the golden sheaves were being reaped, and the mellow clusters gathered, "the poor and stranger" were to be remembered by the Israel of God, because Jehovah was the God of Israel. The reaper and the grape-gatherer were not to be governed by a spirit of grasping covetousness, which would bare the corners of the field and strip the branches of the vine, but rather by a spirit of large-hearted, genuine benevolence, which would leave a sheaf and a cluster "for the poor and stranger," that they too might rejoice in the unbounded goodness of Him whose paths drop fatness, and on whose open hand all the sons of want may confidently wait.

The book of Ruth furnishes a fine example of one who fully acted out this most benevolent statute. "And Boaz said unto her, [Ruth,] 'At meal-time, come thou hither, and eat of the bread, and dip thy morsel in the vinegar.' And she sat beside the reapers: and he reached her parched corn, and she did eat, and was sufficed, and left. And when she was risen up to glean, Boaz commanded his young men, saying, 'Let her glean even among the sheaves, and reproach her not; *and let fall also some of the handfuls of purpose for her,* and leave them, that she may glean them, and rebuke her not' " (Ruth 2:14-16). Most touching and beautiful grace! Truly, it is good for our poor selfish hearts to be brought in contact with such principles and such practices. Nothing can surpass the exquisite refinement of the words, "let fall also some of the handfuls of purpose for her." It was evidently the desire of this noble Israelite that "the stranger" might have abundance, and have it, too, rather as the fruit of her own gleaning than of his benevolence. This was the very essence of refinement. It was putting her in immediate connection with, and dependence upon, the God of Israel, who had fully recognized and provided for "the gleaner." Boaz was merely acting out that gracious ordinance of which Ruth was reaping the benefit. The same grace that had given him the field gave her the gleanings. They were both debtors to grace. She was the happy recipient of Jehovah's goodness: he was the honored exponent of Jehovah's most gracious institution. All was in most lovely moral order. The creature was blessed and God was glorified. Who would not own that it is good for us to be allowed to breathe such an atmosphere?

Let us now turn to another statute of our section. "Thou shalt not defraud thy neighbor, neither rob him: the wages of him that is hired shall not abide with thee all night until the morning" (chap. 19:13). What tender care is here! The High and Mighty One that inhabiteth eternity can take knowledge of the thoughts and feelings that spring up in the heart of a poor laborer. He knows and takes into account the expectations of such an one in reference to the fruit of his day's toil. The wages will naturally be looked for. The laborer's heart counts upon them: the family meal depends upon them. Oh! let them not be held back: send not the laborer home with a heavy heart, to make the heart of his wife and family heavy likewise. By all means, give him that for which he has wrought, to which he has a right, and on which his heart is set. He is a husband, he is a father, and he has borne the burden and heat of the day that his wife and children may not go hungry to bed. Disappoint him not: give him his due. Thus does our God take notice of the very throbbings of the laborer's heart, and make provision for his rising expectations. Precious grace! Most tender, thoughtful, touching, condescending love! The bare contemplation of such statutes is sufficient to throw one into a flood of tenderness. Could any one read such passages and not be melted? Could any one read them and thoughtlessly dismiss a poor laborer, not knowing whether he and his family have wherewithal to meet the cravings of hunger?

Nothing can be more painful to a tender heart than the lack of kindly consideration for the poor so often manifested by the rich. These latter can sit down to their sumptuous repast after dismissing from their door some poor industrious creature who had come seeking the just reward of his honest labor. They think not of the aching heart with which that man returns to his family, to tell them of the disappointment to himself and to them. Oh, it is terrible! It is most offensive to God and to all who have drunk, in any measure, into His grace. If we would know what God thinks of such acting, we have only to hearken to the following accents of holy indignation: "Behold, the hire of the laborers who have reaped down your fields, which is of you kept back by fraud, crieth; and the cries of them that have reaped have entered into the ears of the Lord of Sabaoth" (James 5:4). "The Lord of Sabaoth" hears the cry of the aggrieved and disappointed laborer. His tender love tells itself forth in the institutions of His moral government; and even though the heart should not be melted by the grace of those institutions, the conduct should, at least, be governed by the righteousness thereof. God will not suffer the claims of the poor to be heartlessly tossed aside by those who are so hardened by the influence of wealth as to be insensible to the appeals of tenderness, and who are so far removed beyond the region of personal need as to be incapable of feeling for those whose lot it is to spend their days amid exhausting toil or pinching poverty. The poor are the special objects of God's care. Again and again He makes provision for them in the statutes of His moral administration; and it is particularly declared of Him who shall ere long assume, in manifested glory, the reins of government, that "He shall deliver the needy when he crieth; the poor also, and him that hath no helper. He shall spare the poor and needy, and shall save the souls of the needy. He shall redeem their souls from deceit and violence; and precious shall their blood be in His sight" (Ps. 72:12-14).

May we profit by the review of those precious and deeply practical truths. May our hearts be affected, and our conduct influenced by them. We live in a heartless world; and there is a vast amount of selfishness in our own hearts. We are not sufficiently affected by the thought of the need of others. We are apt to forget the poor in the midst of our abundance. We often forget that the very persons whose labor ministers to our personal comfort are living, it may be, in the deepest poverty. Let us think of these things. Let us beware of "grinding the faces of the poor." If the Jews of old were taught, by the statutes and ordinances of the Mosaic economy, to entertain kindly feelings toward the poor, and to deal tenderly and graciously with the sons of toil, how much more ought the higher and more spiritual ethics of the gospel dispensation produce in the hearts and lives of Christians a large-hearted benevolence toward every form of human need.

True, there is urgent need of prudence and caution, lest we take a man out of the honorable position in which he was designed and fitted to move, namely, a position of dependence upon the fruits—the precious and fragrant fruits—of honest industry. This would be a grievous injury instead of a benefit. The example of Boaz should instruct in this matter. He allowed Ruth to glean; but he took care to make her gleaning profitable. This is a very safe and a very simple principle. God intends that man should work at something or another, and we run counter to Him when we draw our fellow out of the place of dependence upon the results of patient industry, into that of dependence upon the results of false benevolence. The former is as honorable and elevating as the latter is contemptible and demoralizing. There is no bread so sweet to the taste as that which is nobly earned; but then those who earn their bread should get enough. A man will feed and care for his horses; how much more his fellow, who yields him the labor of his hands from Monday morning till Saturday night.

There are two sides to this question, and no doubt one meets with a great deal amongst the poor which is calculated to dry up the springs of benevolence and genuine sympathy. There is much which tends to steel the heart and close the hand; but one thing is certain, it is better to be deceived in ninety-nine cases out of a hundred than to shut up the bowels of compassion against a single worthy object. Our heavenly Father causes His sun to shine upon the evil and on the good; and sendeth rain upon the just and upon the unjust. The same sunbeams that gladden the heart of some devoted servant of Christ are poured upon the path of some ungodly sinner; and the self-same shower that falls upon the tillage of a true believer, enriches also the furrows of some blasphem-ing infidel. This is to be our model. "Be ye therefore perfect, even as your Father which is in heaven is perfect" (Matt. 5:48). It is only as we set the Lord before us, and walk in the power of His grace, that we shall be able to go on from day to day, meeting, with a tender heart and an open hand, every possible form of human misery. It is only as we ourselves are drinking at the exhaustless fountain of divine love and tenderness, that we shall be able to go on ministering to human need unchecked by the oft-repeated manifestation of human depravity. Our tiny springs would soon be dried up were they not maintained in unbroken connection with that ever-gushing source.

The statute which next presents itself for our consideration, exemplifies most touch-ingly the tender care of the God of Israel. "Thou shalt not curse the deaf, nor put a stumbling-block before the blind, but shalt fear thy God: I am the Lord" (ver. 14). Here a barrier is erected to stem the rising tide of irritability with which uncontrolled nature would be almost sure to meet the personal infirmity of deafness. How well we can understand this! Nature does not like to be called upon to repeat its words again and again, in order to meet the deaf man's infirmity. Jehovah thought of this, and provided for it. And what is the provision? "Thou shalt fear thy God." When tried by a deaf person, remember the Lord, and look to Him for grace to enable you to govern your temper.

The second part of this statute reveals a most humiliating amount of wickedness in human nature. The idea of laying a stumbling-block in the way of the blind is about the most wanton cruelty imaginable; and yet man is capable of it, else he would not be warned against it. No doubt this, as well as many other statutes, admits of a spiritual application; but that in no wise interferes with the plain literal principle set forth in it. Man is capable of placing a stumbling-block in the way of a fellow-creature afflicted with blindness. Such is man! Truly, the Lord knew what was in man when He wrote the statutes and judgments of the book of Leviticus.

I shall leave my reader to meditate alone upon the remainder of our section. He will find that each statute teaches a double lesson, namely, a lesson with respect to nature's evil tendencies, and also a lesson as to Jehovah's tender care.*

---

## *CHAPTERS 21–22*

THESE chapters unfold, with great minuteness of detail, the divine requirements in reference to those who were privileged to draw near as priests to "offer the bread of their God." In this, as in the preceding section, we have conduct as the *result,* not the procuring *cause* of the relationship. This should be carefully borne in mind. The sons of Aaron were, in virtue of their birth, priests unto God. They all stood in this relationship, one as well as another. It was not a matter of attainment, a question of progress, something which one had and another had not. All the sons of Aaron were priests; they were born into a priestly place. Their capacity to understand and enjoy their position and its attendant privileges was obviously a different thing altogether. One might be a babe, and another might have reached the point of mature and vigorous manhood. The former would, of necessity, be unable to eat of the priestly food, being a babe, for whom "milk," and not "strong meat," was adapted; but he was as truly a member of the priestly house as the man who could tread, with firm step, the courts of the Lord's house, and feed upon "the wave breast" and "heave shoulder" of the sacrifice.

This distinction is easily understood in the case of the sons of Aaron, and hence it will serve to illustrate, in a very simple manner, the truth as to the members of the true priestly house, over which our great High-Priest presides, and to which all true believers belong (Heb. 3:6). Every child of God is a priest. He is enrolled as a member of Christ's priestly house. He may be very ignorant, but his position as a priest is not founded upon knowledge, but upon life; his experience may be very shallow, but his place as a priest does not depend upon experience, but upon life; his capacity may be very limited, but his relationship as a priest does not rest upon an enlarged capacity, but upon life. He was born into the position and relationship of a priest: he did not work himself thereinto. It was not by any efforts of his own that he became a priest: he became a priest by birth. The spiritual priesthood, together with all the spiritual functions attaching thereunto, is

*Verses 16 and 17 demand special attention. "Thou shalt not go up and down as a talebearer among thy people." This is a most seasonable admonition for the people of God in every age. A talebearer is sure to do incalculable mischief. It has been well remarked that a talebearer injures three persons—he injures himself, he injures his hearer, and he injures the subject of his tale. All this he does directly; and as to the indirect consequences, who can recount them? Let us carefully guard against this horrible evil. May we never suffer a tale to pass our lips; and let us never stand to hearken to a talebearer. May we always know how to drive away a backbiting tongue with an angry countenance, as the north wind driveth away rain.

In verse 17, we learn what ought to take the place of talebearing. "Thou shalt in any wise rebuke thy neighbor, and not suffer sin upon him." In place of carrying to another a tale about my neighbor, I am called upon to go directly to himself and rebuke him, if there is any thing wrong. This is the divine method. Satan's method is to act the talebearer.

the necessary appendage to spiritual birth. The capacity to enjoy the privileges and to discharge the functions of a position must not be confounded with the position itself: they must ever be kept distinct. Relationship is one thing; capacity is quite another.

Furthermore, in looking at the family of Aaron, we see that nothing could break the relationship between him and his sons. There were many things which would interfere with the full enjoyment of the privileges attaching to the relationship. A son of Aaron might "defile himself by the dead"; he might defile himself by forming an unholy alliance; he might have some bodily "blemish"; he might be "blind or lame"; he might be "a dwarf." Any of these things would have interfered very materially with his enjoyment of the privileges and his discharge of the functions pertaining to his relationship, as we read, "No man that hath a blemish of the seed of Aaron the priest shall come nigh to offer the offerings of the Lord made by fire: he hath a blemish: he shall not come nigh to offer the bread of his God. He shall eat the bread of his God, both of the most holy and the holy; only he shall not go in unto the vail, nor come nigh unto the altar, because he hath a blemish; that he profane not my sanctuaries; for I the Lord do sanctify them" (chap. 21:21-23). But none of these things could possibly touch the fact of a relationship founded upon the established principles of human nature. Though a son of Aaron were a dwarf, that dwarf was a son of Aaron. True, he was, as a dwarf, shorn of many precious privileges and lofty dignities pertaining to the priesthood, but he was a son of Aaron all the while. He could neither enjoy the same measure or character of communion, nor yet discharge the same elevated functions of priestly service, as one who had reached to manhood's appointed stature; but he was a member of the priestly house, and as such, permitted to "eat the bread of his God." The relationship was genuine, though the development was so defective.

The spiritual application of all this is as simple as it is practical. To be a child of God is one thing; to be in the enjoyment of priestly communion and priestly worship is quite another. The latter is, alas! interfered with by many things. Circumstances and associations are allowed to act upon us by their defiling influence. We are not to suppose that all Christians enjoy the same elevation of walk, the same intimacy of fellowship, the same felt nearness to Christ. Alas! they do not. Many of us have to mourn over our spiritual defects. There is lameness of walk, defective vision, stunted growth; or we allow ourselves to be defiled by contact with evil, and to be weakened and hindered by unhallowed associations. In a word, as the sons of Aaron, though being priests by birth, were nevertheless deprived of many privileges through ceremonial defilement and physical defects; so we, though being priests unto God by spiritual birth, are deprived of many of the high and holy privileges of our position by moral defilement and spiritual defects. We are shorn of many of our dignities through defective spiritual development. We lack singleness of eye, spiritual vigor, whole-hearted devotedness. Saved we are, through the free grace of God, on the ground of Christ's perfect sacrifice. "We are all the children of God, by faith in Christ Jesus;" but then, salvation is one thing; communion is quite another: sonship is one thing; obedience is quite another.

These things should be carefully distinguished. The section before us illustrates the distinction with great force and clearness. If one of the sons of Aaron happened to be "broken-footed or broken-handed," was he deprived of his sonship? Assuredly not. Was he deprived of his priestly position? By no means. It was distinctly declared, "He shall eat the bread of his God, both of the most holy and of the holy." What, then, did he lose by his physical blemish? He was forbidden to tread some of the higher walks of priestly service and worship. "Only he shall not go in unto the vail, nor come nigh unto the altar." These were very serious privations; and though it may be objected that a man could not help many of these physical defects, that did not alter the matter. Jehovah could not have a blemished priest at His altar, or a blemished sacrifice thereon. Both the priest and the sacrifice should be perfect. "No man that hath a blemish of the seed of Aaron the priest shall come nigh to offer the offerings of the Lord made by fire" (chap. 21:22). "But whatsoever hath a blemish, that shall ye not offer; for it shall not be acceptable for you" (chap. 22:20).

Now, we have both the perfect priest and the perfect sacrifice in the Person of our blessed Lord Jesus Christ. He having "offered Himself without spot to God," passed into the heavens as our great High-Priest, where He ever liveth to make intercession for us. The Epistle to the Hebrews dwells elaborately upon these two points. It throws into vivid contrast the sacrifice and priesthood of the Mosaic system and the Sacrifice and Priesthood of Christ. In Him we have divine perfectness, whether as the Victim or as the Priest. We have all that God could require, and all that man could need. His precious blood has put away all our sins, and His all-prevailing intercession ever maintains us in all the perfectness of the place into which His blood has introduced us. "We are complete in Him" (Col. 2), and yet, so feeble and so faltering are we in ourselves; so full of failure and infirmity; so prone to err and stumble in our onward way, that we could not stand for a moment were it not that "He ever liveth to make intercession for us." These things have been dwelt upon in the earlier chapters of this volume, and it is therefore needless to enter further upon them here. Those who have any thing like correct apprehensions of the grand foundation-truths of Christianity, and any measure of experience in the Christian life, will be able to understand how it is that though "complete in Him who is the head of all principality and power," they nevertheless need, while down here amid the infirmities, conflicts, and buffetings of earth, the powerful advocacy of their adorable and divine High-Priest. The believer is "washed, sanctified, and justified" (1 Cor. 6); he is "accepted in the Beloved" (Eph. 1:6); he can never come into judgment, as regards his person (see John 5:24, where the word is *κρισιν* and not *κατακρισιν*); death and judgment are behind him, because he is united to Christ, who has passed through them both on his behalf and in his stead. All these things are divinely true of the very weakest, most unlettered, and inexperienced member of the family of God; but yet, inasmuch as he carries about with him a nature so incorrigibly bad and so irremediably ruined that no discipline can correct it and no medicine cure it, inasmuch as he is the tenant of a body of sin and death—as he is surrounded on all sides by hostile influences—as he is called to cope perpetually with the combined forces of the world, the flesh, and the devil, he could never keep his ground, much less make progress, were he not upheld by the all-prevailing intercession of his great High-Priest, who bears the names of His people upon His breast and upon His shoulder.

Some, I am aware, have found great difficulty in reconciling the idea of the believer's perfect standing in Christ with the need of priesthood. "If," it is argued, "he is perfect, what need has he of a priest?" The two things are as distinctly taught in the Word as they are compatible one with another, and understood in the experience of every rightly instructed Christian. It is of the very last importance to apprehend, with clearness and accuracy, the perfect harmony between these two points. The believer is perfect in Christ; but in himself, he is a poor feeble creature, ever liable to fall. Hence the unspeakable blessedness of having One who can manage all his affairs for him, at the right hand of the Majesty in the heavens—One who upholds him continually by the right hand of His righteousness—One who will never let him go—One who is able to save to the uttermost—One who is "the same yesterday, to-day, and forever"—One who will bear him triumphantly through all the difficulties and dangers which surround him, and finally "present him faultless before the presence of His glory with exceeding joy." Blessed forever be the grace that has made such ample provision for all our need in the blood of a Spotless Victim and the intercession of a divine High-Priest.

Let it be our care so to walk, so to "keep ourselves unspotted from the world," so to stand apart from all unhallowed associations, that we may enjoy the highest privileges and discharge the most elevated functions of our position as members of the priestly house of which Christ is the Head. We have "boldness to enter into the holiest through the blood of Jesus:" "we have a great High-Priest over the house of God" (Heb. 10). Nothing can ever rob us of these privileges. But then our communion may be marred, our worship may be hindered, our holy functions may remain undischarged. Those ceremonial matters against which the sons of Aaron were warned in the section before us, have their antitypes in the Christian economy. Had they to be warned against unholy contact? So have we. Had they to be warned against unholy alliance? So have we. Had they to be warned against all manner of ceremonial uncleanness? So have we to be warned against "all filthiness of the flesh and spirit" (1 Cor. 7). Were they shorn of many of their loftiest priestly privileges by bodily blemish and imperfect natural growth? So are we by moral blemish and imperfect spiritual growth.

Will any one venture to call in question the practical importance of such principles as these? Is it not obvious that the more highly we estimate the blessings which attach to that priestly house of which we have been constituted members, in virtue of our spiritual birth, the more carefully shall we guard against every thing which might tend in any wise to rob us of their enjoyment? Undoubtedly. And this it is which renders the close study of our section so pre-eminently practical. May we feel its power, through the application of God the Holy Ghost. Then shall we *enjoy* our priestly place; then shall we faithfully discharge our priestly functions. We shall be able "to present our bodies a living sacrifice, holy and acceptable unto God" (Rom. 12:1); we shall be able to "offer the sacrifice of praise to God continually, that is, the fruit of our lips, giving thanks to His name" (Heb. 13:15); we shall be able, as members of the "spiritual house" and the "holy priesthood," to "offer up spiritual sacrifices, acceptable to God by Jesus Christ" (1 Pet. 2:5); we shall be able, in some small degree, to anticipate that blissful time when, from a redeemed creation, the halleluiahs of intelligent and fervent praise shall ascend to the throne of God and the Lamb throughout the everlasting ages.

---

## *CHAPTER 23*

ONE of the most profound and comprehensive chapters in the inspired volume now lies before us, and claims our prayerful study. It contains the record of the seven great feasts or periodical solemnities into which Israel's year was divided. In other words, it furnishes us with a perfect view of God's dealings with Israel during the entire period of their most eventful history.

Looking at the feasts separately, we have the Sabbath, the Passover, the feast of unleavened bread, the first-fruits, Pentecost, the feast of trumpets, the day of atonement, and the feast of tabernacles. This would make eight, altogether; but it is very obvious that the Sabbath occupies quite a unique and independent place. It is first presented, and its proper characteristics and attendant circumstances fully set forth; and then we read, "These are the feasts of the Lord, even holy convocations, which ye shall proclaim in their seasons" (ver. 4).

So that, strictly speaking, as the attentive reader will observe, Israel's *first* great feast was the Passover, and their *seventh* was the feast of tabernacles. That is to say, divesting them of their typical dress, we have, first, redemption; and last of all, we have the millennial glory. The paschal lamb typified the death of Christ (1 Cor. 5:7); and the feast of tabernacles typified "the times of the restitution of all things, of which God hath spoken by the mouth of all His holy prophets since the world began" (Acts 3:21).

Such was the opening and such the closing feast of the Jewish year. Atonement is the foundation, glory the top-stone; while between these two points we have the resurrection of Christ (ver. 10-14), the gathering of the Church (ver. 15-21), the waking up of Israel to a sense of their long-lost glory (ver. 24-25), their repentance and hearty reception of their Messiah (ver. 27-32), and, that not one feature might be lacking in this grand typical representation, we have provision made for the Gentiles to come in at the close of the harvest and glean in Israel's fields (ver. 22). All this renders the picture divinely perfect, and evokes from the heart of every lover of Scripture the most intense admiration. What could be more complete? The blood of the Lamb, and practical holiness founded thereon; the resurrection of Christ from the dead, and His ascension into heaven; the descent of the Holy Ghost, in pentecostal power, to form the Church; the awakening of the remnant; their repentance and restoration; the blessing of "the poor and the stranger;" the manifestation of the glory; the rest and blessedness of the kingdom,—such are the contents of this truly marvelous chapter, which we shall now proceed to examine in detail. May God the Holy Ghost be our Teacher.

"And the Lord spake unto Moses, saying, 'Speak unto the children of Israel, and say unto them, Concerning the feasts of the Lord, which ye shall proclaim to be holy convocations, even these are My feasts. Six days shall work be done; but the seventh day is the Sabbath of rest, a holy convocation; ye shall do no work therein: it is the Sabbath of the Lord in all your dwellings.' " The place which the Sabbath here gets is full of interest. The Lord is about to furnish a type of all His dealings in grace with His people; and ere He does so, He sets forth the Sabbath as the significant expression of that rest which remaineth for the people of God. It was an actual solemnity to be observed by Israel, but it was also a type of what is yet to be when all that great and glorious work which this chapter foreshadows shall have been accomplished. It is God's rest, into which all who believe can enter now in spirit; but which, as to its full and actual accomplishment, yet remains (Heb. 4). We work now: we shall rest by and by. In one sense, the believer enters into rest; in another sense, he labors to enter into it. He has found his rest in Christ; he labors to enter into his rest in glory. He has found his full mental repose in what Christ has wrought for him, and his eye rests on that everlasting Sabbath upon which he shall enter when all his desert toils and conflicts are over. He cannot rest in the midst of a scene of sin and wretchedness; "he rests in Christ, the Son of God, who took the servant's form;" and while thus resting, he is called to labor as a worker together with God, in the full assurance that when all his toil is over, he shall enjoy unbroken, eternal repose in those mansions of unfading light and unalloyed blessedness where labor and sorrow can never enter. Blessed prospect! May it brighten more and more each hour in the vision of faith. May we labor all the more earnestly and faithfully, as being sure of this most precious rest at the end. True, there are foretastes of the eternal Sabbath; but these foretastes only cause us to long more ardently for the blessed reality—that Sabbath which shall never be broken—that "holy convocation" which shall never be dissolved.

We have already remarked that the Sabbath occupies quite a unique and independent place in this chapter. This is evident from the wording of the fourth verse, where the Lord seems to begin afresh with the expression, "These are the feasts of the Lord," as if to leave the Sabbath quite distinct from the seven feasts which follow, though it be, in reality, the type of that rest to which those feasts so blessedly introduce the soul.

"These are the feasts of the Lord, even holy convocations, which ye shall proclaim in their seasons. In the fourteenth day of the first month at even is the Lord's passover" (ver. 4-5). Here, then, we have the first of the seven periodical solemnities—the offering of that paschal lamb whose blood it was that screened the Israel of God from the sword of the destroying angel on that terrible night when Egypt's first-born were laid low. This is the acknowledged type of the death of Christ, and hence its place in this chapter is divinely appropriate. It forms the foundation of all. We can know nothing of rest, nothing of holiness, nothing of fellowship, save on the ground of the death of Christ. It is peculiarly striking, significant, and beautiful to observe that, directly God's rest is spoken of, the next thing introduced is the blood of the paschal lamb. As much as to say, There is the *rest* but here is your *title.* No doubt labor will *capacitate* us, but it is the blood that *entitles* us, to enjoy the rest.

"And on the fifteenth day of the same month is the feast of unleavened bread unto the Lord: seven days ye must eat unleavened bread. In the first day ye shall have a holy convocation: ye shall do no servile work therein. But ye shall offer an offering made by fire unto the Lord seven days: in the seventh day is a holy convocation: ye shall do no servile work therein" (ver. 6-8). The people are here assembled around Jehovah in that practical holiness which is founded upon accomplished redemption; and while thus assembled, the fragrant odor of the sacrifice ascends from the altar of Israel to the throne of Israel's God. This gives us a fine view of that holiness which God looks for in the life of His redeemed. It is based upon the sacrifice, and it ascends in immediate connection with the acceptable fragrance of the Person of Christ. "Ye shall do no *servile work* therein; but ye shall offer *an offering made by fire.*" What a contrast! —the servile work of man's hands, and the sweet savor of Christ's sacrifice! The practical holiness of God's people is not servile labor; it is the living unfolding of Christ through them, by the power of the Holy Ghost. "To me to live is Christ." This is the true idea. Christ is our life; and every exhibition of that life is, in the divine judgment, redolent with all the fragrance of Christ. It may be a very trifling matter in man's judgment, but, insofar as it is the outflow of Christ our life, it is unspeakably precious to God. It ascends to Him and can never be forgotten. "The fruits of righteousness which are by Jesus Christ" are produced in the life of the believer, and no power of earth or hell can prevent their fragrance ascending to the throne of God.

It is needful to ponder deeply the contrast between "servile work" and the outflow of the life of Christ. The type is very vivid. There was a total cessation of manual labor throughout the whole assembly; but the sweet savor of the burnt-offering ascended to God. These were to be the two grand characteristics of the feast of unleavened bread. Man's labor ceased, and the odor of the sacrifice ascended; and this was the type of a believer's life of practical holiness. What a triumphant answer is here to the legalist on the one side, and the antinomian on the other! The former is silenced by the words, "no servile work"; and the latter is confounded by the words, "Ye shall offer an offering made by fire." The most elaborate works of man's hands are "servile"; but the smallest cluster of "the fruits of righteousness" is to the glory and praise of God. Throughout the entire period of the believer's life there must be no servile work—nothing of the hateful and degrading element of legality. There should be only the continual presentation of the life of Christ, wrought out and exhibited by the power of the Holy Ghost. Throughout the "seven days" of Israel's second great periodical solemnity there was to be "no leaven"; but instead thereof, the sweet savor of "an offering made by fire" was to be presented to the Lord. May we fully enter into the practical teaching of this most striking and instructive type.

"And the Lord spake unto Moses, saying, 'Speak unto the children of Israel, and say unto them, When ye be come into the land which I give unto you, and shall reap the harvest thereof, then ye shall bring a sheaf of the first-fruits of your harvest unto the priest; and ye shall wave the sheaf before the Lord, to be accepted for you: on the morrow after the Sabbath the priest shall wave it. And ye shall offer that day when ye wave the sheaf, a he lamb without blemish of the first year, for a burnt-offering unto the Lord. And the meat-offering thereof shall be two tenth deals of fine flour mingled with oil, an offering made by fire unto the

Lord for a sweet savor: and the drink-offering thereof shall be of wine, the fourth part of a hin. And ye shall eat neither bread, nor parched corn, nor green ears, until the self-same day that ye have brought an offering unto your God: it shall be a statute forever throughout your generations, in all your dwellings" (ver. 9-14).

"But now is Christ risen from the dead, and become the *first-fruits* of them that slept" (1 Cor. 15:20). The beautiful ordinance of the presentation of the sheaf of first-fruits typified the resurrection of Christ, who, "at the end of the Sabbath, as it began to dawn toward the first day of the week," rose triumphant from the tomb, having accomplished the glorious work of redemption. His was a "resurrection *from among* the dead;" and in it we have at once the earnest and the type of the resurrection of His people. "Christ the first-fruits; afterwards they that are Christ's at His coming." When Christ comes, His people will be raised "from among the dead [*εκ νεκρων*]," that is, those of them that sleep in Jesus; "but the rest of the dead lived not again until the thousand years were finished" (Rev. 20:5). When, immediately after the transfiguration, our blessed Lord spoke of His rising *"from among the dead,"* the disciples questioned among themselves what that could mean (see Mark 9). Every orthodox Jew believed in the doctrine of the "resurrection of the dead [*αναστασις νεκρων*]," but the idea of a "resurrection from among the dead [*αναστασις εκ νεκρων*]" was what the disciples were unable to grasp; and no doubt many disciples since then have felt considerable difficulty with respect to a mystery so profound.

However, if my reader will prayerfully study and compare 1 Cor. 15 with 1 Thess. 4:13-18, he will get much precious instruction upon this most interesting and practical truth. He can also look at Romans 8:11 in connection: "But if the Spirit of Him that raised up Jesus from the dead [*εκ νεκρων*] dwell in you, He that raised up Christ from the dead shall also quicken your mortal bodies by His Spirit that dwelleth in you." From all these passages it will be seen that the resurrection of the Church will be upon precisely the same principle as the resurrection of Christ. Both the Head and the body are shown to be raised "from among the dead." The first sheaf and all the sheaves that follow after are morally connected.

It must be evident to any one who carefully ponders the subject in the light of Scripture, that there is a very material difference between the resurrection of the believer and the resurrection of the unbeliever. Both shall be raised; but Revelation 20:5 proves that there will be a thousand years between the two, so that they differ both as to the principle and as to the time. Some have found difficulty in reference to this subject, from the fact that in John 5:28 our Lord speaks of "the *hour* in the which *all* that are in the graves shall hear His voice." How, it may be asked, can there be a thousand years between the two resurrections, when both are spoken of as occurring in an "hour"? The answer is very simple. In verse 28, the quickening of dead souls is spoken of as occurring in an "hour"; and this work has been going on for over eighteen hundred years. Now, if a period of nearly *two* thousand years can be represented by the word "hour," what objection can there be to the idea of *one* thousand years being represented in the same way? Surely, none whatever, especially when it is expressly stated that "the rest of the dead lived not again until the thousand years were finished."

But furthermore, when we find mention made of "a *first* resurrection," is it not evident that all are not to be raised together? Why speak of a "first" if there is but the one? It may be said that "the first resurrection" refers to the soul; but where is the Scripture warrant for such a statement? The solemn fact is this: when the "shout of the archangel and the trump of God" shall be heard, the redeemed who sleep in Jesus will be raised to meet Him in the glory; the wicked dead, whoever they be, from the days of Cain down, will remain in their graves during the thousand years of millennial blessedness, and at the close of that bright and blissful period, they shall come forth and stand before "the great white throne," there to be "judged every man according to his works," and to pass from the throne of judgment into the lake of fire. Appalling thought!

How is it in reference to your precious soul? Have you seen, by the eye of faith, the blood of the paschal Lamb shed to screen you from this terrible hour? Have you seen the precious Sheaf of first-fruits reaped and gathered into the heavenly garner, as the earnest of your being gathered in due time? These are solemn questions. Do not put them aside. See that you are *now* under the cover of the blood of Jesus. Remember, you cannot glean so much as a single ear in the fields of redemption until you have seen the true Sheaf waved before the Lord. "Ye shall eat neither bread, nor parched corn, nor green ears, until *the self-same day* that ye have brought an offering unto your God." The harvest could not be touched until the sheaf of first-fruits had been presented, and, with the sheaf, a burnt-offering and a meat-offering.

"And ye shall count unto you from the morrow after the Sabbath, from the day that ye brought the sheaf of the wave-offering; seven Sabbaths shall be complete: even unto the morrow after the seventh Sabbath shall ye number fifty days; and ye shall offer a new meat-offering unto the Lord. Ye shall bring out of your habitations two wave-loaves of two tenth deals: they shall be of fine flour; they shall be baken with leaven; they are the first-fruits unto the Lord" (ver. 15-17). This is the feast of Pentecost—the type of God's people, gathered by the Holy Ghost, and presented before Him, in connection with all the preciousness of Christ. In the passover we have the death of Christ, in the sheaf of first-fruits we have the resurrection of Christ, and in the feast of Pentecost we have the descent of the Holy Ghost to form the Church. All this is divinely perfect. The death and resurrection of Christ had to be accomplished ere the Church could be formed. The sheaf was offered and then the loaves were baked.

And, observe, "they shall be baken *with leaven.*" Why was this? Because they were intended to foreshadow those who, though filled with the Holy Ghost, and adorned with His gifts and graces, had, nevertheless, *evil* dwelling in them. The assembly, on the day of Pentecost, stood in the full value of the blood of Christ, was crowned with the gifts of the Holy Ghost; but there was leaven there also. No power of the Spirit could do away with the fact that there was evil dwelling in the people of God. It might be suppressed and kept out of view, but it was there. This fact is foreshadowed in the type by the leaven in the two loaves, and it is set forth in the actual history of the Church; for albeit God the Holy Ghost was present in the assembly, the flesh was there likewise to lie unto Him. Flesh is flesh, nor can it ever be made aught else than flesh. The Holy Ghost did not come down on the day of Pentecost to improve nature or do away with the fact of its incurable evil, but to baptize believers into one body, and connect them with their living Head in heaven.

Allusion has already been made, in the chapter on the peace-offering, to the fact that leaven was permitted in connection therewith. It was the divine recognition of the evil in the worshiper. Thus is it also in the ordinance of the "two wave-loaves;" they were made to be "baken with *leaven,*" because of the *evil* in the antitype.

But, blessed be God, the evil which was divinely recognized was divinely provided for. This gives great rest and comfort to the heart. It is a comfort to be assured that God knows the worst of us; and, moreover, that He has made provision according to *His* knowledge, and not merely according to *ours.* "And ye shall offer *with the bread* seven lambs *without blemish* of the first year, and one young bullock, and two rams; they shall be for a burnt-offering unto the Lord, with their meat-offering and their drink-offerings, even an offering made by fire, of sweet savor unto the Lord" (ver. 18). Here, then, we have, in immediate connection with the leavened loaves, the presentation of an unblemished sacrifice, typifying the great and all-important truth that it is Christ's perfectness, and not our sinfulness, that is ever before the view of God. Observe particularly the words, "ye shall offer *with the bread* seven lambs *without blemish.*" Precious truth though clothed in typic dress! May the reader be enabled to enter into it, to make his own of it, to stay his conscience upon it, to feed and refresh his heart with it, to delight his whole soul in it. Not I, but Christ.

It may, however, be objected that the fact of Christ's being a spotless Lamb is not sufficient to roll the burden of guilt from a sin-stained conscience—a sweet-savor offering would not, of itself, avail for a guilty sinner. This objection might be urged, but our type fully meets and entirely removes it. It is quite true that a burnt-offering would not have been sufficient where "leaven" was in question; and hence we read, "Then ye shall sacrifice one kid of the goats for a *sin-offering,* and two lambs of the first year for a sacrifice of peace-offerings" (ver. 19). The "sin-offering" was the answer to the "leaven" in the loaves: "peace" was established, so that communion could be enjoyed, and all went up in immediate connection with the "sweet savor" of the "burnt-offering" unto the Lord.

Thus, on the day of Pentecost, the Church was presented in all the value and excellency of Christ, through the power of the Holy Ghost. Though having in itself the leaven of the old nature, that leaven was not reckoned, because the divine Sin-offering had perfectly answered for it. The power of the Holy Ghost did not remove the leaven, but the blood of the Lamb had atoned for it. This is a most interesting and important distinction. The work of the Spirit in the believer does not remove indwelling evil. It enables him to detect, judge, and subdue the evil; but no amount of spiritual power can do away with the fact that the evil is there—though, blessed be God, the conscience is at perfect ease, inasmuch as the blood of our Sin-offering has eternally settled the whole question; and therefore, instead of our evil being under the eye of God, it has been put out of sight forever, and we are accepted in all the acceptableness of Christ, who offered Himself to God as a sweet-smelling sacrifice, that He might perfectly glorify Him in all things, and be the food of His people forever.

Thus much as to Pentecost—after which a long period is suffered to roll on ere we have any movement amongst the people. There is, however, the notice of "the poor and stranger" in that beautiful ordinance which has already been referred to in its moral aspect. Here we may look at it in a dispensational point of view. "And when ye reap the harvest of your land, thou shalt not make clean riddance of the corners of thy field when thou reapest, neither shalt thou gather any gleaning of thy harvest; thou shalt leave them unto the poor, and to the stranger: I am the Lord your God" (ver. 22). Provision is here made for the stranger to glean in Israel's fields. The Gentile is to be brought in to participate in the overflowing goodness of God. When Israel's storehouse and wine-press have been fully furnished, there will be precious sheaves and rich clusters for the Gentile to gather.

We are not, however, to suppose that the spiritual blessings with which the Church is endowed in the heavenlies with Christ are set forth under the figure of a stranger gleaning in Israel's fields. These blessings are as new to the seed of Abraham as they are to the Gentile. They are not the gleanings of Canaan, but the glories of heaven—the glories of Christ. The Church is not merely blessed *by* Christ, but *with* and *in* Christ. The bride of Christ will not be sent forth to gather up, as a stranger, the sheaves and clusters in the corners of Israel's fields and from the branches of Israel's vines. No; she tastes of higher blessings, richer joys, nobler dignities, than aught that Israel ever knew. She is not to glean as a stranger on earth, but to enjoy her own wealthy and happy home in heaven, to which she belongs. This is the "better thing" which God hath, in His manifold wisdom and grace, "reserved" for her. No doubt it will be a gracious privilege for "the stranger" to be permitted to glean after Israel's harvest is reaped; but the Church's portion is incomparably higher, even to be the bride of Israel's King, the partner of His throne, the sharer of His joys,

His dignities, and His glories; to be like Him and with Him forever. The eternal mansions of the Father's house on high, and not the ungleaned corners of Israel's fields below, are to be the Church's portion. May we ever bear this in mind, and live, in some small degree, worthy of such a holy and elevated destination.

"And the Lord spake unto Moses, saying, 'Speak unto the children of Israel, saying, In the seventh month, in the first day of the month, shall ye have a Sabbath, a memorial of blowing of trumpets, a holy convocation. Ye shall do no servile work; but ye shall offer an offering made by fire unto the Lord' " (ver. 23-25). A new subject is introduced here by the words, "the Lord spake unto Moses," which, let me remark in passing, affords an interesting help in classifying the subjects of the entire chapter. Thus, the Sabbath, the passover, and the feast of unleavened bread are given under the first communication; the wave-sheaf, the wave-loaves, and the ungleaned corners are given under the second; after which we have a long unnoticed interval; and then comes the soul-stirring feast of trumpets, on the first day of the seventh month. This ordinance leads us on to the time, now fast approaching, when the remnant of Israel shall "blow the trumpet" for a memorial, calling to remembrance their long-lost glory, and stirring up themselves to seek the Lord.

The feast of trumpets is intimately connected with another great solemnity, namely, "the day of atonement." "*Also* on the tenth day of this seventh month there shall be a day of atonement: it shall be a holy convocation unto you; and ye shall afflict your souls, and offer an offering made by fire unto the Lord. And ye shall do no work in that same day; for it is a day of atonement, to make an atonement for you before the Lord your God. . . . It shall be unto you a Sabbath of rest, and ye shall afflict your souls: in the ninth day of the month at even, from even unto even, shall ye celebrate your Sabbath" (ver. 27-32). Thus, after the blowing of the trumpets, an interval of eight days elapses, and then we have the day of atonement, with which these things are connected, namely, affliction of soul, atonement for sin, and rest from labor. All these things will find their due place in the experience of the Jewish remnant by and by. "The harvest is past, the summer is ended, and we are not saved" (Jer. 8:20). Such will be the pathetic lament of the remnant when the Spirit of God shall have begun to touch their heart and conscience. "And they shall look upon Me whom they have pierced, and they shall mourn for Him, as one mourneth for his only son, and shall be in bitterness for Him, as one that is in bitterness for her first-born. In that day shall there be a great mourning in Jerusalem, as the mourning of Hadadrimmon in the valley of Megiddon. And the land shall mourn, every family apart" (Zech. 12:10-14).

What deep mourning, what intense affliction, what genuine penitence, there will be, when, under the mighty action of the Holy Ghost, the conscience of the remnant shall recall the sins of the past—the neglect of the Sabbath, the breach of the law, the stoning of the prophets, the piercing of the Son, the resistance of the Spirit! All these things will come in array on the tablets of an enlightened and exercised conscience, and produce keen affliction of soul.

But the blood of atonement will meet all. "In that day there shall be a fountain opened to the house of David and to the inhabitants of Jerusalem for sin and for uncleanness" (Zech. 13:1). They will be made to feel their guilt and be afflicted, and they will also be led to see the efficacy of the blood, and find perfect peace—a Sabbath of rest unto their souls.

Now, when such results shall have been reached in the experience of Israel in the latter day, for what should we look? Surely, *the glory.* When the "blindness" is removed and "the vail" taken away, when the heart of the remnant is turned to Jehovah, then shall the bright beams of the "Sun of righteousness" fall, in healing, restoring, and saving power, upon a truly penitent, afflicted, and poor people. To enter elaborately upon this subject would demand a volume in itself. The exercises, the experiences, the conflicts, the trials, the difficulties, and the ultimate blessings of the Jewish remnant are fully detailed throughout the psalms and prophets. The existence of such a body must be clearly seen ere the psalms and prophets can be studied with intelligence and satisfaction. Not but that we may learn much from those portions of inspiration, for "all Scripture is profitable"; but the surest way to make a right use of any portion of the Word of God, is to understand its primary application. If, then, we apply Scriptures to the Church, or heavenly body, which belong, strictly speaking, to the Jewish remnant, or earthly body, we must be involved in serious error as to both the one and the other. In point of fact, it happens in many cases that the existence of such a body as the remnant is completely ignored, and the true position and hope of the Church are entirely lost sight of. These are grave errors, which my reader should sedulously seek to avoid. Let him not suppose for a moment that they are mere speculations, fitted only to engage the attention of the curious, and possessing no practical power whatever. There could not be a more erroneous supposition. What! is it of no practical value to us to know whether we belong to earth or heaven? is it of no real moment to us to know whether we shall be at rest in the mansions above or passing through the apocalyptic judgments down here? Who could admit aught so unreasonable? The truth is, it would be difficult to fix on any line of truth more practical than that which unfolds the distinctive destinies of the earthly remnant and the heavenly Church. I shall not pursue the subject further here; but the reader will find it well worthy of his calm and prayerful study. We shall close this section with a view of the feast of tabernacles—the last solemnity of the Jewish year.

"And the Lord spake unto Moses, saying, 'Speak unto the children of Israel, saying, The fifteenth day of this seventh month shall be the feast of tabernacles for seven days unto the Lord. . . . Also in the fifteenth day of the seventh month, when ye have gathered in the fruit of the land, ye shall keep a feast unto the Lord seven days: on the first day shall be a Sabbath, and on the eighth shall be a Sabbath. And ye shall take you on the first day the boughs of goodly trees, branches of palm-trees, and boughs of thick trees, and willows of the brook; and ye shall rejoice before the Lord your God seven days. And ye shall keep it a feast unto the Lord seven days in the year: it shall be a statute forever in your generations; ye shall celebrate it in the seventh month. Ye shall dwell in booths seven days: all that are Israelites born shall dwell in booths; that your generations may know that I made the children of Israel to dwell in booths, when I brought them out of the land of Egypt: I am the Lord your God' " (ver. 33-43).

This feast points us forward to the time of Israel's glory in the latter day, and therefore it forms a most lovely and appropriate close to the whole series of feasts. The harvest was gathered in, all was done, the storehouses were amply furnished, and Jehovah would have His people to give expression to their festive joy. But, alas! they seem to have had but little heart to enter into the divine thought in reference to this most delightful ordinance. They lost sight of the fact that they had been strangers and pilgrims, and hence their long neglect of this feast. From the days of Joshua down to the time of Nehemiah, the feast of tabernacles had never once been celebrated. It was reserved for the feeble remnant that returned from the Babylonish captivity to do what had not been done even in the bright days of Solomon. "And all the congregation of them that were come again out of the captivity made booths, and sat under the booths: for since the days of Joshua the son of Nun, unto that day, had not the children of Israel done so. And there was very great gladness" (Neh. 8:17). How refreshing it must have been to those who had hung their harps on the willows of Babylon, to find themselves beneath the shade of the willows of Canaan! It was a sweet foretaste of that time of which the feast of tabernacles was the type, when Israel's restored tribes shall repose within those millennial bowers which the faithful hand of Jehovah will erect for them in the land which He sware to give unto Abraham and to his seed forever. Thrice-happy moment when the heavenly and the earthly shall meet as intimated in "the first day" and "the eighth day" of the feast of tabernacles! "The heavens shall hear the earth, and the earth shall hear the corn and the wine and the oil, and they shall hear Jezreel."

There is a fine passage in the last chapter of Zechariah which goes to prove very distinctly that the true celebration of the feast of tabernacles belongs to the glory of the latter day. "And it shall come to pass that every one that is left of all the nations which came against Jerusalem, shall even go up from year to year to worship the King, the Lord of hosts, and to keep the feast of tabernacles" (chap. 14:16). What a scene! Who would seek to rob it of its characteristic beauty by a vague system of interpretation falsely called spiritualizing? Surely, Jerusalem means Jerusalem, nations mean nations, and the feast of tabernacles means the feast of tabernacles. Is there any thing incredible in this? Surely, nothing, save to man's reason, which rejects all that lies beyond its narrow range. The feast of tabernacles shall yet be celebrated in the land of Canaan, and the nations of the saved shall go up thither to participate in its glorious and hallowed festivities. Jerusalem's warfare shall then be accomplished; the roar of battle shall cease; the sword and the spear shall be transformed into the implements of peaceful agriculture; Israel shall repose beneath the refreshing shade of their vines and fig-trees; and all the earth shall rejoice in the government of "the Prince of Peace." Such is the prospect presented in the unerring pages of inspiration. The types foreshadow it, the prophets prophesy of it, faith believes it, and hope anticipates it.

*Note:* At the close of our chapter we read, "And Moses declared unto the children of Israel *the feasts of the Lord.*" This was their true character, their original title; but in the Gospel of John they are called *"feasts of the Jews."* They had long ceased to be Jehovah's feasts. He was shut out. They did not want Him; and hence, in John 7, when Jesus was asked to go up to *"the Jews' feast of tabernacles,"* He answered, "My time is not yet come"; and when He did go up, it was "privately," to take His place outside of the whole thing, and to call upon every thirsty soul to come unto Him and drink. There is a solemn lesson in this. Divine institutions are speedily marred in the hands of man; but how deeply blessed to know that the thirsty soul that feels the barrenness and drought connected with a scene of empty religious formality, has only to flee to Jesus and drink freely of His exhaustless springs, and so become a channel of blessing to others.

---

## *CHAPTER 24*

THERE is very much to interest the spiritual mind in this brief section. We have seen in chapter 23 the history of the dealings of God with Israel, from the offering up of the true paschal Lamb, until the rest and glory of the millennial kingdom. In the chapter now before us, we have two grand ideas, namely, first, the unfailing record and memorial of the twelve tribes, maintained before God by the power of the Spirit and the efficacy of Christ's priesthood; and secondly, the apostacy of Israel after the flesh, and divine judgment executed thereon. It is the clear apprehension of the former that will enable us to contemplate the latter.

"And the Lord spake unto Moses, saying, 'Command the children of Israel, that they bring unto thee *pure* oil olive, *beaten* for the light, to cause the lamps to burn *continually.* Without the vail of the testimony, in the tabernacle of the congregation, shall Aaron order it *from the evening unto the morning,* before the Lord *continually;* it shall be a statute forever in your generations. He shall order the lamps upon the *pure* candlestick before the Lord *continually*' " (ver. 1-4). The "pure oil" represents the grace of the Holy Spirit, founded upon the work of Christ, as exhibited by the candlestick of "beaten gold." The "olive" was *pressed* to yield the "oil," and the gold was *"beaten"* to form the candlestick. In other words, the grace and light of the Spirit are founded upon the death of Christ, and maintained in clearness and power by the priesthood of Christ. The golden lamp diffused its light throughout the precincts of the sanctuary during the dreary hours of night, when darkness brooded over the nation and all were wrapped in slumber. In all this we have a vivid presentation of God's faithfulness to His people whatever might be their outward condition. Darkness and slumber might settle down upon them, but the lamp was to burn "continually." The high-priest was responsible to keep the steady light of testimony burning during the tedious hours of the night. "Without the vail of the testimony, in the tabernacle of the congregation, shall Aaron order it from the evening unto the morning, before the Lord continually." The maintenance of this light was not left dependent upon Israel: God had provided one whose office it was to look after it and order it continually.

But further, we read, "And thou shalt take fine flour, and bake twelve cakes thereof: two tenth deals shall be in one cake. And thou shalt set them in two rows, six in a row, upon the *pure* table before the Lord. And thou shalt put *pure* frankincense upon each row, that it may be on the bread for a memorial, even an offering made by fire unto the Lord. Every Sabbath he shall set it in order before the Lord *continually,* being taken from the children of Israel by an everlasting covenant. And it shall be Aaron's and his sons'; and they shall eat it in the holy place: for it is most holy unto him of the offerings of the Lord made by fire, by a perpetual statute" (ver. 5-9). There is no mention of leaven in these loaves. They represent, I doubt not, Christ in immediate connection with "the twelve tribes of Israel." They were laid up in the sanctuary before the Lord, on the pure table, for seven days, after which they became the food of Aaron and his sons, furnishing another striking figure of Israel's condition in the view of Jehovah, whatever might be their outward aspect. The twelve tribes are ever before Him. Their memorial can never perish. They are ranged in divine order in the sanctuary, covered with the fragrant incense of Christ, and reflected from the pure table whereon they rest beneath the bright beams of that golden lamp which shines with undimmed lustre through the darkest hour of the nation's moral night.

Now, it is well to see that we are not sacrificing sound judgment or divine truth on the altar of fancy, when we venture to interpret, after such a fashion, the mystic furniture of the sanctuary. We are taught in Hebrews 9 that all these things were "the patterns of things in the heavens;" and again, in Hebrews 10:1, that they were "a shadow of good things to come." We are therefore warranted in believing that there are "things in the heavens" answering to the "patterns" —that there is a substance answering to the "shadow." In a word, we are warranted in believing that there is that "in the heavens" which answers to "the seven lamps," "the pure table," and the "twelve loaves." This is not human imagination, but divine truth, on which faith has fed in all ages. What was the meaning of Elijah's altar of "twelve stones" on the top of Carmel? It was nothing else than the expression of his faith in that truth of which the "twelve loaves" were "the pattern" or "the shadow." He believed in the unbroken unity of the nation, maintained before God in the eternal stability of the promise made to Abraham, Isaac, and Jacob, whatever might be the external condition of the nation. Man might look in vain for the manifested unity of the twelve tribes; but faith could always look within the hallowed inclosure of the sanctuary, and there see the twelve loaves, covered with pure frankincense, ranged in divine order on the pure table; and even though all without were wrapped in midnight's gloomy shades, yet could faith discern, by the light of the *seven* golden lamps, the same grand truth foreshadowed, namely, the indissoluble unity of Israel's twelve tribes.

Thus it was then, and thus it is now. The night is dark and gloomy. There is not, in all this lower world, so much as a single ray by which the human eye can trace the unity of Israel's tribes. They are scattered among the nations, and lost to man's vision; but their memorial is before the Lord. Faith owns this, because it knows that "all the promises of God are yea and amen in Christ Jesus." It sees in the upper sanctuary, by the Spirit's perfect light, the twelve tribes faithfully memorialized. Hearken to the following noble accents of faith: "And now I stand and am judged for the hope of the promise made of God unto our fathers: unto which promise *our twelve tribes,* instantly serving God night and day [νυκτα και ημεραν], hope to come" (Acts 26:6-7). Now, if King Agrippa had asked Paul, Where are the twelve tribes? could he have shown them to him? No. But why not? Was it because they were not to be seen? No; but because Agrippa had not eyes to see them. The twelve tribes lay far beyond the range of Agrippa's vision. It needed the eye of faith and the gracious light of the Spirit of God to be able to discern the twelve loaves, ordered upon the pure table in the sanctuary of God. There they were, and Paul saw them there, though the moment in which he gave utterance to his sublime conviction was as dark as it well could be. Faith is not governed by appearances. It takes its stand upon the lofty rock of God's eternal Word, and, in all the calmness and certainty of that holy elevation, feeds upon the immutable word of Him who cannot lie. Unbelief may stupidly stare about and ask, Where are the twelve tribes? or how can they be found and restored? It is impossible to give an answer. Not because there is no answer to be given, but because unbelief is utterly incapable of rising to the elevated point from which the answer can be seen. Faith is as sure that the memorial of the twelve tribes of Israel is before the eye of Israel's God, as it is that the twelve loaves were laid on the golden table every Sabbath day. But who can convince the skeptic or the infidel of this? who can secure credence for such a truth from those who are governed, in all things, by reason or sense, and know nothing of what it is to hope against hope? Faith finds divine certainties and eternal realities in the midst of a scene where reason and sense can find nothing. Oh for a more profound faith! May we grasp, with more intense earnestness, every word that proceedeth out of the mouth of the Lord, and feed upon it in all the artless simplicity of a little child.

We shall now turn to the second point in our chapter, namely, the apostacy of Israel after the flesh, and the divine judgment thereon.

"And the son of an Israelitish woman, whose father was an Egyptian, went out among the children of Israel: and this son of an Israelitish woman and a man of Israel strove together in the camp; and the Israelitish woman's son blasphemed the name of the LORD, and cursed. And they brought him unto Moses . . . and they put him in ward, that the mind of the Lord might be showed them. And the Lord spake unto Moses, saying, 'Bring forth him that hath cursed without the camp; and let all that heard him lay their hands upon his head, and let all the congregation stone him.' . . . And Moses spake to the children of Israel, that they should bring forth him that had cursed out of the camp, and stone him with stones. And the children of Israel did as the Lord commanded Moses" (ver. 10-23).

The peculiar place assigned by the inspired penman to this narrative is striking and interesting. I have no doubt whatever but that it is designed to give us the opposite side of the picture presented in the opening verses of the chapter. Israel after the flesh has grievously failed, and sinned against Jehovah; the name of the Lord has been blasphemed amongst the Gentiles; wrath has come upon the nation; the judgments of an offended God have fallen upon them; but the day is coming when the dark and heavy cloud of judgment shall roll away, and then shall the twelve tribes, in their unbroken unity, stand forth before all the nations as the amazing monument of Jehovah's faithfulness and loving-kindness. "And in that day thou shalt say, O Lord, I will praise Thee; though Thou wast angry with me, Thine anger is turned away, and Thou comfortedst me. Behold, God is my salvation; I will trust, and not be afraid: for the Lord JEHOVAH is my strength and my song, He also is become my salvation. Therefore with joy shall ye draw water out of the wells of salvation. And in that day shall ye say, Praise the Lord, call upon His name, declare His doings among the people, make mention that His name is exalted. Sing unto the Lord; for He hath done excellent things: this is known in all the earth. Cry out and shout, thou inhabitant of Zion; for great is the Holy One of Israel in the midst of thee" (Isa. 12). "For I would not, brethren, that ye should be ignorant of this mystery, lest ye should be wise in your own conceits, that blindness in part is happened to Israel, until the fullness of the Gentiles be come in. And so all Israel shall be saved: as it is written, 'There shall come out of Sion the Deliverer, and shall turn away ungodliness from Jacob. For this is My covenant unto them, when I shall take away their sins.' As concerning the gospel, they are enemies for your sakes; but as touching the election, they are beloved for the fathers' sakes. For the gifts and calling of God are without repentance. For as ye in times past have not believed God, yet have now obtained mercy through their unbelief; even so have these also now not believed in your mercy, that they also may obtain mercy. For God hath concluded them all in unbelief, that He might have mercy upon all. O the depth of the riches both of the wisdom and knowledge of God! how unsearchable are His judgments, and His ways past finding out! For who hath known the mind of the Lord? or who hath been His counselor? or who hath first given to Him, and it shall be recompensed to him again? For of Him and through Him and to Him are all things; to whom be glory forever. Amen" (Rom. 11:25-36).

Passages might be multiplied to prove that though Israel is suffering the divine judgment because of sin, yet "the gifts and calling of God are without repentance"—that though the blasphemer is being stoned without the camp, the twelve loaves are undisturbed within the sanctuary. "The voices of the prophets" declare, and the voices of apostles re-echo the glorious truth that "all Israel shall be saved;" not because they have not sinned, but because "the gifts and calling of God are without repentance." Let Christians beware how they tamper with "the promises made unto the fathers." If these promises be explained away or misapplied, it must necessarily weaken our moral sense of the divine integrity and accuracy of Scripture as a whole. If one part may be explained away, so may another; if one passage may be vaguely interpreted, so any another; and thus it would come to pass that we should be deprived of all that blessed certainty which constitutes the foundation of our repose in reference to all that the Lord hath spoken. But more of this as we dwell upon the remaining chapters of our book.

---

## *CHAPTER 25*

THE intelligent reader will discern a strong moral link between this and the preceding chapter. In chapter 24 we learn that the house of Israel is preserved for the land of Canaan; in chapter 25, we learn that the land of Canaan is preserved for the house of Israel. Taking both together, we have the record of a truth which no power of earth or hell can obliterate—"All Israel shall be saved," and "the land shall not be sold forever." The former of these statements enunciates a principle which has stood like a rock amid the ocean of conflicting interpretations, while the latter declares a fact which many nations of the uncircumcised have sought in vain to ignore.

The reader will observe the peculiar way in which our chapter opens: "And the Lord spake unto Moses *in Mount Sinai.*" The principal part of the communications contained in the book of Leviticus is characterized by the fact of its emanating "from the tabernacle of the congregation." This is easily accounted for. Those communications have special reference to the service, communion, and worship of the priests, or to the moral condition of the people, and hence they are issued, as might be expected, from "the tabernacle of the congregation," that grand centre of all that appertained in any way to priestly service. Here, however, the communication is made from quite a different point. "The Lord spake unto Moses *in Mount Sinai.*" Now, we know that every expression in Scripture has its own special meaning, and we are justified in expecting a different line of communication from "Mount Sinai" from that which reaches us from "the tabernacle of the congregation." And so it is. The chapter at which we have now arrived treats of Jehovah's claims as Lord of all the earth. It is not the worship and communion of a priestly house, or the internal ordering of the nation; but the claims of God in government, His right to give a certain portion of the earth to a certain people to hold as tenants under Him. In a word, it is not to Jehovah in "the tabernacle"—the place of *worship;* but Jehovah in "Mount Sinai"—the place of *government.*

"And the Lord spake unto Moses in Mount Sinai, saying, 'Speak unto the children of Israel, and say unto them, When ye come into the land which I give you, then shall the land keep a Sabbath unto the Lord. Six years thou shalt sow thy field, and six years thou shalt prune thy vineyard. That which groweth of its own accord of thy harvest thou shalt not reap, neither gather the grapes of thy vine undressed; for it is a year of rest unto the land. And the Sabbath of the land shall be meat for you; for thee, and for thy servant, and for thy maid, and for thy hired servant, and for thy stranger that sojourneth with thee, and for thy cattle, and for the beast that are in thy land, shall all the increase thereof be meat' " (ver. 1-7).

Here, then, we have the special feature of the Lord's land. He would have it to enjoy a sabbatic year, and in that year there was to be the evidence of the rich profusion with which He would bless those who held as tenants under Him. Happy, highly privileged tenantry! What an honor to hold immediately under Jehovah! No rent! no taxes! no burdens! Well might it be said, "Happy is the people that is in such a case; yea, happy is the nation whose God is Jehovah." We know, alas! that Israel failed to take full possession of that wealthy land of which Jehovah made them a present. He had given it *all;* He had given it *forever.* They took but *a part,* and that *for a time.* Still, there it is. The property is there, though the tenants are ejected for the present. "The land shall not be sold *forever:* for *the land is Mine;* for ye are strangers and sojourners *with Me.*" What does this mean, but that Canaan belongs specially to Jehovah, and that He will hold it through the tribes of Israel? True, "the earth is the Lord's," but that is quite another thing. It is plain that He has been pleased, for His own unsearchable purposes, to take special possession of the land of Canaan, and to submit that land to a peculiar line of treatment, to mark it off from all other lands, by calling it His own, and to distinguish it by judgments and ordinances and periodical solemnities, the mere contemplation of which enlightens the understanding and affects the heart.

Where, throughout all the earth, do we read of a land enjoying a year of unbroken repose—a year of richest abundance? The rationalist may ask, How can these things be? the skeptic may doubt if they could be; but faith finds a satisfying answer from the lips of Jehovah—"And if ye shall say, What shall we eat the seventh year? behold, we shall not sow, nor gather in our increase: then I will command My blessing upon you in the sixth year, and it shall bring forth fruit for three years. And ye shall sow the eighth year, and eat yet of old fruit until the ninth year; until her fruits come in ye shall eat of the old store" (ver. 20-22). Nature might say, What shall we do for *our sowing?* God's answer is, "I will command *My blessing.*" God's "blessing" is better far than man's "sowing." He was not going to let them starve in His sabbatic year. They were to feed upon the fruits of His blessing, while they celebrated His year of rest—a year which pointed forward to that eternal Sabbath that remains for the people of God.

"And thou shalt number seven Sabbaths of years unto thee, seven times seven years; and the space of the seven Sabbaths of years shall be unto thee forty and nine years. Then shalt thou cause the trumpet of the jubilee to sound on the tenth day of the seventh month; in the day of atonement shall ye make the trumpet sound throughout all your land" (ver. 8-9). It is peculiarly interesting to note the various methods in which the millennial rest was held up to view in the Jewish economy. Every seventh day was a sabbatic day; every seventh year was a sabbatic year; and every seven times seven years there was a jubilee. Each and all of these typical solemnities held up to the vision of faith the blessed prospect of a time when labor and sorrow should cease; when "the sweat of the brow" would no longer be needed to satisfy the cravings of hunger; but when a millennial earth, enriched by the copious showers of divine grace, and fertilized by the bright beams of the Sun of righteousness, should pour its abundance into the storehouse and wine-press of the people of God. Happy time! happy people! How blessed to be assured that these things are not the pencilings of imagination or the flights of fancy, but the substantial verities of divine revelation, to be enjoyed by faith, which is "the substance of things hoped for, the conviction of things not seen."

Of all the Jewish solemnities the jubilee would seem to have been the most soul-stirring and enrapturing. It stood immediately connected with the great day of atonement. It was when the blood of the victim was shed that the emancipating sound of the jubilee trump was heard through the hills and valleys of the land of Canaan. That longed-for note was designed to wake up the nation from the very centre of its moral being—to stir the deepest depths of the soul, and to send a shining river of divine and ineffable joy through the length and breadth of the land. "In the day of atonement shall ye make the trumpet sound throughout *all* your land." Not a corner was to remain unvisited by "the joyful sound." The aspect of the jubilee was as wide as the aspect of the atonement on which the jubilee was based.

"And ye shall hallow the fiftieth year, and proclaim liberty throughout all the land unto all the inhabitants thereof: it shall be a jubilee unto you; and ye shall return every man unto his possession, and ye shall return every man unto his family. A jubilee shall that fiftieth year be unto you: ye shall not sow, neither reap that which groweth of itself in it, nor gather the grapes in it of thy vine undressed. For it is the jubilee; it shall be holy unto you: ye shall eat the increase thereof out of the field. In the year of this jubilee ye shall return every man unto his possession" (ver. 8-13). All estates and conditions of the people were permitted to feel the hallowed and refreshing influence of this most noble institution. The exile returned; the captive was emancipated; the debtor set free; each family opened its bosom to receive once more its long-lost members; each inheritance received back its exiled owner. The sound of the trumpet was the welcome and soul-stirring signal for the captive to escape, for the slave to cast aside the chains of his bondage, for the man-slayer to return to his home, for the ruined and poverty-stricken to rise to the possession of their forfeited inheritance. No sooner had the trumpet's thrice-welcome sound fallen upon the ear than the mighty tide of blessing rose majestically and sent its refreshing undulations into the most remote corners of Jehovah's highly favored land.

"And if thou sell aught unto thy neighbor, or buyest aught of thy neighbor's hand, ye shall not oppress one another: according to the number of years after the jubilee thou shalt buy of thy neighbor, and according unto the number of years of the fruits he shall sell unto thee. According to the multitude of years thou shalt increase the price thereof, and according to the fewness of years thou shalt diminish the price of it; for according to the number of the years of the fruits doth he sell unto thee. Ye shall not therefore oppress one another; but thou shalt fear thy God: for I am the Lord your God" (ver. 14-17). The year of jubilee reminded both buyer and seller that the land belonged to Jehovah and was not to be sold. "The fruits" might be sold, but that was all: Jehovah could never give up the land to any one. It is important to get this point well fixed in the mind; it may open up a very extensive line of truth. If the land of Canaan is not to be sold—if Jehovah declares it to be His forever, then for whom does He want it? who is to hold it under Him? Those to whom He gave it by an everlasting covenant, that they might have it in possession as long as the moon endureth—even to all generations.

There is no spot in all the earth like unto the land of Canaan in the divine estimation. There Jehovah set up His throne and His sanctuary; there His priests stood to minister continually before Him; there the voices of His prophets were heard testifying of present ruin and future restoration and glory; there the Baptist began, continued, and ended his career as the forerunner of the Messiah; there the blessed One was born of a woman; there He was baptized; there He preached and taught; there He labored and died; from thence He ascended in triumph to the right hand of God; thither God the Holy Ghost descended, in Pentecostal power; from thence the overflowing tide of gospel testimony emanated to the ends of the earth; thither the Lord of glory will descend ere long, and plant His foot "on the Mount of Olives;" there His throne will be re-established and His worship restored. In a word, His eyes and His heart are there continually; its dust is precious in His sight; it is the centre of all His thoughts and operations as touching this earth; and it is His purpose to make it an eternal excellency, the joy of many generations.

It is, then, I repeat, immensely important to get a firm hold of this interesting line of truth with respect to the land of Canaan. Of that land Jehovah hath said, *"It is Mine."* Who shall take it from Him? Where is the king or the emperor—where the power, human or diabolical, that can wrest "the pleasant land" out of Jehovah's omnipotent grasp? True, it has been a bone of contention, an apple of discord, to the nations. It has been, and it will yet be, the scene and centre of cruel war and bloodshed. But far above all the din of battle and the strife of nations, these words fall with divine clearness, fullness, and power upon the ear of faith: *"The land is Mine!"* Jehovah can never give up the land, nor those "twelve tribes" through whom He is to inherit it forever. Let my reader think of this; let him ponder it deeply; let him guard against all looseness of thought and vagueness of interpretation as to this subject. God hath not cast away His people, or the land which He sware to give unto them for an everlasting possession. "The twelve loaves" of Leviticus 24 bear witness to the former, and "the jubilee" of Leviticus 25 bears witness to the latter. The memorial of the "twelve tribes of Israel" is ever before the Lord, and the moment is rapidly approaching when the trump of jubilee shall be heard upon the mountains of Palestine. Then, in reality, the captive shall cast off the ignominious chain which for ages has bound him; then shall the exile return to that happy home from which he has so long been banished; then shall every debt be canceled, every burden removed, and every tear wiped away. "For thus saith the Lord, 'Behold, I will extend peace to her [Jerusalem] like a river, and the glory of the Gentiles like a flowing stream: then shall ye suck, ye shall be borne upon her sides, and be dandled upon her knees. As one whom his mother comforteth, so will I comfort you; and ye shall be comforted in Jerusalem. And when ye see this, your heart shall rejoice, and your bones shall flourish like an herb; and the hand of the Lord shall be known toward His servants, and His indignation toward His enemies. For, behold, the Lord will come with fire, and with His chariots like a whirlwind, to render His anger with fury, and His rebuke with flames of fire. For by fire and by His sword will the Lord plead with all flesh: and the slain of the Lord shall be many. . . . For I know their works and their thoughts; it shall come that I will gather all nations and tongues; and they shall come and see My glory. And I will set a sign among them, and I will send those that escape of them unto the nations, to Tarshish, Pul, and Lud, that draw the bow, to Tubal and Javan, to the isles afar off, that have not heard My fame, neither have seen My glory; and they shall declare My glory among the Gentiles. And they shall bring all your brethren for an offering unto the Lord, out of all nations, upon horses, and in chariots, and in litters, and upon mules, and upon swift beasts, to My holy mountain Jerusalem, saith the Lord, as the children of Israel bring an offering in a clean vessel into the house of the Lord. And I will also take of them for priests and for Levites, saith the Lord. For as the new heavens and the new earth, which I will make, shall remain before Me, saith the Lord, so shall your seed and your name remain. And it shall come to pass, that from one new moon to another, and from one Sabbath to another, shall all flesh come to worship before Me, saith the Lord' " (Isaiah 66:12-23).

Now let us look for a moment at the practical effect of the jubilee—its influence upon the transactions between man and man.—"And if thou sell aught unto thy neighbor, or buyest aught of thy neighbor's hand, ye shall not oppress one another. According to the number of years after the jubilee thou shalt buy of thy neighbor, and according to the number of years of the fruits he shall sell unto thee." The scale of prices was to be regulated by the jubilee. If that glorious event were at hand, the price was low; if far off, the price was high. All human compacts as to land were broken up the moment the trump of jubilee was heard, for the land was Jehovah's; and the jubilee brought all back to its normal condition.

This teaches us a fine lesson. If our hearts are cherishing the abiding hope of the Lord's return, we shall set light by all earthly things. It is morally impossible that we can be in the attitude of waiting for the Son from heaven, and not be detached from this present world. "Let your moderation be known unto all men: the Lord is at hand" (Phil. 4). A person may hold "the doctrine of the millennium," as it is called, or the doctrine of "the second advent," and be a thorough man of the world; but one who lives in the habitual expectation of Christ's appearing must be separated from that which will be judged and broken up when He comes. It is not a question of the shortness and uncertainty of human life, which is quite true; or of the transitory and unsatisfying character of the things of time, which is equally true. It is far more potent and influential than either or both of these,—it is this: *"The Lord is at hand."* May our hearts be affected and our conduct in all things influenced by this most precious and sanctifying truth.

---

## *CHAPTER 26*

THIS chapter requires little in the way of note or exposition. It contains a most solemn and affecting record of the blessings of obedience on the one hand, and the terrible consequences of disobedience on the other. Had Israel walked in obedience, they would have been invincible. "I will give peace in the land, and ye shall lie down, and none shall make you afraid; and I will rid evil beasts out of the land, neither shall the sword go through your land. And ye shall chase your enemies, and they shall fall before you by the sword. And five of you shall chase a hundred, and a hundred of you shall put ten thousand to flight; and your enemies shall fall before you by the sword. For I will have respect unto you, and make you fruitful, and multiply you, and establish My covenant with you. And ye shall eat old store, and bring forth the old because of the new. And I will set My tabernacle among you; and My soul shall not abhor you. And I will walk among you, and will be your God, and ye shall be My people. I am the Lord your God, which brought you forth out of the land of Egypt, that ye should not be their bondsmen; and I have broken the bands of your yoke, and made you go upright" (ver. 6-13).

The presence of God should ever have been their shield and buckler. No weapon formed against them could prosper. But then the divine presence was only to be enjoyed by an obedient people. Jehovah could not sanction by His presence disobedience or wickedness. The uncircumcised nations around might depend upon their prowess and their military resources: Israel had only the arm of Jehovah to depend upon, and that arm could never be stretched forth to shield unholiness or disobedience. Their strength was, to walk with God in a spirit of dependence and obedience. So long as they walked thus, there was a wall of fire round about them, to protect them from every enemy and every evil.

But, alas! Israel failed altogether. Notwithstanding the solemn and appalling picture placed before their eyes, in verses 14-33 of this chapter, they forsook the Lord and served other gods, and thus brought upon themselves the sore judgments threatened in this section, the bare record of which is sufficient to make the ears tingle. Under the heavy weight of these judgments they are suffering at this very hour. Scattered and peeled, wasted and outcast, they are the monuments of Jehovah's inflexible truth and justice. They read aloud, to all the nations of the earth, a most impressive lesson on the subject of the moral government of God—a lesson which it would be profitable for these nations to study deeply—yea, and a lesson which it would be salutary for our own hearts to ponder likewise.

We are very prone to confound two things which are clearly distinguished in the Word, namely, God's *government* and God's *grace.* The evils which result from this confusion are various. It is sure to lead to an enfeebled sense of the dignity and solemnity of government, and of the purity, fullness, and elevation of grace. It is quite true that God in government reserves to Himself the sovereign right to act in patience, long-suffering, and mercy; but the exercise of these attributes, in connection with His throne of government, must never be confounded with the unconditional actings of pure and absolute grace.

The chapter before us is a record of divine government, and yet, in it we find such clauses as the following: "If they shall confess their iniquity, and the iniquity of their fathers, with their trespass which they trespassed against Me; and that also they have walked contrary unto Me, and that I also have walked contrary unto them, and have brought them into the land of their enemies; if then their uncircumcised hearts be humbled, and they then accept of the punishment of their iniquity: then will I remember My covenant with Jacob, and also My covenant with Isaac, and also My covenant with Abraham will I remember; and I will remember the land. The land also shall be left of them, and shall enjoy her Sabbaths, while she lieth desolate without them; and they shall accept of the punishment of their iniquity: because, even because they despised My judgments, and because their soul abhorred My statutes. And yet, for all that, when they be in the land of their enemies, I will not cast them away, neither will I abhor them, to destroy them utterly, and to break My covenant with them; for I am the Lord their God. But I will for their sakes remember the covenant of their ancestors, whom I brought forth out of the land of Egypt in the sight of the heathen, that I might be their God: I am the Lord" (ver. 40-45).

Here we find God in government, meeting, in long-suffering mercy, the very earliest and faintest breathings of a broken and penitent spirit. The history of the judges and of the kings presents many instances of the exercise of this blessed attribute of the divine government. Again and again the soul of Jehovah was grieved for Israel (Judges 10:16), and He sent them one deliverer after another, until at length there remained no hope, and the righteous claims of His throne demanded their expulsion from that land which they were wholly incompetent to keep.

All this is *government.* But by and by, Israel will be brought into possession of the land of Canaan on the ground of unqualified and unchangeable *grace*—grace exercised in divine righteousness, through the blood of the cross. It will not be by works of law, nor yet by the institutions of an evanescent economy, but by that grace which "reigns through righteousness, by Jesus Christ our Lord." Wherefore, they shall never again be driven forth from their possession. No enemy shall ever molest them. They shall enjoy undisturbed repose behind the shield of Jehovah's favor. Their tenure of the land will be according to the eternal stability of divine grace and the efficacy of the blood of the everlasting covenant. "They shall be saved in the Lord with an everlasting salvation"

May the Spirit of God lead us into more enlarged apprehensions of divine truth, and endow us with a greater capacity to try the things that differ, and rightly to divide the Word of truth.

---

## *CHAPTER 27*

THIS closing section of our book treats of the "singular vow," or the voluntary act whereby a person devoted himself or his property unto the Lord. "And the Lord spake unto Moses, saying, 'Speak unto the children of Israel, and say unto them, When a man shall make a singular vow, the persons shall be for the Lord by thy estimation. And thy estimation shall be . . . after the shekel of the sanctuary.' "

Now, in the case of a person devoting himself or his beast, his house or his field, unto the Lord, it was obviously a question of capacity or worth; and hence there was a certain scale of valuation, according to age. Moses, as the representative of the claims of God, was called upon to estimate, in each case, according to the standard of the sanctuary. If a man undertakes to make a vow, he must be tried by the standard of righteousness; and, moreover, in all cases, we are called upon to recognize the difference between *capacity* and *title.* In Exodus 30:15, we read, in reference to the atonement money, "The rich shall not give more, and the poor shall not give less, than half a shekel, when they give an offering unto the Lord, to make an atonement for your souls." In the matter of atonement, all stood upon one common level. Thus it must ever be. High and low, rich and poor, learned and ignorant, old and young—all have one common title. "There is no difference." All stand alike on the ground of the infinite preciousness of the blood of Christ. There may be a vast difference as to capacity; as to title, there is none: there may be a vast difference as to experience; as to title, there is none: there may be a vast difference as to knowledge, gift, and fruitfulness; as to title, there is none. The sapling and the tree, the babe and the father, the convert of yesterday and the matured believer, are all on the same ground. "The rich shall not give more, and the poor shall not give less." Nothing more could be given; nothing less could be taken.

"We have boldness to enter into the holiest by the blood of Jesus." This is our title to enter. Our capacity to worship, when we have entered, will depend upon our spiritual energy. Christ is our title: the Holy Ghost is our capacity. Self has nothing to do with either the one or the other. What a mercy! We get in by the blood of Jesus; we enjoy what we find there by the Holy Ghost. The blood of Jesus opens the door; the Holy Ghost conducts us through the house: the blood of Jesus opens the casket; the Holy Ghost unfolds the precious contents: the blood of Jesus makes the casket ours; the Holy Ghost enables us to appreciate its rare and costly gems.

But in Leviticus 27 it is entirely a question of ability, capacity, or worth. Moses had a certain standard, from which he could not possibly descend; he had a certain rule, from which he could not possibly swerve. If any one could come up to that, well; if not, he had to take his place accordingly.

What, then, was to be done in reference to the person who was unable to rise to the height of the claims set forth by the representative of divine righteousness? Hear the consolatory answer—"But if he be *poorer* than thy estimation, then he shall present himself before *the priest*, and the priest shall value him; *according to his ability* that vowed shall the priest value him" (ver. 8). In other words, if it be a question of man's undertaking to meet the claims of *righteousness,* then he must meet them; but if, on the other hand, a man feels himself wholly unable to meet those claims, he has only to fall back upon *grace,* which will take him up just as he is. Moses is the representative of the claims of divine righteousness: the priest is the exponent of the provisions of divine grace. The poor man who was unable to stand before Moses, fell back into the arms of the priest. Thus it is ever. If we cannot *"dig,"* we can *"beg;"* and directly we take the place of beggar, it is no longer a question of what we are able to *earn,* but of what God is pleased to *give.*

Grace all the work shall crown
Through everlasting days.

How happy it is to be debtors to grace! how happy to take, when God is glorified in giving! When man is in question, it is infinitely better to dig than to beg; but when God is in question, the case is the very reverse.

I would just add that I believe this entire chapter bears, in an especial manner, upon the nation of Israel. It is intimately connected with the two preceding chapters. Israel made "a singular vow" at the foot of Mount Horeb; but they were quite unable to meet the claims of law—they were far "poorer than Moses' estimation." But, blessed be God, they will come in under the rich provisions of divine grace. Having learnt their total inability "to dig," they will not be "ashamed to beg"; and hence they shall experience the deep blessedness of being cast upon the sovereign mercy of Jehovah, which stretches, like a golden chain, "from everlasting to everlasting." It is well to be poor, when the knowledge of our poverty serves but to unfold to us the exhaustless riches of divine grace. That grace can never suffer any one to go empty away. It can never tell any one that he is too poor. It can meet the very deepest human need; and not only so, but it is glorified in meeting it. This holds good in every case. It is true of any individual sinner, and it is true with respect to Israel, who, having been valued by the lawgiver, have proved "poorer than his estimation." Grace is the grand and only resource for all. It is the basis of our salvation, the basis of a life of practical godliness, and the basis of those imperishable hopes which animate us amid the trials and conflicts of this sin-stricken world. May we cherish a deeper sense of grace, and more ardent desire for the glory.

We shall here close our meditations upon this most profound and precious book. If the foregoing pages should be used of God to awaken an interest in a section of inspiration which has been so much neglected by the Church in all ages, they shall not have been written in vain.

# NOTES

*on the book of*

# NUMBERS

*"So He led them through the depths,*
*as through the wilderness"*

## *PREFACE*

HAVING read the proof-sheets of the following *Notes on Numbers,* I am prepared, so far, to write a preface. It is with no view of praising the book that I do so, but to show my fellowship with the well-known author in all his labors. The book will speak for itself, and the reader must judge.

After twelve years of joint-editorship in the monthly issue of *"Things New and Old,"* the reader will not be surprised at this mutual love of identification in sending forth another volume of *Notes.* But for this, there is no reason why I should appear.

We will now glance for a moment at the *character* of the book of Numbers. Fuller details will be found in the *Notes*.

It may be regarded as a divine history of the wanderings of the Israelites in the wilderness for about thirty-eight years and ten months, commencing with the first movement of the camp after the tabernacle was reared; and also as a perpetual memorial of Jehovah's patient, tender, and unwearied care of His murmuring and rebellious people. It is emphatically a wilderness book, and characterized by journeyings, service, and all the vicissitudes of wilderness life. As such, it is deeply interesting, most instructive, and easily applied to the Christian in this present evil world (compare Numbers 1 and 36:13 with Deuteronomy 1:3).

The first thing that attracts our attention in reading the book, is sweet and precious to the heart beyond all expression—*God has His people numbered and gathered around Himself.* He dwelt in the camp—*"In the midst whereof I dwell."* Could love do more? Impossible! The twelve tribes guarded the tabernacle of the Lord. The Levites encamped directly around the court; and Moses, Aaron, and the priests guarded the entrance whereby God was approached. The circumference of the camp, thus arranged, and all facing the tabernacle, is generally supposed to have been at least twelve miles. But that which gave unity, strength, and glory to the camp in the wilderness, was the presence of God in His tabernacle, as the centre of His chosen people. Blessed shadow of good things to come—of Christ as the centre, life, and glory of His Church now!

Rather more than a year from the epoch of the Exodus, Jehovah commanded Moses to number the people that were able to bear arms, from twenty years old and upwards. The tribe of Levi, being exempt from military service, was numbered separately. But the complete number, *twelve,* was made up by the division of Joseph into Ephraim and Manasseh (chapters 1,2,3).

Every thing was now in its right place, and every one knew for certain what he had to do, both when the cloud moved and when it rested. The tabernacle set up, the priests consecrated, the people numbered, they were now to leave Horeb. "The Lord God spake unto us in Horeb, saying, 'Ye have dwelt long enough in this mount.' " "And it came to pass on the twentieth day of the second month, in the second year, that the cloud was taken up from off the tabernacle of the testimony. And the children of Israel took their journeys out of the wilderness of Sinai; and the cloud rested in the wilderness of Paran" (Deut. 1:6; Num. 10:11-12).

The pillar of cloud by day, and the pillar of fire by night, guided all the movements of the camp (Num. 9:17-23). The moment the cloud ascended from off the tabernacle, the silver trumpets sounded the alarm, and the whole camp was instantly in motion. Then Moses uttered the prayer, "Rise up, Lord, and let Thine enemies be scattered; and let them that hate Thee flee before Thee." When the cloud rested, the whole camp rested, and every man knew his place and his work. And then Moses prayed, "Return, O Lord, unto the many thousands of Israel" (Num. 10:35-36).

How imposing to the outward eye the sight of this great camp must have been in the midst of the desert! Well might Balaam say, "How goodly are thy tents, O Jacob, and thy tabernacles, O Israel!" But its true loveliness is only seen by the eye of faith. It was the brightest spot in the world, though on the sand of the desert, and the richest in blessing. Far, far above all its other attractions is the knowledge that God Himself is there, thinking of every one and providing for their every need. Day by day, He spread a table for them in the wilderness, and gave them water from the flinty rock. The foot of the traveler was never swollen, and his raiment waxed not old these forty years (Deut. 8:4).

There were upwards of six hundred thousand men above the age of twenty, besides the Levites and women and children, probably more than two millions altogether. But Jehovah gathered them all around Himself, as a father would gather his children, and covered them with the skirts of His cloud, both by night and by day. "He spread a cloud for a covering; and fire to give light in the night" (Ps. 105:39). Thus was the Lord's family in the place of rest, peace, and blessing. The blood of the everlasting covenant had been sprinkled on the mercy-seat within the vail, and judgment had been executed on the sin-offering outside the camp. God was now a wall of fire around His people, and the glory in the midst of them. Oh that Israel had known—oh that Israel had understood the loving-kindness of the Lord, and so put all their trust in Him (see Deut. 32—33)!

In the position and service of the Levites there is always much that is interesting to the Christian. They were typical of the Church (or of the individual Christian) in service, just as the priests were typical of the Church in worship. The fact of the Levites being taken for the service of the Lord in place of the first-born, gave them a very special character. They were first-fruits unto the Lord. Thus it is that the Church is, as the first-fruits, holy to the Lord—"the church of the first-born ones" (Jas. 1; Heb. 12).

As the Levites thus became God's possession for service, and belonged wholly to Him, so it is with the Church. We are redeemed—we are not our own—we are bought with a price; therefore we are to glorify God in our bodies and in our spirits, which are His. We are to serve the living God, in communion with Christ our great High-Priest above. The calling of the Church, however, is a much higher thing than the position of the Levites; for she is one with Christ, and the Holy Ghost gives the capacity and the gift for Christian service.

In conclusion, we may safely affirm that there is no truth in Christianity of such importance, or of such practical power, as the blessed truth of the Church's relationship to Christ. "For in Him dwelleth all the fullness of the Godhead bodily. And ye are complete in Him, which is the head of all principality and power" (Col. 2:9-10). We can only be men of war, worshiping priests, serving Levites, in the highest and truest sense, in the proportion that we live in the power of this great truth. We are joined to the Lord by the one Spirit; our life is hid with Christ in God. May we be content to be the Lord's hidden ones as to this world, and only to be seen and known as His servants, until He come, then shall we also appear with Him in glory.

May the Lord accompany with His own rich blessing, and clothe with His own divine power, this volume of *Notes on Numbers;* and may He accept it as service to Himself, and use it for His own glory, and to His name alone be undivided praise. Amen.

*London, Dec.* 1, 1869. *A.M.*

# NOTES

## *on*

# *THE BOOK OF NUMBERS*

---

## *CHAPTERS 1–2*

WE now enter upon the study of the fourth grand division of the Pentateuch, or five books of Moses; and we shall find the leading characteristic of this book quite as strongly marked as that of any of the three books which have already engaged our attention. In the book of Genesis, after the record of creation, the deluge, and the Babel dispersion, we have God's election of the seed of Abraham; in the book of Exodus, we have redemption; Leviticus gives us priestly worship and communion; in Numbers, we have the walk and warfare of the wilderness. Such are the prominent subjects of these most precious sections of inspiration, while, as might be expected, many other points of deepest interest are collaterally introduced. The Lord, in His great mercy, has led us through the study of Genesis, Exodus, and Leviticus; and we can reckon on Him with confidence to conduct us through the book of Numbers. May His Spirit lead the thoughts and guide the pen, so that not a sentence may be committed to writing that is not in strict accordance with His holy mind. May every page and every paragraph bear the stamp of His approval, and be at once conducive to His glory and the permanent profit of the reader.

"And the Lord spake unto Moses *in the wilderness* of Sinai, in the tabernacle of the congregation, on the first day of the second month, in the second year after they were come out of the land of Egypt, saying, 'Take ye the sum of all the congregation of the children of Israel, after their families, by the house of their fathers, with the number of their names, every male by their polls; from twenty years old and upward, all that are *able to go forth to war* in Israel; thou and Aaron shall number them by their armies' " (chap. 1:1-3).

Here we find ourselves at once "in the wilderness," where those only are to be taken account of who are "able to go forth to war." This is strongly marked. In the book of Genesis, the seed of Israel were in the loins of their father Abraham; in the book of Exodus, they were in the brick-kilns of Egypt; in Leviticus, they were gathered around the tabernacle of the congregation; in Numbers, they are seen in the wilderness. Then, again, in full keeping with above, and in confirmation thereof, in Genesis, we hearken to the call of God in election; in Exodus, we gaze upon the blood of the lamb in redemption; in Leviticus, we are almost entirely occupied with the worship and service of the sanctuary; but no sooner have we opened the book of Numbers than we read of men of war, of armies, of standards, of camps, and trumpets sounding alarm.

All this is highly characteristic, and marks off the book on which we are now entering as one of special interest, value, and importance to the Christian. Each book of the Bible, each section of the inspired canon, has its own distinct place and object: each has its own niche assigned to it by its divine Author. We must not entertain for a moment the thought of instituting any comparison in point of intrinsic value, interest, and importance. All is divine, and therefore perfect. The Christian reader fully and heartily believes this. He reverently sets his seal to the truth of the plenary inspiration of holy Scripture—of all Scripture, and of the Pentateuch amongst the rest; nor is he to be moved one hair's breadth from this by the bold and impious attacks of infidels, ancient, mediaeval, or modern. Infidels and rationalists may traffic in their unhallowed reasonings; they may exhibit their enmity against the book and its Author; but the pious Christian rests, notwithstanding all, in the simple and happy belief that "all Scripture is given by inspiration of God."

But while we must utterly reject the idea of any comparison as to authority and value, we may, with very much profit, compare the contents, design, and scope of the various books of the Bible. And the more profoundly we meditate upon these, the more forcibly shall we be struck with the exquisite beauty, infinite wisdom, and wonderful precision of the volume as a whole, and of each distinct division thereof. The inspired writer never swerves from the direct object of the book, whatever that object may be. You will never find aught in any one book of the Bible which is not in the most perfect harmony with the main design of that book. To prove and illustrate this statement would lead us through the entire canon of holy Scripture, and hence we shall not attempt it. The intelligent Christian does not need the proof, however much he might be interested in the illustration. He takes his stand upon the great fact that the book as a whole, and in all its parts, is from God; and his heart reposes in the conclusion that in that whole, and in each of those parts, there is not a jot or a tittle which is not in every way worthy of the divine Author.

Hear the following words from the pen of one who expresses himself as "deeply convinced of the divine inspiration of the Scriptures, given to us of God, and confirmed in this conviction by daily and growing discoveries of their fullness, depth, and perfectness, ever more sensible, through grace, of the admirable perfection of the parts, and the wonderful connection of the whole": "The Scriptures," says this writer, "have a living source, and living power has pervaded their composition: hence their infiniteness of bearing, and the impossibility of separating any one part from its connection with whole, because one God is the living centre from which all flows; one Christ the living centre around which all its truth circles, and to which it refers, though in various glory; and one Spirit the divine sap which carries its power from its source in God to the minutest branches of the all-uniting truth, testifying of the glory, the grace, and the truth of Him whom God sets forth as the object and centre and head of all that is in connection with Himself, of Him who is, withal, God over all, blessed for evermore. . . . The more—beginning from the utmost leaves and branches of this revelation of the mind of God, by which we have been reached when far from Him—we have traced it up towards its centre, and thence looked down again towards its extent and diversity, the more we learn its infiniteness, and our own feebleness of apprehension. We learn, blessed be God, this, that the love which is its source is found in unmingled perfectness and fullest display of those manifestations of it which have reached us even in our ruined state. The same perfect God of love is in it all. But the unfoldings of divine wisdom in the counsels in which God has displayed Himself, remain ever to us a subject of research, in which every new discovery, by increasing our spiritual intelligence, makes the infiniteness of the whole, and the way in which it surpasses all our thoughts, only more and more clear to us."

It is truly refreshing to transcribe such lines from the pen of one who has been a profound student of Scripture for forty years. They are of unspeakable value, at a moment when so many are ready to cast a slight upon the sacred volume. Not that we are in any wise dependent upon human testimony in forming our conclusions as to the divine origin of the Bible, inasmuch as these conclusions rest upon a foundation furnished by the Bible itself. God's Word, as well as His work, speaks for itself; it carries its own credentials with it; it speaks to the heart; it reaches down to the great moral roots of our being; it penetrates the very innermost chambers of the soul; it shows us what we are; it speaks to us as no other book can speak; and as the woman of Sychar argued that Jesus must be the Christ because He told her all things that ever she did, so may we say, in reference to the Bible, It tells us all that ever we did, is not this the Word of God? No doubt it is only by the Spirit's teaching that we can discern and appreciate the evidence and credentials with which holy Scripture presents itself before us; but still it does speak for itself, and needs not human testimony to make it of value to the soul. We should no more think of having our faith in the Bible established upon man's testimony in its favor, than we should think of having it shaken by his testimony against it.

It is of the very last possible importance, at all times, but more especially at a moment like the present, to have the heart and mind established in the grand truth of the divine authority of holy Scripture—its plenary inspiration—its all-sufficiency for all purposes, for all people, at all times. There are two hostile influences abroad, namely, infidelity on the one hand, and superstition on the other. The former denies that God has spoken to us in His Word; the latter admits that He has spoken, but it denies that we can understand what He says, save by the interpretation of the church.

Now, while there are very many who recoil with horror from the impiety and audacity of infidelity, they do not see that superstition just as completely deprives them of the Scriptures. For wherein, let us ask, lies the difference between denying that God has spoken and denying that we can understand what He says? In either case, are we not deprived of the Word of God? Unquestionably. If God cannot make me understand what He says—if He cannot give me the assurance that it is He Himself who speaks, I am in no wise better off than if He had not spoken at all. If God's Word is not sufficient without human interpretation, then it cannot be God's Word at all. That which is insufficient is not God's Word. We must admit either of two things, namely, that God has not spoken at all, or if He has spoken, His Word is perfect. There is no neutral ground in reference to this question. Has God given us a revelation? Infidelity says, "No." Superstition says, "Yes, but you cannot understand it without human authority." Thus are we, in the one case as well as in the other, deprived of the priceless treasure of God's own precious Word; and thus, too, infidelity and superstition, though apparently so unlike, meet in the one point of depriving us of a divine revelation.

But, blessed be God, He has given us a revelation—He has spoken, and His Word is able to reach the heart and the understanding also. God is able to give the certainty that it is He who speaks, and we do not want any human authority to intervene. We do not want a poor rush-light to enable us to see that the sun is shining. The beams of that glorious luminary are quite enough without any such miserable addition. All we want is to stand in the sunshine, and we shall be convinced that the sun shines. If we retire into a vault, or into a tunnel, we shall not feel his influence; and just so is it with regard to Scripture—if we place ourselves beneath the chilling and darkening influences of superstition or infidelity, we shall not experience the genial and enlightening power of that divine revelation.

Having said thus much as to the divine volume as a whole, we shall now proceed to consider the contents of the section which lies open before us. In chapter 1, we have the declaration of the *"pedigree;"* and in chapter 2, the recognition of the *"standard."* "And Moses and Aaron took these men which are expressed by their names: and they assembled all the congregation together on the first day of the second month, and *they declared their pedigrees* after their families, by the house of their fathers; according to the number of the names, from twenty years old and upward, by their polls. As the Lord commanded Moses, so he numbered them in the wilderness of Sinai" (chap. 1:17-19).

Has this any voice for us? does it convey any great spiritual lesson to our understanding? Assuredly it does. In the first place, it suggests this important question to the reader: Can I declare my pedigree? It is greatly to be feared there are hundreds, if not thousands, of professing Christians who are wholly incompetent to do so. They cannot say, with clearness and decision, "*Now are* we the sons of God" (1 John 3:2)—"Ye *are* all the children of God by faith in Christ Jesus. . . . And if ye are Christ's, then *are* ye Abraham's seed, and heirs according to the promise" (Gal. 3:26,29). "For as many as are led by the Spirit of God, they *are* the sons of God. . . .

The Spirit itself beareth witness with our spirit, that we *are* the sons of God" (Rom. 8:14,16).

This is the Christian's "pedigree," and it is his privilege to be able to "declare" it. He is born from above—born again—born of water and the Spirit, *i.e.,* by the Word and by the Holy Ghost (compare diligently, John 3:5; Jas. 1:18; 1 Pet. 1:23; Eph. 5:26). The believer traces his pedigree directly up to a risen Christ in glory. This is Christian genealogy. So far as our natural pedigree is concerned, if we trace it up to its *source,* and then declare it honestly, we must see and admit that we are sprung from a ruined stock. Ours is a fallen family. Our fortunes are gone; our very blood attainted; we are irrecoverably ruined; we can never regain our original position; our former *status* and the inheritance which belonged to it are irretrievably lost. A man may be able to trace his genealogical line through a race of nobles, of princes, or of kings; but if he is fully to "declare his pedigree," he cannot stop short of a fallen, ruined, outcast head. We must get to the *source* of a thing to know what it really is. It is thus God looks at and judges of things, and we must think with Him if we would think aright. His judgment of men and things must be dominant forever. Man's judgment is only ephemeral, it lasts but for a day; and hence, according to faith's estimate, the estimate of sound sense, "it is a *small* thing to be judged of man's day" (1 Cor. 4:3). Oh, how small! Would that we felt more deeply how small a thing it is to be judged of man's judgment, or, as the margin reads it, of man's day! Would that we walked habitually in the real sense of the smallness thereof! It would impart a calm elevation and a holy dignity which would lift us above the influence of the scene through which we are passing. What is rank in this life? What importance can attach to a pedigree which, if honestly traced and faithfully declared, is derived from a ruined stock? A man can only be proud of his birth when he stops short of his real origin—"born in sin and shapen in iniquity." Such is man's origin—such his birth. Who can think of being proud of such a birth—of such an origin? who but one whose mind the god of this world hath blinded?

But how different with the Christian! His pedigree is heavenly; his genealogical tree strikes its roots into the soil of the new creation. Death can never break the line, inasmuch as it is formed in resurrection. We cannot be too simple as to this. It is of the utmost importance that the reader should be thoroughly clear on this foundation-point. We can easily see, from this first chapter of Numbers, how essential it was that every member of the congregation of Israel should be able to declare his pedigree. Uncertainty on this point would have proved disastrous; it would have produced hopeless confusion. We can hardly imagine an Israelite, when called to declare his pedigree, expressing himself in the doubtful manner adopted by many Christians nowadays. We cannot conceive his saying, Well, I am not quite sure. Sometimes I cherish the hope that I am of the stock of Israel; but at other times, I am full of fear that I do not belong to the congregation of the Lord at all. I am all in uncertainty and darkness. Can we conceive such language? Assuredly not. Much less could we imagine any one maintaining the monstrous notion that no one could possibly be sure as to whether he was a true Israelite or not until the day of judgment.

All such ideas and reasonings—all such doubts, fears, and questions, we may rest assured, were foreign to the mind of the Israelite. Every member of the congregation was called to declare his pedigree ere taking his place in the ranks as a man of war. Each one was able to say, like Saul of Tarsus, "Circumcised the eighth day, of the stock of Israel," etc. All was settled and clear, and necessarily so if there was to be any real entrance upon the walk and warfare of the wilderness.

Now, may we not legitimately ask, If a Jew could be certain as to his pedigree, why may not a Christian be certain as to his? Weigh this question; and if you are one of that large class of persons who are never able to arrive at the blessed certainty of their heavenly lineage—their spiritual birth, pause, we beseech you, and let us reason with you on this momentous point. It may be you are disposed to ask, How can I be sure that I am, really and truly, a child of God, a member of Christ, born of the Word and Spirit of God? I would give worlds, were they mine, to be certain as to this most weighty question.

Well, then, we would earnestly desire to help you in this matter. Indeed, one special object before us in penning these *Notes* is, to assist anxious souls, by answering, as the Lord may enable us, their questions, solving their difficulties, and removing the stumbling-blocks out of their way.

And first of all, let us point out one special feature which belongs to all the children of God without exception. It is a very simple, but a very blessed feature. If we do not possess it in some degree, it is most certain we are not of the heavenly race; but if we do possess it, it is just as certain that we are, and we may, therefore, without any difficulty or reserve, "declare our pedigree." Now what is this feature? what is this great family characteristic? Our Lord Jesus Christ supplies the answer. He tells us that "Wisdom is justified of *all* her children" (Luke 7:35; Matt. 11:19). All the children of Wisdom, from the days of Abel down to the present moment, have been marked by this great family trait. There is not so much as a single exception. All God's children—all the sons of Wisdom have always exhibited, in some degree, this moral feature—they have justified God.

Let the reader consider this. It may be he finds it hard to understand what is meant by justifying God; but a passage or two of holy Scripture will, we trust, make it quite plain. We read in Luke 7 that "all the people that heard Jesus, and the publicans, *justified God*, being baptized with the baptism of John. But the Pharisees and lawyers rejected the counsel of God against themselves, being not baptized of him" (ver. 29-30). Here we have the two generations brought, as it were, face to face. The publicans justified God and condemned themselves: the Pharisees justified themselves and judged God. The former submitted to the baptism of John—the baptism of repentance: the latter refused that baptism—refused to repent—refused to humble and to judge themselves.

Here we have the two great classes into which the whole human family has been divided, from the days of Abel and Cain down to the present day; and here, too, we have the simplest possible test by which to try our "pedigree." Have we taken the place of self-condemnation? have we bowed in true repentance before God? This is to justify God. The two things go together—yea, they are one and the same. The man who condemns himself justifies God; and the man who justifies God condemns himself. On the other hand, the man who justifies himself judges God; and the man who judges God justifies himself.

Thus it stands in every case. And be it observed that the very moment we take the ground of repentance and self-judgment, God takes the ground of a Justifier. God always justifies those who condemn themselves. All His children justify Him, and He justifies all His children. The moment David said, "I have sinned against the Lord," the answer was, "The Lord hath put away thy sin." Divine forgiveness follows, with the most intense rapidity, human confession.

Hence it follows that nothing can be more foolish than for any one to justify himself, inasmuch as God must be justified in His sayings, and overcome when He is judged (comp. Ps. 51:4; Rom. 3:4). God must have the upper hand in the end, and then all self-justification shall be seen in its true light. The wisest thing, therefore, is to condemn ourselves. This is what all the children of Wisdom do. Nothing is more characteristic of the true members of Wisdom's family than the habit and spirit of self-judgment. Whereas, on the other hand, nothing so marks all those who are not of this family as a spirit of self-vindication.

These things are worthy of our most earnest attention. Nature will blame any thing and every thing, any one and every one, but itself; but where grace is at work, there is ever a readiness to judge self, and take the lowly place. This is the true secret of blessing and peace. All God's children have stood on this blessed ground, exhibited this lovely moral trait, and reached this grand result. We cannot find so much as a single exception in the entire history of Wisdom's happy family; and we may safely say that if the reader has been led, in truth and reality, to own himself lost—to condemn himself—to take the place of true repentance, then is he, in very deed, one of the children of Wisdom, and he may therefore, with boldness and decision, "declare his pedigree."

We would urge this point at the outset. It is impossible for any one to recognize and rally around the proper "standard" unless he can declare his "pedigree." In short, it is impossible to take up a true position in the wilderness so long as there is any uncertainty as to this great question. How could an Israelite of old have taken his place in the assembly—how could he have stood in the ranks—how could he expect to make any progress through the wilderness, if he could not distinctly declare his pedigree? Impossible. Just so is it with Christians now. Progress in wilderness life—success in spiritual warfare, is out of the question if there be any uncertainty as to the spiritual pedigree. We must be able to say, *"We know* that we have passed from death unto life"—*"We know* that we are of God"—"We believe and are sure," ere there can be any real advance in the life and walk of a Christian.

Can you declare your pedigree? Is this a thoroughly settled point with you? Are you clear as to this in the very depths of your soul? When you are all alone with God is it a perfectly settled question between you and Him? Search and see. Make sure work of it. Do not slur the matter over. Build not upon mere profession. Say not, I am a member of such a church; I receive the Lord's supper; I hold such and such doctrines; I have been religiously brought up; I live a moral life; I have done nobody any harm; I read the Bible and say my prayers; I have family worship in my house; I give largely in the cause of philanthropy and religion. All this may be perfectly true of you, and yet you may not have a single pulse of divine life, a single ray of divine light. Not one of these things, not all of them put together, could be accepted as a declaration of spiritual pedigree. There must be the witness of the Spirit that you are a child of God, and this witness always accompanies simple faith in the Lord Jesus Christ. "He that believeth in the Son of God hath the witness in himself" (1 John 5:10). It is not by any means a question of looking into your own heart for evidences; it is not a building upon frames, feelings, and experiences—nothing of the sort. It is a childlike faith in Christ; it is having eternal life in the Son of God; it is the imperishable record of the Holy Ghost; it is taking God at His word. "Verily, verily, I say unto you, He that heareth My word, and believeth on Him that sent Me, *hath* everlasting life, and shall not come into judgment [κρισιν], but *is passed* from death unto life" (John 5:24).

This is the true way to declare your pedigree; and be assured of it, you must be able to declare it ere you can "go forth to war." We do not mean to say you cannot be saved without this. God forbid we should say any such thing. We believe there are hundreds of the true spiritual Israel who are not able to declare their pedigree; but we ask, Are such able to go forth to war? are they vigorous military men? Far from it. They cannot even know what true conflict is: on the contrary, persons of this class mistake their doubts and fears—their dark and cloudy seasons for true Christian conflict. This is a most serious mistake, but, alas! a very common one. We continually find a low, dark, legal condition of soul defended on the ground of Christian conflict, whereas, according to the New Testament, true Christian conflict, or warfare, is carried on in a region where doubts and fears are unknown. It is when we stand in the clear daylight of God's full salvation—salvation in a risen Christ—that we really enter upon the warfare proper to us as Christians. Are we to suppose for a moment that our legal struggles, our culpable unbelief, our refusal to submit to the righteousness of God, our questionings and reasonings, can be viewed as Christian conflict? By no means. All these things must be regarded as conflict with God; whereas Christian conflict is carried on with Satan. "We wrestle not against flesh and blood, but against principalities, against powers, against the rulers of the darkness of this world, against wicked spirits in high place" (Eph. 6:12).

This is Christian conflict. But can such conflict be waged by those who are continually doubting whether they are Christians or not? We do not believe it. Could we imagine an Israelite in conflict with Amalek in the wilderness, or with the Canaanites in the land of promise, while yet unable to "declare his pedigree" or recognize his "standard"? The thing is inconceivable. No, no; every member of the congregation who was able to go forth to war was perfectly clear and settled as to those two points. Indeed, he could not go forth if he were not so.

While on the important subject of Christian conflict, it may be well to call attention to the three portions of New Testament Scripture in which we have three distinct characters of conflict presented, namely, Romans 7:7-24; Galatians 5:17; Ephesians 6:10-17. If the reader will just turn for a moment to the above Scriptures, we shall seek to point out the true character of each.

In Romans 7:7-24, we have the struggle of a soul quickened but not emancipated—a regenerated soul under the law. The proof that we have before us here a quickened soul, is found in such utterances as these: "That which I do, I allow not." "To will is present with me." *"I delight in the law of God after the inward man."* None but a regenerated soul could speak thus. The disallowance of the wrong, the *will* to do right, the inward delight in the law of God—all these are the distinct marks of the new life—the precious fruits of regeneration. No unconverted person could truthfully use such language.

But on the other hand, the proofs that we have before us in this Scripture a soul not fully emancipated, not in the joy of known deliverance, not in the full consciousness of victory, not in the assured possession of spiritual power—the plain proofs of all this we have in such utterances as the following: "I am carnal, sold under sin." "What I would, that do I not; but what I hate, that do I." "O wretched man that I am! who shall deliver me?" Now, we know that a Christian is not "carnal," but spiritual; he is not "sold under sin," but redeemed from its power; he is not a "wretched man," sighing for deliverance, but a happy man, who knows himself delivered. He is not an impotent slave, unable to do the right thing, and ever compelled to do the wrong; he is a free man, endowed with power in the Holy Ghost, and able to say, "I can do *all* things through Christ that strenghteneth me" (Phil. 4).

We cannot here attempt to enter upon a full exposition of this most important Scripture; we merely offer a suggestion or two which may help the reader to seize its scope and import. We are fully aware that many Christians differ widely as to the interpretation of this chapter. Some deny that it presents the exercises of a quickened soul; others maintain that it sets forth the experiences proper to a Christian. We cannot accept either conclusion. We believe it exhibits to our view the exercises of a truly regenerated soul, but of a soul not set free by the knowledge of its union with a risen Christ, and the power of the Holy Ghost. Hundreds of Christians are actually in the seventh of Romans; but their proper place is in the eighth. They are, as to their experience, under the law; they do not know themselves as sealed by the Holy Ghost; they are not in possession of full victory in a risen and glorified Christ; they have doubts and fears, and are ever disposed to cry out, "O wretched man that I am! who shall deliver me?" But is not a Christian delivered? is he not saved? is he not accepted in the Beloved? is he not sealed by that Holy Spirit of promise? is he not united to Christ? ought he not to know, to enjoy, and to confess all this? Unquestionably. Well, then, he is no longer, as to his standing, in the seventh of Romans. It is his privilege to sing the song of victory, at heaven's side of the empty tomb of Jesus, and to walk in the holy liberty wherewith Christ makes His people free. The seventh of Romans is not liberty at all, but bondage—except, indeed, at the very close, where the soul is able to say, "I thank God." No doubt, it may be a very wholesome exercise to pass through all that is here detailed for us with such marvelous vividness and power; and furthermore, we must declare that we should vastly prefer being honestly in the seventh of Romans to being falsely in the eighth. But all this leaves wholly untouched the question as to the proper application of this profoundly interesting passage of Scripture.

We shall now glance for a moment at the conflict in Galatians 5:17. We shall quote the passage. "For the flesh lusteth against the Spirit, and the Spirit against the flesh: and these are contrary the one to the other: so that ye cannot do the things that ye would."* This passage is often quoted to account for continual *defeat,* whereas it really contains the secret of perpetual *victory.* In verse 16, we read, "This I say, then, walk in the Spirit, and *ye shall not fulfill* the lust of the flesh." This makes it all so clear. The presence of the Holy Ghost secures power. We are assured that God is stronger than "the flesh," and therefore where He is in conflict, the triumph is secured. And be it carefully noted that Galatians 5:17 does not speak of the conflict between the two natures—the old and the new, but between the Holy Ghost and the flesh. This is the reason why it is added, "In order that ye may not do the things that ye would." If the Holy Ghost were not dwelling in us, we should be sure to fulfill the lust of the flesh; but inasmuch as He is in us to carry on the warfare, we are no longer obliged to do wrong, but blessedly enabled to do right.

Now this precisely marks the point of difference between Romans 7:14-15 and Galatians 5:17. In the former, we have the new nature, but not the power of the indwelling Spirit; in the latter, we have not only the new nature, but also the power of the Holy Ghost. We must ever bear in mind that the new nature in a believer is dependent. It is dependent upon the Spirit for power, and upon the Word for guidance. But clearly, where God the Holy Ghost is, there must be power. He may be grieved and hindered, but Galatians 5:16 distinctly teaches that if we walk in the Spirit, we shall have sure and constant victory over the flesh. Hence, therefore, it would be a very serious mistake indeed to quote Galatians 5:17 as a reason for a low and carnal walk. Its teaching is designed to produce the direct opposite.

And now one word on Ephesians 6:10-17. Here we have the conflict between the Christian and wicked spirits in heavenly places. The Church belongs to heaven, and should ever maintain a heavenly walk and conversation. It should be our constant aim to make good our heavenly standing—to plant the foot firmly upon our heavenly inheritance, and keep it there. This, the devil seeks to hinder in every possible way, and hence the conflict; hence, too, "the whole armor of God," by which alone we can stand against our powerful spiritual foe.

It is not our purpose to dwell upon the armor, as we have merely called the reader's attention to the above three Scriptures in order that he may have the subject of conflict, in all its phases, fully before his mind, in connection with the opening lines of the book of Numbers. Nothing can be more interesting; nor can we possibly overestimate the importance of being clear as to the real nature and ground of Christian conflict. If we go forth to war without knowing what the war is about, and in a state of uncertainty as to whether our "pedigree" is all right, we shall not make much headway against the enemy. But, as has been already remarked, there was another thing quite as necessary for the man of war as the clear declaration of his pedigree, and that was, the distinct recognition of his standard. The two things were essential for the walk and warfare of the wilderness. Moreover, they were inseparable. If a man did not know his pedigree, he could

*We ought perhaps to inform the reader that many able scholars render the last clause of Galatians 5:17 thus: "In order that ye may not do the things that ye would." We assuredly believe this rendering to be in full keeping with the spirit of the context; though we are each day more convinced of the unrivaled excellence of our precious English Bible.

not recognize his standard, and thus all would have been plunged in hopeless confusion. In place of keeping rank, and making steady progress, they would have been in each other's way, and treading one upon another. Each had to know his post and keep it—to know his standard and abide by it. Thus they moved on together; thus progress was made, work done, and warfare carried on. The Benjamite had his post, and the Ephraimite had his, and neither was to interfere with or cross the path of the other. Thus with all the tribes throughout the camp of the Israel of God. Each had his pedigree, and each had his post; and neither the one nor the other was according to their own thoughts: all was of God. He gave the pedigree, and He assigned the standard; nor was there any need of comparing one with another, or any ground of jealousy one of another; each had his place to fill and his work to do, and there was work enough and room enough for all. There was the greatest possible variety, and yet the most perfect unity. "Every man of the children of Israel shall pitch by his own standard, with the ensign of their father's house." "And the children of Israel did according to all that the Lord commanded Moses: so they pitched by their standards, and so they set forward, every one after their families, according to the house of their fathers" (chap. 2:2,34).

Thus, in the camp of old, as well as in the Church now, we learn that "God is not the Author of confusion." Nothing could be more exquisitely arranged than the four camps, of three tribes each, forming a perfect square, each side of the square exhibiting its own specific standard. "Every man of the children of Israel shall pitch by his own standard, with the ensign of their father's house: over against the tabernacle of the congregation shall they pitch." The God of the armies of Israel knew how to marshal His hosts. It would be a great mistake to suppose that God's warriors were not ordered according to the most perfect system of military tactics. We may plume ourselves upon our progress in arts and sciences, and we may fancy that the host of Israel presented a spectacle of rude disorder and wild confusion, compared with what may be seen in modern times; but this would be an empty conceit. We may rest assured that the camp of Israel was ordered and furnished in the most perfect manner, for the simplest and most conclusive of all reasons, namely, that it was ordered and furnished by the hand of God. Grant us but this, that God has done any thing, and we argue, with the most perfect confidence, that it has been perfectly done.

This is a very simple, but a very blessed principle. Of course it would not satisfy an infidel or a skeptic; what would? It is the province and prerogative of a skeptic to doubt every thing, to believe nothing. He measures every thing by his own standard, and rejects whatever he cannot reconcile with his own notions. He lays down, with marvelous coolness, his own premises, and then proceeds to draw his own conclusions; but if the premises are false, the conclusions must be false likewise. And there is this invariable feature attaching to the premises of all skeptics, rationalists, and infidels—*they always leave out God;* and hence all their conclusions must be fatally false. On the other hand, the humble believer starts with this great first principle, that *God is;* and not only that He is, but that He has to do with His creatures; that He interests Himself in, and occupies Himself about, the affairs of men.

What consolation for the Christian! But infidelity will not allow this at all. To bring God in is to upset all the reasonings of the skeptic, for they are based upon the thorough exclusion of God.

However, we are not now writing in order to meet infidels, but for the edification of believers; and yet it is sometimes well to call attention to the thorough rottenness of the whole system of infidelity; and surely, in no way can this be more clearly or forcibly shown than by the fact that it rests entirely upon the exclusion of God. Let this fact be seized, and the whole system crumbles into dust at our feet. If we believe that God is, then assuredly every thing must be viewed in relation to Him. We must look at all from

His point of view. Nor is this all. If we believe that God is, then we must see that man cannot judge Him. God must be the judge of right or wrong, of what is and what is not worthy of Himself. So also in reference to God's Word. If it be true that God is, and that He has spoken to us—He has given us a revelation, then assuredly that revelation is not to be judged by man's reason. It is above and beyond any such tribunal. Only think of measuring God's Word by the rules of human arithmetic! And yet this is precisely what has been done, in our own day, with this blessed book of Numbers, with which we are now engaged, and with which we shall proceed, leaving infidelity and its arithmetic aside.

We feel it very needful, in our notes and reflections on this book, as well as on every other book, to remember two things, namely, first, the *book;* and secondly, the *soul*—the book and its contents; the soul and its necessities. There is a danger of becoming so occupied with the former as to forget the latter; and on the other hand, there is the danger of becoming so wholly engrossed with the latter as to forget the former. Both must be attended to. And we may say that what constitutes an efficient ministry, whether written or oral, is the proper adjustment of these two things. There are some ministers who study the Word very diligently, and, it may be, very profoundly; they are well versed in Biblical knowledge; they have drunk deeply at the fountain of inspiration. All this is of the utmost importance, and of the very highest value. A ministry without this will be barren indeed. If a man does not study his Bible diligently and prayerfully, he will have little to give to his readers or his hearers—at least, little worth their having. Those who minister in the Word must dig for themselves, and *"dig deep."*

But then the *soul* must be considered—its condition anticipated, and its necessities met. If this be lost sight of, the ministry will lack point, pungency, and power. It will be inefficient and unfruitful. In short, the two things must be combined and properly adjusted. A man who merely studies the *book* will be unpractical; a man who merely studies the *soul* will be unfurnished; a man who duly studies *both* will be a good minister of Jesus Christ.

Now, we desire, in our measure, to be this to the reader; and hence, as we travel, in his company, through the marvelous book which lies open before us, we would not only seek to point out its moral beauties and unfold its holy lessons, but we would also feel it to be our bounden duty to put an occasional question to him or her, as to how far those lessons are being learnt and those beauties appreciated. We trust the reader will not object to this, and hence, ere we close this our first section, we would ask him a question or two thereon.

And first, then, Art thou clear and settled as to thy "pedigree"? is it a settled thing that thou art on the Lord's side? Do not, we beseech thee, leave this grand question unsettled. We have asked it before, and we ask it again. Dost thou know, canst thou declare, thy spiritual pedigree? It is the first thing for God's warrior. It is of no use to think of entering the militant host so long as you are unsettled as to this point. We say not that a man cannot be saved without this. Far be the thought. But he cannot take rank as a man of war. He cannot do battle with the world, the flesh, and the devil so long as he is filled with doubts and fears as to whether he belongs to the true spiritual stock. If there is to be any progress, if there is to be that decision so essential to a spiritual warrior, we must be able to say, *"We know* that we have passed from death unto life"—*"We know* that we are of God."

This is the proper language of a man of war. Not one of that mighty host that mustered "over against the tabernacle of the congregation" would have understood such a thing as a single doubt, or shadow of a doubt, as to *his own very pedigree.* Doubtless, he would have smiled had any one raised a question on the subject. Each one of the six hundred thousand knew well whence he had sprung, and therefore where he was to take his stand. And just so with God's militant host now. Each member thereof will need to possess the most unclouded confidence as to his relationship, else he will not be able to stand in the battle.

And then as to the "standard." What is it? Is it a doctrine? Nay. Is it a theological system? Nay. Is it an ecclesiastical polity? Nay. Is it a system of ordinances, rites, or ceremonies? Nothing of the sort. God's warriors do not fight under any such banner. What is the standard of God's militant host? Let us hear and remember. It is Christ. This is the only standard of God, and the only standard of that warrior-band which musters in this wilderness-world to wage war with the hosts of evil and fight the battles of the Lord. Christ is the standard for every thing. To have any other would only unfit us for that spiritual conflict to which we are called. What have we, *as Christians,* to do with contending for any system of theology or church organization? Of what account, in our estimation, are ordinances, ceremonies, or ritualistic observances? Are we going to fight under such banners as these? God forbid! Our theology is the Bible; our church-organization is the one Body, formed by the presence of the Holy Ghost, and united to the living and exalted Head in the heavens. To contend for any thing less than these is entirely below the mark of a true spiritual warrior.

Alas! that so many who profess to belong to the Church of God should so forget their proper standard, and be found fighting under another banner. We may rest assured it superinduces weakness, falsifies the testimony, and hinders progress. If we would stand in the day of battle, we must acknowledge no standard whatsoever but Christ and His word—the living Word and the written Word. Here lies our security in the face of all spiritual foes. The more closely we adhere to Christ, and to Him *alone,* the stronger and the safer we shall be. To have Him as a perfect covering for our eyes, to keep close to Him—fast by His side, this is our grand moral safeguard. "The children of Israel shall pitch their tents, every man by his own camp, and every man by his own standard, throughout their hosts."

Oh that thus it may be throughout all the host of the Church of God! May all be laid aside for Christ. May He be enough for our hearts. As we trace our "pedigree" up to Him, may His name be inscribed on the "standard" around which we encamp in this wilderness, through which we are passing home to our eternal rest above. See to it, we beseech thee, that there be not one jot or tittle inscribed on thy banner save Jesus Christ—that name which is above every name, and which shall yet be exalted forever throughout the wide universe of God.

---

## *CHAPTERS 3–4*

WHAT a marvelous spectacle was the camp of Israel in that waste howling wilderness! What a spectacle to angels, to men, and to devils! God's eye ever rested upon it. His presence was there. He dwelt in the midst of His militant people. It was there He found His habitation. He did not, He could not, find His abode amid the splendors of Egypt, of Assyria, or of Babylon. No doubt those nations presented much that was attractive to nature's eye. The arts and sciences were cultivated amongst them. Civilization had reached a far loftier point amongst those ancient nations than we moderns are disposed to admit. Refinement and luxury were probably carried to as great an extent there as amongst those who put forth very lofty pretensions.

But, be it remembered, Jehovah was not known among those nations; His name had never been revealed to them; He did not dwell in their midst. True, there were the ten thousand testimonies to His creative power; and moreover, His superintending providence was over them: He gave them rain and fruitful seasons, filling their hearts with food and gladness; the blessings and benefits of His liberal hand were showered upon them from day to day and year to year; His showers fertilized their fields, His sunbeams gladdened their hearts: but they knew Him not, and cared not for Him. His dwelling was not there. Not one of those nations could say, "Jehovah is my strength and song, and

He is become my salvation: He is my God, and I will prepare Him a habitation; my father's God, and I will exalt Him" (Exod. 15:2).

Jehovah found His abode in the bosom of His redeemed people, and no where else. Redemption was the necessary basis of God's habitation amongst men. Apart from redemption, the divine presence could only prove the destruction of man; but redemption being known, that presence secures man's highest privilege and brightest glory.

God dwelt in the midst of His people Israel. He came down from heaven, not only to redeem them out of the land of Egypt, but to be their traveling-companion through the wilderness. What a thought! The Most High God taking up His abode on the sand of the desert, and in the very bosom of His redeemed congregation! Truly, there was nothing like that throughout the wide, wide world. There was that host of six hundred thousand men, beside women and children, in a sterile desert, where there was not a blade of grass, not a drop of water—no visible source of subsistence. How were they to be fed? God was there! How were they to be kept in order? God was there! How were they to track their way through a howling wilderness, where there was no way? God was there!

In a word, God's presence secured every thing. Unbelief might say, What! are three millions of people to be fed on air? Who has charge of the commissariat? where are the military stores? where is the baggage? who is to attend to the clothing? Faith alone could answer, and its answer is simple, brief, and conclusive—God was there! And that was quite sufficient. All is comprehended in that one sentence. In faith's arithmetic, God is the only significant figure; and having Him, you may add as many ciphers as you please. If all your springs are in the living God, it ceases to be a question of your need, and resolves itself into a question of His sufficiency.

What were six hundred thousand footmen to the Almighty God? what the varied necessities of their wives and children? In man's estimation, these things might seem overwhelming. England has just sent out ten thousand troops to Abyssinia; but only think of the enormous expense and labor—think of the number of transports required to convey provisions and other necessaries for that small army. But imagine an army sixty times the size, together with the women and children; conceive this enormous host entering upon a march that was to extend over the space of forty years, through "a great and terrible wilderness," in which there was no corn, no grass, no water-spring. How were they to be sustained? No supplies with them, no arrangements entered into with friendly nations to forward supplies, no transports dispatched to meet them at various points along their route; in short, not a single visible source of supply—nothing that nature would consider available.

All this is something worth pondering. But we must ponder it in the divine presence. It is of no possible use for reason to sit down and try to solve this mighty problem by human arithmetic. No; it is only faith that can solve it, and that, moreover, by the Word of the living God. Here lies the precious solution. Bring God in, and you want no other factors to work out your answer; leave Him out, and the more powerful your reason, and the more profound your arithmetic, the more hopeless must be your perplexity.

Thus it is that faith settles the question. God was in the midst of His people. He was there in all the fullness of His grace and mercy—there in His perfect knowledge of His people's wants, and of the difficulties of their path—there in His almighty power and boundless resources, to meet these difficulties and supply these wants. And so fully did He enter into all these things, that He was able, at the close of their long wilderness-wanderings, to appeal to their hearts in the following touching accents: "For the Lord thy God hath blessed thee in all the works of thy hand; He knoweth thy walking through this great wilderness: these forty years the Lord thy God hath been with thee; *thou hast lacked nothing.*" And again, "Thy raiment waxed not old upon thee, neither did thy foot swell, these forty years" (Deut. 2:7; 8:4).

Now, in all these things, the camp of Israel was a type—a vivid, striking type. A type of what? A type of the Church of God passing through this world. The testimony of Scripture is so distinct on this point, as to leave no room and no demand for the exercise of imagination. "All these things happened unto them for ensamples; and they are written for our admonition, upon whom the ends of the world are come" (1 Cor. 10:11).

Hence, therefore, we may draw near and gaze, with intense interest, upon that marvelous spectacle, and seek to gather up the precious lessons which it is so eminently fitted to teach. And, oh, what lessons! Who can duly estimate them? Look at that mysterious camp in the desert, composed, as we have said, of warriors, workers, and worshipers. What separation from all the nations of the world! what utter hopelessness! what exposure! what absolute dependence upon God! They had nothing, could do nothing, could know nothing. They had not a morsel of food nor a drop of water, but as they received it day by day from the immediate hand of God. When they retired to rest at night, there was not a single atom of provision for the morrow. There was no storehouse, no larder, no visible source of supply—nothing that nature could take any account of.

But God was there, and that, in the judgment of faith, was quite enough. *They were shut up to God.* This is the one grand reality. Faith owns nothing real, nothing solid, nothing true, but the one true, living, eternal God. Nature might cast a longing look at the granaries of Egypt, and see something tangible, something substantial there: faith looks up to heaven and finds *all* its springs there.

Thus it was with the camp in the desert, and thus it is with the Church in the world. There was not a single exigency, not a single contingency, not a single need of any sort whatsoever, for which the Divine Presence was not an all-sufficient answer. The nations of the uncircumcised might look on and marvel; they might, in the bewilderment of blind unbelief, raise many a question as to how such a host could ever be fed, clothed, and kept in order. Most certainly they had no eyes to *see* how it could be done. They knew not Jehovah, the Lord God of the Hebrews; and therefore to tell them that He was going to undertake for that vast assembly would indeed seem like idle tales.

And so it is now, in reference to the assembly of God, in this world, which may truly be termed a moral wilderness. Looked at from God's point of view, that assembly is not of the world; it is in complete separation. It is as thoroughly apart from the world as the camp of Israel was apart from Egypt. The waters of the Red Sea rolled between that camp and Egypt; and the deeper and darker waters of the death of Christ roll between the Church of God and this present evil world. It is impossible to conceive separation more complete. "They," says our Lord Christ, "are not of the world, even as I am not of the world" (John 17).

Then, as to entire dependence, what can be more dependent than the Church of God in this world? She has nothing in or of herself. She is set down in the midst of a moral desert, a dreary waste, a vast howling wilderness, in the which there is literally nothing on which she can live. There is not one drop of water, not a single morsel of suited food, for the Church of God throughout the entire compass of this world.

So also as to the matter of exposure to all sorts of hostile influences. Nothing can exceed it. There is not so much as one friendly influence. All is against her. She is in the midst of this world like an exotic—a plant belonging to a foreign clime, and set down in a sphere where both the soil and the atmosphere are uncongenial.

Such is the Church of God in the world—a separated, dependent, defenseless thing, wholly cast upon the living God. It is calculated to give great vividness, force, and clearness to our thoughts about the Church to view it as the antitype of the camp in the desert; and that it is in no wise fanciful or far-fetched to view it thus, 1 Corinthians 10:11 does most clearly show. We are fully warranted in saying that what the camp of Israel was literally, that the Church is morally and spiritually. And further, that what the wilderness was literally to Israel, that the world is morally and spiritually to the Church of God. The wilderness was the sphere of Israel's toil and danger, not of their supplies or their enjoyment; and the world is the sphere of the Church's toil and danger, not of its supplies or its enjoyment.

It is well to seize this fact, in all its moral power. The assembly of God in the world, like "the congregation in the wilderness," is wholly cast upon the living God. We speak, be it remembered, from the divine standpoint—of what the Church is in God's sight. Looked at from man's point of view—looked at as she is in her own actual practical state, it is, alas! another thing. We are now only occupied with the normal, the true, the divine idea of God's assembly in this world.

And let it not be forgotten for one moment, that as truly as there was a camp in the desert of old—a congregation in the wilderness, so truly is there the Church of God—the body of Christ—in the world now. Doubtless, the nations of the world knew little and cared less about that congregation of old; but that did not weaken or touch the great living fact. So now, the men of the world know little and care less about the assembly of God—the body of Christ; but that in no wise touches the grand living truth that there *is* such a thing actually existing in this world, and *has been* ever since the Holy Ghost descended on the day of Pentecost. True, the congregation of old had its trials, its conflicts, its sorrows, its temptations, it strifes, its controversies, its internal commotions, its numberless and nameless difficulties, calling for the varied resources that were in God—the precious ministrations of prophet, priest, and king which God had provided; for, as we know, Moses was there as "king in Jeshurun," and as the prophet raised up of God; and Aaron was there to exercise all the priestly functions.

But in spite of all these things that we have named—in spite of the weakness, the failure, the sin, the rebellion, the strife—still there was the striking fact, to be taken cognizance of by men, by devils, and by angels, namely, a vast congregation, amounting to something like three millions of people (according to the usual mode of computation) journeying through a wilderness, wholly dependent upon an unseen arm, guided and cared for by the eternal God, whose eye was never for one moment withdrawn from that mysterious typical host; yea, He dwelt in their midst, and never left them, in all their unbelief, their forgetfulness, their ingratitude, and rebellion. God was there to sustain and guide, to guard and keep them day and night. He fed them with bread from heaven day by day, and He brought them forth water out of the flinty rock.

This, assuredly, was a stupendous fact—a profound mystery. God had a congregation in the wilderness—apart from the nations around, shut up to Himself. It may be the nations of the world knew nothing, cared nothing, thought nothing, about this assembly. It is certain the desert yielded nothing in the way of sustenance or refreshment. There were serpents and scorpions—there were snares and dangers—drought, barrenness, and desolation; but there was that wonderful assembly maintained in a manner that baffled and confounded human reason.

Remember, this was a type. A type of what? A type of something that has been in existence for over eighteen centuries; is in existence still; and shall be in existence until the moment that our Lord Christ rises from His present position and descends into the air. In one word, a type of the Church of God in the world. How important to recognize this fact! How sadly it has been lost sight of! how little understood, even now! And yet every Christian is solemnly responsible to recognize, and practically to confess it. There is no escaping it. Is it true that there is something in this world at this very moment answering to the camp in the desert? Yes, verily; there is, in very truth, the Church in the wilderness. There is an assembly passing through this world, just as the literal Israel passed through the literal desert. And moreover, the world is morally and spiritually to that Church what the desert was literally and practically to Israel of old. Israel found no springs in the desert; and the Church of God should find no springs in the world. If she does, she proves false to her Lord. Israel was not of the desert, but passing through it; and the Church of God is not of the world, but passing through it.

If this be thoroughly entered into by the reader, it will show him the place of complete separation which belongs to the Church of God as a whole, and to each individual member thereof. The Church, *in God's view of her,* is as thoroughly marked off from this present world as the camp of Israel was marked off from the surrounding desert. There is as little in common between the Church and the world as there was between Israel and the sand of the desert. The most brilliant attractions and bewitching fascinations of the world are to the Church of God what the serpents and scorpions and the ten thousand other dangers of the wilderness were to Israel.

Such is the divine idea of the Church; and it is with this idea that we are now occupied. Alas! how different it is with that which calls itself the Church! But we want the reader to dwell, for the present, on the true thing; we want him to place himself, by faith, at God's stand-point, and view the Church from thence. It is only by so doing that he can have any thing like a true idea of what the Church is, or of his own personal responsibility with respect to it. God *has* a Church in the world. There *is* a body now on the earth, indwelt by God the Spirit, and united to Christ the Head. This Church—this body—is composed of all those who truly believe on the Son of God, and who are united by the grand fact of the presence of the Holy Ghost.

And be it observed, this is not a matter of opinion—a certain thing which we may take up or lay down at pleasure. It is a divine fact; it is a grand truth, whether we will hear or whether we will forbear. The Church is an existing thing, and we, if believers, are members thereof. We cannot avoid this: we cannot ignore it. We are actually in the relationship—baptized into it by the Holy Ghost. It is as real and as positive a thing as the birth of a child into a family. The birth has taken place, the relationship is formed, and we have only to recognize it, and walk in the sense of it from day to day. The very moment in which a soul is born again—born from above, and sealed by the Holy Ghost, he is incorporated into the body of Christ. He can no longer view himself as a solitary individual, an independent person, an isolated atom; he is a member of a body, just as the hand or the foot is a member of the human body. He is a member of *the* Church of God, and cannot, properly and truly, be a member of any thing else. How could my arm be a member of any other body? And on the same principle, we may ask, How could a member of the body of Christ be a member of any other body?

What a glorious truth is this respecting the Church of God—the antitype of the camp in the desert—"the congregation in the wilderness"! What a fact to be governed by! There *is* such a thing as the Church of God amid all the ruin and the wreck, the strife and the discord, the confusion and division, the sects and parties. This, surely, is a most precious truth. But not only is it most precious, it is also most practical and formative. We are as bound to recognize, by faith, this Church in the world, as the Israelite was bound to recognize, by sight, the camp in the desert. There *was* one camp—one congregation, and the true Israelite belonged thereto; there *is* one Church—one body, and the true Christian belongs to it.

But how is this body organized? By the Holy Ghost, as it is written, "By one Spirit are we all baptized into one body" (1 Cor. 12:13). How is it maintained? By its living Head, through the Spirit, and by the Word, as it is written, "No man ever yet hated his own flesh; but nourisheth and cherisheth it, even as the Lord the Church" (Eph. 5:29). Is not this enough? Is not the Lord Christ sufficient? Doth not the Holy Ghost suffice? Do we want any thing more than the varied virtues that are lodged in the name of Jesus? Are not the gifts of the Eternal Spirit quite sufficient for the growth and maintenance of the Church of God? Doth not the fact of the divine presence in the Church, secure *all* that the Church can possibly need? Is it not sufficient for "exigence of every hour"? Faith says—and says it with emphasis and decision—Yes! Unbelief—human reason, says, No; we want a great many things as well. What is our brief reply? Simply this: If God be not sufficient, we know not whither to turn; if the name of Jesus doth not suffice, we know not what to do; if the Holy Ghost cannot meet all our need, in communion, in ministry, and in worship, we know not what to say.

It may, however, be said that "things are not as they were in apostolic times. The professing church has failed; pentecostal gifts have ceased; the palmy days of the Church's first love have passed away; and therefore we must adopt the best means in our power for the organization and maintenance of our churches." To all this we reply, God has not failed; Christ, the Head of the Church, has not failed; the Holy Spirit has not failed; not one jot or tittle of God's Word has failed. This is the true ground of faith. "Jesus Christ is the same yesterday, to-day, and forever." He has said, "Lo, I am with you." How long? During the days of first love? during apostolic times? so long as the Church shall continue faithful? No; "I am with you *always,* even unto the end of the age" (Matt. 28). So also, at an earlier moment, when, for the first time in the whole canon of Scripture, the Church, properly so called, is named, we have those memorable words, "On this Rock [the Son of the living God] I will build My Church, and the gates of hell shall not prevail against it" (Matt. 16).

Now, the question is, Is that Church on the earth at this moment? Most assuredly. It is as true that there is a Church now on this earth as that there was a camp in the desert of old. Yes; and as truly as God was in that camp to meet every exigence, so truly is He now in the Church to order and guide in every thing, as we read, "Ye are builded together for a habitation of God through the Spirit" (Eph. 2). This is quite sufficient. All we want is to lay hold, by a simple faith, of this grand reality. The name of Jesus is as sufficient for all the exigencies of the Church of God as it is for the soul's salvation. The one is as true as the other. "Where two or three are gathered together in [or, unto] My name, there am I in the midst" (Matt. 18). Has this ceased to be true? and if not, is not Christ's presence quite enough for His Church? Do we need to set about planning or working for ourselves in church matters? No more than in the matter of the soul's salvation. What do we say to the sinner? Trust Christ. What do we say to the saint? Trust Christ. What do we say to an assembly of saints, few or many? Trust Christ. Is there aught that He cannot manage? "Is there a thing too hard for Him?" Has His treasury of gift and grace become exhausted? Is He not able to supply ministerial gifts? Can He not furnish evangelists, pastors, and teachers? Can He not perfectly meet all the manifold necessities of His Church in the wilderness? If not, where are we? What shall we do? whither shall we turn? What had the congregation of old to do? To look to Jehovah. For every thing? Yes; for every thing—for food, for water, for clothing, for guidance, for protection, for all. All their springs were in Him. Must we turn to some one else? Never. Our Lord Christ is amply sufficient, in spite of all our failure and ruin, our sin and unfaithfulness. He has sent down the Holy Ghost, the blessed Paraclete, to dwell with and in His people—to form them into one body, and unite them to their living head in heaven. He is the power of unity, of communion, of ministry, and of worship. He has not left us, and He never will. Only let us trust Him; let us use Him; let us give Him room to act. Let us carefully guard against every thing that might tend to quench, to hinder, or to grieve Him. Let us acknowledge Him, in His own proper place in the assembly, and yield ourselves, in all things, to His guidance and authority.

Here, we are persuaded, lies the true secret of power and blessing. Do we deny the ruin? How could we? Alas! it stands forth as a fact too palpable and glaring to admit of denial. Do we seek to deny our share in the ruin—our folly and sin? Would to God we felt it more deeply! But shall we add to our sin by denying our Lord's grace and power to meet us in our folly and ruin? Shall we forsake Him, the Fountain of living waters, and hew out for ourselves broken cisterns that can hold no water? Shall we turn from the Rock of Ages and lean upon the broken reeds of our own devising? God forbid! Rather let the language of our hearts be, as we think of the name of Jesus:

> Salvation in that name is found,
> Cure for my grief and care;
> A healing balm for every wound,
> *All, all I want is there.*

But let not the reader suppose that we want to lend the smallest countenance to ecclesiastical pretention. We perfectly abhor any such thing. We look upon it as utterly contemptible. We believe we cannot possibly take too low a place. A low place and a lowly spirit are what alone become us in view of our common sin and shame. All we seek to maintain is this, the all-sufficiency of the name of Jesus for all the exigencies of the Church of God, at all times and under all circumstances. There was all power in that name in apostolic times, and why not now? Has any change passed over that glorious name? No, blessed be God. Well, then, it is sufficient for us at this moment, and all we want is to confide in it fully, and to show that we so confide by discarding thoroughly every other ground of confidence, and coming out, with bold decision, to that peerless and precious name. He has, blessed be His name, come down to the smallest congregation—the smallest plurality, inasmuch as He has said, "Where *two* or three are gathered together in My name, there am I." Does this still hold good? has it lost its power? does it no longer apply? Where has it been repealed?

Oh, Christian reader, we call upon you, by every argument which ought to weigh with your heart, to give your cordial assent and consent to this one eternal truth, namely, *The all-sufficiency of the name of the Lord Jesus Christ for the assembly of God, in every possible condition in which it can be found, throughout its entire history.** We call upon you not merely to hold this as a true theory, but to confess it practically; and then, assuredly, you will taste the deep blessedness of the presence of Jesus in the outside place—a blessedness which must be tasted in order to be known; but when once really tasted, it can never be forgotten or surrendered for aught beside.

But we had no intention of pursuing the foregoing line of thought so far, or of penning such a lengthened introduction to the section of our book which lies open before us, and to which we shall now invite the reader's particular attention.

On looking attentively at "the congregation in the wilderness" (Acts 7:38), we find it composed of three distinct elements, namely, *warriors, workers,* and *worshipers.* There was a *nation* of warriors, a *tribe* of workers, a *family* of worshipers, or priests. We have glanced at the first of these, and seen each one, according to his "pedigree," taking up his position by his "standard," according to the direct appointment of Jehovah; and we shall now dwell for a few moments on the second, and see each one at his work and service, according to the same appointment. We have considered the warriors; let us meditate on the workers.

The Levites were distinctly marked off from all the other tribes, and called to a very specific place and service. Thus we read of them, "But the Levites after the tribe of their fathers were not numbered among them. For the Lord had spoken unto Moses, saying, 'Only thou shalt not number the tribe of Levi, neither take the sum of them among the children of Israel. But thou shalt appoint the Levites over the tabernacle of testimony, and over all the vessels thereof, and over all things that belong to it: they shall bear the tabernacle, and all the vessels thereof; and they shall minister unto it, and shall encamp round about the tabernacle.

*In using the expression, "The all-sufficiency of the name of the Lord Jesus Christ," we understand by it all that is secured to His people in that name—life, righteousness, acceptance, the presence of the Holy Ghost with all His varied gifts, a divine centre or gathering-point. In a word, we believe that every thing that the Church can possibly need, for time or eternity, is comprehended in that one glorious name—The Lord Jesus Christ.

And when the tabernacle setteth forward, the Levites shall take it down; and when the tabernacle is to be pitched, the Levites shall set it up: and the stranger that cometh nigh shall be put to death. And the children of Israel shall pitch their tents, every man by his own camp, and every man by his own standard, throughout their hosts. But the Levites shall pitch round about the tabernacle of testimony, that there be no wrath upon the congregation of the children of Israel; and the Levites shall keep the charge of the tabernacle of testimony' " (chap. 1:47-53). And again we read, "But the Levites were not numbered among the children of Israel, as the Lord commanded Moses" (chap. 2:33).

But why the Levites? Why was this tribe specially marked off from all the others, and set apart for so holy and elevated a service? Was there any special sanctity or goodness about them to account for their being so distinguished? Not by nature, certainly, nor yet by practice, as we may see by the following words: "Simeon and Levi are brethren; instruments of cruelty are in their habitations. O my soul, come not thou into their secret; unto their assembly, mine honor, be not thou united; for in *their anger they slew a man,* and in their self-will they digged down a wall. Cursed by their anger, for it was fierce; and their wrath, for it was cruel: I will divide them in Jacob, and scatter them in Israel" (Gen. 49).

Such was Levi by nature and by practice—self-willed, fierce, and cruel. How remarkable that such an one should be singled out and brought into a place of such high and holy privilege! Surely, we may say, it was grace from first to last. It is the way of grace to take up the very worst cases. It stoops to the lowest depths and gathers up its brightest trophies from thence. "This is a faithful saying, and worthy of all acceptation, that Christ Jesus came into the world to save sinners, of whom I am chief" (1 Tim. 1:16). "Unto me, who am less than the least of all saints, is this grace given, that I should preach among the Gentiles the unsearchable riches of Christ" (Eph. 3).

But how striking the language, "O my soul, come not thou into their secret; unto their assembly, mine honor, be not thou united." God is of purer eyes than to behold evil, and cannot look on iniquity. God could not come into Levi's secret, or be united unto his assembly. That was impossible. God could have naught to do with self-will, fierceness, and cruelty. But yet He could bring Levi into His secret, and unite him to His assembly. He could take him out of his habitation, wherein were instruments of cruelty, and bring him into the tabernacle, to be occupied with the holy instruments and vessels that were there. This was grace—free, sovereign grace; and herein must be sought the basis of all Levi's blessed and elevated service. So far as he was personally concerned, there was an immeasurable distance between him and a holy God—a chasm which no human art or power could bridge. A holy God could have nothing to do with self-will, fierceness, and cruelty; but a God of grace could have to do with Levi. He could visit such an one in sovereign mercy, and raise him up from the depths of his moral degradation, and bring him into a place of nearness to Himself.

And, oh, what a marvelous contrast between Levi's position by nature and his position by grace! between the instruments of cruelty and the vessels of the sanctuary! between Levi in Genesis 34 and Levi in Numbers 3 and 4.

But let us look at the mode of God's dealing with Levi—the ground on which he was brought into such a place of blessing. In doing this, it will be needful for us to refer to chapter 8 of our book, and there we are let into the secret of the whole matter. We shall see that there was and could be no allowance of aught that belonged to Levi—no sanction of any of his ways; and yet there was the most perfect display of grace—grace reigning through righteousness. We speak of the type and its significance. We do so in view of that statement already referred to—"Now, all these things happened unto them for types." It is not a question of how far the Levites saw through these things. This is not at all the point. We are not to ask, What did the Levites see in God's dealing with them? but, What do we learn?

"And the Lord spake unto Moses, saying, 'Take the Levites from among the children of Israel, and cleanse them. And thus shalt thou do unto them, to cleanse them: Sprinkle water of purifying upon them, and let them shave all their flesh, and let them wash their clothes, and so make themselves clean" (chap. 8:5-7).

Here we have, in type, the only divine principle of cleansing. It is the application of death to nature and all its habits: it is the Word of God brought to bear upon the heart and conscience, in a living way. Nothing can be more expressive than the double action presented in the above passage. Moses was to sprinkle water of purifying upon them; and then they were to shave off all their hair, and wash their garments. There is great beauty and precision here. Moses, as representing the claims of God, cleanses the Levites according to those claims; and they, being cleansed, are able to bring the sharp razor to bear upon all that was the mere growth of nature, and to wash their garments, which expresses, in typic form, the cleansing their habits according to the Word of God. This was God's way of meeting all that appertained to Levi's natural state—the self-will, the fierceness, and the cruelty. The pure water and the sharp razor were called into action—the washing and shaving had to go on ere Levi was fit to approach the vessels of the sanctuary.

Thus it is in every case. There is, there can be, no allowance of nature among God's workers. There never was a more fatal mistake than to attempt to enlist nature in the service of God. It matters not how you may endeavor to improve or regulate it; it is not improvement, but death that will avail. It is of the very last possible importance for the reader to lay hold, with clearness and force, of this great practical truth. Man has been weighed in the balance and found wanting: the plummet has been applied to him, and he has been found crooked. It is of no possible use seeking to reform. Nothing will do save the *water* and the *razor.* God has closed up man's history; He has brought it to an end in the death of Christ. The first grand fact that the Holy Ghost presses upon the human conscience is, that God has delivered His solemn verdict upon human nature, and that each one must accept that verdict against himself personally. It is not a matter of opinion, or a matter of feeling. A person may say, I do not see, or I do not feel, that I am so bad as you seem to make out. We reply, That does not affect the question in the least. God has declared His judgment about us, and it is man's first duty to fall in with and bow to that. Of what use would it have been for Levi to say that he did not agree with what God's Word had said about him? Would that, could that, have altered the question as to him? In no wise. The divine record remained the same whether Levi felt it or not; but clearly it was the first step in wisdom's pathway to bow down under the weight of that record.

All this is expressed, in type, in the "water" and the "razor"—the "washing" and the "shaving." Nothing could be more significant or impressive. These acts set forth the solemn truth of the sentence of death upon nature, and the execution of judgment upon all that nature produces.

And what, let us ask, is the meaning of the initiatory act of Christianity—the act of baptism? Does it not set forth the blessed fact that "our old man"—our fallen nature—is completely set aside, and that we are introduced into an entirely new position? Truly so. And how do we use the razor? By rigid self-judgment, day by day; by the stern disallowance of all that is of nature's growth. This is the true path for all God's workers in the wilderness. When we look at Levi's conduct at Shechem, in Genesis 34, and the record concerning him in Genesis 49, we may ask, How can such an one ever be allowed to carry the vessels of the sanctuary? The answer is, Grace shines in Levi's call, and holiness shines in Levi's cleansing. He was called to the work according to the riches of divine grace; but he was fitted for the work according to the claims of divine holiness.

Thus it must be with all God's workers. We are most thoroughly convinced that we are fit for God's work just so far as nature is brought under the power of the cross and the sharp razor of self-judgment. Self-will can never be made available in the service of God; nay, it must be set aside, if we would know what true service is. There is, alas! a large amount of that which passes for service which, if judged in the light of the divine presence, would be seen to be but the fruit of a restless will. This is most solemn, and demands our most earnest attention. We cannot exercise too severe a censorship over ourselves in this very thing. The heart is so deceitful that we may be led to imagine that we are doing the Lord's work, when in reality we are only pleasing ourselves; but if we would tread the path of true service, we must seek to be more and more apart from nature. The self-willed Levi must pass through the typic process of washing and shaving ere he can be employed in that elevated service assigned him by the direct appointment of the God of Israel.

But ere proceeding to examine particularly the work and service of the Levites, we must look for a moment at a scene in Exodus 32, in which they act a very prominent and a very remarkable part. We allude, as the reader will at once perceive, to the golden calf. During the absence of Moses, the people so completely lost sight of God and His claims as to set up a molten calf and bow down thereto. This terrible act called for summary judgment. "And when Moses saw that the people were naked, (for Aaron had made them naked to their shame among their enemies,) then Moses stood in the gate of the camp, and said, 'Who is on the Lord's side? let him come unto me.' And all the sons of Levi gathered themselves together unto him. And he said unto them, 'Thus saith the Lord God of Israel, Put every man his sword by his side, and go in and out from gate to gate throughout the camp, and slay every man his brother, and every man his companion, and every man his neighbor.' And the children of Levi did according to the word of Moses: and there fell of the people that day about three thousand men. For Moses had said, 'Consecrate yourselves to-day to the Lord, even every man upon his son, and upon his brother; that He may bestow upon you a blessing this day' " (Exod. 32:25-29).

This was a testing moment. It could not be otherwise, when this great question was pressed home upon the heart and conscience, *"Who is on the Lord's side?"* Nothing could be more searching. The question was not, Who is willing to work? No; it was a far deeper and more searching question. It was not Who will go here or there—do this or that? There might be a vast amount of doing and going, and all the while it might be but the impulse of an unbroken will, which, acting upon religious nature, gave an appearance of devotedness and piety eminently calculated to deceive one's self and others.

But to be "on the Lord's side" implies the surrender of one's own will—yea, the surrender of one's self, and this is essential to the true servant—the real workman. Saul of Tarsus was on this ground when he exclaimed, "Lord, what wilt *Thou* have *me* to do?" What words, from the self-willed, fierce, and cruel persecutor of the Church of God!

"Who is on the Lord's side?" Reader, art thou? Search and see. Examine thyself closely. Remember, the question is not at all What art thou doing? No; it is far deeper. If thou art on the Lord's side, thou art ready for any thing and every thing. Thou art ready to stand still, or ready to go forward; ready to go to the right or to the left; ready to be active, and ready to be quiet; ready to stand on thy feet, and ready to lie on thy back. The grand point is this, namely, the surrender of thyself to the claims of another, and that other the Lord Christ.

This is an immense point. Indeed we know of nothing more important at the present moment than this searching question, "Who is on the Lord's side?" We live in days of immense self-will. Man exults in his liberty. And this comes out very prominently in religious matters. Just as it was in the camp of Israel in the days of the thirty-second of Exodus—the days of the golden calf. Moses was out of sight, and the human will was at work; the graving-tool was called into operation; and what was the result? The molten calf; and when Moses returned, he found the people in idolatry and nakedness. Then came forth the solemn and testing question, "Who is on the Lord's side?" This brought things to an issue, or rather it put people to the test. Nor is it otherwise now. Man's will is rampant, and that, too, in matters of religion. Man boasts of his rights, of the freedom of his will, the freedom of his judgment. There is the denial of the lordship of Christ; and therefore it behooves us to look well to it, and see that we really are taking sides with the Lord against ourselves; that we are in the attitude of simple subjection to His authority. Then we shall not be occupied with the amount or character of our service; it will be our one object to do the will of our Lord.

Now, to act thus under the Lord may often give an appearance of narrowness to our sphere of action; but with this we have nothing whatever to do. If a master tells his servant to stand in the hall, and not to stir until he rings the bell, what is the servant's duty? Clearly to stand still; nor should he be moved from this position or attitude, even though his fellow-servants should find fault with his apparent inactivity and good-for-nothingness; he may rest assured his master will approve and vindicate. This is enough for any true-hearted servant, whose one desire will ever be not so much to do a great deal, as to do the will of his Lord.

In a word, then, the question for the camp of Israel in the day of the golden calf, and the question for the Church in this day of human will, is this: "Who is on the Lord's side?" Momentous question! It is not, Who is on the side of religiousness, philanthropy, or moral reform? There may be a large amount of any or all of these things, and yet the will be thoroughly unbroken. Let us not forget this; nay, rather we should say, let us continually bear it in mind. We may be very zealous in promoting all the various schemes of philanthropy, religiousness, and moral reform, and all the while be ministering to self, and feeding self-will. This is a most solemn and weighty consideration; and it behooves us to give earnest heed to it. We are passing through a moment in the which man's will is being pampered with unparalleled diligence. We believe, most assuredly, that the true remedy for this evil will be found wrapped up in this one weighty question, "Who is on the Lord's side?" There is immense practical power in this question. To be really on *the Lord's* side is to be ready for aught to which He may see fit to call us, no matter what. If the soul is brought to say, in real truth, *"Lord,* what wilt Thou have me to do?" "Speak, *Lord,* for *Thy servant heareth,"* then we are ready for every thing. Hence, in the case of the Levites, they were called to "slay every man his brother, and every man his companion, and every man his neighbor." This was terrible work for flesh and blood; but the moment demanded it. God's claims had been openly and grossly dishonored; human invention had been at work, with the graving-tool, and a calf had been set up; the glory of God had been changed into the similitude of an ox that eateth grass; and therefore all who were on the Lord's side were called to gird on the sword. Nature might say, No; let us be tender and gentle and gracious. We shall accomplish more by kindness than by severity. It can do no good to wound people. There is far more power in love than in harshness. Let us love one another. Thus might nature throw out its suggestions—thus it might reason and argue; but the command was distinct and decisive, "Put every man his sword by his side." The sword was the only thing when the golden calf was there. To talk of love at such a moment would be to fling overboard the just claims of the God of Israel. It belongs to the true spirit of obedience to render the very service which suits the occasion. A servant has no business to reason; he is simply to do as he is bid. To raise a question, or put forth a demur, is to abandon our place as a servant. It might seem most dreadful work to have to slay a brother, a companion, or a neighbor; but the word of the Lord was imperative. It left no room for evasion; and the Levites, through grace, yielded a full and ready obedience. "The children of Levi did according to the word of Moses."

This is the only true path for those who

will be God's workers, and Christ's servants, in this world where self-will is dominant. It is immensely important to have the truth of the lordship of Christ deeply engraved upon the heart. It is the only regulator of the course and conduct. It settles a thousand questions. If the heart be really subject to the authority of Christ, it is in readiness for any thing and every thing to which He calls us, be it to stand still or to go forward, to do little or much, to be active or passive. To a really obedient heart the question is not at all, What am I doing? or Where am I going? It is simply, Am I doing the will of my Lord?

Such was the ground occupied by Levi. And mark the divine comment on this, as given in Malachi. "And ye shall know that I have sent this commandment unto you, that My covenant might be with Levi, saith the Lord of hosts. My covenant was with him of life and peace; and I gave them to him for the fear wherewith he feared Me, and was afraid before My name. The law of truth was in his mouth, and iniquity was not found in his lips: he walked with Me in peace and equity, and did turn many away from iniquity" (Mal. 2:4-6). Mark also the blessing pronounced by the lips of Moses, "And of Levi he said, 'Let thy Thummim and thy Urim be with thy holy one, whom thou didst prove at Massah, and with whom thou didst strive at the waters of Meribah; who said unto his father and to his mother, I have not seen him; neither did he acknowledge his brethren, nor knew his own children; for they have observed thy word and kept thy covenant. They shall teach Jacob thy judgments, and Israel thy law; they shall put incense before thee, and whole burnt-sacrifice upon thine altar. Bless, Lord, his substance, and accept the work of his hands: smite through the loins of them that rise against him, and of them that hate him, that they rise not again' " (Deut. 33:8-11).

It might have appeared unwarrantably harsh and severe in Levi not to have seen his parents, or known or acknowledged his brethren. But God's claims are paramount, and our Lord Christ hath declared these solemn words, "If any man come to Me, and hate not his father and mother and wife and children and brethren and sisters, yea, and his own life also, he cannot be My disciple" (Luke 14:26).

These are plain words, and they let us into the secret of what it is which lies at the bottom of all true service. Let no one imagine that we are to be without natural affection. Far be the thought. To be so would be to connect us, morally, with the apostasy of the last days (see 2 Tim. 3:3). But when the claims of natural affection are allowed to stand in the way of whole-hearted service to Christ, and when the so-called love of our brethren receives a higher place than faithfulness to Christ, then are we unfit for His service and unworthy of the name of His servants. Let it be carefully noted that what formed the *moral* ground of Levi's title to be employed in the Lord's service was the fact that he did not *see* his parents, *acknowledge* his brethren, or *know* his children. In a word, he was enabled to set the claims of nature completely aside, and to give the claims of Jehovah the paramount place in his heart. This, we repeat, is the only true basis of the servant's character.

This is a most weighty consideration, and one which demands the most serious attention of the Christian reader. There may be a vast amount of what looks like service—a great deal of activity, of coming and going, of doing and saying—and, all the while, there may not be a single atom of true Levite service—yea, it may, in God's estimation, be only the restless activity of the will. What, it may be said, can the will show itself in the service of God—in matters of religion? Alas! it can, and does. And very often the apparent energy and fruitfulness in work and service is just in proportion to the energy of the will. This is peculiarly solemn. It calls for the most rigid self-judgment, in the light of the divine presence. True service doth not consist in great activity, but in profound subjection to the will of our Lord; and where this exists, there will be a readiness to sink the claims of parents, brethren, and children, in order to carry out the will of Him whom we own as Lord. True, we should love our parents, our brethren, and our children. It is not that we should love these less, but we should love Christ more. He and His claims must ever have the paramount place in the heart, if we would be true workers for God, true servants for Christ, true Levites in the wilderness. It was this that marked the actings of Levi on the occasion to which we are referring. God's claims were in question, and hence the claims of nature were not to be entertained for a moment. Parents, brethren, and children, how dear soever these might be, were not to stand in the way when the glory of the God of Israel had been changed into the similitude of an ox that eateth grass.

Here lies the whole question, in all its weight and magnitude. The ties of natural relationship, with all the claims, duties, and responsibilities arising out of such ties, will ever get their proper place, their due respect, from those whose hearts and minds and consciences have been brought under the adjusting power of the truth of God. Naught, save what is really due to God and His Christ, should ever be suffered to infringe those rights which are founded upon natural relationship. This is a most necessary and wholesome consideration, and one which we would particularly press upon the young Christian reader. We have ever to be on our guard against a spirit of self-will and self-pleasing, which is never so dangerous as when it clothes itself in the garb of religious service and work so called. It behooves us to be *very sure indeed* that we are directly and simply governed by the claims of God when we disregard the claims of natural relationship. In Levi's case, the matter was as clear as a sunbeam, and hence *the "sword"* of judgment, not the kiss of affection, befitted the critical moment. So also in our history, there are moments in which it would be open disloyalty to our Lord Christ to hearken for one instant to the voice of natural relationship.

The above remarks may help the reader to understand the actings of the Levites in Exodus 32, and the words of our Lord in Luke 14:26. May God's Spirit enable us to realize and exhibit the adjusting power of truth.

We shall now dwell for a few moments on the consecration of the Levites, in Numbers 8, in order that we may have the whole subject before our minds. Truly it is a theme full of instruction for all who desire to be workers for God.

After the ceremonial acts of "washing" and "shaving" already referred to, we read, "Then let them [*i.e.,* the Levites] take a young bullock with his meat-offering, even fine flour mingled with oil, and another young bullock shalt thou take for a sin-offering. And thou shalt bring the Levites before the tabernacle of the congregation: and thou shalt gather the whole assembly of the children of Israel together: and thou shalt bring the Levites before the Lord: and the children of Israel shall put their hands upon the Levites: and Aaron shall offer the Levites before the Lord for an offering of the children of Israel, that they may execute the service of the Lord. And the Levites shall lay their hands upon the heads of the bullocks; and thou shalt offer the one for a sin-offering, and the other for a burnt-offering, unto the Lord, to make an atonement for the Levites."

Here we have presented to us, in type, the two grand aspects of the death of Christ. The sin-offering furnishes the one, the burnt-offering furnishes the other. Into the details of those offerings we do not enter here, having sought to do so in the opening chapters of our *Notes on Leviticus.* We would merely observe here that in the sin-offering we see Christ bearing sin in His own body on the tree, and enduring the wrath of God against sin; in the burnt-offering, we see Christ glorifying God even in the very matter of making atonement for sin. Atonement is made in both; but in the former, it is atonement according to the depth of the sinner's need; in the latter, it is atonement according to the measure of Christ's devotedness to God. In that, we see the hatefulness of sin; in this, the preciousness of Christ. It is, we need hardly say, the same atoning death of Christ, but presented in two distinct aspects.*

*For further instruction on the doctrine of the sin-offering and the burnt-offering, the reader is referred to *Notes on Leviticus,* chapters 1 and 4.

Now, the Levites laid their hands on both the sin-offering and the burnt-offering; and this act of the imposition of hands expressed the simple fact of identification. But how different the result in each case! When Levi laid his hands on the head of the sin-offering, it involved the transfer of all his sins, of all his guilt, of all his fierceness, cruelty, and self-will to the victim; and on the other hand, when he laid his hands on the head of the burnt-offering, it involved the transfer of all the acceptableness of the sacrifice, of all its perfectness, to Levi. Of course, we speak of what the type set forth. We do not undertake to state aught as to Levi's intelligent entrance into these things; we merely seek to unfold the meaning of the ceremonial figure; and, most assuredly, no figure could be more expressive than the imposition of hands, whether we view it in the case of the sin-offering or in the case of the burnt-offering. The doctrine of all this is embodied in that most weighty passage at the close of 2 Cor. 5, "He hath made Him [Christ] to be sin for us, who knew no sin, that we might become the righteousness of God in Him." " 'And thou shalt set the Levites before Aaron, and before his sons, and offer them for an offering unto the Lord. Thus shalt thou separate the Levites from among the children of Israel; and the Levites shall be Mine. And after that shall the Levites go in to do the service of the tabernacle of the congregation; and thou shalt cleanse them, and offer them for an offering. For they are wholly given unto Me from among the children of Israel; instead of such as open every womb, even instead of the first-born of all the children of Israel, have I taken them unto Me. For all the first-born of the children of Israel are Mine, both man and beast: on the day that I smote every first-born in the land of Egypt I sanctified them for Myself. And I have taken the Levites for all the first-born of the children of Israel. And I have given the Levites as a gift to Aaron and to his sons from among the children of Israel, to do the service of the children of Israel in the tabernacle of the congregation, and to make an atonement for the children of Israel: that there be no plague among the children of Israel, when the children of Israel come nigh unto the sanctuary.' And Moses and Aaron and all the congregation of the children of Israel did to the Levites according unto all that the Lord commanded Moses concerning the Levites, so did the children of Israel unto them" (Num. 8:13-20).

How forcibly are we reminded, by the foregoing lines, of the words of our Lord in John 17—"I have manifested Thy name unto the men which Thou gavest Me out of the world: Thine they were, and Thou gavest them Me; and they have kept Thy word. . . . I pray for them: I pray not for the world, but for them which Thou hast given Me; for they are Thine. And all Mine are Thine, and Thine are Mine; and I am glorified in them" (ver. 6-10).

The Levites were a separated people—God's special possession. They took the place of all the first-born in Israel—of those who were saved from the sword of the destroyer by the blood of the lamb. They were, typically, a dead and risen people, set apart to God, and by Him presented as a gift to Aaron the high-priest, to do the service of the tabernacle.

What a place for the self-willed, fierce, and cruel Levi! What a triumph of grace! What an illustration of the efficacy of the blood of atonement and the water of purification! They were, by nature and by practice, far off from God; but the "blood" of atonement, and the "water" of cleansing, and the "razor" of self-judgment, had done their blessed work, and hence the Levites were in a condition to be presented as a gift to Aaron and to his sons, to be associated with them in the hallowed services of the tabernacle of the congregation.

In all this the Levites were a striking type of God's people now. These latter have been lifted from the depths of their degradation and ruin as sinners. They are washed in the precious blood of Christ, purified by the application of the Word, and called to the exercise of habitual and rigid self-judgment. Thus are they fitted for that holy service to the which they are called. God has given them to His Son, in order that they may be

His workers in this world. "Thine they were, and Thou gavest them Me." Wondrous thought! To think that such as we could be thus spoken of! To think of our being God's property and God's gift to His Son! Well may we say it surpasses all human thought. It is not merely that we are saved from hell; that is true: it is not merely that we are pardoned, justified, and accepted; all this is true: but we are called to the high and holy work of bearing through this world the name, the testimony, the glory, of our Lord Jesus Christ. This is our work as true Levites. As men of war, we are called to fight; as priests, we are privileged to worship; but as Levites, we are responsible to serve, and our service is to carry through this dreary desert scene the Antitype of the tabernacle, and that tabernacle was the figure of Christ. This is our distinct line of service. To this we are called; to this we are set apart.

The reader will, we doubt not, notice, with interest, the fact that it is in this book of Numbers, and here alone, that we are furnished with all the precious and deeply instructive details respecting the Levites. In this we have a fresh illustration of the character of our book. It is from a wilderness stand-point that we get a full and proper view of God's workers as well as of God's warriors.

And now, let us examine, for a few moments, the service of the Levites, as detailed in Numbers 3 and 4. "And the Lord spake unto Moses, saying, 'Bring the tribe of Levi near, and present them before Aaron the priest, that they may minister unto him. And they shall keep his charge, and the charge of the whole congregation before the tabernacle of the congregation, to do the service of the tabernacle. And they shall keep all the instruments of the tabernacle of the congregation, and the charge of the children of Israel, to do the service of the tabernacle. And thou shalt give the Levites unto Aaron and to his sons: they are wholly given unto him out of the children of Israel' " (chap. 3:5-9).

The Levites represented the whole congregation of Israel, and acted on their behalf. This appears from the fact that the children of Israel laid their hands on the heads of the Levites, just as the Levites laid their hands on the heads of the sacrifices (see chap. 8:10). The act of imposition expressed identification, so that, according to this, the Levites furnish a distinct view of the people of God in the wilderness. They present them to us as a company of earnest workers, and that, too, be it noted, not as mere desultory laborers, running to and fro, and doing each one what seemed right in his own eyes. Nothing of the sort. If the men of war had their pedigree to show, and their standard to adhere to, so had the Levites their centre to gather around and their work to do. All was as clear, distinct, and defined as God could make it; and moreover, all was under the immediate authority and direction of the high-priest.

It is most needful for all who would be true Levites, proper workmen, intelligent servants, to weigh, with all seriousness, this point. Levite service was to be regulated by the appointment of the priest. There was no more room for the exercise of self-will in the service of the Levites than there was in the position of the men of war. All was divinely settled; and this was a signal mercy to all whose hearts were in a right condition. To one whose will was unbroken, it might seem a hardship and a most irksome task to be obliged to occupy the same position, or to be engaged in precisely the same line of work. Such an one might sigh for something fresh—some variety in his work; but, on the contrary, where the will was subdued, and the heart adjusted, each one would say, My path is perfectly plain; I have only to obey. This is ever the business of the true servant. It was pre-eminently so with Him who was the only perfect servant that ever trod the earth. He could say, "I came down from heaven, not to do Mine own will, but the will of Him that sent Me." And again, "My meat is to do the will of Him that sent Me, and to finish His work."

But there is another fact which claims our attention, in reference to the Levites, and that is, their service had exclusively to do with the tabernacle and its belongings. They had nothing else to do. For a Levite to think of putting his hand to aught beside would have been to deny his calling, to abandon his divinely appointed work, and to fly in the face of God's commandments.

Just so is it with Christians now. Their exclusive business—their one grand work—their absorbing service, is Christ and His belongings. They have nothing else to do. For a Christian to think of putting his hand to aught beside is to deny his calling, to abandon his divinely appointed work, and to fly in the face of the divine commandments. A true Levite of old could say, To me to live is the tabernacle; and a true Christian now can say, "To me to live is Christ." The grand question, in every matter which may present itself before the Christian, is this, Can I connect Christ with it? If not, I have nothing whatever to do with it.

This is the true way to look at things. It is not a question as to the right or wrong of this or that. No; it is simply a question as to how far it concerns the name and glory of Christ. This simplifies every thing amazingly. It answers a thousand questions, solves a thousand difficulties, and makes the path of the true and earnest Christian as clear as a sunbeam. A Levite had no difficulty as to his work. It was all settled for him with divine precision. The burden that each had to carry, and the work that each had to do, was laid down with a clearness which left no room for the questionings of the heart. Each man could know his work and do it; and, let us add, the work was done by each one discharging his own specific functions. It was not by running hither and thither, and doing this or that, but by each man sedulously adhering to his own particular calling, that the service of the tabernacle was duly discharged.

It is well to bear this in mind. We, as Christians, are very apt to jostle one another; indeed, we are sure to do so if we do not each one pursue his own divinely appointed line of work. We say "*divinely* appointed," and would press the word; we have no right to choose our own work. If the Lord has made one man an evangelist, another a teacher, another a pastor, and another an exhorter, how is the work to go on? Surely, it is not by the evangelist trying to teach, and the teacher to exhort, or one who is not fitted for either trying to do both. No; it is by each one exercising his own divinely imparted gift. No doubt, it may please the Lord to endow one individual with a variety of gifts; but this does not, in the smallest degree, touch the principle on which we are dwelling, which is simply this, every one of us is responsible to know his own special line and pursue it. If this be lost sight of, we shall get into hopeless confusion. God has His quarry-men, His stone-squarers, and His masons. The work progresses by each man attending diligently to his own work. If all were quarry-men, where were the stone-squarers? if all were stone-squarers, where were the masons? The greatest possible damage is done to the cause of Christ, and to God's work in the world, by one man aiming at another's line of things, or seeking to imitate another's gift. It is a grievous mistake, against which we would solemnly warn the reader. Nothing can be more senseless. God never repeats Himself. There are not two faces alike, not two leaves in the forest alike, not two blades of grass alike. Why, then, should any one aim at another's line of work, or affect to possess another's gift? Let each one be satisfied to be just what his Master has made him. This is the secret of real peace and progress.

All this finds a very vivid illustration in the inspired record concerning the service of the three distinct classes of the Levites, which we shall now proceed to quote at length for the reader. There is nothing, after all, to be compared wih the veritable language of holy Scripture.

"And the Lord spake unto Moses in the wilderness of Sinai, saying, 'Number the children of Levi after the house of their fathers, by their families every male from a month old and upward shalt thou number them.' And Moses numbered them *according to the word of the Lord, as he was commanded.* And these were the sons of Levi by their names: Gershon and Kohath and Merari. And these are the names of the sons of Gershon by their families: Libni and Shimei. And the sons of Kohath by their families: Amram and Izehar, Hebron and Uzziel. And the sons of Merari by their families: Mahli and Mushi. These are the families of the Levites according to the house of their fathers. Of Gershon was the family of the Libnites, and the family of the Shimites: these are the families of the Gershonites. Those that were numbered of them, according to the number of all the males, from a month old and upward, even those that were numbered of them were seven thousand and five hundred. The families of the Gershonites shall pitch behind the tabernacle westward. And the chief of the house of the father of the Gershonites shall be Eliasaph the son of Lael. And the charge of the sons of Gershon in the tabernacle of the congregation shall be the tabernacle, and the tent, the covering thereof, and the hanging for the door of the tabernacle of the congregation, and the hangings of the court, and the curtain for the door of the court, which is by the tabernacle, and by the altar round about, and the cords of it for all the service thereof" (chap. 3:14-26). And again, we read, "And the Lord spake unto Moses, saying, 'Take also the sum of the sons of Gershon, throughout the houses of their fathers, by their families; from thirty years old and upward until fifty years old shalt thou number them; all that enter in to perform the service, to do the work in the tabernacle of the congregation. This is the service of the families of the Gershonites, to serve, and for burdens: and they shall bear the curtains of the tabernacle, and the tabernacle of the congregation, his covering, and the covering of the badgers' skins that is above upon it, and the hanging for the door of the tabernacle of the congregation, and the hangings of the court, which is by the tabernacle and by the altar round about, and their cords, and all the instruments of their service, and all that is made for them: so shall they serve. At the appointment of Aaron and his sons shall be all the service of the sons of the Gershonites, in all their burdens, and in all their service: and ye shall appoint unto them in charge all their burdens. This is the service of the families of the sons of Gershon in the tabernacle of the congregation: and their charge shall be under the hand of Ithamar the son of Aaron the priest" (chap. 4:21-28).

Thus much as to Gershon and his work. He, with his brother Merari, had to carry "the tabernacle"; whereas Kohath was called to bear "the sanctuary," as we read in chapter 10. "And the tabernacle was taken down; and the sons of Gershon, and the sons of Merari set forward, bearing *the tabernacle*. . . . And the Kohathites set forward, bearing *the sanctuary;* and the other [*i.e.*, the Gershonites and the Merarites] did set up the tabernacle against they came" (ver. 17,21). There was a strong moral link connecting Gershon and Merari in their service, although their work was perfectly distinct, as we shall see from the following passage:

"As for the sons of Merari, thou shalt number them after their families, by the house of their fathers; from thirty years old and upward, even unto fifty years old, shalt thou number them, every one that entereth into the service, to do the work of the tabernacle of the congregation. And this is the charge of their burden, according to all their service in the tabernacle of the congregation: the boards of the tabernacle, and the bars thereof, and the pillars thereof, and sockets thereof, and the pillars of the court round about, and their sockets, and their pins, and their cords, with all their instruments, and with all their service: and by name ye shall reckon the instruments of the charge of their burden. This is the service of the families of the sons of Merari, according to all their service in the tabernacle of the congregation, under the hand of Ithamar, the son of Aaron the priest" (chap. 4:29-33).

All this was clear and distinct. Gershon had nothing to do with the boards and pins, and Merari had nothing to do with the curtains or the coverings. And yet they were very intimately connected, as they were mutually dependent. "The boards and sockets" would not do without "the curtains," and the curtains would not do without the boards and sockets. And as to "the *pins,*" though apparently so insignificant, who could estimate their importance in keeping things together, and maintaining the visible unity of the whole? Thus all worked together to one common end, and that end was gained by each attending to his own special line. If a Gershonite had taken it into his head to abandon "the curtains" and address himself to "the pins," he would have left his own work undone and interfered with the work of the Merarite. This would never do. It would have thrown every thing into hopeless confusion; whereas by adhering to the divine rule, all was maintained in the most exquisite order.

It must have been perfectly beautiful to mark God's workers in the wilderness. Each one was at his post, and each moved in his divinely appointed sphere. Hence, the moment the cloud was lifted up and the order issued to strike, every man knew what he had to do, and he addressed himself to that and to nothing else. No man had any right to think for himself: Jehovah thought for all. The Levites had declared themselves "on the Lord's side"; they had yielded themselves to His authority; and this fact lay at the very base of all their wilderness work and service. Looked at in this light, it would be deemed a matter of total indifference whether a man had to carry a pin, a curtain, or a golden candlestick. The grand question for each and for all was simply, Is this my work? is this what the Lord has given me to do?

This settled every thing. Had it been left to human thinking or human choosing, one man might like this, another might like that, and a third might like something else. How then could the tabernacle ever be borne along through the wilderness, or set up in its place? Impossible! There could be but one supreme authority, namely, Jehovah Himself. He arranged for all, and all had to submit to Him. There was no room at all for the exercise of the human will. This was a signal mercy; it prevented a world of strife and confusion. There must be subjection—there must be a broken will—there must be a cordial yielding to divine authority, otherwise it will turn out to be like the book of Judges—"every man doing that which is right in his own eyes." A Merarite might say—or think, if he did not say it,"What! am I to spend the very best portion of my life upon earth—the days of my prime and vigor—in looking after a few pins? Was this the end for which I was born? Am I to have nothing higher before me as an object in life? Is this to be my occupation from the age of thirty to fifty?"

To such questions there was a twofold reply. In the first place, it was enough for the Merarite to know that Jehovah had assigned him his work. This was sufficient to impart dignity to what nature might esteem the smallest and meanest matter. It does not matter what we are doing, provided always we are doing our divinely appointed work. A man may pursue what his fellows would deem a most brilliant career; he may spend his energies, his time, his talents, his fortune, in pursuits which the men of this world esteem grand and glorious, and, all the while, his life may prove to be but a splendid bubble. But on the other hand, the man that simply does the will of God, whatever that may be—the man who executes his Lord's commands, whatever such commands may enjoin—that is the man whose path is illuminated by the beams of divine approbation, and whose work shall be remembered when the most splendid schemes of the children of this world have sunk in eternal oblivion.

But, besides the moral worth attaching always to the act of doing what we are told to do, there was also a special dignity belonging to the work of a Merarite, even though that work was merely attending to a few "pins" or "sockets." Every thing connected with the tabernacle was of the very deepest interest and highest value. There was not, in the whole world, any thing to be compared with that boarded tent with all its mystic belongings. It was a holy dignity and privilege to be allowed to touch the smallest pin that formed a part of that wonderful tabernacle in the wilderness. It was more glorious, by far, to be a Merarite looking after the pins of the tabernacle, than to wield the sceptre of Egypt or Assyria. True, that Merarite, according to the import of his name, might seem a poor "sorrowful" laboring man; but oh! his labor stood connected with the dwelling-place of the Most High God, the possessor of heaven and earth. His hands handled the things which were the patterns of things in the heavens. Every pin, every socket, every curtain, and every covering was a shadow of good things to come—a foreshadowing of Christ.

We do not mean to assert that the poor laboring Merarite or Gershonite understood these things. This is not, by any means, the point. *We* can understand them. It is our privilege to bring all these things—the tabernacle and its mystic furniture—under the brilliant light of the New Testament, and there read Christ in all.

While, therefore, we predicate nothing as to the measure of intelligence possessed by the Levites in their respective work, we, at the same time, may say, with confidence, that it was a very precious privilege to be allowed to touch and handle, and bear through the wilderness, the earthly shadows of heavenly realities. Moreover, it was a special mercy to have the authority of a "Thus saith the Lord" for every thing they put their hand to. Who can estimate such a mercy—such a privilege? Each member of that marvelous tribe of workers had his own particular line of things marked out by God's hand and superintended by God's priest. It was not each doing what he liked himself, nor one man running in the wake of another, but all bowing to the authority of God, and doing precisely what they were told to do. This was the secret of order throughout the eight thousand five hundred and eighty workers (chap. 4:48); and, we may say, with all possible confidence, it is the only true secret of order still. Why is it that we have so much confusion in the professing church? why such conflicting thoughts, feelings, and opinions? why such clashing one with another? why such crossing of each other's path? Simply from the lack of entire and absolute submission to the Word of God. Our *will* is at work. We choose our own ways, instead of allowing God to choose for us. We want that attitude and temper of soul in the which *all* human thoughts (our own amongst them) shall be put down at what they are really worth, and God's thoughts shall rise into full unqualified dominion.

This, we feel persuaded, is the grand desideratum—the crying want of the day in which our lot is cast. Man's will is every where gaining the ascendant. It is rising like a mighty tide, and bearing away those ancient barriers which have, in some measure, kept it in check. Many an old and time-honored institution is, at this moment, giving way before the torrent; many an edifice, whose foundations, as we supposed, were laid deep down in the fond and reverent affections of the people, is giving way beneath the battering-ram of popular feeling. "Let us break their bands asunder, and cast away their cords from us."

Such is, pre-eminently, the spirit of the age. What is the antidote? *Subjection!* Subjection to what? Is it to what is called the authority of the church? Is it to the voice of tradition? Is it to the commandments and doctrines of men? No, blessed be God; it is not to any of these things, nor to all of them put together. To what, then? To the voice of the living God—the voice of holy Scripture. This is the grand remedy for self-will on the one hand, and submission to human authority on the other. "We must *obey*"—this is the answer to self-will; "We must obey *God,*"—this is the answer to mere bowing down to human authority. We see these two elements all around us. The former—self-will, resolves itself into infidelity; the latter—subjection to man, resolves itself into superstition. These two will bear sway over the whole civilized world. They will carry away all, save those who are divinely taught to say and feel and act upon that immortal sentence, "We must obey God rather than man."

It was this that enabled the Gershonite in the wilderness to look after those rough, unattractive-looking "badger-skins," and that enabled the Merarite to look after these apparently insignificant "pins." Yes, and it is this which will enable the Christian now to address himself to that special line of service to which his Lord may see fit to call him.

What though, to human eyes, it seems rough and unattractive, mean and insignificant; it is enough for us that our Lord has assigned us our post and given us our work, and that our work has direct reference to the Person and glory of Him who is the chiefest among ten thousand and altogether lovely. We, too, may have to confine ourselves to the antitype of the rough, unsightly badger-skin, or the insignificant pin. But let us remember that whatever has reference to Christ—His name, His Person, His cause—in the world, is unspeakably precious to God. It may be very small in man's account, but what of that? We must look at things from God's point of view, we must measure them by His standard, and that is, Christ. God measures every thing by Christ. Whatever has even the very smallest reference to Christ is interesting and important in God's account; whereas the most splendid undertakings, the most gigantic schemes, the most astonishing enterprises, of the men of this world, all pass away like the morning cloud and the early dew. Man makes *self* his centre, his object, his standard. He values things according to the measure in which they exalt himself and further his interests. Even religion itself, so called, is taken up in the same way, and made a pedestal on which to display himself. Every thing, in short, is worked up as capital for self, and used as a reflector to throw light upon and call attention to that one object. Thus there is a mighty gulf between God's thoughts and man's thoughts, and the shores of that gulf are as far apart as *Christ* and *self*. All that belongs to Christ is of eternal interest and moment: all that belongs to self shall pass away and be forgotten. Hence, therefore, the most fatal mistake into which any man can fall is to make *self* his object. It must issue in everlasting disappointment. But on the other hand, the very wisest, safest, best thing that any man can do, is to make Christ his one absorbing object. This must infallibly issue in everlasting blessedness and glory.

Pause here a moment, and commune with thine own heart and conscience. It seems to us, at this point, that we have a sacred responsibility to discharge in reference to thy soul. We are penning these lines in the solitude of our chamber at Bristol, and you may, perchance, read them in the solitude of thy chamber in New Zealand, Australia, or some other distant spot. We would therefore remember that our object is not to write a book, nor yet merely to expound Scripture. We desire to be used of God in the blessed work of dealing with thy very inmost soul. Permit us, therefore, to put this solemn and pointed question home to thee: *What is thy object?* Is it Christ, or self? Be honest with thyself before the almighty and all-seeing Searcher of hearts. Sit in stern judgment upon thyself, as in the very light of the divine presence. Be not deceived by any gilded or false coloring. God sees below the surface of things, and He would have thee to do so likewise. He presents Christ to thee, in contrast with all beside. Hast thou accepted Him? Is He thy wisdom, thy righteousness, thy sanctification, and thy redemption? Canst thou say, without hesitation, "My Beloved is mine, and I am His"? Search and see. Is this a thoroughly settled point, deep down in the very depths of thy soul? If so, art thou making Christ thy exclusive object? art thou measuring every thing by Him?

Ah, these are searching questions. Be assured we do not put them to thee without feeling their edge and power for ourselves. As God is our witness, we do feel, though in a very small degree, their weight and seriousness. We are deeply and thoroughly convinced that nothing will stand save that which is connected with Christ; and moreover, that the very smallest matter which refers, however remotely, to Him is of commanding interest in the judgment of heaven. If we may be permitted to awaken a sense of this in any heart, or to deepen the sense where it has been awakened, we shall feel we have not penned this volume in vain.

We must now, ere closing this lengthened section, glance for a few moments at the Kohathites and their work.

"And the Lord spake unto Moses and unto Aaron, saying, 'Take the sum of the sons of Kohath from among the sons of Levi, after their families, by the house of their fathers, from thirty years old and upward even until fifty years old, all that enter into the host, to do the work in the tabernacle of the congregation. This shall be the service of the sons of Kohath in the tabernacle of the congregation, about the most holy things: and when the camp setteth forward, Aaron shall come, and his sons, and they shall take down the covering vail, and cover *the ark* of testimony with it: and shall put thereon the covering of badgers' skins, and shall spread over it a cloth wholly of blue, and shall put in the staves thereof. And upon *the table* of show-bread they shall spread a cloth of blue, and put thereon the dishes, and the spoons, and the bowls, and covers to cover withal: and the continual bread shall be thereon: and they shall spread upon them a cloth of scarlet, and cover the same with a covering of badgers' skins, and shall put in the staves thereof. And they shall take a cloth of blue, and cover the candlestick of the light, and his lamps, and his tongs, and his snuff-dishes, and all the oil vessels thereof, wherewith they minister unto it; and they shall put it and all the vessels thereof within a covering of badgers' skins, and shall put it upon a bar. And upon *the golden altar* they shall spread a cloth of blue, and cover it with a covering of badgers' skins, and shall put to the staves thereof: and they shall take all the instruments of ministry, wherewith they minister in the sanctuary, and put them in a cloth of blue, and cover them with a covering of badgers' skins, and shall put them on a bar: and they shall take away the ashes from *the altar,* and spread a purple cloth thereon: and they shall put upon it all the vessels thereof, wherewith they minister about it, even the censers, the flesh-hooks, and the shovels, and the basons, all the vessels of the altar; and they shall spread upon it a covering of badgers' skins, and put to the staves of it. And when Aaron and his sons have made an end of covering the sanctuary, and all the vessels of the sanctuary, as the camp is to set forward; after that, the sons of Kohath shall come to bear it: but they shall not touch any holy thing, lest they die. These things are the burden of the sons of Kohath in the tabernacle of the congregation' " (4:1-15).

Here we see what precious mysteries were committed to the charge of the Kohathites. The ark, the golden table, the golden candlestick, the golden altar, and the altar of burnt-offering—all these were shadows of good things to come—the patterns of things in the heavens—the figures of the true—the types of Christ, in His Person, His work, and His offices, as we have sought to show in our *Notes on Exodus* (chap. 24–30). They are here presented in the wilderness, and, if we may be allowed the expression, in their traveling-dress. With the exception of the ark of the covenant, all these things presented the one unvarying appearance to the human eye, namely, the rough covering of the badgers' skins. With the ark there was this difference, that above the badgers' skins there was "a cloth wholly of blue," setting forth, doubtless, the entirely heavenly character of the Lord Jesus Christ in His own divine Person. That which was essentially heavenly in Him lay upon the very surface of His blessed life here below. He was the entirely heavenly Man—"the Lord from heaven." Underneath this covering of blue were the badgers' skins, which may be viewed as the expression of that which protects from evil. The ark was the only thing that was covered in this peculiar manner.

With regard to "the table of show-bread," which was a type of our Lord Jesus Christ in His connection with the twelve tribes of Israel, there was first "a cloth of *blue,*" and then "a cloth of *scarlet*"; and over all, the badgers' skins. In other words, there was that which is essentially heavenly; then that which expresses human splendor; and above all, that which protects from evil. It is the purpose of God that Israel's twelve tribes shall be pre-eminent in the earth—that in them the very highest type of human splendor shall be exhibited. Hence the appropriateness of the "scarlet" covering on the table of show-bread. The twelve loaves evidently point to the twelve tribes; and as to the scarlet color, the reader has only to look through Scripture in order to see that it sets forth that which man considers splendid.

The coverings of the golden candlestick and of the golden altar were identical, namely, first, the heavenly covering, and then the external badgers' skin. In the candlestick we see our Lord Christ in connection with the work of the Holy Ghost in light and testimony. The golden altar shows us Christ and the preciousness of His intercession—the fragrance and value of what He is before God. Both these, when passing along the sand of the desert, were wrapped up in that which was heavenly, and protected above by the badgers' skins.

Finally, in reference to the brazen altar, we observe a marked distinction. It was covered with "purple" instead of "blue" or "scarlet." Why was this? Doubtless because the brazen altar prefigured Christ as the One who "*suffered* for sins," and who shall therefore wield the sceptre of royalty. "Purple" is the royal color. The One who suffered in this world shall reign; the One who wore the crown of thorns shall wear the crown of glory. Hence the moral fitness of the "purple" covering on the brazen altar—for on that altar the victim was offered. We know there is nothing in Scripture without its own divine meaning, and it is our privilege as well as our duty to seek to know the meaning of all that our God has graciously written for our learning. This, we believe, can only be reached by humble, patient, prayerful waiting upon Him. The One who has penned the book knows perfectly the scope and object of the book as a whole, and of each division of the book in particular. This will have the effect of checking the unhallowed flights of the imagination. The Spirit of God alone can open Scripture to our souls. "God is His own interpreter" in revelation as well as in providence, and the more we lean on Him, in true self-emptiness, the deeper insight we shall have both into His Word and ways.

We would therefore say to the Christian reader: Take the first fifteen verses of Numbers 4, and read them in the presence of God. Ask Him to explain to thee the meaning of each clause—the meaning of the ark, and why it alone was covered with "a cloth wholly of blue." And so of all the rest. We have ventured, we trust in humility of mind, to suggest the meaning; but we earnestly desire that thou shouldst get it directly from God for thyself, and not accept it merely from man. We confess we are terribly afraid of imagination; and we know not that we have ever sat down to write on sacred Scripture with a deeper sense of this, that none but the Holy Ghost can really explain it.

Thou wilt say, then, Why sit down to write at all? Well, it is with the fond hope of being permitted, in some feeble manner, to help the earnest student of Scripture to catch sight of the rare and exquisite gems that lie scattered along the inspired page, so that he may pick them up for himself. Thousands of readers might read, again and again, the fourth of Numbers, and not even perceive the fact that the ark was the only part of the mystic furniture of the tabernacle that did not exhibit the badger-skin. And if the simple fact be not laid hold of, how can its import be seen? So also as to the brazen altar, how many have failed to notice that it alone put on the "purple"!

Now, we may rest assured that both these facts are full of spiritual meaning. The ark was the very highest manifestation of God, and therefore we may understand why it should exhibit, at first sight, that which was purely heavenly. The brazen altar was the place where sin was judged—it typified Christ in His work as a Sin-bearer—it set forth that most distant place to which He traveled for us; and yet that brazen altar was the only thing that was wrapped in *royal* covering. Can aught be more exquisite than the teaching here? What infinite wisdom in all these fine distinctions! The ark conducts us to the very highest point in heaven; the brazen altar conducts us to the lowest point on earth. They stood at extreme points in the tabernacle. In the former, we see the One who magnified the law; in the latter, we see the One who was made sin. In the one, that which was heavenly was seen at the first sight; and it was only when you looked deeper, you saw the badger-skin; and deeper still, that mysterious vail, the type of

Christ's flesh: but in the other, the first thing you saw was the badger-skin; and deeper down, the royal covering. We see Christ in each, though in a different aspect. In the ark, we have Christ maintaining the glory of God; in the brazen altar, we have Christ meeting the sinner's need. Blessed combination for us!

But further, has the reader noticed that in the entire of this marvelous passage to which we have been calling his particular attention there is no mention of a certain piece of furniture which we know, from Exodus 30 and other Scriptures, occupied a very important place in the tabernacle? We allude to the brazen laver. Why is this omitted in Numbers 4? It is more than probable that some of our keen-eyed rationalists would find here what they would pronounce an error—a defect—a discrepancy. But is it so? No, thank God! The devout Christian student knows full well that such things are wholly incompatible with the volume of God. He knows and confesses this, even though he may not be able to account for the absence of this or the presence of that particular thing in any given passage. But just insofar as we are enabled, through the mercy of God, to see the spiritual reason of things, do we always find that where the rationalist sees or affects to see flaws, the pious student sees brilliant gems.

Thus it is, we doubt not, in reference to the omission of the brazen laver from the catalogue in Numbers 4. It is only one of the ten thousand illustrations of the beauty and perfectness of the inspired volume.

But, the reader may inquire, why is the laver omitted? The reason may be found in the double fact of what that laver was made from, and what it was made for. This double fact we have noticed in Exodus. The laver was made of the looking-glasses of the women who assembled at the door of the tabernacle of the congregation (Exod. 38:8). This was its material. And as to its object, it was provided as a means of purification for man. Now, in all those things which formed the special burden and charge of the Kohathites, we see only the varied manifestations of God in Christ, from the ark, in the holiest of all, to the brazen altar, in the court of the tabernacle; and inasmuch as the laver was not a manifestation of God, but a purification for man, it is therefore not found in the custody and charge of the Kohathites.

But we must now leave the reader to meditate alone on this most profound section of our book (chap. 3 and 4). It is really inexhaustible. We might go on expatiating upon it until we had filled volumes instead of pages, and after all, we should feel as though we had barely penetrated the surface of a mine whose depth never can be sounded—whose treasures never can be exhausted. What human pen can bring out the marvelous instruction contained in the inspired account of the tribe of Levi? Who can attempt to unfold that sovereign grace which shines in the fact that the self-willed Levi should be the very first to respond to that soul-stirring call, "Who is on the Lord's side?" Who can speak aright of that rich, abounding, distinguishing mercy illustrated in the fact that those whose hands had been imbued in blood should be permitted to handle the vessels of the sanctuary; and that those into whose assembly God's Spirit could not enter should be brought into the very bosom of the congregation of God, there to be occupied with that which was so precious to Him?

And then those three divisions of workers —Merarites, Gershonites, and Kohathites; what instruction is here! what a type of the various members of the Church of God, in their various service! what depth of mysterious wisdom in all this! Is it speaking too strongly—is it too much, to say that nothing, at this moment, so deeply impresses us as the sense of the utter feebleness and poverty of all that we have advanced on one of the very richest sections of the inspired volume? Still we have conducted the reader to a mine of infinite depth and richness, and we must leave him to penetrate thereinto by the gracious aid of Him to whom the mine belongs, and who alone is able to evolve its wealth. All that man can write or say on any portion of God's Word can, at best, be but suggestive: to speak of it as exhaustive would be to cast a slight upon the sacred canon. May we tread the holy place with unshod feet, and be as those who inquire in the temple, and whose studies are perfumed by the spirit of worship.*

---

## *CHAPTER 5*

"AND the Lord spake unto Moses, saying, 'Command the children of Israel that they put out of the camp every leper, and every one that hath an issue, and whosoever is defiled by the dead: both male and female shall ye put out, without the camp shall ye put them; that they defile not their camps, *in the midst whereof I dwell.'* And the children of Israel did so, and put them out without the camp: as the Lord spake unto Moses, so did the children of Israel" (Num. 5:1-4).

Here we have unfolded to us, in few words, the great foundation-principle on which the discipline of the assembly is founded—a principle, we may say, of the very last importance, though, alas! so little understood or attended to. It was the presence of God in the midst of His people Israel that demanded holiness on their part. "That they defile not their camps, in the midst of which I dwell." The place where the Holy One dwells must be holy. This is a plain and a necessary truth.

We have already remarked that *redemption* was the *basis* of God's dwelling in the midst of His people; but we must remember that *discipline* was essential to His continuance amongst them. He could not dwell where evil was deliberately and avowedly sanctioned. Blessed be His name, He can and does bear with weakness and ignorance; but He is of purer eyes than to behold evil, and cannot look on iniquity. Evil cannot dwell with Him, nor can He have fellowship with it. It would involve a denial of His very nature; and He cannot deny Himself.

It may, however, be said, in reply, Does not God the Holy Ghost dwell in the individual believer, and yet there is much evil in him? True, the Holy Ghost dwells in the believer, on the ground of accomplished redemption. He is there, not as the sanction of what is of nature, but as the seal of what is of Christ; and His presence and fellowship are enjoyed just in proportion as the evil in us is habitually judged. Will any one assert that we can realize and delight in the Spirit's indwelling while allowing our indwelling pravity, and indulging the desires of the flesh and of the mind? Far away be the impious thought! No; we must judge ourselves, and put away every thing inconsistent with the holiness of the One who dwells in us. Our "old man" is not recognized at all; it has no existence before God; it has been condemned utterly in the cross of Christ. We feel its workings, alas! and have to mourn over them, and judge ourselves on account of them; but God sees us in Christ—in the Spirit—in the new creation. And, moreover, the Holy Ghost dwells in the body of the believer, on the ground of the blood of Christ; and this indwelling demands the judgment of evil in every shape and form.

So, also in reference to the assembly. No doubt there is evil there—evil in each individual member, and therefore evil in the body corporate. But it must be judged; and if judged, it is not allowed to act—it is rendered null. But to say that an assembly is not to judge evil, is nothing more or less than corporate antinomianism. What should we say to a professing Christian who maintained that he was not solemnly responsible to judge evil in himself and in his ways? We should, with great decision, pronounce him an antinomian. And if it be wrong for a single individual to take such ground, must it not be proportionably wrong for an assembly? We cannot see how this can be called in question.

What would have been the result had Israel refused to obey the peremptory "command" given at the opening chapter

---

*For further suggestions on the subjects touched upon in the foregoing section, the reader is referred to *Notes on Exodus,* chapters 24—30; also to "The History of the Tribe of Levi Considered," in *Miscellaneous Writings,* vol. 4.

before us? Supposing they had said, We are not responsible to judge evil; and we do not feel that it becomes poor failing, erring mortals such as we to judge any body. These people with the leprosy, and the issue, and so forth, are as much Israelites as we are, and have as good a right to all the blessings and privileges of the camp as we have; we do not therefore feel it would be right for us to put them out.

Now, what, we ask, would have been God's rejoinder to such a reply? If the reader will just turn for an instant to Joshua 7, he will find as solemn an answer as could well be given. Let him draw near and carefully inspect that "great heap of stones" in the valley of Achor. Let him read the inscription thereon. What is it? "God is greatly to be feared in the assembly of His saints, and to be had in reverence of all them that are round about Him." "*Our* God is a consuming fire." What is the meaning of all this? Let us hear it and consider it. Lust had conceived in the heart of one member of the congregation, and brought forth sin. What then? Did this involve the whole congregation? Yes, verily; this is the solemn truth. "*Israel* [not merely Achan,] hath sinned, and *they* have also transgressed My covenant which I commanded them: for *they* have even taken of the accursed thing, and have also stolen, and dissembled also, and *they* have put it even among their own stuff. Therefore the children of Israel could not stand before their enemies, but turned their backs before their enemies, because *they* were accursed: *neither will I be with you any more, except ye destroy the accursed thing from among you*" (Josh. 7:11-12).

This is peculiarly solemn and searching. It most assuredly utters a loud voice in our ears, and conveys a holy lesson to our hearts. There were, so far as the narrative informs us, many hundreds of thousands, throughout the camp of Israel, as ignorant as Joshua himself seems to have been of the fact of Achan's sin, and yet the word was, "*Israel* hath sinned—transgressed—taken the accursed thing—stolen and dissembled." How was this? The assembly was one. God's presence in the midst of the congregation constituted it one—so one, that the sin of each was the sin of all. "A little leaven leaveneth the whole lump." Human reason may demur to this, as it is sure to demur to every thing that lies beyond its narrow range. But God says it, and this is enough for the believing mind. It doth not become us to ask, Why? How? or Wherefore? The testimony of God settles every thing, and we have only to believe and obey. It is enough for us to know that the fact of God's presence demands holiness, purity, and the judgment of evil. Let us remember this. It is not upon the principle so justly repudiated by every lowly mind, "Stand by thyself; I am holier than thou." No; it is entirely on the ground of what God is. "Be ye holy, for I am holy." God could not give the sanction of His holy presence to unjudged wickedness. What! give a victory at Ai with an Achan in the camp? Impossible! A victory under such circumstances would have been a dishonor to God, and the very worst thing that could have happened to Israel. It could not be. Israel must be chastised; they must be humbled and broken; they must be brought down to the valley of Achor—the place of trouble, for there alone can "a door of hope" be opened when evil has come in.

Let not the reader misunderstand this great practical principle. It has, we fear, been greatly misunderstood by many of God's people. Many there are who seem to think that it can never be right for those who are saved by grace, and who are themselves signal monuments of mercy, to exercise discipline in any form, or on any ground whatsoever. To such persons, Matthew 7:1 seems to condemn utterly the thought of our undertaking to judge. "Are we not," say they, "expressly told by our Lord not to judge? Are not these His own veritable words—'Judge not, that ye be not judged'?" No doubt; but what do these words mean? Do they mean that we are not to judge the doctrine and manner of life of such as present themselves for Christian fellowship? Do they lend any support to the idea that no matter what a man holds, or what he teaches, or what he does, we are to receive him all the same? Can this be the force and meaning of our Lord's words? Who could, for one moment, cede aught so monstrous as this? Does not our Lord, in this very same chapter, tell us to "beware of false prophets"? But how can we beware of any one if we are not to judge? If judgment is not to be exercised in any case, why tell us to beware?

The truth is as simple as possible. God's assembly is responsible to judge the doctrine and morals of all who claim entrance at the door. We are not to judge motives, but we are to judge ways. We are directly taught, by the inspired apostle, in the fifth chapter of 1 Corinthians, that we are bound to judge all who take the ground of being inside the assembly. "For what have I to do to judge them also that are without? Do not ye judge them that are within? But them that are without God judgeth. *Therefore* put away from among yourselves that wicked person" (ver. 12-13).

This is most distinct. We are not to judge those "without," but we are to judge those "within." That is, those who take the ground of being Christians—of being members of God's assembly—all such come within the range of judgment. The very moment a man enters the assembly, he takes his place in that sphere where discipline is exercised upon every thing contrary to the holiness of the One who dwells there.

And let not the reader suppose for a moment that the unity of the *body* is touched when the discipline of the *house* is maintained. This would be a very serious mistake indeed; and yet, alas! it is a very common one. We frequently hear it said of those who rightly seek to maintain the discipline of the house of God, that they are rending the body of Christ. There could hardly be a greater mistake. The fact is, the former is our bounden duty; the latter, an utter impossibility. The discipline of God's house must be carried out; but the unity of Christ's body can never be dissolved.

Again, we sometimes hear people speak of cutting off the limbs of the body of Christ. This also is a mistake. Not a single limb of the body of Christ can ever be disturbed. Each member has been incorporated into its place by the Holy Ghost, in pursuance of the eternal purpose of God, and on the ground of the accomplished atonement of Christ; nor can any power of men or devils ever sever a single limb from the body. All are indissolubly joined together in a perfect unity, and maintained therein by divine power. The unity of the Church of God may be compared to a chain stretching across a river: you see it at either side, but it dips in the middle; and if you were to judge by the sight of your eyes, you must suppose that the chain had given way at the centre. So is it with the Church of God: it was seen to be one at the beginning; it will be seen to be one by and by; and it is, in God's sight, one now, though the unity be not visible to mortal eyes.

It is of the very last moment that the Christian reader should be thoroughly clear on this great Church-question. The enemy has sought, by every means in his power, to cast dust into the eyes of God's dear people, in order that they might not see the truth in this matter. We have on the one side, the boasted unity of Roman Catholicism; and on the other hand, the deplorable divisions of Protestantism. Rome points, with an air of triumph, to the numerous sects of Protestants; and Protestants likewise point to the numerous errors, corruptions, and abuses of Romanism. Thus the earnest seeker after truth hardly knows where to turn or what to think; while, on the other hand, the careless, the indifferent, the self-indulgent, and the world-loving are only too ready to draw a plea, from all that they see around them, for flinging aside all serious thought and concern about divine things; and even if, like Pilate, they sometimes flippantly ask the question, "What is truth?" they, like him, turn on their heel without waiting for an answer.

Now, we are firmly persuaded that the true secret of the whole matter—the grand solution of the difficulty—the real relief for the hearts of God's beloved saints, will be found in the truth of the indivisible unity of the Church of God, the body of Christ, on the earth. This truth is not merely to be held as a doctrine, but to be confessed, maintained, and carried out, at all cost to ourselves. It is a great formative truth for the soul, and contains in it the only answer to Rome's boasted unity on the one hand, and to Protestant divisions on the other. It will enable us to testify to Protestantism that we have found unity, and to Roman Catholicism that we have found the unity of the Spirit.

It may, however, be argued, in reply, that it is the veriest Utopianism to seek to carry out such an idea in the present condition of things. Every thing is in such ruin and confusion that we are just like a number of children who have lost their way in a wood, and are trying to make the best of their way home, some in large parties, some in groups of two or three, and some all alone.

Now this may seem very plausible; and we do not doubt in the least but that it would carry immense weight with a large number of the Lord's people at the present moment; but in the judgment of faith, such a mode of putting the matter possesses no weight whatever. And for this simple reason, that the one all-important question for faith is this, namely, Is the unity of the Church a human theory or a divine reality? A divine reality most surely, as it is written, "There is one body, and one Spirit" (Eph. 4:4). If we deny that there is "one body," we may, with equal force, deny that there is "one Lord, one faith, one baptism, one God and Father of all," inasmuch as all lie side by side on the page of inspiration, and if we disturb one, we disturb all.

Nor are we confined to one solitary passage of Scripture on this subject; though had we but one, it were amply sufficient. But we have more than one. Hearken to the following: "The cup of blessing which we bless, is it not the communion of the blood of Christ? The bread which we break, is it not the communion of the body of Christ? For we being many are one bread, and one body; for we are all partakers of that one bread" (1 Cor. 10:16-17). Read also 1 Corinthians 12:12-27, where this whole subject is unfolded and applied.

In a word, then, the Word of God doth most clearly and fully establish the truth of the indissoluble unity of the body Christ; and, moreover, it establishes, as clearly and as fully, the truth of the discipline of God's house. But, be it observed, the proper carrying out of the latter will never interfere with the former. The two things are perfectly compatible. Are we to suppose that when the apostle commanded the church of Corinth to put away from amongst them "that wicked person," the unity of the body was touched? Surely not. And yet was not that man a member of the body of Christ? Truly so, for we find him restored in the second Epistle. The discipline of the house of God had done its work with a member of the body of Christ, and the erring one was brought back. Such was the object of the Church's act.

All this may help to clear the mind of the reader as to the deeply interesting subject of reception at the Lord's table and exclusion from it. There seems to be a considerable amount of confusion in the minds of many Christians as to these things. Some there are who seem to think that provided a person be a Christian, he should on no account be refused a place at the Lord's table. The case in 1 Corinthians 5 is quite sufficient to settle this question. Evidently that man was not put away on the ground of his not being a Christian. He was, as we know, spite of his failure and sin, a child of God; and yet was the assembly at Corinth commanded to put him away; and had they not done so, they would have brought down the judgment of God upon the whole assembly. God's presence is in the assembly, and therefore evil must be judged.

Thus, whether we look at the fifth chapter of Numbers or at the fifth chapter of 1 Corinthians, we learn the same solemn truth, namely, that "holiness becometh God's house forever." And further, we learn that it is with God's own people that discipline must be maintained, and not with those outside. For what do we read in the opening lines of Numbers 5? Were the children of Israel commanded to put out of the camp every one that was not an Israelite—every one that was not circumcised—every one who could not trace his pedigree, in an unbroken line, up to

Abraham? were these the ground of exclusion from the camp? Not at all. Who, then, were to be put out? "Every leper," that is, every one in whom sin is *allowed* to work; "every one that hath an issue," that is, every one from whom a defiling influence is emanating; and "whosoever is defiled by the dead." These were the persons that were to be separated from the camp in the wilderness, and their antitypes are to be separated from the assembly now.

And why, we may ask, was this separation demanded? Was it to uphold the reputation or respectability of the people? Nothing of the sort. What then? "That they defile not their camps in the midst whereof *I dwell.*" And so is it now. We do not judge and put away bad doctrine in order to maintain *our* orthodoxy; neither do we judge and put away moral evil in order to maintain *our* reputation and respectability. The only ground of judgment and putting away is this: "Holiness becometh Thine house, O Lord, forever." God dwells in the midst of His people. "Where two or three are gathered together in My name, there am I." "Know ye not that ye are the temple of God, and that the Spirit of God dwelleth in you?" (1 Cor. 3:16) And again, "Now therefore ye are no more strangers and foreigners, but fellow-citizens with the saints, and of the household of God; and *are* built upon the foundation of the apostles and prophets, Jesus Christ Himself being the chief corner stone; in whom all the building fitly framed together, groweth unto *a holy temple* in the Lord: in whom ye also *are* builded together for a habitation of God through the Spirit" (Eph. 2:19-22).

But it may be that the reader feels disposed to put some such questions as the following: How is it possible to find a pure, a perfect church? Is there not—will there not—must there not be some evil in every assembly, in spite of the most intense pastoral vigilance and corporate faithfulness? How, then, can this high standard of purity be maintained? No doubt, there is evil in the assembly, inasmuch as there is indwelling sin in each member of the assembly. But it must not be allowed; it must not be sanctioned; it must be judged and kept under. It is not the presence of judged evil that defiles, but the allowance and sanction of evil. It is with the Church, in its corporate character, as with the members in their individual character.—"If we would judge ourselves, we should not be judged" (1 Cor. 11:31). Hence, therefore, no amount of evil should lead a man to separate from the Church of God; but if an assembly denies its solemn responsiblity to judge evil, both in doctrine and morals, it is no longer on the ground of the Church of God at all, and it becomes your bounden duty to separate from it. So long as an assembly is on the ground of the Church of God, however feeble it be, and few in number, to separate from it is schism. But if an assembly be not on God's ground (and most certainly it is not if it denies its duty to judge evil), then it is schism to continue in association with it.

But will not this tend to multiply and perpetuate divisions? Most assuredly not. It may tend to break up mere human associations; but this is not schism, but the very reverse, inasmuch as all such associations, however large, powerful, and apparently useful, are positively antagonistic to the unity of the body of Christ—the Church of God.

It cannot fail to strike the thoughtful reader that the Spirit of God is awakening attention, on all hands, to the great question of the Church. Men are beginning to see that there is very much more in this subject than the mere notion of an individual mind, or the dogma of a party. The question, "What is the Church?" is forcing itself upon many hearts, and demanding an answer. And what a mercy to have an answer to give! an answer as clear, as distinct, and as authoritative as the voice of God—the voice of holy Scripture—can give. Is it not an unspeakable privilege, when assailed on all sides by the claims of churches—"High-Church," "Low-Church," "Broad-Church," "State-Church," "Free-Church,"—to be able to fall back upon the one true Church of the living God—the body of Christ? We most assuredly esteem it as such; and we are firmly persuaded that here alone is the divine solution of the difficulties of thousands of the people of God.

But where is this Church to be found? Is it not a hopeless undertaking to set out to look for it amid the ruin and confusion which surround us? No, blessed be God; for albeit we may not *see* all the members of the Church gathered together, yet it is our privilege and holy duty to know and occupy *the ground* of the Church of God, and no other. And how is this ground to be discerned? We believe that the first step towards discerning the true ground of the Church of God is, to stand apart from every thing that is contrary thereto. We need not expect to discover what is true while our minds are beclouded by what is false. The divine order is, "Cease to do evil: learn to do well." God does not give us light for two steps at a time. Hence, the moment we discover that we are on wrong ground, it is our duty to abandon it, and wait on God for further light, which He will most surely give.

But we must proceed with our chapter.

"The Lord spake unto Moses, saying, 'Speak unto the children of Israel: When a man or woman shall commit any sin that men commit, to do a trespass against the Lord, and that person be guilty; then they shall confess their sin which they have done; and he shall recompense his trespass with the principal thereof, and add unto it the fifth part thereof, and give it unto him against whom he hath trespassed. But if the man have no kinsman to recompense the trespass unto, let the trespass be recompensed unto the Lord, even to the priest; beside the ram of the atonement, whereby an atonement shall be made for him.' "

The doctrine of the trespass-offering has been considered in our *Notes on Leviticus*, chapter 5; and to that we must refer our reader, as we do not mean to occupy his time or our own in going into any points which have been already considered. We shall merely notice here the very important questions of confession and restitution. Not only is it true that both God and man are gainers by the great Trespass-Offering presented on the cross at Calvary, but we also learn, from the foregoing quotation, that God looked for confession and restitution, when any trespass had been committed. The sincerity of the former would be evidenced by the latter. It was not sufficient for a Jew who had trespassed against his brother to go and say, I am sorry. He had to restore the thing wherein he had trespassed, and add a fifth thereto. Now, although we are not under the law, yet may we gather much instruction from its institutions; although we are not under the schoolmaster, we may learn some good lessons from him. If, then, we have trespassed against any one, it is not enough that we confess our sin to God and to our brother, we must make restitution; we are called upon to give practical proof of the fact that we have judged ourselves on account of that thing in which we have trespassed.

We question if this is felt as it ought to be. We fear there is a light, flippant, easy-going style in reference to sin and failure, which must be very grievous indeed to the Spirit of God. We rest content with the mere lip-confession, without the deep, heartfelt sense of the evil of sin in God's sight. The thing itself is not judged in its moral roots, and, as a consequence of this trifling with sin, the heart becomes hard, and the conscience loses its tenderness. *This is very serious.* We know of few things more precious than a tender conscience. We do not mean a *scrupulous* conscience, which is governed by its own crotchets; or a *morbid* conscience, which is governed by its own fears. Both these are most troublesome guests for any one to entertain. But we mean a *tender* conscience, which is governed, in all things, by the Word of God, and which refers, at all times, to His authority. This sound description of conscience we consider an inestimable treasure. It regulates every thing, takes cognizance of the very smallest matter connected with our daily walk and habits—our mode of dress, our houses, our furniture, our table, our entire deportment, spirit, and style, our mode of conducting our business, or if it be our lot to serve others, the mode in which we discharge the service, whatever it be. In short, every thing falls under the healthful moral influence of a tender conscience. "Herein," says the blessed apostle, "do I exercise myself, to have *always* a conscience void of offense toward God and men" (Acts 24:16).

This is what we may well covet. There is something morally beautiful and attractive in this exercise of the greatest and most gifted servant of Christ. He, with all his splendid gifts, with all his marvelous powers, with all his profound insight into the ways and counsels of God, with all he had to speak of and glory in, with all the wonderful revelations made to him in the third heavens; in a word, he, the most honored of apostles and privileged of saints, gave holy diligence to keep always a conscience void of offense both toward God and man; and if, in an unguarded moment, he uttered a hasty word, as he did to Ananias the high-priest, he was ready, the very next moment, to confess and make restitution, so that the hasty utterance, "God shall smite thee, thou whited wall," was withdrawn, and God's Word given instead—"Thou shalt not speak evil of the ruler of thy people."

Now, we do not believe that Paul could have retired to rest that night with a conscience void of offense if he had not withdrawn his words. There must be confession when we do or say what is wrong; and if there be not the confession, our communion will assuredly be interrupted. Communion, with unconfessed sin upon the conscience, is a moral impossibility. We may talk of it, but it is all the merest delusion. We must keep a clean conscience if we would walk with God. There is nothing more to be dreaded than moral insensibility, a slovenly conscience, an obtuse moral sense that can allow all sorts of things to pass unjudged—that can commit sin, pass on, and coolly say, "What evil have I done?"

Let us, with holy vigilance, watch against all this; let us seek to cultivate a tender conscience. It will demand from us what it demanded from Paul, namely, "exercise." But it is blessed exercise, and it will yield most precious fruits. Do not suppose that there is aught that savors of the legal in this exercise; nay, it is most thoroughly Christian; indeed we look upon those noble words of Paul as the very embodiment, in a condensed form, of the whole of a Christian's practice. "To have *always* a conscience void of offense toward God and men" comprehends every thing.

But, alas! how little do we habitually ponder the claims of God, or the claims of our fellow-man! How little is our conscience up to the mark! Claims of all sorts are neglected, yet we feel it not. There is no brokenness and contrition before the Lord. We commit trespass in a thousand things, yet there is no confession or restitution. Things are allowed to pass that ought to be judged, confessed, and put away. There is sin in our holy things; there is lightness and indifference of spirit in the assembly and at the Lord's table; we rob God, in various ways; we think our own thoughts, speak our own words, do our own pleasure; and what is all this but robbing God, seeing that we are not our own, but bought with a price?

Now, we cannot but think that all this must sadly hinder our spiritual growth. It grieves the Spirit of God, and hinders His gracious ministry of Christ to our souls whereby alone we grow up into Him. We know, from various parts of God's Word, how much He prizes a tender spirit, a contrite heart. "To this man will I look, even to him that is of a contrite spirit and trembles at My word." With such an one God can dwell; but with hardness and insensibility, coldness and indifference, He can have no fellowship. Oh, then, let us exercise ourselves to have always a pure and uncondemning conscience, both as to God and as to our fellow-man.

The third and last section of our chapter, which we need not quote at length, teaches us a deeply solemn lesson, whether we view it from a dispensational or a moral point of view. It contains the record of the great ordinance designed for the trial of jealousy. Its place here is remarkable. In the first section, we have the corporate judgment of evil; in the second, we have individual self-judgment, confession, and restitution; and in the third, we learn that God cannot endure even the mere suspicion of evil.

Now, we fully believe that this very

impressive ordinance has a dispensational bearing upon the relationship between Jehovah and Israel. The prophets dwell largely upon Israel's conduct as a wife, and upon Jehovah's jealousy on that score. We do not attempt to quote the passages, but the reader will find them throughout the pages of Jeremiah and Ezekiel. Israel could not abide the searching trial of the bitter water. Her unfaithfulness has been made manifest; she has broken her vows; she has gone aside from her Husband, the Holy One of Israel, whose burning jealousy has been poured forth upon the faithless nation. He is a jealous God, and cannot bear the thought that the heart that He claims as His own should be given to another.

Thus we see that this ordinance for the trial of jealousy bears very distinctly upon it the impress of the divine character. In it He most fully enters into the thoughts and feelings of an injured husband, or of one who even suspected an injury. The bare suspicion is perfectly intolerable, and where it takes possession of the heart, the matter must be sifted to the very bottom. The suspected one must undergo a process of such a searching nature that only the faithful one can endure. If there was a trace of guilt, the bitter water would search down into the very depths of the soul and bring it all out. There was no escape for the guilty one; and we may say that the very fact of there being no possible escape for the guilty, only made the vindication of the innocent more triumphant. The self-same process that declared the guilt of the guilty, made manifest the innocence of the faithful. To one who is thoroughly conscious of integrity, the more searching the investigation the more welcome it is. If there were a possiblity of a guilty one escaping, through any defect in the mode of trial, it would only make against the innocent. But the process was divine, and therefore perfect; and hence, when the suspected wife had gone through it in safety, her fidelity was perfectly manifested, and full confidence restored.

What a mercy, then, to have had such a perfect mode of settling all suspected cases! Suspicion is the death-blow to all loving intimacy, and God would not have it in the midst of His congregation. He would not only have His people collectively to judge evil, and individually to judge themselves; but where there was even the suspicion of evil, and no evidence forthcoming, He Himself devised a method of trial which perfectly brought the truth to light. The guilty one had to drink death, and found it to be judgment:* the faithful one drank death, and found it victory.

---

## *CHAPTER 6*

"AND the Lord spake unto Moses, saying, 'Speak unto the children of Israel, and say unto them, When either man or woman shall separate themselves to vow a vow of a Nazarite, to separate themselves unto the Lord; he shall separate himself from wine and strong drink, and shall drink no vinegar of wine, or vinegar of strong drink, neither shall he drink any liquor of grapes, nor eat moist grapes, or dried. All the days of his separation shall he eat nothing that is made of the vinetree, from the kernels even to the husk. All the days of the vow of his separation there shall no razor come upon his head: until the days be fulfilled, in the which he separateth himself unto the Lord, he shall be holy, and shall let the locks of the hair of his head grow. All the days that he separateth himself unto the Lord he shall come at no dead body. He

*The *"dust"* lifted from the floor of the tabernacle may be viewed as the figure of death.—"Thou hast brought me into the dust of death." The *"water"* prefigures the Word, which, being brought to bear upon the conscience, by the power of the Holy Ghost, makes every thing manifest. If there has been any unfaithfulness to Christ, the true Husband of His people, it must be thoroughly judged. This holds good with regard to the nation of Israel, to the Church of God, and to the individual believer. If the heart be not true to Christ, it will not be able to stand the searching power of the Word; but if there be truth in the inward parts, the more one is searched and tried, the better. How blessed it is when we can truly say, "Search me, O God, and know my heart: try me, and know my thoughts; and see if there be any wicked way in me, and lead me in the way everlasting" (Ps. 139:23-24).

shall not make himself unclean for his father, or for his mother, for his brother, or for his sister, when they die; because the consecration of his God is upon his head. All the days of his separation he is holy unto the Lord" (ver. 1-8).

The ordinance of Nazariteship is full of interest and practical instruction. In it we see the case of one setting himself apart, in a very special manner, from things which, though not absolutely sinful in themselves, were nevertheless calculated to interfere with that intense consecration of heart which is set forth in true Nazariteship.

In the first place, the Nazarite was not to drink wine. The fruit of the vine, in every shape and form, was to him a forbidden thing. Now, wine, as we know, is the apt symbol of earthly joy—the expression of that social enjoyment which the human heart is so fully capable of entering into. From this the Nazarite in the wilderness was sedulously to keep himself. With him it was a literal thing. He was not to excite nature by the use of strong drink. All the days of his separation he was called to exercise the strictest abstinence from wine.

Such was the type, and it is written for our learning—written, too, in this marvelous book of Numbers, so rich in its wilderness lessons. This is only what we might expect. The impressive institution of the Nazarite finds its appropriate place in the book of Numbers. It is in perfect keeping with the character of the book, which, as has been already remarked, contains all that specially belongs to life in the wilderness.

Let us then inquire into the nature of the lesson taught us in the Nazarite's abstinence from every thing pertaining to the vine, from the kernel even to the husk.

There has been but one true and perfect Nazarite in this world—but one who maintained, from first to last, the most complete separation from all mere earthly joy. From the moment He entered upon His public work, He kept Himself apart from all that was of this world. His heart was fixed upon God and His work, with a devotion that nothing could shake. No claims of earth or nature were ever allowed, for a single moment, to come in between His heart and that work which He came to do. "Wist ye not that I must be about My Father's business?" And again, "Woman, what have I to do with thee?" With such words did the true Nazarite seek to adjust the claims of nature. He had one thing to do, and to that He separated Himself perfectly. His eye was single and His heart undivided. This is apparent from first to last. He could say to His disciples, "I have meat to eat that ye know not of"; and when they, not knowing the deep significance of His words, said, "Hath any man brought Him aught to eat?" He replied, "My meat is to do the will of Him that sent Me, and to finish His work" (John 4). So also at the close of His course here below, we hear Him giving utterance to such words as these, as He took into His hand the paschal cup: "Take this, and divide it among yourselves; for I say unto you, I will not drink of the fruit of the vine until the kingdom of God shall come" (Luke 22:17-18).

Thus we see how the perfect Nazarite carried Himself throughout. He could have no joy in the earth, no joy in the nation of Israel. The time had not come for that, and therefore He detached Himself from all that which mere human affection might find in association with His own, in order to devote Himself to the one grand object which was ever before His mind. The time will come when He, as the Messiah, will rejoice in His people and in the earth; but until that blissful moment arrives, He is apart as the true Nazarite, and His people are linked with Him. "They are not of the world, even as I am not of the world. Sanctify them through Thy truth: Thy word is truth. As Thou hast sent Me into the world, even so have I also sent them into the world. And for their sakes I sanctify Myself, that they also might be sanctified through the truth" (John 17:16-19).

Let us deeply ponder this first grand feature of the Nazarite character. It is important we should faithfully examine ourselves in the light of it. It is a very grave question indeed how far we, as Christians, are really entering into the meaning and power of this intense separation from all the excitement of nature, and from all merely earthly joy. It may perhaps be said, What harm is there in having a little amusement or recreation? Surely, we are not called to be monks. Has not God given us richly all things to enjoy? And while we are in the world, is it not right we should enjoy it?

To all this we reply, It is not a question of the harm of this, that, or the other. There was no harm, as a general rule, in wine; nothing abstractedly wrong in the vine-tree: but the point is this, if any one aimed at being a Nazarite, if he aspired to this holy separation unto the Lord, then was he to abstain *wholly* from the use of wine and strong drink. Others might drink wine; but the Nazarite was not to touch it.

Now, the question for us is this: Do we aim at being Nazarites? do we sigh after thorough separation and devotement of ourselves, in body, soul, and spirit, unto God? If so, we must be apart from all these things in which mere nature finds its enjoyment. It is upon this one hinge that the whole question turns. The question most assuredly is not "Are we to be monks?" but, Do we want to be Nazarites? Is it our heart's desire to be apart, with our Lord Christ, from all mere earthly joy—to be separated unto God from those things which, though not absolutely sinful in themselves, do nevertheless tend to hinder that entire consecration of heart which is the true secret of all spiritual Nazariteship? Is not the Christian reader aware that there are, in very deed, many such things? Is he not conscious that there are numberless things which exert a distracting and weakening influence upon his spirit, and yet were they to be tried by the standard of ordinary morality, they might be allowed to pass as harmless?

But we must remember that God's Nazarites do not measure things by any such standard. Theirs is not an ordinary morality at all. They look at things from a divine and heavenly stand-point, and hence they cannot suffer aught to pass as harmless which tends in any wise to interfere with that high tone of consecration to God after which their souls are fervently breathing.

May we have grace to weigh these things, and to watch against every defiling influence. Each one must be aware of what it is which, in his case, would prove to be wine and strong drink. It may seem to be a trifle; but we may rest assured that nothing is a trifle which breaks the current of our soul's communion with God, and robs us of that holy intimacy which it is our privilege ever to enjoy.

But there was another thing which marked the Nazarite. He was not to shave his head. "All the days of the vow of his separation there shall no razor come upon his head: until the days be fulfilled in the which he separateth himself unto the Lord, he shall be holy, and shall let the locks of the hair of his head grow."

In 1 Corinthians 11:14, we learn that it argues a lack of dignity for a man to have long hair. "Doth not even nature itself teach you, that if a man have long hair, it is a shame unto him?" From this we learn that if we really desire to live a life of separation to God, we must be prepared to surrender our dignity in nature. This our Lord Jesus Christ did perfectly. He made Himself of no reputation; He surrendered His rights in every thing; He could say, "I am a worm and no man"; He emptied Himself thoroughly, and took the very lowest place; He neglected Himself, while He cared for others. In a word, His Nazariteship was perfect in this as in all beside.

Now, here is just the very thing which we so little like to do. We naturally stand up for our dignity and seek to maintain our rights. It is deemed manly so to do. But the perfect Man never did so; and if we aim at being Nazarites, we shall not do so either. We must surrender the dignities of nature, and forego the joys of earth, if we would tread a path of thorough separation to God in this world. By and by both will be in place, but not now.

Here again, be it remarked, the question is not as to the right and wrong of the case. As a general rule, it was right for a man to shave his locks; but it was not right, nay, it was altogether wrong, for a Nazarite to do so. This made all the difference. It was quite right for an ordinary man to shave and drink wine; but the Nazarite was not an ordinary man; he was one set apart from all that was ordinary, to tread a path peculiar to himself; and to use a razor or taste wine would involve the entire surrender of that peculiar path. Hence, if any inquire, Is it not right to enjoy the pleasures of earth, and maintain the dignities of nature? We reply, Quite right, if we are to walk as men; but wholly wrong, yea, absolutely fatal, if we want to walk as Nazarites.

This simplifies the matter amazingly. It answers a thousand questions and solves a thousand difficulties. It is of little use to split hairs about the harm of this or that particular thing. The question is, What is our real purpose and object? do we merely want to get on as men, or do we long to live as true Nazarites? According to the language of 1 Corinthians 3:3, to "walk as men" and to be "carnal" are synonymous. Does such language really govern us? do we drink into the spirit and breathe the atmosphere of such a Scripture? or are we ruled by the spirit and principles of a godless, Christless world? It is useless to spend our time arguing points which would never be raised at all if our souls were in the right temper and attitude. No doubt, it is perfectly right, perfectly natural, perfectly consistent, for the men of this world to enjoy all that it has to offer them, and to maintain their rights and their dignities to the very utmost of their power. It were childish to question this. But on the other hand, what is right and natural and consistent for the men of this world, is wrong, unnatural, and inconsistent for God's Nazarites. Thus the matter stands, if we are to be governed by the simple truth of God. We learn from the sixth chapter of Numbers that if a Nazarite drank wine or shaved his locks, he defiled the head of his consecration. Has this no voice, no lesson for us? Assuredly it has. It teaches us that if our souls desire to pursue a path of whole-hearted consecration to God, we must abstain from the joys of earth, and surrender the dignities and the rights of nature. It must be thus, seeing that God and the world, flesh and spirit, do not and cannot coalesce. The time will come when it will be otherwise; but just now, all who *will* live to God, and walk in the Spirit, must live apart from the world and mortify the flesh. May God, of His great mercy, enable us so to do.

One other feature of the Nazarite remains to be noticed. He was not to touch a dead body. "All the days that he separateth himself unto the Lord, he shall come at no dead body. He shall not make himself unclean for his father, or for his mother, for his brother, or for his sister, when they die; because the consecration of his God is upon his head."

Thus we see that whether it was drinking wine, shaving his locks, or touching a dead body, the effect was the same; any one of the three involved the defilement of the head of the Nazarite's consecration. Wherefore it is plain that it was as defiling to the Nazarite to drink wine or to shave his head, as it was to touch a dead body. It is well to see this. We are prone to make distinctions which will not stand for a moment in the light of the divine presence. When once the consecration of God rested upon the head of any one, that great and important fact became the standard and touchstone of all morality. It placed the individual on entirely new and peculiar ground, and rendered it imperative upon him to look at every thing from a new and peculiar point of view. He was no longer to ask what became him as a man, but what became him as a Nazarite. Hence, if his dearest friend lay dead by his side, he was not to touch him. He was called to keep himself apart from the defiling influence of death, and all because "the consecration of God was upon his head."

Now, in this entire subject of Nazariteship, it is needful for the reader to understand very distinctly that it is not by any means a question of the soul's salvation, of eternal life, or of the believer's perfect security in Christ. If this be not clearly seen, it may lead the mind into perplexity and darkness. There are two grand links in Christianity which, though very intimately connected, are perfectly distinct, namely, the link of eternal life, and the link of personal communion. The former can never be snapped by any thing; the latter can be snapped in a moment, by the weight of a feather. It is to the second of these that the doctrine of Nazariteship pertains.

We behold in the person of the Nazarite a type of one who sets out in some special path of devotedness or consecration to Christ. The power of continuance in this path consists in secret communion with God; so that if the communion be interrupted, the power is gone. This renders the subject peculiarly solemn. There is the greatest possible danger of attempting to pursue the path in the absence of that which constitutes the source of its power. This is most disastrous, and demands the utmost vigilance. We have briefly glanced at the various things which tend to interrupt the Nazarite's communion; but it would be wholly impossible, by any words of ours, to set forth the moral effect of any attempt to keep up the appearance of Nazariteship when the inward reality is gone. It is dangerous in the extreme. It is infinitely better to confess our failure, and take our true place, than to keep up a false appearance. God will have reality; and we may rest assured that, sooner or later, our weakness and folly will be made manifest to all. It is very deplorable and very humbling when "the Nazarites, that were purer than snow," become "blacker than a coal"; but it is far worse when those who have become thus black, keep up the pretense of being white.

Let us look at the solemn case of Samson, as set before us in the sixteenth chapter of Judges. He, in an evil hour, betrayed his secret and lost his power—lost it though he knew it not. But the enemy soon knew it. It was soon made manifest to all that the Nazarite had defiled the head of his consecration. "And it came to pass, when Delilah pressed him daily with her words, and urged him, so that his soul was vexed unto death, that he told her all his heart, and said unto her, 'There hath not come a razor upon mine head; for I have been a Nazarite unto God from my mother's womb: if I be shaven, then my strength will go from me, and I shall become weak, and be like any other man' " (ver. 16-17).

Here, alas! was the betrayal of the deep and holy secret of all his power. Up to this, his path had been one of strength and victory, simply because it had been one of holy Nazariteship. But the lap of Delilah proved too much for the heart of Samson, and what a thousand Philistines could not do was done by the insnaring influence of a single woman. Samson fell from the lofty elevation of the Nazarite down to the level of an ordinary man.

"And when Delilah saw that he had told her all his heart, she sent and called for the lords of the Philistines, saying, 'Come up this once, for he hath showed me all his heart.' Then the lords of the Philistines came up unto her, and brought money in their hand. And she made him sleep upon her knees [alas! a fatal sleep to God's Nazarite!]; and she called for a man, and she caused him to shave off the seven locks of his head; and she began to afflict him, and his strength went from him. And she said, 'The Philistines be upon thee, Samson.' And he awoke out of his sleep, and said, 'I will go out as at other times before, and shake myself.' And he wist not that the Lord was departed from him. But the Philistines took him, and put out his eyes, and brought him down to Gaza, and bound him with fetters of brass; and he did grind in the prison-house" (Judges 16:18-21).

Oh, what a picture! How solemn! how admonitory! What a melancholy spectacle was Samson—going out to shake himself, *"as* at other times"! Alas! the *"as"* was out of place. He might shake himself, but it was no longer "as at other times," for the power was gone; the Lord was departed from him, and the once-powerful Nazarite became a blind prisoner; and instead of triumphing over the Philistines, he had to grind in their prison-house. So much for yielding to mere nature. Samson never regained his liberty. He was permitted, through the mercy of God, to gain one more victory over the uncircumcised; but that victory cost him his life. God's Nazarites must keep themselves pure or lose their power. In their case, power and purity are inseparable. They cannot get on without inward holiness; and hence the urgent need of being ever on the watch against the various things which tend to draw away the heart, distract the mind, and lower the tone of spirituality. Let us ever keep before our souls those words of our chapter, "All the days of his separation he is holy unto the Lord." Holiness is the grand and indispensable characteristic of all the days of Nazariteship; so that when once holiness is forfeited, Nazariteship is at an end.

What, then, it may be asked, is to be done? The Scripture before us supplies the answer.—"And if any man die very suddenly by him, and he hath defiled the head of his consecration, then he shall shave his head in the day of his cleansing; on the seventh day shall he shave it. And on the eighth day he shall bring two turtles, or two young pigeons, to the priest, to the door of the tabernacle of the congregation; and the priest shall offer the one for a sin-offering, and the other for a burnt-offering, and make an atonement for him, for that he sinned by the dead, and shall hallow his head that same day. And he shall consecrate unto the Lord the days of his separation, and shall bring a lamb of the first year for a trespass-offering; but the days that were before shall be lost, because his separation was defiled" (Num. 6:9-12).

Here we find atonement, in its two grand aspects, as the only ground on which the Nazarite could be restored to communion. He had contracted defilement, and that defilement could only be removed by the blood of the sacrifice. We might deem it a very trifling matter to touch a dead body, and particularly under such circumstances. It might be said, How could he help touching it, when the man had suddenly dropped dead by his side? To all this the reply is at once simple and solemn. God's Nazarites must maintain personal purity; and, moreover, the standard by which their purity is to be regulated is not human, but divine. The mere touch of death was sufficient to break the link of communion; and had the Nazarite presumed to go on as though nothing had happened, he would have been flying in the face of God's commandments, and bringing down heavy judgment upon himself.

But, blessed be God, grace had made provision. There was the burnt-offering—the type of the death of Christ to Godward; there was the sin-offering—the type of that same death to usward; and there was the trespass-offering—the type of the death of Christ, not only in its application to the root or principle of sin in the nature, but also to the actual sin committed. In a word, it needed the full virtue of the death of Christ to remove the defilement caused by the simple touch of a dead body. This is peculiarly solemnizing. Sin is a dreadful thing in God's sight—most dreadful. A single sinful thought, a sinful look, a sinful word, is enough to bring a dark, heavy cloud over the soul, which will hide from our view the light of God's countenance, and plunge us into deep distress and misery.

Let us, then, beware how we trifle with sin. Let us remember that ere one stain of the guilt of sin—even the very smallest—could be removed, the blessed Lord Jesus Christ had to pass through all the unutterable horrors of Calvary. That intensely bitter cry, "My God, My God, why hast Thou forsaken Me?" is the only thing that can give us any proper idea of what sin is; and into the profound depths of that cry no mortal or angel can ever enter. But though we can never fathom the mysterious depths of the sufferings of Christ, we should at least seek to meditate more habitually upon His cross and passion, and, in this way, reach a much deeper view of the awfulness of sin in the sight of God. If, indeed, sin was so dreadful, so abhorrent to a holy God, that He was constrained to turn away the light of His countenance from that blessed One who had dwelt in His bosom from all eternity; if He had to forsake Him because He was bearing sin in His own body on the tree, then what must sin be?

Oh, let us seriously consider these things. May they ever have a place deep down in these hearts of ours, that are so easily betrayed into sin. How lightly, at times, do we think of that which cost the Lord Jesus every thing—not only life, but that which is better and dearer than life, even the light of God's countenance! May we have a far deeper sense of the hatefulness of sin. May we most sedulously watch against the bare movement of the eye in a wrong direction; for we may rest assured that the heart will follow the eye, and the feet will follow the heart, and thus we get away from the Lord, lose the sense of His presence and His love, and become miserable, or, if not miserable, what is far worse, dead, cold, and callous—"hardened through the deceitfulness of sin."

May God, in His infinite mercy, keep us from falling. May we have grace to watch more jealously against every thing, no matter what, that might defile the head of our consecration. It is a serious thing to get out of communion, and a most perilous thing to attempt to go on in the Lord's service with a defiled conscience. True it is that grace pardons and restores, but we never regain what we have lost. This latter is set forth with solemn emphasis in the passage of Scripture before us: "He shall consecrate unto the Lord the days of his separation, and shall bring a lamb of the first year for a trespass-offering; *but the days that were before shall be lost* [or, shall fall, as the margin reads it], because his separation was defiled."

This is a point, in our subject, full of instruction and admonition for our souls. When the Nazarite became defiled by any means, even by the touch of a dead body, he had to begin over again. It was not merely the days of his defilement that were lost, or let fall, but actually all the days of his previous Nazariteship. All went for nothing, and this simply by reason of touching a dead body.

What does this teach us? It teaches this, at least, that when we diverge, the breadth of a hair, from the narrow path of communion, and get away from the Lord, we must return to the very point from which we set out, and begin *de novo.* We have many examples of this in Scripture, and it would be our wisdom to consider them, and also to weigh the great practical truth which they illustrate.

Take the case of Abraham, in his descent into Egypt, and recorded in Genesis 12. This was very evidently a divergence from his proper path. And what was the consequence? The days were lost, or let fall, and he had to get back to the point whence he had swerved, and begin over again. Thus, in Genesis 12:8, we read, "And he removed from thence unto a mountain on the east of Bethel, and pitched his tent, having Bethel on the west, and Hai on the east; and there he builded an altar unto the Lord, and called on the name of the Lord." Then, after his return out of the land of Egypt, we read, "He went on his journeys from the south even to Bethel, unto the place where his tent had been *at the beginning,* between Bethel and Hai, unto the place of the altar which he had made there *at the first;* and there Abram called on the name of the Lord" (Gen. 13:3-4). All the time spent in Egypt went for nothing. There was no altar there, no worship, no communion; and Abraham had to get back to the self-same point from which he had diverged, and begin on the new.

Thus it is in every case; and this will account for the miserably slow progress which some of us make in our practical career. We fail, turn aside, get away from the Lord, are plunged in spiritual darkness; and then His voice of love reaches us, in restoring power, and brings us back to the point from which we had wandered; our souls are restored, but we have lost time and suffered incalculably. This is most serious, and it should lead us to walk with holy vigilance and circumspection, so that we may not have to double back upon our path, and lose what can never be regained. True it is that our wanderings and our stumblings and our failings give us an insight into our own hearts, teach us to distrust ourselves, and illustrate the boundless and unchangeable grace of our God. All this is quite true; but still there is a very much higher way of learning both ourselves and God, than by wandering, stumbling, or failing. *Self,* in all the terrible depths of that word, should be judged in the light of the divine presence; and there, too, our souls should grow in the knowledge of God as He unfolds Himself, by the Holy Ghost, in the face of Jesus Christ, and in the precious pages of holy Scripture. This surely is the more excellent way of learning both ourselves and God; and this, too, is the power of all true Nazarite separation. The soul that habitually lives in the sanctuary of God, or, in other words, that walks in unbroken communion with God, is the one who will have a just sense of what nature is, in all its phases, though it be not learnt by sad experience. And not only so, but he will have a deeper and juster sense of what God is in Himself and to all who put their trust in Him. It is poor work to be learning self by experience. We may depend upon it, the true way to learn it is in communion; and when we learn it thus, we shall not be characterized by perpetually dwelling upon our personal vileness, but rather we shall be occupied with that which is outside and above self altogether, even the excellency of the knowledge of Christ Jesus our Lord.

We shall, in closing this section, quote, at length, the statements of "the law of the Nazarite, when the days of his separation are fulfilled: he shall be brought unto the door of the tabernacle of the congregation; and he shall offer his offering unto the Lord, one he lamb of the first year without blemish for a burnt-offering, and one ewe lamb of the first year without blemish, for a sin-offering, and one ram without blemish for peace-offerings; and a basket of unleavened bread, cakes of fine flour mingled with oil, and wafers of unleavened bread anointed with oil, and their meat-offering, and their drink-offering. And the priest shall bring them before the Lord, and shall offer his sin-offering and his burnt-offering. And he shall offer the ram for a sacrifice of peace-offerings unto the Lord, with the basket of unleavened bread: the priest shall offer also his meat-offering and his drink-offering. And the Nazarite shall shave the head of his separation at the door of the tabernacle of the congregation, and shall take the hair of the head of his separation, and put it in the fire which is under the sacrifice of the peace-offerings. And the priest shall take the sodden shoulder of the ram, and one unleavened cake out of the basket, and one unleavened wafer, and shall put them upon the hands of the Nazarite, after the hair of his separation is shaven; and the priest shall wave them for a wave-offering before the Lord: this is holy for the priest, with the wave breast and the heave shoulder; *and after that the Nazarite may drink wine.* This is the law of the Nazarite who hath vowed, and of his offering unto the Lord for his separation, beside that his hand shall get: according to the vow which he vowed, so he must do after the law of his separation" (Num. 6:13-21).

This marvelous "law" leads us onward to something future, when the full result of Christ's perfect work shall appear, and when He, as the Messiah of Israel, shall, at the close of His Nazarite separation, taste true joy in His beloved people, and in this earth. The time will then have come for the Nazarite to drink wine. From all this He set Himself apart, for the accomplishment of that great work, so fully set forth, in all its aspects and in all its bearings, in the foregoing "law." He is apart from the nation, and apart from this world, in the power of true Nazariteship, as He said to His disciples on that memorable night, "I will not drink henceforth [απ' αρτι] of this fruit of the vine until *that day* when I drink it new with you in My Father's kingdom" (Matt. 26:29).

But there is a bright day coming, when Jehovah-Messiah shall rejoice in Jerusalem and joy in His people. The prophets, from Isaiah to Malachi, are full of the most glowing and soul-stirring allusions to that bright and blissful day. To quote the passages would literally fill a volume. But if the reader will turn to the closing section of Isaiah's prophecy, he will find a sample of that to which we refer, and he will find many similar passages throughout the various books of the prophets.

We must not attempt to quote, but we would warn the reader against the danger of being led astray by the uninspired headings attached to those magnificent passages which refer to Israel's future, such, for example, as "The blessings of the gospel"—"The enlargement of the Church." These expressions are calculated to mislead many pious readers, who are apt to take for granted that the headings are as much inspired as the text; or, if not inspired, that they at least contain a correct statement of what the text sets forth. The fact is, there is not a syllable about the Church from beginning to end of the prophets. That the Church can find most precious instruction, light, comfort, and edification from this grand division of the inspired volume is blessedly true; but she will do this just in proportion as she is enabled, by the Spirit's teaching, to discern the real scope and object of this portion of the book of God. To suppose for a moment that we can only derive comfort and profit from that which exclusively or primarily refers to ourselves, would be to take a very narrow, if not an egotistical, view of things. Can we not learn from the book of Leviticus? and yet who would assert that that section refers to the Church?

No, reader; you may rest assured that a calm, unprejudiced, prayerful study of "the law and the prophets" will convince you that the great theme of both the one and the other is, God's government of the world in immediate connection with Israel. True it is that throughout "Moses and all the prophets" there are things concerning (the Lord) Himself. This is plain, from Luke 24:27; but it is "Himself" in His government of this world and of Israel in particular. If this fact be not distinctly seized, we shall study the Old Testament with little intelligence or profit.

It may seem, to some of our readers, a strong statement to assert that there is nothing about the Church, properly so called, throughout the prophets, or indeed in the Old Testament; but a statement or two from the inspired pen of St. Paul will settle the whole question for any one who is really willing to submit to the authority of holy Scripture. Thus in Romans 16 we read, "Now to Him that is of power to stablish you according to my gospel, and the preaching of Jesus Christ, according to the revelation of the mystery, *which was kept secret since the world began,* but *now is made manifest,* and by the Scriptures of the prophets [evidently of the New Testament], according to the commandment of the everlasting God, made known to all nations for the obedience of faith" (ver. 25-26).

So also in Ephesians 3 we read, "For this cause I Paul, the prisoner of Jesus Christ for you Gentiles, if ye have heard of the dispensation of the grace of God, which is given me to you-ward; how that by revelation He made known unto me the mystery; (as I wrote afore in few words, whereby, when ye read, ye may understand my knowledge in the mystery of Christ;) *which in other ages was not made known unto the sons of men, as it is now revealed unto His holy apostles and prophets by the Spirit;** that the Gentiles should be fellow-heirs, and of the same body, and partakers of His promise in Christ by the gospel. . . . And to make all men see what is the fellowship of the mystery, which *from the beginning of the world hath been hid in God,* who created all things by Jesus Christ: to the intent that now unto the principalities and powers in heavenly places might be known by the Church the manifold wisdom of God" (ver. 1-10).

But we must not pursue this deeply interesting subject of the Church; we have merely referred to the foregoing plain passages of Scripture, in order to settle the reader's mind as to the fact that the doctrine of the Church, as taught by Paul, finds no place in the pages of the Old Testament; and therefore, when he reads the prophets and meets the words "Israel," "Jerusalem," "Zion," he is not to apply such terms to the Church of God, inasmuch as they belong to the literal people of Israel, the seed of Abraham, the land of Canaan, and the city

*The "prophets," in the above quotations, are those of the New Testament, as is evident from the form of expression. Had the apostle meant Old Testament prophets, he would have said, His holy prophets and apostles. But the point he is insisting upon is, that the mystery had never been revealed until his time—that it had not been made known to the sons of men in other ages—that it was hid in God; not hid in the Scriptures, but in the infinite mind of God.

of Jerusalem.* God means what He says, and therefore we must not countenance aught that borders upon or looks like a loose and irreverent mode of handling the Word of God. When the Spirit speaks of Jerusalem, He means Jerusalem; if He meant the Church, He would say so. We should not attempt to treat a respectable human document as we treat the inspired volume. We take it for granted that a man not only knows what he means to say, but says what he means; and if this be so in regard to a poor fallible mortal, how much more so in regard to the only wise and living God, who cannot lie?

But we must draw this section to a close, and leave the reader to meditate alone upon the ordinance of the Nazarite, so pregnant with sacred teaching for the heart. We wish him to ponder, in a special way, the fact that the Holy Ghost has given us the full statement of the law of Nazariteship in the book of Numbers—the wilderness book. And not only so, but let him carefully consider the institution itself. Let him see that he understands why the Nazarite was not to drink wine, why he was not to shave his locks, and why he was not to touch a dead body. Let him meditate upon these three things, and seek to gather up the instruction contained therein. Let him ask himself, Do I really long to be a Nazarite—to walk along the narrow path of separation unto God? and if so, am I prepared to surrender all those things which tend to defile, to distract, and to hinder God's Nazarites? And finally, let him remember that there is a time coming when "the Nazarite may drink wine"; or, in other words, when there will be no need to watch against the varied forms of evil within or around; all will be pure; the affections may flow out without check; the garments may flow around us without a girdle; there will be no evil to be separated from, and therefore there will be no need of separation. In a word, there will be "a new heaven and a new earth wherein *dwelleth* righteousness." May God, in His infinite mercy, keep us until that blessed time, in true consecration of heart unto Himself.

---

Observe that we here reach the close of a very distinct section of our book. The camp is duly arranged; every warrior is set in his proper place (chap. 1–2); every workman is set to his proper work (chap. 3–4); the congregation is purified from defilement (chap. 5); provision is made for the highest character of separation to God (chap. 6). All this is very marked. The order is strikingly beautiful. We have before us not only a cleansed and well-ordered camp, but also a character of consecration to God beyond which it is impossible to go, inasmuch as it is that which is only seen in its integrity in the life of our blessed Lord Jesus Christ Himself. Having then reached this lofty point, nothing remains but for Jehovah to pronounce His blessing upon the whole congregation, and accordingly we get that blessing at the close of chapter 6; and surely we may say, a right royal blessing it is. Let us read and consider.

"And the Lord spake unto Moses, saying, 'Speak unto Aaron and unto his sons, saying, On this wise ye shall bless the children of Israel, saying unto them, The Lord bless thee and keep thee; the Lord make His face shine upon thee, and be gracious unto thee. The Lord lift up His countenance upon thee, and give thee peace. And they shall put My name upon the children of Israel; and I will bless them.' "

This copious blessing flows through the channel of priesthood. Aaron and his sons are commissioned to pronounce this wonderful benediction. God's assembly is to be blessed and kept of Him continually; it is ever to bask in the sunlight of His gracious countenance; its peace is to flow as a river; Jehovah's name is to be called upon it; He is ever there to bless.

*The statement in the text refers, of course, to the Old Testament prophecies. There are passages in the Epistles to the Romans and Galatians in which all believers are viewed as the seed of Abraham (see Rom. 4:9-17; Gal. 3:7,9,21; 6:16), but this is obviously a different thing altogether. We have no revelation of "the Church," properly so called, in the Old Testament Scriptures.

What a provision! Oh that Israel had entered into it, and lived in the power of it! But they did not. They quickly turned aside, as we shall see. They exchanged the light of God's countenance for the darkness of Mount Sinai; they abandoned the ground of grace and placed themselves under law. In place of being satisfied with their portion in the God of their fathers, they lusted after other things (compare Psalm 105 and 106). In place of the order, the purity, and the separation to God with which our book opens, we have disorder, defilement, and giving themselves to idolatry.

But, blessed be God, there is a moment approaching in the which the magnificent benediction of Numbers 6 shall have its full application; when Israel's twelve tribes shall be ranged around that imperishable standard, "Jehovah-shammah" (Ezek. 48:35); when they shall be purified from all their defilements, and consecrated unto God in the power of true Nazariteship. These things are set forth in the fullest and clearest manner throughout the pages of the prophets. All these inspired witnesses, without so much as one dissentient voice, bear testimony to the glorious future in store for the literal Israel. They all point forward to that time when the heavy clouds which have gathered and still hang upon the nation's horizon shall be chased away before the bright beams of "the Sun of Righteousness;" when Israel shall enjoy a cloudless day of bliss and glory, beneath the vines and fig-trees of that very land which God gave as an everlasting possession unto Abraham, Isaac, and Jacob.

If we deny the foregoing, we may as well cut out a large portion of the Old Testament, and not a small part of the New, for in both the one and the other the Holy Ghost doth most clearly and unequivocally bear testimony to this precious fact, namely, mercy, salvation, and blessing to the seed of Jacob. We hesitate not to declare our conviction that no one can possibly understand the prophets who does not see this. There is a bright future in store for God's beloved, though now rejected people. Let us beware how we deal with this fact. It is a very grave matter to attempt to interfere, in any wise, with the true and proper application of the Word of God. If He has pledged Himself to bless the nation of Israel, let us have a care how we seek to force the stream of blessing to flow in a different channel. It is a serious thing to tamper with the declared purpose of God. He has declared it to be His purpose to give the land of Canaan an everlasting possession to the seed of Jacob; and if this be called in question, we do not see how we can hold fast the integrity of any one portion of the Word of God. If we allow ourselves to trifle with a large division of the inspired canon—and most assuredly it is trifling with it when we seek to divert it from its true object—then what security have we in reference to the application of Scripture at all? If God does not mean what He says when He speaks of Israel and the land of Canaan, how do we know that He means what He says when He speaks of the Church and her heavenly portion in Christ? If the Jew be robbed of his glorious future, what security has the Christian as to his?

Let us remember that "*all* [not merely some of] the promises of God are yea and Amen in Christ Jesus"; and while we rejoice in the application of this precious statement to ourselves, let us not seek to deny its application to others. We most fully believe that the children of Israel shall yet enjoy the full tide of blessing presented in the closing paragraph of Numbers 6; and until then, the Church of God is called to partake of blessings peculiar to herself. She is privileged to know the presence of God with her and in her midst continually—to dwell in the light of His countenance—to drink of the river of peace—to be blessed and kept, from day to day, by Him who never slumbers nor sleeps. But let us never forget—yea, let us deeply and constantly remember—that the practical sense and experimental enjoyment of these immense blessings and privileges will be in exact proportion to the measure in which the Church seeks to maintain the order, the purity, and the Nazarite separation to which she is called as the dwelling-place of God—the body of Christ—the habitation of the Holy Ghost.

May these things sink down into our hearts, and exert their sanctifying influence upon our whole life and character.

---

## CHAPTER 7

THIS is the very longest section in the entire book of Numbers. It contains a detailed statement of the names of the twelve princes of the congregation, and of their respective offerings on the occasion of the setting up of the tabernacle. "It came to pass on the day that Moses had fully set up the tabernacle, and had anointed it, and sanctified it, and all the instruments thereof, both the altar and all the vessels thereof, and had anointed them, and sanctified them; that the princes of Israel, heads of the house of their fathers, who were the princes of the tribes, and were over them that were numbered, offered: and they brought their offering before the Lord, six covered wagons, and twelve oxen; a wagon for two of the princes, and for each one an ox; and they brought them before the tabernacle. And the Lord spake unto Moses, saying, 'Take it of them, that they may be to do the service of the tabernacle of the congregation; and thou shalt give them unto the Levites, to every man according to his service.' And Moses took the wagons and the oxen, and gave them unto the Levites. Two wagons and four oxen he gave unto the sons of Gershon, according to their service; and four wagons and eight oxen he gave unto the sons of Merari, according unto their service, under the hand of Ithamar, the son of Aaron the priest. But unto the sons of Kohath he gave none, because the service of the sanctuary belonging unto them was that they should bear upon their shoulders" (ver. 1-9).

We noticed, when meditating on chapters 3 and 4, that the sons of Kohath were privileged to carry all that was most precious of the instruments and furniture of the sanctuary; hence they did not receive any of the princes' offering. It was their high and holy service to bear upon their shoulders, and not to make use of wagons or oxen. The more closely we examine those things which were committed to the custody and charge of the Kohathites, the more we shall see that they set forth, in type, the deeper and fuller manifestations of God in Christ. The Gershonites and Merarites, on the contrary, had to do with those things which were more external. Their work was rougher and more exposed, and therefore they were furnished with the needed help which the liberality of the princes placed at their disposal. The Kohathite did not want the aid of a wagon or an ox in his elevated service. His own shoulder was to bear the precious mystic burden.

"And the princes offered for dedicating of the altar in the day that it was anointed, even the princes offered their offering before the altar. And the Lord said unto Moses, 'They shall offer their offering, *each prince on his day,* for the dedicating of the altar.' "

An unspiritual reader, in running his eye over this unusually long chapter, might feel disposed to ask why so much space is occupied, in an inspired document, with what might be given in the compass of a dozen lines. If a man were giving an account of the transaction of those twelve days, he would, in all probability, have very briefly summed up all in one statement, and told us that the twelve princes offered each such and such things.

But that would not have suited the divine mind at all. God's thoughts are not as our thoughts, nor His ways as our ways. Nothing could satisfy Him but the fullest and most detailed account of each man's name, of the tribe which he represented, and of the offering which he made to the sanctuary of God. Hence this long chapter of eighty-nine verses. Each name shines out in its own distinctness: each offering is minutely described and duly estimated. The names and the offerings are not huddled promiscuously together. This would not be like our God; and He can only act like Himself in whatever He does, and speak like Himself in whatever He says. Man may pass hastily or carelessly over gifts and offerings; but God never can, never does, and never will. He delights to record every little act of service, every little loving gift. He never forgets the smallest thing; and not only does He not forget it Himself, but He takes special pains that untold millions shall read the record. How little did those twelve princes imagine that their names and their offerings were to be handed down, from age to age, to be read by countless generations! Yet so it was, for God would have it so. He will enter upon what might seem to us tedious detail—yea, if you please, what man might deem tautology, rather than omit a single name of any of His servants, or a single item of their work.

Thus, in the chapter before us, "each prince" gets his own appointed day for the presenting of his offering, and his own allotted space on the eternal page of inspiration, in the which the most complete record of his gifts is inscribed by God the Holy Ghost.

This is divine. And may we not say that this seventh chapter of Numbers is one of those specimen-pages from the book of eternity, on which the finger of God has engraved the names of His servants, and the record of their work? We believe it is; and if the reader will turn to the twenty-third of second Samuel, and the sixteenth of Romans, he will find two similar pages. In the former, we have the names and the deeds of David's worthies; in the latter, the names and the deeds of Paul's friends at Rome. In both, we have an illustration of what, we feel persuaded, is true of all the saints of God and the servants of Christ from first to last. Each one has his own special place on the roll, and each one his place in the Master's heart, and all will come out by and by. Amongst David's mighty men we have "the first three," "the three," and "the thirty." Not one of "the thirty" ever attained a place among "the three," nor did one of "the three" ever reach to "the first three."

Nor this only. Every act is faithfully set down, and the substance and style most accurately put before us. We have the name of the man, *what* he did, and *how* he did it. All is recorded, with sedulous care and minuteness, by the unerring and impartial pen of the Holy Ghost.

So also, when we turn to that remarkable sample-page furnished in Romans 16, we have all about Phebe—what she was and what she did, and what a solid basis she had on which to rest her claim upon the sympathy and succor of the assembly at Rome. Then we have Priscilla and Aquila—the wife put first,—and how they had laid down their own necks for the life of the blessed apostle, and earned his thanks and that of all the churches of the Gentiles. Next we have "the *well*-beloved Epaenetus"; and "Mary, who bestowed," not merely labor, but *"much* labor" on the apostle. It would not have expressed the mind of the Spirit, or the heart of Christ, merely to say that Epaenetus was "beloved," or that Mary had bestowed "labor." No; the little adjuncts, "well" and "much," were necessary in order to set forth the exact *status* of each.

But we must not enlarge, and we shall merely call attention to verse 12. Why does not the inspired penman place "Tryphena, Tryphosa," and "the beloved Persis" under one head? Why does he not assign them one and the same position? The reason is perfectly beautiful—because he could only say of the two former that they had "labored in the Lord," whereas it was due to the latter to add that she had "labored *much* in the Lord," Can aught be more discriminating? It is "the three," "the first three," and "the thirty" over again. There is no promiscuous jumbling of names and services together—no haste—no inaccuracy. We are told what each one was, and what he did. Each one gets his own place, and receives his own meed of praise.

And this, be it observed, is a specimen-page from the book of eternity. How solemn! and yet how encouraging! There is not a single act of service which we render to our Lord that will not be set down in His book; and not only the *substance* of the act, but the *style* of it also; for God appreciates style as well as we do. He loves a cheerful giver and a cheerful worker, because that is precisely what He is Himself. It was grateful to His heart to see the tide of liberality flowing around His sanctuary from the representatives of the twelve tribes; it was grateful to His heart to mark the actings of David's worthies, in the day of his rejection; it was grateful to His heart to trace the devoted path of the Priscillas, the Aquilas, and the Phebes of a later date; and, we may add, it is grateful to His heart, in this day of so much lukewarmness and vapid profession, to behold, here and there, a true-hearted lover of Christ, and a devoted worker in His vineyard.

May God's Spirit stir up our hearts to more thorough devotedness. May the love of Christ constrain us, more and more, to live, not unto ourselves, but unto Him who loved us and washed us from our scarlet sins in His most precious blood, and made us all we are, or ever hope to be.

---

## *CHAPTER 8*

"AND the Lord spake unto Moses, saying, 'Speak unto Aaron, and say unto him, When thou lightest the lamps, the seven lamps shall give light over against the candlestick.' And Aaron did so; he lighted the lamps thereof over against the candlestick, as the Lord commanded Moses. And this work of the candlestick was of beaten gold, unto the shaft thereof, unto the flowers thereof, was beaten work: according unto the pattern which the Lord had showed Moses, so he made the candlestick" (ver. 1-4).

On reading the foregoing paragraph, two things claim the reader's attention, namely, first, the position which the type of the golden candlestick occupies; and secondly, the instruction which the type conveys.

It is not a little remarkable that the candlestick is the only part of the furniture of the tabernacle introduced in this place. We have nothing about the golden altar, nothing about the golden table. The candlestick alone is before us, and that not in its covering of blue and of badgers' skins, as in chapter 4, where it, like all the rest, is seen in its traveling-dress. It is here seen lighted, not covered. It comes in between the offerings of the princes and the consecration of the Levites, and sheds forth its mystic light according to the commandment of the Lord. Light cannot be dispensed with in the wilderness, and therefore the golden candlestick must be stripped of its covering, and allowed to shine in testimony for God, which, be it ever remembered, is the grand object of every thing, whether it be the offering of our *substance*, as in the case of the princes; or the dedication of our *persons*, as in the case of the Levites. It is only in the light of the sanctuary that the true worth of any thing or any one can be seen.

Hence, the moral order of the whole of this part of our book is striking and beautiful; indeed, it is divinely perfect. Having read, in chapter 7, the lengthened statement of the princes' liberality, *we*, in our wisdom, might suppose that the next thing in order would be the consecration of the Levites, thus presenting, in unbroken connection, "our persons and offerings." But no; the Spirit of God causes the light of the sanctuary to intervene, in order that we may learn in it the true object of all liberality and service in the wilderness.

Is there not lovely moral appropriateness in this? Can any spiritual reader fail to see it? Why have we not the golden altar, with its cloud of incense, here? why not the pure table, with its twelve loaves? Because neither of these would have the least moral connection with what goes before or what follows after; but the golden candlestick stands connected with both, inasmuch as it shows us that all liberality and all work must be viewed in the light of the sanctuary, in order to ascertain its real worth. This is a grand wilderness-lesson, and it is taught us here as blessedly as type can teach us. In our progress through the book of Numbers, we have just read the account of the large-hearted liberality of the great heads of the congregation, on the occasion of the dedication of the altar; and we are about to read the record of the consecration of the Levites; but between the one and the other the inspired penman pauses, in order to let the light of the sanctuary shine on both.

This is divine order. It is, we are bold to say, one of the ten thousand illustrations which lie scattered over the surface of Scripture, tending to demonstrate the divine perfectness of the volume as a whole, and of each book, section, and paragraph therein. And we are glad—intensely glad to point out these precious illustrations to our reader, as we pass along in his company. We consider we are doing him good service herein; and, at the same time, presenting our humble tribute of praise to that book which our Father has graciously penned for us. Well indeed we know it does not need our poor testimony, nor that of any mortal pen or mortal tongue; but still it is our joy to render the testimony, in the face of the enemy's manifold but futile attacks upon its inspiration. The true source and character of all such attacks will become more and more manifest as we become more deeply, livingly, and experimentally acquainted with the infinite depths and divine perfections of the Volume. And hence it is that the internal evidences of holy Scripture—its powerful effect upon *ourselves,* no less than its intrinsic moral glories—its ability to judge the very roots of character and conduct, no less than its admirable structure, in all its parts—are the most powerful arguments in defense of its divinity. A book that exposes me to myself—that tells me all that is in my heart—that lays bare the very deepest moral springs of my nature—that judges me thoroughly, and at the same time reveals to me One who meets my every need—such a book carries its own credentials with it. It craves not and needs not letters of commendation from man. It stands in no need of his favor, in no dread of his wrath. It has often occurred to us that were we to reason about the Bible as the woman of Sychar reasoned about our Lord, we should reach as sound a conclusion about *it* as she reached about *Him.* "Come," said this simple and happy reasoner, "see a Man which told me all things that ever I did: is not this the Christ?" May we not, with equal force of reasoning, say, Come, see a book which told me all things that ever I did: is not this the Word of God? Yes, truly; and not only so, but we may argue, *a fortiori,* inasmuch as the book of God not only tells us all that ever we did, but all we think, and all we say, and all we are (see Rom. 3:10-18; Matt. 15:19).

But is it that we despise external evidences? Far from it. We delight in them. We value every argument and every evidence calculated to strengthen the foundations of the heart's confidence in the divine inspiration of holy Scripture; and most assuredly we have abundance of such material. The very history of the book itself, with all its striking facts, furnishes a broad tributary stream to swell the tide of evidence. The history of its composition, the history of its preservation, the history of its translation from tongue to tongue, the history of its circulation throughout earth's wide domain —in a word, its entire history, "surpassing fable, and yet true," forms a powerful argument in defense of its divine origin. Take, for example, that one fact of most commanding interest, namely, its having been kept for over a thousand years, in the custody of those who would have gladly consigned it, if they could, to eternal oblivion. Is not this a telling fact? Yes; and there are many such facts in the marvelous history of this peerless, priceless Volume.

But after allowing as wide a margin as may be desired, in the which to insert the value of external evidences, we return, with unshaken decision, to our statement, that the internal evidences—the proofs to be gleaned from the book itself—form as powerful a defense as can be erected with which to stem the tide of skeptical and infidel opposition.

We shall not, however, pursue any further this line of thought into which we have been led, while contemplating the remarkable position assigned to the golden candlestick in the book of Numbers. We felt constrained to say thus much in testimony to our most precious Bible, and having said it, we shall return to our chapter, and seek to gather up the instruction contained in its opening paragraph.

"And the Lord spake unto Moses, saying, 'Speak unto Aaron, and say unto him, When thou lightest the lamps, the seven lamps shall give light over against the candlestick.'" Those "seven lamps" express the light of the Spirit in testimony. They were connected with the beaten shaft of the candlestick, which typifies Christ, who, in His Person and work, is the foundation of the Spirit's work in the Church. All depends upon Christ. Every ray of light in the Church, in the individual believer, or in Israel by and by, all flows from Christ.

Nor is this all we learn from our type. "The seven lamps shall give light over against the candlestick." Were we to clothe this figure in New Testament language, we should quote our Lord's words when He says to us, "Let your light so shine before men, that they may see your good works, and glorify your Father which is in heaven" (Matt. 5:16). Wherever the true light of the Spirit shines, it will always yield a clear testimony to Christ. It will call attention not to itself, but to Him; and this is the way to glorify God. "The seven lamps shall give light over against the candlestick."

This is a great practical truth for all Christians. The very finest evidence which can be afforded of true spiritual work is, that it tends directly to exalt Christ. If attention be sought for the work or the workman, the light has become dim, and the Minister of the sanctuary must use the snuffers. It was Aaron's province to light the lamps, and he it was who trimmed them likewise. In other words, the light which, as Christians, we are responsible to yield, is not only founded upon Christ, but maintained by Him, from moment to moment, throughout the entire night. Apart from Him we can do nothing. The golden shaft sustained the lamps; the priestly hand supplied the oil and applied the snuffers. It is all *in* Christ, *from* Christ, and *by* Christ.

And more, it is all *to* Christ. Wherever the light of the Spirit—the true light of the sanctuary—has shone in this wilderness world, the object of that light has been to exalt the name of Jesus. Whatever has been done by the Holy Ghost, whatever has been said, whatever has been written, has had for its aim the glory of that blessed One; and we may say with confidence, that whatever has not that tendency—that aim, is not of the Holy Ghost, be it what it may. There may be an immense amount of work done, a great deal of apparent result reached, a quantity of that which is calculated to attract human attention, and elicit human applause, and yet not one ray of light from the golden candlestick. And why? Because attention is *sought* for the work, or for those engaged in it. *Man* and his doings and sayings are exalted, instead of Christ. The light has not been produced by the oil which the hand of the great High-Priest supplies; and, as a consequence, it is false light; it is a light which shines not over against the candlestick, but over against the name or the actings of some poor mortal.

All this is most solemn, and demands our deepest attention. There is always the utmost danger when a man or his work becomes remarkable. He may be sure Satan is gaining his object, when attention is drawn to aught or to any one but the Lord Jesus Himself. A work may be commenced in the greatest possible simplicity, but, through lack of holy watchfulness and spirituality on the part of the workman, he himself, or the results of his work, may attract general attention, and he may fall into the snare of the devil. Satan's grand and ceaseless object is to dishonor the Lord Jesus; and if he can do this by what seems to be Christian service, he has achieved all the greater victory for the time. He has no objection to work, as such, provided he can detach that work from the name of Jesus. He will ever mingle himself, if he can, with the work; he will present himself amongst the servants of Christ, as he once presented himself amongst the sons of God; but his object is ever one and the same, namely, to dishonor the Lord. He permitted the damsel in Acts 16 to bear testimony to Christ's servants, and say, "These men are the servants of the Most High God, which show unto us the way of salvation"; but this was simply with a view to insnare those servants and mar their work. He was defeated, however, because the light that emanated from Paul and Silas was the genuine light of the sanctuary, and it *shone* only for Christ. They sought not a name for themselves; and inasmuch as it was to them and not to their Master that the damsel bore witness, they refused the witness, and chose rather to suffer for their Master's sake than to be exalted at His expense.

This is a fine example for all the Lord's workmen; and if we turn, for an instant, to Acts 3, we shall find another very striking illustration. There, the light of the sanctuary shone out in the healing of the lame man, and when attention was drawn, *unsought,* to the workmen, we find Peter and John, at once, with holy jealousy, retiring behind their glorious Master and giving all the praise to Him. "And as the lame man which was healed held Peter and John, all the people ran together unto them in the porch that is called Solomon's, greatly wondering. And when Peter saw it, he answered unto the people, 'Ye men of Israel, why marvel ye at this? or why look ye so earnestly *on us* as though by *our own* power or holiness *we* had made this man to walk? The God of Abraham, and of Isaac, and of Jacob, the God of our fathers, hath glorified *His Son Jesus.*' "

Here we have, in very deed, "the seven lamps giving their light over against the candlestick"; or, in other words, the sevenfold or perfect display of the Spirit's light in distinct testimony to the name of Jesus. "Why," said these faithful vessels of the Spirit's light, "look ye so earnestly on *us?*" No need of the snuffers here!—the light was undimmed. It was, no doubt, an occasion which the apostles might have turned to their own account had they been so disposed. It was a moment in the which they might have surrounded their own names with a halo of glory. They might have raised themselves to a pinnacle of fame, and drawn around them the respect and veneration of wondering, if not worshiping, thousands; but had they done so, they would have robbed their Master, falsified the testimony, grieved the Holy Ghost, and brought down upon themselves the just judgment of Him who will not give His glory to another.

But no; the seven lamps were shining brightly in Jerusalem at this interesting moment. The true candlestick was in Solomon's porch just then, and not in the temple; at least, the seven lamps were there, and doing their appointed work most blessedly. Those honored servants sought no glory for themselves; yea, they instantly put forth all their energies in order to avert the wondering gaze of the multitude from themselves, and fix it upon the only worthy One, who, though He had passed into the heavens, was still working by His Spirit on earth.

Many other illustrations might be drawn from the pages of the Acts of the Apostles, but the above will suffice to impress upon our hearts the great practical lesson taught in the golden candlestick, with its seven lamps. We are deeply sensible of our need of the lesson at this very moment. There is always a danger of the work and the workman being more the object than the Master. Let us be on our guard against this. It is a sad evil. It grieves the blessed Spirit, who ever labors to exalt the name of Jesus. It is offensive to the Father, who would ever be sounding in our ears and deep down in our hearts those words heard from an open heaven, on the mount of transfiguration, "This is My beloved Son, in whom I am well pleased, hear ye Him." It is in the most direct and positive hostility to the mind of heaven, where every eye is fixed on Jesus, every heart occupied with Jesus, and where the one eternal, universal, unanimous cry shall be, *"Thou art worthy."*

Let us think of all this—think deeply—think habitually, that so we may shrink from every thing bordering upon or savoring of the exaltation of man—of self—our doings and sayings and thinkings. May we all more earnestly seek the quiet, shady, unobtrusive path where the spirit of the meek and lowly Jesus will ever lead us to walk and serve. In a word, may we so abide in Christ, so receive from Him, day by day and moment by moment, the pure oil, that our light may shine, without our thinking of it, to His praise, in whom alone we have *all,* and apart from whom we can do absolutely *nothing.*

The remainder of the eighth chapter of Numbers contains the record of the ceremonial connected with the consecration of the Levites, to which we have already referred in our notes on chapters 3 and 4.

---

## *CHAPTER 9*

"AND the Lord spake unto Moses in the wilderness of Sinai, in the first month of the second year after they were come out of the land of Egypt, saying, 'Let the children of Israel also keep the passover at his appointed season. In the fourteenth day of this month, at even, ye shall keep it in his appointed season: according to all the rites of it, and according to all the ceremonies thereof, shall ye keep it.' And Moses spake unto the children of Israel, that they should keep the passover. And they kept the passover on the fourteenth day of the first month, at even, in the wilderness of Sinai: according to all that the Lord commanded Moses, so did the children of Israel" (ver. 1-5).

There are three distinct positions in which we find this great redemption-feast celebrated, namely, in Egypt (Exod. 12), in the wilderness (Num. 9), in the land of Canaan (Josh. 5). Redemption lies at the foundation of every thing connected with the history of God's people. Are they to be delivered from the bondage, the death, and the darkness of Egypt? it is by redemption. Are they to be borne along through all the difficulties and dangers of the desert? it is on the ground of redemption. Are they to walk across the ruins of the frowning walls of Jericho, and plant their feet upon the necks of the kings of Canaan? it is in virtue of redemption.

Thus the blood of the paschal lamb met the Israel of God amid the deep degradation of the land of Egypt, and delivered them out of it. It met them in the dreary desert, and carried them through it: it met them on their entrance into the land of Canaan, and established them in it.

In a word, then, the blood of the lamb met the people in Egypt, it accompanied them through the desert, and planted them in Canaan. It was the blessed basis of all the divine actings in them, with them, and for them. Was it a question of the judgment of God against Egypt? the blood of the lamb screened them from it. Was it a question of the numberless and nameless wants of the wilderness? the blood of the lamb secured a full provision for them. Was it a question of the dreaded power of the seven nations of Canaan? the blood of the lamb was the sure and certain pledge of complete and glorious victory. The moment we behold Jehovah coming forth to act on behalf of His people, on the ground of the blood of the lamb, all is infallibly secured, from first to last. The whole of that mysterious and marvelous journey, from the brick-kilns of Egypt to the vine-clad hills and honeyed plains of Palestine, served but to illustrate and set forth the varied virtues of the blood of the lamb.

However, the chapter which now lies open before us presents the passover entirely from a wilderness stand-point; and this will account, to the reader, for the introduction of the following circumstance: "There were certain men which were defiled by the dead body of a man, that they could not keep the passover on that day; and they came before Moses and before Aaron on that day."

Here was a practical difficulty—something abnormal, as we say—something not anticipated, and therefore the question was submitted to Moses and Aaron. "They came before Moses"—the exponent of the claims of God, "and before Aaron"—the exponent of the provisions of the grace of God. There seems something distinct and emphatic in the way in which both these functionaries are referred to. The two elements of which they are the expression would be deemed essential in the solving of such a difficulty as that which here presented itself.

"And those men said unto him, 'We are defiled by the dead body of a man; wherefore are we kept back, that we may not offer an offering of the Lord in his appointed season among the children of Israel?' " There was the plain confession as to the defilement, and the question raised was this: Were they to be deprived of the holy privilege of coming before the Lord in His appointed way? Was there no resource—

no provision for such a case?

A deeply interesting question, surely, but one for which no answer had as yet been provided. We have no such case anticipated in the original institution, in Exodus 12, although we have there a very full statement of all the rites and all the ceremonies of the feast. It was reserved for the wilderness to evolve this new point. It was in the actual walk of the people—in the real practical details of desert life, that the difficulty presented itself for which a solution had to be provided. Hence it is that the record of this entire affair is appropriately given in Numbers, the book of the wilderness.

"And Moses said unto them, 'Stand still, and I will hear what the Lord will command concerning you.' " Lovely attitude! Moses had no answer to give; but he knew who had, and he waited on Him. This was the very best and wisest thing for Moses to do. He did not pretend to be able to give an answer. He was not ashamed to say, *"I do not know."* With all his wisdom and knowledge, he did not hesitate to show his ignorance. This is true knowledge—true wisdom. It might be humiliating to one in Moses' position to appear before the congregation or any members of it, in the light of one ignorant on any question. He who had led the people out of Egypt, he who had conducted them through the Red Sea, he who had conversed with Jehovah and received his commission from the great "I am," could it be possible that he was unable to meet a difficulty arising out of such a simple case as that which was now before him? was it indeed true that such an one as Moses was ignorant as to the right course in reference to men defiled by a dead body?

How few there are who, though not occupying such a lofty position as Moses, would not have attempted a reply of some sort to such a query. But Moses was the meekest man in all the earth. He knew better than to presume to speak when he had nothing to say. Would that we more faithfully followed his example in this matter! It would save us many a sad exhibition, from many a blunder, from many a false attempt. Moreover, it would tend to make us very much more real, more simple, more unaffected. We are ofttimes so silly as to be ashamed to expose our ignorance. We foolishly imagine that our reputation for wisdom and intelligence is touched when we give utterance to that fine sentence, so expressive of true moral greatness, "I don't know." It is a total mistake. We always attach much more weight and importance to the words of a man who never pretends to knowledge which he does not possess; but a man who is always ready to speak, in flippant self-confidence, we are never ready to hear. Oh, to walk, at all times, in the spirit of these lovely words, "Stand still, and I will hear what the Lord will command"!

"And the Lord spake unto Moses, saying, 'Speak unto the children of Israel, saying, If any man of you or of your posterity shall be unclean by reason of a dead body, or be in a journey afar off, yet he shall keep the passover unto the Lord. The fourteenth day of *the second month,* at even, they shall keep it, and eat it with unleavened bread and bitter herbs.' "

There are two grand foundation-truths set forth in the passover, namely, redemption, and the unity of God's people. These truths are unchangeable: nothing can ever do away with them. Failure there may be, and unfaithfulness, in various forms; but those glorious truths of the eternal redemption and perfect unity of God's people remain in all their force and value. Hence that impressive ordinance which so vividly shadowed forth those truths was of perpetual obligation. Circumstances were not to interfere with it; death or distance was not to interrupt it. "If any man of you or of your posterity shall be unclean by reason of a dead body, or be in a journey afar off, yet shall he keep the passover unto the Lord." So imperative, indeed, was it upon every member of the congregation to celebrate this feast, that a special provision is made in Numbers 9, for those who were not up to the mark of keeping it according to the due order. Such persons were to observe it "on the fourteenth day of the *second* month." This was the provision of grace for all cases of unavoidable defilement or distance.

If the reader will turn to 2 Chronicles 30, he will see that Hezekiah, and the congregation in his day, availed themselves of this gracious provision. "And there assembled at Jerusalem much people to keep the feast of unleavened bread in the *second* month, a very great congregation. . . . Then they killed the passover on the fourteenth day of the second month" (ver. 13,15).

The grace of God can meet us in our greatest possible weakness, if only that weakness be felt and confessed.* But let not this most precious and comfortable truth lead us to trifle with sin or defilement. Though grace permitted the second month, instead of the first, it did not, on that account, allow any laxity as to the rites and ceremonies of the feast. "The unleavened bread and bitter herbs" were always to have their place; none of the sacrifice was to remain till the morning, nor was a single bone of it to be broken. God cannot allow any lowering of the standard of truth or holiness. Man, through weakness, failure, or the power of circumstances, might be behind the time; but he must not be below the mark. Grace permitted the former; holiness forbids the latter: and if any one had presumed upon the grace to dispense with the holiness, he would have been cut off from the congregation.

Has this no voice for us? Assuredly it has. We must ever remember, as we pass along through the pages of this marvelous book of Numbers, that the things which happened unto Israel are our types, and that it is at once our duty and our privilege to hang over these types and seek to understand the holy lessons which they are designed of God to teach.

What, then, are we to learn from the regulations with respect to the passover in the second month? Why was Israel so specially enjoined not to omit a single rite or ceremony on that particular occasion? why is it that in this ninth chapter of Numbers the directions for the second month are much more minute than those for the first? It is not, surely, that the ordinance was more important in the one case than in the other, for its importance, in God's judgment, was ever the same; neither is it that there was a shade of difference in the order in either case, for that, too, was ever the same. Still the fact must strike the reader who ponders the chapter before us that where reference is made to the celebration of the passover in the first month, we simply read the words, "according to all the rites of it, and according to all the ceremonies thereof, shall ye keep it"; but on the other hand, when reference is made to the second month, we have a most minute statement of what those rites and ceremonies were,—"They shall eat it with unleavened bread and bitter herbs. They shall leave none of it unto the morning, nor break any bone of it: according to all the ordinances of the passover they shall keep it." (Compare verse 3 with 11-12.)

What, we ask, does this plain fact teach us? We believe it teaches us, most distinctly, that we are never to lower the standard, in the things of God, because of failure and weakness on the part of God's people; but rather, on that very account, to take special pains to hold the standard up, in all its divine integrity. No doubt, there should be the deep sense of failure—the deeper the better; but God's truth is not to be surrendered. We can always reckon, with confidence, upon the resources of divine grace, while seeking to maintain, with unwavering decision, the standard of divine truth.

Let us seek to keep this ever in the remembrance of the thoughts of our hearts. We are in danger, on the one hand, of forgetting the fact that failure has come in—yea, gross failure, unfaithfulness, and sin; and on the other hand, we are in danger of forgetting, in view of that failure, the unfailing faithfulness of God in spite of

*The reader will note, with interest and profit, the contrast between the acting of Hezekiah in 2 Chronicles 30, and the acting of Jeroboam in 1 Kings 12:32. The former availed himself of the provisions of divine grace; the latter followed his own device. The second month was permitted of God; the eighth month was invented by man. Divine provisions meeting man's need, and human inventions opposing God's Word, are totally different things.

everything. The professing church has failed, and become a perfect ruin; and not only so, but we ourselves have individually failed and helped on the ruin. We should feel all this—feel it deeply—feel it constantly. We should ever bear upon our spirits before our God the deep and heart-subduing consciousness of how sadly and how shamefully we have behaved ourselves in the house of God. It would be adding immensely to our failure were we ever to forget that we have failed. The most profound humility and the deepest brokenness of spirit become us in the remembrance of all this; and these inward feelings and exercises will surely express themselves in a lowly walk and carriage in the midst of the scene in which we move.

"Nevertheless the foundation of God standeth sure, having this seal, 'The Lord knoweth them that are His.' And, 'Let every one that nameth the name of Christ depart from iniquity' " (2 Tim. 2:19). Here is the resource of the faithful, in view of the ruins of christendom. God never fails, never changes, and we have simply to depart from iniquity and cling to Him. We are to do what is right, and follow it diligently, and leave results to Him.

We would earnestly beg of the reader to give the foregoing line of thought his entire attention. We want him to pause, for a few moments, and prayerfully consider the whole subject. We are convinced that a due consideration of it, in its two sides, would greatly help us to pick our steps amid the surrounding ruins. The remembrance of the Church's condition, and of our own personal unfaithfulness, would keep us humble; while, at the same time, the apprehension of God's unchanging standard, and of His unswerving faithfulness, would detach us from the evil around, and keep us steady in the path of separation. Both together would effectually preserve us from empty pretension on the one hand, and from laxity and indifference on the other. We have ever to keep before our souls the humbling fact that we have failed, and yet to hold fast that grand truth that God is faithful.

These are, pre-eminently, lessons for the wilderness—lessons for this very day—lessons for *us.* They are suggested, very forcibly, by the inspired record of the passover in the second month—a record peculiar to the book of Numbers—the great wilderness-book. It is in the wilderness that human failure comes so fully out, and in the wilderness the infinite resources of divine grace are displayed. But once more, let us reiterate the statement—and may it be engraved, in characters deep and broad, on our hearts—the richest provisions of divine grace and mercy afford no warrant whatever for lowering the standard of divine truth. If any had pleaded defilement or distance as an excuse for not keeping the passover, or for keeping it otherwise than as God had enjoined, he would, most assuredly, have been cut off from the congregation. And so with us; if we consent to surrender any truth of God because failure has come in—if we, in sheer unbelief of heart, give up God's standard and abandon God's ground—if we draw a plea from the condition of things around us to shake off the authority of God's truth over the conscience, or its formative influence upon our conduct and character, it is very evident that our communion is suspended.*

We would gladly pursue this great practical line of truth somewhat further, but we must forbear, and close this part of our subject by quoting the remainder of this wilderness record concerning the passover.

"But the man that is clean, and is not in a journey, and forbeareth to keep the passover, even the same soul shall be cut off from among his people; because he brought not the offering of the Lord in his appointed season, that man shall bear his sin. And if a stranger shall sojourn among you, and will keep the passover unto the Lord; according to the ordinance of the passover, and according to the manner thereof, so shall he do: ye shall have one ordinance, both for the

*Let it be noted here once for all, that the cutting off of any one from the congregation of Israel answers to the suspension of a believer's communion because of unjudged sin.

stranger and for him that was born in the land" (ver. 13-14).

The willful neglect of the passover would argue, on the part of an Israelite, a total want of appreciation of the benefits and blessings flowing out of his redemption and deliverance from the land of Egypt. The more deeply any one entered into the divine reality of that which had been accomplished on that memorable night, in the which the congregation of Israel found refuge and repose beneath the shelter of the blood, the more earnestly would he long for the return of "the fourteenth day of the first month," that he might have an opportunity of commemorating that glorious occasion; and if there was aught preventing his enjoying the ordinance in "the first month," the more gladly and thankfully would he avail himself of "the second." But the man who could be satisfied to go on, from year to year, without keeping the passover, only proved that his heart was far away from the God of Israel. It were worse than vain for any one to speak of loving the God of his fathers, and of enjoying the blessings of redemption, while the very ordinance which God had appointed to set forth that redemption lay neglected from year to year.

And may we not, to a certain extent, apply all this to ourselves, in reference to the matter of the Lord's supper? Doubtless we may, and that with very much profit. There is this connection between the passover and the Lord's supper, that the former was the type, the latter the memorial, of the death of Christ. Thus we read in 1 Corinthians 5, "Christ our passover is sacrificed for us." This sentence establishes the connection. The passover was the memorial of Israel's redemption from the bondage of Egypt, and the Lord's supper is the memorial of the Church's redemption from the heavier and darker bondage of sin and Satan. Hence, as every true and faithful Israelite would surely be found keeping the passover, in the appointed season, according to all the rites and ceremonies thereof, so will every true and faithful Christian be found celebrating the Lord's supper, in its appointed season, and according to all the principles laid down in the New Testament respecting it. If an Israelite had neglected the passover, even on one single occasion, he would have been cut off from the congregation. Such neglect was not to be tolerated in the assembly of old. It was instantly visited with divine displeasure.

And may we not ask, in the face of this solemn fact, Is it nothing now—is it a matter of no moment for Christians to neglect, from week to week and month to month, the supper of their Lord? Are we to suppose that the One who, in Numbers 9, declared that the neglecter of the passover should be cut off, takes no account of the neglecter of the Lord's table? We cannot believe it for a moment. For albeit it is not a question of being cut off from the Church of God—the body of Christ, are we, on that account to be negligent? Far be the thought. Yea, rather should it have the blessed effect of stirring us up to greater diligence in the celebration of that most precious feast wherein we "do show the Lord's death till He come."

To a pious Israelite, there was nothing like the passover, because it was the memorial of his redemption; and to a pious Christian, there is nothing like the Lord's supper, because it is the memorial of his redemption and of the death of his Lord. Of all the exercises in which the Christian can engage, there is nothing more precious, nothing more expressive, nothing that brings Christ more touchingly or solemnly before his heart, than the Lord's supper. He may sing about the Lord's death, he may pray about it, he may read about it, he may hear about it; but it is only in the supper that he *"shows"* it forth. "And He took bread, and gave thanks, and brake it, and gave unto them, saying, 'This is My body, which is given for you: this do in remembrance of Me.' Likewise also the cup after supper, saying, 'This cup is the new testament in My blood, which is shed for you' " (Luke 22:19-20).

Here we have the feast *instituted;* and when we turn to the Acts of the Apostles, we read that, "upon the first day of the week, the disciples came together to break bread" (Acts 20:7).

Here we have the feast *celebrated;* and

lastly, when we turn to the Epistles, we read, "The cup of blessing which we bless, is it not the communion of the blood of Christ? The bread which we break, is it not the communion of the body of Christ? For we being many are one loaf, and one body; for we are all partakers of that one loaf" (1 Cor. 10:16-17). And again, "For I have received of the Lord that which also I delivered unto you, That the Lord Jesus the same night in which He was betrayed took bread; and when He had given thanks, He brake it, and said, 'Take, eat: this is My body, which is broken for you: this do in remembrance of Me.' After the same manner also He took the cup, when He had supped, saying, 'This cup is the new testament in My blood: this do ye, as oft as ye drink it, in remembrance of Me.' For as often as ye eat this bread, and drink this cup, ye do show the Lord's death till He come" (1 Cor. 11:23-26).

Here we have the feast *expounded.* And may we not say that in the institution, the celebration, and the exposition, we have a threefold cord, not easily broken, to bind our souls to this most precious feast?

How is it, then, that, in the face of all this holy authority, any of God's people should be found neglecting the Lord's table? or, looking at it in another aspect, how is it that any of Christ's members can be satisfied to go on for weeks, and months, and some all their days, without ever remembering their Lord in the way of His own direct and positive appointment? We are aware that some professing Christians regard this subject in the light of a return to Jewish ordinances, and as a coming down from the high ground of the Church. They look upon the Lord's supper and baptism as inward spiritual mysteries, and they consider that we are departing from true spirituality in insisting upon the literal observance of these ordinances.

To all this we very simply reply that God is wiser than we are. If the Lord Christ instituted the supper; if God the Holy Ghost led the early Church to celebrate it; and if He has also expounded it unto us, who are we that we should set up our ideas in opposition to God? No doubt, the Lord's supper should be an inward spiritual mystery to all who partake of it; but it is also an outward, literal, tangible thing. There is literal bread, and literal wine—literal eating, and literal drinking. If any deny this, they may, with equal force, deny that there are literal people gathered together. We have no right to explain away Scripture after such a fashion. It is our happy and holy duty to submit to Scripture—to bow down, absolutely and implicitly, to its divine authority.

Nor is it merely a question of subjection to the authority of Scripture. It is that, most assuredly, as we have abundantly proved by quotation after quotation from the divine Word; and that alone is amply sufficient for every pious mind. But there is more than this. There is such a thing as the response of love in the heart of the Christian, answering to the love of the heart of Christ. Is not this something? Ought we not to seek, in some small degree, to meet the love of such a heart? If our blessed and adorable Lord has, in very deed, appointed the bread and the wine, in the supper, as memorials of His broken body and shed blood; if He has ordained that we should eat of that bread and drink of that cup, in remembrance of Him, ought we not, in the power of responsive affection, to meet the desire of His loving heart? Surely no earnest Christian will question this. It ought ever to be the very joy of our hearts to gather around the table of our loving Lord, and remember Him in the way of His appointment—to show forth His death till He come. It is only marvelous to think that He should seek a place in the remembrance of such hearts as ours; but so it is; and it would be sad indeed if we, on any ground, and for any reason whatsoever, should neglect that very feast with which He has linked His precious name.

This, of course, would not be the place to enter upon any thing like an elaborate exposition of the ordinance of the Lord's supper. We have sought to do this elsewhere.* What we specially desire here is, to

*"Thoughts on the Lord's Supper," in the author's *Miscellaneous Writings,* vol. 3.

urge upon the Christian reader the immense importance and deep interest of the ordinance as viewed on the double ground of subjection to the authority of Scripture, and responsive love to Christ Himself. And furthermore, we are anxious to impress all who may read these lines with a sense of the seriousness of neglecting to eat the Lord's supper, according to the Scriptures. We may depend upon it it is dangerous ground for any to attempt to set aside this positive institution of our Lord and Master. It argues a wrong condition of soul altogether. It proves that the conscience is not subject to the authority of the Word, and that the heart is not in true sympathy with the affections of Christ. Let us therefore see to it that we are honestly endeavoring to discharge our holy responsibilities to the table of the Lord—that we forbear not to keep the feast—that we celebrate it according to the order laid down by God the Holy Ghost.

Thus much as to the passover in the wilderness, and the impressive lessons which it conveys to our souls.

We shall now dwell for a few moments on the closing paragraph of our chapter, which is as truly characteristic as any portion of the book. In it we are called to contemplate a numerous host of men, women, and children, traveling through a trackless wilderness, "where there was no way"—passing over a dreary waste, a vast sandy desert, without compass or human guide.

What a thought! what a spectacle! There were those millions of people moving along without any knowledge of the route by which they were to travel, as wholly dependent upon God for guidance as for food and all beside; a thoroughly helpless pilgrim host. They could form no plans for the morrow. When encamped, they knew not when they were to march, they knew not when or where they were to halt. Theirs was a life of daily and hourly dependence. They had to look up for guidance. Their movements were controlled by the wheels of Jehovah's chariot.

This, truly, was a wondrous spectacle. Let us read the record of it, and drink into our souls its heavenly teaching.

"And on the day that the tabernacle was reared up, the cloud covered the tabernacle, namely, the tent of the testimony: and at even, there was upon the tabernacle as it were the appearance of fire, until the morning. *So it was alway:* the cloud covered it by day, and the appearance of fire by night. And when the cloud was taken up from the tabernacle, then after that the children of Israel journeyed: and in the place where the cloud abode, there the children of Israel pitched their tents. At the commandment of the Lord the children of Israel journeyed, and at the commandment of the Lord they pitched: as long as the cloud abode upon the tabernacle, they rested in their tents. And when the cloud tarried along upon the tabernacle many days, then the children of Israel kept the charge of the Lord, and journeyed not. And so it was, when the cloud was a few days upon the tabernacle; according to the commandment of the Lord they abode in their tents, and according to the commandment of the Lord they journeyed. And so it was, when the cloud abode from even unto the morning, and that the cloud was taken up in the morning, then they journeyed; whether it was by day or by night that the cloud was taken up, they journeyed. Or whether it were two days, or a month, or a year, that the cloud tarried upon the tabernacle, remaining thereon, the children of Israel abode in their tents, and journeyed not; but when it was taken up, they journeyed. At the commandment of the Lord they rested in the tents, and at the commandment of the Lord they journeyed: they kept the charge of the Lord, at the commandment of the Lord by the hand of Moses" (ver. 15-23).

A more lovely picture of absolute dependence upon and subjection to divine guidance it were impossible to conceive than that presented in the foregoing paragraph. There was not a footprint or a landmark throughout that "great and terrible wilderness." It was therefore useless to look for any guidance from those who had gone before. They were wholly cast upon God for every step of the way; they were in a position of constant waiting upon Him. This, to an unsubdued mind—an unbroken will, would be intolerable; but to a soul knowing, loving, confiding, and delighting in God, nothing could be more deeply blessed.

Here lies the real gist of the whole matter. Is God known, loved, and trusted? If He be, the heart will delight in the most absolute dependence upon Him; if not, such dependence would be perfectly insufferable. The unrenewed man loves to think himself independent—loves to fancy himself free—loves to believe that he may do what he likes, go where he likes, say what he likes. Alas! it is the merest delusion. Man is not free: he is the slave of Satan. It is now well-nigh six thousand years since he sold himself into the hands of that great spiritual slaveholder, who has held him ever since, and who holds him still. Yes, Satan holds the natural man—the unconverted, unrepentant man in terrible bondage. He has him bound hand and foot with chains and fetters which are not seen in their true character, because of the gilding wherewith he has so artfully covered them. Satan rules man by means of his lusts, his passions, and his pleasures. He forms lusts in the heart, and then gratifies them with the things that are in the world; and man vainly imagines himself free because he can gratify his desires. But it is a melancholy delusion, and sooner or later it will be found to be such. There is no freedom save that with which Christ makes His people free. He it is who says, "Ye shall know the truth, and the truth shall make you free." And again, "If the Son shall make you free, ye shall be free indeed" (John 8).

Here is true liberty. It is the liberty which the new nature finds in walking in the Spirit, and doing those things that are pleasing in the sight of God. "The service of the Lord is perfect freedom." But this service, in all its departments, involves the most simple dependence upon the living God. Thus it was with the only true and perfect Servant that ever trod this earth. He was ever dependent. Every movement, every act, every word—all He did, and all He left undone—was the fruit of the most absolute dependence upon and subjection to God. He moved when God would have Him move, and stood still when God would have Him stand; He spoke when God would have Him speak, and was silent when God would have Him silent.

Such was Jesus when He lived in this world; and we, as partakers of His nature—His life, and having His Spirit dwelling in us, are called to walk in His steps, and live a life of simple dependence upon God, from day to day. Of this life of dependence, in one special phase of it, we have a graphic and beautiful type at the close of our chapter. The Israel of God—the camp in the desert—that pilgrim host—followed the movement of the cloud. They had to *look up* for guidance. This is man's proper work. He was made to turn his countenance upward, in contrast with the brute, who is formed to look downward.* Israel could form no plans. They could never say, "To-morrow we shall go to such a place." They were entirely dependent upon the movement of the cloud.

Thus it was with Israel, and thus it should be with us. We are passing through a trackless desert—a moral wilderness. There is absolutely no way. We should not know how to walk, or where to go, were it not for that one most precious, most deep, most comprehensive sentence which fell from the lips of our blessed Lord, *"I am the way."* Here is divine, infallible guidance. We are to follow Him. "I am the light of the world: he that followeth Me shall not walk in darkness, but shall have the light of life" (John 8). This is living guidance. It is not acting according to the letter of certain rules and regulations; it is following a living Christ—walking as He walked, doing as He did, imitating His example in all things. This is Christian movement—Christian action. It is keeping the eye fixed upon Jesus, and having the features, traits, and lineaments of His character imprinted on our new nature, and reflected back or reproduced in our daily life and ways.

Now this will assuredly involve the

---

*The Greek word for man (ανθρωπος) signifies to turn the face upwards.

surrender of our own will, our own plans, our own management, altogether. We must follow the cloud: we must wait *ever,* wait *only,* upon God. We cannot say, We shall go here or there, do this or that, tomorrow, or next week. All our movements must be placed under the regulating power of that one commanding sentence (often, alas! lightly penned and uttered by us), *"If the Lord will."*

Oh that we better understood all this! Would that we knew more perfectly the meaning of divine guidance! How often do we vainly imagine, and confidently assert, that the cloud is moving in that very direction which suits the bent of our inclination! We want to do a certain thing, or make a certain movement, and we seek to persuade ourselves that our will is the will of God. Thus, instead of being divinely guided, we are self-deceived. Our will is unbroken, and hence we cannot be guided aright; for the real secret of being rightly guided—guided of God—is to have our own will thoroughly subdued. "The meek will He guide in judgment; and the meek will He teach *His way.*" And again, "I will guide thee with Mine eye." But let us ponder the admonition, "Be ye not as the horse, or as the mule, which have no understanding; whose mouth must be held in with bit and bridle, lest they come near unto thee" (Ps. 32). If the countenance be turned upwards, to catch the movement of the divine "eye," we shall not need the "bit and bridle." But here is precisely the point in which we so sadly fail. We do not live sufficiently near to God to discern the movement of His eye. The *will* is at work. We want to have our own way, and hence we are left to reap the bitter fruits thereof. Thus it was with Jonah. He was told to go to Nineveh, but he wanted to go to Tarshish; and circumstances seemed to favor; providence seemed to point in the direction of his will. But, ah! he had to find his place in the belly of the whale—yea, in "the belly of hell" itself, where "the weeds were wrapped about his head." It was there he learnt the bitterness of following his own will. He had to be taught in the depths of the ocean the true meaning of the "bit and bridle," because he would not follow the gentler guidance of the eye.

But our God is so gracious, so tender, so patient! He will teach and He will guide His poor feeble, erring children. He spares not pains with us. He occupies Himself continually about us, in order that we may be kept from our own ways, which are full of thorns and briars, and walk in His ways, which are pleasantness and peace.

There is nothing in all this world more deeply blessed than to lead a life of habitual dependence upon God; to hang upon Him moment by moment, to wait on Him and cling to Him for every thing, to have all our springs in Him; it is the true secret of peace, and of holy independence of the creature. The soul that can really say, *"All* my springs are in Thee" is lifted above all creature-confidences, human hopes, and earthly expectations. It is not that God does not use the creature, in a thousand ways, to minister to us; we do not at all mean this. He does use the creature; but if we *lean* upon the creature, instead of leaning upon Him, we shall very speedily get leanness and barrenness into our souls. There is a vast difference between God's using the creature to bless us, and our leaning on the creature to the exclusion of Him. In the one case, we are blessed and He is glorified; in the other, we are disappointed and He is dishonored.

It is well that the soul should deeply and seriously consider this distinction. We believe it is constantly overlooked. We imagine, ofttimes, that we are leaning upon and looking to God, when, in reality, if we would only look honestly at the roots of things, and judge ourselves in the immediate presence of God, we should find an appalling amount of the leaven of creature-confidence. How often do we speak of living by faith, and of trusting only in God, when, at the same time, if we would only look down into the depths of our hearts, we should find there a large measure of dependence upon circumstances, references to second causes, and the like.

Christian reader, let us look well to this. Let us see to it that our eye is fixed upon the living God alone, and not upon man whose breath is in his nostrils. Let us wait on Him—wait patiently—wait constantly. If we are at a loss for any thing, let our direct and simple reference be to Him. Are we at a loss to know our way, to know whither we should turn, what step we should take? let us remember that He has said, "I am the way;" let us follow Him. He will make all clear, bright, and certain. There can be no darkness, no perplexity, no uncertainty, if we are following Him; for He has said, and we are bound to believe, "He that followeth Me shall not walk in darkness." Hence, therefore, if we are in darkness, it is certain that we are not following Him. No darkness can ever settle down upon that blessed path along which God leads those who, with a single eye, seek to follow Jesus.

But some one whose eye scans these lines may say, or at least may feel disposed to say, Well, after all, I am in perplexity as to my path. I really do not know which way to turn, or what step to take. If this be the language of the reader, we would simply ask him this one question, Art thou following Jesus? If so, thou canst not be in perplexity. Art thou following the cloud? If so, thy way is as plain as God can make it. Here lies the root of the whole matter. Perplexity and uncertainty is very often the fruit of the working of the *will.* We are bent upon doing something which God does not want us to do at all—upon going somewhere that God does not want us to go. We pray about it, and get no answer; we pray again and again, and get no answer. How is this? Why, the simple fact is that God wants us to be quiet—to stand still—to remain just where we are. Wherefore, instead of racking our brain and harassing our souls about what we ought to do, let us do nothing, but simply wait on God.

This is the secret of peace and calm elevation. If an Israelite in the desert had taken it into his head to make some movement independent of Jehovah; if he took it upon him to move when the cloud was at rest, or to halt while the cloud was moving, we can easily see what the result would have been. And so it will ever be with us. If we move when we ought to rest, or rest when we ought to move, we shall not have the divine presence with us. "At the commandment of the Lord they rested in the tents, and at the commandment of the Lord they journeyed." They were kept in constant waiting upon God—the most blessed position that any one can occupy; but it must be occupied ere its blessedness can be tasted. It is a reality to be known, not a mere theory to be talked of. May it be ours to prove it all our journey through.

---

## *CHAPTER 10*

"AND the Lord spake unto Moses, saying, 'Make thee two trumpets of silver; of a whole piece shalt thou make them; that thou mayest use them for the calling of the assembly, and for the journeying of the camp. And when they shall blow with them, all the assembly shall assemble themselves to thee at the door of the tabernacle of the congregation. And if they blow but with one trumpet, then the princes, which are heads of the thousands of Israel, shall gather themselves unto thee. When ye blow an alarm, then the camps that lie on the east parts shall go forward. When ye blow an alarm the second time, then the camps that lie on the south side shall take their journey: they shall blow an alarm for their journeys. But when the congregation is to be gathered together, ye shall blow, but ye shall not sound an alarm. And the sons of Aaron, the priests, shall blow with the trumpets; and they shall be to you for an ordinance forever throughout your generations. And if ye go to war in your land against the enemy that oppresseth you, then ye shall blow an alarm with the trumpets; and ye shall be remembered before the Lord your God, and ye shall be saved from your enemies. Also in the day of your gladness, and in your solemn days, and in the beginnings of your months, ye shall blow with the trumpets over your burnt-offerings, and over the sacrifices of your peace-offerings; that they may be to you for a memorial before your God. I am the Lord your God.' " (ver. 1-10).

We have quoted the entire of this interesting passage for the reader in order that he may have before him, in the veritable language of inspiration, the lovely institution of "the silver trumpets." It comes in, with striking fitness, immediately after the instruction respecting the movement of the cloud, and is bound up, in a very marked way, with the entire history of Israel, not only in the past, but also in the future. The sound of the trumpet was familiar to every circumcised ear. It was the communication of the mind of God, in a form distinct and simple enough to be understood by every member of the congregation, however distant he might be from the source whence the testimony emanated. God took care that each one in that vast assembly, however far away, should hear the silvery tones of the trumpet of testimony.

Each trumpet was to be made of *one* piece, and they fulfilled a double purpose. In other words, the source of the testimony was one, however the object and practical result might vary. Every movement in the camp was to be the result of the sound of the trumpet. Was the congregation to be gathered in festive joy and worship? it was by a certain sound of the trumpet. Were the tribes to be gathered in hostile array? it was by a blast of the trumpet. In a word, the solemn assembly and the warlike host, the instruments of music and the weapons of war—all—all was regulated by the silver trumpet. Any movement, whether festive, religious, or hostile, that was not the result of that familiar sound, could be but the fruit of a restless and unsubdued will, which Jehovah could by no means sanction. The pilgrim host in the wilderness was as dependent upon the sound of the trumpet as upon the movement of the cloud. The testimony of God, communicated in that particular manner, was to govern every movement throughout the many thousands of Israel.

Moreover, it pertained to the sons of Aaron, the priests, to blow with the trumpets, for the mind of God can only be known and communicated in priestly nearness and communion. It was the high and holy privilege of the priestly family to cluster around the sanctuary of God, there to catch the first movement of the cloud, and communicate the same to the most distant parts of the camp. They were responsible to give a certain sound, and every member of the militant host was equally responsible to yield a ready and an implicit obedience. It would have been at once positive rebellion for any to attempt to move without the word of command, or to refuse to move when once that word was given. All had to wait upon the divine testimony, and walk in the light thereof the very moment it was given. To move without testimony would be to *move in the dark;* to refuse to move, when the testimony was given, would be *to remain in the dark.*

This is most simple and deeply practical. We can have no difficulty in seeing its force and application in the case of the congregation in the wilderness. But let us remember that all this was a type; and further, that it is written for our learning. We are solemnly bound, therefore, to look into it; we are imperatively called upon to seek to gather up and treasure up the great practical instruction contained in the singularly beautiful ordinance of the silver trumpet. Nothing could be more seasonable for the present moment. It teaches a lesson to which the Christian reader should give his most profound attention. It sets forth, in the most distinct manner possible, that God's people are to be absolutely dependent upon and wholly subject to divine testimony in all their movements. A child may read this in the type before us. The congregation in the wilderness dared not assemble for any festive or religious object until they heard the sound of the trumpet; nor could the men of war buckle on their armor till summoned forth by the signal of alarm to meet the uncircumcised foe. They worshiped and they fought, they journeyed and they halted, in simple obedience to the trumpet-call. It was not, by any means, a question of their likings or dislikings, their thoughts, their opinions, or their judgment. It was simply and entirely a question of implicit obedience. Their every movement was dependent upon the testimony of God, as given by the priests from the sanctuary. The song of the worshiper and the shout of the warrior were each the simple fruit of the testimony of God.

How beautiful! how striking! how instructive! and, let us add, how deeply practical! Why do we dwell upon it? Because we firmly believe it contains a needed lesson for the day in which our lot is cast. If there is one feature more characteristic than another of the present hour, it is insubjection to divine authority—positive resistance of the truth when it demands unqualified obedience and self-surrender. It is all well enough so long as it is truth setting forth, with divine fullness and clearness, *our* pardon, *our* acceptance, *our* life, *our* righteousness, *our* eternal security in Christ. This will be listened to and delighted in; but the very moment it becomes a question of the claims and authority of that blessed One who gave His life to save us from the flames of hell and introduce us to the everlasting joys of heaven, all manner of difficulties are started; all sorts of reasonings and questions are raised; clouds of prejudice gather around the soul, and darken the understanding. The sharp edge of truth is blunted or turned aside, in a thousand ways. There is no *waiting* for the sound of the trumpet; and when it sounds, with a blast as clear as God Himself can give, there is no response to the summons. We move when we ought to be still, and we halt when we ought to be moving.

What must be the result of all this? Either no progress at all, or progress in a wrong direction, which is worse than none. It is utterly impossible that we can advance in the divine life unless we yield ourselves, without reserve, to the word of the Lord. Saved we may be, through the rich aboundings of divine mercy, and through the atoning virtues of a Saviour's blood; but shall we rest satisfied with being saved by Christ, and not seek, in some feeble measure, to walk with Him and live for Him? Shall we accept of salvation through the work which He has wrought, and not long after deeper intimacy of communion with Himself and more complete subjection to His authority in all things? How would it have been with Israel in the wilderness had they refused attention to the sound of the trumpet? We can see it at a glance. If, for example, they had presumed, at any time, to assemble for a festive or religious object, without the divinely appointed summons, what would have been the result? or, further, had they taken it upon themselves to move forward on their journey, or go forth to war, ere the trumpet had sounded an alarm, how would it have been? or, finally, had they refused to move when called by the sound of the trumpet, either to the solemn assembly, the onward march, or to the battle, how would they have fared?

The answer is as plain as a sunbeam. Let us ponder it: it has a lesson for us. Let us apply our hearts to it. The silver trumpet settled and ordered every movement for Israel of old: the testimony of God ought to settle and order every thing for the Church now. That silver trumpet was blown by the priests of old: that testimony of God is known in priestly communion now. A Christian has no right to move or act apart from divine testimony: he must wait upon the word of his Lord. Till he gets that, he must stand still: when he has gotten it, he must *go forward.* God can and does communicate His mind to His militant people now, just as distinctly as He did to His people of old. True, it is not now by the sound of the trumpet, or the movement of a cloud, but by His Word and Spirit. It is not by aught that strikes the sense that our Father guides us; but by that which acts on the heart, the conscience, and the understanding. It is not by that which is natural, but by that which is spiritual, that He communicates His mind.

But let us be well assured of this, that our God can and does give our hearts full certainty both as to what we should do and what we should not do, as to where we should go and where we should not go. It seems strange to be obliged to insist upon this—passing strange that any Christian should doubt, much less deny it; and yet so it is. We are often in doubt and perplexity; and some there are who are ready to deny that there can be any such thing as certainty as to the details of daily life and action. This surely is wrong. Cannot an earthly father communicate his mind to his child as to the most minute particulars of his conduct? Who will deny this? And cannot our Father communicate His mind to us, as to all our ways, from day to day? Unquestionably He can; and let not the Christian reader be robbed of the holy privilege of knowing his Father's mind in reference to every circumstance of his daily life.

Are we to suppose, for a moment, that the Church of God is worse off in the matter of guidance than the camp in the desert? Impossible. How is it, then, that one often finds Christians at a loss as to their movements? It must be owing to the lack of a circumcised ear to hear the sound of the silver trumpet, and of a subject will to yield a response to the sound. It may, however, be said that we are not to expect to hear a voice from heaven telling us to do this or that, or to go hither or thither; nor yet to find a literal text of Scripture to guide us in the minor matters of our every-day history. How, for example, is one to know whether he ought to visit a certain town, and remain there a certain time? We reply, If the ear is circumcised, you will assuredly hear the silver trumpet. Till that sounds, never stir: when it sounds, never tarry. This will make all so clear, so simple, so safe, so certain. It is the grand cure for doubt, hesitancy, and vacillation. It will save us from the necessity of running for advice to this one and that one, as to how we should act, or where we should go. And furthermore, it will teach us that it is none of our business to attempt to control the actions or movements of others. Let each one have his ear open, and his heart subject, and then, assuredly, he will possess all the certainty that God can give him, as to his every act and movement, from day to day. Our ever-gracious God can give clearness and decision as to every thing. If He does not give it, no one can: if He does, no one need.

Thus much as to the beautiful institution of the silver trumpet, which we shall not pursue further now, though, as we have noticed above, it is not confined, in its application, to Israel in the wilderness, but is bound up with their entire history right onward to the end. Thus we have the feast of trumpets, the trumpet of the jubilee, the blowing of trumpets over their sacrifices, upon which we do not now dwell, as our immediate object is to help the reader to seize the grand idea presented in the opening paragraph of our chapter. May the Holy Spirit impress upon our hearts the needed lesson of "the silver trumpets."

We have now reached, in our meditations on this precious book, the moment in the which the camp is called to move forward. All is duly ordered, according to that grand regulator, "the commandment of the Lord." Each man according to his pedigree, and each tribe according to the standard thereof, is in the divinely appointed place. The Levites are at their post, each with his own clearly defined work to do. Full provision is made for the cleansing of the camp from every species of defilement; and not only so, but the lofty standard of personal holiness is unfurled, and the fruits of active benevolence are presented. Then we have the golden candlestick and its seven lamps, giving forth their pure and precious light. We have the pillar of fire and of cloud; and finally, the double testimony of the silver trumpet. In short, nothing is lacking to the pilgrim host. A vigilant eye, a powerful hand, and a loving heart have provided for every possible contingency, so that the whole congregation in the wilderness, and each member in particular, might be "thoroughly furnished."

This is only what we might expect. If God undertakes to provide for any one, or for any people, the provision must, of necessity, be perfect. It is wholly impossible that God could omit any one thing needful. He knows all things and can do all things. Nothing can escape His vigilant eye; nothing is beyond His omnipotent hand. Hence, therefore, all those who can truly say, "The Lord is my Shepherd," may add, without hesitancy or reserve, "I shall not want." The soul that is, in truth and reality, leaning on the arm of the living God can never—shall never—want any *good* thing. The poor foolish heart may imagine a thousand wants; but God knows what we really want, and He will provide for *all.*

Thus, then, the camp is ready to move; but, strange to say, there is a departure from the order laid down in the opening of the book. The ark of the covenant, instead of reposing in the bosom of the camp, goes in the very front. In other words, Jehovah, instead of remaining in the center of the congregation to be waited upon there, actually condescends, in His marvelous, illimitable grace, to do the work of an *avant-courier* for His people.

But let us see what it is that leads to this touching display of grace. "And Moses said unto Hobab, the son of Raguel the Midianite, Moses' father-in-law, 'We are journeying unto the place of which the Lord said, I will give it you; come thou with us and we will do thee good; for the Lord hath spoken good concerning Israel.' And he said unto him, 'I will not go; but I will depart to mine own land, and to my kindred.' And he said, 'Leave us not, I pray thee, forasmuch as thou knowest how we are to encamp in the wilderness, and thou mayest be to us instead of eyes.' "

Now, if we did not know something of our own hearts, and the tendency thereof to lean on the creature rather than upon the living God, we might well marvel at the above. We might feel disposed to inquire, What could Moses possibly want with Hobab's eyes? Was not Jehovah sufficient? Did not He know the wilderness? Would He suffer them to go astray? What of the cloud and the silver trumpet? were they not better than Hobab's eyes? Why, then, did Moses seek for human aid? Alas! we can but too well understand the reason. We all know, to our sorrow and loss, the tendency of the heart to lean upon something that our eyes can see. We do not like to occupy the ground of absolute dependence upon God for every step of the journey. We find it hard to lean upon an unseen arm. A Hobab that we can see inspires us with more confidence than the living God whom we cannot see. We move on with comfort and satisfaction when we possess the countenance and help of some poor fellow-mortal; but we hesitate, falter, and quail when called to move on in naked faith in God.

These statements may seem strong; but the question is, are they true? Is there a Christian who reads these lines that will not freely own that it is even so? We are all prone to lean upon an arm of flesh, and that, too, in the face of a thousand and one examples of the folly of so doing. We have proved, times without number, the vanity of all creature-confidences, and yet we *will* confide in the creature. On the other hand, we have, again and again, proved the reality of leaning upon the Word and upon the arm of the living God. We have found that He has never failed us, never disappointed us—nay, that He has always done exceeding abundantly above all that we ask or think; and yet we are ever ready to distrust Him, ever ready to lean upon any broken reed, and betake ourselves to any broken cistern.

Thus it is with us; but, blessed be God, His grace abounds toward us, as it did toward Israel on the occasion to which we are now referring. If Moses will look to Hobab for guidance, Jehovah will teach His servant that He Himself is all-sufficient as a guide. "And they departed from the mount of the Lord three days' journey; and the ark of the covenant of the Lord went before them in the three days' journey, *to search out a resting-place for them.*"

What rich, what precious grace! In place of their finding a resting-place for Him, He would find a resting-place for them. What a thought! The mighty God, the Creator of the ends of the earth, going through the wilderness to look out for a suitable camping-ground for a people who were ready, at every turn in their path, to murmur and rebel against Him!

Such is our God—ever "patient, gracious, powerful, holy"—ever rising, in the magnificence of His grace, above all our unbelief and failure, and proving Himself superior, in His love, to all the barriers which our unfaithfulness would erect. He most assuredly proved to Moses and to Israel that He was far better as a guide than ten thousand Hobabs. We are not told in this place whether Hobab went or not. He certainly refused the first appeal, and perhaps the second likewise. But we are told that the Lord went with them. "The cloud of the Lord was upon them by day, when they went out of the camp." Blessed shelter in the wilderness! Blessed, unfailing resource, in every thing! He went before His people to search them out a resting-place, and when He had found a spot suited to their need, He halted with them, and spread a sheltering wing over them, to protect them from every foe. "He found him in a desert land, and in the waste howling wilderness; He led him about, He instructed him, He kept him as the apple of His eye. As an eagle stirreth up her nest, fluttereth over her young, spreadeth abroad her wings, taketh them, beareth them on her wings; so the Lord alone did lead him, and there was no strange god with him" (Deut. 32:10-12). "He spread a cloud for a covering, and fire to give light in the night" (Ps. 105:39).

Thus, then, all was provided for, according to the wisdom, power, and goodness of God. Nothing was or could be lacking, inasmuch as God Himself was there. "And it came to pass, when the ark set forward, that Moses said, 'Rise up, Lord, and let Thine enemies be scattered, and let them that hate Thee flee before Thee.' And when it rested, he said, 'Return, O Lord, unto the many thousands of Israel.' "

---

## *CHAPTER 11*

HITHERTO we have been occupied, in our study of this book, with God's mode of ordering and providing for His people in the wilderness. We have traveled over the first ten chapters, and seen in them the illustration of the wisdom, goodness, and forethought of Jehovah, the God of Israel. But now we reach a point at which dark clouds gather around us. Up to this, God and His actings have been before us; but now we are called to contemplate man and his miserable ways. This is ever sad and humiliating. Man is the same every where. In Eden, in the restored earth, in the wilderness, in the land of Canaan, in the Church, in the millennium, man is proved to be a total failure. The very moment he moves, he breaks down. Thus, in the first two chapters of Genesis God is seen acting as Creator; every thing is done and ordered in divine perfection, and man is placed in the scene to enjoy the fruit of divine wisdom, goodness, and power. But in chapter 3, all is changed. The moment man acts, it is to disobey and bring in ruin and desolation. So after the deluge, when the earth had passed through that deep and dreadful baptism, and when man again takes his place therein, he exposes himself, and proves that, so far from being able to subdue and govern the earth, he cannot even govern himself (Gen. 9). Hardly had Israel been brought out of Egypt, when they made the golden calf: no sooner had the priesthood been set up, than the sons of Aaron offered strange fire: directly Saul was made king, he proved willful and disobedient.

So also when we turn to the pages of the New Testament, we find the same thing. No sooner is the Church set up and adorned with Pentecostal gifts, than we hear the sad accents of murmuring and discontent. In short, man's history, from first to last, here, there, and every where, is marked with failure. There is not so much as a single exception from Eden down to the close of the millennial day.

It is well to consider this solemn and weighty fact, and to give it a deep place in the heart. It is eminently calculated to correct all false notions as to man's real character and condition. It is well to bear in mind that the awful sentence which struck terror into the heart of the voluptuous king of Babylon has, in point of fact, been passed upon the entire human race, and upon each individual son and daughter of fallen Adam, namely, *"Thou art weighed in the balance and found wanting."* Has the reader fully accepted this sentence against himself? This is a serious inquiry. We feel imperatively called to press it home. Art thou one of Wisdom's children? Dost thou justify God and condemn thyself? Hast thou taken thy place as a self-destroyed, guilty, hell-deserving sinner? If so, Christ is for thee. He died to put away sin and to bear your many sins. Only trust Him, and all He is and has is thine. He is thy wisdom, thy righteousness, thy sanctification, and thy redemption. All who simply and heartily believe in Jesus have passed clean off the old ground of guilt and condemnation, and are seen by God on the new ground of eternal life and divine righteousness. They are accepted in the risen and victorious Christ. "As He is, so are we in this world" (1 John 4:17).

We would earnestly entreat the reader not to rest until this most momentous question is clearly and thoroughly settled in the light of God's own Word and presence. We pray that God the Holy Ghost may deeply exercise the heart and conscience of the unconverted and undecided reader, and lead such to the Saviour's feet.

We shall now proceed with our chapter.

"And when the people complained, it displeased the Lord; and the Lord heard it; and His anger was kindled; and the fire of the Lord burnt among them, and consumed them that were in the uttermost parts of the camp. And the people cried unto Moses; and when Moses prayed unto the Lord, the fire was quenched. And he called the name of the place Taberah: because the fire of the Lord burnt among them. And the mixed multitude that was among them fell a lusting: and the children of Israel also wept again, and said, 'Who shall give us flesh to eat? We remember the fish which we did eat in Egypt freely; the cucumbers and the melons and the leeks and the onions and the garlic. But now our soul is dried away; there is nothing at all, beside this manna, before our eyes.' "

Here the poor human heart lets itself thoroughly out. Its tastes and its tendencies are made manifest. The people sigh after the land of Egypt, and cast back wistful looks after its fruits and its fleshpots. They do not say aught about the lash of the taskmaster and the toil of the brick-kilns. There is total silence as to these things. Nothing is remembered now save those resources by which Egypt had ministered to the lusts of nature.

How often is this the case with us! When once the heart loses its freshness in the divine life—when heavenly things begin to lose their savor—when first love declines—when Christ ceases to be a satisfying and altogether precious portion for the soul—when the Word of God and prayer lose their charm, and become heavy, dull, and mechanical, then the eye wanders back toward the world, the heart follows the eye, and the feet follow the heart. We forget, at such moments, what the world was to us when we were in it and of it. We forget what toil and slavery, what misery and degradation, we found in the service of sin and Satan, and think only of the gratification and ease, the freedom from those painful exercises, conflicts, and anxieties which attend upon the wilderness path of God's people.

All this is most sad, and should lead the soul into the most profound self-judgment. It is terrible when those who have set out to follow the Lord begin to grow weary of the way and of God's provision. How dreadful must those words have sounded in the ear of Jehovah, "But now our soul is dried away: there is nothing at all, beside this manna, before our eyes." Ah! Israel, what more didst thou need? Was not that heavenly food enough for thee? Couldst thou not live upon that which the hand of thy God had provided for thee?

Do we count ourselves free to ask such questions? Do we always find *our* heavenly Manna sufficient for us? What means the frequent inquiry raised by professing Christians as to the right or wrong of such and such worldly pursuits and pleasures? Have we not even heard from the lips of persons making the very highest profession such words as these: "How are we to fill up the day? We cannot be always thinking about Christ and heavenly things: we must have some little recreation." Is not this somewhat akin to Israel's language in Numbers 11?

Yes, truly; and as is the language, so is the acting. We prove, alas! that Christ is not enough for the heart, by the palpable fact of our betaking ourselves to other things. How often, for example, does the Bible lie neglected for hours, while the light and worthless literature of the world is greedily devoured. What mean the well-thumbed newspaper and the almost dust-covered Bible? Do not these things tell a tale? Is not this despising the manna, and sighing after—nay, devouring—the leeks and onions?

We specially call the attention of young Christians to that which is now before us. We are deeply impressed with a sense of their danger of falling into the very sin of Israel as recorded in our chapter. No doubt we are all in danger, but the young amongst us are peculiarly so. Those of us who are advanced in life are not so likely to be drawn away by the frivolous pursuits of the world—by its concerts, its flower-shows, its pleasure-parties, its vain songs and light literature. But the young *will* have a dash of the world. They long to taste it for themselves. They do not find Christ an all-sufficient portion for the heart. They want recreation.

Alas! what a thought! How sad to hear a Christian say, "I want some recreation. How can I fill up the day? I cannot be always thinking of Jesus." We should like to ask all who speak thus, How will you fill up eternity? Shall not Christ be sufficient to fill up its countless ages? Shall you want recreation there? Will you sigh for light literature, vain songs, and frivolous pursuits there?

It will perhaps be said, We shall be different then. In what respect? We have the divine nature; we have the Holy Ghost; we have Christ for our portion; we belong to heaven; we are brought to God. But we have an evil nature in us. Well, are we to cater for that? is it for that we crave recreation? Must we try to help our wretched flesh—our corrupt nature—to fill up the day? Nay, we are called to deny it, to mortify it, to reckon it dead. This is Christian recreation. This is the mode in which the saint is called to fill up his day. How is it possible for us to grow in the divine life if we are only making provision for the flesh? Egypt's food cannot nourish the new nature; and the great question for us is this: Which do we really mean to nourish and cherish? the new, or the old? It must be obvious that the divine nature cannot possibly feed upon newspapers, vain songs, and light literature; and hence, if we give ourselves, in any measure, to these latter, our souls must wither and droop.

May we have grace to think of these things—to think seriously. May we so walk in the Spirit that Christ may ever be a satisfying portion for our hearts. Had Israel in the wilderness walked with God, they never could have said, "Our soul is dried away: there is nothing at all, beside this manna, before our eyes." That manna would have been quite enough for them. And so with us. If we really walk with God in this wilderness world, our souls shall be satisfied with the portion which He gives, and that portion is, a heavenly Christ. Can He ever fail to satisfy? Does He not satisfy the heart of God? Does He not fill all heaven with His glory? Is He not the theme of angels' song, and the object of their adoring homage and wondering worship? Is He not the one grand subject of everlasting counsels and purposes? Doth not the history of His ways overlap eternity?

What answer have we to give to all these queries? What but a hearty, unreserved, unhesitating *Yes?* Well, then, is not this blessed One, in the deep mystery of His Person, in the moral glory of His ways, in the brightness and blessedness of His character—is not He enough for our hearts? Do we want aught beside? Must we get the newspaper, or some light magazine, to fill up the vacuum in our souls? Must we turn from Christ to a flower-show or a concert?

Alas, that we should have to write thus. It is most sad; but it is most needful; and we here put this question most pointedly to the reader: Dost thou really find Christ insufficient to satisfy thy heart? Hast thou cravings which He does not fully meet? If so, thou art in a very alarming condition of soul, and it behooves thee to look at once, and to look closely, into this solemn matter. Get down on thy face before God, in honest self-judgment. Pour out thy heart to Him. Tell Him all. Own to Him how thou hast fallen and wandered—as surely thou must have done when God's Christ is not enough for thee. Have it all out in secret with thy God, and take no rest until thou art fully and blessedly restored to communion with Himself—to heart-fellowship with Him about the Son of His love.

But we must return to our chapter; and in so doing, we call the reader's attention to an expression full of weighty admonition for us: "And *the mixed multitude* that was among them fell a lusting; and the children of Israel also wept again." There is nothing more damaging to the cause of Christ or to the souls of His people than association with men of *mixed* principles. It is very much more dangerous than having to do with open and avowed enemies. Satan knows this well, and hence his constant effort to lead the Lord's people to link themselves with those who are only half-and-half; or, on the other hand, to introduce spurious materials—false professors—into the midst of those who are seeking, in any measure, to pursue a path of separation from the world. We have repeated allusions to this special character of evil in the New Testament. We have it both prophetically, in the Gospels, and historically, in the Acts and in the Epistles. Thus we have the tares and the leaven in Matthew 13; then, in the Acts, we find persons attaching themselves to the assembly who were like the "mixed multitude" of Numbers 11; and finally, we have apostolic reference to spurious materials introduced by the enemy for the purpose of corrupting the testimony and subverting the souls of God's people. Thus the apostle Paul speaks of "false brethren unawares brought in" (Gal. 2:4). Jude also speaks of "certain men crept in unawares" (ver. 4).

From all this we learn the urgent need of vigilance on the part of God's people; and not only of vigilance, but also of absolute dependence upon the Lord, who alone can preserve them from the entrance in of false materials, and keep them free from all contact with men of mixed principles and doubtful character. "The mixed multitude" is sure to "fall a lusting," and the people of God are in imminent danger of being drawn away from their proper simplicity, and of growing weary of the heavenly Manna—their proper food. What is needed is, plain decision for Christ; thorough devotedness to Him and to His cause. Where a company of believers are enabled to go on in wholeheartedness for Christ, and in marked separation from this present world, there is not so much danger of persons of equivocal character seeking a place among them; though doubtless Satan will always seek to mar the testimony by the introduction of hypocrites. Such persons do obtain an entrance, and then by their evil ways bring reproach on the Lord's name. Satan knew full well what he was doing when he led the mixed multitude to attach themselves to the congregation of Israel. It was not all at once that the effect of this admixture was made manifest. The people had come forth with a high hand; they had passed through the Red Sea, and raised the song of victory on its banks. All looked bright and promising; but "the mixed multitude" were there notwithstanding, and the effect of their presence was very speedily made apparent.

Thus it is ever, in the history of God's people. We may notice, in those great spiritual movements which have taken place from age to age, certain elements of decay which at the first were hidden from view by the flowing tide of grace and *energy;* but when that tide began to ebb, then those elements made their appearance. This is very serious, and calls for much holy watchfulness. It applies to individuals just as forcibly as to the people of God collectively. In our early moments—our young days, when zeal and freshness characterized us, the spring-tide of grace rose so blessedly that many things were allowed to escape unjudged which were, in reality, seeds flung into the ground by the enemy's hand, and which, in due season, are sure to germinate and fructify. Hence it follows that both assemblies of Christians and individual Christians should ever be on the watch-tower—ever keeping jealous guard lest the enemy gain an advantage in this matter. Where the heart is true to Christ, all is sure to come right in the end. Our God is so gracious, He takes care of us and preserves us from a thousand snares. May we learn to trust Him and to praise Him.

But we have further lessons to draw from the weighty section which lies open before us. Not only have we to contemplate failure on the part of the congregation of Israel, but even Moses himself is seen faltering and almost sinking beneath the weight of his responsibility. "And Moses said unto the Lord, 'Wherefore hast Thou afflicted Thy servant? and wherefore have I not found favor in Thy sight, that Thou layest the burden of all this people upon me? Have I conceived all this people? have I begotten them, that Thou shouldest say unto me, Carry them in thy bosom, as a nursing father beareth the sucking child, unto the land which Thou swarest unto their fathers? Whence should I have flesh to give unto all this people? for they weep unto me, saying, Give us flesh, that we may eat. I am not able to bear all this people alone, because it is too heavy for me. And if Thou deal thus with me, kill me, I pray Thee out of hand, if I have found favor in Thy sight; and let me not see my wretchedness" (ver. 11-15).

This is truly wonderful language. It is not that we should think for a moment of dwelling upon the failures and infirmities of so dear and so devoted a servant as Moses. Far be the thought. It would ill become us to comment upon the actings or the sayings of one of whom the Holy Ghost has declared that "he was faithful in all his house" (Heb. 3:2). Moses, like all the Old Testament saints, has taken his place amongst the "spirits of just men made perfect," and every inspired allusion to him throughout the pages of the New Testament tends only to put honor upon him, and to set him forth as a most precious vessel.

But still we are bound to ponder the inspired history now before us—history penned by Moses himself. True it is—blessedly true—that the defects and failures of God's people in Old Testament times are not commented upon in the New Testament, yet are they recorded with faithful accuracy in the Old. And wherefore? is it not for our learning? Unquestionably. "Whatsoever things were written aforetime were written for our learning, that we through patience and comfort of the Scriptures might have hope" (Rom. 15:4).

What, then, are we to learn from the remarkable outburst of feeling recorded in Numbers 11:11-15? We learn this at least, that it is the wilderness that really brings out what is in the very best of us. It is there we prove what is in our hearts. And inasmuch as the book of Numbers is emphatically the book of the wilderness, it is just there we might expect to find all sorts of failure and infirmity fully unfolded. The Spirit of God faithfully chronicles every thing. He gives us men as they are; and even though it be a Moses that "speaks unadvisedly with his lips," that very unadvised speaking is recorded for our admonition and instruction. Moses "was a man subject to like passions as we are"; and it is very evident that in the portion of his history now before us, his heart sinks under the tremendous weight of his responsibilities.

It will perhaps be said, "No wonder his heart should sink." No wonder, surely, for his burden was far too heavy for human shoulders. But the question is, Was it too heavy for divine shoulders? Was it really the case that Moses was called to bear the burden alone? Was not the living God with him? and was not He sufficient? What did it matter whether God were pleased to act by one man or by ten thousand? All the power, all the wisdom, all the grace, was in Him. He is the fountain of all blessedness, and, in the judgment of faith, it makes not one whit of difference as to the channel, or whether there is one channel or a thousand and one.

This is a fine moral principle for all the servants of Christ. It is most needful for all such to remember that whenever the Lord places a man in a position of responsibility, He will both fit him for it and maintain him in it. It is, of course, another thing altogether if a man *will* rush unsent into any field of work, or any post of difficulty or danger. In such a case, we may assuredly look for a thorough breakdown, sooner or later. But when God calls a man to a certain position, He will endow him with the needed grace to occupy it. He never sends any one a warfare at his own charges, and therefore all we have to do is to draw upon Him for all we need. This holds good in every case. We can never fail if we only cling to the living God: we can never run dry if we are drawing from the fountain. Our tiny springs will soon dry up; but our Lord Jesus Christ declares that "he that believeth in Me, as the Scripture hath said, 'out of his belly shall flow rivers of living water.' "

This is a grand lesson for the wilderness. We cannot get on without it. Had Moses fully understood it, he never would have given utterance to such words as these: "Whence should *I* have flesh to give unto all this people?" He would have fixed his eye *only* upon God. He would have known that he was but an instrument in the hands of God, whose resources were illimitable. Assuredly, Moses could not supply that vast assembly with food even for a single day; but Jehovah could supply the need of every living thing, and supply it forever.

Do we really believe this? Does it not sometimes appear as though we doubted it? Do we not sometimes feel as though *we* were to supply instead of God? and then is it any marvel if we quail and falter and sink? Well indeed might Moses say, "I am not able to bear all this people alone, because it is too heavy for me." There was only one heart that could bear with such a company, namely, the heart of that blessed One who, when they were toiling amid the brick-kilns of Egypt, had come down to deliver them, and who, having redeemed them out of the hand of the enemy, had taken up His abode in their midst. He was able to bear them, and He alone. His loving heart and mighty hand were alone adequate to the task; and if Moses had been in the full power of this great truth, he would not and could not have said, "If Thou deal thus with me, kill me, I pray Thee, out of hand, if I have found favor in Thy sight; and let me not see my wretchedness."

This surely was a dark moment in the history of this illustrious servant of God. It reminds us somewhat of the prophet Elijah, when he flung himself at the base of the juniper tree and entreated the Lord to take away his life. How wonderful to see those two men together on the mount of transfiguration! It proves, in a very marked way, that God's thoughts are not as ours, nor His ways as ours. He had something better in store for Moses and Elias than aught that they contemplated. Blessed be His name, He rebukes our fears by the riches of His grace, and when our poor hearts would anticipate death and wretchedness, He gives life, victory, and glory.

However, we cannot but see that, in shrinking from a position of weighty responsibility, Moses was really giving up a place of high dignity and holy privilege. This seems most evident from the following passage: "And the Lord said unto Moses, 'Gather unto Me seventy men of the elders of Israel, whom thou knowest to be the elders of the people, and officers over them; and bring them unto the tabernacle of the congregation, *that they may stand there with thee.* And I will come down and talk with thee there; and *I will take of the spirit which is upon thee and will put it upon them;* and they shall bear the burden of the people with thee, that thou bear it not thyself alone' " (ver. 16-17).

Was there any additional power gained by the introduction of seventy men? Not spiritual power, certainly, inasmuch as it was only the spirit that was upon Moses after all. True, there were seventy men instead of one, but the multiplication of men was no increase of spiritual power. It saved Moses trouble, but it lost him dignity. He was henceforth to be a joint-instrument instead of the sole one. It may be said that Moses (blessed servant as he was!) did not want dignity for himself, but rather sought a shady, retired, humble path. No doubt; but this does not touch the question before us. Moses, as we shall see presently, was the meekest man upon the face of the earth; nor do we mean even to hint that any mere man would have done better under the circumstances. But then we must seek to bear away with us the great practical lesson which our chapter so impressively teaches. The very best of men fail; and it seems exceedingly plain that Moses, in the eleventh chapter of Numbers, was not in the calm elevation of faith. He appears, for the moment, to have lost that even balance of soul which is the sure result of finding one's centre in the living God. We gather this, not merely from the fact of his tottering beneath the weight of his responsibility; but let us ponder the following paragraph:

"And say thou unto the people, Sanctify yourselves against to-morrow, and ye shall eat flesh; for ye have wept in the ears of the Lord, saying, 'Who shall give us flesh to eat? for it was well with us in Egypt:' therefore the Lord will give you flesh, and ye shall eat. Ye shall not eat one day, nor two days, nor five days, neither ten days, nor twenty days; but even a whole month, until it come out at your nostrils, and it be loathsome unto you: because that ye have despised the Lord which is among you, and have wept before Him, saying, 'Why came we forth out of Egypt?' And Moses said, 'The people, among whom I am, are six hundred thousand footmen; and Thou hast said, I will give them flesh, that they may eat a whole month. Shall the flocks and the herds be slain for them to suffice them? or shall all the fish of the sea be gathered together for them to suffice them?' And the Lord said unto Moses, 'Is the Lord's hand waxed short? thou shalt see now whether My word will come to pass unto thee or not' " (ver. 18-23).

In all this we see the working of that spirit of unbelief which ever tends to limit the Holy One of Israel. Could not the almighty God, the possessor of heaven and earth, the Creator of the ends of the earth—could not He provide flesh for six hundred thousand footmen? Alas! it is just here we all so sadly fail. We do not enter, as we ought, into the reality of having to do with the living God. Faith brings God into the scene, and therefore it knows absolutely nothing of difficulties—yea, it laughs at impossibilities. In the judgment of faith, God is the grand answer to every question—the grand solution of every difficulty. It refers all to Him; and hence it matters not in the least to faith whether it be six hundred thousand or six hundred millions; it knows that God is all-sufficient. It finds all its resources in Him. Unbelief says, *"How* can such and such things be?" It is full of "Hows"; but faith has one great answer to ten thousand "hows," and that answer is—*God.*

"And Moses went out, and told the people the words of the Lord, and gathered the seventy men of the elders of the people, and set them round about the tabernacle. And the Lord came down in a cloud, and spake unto him, *and took of the spirit that was upon him, and gave it unto the seventy elders;* and it came to pass, that when the spirit rested upon them, they prophesied, and did not cease."

The true secret of all ministry is spiritual power. It is not man's genius, or man's intellect, or man's energy; but simply the power of the Spirit of God. This was true in the days of Moses, and it is true now. "Not by might, nor by power, but by My Spirit, saith the Lord of hosts" (Zech. 4:6). It is well for all ministers to bear this ever in mind. It will sustain the heart and give constant freshness to their ministry. A ministry which flows from abiding dependence upon the Holy Ghost can never become barren. If a man is drawing upon his own resources, he will soon run dry. It matters not what his powers may be, or how extensive his reading, or how vast his stores of information; if the Holy Ghost be not the spring and power of his ministry, it must, sooner or later, lose its freshness and its effectiveness.

How important, therefore, that all who minister, whether in the gospel or in the Church of God, should lean continually and exclusively on the power of the Holy Ghost! He knows what souls need, and He can supply it. But He must be trusted and used. It will not do to lean partly on self and partly on the Spirit of God. If there be aught of self-confidence, it will soon be made apparent. We must really get at the bottom of all that belongs to self if we are to be the vessels of the Holy Ghost.

It is not—need we say it?—that there should not be holy diligence and earnestness in the study of God's Word, and in the study, too, of the exercises, the trials, the conflicts, and the varied difficulties of souls. Quite the reverse. We feel persuaded that the more absolutely we lean, in self-emptiness, upon the mighty power of the Holy Ghost, the more diligently and earnestly we shall study both *the Book* and *the soul.* It would be a fatal mistake for a man to use professed dependence upon the Spirit as a plea for neglecting prayerful study and meditation. "Meditate upon these things: give thyself *wholly* to them; that thy profiting may appear to all" (1 Tim. 4:15).

But after all, let it ever be remembered that the Holy Ghost is the ever-living, never-failing spring of ministry. It is He alone that can bring forth, in divine freshness and fullness, the treasures of God's Word, and apply them, in heavenly power, to the soul's present need. It is not a question of bringing forth new truth, but simply of unfolding the Word itself, and bringing it to bear upon the moral and spiritual condition of the people of God. This is true ministry. A man may speak a hundred times on the same portion of Scripture, to the same people, and on each occasion he may minister Christ in spiritual freshness to their souls. And on the other hand, a man may rack his brain to find out new subjects, and new modes of handling old themes, and all the while there may not be one atom of Christ or of spiritual power in his ministry.

All this holds good in reference to the evangelist, as well as to the teacher or pastor. A man may be called to preach the gospel in the same place for years, and he may, at times, feel burdened by the thought of having to address the same audience, on the same theme, week after week, month after month, year after year. He may feel at a loss for something new—something fresh—some variety: he may wish to get away into some new sphere, where the subjects which are familiar to him will be new to the people. It will greatly help such to remember that the one grand theme of the evangelist is Christ; the power to handle that theme is the Holy Ghost; and the one to whom that theme is to be unfolded is the poor lost sinner. Now, Christ is ever new; the power of the Spirit is ever fresh; the soul's condition and destiny ever intensely interesting. Furthermore, it is well for the evangelist to bear in mind, on every fresh occasion of rising to preach, that those to whom he preaches are really ignorant of the gospel, and hence he should preach as though it were the very first time his audience had ever heard the message, and the first time he had ever delivered it. For, be it remembered, the preaching of the gospel, in the divine acceptation of the phrase, is not a barren statement of mere evangelical doctrine—a certain form of words enunciated over and over again in wearisome routine. Far from it. To preach the gospel is really to unfold the heart of God, the Person and work of Christ; and all this by the present energy of the Holy Ghost, from that exhaustless treasury of holy Scripture.

May all preachers keep these things before the mind, and then it will not matter whether it be *one* preacher or *seventy,* one man in the same place for fifty years, or the same man in fifty different places in one year. The question is not at all as to new men or new places, but simply and entirely as to the power of the Holy Ghost unfolding Christ to the soul. Thus in the case of Moses, as recorded in our chapter, there was no increase of power: it was the spirit that was upon him given to the seventy elders. God can act by one man just as well as by seventy; and if He does not act, seventy are no more than one. It is of the very utmost importance to keep God ever before the soul. This is the true secret of power and freshness, whether for the evangelist, the teacher, or any one else. When a man can say, "All my springs are in God," he need not be troubled as to a sphere of work, or competency to fill it; but when this is not so, we can well understand why a man would sigh for a division of labor and responsibility. We may remember, at the opening of the book of Exodus, how unwilling Moses was to go into Egypt, in simple dependence upon God, and how readily he went in company with Aaron. Thus it is ever. We like something tangible—something that the eye can see and the hand can handle. We find it hard to endure as seeing Him who is invisible; and yet the very props we lean upon often prove to be broken reeds that pierce the hand. Aaron proved to be a fruitful source of sorrow to Moses; and those whom we, in our folly, imagine to be indispensable coadjutors, frequently turn out the very reverse. Oh that we may all learn to lean, with an undivided heart and unshaken confidence, upon the living God!

But we must draw this section to a close, and ere doing so, we shall just glance for a moment at the truly excellent spirit in which Moses meets the new circumstances in which he had placed himself. It is one thing to shrink from the weight of responsibility and care, and it is quite another thing to carry one's self with grace and genuine humility toward those who are called to share that weight with us. The two things are totally different, and we may often see the difference strikingly illustrated. In the scene now before us, Moses manifests that exquisite meekness which so specially characterized him. "But there remained two of the [seventy] men in the camp, the name of the one was Eldad, and the name of the other Medad: and the spirit rested upon them; and they were of them that were written, but went not out unto the tabernacle: and they prophesied in the camp. And there ran a young man, and told Moses, and said, 'Eldad and Medad do prophesy in the camp.' And Joshua the son of Nun, the servant of Moses, one of his young men, answered and said, 'My lord Moses, forbid them.' And Moses said unto him, 'Enviest thou for my sake? Would God that all the Lord's people were prophets, and that the Lord would put His Spirit upon them!' "

This is perfectly beautiful. Moses was far removed from that wretched spirit of envy which would let no one speak but himself. He was prepared, by grace, to rejoice in any and every manifestation of true spiritual power, no matter where or through whom. He knew full well that there could be no right prophesying save by the power of the Spirit of God; and wherever that power was exhibited, who was he that he should seek to quench or hinder?

Would there were more of this excellent spirit! May we each cultivate it. May we have grace to rejoice unfeignedly in the testimony and service of all the Lord's people, even though we may not see eye to eye with them, and though our mode and our measure may vary. Nothing can be more contemptible than that petty spirit of envy and jealousy which will not permit a man to take an interest in any work but his own. We may rest assured that where the spirit of Christ is in action in the heart, there will be the ability to go out and embrace the wide field of our blessed Master's work and all His beloved workmen: there will be the hearty rejoicing in having the work done, no matter who is the doer of it. A man whose heart is full of Christ will be able to say—and to say it without affectation, provided the work is done—provided Christ is glorified—provided souls are saved—provided the Lord's flock is cared for and fed, it matters nothing to me who does the work.

This is the right spirit to cultivate, and it stands out in bright contrast with the narrowness and self-occupation which can only rejoice in work in which *"I, myself,"* have a prominent place. May the Lord deliver us from all this, and enable us to cherish that temper of soul expressed by Moses when he said, "Enviest thou for my sake? Would God that all the Lord's people were prophets, and that the Lord would put His Spirit upon them!"

The closing paragraph of our chapter shows us the people in the miserable and fatal enjoyment of that for which their hearts had lusted. "He gave them their request, but sent leanness into their soul." They got what they longed for, and found it death. They *would* have flesh, and with the flesh came the judgment of God. This is most solemn. May we heed the warning. The poor heart is full of vain desires and hateful lusts. The heavenly Manna fails to satisfy. There must be something else. God allows us to have it. But what then? Leanness—barrenness—judgment! O Lord, keep our hearts fixed on Thyself alone and at all times! Be Thou the ever-satisfying portion of our souls, while we tread this desert, and till we see Thy face in glory!

---

## *CHAPTER 12*

THE brief section of our book to which we now approach may be viewed in two distinct aspects: in the first place, it is typical or dispensational; and in the second, moral or practical.

In the union of Moses with "the Ethiopian woman," we have a type of that great and marvelous mystery, the union of the Church with Christ her Head. This subject has come before us in our study of the book of Exodus; but we see it here in a peculiar light—as that which evokes the enmity of Aaron and Miriam. The sovereign actings of grace draw forth the opposition of those who stand upon the ground of natural relationship and fleshly privilege. We know, from the teaching of the New Testament, that the extension of grace to the Gentiles was that which ever elicited the fiercest and most terrible hatred of the Jews. They would not have it; they would not believe in it; nay, they would not even hear of it. There is a very remarkable allusion to this in the eleventh chapter of Romans, where the apostle, referring to the Gentiles, says, "For as ye in times past have not believed God, yet have now obtained mercy through their unbelief: even so have these [Jews] also now not believed in your mercy [or, in mercy to you], that they also may obtain mercy" (ver. 30-31—*see Greek).*

This is precisely what we have typically presented in the history of Moses. He, first of all, presented himself to Israel, his brethren according to the flesh; but they, in unbelief, rejected him. They thrust him from them, and would not have him. This became, in the sovereignty of God, the occasion of mercy to the stranger; for it was during the period of Moses' rejection by Israel that he formed the mystic and typical union with a Gentile bride. Against this union Miriam and Aaron speak, in the chapter before us, and their opposition brings down the judgment of God. Miriam becomes leprous—a poor defiled thing—a proper subject of mercy, which flows out to her through the intercession of the very one against whom she had spoken.

The type is complete and most striking. The Jews have not believed in the glorious truth of mercy to the Gentiles, and therefore wrath has come upon them to the uttermost. But they will be brought in by and by, on the ground of simple mercy, just as the Gentiles have come in. This is very humiliating to those who sought to stand on the ground of promise and national privilege; but thus it is in the dispensational wisdom of God, the very thought of which draws forth from the inspired apostle that magnificent doxology, "O the depth of the riches both of the wisdom and knowledge of God! how unsearchable are His judgments, and His ways past finding out! For who hath known the mind of the Lord? or who hath been His counselor? or who hath first given to Him, and it shall be recompensed unto him again? For of Him, and through Him, and to Him, are all things: to whom be glory forever. Amen."

Thus much as to the typical bearing of our chapter. Let us now look at it in its moral and practical bearing. "And Miriam and Aaron spake against Moses because of the Ethiopian woman whom he had married: for he had married an Ethiopian woman. And they said: 'Hath the Lord indeed spoken only by Moses? hath He not spoken also by us?' And the Lord heard it. (Now the man Moses was very meek, above all the men which were upon the face of the earth.) And the Lord spake suddenly unto Moses, and unto Aaron, and unto Miriam, 'Come out, ye three, unto the tabernacle of the congregation.' And they three came out. And the Lord came down in the pillar of the cloud, and stood in the door of the tabernacle, and called Aaron and Miriam; and they both came forth. And He said, 'Hear now My words: If there be a prophet among you, I the Lord will make Myself known unto him in a vision, and will speak unto him in a dream. My servant Moses is not so, who is faithful in all Mine house. With him will I speak mouth to mouth, even apparently, and not in dark speeches; and the similitude of the Lord shall he behold: wherefore then were ye not afraid to speak against My servant Moses?' And the anger of the Lord was kindled against them; and He departed. And the cloud departed from off the tabernacle; and, behold, Miriam became leprous, white as snow: and Aaron looked upon Miriam, and, behold, she was leprous" (ver. 1-10).

It is a most serious thing for any one to speak against the Lord's servant. We may rest assured that God will deal with it, sooner or later. In the case of Miriam, the divine judgment came down suddenly and solemnly. It was a grievous wrong, yea, it was positive rebellion, to speak against the one whom God had so markedly raised up and clothed with a divine commission; and who, moreover, in the very matter of which they complained, had acted in full consonance with the counsels of God, and furnished a type of that glorious mystery which was hidden in His eternal mind, even the union of Christ and the Church.

But in any case, it is a fatal mistake to speak against the very feeblest and humblest of God's servants. If the servant does wrong—if he is in error, if he has failed in any thing—the Lord Himself will deal with him; but let the fellow-servants beware how they attempt to take the matter into their hands, lest they be found like Miriam, meddling to their own hurt.

It is very awful to hear, at times, the way in which people allow themselves to speak and write about Christ's servants. True, these latter may give occasion; they may have made mistakes, and manifested a wrong spirit and temper; but we must confess we feel it to be a very dreadful sin against Christ to speak evil of His dear servants. Surely, we ought to feel the weight and solemnity of these words: *"Wherefore then were ye not afraid to speak against My servant?"*

May God give us grace to watch against this sore evil. Let us see to it that we be not found doing that which is so offensive to Him, even speaking against those who are dear to His heart. There is not a single one of God's people in whom we cannot find some good thing, provided only we look for it in the right way. Let us be occupied *only* with the good; let us dwell upon that, and seek to strengthen and develop it in every possible way. And on the other hand, if we have not been able to discover the good thing in our brother and fellow-servant, if our eye has only detected the crooked thing, if we have not succeeded in finding the vital spark amid the ashes—the precious gem among the surrounding rubbish, if we have only seen what was of mere nature, why then let us, with a loving and delicate hand, draw the curtain of silence around our brother, or speak of him only at the throne of grace.

So also when we happen to be in company with those who indulge in the wicked practice of speaking against the Lord's people, if we cannot succeed in changing the current of the conversation, let us rise and leave the place, thus bearing testimony against that which is so hateful to Christ. Let us never sit by and listen to a backbiter. We may rest assured he is doing the work of the devil, and inflicting positive injury upon three distinct parties, namely, himself, his hearer, and the subject of his censorious remarks.

There is something perfectly beautiful in the way in which Moses carries himself in the scene before us. Truly, he proved himself a meek man, not only in the matter of Eldad and Medad, but also in the more trying matter of Miriam and Aaron. As to the former, instead of being jealous of those who were called to share his dignity and responsibility, he rejoiced in their work, and prayed that all the Lord's people might taste the same holy privilege; and as to the latter, instead of cherishing any feeling of resentment against his brother and sister, he was ready at once to take the place of intercession. "And Aaron said unto Moses, 'Alas! my lord, I beseech thee, lay not the sin upon us, wherein we have done foolishly, and wherein we have sinned. Let her not be as one dead, of whom the flesh is half consumed when he cometh out of his mother's womb.' And Moses cried unto the Lord, saying, 'Heal her now, O God, I beseech Thee' " (ver. 11-13).

Here Moses breathes the spirit of his Master, and prays for those who had spoken so bitterly against him. This was victory—the victory of a meek man—the victory of grace. A man who knows his right place in the presence of God is able to rise above all evil-speaking. He is not troubled by it, save for those who practice it; he can afford to forgive it; he is not touchy, tenacious, or self-occupied. He knows that no one can put him lower than he deserves to be; and hence if any speak against him, he can meekly bow his head and pass on, leaving himself and his cause in the hands of Him who judgeth righteously, and who will assuredly reward every man according to his works.

This is true dignity. May we understand it somewhat better, and then we shall not be so ready to take fire if any one thinks proper to speak disparagingly of us or of our work—nay, more, we shall be able to lift up our hearts in earnest prayer for them, and thus draw down blessing on them and on our own souls. The few closing lines of our chapter confirm the typical or dispensational view which we have ventured to suggest. "And the Lord said unto Moses, 'If her father had but spit in her face, should she not be ashamed seven days? let her be shut out from the camp seven days, and after that let her be received in again.' And Miriam was shut out from the camp seven days: and the people journeyed not till Miriam was brought in again. And afterward the people removed from Hazeroth and pitched in the wilderness of Paran" (ver. 14-16). We may regard Miriam, thus shut out of the camp, as a figure of the present condition of the nation of Israel, who, in consequence of their implacable opposition to the divine thought of mercy to the Gentile, are set aside; but when the "seven days" have run their course, Israel shall be restored, on the ground of sovereign mercy exercised toward them through the intercession of Christ.

## *CHAPTER 13*

"AND the Lord spake unto Moses, saying, 'Send thou men that they may search the land of Canaan, which I give unto the children of Israel: of every tribe of their fathers shall ye send a man, every one a ruler among them.' And Moses by the commandment of the Lord sent them from the wilderness of Paran" (ver. 1-3).

In order fully to understand the foregoing commandment, we must look at it in connection with a passage in the book of Deuteronomy, where Moses, in going over the facts of Israel's marvelous history in the wilderness, reminds them of the following important and interesting circumstance: "And when we departed from Horeb, we went through all that great and terrible wilderness, which ye saw by the way of the mountain of the Amorites, as the Lord our God commanded us; and we came to Kadesh-barnea. And I said unto you, 'Ye are come unto the mountain of the Amorites, which the Lord our God doth give unto us. Behold, the Lord thy God hath set the land before thee; go up and possess it, as the Lord God of thy fathers hath said unto thee; fear not, neither be discouraged.' *And ye came near unto me every one of you,* and said, *'We will send men before us,* and they shall search us out the land, and bring us word again by what way we must go up, and into what cities we shall come' " (Deut. 1:19-22).

Now here we have the moral root of the fact stated in Numbers 13:2. It is evident that the Lord gave the commandment concerning the spies because of the moral condition of the people. Had they been governed by simple faith, they would have acted on those soul-stirring words of Moses, "Behold, the Lord thy God hath set the land before thee: *go up and possess it,* as the Lord God of thy fathers hath said unto thee; *fear not, neither be discouraged.*" There is not a single syllable about spies in this splendid passage. What does faith want of spies, when it has the word and the presence of the living God? If Jehovah had given them a land, it must be worth having. And had He not? Yes, truly; and not only so, but He had borne testimony to the nature and character of that land in the following glowing words: "For the Lord thy God bringeth thee into a good land, a land of brooks of water, of fountains and depths that spring out of valleys and hills; a land of wheat and barley and vines and fig-trees and pomegranates; a land of oil olive and honey; a land wherein thou shalt eat bread without scarceness, thou shalt not lack any thing in it; a land whose stones are iron, and out of whose hills thou mayest dig brass" (Deut. 8:7-9).

Should not all this have sufficed for Israel? Ought they not to have been satisfied with the testimony of God? Had not He spied out the land for them, and told them all about it? and was not this enough? What need of sending men to spy the land? Did not God know all about it? Was there a spot "from Dan to Beersheba" with which He was not perfectly acquainted? Had He not selected this land and allotted it, in His own eternal counsels, for the seed of Abraham His friend? Did He not know all about the difficulties? and was He not able to surmount them? Why, then, did they "come near *every one of them,* and say, 'We will send men before us, and they shall search us out the land, and bring us word again' "?

These questions come right home to our hearts. They find us out, and make thoroughly manifest where we are. It is not for us to sit down and coolly animadvert upon the ways of Israel in the wilderness, to point out error here and failure there. We must take all these things as types set before us for our admonition. They are beacons, erected by a friendly and faithful hand, to warn us off from the dangerous shoals, quicksands, and rocks which lie along our course, and threaten our safety. This, we may be sure, is the true way to read every page of Israel's history, if we would reap the profit which our God has designed for us in penning such a record.

But it may be the reader is disposed to ask a question here. Did not the Lord expressly command Moses to send spies? and if so, how was it wrong for Israel to send them? True, the Lord did command Moses to send the spies, in Numbers 13, but this was in consequence of the moral condition of the people, as set forth in Deuteronomy 1. We shall not understand the former unless we read it in the light of the latter. We learn most distinctly from Deuteronomy 1:22 that the idea of sending the spies had its origin in the heart of Israel. God saw their moral condition, and He issued a command in full keeping therewith.

If the reader will turn to the opening pages of the first book of Samuel, he will find something similar in the matter of the appointment of a king. The Lord commanded Samuel to hearken to the voice of the people, and make them a king (1 Sam. 8:22). Was it that He approved of the plan? Most surely not; on the contrary, He declares plainly that it was a positive rejection of Himself. Why then command Samuel to appoint a king? The command was given in consequence of Israel's condition. They were growing weary of the position of entire dependence upon an unseen arm, and they longed for an arm of flesh; they desired to be like the nations around them, and to have a king who should go out before them, and fight their battles for them. Well, God gave them their request, and they were very speedily called to prove the worthlessness of their plan. Their king proved a most complete failure, and they had to learn that it was an evil and a bitter thing to forsake the living God and lean on a broken reed of their own selection.

Now, we see the same thing in the matter of the spies. There can be no question, in the mind of any spiritual person who studies the entire subject, as to the fact that the scheme of sending the spies was the fruit of unbelief. A simple heart that trusted God would never have thought of such a thing. What! are we to send poor mortals to spy out a land which God has graciously given to us, and which He has so fully and faithfully described? Far be the thought. Nay, rather let us say, It is enough: the land is the gift of God, and as such it must be good. His word is enough for our hearts: we want no spies; we seek for no mortal testimony to confirm the word of the living God. He has given; He has spoken; this is enough.

But, alas! Israel was not in a condition to adopt such language. They *would* send spies. They wanted them; their hearts craved them; the desire for them lay in the very depths of the soul. Jehovah knew this, and hence He issued a commandment in direct reference to the moral state of the people.

The reader would do well to ponder this subject, in the light of Scripture. He will need to compare Deuteronomy 1 with Numbers 13. It is possible he may find difficulty in judging of the true nature and moral roots of the act of sending the spies, from the fact that the thing was ultimately done in pursuance of "the commandment of the Lord." But we must ever remember that the fact of the Lord's commanding the thing to be done does not, by any means, prove that the people were right in seeking it. The giving of the law at Mount Sinai, the sending of the spies, and the appointment of a king are all proofs of this. No doubt God overruled all these things for His own glory and for man's ultimate blessing, but still the law could not be viewed as the expression of the heart of God. The setting up of a king was a positive rejection of Himself; and we may say that the sending of men to spy out the land of promise proved, very distinctly, that the heart of Israel was not fully satisfied with Jehovah. The whole affair was the fruit of their weakness and unbelief, though acquiesced in by God because of their condition, and overruled by Him, in His infinite goodness and unerring wisdom, for the unfolding of His ways and the display of His glory.

"And Moses sent them [the spies] to spy out the land of Canaan, and said unto them, 'Get you up this way southward, and go up into the mountain: and see the land what it is; and the people that dwell therein, whether they be strong or weak, few or many; and what the land is that they dwell in, whether it be good or bad; and what cities they be that they dwell in, whether in tents or in strongholds; and what the land is, whether it be fat or lean, whether there be wood therein or not. And be ye of good courage, and bring of the fruit of the land.' Now the time was the time of the first-ripe grapes. So they went up, and searched the land from the wilderness of Zin unto Rehob, as men come to Hamath. . . . And they came unto the brook of Eshcol, and cut down from thence a branch with one cluster of grapes, and they bare it between two upon a staff; and they brought of the pomegranates, and of the figs. The place was called the brook Eshcol, because of the cluster of grapes which the children of Israel cut down from thence. And they returned from searching of the land after forty days. And they went and came to Moses, and to Aaron, and to all the congregation of the children of Israel, unto the wilderness of Paran, to Kadesh; and brought back word unto them, and unto all the congregation, and showed them the fruit of the land. And they told him, and said, 'We came unto the land whither thou sentest us, and surely it floweth with milk and honey; and this is the fruit of it' " (chap. 13:17-27).

Here, then, was the fullest confirmation of all that the Lord had said concerning the land—the testimony of twelve men as to the fact that the land flowed with milk and honey—the testimony of their own senses as to the character of the fruit of the land. Furthermore, there was the telling fact that twelve men had actually been in the land, had spent forty days in traveling up and down therein, had drunk of its springs and eaten of its fruits. And what, according to the judgment of faith, would have been the plain inference to be drawn from such a fact? Why, simply, that the same hand which had conducted twelve men into the land could conduct the whole congregation.

But, alas! the people were not governed by faith, but by dark and depressing unbelief; and even the spies themselves—the very men who had been sent for the purpose of assuring and confirming the congregation —even they, with two brilliant exceptions, were under the power of the same God-dishonoring spirit. In short, the whole scheme proved a failure. The issue only made manifest the true condition of the hearts of the people. Unbelief was dominant. The testimony was plain enough—"We came unto the land whither thou sentest us, and surely it floweth with milk and honey; and this is the fruit of it." There was nothing whatever lacking on God's side of the question. The land was all that He had said, the spies themselves being witnesses; but let us hearken to what follows. "Nevertheless the people be strong that dwell in the land, and the cities are walled, and very great: and moreover we saw the children of Anak there" (ver. 28).

There is always sure to be a "nevertheless" where man is concerned, and when unbelief is at work. The unbelieving spies *saw* the difficulties—great cities, high walls, tall giants. All these things they saw, but they did not see Jehovah at all. They looked at the things that were seen, rather than at the things that were unseen. Their eye was not fixed upon Him who is invisible. Doubtless, the cities were great, but God was greater; the walls were high, but God was higher; the giants were strong, but God was stronger.

Thus it is that faith ever reasons. Faith reasons from God to the difficulties,—it begins with Him: unbelief, on the contrary, reasons from the difficulties to God,—it begins with them. This makes all the difference. It is not that we are to be insensible to the difficulties; neither are we to be reckless. Neither insensibility nor yet recklessness is faith. There are some easy-going people who seem to get along through life on the principle of taking things by the smooth handle. This is not faith. Faith looks the difficulties straight in the face; it is fully alive to the roughness of the handle. It is not ignorant, not indifferent, not reckless; but—what? *It brings in the living God.* It looks to Him; it leans on Him; it draws from Him. Here lies the grand secret of its power. It cherishes the calm and deep conviction that there never was a wall too high for the almighty God—never a city too great—never a giant too strong. In short, faith is the only thing that gives God His proper place; and, as a consequence, is the only thing that lifts the soul completely above the influences of surrounding circumstances, be they what they may. Of this precious faith, Caleb was the exponent, when he said, "Let us go up at once, and possess it; for we are well able to overcome it." These are the pure accents of that lively faith that glorifies God and makes nothing of circumstances.

But, alas! the great majority of the spies were no more governed by this lively faith than the men who sent them; and hence, the one believer was talked down by the ten infidels. "The men that went up with him said, 'We be not able to go up against the people.' " The language of infidelity was flatly opposed to the language of faith. The latter, looking at God, said, "We are *well* able"; the former, looking at the difficulties, said, "We are *not* able." Thus it was and thus it is. The eyes of faith are ever covered by the living God, and therefore difficulties are not seen: the eyes of unbelief are covered with the circumstances, and therefore God is not seen. Faith brings in God, and therefore all is bright and easy: unbelief always shuts God out, and therefore all is dark and difficult.

"And they brought up an evil report of the land which they had searched unto the children of Israel, saying, 'The land, through which we have gone to search it, is a land that eateth up the inhabitants thereof; and all the people that we saw in it are men of a great stature. And there we saw the giants, the sons of Anak, which come of the giants; and we were in our own sight as grasshoppers, and so we were in their sight.' " Not a word about God. He is entirely shut out. Had they thought of Him—had they brought the giants into comparison with Him, then it would have made not one whit of difference as to whether they themselves were grasshoppers, or whether they were men; but in point of fact, they, by their shameful unbelief, reduced the God of Israel to the level of a grasshopper.

It is very remarkable that wherever infidelity is at work it will always be found characterized by this one fact, namely, it shuts out God. This will be found true in all ages, in all places, and under all circumstances. There is no exception. Infidelity can take account of human affairs, it can reason upon them, and draw conclusions from them; but all its reasonings and all its conclusions are based upon the exclusion of God. The force of its arguments depends upon shutting Him out, and keeping Him out. Only introduce God, and all the reasonings of infidelity crumble into dust beneath your feet. Thus, in the scene before us, what is faith's reply to all the objections advanced by those ten unbelievers? Its one, simple, all-satisfying reply, to which there can be no rejoinder, is, *God!*

Do you know aught of the force and value of this most blessed answer? Do you know God? Does He fill the entire range of your soul's vision? Is He the answer to your every question? the solution of your every difficulty? Do you know the reality of walking, day by day, with the living God? Do you know the tranquilizing power of leaning upon Him, "through all the changes and chances of this mortal life"? If not, let me entreat of you not to go on for one hour in your present state. The way is open. God has revealed Himself in the face of Jesus Christ, as the relief, the resource, and the refuge of every needy soul. Look to Him now, even now, "while He may be found; call upon Him while He is near." "Whosoever shall call upon the name of the Lord shall be saved," and "he that believeth shall never be confounded."

But if, on the other hand, you do, through grace, know God as your Saviour—your Father, then seek to glorify Him in all your ways, by a childlike, unquestioning confidence in all things. Let Him be a perfect covering for your eyes, under all circumstances; and thus, in spite of all difficulties, your soul shall be kept in perfect peace.

---

## *CHAPTER 14*

"AND all the congregation lifted up their voice and cried; and the people wept that night." Need we wonder? What else could be expected from a people who had nothing before their eyes but mighty giants, lofty walls, and great cities? What but tears and sighs could emanate from a congregation who saw themselves as grasshoppers in the presence of such insuperable difficulties, and having no sense of the divine power that could carry them victoriously through all? The whole assembly was abandoned to the absolute dominion of infidelity. They were surrounded by the dark and chilling clouds of unbelief. God was shut out. There was not so much as a single ray of light to illumine the darkness with which they had surrounded themselves. They were occupied with themselves and their difficulties, instead of with God and His resources. What else, therefore, could they do but lift up the voice of weeping and lamentation?

What a contrast between this and the opening of Exodus 15! In this latter, their eyes were only upon Jehovah, and therefore they could sing the song of victory. "Thou in Thy mercy hast led forth the people which Thou hast redeemed; Thou hast guided them in Thy strength unto Thy holy habitation. *The people shall hear and be afraid: sorrow shall take hold on the inhabitants of Palestina.*" Instead of this, it was Israel that was afraid, and sorrow took hold upon them. "Then the dukes of Edom shall be amazed; the mighty men of Moab, *trembling shall take hold upon them:* all the inhabitants of Canaan shall melt away. *Fear and dread shall fall upon them.*" In short, it is the most complete reversing of the picture. The sorrow, the trembling, and the fear take hold upon Israel instead of their enemies. And why? Because the One who filled their vision in Exodus 15 is completely shut out in Numbers 14. This makes all the difference. In the one case, faith is in the ascendant; in the other, infidelity. "By the greatness of *Thine arm* they shall be as still as a stone; till Thy people pass over, O Lord, till the people pass over which Thou hast purchased. Thou shalt bring them in, and plant them in the mountain of Thine inheritance, in the place, O Lord, which

Thou hast made for Thee to dwell in; in the sanctuary, O Lord, which Thy hands have established. The Lord shall reign forever and ever."

Oh, how do these triumphal accents contrast with the infidel cries and lamentations of Numbers 14! Not a syllable about sons of Anak, lofty walls, and grasshoppers in Exodus 15. No; it is all Jehovah. It is His right hand, His mighty arm, His power, His inheritance, His habitation, His actings on behalf of His ransomed people. And then if the inhabitants of Canaan are referred to, they are only thought of as sorrowing, terror-stricken, trembling, and melting away.

But on the other hand, when we come to Numbers 14, all is most sadly reversed. The sons of Anak rise into prominence; the towering walls, the giant cities with frowning bulwarks, fill the vision of the people, and we hear not a word about the almighty Deliverer. There are the difficulties on the one side and grasshoppers on the other, and one is constrained to cry out, Can it be possible that the triumphal singers by the Red Sea have become the infidel weepers at Kadesh?

Alas! it is so; and here we learn a deep and holy lesson. We must continually recur, as we pass along through these wilderness scenes, to those words which tell us that "all these things happened unto Israel for ensamples; and they are written for our admonition, upon whom the ends of the ages are met" (1 Cor. 10:11—*see Greek*). Are not we, too, like Israel, prone to look at the difficulties which surround us, rather than at that blessed One who has undertaken to carry us right through them all and bring us safely into His own everlasting kingdom? Why is it we are sometimes cast down? Why go we mourning? Wherefore are the accents of discontent and impatience heard in our midst, rather than the songs of praise and thanksgiving? Simply because we allow circumstances to shut out God, instead of having God as a perfect covering for our eyes and a perfect object for our hearts.

And further, let us inquire, wherefore is it that we so sadly fail to make good our position as heavenly men?—to take possession of that which belongs to us as Christians?—to plant the foot upon that spiritual and heavenly inheritance which Christ has purchased for us, and on which He has entered as our forerunner? What answer must be given to these inquiries? Just one word—*Unbelief!*

It is declared, concerning Israel, by the voice of inspiration, that "they could not enter in [to Canaan] because of unbelief" (Heb. 3). So is it with us. We fail to enter upon our heavenly inheritance—fail to take possession, practically, of our true and proper portion—fail to walk, day by day, as a heavenly people, having no place, no name, no portion in the earth—having nothing to do with this world save to pass through it as pilgrims and strangers, treading in the footsteps of Him who has gone before and taken His place in the heavens. And why do we fail? Because of unbelief. Faith is not in energy, and therefore the things which are seen have more power over our hearts than the things which are unseen. Oh, may the Holy Spirit strengthen our faith, and energize our souls, and lead us upward and onward, so that we may not merely be found *talking* of heavenly life, but *living* it, to the praise of Him who has, in His infinite grace, called us thereto.

"And all the children of Israel murmured against Moses and against Aaron: and the whole congregation said unto them, 'Would God that we had died in the land of Egypt! or would God we had died in this wilderness! And wherefore hath the Lord brought us unto this land, to fall by the sword, that our wives and our children should be a prey? Were it not better for us to return into Egypt?' And they said one to another, 'Let us make a captain, and let us return into Egypt.' "

There are two melancholy phases of unbelief exhibited in Israel's history in the wilderness: the one at Horeb, the other at Kadesh. At Horeb, they made *a calf,* and said, "These be thy gods, O Israel, that brought thee up out of the land of Egypt." At Kadesh, they proposed to make *a captain* to lead them back into Egypt. The former of these is the *superstition* of unbelief; the latter, the willful *independence* of unbelief; and most surely we need not marvel if those who thought that a calf had brought them out of Egypt should seek a captain to lead them back. The poor human mind is tossed like a ball from one to the other of those sore evils. There is no resource save that which faith finds in the living God. In Israel's case, God was lost sight of. It was either a calf or a captain; either death in the wilderness or return into Egypt.

Caleb stands in bright contrast with all this. To him it was neither death in the wilderness nor return into Egypt, but an abundant entrance into the promised land behind the impenetrable shield of Jehovah. "And Joshua the son of Nun, and Caleb the son of Jephunneh, which were of them that searched the land, rent their clothes; and they spake unto all the company of the children of Israel, saying, 'The land, which we passed through to search it, is an exceeding good land. If the Lord delight in us, then He will bring us into this land, and give it us; a land which floweth with milk and honey. Only rebel not ye against the Lord, neither fear ye the people of the land; for they are bread for us: their defense is departed from them, and the Lord is with us: fear them not.' But all the congregation bade stone them with stones."

And for what were they to be stoned? Was it for telling lies? was it for blasphemy or evil-doing? No; it was for their bold and earnest testimony to the truth. They had been sent to spy the land, and to furnish a true report concerning it. This they did; and for this, "all the congregation bade stone them with stones." The people did not like the truth then any more than now. Truth is never popular. There is no place for it in this world or in the human heart. Lies will be received, and error in every shape, but truth never. Joshua and Caleb had to encounter, in their day, what all true witnesses in every age have experienced and all must expect, namely, the opposition and hatred of the mass of their fellows. There were six hundred thousand voices raised against two men who simply told the truth and trusted in God. Thus it has been, thus it is, and thus it will be until that glorious moment when "the earth shall be full of the knowledge of the Lord, as the waters cover the sea."

But, oh, how important it is to be enabled, like Joshua and Caleb, to bear a full, clear, and uncompromising testimony to the truth of God! How important to maintain the truth as to the proper portion and inheritance of the saints! There is such a tendency to corrupt the truth—to fritter it away—to surrender it—to lower the standard. Hence the urgent need of having the truth in divine power in the soul, of being able, in our little measure, to say, "We speak that we do know, and testify that we have seen." Caleb and Joshua had not only been in the land, but they had been with God about the land. They had looked at it all from faith's point of view. They knew the land was theirs, in the purpose of God; that it was worth having, as the gift of God; and that they should yet possess it, by the power of God. They were men full of faith, full of courage, full of power.

Blessed men! They were living in the light of the divine presence, while the whole congregation were wrapped in the dark shades of their own unbelief. What a contrast! This it is which ever marks the difference between even the people of God. You may constantly find persons of whom you can have no doubt as to their being children of God, but yet they never seem to rise to the height of divine revelation as to their standing and portion as saints of God. They are always full of doubts and fears, always overcast with clouds, always at the dark side of things; they are looking at themselves, or at their circumstances, or at their difficulties; they are never bright and happy, never able to exhibit that joyful confidence and courage which become a Christian, and which bring glory to God.

Now all this is truly lamentable; it ought not to be; and we may rest assured there is some grave defect—something radically wrong. The Christian should always be peaceful and happy, always able to praise God, come what may. His joys do not flow from himself or from the scene through which he is passing; they flow from the living God, and they are beyond the reach of every earthly influence. He can say, "My God, the spring of all my joys." This is the sweet privilege of the very feeblest child of God. But here is just where we so sadly fail and come short. We take our eyes off God, and fix them on ourselves, or on our circumstances, our grievances, or our difficulties; hence all is darkness and discontent, murmuring and complaining. This is not Christianity at all. It is unbelief—dark, deadly, God-dishonoring, heart-depressing unbelief. "God hath not given us the spirit of fear, but of power and of love and of a sound mind."

Such is the language of a true spiritual Caleb—language addressed to one whose heart was feeling the pressure of the difficulties and dangers which surrounded him. The spirit of God fills the soul of the true believer with holy boldness. He gives moral elevation above the chilling and murky atmosphere around, and lifts the soul into the bright sunshine of that region "where storms and tempests never rise."

"And the glory of the Lord appeared in the tabernacle of the congregation before all the children of Israel. And the Lord said unto Moses, 'How long will this people provoke Me? and how long will it be ere they believe Me, for all the signs which I have showed among them? I will smite them with the pestilence and disinherit them, and will make of thee a greater nation, and mightier than they."

What a moment was this in the history of Moses! Here was what nature might well regard as a golden opportunity for him. Never before and never since have we any occasion in the which a mere man had such a door open before him. The enemy and his own heart might say, Now's your time. You have here an offer of becoming the head and founder of a great and mighty nation—an offer made to you by Jehovah Himself. You have not sought it. It is put before you by the living God, and it would be the very height of folly on your part to reject it.

But Moses was not a self-seeker. He had drunk too deeply into the spirit of Christ to seek to be any thing. He had no unholy ambition, no selfish aspirations. He desired only God's glory and His people's good; and in order to reach those ends, he was ready, through grace, to lay himself and his interests on the altar.

Hear his marvelous reply. Instead of jumping at the offer contained in the words, "I will make of thee a greater nation and mightier than they"—instead of eagerly grasping at the golden opportunity of laying the foundation of his personal fame and fortune, he sets himself completely aside, and replies in accents of the most noble disinterestedness. "And Moses said unto the Lord, 'Then the Egyptians shall hear it, (for Thou broughtest up this people in Thy might from among them;) and they will tell it to the inhabitants of this land: for they have heard that Thou, Lord, art among this people; that Thou, Lord, art seen face to face; and that Thy cloud standeth over them; and that Thou goest before them, by day-time in a pillar of a cloud, and in a pillar of fire by night. Now if Thou shalt kill all this people as one man, then the nations which have heard the fame of Thee will speak, saying, Because the Lord was not able to bring this people into the land which He sware unto them, therefore He hath slain them in the wilderness" (ver. 13-16).

Here Moses takes the very highest ground. He is wholly occupied about the Lord's glory. He cannot endure the thought that the lustre of that glory should be tarnished in the view of the nations of the uncircumcised. What though he should become a head and a founder? What though future millions should look back to him as their illustrious progenitor? If all this personal glory and greatness was only to be purchased by the sacrifice of a single ray of divine glory—what then? Away with it all. Let the name of Moses be blotted out forever. He had said as much in the days of the *calf,* and he was ready to repeat it in the days of the *captain.* In the face of the superstition and independence of an unbelieving nation, the heart of Moses throbbed *only* for the glory of God. That must be guarded at all cost. Come what may—cost what it may, the glory of the Lord must be maintained. Moses felt it was impossible for any thing to be right if the basis were not laid firmly down in the strict maintenance of the glory of the God of Israel. To think of himself made great at God's expense was perfectly insufferable to the heart of this blessed man of God. He could not endure that the name which he loved so well should be blasphemed among the nations, or that it should ever be said by any one, "The Lord was not able."

But there was another thing which lay near the disinterested heart of Moses. He thought of the people; he loved and cared for them. Jehovah's glory, no doubt, stood uppermost; but Israel's blessing stood next. "And now," he adds, "I beseech Thee, let the power of my Lord be great, according as Thou hast spoken, saying, 'The Lord is long-suffering, and of great mercy, forgiving iniquity and transgression, and by no means clearing the guilty; visiting the iniquity of the fathers upon the children unto the third and fourth generation.' Pardon, I beseech Thee, the iniquity of this people, according unto the greatness of Thy mercy, and as Thou hast forgiven this people from Egypt even until now" (ver. 17-19).

This is uncommonly fine. The order, the tone, and the spirit of this entire appeal are most exquisite. There is, first and chiefest of all, a jealous care for the Lord's glory. This must be fenced round about on every side. But then it is on this very ground, namely, the maintenance of the divine glory, that pardon is sought for the people. The two things are linked together in the most blessed way in this intercession. "Let the *power* of my Lord be great." To what end? Judgment and destruction? Nay; "The Lord is *long-suffering.*" What a thought! The power of God in long-suffering and pardon! How unspeakably precious! How intimate was Moses with the very heart and mind of God when he could speak in such a strain! and how does he stand in contrast with Elijah, on Mount Horeb, when he made intercession *against* Israel! We can have little question as to which of these two honored men was most in harmony with the mind and spirit of Christ. "Pardon, I beseech Thee, the iniquity of this people, according unto the greatness of Thy mercy." These words were grateful to the ear of Jehovah, who delights in dispensing pardon. "And the Lord said, 'I have pardoned, according to thy word.' " And then He adds, "But as truly as I live, all the earth shall be filled with the glory of the Lord"

Let the reader carefully note these two statements; they are absolute and unqualified. "I have pardoned," and, "All the earth shall be filled with the glory of the Lord." Nothing could, by any possibility, touch these grand facts. The *pardon* is secured, and the *glory* shall yet shine forth over all the earth. No power of earth or hell, men or devils, can ever interfere with the divine integrity of these two precious statements. Israel shall rejoice in the plenary pardon of their God, and all the earth shall yet bask in the bright sunshine of His glory.

But then there is such a thing as government, as well as grace. This must never be forgotten, nor must these things ever be confounded. The whole book of God illustrates the distinction between grace and government; and no part of it, perhaps, more forcibly than the section which now lies open before us. Grace will pardon, and grace will fill the earth with the blessed beams of divine glory; but mark the appalling movement of the wheels of government as set forth in the following burning words: "Because all those men which have seen My glory, and My miracles, which I did in Egypt and in the wilderness, have tempted Me now these ten times, and have not hearkened to My voice; surely they shall not see the land which I sware unto their fathers, neither shall any of them that provoked Me see it: but My servant Caleb, because he had another spirit with him, and hath followed Me fully, him will I bring into the land whereinto he went; and his seed shall possess it. (Now the Amalekites and the Canaanites dwelt in the valley.) To-morrow turn you, and get you into the wilderness by the way of the Red Sea" (ver. 22-25).

This is most solemn. Instead of confiding in God, and going boldly on into the land of promise, in simple dependence upon His omnipotent arm, they provoked Him by their unbelief, despised the pleasant land, and were compelled to turn back again into that great and terrible wilderness. "The Lord spake unto Moses and unto Aaron, saying, 'How long shall I bear with this evil congregation, which murmur against Me? I have heard the murmurings of the children of Israel, which they murmur against Me. Say unto them, As truly as I live, saith the Lord, as ye have spoken in Mine ears, so will I do to you: your carcasses shall fall in this wilderness; and all that were numbered of you, according to your whole number, from twenty years old and upward, which have murmured against Me, doubtless ye shall not come into the land concerning which I sware to make you dwell therein, save Caleb the son of Jephunneh, and Joshua the son of Nun. But your little ones, which ye said should be a prey, them will I bring in, and they shall know the land which ye have despised. But as for you, your carcasses, they shall fall in this wilderness. And your children shall wander in the wilderness forty years, and bear your whoredoms, until your carcasses be wasted in the wilderness. After the number of the days in which ye searched the land, even forty days, each day for a year, shall ye bear your iniquities, even forty years; and ye shall know My breach of promise. I the Lord have said, I will surely do it unto all this evil congregation that are gathered together against Me; in this wilderness they shall be consumed, and there they shall die' " (ver. 26-35).

Such, then was the fruit of unbelief, and such the governmental dealings of God with a people that had provoked Him by their murmurings and hardness of heart.

It is of the utmost importance to note here that it was unbelief that kept Israel out of Canaan on the occasion now before us. The inspired commentary in Hebrews 3 places this beyond all question. "So we see that they could not enter in because of unbelief." It might perhaps be said that the time was not come for Israel's entrance upon the land of Canaan. The iniquity of the Amorites had not yet reached its culminating point. But this is not the reason why Israel refused to enter the land. They knew nothing and thought nothing about the iniquity of the Amorites. Scripture is as plain as possible: "They could not enter in," not because of the iniquity of the Amorites —not because the time was not come, but simply "because of unbelief." They ought to have entered. They were responsible to do so, and they were judged for not doing so. The way was open. The judgment of faith, as uttered by faithful Caleb, was clear and unhesitating—"Let us go up *at once,* and possess it; for we are well able to overcome it." They were as well able at that moment as they could ever be at any moment inasmuch as the One who had given them the land was the spring of their ability to enter upon it and possess it.

It is well to see this, and to ponder it deeply. There is a certain style of speaking of the counsels, purposes, and decrees of God—of the enactments of His moral government, and of the times and seasons which He has put in His own power—which goes far to sweep away the very foundations of human responsiblity. This must be carefully guarded against. We must ever bear in mind that man's responsiblity rests on what is *revealed,* not on what is *secret.* Israel was responsible to go up at once and take possession of the land, and they were judged for not doing so. Their carcasses fell in the wilderness, because they had not faith to enter the land.

And does not this convey a solemn lesson to us? Most surely. How is it that we, as Christians, so fail in making good, practically, our heavenly position? We are delivered from judgment by the *blood* of the Lamb; we are delivered from this present world by the *death* of Christ; but we do not, in spirit and by faith, cross the Jordan, and take possession of our heavenly inheritance. It is generally believed that Jordan is a type of death, as the end of our natural life in this world. This, in one sense, is true; but how was it that when Israel did at length cross the Jordan they had to begin to fight? Assuredly we shall not have any fighting when we actually get to heaven. The spirits of those who have departed in the faith of Christ are not fighting in heaven. They are not in conflict in any shape or form. They are at rest. They are waiting for the morning of the resurrection; but they wait in rest, not in conflict.

Hence, therefore, there is something more typified in Jordan than the end of an individual's life in this world. We must view it as the figure of the death of Christ, in one grand aspect; just as the Red Sea is a figure of it in another, and the blood of the paschal lamb in another. The blood of the lamb sheltered Israel from the judgment of God upon Egypt; the waters of the Red Sea delivered Israel from Egypt itself and all its power; but they had to cross the Jordan,—they had to plant the sole of their foot upon the land of promise, and make good their place there in spite of every foe. They had to fight for every inch of Canaan.

And what is the meaning of this latter? Have we to fight for heaven? When a Christian falls asleep, and his spirit goes to be with Christ in paradise, is there any question of fighting? Clearly not. What, then, are we to learn from the crossing of Jordan and the wars of Canaan? Simply this: Jesus has died. He has passed away out of this world. He has not only died for our sins, but He has broken every link which connected us with this world; so that we are dead to the world as well as dead to sin and dead to the law. We have, in God's sight, and in the judgment of faith, as little to do with this world as a man lying dead on the floor. We are called to reckon ourselves dead to it all, and alive to God through Jesus Christ our Lord. We live in the power of the new life which we possess in union with Christ risen. We belong to heaven; and it is in making good our position as heavenly men that we have to fight with wicked spirits in the heavenlies—in the very sphere which belongs to us, and from which they have not yet been expelled. If we are satisfied to "walk as men"—to live as those who belong to this world—to stop short of Jordan, if we are satisfied to live as "dwellers upon the earth," if we do not aim at our proper heavenly portion and position, then we shall not know aught of the conflict of Ephesians 6:12. It is seeking to live as heavenly men now, on the earth, that we shall enter into the meaning of that conflict which is the antitype of Israel's wars in Canaan. We shall not have to fight when we get to heaven; but if we want to live a heavenly life on the earth, if we seek to carry ourselves as those who are dead to the world and alive in Him who went down into Jordan's cold flood for us, then, assuredly, we must fight. Satan will leave no stone unturned to hinder our living in the power of our heavenly life; and hence the conflict. He will seek to make us walk as those who have an earthly standing, to be citizens of this world, to contend for our rights, to maintain our rank and dignity, to give the lie, practically, to that great foundation Christian truth that we are dead and risen with and in Christ.

If the reader will turn for a moment to Ephesians 6, he will see how this interesting subject is presented by the inspired writer. "Finally, my brethren, be strong in the Lord, and in the power of His might. Put on the whole armor of God, that ye may be able to stand against *the wiles* of the devil. For we wrestle not against flesh and blood [as Israel had to do in Canaan]; but against principalities, against powers, against the rulers of the darkness of this world, against wicked spirits in heavenly places. Wherefore take unto you the whole armor of God, that ye may be able to withstand in the evil day, and having done all, to stand" (ver. 10-13).

Here we have proper Christian conflict. It is not here a question of the lusts of the flesh, or the fascinations of the world—though surely we have to watch against these,—but the "wiles of the devil." Not his power, which is forever broken, but those subtle devices and snares by which he seeks to keep Christians from realizing their heavenly position and inheritance.

Now, it is in carrying on this conflict that we so signally fail. We do not aim at apprehending that for which we have been apprehended. Many of us are satisfied with knowing that we are sheltered from judgment by the blood of the Lamb. We do not enter into the deep significance of the Red Sea and the river Jordan; we do not practically seize their spiritual import. We walk as men, the very thing for which the apostle blamed the Corinthians. We live and act as if we belonged to this world, whereas Scripture teaches, and our baptism expresses, that we are dead to the world, even as Jesus is dead to it; and that we are risen in Him, through the faith of the operation of God, who hath raised Him from the dead (Col. 2:12).

May the Holy Spirit lead our souls into the reality of these things. May He so present to us the precious fruits of that heavenly land which is ours in Christ, and so strengthen us with His own might in the inner man, that we may boldly cross the Jordan and plant the foot upon the spiritual Canaan. We live far below our privileges as Christians. We allow the things that are seen to rob us of the enjoyment of those things that are unseen. Oh, for a stronger faith, to take possession of all that God has freely given to us in Christ!

We must now proceed with our history.

"And the men, which Moses sent to search the land, who returned, and made all the congregation to murmur against him, by bringing up a slander upon the land, even those men that did bring up the evil report upon the land, died by the plague before the Lord. But Joshua the son of Nun, and Caleb the son of Jephunneh, which were of the men that went to search the land, lived still" (ver. 36-38).

It is wonderful to think that out of that vast assembly of six hundred thousand men, besides women and children, there were only two that had faith in the living God. We do not, of course, speak of Moses, but merely of the congregation. The whole assembly, with two very brilliant exceptions indeed, was governed by a spirit of unbelief. They could not trust God to bring them into the land; nay, they thought He had brought them into the wilderness to die there; and surely, we may say, they reaped according to their dark unbelief. The ten false witnesses died by the plague; and the many thousands who received their false witness were compelled to turn back into the wilderness, there to wander up and down for forty years, and then die and be buried.

But Joshua and Caleb stood on the blessed ground of faith in the living God—that faith which fills the soul with most joyful confidence and courage. And of them we may say, they reaped according to their faith. God must always honor the faith which He has implanted in the soul. It is His own gift, and He cannot, we may say with reverence, but own it wherever it exists. Joshua and Caleb were enabled, in the simple power of faith, to withstand a tremendous tide of infidelity. They held fast their confidence in God in the face of every difficulty; and He signally honored their faith in the end, for while the carcasses of their brethren were mouldering in the dust of the wilderness, their feet were treading the vine-clad hills and fertile valleys of the land of Canaan. The former declared that God had brought them forth to die in the wilderness, and they were taken at their word; the latter declared that God was able to bring them into the land, and they were taken at their word.

This is a most weighty principle: "According to your faith, so be it unto you." Let us remember this. God delights in faith. He loves to be trusted; and He will ever put honor upon those who trust Him. On the contrary, unbelief is grievous to Him. It provokes and dishonors Him, and brings darkness and death over the soul. It is a most terrible sin to doubt the living God, who cannot lie, and to harbor questions when He has spoken. The devil is the author of all doubtful questions. He delights in shaking the confidence of the soul; but he has no power whatever against a soul that simply confides in God. His fiery darts can never reach one who is hidden behind the shield of faith. And, oh, how precious it is to live a life of childlike trust in God! It makes the heart so happy, and fills the mouth with praise and thanksgiving; it chases away every cloud and mist, and brightens our path with the blessed beams of our Father's countenance. On the other hand, unbelief fills the heart with all manner of questions, throws us in upon ourselves, darkens our path, and makes us truly miserable. Caleb's heart was full of joyful confidence, while the hearts of his brethren were filled with bitter murmurings and complaints. Thus it must ever be. If we want to be happy, we must be occupied with God and His surroundings: if we want to be miserable, we have only to be occupied with self and its surroundings. Look, for a moment, at the first chapter of Luke. What was it that shut up Zacharias in dumb silence? It was unbelief. What was it that filled the heart and opened the lips of Mary and Elizabeth? Faith. Here lay the difference. Zacharias might have joined those pious women in their songs of praise were it not that dark unbelief had sealed his lips in melancholy silence. What a picture! What a lesson! Oh that we may learn to trust God more simply! May the doubtful mind be far from us. May it be ours, in the midst of an infidel scene, to be strong in faith, giving glory to God.

The closing paragraph of our chapter teaches us another holy lesson—let us apply our hearts to it with all diligence. "And Moses told these sayings unto all the children of Israel: and the people mourned greatly. And they rose up early in the morning, and gat them up into the top of the mountain, saying, 'Lo, we be here, and will go up unto the place which the Lord hath promised: for we have sinned.' And Moses said, 'Wherefore now do ye transgress the commandment of the Lord? but it shall not prosper. Go not up, for the Lord is not among you; that ye be not smitten before your enemies. For the Amalekites and the Canaanites are there before you, and ye shall fall by the sword: because ye are turned away from the Lord, therefore the Lord will not be with you.' But they presumed to go up unto the hill-top: nevertheless the ark of the covenant of the Lord, and Moses, departed not out of the camp. Then the Amalekites came down, and the Canaanites which dwelt in that hill, and smote them, and discomfited them, even unto Hormah."

What a mass of contradictions is the human heart! When exhorted to go up at once, in the energy of faith, and possess the land, they shrank back and refused to go. They fell down and wept when they ought to have gone up and conquered. In vain did the faithful Caleb assure them that the Lord would bring them in and plant them in the mountain of His inheritance—that He was able to do it. They would not go up, because they could not trust God. But now, instead of bowing their heads and accepting the governmental dealings of God, they *would* go up, presumptuously, trusting in themselves.

But, ah! how vain to move without the living God in their midst! Without Him they could do nothing. And yet, when they might have had Him, they were afraid of the Amalekites; but now, they presume to face those very people without Him. "Lo, we be here, and *will* go up unto the place which the Lord hath promised." This was more easily said than done. An Israelite without God was no match for an Amalekite; and it is very remarkable that when Israel refused to act in the energy of faith—when they fell under the power of a God-dishonoring unbelief, Moses points out to them the very difficulties to which they themselves had referred. He tells them *"the Amalekites and the Canaanites are there before you."*

This is full of instruction. They, by their unbelief, had shut out God; and therefore it was obviously a question between Israel and the Canaanites. Faith would have made it a question between God and the Canaanites. This was precisely the way in which Joshua and Caleb viewed the matter when they said, "If the Lord delight in us, then He will bring us into this land, and give it us; a land which floweth with milk and honey. Only rebel not ye against the Lord, *neither fear ye the people of the land;* for they are bread for us: their defense is departed from them, and *the Lord is with us: fear them not."*

Here lay the grand secret. The Lord's presence with His people secures victory over every foe; but if He be not with them, they are as water poured upon the ground. The ten unbelieving spies had declared themselves to be as grasshoppers in the presence of the giants, and Moses, taking them at their word, told them, as it were, that grasshoppers are no match for giants. If, on the one hand, it be true that "according to your faith, so be it unto you," it is also true, on the other hand, that according to your unbelief, so be it unto you.

But the people presumed. They affected to be something when they were nothing. And oh, how miserable to presume to move in our own strength! What defeat and confusion! what exposure and contempt! what humbling and smashing to pieces! It must be so. They abandoned God in their unbelief, and He abandoned them in their vain presumption. They would not go with Him in faith, and He would not go with them in their unbelief. "Nevertheless the ark of the covenant of the Lord, and Moses, departed not out of the camp." They went without God, and hence they fled before their enemies.

Thus it must ever be. It is of no possible use to affect strength, to put forth lofty pretensions, to presume to be any thing. Assumption and affectation are worse than worthless. If God be not with us, we are as the vapor of the morning. But this must be learnt practically. We must be brought down to the very bottom of all that is in self, so as to prove its utter worthlessness. And truly it is the wilderness, with all its varied scenes, and its thousand and one exercises, that leads to this practical result. There we learn what flesh is. There nature comes fully out, in all its phases; sometimes full of cowardly unbelief; at other times, full of false confidence. At Kadesh, refusing to go up when told to go; at Hormah, persisting in going when told not. Thus it is that extremes meet in that evil nature which the writer and the reader bear about from day to day.

But there is one special lesson, beloved Christian reader, which we should seek to learn thoroughly ere we take our departure from Hormah, and it is this: There is immense difficulty in walking humbly and patiently in the path which our own failure has rendered necessary for us. Israel's unbelief, in refusing to go up into the land, rendered it needful, in the governmental dealings of God, that they should turn about and wander in the wilderness for forty years. To this they were unwilling to submit. They kicked against it. They could not bow their necks to the necessary yoke.

How often is this the case with us! We fail; we take some false step; we get into trying circumstances in consequence; and then, instead of meekly bowing down under the hand of God, and seeking to walk with Him in humbleness and brokenness of spirit, we grow restive and rebellious; we quarrel with the circumstances instead of judging ourselves; and we seek, in self-will, to escape from the circumstances, instead of accepting them as the just and necessary consequence of our conduct.

Again, it may happen that through weakness or failure of one kind or another, we refuse to enter a position or path of spiritual privilege, and thereby we are thrown back in our course, and put upon a lower form in the school. Then, instead of carrying ourselves humbly, and submitting, in meekness and contrition, to the hand of God, we presume to force ourselves into the position, and affect to enjoy the privilege, and put forth pretensions to power, and it all issues in the most humiliating defeat and confusion.

These things demand our most profound consideration. It is a great thing to cultivate a lowly spirit—a heart content with a place of weakness and contempt. God resisteth the proud, but He giveth grace to the lowly. A pretentious spirit must sooner or later be brought down, and all hollow assumption of power must be exposed. If there be not faith to take possession of the promised land, there is nothing for it but to tread the wilderness in meekness and lowliness.

And, blessed be God, we shall have Him with us in that wilderness journey, though we shall not and cannot have Him with us in our self-chosen path of pride and assumption. Jehovah refused to accompany Israel into the mountain of the Amorites; but He was ready to turn about, in patient grace, and accompany them through all their desert wanderings. If Israel would not enter Canaan with Jehovah, He would go back into the wilderness with Israel. Nothing can exceed the grace that shines in this. Had they been dealt with according to their deserts, they might, at least, have been left to wander alone through the desert. But, blessed forever be His great name, He does not deal with us after our sins, or reward us according to our iniquities. His thoughts are not as our thoughts, nor His ways as our ways. Notwithstanding all the unbelief, the ingratitude, and the provocation exhibited by the people; notwithstanding that their return back into the desert was the fruit of their own conduct, yet did Jehovah, in condescending grace and patient love, turn back with them to be their traveling-companion for forty long and dreary years in the wilderness.

Thus, if the wilderness proves what man is, it also proves what God is; and further, it proves what faith is; for Joshua and Caleb had to return with the whole congregation of their unbelieving brethren, and remain for forty years out of their inheritance, though they themselves were quite prepared, through grace, to go up into the land. This might seem a great hardship. Nature might judge it unreasonable that two men of faith should have to suffer on account of the unbelief of other people. But faith can afford to wait patiently. And besides, how could Joshua and Caleb complain of the protracted march when they saw Jehovah about to share it with them? Impossible. They were prepared to wait for God's time, for faith is never in a hurry. The faith of the servants might well be sustained by the grace of the Master.

---

## *CHAPTER 15*

THE words with which our chapter opens are peculiarly striking, when taken in connection with the contents of chapter 14. There, all seemed dark and hopeless. Moses had to say to the people, "*Go not up,* for the Lord is not among you; that ye be not smitten before your enemies." And again, the Lord had said to them, "As truly as I live, as ye have spoken in Mine ears, so will I do to you. Your carcasses shall fall in this wilderness. . . . Doubtless *ye shall not come into the land* concerning which I sware to make you dwell therein. . . . As for you, your carcasses, they shall fall in this wilderness."

Thus much as to chapter 14. But no sooner do we open the section now before us, than, just as though nothing had happened, and though all were as calm, as bright, and as certain as God could make it, we read such words as these: "The Lord spake unto Moses, saying, 'Speak unto the children of Israel, and say unto them, *When ye be come into the land of your habitations, which I give unto you,*" etc. This is one of the most remarkable passages in the entire of this most wonderful book. Indeed there is not, in the whole compass of the book, a passage more thoroughly characteristic, not only of Numbers, but of the entire volume of God. When we read the solemn sentence, "Ye shall not come into the land," what is the plain lesson which it reads out to us? The lesson, which we are so slow to learn, of man's utter worthlessness.—"All flesh is grass."

And, on the other hand, when we read such words as these: "When ye be come into the land of your habitations, which I give unto you," what is the precious lesson which they read out to us? This, assuredly, that salvation is of the Lord. In the one, we learn man's failure; in the other, God's faithfulness. If we look at man's side of the question, the sentence is, "Doubtless *ye shall not* come into the land;" but if we look at God's side of the question, we can reverse the matter, and say, "Doubtless *ye shall.*"

Thus it stands in the scene now before us, and thus it stands in the whole volume of inspiration—from beginning to end. Man fails, but God is faithful: man forfeits every thing, but God makes good all. "The things which are impossible with man are possible with God." Need we travel through the inspired canon in order to illustrate and prove this? Need we refer to the history of Adam in paradise? or the history of Noah after the flood? or the history of Israel in the wilderness, Israel under the law, Israel under the Levitical ceremonial? Shall we dwell upon the record of man's failure in the prophetic, priestly, and kingly office? Shall we point out the failure of the professing church as a responsible vessel on the earth? Has not man failed always and in every thing? Alas! it is so.

This is one side of the picture—the dark and humbling side. But, blessed be God, there is the bright and encouraging side also. If there is the "Doubtless ye shall not," there is also the "Doubtless ye shall." And why? Because Christ has entered the scene, and in Him all is infallibly secured for the glory of God and the eternal blessing of man. It is God's eternal purpose to "head up all things in Christ." There is not a single thing in which the first man has failed that the second Man will not make good. All is set up on a new footing in Christ. He is the Head of the new creation; Heir of all the promises made to Abraham, Isaac, and Jacob touching the land; Heir of all the promises made to David concerning the throne. The government shall be upon His shoulders. He shall bear the glory. He is the Prophet, Priest, and King. In a word, Christ makes good all that Adam lost, and brings in much more beside than Adam ever had. Hence, when we look at the first Adam and his doings, whenever and however viewed, the sentence is, "Doubtless *ye shall not.*" Ye shall not remain in paradise—ye shall not retain the government—ye shall not inherit the promises—ye shall not enter the land—ye shall not occupy the throne—ye shall not enter the kingdom.

But, on the other hand, when we look at the last Adam and His doings, wherever and however viewed, the entire category must be gloriously reversed; the "not" must be forever eluded from the sentence, for in Christ Jesus "all the promises of God are yea and Amen, to the glory of God by us." There is no "nay" in the matter when Christ is concerned. All is "yea"—all is divinely settled and established; and because it is so, God has set His seal to it, even the seal of His Spirit, which all believers now possess. "For the Son of God, Jesus Christ, who was preached among you by us, even by me and Silvanus and Timotheus, was not yea and nay, but in Him was yea. For all the promises of God in Him are yea, and in Him Amen, unto the glory of God by us. Now He which stablisheth us with you in Christ, and hath anointed us, is God; who hath also sealed us, and given the earnest of the Spirit in our hearts" (2 Cor. 1:19-22).

Thus, then, the opening lines of Numbers 15 must be read in the light of the whole volume of God. It falls in with the entire history of the ways of God with man, in this world. Israel had forfeited all title to the land. They deserved nothing better than that their carcasses should fall in the wilderness. And yet such is the large and precious grace of God, that He could speak to them of their coming into the land, and instruct them as to their ways and works therein.

Nothing can be more blessed or more establishing than all this. God rises above all human failure and sin. It is utterly impossible that a single promise of God can fail of its accomplishment. Could it be that the conduct of Abraham's seed in the wilderness should frustrate God's eternal purpose, or hinder the fulfillment of the absolute and unconditional promise made to the fathers? Impossible. And therefore, if the generation which came out of Egypt refused to go into Canaan, Jehovah would, of the very stones, raise up a seed to whom His promise should be made good. This will help to explain the opening sentence of our chapter, which comes in with such remarkable force and beauty after the humiliating scenes of chapter 14. In this latter, Israel's sun seems to go down amid dark and angry clouds; but in the former, it rises with serene brightness, revealing and establishing that great truth that "the gifts and calling of God are without repentance." God never repents of His call or His gift; and hence, though an unbelieving generation should murmur and rebel ten thousand times over, He will make good all that He has promised.

Here is the divine resting-place of faith at all times—the sure and safe haven for the soul amid the wreck of all human schemes and undertakings. Every thing goes to pieces in man's hands, but God in Christ remains. Let man be set up in business again and again, under the most favorable circumstances, and he is sure to become a bankrupt; but God has set up Christ in resurrection, and all who believe in Him are placed on a new footing altogether—they are taken into partnership with the risen and glorified Head, and there they stand forever. That wondrous partnership can never be dissolved. All is secured on a basis that no power of earth or hell can ever touch.

Reader, say, dost thou understand the application of all this to thyself? Hast thou discovered, in the light of God's presence, that thou art, in very deed, a bankrupt? that thou hast made shipwreck of every thing? that thou hast not a single plea to urge? Hast thou been led to make a personal application of those two sentences upon which we have been dwelling, namely, "Doubtless thou shalt not," and "Doubtless thou shalt"? Hast thou learnt the force of these words, "Thou hast destroyed thyself; but in Me is thy help"? In one word, hast thou come to Jesus as a lost, guilty, self-destroyed sinner, and found redemption, pardon, and peace in Him?

Do pause and seriously consider these things. We can never lose sight of the weighty fact that we have something more to do than to write *Notes on the Book of Numbers:* we have to consider the soul of the reader. We have a most solemn responsibility to discharge to him or to her; and therefore it is that, from time to time, we feel constrained to turn, for a moment, from the page on which we are meditating, in order to make an appeal to the heart and conscience of the reader, and entreat him, most earnestly, that if he be as yet unconverted, undecided, he would lay aside this volume, and apply his heart seriously to the great question of his present condition and eternal destiny. In comparison with this, all other questions dwindle into utter insignificance. What are all the schemes and undertakings which begin, continue, and end in time, when compared with eternity and the salvation of your never-dying soul? They are as the small dust of the balance. "What shall it profit a man if he shall gain the whole world and lose his own soul?" If you had the wealth of a Rothschild—the money-king, if you stood on the loftiest pinnacle of literary fame or political ambition, if your name were adorned with all the honors which the universities of this world could bestow, if your brow were wreathed with the laurels and your breast covered with the medals of a hundred victories, what would it profit you? You must leave all—you must pass through the narrow arch of time into the boundless ocean of eternity. Men of princely wealth, men of literary fame, men who have ruled by their intellectual power the House of Lords and Commons, who have held thousands hanging entranced upon their lips, men who have reached the very highest point of naval, military, and forensic distinction, have passed away into eternity; and the awful question as to such is, "Where is the soul?"

Beloved reader, we beseech thee, by the most weighty arguments that can possibly be urged upon the soul of man, not to turn away from this subject until thou hast come to a right conclusion. By God's great love, by the cross and passion of Christ, by the powerful testimony of God the Holy Ghost, by the awful solemnity of a never-ending eternity, by the unspeakable value of thy immortal soul, by all the joys of heaven, by all the horrors of hell—by these seven weighty arguments, we urge thee, this moment, to come to Jesus. Delay not! argue not! reason not! but come now, just as you are—with all your sins, with all your misery, with your misspent life, with your dreadful record of mercies slighted, advantages abused, opportunities neglected—come to Jesus, who stands, with open arms and loving heart, ready to receive you, and points to those wounds which attest the reality of His atoning death upon the cross, and tells you to put your trust in Him, and assures you you will never be confounded. May God's Spirit carry home this appeal to thy heart, this moment, and give thee no rest until thou art savingly converted to Christ, reconciled to God, and sealed with the Holy Spirit of promise.

We shall now return, for a moment, to our chapter.

Nothing can be more lovely than the picture here presented. We have vows, and free-will offerings, sacrifices of righteousness, and the wine of the kingdom, all based upon the sovereign grace which shines in the very first verse. It is a fair sample, a beauteous foreshadowing of the future condition of Israel. It reminds us of the marvelous visions which close the book of the prophet Ezekiel. The unbelief, the murmuring, the rebellion, are all over and all forgotten. God retires into His own eternal counsels, and from thence looks forward to the time when His people shall offer an offering in righteousness and pay their vows to Him, and the joy of His kingdom shall fill their hearts forever (ver. 3-13).

But there is a very striking feature in this chapter, and that is, the place which "the stranger" gets. It is most thoroughly characteristic. "And if a stranger sojourn with you, or whosoever be among you in your generations, and will offer an offering made by fire, of a sweet savor unto the Lord; as ye do, so he shall do. One ordinance shall be both for you of the congregation, and also for the stranger that sojourneth with you, *an ordinance forever* in your generations: *as ye are, so shall the stranger be before the Lord.* One law and one manner shall be for you, and for the stranger that sojourneth with you."

What a place for the stranger! What a lesson for Israel! What a standing testimony on the page of their favorite and boasted Moses! The stranger is placed on the very same platform with Israel! *"As* ye are, *so* shall the stranger be;" and this, too, "before the Lord." In Exodus 12:48, we read, "And when a stranger shall sojourn with thee, and will keep the passover to the Lord, let all his males be circumcised, and then let him come near and keep it." But in Numbers 15 there is no allusion to circumcision at all. And why? Is it that such a point could ever be waived? No; but we believe the omission here is full of meaning. Israel had forfeited every thing. The rebellious generation was to be set aside and cut off; but God's eternal purpose of grace must stand, and all His promises be fulfilled. All Israel shall be saved; they shall possess the land; they shall offer pure offerings, pay their vows, and taste the joy of the kingdom. On what ground? On the ground of sovereign mercy. Well, it is on the self-same ground that "the stranger" shall be brought in; and not only brought in, but *"as* ye are, *so* shall the stranger be before the Lord."

Will the Jew quarrel with this? Let him go and study Numbers 13 and 14. And when he has drunk into his inmost soul the wholesome lesson, then let him meditate on chapter 15, and we feel assured he will not seek to push "the stranger" off the platform, for he will be ready to confess himself a debtor to mercy alone, and to acknowledge that the same mercy which has reached him can reach the stranger, and he will rejoice to go in company with that stranger to drink of the wells of salvation thrown open by the sovereign grace of the God of Jacob.

Are we not forcibly reminded, by the teaching of this part of our book, of that profound section of dispensational truth presented in Romans 9–11, particularly of its magnificent close? "The gifts and calling of God are without repentance. For as ye [strangers] in times past have not believed God, yet have now obtained mercy through their unbelief: even so have these also now not believed in your mercy [*i.e.,* mercy shown to the Gentiles–*see Greek*], that they also may obtain mercy [*i.e.,* come in on the ground of mercy like the stranger]. For God hath concluded them all in unbelief, that He might have mercy upon all [Jews and Gentiles–Israel and the stranger]. O the depth of the riches both of the wisdom and knowledge of God! how unsearchable are His judgments, and His ways past finding out! For who hath known the mind of the Lord? or who hath been His counselor? Or who hath first given to Him, and it shall be recompensed unto him again? For of Him, and through Him, and to Him, are all things; to whom be glory forever. Amen" (Rom 11:29-36).

From verses 22-31 of our chapter, we have instructions as to sins of ignorance and presumptuous sins–a very grave and important distinction. For the former, ample provision is made, in the goodness and mercy of God. The *death* of Christ is presented, in this portion of the chapter, in its two grand aspects, namely, the burnt-offering and the sin-offering; that is, its aspect to Godward and its aspect to usward; and we have also all the preciousness, fragrance, and joy of His perfect *life* and service as a man in this world, as typified by the meat-offering and drink-offering. In the burnt-offering, we see atonement wrought according to the measure of Christ's devotedness to God, and of God's delight in Him: in the sin-offering, we see atonement wrought according to the measure of the sinner's necessities and the hatefulness of sin in God's sight. The two offerings, taken together, present the atoning death of Christ in all its fullness. Then, in the meat-offering, we have Christ's perfect life and the reality of His human nature, as manifested in all the details of His path and service in this world; while the drink-offering, typifies His complete surrender of Himself to God.

Into the rich and marvelous instruction conveyed in the different classes of sacrifices presented in this passage, we do not attempt to enter now. The reader who desires to study the subject more fully is referred to *Notes on the Book of Leviticus.* We merely state here, in the very briefest manner, what we judge to be the main import of each offering; to go into details would only be to repeat what we have already written.

We would merely add that the claims of God demand that sins of ignorance should be taken cognizance of. We might feel disposed to say, or at least to think, that such sins ought to be passed over; but God does not think so. His holiness must not be reduced to the standard of our intelligence. *Grace* has made provision for sins of ignorance, but *holiness* demands that such sins should be judged and confessed. Every true heart will bless God for this. For what would become of us if the provisions of divine grace were not adequate to meet the claims of divine holiness? and adequate they most surely could not be if they traveled not beyond the range of our intelligence.

Yet, while all this will, generally speaking, be fully admitted, it is often very sorrowful to hear professing Christians making excuses for ignorance, and justifying unfaithfulness and error on the ground of ignorance. But very often, in such cases, the question may very cogently be urged, why are we ignorant, in reference to any point of conduct, or the claims of Christ upon us? Suppose a question comes before us demanding a positive judgment, and calling for a certain line of action; we plead ignorance. Is this right? will it avail? will it dispose of our responsibility? will God allow us to shirk the question after such a fashion? We may rest assured it will not do. Why are we ignorant? Have we put forth all our energies, have we adopted every available means, have we made every possible effort, to get at the root of the matter and reach a just conclusion? Let us bear in mind that the claims of truth and holiness demand all this of us; nor should we be satisfied with any thing less. We cannot but admit that were it a question involving, in any measure, *our own* interests—*our* name, *our* reputation, *our* property, we should leave no stone unturned in order to make ourselves fully acquainted with all the facts of the case. We should not long plead ignorance in such matters. If information were to be had, we should have it. We should do our very utmost to know all the ins and outs, the *pros* and *cons,* of the question, so that we might form a sound judgment in the matter.

Is this not so? Well, then, why should we plead ignorance when the claims of Christ are in question? Does it not prove that while we are quick, earnest, energetic, all alive, when *self* is concerned, we are indifferent, sluggish, slow-paced, when Christ is concerned? Alas! this is the plain, humbling truth. May we be humbled under a sense of it. May the Spirit of God make us more thoroughly in earnest in things which concern our Lord Jesus Christ. May self and its interests sink, and may Christ and His interests rise in our estimation, every day; and may we at least cordially own our holy responsibility to go diligently into every question in the which the glory of our Lord and Saviour Jesus Christ may, even in the most remote degree, be involved, however we may fail practically in our research. Let us not dare to say or think or act as though we thought that aught that concerns Him is a matter of indifference to us. God, in His mercy, forbid! Let us esteem all that merely concerns ourselves to be comparatively non-essential, but the claims of Christ to be of paramount authority.

We have said thus much on the subject of ignorance, in the sense of our responsibility to the truth of God and to the soul of the reader. We feel its immense practical importance. We believe we very often plead *ignorance,* when *indifference* would be the truer term to use. This is very sad. Surely, if our God, in His infinite goodness, has made ample provision even for sins of ignorance, that is no reason why we should coolly shelter ourselves behind the plea of ignorance, when there is the most abundant information within our reach had we only the energy to make use of it.

We might not, perhaps, have dwelt at such length upon this point were it not for the conviction, which becomes each day more strengthened in the soul, that we have reached a serious moment in our history as Christians. We are not given to croaking: we have no sympathy whatever with it. We believe it is our privilege to be filled with the most joyful confidence, and to have our hearts and minds ever garrisoned by the peace of God that passeth all understanding. "God hath not given us the spirit of fear; but of power, and of love, and of a sound mind" (2 Tim. 1:7).

But it is impossible to close our eyes to the startling fact that the claims of Christ, the value of truth, the authority of holy Scripture, are being more and more set aside each day, each week, each year. We believe we are approaching a moment in the which there will be toleration for any thing and every thing save the truth of God. It behooves us, therefore, to look well to it that God's Word has its own proper place in the heart, and that the conscience is governed in all things by its holy authority. A tender conscience is a most precious treasure to carry about with us from day to day—a conscience that ever yields a true response to the action of the Word of God—that bows down without a question to its plain statements. When the conscience is in this fine condition, there is always a regulating power wherewith to act upon one's practical course and character. Conscience may be compared to the regulator of a watch. It may happen that the hands of the watch get astray; but so long as the regulator has power over the spring, there is always the means of correcting the hands. If that power be gone, the entire watch must be taken to pieces. So with the conscience. So long as it continues true to the touch of Scripture, as applied by the Holy Ghost, there is always a safe and sure regulating power; but if it becomes sluggish, hardened, or perverted—if it refuses to yield a true response to "Thus saith the Lord," there is little, if any, hope. It then becomes a case similar to that referred to in our chapter,—"But the soul that doeth aught *presumptuously,* whether he be born in the land, or a stranger, *the same reproacheth the Lord;* and that soul shall be cut off from among his people. *Because he hath despised the word of the Lord,* and hath broken His commandment, that soul shall utterly be cut off; his iniquity shall be upon him" (ver. 30-31).

This is no sin of ignorance, but a presumptuous, willful sin, for which nothing remained but the unmitigated judgment of God. "Rebellion is as the sin of witchcraft, and stubbornness is as iniquity and idolatry" (1 Sam. 15:23). These are weighty words for a moment like the present, when man's will is developing itself with such extraordinary force. It is deemed manly to assert our will, but Scripture teaches the direct opposite. The two grand elements of human perfection—of perfect manhood—are these, namely, *dependence* and *obedience.* In proportion as any one departs from these, he departs from the true spirit and attitude of a man. Hence, when we turn our eyes to Him who was *the* perfect Man—the Man Christ Jesus, we see these two grand features perfectly adjusted and perfectly developed from first to last. That blessed One was never, for a single moment, out of the attitude of perfect dependence and absolute obedience. To prove and illustrate this fact would take us through the entire gospel narrative. But take the scene of the temptation, and there you will find a sample of the whole of that blessed life. His one unvarying reply to the tempter was, *"It is written."* No reasonings, no arguments, no questions. He lived by the Word of God. He conquered Satan by holding fast the *only* true position of a man—dependence and obedience. He *could* depend upon God, and He *would* obey Him. What could Satan do in such a case? Absolutely nothing.

Well, then, this is our example. We, as having the life of Christ, are called to live in habitual dependence and obedience. This is walking in the Spirit: this is the safe and happy path of the Christian. Independence and disobedience go together: they are utterly unchristian and unmanly. We find these two things in the first man, as we find the two opposites in the second. Adam in the garden sought to be independent. He was not content with being a man, and abiding in the only true place and spirit of a man, and he became disobedient. Here lies the secret of fallen humanity—these are the two elements which make up fallen manhood. Trace it where you will—before the flood, after the flood, without law, under the law, heathen, pagan, Jew, Turk, or nominal Christian,—analyze it as closely as you please, and you will see that it resolves itself into these two component parts—independence and disobedience. And when you reach the close of man's history in this world—when you view him in that last sad sphere in which he is to figure, how do you see him?—in what character does he appear? As "the willful king," and the "lawless man."

May we have grace to ponder these things aright. Let us cultivate a lowly and an obedient spirit. God has said, "To this man will I look, even to him who is of a contrite spirit and trembleth at My word." May these words sink down into our ears and into our hearts; and let the constant breathing of our souls be, "Keep back Thy servant, O Lord, from presumptuous sins, and let them not have dominion over him."*

It only remains for us, ere closing this section, to notice the case of the Sabbath-breaker and the institution of "the ribband of blue."

"And while the children of Israel were in the wilderness, they found a man that gathered sticks upon the Sabbath day. And they that found him gathering sticks brought him to Moses and Aaron, and to all the congregation. And they put him in ward, because it was not declared what should be done to him. And the Lord said unto Moses, 'The man shall be surely put to death: all the congregation shall stone him with stones without the camp.' And all the congregation brought him without the camp, and stoned him with stones, and he died; as the Lord commanded Moses" (ver. 32-36).

This surely was a presumptuous sin—it was flying in the face of a most plain and positive commandment of God. It is this that specially marks a presumptuous sin, and leaves it utterly inexcusable. Ignorance cannot be pleaded in the face of a divine command.

But why, it may be asked, had they to put the man in ward? Because, although the commandment was explicit, yet the breach of it had not been anticipated, nor had any penalty been enacted. To speak after the manner of men, Jehovah had not contemplated such folly on man's part as the interruption of His rest, and therefore He had not formally provided for such an occurrence. We need not say that God knows the end from the beginning; but in the matter now before us, He purposely left the case unnoticed until occasion required. But, alas! occasion did require, for man is

*We would remind the young Christian reader especially, that the true safeguard against sins of ignorance is, the study of the Word; and the true safeguard against presumptuous sins is, subjection to the Word. We all need to bear these things in mind, but our younger brethren particularly. There is a strong tendency amongst young Christians to get into the current of this present age, and to drink in its spirit. Hence the independence, the strong will, the impatience of control, the disobedience to parents, the headiness, high-mindedness, and self-confidence, the pretentious style, the assumption, the setting up to be wiser than elders—all these things so hateful in the sight of God, and so entirely opposed to the spirit of Christianity. We would most earnestly and lovingly entreat all our young friends to guard against these things, and to cultivate a lowly mind. Let them remember that "God resisteth the proud, but giveth grace to the lowly."

capable of any thing. He has no heart for God's rest. To kindle a fire on the Sabbath day was not only a positive breach of the law, but it evidenced the most complete alienation from the mind of the Lawgiver, inasmuch as it introduced into the day of *rest* that which is the apt symbol of *judgment.* Fire is emblematical of judgment, and as such it was wholly out of keeping with the repose of the Sabbath; nothing therefore remained but to visit the Sabbath-breaker with judgment, for "whatsoever a man soweth, that shall he also reap."

"And the Lord spake unto Moses, saying, 'Speak unto the children of Israel, and bid them that they make them fringes in the borders of their garments, throughout their generations, and that they put upon the fringe of the borders a ribband of blue. And it shall be unto you for a fringe, that ye may look upon it, and remember all the commandments of the Lord, and do them; and that ye seek not after your own heart, and your own eyes . . . that ye may remember, and do all My commandments, and be holy unto your God. I am the Lord your God, which brought you out of the land of Egypt, to be your God: I am the Lord your God' " (ver. 37-41).

The God of Israel would keep His people in continual remembrance of His holy commandments. Hence the beautiful institution of "the ribband of *blue,*" which was designed to be a *heavenly* memorial attached to the very borders of their garments, so that the word of God might ever be held fast in the remembrance of the thoughts of their hearts. Whenever an Israelite cast his eyes upon the blue ribband, he was to think of Jehovah, and yield a hearty obedience to all His statutes.

Such was the great practical intention of "the ribband of blue." But when we turn to Matthew 23:5, we learn the sad use which man had made of the divine institution. "But all their works they do for to be seen of men: they make broad their phylacteries, and *enlarge the borders of their garments."* Thus the very thing which had been instituted for the purpose of leading them to remember Jehovah, and to yield a lowly obedience to His precious Word, was turned into an occasion of self-exaltation and religious pride. Instead of thinking of God and His Word, they thought of themselves, and of the place which they held in the estimation of their fellows. *"All* their works they do to be *seen of men."* Not a thought of God. The spirit of the original institution was completely lost, while the outward form was kept up for selfish ends. Can we not see something like this around us and among us? Let us think of it—think deeply and seriously. Let us see to it that we do not turn the heavenly memorial into an earthly badge, and that which ought to lead to lowly obedience into an occasion of self-exaltation.

---

## *CHAPTER 16*

THE chapter on which we have just been dwelling is what may be called a digression from the history of Israel's wilderness life, except indeed the short paragraph respecting the Sabbath-breaker. It looks forward into the future, when, spite of all their sin and folly, their murmuring and rebellion, Israel shall possess the land of Canaan, and offer sacrifices of righteousness and songs of praise to the God of their salvation. In it we have seen Jehovah rising far above all the unbelief and disobedience, the pride and willfulness, exhibited in chapters 13 and 14, and looking on to the full and final accomplishment of His own eternal purpose, and the fulfillment of His promise to Abraham, Isaac, and Jacob.

But in chapter 16 the wilderness story is resumed—that sad and humbling story, so far as man is concerned, but a bright and blessed story of the exhaustless patience and boundless grace of God. These are the two grand lessons of the wilderness. We learn what man is and we learn what God is. The two things lie side by side on the pages of the book of Numbers. Thus in chapter 14 we have man and his ways; in chapter 15 we have God and His ways; and now, in the chapter which opens before us, we come back to man and his ways again. May we reap much deep and solid instruction from the double lesson.

"Now Korah, the son of Izhar, the son of Kohath, the son of Levi, and Dathan and Abiram, the sons of Eliab, and On, the son of Peleth, sons of Reuben, took men; and they rose up before Moses, with certain of the children of Israel, two hundred and fifty princes of the assembly, famous in the congregation, men of renown: and they gathered themselves together against Moses and against Aaron, and said unto them, 'Ye take too much upon you, seeing all the congregation are holy, every one of them, and the Lord is among them: wherefore then lift ye up yourselves above the congregation of the Lord?' " (ver. 1-3)

Here, then, we enter upon the solemn history of what the Holy Ghost, by the apostle Jude, terms, "The gainsaying of Core." The rebellion is attributed to Korah, inasmuch as he was the religious leader in it. He seems to have possessed sufficient influence to gather around him a large number of influential men—"princes, famous men, and men of renown." In short, it was a very formidable and serious rebellion; and we shall do well to look closely at its source and moral features.

It is always a most critical moment in the history of an assembly when a spirit of disaffection displays itself, for if it be not met in the right way, the most disastrous consequences are sure to follow. There are materials in every assembly capable of being acted upon, and it only needs some restless masterspirit to arise, in order to work on such materials, and fan into a devouring flame the fire that has been smouldering in secret. There are hundreds and thousands ready to flock around the standard of revolt, when once it has been raised, who have neither the vigor nor the courage to raise it themselves. It is not every one that Satan will take up as an instrument in such work. It needs a shrewd, clever, energetic man—a man of moral power—one possessing influence over the minds of his fellows, and an iron will to carry forward his schemes. No doubt Satan infuses much of all these into the men whom he uses in his diabolical undertakings. At all events, we know, as a fact, that the great leaders in all rebellious movements are generally men of master-minds, capable of swaying, according to their own will, the fickle multitude, which, like the ocean, is acted upon by every stormy wind that blows. Such men know how, in the first place, to stir the passions of the people; and, in the second place, how to wield them when stirred. Their most potent agency—the lever with which they can most effectually raise the masses—is some question as to their liberty and their rights. If they can only succeed in persuading people that their liberty is curtailed, and their *rights* infringed, they are sure to gather a number of restless spirits around them, and do a vast deal of serious mischief.

Thus it was in the matter of Korah and his coadjutors. They sought to make it appear that Moses and Aaron were lording it over their brethren and interfering with their rights and privileges as members of a holy congregation, in which, according to their judgment, all were on a dead level, and one had as much right to be active as another.

"Ye take too much upon you." Such was their charge against "the meekest man in all the earth." But what had Moses taken upon him? Surely, the most cursory glance back at the history of that dear and honored servant would have been sufficient to convince any impartial person that, so far from taking dignity and responsibility upon him, he had shown himself only too ready to shrink from them when presented, and sink under them when imposed. Hence, therefore, any one who could think of accusing Moses of taking upon him, only proved himself totally ignorant of the man's real spirit and character. Assuredly, the one who could say to Joshua, "Enviest thou for my sake? Would God that all the Lord's people were prophets, and that the Lord would put His Spirit upon them!" was not very likely to take much upon him.

But on the other hand, if God calls out a man into prominence, if He qualifies him for work, if He fills and fits the vessel for special service, if He assigns a man his position, then of what possible use can it be for any one to quarrel with divine gift and divine appointment? In truth, nothing can be more absurd. "A man can receive nothing except it be given him from heaven." And therefore it must prove worse than useless for any one to assume to be or have aught, for all such assumption must prove hollow in the end. Men will, sooner or later, find their level; and nothing will stand but what is of God.

Korah and his company, therefore, were quarreling with God, and not with Moses and Aaron. These latter had been called of God to occupy a certain position and to do a certain work, and woe be to them if they refused. It was not they who had aimed at the position or assumed the work; they were ordained of God. This ought to have settled the question; and it would have settled it for all save restless, self-occupied rebels, who sought to undermine the true servants of God in order to exalt themselves. This is always the way with the promoters of sedition or disaffection. Their real object is to make themselves somebody. They talk loudly and very plausibly about the common rights and privileges of God's people; but in reality, they themselves are aiming at a position for which they are in no way qualified, and at privileges to which they have no right.

In point of fact, the matter is as simple as possible. Has God given a man his place to fill—his work to do? Who will question this? Well, then, let each one know his place and fill it—know his work and do it. It is the most senseless thing in the world for one to attempt to occupy another's post or do another's work. We were led to see this very distinctly when meditating on chapters 3 and 4 of this book. It must ever hold good. Korah had his work; Moses had his. Why should one envy another? It would be quite as reasonable to charge the sun, moon, and stars with taking too much upon them when they shine in their appointed spheres, as to charge any gifted servant of Christ therewith when he seeks to discharge the responsibility which his gift most surely imposes upon him. These luminaries serve in the place assigned them by the hand of the almighty Creator, and so long as Christ's servants do the same, it is charging them falsely to say that they take too much upon them.

Now this principle is of immense, importance in every assembly, large or small, under all circumstances where Christians are called to work together. It is a mistake to suppose that all the members of the body of Christ are called to places of prominence, or that any member can select his place in the body. It is wholly and absolutely a matter of divine appointment.

This is the clear teaching of 1 Corinthians 12. "The body is not one member, but many. If the foot shall say, Because I am not the hand, I am not of the body; is it therefore not of the body? And if the ear shall say, Because I am not the eye, I am not of the body; is it therefore not of the body? If the whole body were an eye, where were the hearing? If the whole were hearing, where were the smelling? But now *hath God set the members every one of them in the body, as it hath pleased Him*" (ver. 14-18).

Here lies the true, the *only* true source of ministry in the Church of God—the body of Christ. "God hath set the members." It is not one man appointing another; still less is it a man appointing himself. It is divine appointment or nothing, yea, worse than nothing—a daring usurpation of divine rights.

Now, looking at the subject in the light of that marvelous illustration of 1 Corinthians 12, what sense would there be in the feet charging the hands, or the ears charging the eyes, with taking too much upon them? Would not the notion be preposterous in the extreme? True, those members occupy a prominent place in the body; but why do they? Because "God has set them there as it pleased Him." And what are they doing in that prominent place? They are doing the work which God has given them to do. And to what end? The good of the whole body. There is not a single member, however obscure, that does not derive positive benefit from the duly discharged functions of the prominent member. On the other hand, the prominent member is a debtor to the duly discharged functions of the obscure one. Let the eyes lose their power of vision, and every member will feel it; let there be functional derangement in the most trivial member, and the most honorable member will suffer.

Hence, therefore, it is not a question of taking upon us much or little, but of doing our appointed work, and filling our appointed place. It is by the effectual working of all the members, according to the measure of every part, that the edification of the whole body is promoted. If this great truth be not seized and carried out, edification, so far from being promoted, is most positively hindered; the Holy Ghost is quenched and grieved; the sovereign rights of Christ are denied; and God is dishonored. Every Christian is responsible to act on this divine principle, and to testify against every thing that practically denies it. The fact of the ruin of the professing church is no reason whatever for abandoning the truth of God, or sanctioning any denial of it. The Christian is always solemnly bound to submit himself to the revealed mind of God. To plead circumstances as an excuse for doing wrong, or for neglecting any truth of God, is simply flying in the face of divine authority, and making God the author of our disobedience.

But we cannot pursue this subject further. We have merely referred to it here in connection with our chapter, with which we must now proceed. It is undoubtedly a most solemn page of Israel's wilderness story.

Korah and his company were very speedily taught the folly and sin of their rebellious movement. They were awfully wrong in daring to set themselves up against the true servants of God. As to Moses, the man against whom they were gathered together, when he heard their seditious words, "he fell upon his face." This was a very good way to meet rebels. We have seen this beloved servant of God on his face when he ought to have been on his feet (Exod. 14), but here it was about the best and safest thing he could do. There is never much use in contending with restless and disaffected people; better far leave them in the Lord's hands; for with Him, in reality, is their controversy. If God sets a man in a certain position, and gives him a certain work to do, and his fellows think proper to quarrel with him, simply on the score of his doing that work, and filling that position, then is their quarrel really with God, who knows how to settle it, and will do it in His own way. The assurance of this gives holy calmness and moral elevation to the Lord's servant in moments when envious and turbulent spirits rise up against him. It is hardly possible for any one to occupy a prominent place of service, or to be pre-eminently used of God, without, at some time or another, having to encounter the attacks of certain radical and discontented men, who cannot bear to see any one more honored than themselves. But the true way to meet such is to take the place of utter prostration and nothingness, and allow the tide of disaffection to roll over one.

"And when Moses heard it, he fell upon his face: and he spake unto Korah and all his company, saying, 'Even to-morrow *the Lord will show* [not Moses will show] who are His, and who is holy; and will cause him to come near unto Him: even him whom *He hath chosen* will He cause to come near unto Him. This do: Take you censers, Korah, and all his company; and put fire therein, and put incense in them *before the Lord* to-morrow: and it shall be that the man whom *the Lord doth choose,* he shall be holy: ye take too much upon you, ye sons of Levi' " (ver. 4-7).

This was placing the matter in the proper hands. Moses gives great prominence to the sovereign rights of Jehovah. "The Lord will show," and, "The Lord will choose." There is not a syllable about himself or Aaron. The whole question hinges upon the Lord's choice and the Lord's appointment. The two hundred and fifty rebels are brought face to face with the living God. They are summoned into His presence, with their censers in their hands, in order that the whole matter may be thoroughly gone into and definitely settled before that grand tribunal from which there can be no appeal. It would, obviously, have been of no possible use for Moses and Aaron to attempt to give judgment, inasmuch as they were defendants in the cause; but Moses was blessedly willing to have all parties summoned into the divine presence, there to have their matters judged and determined.

This was true humility and true wisdom. It is always well, when people are seeking a place, to let them have it, to their heart's content; for, most assuredly, the very place after which they have foolishly aspired will be the scene of their signal defeat and deplorable confusion. You may sometimes see men envying others in a certain sphere of service, and longing to occupy that sphere themselves. Let them try it; and they are sure, in the end, to break down and retire covered with shame and confusion of face. The Lord will surely confound all such. There is no use in man trying to do it; and hence it is always best for such as may happen to be the objects of envious attack just to fall on their faces before God, and let Him settle the question with the malcontents. It is most sad when such scenes occur in the history of God's people; but they have occurred, they do occur, and they may occur again and again; and we feel assured that the very best plan is, to let men of a restless, ambitious, disaffected spirit run to the full length of their tether, and then they are sure to be pulled up. It is, in point of fact, to leave them in the hands of God, who will most surely deal with them in His own perfect way.

"And Moses said unto *Korah*, 'Hear, I pray you, ye sons of Levi: Seemeth it but a small thing unto you that the God of Israel hath separated you from the congregation of Israel, to bring you near to Himself to do the service of the tabernacle of the Lord, and to stand before the congregation to minister unto them? And He hath brought *thee* near unto Him, and all thy brethren the sons of Levi with thee; and *seek ye the priesthood* also? For which cause both thou and all thy company are gathered together against the Lord: and what is Aaron, that ye murmur against him?' " (ver 8-11)

Here we are conducted to the very root of this terrible conspiracy. We see the man who originated it, and the object at which he aimed. Moses addresses Korah, and charges him with aiming at the priesthood. Let the reader carefully note this. It is important that he should have this point clearly before his mind, according to the teaching of Scripture. He must see what Korah was, what his work was, and what the object of his restless ambition was,—he must see all these things if he would understand the true force and meaning of Jude's expression—"The gainsaying of Core."

What, then, was Korah? He was a Levite, and as such, he was entitled to minister and to teach. "They shall teach Jacob Thy judgments, and Israel Thy law." "The God of Israel hath brought you near to Himself, to do the service of the tabernacle of the Lord, and to stand before the congregation to minister unto them." Such was Korah, and such his sphere of work. At what did he aim? *At the priesthood.* "Seek ye the priesthood also?"

Now, to a cursory observer it might not have appeared that Korah was seeking any thing for himself. He seemed to be contending for the rights of the whole assembly. But Moses, by the Spirit of God, unmasks the man, and shows that, under the plausible pretext of standing up for the common rights of the congregation, he was audaciously seeking the priesthood for himself. It is well to note this. It will most generally be found that loud talkers about the liberties, rights, and privileges of God's people are, in reality, seeking their own exaltation and advantage. Not content with doing their proper work, they are seeking an improper place. This is not always apparent; but God is sure to make it manifest, sooner or later, for "by Him actions are weighed." Nothing can be more worthless than seeking a place for one's self. It is sure to end in disappointment and confusion. The grand thing for each one is, to be found filling his appointed place, and doing his appointed work; and the more humbly, quietly, and unpretendingly, the better.

But Korah had not learnt this simple, but wholesome, principle. He was not content with his divinely appointed place and service, but aimed at something which did not belong to him at all,—he aimed at being a priest. His sin was the sin of rebellion against God's high-priest. This was "the gainsaying of Core."

It is important to seize this fact in Korah's history. It is not generally understood; and hence it is that his sin is charged, nowadays, upon those who seek to exercise any gift which may have been bestowed upon them by the Head of the Church. But a moment's calm reflection upon the subject in the light of Scripture would be quite sufficient to show how utterly baseless is such a charge. Take, for example, a man to whom Christ has manifestly given the gift of an evangelist. Are we to suppose him guilty of the sin of Korah because, in pursuance of the divine gift and the divine commission, he goes forth to preach the gospel? Should he preach? or should he not preach? Is the divine gift—the divine call—sufficient? Is he acting as a rebel when he preaches the gospel?

So also as regards a pastor or teacher. Is he guilty of the sin of Korah because he exercises the special gift imparted to him by the Head of the Church? Does not Christ's gift make a man a minister? is any thing further necessary? Is it not plain, to any unprejudiced mind—to any one willing to be taught by Scripture, that the possession of a divinely imparted gift makes a man a minister, without any thing further whatsoever? And is it not equally plain that though a man had every thing else that could be had, and yet had no gift from the Head of the Church, he is no minister? We confess we do not see how these plain propositions can be called in question.

We are speaking, be it remembered, of special gifts of ministry in the Church. No doubt, every member in the body of Christ has some ministry to fulfill, some work to do. This is understood by every well-instructed Christian; and, moreover, it is clear that the edification of the body is carried on, not merely by some special prominent gifts, but by the effectual working of all the members in their respective places, as we read in the Epistle to the Ephesians—"But speaking the truth in love, may grow up into Him in all things, which is the head, even Christ: from whom the whole body fitly joined together, and compacted by that which *every joint supplieth,* according to *the effectual working in the measure of every part,* maketh increase of the body unto the edifying of itself in love" (chap. 4:15-16).

All this is as plain as Scripture can make it. But as to any special gifts, such as that of evangelist, pastor, prophet, or teacher, it must be received from Christ alone; and the possession of it makes a man a minister, without any thing further. And, on the other hand, all the education and all the human authority under the sun could not make a man an evangelist, a pastor, or teacher, unless he has a *bona-fide* gift from the Head of the Church.

Thus much as to ministry in the Church of God. We trust enough has been said to prove to the reader that it is a very grave mistake indeed to charge men with the awful sin of Korah because they exercise those gifts which have been imparted to them by the great Head of the Church. In point of fact, it would be a sin not to exercise them.

But there is a very material difference between ministry and priesthood. Korah did not aim at being a minister, for that he was. He aimed at being a priest, which he could not be. The priesthood was vested in Aaron and his family; and it was a daring usurpation for any one else, no matter who, to attempt to offer sacrifice, or discharge any other priestly function. Now, Aaron was a type of our great High-Priest, who is passed into the heavens—Jesus, the Son of God. Heaven is the sphere of His ministry. "If He were on earth, He should not be a priest" (Heb. 8:4). "Our Lord sprang out of Juda; of which tribe Moses spake nothing concerning priesthood." There is no such thing as a priest on earth now, save in the sense in which all believers are priests. Thus we read in Peter, "But ye are a chosen generation, a royal priesthood" (chap. 2:9). Every Christian is a priest in this sense of the term. The very feeblest saint in the Church of God is as much a priest as Paul was. It is not a question of capacity, or spiritual power, but simply of position. All believers are priests, and they are called to offer spiritual sacrifices, according to Hebrews 13:

15-16—"By Him therefore let us offer the *sacrifice of praise* to God continually, that is, the fruit of our lips, giving thanks to His name. But to do good and to communicate forget not; for with *such sacrifices* God is well pleased."

This is the Christian priesthood. And let the reader note it carefully, that to aim at any other form of priesthood than this—to assume any other priestly function—to set up a certain priestly class—a sacerdotal *caste*—a number of men to act on behalf of their fellows, or discharge priestly service for them before God,—this is, in principle, the sin of Korah. We only speak of the principles, not of persons. The germ of the sin is as distinct as possible. By and by there will be the full-blown fruit.

The reader cannot possibly be too simple in apprehending this entire subject. It is, we may truly say, of capital importance at this moment. Let him examine it only in the light of holy Scripture. Tradition will not do; ecclesiastical history will not do: it must be God's Word alone. In the light of that Word, let the question be asked and answered, Who are justly chargeable with the sin of Korah? Is it those who seek to exercise whatever gifts the Head of the Church has bestowed, or those who assume a priestly office and work which only belong to Christ Himself? This is a very weighty and solemn question. May it be calmly pondered, in the divine presence; and may we seek grace to be faithful to Him who is not only our gracious Saviour, but our sovereign Lord.

The remainder of our chapter presents a most solemn picture of divine judgment executed upon Korah and his company. The Lord very speedily settled the question raised by those rebellious men. The very record of it is appalling beyond expression. What must the fact have been? The earth opened her mouth and swallowed up the three principal movers in the rebellion, and the fire of the Lord went forth and consumed the two hundred and fifty men who undertook to offer incense.

"And Moses said, 'Hereby ye shall know that the Lord hath sent me to do all these works; for *I have not done them of mine own mind.* If these men die the common death of all men or if they be visited after the visitation of all men; then the Lord hath not sent me. But if the Lord make a new thing, and the earth open her mouth, and swallow them up, with all that appertain unto them, and they go down quick into the pit; then ye shall understand that these men have provoked the Lord' " (ver. 28-30).

Moses, in these words, makes it a question simply between Jehovah and the rebels. He can appeal to God, and leave all in His hands. This is the true secret of moral power. A man who has nothing of his own to seek—no aim or object but the divine glory—can confidently wait the issue of things. But in order to do this, the eye must be single, the heart upright, the purpose pure. It will not do to assume or affect any thing. If God is going to judge, He most assuredly will expose all assumption and affectation. These things can have no place when the earth is opening her mouth, and the fire of the Lord is devouring all around. It is all very well to swagger and boast, and speak great swelling words when all is at rest; but when God enters the scene, in terrible judgment, the aspect of things is speedily changed.

"And it came to pass, as he had made an end of speaking all these words, that the ground clave asunder that was under them; and the earth opened her mouth, and swallowed them up, and their houses, and all the men that appertained unto Korah, and all their goods. They, and all that appertained to them, went down alive into the pit, and the earth closed upon them; and they perished from among the congregation. And all Israel that were round about them fled at the cry of them: for they said, 'Lest the earth swallow us up also' " (ver. 31-34).

Truly, "it is a fearful thing to fall into the hands of the living God." "God is greatly to be feared in the assembly of His saints, and to be had in reverence of all them that are round about Him." "Our God is a consuming fire." How much better it would have been for Korah had he rested content with his Levite service, which was of the very highest order. His work, as a Kohathite, was to carry some of the most precious vessels of the sanctuary; but he aimed at the priesthood, and fell into the pit.

Nor was this all. Hardly had the ground closed over the rebels when "there came out a fire from the Lord, and consumed the two hundred and fifty men that offered incense." It was a most terrific scene altogether—a signal and soul-subduing exhibition of divine judgment upon human pride and pretension. It is vain for a man to exalt himself against God, for He resisteth the proud, but giveth grace to the humble. What consummate folly for worms of the dust to lift themselves up against the almighty God! Poor man! he is more silly, by far, than the moth that rushes against the blaze that consumes it.

Oh to walk humbly with our God! to be content with His will! to be satisfied to fill a very humble niche, and to do the most unpretending work! This is true dignity and true happiness. If God gives us a crossing to sweep, let us sweep it, as under His eye and to His praise. The grand and all-essential point is, to be found doing the very work which He gives us to do, and occupying the very post to which He appoints us. Had Korah and his company learnt this, their piercing wail would never have terrified the hearts of their brethren. But no; they would be something, when they were nothing, and hence they went down into the pit. Pride and destruction are inseparably linked together in the moral government of God. This principle always holds good, however the measure may vary. Let us remember it. Let us seek to rise from the study of Numbers 16 with a deepened sense of the value of a humble and contrite spirit. We live at a moment in which man is pushing himself upward and onward. *"Excelsior"* is a very popular motto just now. Let us look well to our mode of interpreting and applying it. "He that exalteth himself shall be abased." If we are to be governed by the rule of God's kingdom, we shall find that the only way to get up is to go down. The One who now occupies the very highest place in heaven is the One who voluntarily took the very lowest place on earth (see Phil. 2:5-11).

Here is our example, as Christians; and here, too, the divine antidote against the pride and restless ambition of the men of this world. Nothing is more sad than to witness a pushing, bustling, forward, self-confident, spirit and style in those who profess to be followers of Him who was meek and lowly in heart. It is such a flagrant contradiction of the spirit and precepts of Christianity, and is a sure accompaniment of an unbroken condition of soul. It is utterly impossible for any one to indulge in a boastful, pretentious, self-confident spirit if ever he has really measured himself in the presence of God. To be much alone with God is the sovereign remedy for pride and self-complacency. May we know the reality of this in the secret of our own souls. May the good Lord keep us truly humble, in all our ways, simply leaning on Himself, and very, very little in our own eyes.

The closing paragraph of our chapter illustrates, in a most striking manner, the incorrigible evil of the natural heart. One might fondly hope that after the impressive scenes enacted in the presence of the congregation, deep and permanent lessons would be learnt. Having seen the earth open her mouth, having heard the heart-rending cry of the rebels as they descended into the pit, having seen the fire of the Lord coming forth and consuming, as in a moment, two hundred and fifty princes of the congregation—having witnessed such tokens of the divine judgment—such a display of divine power and majesty, one might suppose that the people would henceforth walk softly and humbly, and that the accents of discontent and rebellion would no more be heard in their tents.

Alas! man is not to be so taught. The flesh is utterly incurable. This truth is taught in every section and on every page of the volume of God. It is illustrated in the closing lines of Numbers 16: "But on the morrow." Think of that! It was not in a year, or a month, or even a week after the appalling scenes on which we have been dwelling, "but on the morrow, *all the congregation* [no longer a few daring spirits merely] murmured against Moses and against Aaron, saying, 'Ye have killed the people of the Lord.' And it came to pass, when the congregation was gathered against Moses and against Aaron, that they looked toward the tabernacle of the congregation; and, behold, the cloud covered it, and the glory of the Lord appeared. And Moses and Aaron came before the tabernacle of the congregation. And the Lord spake unto Moses, saying, 'Get you up from among this congregation, that I may consume them as in a moment'' (ver. 41-45).

Here is another opportunity for Moses. The whole congregation is again threatened with immediate destruction. All seems hopeless. The divine long-suffering seems at an end, and the sword of judgment is about to fall on the whole assembly. And now it appears that in that very priesthood which the rebels had despised lies the only hope for the people; and that the very men whom they had charged with killing the Lord's people, were God's instruments in saving their lives. "And Moses and Aaron fell upon their faces. And Moses said unto Aaron, 'Take a censer, and put fire therein from off the altar, and put on incense, and go quickly unto the congregation, and make an atonement for them: for there is wrath gone out from the Lord; the plague is begun.' And Aaron took as Moses commanded, and ran into the midst of the congregation; and, behold, the plague was begun among the people: and he put on incense, and made an atonement for the people. And he stood between the dead and the living; and the plague was stayed" (ver. 46-48).

It is here made very apparent that nothing but priesthood—even that very priesthood which had been so despised—could avail for a rebellious and stiff-necked people. There is something unspeakably blessed in this closing paragraph. There stands Aaron, God's high-priest, between the dead and the living, and from his censer a cloud of incense goes up before God. Impressive type of One greater than Aaron, who, having made a full and perfect atonement for the sins of His people, is ever before God in all the fragrance of His Person and work! Priesthood alone could bring the people through the wilderness. It was the rich and suited provision of divine grace. The people were indebted to intercession for their preservation from the just consequences of their rebellious murmurings. Had they been dealt with merely on the ground of justice, all that could be said was, "Let Me alone, that I may consume them in a moment."

This is the language of pure and inflexible justice. Immediate destruction is the work of justice: full and final preservation is the glorious and characteristic work of divine grace—grace reigning through righteousness. Had God dealt in mere justice with the people, His name would not have been declared, inasmuch as there is far more in His name than justice. There is love, mercy, goodness, kindness, long-suffering, deep and unfailing compassion. But none of these things could be seen had the people been consumed in a moment, and hence the name of Jehovah would not have been declared or glorified. "For My name's sake will I defer Mine anger, and for My praise will I refrain from thee, that I cut thee not off. . . . For Mine own sake, even for Mine own sake, will I do it; for how should My name be polluted? and I will not give My glory unto another" (Isa. 48:9,11).

How well it is for us that God acts towards us and for us and in us for the glory of His own name! How wonderful, too, that His glory should most fully shine—yea, could only be seen in that vast plan which His own heart has devised, in which He is revealed as "a just God and a Saviour." Precious title for a poor lost sinner! In it is wrapped up all that such an one can possibly need for time and eternity. It meets him in the depth of his need, as a guilty, hell-deserving one; bears him along through all the varied exigencies, trials, and sorrows of the wilderness; and, finally, conducts him to that bright and blessed world above, where sin and sorrow can never enter.

## *CHAPTERS 17–18*

THESE two chapters form a distinct section, in which we have presented to us the source, the responsibilities, and the privileges of priesthood. Priesthood is a divine institution. "No man taketh this honor unto himself, but he that is called of God, as was Aaron." This is made manifest in a most striking manner in chapter 17: "The Lord spake unto Moses, saying, 'Speak unto the children of Israel, and take of every one of them a rod according to the house of their fathers, of all their princes according to the house of their fathers twelve rods: write thou every man's name upon his rod. And thou shalt write Aaron's name upon the rod of Levi; for one rod shall be for the head of the house of their fathers. And thou shalt lay them up in the tabernacle of the congregation before the testimony, where I will meet with you. And it shall come to pass that the man's rod whom I shall choose shall blossom; and I will make to cease from Me the murmurings of the children of Israel, whereby they murmur against you.' And Moses spake unto the children of Israel, and every one of their princes gave him a rod apiece, for each prince one, according to their father's houses, even twelve rods; and the rod of Aaron was among their rods" (ver. 1-6).

What matchless wisdom shines in this arrangement! How completely is the matter taken out of man's hands and placed where alone it ought to be, namely, in the hands of the living God! It was not to be a man appointing himself, or a man appointing his fellow; but God appointing the man of His own selection. In a word, the question was to be definitively settled by God Himself, so that all murmurings might be silenced forever, and no one be able again to charge God's high-priest with taking too much upon him. The human will had nothing whatever to do with this solemn matter. The twelve rods, all in a like condition, were laid up before the Lord: man retired, and left God to act. There was no room, no opportunity, because there was no occasion, for human management. In the profound retirement of the sanctuary, far away from all man's thinkings, was the grand question of priesthood settled by divine decision; and being thus settled, it could never again be raised.

"And Moses laid up the rods before the Lord in the tabernacle of witness. And it came to pass that on the morrow, Moses went into the tabernacle of witness; and, behold, the rod of Aaron for the house of Levi was budded, and brought forth buds, and bloomed blossoms, and yielded almonds." Striking and beautiful figure of Him who was "declared to be the Son of God with power by resurrection from the dead"! The twelve rods were all alike lifeless; but God—the living God—entered the scene, and by that power peculiar to Himself, infused life into Aaron's rod, and brought it forth to view, bearing upon it the fragrant fruits of resurrection.

Who could gainsay this? The rationalist may sneer at it, and raise a thousand questions. Faith gazes on that fruit-bearing rod, and sees in it a lovely figure of the new creation, in the which all things are of God. Infidelity may argue on the ground of the apparent impossibility of a dry stick budding, blossoming, and bearing fruit in the course of one night. But to whom does it appear impossible? To the infidel—the rationalist—the skeptic. And why? Because he always shuts out God. Let us remember this. *Infidelity invariably shuts out God.* Its reasonings are carried on and its conclusions reached in midnight darkness. There is not so much as a single ray of true light in the whole of that sphere in which infidelity operates. It excludes the only source of light, and leaves the soul wrapped in the shades and deep gloom of a darkness that may be felt.

It is well for the young reader to pause here, and deeply ponder this solemn fact. Let him calmly and seriously reflect on this special feature of infidelity—rationalism—or skepticism. It begins, continues, and ends with shutting out God. It would approach the mystery of Aaron's budding, blossoming, fruit-bearing rod with a godless, audacious *"How?"* This is the infidel's great argument? He can raise ten thousand questions, but never settle one. He will teach you how to doubt, but never how to believe. He will lead you to doubt every thing, but gives you nothing to believe.

Such is infidelity. It is of Satan, who ever has been, is, and will be the great question-raiser. Wherever you trace Satan, you will always find him raising questions. He fills the heart with all sorts of "ifs" and "hows," and thus plunges the soul in thick darkness. If he can only succeed in raising a question, he has gained his point; but he is perfectly powerless with a simple soul that just believes that *God is,* and *God has spoken.* Here is faith's noble answer to the infidel's questions—its divine solution of all the infidel's difficulties. Faith always brings in the very One that infidelity always shuts out. It thinks with God; infidelity thinks without Him.

Hence, then, we would say to the Christian reader, and specially to the young Christian, never admit questions when God has spoken. If you do, Satan will have you under his foot in a moment. Your only security against him is found in that one impregnable, immortal sentence, "It is written." It will never do to argue with him on the ground of experience, of feeling, or of observation; it must be absolutely and exclusively on the ground of this, that God is, and that God has spoken. Satan can make no hand of this weighty argument at all. It is invincible. Every thing else he can shiver to pieces, but this confounds him and puts him to flight at once.

We see this very strikingly illustrated in the temptation of our Lord. The enemy, according to his usual way, approached the blessed One with *a question: "If* Thou be the Son of God." How did the Lord answer him? Did He say, I know I am the Son of God—I have had a testimony from the opened heavens, and from the descending and anointing Spirit—I feel and believe and realize that I am the Son of God? No; such was not His mode of answering the tempter. How then? *"It is written."* Such was the thrice-repeated answer of the obedient and dependent Man, and such must be the answer of every one who will overcome the tempter.

Thus, in reference to Aaron's budding rod, if any inquire, How can such a thing be? It is contrary to the laws of nature; and how could God traverse the established principles of natural philosophy? Faith's reply is sublimely simple. God can do as He pleases. The One who called worlds into existence could make a rod to bud, blossom, and bear fruit in a moment. Bring God in, and all is simple and plain as possible: leave God out, and all is plunged in hopeless confusion. The attempt to tie up (we speak with reverence) the almighty Creator of the vast universe by certain laws of nature, or certain principles of natural philosophy, is nothing short of impious blasphemy. It is almost worse than denying His existence altogether. It is hard to say which is the worse—the atheist, who says there is no God, or the rationalist, who maintains that He cannot do as He pleases.

We feel the immense importance of being able to see the real roots of all the plausible theories which are afloat at the present moment. The mind of man is busy forming systems, drawing conclusions, and reasoning in such a manner as virtually to exclude the testimony of holy Scripture altogether, and to shut out God from His own creation. Our young people must be solemnly warned as to this. They must be taught the immense difference between the facts of science and the conclusions of scientific men. A fact is a fact wherever you meet it, whether in geology, astronomy, or any other department of science; but men's reasonings, conclusions, and systems are another thing altogether. Now, Scripture will never touch the facts of science; but the reasonings of scientific men are constantly found in collision with Scripture. Alas! for such men! When such is the case, we must, with plain decision, denounce such reasonings altogether, and exclaim, with the apostle, "Let God be true, and every man a liar."

Gladly would we dwell upon this point, though it be a digression, for we deeply feel its seriousness; but we must, for the present, be content with solemnly urging upon the reader the necessity of giving to holy Scripture the supreme place in his heart and mind. We must bow down, with absolute submission, to the authority of, not "Thus saith the Church"—"Thus say the fathers"—"Thus say the doctors," but *"Thus saith the Lord"—"It is written."* This is our *only* security against the rising tide of infidelity, which threatens to sweep away the foundations of religious thought and feeling throughout the length and breadth of christendom. None will escape save those who are taught and governed by the Word of the Lord. May God increase the number of such.

We shall now proceed with our chapter.

"And Moses brought out all the rods from before the Lord unto all the children of Israel; and they looked, and took every man his rod. And the Lord said unto Moses, 'Bring Aaron's rod again before the testimony, to be kept for a token against the rebels; and thou shalt quite take away their murmurings from Me, that they die not.' And Moses did so; as the Lord commanded him, so did he" (ver. 9-11).

Thus the question was divinely settled. Priesthood is founded upon that precious grace of God which brings life out of death. This is the source of priesthood. It could be of no possible use for man to take any one of the eleven dead rods and make it the badge of priestly office. All the human authority under the sun could not infuse life into a dead stick, or make that stick the channel of blessing to souls. And so of all the eleven rods put together; there was not so much as a single bud or blossom throughout the whole. But where there were precious evidences of quickening power—refreshing traces of divine life and blessing—fragrant fruits of efficacious grace—there, and there alone, was to be found the source of that priestly ministry which could carry, not only a needy, but a murmuring and rebellious people through the wilderness.

Here we may naturally inquire, What about Moses' rod? why was it not amongst the twelve? The reason is blessedly simple. Moses' rod was the expression of power and authority: Aaron's rod was the lovely expression of that grace that quickens the dead, and calls those things that be not as though they were. Now, mere power or authority could not conduct the congregation through the wilderness. Power could crush the rebel,—authority might strike the sinner; but only mercy and grace could avail for an assembly of needy, helpless, sinful men, women, and children. The grace that could bring almonds out of a dead stick could bring Israel through the wilderness. It was only in connection with Aaron's budding rod that Jehovah could say, "Thou shalt *quite* take away the murmurings of the children of Israel from Me, that they die not." The rod of *authority* could not take away the *murmurers,* but the rod of *grace* could take away the *murmurs.*

The reader may refer, with interest and profit, to a passage in the opening of Hebrews 9, in connection with the subject of Aaron's rod. The apostle, in speaking of the ark of the covenant, says, "Wherein was the golden pot that had manna, and Aaron's rod that budded, and the tables of the covenant." This was in the wilderness. The rod and the manna were the provisions of divine grace for Israel's desert wanderings and desert need. But when we turn to 1 Kings 8:9, we read, "There was nothing in the ark save the two tables of stone, which Moses put there at Horeb, when the Lord made a covenant with the children of Israel, when they came out of the land of Egypt." The wilderness wanderings were over, the glory of Solomon's day was sending forth its beams over the land, and hence the budding rod and the pot of manna are omitted, and nothing remains save that law of God which was the foundation of His righteous government in the midst of His people.

Now, in this we have an illustration, not only of the divine accuracy of Scripture as a whole, but also of the special character and object of the book of Numbers. Aaron's rod was in the ark during its wilderness wanderings. Precious fact! Let the reader seek to lay hold of its deep and blessed significance. Let him ponder the difference between the rod of Moses and the rod of Aaron. We have seen the former doing its characteristic work in other days and amid other scenes; we have seen the land of Egypt trembling beneath the heavy strokes of that rod; plague after plague fell upon that devoted scene in answer to that outstretched rod; we have seen the waters of the sea divided in answer to that rod. In short, the rod of Moses was a rod of power—a rod of authority. But it could not avail to hush the murmurings of the children of Israel, nor yet to bring the people through the desert. Grace alone could do that; and we have the expression of pure grace—free, sovereign grace—in the budding of Aaron's rod.

Nothing can be more forcible, nothing more lovely. That dry, dead stick was the apt figure of Israel's condition, and indeed of the condition of every one of us by nature. There was no sap, no life, no power. One might well say, "What good can ever come of it?" None whatever, had not grace come in and displayed its quickening power. So was it with Israel in the wilderness, and so is it with us now. How were they to be led along from day to day? how were they to be sustained in all their weakness and need? how were they to be borne with in all their sin and folly? The answer is found in Aaron's budding rod. If the dry, dead stick was the expression of nature's barren and worthless condition, the buds, blossoms, and fruit set forth that living and life-giving grace and power of God on which was based the priestly ministry that alone could bear the congregation through the wilderness. Grace alone could answer the ten thousand necessities of the militant host. Power could not suffice, authority could not avail: priesthood alone could supply what was needed, and this priesthood was instituted on the foundation of that efficacious grace which could bring fruit out of a dry rod.

Thus it was as to priesthood of old, and thus it is as to ministry now. All ministry in the Church of God is the fruit of divine grace—the gift of Christ, the Church's Head. There is no other source of ministry whatsoever. From apostles down to the very lowest gifts—all proceed from Christ. The grand root-principle of all ministry is embodied in those words of Paul to the Galatians in which he speaks of himself as "an apostle, not of men, neither by man, but by Jesus Christ, and God the Father, who raised Him from the dead" (Gal. 1:1).

Here, be it noted, is the sublime source from whence all ministry emanates. It is not of man, or by man, in any shape or form. Man may take up dry sticks and shape and fashion them according to his own will, and he may ordain and appoint, and call them by certain high-sounding, official titles; but of what use is it? they are only dry, dead sticks. We may justly say, "Where is there a single cluster of fruit? where is there a single blossom? nay, where is there one solitary bud?" Even one bud will suffice to prove that there is something divine; but in the absence of this, there can be no living ministry in the Church of God. It is the gift of Christ, and that alone, that makes a man a minister. Without this, it is an empty assumption for any one to set himself up, or be set up by others, to be a minister.

Does the reader thoroughly own this great principle? is it as clear as a sunbeam to his soul? Has he any difficulty respecting it? If so, we entreat him to seek to divest his mind of all preconceived thoughts, from what source soever derived; let him rise above the hazy mists of traditional religion; let him take the New Testament, and study, as in the immediate presence of God, the twelfth and fourteenth chapters of 1 Corinthians, and also Ephesians 4:7-12. In these passages he will find the whole subject of ministry unfolded, and from them he will learn that all true ministry, whether it be apostles, prophets, teachers, pastors, or evangelists,—all is of God—all flows down from Christ, the exalted Head of the Church. If a man be not possessed of a *bona-fide* gift from Christ, he is not a minister. Every member of the body has a work to do. The edification of the body is promoted by the proper action of all the members, whether prominent or obscure, "comely" or "uncomely." In short, all ministry is from God, and not from man; it is by God, and not by man. There is no such thing in Scripture as a humanly ordained ministry. All is of God.

We must not confound ministerial gifts with office or local charge. We find the apostles, or their delegates, ordaining elders and appointing deacons; but this was quite a distinct thing from ministerial gifts. Those elders and deacons might possess and exercise some specific gift in the body; the apostle did not ordain them to exercise such gift, but only to fulfill the local charge. The spiritual gift was from the Head of the Church, and was independent of the local charge altogether.

It is most necessary to be clear as to the distinction between gift and local charge. There is the utmost confusion of the two things throughout the entire professing church, and the consequence is that ministry is not understood. The members of the body of Christ do not understand their place or their functions. Human election, or human authority in some shape or another, is deemed essential to the exercise of ministry in the Church. But there is really no such thing in Scripture. If there be, nothing is easier than to produce it. We ask the reader to find a single line, from cover to cover of the New Testament, in which a human call, human appointment, or human authority has any thing whatsoever to do with the exercise of ministry in its very fullest range. We boldly assert there is no such thing.* Ah! no; blessed be God, ministry in His Church is "not of men, neither by man, but by Jesus Christ, and God the Father, who raised Him from the dead." "*God hath set* the members *every one of them* in the body, *as it hath pleased Him*" (1 Cor. 12:18). "But unto every one of us is given grace according to the measure of the gift of Christ. Wherefore He saith, 'When He ascended up on high, He led captivity captive, and gave gifts unto men.' . . . And He gave some, apostles; and some, prophets; and some, evangelists; and some, pastors and teachers; for the perfecting of the saints, for the work of the ministry, for the edifying of the body of Christ: till we all come in the unity of the faith, and of the knowledge of the Son of God, unto a perfect man, unto the measure of the stature of the fullness of Christ" (Eph. 4:7-13).

Here, all the grades of ministerial gift are placed on one and the same ground, from apostles down to evangelists and teachers. They are all given by the Head of the Church; and when bestowed, they render the possessors responsible at once to the Head in heaven and to the members on earth. The idea of any possessor of a positive gift from God waiting for human authority is as great an insult to the Divine Majesty as if Aaron had gone, with his blooming rod in his hand, to be ordained to the priesthood by some of his fellows. Aaron knew better. He was called of God, and that was quite enough for him. And so now, all who possess a divine gift are called of God to the ministry, and they need nothing more, save to wait on their ministry and cultivate their gift.

Need we add that it is vain for men to set up to be ministers unless they really do possess the gift? A man may fancy he has a gift, and it may be only a vain conceit of his own mind. It is quite as bad, if not worse, for one man to go to work on the strength of his own foolish imagination, as for another to go on the strength of the unwarrantable authority of his fellows. What we contend for is this: Ministry is of God, as to its source, power, and responsibility. We do not think that this statement will be called in question by any who are disposed to be taught exclusively by Scripture. Every minister, whatever be his gift, should be able, in his measure, to say, "God has put me into the ministry." But for a man to use this language without possessing any gift, is, to say the least of it, worse than worthless. The people of God can easily tell where

---

*Even in the matter of appointing deacons, in Acts 6 we see it was an apostolic act. "Wherefore, brethren, look ye out among you seven men of honest report, full of the Holy Ghost and wisdom, whom *we may appoint* over this business." The brethren were allowed to *select* the men, inasmuch as it was their money that was in question; but the *appointment* was divine; and this, be it remembered, had reference merely to the business of deacons who were to manage the Church's temporal affairs. But as regards the work of evangelists, pastors, and teachers, it is wholly independent of human choice and human authority, and rests simply upon the gift of Christ (Eph. 4:11).

there is real spiritual gift. Power is sure to be felt. But if men pretend to gift or power without the reality, their folly shall speedily be manifest to all. All pretenders are sure to find their true level, sooner or later.

Thus much as to ministry and priesthood. The source of each is divine. The true foundation of each lies in the budding rod. Let this be ever borne in mind. Aaron could say, "God put me into the priesthood;" and if challenged for his proof, he could point to the fruit-bearing rod. Paul could say, "God put me into the ministry;" and when challenged for his proof, could point to the thousands of living seals of his work. Thus it must ever be in principle, whatever be the measure. Ministry must not be merely in word or in tongue, but in deed and in truth. God will not know the speech, but the power.

But ere we turn from this subject, we deem it most necessary to impress upon the reader the importance of distinguishing between ministry and priesthood. The sin of Korah consisted in this: that, not content with being a minister, he aimed at being a priest; and the sin of christendom is of the same character. Instead of allowing ministry to rest upon its own proper New Testament basis, to exhibit its proper characteristics and discharge its proper functions, it is exalted into a priesthood, a sacerdotal caste, the members of which are distinguished from their brethren by their style of dress and certain titles. There is no foundation whatsoever for these things in the New Testament. According to the plain teaching of that blessed book, all believers are priests. Thus, in Peter, we read, "But *ye* [not merely the apostles, but all believers] are a chosen generation, *a royal priesthood*" (1 Pet. 2:9). So also in Revelation—"Unto Him that loved us, and washed us from our sins in His own blood, and hath made us kings and *priests* unto God and His Father" (chap. 1:5-6). And, in pursuance of the truth set forth in the foregoing passages, we find the apostle Paul, by the Holy Ghost, exhorting the Hebrew believers to draw nigh, and enter with boldness into the very holiest of all" (chap. 10:19-22). And further on he says, "By Him therefore [*i.e.*, Jesus] let us *offer the sacrifice* of praise to God continually, that is, the fruit of our lips giving thanks to His name. But to do good and to communicate forget not; for with *such sacrifices* God is well pleased" (Heb. 13:15-16).

How marvelous it must have appeared to Jewish saints—to those trained amid the institutions of the Mosaic economy, to be exhorted to enter into a place to which the very highest functionary in Israel could only approach once a year, and that but for a moment! and then to be told that they were to offer sacrifice—that they were to discharge the peculiar functions of the priesthood! All this was wonderful. But thus it is, if we are to be taught by Scripture, and not by the commandments, the doctrines, and the traditions of men. All Christians are priests. They are not all apostles, prophets, teachers, pastors, or evangelists; but they are all priests. The very feeblest member of the Church was as much a priest as Peter, Paul, James, or John. We speak not of capacity or spiritual power, but of the position which all occupy in virtue of the blood of Christ. There is no such thing in the New Testament as a certain class of men, a certain privileged caste, brought into a higher or nearer position than their brethren. All this is flatly opposed to Christianity—a bold traversing of all the precepts of the Word of God, and the special teachings of our blessed Lord and Master.

Let no one suppose that these things are unimportant. Far from it. They affect the very foundations of Christianity. We have only to open our eyes and look around us in order to see the practical results of this confounding of ministry and priesthood. And we may rest assured that the moment is rapidly approaching when these results shall assume a far more awful character, and bring down the very heaviest judgments from the living God. We have not yet seen the full antitype of "the gain-saying of Core," but it will soon be manifested; and we solemnly warn the Christian reader to take heed how he lends his sanction to the serious error of mixing up two things so entirely distinct as ministry and priesthood. We would exhort him to take this whole subject up in the light of Scripture. We want him to submit to the authority of God's Word, and to abandon every thing that is not founded thereon. It matters not what it is—it may be a time-honored institution, an expedient arrangement, a decent ceremony supported by tradition and countenanced by thousands of the very best of men. It matters not. If the thing has no foundation in holy Scripture, it is an error and an evil and a snare of the devil, to entrap our souls and lead us away from the simplicity that is in Christ. For example, if we are taught that there is, in the Church of God, a sacerdotal caste—a class of men more holy, more elevated, nearer to God, than their brethren—than ordinary Christians, what is this but Judaism revived and tacked on to Christian forms? and what must be the effect of this, but to rob the children of God of their proper privileges as such, and to put them at a distance from Him, and place them under bondage?

We shall not pursue this subject any further just now. Enough, we trust, has been suggested to lead the reflecting reader to follow it up for himself. We only add, and that with special emphasis, let him follow it up *only* in the light of Scripture. Let him resolve, by the grace of God, to lay aside every thing which rests not upon the solid and sacred basis of the written Word. Thus, and thus alone, can he be preserved from every form of error, and led to a sound conclusion on this most important and interesting question.

The closing lines of chapter 17 furnish a remarkable illustration of how quickly the human mind passes from one extreme to another. "The children of Israel spake unto Moses, saying, 'Behold, we die, we perish, we all perish. Whosoever cometh any where near unto the tabernacle of the Lord shall die: shall we be consumed with dying?' " In the preceding chapter, we see bold presumption in the very presence of the majesty of Jehovah, where there should have been profound humility. Here, in the presence of divine grace and its provisions, we observe legal fear and distrust. Thus it is ever. Mere nature neither understands holiness nor grace. At one moment we hearken to such accents as these: "*All* the congregation are holy;" and the next moment, the word is, "Behold, we die, we perish, we all perish." The carnal mind presumes where it ought to retire; it distrusts where it ought to confide.

However, all this becomes the occasion, through the goodness of God, of unfolding to us, in a very full and blessed manner, the holy responsibilities, as well as the precious privileges, of the priesthood. How gracious it is—how like our God, to turn His people's mistakes into an occasion of furnishing deeper instruction as to His ways! It is His prerogative, blessed be His name, to bring good out of evil—to make the eater yield meat, and the strong, sweetness. Thus "the gainsaying of Core" gives occasion for the copious volume of instruction furnished by Aaron's rod, and the closing lines of chapter 17 call forth an elaborate statement of the functions of Aaron's priesthood. To this latter we shall now proceed to direct the reader's attention.

"And the Lord said unto Aaron, 'Thou and thy sons and thy father's house with thee, shall bear the iniquity of the sanctuary; and thou and thy sons with thee shall bear the iniquity of your priesthood. And thy brethren also of the tribe of Levi, the tribe of thy father, bring thou with thee, that they may be joined unto thee, and minister unto thee: but thou and thy sons with thee shall minister before the tabernacle of witness. And they shall keep thy charge, and the charge of all the tabernacle: only they shall not come nigh the vessels of the sanctuary and the altar, that neither they nor ye also die. And they shall be joined unto thee, and keep the charge of the tabernacle of the congregation, for all the service of the tabernacle: and a stranger shall not come nigh unto you. And ye shall keep the charge of the sanctuary, and the charge of the altar: *that there be no wrath any more upon the children of Israel.* And I, behold, I have taken your brethren the Levites from among the children of Israel: to you they are given as a gift for the Lord, to do the service of the tabernacle of the congregation. Therefore thou and thy sons with thee shall keep your priest's office for every thing of the altar, and within the vail; and ye shall serve: I have given your priest's office unto you as a service of gift: and the stranger that cometh nigh shall be put to death' " (chap. 18:1-7).

Here we have a divine answer to the question raised by the children of Israel—"Shall we be consumed with dying?" "No," says the God of all grace and mercy. And why not? Because "Aaron and his sons with him shall keep the charge of the sanctuary, and the charge of the altar; that there be *no wrath any more* upon the children of Israel." Thus the people are taught that in that very priesthood which had been so despised and spoken against, they were to find their security.

But we have to notice particularly that Aaron's sons, and his father's house, are associated with him in his high and holy privileges and responsibilities. The Levites were given as a gift to Aaron, to do the service of the tabernacle of the congregation. They were to serve under Aaron, the head of the priestly house. This teaches us a fine lesson, and one much needed by Christians at the present moment. We all want to bear in mind that service, to be intelligent and acceptable, must be rendered in subjection to priestly authority and guidance. "And thy brethren also of the tribe of Levi, the tribe of thy father, bring thou with thee, that they may be *joined unto thee,* and *minister unto thee.*" This stamped its distinct character upon the entire range of Levite service. The whole tribe of workers were associated with and subject to the great high-priest. All was under his immediate control and guidance. So must it be now, in reference to all God's workers. All Christian service must be rendered in fellowship with our great High-Priest, and in holy subjection to His authority. It is of no value otherwise. There may be a great deal of work done, there may be a great deal of activity; but if Christ be not the immediate object before the heart, if His guidance and authority be not fully owned, the work must go for nothing.

But, on the other hand, the smallest act of service, the meanest work done under the eye of Christ—done with direct reference to Him, has its value in God's estimation, and shall most assuredly receive its due reward. This is truly encouraging, and consolatory to the heart of every earnest worker. The Levites had to work under Aaron: Christians have to work under Christ—we are responsible to Him. It is very well and very beautiful to walk in fellowship with our dear fellow-workmen, and to be subject one to another, in the fear of the Lord. Nothing is further from our thoughts than to foster or countenance a spirit of haughty independence, or that temper of soul which would hinder our genial and hearty co-operation with our brethren in every good work. All the Levites were "joined unto Aaron" in their work, and therefore they were joined one to another; hence they had to work together. If a Levite had turned his back upon his brethren, he would have turned his back upon Aaron. We may imagine a Levite taking offense at something or other in the conduct of his fellows, and saying to himself, I cannot get on with my brethren. I must walk alone. I can serve God, and work under Aaron; but I must keep aloof from my brethren, inasmuch as I find it impossible to agree with them as to the mode of working. But we can easily see through the fallacy of all this. For a Levite to adopt such a line of action would have produced nothing but confusion. All were called to work together, how varied soever their work might be.

Still, be it ever borne in mind, their work did vary; and, moreover, each was called to work under Aaron. There was individual responsibility with the most harmonious corporate action. We certainly desire, in every possible way, to promote unity in action; but this must never be suffered to trench upon the domain of personal service, or to interfere with the direct reference of the individual workman to his Lord. The Church of God affords a very extensive platform to the Lord's workers. There is ample space thereon for all sorts of laborers. We must not attempt to reduce all to a dead level, or cramp the varied energies of Christ's servants by confining them to certain old ruts of our own formation. This will never do. We must, all of us, diligently seek to combine the most cordial unanimity with the greatest possible variety in action. Both will be healthfully promoted by each and all remembering that we are called to serve together under Christ.

Here lies the grand secret. *Together, under Christ!* May we bear this in mind. It will help us to recognize and appreciate another's line of work though it may differ from our own; and, on the other hand, it will preserve us from an overweening sense of our own department of service, inasmuch as we shall see that we are, one and all, but co-workers in the one wide field, and that the great object before the Master's heart can only be attained by each worker pursuing his own special line, and pursuing it in happy fellowship with all.

There is a pernicious tendency in some minds to depreciate every line of work save their own. This must be carefully guarded against. If all were to pursue the same line, where were that lovely variety which characterizes the Lord's work and workmen in the world? Nor is it merely a question of the line of work, but actually of the peculiar style of each workman. You may find two evangelists, each marked by an intense desire for the salvation of souls, each preaching substantially the same truth, and yet there may be the greatest possible variety in the mode in which each one seeks to gain the self-same object. We should be prepared for this; indeed we should fully expect it. And the same holds good in reference to every other branch of Christian service. We should strongly suspect the ground occupied by a Christian assembly if there were not ample space allowed for every branch and style of Christian service—for every line of work capable of being taken up in individual responsibility to the great Head of the priestly house. We ought to do nothing which we cannot do under Christ, and in fellowship with Him; and all that can be done in fellowship with Christ can surely be done in fellowship with those who are walking with Him.

Thus much as to the special manner in which the Levites are introduced in our chapter, in connection with Aaron and his sons. To these latter we shall now turn for a few moments, and meditate on the rich provision made for them, in the goodness of God, as well as the solemn functions devolving upon them in their priestly place.

"And the Lord spake unto Aaron, 'Behold, I also have given thee the charge of My heave-offerings of all the hallowed things of the children of Israel; unto thee have I given them, *by reason of the anointing,* and to thy sons, by an ordinance forever. This shall be thine of the most holy things, reserved from the fire: every oblation of theirs, every meat-offering of theirs, and every sin-offering of theirs, and every trespass-offering of theirs, which they shall render unto Me, shall be most holy for thee and for thy sons. In the most holy place shalt thou eat it; *every male* shall eat it: it shall be holy unto thee' " (ver. 8-10).

Here we have a type of the people of God looked at in another aspect. They are here presented, not as workers, but as worshipers—not as Levites, but as priests. All believers—all Christians—all the children of God—are priests. There is, according to the teaching of the New Testament, no such thing as a priest upon earth, save in the sense in which all believers are priests. A special priestly *caste*—a certain class of men set apart as priests—is a thing not only unknown in Christianity, but most positively hostile to the spirit and principles thereof. We have already referred to this subject, and quoted the various passages of Scripture bearing upon it. We have a great High-Priest who has passed into the heavens, for if He were on earth, He should not be a priest. (Compare Heb. 4:14 and 8:4.) "Our Lord sprang out of Juda; of which tribe Moses spake nothing concerning priesthood." Hence, therefore, a sacrificing priest on the earth is a direct denial of the truth of Scripture, and a complete setting aside of the glorious fact on which Christianity is based, namely, accomplished redemption. If there is any need of a priest now, to offer sacrifice for sins, then, most assuredly, redemption is not an accomplished fact. But Scripture, in hundreds of places, declares that it is, and therefore we need no more offering for sin. "But Christ being come a High-Priest of good things to come, by a greater and more perfect tabernacle, *not made with hands,* that is to say, not of this building; neither by the blood of goats and calves, but by His own blood, He entered in once into the holy place, *having obtained eternal redemption*" (Heb. 9:11-12). So also, in chapter 10 we read, "By one offering He hath perfected forever them that are sanctified." And again, "Their sins and iniquities will I remember no more. Now where remission of these is, there is no more offering for sin."

This settles the great question as to priesthood and sacrifice for sin. Christians cannot be too clear or decided in reference to it. It lies at the very foundation of true Christianity, and demands the deep and serious attention of all who desire to walk in the clear light of a full salvation, and to occupy the true Christian position. There is a strong tendency towards Judaism—a vigorous effort to ingraft Christian forms upon the old Jewish stem. This is nothing new; but just now the enemy seems peculiarly busy. We can perceive a great leaning towards Romanism throughout the length and breadth of christendom; and in nothing is this leaning more strikingly apparent than in the institutions of a special priestly order in the Church of God. We believe it to be a thoroughly antichristian institution. It is the denial of the common priesthood of all believers. If a certain set of men are ordained to occupy a place of peculiar nearness and sanctity, then where are the great mass of Christians to stand?

This is the question. It is precisely here that the great importance and gravity of this whole subject are made apparent. Let not the reader suppose that we are contending for some peculiar theory of any particular class or sect of Christians. Nothing is further from our thoughts. It is because we are convinced that the very foundations of the Christian faith are involved in this question of priesthood that we urge its consideration upon all with whom we have to do. We believe it will invariably be found that in proportion as Christians become clear and settled on the divine ground of accomplished redemption, they get further and further away from the Romanism and Judaism of an order of priests in the Church of God. And, on the other hand, where souls are not clear, not settled, not spiritual—where there is legality, carnality, and worldliness, there you will find a hankering after a humanly appointed priesthood. Nor is it difficult to see the reason of this. If a man is not himself in a fit state to draw nigh to God, it will be a relief to him to employ another to draw nigh for him. And most certainly, no man is in a fit state to draw nigh to a holy God who does not know that his sins are forgiven—has not got a perfectly purged conscience—is in a dark, doubting, legal state of soul. In order to come boldly into the holiest of all, we must know what the blood of Christ has done for us; we must know that we ourselves are made priests to God; and that, in virtue of the atoning death of Christ, we are brought so near to God that it is impossible for any order of men to come between. "He hath loved us, and washed us from our sins in His own blood, and made us priests unto God and His Father" (Rev. 1). "But ye are a chosen generation, *a royal priesthood,* a holy nation, a peculiar people; that ye should show forth the praises of Him who hath called you out of darkness into His marvelous light." And again, "Ye also, as lively stones, are built up a spiritual house, *a holy priesthood,* to offer up *spiritual sacrifices,* acceptable to God by Jesus Christ" (1 Pet. 2:5,9). "By Him therefore let us offer the *sacrifice of praise* to God continually, that is, the fruit of our lips giving thanks to His name. But to do good and to communicate forget not, for with such sacrifices God is well pleased" (Heb. 13:15-16).

Here we have the two great branches of spiritual sacrifice which, as priests, we are privileged to offer, namely, praise to God, doing good to men. The very youngest, the most inexperienced, the most unlettered Christian is capable of understanding these things. Who is there in all the family of

God—in all the priestly household of our divine High-Priest, who cannot, with his *heart,* say, "The Lord be praised"? and who cannot, with his *hand,* do good to his fellow? And this is priestly worship and priestly service—the common worship and service of all true Christians. True, the measure of spiritual power may vary; but all the children of God are constituted priests, one as much as another.

Now, in the eighteenth chapter of Numbers we are presented with a very full statement of the provision made for Aaron and his house, and in that provision, a type of the spiritual portion of the Christian priesthood. And surely we cannot read the record without seeing what a royal portion is ours. "Every oblation of theirs, every meat-offering of theirs, and every sin-offering of theirs, and every trespass-offering of theirs, which they shall render unto Me, shall be most holy for thee and for *thy sons. In the most holy place* shalt thou eat it; *every male* shall eat it: it shall be holy unto thee."

It demands a very large measure of spiritual capacity to enter into the depth and meaning of this marvelous passage. To eat the sin-offering or the trespass-offering is, in figure, to make another's sin or trespass one's own. This is very holy work. It is not every one who can, in spirit, identify himself with the sin of his brother. To do so in fact, in the way of atonement, is, we need hardly say, wholly out of question. There was but one who could do this, and He—adored forever be His name!—has done it perfectly.

But there is such a thing as making my brother's sin my own, and bearing it in spirit before God, as though it were my own. This is shadowed forth by Aaron's sons eating the sin-offering in the most holy place. It was only the *sons* who did so.—"Every *male* shall eat it.* It was the very highest order of priestly service. "In the most holy place shalt thou eat it." We need to be very near to Christ in order to enter into the spiritual meaning and application of all this. It is a wonderfully blessed and holy exercise, and it can only be known in the immediate presence of God. How little we really know of this the heart can testify. Our tendency is, when a brother has sinned, to sit in judgment upon him—to take the place of a severe censor—to look upon his sin as a something with which we have nothing whatever to do. This is to fail sadly in our priestly functions—it is refusing to eat the sin-offering in the most holy place. It is a most precious fruit of grace to be able so to identify one's self with an erring brother as to make his sin one's own—to bear it, in spirit, before God.

This, truly, is a very high order of priestly service, and demands a large measure of the spirit and mind of Christ. It is only the spiritual who really enter into this; and, alas! how few of us are truly spiritual! "Brethren, if a man be overtaken in a fault, *ye which are spiritual,* restore such an one in the spirit of meekness; considering thyself, lest thou also be tempted. Bear ye one another's burdens, and so fulfill the law of Christ" (Gal. 6:1-2). May the Lord give us grace to fulfill this blessed "law." How unlike it is to every thing in us! How it rebukes our harshness and selfishness! Oh to be more like Christ in this as in all beside!

But there was another order of priestly privilege, not so high as that which we have been considering. "And this is thine: the heave-offering of their *gift,* with all the wave-offerings of the children of Israel: I have given them unto thee, and to thy sons and to thy *daughters* with thee, by a statute forever: *every one that is clean* in thy house shall eat of it" (ver. 11).

The daughters of Aaron were not to eat of the sin-offerings or the trespass-offerings. They were provided for according to the utmost limit of their capacity; but there were certain functions which they could not discharge—certain privileges which lay beyond their range—certain responsibilities too weighty for them to sustain. It is far easier to have fellowship with another in the presentation of a thank-offering than it is to

*As a general principle, the "son" presents the divine idea; the "daughter," the human apprehension thereof: the "male" sets forth the thing as God gives it; the "female," as we realize and exhibit it.

make his sin our own. This latter demands a measure of priestly energy which finds its type in Aaron's "sons," not in his "daughters." We must be prepared for those varied measures amongst the members of the priestly household. We are all, blessed be God, on the same ground; we all stand in the same title; we are all in the same relationship, but our capacities vary; and while we should all aim at the very highest standard of priestly service, and the very highest measure of priestly capacity, it is of no possible use to pretend to what we do not possess.

One thing, however, is clearly taught in verse 11, and that is, we must be *"clean"* in order to enjoy any priestly food—clean, through the precious blood of Christ applied to our conscience—clean, through the application of the Word, by the Spirit, to our habits, associations, and ways. When thus clean, whatever be our capacity, we have the richest provision made for our souls, through the precious grace of God. Hearken to the following words: *"All the best* of the oil, and *all the best* of the wine, and of the wheat, the first-fruits of them which they shall offer unto the Lord, them have I given thee. And whatsoever is *first ripe* in the land, which they shall bring unto the Lord, shall be thine; *every one that is clean* in thy house shall eat of it" (ver. 12-13).*

Here, assuredly, we have a princely portion provided for those who are made priests unto God. They were to have the very best and the very first of every thing which the Lord's land produced. There was "the wind which maketh glad the heart of man, and oil to make his face to shine, and bread which strengtheneth man's heart" (Ps. 104:15).

What a figure have we in all this of our portion in Christ! The olive, the grape, and the finest of the wheat were pressed and bruised, in order to feed and gladden the priests of God; and the blessed Antitype of all these has, in infinite grace, been bruised and crushed in death, in order that, by His flesh and blood, He might minister life, strength, and gladness to His household. He, the precious Corn of wheat, fell into the ground and died, that we might live; and the juices of the living Vine were pressed to fill that cup of salvation of which we drink now, and shall drink forever, in the presence of our God.

What, therefore, remains? What do we want, save an enlarged capacity to enjoy the fullness and blessedness of our portion in a crucified, risen, and glorified Saviour? We may well say, "We have all and abound." God has given us all that even He could give—the very best He had; He has given us His own portion; He has called us to sit down with Himself, in holy, happy fellowship, and feast upon the fatted calf; He has caused our ears to hear, and our hearts, in some small degree, to enter into these most marvelous words, "Let *us* eat and be merry."

How wonderful to think that nothing could satisfy the heart and mind of God but to gather His people around Himself and feed them with that in which He Himself delights! "Truly our fellowship is with the Father, and with His Son Jesus Christ" (1 John 1). What more could even the love of God do for us than this? And for whom has He done it? For those who were dead in trespasses and sins—for aliens, enemies, guilty rebels—for dogs of the Gentiles—for those who were far from Him, having no hope, and without God in the world—for those who, had we our deserts, should be now burning in the eternal flames of hell. Oh, what wondrous grace! what profound depths of sovereign mercy! and, we must add, what a divinely precious atoning sacrifice, to bring poor, self-destroyed, guilty, hell-deserving sinners into such ineffable blessedness!—to pluck us as brands from everlasting burnings, and make us priests to God!—to take away all our "filthy garments" from us, and cleanse, clothe, and crown us, in His own presence, and to His own praise! May we praise Him. May our

*Let the reader consider what the moral effect must be of taking the above passage literally and applying it to a certain priestly class in the Church of God. Take it typically and spiritually, and you have a striking and beautiful figure of the spiritual food provided for all the members of the priestly family, which is, in one word, Christ in all His preciousness and fullness.

hearts and lives praise Him. May we know how to enjoy our priestly place and portion, and to wear our mitre well. We can do nothing better than praise God—nothing higher than to present to Him, by Jesus Christ, the fruit of our lips giving thanks to His name. This shall be our everlasting employment in that bright and blessed world to which we are hastening, and where we shall soon be, to dwell forever with Him who has loved us and given Himself for us—our own blessed Saviour-God—to go no more out for evermore.

In verses 14-19 of our chapter we have instruction as to "the first-born of man and beast." We may remark that man is placed on a level with the unclean beast: both had to be redeemed. The unclean beast was unfit for God, and so was man, unless redeemed by blood. The clean animal was not to be redeemed; it was fit for God's use, and was given to be the food of the entire priestly household—sons and daughters alike. In this we have a type of Christ, in whom God can find His perfect delight—the full joy of His heart—the only object, throughout the wide universe, in which He could find perfect rest and satisfaction. And—wondrous thought!—He has given Him to us, His priestly household, to be our food, our light, our joy, our all in all, forever.*

Jesus, of Thee we ne'er would tire:
The new and living food
Can satisfy our heart's desire,
And life is in Thy blood.

The reader will notice, in this chapter as elsewhere, that every fresh subject is introduced by the words, "And the Lord spake unto Moses," or "unto Aaron." Thus, from verses 20-32 we are taught that the priests and Levites—God's worshipers and workers—were to have no inheritance among the children of Israel, but were to be absolutely shut up to God Himself for the supply of all their need. Most blessed position! Nothing can be more lovely than the picture here presented. The children of Israel were to bring their offerings and lay them down at the feet of Jehovah, and He, in His infinite grace, commanded His workers to pick up these precious offerings—the fruit of His people's devotedness—and feed upon them, in His own blessed presence, with thankful hearts. Thus the circle of blessing went round. God ministered to all the wants of His people, His people were privileged to share the rich fruits of His bounty with the priests and Levites, and these latter were permitted to taste the rare and exquisite pleasure of giving back to God of that which had flown from Him to them.

All this is divine. It is a striking figure of that which we should look for in the Church of God now. As we have already remarked, God's people are presented, in this book, under three distinct phases, namely, as warriors, workers, and worshipers; and in all three they are viewed as in the attitude of the most absolute dependence upon the living God. In our warfare, in our work, and in our worship we are *shut up to God.* Precious fact! "All our springs are in Him." What more do we want? Shall we turn to man or to this world for relief or resource? God forbid! Nay, rather let it be our one grand object to prove, in our entire history, in every phase of our character, and in every department of our work, that God is enough for our hearts.

It is truly deplorable to find God's people and Christ's servants looking to the world for support, and trembling at the thought of that support being withheld. Only let us try to imagine the Church of God in the days of Paul relying upon the Roman government for the support of its bishops, teachers, and evangelists. Ah, no; the Church looked to its divine Head in the heavens, and to the divine Spirit upon earth, for all its need. Why should it be otherwise now? The world is the world still; and the Church is not of the world, and should not look for the world's gold and silver. God will take care of His people and of His servants, if they will only trust Him. We may depend upon it, the

---

*For further remarks on the subject presented in Numbers 18:14-19, the reader is referred to *Notes on Exodus,* chapter 13. We are anxious to avoid, as much as possible, any repetition of what has been gone into in previous comments.

*divinum donum* (God's gift) is far better for the Church than the *regium donum* (the government gift)—no comparison in the estimation of a spiritual mind.

May all the saints of God, and all the servants of Christ, in every place, apply their hearts earnestly to the consideration of these things; and may we have grace to confess practically, in the face of a godless, Christless, infidel world, that the living God is amply sufficient for our every need, not only while passing through the narrow archway of time, but also for the boundless ocean of eternity. God grant it for Christ's sake.

---

## *CHAPTER 19*

ONE of the most important sections of the book of Numbers now lies open before us, presenting for our consideration the deeply interesting and instructive ordinance of "the red heifer." A thoughtful student of Scripture would naturally feel disposed to inquire why it is that we get this type in Numbers and not in Leviticus. In the first seven chapters of the latter book we have a very elaborate statement of the doctrine of sacrifice, and yet we have no allusion whatever to the red heifer. Why is this? What are we to learn from the fact that this beautiful ordinance is presented in the book of Numbers and no where else? We believe it furnishes another striking illustration of the distinctive character of our book. The red heifer is pre-eminently a wilderness-type. It was God's provision for defilements by the way, and it prefigures the death of Christ as a purification for sin, to meet our need in passing through a defiling world home to our eternal rest above. It is a most instructive figure, and unfolds most precious and needed truth. May the Holy Ghost, who has penned the record, be graciously pleased to expound and apply it to our souls.

"And the Lord spake unto Moses and unto Aaron, saying, 'This is the ordinance of the law which the Lord hath commanded, saying, Speak unto the children of Israel that they bring thee a red heifer without spot, wherein is no blemish, and upon which never came yoke' " (ver. 1-2).

When, with the eye of faith, we gaze upon the Lord Jesus, we not only see Him to be the spotless One in His own holy Person, but also One who never bore the yoke of sin. The Holy Ghost is ever the jealous Guardian of the Person of Christ, and He delights to present Him to the soul in all His excellency and preciousness. Hence it is that every type and every shadow designed to set Him forth exhibits the same careful guardianship. Thus, in the red heifer we are taught that not only was our blessed Saviour as to His human nature intrinsically and inherently pure and spotless, but that as to His birth and relationships He stood perfectly clear from every mark and trace of sin. No yoke of sin ever came upon His sacred neck. When He speaks of "My yoke" (Matt. 11:29), it was the yoke of implicit subjection to the Father's will in all things. This was the only yoke He ever wore; and this yoke was never off for one moment during the entire of His spotless and perfect career—from the manger, where He lay a helpless babe, to the cross, where He expired as a victim.

But He wore no yoke of sin. Let this be distinctly understood. He went to the cross to expiate our sins, to lay the ground-work of our perfect purification from all sin; but He did this as One who had never, at any time during His blessed life, worn the yoke of sin. He was "without sin," and as such, was perfectly fitted to do the great and glorious work of expiation. To think of Him as bearing the yoke of sin in His life, would be to think of Him as unfit to atone for it in His death. "*Wherein* is no blemish, and *whereon* never came yoke." It is quite as needful to remember and weigh the force of the word "whereon" as of the word "wherein." Both expressions are designed by the Holy Ghost to set forth the perfection of our Lord and Saviour Jesus Christ, who was not only internally spotless, but also externally free from every trace of sin. Neither in His Person nor yet in His relationships was

He in any wise obnoxious to the claims of sin or death. He—adored forever be His blessed name!—entered into all the reality of our circumstances and condition; but *in* Him was no sin, and *on* Him no yoke of sin.

Touched with a sympathy within,
He knows our feeble frame;
He knows what sore temptations mean,
For He has felt the same.

But spotless, undefiled, and pure,
The great Redeemer stood,
While Satan's fiery darts He bore,
And did resist to blood.

"And ye shall give her unto Eleazar the priest, that he may bring her forth without the camp, and one shall slay her before his face" (ver. 3).

The thoughtful reader of Scripture will not pass over any expression, how trivial soever it may seem to be. Such an one will ever bear in mind that the book which lies open before him is from God, and therefore perfect—perfect as a whole—perfect in all its parts. Every little word is pregnant with meaning; each little point, feature, and circumstance contains some spiritual teaching for the soul. No doubt, infidels and rationalists altogether fail in seizing this weighty fact, and, as a consequence, when they approach the divine volume, they make the saddest havoc. They see flaws where the spiritual student sees only gems; they see incongruities and contradictions where the devout, self-distrusting, Spirit-taught disciple beholds divine harmonies and moral glories.

This is only what we might expect, and it is well to remember it nowadays. "God is His own interpreter" in Scripture as well as in providence; and if we wait on Him, He will assuredly make it plain. But as in providence "blind unbelief is sure to err, and scan His ways in vain," so in Scripture it is sure to err, and scan His lines in vain. And the devout poet might have gone farther; for, most surely, unbelief will not only scan God's ways and God's Word in vain, but turn both the one and the other into an occasion of making a blasphemous attack upon God Himself—upon His nature, and upon His character, as well as upon the revelation which He has been pleased to give us. The infidel would rudely smash the lamp of inspiration, quench its heavenly light, and involve us all in that deep gloom and moral darkness which inwrap his misguided mind.

We have been led into the foregoing train of thought while meditating upon the third verse of our chapter. We are exceedingly desirous to cultivate the habit of profound and careful study of holy Scripture. It is of immense importance. To say or think that there is so much as a single clause, or a single expression, from cover to cover of the inspired volume, unworthy of our prayerful meditation, is to imply that God the Holy Ghost has thought it worth His while to write what we do not think it worth our while to study. "All Scripture is given by inspiration of God" (2 Tim. 3:16). This commands our reverence. "Whatsoever things were written aforetime were written for our learning" (Rom. 15:4). This awakens our personal interest. The former of these quotations proves that Scripture comes *from God;* the latter proves that it comes *to us.* That and this, taken together, bind us to God by the divine link of holy Scripture—a link which the devil, in this our day, is doing his very utmost to snap; and that, too, by means of agents of acknowledged moral worth and intellectual power. The devil does not select an ignorant or immoral man to make his grand and special attacks upon the Bible, for he knows full well that the former could not speak, and the latter would not get a hearing; but he craftily takes up some amiable, benevolent, and popular person—some one of blameless morals—a laborious student, a profound scholar, a deep and original thinker. Thus he throws dust in the eyes of the simple, the unlearned, and the unwary.

We pray you to remember this. If we can deepen in your soul the sense of the unspeakable value of your Bible, if we can warn you off from the dangerous rocks and quicksands of rationalism and infidelity, if we are made the means of stablishing and strengthening you in the assurance that when you are hanging over the sacred page of Scripture you are drinking at a fountain every drop of which has flowed into it from the very bosom of God Himself,—if we can reach all or any of these results, we shall not regret the digression from our chapter, to which we now return.

"And ye shall give her unto Eleazar the priest, that he may bring her forth without the camp, and one shall slay her before his face." We have, in the priest and the victim, a joint type of the Person of Christ. He was at once the Victim and the Priest. But He did not enter upon His priestly functions until His work as a victim was accomplished. This will explain the expression in the last clause of the third verse—*"one shall slay her before his face."* The death of Christ was accomplished on earth, and could not, therefore, be represented as the act of priesthood. Heaven, not earth, is the sphere of His priestly service. The apostle, in the Epistle to the Hebrews, expressly declares, as the sum of a most elaborate and amazing piece of argument, that "we have such a High-Priest, who is set on the right hand of the throne of the Majesty in the heavens; a Minister of the sanctuary, and of the true tabernacle, which the Lord pitched, and not man. For every high-priest is ordained to offer gifts and sacrifices: wherefore it is of necessity that this Man have somewhat also to offer. *For if He were on earth, He should not be a priest,* seeing that there are priests that offer gifts according to the law" (Heb. 8:1-4). "But Christ being come a High-Priest of good things to come, by a greater and more perfect tabernacle, not made with hands, that is to say, not of this building; neither by the blood of goats and calves, but by His own blood He entered in once into the holy place, having obtained eternal redemption." "For Christ is not entered into the holy places made with hands, the figures of the true, but *into heaven itself,* now to appear in the presence of God for us" (chap. 9:11-12,24). "But this Man, after He had offered one sacrifice for sins, forever *sat down on the right hand of God"* (chap. 10:12).

From all these passages, taken in connection with Numbers 19:3, we learn two things, namely, that the death of Christ is not presented as the proper, ordinary act of priesthood; and further, that heaven, not earth, is the sphere of His priestly ministry. There is nothing new in these statements —others have advanced them repeatedly, but it is important to notice every thing tending to illustrate the divine perfection and precision of holy Scripture. It is deeply interesting to find a truth which shines brightly in the pages of the New Testament wrapped up in some ordinance or ceremony of Old Testament times. Such discoveries are ever welcome to the intelligent reader of the Word. The truth, no doubt, is the same wherever it is found; but when it bursts upon us, with meridian brightness, in the New Testament Scriptures, and is divinely shadowed forth in the Old, we not only have the truth established, but the unity of the volume illustrated and enforced.

But we must not pass over unnoticed the place where the death of the victim was accomplished. "That he may bring her forth without the camp." As has already been remarked, the priest and the victim are identified, and form a joint type of Christ; but it is added, "one shall slay her before his face," simply because the death of Christ could not be represented as the act of priesthood. What marvelous accuracy! And yet it is not marvelous, for what else should we look for in a book every line of which is from God Himself? Had it been said, He shall slay her, then Numbers 19 would be at variance with the Epistle to the Hebrews. But no; the harmonies of the volume shine forth among its brightest glories. May we have grace to discern and appreciate them.

Jesus, then, suffered without the gate. "Wherefore Jesus also, that He might sanctify the people with His own blood, suffered without the gate" (Heb. 13:12). He took the outside place, and His voice falls on the ear from thence. Do we listen to it; do we understand it? Should we not consider more seriously the place where Jesus died? Are we to rest satisfied with reaping the benefits of Christ's death, without seeking fellowship with Him in His rejection? God forbid! "Let us *go forth,* therefore, unto Him without the camp, bearing His reproach."* There is immense power in these words. They should rouse our whole moral being to seek more complete identification with a rejected Saviour. Shall we see Him die outside, while we reap the benefits of His death and remain within? Shall we seek a home and a place and a name and a portion in that world from which our Lord and Master is an outcast? Shall we aim at getting on in a world which could not tolerate that blessed One to whom we owe our present and everlasting felicity? Shall we aspire after honor, position, and wealth where our Master found only a manger, a cross, a borrowed grave? May the language of our *hearts* be, "Far be the *thought!*" and may the language of our *lives* be, "Far be the *thing!*" May we, by the grace of God, yield a more hearty response to the Spirit's call to *"go forth."*

Let us never forget that when we look at the death of Christ, we see two things, namely, the death of a victim and the death of a martyr—a victim for sin, a martyr for righteouness—a victim under the hand of God, a martyr under the hand of man. He suffered for sin that we might never suffer. Blessed be His name for evermore! But then, His martyr-sufferings—His sufferings for righteousness under the hand of man, these we may know; "for unto you *it is given,* in the behalf of Christ, not only to believe on Him, but also to *suffer* for His sake" (Phil. 1:29). It is a positive *gift* to be allowed to suffer with Christ. Do we so esteem it?

In contemplating the death of Christ, as typified by the ordinance of the red heifer, we see not only the complete putting away of sin, but also the judgment of this present evil world. "He gave Himself for our sins that He might deliver us from this present evil world, according to the will of God and our Father" (Gal. 1:4). Here the two things are put together by God; and, most surely, they should never be separated by us. We have the judgment of sin, root and branch, and the judgment of this world. The former should give perfect repose to the exercised conscience, while the latter should deliver the heart from the insnaring influence of the world, in all its multiplied forms. That purges the conscience from all sense of guilt; this snaps the link which binds the heart and the world together.

Now, it is most needful for the reader to understand and enter experimentally into the connection existing between these two things. It is quite possible to miss this grand link, even while holding and contending for a vast amount of evangelical truth; and it may be confidently affirmed that where this link is missing, there must be a very serious defect in the Christian character. We frequently meet with earnest souls who have been brought under the convicting and awakening power of the Holy Spirit, but who have not yet known, for the ease of their troubled consciences, the full value of the atoning death of Christ, as putting away forever all their sins, and bringing them nigh to God, without a stain upon the soul or a sting in the conscience. If this be the present actual condition of the reader, he would need to consider the first clause of the verse just quoted—"He gave Himself for our sins." This is a most blessed statement for a troubled soul. It settles the whole question of sin. If it be true that Christ gave Himself for my sins, what remains for me but to rejoice in the precious fact that my sins are all gone? The One who took my place, who stood charged with my sins, who suffered in my room and stead, is now at the right hand of God, crowned with glory and honor. This is enough. My sins are all gone forever. If they were not, *He* could not be where He now is. The crown of glory which wreathes His blessed brow is the proof that my sins are perfectly atoned for, and therefore perfect peace is my portion—a peace as perfect as the work of Christ can make it.

But then let us never forget that the very same work that has forever put away our sins has delivered us from this present evil world. The two things go together. Christ has not only delivered me from the consequences of my sins, but also from the present power of sin, and from the claims

*"The camp," in the above passage, refers primarily to Judaism; but it has a very pointed moral application to every system of religion set up by man, and governed by the spirit and principles of this present evil world.

and influences of that thing which Scripture calls "the world." All this, however, will come more fully out as we proceed.

"And Eleazar the priest shall take of her blood with his finger, and sprinkle of her blood directly before the tabernacle of the congregation seven times." Here we have the solid ground-work of all real purification. We know that in the type before us it is only, as the inspired apostle tells us, a question of "sanctifying to the purifying of the flesh" (Heb. 9:13). But we have to look beyond the type to the Antitype—beyond the shadow to the substance. In the sevenfold sprinkling of the blood of the red heifer before the tabernacle of the congregation, we have a figure of the perfect presentation of the blood of Christ to God, as the only ground of the meeting-place between God and the conscience. The number "seven," as had frequently been observed, is expressive of perfection; and in the figure before us, we see the perfection attaching to the death of Christ as an atonement for sin, presented to and accepted by God. All rests upon this divine ground. The blood has been shed and presented to a holy God as a perfect atonement for sin. This, when simply received by faith, must relieve the conscience from all sense of guilt, and all fear of condemnation. There is nothing before God save the perfection of the atoning work of Christ. Sin has been judged, and our sins put away; they have been completely obliterated by the precious blood of Christ. To believe this, is to enter into perfect repose of conscience.

And here let the reader carefully note that there is no further allusion to the sprinkling of blood throughout the entire of this singularly interesting chapter. This is precisely in keeping with the doctrine of Hebrews 9–10. It is but another illustration of the divine harmony of the volume. The sacrifice of Christ, being divinely perfect, needs not to be repeated. Its efficacy is divine and eternal. "But Christ being come a High-Priest of good things to come, by a greater and more perfect tabernacle, not made with hands, that is to say, not of this building; neither by the blood of goats and calves, but by His own blood, He entered in once into the holy place, having obtained *eternal* redemption. For if the blood of bulls and of goats, and *the ashes of a heifer* sprinkling the unclean, sanctifieth to the purifying of the flesh; how much more shall the blood of Christ, who through the eternal Spirit offered Himself without spot to God, purge your conscience from dead works to serve the living God?" (Heb. 9:11-14) Observe the force of these two words, *"once"* and *"eternal."* See how they set forth the completeness and divine efficacy of the sacrifice of Christ. The blood was shed once and forever. To think of a repetition of that great work would be to deny its everlasting and all-sufficient value, and reduce it to the level of the blood of bulls and goats.

But further—"It was therefore necessary that the patterns of things in the heavens should be purified with these; but the heavenly things themselves with better sacrifices than these. For Christ is not entered into the holy places made with hands, which are the figures of the true; but into heaven itself, now to appear in the presence of God for us: nor yet *that He should offer Himself often,* as the high-priest entereth into the holy place every year with blood of others; for then *must He often have suffered* since the foundation of the world; but now *once* in the end of the world hath He appeared *to put away sin* by the sacrifice of Himself." Sin, therefore, has been put away. It cannot be put away and at the same time be on the believer's conscience. This is plain. It must either be admitted that the believer's sins are blotted out, and his conscience perfectly purged, or that Christ must die over again. But this latter is not only needless, but wholly out of the question; for, as the apostle goes on to say, "as it is appointed unto men *once* to die, but after this the judgment; so Christ was once offered to bear the sins of many; and unto them that look for Him shall He appear the second time, without sin, unto salvation."

There is something most marvelous in the patient elaborateness with which the Holy Ghost argues out this entire subject. He expounds, illustrates, and enforces the great doctrine of the completeness of the sacrifice in such a way as to carry conviction to the soul, and relieve the conscience of its heavy burden. Such is the exceeding grace of God, that He has not only accomplished the work of eternal redemption for us, but, in the most patient and painstaking manner, has argued and reasoned, and proved the whole point in question, so as not to leave one hair's breadth of ground on which to base an objection. Let us hearken to His further powerful reasonings, and may the Spirit apply them in power to the heart of the anxious reader.

"For the law having a shadow of good things to come, and not the very image of the things, can never with those sacrifices which they offered year by year continually make the comers thereunto *perfect.* For then would they not have *ceased to be offered?* because that the worshipers *once purged* should have had *no more conscience of sins.* But in those sacrifices there is a remembrance again made of sins every year. For it is not possible that the blood of bulls and of goats should take away sins." But that which the blood of bulls could never do, the blood of Jesus has forever done. This makes all the difference. All the blood that ever flowed around Israel's altars—the millions of sacrifices offered according to the requirements of the Mosaic ritual—could not blot out one stain from the conscience, or justify a sin-hating God in receiving a sinner to Himself. "It is not possible that the blood of bulls and of goats should take away sins." "Wherefore when He cometh into the world He saith, 'Sacrifice and offering Thou wouldest not, but a body hast Thou prepared Me: in burnt-offerings and sacrifices for sin Thou hast had no pleasure. Then said I, Lo, I come (in the volume of the book it is written of Me,) to do Thy will, O God.' . . . By the which will we are sanctified through the offering of the body of Jesus Christ *once.*" Mark the contrast. God had no pleasure in the endless round of sacrifices under the law,—they did not please Him. They left wholly unaccomplished that which He had in His loving heart to do for His people, namely, to rid them completely of sin's heavy load, and bring them unto Himself, in perfect peace of conscience and liberty of heart. This, Jesus, by the one offering of His blessed body, did. He did the will of God; and, blessed forever be His name, He has not to do His work over again. We may refuse to believe that the work is done, refuse to commit our souls to its efficacy—to enter into the rest which it is calculated to impart—to enjoy the holy liberty of spirit which it is fitted to yield; but there stands the work in its own imperishable virtue; and there, too, stand the Spirit's arguments respecting that work, in their own unanswerable force and clearness; and neither Satan's dark suggestions nor our own unbelieving reasonings can ever touch either the one or the other. They can, and, alas! they do, most sadly interfere with our soul's enjoyment of the truth; but the truth itself remains ever the same.

"And every priest *standeth daily* ministering and *offering oftentimes the same sacrifices, which can never take away sins:* but this Man, after He had offered *one sacrifice* for sins, *forever sat down* on the right hand of God; from henceforth expecting till His enemies be made His footstool. For *by one offering* He hath perfected forever them that are sanctified." It is due to the blood of Christ that it should impart eternal perfection; and, we may surely add, it is due to it likewise that our souls should taste that perfection. No one need ever imagine that he is doing honor to the work of Christ, or to the Spirit's testimony respecting that work, when he refuses to accept that perfect remission of sins which is proclaimed to him through the blood of the cross. It is no sign of true piety, or of pure religion, to deny what the grace of God has done for us in Christ, and what the record of the Eternal Spirit has presented to our souls on the page of inspiration.

Does it not seem strange that when the Word of God presents to our view Christ seated at the right hand of God, in virtue of accomplished redemption, we should be virtually in no wise better off than those who had merely a human priest standing daily ministering, and offering the same round of sacrifices? We have a divine Priest, who has sat down forever. They had a merely human priest, who could never, in his official capacity, sit down at all; and yet are we, in the state of the mind, in the apprehension of the soul, in the actual condition of the conscience, in no respect better off than they? Can it be possible that, with a perfect work to rest upon, our souls should never know perfect rest? The Holy Ghost, as we have seen in these various quotations taken from the Epistle to the Hebrews, has left nothing unsaid to satisfy our souls as to the question of the complete putting away of sin by the precious blood of Christ. Why, then, should you not this moment enjoy full, settled peace of conscience? Has the blood of Jesus done nothing more for you than the blood of a bullock did for a Jewish worshiper?

It may be, however, that the reader is ready to say, in reply to all that we have been seeking to urge upon him, I do not, in the least, doubt the efficacy of the blood of Jesus. I believe it cleanseth from all sin. I believe, most thoroughly, that all who simply put their trust in that blood are perfectly safe, and will be eternally happy. My difficulty does not lie here at all. What troubles me is not the efficacy of the blood, in which I fully believe, but *my own personal interest in that blood,* of which I have no satisfactory evidence. This is the secret of all my trouble. The doctrine of the blood is as clear as a sunbeam, but the question of *my* interest therein is involved in hopeless obscurity."

Now, if this be at all the embodiment of the reader's feelings on this momentous subject, it only proves the necessity of his deeply pondering the fourth verse of the nineteenth of Numbers. There he will see that the true basis of all purification is found in this, that the blood of atonement has been presented to God, and accepted by Him. This is a most precious truth, but one little understood. It is of all importance that the really anxious soul should have a clear view of the subject of atonement. It is so natural to us all to be occupied with our thoughts and feelings about the blood of Christ, rather than with the blood itself, and with God's thoughts respecting it. If the blood has been perfectly presented to God, if He has accepted it, if He has glorified Himself in the putting away of sin, then what remains for the divinely exercised conscience but to find perfect repose in that which has met all the claims of God, harmonized His attributes, and laid the foundations of that marvelous platform whereon a sin-hating God and a poor sin-destroyed sinner can meet? Why introduce the question of my interest in the blood of Christ, as though that work were not complete without aught of mine, call it what you will—my interest, my feelings, my experience, my appreciation, my appropriation, my any thing? Why not rest in Christ alone? This would be really having an interest in Him. But the very moment the heart gets occupied with the question of its own interest, the moment the eye is withdrawn from that divine object which the Word of God and the Holy Ghost present, then spiritual darkness and perplexity must ensue, and the soul, instead of rejoicing in the perfection of the work of Christ, is tormented by looking at its own poor, imperfect feelings.

> Th'atoning work is done,
> The Victim's blood is shed,
> And Jesus now is gone
> *His* people's cause to plead
> He stands in Heav'n their great High-Priest,
> And bears their names upon His breast.

Here, blessed be God, we have the stable ground-work of "purification for sin," and of perfect peace for the conscience. "The atoning work is done." All is finished. The great Antitype of the red heifer has been slain. He gave Himself up to death, under the wrath and judgment of a righteous God, that all who simply put their trust in Him might know, in the deep secret of their own souls, divine purification and perfect peace. We are purified, as to the conscience, not by our thoughts about the blood, but by the blood itself. We must insist upon this. God Himself has made out our title for us, and that title is found in the blood *alone.* Oh, that most precious blood of Jesus, that speaks profound peace to every troubled soul that will simply lean upon its eternal efficacy! Why, we may ask, is it that the blessed doctrine of the blood is so little understood and appreciated? Why will people persist in looking to aught else, or in mingling aught else with it? May the Holy Ghost lead the anxious reader, as he reads these lines, to stay his heart and conscience upon the atoning sacrifice of the Lamb of God.

Having thus endeavored to present to the reader the precious truth unfolded to us in the *death* of the red heifer, we shall now ask him to meditate for a few moments upon the *burning* of the heifer. We have looked at the *blood,* let us now gaze upon the *ashes.* In the former, we have the sacrificial death of Christ as the only purification for sin; in the latter, we have the remembrance of that death applied to the heart by the Spirit, through the Word, in order to remove any defilement contracted in our walk from day to day. This gives great completeness and beauty to this most interesting type. God has not only made provision for past sins, but also for present defilement, so that we may be ever before Him in all the value and credit of the perfect work of Christ. He would have us treading the courts of His sanctuary, the holy precincts of His presence, "clean every whit." And not only does He Himself see us thus, but, blessed forever be His name, He would have us thus in our own inward self-consciousness. He would give us, by His Spirit, through the Word, the deep inward sense of cleanness in His sight, so that the current of our communion with Him may flow on without a ripple and without a curve. "If we walk in the light, as He is in the light, we have fellowship one with another, and the blood of Jesus Christ His Son cleanseth us from all sin" (1 John 1). But if we fail to walk in the light—if we forget, and, in our forgetfulness, touch the unclean thing, how is our communion to be restored? Only the removal of the defilement. And how is this to be effected? By the application to our hearts and consciences of the precious truth of the death of Christ. The Holy Ghost produces self-judgment, and brings to our remembrance the precious truth that Christ suffered death for that defilement which we so lightly and indifferently contract. It is not a fresh sprinkling of the blood of Christ—a thing unknown in Scripture—but the remembrance of His death brought home, in fresh power, to the contrite heart, by the ministry of the Holy Ghost.

"And one shall burn the heifer in his sight. . . . And the priest shall take cedarwood and hyssop and scarlet, and cast it into the midst of the burning of the heifer. . . . And a man that is clean shall gather up the ashes of the heifer, and lay them up without the camp in a clean place, and it shall be kept for the congregation of the children of Israel for a water of separation: it is a purification for sin."

It is the purpose of God that His children should be purified from all iniquity, and that they should walk in separation from this present evil world, where all is death and defilement. This separation is effected by the action of the Word on the heart, by the power of the Holy Ghost. "Grace to you and peace from God the Father, and our Lord Jesus Christ, who gave Himself for our sins, that He might deliver us from this present evil world, according to the will of God and our Father" (Gal. 1:4). And again, "Looking for that blessed hope, and the glorious appearing of the great God and our Saviour Jesus Christ; who gave Himself for us, that He might *redeem* us from all iniquity, and *purify* unto Himself a peculiar people, zealous of good works" (Titus 2:13-14).

It is remarkable how constantly the Spirit of God presents, in intimate connection, the full relief of the conscience from all sense of guilt, and the deliverance of the heart from the moral influence of this present evil world. Now, it should be our care, beloved Christian reader, to maintain the integrity of this connection. Of course, it is only by the gracious energy of the Holy Ghost that we can do so; but we ought to seek earnestly to understand and practically carry out the blessed link of connection between the death of Christ as an atonement for sin and as the moral power of separation from this world. Many of the people of God never get beyond the former, if they even get that length. Many seem to be quite satisfied with the knowledge of the forgiveness of sins through the atoning work of Christ, while, at the same time, they fail to realize deadness to the world in virtue of the death of Christ and their identification with Him therein.

Now, when we stand and gaze upon the burning of the red heifer in Numbers 19, when we examine that mystic heap of ashes, what do we find? It may be said, in reply, We find our sins there. True, thanks be to God and to the Son of His love, we do indeed find our sins, our iniquities, our trespasses, our deep crimson guilt, all reduced to ashes; but is there nothing more? can we not, by a careful analysis, discover more? Unquestionably. We find nature there, in every stage of its existence—from the highest to the lowest point in its history. Moreover, we find all the glory of this world there. The cedar and the hyssop represent nature in its widest extremes; and in giving its extremes, they take in all that lies between. "Solomon spake of trees, from the cedar-tree that is in Lebanon even unto the hyssop that springeth out of the wall."

"Scarlet" is viewed, by those who have carefully examined Scripture on the point, as the type or expression of human splendor, worldly grandeur, the glory of this world, the glory of man. Hence, therefore, we see in the burning of the heifer, the end of all worldly greatness, human glory, and the complete setting aside of the flesh with all its belongings. This renders the burning of the heifer deeply significant. It shadows forth a truth too little known, and when known, too readily forgotten—a truth embodied in these memorable words of the apostle, "God forbid that I should glory save in the cross of our Lord Jesus Christ, whereby the world is crucified unto me, and I unto the world."

We are all far too prone to accept the cross as the ground of escape from all the consequences of our sins, and of full acceptance with God, and, at the same time, refuse it as the ground of our complete separation from the world. True it is, thanks and praise be to our God, the solid ground of our deliverance from guilt and consequent condemnation; but it is more than this. It has severed us forever from all that pertains to this world, through which we are passing. Are my sins put away? Yes, blessed be the God of all grace. According to what? According to the perfection of Christ's atoning sacrifice as estimated by God Himself. Well, then, such precisely is the measure of our deliverance from this present evil world—from its fashions, its maxims, its habits, its principles. The believer has absolutely nothing in common with this world, insofar as he enters into the spirit and power of the cross of the Lord Jesus Christ. That cross has dislodged him from every thing here below, and made him a pilgrim and a stranger in this world. The truly devoted heart sees the dark shadow of the cross looming over all the glitter and glare, the pomp and fashion of this world. Paul saw this, and the sight of it caused him to esteem the world, in its very highest aspect, in its most attractive forms, in its brightest glories, as dross.

Such was the estimate formed of this world by one who had been brought up at the feet of Gamaliel. "The world is crucified unto me," said he, "and I unto the world." Such was Paul, and such should every Christian be—a stranger on earth, a citizen of heaven, and this not merely in sentiment and theory, but in downright fact and reality; for as surely as our deliverance from hell is more than a mere sentiment or theory, so surely is our separation from this present evil age. The one is as positive and as real as the other.

But here let us ask, Why is not this great practical truth more pressed home upon the hearts of evangelical Christians at the present moment? why are we so slow to urge upon one another the separating power of the cross of Christ? If my heart loves Jesus, I shall not seek a place, a portion, or a name where He only found a malefactor's cross. This, dear reader, is the simple way to look at the matter. Do you really love Christ? has your heart been touched and attracted by His wondrous love to you? If so, remember that He was cast out by this world. Yes, Jesus was and still is an outcast from this world. There is no change. The world is the world still; and be it remembered that one of Satan's special devices is to lead people to accept salvation from Christ, while at the same time they refuse to be identified with Him in His rejection—to avail themselves of the atoning work of the cross, while abiding comfortably in the world that is stained with the guilt of nailing Christ thereto. In other words, he leads people to think and to say that the offense of the cross has ceased; that the world of the nineteenth century is totally different from the world of the first; that if the Lord Jesus were on earth now, He would meet with very different treatment from that which He received then; that it is not now a pagan world, but a Christian one, and this makes a material and a fundamental difference; that now it is quite right for a Christian to accept of citizenship in this world—to have a name, a place, and a portion here, seeing it is not the same world at all as that which nailed the Son of God to Calvary's cursed tree.

Now, we feel it incumbent on us to press upon all who read these lines that this is, in very deed, a lie of the arch-enemy of souls. The world is not changed. It may have changed its dress, but it has not changed its nature, its spirit, its principles. It hates Jesus as cordially as when the cry went forth, "Away with Him! Crucify Him!" There is really no change. If only we try the world by the same grand test, we shall find it to be the same evil, God-hating, Christ-rejecting world as ever. And what is that test? Christ crucified. May this solemn truth be engraved on our hearts. May we realize and manifest its formative power. May it detach us more completely from all that belongs to the world. May we be enabled to understand more fully the truth presented in the ashes of the red heifer. Then shall our separation from the world, and our dedication to Christ, be more intense and real. The Lord, in His exceeding goodness, grant that thus it may be, with all His people, in this day of hollow, worldly, half-and-half profession.

Let us now consider for a moment how the ashes were to be applied.

"He that toucheth the dead body of any man shall be unclean seven days. He shall purify himself with it on the third day, and on the seventh day he shall be clean; but if he purify not himself the third day, then the seventh day he shall not be clean. Whosoever toucheth the dead body of any man that is dead, and purifieth not himself, defileth the tabernacle of the Lord; and that soul shall be cut off from Israel; because the water of separation was not sprinkled upon him, he shall be unclean; his uncleanness is yet upon him."

It is a solemn thing to have to do with God—to walk with Him, from day to day, in the midst of a defiled and defiling scene. He cannot tolerate any uncleanness upon those with whom He deigns to walk, and in whom He dwells. He can pardon and blot out; He can heal, cleanse, and restore; but He cannot sanction unjudged evil, or suffer it upon His people. It would be a denial of His very name and nature were He to do so. This, while deeply solemn, is truly blessed. It is our joy to have to do with One whose presence demands and secures holiness. We are passing through a world in which we are surrounded with defiling influences. True, defilement is not now contracted by touching "a dead body, or a bone of a man, or a grave." These things were, as we know, types of things moral and spiritual, with which we are in danger of coming in contact every day and every hour. We doubt not but those who have much to do with the things of this world are most painfully sensible of the immense difficulty of escaping with unsoiled hands. Hence the need of holy diligence in all our habits and associations, lest we contract defilement, and interrupt our communion with God. He must have us in a condition worthy of Himself. "Be ye holy, for I am holy."

But the anxious reader, whose whole soul breathes after holiness, may eagerly inquire, What, then, are we to do, if it be true that we are thus surrounded, on all hands, with defiling influences, and if we are so prone to contract that defilement? Furthermore, if it is impossible to have fellowship with God with unclean hands and a condemning conscience, what are we to do? First of all, then, we should say, be watchful; wait much and earnestly on God. He is faithful and gracious—a prayer-hearing and a prayer-answering God—a liberal and an unupbraiding Giver. "He giveth *more* grace." This is positively a blank check, which faith can fill up to any amount. Is it the real purpose of your soul to get on—to advance in the divine life—to grow in personal holiness? Then beware how you continue, for a single hour, in contact with what soils your hands and wounds your conscience, grieves the Holy Ghost and mars your communion. Be decided: be wholehearted. Give up at once the unclean thing, whatever it be—habit, or association, or any thing else. Cost what it may, give it up; entail what loss it may, abandon it. No worldly gain, no earthly advantage, could compensate for the loss of a pure conscience, an uncondemning heart, and the light of your Father's countenance. Are you not convinced of this? If so, seek grace to carry out your conviction.

But it may be further asked, What is to be done when defilement is actually contracted? How is the defilement to be removed? Hear the reply in the figurative language of Numbers 19: "And for an unclean person, they shall take of the *ashes* of the burnt heifer of purification for sin, and running water shall be put thereto in a vessel: and a clean person shall take hyssop, and dip it in the water, and sprinkle it upon the tent, and upon all the vessels, and upon the persons that were there, and upon him that touched a bone, or one slain, or one dead, or a grave: and the clean person shall sprinkle upon the unclean on the third day and on the seventh day; and on the seventh day he shall purify himself, and wash his clothes, and bathe himself in water, and shall be clean at even."

The reader will remark that in the twelfth and eighteenth verses there is a double action set forth. There is the action of the third day and the action of the seventh day. Both were essentially necessary to remove the ceremonial defilement caused by contact with the varied forms of death above specified. Now, what did this double action typify? what is it that, in our spiritual history, answers thereto? We believe it to be this: When we, through lack of watchfulness and spiritual energy, touch the unclean thing and get defiled, we may be ignorant of it, but God knows all about it. He cares for us, and is looking after us; not, blessed be His name, as an angry judge, or stern censor, but as a loving Father, who will never impute any thing to us, because it was all, long ago, imputed to the One who died in our stead. But though He will never impute it to us, He will make us feel it deeply and keenly. He will be a faithful reprover of the unclean thing; and He can reprove all the more powerfully simply because He will never reckon it against us. The Holy Spirit brings our sin to remembrance, and this causes unutterable anguish of heart. This anguish may continue for some time; it may be moments, days, months, or years. We once met with a young Christian who was rendered miserable for three years by having gone with some worldly friends on an excursion. This convicting operation of the Holy Ghost we believe to be shadowed forth by the action of the third day. He first brings our sin to remembrance; and then He graciously brings to our remembrance, and applies to our souls, through the written Word, the value of the death of Christ as that which has already met the defilement which we so easily contract. This answers to the action of the seventh day—removes the defilement and restores our communion.

And be it carefully remembered that we can never get rid of defilement in any other way. We may seek to forget, to slur over, to heal the wound slightly, to make little of the matter, to let time obliterate it from the tablet of memory. It will never do; nay, it is most dangerous work. There are few things more disastrous than trifling with conscience or the claims of holiness. And it is as foolish as it is dangerous; for God has, in His grace, made full provision for the removal of the uncleanness which His holiness detects and condemns. But the uncleanness must be removed, else communion is impossible. "If I wash thee not, thou hast no part *with* Me." The suspension of a believers's communion is what answers to the cutting off of a member from the congregation of Israel. The

Christian can never be cut off from Christ; but his communion can be interrupted by a single sinful thought, and that sinful thought must be judged and confessed, and the soil of it removed, ere the communion can be restored. It is well to remember this. It is a serious thing to trifle with sin. We may rest assured we cannot possibly have fellowship with God and walk in defilement. To think so, is to blaspheme the very name, the very nature, the very throne and majesty of God. No; we must keep a clean conscience, and maintain the holiness of God, else we shall very soon make shipwreck of faith, and break down altogether. May the Lord keep us walking softly and tenderly, watchfully and prayerfully, until we have laid aside our bodies of sin and death, and entered upon that bright and blessed world above, where sin, death, and defilement are unknown.

In studying the ordinances and ceremonies of the Levitical economy, nothing is more striking than the jealous care with which the God of Israel watched over His people, in order that they might be preserved from every defiling influence. By day and by night, awake and asleep, at home and abroad, in the bosom of the family and in the solitary walk, His eyes were upon them. He looked after their food, their raiment, their domestic habits and arrangements. He carefully instructed them as to what they might and what they might not eat, what they might and what they might not wear. He even set forth distinctly His mind as to the very touching and handling of things. In short, He surrounded them with barriers amply sufficient, had they only attended to them, to resist the whole tide of defilement to which they were exposed on every side.

In all this, we read, in unmistakable characters, the holiness of God; but we read also, as distinctly, the grace of God. If divine holiness could not suffer defilement upon the people, divine grace made ample provision for the removal thereof. This provision is set forth in our chapter under two forms, namely, the blood of atonement and the water of separation. Precious provision! a provision illustrating at once the holiness and the grace of God. Did we not know the ample provisions of divine grace, the lofty claims of divine holiness would be perfectly overwhelming; but being assured of the former, we can heartily rejoice in the latter. Could we desire to see the standard of divine holiness lowered a single hair's breadth? Far be the thought! How could we? or why should we? seeing that divine grace has fully provided what divine holiness demands. An Israelite of old might shudder as he hearkened to such words as these: "He that toucheth the dead body of any man shall be unclean seven days;" and again, "Whosoever toucheth the dead body of any man that is dead, and purifieth not himself, defileth the tabernacle of the Lord; and that soul shall be cut off from Israel." Such words might indeed terrify his heart. He might feel led to exclaim, What am I to do? How can I ever get on? It seems perfectly impossible for me to escape defilement. But then, what of the ashes of the burnt heifer? what of the water of separation?—what could these mean? They set forth the memorial of the sacrificial death of Christ applied to the heart by the power of the Spirit of God. "He shall purify himself with it the third day, and on the seventh day he shall be clean; but if he purify not himself the third day, then the seventh day he shall not be clean." If we contract defilement, even though it be through negligence, that defilement must be removed ere our communion can be restored. But we cannot get rid of the soil by any effort of our own; it can only be by the use of God's gracious provision, even the water of purification. An Israelite could no more remove, by his own efforts, the defilement caused by the touch of a dead body, than he could have broken Pharaoh's yoke, or delivered himself from the lash of Pharaoh's taskmasters.

Observe that it was not a question of offering a fresh sacrifice, nor yet of a fresh application of the blood. It is of special importance that this should be distinctly seen and understood. The death of Christ cannot be repeated. "Christ being raised from the dead dieth no more; death hath no more dominion over Him. For in that He died, He died unto sin once; but in that He liveth, He liveth unto God." We stand, by the grace of God, in the full credit and value of the death of Christ; but, inasmuch as we are surrounded on all sides by temptations and snares, and as we have within us such capabilities and tendencies, and further, seeing we have a powerful adversary who is ever on the watch to insnare us, and lead us off the path of truth and purity, we could not get on for a single moment were it not for the gracious way in which our God has provided for all our exigencies in the precious death and all-prevailing advocacy of our Lord Jesus Christ. It is not merely that the blood of Jesus Christ has washed away all our sins, and reconciled us to a holy God, but "we have an advocate with the Father, Jesus Christ the righteous." "He ever liveth to make intercession for us," and "He is able to save them to the uttermost that come unto God by Him." He is ever in the presence of God for us. He represents us there, and maintains us in the divine integrity of the place and relationship in which His atoning death has set us. Our case can never, by any possibility, fall through in the hands of such an advocate. He must cease to live ere the very feeblest of His saints can perish. We are identified with Him and He with us.

Now, then, what should be the practical effect of all this grace upon our hearts and lives? When we think of the death and of the burning—of the blood and of the ashes—of the atoning sacrifice, and the interceding Priest and Advocate, what influence should it exert upon our souls? how should it act upon our consciences? Should it lead us to think little of sin? should it cause us to walk carelessly and indifferently? should it have the effect of making us light and frivolous in our ways? Alas! for the heart that can think so. We may rest assured of this, that the man who can draw a plea from the rich provisions of divine grace for lightness of conduct or levity of spirit, knows very little, if indeed he knows any thing at all, of the true nature of proper influence of grace and its provisions. Could we imagine for a moment that the ashes of the heifer or the water of separation would have had the effect of making an Israelite careless as to his walk? Assuredly not. On the contrary, the very fact of such careful provision being made, by the goodness of God, against defilement, would make him feel what a serious thing it was to contract it. Such, at least, would be the proper effect of the provisions of divine grace. The heap of ashes, laid up in a clean place, gave forth a double testimony; it testified of the goodness of God, and it testified of the hatefulness of sin. It declared that God could not suffer uncleanness upon His people; but it declared also that He had provided the means of removing it. It is utterly impossible that the blessed doctrine of the sprinkled blood, of the ashes, and of the water of separation can be understood and enjoyed without its producing a holy horror of sin in all its defiling forms. And we may further assert that no one who has ever felt the anguish of a defiled conscience could lightly contract defilement. A pure conscience is far too precious a treasure to be lightly parted with, and a defiled conscience is far too heavy a burden to be lightly taken up. But, blessed be the God of all grace, He has met all our need, in His own perfect way, and He has met it, too, not to make us careless, but to make us watchful. "My little children, these things write I unto you, that ye sin not." But then He adds, "If any man sin, we have an advocate with the Father, Jesus Christ the righteous. And He is the propitiation for our sins; and not for ours only, but for the whole world" (1 John).

But we must draw this section to a close, and shall merely add a word on the closing verses of our chapter. "And it shall be a perpetual statute unto them, that he that sprinkleth the water of separation shall wash his clothes, and he that toucheth the water of separation shall be unclean until even. And whatsoever the unclean person toucheth shall be unclean, and the soul that toucheth it shall be unclean until even" (chap. 19:21-22). In verse 18 we are taught that it needed a clean person to sprinkle the unclean, and in verse 21 we are taught that the act of sprinkling another defiled one's self.

Putting both these together, we learn, as another has said, "that any one who has to do with the sin of another, though it be in the way of duty, to cleanse it, is defiled; not as the guilty person, it is true, but we cannot touch sin without being defiled." And we learn also that in order to lead another into the enjoyment of the cleansing virtue of Christ's work, I must be in the enjoyment of that cleansing work myself. It is well to remember this. Those who applied the water of separation to others had to use that water for themselves. May our souls enter into this. May we ever abide in the sense of the perfect cleanness into which the death of Christ introduces us, and in which His priestly work maintains us; and, oh, let us never forget that *contact with evil defiles!* It was so under the Mosaic economy, and it is so now.

---

## *CHAPTER 20*

"THEN came the children of Israel, even the whole congregation, into the desert of Zin, in the first month: and the people abode in Kadesh; and Miriam died there, and was buried there" (ver. 1).

The chapter which now opens before us furnishes a very remarkable record of wilderness life and experience. In it we see Moses, the servant of God, passing through some of the most trying scenes of his eventful life. First of all, Miriam dies. The one whose voice was heard, amid the brilliant scenes of Exodus 15, chanting a hymn of victory, passes away, and her ashes are deposited in the wilderness of Kadesh. The timbrel is laid aside. The voice of song is hushed in the silence of death. She can no longer lead in the dance. She had sung sweetly in her day; she had very blessedly seized the keynote of that magnificent song of praise sung on the resurrection side of the Red Sea. Her chorus embodied the great central truth of redemption.—"Sing ye to the Lord, for He hath triumphed gloriously: the horse and his rider hath He thrown into the sea." This was truly a lofty strain; it was the suited utterance for the joyous occasion.

But now the prophetess passes off the scene, and the voice of melody is exchanged for the voice of murmuring. Wilderness life is becoming irksome. The trials of the desert put nature to the test; they bring out what is in the heart. Forty years' toil and travail make a great change in people. It is very rare indeed to find a case in which the verdure and freshness of spiritual life are kept up, much less augmented, throughout all the stages of Christian life and warfare. It ought not to be such a rarity; it ought to be the very reverse, inasmuch as it is in the actual details, the stern realities of our path through this world, that we prove what God is. He, blessed be His name, takes occasion from the very trials of the way to make Himself known to us in all the sweetness and tenderness of love that knows no change. His loving-kindness and tender mercy never fail. Nothing can exhaust those springs which are in the living God. He will be what He is spite of all our naughtiness: God will be God, let man prove himself ever so faithless and faulty.

This is our comfort, our joy, and the source of our strength. We have to do with the living God. What a reality! Come what may, He will prove Himself equal to every emergency—amply sufficient "for exigence of every hour." His patient grace can bear with our manifold infirmities, failures, and shortcomings, and His strength is made perfect in our utter weakness. His faithfulness never fails; His mercy is from everlasting to everlasting. Friends fail or pass away; links of fond friendship are snapped in this cold, heartless world; fellow-laborers part company; Miriams and Aarons die; but God remaineth. Here lies the deep secret of all true and solid blessedness. If we have the hand and heart of the living God with us, we need not fear. If we can say, "The Lord is my Shepherd," we can assuredly add, "We shall not want."

Still there are the scenes of sorrow and trial in the desert, and we have to go through them. Thus it was with Israel in the chapter before us. They were called to meet the keen blasts of the wilderness, and they met them with accents of impatience and discontent. "And there was no water for the congregation: and they gathered themselves together against Moses and against Aaron. And the people chode with Moses, and spake, saying, 'Would God that we had died when our brethren died before the Lord! And why have ye brought up the congregation of the Lord into this wilderness, that we and our cattle should die there? And wherefore have ye made us to come up out of Egypt, to bring us unto this evil place? It is no place of seed, or of figs, or of vines, or of pomegranates; neither is there any water to drink' " (ver. 2-5).

This was a deeply trying moment to the spirit of Moses. We can form no conception of what it must have been to encounter six hundred thousand murmurers, and to be obliged to listen to their bitter invectives, and to hear himself charged with all the misfortunes which their own unbelief had conjured up before them. All this was no ordinary trial of patience; and most assuredly *we* need not marvel if that dear and honored servant found the occasion too much for him. "And Moses and Aaron went from the presence of the assembly unto the door of the tabernacle of the congregation, and they fell upon their faces: and the glory of the Lord appeared unto them" (ver. 6).

It is deeply touching to find Moses, again and again, on his face before God. It was a sweet relief to make his escape from a tumultuous host and betake himself to the only One whose resources were adequate to meet such an occasion. "They fell upon their faces; and the glory of the Lord appeared unto them." They do not appear, on this occasion, to have attempted any reply to the people; "they went from the presence of the assembly" and cast themselves upon the living God. They could not possibly have done better. Who but the God of all grace could meet the ten thousand necessities of wilderness life? Well had Moses said, at the very beginning, "If Thy prsence go not with us, carry us not up hence." Assuredly, he was right and wise in so expressing himself. The divine presence was the *only* answer to the demand of such a congregation; but that presence *was* an all-sufficient answer. God's treasury is absolutely inexhaustible. He can never fail a trusting heart. Let us remember this. God delights to be used; He never grows weary of ministering to the need of His people. If this were ever kept in the remembrance of the thoughts of our hearts, we should hear less of the accents of impatience and discontent, and more of the sweet language of thankfulness and praise; but, as we have had frequent occasion to remark, desert life tests every one. It proves what is in us, and, thanks be to God, it brings out what is in *Him* for us.

"And the Lord spake unto Moses, saying, 'Take *the* rod, and gather thou the assembly together, thou and Aaron thy brother, and speak ye unto the rock before their eyes; and it shall give forth his water, and thou shalt bring forth to them water out of the rock: so thou shalt give the congregation and their beasts drink.' And Moses took *the* rod from before the Lord as He commanded him. And Moses and Aaron gathered the congregation together before the rock, and he said unto them, 'Hear, now, ye rebels; must we fetch you water out of this rock?' And Moses lifted up his hand, and with *his* rod he smote the rock twice: and the water came out abundantly; and the congregation drank, and their beasts also" (ver. 7-11).

Two objects in the foregoing quotation demand the reader's attention, namely, "The rock" and "the rod." They both present Christ most blessedly to the soul, but in two distinct aspects. In 1 Corinthians 10:4, we read, "They drank of that spiritual Rock that followed them: and that Rock was Christ." This is plain and positive. It leaves no room whatever for the exercise of imagination. "That Rock was Christ"—Christ smitten for us.

Then as regards "the rod," we must remember that it was not the rod of Moses—the rod of authority—the rod of power. This would not suit the occasion before us. It had done its work; it had smitten the rock once, and that was enough. This we learn from Exodus 17, where we read, "The Lord said unto Moses, 'Go on before the people, and take with thee of the elders of Israel; and *thy* rod, *wherewith thou smotest the river* (see Exodus 7:20), take in thy hand and go.

Behold, I will stand before thee there upon the rock in Horeb; and thou shalt smite the rock, and there shall come water out of it, that the people may drink.' And Moses did so in the sight of the elders of Israel."

Here we have a type of Christ smitten for us, by the hand of God, in judgment. The reader will note the expression, "Thy rod wherewith thou smotest the river." Why the river? why should this particular stroke of the rod be referred to? Exodus 7:20 furnishes the reply.—"And he [Moses] lifted up the rod, and smote the waters that were in the river, in the sight of Pharaoh, and in the sight of his servants; and all the waters that were in the river were *turned to blood.*" It was the rod which turned the water into blood that was to smite "that Rock which was Christ," in order that streams of life and refreshment might flow for us.

Now, this smiting could only take place once; it is never to be repeated. "Knowing that Christ being raised from the dead dieth no more; death hath no more dominion over Him. For in that He died, He died unto sin *once;* but in that He liveth, He liveth unto God" (Rom. 6:9-10). "But now *once* in the end of the world hath He appeared to put away sin by the sacrifice of Himself . . . so Christ was *once* offered to bear the sins of many" (Heb. 9:26,28). "For Christ also hath *once* suffered for sins, the just for the unjust, that He might bring us to God" (1 Pet. 3:18).

There can be no repetition of the death of Christ, and hence Moses was wrong in smiting the rock twice with *his* rod—wrong in smiting it at all. He was commanded to take *"the rod"*—Aaron's rod—the priestly rod, and speak to the rock. The atoning work is done, and now our great High-Priest has passed into the heavens, there to appear in the presence of God for us, and the streams of spiritual refreshment flow to us on the ground of accomplished redemption and in connection with Christ's priestly ministry, of which Aaron's budding rod is the exquisite figure.

Hence, then, it was a grave mistake for Moses to smite the rock a second time—a mistake to use his rod in the matter at all. To have smitten with Aaron's rod would, as we can easily understand, have spoiled its lovely blossom. A word would have sufficed in connection with the rod of priesthood—the rod of grace. Moses failed to see this—failed to glorify God. He spoke unadvisedly with his lips, and as a consequence, he was prohibited going over Jordan. His rod could not take the people over—for what could mere authority do with a murmuring host—and he was not suffered to go over himself, because he failed to sanctify Jehovah in the eyes of the congregation.

But Jehovah took care of His own glory. He sanctified Himself before the people, and notwithstanding their rebellious murmurings, and Moses' sad mistake and failure, the congregation of the Lord received a gushing stream from the smitten rock.

Nor was this all. It was not merely that grace triumphed in furnishing Israel's murmuring hosts with drink, but even in reference to Moses himself it shines out most brilliantly, as we may see in Deuteronomy 34. It was grace that brought Moses to the top of Pisgah and showed him the land of Canaan from thence. It was grace that led Jehovah to provide a grave for His servant and bury him therein. It was better to see the land of Canaan in company with God than to enter it in company with Israel. And yet we must not forget that Moses was prevented entering the land because of the unadvised speaking. God in government kept Moses out of Canaan: God in grace brought Moses up to Pisgah. These two facts in the history of Moses illustrate very forcibly the distinction between grace and government—a subject of the deepest interest, and of great practical value. Grace pardons and blesses, but government takes its course. Let us ever remember this. "Whatsoever a man soweth, that shall he also reap." This principle runs through all the ways of God in government, and nothing can be more solemn; nevertheless, "grace reigns through righteousness, unto eternal life, by Jesus Christ our Lord." All praise to Him who is at once the fountain and the channel of this grace!

From verses 14-20 of our chapter, we have the correspondence between Moses and the king of Edom. It is instructive and interesting to notice the style of each, and to compare it with the history given in Genesis 32–33. Esau had a serious grudge against Jacob; and albeit, through the direct interposition of God, he was not suffered to touch a hair of his brother's head, still, on the other hand, Israel must not meddle with Esau's possessions. Jacob had supplanted Esau, and Israel must not molest Edom. "Command thou the people, saying, Ye are to pass through the coast of your brethren the children of Esau, which dwell in Seir; and they shall be afraid of you: take ye good heed unto yourselves therefore. Meddle not with them; for I will not give you of their land—no, not so much as a foot-breadth, because I have given Mount Seir unto Esau for a possession. Ye shall buy meat of them for money, that ye may eat; and ye shall also buy water of them for money, that ye may drink" (Deut. 2:4-6). Thus we see that the same God who would not suffer Esau to touch Jacob, in Genesis 33, now will not suffer Israel to touch Edom, in Numbers 20.

The closing paragraph of Numbers 20 is deeply touching. We shall not quote it, but the reader should refer to it, and compare it carefully with the scene in Exodus 4:1-17. Moses had deemed Aaron's companionship indispensable; but he afterwards found him to be a sore thorn in his side, and here he is compelled to strip him of his robes and see him gathered to his fathers. All this is very admonitory, in whatever way we view it, whether as regards Moses or Aaron. We have already referred to this instructive piece of history, and therefore we shall not dwell upon it here; but may the good Lord engrave its solemn lesson deeply upon the tablets of our hearts.

---

## *CHAPTER 21*

THIS chapter brings prominently before us the familiar and beautiful ordinance of the brazen serpent—that great evangelical type. "And they journeyed from Mount Hor by the way of the Red Sea, to compass the land of Edom: and the soul of the people was much discouraged because of the way. And the people spake against God, and against Moses, "Wherefore have ye brought us up out of Egypt to die in the wilderness? for there is no bread, neither is there any water; and our soul loatheth this light bread" (ver. 4-5).

Alas! it is the same sad story over and over again—"The murmurs of the wilderness." It was all well enough to escape out of Egypt when the terrific judgments of God were falling upon it in rapid succession. At such a moment, there was but little attraction in the flesh-pots, the leeks, the onions, and the garlic, when they stood connected with the heavy plagues sent forth from the hand of an offended God. But now, the plagues are forgotten, and the flesh-pots alone remembered. "Would to God we had died by the hand of the Lord in the land of Egypt, when we sat by the flesh-pots, and when we did eat bread to the full."

What language! Man would rather sit by the flesh-pots, in a land of death and darkness, than walk with God through the wilderness and eat bread from heaven. The Lord Himself had brought His glory down into connection with the very sand of the desert, because His redeemed were there. He had come down to bear with all their provocation—to "suffer their manners in the wilderness." All this grace and exceeding condescension might well have called forth in them a spirit of grateful and humble subjection. But no; the very earliest appearance of trial was sufficient to elicit from them the cry, "Would to God we had died in the land of Egypt!"

However, they were very speedily made to taste the bitter fruits of their murmuring spirit. "The Lord sent fiery serpents among the people, and they bit the people; and much people of Israel died" (ver. 6). The serpent was the *source* of their discontent; and their condition, when bitten of the serpents, was well calculated to reveal to them the true *character* of their discontent. If the Lord's people will not walk happily and contentedly with Him, they must taste the power of the serpent—alas! a terrible power, in whatever way it may be experienced.

The serpents' bite brought Israel to a sense of their sin. "Therefore the people came to Moses, and said, 'We have sinned, for we have spoken against the Lord, and against thee: pray unto the Lord, that He take away the serpents from us' " (ver. 7).

Here, then, was the moment for divine grace to display itself. Man's need has ever been the occasion for the display of God's grace and mercy. The moment Israel could say, "We have sinned," there was no further hindrance. God could act, and this was enough. When Israel murmured, the serpents' bite was the answer: when Israel confessed, God's grace was the answer. In the one case, the serpent was the instrument of their wretchedness; in the other, it was the instrument of their restoration and blessing. "And the Lord said unto Moses, 'Make thee a fiery serpent, and set it upon a pole: and it shall come to pass, that every one that is bitten, when he looketh upon it, shall live" (ver. 8). The very image of that which had done the mischief was set up to be the channel through which divine grace might flow down, in rich abundance, to poor wounded sinners. Striking and beautiful type of Christ on the cross!

It is a very common error to view the Lord Jesus rather as the averter of God's wrath, than as the channel of His love. That He endured the wrath of God against sin is most preciously true; but there is more than this. He has come down into this wretched world to die upon the cursed tree, in order that, by dying, He might open up the everlasting springs of the love of God to the heart of poor rebellious man. This makes a vast difference in the presentation of God's nature and character to the sinner, which is of the very last importance. Nothing can ever bring a sinner back to a state of true happiness and holiness but his being fully established in the faith and enjoyment of the love of God. The very first effort of the serpent, when, in the garden of Eden, he assailed the creature, was to shake his confidence in the kindness and love of God, and thus produce discontent with the place in which God had set him. Man's fall was the result—the immediate result of his doubting the love of God: man's recovery must flow from his belief of that love; and it is the Son of God Himself who says, "God so loved the world, that He gave His only begotten Son, that whosoever believeth in Him should not perish, but have everlasting life" (John 3:16).

Now, it is in close connection with the foregoing statement that our Lord expressly teaches that He was the antitype of the brazen serpent. As the Son of God sent forth from the Father, He was, most assuredly, the gift and expression of God's love to a perishing world. But He was also to be lifted up upon the cross in atonement for sin, for *only* thus could divine love meet the necessities of the dying sinner. "As Moses lifted up the serpent in the wilderness, even so *must* the Son of Man be lifted up; that whosoever believeth in Him should not perish, but have eternal life." The whole human family have felt the serpent's deadly sting; but the God of all grace has found a remedy in the One who was lifted up on the cursed tree; and now, by the Holy Ghost sent down from heaven, He calls on all those who feel themselves bitten, to look to Jesus for life and peace. Christ is God's great ordinance, and through Him a full, free, present, and eternal salvation is proclaimed to the sinner—a salvation so complete, so well based, so consistent with all the attributes of the divine character and all the claims of the throne of God, that Satan cannot raise a single question about it. Resurrection is the divine vindication of the work of the cross, and the glory of Him who died thereon, so that the believer may enjoy the most profound repose in reference to sin. God is well pleased in Jesus; and inasmuch as He views all believers in Him, He is well pleased in them also.

And be it noted, faith is the instrument whereby the sinner lays hold of Christ's salvation. The wounded Israelite had simply to *look and live*—look, not at himself, not at his wounds, not at others around him, but, directly and exclusively, to God's remedy. If he refused or neglected to look to that, there was nothing for him but death. He was called to fix his earnest gaze upon God's remedy, which was so placed that all might see it. There was no possible use in looking any where else, for the word was, *"Every one* that is bitten, *when* he looketh upon *it,* shall live." The bitten Israelite was shut up to the brazen serpent; for the brazen serpent was God's exclusive remedy for the bitten Israelite. To look any where else, was to get nothing: to look at God's provision, was to get life.

Thus it is now. The sinner is called simply to look to Jesus. He is not told to look to ordinances—to look to churches—to look to men or angels. There is no help in any of these, and therefore he is not called to look to them, but exclusively to Jesus, whose death and resurrection form the eternal foundation of the believer's peace and hope. God assures him that "whosoever believeth in Him shall not perish, but have everlasting life." This should fully satisfy the heart and conscience. God is satisfied, and so ought we to be. To raise doubt, is to deny the record of God. If an Israelite had said, How do I know that looking to that serpent of brass will restore me? or if he had begun to dwell upon the greatness and hopeless nature of his malady, and to reason upon the apparent uselessness of looking up to God's ordinance; in short, if any thing, no matter what, had prevented his looking to the brazen serpent, it would have involved a positive rejection of God, and death would have been the inevitable result.

Thus in the case of the sinner, the moment he is enabled to cast a look of faith to Jesus, his sins vanish. The blood of Jesus, like a mighty cleansing stream, flows over his conscience, washes away every stain, and leaves him without spot or wrinkle, or any such thing; and all this, too, in the very light of the holiness of God, where not one speck of sin can be tolerated.

But ere closing our meditation on the brazen serpent, it may be well just to observe what we may call the intense individuality which marked the bitten Israelite's look at the serpent. Each one had to look for himself. No one could look for another. It was a personal question. No one could be saved by proxy. There was life in a look, but the look must be given. There needed to be a personal link—direct individual contact with God's remedy.

Thus it was then, and thus it is now. We must have to do with Jesus for ourselves. The Church cannot save us—no order or priests or ministers can save us. There must be the personal link with the Saviour, else there is no life. "It came to pass, that if a serpent had bitten *any man,* when *he* beheld the serpent of brass, he lived." This was God's order then, and this is His order now; for *"as* Moses lifted up the serpent in the wilderness, even *so* must the Son of Man be lifted up." Let us remember the two little words *"as"* and *"so,"* for they apply to every particular in the type and the Antitype. Faith is an individual thing; repentance is an individual thing; salvation is an individual thing. Let us never forget this. True, there is, in Christianity, union and communion; but we must have to do with Christ for ourselves, and we must walk with God for ourselves. We can neither get life nor live by the faith of another. There is, we repeat with emphasis, an intense individuality in every stage of the Christian's life and practical career.

We shall not dwell further upon the familiar type of "the serpent of brass," but we pray God to enable the reader to meditate upon it for himself, and to make a direct personal application of the precious truth unfolded in one of the most striking figures of Old Testament times. May he be led to gaze, with a more profound and soul-subduing faith, upon the cross, and to drink into his inmost soul the precious mystery there presented. May he not be satisfied with merely getting life by a look at that cross, but seek to enter, more and more, into its deep and marvelous meaning, and thus be more devotedly knit to Him who, when there was no other way of escape possible, did voluntarily surrender Himself to be bruised on that cursed tree for us and for our salvation.

We shall close our remarks on Numbers 21 by calling the reader's attention to verses

16-18. "And from thence they went to Beer: that is the well whereof the Lord spake unto Moses, 'Gather the people together, and I will give them water.' Then Israel sang this song, 'Spring up, O well; sing ye unto it. The princes digged the well, the nobles of the people digged it, by the direction of the law-giver, with their staves.' "

This is a remarkable passage coming in at such a moment and in such a connection. The murmurings are hushed, the people are nearing the borders of the promised land, the effects of the serpents' bite have passed away, and now, without any rod, without any smiting, the people are supplied with refreshment. What though the Amorites, Moabites, and Ammonites are about them? what though the power of Sihon stands in the way? God can open a well for His people and give them a song in spite of all. Oh, what a God is our God! How blessed it is to trace His actings and ways with His people in all these wilderness scenes! May we learn to trust Him more implicitly, and to walk with Him, from day to day, in holy and happy subjection. This is the true path of peace and blessing.

---

## *CHAPTERS 22–24*

THESE three chapters form a distinct section of our book—a truly marvelous section, abounding in rich and varied instruction. In it we have presented to us, first, the covetous prophet, and secondly, his sublime prophecies. There is something peculiarly awful in the case of Balaam. He evidently loved money—no uncommon love, alas! in our own day. Balak's gold and silver proved a very tempting bait to the wretched man—a bait too tempting to be resisted. Satan knew his man, and the price at which he could be purchased.

If Balaam's heart had been right with God, he would have made very short work with Balak's message; indeed it would not have cost him a moment's consideration to send a reply. But Balaam's heart was all wrong, and we see him in chapter 22 in the melancholy condition of one acted upon by conflicting feelings. His heart was bent upon going, because it was bent upon the silver and gold; but at the same time, there was a sort of reference to God—an appearance of religiousness, put on as a cloak to cover his covetous practices. He longed for the money, but he would fain lay hold of it after a religious fashion. Miserable man!—most miserable! His name stands on the page of inspiration as the expression of one very dark and awful stage of man's downward history. "Woe unto them!" says Jude; "for they have gone in the way of Cain, and ran greedily after *the error of Balaam for reward,* and perished in the gainsaying of Core." Peter, too, presents Balaam as a prominent figure in one of the very darkest pictures of fallen humanity—a model on which some of the vilest characters are formed. He speaks of those "having eyes full of adultery, and that cannot cease from sin; beguiling unstable souls; a heart they have exercised with covetous practices; cursed children: which have forsaken the right way, and are gone astray, following the way of Balaam the son of Bosor, *who loved the wages of unrighteousness;* but was rebuked for his iniquity: the dumb ass speaking with man's voice forbad the madness of the prophet" (2 Peter 2:14-16).

These passages are solemnly conclusive as to the true character and spirit of Balaam. His heart was set upon money—"he loved the wages of unrighteousness," and his history has been written by the pen of the Holy Ghost as an awful warning to all professors to beware of covetousness, which is idolatry. We shall not dwell further upon the sad story. The reader may pause for a few moments, and gaze upon the picture presented in Numbers 22. He may study the two prominent figures—the crafty king and the covetous, self-willed prophet; and we doubt not he will rise up from the study with a deepened sense of the evil of covetousness, the great moral danger of setting the heart's affections upon this world's riches, and the deep blessedness of having the fear of God before our eyes.

We shall now proceed to examine those marvelous prophecies delivered by Balaam in the audience of Balak, king of the Moabites.

It is profoundly interesting to witness the scene enacted on the high places of Baal, to mark the grand question at stake, to listen to the speakers, to be admitted behind the scenes on such a momentous occasion. How little did Israel know or imagine what was going on between Jehovah and the enemy. It may be they were murmuring in their tents at the very moment in the which God was setting forth their perfection by the tongues of the covetous prophet. Balak would fain have Israel cursed, but, blessed be God, He will not suffer any one to curse His people. He may have to deal with them Himself, in secret, about many things; but He will not suffer another to move his tongue against them. He may have to expose them to themselves, but He will not allow a stranger to expose them.

This is a point of deepest interest. The great question is not so much what the enemy may think of God's people, or what they may think about themselves, or what they may think of one another. The real, the all-important question is, What does God think about them? He knows exactly all that concerns them, all that they are, all that they have done, all that is in them. Every thing stands clearly revealed to His all-penetrating eye. The deepest secrets of the heart, of the nature, and of the life are all known to Him. Neither angels, men, nor devils know us as God knows us. God knows us perfectly, and it is with Him we have to do; and we can say, in the triumphant language of the apostle, "If God be for us, who can be against us?" (Rom. 8) God sees us, thinks of us, speaks about us, acts towards us, according to what He Himself has made us and wrought for us, according to the perfection of His own work. "Beholders many faults may find;" but, as regards our standing, our God sees us only in the comeliness of Christ: we are perfect in Him. When God looks at His people, He beholds in them His own workmanship; and it is to the glory of His holy name, and to the praise of His salvation, that not a blemish should be seen on those who are His—those whom He, in sovereign grace, has made His own. His character, His name, His glory, and the perfection of His work are all involved in the standing of those with whom He has linked Himself.

Hence, therefore, the moment any enemy or accuser enters the scene, Jehovah places Himself in front to receive and answer the accusation; and His answer is always founded, not upon what His people are in themselves, but upon what He had made them through the perfection of His own work. His glory is linked with them, and in vindicating them, He maintains His own glory. He places Himself between them and every accusing tongue. His glory demands that they should be presented in all the comeliness which He has put upon them. If the enemy comes to curse and accuse, Jehovah answers him by pouring forth the rich current of His everlasting complacency in those whom He has chosen for Himself, and whom He has made fit to be in His presence forever.

All this is strikingly illustrated in the third chapter of the prophet Zechariah. There, too, the enemy presents himself to resist the representative of the people of God. How does God answer him? Simply by cleansing, clothing, and crowning the one whom Satan would fain curse and accuse, so that Satan has not a word to say. He is silenced forever. The filthy garments are gone, and he that was a brand is become a *mitred* priest—he who was only fit for hell is now fitted to walk up and down in the courts of the Lord.

So also when we turn to the book of Canticles, we see the same thing. There, the bridegroom, in contemplating the bride, declares to her, "Thou art *all fair,* my love; there is *no spot* in thee" (chap. 4:7). She, in speaking of herself, can only exclaim, *"I am black"* (chap. 1:5-6). So also in John 13, the Lord Jesus looks at His disciples and pronounces them "clean every whit," although, in a few hours afterwards, one of them was to curse and swear that he did not know Him. So vast is the difference between what we are in ourselves and what we are in Christ—between our positive standing and our possible state.

Should this glorious truth as to the perfection of our standing make us careless as to our practical state? Far away be the monstrous thought! Nay, the knowledge of our absolutely settled and perfect position in Christ is the very thing which the Holy Ghost makes use of in order to raise the standard of practice. Hearken to those powerful words from the pen of the inspired apostle—"If ye then be risen with Christ, seek those things which are above, where Christ sitteth on the right hand of God. Set your affection on things above, not on things on the earth. For ye are dead, and your life is hid with Christ in God. When Christ our life shall appear, then shall ye also appear with Him in glory. Mortify *therefore* your members" (Col. 3:1-5). We must never measure the standing by the state, but always judge the state by the standing. To lower the standing because of the state, is to give the death-blow to all progress in practical Christianity.

The foregoing line of truth is most forcibly illustrated in Balaam's four parables. To speak after the manner of men, we never should have had such a glorious view of Israel as seen in "the vision of the Almighty"—"from the top of the rocks"—by one "having his eyes open," had not Balak sought to curse them. Jehovah, blessed be His name, can very speedily open a man's eyes to the true state of the case, in reference to the standing of His people and His judgment respecting them. He claims the privilege of setting forth *His* thoughts about them. Balak and Balaam, with "all the princes of Moab," may assemble to hear Israel cursed and defied; they may "build seven altars," and "offer a bullock and a lamb on every altar;" Balak's silver and gold may glitter under the covetous gaze of the false prophet; but not all the powers of earth and hell—men and devils combined, in their dark and terrible array, can evoke a single breath of curse or accusation against the Israel of God. As well might the enemy have sought to point out a flaw in that fair creation which God had pronounced "very good," as to fasten an accusation upon the redeemed of the Lord. Oh, no; they shine in all the comeliness which He has put upon them, and all that is needed in order to see them thus, is to mount to "the top of the rocks"—to have "the eyes open" to look at them from His point of view, so that we may see them in "the vision of the Almighty."

Having thus taken a general survey of the contents of these remarkable chapters, we shall briefly glance at each of the four parables in particular. We shall find a distinct point in each—a distinct feature in the character and condition of the people as seen in "the vision of the Almighty."

In the first of Balaam's wonderful parables, we have the marked separation of God's people from all the nations most distinctly set forth. "How shall I curse whom God hath not cursed? or how shall I defy whom the Lord hath not defied? for from the top of the rocks I see him, and from the hills I behold him: lo, the people shall dwell alone, and shall not be reckoned among the nations. Who can count the dust of Jacob, and the number of the fourth part of Israel? Let me die the death of the righteous, and let my last end be like his."*

Here we have Israel singled out, and partitioned off to be a separated and peculiar people—a people who, according to the divine thought concerning them, were never, at any time, on any ground, or for any object whatsoever, to be mingled with or reckoned amongst the nations. "The people shall dwell *alone.*" This is distinct and emphatic. It is true of the literal seed of Abraham, and true of all believers now. Immense practical results flow out of this great principle. God's people are to be separated unto Him, not on the ground of being better than others, but simply on the ground of what God is, and what He would ever have His people to be. We shall not pursue this point

*Poor, wretched Balaam! Miserable man! He would fain die the death of the righteous. Many there are who would say the same; but they forget that the way "to die the death of the righteous" is to possess and exhibit the *life* of the righteous. Many—alas! how many—would like to die the death who do not live the life. Many would like to possess Balak's silver and gold and yet be enrolled amongst the Israel of God. Vain thought! Fatal delusion! We cannot serve God and mammon.

further just now; but the reader would do well to examine it thoroughly in the light of the divine Word. *"The people shall dwell alone, and shall not be reckoned among the nations"* (chap. 23:8-9).

But if Jehovah, in His sovereign grace, is pleased to link Himself with a people; if He calls them out to be a separate people in the world—to "dwell alone," and shine for Him in the midst of those who are still "sitting in darkness and the shadow of death," He can only have them in such a condition as suits Himself. He must make them such as He would have them to be—such as shall be to the praise of His great and glorious name. Hence, in the second parable, the prophet is made to tell out, not merely the negative, but the positive condition of the people. "And he took up his parable and said, 'Rise up, Balak, and hear; hearken unto me, thou son of Zippor: God is not a man, that He should lie; neither the son of man, that He should repent: hath He said, and shall He not do it? or hath He spoken, and shall He not make it good? Behold, I have received commandment to bless; and *He hath blessed;* and I *cannot* reverse it. He hath not beheld iniquity in Jacob, neither hath He seen perverseness in Israel: the Lord his God is with him, and the shout of a King is among them. God brought them out of Egypt; he hath as it were the strength of a unicorn. Surely there is no enchantment against Jacob, neither is there any divination against Israel: according to this time it shall be said of Jacob and of Israel, What hath *God wrought!* [not, What hath Israel wrought!] Behold, the people shall rise up as a great lion, and lift up himself as a young lion: he shall not lie down until he eat of the prey, and drink the blood of the slain' " (chap. 23:18-24).

Here we find ourselves on truly elevated ground, and on ground as solid as it is elevated. This is, in truth, "the top of the rocks"—the pure air and wide range of "the hills," where the people of God are seen only in "the vision of the Almighty"—seen as He sees them, without spot or wrinkle or any such thing—all their deformities hidden from view—all His comeliness seen upon them.

In this very sublime parable, Israel's blessedness and security are made to depend, not on themselves, but upon the truth and faithfulness of Jehovah. "God is not a man, that He should lie; neither the son of man, that He should repent." This places Israel upon safe ground. God must be true to Himself. Is there any power that can possibly prevent Him from fulfilling His word and oath? Surely not. *"He hath blessed;* and I cannot reverse it." God *will* not, and Satan *cannot* reverse the blessing.

Thus all is settled. "It is ordered in all things and sure." In the previous parable, it was, "God hath *not cursed;*" here, it is, "He *hath blessed.*" There is very manifest advance. As Balak conducts the money-loving prophet from place to place, Jehovah takes occasion to bring out fresh features of beauty in His people, and fresh points of security in their position. Thus it is not merely that they are a separated people dwelling alone; but they are a justified people, having the Lord their God *with* them, and the shout of a King *among* them. "He hath not beheld iniquity in Jacob, neither hath He seen perverseness in Israel." The enemy may say, There is iniquity and perverseness there all the while. Yes, but who can make Jehovah behold it, when He Himself has been pleased to blot it all out as a thick cloud for His name's sake? If He has cast it behind His back, who can bring it before His face? "It is God that justifieth; who is he that condemneth?" God sees His people so thoroughly delivered from all that could be against them, that He can take up His abode in their midst, and cause His voice to be heard amongst them.

Well, therefore, may we exclaim, " 'What hath God wrought!' It is not, What hath Israel wrought!" Balak and Balaam would have found plenty to do in the way of cursing had Israel's work been in question. The Lord be praised, it is on what He hath wrought that His people stand, and their foundation is as stable as the throne of God. "If God be for us, who can be against us?" If God stands right between us and every foe, what have we to *fear?* If He undertakes, on our behalf, to answer every accuser, then assuredly perfect peace is our portion.

However, the king of Moab still fondly hoped and sedulously sought to gain his end. And doubtless Balaam did the same, for they were leagued together against the Israel of God, thus reminding us forcibly of the beast and the false prophet, who are yet to arise and play an awfully solemn part in connection with Israel's future, as presented on the apocalyptic page.

"And when Balaam saw that it pleased the Lord to bless Israel, he went not, as at other times, to seek for enchantments [what a dreadful disclosure is here!], but he set his face toward the wilderness. And Balaam lifted up his eyes, and he saw Israel abiding in his tents, according to their tribes; and the Spirit of God came upon him. And he took up his parable, and said, 'Balaam the son of Beor hath said, he hath said, which heard *the words of God,* which saw *the vision of the Almighty,* falling into a trance, but having his eyes open: How goodly are thy tents, O Jacob, and thy tabernacles, O Israel! As the valleys are they spread forth, as the gardens by the river's side, as the trees of lign aloes which the Lord hath planted, and as cedar-trees beside the waters. He shall pour the water out of his buckets, and his seed shall be in many waters, and his King shall be higher than Agag, and his kingdom shall be exalted. God brought him forth out of Egypt; he hath as it were the strength of a unicorn: he shall *eat up the nations* his enemies, [terrible announcement for Balak!] and shall break their bones, and pierce them through with his arrows. He couched, he lay down as a lion, and as a great lion: who shall stir him up? Blessed is he that blesseth thee, and cursed is he that curseth thee' " (chap. 24:1-9).

"Higher and higher yet" is surely the motto here. We may well shout, "Excelsior!" as we mount up to the top of the rocks, and hearken to those brilliant utterances which the false prophet was forced to give out. It was better and better for Israel, worse and worse for Balak. He had to stand by and not only hear Israel "blessed," but hear himself "cursed" for seeking to curse them.

But let us particularly notice the rich grace that shines in this third parable. "How goodly are thy tents, O Jacob, and thy tabernacles, O Israel!" If one had gone down to examine those tents and tabernacles in "the vision" of man, they might have appeared "black as the tents of Kedar;" but looked at in "the vision of the Almighty," they were "goodly," and whoever did not see them thus needed to have *"his eyes opened."* If I am looking at the people of God "from the top of the rocks," I shall see them as God sees them, and that is, as clothed with all the comeliness of Christ—complete in Him—accepted in the Beloved. That is what will enable me to get on with them, to walk with them, to have fellowship with them, to rise above their points and angles, blots and blemishes, failures and infirmities.* If I do not contemplate them from this lofty—this divine ground, I shall be sure to fix my eye on some little flaw or other, which will completely mar my communion, and alienate my affections.

In Israel's case, we shall see, in the very next chapter, what terrible evil they fell into. Did this alter Jehovah's judgment? Surely not. "He is not the son of man, that He should repent." He judged and chastened them for their evil, because He is holy, and can never sanction, in His people, aught that is contrary to His nature. But He could never reverse His judgment respecting them. He knew all about them, He knew what they were and what they would do; but yet He said, "I have not beheld iniquity in Jacob, neither have I seen perverseness in Israel." "How goodly are thy tents, O Jacob, and thy tabernacles, O Israel!" Was this making light of their evil? The thought were blasphemy. He could chasten them for their sins; but the moment an enemy comes forth to curse or accuse, He stands in front of His people and says, "I see no iniquity." "How goodly are thy tents!"

Dost thou think that such views of divine grace will minister to a spirit of antinomianism? Far be the thought! We may rest

*The statement in the text does not, by any means, touch the question of discipline in the house of God. We are bound to judge moral evil and doctrinal error (1 Cor. 5:12-13).

assured we are never farther away from the region of that terrible evil than when we are breathing the pure and holy atmosphere of "the top of the rocks"—that high ground from whence God's people are viewed, not as they are in themselves, but as they are in Christ—not according to the thoughts of man, but according to the thoughts of God. And furthermore, we may say that the only true and effectual mode of raising the standard of moral conduct is to abide in the faith of this most precious and tranquilizing truth, that God sees us perfect in Christ.

But we must take one more glance at our third parable. Not only are Israel's tents seen to be goodly in the eyes of Jehovah, but the people themselves are presented to us as abiding fast by those ancient sources of grace and living ministry which are found in God. "As the valleys are they spread forth, as gardens by the river's side, as the trees of lign aloes which the Lord hath planted, and as cedar-trees beside the waters." How exquisite! how perfectly beautiful! And only to think that we are indebted to the godless confederacy between Balak and Balaam for those sublime utterances!

But there is more than this. Not only is Israel seen drinking at those everlasting well-springs of grace and salvation, but, as must ever be the case, as a channel of blessing to others. "He shall pour the water out of his buckets." It is the fixed purpose of God that Israel's twelve tribes shall yet be a medium of rich blessing to all the ends of the earth. This we learn from such Scriptures as Ezekiel 47 and Zechariah 14, on which we do not now attempt to dwell; we merely refer to them as showing the marvelous fullness and beauty of these glorious parables. The reader may meditate with much spiritual profit upon these and kindred Scriptures, but let him carefully guard against the fatal system falsely called spiritualizing, which, in fact, consists mainly in applying to the professing church all the special blessings of the house of Israel, while to the latter are left only the curses of a broken law. We may rest assured that God will not sanction any such system as this. Israel is beloved for the fathers' sakes, and "the gifts and calling of God are without repentance" (Rom. 11).

We shall close this section by a brief reference to Balaam's last parable. Balak, having heard such a glowing testimony to Israel's future, and the overthrow of all their enemies, was not only sorely disappointed, but greatly enraged. "And Balak's anger was kindled against Balaam, and he smote his hands together: and Balak said unto Balaam, 'I called thee to curse mine enemies, and, behold, thou hast altogether blessed them these three times. Therefore now flee thou to thy place: I thought to promote thee unto *great honor* [?]; but, lo, the Lord hath kept thee back from honor.' And Balaam said unto Balak, 'Spake I not also to thy messengers which thou sentest unto me, saying, If Balak would give me his full of silver and gold [the very thing his poor heart craved intensely], I *cannot* go beyond the commandment of the Lord, to do either good or bad of mine own mind; but what the Lord saith, that will I speak. And now, behold, I go unto my people: come, therefore, and I will advertise thee what *this people* shall do to *thy people* in the latter days.' [This was coming to close quarters.] And he took up his parable, and said, 'Balaam the son of Beor hath said, and the man whose eyes are open hath said: he hath said, which heard the words of God, and knew the knowledge of the Most High, which saw the vision of the Almighty, falling into a trance, but having his eyes open: I shall see Him, but not now: I shall behold Him, but not nigh: [tremendous fact for Balaam!] there shall come a Star out of Jacob, and a Sceptre shall rise out of Israel, and shall smite the corners of Moab, and destroy all the children of Sheth' " (ver. 10-17).

This gives great completeness to the subject of these parables. The top-stone is here laid on the magnificent superstructure. It is, in good truth, grace and glory. In the first parable, we see the absolute separation of the people; in the second, their perfect justification; in the third, their moral beauty and fruitfulness; and now, in the fourth, we stand on the very summit of the hills—on the loftiest crag of the rocks, and survey the wide plains of glory in all their length and breadth, stretching away into a boundless future. We see the Lion of the tribe of Judah crouching; we hear His roar; we see Him seizing upon all His enemies, and crushing them to atoms. The Star of Jacob rises to set no more. The true David ascends the throne of His Father, Israel is pre-eminent in the earth, and all his enemies are covered with shame and everlasting contempt.

It is impossible to conceive any thing more magnificent than these parables, and they are all the more remarkable as coming at the very close of Israel's desert wanderings, during which they had given such ample proof of what they were—of what materials they were made, and what their capabilities and tendencies were. But God was above all, and nothing changeth His affection. Whom He loves, and as He loves, He loves to the end; and hence the league between the typical "beast and false prophet" proved abortive. Israel was blessed of God and not to be cursed of any. "And Balaam rose up, and went and returned to his place; and Balak also went his way."

---

## *CHAPTER 25*

HERE a new scene opens upon our view. We have been on the top of Pisgah, hearkening to God's testimony respecting Israel, and there, all was bright and fair—without a cloud, without a spot; but now we find ourselves in the plains of Moab, and all is changed. There, we had to do with God and His thoughts; here, we have to do with the people and their ways. What a contrast! It reminds us of the opening and the close of 2 Corinthians 12. In the former, we have the *positive standing* of the Christian; in the latter, the *possible state* into which he may fall if not watchful. That shows us "a man in Christ" capable of being caught up into paradise at any moment; this shows us saints of God capable of plunging into all manner of sin and folly.

Thus it is with Israel as seen from "the top of the rocks" in "the vision of the Almighty," and Israel as seen in the plains of Moab. In the one case, we have their perfect standing; in the other, their imperfect state. Balaam's parable gives us God's estimate of the former; the javelin of Phinehas, His judgment upon the latter. God will never reverse His decision as to what His people are as to standing, but He must judge and chasten them when their ways comport not with that standing. It is His gracious will that their state should correspond with their standing. But here is, alas! where failure comes in. Nature is allowed to act in various ways, and our God is constrained to take down the rod of discipline, in order that the evil thing which we have suffered to manifest itself may be crushed and subdued.

Thus it is in Numbers 25. Balaam, having failed in his attempt to curse Israel, succeeds in seducing them, by his wiles, to commit sin, hoping thereby to gain his end. "And Israel joined himself unto Baal-peor: and the anger of the Lord was kindled against Israel. And the Lord said unto Moses, 'Take all the heads of the people, and hang them up before the Lord against the sun, that the fierce anger of the Lord may be turned away from Israel' " (ver. 3-4). Then we have the striking record of the zeal and faithfulness of Phinehas. "And the Lord spake unto Moses, saying, 'Phinehas, the son of Eleazar, the son of Aaron the priest, hath turned My wrath away from the children of Israel, while he was zealous for My sake among them, that I consumed not the children of Israel in My jealousy. Wherefore say, Behold, I give unto him My covenant of peace: and he shall have it, and his seed after him, even the covenant of an everlasting priesthood; because he was zealous for his God, and made an atonement for the children of Israel' " (ver. 10-13).

God's glory and Israel's good were the objects that ruled the conduct of the faithful Phinehas on this occasion. It was a critical moment. He felt there was a demand for the most stern action. It was not time for false tenderness. There are moments in the history of God's people in the which tenderness to man becomes unfaithfulness to God; and it is of the utmost importance to be able to discern such moments. The prompt acting of

Phinehas saved the whole congregation, glorified Jehovah in the midst of His people, and completely frustrated the enemy's design. Balaam fell among the judged Midianites, but Phinehas became the possessor of an everlasting priesthood.

Thus much as to the solemn instruction contained in this brief section of our book. May we profit by it. May God's Spirit give us such an abiding sense of the perfection of our standing in Christ that our practical ways may be more in accordance with it.

---

## *CHAPTER 26*

THIS, though one of the longest chapters in our book, does not call for much in the way of remark or exposition. In it we have the record of the second numbering of the people, as they were about to enter upon the promised land. How sad to think that out of the six hundred thousand men of war which were numbered at first, only two remain—Joshua and Caleb! All the rest lay mouldering in the dust, buried beneath the sand of the desert, all passed away. The two men of simple faith remained to have their faith rewarded. As for the men of unbelief, the inspired apostle tells us, "Their carcasses fell in the wilderness."

How solemn! How full of instruction and admonition for us! Unbelief kept the first generation from entering the land of Canaan, and caused them to die in the wilderness. This is the fact on which the Holy Ghost grounds one of the most searching warnings and exhortations any where to be found in the compass of the inspired volume. Let us hear it. "Wherefore . . . take heed, brethren, lest there be in any of you an evil heart of unbelief, in departing from the living God. But exhort one another daily, while it is called, 'To-day'; lest any of you be hardened through the deceitfulness of sin. For we are made partakers of Christ, if we hold the beginning of our confidence steadfast unto the end; while it is said, 'To-day, if ye will hear His voice, harden not your hearts, as in the provocation.' For some, when they had heard, did provoke: howbeit not all that came out of Egypt by Moses. But with whom was He grieved forty years? was it not with them that had sinned, whose carcasses fell in the wilderness? And to whom sware He that they should not enter into His rest, but to them that believed not? So we see that they could not enter in because of unbelief. Let us therefore fear, lest a promise being left us of entering into His rest, any of you should seem to come short of it. For unto us was the gospel preached, as well as unto them; but the Word preached did not profit them, not being mixed with faith in them that heard" (Heb. 3:7—4:1-2).

Here lies the great practical secret. The Word of God mixed with faith. Precious mixture! The only thing that can really profit any one. We may hear a great deal, we may talk a great deal, we may profess a great deal, but we may rest assured that the measure of real spiritual power—power to surmount difficulties—power to overcome the world—power to get on—power to possess ourselves of all that God has bestowed upon us,—the measure of this power is simply the measure in which God's Word is mixed with faith. That Word is settled forever in heaven; and if it is fixed in our hearts, by faith, there is a divine link connecting us with heaven and all that belongs to it; and in proportion as our hearts are thus livingly linked with heaven and the Christ who is there, shall we be practically separated from this present world, and lifted above its influence. Faith takes possession of all that God has given. It enters into that within the vail; it endures as seeing Him who is invisible; it occupies itself with the unseen and eternal, not with the seen and the temporal. Men think possession sure; faith knows nothing sure but God and His Word. Faith takes God's Word and locks it up in the very innermost chamber of the heart, and there it remains as hid treasure—the only thing that deserves to be called treasure. The happy possessor of this treasure is rendered thoroughly independent of the world. He may be poor as regards the riches of this perishing scene; but if only he is rich in faith, he is the possessor of untold wealth—"durable riches and righteousness"

—"the unsearchable riches of Christ."

These are not the pencilings of fancy—the mere visions of the imagination. No; they are substantial verities—divine realities, which you may now enjoy in all their preciousness. If you will only take God at His word—only believe what He says because He says it—for this is faith—then verily you have this treasure, which renders its possessor entirely independent of this scene where men live only by the sight of their eyes. The men of this world speak of *"the positive"* and *"the real,"* meaning thereby what they can see and experience; in other words, the things of time and sense—the tangible—the palpable. Faith knows nothing positive, nothing real, but the word of the living God.

Now, it was the lack of this blessed faith that kept Israel out of Canaan, and caused six hundred thousand carcasses to fall in the wilderness; and it is the lack of this faith that keeps thousands of God's people in bondage and darkness, when they ought to be walking in liberty and light—that keeps them in depression and gloom, when they ought to be walking in the joy and strength of God's full salvation—that keeps them in fear of judgment, when they ought to be walking in the hope of glory—that keeps them in doubt as to whether they shall escape the sword of the destroyer in Egypt, when they ought to be feasting on the old corn of the land of Canaan.

Oh that God's people would consider these things in the secret of His presence and in the light of His Word! Then, indeed, they would better know and more fully appreciate the fair inheritance which faith finds in the eternal Word of God—they would more clearly apprehend the things which are freely given to us of God in the Son of His love. May the Lord send out His light and His truth, and lead His people into the fullness of their portion in Christ, so that they may take their true place, and yield a true testimony for Him, while waiting for His glorious advent.

---

## *CHAPTER 27*

THE conduct of the daughters of Zelophehad, as recorded in the opening section of this chapter, presents a striking and beautiful contrast to the unbelief on which we have just been commenting. They most assuredly belonged not to the generation of those who are ever ready to abandon divine ground, lower the divine standard, and forego the privileges conferred by divine grace. No; those five noble women had no sympathy with such. They were determined, through grace, to plant the foot of faith on the very highest ground, and, with holy yet bold decision, to make their own of that which God had given. Let us read the refreshing record.

"Then came the daughters of Zelophehad, the son of Hepher, the son of Gilead, the son of Machir, the son of Manasseh, of the families of Manasseh the son of Joseph: and these are the names of his daughters; Mahlah, Noah, and Hoglah, and Milcah, and Tirzah. And they stood before Moses, and before Eleazar the priest, and before the princes and all the congregation, by the door of the tabernacle of the congregation, saying, 'Our father died in the wilderness, and he was not in the company of them that gathered themselves together against the Lord in the company of Korah; but died in his own sin, and had no sons. Why should the name of our father be done away from among his family because he hath no sons? Give unto us, therefore, a possession among the brethren of our father' " (ver. 1-4).

This is uncommonly fine. It does the heart good to read such words as these at a time like the present, when so little is made of the proper standing and portion of God's people, and when so many are content to go on from day to day and year to year without caring even to inquire into the things which are freely given to them of God. Nothing is more sad than to see the carelessness, the utter indifference, with which many professing Christians treat such great and all-important questions as the standing, walk, and hope of the believer and the Church of God. It is not, by any means, our purpose to go into these questions here. We merely desire to call the reader's attention to the fact that it is at once sinning against our own rich mercies, and dishonoring the Lord, when we evince a spirit of indifferentism in reference to any one point of divine revelation as to the position and portion of the Church or of the individual believer. If God, in the aboundings of His grace, has been pleased to bestow upon us precious privileges, as Christians, ought we not to seek earnestly to know what these privileges are? ought we not to seek to make them our own, in the artless simplicity of faith? Is it treating our God and His revelation worthily to be indifferent as to whether we are servants or sons —as to whether we have the Holy Ghost dwelling in us or not—as to whether we are under law or under grace—whether ours is a heavenly or an earthly calling?

Surely not. If there be one thing plainer than another in Scripture, it is this, that God delights in those who appreciate and enjoy the provision of His love—those who find their joy in Himself. The inspired volume teems with evidence on this point. Look at the case now before us in our chapter. Here were those daughters of Joseph—for such we must call them—bereaved of their father—helpless and desolate, as viewed from nature's stand-point. Death had snapped the apparent link which connected them with the proper inheritance of God's people. What then? Were they content to give up?—to fold their arms in cold indifference? Was it nothing to them whether or not they were to have a place and a portion with the Israel of God? Ah! no; these illustrious women exhibit something totally different from all this—something which we may well study and seek to imitate—something which, we are bold to say, refreshed the heart of God. They felt sure there was a portion for them in the land of promise, of which neither death nor any thing that happened in the wilderness could ever deprive them. "Why should the name of our father be done away from among his people because he hath no son?" Could death, could failure of male issue, could any thing, frustrate the goodness of God? Impossible. "Give unto us, therefore, a possession among the brethren of our father."

Noble words! words that went right up to the throne and to the heart of the God of Israel. It was a most powerful testimony delivered in the ears of the whole congregation. Moses was taken aback. Here was something beyond the range of the lawgiver. Moses was a servant, and a blessed and honored servant too; but again and again, in the course of this marvelous book of Numbers—this wilderness volume, questions arise with which he is unable to deal, as for example, the defiled men in chapter 9, and the daughters of Zelophehad in the section before us.

"And Moses brought their cause before the Lord. And the Lord spake unto Moses, saying, '*The daughters of Zelophehad speak right: thou shalt surely give them a possession of an inheritance among their father's brethren; and thou shalt cause the inheritance of their father to pass unto them*' " (ver. 5-7).

Here was a glorious triumph, in the presence of the whole assembly. A bold and simple faith is always sure to be rewarded. It glorifies God, and God honors it. Need we travel from section to section and from page to page of the holy volume to prove this? Need we turn to the Abrahams, the Hannahs, the Deborahs, the Rahabs, the Ruths, of Old Testament times? or to the Marys, the Elizabeths, the centurions, and the Syrophenicians of the New Testament times? Wherever we turn, we learn the same great practical truth, that God delights in a bold and simple faith—a faith that artlessly seizes and tenaciously holds all that He has given—that positively refuses, even in the very face of nature's weakness and death, to surrender a single hair's breadth of the divinely given inheritance. What though Zelophehad's bones lay mouldering in the dust of the wilderness? what though no male issue appeared to sustain his name? faith could rise above all these things, and count on God's faithfulness to make good all that His Word had promised.

"The daughters of Zelophehad speak right." They always do so. Their words are words of faith, and as such, are always right in the judgment of God. It is a terrible thing to limit "the Holy One of Israel." He delights to be trusted and used. It is utterly impossible for faith to overdraw its account in God's bank. God could no more disappoint faith than He could deny Himself. He can never say to faith, You have miscalculated; you take too lofty—too bold a stand; go lower down, and lessen your expectations. Ah! no; the only thing in all this world that truly delights and refreshes the heart of God is the faith that can simply trust Him; and we may rest assured of this, that the faith that can trust Him is also the faith that can love Him and serve Him and praise Him.

Hence, then, we are deeply indebted to the daughters of Zelophehad. They teach us a lesson of inestimable value. And more than this—their acting gave occasion to the unfolding of a fresh truth, which was to form the basis of a divine rule for all future generations. The Lord commanded Moses, saying, "If a man die, and have no son, then ye shall cause his inheritance to pass unto his daughter."

Here we have a great principle laid down, in reference to the question of inheritance, of which, humanly speaking, we should have heard nothing had it not been for the faith and faithful conduct of these remarkable women. If they had listened to the voice of timidity and unbelief—if they had refused to come forward, before the whole congregation, in the assertions of the claims of faith; then, not only would they have lost their own inheritance and blessing, but all future daughters of Israel in a like position would have been deprived of their portion likewise. Whereas, on the contrary, by acting in the precious energy of faith, they preserved their inheritance; they got the blessing; they received testimony from God; their names shine on the page of inspiration; and their conduct furnished, by divine authority, a precedent for all future generations.

Thus much as to the marvelous results of faith. But then we must remember that there is moral danger arising out of the very dignity and elevation which faith confers on those who, through grace, are enabled to exercise it; and this danger must be carefully guarded against. This is strikingly illustrated in the further history of the daughters of Zelophehad, as recorded in the last chapter of our book. "And the chief fathers of the families of the children of Gilead, the son of Machir, the son of Manasseh, of the families of the sons of Joseph, came near, and spake before Moses, and before the princes, the chief fathers of the children of Israel: and they said, 'The Lord commanded my lord to give the land for an inheritance by lot to the children of Israel; and my lord was commanded by the Lord to give the inheritance of Zelophehad our brother unto his daughters. And if they be married to any of the sons of the other tribes of the children of Israel, then shall their inheritance be taken from the inheritance of our fathers, and shall be put to the inheritance of the tribe whereunto they are received: so shall it be taken from the lot of our inheritance. And when the jubilee of the children of Israel shall be, then shall their inheritance be put unto the inheritance of the tribe whereunto they are received: so shall their inheritance be taken away from the inheritance of the tribe of our fathers.' And Moses commanded the children of Israel according to the word of the Lord, saying, 'The tribe of the sons of Joseph hath said well' " (Num. 36:1-5).

The "fathers" of the house of Joseph must be heard as well as the "daughters." The faith of the latter was most lovely; but there was just a danger lest, in the elevation to which that faith had raised them, they might forget the claims of others, and remove the landmarks which guarded the inheritance of their fathers. This had to be thought of and provided for. It was natural to suppose that the daughters of Zelophehad would marry; and moreover, it was possible they might form an alliance outside the boundaries of their tribe; and thus in the year of jubilee—that grand adjusting institution—instead of adjustment, there would be confusion, and a permanent breach in the inheritance of Manasseh. This would never do; and therefore the wisdom of those ancient fathers is very apparent. We need to be guarded on every side, in order that the integrity of faith and the testimony may be duly maintained. We are not to carry things with a high hand and a strong will though we have ever such strong faith, but be ever ready to yield ourselves to the adjusting power of the whole truth of God.

"This is the thing which the Lord doth command concerning the daughters of Zelophehad, saying, 'Let them marry to whom they think best, only to the family of the tribe of their father shall they marry; so shall not the inheritance of the children of Israel remove from tribe to tribe; for every one of the children of Israel shall keep himself to the inheritance of the tribe of his fathers. . . . Even as the Lord commanded Moses, so did the daughters of Zelophehad; for they [the five daughters] were married unto their father's brothers' sons. And they were married into the families of the sons of Manasseh, the son of Joseph; and their inheritance remained in the tribe of the family of their father" (Num. 36:6-12).

Thus all is settled. The activities of faith are governed by the truth of God, and individual claims are adjusted in harmony with the true interests of all; while at the same time the glory of God is so fully maintained that at the time of the jubilee, instead of any confusion in the landmarks of Israel, the integrity of the inheritance is secured according to the divine grant.

Nothing can be more instructive than this entire history of the daughters of Zelophehad. May we really profit by it.

The closing paragraph of our chapter is full of deep solemnity. The governmental dealings of God are displayed before our eyes in a manner eminently calculated to impress the heart. "The Lord said unto Moses, 'Get thee up into this mount Abarim, and see the land which I have given unto the children of Israel. And when thou hast seen it, thou also shalt be gathered unto thy people, as Aaron thy brother was gathered. For ye rebelled against My commandment in the desert of Zin, in the strife of the congregation, to sanctify Me at the water before their eyes: that is the water of Meribah in Kadesh in the wilderness of Zin'" (ver. 12-14).

Moses must not go over Jordan. It is not only that he cannot officially bring the people over, but he cannot even go himself. Such was the enactment of the government of God. But on the other hand, we see grace shining out, with uncommon lustre, in the fact that Moses is conducted by God's own hand to the top of Pisgah, and from thence he sees the land of promise, in all its magnificence, not merely as Israel afterwards possessed it, but as God had originally given it.

Now this was the fruit of grace, and it comes out more fully in the close of Deuteronomy, where we are also told that God buried His dear servant. This is wonderful. Indeed there is nothing like it in the history of the saints of God. We do not dwell upon this subject here, having done so elsewhere;* but it is full of the deepest interest. Moses spake unadvisedly with his lips, and for that he was forbidden to cross the Jordan. This was God in *government.* But Moses was taken up to Pisgah, there, in company with Jehovah, to get a full view of the inheritance; and then Jehovah made a grave for His servant and buried him therein. This was God in *grace*—marvelous, matchless grace!—grace that has ever made the eater yield meat and the strong sweetness. How precious to be the subjects of such grace! May our souls rejoice in it more and more, in the eternal fountain whence it emanates, and in the channel through which it flows.

We shall close this section by a brief reference to the lovely unselfishness of Moses in the matter of appointing a successor. That blessed man of God was ever characterized by a most exquisite spirit of self-surrender—that rare and admirable grace. We never find him seeking his own things; on the contrary, again and again, when opportunity was afforded him of building up his own fame and fortune, he proved very distinctly that the glory of God and the good of His people so occupied and filled his heart that there was no room for a single selfish consideration.

Thus it is in the closing scene of our

*See "Grace and Government," in the author's *Miscellaneous Writings,* vol. 5.

chapter. When Moses hears that he is not to go over Jordan, instead of being occupied in regrets as to himself, he only thinks of the interests of the congregation. "And Moses spake unto the Lord, saying, 'Let the Lord, the God of the spirits of all flesh, set a man over the congregation, which may go out before them, and which may go in before them, and which may lead them out, and which may bring them in; that the congregation of the Lord be not as sheep which have no shepherd.' "

What unselfish breathings are here! How grateful they must have proved to the heart of that One who so loved and cared for His people! Provided that Israel's need were met, Moses was content. If only the work was done, he cared not who did it. As to himself—his interests and his destinies, he could calmly leave all in the hand of God. He would take care of him, but, oh! his loving heart yearns over the beloved people of God; and the very moment he sees Joshua ordained as their leader, he is ready to depart and be at rest forever. Blessed servant! happy man! Would there were even a few amongst us characterized, in some small degree, by his excellent spirit of self-abnegation, and jealous care for God's glory and His people's good. But alas! we have to repeat, with deepening emphasis, the words of the apostle, "All seek their own, not the things that are Jesus Christ's." O Lord, stir up all our hearts to desire a more earnest consecration of ourselves, in spirit, soul, and body, to Thy blessed service. May we, in good truth, learn to live, not unto ourselves, but unto Him who died for us—who came from heaven to earth about our sins, and is gone back from earth to heaven about our infirmities, and who is coming again for our eternal salvation and glory.

---

## *CHAPTERS 28–29*

THESE two chapters must be read together; they form a distinct section of our book—a section pregnant with interest and instruction. The second verse of chapter 28 gives us a condensed statement of the contents of the entire section. "And the Lord spake unto Moses, saying, 'Command the children of Israel, and say unto them, My offering, and My bread for My sacrifices made by fire, for a sweet savor unto Me, shall ye observe to offer unto Me in their due season.' "

In these words the reader is furnished with a key with which to unlock the whole of this portion of the book of Numbers. It is as distinct and simple as possible. "*My* offering," "*My* bread," "*My* sacrifices," "*A sweet savor unto Me.*" All this is strongly marked. We may learn here, without an effort, that the grand leading thought is, Christ to Godward. It is not so much Christ as meeting our need—though surely He does most blessedly meet that—as Christ feeding and delighting the heart of God. It is God's bread—a truly wonderful expression, and one little thought of or understood. We are all sadly prone to look at Christ merely as the procuring cause of our salvation, the One through whom we are forgiven and saved from hell, the channel through which all blessing flows to us. He is all this, blessed forever be His name. He is the Author of eternal salvation to all them that obey Him; He bore our sins in His own body on the tree; He died, the just for the unjust, to bring us to God; He saves us from our sins, from their present power, and from their future consequences.

All this is true; and consequently, throughout the whole of the two chapters which lie open before us, and in each distinct paragraph, we have the sin-offering introduced (see chap. 28:15,22,30; 29:5, 11,16,19,22,25,28,31,34,38). Thirteen times over is mention made of the sin-offering of atonement, and yet for all that it remains true and obvious that sin or atonement for sin is not by any means the great prominent subject. There is no mention of it in the verse which we have quoted for the reader, although that verse plainly gives a summary of the contents of the two chapters; nor is there any allusion to it until we reach the fifteenth verse.

Need we say that the sin-offering is essential, inasmuch as man is in question, and man is a sinner? It would be impossible to treat of the subject of man's approach to God, his worship, or his communion without introducing the atoning death of Christ as the necessary foundation. This the whole heart confesses with supreme delight. The mystery of Christ's precious sacrifice shall be the well-spring of our souls throughout the everlasting ages.

But shall we be deemed Socinian in our thoughts if we assert that there is something in Christ and in His precious death beyond the bearing of our sins and the meeting of our necessities? We trust not. Can any one read Numbers 28 and 29 and not see this? Look at one simple fact, which might strike the mind of a child. There are seventy-one verses in the entire section, and out of these, thirteen allude to the sin-offering, and the remaining fifty-eight are occupied with sweet-savor offerings.

In a word, then, the special theme here is, God's delight in Christ. Morning and evening, day by day, week after week, from one new moon to another, from the opening to the close of the year, it is Christ in His fragrance and preciousness to Godward. True it is—thanks be to God, and to Jesus Christ His Son—our sin is atoned for, judged, and put away forever—our trespasses forgiven and guilt canceled; but above and beyond this, the heart of God is fed, refreshed, and delighted by Christ. What was the morning and evening lamb? was it a sin-offering, or a burnt-offering? Hear the reply in God's own words: "And thou shalt say unto them, 'This is the offering made by fire which ye shall offer unto the Lord; two lambs of the first year without spot day by day, for *a continual burnt-offering.* The one lamb shalt thou offer in the morning, and the other lamb shalt thou offer at even; and a tenth part of an ephah of flour for a meat-offering, mingled with the fourth part of a hin of beaten oil. It is a continual burnt-offering, which was ordained in Mount Sinai, for a sweet savor, a sacrifice made by fire unto the Lord.' "

Again, what were the two lambs for the Sabbath? a sin-offering, or a burnt-offering? "This is *the burnt-offering* of every Sabbath." It was to be double, because the Sabbath was a type of the rest that remaineth for God's people, when there will be a twofold appreciation of Christ. But the character of the offering is as plain as possible—it was Christ to Godward. This is the special point in the burnt-offering. The sin-offering is Christ to usward. In this, it is a question of the hatefulness of sin; in that, it is a question of the preciousness and excellency of Christ.

So also at the beginnings of their months (ver. 11), in the feast of the passover and unleavened bread (ver. 16-25), in the feast of first-fruits (ver. 26-31), in the feast of trumpets (chap. 29:1-6), in the feast of tabernacles (ver. 7-38). In a word, throughout the entire range of feasts, the leading idea is, Christ as a sweet savor. The sin-offering is never lacking; but the sweet-savor offerings get *the* prominent place, as is evident to the most cursory reader. We do not think it possible for any one to read this remarkable portion of Scripture and not observe the contrast between the place of the sin-offering and that of the burnt-offering. The former is only spoken of as "*one* kid of the goats," whereas the latter comes before us in the form of "fourteen lambs," "thirteen bullocks," and such like. Such is the large place which the sweet-savor offerings get in this Scripture.

But why dwell upon this? why insist upon it? Simply to show to the Christian reader the true character of the worship God looks for, and in which He delights. God delights in Christ, and it should be our constant aim to present to God that in which He delights. Christ should ever be the material of our worship; and He will be, in proportion as we are led by the Spirit of God. How often, alas! it is otherwise with us, the heart can tell. Both in the assembly and in the closet, how often is the tone low, and the spirit dull and heavy. We are occupied with self instead of with Christ; and the Holy Ghost, instead of being able to do His own proper work, which is, to take of the things of Christ and show them unto us, is obliged to occupy us with ourselves, in self-judgment, because our ways have not been right.

All this is to be deeply deplored. It demands our serious attention, both as assemblies and as individuals—in our public reunions and in our private devotions. Why is the tone of our public meetings frequently so low? Why such feebleness, such barrenness, such wandering? Why are the hymns and prayers so wide of the mark? Why is there so little that really deserves the name of worship? Why is there such restlessness and aimless activity? Why is there so little in our midst to refresh the heart of God?—so little that He can really speak of as *"His* bread, for *His* sacrifices made by fire, for a sweet savor unto Him"? We are occupied with self and its surroundings—our wants, our weakness, our trials and difficulties; and we leave God without the bread of His sacrifice. We actually rob Him of His due, and of that which His loving heart desires.

Is it that we can ignore our trials, our difficulties, and our wants? No; but we can commit them to Him. He tells us to cast *all* our care upon Him, in the sweet and tranquilizing assurance that He careth for us. He invites us to cast our burdens upon Him, in the assurance that He will sustain us. He is mindful of us. Is not this enough? Ought we not to be sufficiently at leisure from ourselves, when we assemble in His presence, to be able to present to Him something besides our own things? He has provided for us; He has made all right for us; our sins and our sorrows have all been divinely met; and most surely we cannot suppose that such things are the food of God's sacrifice. He has made them His care, blessed be His name; but they cannot be said to be His food.

Ought we not to think of these things?—think of them in reference both to the assembly and the closet? for the same remarks apply both to the one and the other. Ought we not to cultivate such a condition of soul as would enable us to present to God that which He is pleased to call "His bread"? The truth is, we want more entire and habitual occupation of heart with Christ as a sweet savor to God. It is not that we should value the Sin-offering less (far be the thought!); but let us remember that there is something more in our precious Lord Jesus Christ than the pardon of our sins and the salvation of our souls. What do the burnt-offering, the meat-offering, and the drink-offering set forth? Christ as a sweet savor, Christ the food of God's offering, the joy of His heart. Need we say it is one and the same Christ? Need we insist upon it that it is the same One who was made a curse for us that is a sweet savor to God? Surely every Christian owns this. But are we not prone to confine our thoughts of Christ to what *He did for us* to the virtual exclusion of what *He is to God?* It is this we have to mourn over and judge—this we must seek to have corrected; and we cannot but think that a careful study of Numbers 28—29 would prove a very excellent corrective. May God, by His Spirit, use it to this end.

Having, in our *Notes on the Book of Leviticus* offered to the reader what God has given to us in the way of light on the sacrifices and feasts, we do not feel led to dwell upon them here. The reader will find in chapters 1—8, and chapter 33, what may interest and help him in reference to the subjects treated of in the two chapters on which we have been dwelling.

---

## *CHAPTER 30*

THIS brief section has what we may term a dispensational bearing. It applies specially to Israel, and treats of the question of vows and bonds. The man and the woman stand in marked contrast in relation to this subject. "If a man vow a vow unto the Lord, or swear an oath to bind his soul with a bond; he shall not break his word, he shall do according to all that proceedeth out of his mouth" (ver. 2).

In reference to the woman, the case was different. "If a woman also vow a vow unto the Lord, and bind herself by a bond, being in her father's house in her youth; and her father hear her vow, and her bond wherewith she hath bound her soul, and her father shall hold his peace at her: then all her vows shall stand, and every bond wherewith she hath bound her soul shall stand. But if her father disallow her in the day that he heareth; not any of her vows, or of her bonds wherewith she hath bound her soul, shall stand: and the Lord shall forgive her, because her father disallowed her" (ver. 3-5). The same thing applied in the case of a wife. Her husband could either confirm or annul all her vows and bonds.

Such was the law with regard to vows. There was no relief for the man. He was bound to go right through with whatever had proceeded out of his mouth. Whatever he undertook to do, he was solemnly and irreversibly held to it. There was no back door, as we say—no way of getting out of it.

Now, we know who, in perfect grace, took this position, and voluntarily bound Himself to accomplish the will of God, whatever that will might be. We know who it is that says, "I will pay My vows unto the Lord now in the presence of all His people." "The Man Christ Jesus," who, having taken the vows upon Him, discharged them perfectly to the glory of God and the eternal blessing of His people. There was no escape for Him. We hear Him exclaiming, in the deep anguish of His soul, in the garden of Gethsemane, "If it be possible, let this cup pass from Me." But it was not possible. He had undertaken the work of man's salvation, and He had to go through the deep and dark waters of death, judgment, and wrath, and perfectly meet all the consequences of man's condition. He had a baptism to be baptized with, and was straitened until it was accomplished. In other words, He had to die, in order that, by death, He might open the pent-up floodgates, and allow the mighty tide of divine and everlasting love to flow down to His people. All praise and adoration be to His peerless name forever!

Thus much as to the man and his vows and bonds. In the case of the woman, whether as the daughter or the wife, we have the nation of Israel, and that in two ways, namely, under government and under grace. Looked at from a governmental point of view, Jehovah, who is at once the Father and the Husband, has held His peace at her, so that her vows and bonds are allowed to stand; and she is, to this day, suffering the consequences, and made to feel the force of those words, "Better that thou shouldest not vow, than that thou shouldest vow and not pay."

But on the other hand, as viewed from the blessed stand-point of grace, the Father and the Husband has taken all upon Himself, so that she shall be forgiven and brought into the fullness of blessing by and by, not on the ground of accomplished vows and ratified bonds, but on the ground of sovereign grace and mercy, through the blood of the everlasting covenant. How precious to find Christ every where! He is the centre and foundation, the beginning and the end, of all the ways of God. May our hearts be ever filled with Him; may our lips and lives speak His praise; may we, constrained by His love, live to His glory all our days upon earth, and then go home to be with Himself forever, to go no more out.

We have here given what we believe to be the primary thought of this chapter. That it may be applied, in a secondary way, to individuals, we do not by any means question; and further, that, like all Scripture, it has been written for our learning, we most thankfully own. It must ever be the delight of the devout Christian to study all the ways of God, whether in grace or government—His ways with Israel, His ways with the Church, His ways with all, His ways with each. Oh to pursue this study with an enlarged heart and an enlightened understanding!

---

## *CHAPTER 31*

WE have here the closing scene of Moses' *official* life, as in Deuteronomy 34 we have the closing scene of his *personal* history. "And the Lord spake unto Moses, saying, 'Avenge the children of Israel of the Midianites; afterward shalt thou be gathered unto thy people.' And Moses spake unto the people, saying, 'Arm some of yourselves unto the war, and let them go against the Midianites, and avenge the Lord of Midian.

Of every tribe a thousand, throughout all the tribes of Israel, shall ye send to the war.' So there were delivered out of the thousands of Israel, a thousand of every tribe, twelve thousand armed for war. And Moses sent them to the war, a thousand of every tribe, them and *Phinehas the son of Eleazar the priest,* to the war, *with the holy instruments,* and the trumpets to blow in his hand. And they warred against the Midianites, as the Lord commanded Moses; *and they slew all the males"* (ver. 3-7).

This is a very remarkable passage. The Lord says to Moses, *"Avenge the children of Israel* of the Midianites," and Moses says to Israel, *"Avenge the Lord* of Midian." The people had been insnared by the wiles of the daughters of Midian, through the evil influence of Balaam the son of Beor; and they are now called upon to clear themselves thoroughly from all the defilement which, through want of watchfulness, they had contracted. The sword is to be brought upon the Midianites, and all the spoil is to be made to pass either through the fire of judgment or through the water of purification. Not one jot or tittle of the evil thing is to be suffered to pass unjudged.

Now, this war was what we may call abnormal. By right, the people ought not to have had any occasion to encounter it at all. It was not one of the wars of Canaan; it was simply the result of their own unfaithfulness—the fruit of their own unhallowed commerce with the uncircumcised. Hence, although Joshua, the son of Nun, had been duly appointed to succeed Moses as leader of the congregation, we find no mention whatever of him in connection with this war. On the contrary, it is to Phinehas, the son of Eleazar the priest, that the conduct of this expedition is committed; and he enters upon it "with the holy instruments and the trumpets."

All this is strongly marked. *The priest* is the prominent person, and *the holy instruments* the prominent instrumentality. It is a question of wiping away the stain caused by their unholy association with the enemy; and therefore, instead of a general officer with sword and spear, it is a priest with holy instruments that appears in the foreground. True, the sword is here, but it is not the prominent thing. It is the priest with the vessels of the sanctuary, and that priest the self-same man who first executed judgment upon that very evil which has here to be avenged.

The moral of all this is at once plain and practical. The Midianites furnish a type of that peculiar kind of influence which the world exerts over the hearts of the people of God—the fascinating and insnaring power of the world used by Satan to hinder our entrance upon our proper heavenly portion. Israel should have had nothing to do with these Midianites; but having, in an evil hour —an unguarded moment, been betrayed into association with them, nothing remains but war and utter extermination.

So with us as Christians. Our proper business is, to pass through the world as pilgrims and strangers; having nothing to do with it, save to be the patient witnesses of the grace of Christ, and thus shine as lights in the midst of the surrounding moral gloom. But, alas! we fail to maintain this rigid separation; we suffer ourselves to be betrayed into alliance with the world, and in consequence, we get involved in trouble and conflict which does not properly belong to us at all. War with Midian formed no part of Israel's proper work. They had to thank themselves for it. But God is gracious; and hence, through a special application of priestly ministry, they were enabled, not only to conquer the Midianites, but to carry away much spoil. God, in His infinite goodness, brings good out of evil. He will cause the eater to yield meat, and the strong sweetness. His grace shines out, with exceeding brightness, in the scene before us, inasmuch as He actually deigns to accept a portion of the spoils taken from the Midianites. But the evil had to be thoroughly judged. "Every male" had to be put to death—all in whom there was the energy of the evil had to be completely exterminated; and finally, the fire of judgment and the water of purification had to do their work on the spoil ere God or His people could touch an atom of it.

What holy lessons are here! May we apply

our hearts to them. May we be enabled to pursue a path of more intense separation, and to press on our heavenly road as those whose portion and whose home is on high. God in His mercy grant it.

---

## *CHAPTER 32*

THE fact recorded in this chapter has given rise to considerable discussion. Various have been the opinions advanced in reference to the conduct of the two tribes and a half. Were they right, or were they wrong in choosing their inheritance on the wilderness side of Jordan? This is the question. Was their acting in this matter the expression of power, or of weakness? How are we to form a sound judgment in this case?

In the first place, where was Israel's proper portion—their divinely destined inheritance? Most surely on the other side of Jordan, in the land of Canaan. Well, then, ought not this fact to have sufficed? Would or could a really true heart—a heart that thought and felt and judged with God—have entertained the idea of selecting a portion other than that which God had allotted and bestowed? Impossible. Hence, then, we need not to go further in order to have a divine judgment on this subject. It was a mistake, a failure, a stopping short of the divine mark, on the part of Reuben and Gad and the half tribe of Manasseh, to choose any boundary-line short of the river Jordan. They were governed, in their conduct, by worldly and selfish considerations—by the sight of their eyes—by carnal motives. They surveyed "the land of Jazer and the land of Gilead," and they estimated it entirely according to their own interests, and without any reference to the judgment and will of God. Had they been simply looking to God, the question of settling down short of the river Jordan would never have been raised at all.

But when people are not simple, not true-hearted, they get into circumstances which give rise to all sorts of questions. It is a great matter to be enabled, by divine grace, to pursue a line of action, and to tread a path so unequivocal, as that no question can be raised. It is our holy and happy privilege so to carry ourselves as that no complication may ever arise. The secret of so doing is to walk with God, and thus to have our conduct wholly governed by His Word.

But that Reuben and Gad were not thus governed is manifest from the entire history. They were half-and-half men; men of mixed principles; mere borderers; men that sought their own things, and not the things of God. Had these latter engrossed their hearts, nothing would have induced them to take up their position short of the true boundary-line.

It is very evident that Moses had no sympathy with their proposal. It was a judgment upon his conduct that he was not allowed to go over. His heart was in the promised land, and he longed to go thither in person. How could he, then, approve of the conduct of men who were not only prepared, but actually desirous, to take up their abode somewhere else? Faith can never be satisfied with any thing short of the true position and portion of God's people. A single eye can only see, a faithful heart only desire, the inheritance given of God.

Hence, therefore, Moses at once condemned the proposition of Reuben and Gad. True, he afterwards relaxed his judgment and gave his consent. Their promise to cross the Jordan, ready-armed, before their brethren, drew from Moses a kind of assent. It seemed an extraordinary manifestation of unselfishness and energy to leave all their loved ones behind, and cross the Jordan, only to fight for their brethren. But where had they left those loved ones? They had left them short of the divine mark. They had deprived them of a place and portion in the true land of promise—that inheritance of which God had spoken to Abraham, Isaac, and Jacob. And for what? Just to get good pasture for their cattle. For an object like this did the two tribes and a half abandon their place within the true limits of the Israel of God.

And now let us look at the consequences

of this line of action. Let the reader turn to Joshua 22. Here we have the first sorrowful effect of the equivocal conduct of Reuben and Gad. They must needs build an altar—"a great altar to see to," lest in time to come their brethren might disown them. What does all this prove? It proves that they were all wrong in taking up their position on this side of Jordan. And only mark the effect upon the whole assembly—the disturbing, alarming effect of this altar. At the first blush, it wore the aspect of actual rebellion. "And when the children of Israel heard it, *the whole congregation of the children of Israel* gathered themselves together at Shiloh, to go up to war against them. And *the children of Israel* sent unto *the children of Reuben,* and to the children of Gad, and to the half tribe of Manasseh,* into the land of Gilead, Phinehas the son of Eleazar the priest, and with him ten princes, of each chief house a prince throughout all the tribes of Israel; and each one was a head of the house of their fathers among the thousands of Israel. And they came unto the children of Reuben, and to the children of Gad, and to the half tribe of Manasseh, unto the land of Gilead, and they spake with them, saying, 'Thus saith *the whole congregation of the Lord* [did not the two and a half belong to it?], What trespass is this that ye have committed against the God of Israel, to turn away this day from following the Lord, in that ye have builded you an altar, that ye might rebel this day against the Lord? Is the iniquity of Peor too little for us, from which we are not cleansed until this day, although there was a plague in the congregation of the Lord, but that ye must turn away this day from following the Lord? and it will be, seeing ye rebel to-day against the Lord, that to-morrow He will be wroth with the whole congregation of Israel. Notwithstanding, if the land of *your possession* be unclean, then pass ye over unto *the land of the possession of the Lord,* wherein the Lord's tabernacle dwelleth [what burning words!], and take possession among us; but rebel not against the Lord, nor rebel against us, in building you an altar beside the altar of the Lord our God' " (Joshua 22:12-19).

Now all this serious misunderstanding, all this trouble and alarm, was the result of failure on the part of Reuben and Gad. True, they were able to explain themselves and satisfy their brethren in reference to the altar; but then there would have been no need of the altar, no demand for explanation, no cause of alarm, had they not taken up an equivocal position.

Here was the source of all the mischief; and it is important for the Christian reader to seize this point with clearness, and to deduce from it the great practical lesson which it is designed to teach. It can hardly be questioned by any thoughtful, spiritually minded person who fully weighs all the evidence in the case, that the two tribes and a half were wrong in stopping short of the Jordan, in taking up their position. This seems to us unquestionable, even on the ground of what has already come before us; and if further proof were needed, it is furnished by the fact that they were the very first to fall into the enemy's hands (see 1 Kings 22:3).

But it may be that the reader is disposed to ask, What has all this to say to us? has this piece of history any voice—any instruction for us? Unquestionably. It sounds in our ears, with accents of deep solemnity, Beware of falling short of your proper position—your proper portion—of being content with the things which belong to this world—of taking any stand short of death and resurrection—the true, the spiritual Jordan.†

Such, we conceive, is the teaching of this portion of our book. It is a grand point to be wholehearted, decided, and unequivocal in taking our stand for Christ. Serious damage

* As though the two tribes and a half were actually detached from the nation of Israel.

†No doubt there are many sincere Christians who do not see the heavenly calling and position of the Church—who do not enter into the special character of truth taught in the Epistle to the Ephesians—who are, nevertheless, according to their light, earnest, devoted, and true-hearted; but we feel persuaded that such persons lose incalculable blessing to their own souls, and fall very short of the true Christian testimony.

is done to the cause of God and the testimony of Christ by those who profess to be Christians denying their heavenly calling and character, and acting as though they were citizens of this world. This is a powerful engine in the hands of Satan. An undecided, half-and-half Christian is more inconsistent than an open, out-and-out worldling or infidel. The unreality of professors is more injurious by far to the cause of God than all the forms of moral pravity put together. This may seem a strong statement, but it is too true. Christian professors who are only mere borderers—men of mixed principles—persons of doubtful deportment—these are the men who most seriously damage the blessed cause, and promote the designs of the enemy of Christ. What we want, just now, is a band of whole-hearted, thorough-going, unmistakable witnesses for Jesus Christ—men who shall declare plainly that they seek a country—earnest, unworldly men.

These are the men for the present crisis. What can be more deplorable, more saddening and discouraging, than to find those who make a lofty profession, who talk loudly of death and resurrection, who boast of their high doctrines and heavenly privileges, but whose walk and ways give the lie to their words? They love the world and the things of the world; they love money, and are eager to grasp and hoard as much as possible.

Beloved Christian reader, let us see to these things; let us honestly judge ourselves as in the very presence of God, and put away from us every thing, no matter what, that tends to hinder the complete devotion of ourselves, in spirit and soul and body, to Him who loved us and gave Himself for us. May we, to use the language of Joshua 22, so carry ourselves as not to need any altar to see to, nor any thing to declare where we belong to, where we worship, whose we are, and whom we serve. Thus shall every thing about us be transparent and unquestionable, our testimony shall be distinct, and the sound of our trumpet certain; our peace, too, shall flow like an even river, and the entire bent of our course and character shall be to the praise of Him whose name is called upon us. May the good Lord stir up the hearts of His people, in this day of hateful indifferentism, lukewarmness, and easy-going profession, to more genuine self-surrender, true consecration to the cause of Christ, and unshaken faith in the living God. Will the reader join us in pleading for all this?

---

## *CHAPTERS 33–34*

THE first of these sections gives us a wonderfully minute description of the desert wanderings of the people of God. It is impossible to read it without being deeply moved by the tender love and care of God so signally displayed throughout the whole. To think of His deigning to keep such a record of the journeyings of His poor people, from the moment they marched out of Egypt until they crossed the Jordan—from the land of death and darkness to the land flowing with milk and honey. "He knoweth thy walking through this great wilderness: these forty years the Lord thy God hath been with thee; thou hast lacked nothing." He went before them every step of the way; He traveled over every stage of the wilderness; in all their afflictions He was afflicted. He took care of them like a tender nurse. He suffered not their garments to wax old, or their feet to swell, for these forty years; and here He retraces the entire way by which His hand had led them, carefully noting down each successive stage of that marvelous pilgrimage, and every spot in the desert at which they had halted. What a journey! What a Traveling Companion!

It is very consolatory to the heart of the poor weary pilgrim to be assured that every stage of his wilderness journey is marked out by the infinite love and unerring wisdom of God. He is leading His people by a right way, home to Himself; and there is not a single circumstance in their lot, or a single ingredient in their cup, which is not carefully ordered by Himself, with direct reference to their present profit and their everlasting felicity. Let it only be our care to walk with Him, day by day, in simple confidence, casting all our care upon Him, and leaving ourselves and all our belongings absolutely in His hands. This is the true source of peace and blessedness all the journey through; and then, when our desert wanderings are over—when the last stage of the wilderness has been trodden, He will take us home to be with Himself forever.

> There with what joy reviewing
> Past conflicts, dangers, fears—
> Thy hand our foes subduing,
> And drying all our tears—
> Our hearts with rapture burning,
> The path we shall retrace,
> Where now our souls are learning
> The riches of Thy grace.

Chapter 34 gives the boundaries of the inheritance, as drawn by the hand of Jehovah. The self-same hand which had guided their wanderings, here fixes the bounds of their habitation. Alas! they never took possession of the land as given of God. He gave them the whole land, and gave it forever: they took but a part, and that for a time. But, blessed be God, the moment is approaching when the seed of Abraham shall enter upon the full and everlasting possession of that fair inheritance, from which they are for the present excluded. Jehovah will assuredly accomplish all His promises, and lead His people into all the blessings secured to them in the everlasting covenant—that covenant which has been ratified by the blood of the Lamb. Not one jot or tittle shall fail of all that He has spoken. His promises are all yea and Amen in Christ Jesus, who is the same yesterday, to-day, and forever. All praise to the Father, and unto the Son, and to the Holy Spirit!

---

## *CHAPTER 35*

THE opening lines of this most interesting chapter set before us the gracious provision which Jehovah made for His servants the Levites. Each of the tribes of Israel was privileged—that we say not bound—to furnish the Levites with a certain number of cities with their suburbs, according to their ability. "All the cities which ye shall give to the Levites shall be forty and eight cities: them shall ye give with their suburbs. And the cities which ye shall give shall be of the possession of the children of Israel: from them that have many ye shall give many, but from them that have few ye shall give few: every one shall give of his cities unto the Levites, according to his inheritance which he inheriteth" (ver. 7-8).

The Lord's servants were wholly cast upon Him for their portion. They had no inheritance or possession save in Himself. Blessed inheritance! Precious portion! None like it, in the judgment of faith. Blessed are all those who can truly say to the Lord, "Thou art the portion of my cup, and the lot of my inheritance." God took care of His dependent servants, and permitted the whole congregation of Israel to taste the hallowed privilege—for such it most assuredly was—of being co-workers with Him in providing for those who had willingly devoted themselves to His work, abandoning all besides.

Thus, then, we learn that, out of the twelve tribes of Israel, forty and eight cities, with their suburbs, were to be given over to the Levites; and out of these, again, the Levites had the privilege of furnishing six cities to be a refuge for the poor manslayer. Most lovely provision! lovely in its origin! lovely in its object!

The cities of refuge were situated three on the eastern and three on the western side of Jordan. Whether Reuben and Gad were right or wrong in settling east of that significant boundary, God in His mercy would not leave the slayer without a refuge from the avenger of blood. On the contrary, like Himself, He ordained that those cities which were designed as a merciful provision for the slayer should be so situated that wherever there was need of a shelter that shelter might be near at hand. There was always a city within reach of any who might be exposed to the sword of the avenger. This was worthy of our God. If any slayer happened to fall into the hands of the avenger of blood, it was not for want of refuge near at hand, but because he had failed to avail himself of it. All necessary provision was made; the cities were named, and well defined, and publicly known. Every thing was made as plain, as simple, and as easy as possible. Such was God's gracious way.

No doubt, the slayer was responsible to put forth all his energy to reach the sacred precincts; and no doubt he would. It is not at all likely that any one would be so blind or so infatuated as to fold his arms, in cool indifference, and say, If I am fated to escape, I shall escape; my efforts are not needed: if I am not fated to escape, I cannot escape; my efforts are of no use. We cannot fancy a manslayer using such silly language, or being guilty of such blind fatuity as this. He knew too well that if the avenger could but lay his hand upon him, all such notions would be of small account. There was but the one thing to be done, and that was, to escape for his life—to flee from impending judgment—to find his safe abode within the gates of the city of refuge. Once there, he could breathe freely. No evil could overtake him there. The moment he crossed the threshold of the gate, he was as safe as God's provision could make him. If a hair of his head could be touched within the bounds of the city, it could but be a dishonor and a reproach upon the ordinance of God. True, he had to keep close; he dared not venture outside the gate. Within, he was perfectly safe; without, he was thoroughly exposed. He could not even visit his friends; he was an exile from his father's house; he was a prisoner of hope. Absent from the home of his heart's affections, he waited for the death of the high-priest, which was to set him perfectly free and restore him, once more, to his inheritance and to his people.

Now, we believe that this beautiful ordinance had special reference to Israel. They have killed the Prince of Life; but the question is, As which are they viewed by God? as the murderer, or as the slayer? If the former, there is no refuge—no hope. No murderer could be sheltered within the city of refuge. Here is the law of the case, as stated in Joshua 20: "The Lord also spake unto Joshua, saying, 'Speak to the children of Israel, saying, Appoint out for you cities of refuge, whereof I spake unto you by the hand of Moses: that the slayer that killeth any person unawares and unwittingly may flee thither; and they shall be your refuge from the avenger of blood. And when he that doth flee unto one of those cities shall stand at the entering of the gate of the city, and shall declare his cause in the ears of the elders of that city, they shall take him into the city unto them, and give him a place, that he may dwell among them. And if the avenger of blood pursue after him, then they shall not deliver the slayer up into his hand, *because he smote his neighbor unwittingly,* and hated him not aforetime. And he shall dwell in that city until he stand before the congregation for judgment, and until the death of the high-priest that shall be in those days; then shall the slayer return, and come unto his own city, and unto his own house, unto the city from whence he fled' " (ver. 1-6).

But with respect to the murderer, the law was rigid and unbending—"The murderer shall surely be put to death. The revenger of blood himself shall slay the murderer, when he meeteth him" (Num. 35).

Israel, then, through the marvelous grace of God, will be treated as a slayer and not as a murderer. "Father, forgive them, for they know not what they do." These potent words ascended to the ear and to the heart of the God of Israel. They were heard and answered; nor are we to suppose that the answer was exhausted in its application on the day of Pentecost. No; it still holds good, and its efficacy will be illustrated in the future history of the house of Israel. That people are now under God's keeping. They are exiles from the land and the home of their fathers; but the time is coming when they shall be restored to their own land, not by the death of the High-Priest—blessed be His deathless name! He can never die—but He will leave His present position, and come forth, in a new character, as the Royal Priest, to sit upon His throne. Then shall the exile return to his long-lost home and his forfeited inheritance. But not till then, else it would be ignoring the fact that they killed the Prince of Life, which were impossible. The man-slayer must remain out of his possession until the appointed time; but he is not to be treated as a murderer, because he did it unwittingly. "I obtained mercy," says the Apostle Paul, speaking as a pattern to Israel, "because I did it ignorantly in unbelief." "And now, brethren," says Peter, "I wot that through ignorance ye did it, as did also your rulers."

These passages, together with the precious intercession of the slain One, do, in the most distinct manner, place Israel on the ground of the manslayer, and not on the ground of the murderer. God has provided a refuge and a shelter for His much-loved people, and in due time they shall return to their long-lost dwellings, in that land which Jehovah gave as a gift to Abraham His friend forever.

Such we believe to be the true interpretation of the ordinance of the city of refuge. Were we to view it as bearing upon the case of a sinner taking refuge in Christ, it could only be in a very exceptional way, inasmuch as we should find ourselves surrounded, on all hands, by points of contrast, rather than by points of similarity. For in the first place, the man-slayer in the city of refuge was not exempt from judgment, as we learn from Joshua 20:6; but for the believer in Jesus there is and can be no judgment, for the simplest of all reasons, that Christ has borne the judgment instead.

Again, there was a possibility of the slayer's falling into the hands of the avenger if he ventured outside the gates of the city. The believer in Jesus can never perish; he is as safe as the Saviour Himself.

Finally, as regards the slayer, it was a question of temporal safety and life in this world: as regards the believer in Jesus, it is a question of eternal salvation and life everlasting in the world to come. In fact, in almost every particular, it is striking contrast rather than similarity.

One grand point there is common to both, and that is, the point of exposure to imminent danger, and the urgent need of fleeing for refuge. If it would have been wild folly on the part of the slayer to linger or hesitate for a moment, until he found himself safely lodged in the city of refuge, it is surely still wilder folly, yea, the very height of madness, on the part of the sinner, to linger or hesitate in coming to Christ. The avenger might perhaps fail to lay hold on the slayer even though he were not in the city, but judgment *must* overtake the sinner out of Christ. There is no possibility of escape, if there is the thickness of a gold leaf between the soul and Christ. Solemn thought! May it have its due weight in the heart of the reader who is yet in his sins. May he find no rest—not one moment's rest—until he has fled for refuge to lay hold on the hope set before him in the gospel. Judgment impends—sure, certain, solemn judgment. It is not only that the avenger may come, but judgment must come upon all who are out of Christ.

O unconverted, thoughtless, careless reader—should this volume fall into the hands of such—hear the warning voice! Flee for thy life! Tarry not, we entreat thee! Delay is madness. Every moment is precious. You know not the hour in the which you may be cut down, and consigned to that place in the which not a single ray of hope, not even the faintest glimmer, can ever visit you—the place of eternal night, eternal woe, eternal torment—the place of a deathless worm and an unquenchable flame. Beloved friend, do let us entreat thee to come now, just as thou art, to Jesus, who stands with open arms and loving heart, ready to receive thee, to shelter, to save, and to bless, according to all the love of His heart and the perfect efficacy of His name and His sacrifice. May God the Holy Spirit, by His own resistless energy, lead thee, just now, to come. "Come unto Me," says the loving Lord and Saviour, "all ye that labor and are heavy-laden, and I will give you rest." Precious words! May they fall, with divine power, upon many a weary heart!

Here we close our meditations upon this marvelous section of the volume of God;* and in doing so, we are impressed with a

*Chapter 36 has been referred to in our meditation on chapter 27.

profound sense of the depth and richness of the mine to which we have sought to conduct the reader, and also of the excessive feebleness and poverty of the suggestions which we have been enabled to offer. However, our confidence is in the living God, that He will, by His Holy Spirit, lead the heart and mind of the Christian reader into the enjoyment of His own precious truth, and thus fit him, more and more, for His service in these last evil days, that the name of our Lord Jesus Christ may be magnified, and His truth maintained in living power. May God, in His abounding mercy, grant this, for Jesus Christ's sake.

# NOTES

*on the book of*

# DEUTERONOMY

*"Forever, O Lord, Thy Word is settled in heaven"*

*"Thy Word have I hid in my heart,
that I might not sin against Thee"*

THE value and importance of the Word of God cannot be over-estimated at the present moment. Its integrity and authority are being assailed from almost every quarter and in every form of attack. "If the foundations be destroyed, what can the righteous do?" (Ps. 11:3)

Infidel thoughts and principles are not limited to a few literary and speculative minds, as they were fifty years ago, but are now asserted by many who ought to be the true guardians of Christianity and the defenders of the Bible as a revelation from God.

In this way the multitude of the simple and unsuspecting are deceived. If the style of address be pleasing, few care to compare what they have been hearing with the holy Scriptures. The conscience not being aroused, they take no further trouble.

But what of the state of immortal souls, under such a ministry, in view of eternity? On whom does the weight of responsibility rest? Fine-spun theories will never awaken a soul asleep in sin: the lost sinner must be brought face to face with the plain Word of God and the solemn realities of eternity. His voice must be heard. All is absolute, positive, and definite here, whatever infidelity may say. "The Word of the Lord endureth forever."

The burden of the following pages, I am thankful to find, is well calculated to meet and counteract the looseness and indefiniteness of the prevailing teaching of the present day.

And this, I may also say, is the burden of the book of Deuteronomy. The Jewish lawgiver presses with great earnestness the Word of Jehovah on the heart of Israel. It is not a book of ceremonials, but the reminding of the people of their obligation to keep the commandments, the statutes, and the judgments of the Lord.

This is the first moral duty of man in every age—implicit obedience and submission to the revealed will of God. Moses speaks to the children of Israel as a father, and appeals to them in the most tender and loving way. "Hearken, O Israel," he says, "unto the statutes and unto the judgments which I teach you . . . ye shall not add unto the word which I command you, neither shall ye diminish aught from it, that ye may keep the commandments of the Lord your God which I command you." And again, he says, "Thou shalt bind them for a sign upon thine hand, and they shall be as frontlets between thine eyes. And thou shalt write them upon the posts of thy houses, and on thy gates."

The welfare of the people individually and nationally depended on their faithfully observing these oft-repeated laws. To neglect them was to bring upon themselves the displeasure and chastening of the God of Israel.

But more need not be said here on these subjects. The reader will find in the following pages the most ample unfolding and practical application of these divine exhortations and warnings. But the writer has not confined himself to what Deuteronomy teaches, but has enlarged on what it suggests. In this way we have brought before us the grand cardinal truths of Christianity: a wide circle of truth is embraced, and much that applies to the individual Christian, the family, the household, and the Church of God will be found in the accompanying book.

It now goes forth with the earnest desire that the Lord may be graciously pleased to use it for the glory of His own name, the help of His people, and the eternal blessing of many precious souls.

*A.M.*

*London, November, 1880.*

## *NOTES*

*on*

## *THE BOOK OF DEUTERONOMY*

---

### *INTRODUCTION*

THE character of the book on which we now enter is quite as distinct as that of any of the four preceding sections of the Pentateuch. Were we to judge from the title of the book, we might suppose that it is a mere repetition of what we find in previous books. This would be a very grave mistake. There is no such thing as mere repetition in the Word of God. Indeed, God never repeats Himself, either in His Word or in His works. Wherever we trace our God, whether on the page of holy Scripture or in the vast fields of creation, we see divine fullness, infinite variety, marked design; and just in proportion to our spirituality of mind will be our ability to discern and appreciate these things. Here, as in all beside, we need the eye anointed with heavenly eye-salve. What a poor idea must the man entertain of inspiration who could imagine for a moment that the fifth book of Moses is a barren repetition of what is to be found in Exodus, Leviticus, and Numbers! Why, even in human composition we should not expect to find such a flagrant imperfection, much less in the perfect revelation which God has so graciously given us in His holy Word. The fact is, there is not, from cover to cover of the inspired volume, a single superfluous sentence, not one redundant clause, not one statement without its own distinct meaning—its own direct application. If we do not see this, we have yet to learn the depth, force, and meaning of the words, "All scripture is given by inspiration of God."

Precious words! Would they were more thoroughly understood in this our day! It is of the utmost possible importance that the Lord's people should be rooted, grounded, and settled in the grand truth of the plenary inspiration of holy Scripture. It is to be feared that laxity as to this most weighty subject is spreading in the professing church to an appalling extent. In many quarters it has become fashionable to pour contempt upon the idea of plenary inspiration. It is looked upon as the veriest childishness and ignorance. It is regarded by many as a great proof of profound scholarship, breadth of mind, and original thinking to be able, by free criticism, to find out flaws in the precious volume of God. Men presume to sit in judgment upon the Bible as though it were a mere human composition. They undertake to pronounce upon what is and what is not worthy of God. In fact, they do virtually sit in judgment upon God Himself. The present result is, as might be expected, utter darkness and confusion, both for those learned doctors themselves and for all who are so foolish as to listen to them. And as for the future, who can conceive the eternal destiny of all those who shall have to answer before the judgment-seat of Christ for the sin of blaspheming the Word of God, and leading hundreds astray by their infidel teaching?

We shall not, however, occupy time in dwelling upon the sinful folly of infidels and skeptics (even though called Christians), or their puny efforts to cast dishonor upon that peerless volume which our gracious God has caused to be written for our learning. They will some day or other find out their fatal mistake. God grant it may not be too late! And as for us, let it be our deep joy and consolation to meditate upon the Word of God, that so we may ever be discovering some fresh treasure in that exhaustless mine —some new moral glories in that heavenly revelation!

The book of Deuteronomy holds a very distinct place in the inspired canon. Its opening lines are sufficient to prove this. "These be the words which Moses spake unto all Israel on this side Jordan in the wilderness, in the plain over against the Red Sea, between Paran, and Tophel, and Laban, and Hazeroth, and Dizahab."

Thus much as to the place in which the lawgiver delivered the contents of this marvelous book. The people had come up to the eastern bank of the Jordan, and were about to enter upon the land of promise. Their desert wanderings were nearly ended, as we learn from the third verse, in which the point of time is as distinctly marked as is the geographical position in verse 1.—"It came to pass in the fortieth year, in the eleventh month, on the first day of the month, that Moses spake unto the children of Israel, according unto all that the Lord had given him in commandment unto them."

Thus, not only have we both time and place set forth with divine precision and minuteness, but we also learn, from the words just quoted, that the communications made to the people in the plains of Moab were very far indeed from being a repetition of what has come before us in our studies on the books of Exodus, Leviticus, and Numbers. Of this we have further and very distinct proof in a passage in chapter 29 of the book on which we are now entering.—"These are the words of the covenant which the Lord commanded Moses to make with the children of Israel in the land of Moab, *beside the covenant which He made with them in Horeb.*"

Let the reader note particularly these words. They speak of two covenants—one at Horeb and one in Moab; and the latter, so far from being a mere repetition of the former, is as distinct from it as any two things can be. Of this we shall have the fullest and clearest evidence in our study of the profound book which now lies open before us.

True, the Greek title of the book, signifying the law a second time, might seem to give rise to the idea of its being a mere recapitulation of what has gone before; but we may rest assured it is not so. Indeed, it would be a very grave error to think so. The book has its own specific place. Its scope and object are as distinct as possible. The grand lesson which it inculcates, from first to last, is *obedience;* and that, too, not in the mere letter, but in the spirit of love and fear—an obedience grounded upon a known and enjoyed relationship—an obedience quickened by the sense of moral obligations of the weightiest, most influential character.

The aged lawgiver—the faithful, beloved, and honored servant of the Lord was about to take leave of the congregation. He was going to heaven and they were about to cross the Jordan, and hence his closing discourses are solemn and affecting in the very highest degree. He reviews the whole of their wilderness history, and that, too, in a manner most touching and impressive. He recounts the scenes and circumstances of their forty eventful years of desert life, in a style eminently calculated to touch the deepest moral springs of the heart. We hang over these most precious discourses with wonder and delight. They possess an incomparable charm, arising from the circumstances under which they were delivered, as well as from their own divinely powerful contents. They speak to us no less effectively than to those for whom they were specially intended. Many of the appeals and exhortations come home to us with a power of application as if they had been uttered but yesterday.

And is it not thus with all Scripture? Are we not continually struck with its marvelous power of adaptation to our own very state, and to the day in which our lot is cast? It speaks to us with a point and freshness as if it were written expressly for us—written this very day. There is nothing like Scripture. Take any human writing of the same date as the book of Deuteronomy; if you could lay your hand on some volume written three thousand years ago, what would you find? A curious relic of antiquity—something to be placed in the British Museum, side by side with an Egyptian mummy, having no application whatever to us or to our time—a musty document—a piece of obsolete writing, practically useless to us, referring only to a state of society and to a condition of things long since passed away and buried in oblivion.

The Bible, on the contrary, is the book for to-day. It is God's own book—His perfect revelation. It is His own very voice speaking to each one of us. It is a book for every age, for every clime, for every class, for every condition—high and low, rich and poor, learned and ignorant, old and young. It speaks in a language so simple that a child can understand it, and yet so profound that the most gigantic intellect cannot exhaust it. Moreover, it speaks right home to the heart; it touches the deepest springs of our moral being; it goes down to the hidden roots of thought and feeling in the soul; it judges us thoroughly. In a word, it is, as the inspired apostle tells us, "quick and powerful, and sharper than any two-edged sword, piercing even to the dividing asunder of soul and spirit, and of the joints and marrow, and is a discerner of the thoughts and intents of the heart" (Heb. 4:12).

And then mark the marvelous comprehensiveness of its range. It deals as accurately and as forcibly with the habits and customs, the manners and maxims of the nineteenth century of the Christian era as with those of the very earliest ages of human existence. It displays a perfect acquaintance with man in every stage of his history. The London of today and the Tyre of three thousand years ago are mirrored, with like precision and faithfulness, on the sacred page. Human life, in every stage of its development, is portrayed by a master-hand in that wonderful volume which our God has graciously penned for our learning.

What a privilege to possess such a book!—to have in our hands a divine revelation!—to have access to a book, every line of which is given by inspiration of God!—to have a divinely given history of the past, the present, and the future! Who can estimate aright such a privilege as this?

But then, this book judges man—judges his ways—judges his heart. It tells him the truth about himself. Hence man does not like God's book. An unconverted man would vastly prefer a newspaper or a sensational novel to the Bible. He would rather read the report of a trial in one of our criminal courts than a chapter in the New Testament.

Hence, too, the constant effort to pick holes in God's blessed book. Infidels in every age and of every class have labored hard to find out flaws and contradictions in holy Scripture. The determined enemies of the Word of God are to be found, not only in the ranks of the vulgar, the coarse, and the demoralized, but amongst the educated, the refined, and the cultivated. Just as it was in the days of the apostles, "certain lewd fellows of the baser sort," and "devout and honorable women"—two classes so far removed from each other socially and morally—found one point in which they could heartily agree, namely, the utter rejection of the Word of God and of those who faithfully preached it. (Comp. Acts 13:50 with 17:5). So we ever find that men who differ in almost every thing else, agree in their determined opposition to the Bible. Other books are let alone. Men care not to point out defects in Virgil, in Horace, in Homer, or Herodotus; but the Bible they cannot endure, because it exposes them and tells them the truth about themselves and the world to which they belong.

And was it not exactly the same with the living Word—the Son of God—the Lord Jesus Christ when He was here among men? Men hated Him because He told them the truth. His ministry, His words, His ways—His whole life was a standing testimony against the world; hence their bitter and persistent opposition. Other men were allowed to pass on, but He was watched and waylaid at every turn of His path. The great leaders and guides of the people "sought to entangle Him in His talk," to find occasion against Him, in order that they might deliver Him to the power and authority of the governor. Thus it was during His marvelous life; and at the close, when the blessed One was nailed to the cross between two malefactors, these latter were let alone; there were no insults heaped upon them—the chief priests and elders did not wag their heads at them. No; all the insults, all the mockery, all the coarse and heartless vulgarity—all was heaped upon the divine Occupant of the centre cross.

Now, it is well we should thoroughly understand the real source of all the opposition to the Word of God—whether it be the living Word or the written Word. It will enable us to estimate it at its real worth. The devil hates the Word of God—hates it with a perfect hatred; and hence he employs learned infidels to write books to prove that the Bible is not the Word of God, that it cannot be, inasmuch as there are mistakes and discrepancies in it; and not only so, but in the Old Testament we find laws and institutions, habits and practices, unworthy of a gracious and benevolent Being.

To all this style of argument we have one brief and pointed reply. Of all these learned infidels we simply say, They know nothing whatever about the matter. They may be very learned, very clever, very deep and original thinkers, well made up in general literature, very competent to give an opinion on any subject within the domain of natural and moral philosophy, very able to discuss any scientific question; moreover, they may be very amiable in private life—truly estimable characters—kind, benevolent, philanthropic, beloved in private and respected in public—all this they may be, but being unconverted, and not having the Spirit of God, they are wholly unfit to form, much less to give, a judgment on the subject of holy Scripture. If any one wholly ignorant of astronomy were to presume to sit in judgment on the principles of the Copernican system, these very men of whom we speak would at once pronounce him utterly incompetent to speak, and unworthy to be heard on such a subject. In short, no one has any right whatever to offer an opinion on a matter with which he is unacquainted. This is an admitted principle on all hands; and therefore its application in the case now before us cannot justly be called in question.

Now, the inspired apostle tells us, in his first Epistle to the Corinthians, that "the natural man receiveth not the things of the Spirit of God; for they are foolishness unto him; *neither can he know them,* because they are spiritually discerned." This is conclusive. He speaks of man in his natural state, be he ever so learned, ever so cultivated. He is not speaking of any special class of men, but simply of man in his unconverted state—man destitute of the Spirit of God. Some may imagine that the apostle refers to man in a state of barbarism, or savage ignorance. By no means; it is simply man in nature, be he a learned philosopher or an ignorant clown. "He cannot know the things of the Spirit of God." How, then, can he form or give a judgment as to the Word of God? How can he take it upon him to say what is or what is not worthy of God to write? And if he is audacious enough to do so (as, alas! he is), who will be foolish enough to listen to him? His arguments are baseless, his theories worthless, his books only fit for the wastepaper basket; and all this, be it observed, on the universally admitted principle above stated, that no one has any title to be heard on a subject of which he is wholly ignorant.

In this way we dispose of the whole tribe of infidel writers. Who would think of listening to a blind man on the subject of light and shade? And yet such a man has much more claim to be heard than an unconverted man on the subject of inspiration. Human learning, however extensive and varied—human wisdom, however profound, cannot qualify a man to form a judgment upon the Word of God. No doubt a scholar may examine and collate mss. simply as a matter of criticism; he may be able to form a judgment as to the question of authority for any particular reading of a passage; but this is a different matter altogether from an infidel writer undertaking to pronounce judgment upon the revelation which God has, in His infinite goodness, given to us. We maintain that no man can do this. It is only by the Spirit, who Himself inspired the holy Scriptures, that those Scriptures can be understood and appreciated. The Word of God must be received upon its own authority. If man can judge it or reason upon it, it is not the Word of God at all. Has God given us a revelation, or has He not? If He has, it must be absolutely perfect in every respect; and being such, it must be entirely beyond the range of human judgment. Man is no more competent to judge Scripture than he is to judge God. The Scriptures judge man; not man the Scriptures.

This makes all the difference. Nothing can be more miserably contemptible than the books which infidels write against the Bible. Every page, every paragraph, every sentence, only goes to illustrate the truth of the apostle's statement, that "the natural man receiveth not the things of the Spirit of God . . . *neither can he know them,* because they are spiritually discerned." Their gross ignorance of the subject with which they undertake to deal is only equaled by their self-confidence. Of their irreverence we say nothing; for who would think of looking for reverence in the writings of infidels? We might perhaps look for a little modesty were it not that we are fully aware of the bitter *animus* which lies at the root of all such writings, and renders them utterly unworthy of a moment's consideration. Other books may have a dispassionate examination; but the precious book of God is approached with the foregone conclusion that it is not a divine revelation, because, forsooth, infidels tell us that God could not give us a written revelation of His mind.

How strange! Men can give us a revelation of their thoughts (and infidels have done so pretty plainly), but God cannot! What folly! What presumption! Why, we may lawfully inquire, could not God reveal His mind to His creatures? Why should it be thought a thing incredible? For no reason whatever, but because infidels would have it so. The wish is, in this case assuredly, father to the thought. The question raised by the old serpent in the garden of Eden nearly six thousand years ago, has been passed on from age to age by all sorts of skeptics, rationalists, and infidels, namely, "Hath God said?" We reply, with intense delight, Yes; blessed be His holy name, He has spoken—spoken to us. He has revealed His mind; He has given us the holy Scriptures. "*All scripture is given by inspiration of God,* and is profitable for doctrine, for reproof, for correction, for instruction in righteousness; that the man of God may be perfect [αρτιος], thoroughly furnished unto all good works." And again, "Whatsoever things were written aforetime were written for our learning, that we through patience and comfort of the Scriptures might have hope" (2 Tim. 3:16-17; Rom. 15:4).

The Lord be praised for such words! They assure us that all Scripture is given of God, and that all Scripture is given to us. Precious link between the soul and God! What tongue can tell the value of such a link? God has spoken—spoken to us. His Word is a rock against which all the waves of infidel thought dash themselves in contemptible impotency, leaving it in its own divine strength and eternal stability. Nothing can touch the Word of God. Not all the powers of earth and hell, men and devils combined can ever move the Word of God. There it stands, in its own moral glory, spite of all the assaults of the enemy, from age to age. "Forever, O Lord, Thy Word is settled in heaven." "Thou hast magnified Thy Word above all Thy name." What remains for us? Just this: "Thy Word have I hid in my heart, that I might not sin against Thee." Here lies the deep secret of peace. The heart is linked to the throne—yea, to the very heart of God by means of His most precious Word, and is thus put in possession of a peace which the world can neither give nor take away. What can all the theories, the reasonings, and the arguments of infidels effect? Just nothing. They are esteemed as the dust of the summer threshing-floor. To one who has really learnt, through grace, to confide in the Word of God—to rest on the authority of holy Scripture, all the infidel books that ever were written are utterly worthless, pointless, powerless; they display the ignorance and terrible presumption of the writers; but as to Scripture, they leave it just where it ever has been and ever will be—"settled in heaven," as immovable as the throne of God.* The assaults of infidels cannot touch the throne of God, neither can they touch His Word; and, blessed be His name, neither can they touch the peace that flows through the heart

*In referring to infidel writers, we should bear in mind that by far the most dangerous of such are those calling themselves Christians. In our young days, whenever we heard the word "infidel," we at once thought of a Tom Paine or a Voltaire; now, alas! we have to think of so-called bishops and doctors of the professing church. Tremendous fact!

that rests on that imperishable foundation. "Great peace have they that love Thy law, and nothing shall offend them." "The Word of our God shall stand forever." "All flesh is as grass, and all the glory of man as the flower of grass. The grass withereth, and the flower thereof falleth away; but the Word of the Lord endureth forever. And this is the Word which by the gospel is preached unto you" (1 Pet. 1:24-25).

Here we have the same precious golden link again. The Word which has reached us in the form of glad tidings is the Word of the Lord which endureth forever; and hence our salvation and our peace are as stable as the Word on which they are founded. If *all* flesh is as grass, and *all* the glory of man as the flower of grass, then what are the arguments of infidels worth? They are as worthless as withered grass or a faded flower; and the men who put them forth and those who are moved by them will find them to be so, sooner or later. Oh, the sinful folly of arguing against the Word of God—arguing against the only thing in all this world that can give rest and consolation to the poor, weary human heart—arguing against that which brings the glad tidings of salvation to poor lost sinners—brings them fresh from the heart of God!

But we may perhaps here be met by the question so often raised, and which has troubled many and led them to fly for refuge to what is called "the authority of the church." The question is this: "How are we to know that the book which we call the Bible is the Word of God?" Our answer to this question is a very simple one—it is this: The One who has graciously given us the blessed book can give us also the certainty that the book is from Him. The same Spirit who inspired the various writers of the holy Scriptures can make us know that those Scriptures are the very voice of God speaking to us. It is only by the Spirit that any one can discern this. As we have already seen, "the natural man receiveth not the things of the Spirit of God . . . neither can he know them, because they are spiritually discerned." If the Holy Spirit does not make us know, and give us the certainty that the Bible is the Word of God, no man or body of men can possibly do it; and on the other hand, if He does give us the blessed certainty, we do not need the testimony of man.

We freely admit that on this great question a shadow of uncertainty would be positive torture and misery; but who can give us certainty? God alone. If all the men upon earth were to agree in their testimony to the authority of holy Scripture—if all the councils that ever sat, all the doctors that ever taught, all the fathers that ever wrote, were in favor of the dogma of plenary inspiration—if the universal church, if every denomination in christendom were to assent to the truth that the Bible is, in very deed, the Word of God—in a word, if we had all the human authority that could possibly be had in reference to the integrity of the Word of God, it would be utterly insufficient as a ground of certainty; and if our faith were founded on that authority, it would be perfectly worthless. God alone can give us the certainty that He has spoken in His Word; and blessed be His name, when He gives it, all the arguments, all the cavilings, all the quibblings, all the questionings of infidels, ancient and modern, are as the foam on the water, the smoke from the chimney-top, or the dust on the floor. The true believer rejects them as so much worthless rubbish, and rests in holy tranquility in that peerless revelation which our God has graciously given us.

It is of the very last possible importance for the reader to be thoroughly clear and settled as to this grave question, if he would be raised above the influence of infidelity on the one hand and superstition on the other. Infidelity undertakes to tell us that God has not given us a book-revelation of His mind—could not give it: Superstition undertakes to tell us that even though God has given us a revelation, yet we cannot be assured of it without man's authority, nor understand it without man's interpretation. Now it is well to see that by both alike we are deprived of the precious boon of holy Scripture. And this is precisely what the devil aims at. He wants to rob us of the Word of God; and he can do this quite as effectually by the apparent self-distrust that humbly and reverently looks to wise and learned men for authority, as by an audacious infidelity that boldly rejects all authority, human or divine.

Take a case. A father writes a letter to his son at Canton—a letter full of the affection and tenderness of a father's heart. He tells him of his plans and arrangements, tells him of every thing that he thinks would interest the heart of a son—every thing that the love of a father's heart could suggest. The son calls at the post-office in Canton to inquire if there is a letter from his father. He is told by one official that there is no letter, that his father has not written and could not write—could not communicate his mind by such a medium at all, that it is only folly to think of such a thing. Another official comes forward, and says, Yes; there is a letter here for you, but you cannot possibly understand it; it is quite useless to you, indeed it can only do you positive mischief inasmuch as you are quite unable to read it aright. You must leave the letter in our hands, and we will explain to you such portions of it as we consider suitable for you. The former of these two officials represents Infidelity; the latter, Superstition. By both alike would the son be deprived of the longed-for letter—the precious communication from his father's heart. But what, we may inquire, would be his answer to these unworthy officials? A very brief and pointed one we may rest assured. He would say to the first, I know my father can communicate his mind to me by letter, and that he has done so. He would say to the second, I know my father can make me understand his mind far better than you can. He would say to both, and that, too, with bold and firm decision, Give me at once my father's letter; it is addressed to me, and no man has any right to withhold it from me.

Thus, too, should the simple-hearted Christian meet the *insolence* of Infidelity and the *ignorance* of Superstition—the two special agencies of the devil, in this our day, in setting aside the precious Word of God. "My Father has communicated His mind, and He can make me understand the communication." "All Scripture is given *by inspiration of God;*" and, "Whatsoever things were written aforetime were written *for our learning.*" Magnificent answer to every enemy of God's precious and peerless revelation, be he rationalist or ritualist!

We do not attempt to offer any apology to the reader for this lengthened introduction to the book of Deuteronomy. Indeed we are only too thankful for an opportunity of bearing our feeble testimony to the grand truth of the divine inspiration of the holy Scriptures. We feel it to be our sacred duty, as most surely it is our high privilege, to press upon all to whom we have access, the immense importance—yea, the absolute necessity of the most uncompromising decision on this point. We must faithfully maintain, at all cost, the divine authority, and therefore the absolute supremacy and all-sufficiency, of the Word of God at all times, in all places, for all purposes. We must hold to it that the Scriptures, having been given of God, are complete, in the very highest and fullest sense of the word; that they do not need any human authority to accredit them, or any human voice to make them available: they speak for themselves, and carry their own credentials with them. All we have to do is to believe and obey, not to reason or discuss. God has spoken it: it is ours to hearken, and yield an unreserved and reverent obedience.

This is one grand leading point throughout the book of Deuteronomy, as we shall see in the progress of our meditations; and never was there a moment, in the history of the Church of God, in which it was more needful to urge home on the human conscience the necessity of implicit obedience to the Word of God. It is, alas! but little felt. Professing Christians, for the most part, seem to consider that they have a right to think for themselves—to follow their own reason, their own judgment, or their own conscience. They do not believe that the Bible is a divine and universal guide-book. They think there are very many things in which we are left to choose for ourselves; hence the almost numberless sects, parties, creeds, and schools of thought. If human opinion be allowed at all, then, as a matter of course, one man has as good a right to think as another; and thus it has come to pass that the professing church has become a proverb and a by-word for division.

And what is the sovereign remedy for this wide-spread disease? Here it is: *Absolute and complete subjection to the authority of holy Scripture.* It is not men going to Scripture to get *their* opinions and *their* views confirmed; but going to Scripture to get the mind of God as to every thing, and bowing down their whole moral being to divine authority. This is the one pressing need of the day in which our lot is cast—reverent subjection, in all things, to the supreme authority of the Word of God. No doubt, there will be variety in our measure of intelligence, in our apprehension and appreciation of Scripture; but what we specially urge upon all Christians is that condition of soul, that attitude of heart expressed in those precious words of the psalmist, "Thy Word have I hid in mine heart, that I might not sin against Thee." This, we may rest assured, is grateful to the heart of God. "To this man will I look, even to him that is poor and of a contrite spirit, and trembleth at My Word."

Here lies the true secret of moral security. Our knowledge of Scripture may be very limited; but if our reverence for it be profound, we shall be preserved from a thousand errors—a thousand snares. And then there will be steady growth. We shall grow in the knowledge of God, of Christ, and of the written Word; we shall delight to draw from those living and exhaustless depths of holy Scripture, and to range through those green pastures which infinite grace has so freely thrown open to the flock of Christ. Thus shall the divine life be nourished and strengthened; the Word of God will become more and more precious to our souls, and we shall be led, by the powerful ministry of the Holy Ghost, into the depth, fullness, majesty, and moral glory of holy Scripture. We shall be delivered completely from the withering influences of all mere systems of theology, high, low, or moderate—a most blessed deliverance! We shall be able to tell the advocates of all the schools of divinity under the sun that whatever elements of truth they may have in their systems we have in divine perfectness in the Word of God; not twisted and tortured to make them fit into a system, but in their right place in the wide circle of divine revelation which has its eternal centre in the blessed Person of our Lord and Saviour Jesus Christ.

---

## *CHAPTER 1*

"THESE be the words which Moses spake unto all Israel on this side Jordan in the wilderness, in the plain over against the Red Sea, between Paran, and Tophel, and Laban, and Hazeroth, and Dizahab. (There are eleven days' journey from Horeb, by the way of Mount Seir, unto Kadesh-barnea.)"

The inspired writer is careful to give us, in the most precise manner, all the bearings of the place in which the words of this book were spoken in the ears of the people. Israel had not yet crossed the Jordan; they were just beside it, and over against the Red Sea where the mighty power of God had been so gloriously displayed nearly forty years before. The whole position is described with a minuteness which shows how thoroughly God entered into every thing that concerned His people. He was interested in all their movements and in all their ways. He kept a faithful record of all their encampments. There was not a single circumstance connected with them, however trifling, beneath His gracious notice. He attended to every thing. His eye rested continually on that assembly as a whole, and on each member in particular. By day and by night He watched over them. Every stage of their journey was under His immediate and most gracious superintendence. There was nothing, however small, beneath His notice; nothing, however great, beyond His power.

Thus it was with Israel in the wilderness of old, and thus it is with the Church now—the Church as a whole, and each member in particular. A Father's eye rests upon us continually, His everlasting arms are around and underneath us day and night.

"He withdraweth not His eyes from the righteous." He counts the hairs of our heads, and enters, with infinite goodness, into every thing that concerns us. He has charged Himself with all our wants and all our cares. He would have us to cast our every care on Him, in the sweet assurance that He careth for us. He most graciously invites us to roll our every burden over on Him, be it great or small.

All this is truly wonderful. It is full of deepest consolation. It is eminently calculated to tranquilize the heart, come what may. The question is, Do we believe it? are our hearts governed by the faith of it? Do we really believe that the almighty Creator and Upholder of all things, who bears up the pillars of the universe, has graciously undertaken to do for us all the journey through? Do we thoroughly believe that "the Possessor of heaven and earth" is our Father? and that He has charged Himself with all our wants from first to last? Is our whole moral being under the commanding power of those words of the inspired apostle, "He that spared not His own Son, but delivered Him up for us all, how shall He not with Him also freely give us all things?" Alas! it is to be feared that we know but little of the power of these grand yet simple truths. We talk about them, we discuss them, we profess them, we give a nominal assent to them; but with all this, we prove, in our daily life—in the actual details of our personal history, how feebly we enter into them. If we truly believed that our God has charged Himself with all our necessities—if we were finding all our springs in Him—if He were a perfect covering for our eyes and a resting-place for our hearts, could we possibly be looking to poor creature-streams, which so speedily dry up and disappoint our hearts? We do not and cannot believe it. It is one thing to hold the theory of the life of faith, and another thing altogether to live that life. We constantly deceive ourselves with the notion that we are living by faith, when in reality we are leaning on some human prop, which sooner or later is sure to give way.

Is it not so? Are we not constantly prone to forsake the Fountain of living waters, and hew out for ourselves broken cisterns, which can hold no water? And yet we speak of living by faith! We profess to be looking only to the living God for the supply of our need, whatever that need may be, when, in point of fact, we are sitting beside some creature-stream and looking for something there. Need we wonder if we are disappointed? How could it possibly be otherwise? Our God will not have us dependent upon aught or any one but Himself. He has, in manifold places in His Word, given us His judgment as to the true character and sure result of all creature-confidence. Take the following most solemn passage from the prophet Jeremiah: "Cursed be the man that trusteth in man, and maketh flesh his arm, and whose heart departeth from the Lord. For he shall be like the heath in the desert, and shall not see when good cometh; but shall inhabit the parched places in the wilderness, in a salt land and not inhabited." And then mark the contrast—"Blessed is the man that trusteth in the Lord, and whose hope the Lord is: for he shall be as a tree planted by the waters, and that spreadeth out her roots by the river, and shall not see when heat cometh, but her leaf shall be green; and shall not be careful in the year of drought, neither shall cease from yielding fruit" (Jer. 17:5-8).

Here we have, in language divinely forcible, clear, and beautiful, both sides of this most weighty subject put before us. Creature-confidence brings a certain curse; it can only issue in barrenness and desolation. God, in very faithfulness, will cause every human stream to dry up—every human prop to give way, in order that we may learn the utter folly of turning away from Him. What figure could be more striking or impressive than those used in the above passage? "A heath in the desert," "parched places in the wilderness," "a salt land not inhabited." Such are the figures used by the Holy Ghost to illustrate all mere human dependence—all confidence in man.

But on the other hand, what can be more lovely or more refreshing than the figures used to set forth the deep blessedness of simple trust in the Lord? "A tree planted by the waters," "spreading out her roots by the rivers," the leaf ever green, the fruit never ceasing. Perfectly beautiful! Thus it is with the man who trusteth in the Lord, and whose hope the Lord is. He is nourished by those eternal springs that flow from the heart of God. He drinks at the Fountain, life-giving and free. He finds all his resources in the living God. There may be "heat," but he does not see it; "the year of drought" may come, but he is not careful. Ten thousand creature-streams may dry up, but he does not perceive it, because he is not dependent upon them; he abides hard by the ever-gushing Fountain. He can never want any good thing. He lives by faith.

And here, while speaking of the life of faith—that most blessed life, let us clearly understand what it is, and carefully see that we are living it. We sometimes hear this life spoken of in a way by no means intelligent. It is not unfrequently applied to the mere matter of trusting God for food and raiment. Certain persons who happen to have no visible source of temporal supplies—no settled income—no property of any kind, are singled out and spoken of as "living by faith," as if that marvelous and glorious life had no higher sphere or wider range than temporal things—the mere supply of our bodily wants.

Now, we cannot too strongly protest against this most unworthy view of the life of faith. It limits its sphere and lowers its range in a manner perfectly intolerable to any one who understands aught of its most holy and precious mysteries. Can we for a moment admit that a Christian who happens to have a settled income of any kind is to be deprived of the privilege of living by faith? Or, further, can we permit that life to be limited and lowered to the mere matter of trusting God for the supply of our bodily wants? Does it soar no higher than food and raiment? Does it give no more elevated thought of God than that He will not let us starve or go naked?

Far away, and away forever, be the unworthy thought! The life of faith must not be so treated. We cannot allow such a gross dishonor to be offered to it, or such a grievous wrong done to those who are called to live it. What, we would ask, is the meaning of those few but weighty words, "The just shall live by faith"? They occur, first of all, in Habakkuk 2. They are quoted by the apostle in Romans 1, where he is, with a master-hand, laying the solid foundations of Christianity. He quotes them again in Galatians 3 where he is, with intense anxiety, recalling those bewitched assemblies to those solid foundations which they, in their folly, were abandoning. Finally, he quotes them again in chapter 10 of his Epistle to the Hebrews, where he is warning his brethren against the danger of casting away their confidence and giving up the race.

From all this we may assuredly gather the immense importance and practical value of the brief but far-reaching sentence, "The just shall live by faith." But to whom does it apply? Is it only for a few of the Lord's servants, here and there, who happen to have no settled income? We utterly reject the thought. It applies to every one of the Lord's people. It is the high and happy privilege of all who come under the title—that blessed title, "The just." We consider it a very grave error to limit it in any way. The moral effect of such limitation is most injurious. It gives undue prominence to one department of the life of faith which, if any distinction be allowable, we should judge to be the very lowest. But in reality, there should be no distinction: the life of faith is one. Faith is the grand principle of the divine life from first to last. By faith we are justified, and by faith we live; by faith we stand, and by faith we walk. From the starting-post to the goal of the Christian course it is all by faith.

Hence, therefore, it is a serious mistake to single out certain persons who trust the Lord for temporal supplies, and speak of them as living by faith, as if they alone did so. And not only so, but such persons are held up to the gaze of the Church of God as something wonderful; and the great mass of Christians are led to think that the privilege of living by faith lies entirely beyond their range. They are led into a complete mistake as to the real character and sphere of the life of faith, and thus they suffer in the inner life.

Let the Christian reader, then, distinctly understand that it is his happy privilege, whoever he be or whatever be his position, to live a life of faith, in all the depth and fullness of that word. He may, according to his measure, take up the language of the blessed apostle, and say, "The life that I live in the flesh, I live by the faith of the Son of God, who loved me, and gave Himself for me." Let nothing rob him of this high and holy privilege which belongs to every member of the household of faith. Alas! we fail. Our faith is weak, when it ought to be strong, bold, and vigorous. Our God delights in a bold faith. If we study the gospels, we shall see that nothing so refreshed and delighted the heart of Christ as a fine bold faith—a faith that understood Him and drew largely upon Him. Look, for example, at the Syrophenician in Mark 7, and the centurion in Luke 7.

True, He could meet a weak faith—the very weakest. He could meet an "If Thou *wilt*" with a gracious "I will"—an "If Thou *canst*" with "If thou canst believe, all things are possible." The faintest look, the feeblest touch, was sure to meet with a gracious response; but the Saviour's heart was gratified and His spirit refreshed when He could say, "O woman, great is thy faith; be it unto thee even as thou wilt"; and again, "I have not found so great faith, no, not in Israel."

Let us remember this. We may rest assured it is the very same to-day as when our blessed Lord was here amongst men. He loves to be trusted, to be used, to be drawn upon. We can never go too far in counting on the love of His heart or the strength of His hand. There is nothing too small, nothing too great for Him; He has all power in heaven and on earth; He is head over all things to His Church; He holds the universe together; He upholds all things by the word of His power. Philosophers talk of the forces and laws of nature: the Christian thinks with delight of Christ, His hand, His Word, His mighty power. By Him all things were created, and by Him all things consist.

And then His love! What rest, what comfort, what joy, to know and remember that the almighty Creator and Upholder of the universe is the everlasting Lover of our souls! that He loves us perfectly; that His eye is ever upon us, His heart ever toward us; that He has charged Himself with all our wants, whatever these wants may be—whether physical, mental, or spiritual! There is not a single thing within the entire range of our necessities that is not treasured up for us in Christ. He is Heaven's treasury—God's storehouse, and all this for us.

Why, then, should we ever turn to another? Why should we ever, directly or indirectly, make known our wants to a poor fellow-mortal? Why not go straight to Jesus? Do we want sympathy? Who can sympathize with us like our most merciful High-Priest, who is touched with the feeling of our infirmities? Do we want help of any kind? Who can help us like our almighty Friend, the Possessor of unsearchable riches? Do we want counsel or guidance? Who can give it like the blessed One who is the very wisdom of God, and who is made of God unto us wisdom? Oh, let us not wound His loving heart, and dishonor His glorious name by turning away from Him. Let us jealously watch against the tendency so natural to us to cherish human hopes, creature-confidences, and earthly expectations. Let us abide hard by the Fountain, and we shall never have to complain of the streams. In a word, let us seek to live by faith, and thus glorify God in our day and generation.

We shall now proceed with our chapter; and in so doing, we would call the reader's attention to verse 2. It is certainly a very remarkable parenthesis. "(There are eleven days' journey from Horeb, by the way of Mount Seir, unto Kadesh-barnea.)" Eleven days! and yet it took them forty years! How was this? Alas! we need not travel far for the answer. It is only too like ourselves. How slowly we get over the ground! What windings and turnings! How often we have to go back and travel over the same ground again and again! We are slow travelers, because we are slow learners. It may be we feel disposed to marvel how Israel could have taken forty years to accomplish a journey of eleven days; but we may, with much greater reason, marvel at ourselves. We, like them, are kept back by our unbelief and slowness of heart; but there is far less excuse for us than for them, inasmuch as our privileges are so very much higher.

Some of us have much reason to be ashamed of the time we spend over our lessons. The words of the blessed apostle do but too forcibly apply to us—"For when for the time ye ought to be teachers, ye have need that one teach you again which be the first principles of the oracles of God; and are become such as have need of milk, and not of strong meat." Our God is a faithful and wise as well as a gracious and patient Teacher. He will not permit us to pass cursorily over our lessons. Sometimes, perhaps, we think we have mastered a lesson, and we attempt to move on to another; but our wise Teacher knows better, and He sees the need of deeper ploughing. He will not have us mere theorists or smatterers: He will keep us, if need be, year after year at our scales until we learn to sing.

Now, while it is very humbling to us to be so slow in learning, it is very gracious of Him to take such pains with us, in order to make us sure. We have to bless Him for His mode of teaching as for all beside—for the wonderful patience with which He sits down with us over the same lesson again and again, in order that we may learn it thoroughly.*

"And it came to pass in the fortieth year, in the eleventh month, on the first day of the month, that Moses spake unto the children of Israel, according unto all that the Lord had given him in commandment unto them" (ver. 3). These few words contain a volume of weighty instruction for every servant of God—for all who are called to minister in the Word and doctrine. Moses gave the people just what he himself had received from God—nothing more, nothing less. He brought them into direct contact with the living Word of Jehovah. This is the grand principle of ministry at all times. Nothing else is of any real value. The Word of God is the only thing that will stand. There is divine power and authority in it. All mere human teaching, however interesting—however attractive at the time, will pass away and leave the soul without any foundation to rest upon.

Hence it should be the earnest, jealous care of all who minister in the assembly of God, to preach the Word in all its purity, in all its simplicity; to give it to the people as they get it from God; to bring them face to face with the veritable language of holy Scripture. Thus will their ministry tell, with living power, on the hearts and consciences of their hearers. It will link the soul with God Himself, by means of the Word, and impart a depth and solidity which no human teaching can ever produce.

Look at the blessed apostle Paul. Hear him express himself on this weighty subject: "And I, brethren, when I came to you, came not with excellency of speech or of wisdom, declaring unto you the testimony of God. For I determined not to know any thing among you, save Jesus Christ, and Him crucified. And I was with you in weakness, and in fear, and in much trembling. And my speech and my preaching was not with enticing words of man's wisdom, but in demonstration of the Spirit and of power." What was the object of all this fear and trembling? "That your faith should not stand in the wisdom of men, but in the power of God" (1 Cor. 2:1-5).

This true-hearted faithful servant of Christ

---

*The journey of Israel from Horeb to Kadesh-barnea illustrates but too forcibly the history of many souls in the matter of finding peace. Many of the Lord's beloved people go on for years, doubting and fearing, never knowing the blessedness of the liberty wherewith Christ makes His people free. It is most distressing, to any one who really cares for souls, to see the sad condition in which some are kept all their days, through legality, bad teaching, false manuals of devotion, and such like. It is a rare thing now-a-days to find in christendom a soul fully established in the peace of the gospel. It is considered a good thing—a sign of humility—to be always doubting. Confidence is looked upon as presumption. In short, things are turned completely upside down. The gospel is not known: souls are under law instead of under grace,—they are kept at a distance instead of being taught to draw nigh. Much of the religion of the day is a deplorable mixture of Christ and self, law and grace, faith and works. Souls are kept in a perfect muddle all their days.

Surely these things demand the grave consideration of all who occupy the responsible place of teachers and preachers in the professing church. There is a solemn day approaching, when all such will be called to render an account of their ministry.

sought only to bring the souls of his hearers into direct personal contact with God Himself. He sought not to link them with Paul. "Who then is Paul, and who is Apollos, but ministers *by whom ye believed?*" All false ministry has for its object the attaching of souls to itself. Thus the minister is exalted, God is shut out, and the soul left without any divine foundation to rest upon. True ministry, on the contrary, as seen in Paul and Moses, has for its blessed object the attaching of the soul to God. Thus the minister gets his true place—simply an instrument, God is exalted, and the soul established on a sure foundation which can never be moved.

But let us hear a little more from our apostle on this most weighty subject. "Moreover, brethren, I declare unto you the gospel which I preached unto you, which also ye have received, and wherein ye stand; by which also ye are saved, if ye keep in memory what I preached unto you, unless ye have believed in vain. *For I delivered unto you first of all that which I also received"*—nothing more, nothing less, nothing different—"how that Christ died for our sins *according to the Scriptures;* and that He was buried, and that He rose again the third day *according to the Scriptures."*

This is uncommonly fine. It demands the serious consideration of all who would be true and effective ministers of Christ. The apostle was careful to allow the pure stream to flow down from its living source—the heart of God, into the souls of the Corinthians. He felt that nothing else was of any value. If he had sought to link them on to himself, he would have sadly dishonored his Master, done them a grievous wrong, and he himself would most assuredly suffer loss in the day of Christ.

But no; Paul knew better. He would not, for worlds, lead any to build upon himself. Hear what he says to his much-loved Thessalonians.—"For this cause also thank we God without ceasing, because, when *ye received the Word of God* which ye heard of us, ye received it *not as the word of men,* but *as it is in truth, the Word of God,* which effectually worketh also in you that believe" (1 Thess. 2:13).

We feel solemnly responsible to commend this grave and important point to the serious consideration of the Church of God. If all the professed ministers of Christ were to follow the example of Moses and Paul, in reference to the matter now before us, we should witness a very different condition of things in the professing church. But the plain and serious fact is, that the Church of God, like Israel of old, has wholly departed from the authority of His Word. Go where you will, and you find things done and taught which have no foundation in Scripture. Things are not only tolerated but sanctioned and stoutly defended which are in direct opposition to the mind of Christ. If you ask for the divine authority for this, that, and the other institution or practice, you will be told that Christ has not given us directions as to matters of church government; that in all questions of ecclesiastical polity, clerical orders, and liturgical services, He has left us free to act according to our consciences, judgment, or religious feelings; that it is simply absurd to demand a "Thus saith the Lord" for all the details connected with our religious institutions: there is a broad margin left to be filled up according to our national customs and our peculiar habits of thought. It is considered that professing Christians are left perfectly free to form themselves into so-called churches, to choose their own form of government, to make their own arrangements, and to appoint their own office-bearers.

Now the question which the Christian reader has to consider is, "Are these things so?" Can it be that our Lord Christ has left His Church without guidance as to matters so interesting and momentous? Can it be possible that the Church of God is worse off, in the matter of instruction and authority, than Israel? In our studies on the books of Exodus, Leviticus, and Numbers, we have seen (for who could help seeing?) the marvelous pains which Jehovah took to instruct His people as to the most minute particulars connected with their public worship and private life. As to the tabernacle, the temple, the priesthood, the ritual, the various feasts and sacrifices, the periodical solemnities, the months, the days, the very hours, all was ordered and settled with divine precision. Nothing was left to mere human arrangement. Man's wisdom, his judgment, his reason, his conscience, had nothing whatever to do in the matter. Had it been left to man, how should we ever have had that admirable, profound, and far-reaching typical system which the inspired pen of Moses has set before us? If Israel had been allowed to do what (as some would fain persuade us) the Church is allowed, what confusion, what strife, what division, what endless sects and parties, would have been the inevitable result!

But it was not so. The Word of God settled every thing. "As the Lord commanded Moses." This grand and influential sentence was appended to every thing that Israel had to do, and to every thing they were not to do. Their national institutions and their domestic habits—their public and their private life, all came under the commanding authority of "Thus saith the Lord." There was no occasion for any member of the congregation to say, I cannot see this, or, I cannot go with that, or, I cannot agree with the other. Such language could only be regarded as the fruit of self-will. He might just as well say, I cannot agree with Jehovah. And why? Simply because the Word of God had spoken as to every thing, and that, too, with a clearness and simplicity which left no room whatever for human discussion. Throughout the whole of the Mosaic economy there was not the breadth of a hair of margin left in which to insert the opinion or the judgment of man. It pertained not to man to add the weight of a feather to that vast system of types and shadows which had been planned by the divine mind, and set forth in language so plain and pointed, that all Israel had to do was to *obey*—not to argue, not to reason, not to discuss, but to obey.

Alas! they failed, as we know. They did their own will: they took their own way; they did "every man that which was right in his own eyes." They departed from the Word of God, and followed the imaginations and devices of their own evil heart, and brought upon themselves the wrath and indignation of offended Deity, under which they suffer till this day, and shall yet suffer unexampled tribulation.

But all this leaves untouched the point on which we are just now dwelling. Israel had the oracles of God, and these oracles were divinely sufficient for their guidance in every thing. There was no room left for the commandments and doctrines of men. The Word of the Lord provided for every possible exigence, and that Word was so plain as to render human comment needless.

Is the Church of God worse off, as regards guidance and authority, than Israel of old? Are Christians left to think and arrange for themselves in the worship and service of God? Are there any questions left open for human discussion? Is the Word of God sufficient, or is it not? Has it left any thing unprovided for? Let us hearken diligently to the following powerful testimony: "All Scripture is given by inspiration of God, and is profitable for doctrine, for reproof, for correction, for instruction in righteousness; that the man of God may be *perfect* [αρτιος] *throughly furnished unto all good works*" (2 Tim. 3).

This is perfectly conclusive. Holy Scripture contains all that the man of God can possibly require to make him perfect, to equip him thoroughly for every thing that can be called a "good work." And if this be true as to the man of God individually, it is equally true as to the Church of God collectively. Scripture is all-sufficient—for each, for all. Thank God that it is so! What a signal mercy to have a divine guide-book! Were it not so, what should we do? whither should we turn? what would become of us? If we were left to human tradition and human arrangement in the things of God, what hopeless confusion! what clashing of opinions! what conflicting judgments! And all this of necessity, inasmuch as one man would have quite as good a right as another to put forth his opinion and to suggest his plan.

We shall perhaps be told that, notwithstanding our possession of the holy Scripture, we have, nevertheless, sects, parties, creeds, and schools of thought almost innumerable. But why is this? Simply because we refuse to submit our whole moral being to the authority of holy Scripture. This is the real secret of the matter—the true source of all those sects and parties which are the shame and sorrow of the Church of God.

It is vain for men to tell us that these things are good in themselves—that they are the legitimate fruit of that free exercise of thought and private judgment which form the very boast and glory of Protestant Christianity. We do not and cannot believe for a moment that such a plea will stand before the judgment-seat of Christ. We believe, on the contrary, that this very boasted freedom of thought and independence of judgment are in direct opposition to that spirit of profound and reverent obedience which is due to our adorable Lord and Master. What right has a servant to exercise his private judgment in the face of his master's plainly expressed will? None whatever. The duty of a servant is simply to obey—not to reason or to question, but to do what he is told. He fails, as a servant, just insofar as he exercises his own private judgment. The most lovely moral trait in a servant's character is implicit, unquestioning, and unqualified obedience. The one grand business of a servant is to do his master's will.

All this will be fully admitted in human affairs; but in the things of God, men think themselves entitled to exercise their private judgment. It is a fatal mistake. God has given us His Word; and that Word is so plain, that wayfaring men, though fools, need not err therein. Hence, therefore, if we were all guided by that Word, if we were all to bow down in a spirit of unquestioning obedience to its divine authority, there could not be conflicting opinions and opposing sects. It is quite impossible that the voice of holy Scripture can teach opposing doctrines. It cannot possibly teach one man Episcopacy; another, Presbyterianism; and another, Independency. It cannot possibly furnish a foundation for opposing schools of thought. It would be a positive insult offered to the divine volume to attempt to attribute to it all the sad confusion of the professing church. Every pious mind must recoil, with just horror, from such an impious thought. Scripture cannot contradict itself; and therefore if two men or ten thousand men are exclusively taught by Scripture, they will think alike.

Hear what the blessed apostle says to the church at Corinth—says to us, "Now I beseech you, brethren, *by the name of our Lord Jesus Christ"* (mark the mighty moral force of this appeal) "that ye all *speak the same thing,* and that there be no divisions among you; but that ye be perfectly joined together in *the same mind,* and in *the same judgment."*

Now the question is, how was this most blessed result to be reached? Was it by each one exercising the right of private judgment? Alas! it was this very thing that gave birth to all the division and contention in the assembly at Corinth, and drew forth the sharp rebuke of the Holy Ghost. Those poor Corinthians thought they had a right to think and judge and choose for themselves, and what was the result? "It hath been declared unto me of you, my brethren, by them which are of the house of Chloe, that there are contentions among you. Now this I say, that *every one of you saith,* I am of Paul; and I of Apollos; and I of Cephas; and I of Christ. Is Christ divided?"

Here we have private judgment and its sad fruit—its necessary fruit. One man has quite as good a right to think for himself as another; and no man has any right whatsoever to force his opinion upon his fellow. Where, then, lies the remedy? In flinging to the winds our private judgments, and reverently submitting ourselves to the supreme and absolute authority of holy Scripture. If it be not thus, how could the apostle beseech the Corinthians to "speak the same thing, and to be perfectly joined together in the same mind, and in the same judgment"? Who was to prescribe the "thing" that all were to "speak"? In whose "mind" or whose "judgment" were all to be "perfectly joined together"? Had any one member of the assembly, however gifted or intelligent, the slightest shadow of a right to set forth what his brethren were to speak, to think or to judge? Most certainly not. There was one absolute, because divine, authority to which all were bound, or rather privileged, to submit themselves. Human opinions, man's private judgment, his conscience, his reason—all these things must go for what they are worth; and most assuredly they are perfectly worthless as authority. The Word of God is the *only* authority; and if we are all governed by that, we shall "all speak the same thing," and "there will be no divisions among us"; but we shall "be perfectly joined together in the same mind, and in the same judgment."

Lovely condition! But, alas! it is not the present condition of the Church of God; and therefore it is perfectly evident that we are not all governed by the one supreme, absolute, and all-sufficient authority—the voice of holy Scripture—that most blessed voice that can never utter one discordant note—a voice ever divinely harmonious to the circumcised ear.

Here lies the root of the whole matter. The Church has departed from the authority of Christ, as set forth in His Word. Until this is seen, it is only lost time to discuss the claims of conflicting systems, ecclesiastical or theological. If a man does not see that it is his sacred duty to test every ecclesiastical system, every liturgical service, and every theological creed by the Word of God, discussion is perfectly useless. If it be allowable to settle things according to expediency—according to man's judgment, his conscience, or his reason, then verily we may as well at once give up the case as hopeless. If we have no divinely settled authority—no perfect standard—no infallible guide, we cannot see how it is possible for any one to possess the certainty that he is treading in the true path. If indeed it be true that we are left to choose for ourselves, amid the almost countless paths which lie around us, then farewell to all certainty—farewell to peace of mind and rest of heart—farewell to all holy stability of purpose and fixedness of aim. If we cannot say of the ground we occupy, of the path we pursue, and of the work in which we are engaged, "This is the thing which the Lord hath commanded," we may rest assured we are in a wrong position, and the sooner we abandon it the better.

Thank God, there is no necessity whatever for His child or His servant to continue for one hour in connection with what is wrong. "Let every one that nameth the name of Christ depart from iniquity." But how are we to know what is iniquity? By the Word of God. Whatever is contrary to Scripture, whether in morals or in doctrines, is iniquity, and I must depart from it, cost what it may. It is an individual matter. *"Let every one." "He* that hath ears." *"He* that overcometh." "If *any* man hear My voice."

Here is the point. Let us mark it well. It is *Christ's* voice. It is not the voice of this good man or that good man; it is not the voice of the church, the voice of the fathers, the voice of general councils, but the voice of our own beloved Lord and Master. It is the individual conscience in direct, living contact with the voice of Christ—the living, eternal Word of God—the holy Scriptures. Were it merely a question of human conscience or judgment or authority, we are at once plunged in hopeless uncertainty, inasmuch as what one man might judge to be iniquity, another might consider to be perfectly right. There must be some fixed standard to go by—some supreme authority from which there can be no appeal; and, blessed be God, there is. God has spoken; He has given us His Word; and it is at once our bounden duty, our high privilege, our moral security, our true enjoyment, to obey that Word.

Not man's interpretation of the Word, but the Word itself. This is all-important. We must have nothing—absolutely nothing between the human conscience and divine revelation. Men talk to us about the authority of the church. Where are we to find it? Suppose a really anxious, earnest, honest soul, longing to know the true way. He is told to listen to the voice of the church. He asks, Which church? Is it the Greek, Latin, Anglican, or Scotch church? Not two of them agree. Nay, more; there are conflicting parties, contending sects, opposing schools of thought, in one and the self-same body. Councils have differed, fathers have disagreed, popes have anathematized one another. In the Anglican Establishment, we have high-church, low-church, and broad-church, each differing from the rest. In the Scotch or Presbyterian church, we have the Established church, the United Presbyterian, and the Free church. And then if the anxious inquirer turns away in hopeless perplexity from those great bodies, in order to seek guidance amid the ranks of Protestant dissenters, is he likely to fare any better?

Ah! it is perfectly hopeless. The whole professing church has revolted from the authority of Christ, and cannot possibly be a guide or an authority for any one. In the second and third chapters of the book of Revelation, the church is seen under judgment, and the appeal, seven times repeated, is, "He that hath an ear, let him hear"—what? The voice of the church? Impossible! The Lord could never direct us to hear the voice of that which is itself under judgment. Hear what, then? "Let him hear what the Spirit saith unto the churches."

And where is this voice to be heard? *Only* in the holy Scriptures, given of God, in His infinite goodness, to guide our souls in the way of peace and truth, notwithstanding the hopeless ruin of the church, and the thick darkness and wild confusion of baptized christendom. It lies not within the compass of human language to set forth the value and importance of having a divine and therefore an infallible and all-sufficient guide and authority for our individual path.

But be it remembered, we are solemnly responsible to bow to that authority, and follow that guide. It is utterly vain, indeed morally dangerous, to profess to have a divine guide and authority unless we are thoroughly subject thereto. This it was that characterized the Jews in the days of our Lord. They had the Scriptures, but they did not obey them. And one of the saddest features in the present condition of christendom is its boasted possession of the Bible, while the authority of that Bible is boldly set aside.

We deeply feel the solemnity of this, and would earnestly press it upon the conscience of the Christian reader. The Word of God is virtually ignored amongst us. Things are practiced and sanctioned, on all hands, which not only have no foundation in Scripture, but are diametrically opposed to it. We are not exclusively taught and absolutely governed by Scripture.

All this is most serious, and demands the attention of all the Lord's people in every place. We feel compelled to raise a warning note in the ears of all Christians in reference to this most weighty subject. Indeed, it is the sense of its gravity and vast moral importance that has led us to enter upon the service of writing these *Notes on the Book of Deuteronomy.* It is our earnest prayer that the Holy Ghost may use these pages to recall the hearts of the Lord's dear people to their true and proper place—even the place of reverent allegiance to His blessed Word. We feel persuaded that what will characterize all those who will walk devotedly in the closing hours of the Church's earthly history will be profound reverence for the Word of God, and genuine attachment to the Person of our Lord and Saviour Jesus Christ. The two things are inseparably bound together by a sacred and imperishable link.

"The Lord our God spake unto us in Horeb, saying, 'Ye have dwelt long enough in this mount: turn you, and take your journey, and go to the mount of the Amorites, and unto all the places nigh thereunto, in the plain, in the hills, and in the vale, and in the south, and by the sea-side, to the land of the Canaanites, and unto Lebanon, unto the great river, the river Euphrates' " (ver. 6-7).

We shall find, throughout the whole of the book of Deuteronomy, the Lord dealing much more directly and simply with the people than in any of the three preceding books; so far is it from being true that Deuteronomy is a mere repetition of what has passed before us in previous sections. For instance, in the passage just quoted there is no mention of the movement of the cloud—no reference to the sound of the trumpet. "The Lord our God spake unto us." We know, from the book of Numbers, that the movements of the camp were governed by the movements of the cloud, as communicated by the sound of the trumpet. But neither the trumpet nor the cloud is alluded to in this book. It is much more simple and familiar. "The Lord our God spake unto us in Horeb, saying, 'Ye have dwelt long enough in this mount.' "

This is very beautiful. It reminds us somewhat of the lovely simplicity of patriarchal times, when the Lord spake unto the fathers as a man speaketh to his friend. It was not by the sound of a trumpet, or by the movement of a cloud, that the Lord communicated His mind to Abraham, Isaac, and Jacob. He was so very near to them that there was no need, no room for an agency characterized by ceremony and distance. He visited them, sat with them, partook of their hospitality, in all the intimacy of personal friendship.

Such is the lovely simplicity of the order of things in patriarchal times; and this it is which imparts a peculiar charm to the narratives of the book of Genesis.

But in Exodus, Leviticus, and Numbers we have something quite different. There, we have set before us a vast system of types and shadows, rites, ordinances, and ceremonies, imposed on the people for the time being, the import of which is unfolded to us in the Epistle to the Hebrews. "The Holy Ghost this signifying, that the way into the holiest of all was not yet made manifest, while as the first tabernacle was yet standing; which was a figure for the time then present, in which were offered both gifts and sacrifices, that could not make him that did the service perfect, as pertaining to the conscience; which stood only in meats and drinks, and divers washings, and carnal ordinances, imposed on them until the time of reformation" (Heb. 9:8-10).

Under this system, the people were at a distance from God. It was not with them as it had been with their fathers in the book of Genesis. God was shut in from them, and they were shut out from Him. The leading features of the Levitical ceremonial, so far as the people were concerned, were bondage, darkness, distance; but on the other hand, its types and shadows pointed forward to that one great Sacrifice which is the foundation of all God's marvelous counsels and purposes, and by which He can, in perfect righteousness, and according to all the love of His heart, have a people near unto Himself, to the praise of the glory of His grace, throughout the golden ages of eternity.

Now, it has been already remarked, we shall find in Deuteronomy comparatively little of rites and ceremonies. The Lord is seen more in direct communication with the people; and even the priests, in their official capacity, come rarely before us; and if they are referred to, it is very much more in a moral than in a ceremonial way. Of this we shall have ample proof as we pass along; it is a marked feature of this beautiful book.

"The Lord our God spake unto us in Horeb, saying, 'Ye have dwelt long enough in this mount: turn you, and take your journey, and go to the mount of the Amorites.' " What a rare privilege for any people to have the Lord so near to them, and so interested in all their movements and in all their concerns, great and small! He knew how long they ought to remain in any one place, and whither they should next bend their steps. They had no need to harass themselves about their journeyings, or about any thing else. They were under the eye and in the hands of One whose wisdom was unerring, whose power was omnipotent, whose resources were inexhaustible, whose love was infinite, who had charged Himself with the care of them, who knew all their need, and was prepared to meet it, according to all the love of His heart and the strength of His holy arm.

What, then, we may ask, remained for them to do? What was their plain and simple duty? Just to obey. It was their high and holy privilege to rest in the love and obey the commandments of Jehovah, their covenant God. Here lay the blessed secret of their peace, their happiness, and their moral security. They had no need whatever to trouble themselves about their movements, no need of planning or arranging. Their journeyings were all ordered for them by One who knew every step of the way from Horeb to Kadesh-barnea, and they had just to live by the day, in happy dependence upon Him.

Happy position! Privileged path! Blessed portion! But it demanded a broken will, an obedient mind, a subject heart. If when Jehovah had said, "Ye have compassed this mountain long enough," they, on the contrary, were to form the plan of compassing it a little longer, they would have had to compass it without Him. His companionship, His counsel, and His aid could only be counted upon in the path of obedience.

Thus it was with Israel in their desert wanderings, and thus it is with us. It is our most precious privilege to leave all our matters in the hands, not merely of a convenant God, but of a loving Father. He arranges our movements for us; He fixes the bounds of our habitation; He tells us how long to stay in a place, and where to go next. He has charged Himself with all our concerns, all our movements, all our wants. His gracious word to us is, "Be careful for nothing; but in every thing by prayer and supplication with thanksgiving let your requests be made known unto God." And what then? "The peace of God, which passeth all understanding, shall keep your hearts and minds through Christ Jesus."

But it may be the reader feels disposed to ask, How does God guide His people now? We cannot expect to hear His voice telling us when to move or where to go. To this we reply, at once, It cannot surely be that the members of the Church of God—the body of Christ—are worse off in the matter of divine guidance than Israel in the wilderness. Cannot God guide His children—cannot Christ guide His servants—in all their movements and in all their service? Who would think, for a moment, of calling in question a truth so plain and so precious? True, we do not expect to hear a voice, or see the movement of a cloud; but we have what is very much better, very much higher, very much more intimate. We may rest assured our God has made ample provision for us in this, as in all beside, according to all the love of His heart.

Now, there are three ways in which we are guided: we are guided by the Word, we are guided by the Holy Ghost, and we are guided by the instincts of the divine nature; and we have to bear in mind that the instincts of the divine nature, the leadings of the Holy Ghost, and the teaching of holy Scripture will always harmonize. This is of the utmost importance to keep before us. A person might fancy himself to be led by the instincts of the divine nature, or by the Holy Spirit, to pursue a certain line of action involving consequences at issue with the Word of God. Thus his mistake would be made apparent. It is a very serious thing for any one to act on mere impulse or impression. By so doing, he may fall into a snare of the devil, and do very serious damage to the cause of Christ. We must calmly weigh our impressions in the balances of the sanctuary, and faithfully test them by the standard of the divine Word. In this way we shall be preserved from error and delusion. It is a most dangerous thing to trust impressions or act on impulse. We have seen the most disastrous consequences produced by so doing. Facts *may be* reliable. Divine authority *is* absolutely infallible. Our own impressions may prove as delusive as a will-o'-the-wisp, or a mirage of the desert: human feelings are most untrustworthy. We must ever submit them to the most severe scrutiny, lest they betray us into some fatally false line of action. We can trust Scripture without a shadow of misgiving; and we shall find, without exception, that the man who is led by the Holy Ghost, or guided by the instincts of the divine nature, will never act in opposition to the Word of God. This is what we may call an axiom in the divine life—an established rule in practical Christianity. Would that it had been more attended to in all ages of the Church's history! Would that it were more pondered in our own day!

But there is another point in this question of divine guidance which demands our serious attention. We not unfrequently hear people speak of "the finger of divine Providence" as something to be relied upon for guidance. This may be only another mode of expressing the idea of being guided by circumstances, which, we do not hesitate to say, is very far indeed from being the proper kind of guidance for a Christian.

No doubt, our Lord may and does, at times, intimate His mind and indicate our path by His providence; but we must be sufficiently near to Him to be able to interpret the providence aright, else we may find that what is called "an opening of Providence" may actually prove an opening by which we slip off the holy path of obedience. Surrounding circumstances, just like our inward impressions, must be weighed in the presence of God, and judged by the light of His Word, else they may lead us into the most terrible mistakes. Jonah might have considered it a remarkable providence to find a ship going to Tarshish; but had he been in communion with God, he would not have needed a ship. In short, the Word of God is the one grand test and perfect touchstone for every thing—for outward circumstances and inward impressions—for feelings, imaginations, and tendencies—all must be placed under the searching light of holy Scripture and there calmly and seriously judged. This is the true path of safety, peace, and blessedness for every child of God.

It may, however, be said, in reply to all this, that we cannot expect to find a text of Scripture to guide us in the matter of our movements, or in the thousand little details of daily life. Perhaps not; but there are certain great principles laid down in Scripture, which, if properly applied, will afford divine guidance even where we might not be able to find a particular text. And not only so, but we have the fullest assurance that our God can and does guide His children in all things. "The steps of a good man are ordered of the Lord." "The meek will He guide in judgment; and the meek will He teach His way." "I will guide thee with Mine eye." He can signify His mind to us as to this or that particular act or movement. If not, where are we? How are we to get on? How are we to regulate our movements? Are we to be drifted hither and thither by the tide of circumstances? Are we left to blind chance, or to the mere impulse of our own will?

Thank God, it is not so. He can, in His own perfect way, give us the certainty of His mind in any given case; and without that certainty we should never move. Our Lord Christ (all homage to His peerless name!) can intimate His mind to His servant as to where He would have him to go and what He would have him to do; and no true servant will ever think of moving or acting without such intimation. We should never act or move in uncertainty. If we are not sure, let us be quiet and wait. Very often it happens that we harass and fret ourselves about movements that God would not have us make at all. A person once said to a friend, "I am quite at a loss to know which way to turn." "Then, don't turn at all," was the friend's wise reply.

But here an all-important moral point comes in, and that is, our whole condition of soul. This, we may rest assured, has very much to do with the matter of guidance. It is "the meek He will guide in judgment, and teach His way." We must never forget this. If only we are humble and self-distrusting—if we wait on our God, in simplicity of heart, uprightness of mind, and honesty of purpose, He will most assuredly guide us. But it will never do to go and ask counsel of God in a matter about which our mind is made up, or our will is at work.

This is a fatal delusion. Look at the case of Jehoshaphat, in 1 Kings 22: "It came to pass in the third year, that Jehoshaphat the king of Judah came down to the king of Israel"—a sad mistake, to begin with. "And the king of Israel said unto his servants, 'Know ye that Ramoth in Gilead is ours, and we be still, and take it not out of the hand of the king of Syria?' And he said unto Jehoshaphat, 'Wilt thou go with me to battle to Ramoth-gilead?' And Jehoshaphat said to the king of Israel, 'I am as thou art, my people as thy people, my horses as thy horses; and, [as we have it in 2 Chronicles 18:3] we will be with thee in the war.' "

Here we see that his mind was made up before ever he thought of asking counsel of God in the matter. He was in a false position and a wrong atmosphere altogether. He had fallen into the snare of the enemy, through lack of singleness of eye, and hence he was not in a fit state to receive or profit by divine guidance. He was bent on his own will, and the Lord left him to reap the fruits of it; and but for infinite and sovereign mercy, he would have fallen by the sword of the Syrians, and been borne a corpse from the battle-field.

True, he did say to the king of Israel,

"Inquire, I pray thee, at the word of the Lord to-day." But where was the use of this, when he had already pledged himself to a certain line of action? What folly for any one to make up his mind and then go and ask for counsel! Had he been in a right state of soul, he never would have sought counsel in such a case at all; but his state of soul was bad, his position false, and his purpose in direct opposition to the mind and will of God. Hence, although he heard, from the lips of Jehovah's messenger, His solemn judgment on the entire expedition, yet he took his own way, and well-nigh lost his life in consequence.

We see the same thing in the forty-second chapter of Jeremiah. The people applied to the prophet to ask counsel as to their going down into Egypt; but they had already made up their minds as to their course—they were bent on their own will. Miserable condition! Had they been meek and humble, they would not have needed to ask counsel in the matter; but they said unto Jeremiah the prophet, " 'Let, we beseech thee, our supplication be accepted before thee, and pray for us unto the Lord *thy* God [Why not say, The Lord *our* God?] even for all this remnant; (for we are left but a few of many, as thine eyes do behold us:) that the Lord *thy* God may show us the way wherein we may walk, and the thing that we may do.' Then Jeremiah the prophet said unto them, 'I have heard you; behold, I will pray unto the Lord *your* God according to your words; and it shall come to pass, that whatsoever thing the Lord shall answer you, I will declare it unto you; I will keep nothing back from you.' Then they said to Jeremiah, 'The Lord be a true and faithful witness between us, if we do not even according to all things for the which the Lord *thy* God shall send thee to us. Whether it be good, or whether it be evil [How could the will of God be aught but good?], we will obey the voice of the Lord our God, to whom we send thee; that it may be well with us, when we obey the voice of the Lord our God.' "

Now, all this seemed very pious and very promising; but mark the sequel. When they found that the judgment and counsel of God did not tally with their will, "then spake . . . *all the proud men,* saying unto Jeremiah, 'Thou speakest falsely: the Lord our God hath not sent thee to say, Go not into Egypt to sojourn there.' "

Here, the real state of the case comes clearly out. Pride and self-will were at work; their vows and promises were false. "Ye dissembled in your hearts," says Jeremiah, "when ye sent me unto the Lord your God, saying, 'Pray for us unto the Lord our God; and according unto all that the Lord our God shall say, so declare unto us, and we will do it.' " It would have been all very well had the divine response fallen in with their will in the matter; but inasmuch as it ran counter, they rejected it altogether.

How often is this the case! The Word of God does not suit man's thoughts; it judges them, it stands in direct opposition to his will, it interferes with his plans, and hence he rejects it. The human will and human reason are ever in direct antagonism to the Word of God, and the Christian must refuse both the one and the other if he really desires to be divinely guided. An unbroken will and blind reason, if we listen to them, can only lead us into darkness, misery, and desolation. Jonah *would* go to Tarshish, when he ought to have gone to Nineveh; and the consequence was that he found himself "in the belly of hell," with "the weeds wrapped about his head." Jehoshaphat *would* go to Ramoth-gilead, when he ought to have been at Jerusalem; and the consequence was that he found himself surrounded by the swords of the Syrians. The remnant, in the days of Jeremiah, *would* go into Egypt, when they ought to have remained at Jerusalem; and the consequence was that they died by the sword, by the famine, and by the pestilence in the land of Egypt, "whither they *desired* to go and to sojourn."

Thus it must ever be. The path of self-will is sure to be a path of darkness and misery; it cannot be otherwise: the path of obedience, on the contrary, is a path of peace, a path of light, a path of blessing, a path on which the beams of divine favor are ever poured in living lustre. It may, to the human eye, seem narrow, rough, and lonely; but the obedient soul finds it to be the path of life, peace, and moral security. "The path of the just is as the shining light, that shineth more and more unto the perfect day." Blessed path! May the writer and the reader ever be found treading it, with a steady step and earnest purpose.

Before turning from this great practical subject of divine guidance and human obedience, we must ask the reader to refer, for a few moments, to a very beautiful passage in the eleventh chapter of Luke. He will find it full of the most valuable instruction.

"The light of the body is the eye: therefore when thine eye is single, thy whole body also is full of light; but when thine eye is evil, thy body also is full of darkness. Take heed, therefore, that the light which is in thee be not darkness. If thy whole body therefore be full of light, having no part dark, the whole shall be full of light, as when the bright shining of a candle doth give thee light" (ver. 34-36).

Nothing can exceed the moral force and beauty of this passage. First of all, we have the "single eye." This is essential to the enjoyment of divine guidance. It indicates a broken will—a heart honestly fixed upon doing the will of God. There is no undercurrent, no mixed motive, no personal end in view. There is the one simple desire and earnest purpose to do the will of God, whatever that will may be.

Now, when the soul is in this attitude, divine light comes streaming in and fills the whole body. Hence it follows that if the body is not full of light, the eye is not single; there is some mixed motive; self-will or self-interest is at work; we are not upright before God. In this case, any light which we profess to have is darkness; and there is no darkness so gross or so terrible as that judicial darkness which settles down upon the heart governed by self-will while professing to have light from God. This will be seen in all its horrors by and by in christendom, when "that Wicked shall be revealed, whom the Lord shall consume with the spirit of His mouth, and shall destroy with the brightness of His coming; even him, whose coming is after the working of Satan with all power and signs and lying wonders, and with all deceivableness of unrighteousness in them that perish; because *they received not the love of the truth,* that they might be saved. And *for this cause* God shall send them strong delusion, that they should believe a lie; that they all might be damned who believed not the truth, but *had pleasure in unrighteousness*" (2 Thess. 2:8-12).

How awful is this! How solemnly it speaks to the whole professing church! How solemnly it addresses the conscience of both the writer and the reader of these lines! Light not acted upon becomes darkness. "If the light which is in thee be darkness, how great is that darkness!" But on the other hand, a little light honestly acted upon is sure to increase; for "to him that hath shall more be given," and "the path of the just is as the shining light, that shineth more and more unto the perfect day."

This moral progress is beautifully and forcibly set forth in Luke 11:36: "If thy whole body therefore be full of light, having *no part dark*"—no chamber kept closed against the heavenly rays—no dishonest reserve—the whole moral being laid open, in genuine simplicity, to the action of divine light; then "the whole shall be full of light, as when the bright shining of a candle doth give thee light." In a word, the obedient soul has not only light for his own path, but the light shines out, so that others see it, like the bright shining of a candle. "Let your light so shine before men, that they may see your good works, and glorify your Father which is in heaven."

We have a very vivid contrast to all this in the thirteenth chapter of Jeremiah. "Give glory to the Lord your God, *before He cause darkness,* and before your feet stumble upon the dark mountains, and while ye look for light, He turn it into the shadow of death, and make it gross darkness." The way to give glory to the Lord our God is to obey His Word. The path of duty is a bright and blessed path; and the one who, through grace, treads that path will never stumble on the dark mountains. The truly humble, the lowly, the self-distrusting, will keep far away from those dark mountains, and walk in that blessed path which is ever illuminated by the bright and cheering beams of God's approving countenance.

This is the path of the just, the path of heavenly wisdom, the path of perfect peace. May we ever be found treading it; and let us never, for one moment, forget that it is our high privilege to be divinely guided in the most minute details of our daily life. Alas! for the one who is not so guided. He will have many a stumble, many a fall, many a sorrowful experience. If we are not guided by our Father's eye, we shall be like the horse or the mule, which have no understanding, whose mouth must be held in with bit and bridle,—like the horse, impetuously rushing where he ought not, or the mule, obstinately refusing to go where he ought. How sad for a Christian to be like these! How blessed to move, from day to day, in the path marked out for us by our Father's eye!—a path which the vulture's eye hath not seen, or the lion's whelp trodden; the path of holy obedience; the path in which the meek and lowly will ever be found, to their deep joy, and the praise and glory of Him who has opened it for them and given them grace to tread it.

In the remainder of our chapter, Moses rehearses in the ears of the people, in language of touching simplicity, the facts connected with the appointment of the judges, and the mission of the spies. The appointment of the judges, Moses here attributes to his own suggestion: the mission of the spies was the suggestion of the people. That dear and most honored servant of God felt the burden of the congregation too heavy for him; and assuredly it was very heavy; though we know well that the grace of God was amply sufficient for the demand, and, moreover, that that grace could act as well by one man as by seventy.

Still, we can well understand the difficulty felt by "the meekest man in all the earth" in reference to the responsibility of so grave and important a charge; and truly the language in which he states his difficulty is affecting in the highest degree.

"And I spake unto you at that time, saying, 'I am not able to bear you myself alone: [Surely not; what mere mortal could? But God was there to be counted upon for exigence of every hour] the Lord your God hath multiplied you, and, behold, ye are this day as the stars of heaven for multitude.' (The Lord God of your fathers make you a thousand times so many more as ye are, and bless you, as He hath promised you.)" Lovely parenthesis! Exquisite breathing of a large and lowly heart! "How can I myself alone bear your cumbrance, and your burden, and *your strife?*"

Alas! here lay the secret of much of the "cumbrance" and the "burden." They could not agree among themselves,—there were controversies, contentions, and questions; and who was sufficient for these things? what human shoulder could sustain such a burden? How different it might have been with them! Had they walked lovingly together, there would have been no cases to decide, and therefore no need of judges to decide them. If each member of the congregation had sought the prosperity, the interest, and the happiness of his brethren, there would have been no "strife," no "cumbrance," no "burden." If each had done all that in him lay to promote the common good, how lovely would have been the result!

But, ah! it was not so with Israel in the desert; and, what is still more humbling, it is not so in the Church of God, although our privileges are so much higher. Hardly had the assembly been formed by the presence of the Holy Ghost ere the accents of murmuring and discontent were heard. And about what? About "neglect," whether fancied or real. Whatever way it was, *self* was at work. If the neglect was merely imaginary, the Grecians were to blame; and if it was real, the Hebrews were to blame. It generally happens, in such cases, that there are faults on both sides; but the true way to avoid all strife, contention, and murmuring is to put self in the dust and earnestly seek the good of others. Had this excellent way been understood and adopted, from the outset, what a different task the ecclesiastical historian would have had to perform! But, alas! it has not been adopted; and hence the history of the professing church, from the very beginning, has been a deplorable and humiliating record of controversy, division, and strife. In the very presence of the Lord Himself, whose whole life was one of complete self-surrender, the apostles disputed about who should be greatest. Such a dispute could never have arisen had each known the exquisite secret of putting self in the dust and seeking the good of others. No one who knows aught of the true moral elevation of self-emptiness could possibly seek a good or a great place for himself. Nearness to Christ so satisfies the lowly heart, that honors, distinctions, and rewards are little accounted of; but where self is at work, there you will have envy and jealousy, strife and contention, confusion and every evil work.

Witness the scene between the two sons of Zebedee and their ten brethren, in the tenth chapter of Mark. What was at the bottom of it? Self. The two were thinking of a good place for themselves in the kingdom, and the ten were angry with the two for thinking of any such thing. Had each set self aside, and sought the good of others, such a scene would never have been enacted; the two would not have been thinking about themselves, and hence there would have been no ground for the "indignation" of the ten.

But it is needless to multiply examples. Every age of the church's history illustrates and proves the truth of our statement that self and its odious workings are the producing cause of strife, contention, and division, always. Turn where you will—from the days of the apostles down to the days in which our lot is cast, and you will find unmortified self to be the fruitful source of strife and schism; and on the other hand, you will find that to sink self and its interests is the true secret of peace, harmony, and brotherly love. If only we learn to set self aside, and seek earnestly the glory of Christ and the prosperity of His beloved people, we shall not have many "cases" to settle.

We must now return to our chapter.

"How can I myself alone bear your cumbrance, and your burden, and your strife? Take you wise men, and understanding, and known among your tribes, and I will make them rulers over you. And ye answered me, and said, 'The thing which thou hast spoken is good for us to do.' So I took the chief of your tribes, *wise* men, and *known*"—men fitted of God, and possessing, because entitled to, the confidence of the congregation —"and made them heads over you, captains over thousands, and captains over hundreds, and captains over fifties, and captains over tens, and officers among your tribes."

Admirable arrangement! If indeed it had to be made, nothing could be better adapted to the maintenance of order than the graduated scale of authority, varying from the captain of ten to the captain of a thousand; the lawgiver himself at the head of all, and he in immediate communication with the Lord God of Israel.

We have no allusion here to the fact recorded in Exodus 18, namely, that the appointment of those rulers was at the suggestion of Jethro, Moses' father-in-law; neither have we any reference to the scene in Numbers 11. We call the reader's attention to this as one of the many proofs which lie scattered along the pages of Deuteronomy that it is very far indeed from being a mere repetition of the preceding sections of the Pentateuch. In short, this delightful book has a marked character of its own, and the mode in which facts are presented is in perfect keeping with that character. It is very evident that the object of the venerable lawgiver, or rather of the Holy Ghost in him, was to bring every thing to bear, in a moral way, upon the hearts of the people, in order to produce that one grand result which is the special object of the book from beginning to end, namely, a loving obedience to all the statutes and judgments of the Lord their God.

We must bear this in mind if we would study aright the book which lies open before us. Infidels, skeptics, and rationalists may impiously suggest to us the thought of discrepancies in the various records given in the different books; but the pious reader will reject, with a holy indignation, every such suggestion, knowing that it emanates directly from the father of lies, the determined and persistent enemy of the precious revelation of God. This, we feel persuaded, is the true way in which to deal with all infidel assaults upon the Bible. Argument is useless, inasmuch as infidels are not in a position to understand or appreciate its force; they are profoundly ignorant of the matter. Nor is it merely a question of profound ignorance, but of determined hostility; so that, in every way, the judgment of all infidel writers on the subject of divine inspiration is utterly worthless and perfectly contemptible. We would pity and pray for the men, while we thoroughly despise and indignantly reject their opinions. The Word of God is entirely above and beyond them. It is as perfect as its Author, and as imperishable as His throne; but its moral glories, its living depths, and its infinite perfections are only unfolded to faith and need. "I thank Thee, O Father, Lord of heaven and earth, because Thou hast hid these things from the wise and prudent, and hast revealed them unto babes."

If we are only content to be as simple as a babe, we shall enjoy the precious revelation of a Father's love, as given by His Spirit in the holy Scriptures; but on the other hand, those who fancy themselves wise and prudent—who build upon their learning, their philosophy, and their reason—who think themselves competent to sit in judgment on the Word of God, and hence of God Himself, are given over to judicial darkness, blindness, and hardness of heart. Thus it comes to pass that the most egregious folly and the most contemptible ignorance that man can display will be found in the pages of those learned writers who have dared to write against the Bible. "Where is the wise? where is the scribe? where is the disputer of this world? hath not God made foolish the wisdom of this world? For after that in the wisdom of God the world by wisdom knew not God, it pleased God by the foolishness of preaching to save them that believe" (1 Cor. 1:20-21).

"If any man will be wise, let him become a fool." Here lies the grand moral secret of the matter. Man must get to the end of his own wisdom, as well as of his own righteousness. He must be brought to confess himself a fool ere he can taste the sweetness of divine wisdom. It is not within the range of the most gigantic human intellect, aided by all the appliances of human learning and philosophy, to grasp the very simplest elements of divine revelation; and therefore, when unconverted men, whatever may be the force of their genius or the extent of their learning, undertake to handle spiritual subjects, and more especially the subject of the divine inspiration of holy Scripture, they are sure to exhibit their profound ignorance, and utter incompetency to deal with the question before them. Indeed, whenever we look into an infidel book, we are struck with the feebleness of their most forcible arguments; and not only so, but in every instance in which they attempt to find a discrepancy in the Bible, we see only divine wisdom, beauty, and perfectness.

We have been led into the foregoing line of thought in connection with the subject of the appointment of the elders, which is given to us in each book according to the wisdom of the Holy Ghost, and in perfect keeping with the scope and object of the book. We shall now proceed with our quotation.

"And I charged your judges at that time, saying, 'Hear the causes between your brethren, and *judge righteously* between your brethren, and *the stranger* that is with him. *Ye shall not respect persons* in judgment; but *ye shall hear the small as well as the great; ye shall not be afraid of the face of man;* for the judgment is God's; and the cause that is too hard for you, bring it unto me, and I will hear it.' "

What heavenly wisdom is here! what even-handed justice! What holy impartiality! In every case of difference, all the facts on both sides were to be fully heard and patiently weighed. The mind was not to be warped by prejudice, predilection, or personal feeling of any kind. The judgment was to be formed, not by impressions, but by facts—clearly established, undeniable facts. Personal influence was to have no weight whatever. The position and circumstances of either party in the cause were not to be considered. The case must be decided entirely upon its own merits. "Ye shall hear the small as well as the great." The poor man was to have the same even-handed justice meted out to him as the rich; the stranger as one born in the land. No difference was to be allowed.

How important is all this! how worthy of our attentive consideration! how full of deep and valuable instruction for us all! True, we are not all called to be judges or elders or leaders; but the great moral principles laid down in the above quotation are of the very utmost value to every one of us, inasmuch as cases are continually occurring which call for their direct application. Wherever our lot may be cast, whatever our line of life or sphere of action, we are liable, alas! to meet with cases of difficulty and misunderstanding between our brethren, cases of wrong, whether real or imaginary; and hence it is most needful to be divinely instructed as to how we ought to carry ourselves in respect to such.

Now, in all such cases, we cannot be too strongly impressed with the necessity of having our judgment based on facts—all the facts on both sides. We must not allow ourselves to be guided by our own impressions, for we all know that mere impressions are most untrustworthy. They may be correct, and they may be utterly false. Nothing is more easily received and conveyed than a false impression, and therefore any judgment based on mere impressions is worthless. We must have solid, clearly established facts—facts established by two or three witnesses, as Scripture so distinctly enforces (Deut. 17:6; Matt. 18:16; 2 Cor. 13:1; 1 Tim. 5:19).

But further, we must never be guided in judgment by an *ex parte* statement. Every one is liable, even with the best intentions, to give a color to his statement of a case. It is not that he would intentionally make a false statement, or tell a deliberate lie; but through inaccuracy of memory, or one cause or another, he may not present the case as it really is. Some fact may be omitted, and that one fact may so affect all the other facts as to alter their bearing completely. "*Audi alteram partem*" ("Hear the other side") is a wholesome motto. And not only hear the other side, but hear all the facts on both sides, and thus you will be able to form a sound and righteous judgment. We may set it down as a standing rule, that any judgment formed without an accurate knowledge of all the facts is perfectly worthless. "Hear the causes between your brethren, and judge righteously between every man and his brother, and the stranger that is with him." Seasonable, needed words, most surely, at all times, in all places, and under all circumstances. May we apply our hearts to them.

And how important the admonition in verse 17! "Ye shall not respect persons in judgment; but ye shall hear the small as well as the great; ye shall not be afraid of the face of man." How these words discover the poor human heart! How prone we are to respect persons—to be swayed by personal influence—to attach importance to position and wealth—to be afraid of the face of man!

What is the divine antidote against all these evils? Just this: the fear of God. If we set the Lord before us, at all times, it will effectually deliver us from the pernicious influence of partiality, prejudice, and the fear of men. It will lead us to wait humbly and patiently on the Lord for guidance and counsel in all that may come before us, and thus we shall be preserved from forming hasty and one-sided judgment of men and things—that fruitful source of mischief amongst the Lord's people in all ages.

We shall now dwell for a few moments on the very affecting manner in which Moses brings before the congregation all the circumstances connected with the mission of the spies, which, like the appointment of the judges, is in perfect keeping with the scope and object of the book. This is only what we might expect. There is not, there could not be, a single sentence of useless repetition in the divine volume; still less could there be a single flaw, a single discrepancy, a single contradictory statement. The Word of God is absolutely perfect—perfect as a whole, perfect in all its parts. We must firmly hold and faithfully confess this in the face of this infidel age.

We speak not of human translations of the Word of God, in which there must be more or less of imperfection; though even here, we cannot but be "filled with wonder, love, and praise" when we mark the way in which our God so manifestly presided over our excellent English translation, so that the poor man at the back of a mountain may be assured of possessing, in his common English Bible, the revelation of God to his soul. And most surely we are warranted in saying that this is just what we might look for at the hands of our God. It is but reasonable to infer that the One who inspired the writers of the Bible would also watch over the translation of it; for inasmuch as He gave it originally, in His grace, to those who could read Hebrew and Greek, so would He not, in the same grace, give it in every language under heaven? Blessed forever be His holy name, it is His gracious desire to speak to every man in the very tongue in which he was born,—to tell us the sweet tale of His grace—the glad tidings of salvation in the very accents in which our mothers whispered into our infant ears those words of love that went right home to our very hearts (see Acts 2:5-8).

Oh that men were more impressed and affected with the truth and power of all this, and then we should not be troubled with so many foolish and unlearned questions about the Bible.

Let us now hearken to the account given by Moses of the mission of the spies—its origin and its result. We shall find it full of most weighty instruction, if only the ear be open to hear and the heart duly prepared to ponder.

"And I commanded you at that time all the things which ye should do." The path of simple obedience was plainly set before them. They had but to tread it with an obedient heart and firm step. They had not to reason about consequences, or weigh the results; all these they had just to leave in the hands of God, and move on with steady purpose in the blessed path of obedience.

"And when we departed from Horeb, we went through all that *great and terrible wilderness,* which ye saw by the way of the mountain of the Amorites, as the Lord our God commanded us; and we came to Kadesh-barnea. And I said unto you, 'Ye are come unto the mountain of the Amorites, which the Lord our God doth give unto us. Behold, the Lord thy God hath set the land before thee: go up and possess it, as the Lord God of thy fathers hath said unto thee; fear not, neither be discouraged.' "

Here was their warrant for entering upon immediate possession. The Lord their God had given them the land and set it before them. It was theirs by His free gift—the gift of His sovereign grace, in pursuance of the covenant made with their fathers. It was His eternal purpose to possess the land of Canaan through the seed of Abraham His friend. This ought to have been enough to set their hearts perfectly at rest, not only as to the character of the land, but also as to their entrance upon it. There was no need of spies. Faith never wants to spy what God has given. It argues that what He has given must be worth having, and that He is able to put us in full possession of all that His grace has bestowed. Israel might have concluded that the same hand that had conducted them "through all that great and terrible wilderness" could bring them in and plant them in their destined inheritance.

So Faith would have reasoned; for it always reasons from God down to circumstances, never from circumstances up to God. "If God be for us, who can be against us?" This is Faith's argument, grand in its simplicity and simple in its moral grandeur. When God fills the whole range of the soul's vision, difficulties are little accounted of. They are either not seen, or, if seen, they are viewed as occasions for the display of divine power. Faith exults in seeing God triumphing over difficulties.

But, alas! the people were not governed by faith on the occasion now before us, and therefore they had recourse to spies. Of this Moses reminds them, and that, too, in language at once most tender and faithful. "And ye came near unto me, *every one of you,* and said, 'We will send men before us, and they shall search us out the land, and bring us word again, by what way we must go up, and into what cities we shall come.' "

Surely, they might well have trusted God for all this. The One who had brought them up out of Egypt, made a way for them through the sea, guided them through the trackless desert, was fully able to bring them into the land. But no; they would send spies, simply because their hearts had not simple confidence in the true, the living, the almighty God.

Here lay the moral root of the matter; and it is well that the reader should thoroughly seize this point. True it is that, in the history given in Numbers, the Lord told Moses to send the spies; but why? Because of the moral condition of the people. And here we see the characteristic difference and yet the lovely harmony of the two books. Numbers gives us the public history, Deuteronomy the secret source of the mission of the spies; and as it is in perfect keeping with Numbers to give us the former, so it is in perfect keeping with Deuteronomy to give us the latter. The one is the complement of the other. We could not fully understand the subject had we only the history given in Numbers. It is the touching commentary given in Deuteronomy which completes the picture. How perfect is Scripture! All we need is the eye anointed to see and the heart prepared to appreciate its moral glories.

It may be, however, that the reader still feels some difficulty in reference to the question of the spies. He may feel disposed to ask how it could be wrong to send them when the Lord told them to do so. The answer is, the wrong was not in the act of sending them when they were told, but in the wish to send them at all. The wish was the fruit of unbelief, and the command to send them was because of that unbelief.

We may see something of the same in the matter of divorce in Matthew 19: "The Pharisees also came unto Him, tempting Him, and saying unto Him, 'Is it lawful for a man to put away his wife for every cause?' And He answered and said unto them, 'Have ye not read, that He which made them at the beginning made them male and female, and said, For this cause shall a man leave father and mother, and shall cleave to his wife; and they twain shall be one flesh? Wherefore they are no more twain, but one flesh. What therefore God hath joined together, let not man put asunder.' They say unto Him, 'Why did Moses, then, command to give a writing of divorcement, and to put her away?' He saith unto them, 'Moses *because of the hardness of your hearts* suffered you to put away your wives; but from the beginning it was not so.' "

It was not in keeping with God's original institution, or according to His heart, that a man should put away his wife; but, in consequence of the hardness of the human heart, divorce was permitted by the lawgiver. Is there any difficulty in this? Surely not; unless the heart is bent on making one. Neither is there any difficulty in the matter of the spies. Israel ought not to have needed them: simple faith would never have thought of them. But the Lord saw the real condition of things and issued a command accordingly; just as, in after ages, He saw the heart of the people bent on having a king, and He commanded Samuel to give them one.—"And the Lord said unto Samuel, 'Hearken unto the voice of the people in all that they say unto thee; for they have not rejected thee, but they have rejected Me, that I should not reign over them. According to all the works which they have done since the day that I brought them up out of Egypt even unto this day, wherewith they have forsaken Me, and served other gods, so do they also unto thee. Now therefore hearken unto their voice: *howbeit yet protest solemnly* unto them, and shew them the manner of the king that shall reign over them' " (1 Sam. 8:7-9).

Thus we see that the mere granting of a desire is no proof whatever that such desire is according to the mind of God. Israel ought not to have asked for a king. Was not Jehovah sufficient? was not He their King? could not He, as He had ever done, lead them forth to battle and fight for them? Why seek an arm of flesh? why turn away from the living, the true, the almighty God to lean on a poor fellow-worm? What power was there in a king but that which God might see fit to bestow upon him? None whatever. All the power, all the wisdom, all real good, was in the Lord their God; and it was there for them—there at all times, to meet their every need. They had but to lean upon His almighty arm—to draw upon His exhaustless resources, to find all their springs in Him.

When they did get a king, according to their hearts' desire, what did he do for them? "All the people followed him trembling." The more closely we study the melancholy history of Saul's reign, the more we see that he was, almost from the very outset, a positive hindrance rather than a help. We have but to read his history, from first to last, in order to see the truth of this. His whole reign was a lamentable failure, aptly and forcibly set forth in two glowing sentences of the prophet Hosea. "I gave thee a king in Mine anger, and took him away in My wrath." In a word, he was the answer to the unbelief and self-will of the people, and therefore all their brilliant hopes and expectations respecting him were most lamentably disappointed. He failed to answer the mind of God, and, as a necessary consequence, he failed to meet the people's need. He proved himself wholly unworthy of the crown and sceptre, and his ignominious fall on Mount Gilboa was in melancholy keeping with his whole career.

Now, when we come to consider the mission of the spies, we find it too, like the appointment of a king, ending in complete failure and disappointment. It could not be otherwise, inasmuch as it was the fruit of unbelief. True, God gave them spies, and Moses, with touching grace, says, "The saying pleased me well; and I took twelve men of you, one of a tribe"—it was Grace coming down to the condition of the people and consenting to a plan which was suited to that condition; but this by no means proves that either the plan or the condition was according to the mind of God. Blessed be His name, He can meet us in our unbelief though He is grieved and dishonored by it. He delights in a bold, artless faith; it is the only thing in all this world that gives Him His proper place. Hence, when Moses said to the people, "Behold, the Lord thy God hath set the land before thee: go up and possess it, as the Lord God of thy fathers hath said unto thee; fear not, neither be discouraged," what would have been the proper response from them? Here we are: lead on, almighty Lord—lead on to victory. Thou art enough. With Thee as our leader, we move on with joyful confidence. Difficulties are nothing to Thee, and therefore they are nothing to us. Thy word and Thy presence are all we want. In these we find at once our authority and power. It matters not in the least to us who or what may be before us: mighty giants, towering walls, frowning bulwarks—what are they all in the presence of the Lord God of Israel, but as withered leaves before the whirlwind; Lead on, O Lord.

This would have been the language of Faith; but, alas! it was not the language of Israel on the occasion before us. God was not sufficient for them. They were not prepared to go up, leaning on His arm alone: they were not satisfied with His report of the land; they would send spies. Any thing for the poor human heart but simple dependence upon the one living and true God. The natural man cannot trust God, simply because he does not know Him. "They that know Thy name will put their trust in Thee."

God must be known, in order to be trusted; and the more fully He is trusted, the better He becomes known. There is nothing in all this world so truly blessed as a life of simple faith; but it must be a reality and not a mere profession. It is utterly vain to talk of living by faith, while the heart is secretly resting on some creature-prop. The true believer has to do exclusively with God. He finds in Him all his resources. It is not that he undervalues the instruments or the channels which God is pleased to use; quite the reverse. He values them exceedingly; and cannot but value them, as the means which God uses for his help and blessing; but he does not allow them to displace God. The language of his heart is, "My soul, wait thou only upon God; for my expectation is from Him. He *only* is my rock."

There is peculiar force in the word "only." It searches the heart thoroughly. To look to the creature, directly or indirectly, for the supply of any need, is, in principle, to depart from the life of faith; and, oh! it is miserable work, this looking, in any way, to creature-streams. It is just as morally degrading as the life of faith is morally elevating. And not only is it degrading, but disappointing. Creature-props give way, and creature-streams run dry; but they that trust in the Lord shall never be confounded, and never want any good thing. Had Israel trusted the Lord instead of sending spies, they would have had a very different tale to tell; but spies they would send, and the whole affair proved a most humiliating failure.

"And they turned, and went up into the mountain, and came unto the valley of Eschol, and searched it out. And they took of the fruit of the land in their hands, and brought it down unto us, and brought us word again, and said, 'It is a good land which the Lord our God doth give us.' " How could it possibly be otherwise when God was giving it? Did they want spies to tell them that the gift of God was good? Assuredly, they ought not. An artless faith would have argued thus: Whatever God gives must be worthy of Himself; we want no spies to assure us of this. But, ah! this artless faith is an uncommonly rare gem in this world; and even those who possess it know but little of its value or how to use it. It is one thing to talk of the life of faith, and another thing altogether to live it—the theory is one thing, the living reality quite another. But let us never forget that it is the privilege of every child of God to live by faith, and, further, that the life of faith takes in every thing that the believer can possibly need, from the starting-post to the goal of his earthly career. We have already touched upon this important point; it cannot be too earnestly or constantly insisted upon.

With regard to the mission of the spies, the reader will note with interest the way in which Moses refers to it. He confines himself to that portion of their testimony which was according to truth; he says nothing about the ten infidel spies. This is in perfect keeping with the scope and object of the book. Every thing is brought to bear, in a moral way, on the conscience of the congregation. He reminds them that they themselves had proposed to send the spies; and yet, although the spies had placed before them the fruit of the land, and borne testimony to its goodness, they would not go up. "Notwithstanding ye would not go up, but rebelled against the commandment of the Lord your God." There was no excuse whatever. It was evident that their hearts were in a state of positive unbelief and rebellion, and the mission of the spies, from first to last, only made this fully manifest.

"And ye murmured in your tents, and said, 'Because the Lord hated us'—a terrible lie on the very face of it!—'He hath brought us forth out of the land of Egypt, to deliver us into the hand of the Amorites, to destroy us.' " What a strange proof of hatred! How utterly absurd are the arguments of unbelief! Surely, had He hated them, nothing was easier than to leave them to die amid the brick-kilns of Egypt, beneath the cruel lash of Pharaoh's taskmasters. Why take so much trouble about them? Why those ten plagues sent upon the land of their oppressors? Why, if He hated them, did He not allow the waters of the Red Sea to overwhelm them as they had overwhelmed their enemies? Why had He delivered them from the sword of Amalek? In a word, why all these marvelous triumphs of grace on their behalf if He hated them? Ah! if they had not been governed by a spirit of dark and senseless unbelief, such a brilliant array of evidence would have led them to a conclusion the direct opposite of that to which they gave utterance. There is nothing beneath the canopy of heaven so stupidly irrational as unbelief; and, on the other hand, there is nothing so sound, clear, and logical as the simple argument of a childlike faith. May the reader ever be enabled to prove the truth of this.

"And ye murmured in your tents." Unbelief is not only a blind and senseless reasoner, but a dark and gloomy murmurer. It neither gets to the right side of things nor the bright side of things. It is always in the dark—always in the wrong, simply because it shuts out God, and looks only at circumstances. They said, "Whither shall we go up? our brethren have discouraged our hearts, saying, 'The people is greater and taller than we'—but they were not greater than Jehovah—'and the cities are great and *walled up to heaven*'—the gross exaggeration of unbelief—'and moreover we have seen the sons of the Anakims there.' "

Now, Faith would say, Well, what though the cities be walled up to heaven, our God is above them, for He is *in* heaven. What are great cities or lofty walls to Him who formed the universe, and sustains it by the Word of His power? What are Anakims in the presence of the almighty God? If the land were covered with walled cities from Dan to Beersheba, and if the giants were as numerous as the leaves of the forest, they would be as the chaff of the threshing-floor before the One who has promised to give the land of Canaan to the seed of Abraham, His friend, for an everlasting possession.

But Israel had not faith, as the inspired apostle tells us in the third chapter of Hebrews, "They could not enter in because of unbelief." Here lay the great difficulty. The walled cities and the terrible Anakims would soon have been disposed of had Israel only trusted God. He would have made very short work of all these; but, ah! that deplorable unbelief! it ever stands in the way of our blessing. It hinders the outshining of the glory of God; it casts a dark shadow over our souls, and robs us of the privilege of proving the all-sufficiency of our God to meet our every need and remove our every difficulty.

Blessed be His name, He never fails a trusting heart. It is His delight to honor the very largest drafts that Faith hands in at His exhaustless treasury. His assuring word to us ever is, "Be not afraid; only believe." And again, "According to your faith be it unto you." Precious soul-stirring words! may we all realize more fully their living power and sweetness. We may rest assured of this, we can never go too far in counting on God; it would be a simple impossibility. Our grand mistake is that we do not draw more largely upon His infinite resources. "Said I not unto thee that if thou wouldest believe, thou shouldest see the glory of God?"

Thus we can see why it was that Israel failed to see the glory of God on the occasion before us—they did not believe. The mission of the spies proved a complete failure. As it began, so it ended—in the most deplorable unbelief. God was shut out: difficulties filled their vision.

"They could not enter in." They could not see the glory of God. Hearken to the deeply affecting words of Moses. It does the heart good to read them. They touch the very deepest springs of our renewed being. "Then I said unto you, 'Dread not, neither be afraid of them. The Lord your God which goeth before you, He shall fight for you'—only think of God fighting for people! think of Jehovah as a Man of war!—'He shall fight for you, according to all that He did for you in Egypt before your eyes; and in the wilderness, where thou hast seen how that *the Lord thy God bare thee, as a man doth bear his son,* in all the way that ye went, until ye came into this place.' Yet in this thing *ye did not believe the Lord your God,* who went in the way before you, to search you out a place to pitch your tents in, in fire by night, to show you by what way ye should go, and in a cloud by day."

What moral force, what touching sweetness in this appeal! How clearly we can see here, as indeed on every page of the book, that Deuteronomy is not a barren repetition of facts, but a most powerful commentary on those facts. It is well that the reader should be thoroughly clear as to this. If in the book of Exodus or Numbers the inspired lawgiver records the actual facts of Israel's wilderness-life, in the book of Deuteronomy he comments on those facts with a pathos that quite melts the heart. And here it is that the exquisite style of Jehovah's acts is pointed out and dwelt upon with such inimitable skill and delicacy. Who could consent to give up the lovely figure set forth in the words, "*As* a man doth bear his son"? Here we have the style of the action. Could we do without this? Assuredly not. It is the style of an action that touches the heart, because it is the style that so peculiarly expresses the heart. If the power of the *hand* or the wisdom or the *mind* is seen in the *substance* of an action, the love of the *heart* comes out in the *style.* Even a little child can understand this, though he might not be able to explain it.

But, alas! Israel could not trust God to bring them into the land. Notwithstanding the marvelous display of His power, His faithfulness, His goodness, and loving-kindness, from the brick-kilns of Egypt to the very borders of the land of Canaan, yet they did not believe. With an array of evidence which ought to have satisfied any heart, they still doubted. "And the Lord heard the voice of your words, and was wroth, and sware, saying, 'Surely there shall not one of these men of this evil generation see that good land, which I sware to give unto your fathers, save Caleb the son of Jephunneh; he shall see it; and to him will I give the land that he hath trodden upon, and to his children, because he hath wholly followed the Lord.' "

"Said I not unto thee that if thou wouldest believe, thou shouldest see the glory of God?" Such is the divine order. Men will tell you that seeing is believing, but in the kingdom of God, believing is seeing. Why was it that not a man of that evil generation was allowed to see the good land? Simply because they did not believe in the Lord their God. On the other hand, why was Caleb allowed to see and take possession? Simply because he believed. Unbelief is ever the great hindrance in the way of our seeing the glory of God. "He did not many mighty works there because of their unbelief." If Israel had only believed, only trusted the Lord their God, only confided in the love of His heart and in the power of His arm, He would have brought them in and planted them in the mountain of His inheritance.

And just so is it with the Lord's people now. There is no limit to the blessings which we might enjoy, could we only count more fully upon God. "All things are possible to him that believeth." Our God will never say, You have drawn too largely; you expect too much. Impossible. It is the joy of His loving heart to answer the very largest expectations of Faith.

Let us, then, draw largely. "Open thy mouth wide, and I will fill it." The exhaustless treasury of heaven is thrown open to Faith. "*All things* whatsoever ye shall ask in prayer, believing, ye shall receive." "If any of you lack wisdom, let him ask of God, who giveth to all men liberally, and upbraideth not; and it shall be given him. But let him ask in faith, *nothing wavering.*"

Faith is the divine secret of the whole matter—the mainspring of Christian life from first to last. Faith wavers not, staggers not: Unbelief is ever a waverer and a staggerer, and hence it never sees the glory of God, never sees His power. It is deaf to His voice and blind to His actions; it depresses the heart and weakens the hands; it darkens the path and hinders all progress. It kept Israel out of the land of Canaan for forty years; and we have no conception of the amount of blessing, privilege, power, and usefulness which we are constantly missing through its terrible influence. If faith were in more lively exercise in our hearts, what a different condition of things we should witness in our midst. What is the secret of the deplorable deadness and barrenness throughout the wide field of Christian profession? How are we to account for our impoverished condition, our low tone, our stunted growth? Why is it that we see such poor results in every department of Christian work? Why are there so few genuine conversions? Why are our evangelists so frequently cast down by reason of the paucity of their sheaves? How are we to answer all these questions? what is the cause? Will any one attempt to say it is not our unbelief?

No doubt, our divisions have much to do with it; our worldliness, our carnality, our self-indulgence, our love of ease. But what is the remedy for all these evils? How are our hearts to be drawn out in genuine love to all our brethren? By faith, that precious principle "that worketh by love." Thus the blessed apostle says to the dear young converts at Thessalonica, "Your faith groweth exceedingly." And what then? "The love of every one of you all toward each other aboundeth." Thus it must ever be. Faith puts us into direct contact with the eternal spring of love in God Himself, and the necessary consequence is that our hearts are drawn out in love to all who belong to Him—all in whom we can, in the very feeblest way, trace His blessed image. We cannot possibly be near the Lord and not love all who in every place call upon His name out of a pure heart. The nearer we are to Christ, the more intensely we must be knit, in true brotherly love, to every member of His body.

Then as to worldliness, in all its varied forms, how is it to be overcome? Hear the reply of another inspired apostle. "For whatsoever is born of God overcometh the world; and this is the victory that overcometh the world, even our faith. Who is he that overcometh the world, but he that believeth that Jesus is the Son of God?" The new man, walking in the power of faith, lives above the world, above its motives, above its objects, its principles, its habits, its fashions; he has nothing in common with it. Though in it, he is not of it; he moves right athwart its current; he draws all his springs from heaven; his life, his hope, his all is there, and he ardently longs to be there himself when his work on earth is done.

Thus we see what a mighty principle faith is. It purifies the heart, it works by love, and it overcomes the world. In short, it links the heart in living power with God Himself, and this is the secret of true elevation, holy benevolence, and divine purity. No marvel, therefore, that Peter calls it "precious faith," for truly it is precious beyond all human thought.

See how this mighty principle acted in Caleb, and the blessed fruit it produced. He was permitted to realize the truth of those words, uttered hundreds of years afterwards, "According to your faith be it unto you." He believed that God was able to bring them into the land, and that all the difficulties and hindrances were simply bread for faith. And God, as He ever does, answered his faith. "Then the children of Judah came unto Joshua in Gilgal; and Caleb the son of Jephunneh the Kenezite said unto him, 'Thou knowest the thing that the Lord said unto Moses the man of God concerning me and thee in Kadesh-barnea. Forty years old was I when Moses the servant of the Lord sent me from Kadesh-barnea to espy out the land; and I brought him word again as it was in my heart'—the simple testimony of a bright and lovely faith. 'Nevertheless my brethren that went up with me made the heart of the people melt; but I wholly followed the Lord my God. And Moses sware on that day, saying, Surely the land whereon thy feet have trodden shall be thine inheritance, and thy children's forever, because thou hast wholly followed the Lord my God. And now, behold, the Lord hath kept me alive, *as He said,* these forty and five years, ever since the Lord spake this word unto Moses, while the children of Israel wandered in the wilderness; and now, lo, I am this day fourscore and five years old. As yet I am as strong this day as I was in the day that Moses sent me; as my strength was then, even so is my strength now, for war, both to go out, and to come in. Now therefore give me this mountain, whereof the Lord spake in that day; for thou heardest in that day how the Anakims were there, and that the cities were great and fenced: if so be the Lord will be with me, then I shall be able to drive them out, as the Lord said."

How refreshing are the utterances of an artless faith! How edifying! how truly encouraging! How vividly they contrast with the gloomy, depressing, withering accents of dark, God-dishonoring unbelief! "And Joshua blessed him, and gave unto Caleb the son of Jephunneh Hebron for an inheritance. Hebron therefore became the inheritance of Caleb the son of Jephunneh the Kenezite unto this day, because that he wholly followed the Lord God of Israel" (Joshua 14). Caleb, like his father Abraham, was strong in faith, giving glory to God; and we may say, with all possible confidence, that inasmuch as faith ever honors God, He ever delights to honor faith; and we feel persuaded that if only the Lord's people could more fully confide in God, if they would but draw more largely upon His infinite resources, we should witness a totally different condition of things from what we see around us. "Said I not unto thee that if thou wouldest believe, thou shouldest see the glory of God?" Oh for a more lively faith in God—a bolder grasp of His faithfulness, His goodness, and His power! Then we might look for more glorious results in the gospel-field; more zeal, more energy, more intense devotedness in the Church of God; and more of the fragrant fruits of righteousness in the life of believers individually.

We shall now, for a moment, look at the

closing verses of our chapter, in which we shall find some very weighty instruction. And, first of all, we see the actings of divine government displayed in a most solemn and impressive manner. Moses refers, in a very touching way, to the fact of his exclusion from the promised land. "Also the Lord was angry with me *for your sakes,* saying, 'Thou also shalt not go in thither.' "

Mark the words, "for your sakes." It was very needful to remind the congregation that it was on their account that Moses, that beloved and honored servant of the Lord, was prevented from crossing the Jordan, and setting his foot upon the land of Canaan. True, "he spake unadvisedly with his lips," but "they provoked his spirit" to do so. This ought to have touched them to the quick. They not only failed, through unbelief, to enter in themselves, but they were the cause of his exclusion, much as he longed to see "that goodly mountain and Lebanon" (see Ps. 106:32).

But the government of God is a grand and awful reality. Let us never for one moment forget this. The human mind may marvel why a few ill-advised words, a few hasty sentences, should be the cause of keeping such a beloved and honored servant of God from that which he so ardently desired; but it is our place to bow the head in humble adoration and holy reverence, not to reason or judge. "Shall not the Judge of all the earth do right?" Most surely. He can make no mistake. "Great and marvelous are Thy works, Lord God Almighty; just and true are Thy ways, Thou King of nations." "God is greatly to be feared in the assembly of the saints; and to be had in reverence of all them that are about Him." "Our God is a consuming fire;" and "it is a fearful thing to fall into the hands of the living God."

Does it in any wise interfere with the action and range of the divine government that we, as Christians, are under the reign of grace? By no means. It is as true to-day as ever it was that "whatsoever *a man* soweth, that shall he also reap." Hence, therefore, it would be a serious mistake for any one to draw a plea from the freedom of divine grace to trifle with the enactments of divine government. The two things are perfectly distinct, and should never be confounded. Grace can pardon—freely, fully, eternally; but the wheels of Jehovah's governmental chariot roll on, in crushing power and appalling solemnity. Grace pardoned Adam's sin; but Government drove him out of Eden, to earn a living by the sweat of his brow, amid the thorns and thistles of a cursed earth: Grace pardoned David's sin, but the sword of Government hung over his house to the end; Bathsheba was the mother of Solomon, but Absalom rose in rebellion.

So with Moses; Grace brought him to the top of Pisgah and showed him the land, but Government sternly and absolutely forbad his entrance thither. Nor does it in the least touch this weighty principle to be told that Moses, in his official capacity as the representative of the legal system, could not bring the people into the land. This is quite true; but it leaves wholly untouched the solemn truth now before us. Neither in the twentieth chapter of Numbers nor in the first chapter of Deuteronomy have we any thing about Moses in his official capacity. It is himself personally we have before us, and he is forbidden to enter the land because of having spoken unadvisedly with his lips.

It will be well for us all to ponder deeply, as in the immediate presence of God, this great practical truth. We may rest assured that the more truly we enter into the knowledge of grace, the more we shall feel the solemnity of government, and entirely justify its enactments. Of this we are most fully persuaded. But there is imminent danger of taking up, in a light and careless manner, the doctrines of grace while the heart and the life are not brought under the sanctifying influence of those doctrines. This has to be watched against with holy jealousy. There is nothing in all this world more awful than mere fleshly familiarity with the theory of salvation by grace. It opens the door for every form of licentiousness. Hence it is that we feel the necessity of pressing upon the conscience of the reader the practical truth of the government of God. It is most salutary at all times, but particularly so in this our day, when there is such a fearful tendency to turn the grace of our God into lasciviousness. We shall invariably find that those who most fully enter into the deep blessedness of being under the reign of grace, do also most thoroughly justify the actings of divine government.

But we learn, from the closing lines of our chapter, that the people were by no means prepared to submit themselves under the governmental hand of God; in short, they would neither have grace nor government. When invited to go up at once and take possession of the land, with the fullest assurances of the divine presence and power with them, they hesitated and refused to go. They gave themselves up completely to a spirit of dark unbelief. In vain did Joshua and Caleb sound in their ears the most encouraging words, in vain did they set before their eyes the rich fruit of the goodly land, in vain did Moses seek to move them by the most soul-stirring words; they would not go up when they were told to go. And what then? They were taken at their word. According to their unbelief, so was it unto them. "Moreover, your little ones, which ye said should be a prey, and your children, which in that day had no knowledge between good and evil, they shall go in thither, and unto them will I give it, and they shall possess it. But as for you, turn you, and take your journey into the wilderness, by the way of the Red Sea."

How sad! and yet how else could it be? If they would not, in simple faith, go up into the land, there remained nothing for them but turning back into the wilderness. But to this they would not submit. They would neither avail themselves of the provisions of grace nor bow to the sentence of judgment. "Then ye answered and said unto me, 'We have sinned against the Lord; we will go up and fight, according to all that the Lord our God commanded us.' And when ye had girded on every man his weapon of war, ye were ready to go up into the hill."

This looked like contrition and self-judgment; but it was hollow and false. It is a very easy thing to *say,* "We have sinned." Saul said it in his day; but he said it without heart, without any genuine sense of what he was saying. We may easily gather the force and value of the words "I have sinned" from the fact that they were immediately followed by *"Honor me* now, I pray thee, before the elders of my people." What a strange contradiction!— "I have sinned," yet "Honor me." If he had really felt his sin, how different his language would have been! how different his spirit, style, and deportment! but it was all a solemn mockery. Only conceive a man full of himself, making use of a form of words, without one atom of true heart feeling; and then, in order to get honor for himself, going through the empty formality of worshiping God. What a picture! Can any thing be more sorrowful? How terribly offensive to Him who desires truth in the inward parts, and who seeks those to worship Him who worship Him in spirit and in truth! The feeblest breathings of a broken and contrite heart are precious to God; but, oh, how offensive to Him are the hollow formalities of a mere religiousness, the object of which is to exalt man in his own eyes and in the eyes of his fellows! How perfectly worthless is the mere lip-confession of sin where the heart does not feel it! As a recent writer has well remarked, "it is an easy thing to say, 'We have sinned,' but how often we have to learn that it is not the quick, abrupt confession of sin which affords evidence that sin is felt! It is rather a proof of hardness of heart. The conscience feels that a certain act of confessing the sin is necessary, but perhaps there is hardly any thing which more hardens the heart than the habit of confessing sin without feeling it. This, I believe, is one of the great snares of christendom from of old and now, that is, the stereotyped acknowledgment of sin—the mere habit of hurrying through a formula of confession to God. I dare say we have almost all done so, without referring to any particular mode; for, alas! there is formality enough; and without having written forms, the heart may frame forms of its own, as we may have observed in our own experience, without finding fault with other people."*

---

**Lectures Introductory to the Pentateuch,* by W. Kelly.

Thus it was with Israel at Kadesh. Their confession of sin was utterly worthless; there was no truth in it. Had they felt what they were saying, they would have bowed to the judgment of God, and meekly accepted the consequence of their sin. There is no finer proof of true contrition than quiet submission to the governmental dealings of God. Look at the case of Moses. See how he bowed his head to the divine discipline. "The Lord," he says, "was angry with me for your sakes, saying, 'Thou also shalt not go in thither. But Joshua the son of Nun, which standeth before thee, he shall go in thither: encourage him; for he shall cause Israel to inherit it.' "

Here, Moses shows them that they were the cause of his exclusion from the land; and yet he utters not a single murmuring word, but meekly bows to the divine judgment, not only content to be superseded by another, but ready to appoint and encourage his successor. There is no trace of jealousy or envy here. It was enough for that beloved and honored servant if God was glorified and the need of the congregation met. He was not occupied with himself or his own interests, but with the glory of God and the blessing of His people.

But the people manifested a very different spirit. "We will go up and fight." How vain! How foolish! When commanded by God and encouraged by His true-hearted servants to go up and possess the land, they replied, "Whither shall we go up?" and when commanded to turn back into the wilderness, they replied, "We will go up and fight."

"And the Lord said unto me, 'Say unto them, Go not up, neither fight; for I am not among you; lest ye be smitten before your enemies.' So I spake unto you; and ye would not hear, but rebelled against the commandment of the Lord, and went presumptuously up into the hill. And the Amorites, which dwelt in that mountain, came out against you, and chased you, as bees do, and destroyed you in Seir, even unto Hormah."

It was quite impossible for Jehovah to accompany them along the path of self-will and rebellion; and, most assuredly, Israel, without the divine presence, could be no match for the Amorites. If God be for us and with us, all must be victory; but we cannot count on God if we are not treading the path of obedience. It is simply the height of folly to imagine that we can have God with us if our ways are not right. "The name of the Lord is a strong tower, the righteous runneth into it and is safe." But if we are not walking in practical righteousness, it is wicked presumption to talk of having the Lord as our strong tower.

Blessed be His name, He can meet us in the very depths of our weakness and failure, provided there be the genuine and hearty confession of our true condition; but to assume that we have the Lord with us while we are doing our own will and walking in palpable unrighteousness, is nothing but wickedness and hardness of heart. "Trust in the Lord, and do good"—this is the divine order; but to talk of trusting in the Lord while doing evil, is to turn the grace of our God into lasciviousness, and place ourselves completely in the hands of the devil, who only seeks our moral ruin. "The eyes of the Lord run to and fro throughout the whole earth, to show Himself strong in the behalf of them whose heart is perfect toward Him." When we have a good conscience, we can lift up the head and move on through all sorts of difficulties; but to attempt to tread the path of faith with a bad conscience, is the most dangerous thing in this world. We can only hold up the shield of faith when our loins are girt with truth, and the breast covered with the breastplate of righteousness.

It is of the utmost importance that Christians should seek to maintain practical righteousness, in all its branches. There is immense moral weight and value in these words of the blessed apostle Paul, "Herein do I exercise myself, to have always a conscience void of offense toward God and men." He ever sought to wear the breastplate, and to be clothed in that white linen which is the righteousness of saints. And so should we. It is our holy privilege to tread, day by day, with firm step, the path of duty, the path of obedience, the path on which the light of God's approving countenance ever shines;

then, assuredly, we can count on God, lean upon Him, draw from Him, find all our springs in Him, wrap ourselves up in His faithfulness, and thus move on, in peaceful communion and holy worship, toward our heavenly home.

It is not, we repeat, that we cannot look to God in our weakness, our failure, and even when we have erred and sinned. Blessed be His name, we can; and His ear is ever open to our cry. "If we confess our sins, He is faithful and just to forgive us our sins, and to cleanse us from all unrighteousness" (1 John 1). "Out of the depths have I cried unto Thee, O Lord. Lord, hear my voice: let Thine ears be attentive to the voice of my supplications. If Thou, Lord, shouldest mark iniquities, O Lord, who shall stand? But there is forgiveness with Thee, that Thou mayest be feared" (Ps. 130). There is absolutely no limit to divine forgiveness, inasmuch as there is no limit to the extent of the atonement, no limit to the virtue and efficacy of the blood of Jesus Christ, God's Son, which cleanseth from all sin; no limit to the prevalency of the intercession of our adorable Advocate, our great High-Priest, who is able to save to the uttermost—right through and through to the end—them that come unto God by Him.

All this is most blessedly true; it is largely taught and variously illustrated throughout the volume of inspiration; but the confession of sin, and the pardon thereof, must not be confounded with practical righteousness. There are two distinct conditions in which we may call upon God: we may call upon Him in deep contrition and be heard, or we may call upon Him with a good conscience and an uncondemning heart and be heard. But the two things are very distinct; and not only are they distinct in themselves, but they both stand in marked contrast with that indifference and hardness of heart which would presume to count on God in the face of positive disobedience and practical unrighteousness. It is this which is so dreadful in the sight of the Lord, and which must bring down His heavy judgment. Practical righteousness He owns and approves; confessed sin He can freely and fully pardon; but to imagine that we can put our trust in God while our feet are treading the path of iniquity, is nothing short of the most shocking impiety. "Trust ye not in lying words, saying, The temple of the Lord, The temple of the Lord, The temple of the Lord, are these. For if ye throughly amend your ways and your doings; if ye throughly execute judgment between a man and his neighbor; if ye oppress not the stranger, the fatherless, and the widow, and shed not innocent blood in this place, neither walk after other gods to your hurt: then will I cause you to dwell in this place, in the land that I gave to your fathers, forever and ever. Behold, ye trust in lying words, that cannot profit. Will ye steal, murder, and commit adultery, and swear falsely, and burn incense unto Baal, and walk after other gods whom ye know not; and come and stand before Me in this house, which is called by My name, and say, 'We are delivered to do all these abominations?' " (Jeremiah 7)

God deals in moral realities. He desires truth in the inward parts; and if men will presume to hold the truth in unrighteousness, they must look out for His righteous judgment. It is the thought of all this that makes us feel the awful condition of the professing church. The solemn passage which we have just culled from the prophet Jeremiah, though bearing primarily upon the men of Judah and the inhabitants of Jerusalem, has a very pointed application to christendom. We find, in the third chapter of 2 Timothy, that all the abominations of heathenism, as detailed in the close of Romans 1, are reproduced in the last days under the garb of the Christian profession, and in immediate connection with "a form of godliness." What must be the end of such a condition of things? Unmitigated wrath. The very heaviest judgments of God are reserved for that vast mass of baptized profession which we call christendom. The moment is rapidly approaching when all the beloved and blood-bought people of God shall be called away out of this dark and sinful, though so-called "Christian world," to be forever with the Lord, in that sweet home of love prepared in the Father's house. Then the "strong delusion" shall be sent upon christendom—upon those very countries where the light of a full-orbed Christianity has shone, where a full and free gospel has been preached, where the Bible has been circulated by millions, and where all, in some way or another, profess the name of Christ and call themselves Christians.

And what then?—what is to follow this "strong delusion"? Any fresh testimony? any further overtures of mercy? any further effort of long-suffering grace? Not for christendom! not for the rejecters of the gospel of God! not for Christless, Godless professors of the hollow and worthless forms of Christianity! The heathen shall hear "the everlasting gospel"—"the gospel of the kingdom;" but as for that terrible thing, that most frightful anomaly called christendom—"the vine of the earth," nothing remains but the wine-press of the wrath of Almighty God, the blackness and darkness forever, the lake that burneth with fire and brimstone.

These are the true sayings of God. Nothing would be easier than to place before your eyes an array of Scripture proof perfectly unanswerable: this would be foreign to our present object. The New Testament, from cover to cover, sets forth the solemn truth above enunciated; and every system of theology under the sun that teaches differently will be found, on this point at least, to be totally false.

---

## *CHAPTER 2*

THE closing lines of chapter 1 show us the people weeping before the Lord. "And ye returned and wept before the Lord; but the Lord would not hearken to your voice, nor give ear unto you. So ye abode in Kadesh many days, according unto the days that ye abode there."

There was no more reality in their tears than in their words—their weeping was no more to be trusted than their confession. It is possible for people to confess and shed tears without any true sense of sin in the presence of God. This is very solemn. It is really mocking God. We know, blessed forever be His name, that a truly contrite heart is His delight. He makes His abode with such. "The sacrifices of God are a broken spirit: a broken and a contrite heart, O God, Thou wilt not despise." The tears that flow from a penitent heart are more precious, by far, to God than the cattle upon a thousand hills, because they prove that there is room in that heart for Him; and this is what He seeks, in His infinite grace. He wants to dwell in our hearts, and fill us with the deep, unspeakable joy of His own most blessed presence.

But Israel's confession and tears at Kadesh were not real, and hence the Lord could not accept them. The feeblest cry of a broken heart ascends directly to the throne of God, and is immediately answered by the soothing, healing balm of His pardoning love; but when tears and confession stand connected with self-will and rebellion, they are not only utterly worthless, but a positive insult to the divine Majesty.

Thus, then, the people had to turn back into the wilderness, and wander there for forty years. There was nothing else for it. They would not go up into the land, in simple faith, with God, and He would not go up with them in their self-will and self-confidence; they had, therefore, simply to accept the consequence of their disobedience. If they would not enter the land, they must fall in the wilderness.

How solemn is all this! and how solemn is the Spirit's commentary upon it in the third chapter of Hebrews! and how pointed and forcible the application to us! "Wherefore, as the Holy Ghost saith, 'To-day if ye will hear His voice, harden not your hearts, as in the provocation, in the day of temptation in the wilderness; when your fathers tempted Me, proved Me, and saw My works forty years. Wherefore I was grieved with that generation, and said, They do alway err *in heart;* and they have not known My ways. So I sware in My wrath, They shall not enter into My rest.' Take heed, brethren, lest there be in any of you an evil heart of unbelief, in departing from the living God. But exhort one another daily, while it is called 'Today'; lest any of you be hardened through the deceitfulness of sin. For we are made partakers of Christ, if we hold the beginning of our confidence steadfast unto the end; while it is said, 'To-day if ye will hear His voice; harden not your hearts, as in the provocation. For some, when they had heard, did provoke; howbeit not all that came out of Egypt by Moses. But with whom was He grieved forty years? was it not with them that had sinned, whose carcases fell in the wilderness? And to whom sware He that they should not enter into His rest, but to them that believed not? So we see that they could not enter in because of unbelief. Let us therefore fear, lest, a promise being left us of entering into His rest, any of you should seem to come short of it. For unto us was the gospel preached, as well as unto them; but the word preached did not profit them, not being mixed with faith in them that heard."

Here, as in every page of the inspired volume, we learn that unbelief is *the* thing that grieves the heart and dishonors the name of God; and not only so, but it robs us of the blessings, the dignities, and the privileges which infinite grace bestows. We have very little idea of how much we lose, in every way, through the unbelief of our hearts. Just as in Israel's case the land was before them, in all its fruitfulness and beauty, and they were commanded to go and take possession, but "they could not enter in because of unbelief;" so with us—we fail to possess ourselves of the fullness of blessing which sovereign grace has put within our reach. The very treasury of heaven is thrown open to us, but we fail to appropriate. We are poor, feeble, empty, and barren when we might be rich, vigorous, full, and fruitful. We are blessed with all spiritual blessings in the heavenlies in Christ, but how shallow is our apprehension! how feeble our grasp! how poor our thoughts!

Then, again, who can calculate how much we lose, through our unbelief, in the matter of the Lord's work in our midst? We read in the gospel of a certain place in which our blessed Lord could not do many mighty works, because of their unbelief. Has this no voice for us? Do we too hinder Him by unbelief? We shall perhaps be told by some that the Lord will carry on His work irrespective of us or our faith; He will gather out His own and accomplish the number of His elect spite of our unbelief. Not all the power of earth and hell—men and devils combined—can hinder the carrying out of His counsels and purposes; and as to His work, It is not by might nor by power, but by His Spirit. Human efforts are in vain; and the Lord's cause can never be furthered by Nature's excitement.

Now, all this is perfectly true; but it leaves wholly untouched the inspired statement quoted above. "He could there do not many mighty works, because of their unbelief." Did not those people lose blessing through their unbelief? did they not hinder much good being done? We must beware how we surrender our minds to the withering influence of a pernicious fatalism, which, with a certain semblance of truth, is utterly false, inasmuch as it denies all human responsibility and paralyzes all godly energy in the cause of Christ. We have to bear in mind that the same One who, in His eternal counsels, has decreed the end, has also designed the means; and if we, in the sinful unbelief of our hearts and under the influence of one-sided truth, fold our arms and neglect the means, He will set us aside and carry on His work by other hands. He will work, blessed be His holy name, but we shall lose the dignity, the privilege, and the blessing of being His instruments.

Look at that striking scene in the second of Mark. It most forcibly illustrates the great principle which we desire to press upon all who may read these lines. It proves the power of faith, in connection with the carrying on of the Lord's work. If the four men whose conduct is here set forth had suffered themselves to be influenced by a mischievous fatalism, they would have argued that it was no use doing any thing—if the palsied man was to be cured he would be cured, without human effort. Why should they busy themselves in climbing up on the house, uncovering the roof, and letting down the sick man into the midst before Jesus?

Ah, it was well for the palsied man and well for themselves that they did not act on such miserable reasoning as this. See how their lovely faith wrought. It refreshed the heart of the Lord Jesus; it brought the sick man into the place of healing, pardon, and blessing; and it gave occasion for the display of divine power, which arrested the attention of all present and gave testimony to the great truth that God was on earth, in the Person of Jesus of Nazareth, healing diseases and forgiving sins.

Many other examples might be adduced, but there is no need. All Scripture establishes the fact that unbelief hinders our blessing, hinders our usefulness, robs us of the rare privilege of being God's honored instruments in the carrying on of His glorious work, and of seeing the operations of His hand and His Spirit in our midst; and, on the other hand, that faith draws down power and blessing, not only for ourselves, but for others—that it both glorifies and gratifies God, by clearing the platform of the creature and making room for the display of divine power. In short, there is no limit to the blessing which we might enjoy at the hand of our God if our hearts were more governed by that simple faith which ever counts on Him, and which He ever delights to honor. "According to your faith, be it unto you." Precious soul-stirring words! May they encourage us to draw more largely upon those exhaustless resources which we have in God. He delights to be used, blessed forever be His holy name. His word to us is, "Open thy mouth *wide,* and I will fill it." We can never expect too much from the God of all grace, who has given us His only begotten Son, and will with Him freely give us all things.

But Israel could not trust God to bring them into the land; they presumed to go in their own strength, and, as a consequence, were put to flight before their enemies. Thus it must ever be. Presumption and faith are two totally different things: the former can only issue in defeat and disaster; the latter, in sure and certain victory.

"Then we turned and took our journey into the wilderness, by the way of the Red Sea, as the Lord spake unto me; and we compassed Mount Seir many days." There is great moral beauty in the little word *"we."* Moses links himself thoroughly with the people. He and Joshua and Caleb had all to turn back into the wilderness, in company with the unbelieving congregation. This might, in the judgment of nature, seem hard; but we may rest assured it was good and profitable. There is always deep blessing in bowing to the will of God, even though we may not always be able to see the why and the wherefore of things. We do not read of a single murmuring word from these honored servants of God at having to turn back into the wilderness for forty years, although they were quite ready to go up into the land. No; they simply turned back. And well they might, when Jehovah turned back also. How could they think of complaining, when they beheld the traveling-chariot of the God of Israel facing round to the wilderness? Surely the patient grace and long-suffering mercy of God might well teach them to accept, with a willing mind, a protracted sojourn in the wilderness, and to wait for the blessed moment of entrance upon the promised land.

It is a great thing always to submit ourselves meekly under the hand of God. We are sure to reap a rich harvest of blessing from the exercise. It is really taking the yoke of Christ upon us, which, as He Himself assures us, is the true secret of rest. "Come unto Me, all ye that labor and are heavy laden, and I will give you rest. Take My yoke upon you, and learn of Me; for I am meek and lowly in heart; and ye shall find rest unto your souls. For My yoke is easy, and My burden is light."

What was this yoke? It was absolute and complete subjection to the Father's will. This we see in perfection in our adorable Lord and Saviour Jesus Christ. He could say, "Even so, Father; for so it seemed good in Thy sight." Here was the point with Him—"good in Thy sight." This settled every thing. Was His testimony rejected? did He seem to labor in vain, and spend His strength for naught and in vain? What then? "I thank Thee, O Father, Lord of heaven and earth." It was all right. Whatever pleased the Father, pleased Him. He never had a thought or wish that was not in perfect consonance with the will of God. Hence He, as a man, ever enjoyed perfect rest. He rested in the divine counsels and purposes. The current of His peace was unruffled, from first to last.

This was the yoke of Christ; and this is what He, in His infinite grace, invites us to take upon us, in order that we too may find rest unto our souls. Let us mark and seek to understand the words, "ye shall *find* rest." We must not confound the "rest" which *He gives* with the "rest" which we find. When the weary, burdened, heavy-laden soul comes to Jesus in simple faith, He gives rest—settled rest—the rest which flows from the full assurance that all is done—sins forever put away; perfect righteousness accomplished, revealed, and possessed; every question divinely and eternally settled; God glorified; Satan silenced; conscience tranquilized.

Such is the rest which Jesus gives when we come to Him. But then we have to move through the scenes and circumstances of our daily life. There are trials, difficulties, exercises, buffetings, disappointments, and reverses of all sorts. None of these can, in the smallest degree, touch the rest which Jesus gives; but they may very seriously interfere with the rest which we are to find. They do not trouble the conscience, but they may greatly trouble the heart; they may make us very restless, very fretful, very impatient. For instance, I want to preach at Glasgow; I am announced to do so; but lo! I am shut up in a sick-room in London. This does not trouble my conscience, but it may greatly trouble my heart; I may be in a perfect fever of restlessness, ready to exclaim, How tiresome! How terribly disappointing! Whatever am I to do? It is most untoward!

And how is this state of things to be met? How is the troubled heart to be tranquilized, and the restless mind to be calmed down? What do I want? I want to find rest; how am I to find it? By stooping down and taking Christ's precious yoke upon me—the very yoke which He Himself ever wore, in the days of His flesh—the yoke of complete subjection to the will of God. I want to be able to say, without one atom of reserve—to say from the very depths of my heart, "Thy will, O Lord, be done." I want such a profound sense of His perfect love to me, and of His infinite wisdom in all His dealings with me, that I would not have it otherwise if I could—yea, that I would not move a finger to alter my position or circumstances, feeling assured that it is very much better for me to be suffering on a sick-bed in London than speaking on a platform in Glasgow.

Here lies the deep and precious secret of rest of heart, as opposed to restlessness. It is the simple ability to thank God for every thing, be it ever so contrary to our own will and utterly subversive of our own plans. It is not a mere assent to the truth that "all things work together for good to them that love God, to them who are the called according to His purpose"; it is the positive sense—the actual realization of the divine fact that the thing which God appoints is the very best thing for us; it is perfect repose in the love, wisdom, power, and faithfulness of the One who has graciously undertaken for us in every thing, and charged Himself with all that concerns us for time and eternity. We know that love will always do its very best for its object. What must it be to have God doing His very best for us? Where is the heart that would not be satisfied with God's best if only it knows aught of Him?

But He must be known ere the heart can be satisfied with His will. Eve, in the garden of Eden, beguiled by the serpent, became dissatisfied with the will of God. She *wished* for something which He had forbidden, and this something the devil undertook to supply. She thought the devil could do better for her than God. She thought to better her circumstances by taking herself out of the hands of God and placing herself in the hands of Satan. Hence it is that no unrenewed heart can ever, by any possibility, rest in the will of God. If we search the human heart to the bottom, if we submit it to a faithful analysis, we shall not find so much as a single thought in unison with the will of God—no, not one. And even in the case of the true Christian—the child of God, it is only as he is enabled, by the grace of God, to mortify his own will, to reckon himself dead, and to walk in the Spirit, that he can delight in the will of God, and give thanks in every thing. It is one of the very finest evidences of the new birth to be able, without a single shade of reserve, to say, in respect to every dealing of the hand of God, "Thy will be done." "Even so, Father; for so it seemed good in Thy sight." When the heart is in this attitude, Satan can make nothing of it. It is a grand point to be able to tell the devil and to tell the world—tell them, not in word and in tongue, but in deed and in truth; not merely with the lips, but in the heart and the life—*I am perfectly satisfied with the will of God.*

This is the way to find rest. Let us see that we understand it. It is the divine remedy for that unrest, that spirit of discontent, that dissatisfaction with our appointed lot and sphere, so sadly prevalent on all hands. It is a perfect cure for that restless ambition so utterly opposed to the mind and spirit of Christ, but so entirely characteristic of the men of this world.

May we cultivate, with holy diligence, that meek and lowly spirit which is, in the sight of God, of great price, which bows to His blessed will in all things, and vindicates His dealings, come what may. Thus shall our peace flow as a river, and the name of our Lord Jesus Christ shall be magnified in our course, character, and conduct.

Ere turning from the deeply interesting and practical subject which has been engaging our attention, we would observe that there are three distinct attitudes in which the soul may be found in reference to the dealings of God, namely, subjection, acquiescence, and rejoicing. When the will is broken, there is subjection; when the understanding is enlightened as to the divine object, there is acquiescence; and when the affections are engaged with God Himself, there is positive rejoicing. Hence we read, in the tenth chapter of Luke, "In that hour Jesus *rejoiced* in spirit, and said, '*I thank Thee,* O Father, Lord of heaven and earth, that Thou hast hid these things from the wise and prudent, and hast revealed them unto babes: even so, Father; for so it seemed good in Thy sight.' " That blessed One found His perfect delight in all the will of God. It was His meat and drink to carry out that will, at all cost. In service or in suffering, in life or in death, He never had any motive but the Father's will. He could say, "I do always the things that please Him." Eternal and universal homage to His peerless name!

We shall now proceed with our chapter.

"And the Lord spake unto me, saying, 'Ye have compassed this mountain long enough; turn you northward.' "

The word of the Lord determined every thing. It fixed how long the people were to remain in any given place, and it indicated with equal distinctness whither they were next to bend their steps. There was no need whatever for them to plan or arrange their movements: it was the province and prerogative of Jehovah to settle all for them; it was theirs to obey. There is no mention here of the cloud and the trumpet; it is simply God's word and Israel's obedience.

Nothing can be more precious to a child of God, if only the heart be in a right condition, than to be guided, in all his movements, by the divine command. It saves a world of anxiety and perplexity. In Israel's case, called as they were to journey through a great and terrible wilderness, where there was no way, it was an unspeakable mercy to have their every movement, their every step, their every halting-place, ordered by an infallible Guide. There was no need whatever for them to trouble themselves about their movements, no need to inquire how long they were to stay in any given place, or where they were to go next; Jehovah settled all for them. It was for them simply to wait on Him for guidance, and to do what they were told.

Yes, here was the grand point—a waiting and an obedient spirit. If this were lacking, they were liable to all sorts of questionings, reasonings, and rebellious activities. When God said, "Ye have compassed this mountain long enough," had Israel replied, No; we want to compass it a little longer: we are very comfortable here, and we do not wish to make any change; or, again, if when God said, "Turn you northward" they had replied, No; we vastly prefer going eastward; what would have been the result? Why, they would have forfeited the divine presence with them, and who could guide or help or feed them then? They could only count on the divine presence with them while they trod the path indicated by the divine command. If they chose to take their own way, there was nothing for them but famine, desolation, and darkness. The stream from the smitten rock and the heavenly manna, were only to be found in the path of obedience.

Now, we Christians have to learn our lesson in all this—a wholesome, needed, valuable lesson. It is our sweet privilege to have our path marked out for us, day by day, by divine authority. Of this we are to be most deeply and thoroughly persuaded. We are not to allow ourselves to be robbed of this rich blessing by the plausible reasonings of unbelief. God has promised to guide us, and His promise is yea and Amen. It is for us to make our own the promise, in the artless simplicity of faith. It is as solid and as real and as true as God can make it. We cannot admit for a moment that Israel in the desert were better off in the matter of guidance than God's heavenly people in their passage through this world. How did Israel know the length of the haltings or the line of their march? By the word of God. Are we worse off? Far be the thought. Yea, we are better off by far than they. We have the Word and Spirit of God to guide us. To us pertains the high and holy privilege of walking in the footsteps of the Son of God.

Is not this perfect guidance? Yes, thank God, it is. Hear what our adorable Lord Jesus Christ saith to us—"I am the light of the world; he that followeth Me shall not walk in darkness, but shall have the light of life." Let us mark these words, "he that *followeth Me.*" He has left us "an example, that we should follow His steps." This is living guidance. How did Jesus walk? Always and only by the commandment of His Father. By that He acted; by that He moved; without it He never acted, moved, or spoke.

Now, we are called to follow Him; and in so doing, we have the assurance of His own word that we shall not walk in darkness, but shall have the light of life. Precious words!—*"the light of life."* Who can sound their living depths? who can duly estimate their worth? "The darkness is past, and the true light now shineth," and it is for us to walk in the full blaze of the light that shines along the pathway of the Son of God. Is there any uncertainty, any perplexity, any ground for hesitation here? Clearly not. How could there be if we are following Him? It is utterly impossible to combine the two ideas.

And be it remarked here that it is not by any means a question of having a literal text of Scripture for every movement or every act. For example, I cannot expect to get a text of Scripture, or a voice from heaven, to tell me to go to London or to Edinburgh; or how long I am to stay when I go. How, then, it may be asked, am I to know where I ought to go, or how long I am to stay? The answer is, Wait on God, in singleness of eye and sincerity of heart, and He will make your path as plain as a sunbeam. This was what Jesus did; and if we follow Him, we shall not walk in darkness. "I will guide thee with Mine eye" is a most precious promise; but in order to profit by it, we must be near enough to Him to catch the movement of His eye, and intimate enough with Him to understand its meaning.

Thus it is, in all the details of our daily life. It would answer a thousand questions, and solve a thousand difficulties, if we did but wait for divine guidance, and never attempt to move without it. If I have not gotten light to move, it is my plain duty to be still. We should never move in uncertainty. It often happens that we harass ourselves about moving or acting, when God would have us to be still and do nothing. We go and ask God about it, but get no answer; we betake ourselves to friends for advice and counsel, but they cannot help us, for it is entirely a question between our own souls and the Lord. Thus we are plunged in doubt and anxiety. And why? Simply because the eye is not single; we are not following Jesus, "the light of the world." We may set it down as a fixed principle, a precious axiom in the divine life, that if we are following Jesus, we shall have the light of life. He has said it, and that is enough for faith.

Hence, then, we deem ourselves perfectly warranted in concluding that the One who guided His earthly people in all their desert wanderings, can and will guide His heavenly people now in all their movements and in all their ways. But, on the other hand, let us see to it that we are not bent on doing our own will, having our own way, and carrying out our own plans. "Be ye not as the horse or as the mule, which have no understanding, whose mouth must be held in with bit and bridle, lest they come near unto thee." Be it our one grand aim to walk in the footsteps of that blessed One who pleased not Himself, but ever moved in the current of the divine will, never acted without divine authority; who, though Himself God over all, blessed forever, yet, having taken His place as a man, on the earth, surrendered completely His own will, and found His meat and His drink in doing the will of His Father. Thus shall our hearts and minds be kept in perfect peace; and we shall be enabled to move on, from day to day, with firm and decided step, along the path indicated for us by our divine and ever-present Guide, who not only knows, as God, every step of the way, but who, as man, has trodden it before us, and left us an example that we should follow His steps. May we follow Him more faithfully in all things, through the gracious ministry of the Holy Ghost, who dwelleth in us.

We have now to invite the reader's attention to a subject of very deep interest, and one which occupies a large place in Old Testament Scripture, and is forcibly illustrated in the chapter which lies open before us, namely, God's government of the world, and His wonderful ordering of the nations of the earth. It is a grand and all-important fact to keep ever before the mind that the One whom we know as "the God and Father of our Lord Jesus Christ," and our God and Father, takes a real, lively, personal interest in the affairs of nations—that He takes cognizance of their movements and of their dealings one with another.

True, all this is in immediate connection with Israel and the land of Palestine, as we read in the thirty-second chapter of our book, and eighth verse—a passage of singular interest and of great suggestive power. "When the Most High divided to the nations their inheritance, when He separated the sons of Adam, He set the bounds of the people according to the number of the children of Israel." Israel was and shall yet be God's earthly centre; and it is a fact of the deepest interest that, from the very outset, as we see in Genesis 10, the Creator and Governor of the world formed the nations and fixed their bounds according to His own sovereign will, and with direct reference to the seed of Abraham, and that narrow strip of land which they are to possess, in virtue of the everlasting covenant made with their fathers.

But in the second chapter of Deuteronomy, we find Jehovah, in His faithfulness and righteousness, interfering to protect three distinct nations in the enjoyment of their national rights, and that, too, against the encroachments of His own chosen people. He says to Moses, "Command thou the people, saying, 'Ye are to pass through the coast of your brethren the children of Esau, which dwell in Seir; and they shall be afraid of you: take ye good heed unto yourselves therefore: meddle not with them; for I will not give you of their land, no, not so much as a foot-breadth, because I have given Mount Seir unto Esau for a possession. Ye shall buy meat of them for money, that ye may eat; and ye shall also buy water of them for money, that ye may drink.' "

Israel might imagine that they had nothing to do but seize upon the lands of the Edomite; but they had to learn something very different—they had to be taught that the Most High is the Governor amongst the nations—that the whole earth belongs to Him, and He portions it out to one or another according to His good pleasure.

This is a very magnificent fact to keep before the mind. The great majority of men think but little of it. Emperors, kings, princes, governors, statesmen, take little account of it. They forget that God interests Himself in the affairs of nations—that He bestows kingdoms, provinces, and lands as He sees fit. They act, at times, as if it were only a question of military conquest, and as if God had nothing to do with the question of national boundaries and territorial possessions. This is their great mistake. They do not understand the meaning and force of this simple sentence, "*I have given* Mount Seir unto Esau for a possession." God will never surrender His rights in this respect. He would not allow Israel to touch a single atom of Esau's property. They were, to use a modern phrase, to pay ready cash for whatever they needed, and go quietly on their way. Indiscriminate slaughter and plunder were not to be thought of by the people of God.

And mark the lovely reason for all this. "For the Lord thy God hath blessed thee in all the works of thy hand; He knoweth thy walking through this great wilderness; these forty years the Lord thy God hath been with thee, thou hast lacked nothing." They could well afford, therefore, to let Esau alone, and leave his possessions untouched. They were the favored objects of Jehovah's tender care. He took knowledge of every step of their weary journey through the desert. He had, in His infinite goodness, charged Himself with all their necessities. He was going to give them the land of Canaan, according to His promise to Abraham; but the self-same hand which was giving them Canaan had given Mount Seir to Esau.

We see the same thing exactly in reference to Moab and Ammon. "The Lord said unto me, 'Distress not the Moabites, neither contend with them in battle; for I will not give thee of their land for a possession, because I have given Ar unto the children of Lot for a possession.' " And again, "And when thou comest nigh over against the children of Ammon, distress them not, nor meddle with them; for I will not give thee of the land of the children of Ammon any possession, because I have given it unto the children of Lot for a possession."

The possessions here alluded to had been, of old time, in the hands of giants; but it was God's purpose to give up their territories to the children of Esau and Lot, and therefore He destroyed these giants; for who or what can stand in the way of the divine counsels? "That also was accounted a land of giants: giants dwelt therein in old time . . . a people great, and many, and tall, as the Anakims; but the Lord destroyed them before them; and they succeeded them, and dwelt in their stead: as He did to the children of Esau which dwelt in Seir, when He destroyed the Horims from before them; and they succeeded them, and dwelt in their stead even unto this day" (ver. 20-23).

Hence, then, Israel were not permitted to meddle with the possessions of any of these three nations—the Edomites, Ammonites, and Moabites; but in the very next sentence, we see another thing altogether in the case of the Amorites. "Rise ye up, take your journey, and pass over the river Arnon: behold, I have given into thine hand Sihon the Amorite, king of Heshbon, and his land: begin to possess it, and contend with him in battle."

The great principle, in all these varied instructions to Israel, is that God's word must settle every thing for His people. It was not for Israel to inquire why they were to leave the possessions of Esau and Lot untouched, and to seize upon those of Sihon. They were simply to do what they were told. God can do as He pleases. He has His eye upon the whole scene: He scans it all. Men may think He has forsaken the earth, but He has not, blessed be His name. He is, as the apostle tells us in his discourse at Athens, "Lord of heaven and earth"; and "He hath made of one blood all nations of men, for to dwell on all the face of the earth; and hath determined the times before appointed, and the bounds of their habitations." And, further, "He hath appointed a day, in the which He will judge the habitable earth [*οἰκουμένην*] in righteousness, by that Man whom He hath ordained; whereof He hath given assurance [given proof] unto all, in that He hath raised Him from the dead."

Here we have a most solemn and weighty truth, to which men of all ranks and conditions would do well to take heed. God is the Sovereign Ruler of the world. He giveth no account of any of His matters. He puts down one and sets up another. Kingdoms, thrones, governments, are all at His disposal. He acts according to His own will in the ordering and arrangement of human affairs. But, at the same time, He holds men responsible for their actings in the various positions in which His providence has placed them. The ruler and the ruled, the king, the governor, the magistrate, the judge—all classes and grades of men will have, sooner or later, to give account to God. Each one, as if he were the only one, will have to stand before the judgment-seat of Christ, and there review his whole course, from first to last. Every act, every word, every secret thought, will there come out with awful distinctness. There will be no escaping in a crowd. The Word declares that they shall be judged *"every man* according to his works." It will be intensely individual, and unmistakably discriminating. In a word, it will be a divine judgment, and therefore absolutely perfect. Nothing will be passed over. "Every idle word that men shall speak, they shall give account thereof at the day of judgment." Kings, governors, and magistrates will have to account for the way in which they have used the power with which they were intrusted, and the wealth which passed through their hands. The noble and the wealthy who have spent their fortune and their time in folly, vanity, luxury, and self-indulgence will have to answer for it all before the throne of the Son of Man, whose eyes are as a flame of fire, to read men through and through; and His feet as fine brass, to crush, in unsparing judgment, all that is contrary to God.

Infidelity may sneeringly inquire, *How* can these things be? *How* could the untold millions of the human race find room before the judgment-seat of Christ? and *how* could there be time to enter so minutely into the details of each personal history? Faith replies, God says it shall be so, and this is conclusive; and as to the "How?" the answer is God! Infinity! Eternity! Bring God in, and all questions are hushed and all difficulties disposed of in a moment. In fact, the one grand, triumphant answer to all the objections of the infidel, the skeptic, the rationalist, and the materialist, is just that one majestic word, *"God!"*

We press this upon the reader; not, indeed to enable him to reply to infidels, but for the rest and comfort of his own heart. As to infidels, we are increasingly persuaded that our highest wisdom is to act on our Lord's words in Matthew 15, "Let them alone." It is perfectly useless to argue with men who despise the Word of God, and have no other foundation to build upon than their own carnal reasonings. But, on the other hand, we deem it to be of the very last possible importance that the heart should ever repose, in all the artless simplicity of a child, in the truth of God's Word. "Hath He said, and shall He not do it? or hath He spoken, and shall He not make it good?"

Here is the sweet and hallowed resting-place of faith, the calm haven where the soul can find refuge from all the conflicting currents of human thought and feeling. "The Word of the Lord endureth forever; and this is the Word which by the gospel is preached unto you." Nothing can touch the Word of our God. It is settled forever in heaven; and all we want is to have it hidden in our hearts, as our own very possession—the treasure which we have received from God—the living fountain where we may ever drink for the refreshment and comfort of our souls. Then shall our peace flow as a river, and our path shall be as the shining light, which shineth more and more unto the perfect day.

Thus may it be, O Lord, with all Thy beloved people, in these days of growing infidelity. May Thy holy Word be increasingly precious to our hearts. May our consciences feel its power. May its heavenly doctrines form our character and govern our conduct in all the relationships of life, that Thy name may be glorified in all things.

---

## *CHAPTER 3*

"THEN we turned, and went up the way to Bashan; and Og the king of Bashan came out against us, he and all his people, to battle at Edrei. And the Lord said unto me, 'Fear him not: for I will deliver him, and all his people, and his land, into thy hand; and thou shalt do unto him as thou didst unto Sihon king of the Amorites, which dwelt at Heshbon.' So the Lord our God delivered into our hands Og also, the king of Bashan, and all his people; and we smote him until none was left to him remaining. And we took all his cities at that time, there was not a city which we took not from them, threescore cities, all the region of Argob, the kingdom of Og in Bashan. All these cities were fenced with high walls, gates, and bars; beside unwalled towns a great many. And we utterly destroyed them, as we did unto Sihon king of Heshbon, utterly destroying the men, women, and children of every city. But all the cattle, and the spoil of the cities, we took for a prey to ourselves" (ver. 1-7).

The divine instructions as to Og, king of Bashan, were precisely similar to those given, in the preceding chapter, with respect to Sihon the Amorite; and in order to understand both, we must look at them purely in the light of the government of God—a subject but little understood, though one of very deep interest and practical importance. We must accurately distinguish between grace and government. When we contemplate God in government, we see Him displaying His power in the way of righteousness—punishing evil-doers, pouring out vengeance upon His enemies, overthrowing empires, upturning thrones, destroying cities, sweeping away nations, tribes, and peoples. We find Him commanding His people to slay men, women, and little children with the edge of the sword; to set fire to their houses, and turn their cities into desolate heaps.

Again, we hear Him addressing the prophet Ezekiel in the following remarkable words: "Son of man, Nebuchadrezzar king of Babylon caused his army to serve a great service against Tyrus: every head was made bald, and every shoulder was peeled; yet had he no wages, nor his army, for Tyrus, for the service that he had served against it. Therefore, thus saith the Lord God, Behold, I will give the land of Egypt unto Nebuchadrezzar king of Babylon; and he shall take her multitude, and take her spoil, and take her prey; and it shall be the wages for his army. I have given him the land of Egypt for his labor wherewith he served against it, because they wrought for Me, saith the Lord God" (Ezek. 29:18-20).

This is a very wonderful passage of Scripture; setting before us a subject which runs through the entire volume of Old Testament Scripture—a subject demanding our profound and reverent attention. Whether we turn to the five books of Moses, to the historical books, to the Psalms, or to the prophets, we find the inspiring Spirit giving us the most minute details of God's actings in government. We have the deluge in the days of Noah, when the whole earth, with all its inhabitants, with the exception of eight persons, was destroyed by an act of divine government. Men, women, children, cattle, fowl, and creeping things were all swept away and buried beneath the billows and waves of God's righteous judgment.

Then we have, in the days of Lot, the cities of the plain, with all their inhabitants —men, women, and children—in a few short hours, consigned to utter destruction, overthrown by the hand of Almighty God, and buried beneath the deep, dark waters of the Dead Sea. Those guilty cities, "Sodom and Gomorrha, and the cities about them in like manner, giving themselves over to fornication, and going after strange flesh, are set forth for an example, suffering the vengeance of eternal fire."

Then, again, as we pass down along the page of inspired history, we see the seven nations of Canaan—men, women, children—given over into the hands of Israel for unsparing judgment; nothing that breathed was to be left alive.

But, we may truly say, time would fail us even to refer to all the passages of holy Scripture which set before our eyes the solemn actings of the divine government. Suffice it to say that the line of evidence runs from Genesis to Revelation—beginning with the deluge and ending with the burning up of the present system of things.

Now, the question is, Are we competent to understand these ways of God in government? Is it any part of our business to sit in judgment upon them? Are we capable of unraveling the profound and awful mysteries of divine providence? Can we—are we called upon to—account for the tremendous fact of helpless babes involved in the judgment of their guilty parents? Impious infidelity may sneer at these things; morbid sentimentality may stumble over them; but the true believer, the pious Christian, the reverent student of holy Scripture, will meet them all with this one simple but safe and solid question, "Shall not the Judge of all the earth do right?"

This, we may rest assured, is the only true way in which to meet such questions. If man is to sit in judgment upon the actings of God in government—if he can take upon himself to decide as to what is and what is not worthy of God to do, then, verily, we have lost the true sense of God altogether. And this is just what the devil is aiming at. He wants to lead the heart away from God; and to this end, he leads men to reason and question and speculate in a region which lies as far beyond their ken as heaven is above the earth. Can we comprehend God? If we could, we should ourselves be God.

> We comprehend Him not,
> Yet earth and heaven tell,
> God sits as Sovereign on the throne,
> And ruleth all things well.

It is at once absurd and impious, in the very highest degree, for puny mortals to dare to question the counsels, enactments, and ways of the almighty Creator and all-wise Governor of the universe. Assuredly, all who do so must sooner or later find out their terrible mistake. Well would it be for all questioners and cavilers to give heed to the pungent question of the inspired apostle in Romans 9: "Nay but, O man, who art thou that repliest against God? Shall the thing formed say to him that formed it, Why hast thou made me thus? Hath not the potter power over the clay, of the same lump to make one vessel unto honor, and another unto dishonor?"

How simple! How forcible! How unanswerable! This is the divine method of meeting all the hows and whys of infidel reason. If the potter has power over the lump of clay which he holds in his hand—a fact which none would think of disputing—how much more has the Creator of all things power over the creatures which His hand has formed! Men may reason and argue interminably as to why God permitted sin to enter; why He did not at once annihilate Satan and his angels; why He allowed the serpent to tempt Eve; why He did not keep her back from eating the forbidden fruit. In short, the hows and whys are endless; but the answer is one—"Who art thou, O man, that repliest against God?" How monstrous for a poor worm of the earth to attempt to sit in judgment upon the unsearchable judgments and ways of the Eternal God! What blind and presumptuous folly for a creature, whose understanding is darkened by sin, and who is thus wholly incapable of forming a right judgment about any thing divine, heavenly, or eternal, to attempt to decide how God should act in any given case! Alas! it is to be feared that thousands who now argue with great apparent cleverness against the truth of God, will find out their fatal mistake when it will be too late to correct it.

And as to all those who, though very far from taking common ground with the infidel, are nevertheless troubled with doubts and misgivings as to some of God's ways in government, and as to the awful question of eternal punishment,* we would earnestly recommend them to study and drink in the spirit of that lovely little psalm, 131: "Lord, my heart is not haughty, nor mine eyes lofty: neither do I exercise myself in great matters, or in things too high for me. Surely I have behaved and quieted myself as a child that is weaned of his mother: my soul is even as a weaned child."

Then, when the heart has in some measure taken in this exquisite breathing, it may turn with real profit to the words of the inspired apostle (2 Cor. 10): "For the weapons of our warfare are not carnal, but mighty through God to the pulling down of strong

*With regard to the solemn subject of eternal punishment, we here offer a few remarks, seeing that so very many, both in England and America, are troubled with difficulties respecting it.

There are three considerations, which, if duly weighed, will, we think, settle every Christian on the doctrine.

I. The first is this: There are seventy passages in the New Testament where the word "everlasting," or "eternal," holds; casting down imaginations, and every high thing that exalteth itself against the knowledge of God, and bringing into captivity every thought to the obedience of Christ."

Doubtless, the philosopher, the scholar, the profound thinker, would smile contemptuously at such a childish mode of dealing with such great questions; but this is a very small matter in the judgment of the devout disciple of Christ. The same inspired apostle makes very short work of all this world's wisdom and learning. He says, "Let no man deceive himself. If any man among you seemeth to be wise in this world, let him become a fool, that he may be wise. For the wisdom of this world is foolishness with God. For it is written, 'He taketh the wise in their own craftiness.' And again, 'The Lord knoweth the thoughts of the wise, that they are vain' " (1 Cor. 3). And again, "It is written, 'I will destroy the wisdom of the wise, and will bring to nothing the understanding of the prudent.' Where is the wise? where is the scribe? where is the disputer of this world? hath not God made foolish the wisdom of this world? For after that in the wisdom of God the world by wisdom knew not God, it pleased God by the foolishness of the preaching *to save them that believe*" (1 Cor. 1:19-21).

Here lies the grand moral secret of the whole matter. Man has to find out that he is simply a fool, and that all the wisdom of the world is foolishness. Humbling but wholesome truth! Humbling, because it puts man in his right place; wholesome, yea, most precious, because it brings in the wisdom of God. We hear a great deal nowadays about science, philosophy, and learning. "Hath not God made foolish the wisdom of this world?"

Do we fully take in the meaning of these words? Alas! it is to be feared they are but little understood. There are not wanting men who would fain persuade us that science has gone far beyond the Bible.* Alas! for the sci-

---

[αιωνιος] occurs. It is applied to the "life" which believers possess, to the "mansions" into which they are to be received, to the "glory" which they are to enjoy; it is applied to God (Rom. 16:26), to the "salvation" of which our Lord Jesus Christ is the Author, to the "redemption" which He has obtained for us, and to the "Spirit."

Then, out of the seventy passages referred to above, which the reader can verify in a few moments by a glance at a Greek Concordance, there are seven in which the self-same word is applied to the "punishment" of the wicked, to the "judgment" which is to overtake them, to the "fire" which is to consume them.

Now, the question is, Upon what principle, or by what authority, can any one mark off these seven passages and say that in them the word αιωνιος does not mean "everlasting," while in the other sixty-three it does? We consider the statement utterly baseless, and unworthy the attention of any sober mind. We fully admit that, had the Holy Spirit thought proper, when speaking of the judgment of the wicked, to make use of a different word from that used in the other passages, reason would that we should weigh the fact. But no; He uses the same word invariably, so that if we deny eternal punishment, we must deny eternal life, eternal glory, an eternal Spirit, an eternal God, an eternal any thing. In short, if punishment be not eternal, nothing is eternal, so far as this argument is concerned. To meddle with this stone in the archway of divine revelation, is to reduce the whole to a mass of ruin around us. And this is just what the devil is aiming at. We are fully persuaded that to deny the truth of eternal punishment is to take the first step on that inclined plane which leads down to the dark abyss of universal skepticism.

II. Our second consideration is drawn from the great truth of the immortality of the soul. We read in the second chapter of Genesis that "the Lord God formed man of the dust of the ground, and breathed into his nostrils the breath of life; and man became a living soul." Upon this one passage, as upon an immovable rock, even if we had not another, we build the great truth of the immortality of the human soul. The fall of man made no difference as to this. Fallen or unfallen, innocent or guilty, converted or unconverted, the soul must live forever.

The tremendous question is, Where is it to live? God cannot allow sin into His presence. "He is of purer eyes than to behold evil, and cannot look upon iniquity." Hence, if a man dies in his sins—dies unrepentant, unwashed, unpardoned, then, most assuredly, where God is he never can come; indeed, it is the very last place to which he would like to come. There is nothing for him but an endless eternity in the lake that burneth with fire and brimstone.

III. And lastly, we believe that the truth of eternal punishment stands intimately connected with the infinite nature of the atonement of our Lord and Saviour Jesus Christ. If nothing short of an infinite sacrifice could deliver us from the consequences of sin, those consequences must be eternal. This consideration may not, perhaps, in the judgment of some, carry much weight with it; but to us its force is absolutely irresistible. We must measure sin and its consequences as we measure divine love and its results—not by the standard of human sentiment or reason, but only by the standard of the cross of Christ.

*We must distinguish between all true science and "science falsely so called." And further, we must distinguish between the *facts* of science, and the *conclusions* of scientific men. The facts are what God has done and is doing; but when men set about drawing their conclusions from the facts, they make the most serious mistakes.

However, it is a real relief to the heart to think that there are many philosophers and men of science who give God His right place, and who love our Lord Jesus Christ in sincerity.

ence, and for all those who give heed to it. If it has gone beyond the Bible, whither has it gone? In the direction of God, of Christ, of heaven, of holiness, of peace? Nay; but quite in the opposite direction. And where must it all end? We tremble to think, and feel reluctant to pen the reply. Still, we must be faithful, and declare solemnly that the sure and certain end of that path along which human science is conducting its votaries is the blackness of darkness forever.

"The world by wisdom knew not God." What did the philosophy of Greece do for its disciples? It made them the ignorant worshipers of *"an unknown God."* The very inscription on their altar published to the universe their ignorance and their shame.

And may we not lawfully inquire if philosophy has done better for christendom than it did for Greece? Has it communicated the knowledge of the true God? Who could dare to say, Yes? There are millions of baptized professors throughout the length and breadth of christendom who know no more of the true God than those philosophers who encountered Paul in the city of Athens.

The fact is this: every one who really knows God, is the privileged possessor of eternal life. So our Lord Jesus Christ declares, in the most distinct manner, in the seventeenth chapter of John. "This is life eternal, that they might know Thee the only true God, and Jesus Christ, whom Thou hast sent." This is most precious to every soul that, through grace, has gotten this knowledge. To know God, is to have life—life eternal.

But how can I know God? where can I find Him? Can science and philosophy tell me? Have they ever told any one? have they ever guided any poor wanderer into this way of life and peace? No; never. "The world by wisdom knew not God." The conflicting schools of ancient philosophy could only plunge the human mind into profound darkness and hopeless bewilderment; and the conflicting schools of modern philosophy are not a whit better. They can give no certainty, no safe anchorage, no solid ground of confidence, to the poor benighted soul. Barren speculation, torturing doubt, wild and baseless theory, is all that human philosophy, in any age or of any nation, has to offer to the earnest inquirer after truth.

How, then, are we to know God? If such a stupendous result hangs on this knowledge, if to know God is life eternal—and Jesus says it is—then how is He to be known? "No man hath seen God at any time; the only begotten Son, which is in the bosom of the Father, He hath declared Him" (John 1:18).

Here we have an answer divinely simple, divinely sure. Jesus reveals God to the soul—reveals the Father to the heart. Precious fact! We are not sent to creation to learn who God is, though we see His power, wisdom, and goodness there; we are not sent to the law, though we see His justice there; we are not sent to providence, though we see the profound mysteries of His government there. No; if we want to know who and what God is, we are to look in the face of Jesus Christ, the only begotten Son of God, who dwelt in His bosom before all worlds, who was His eternal delight, the object of His affections, the centre of His counsels. He it is who reveals God to the soul. We cannot have the slightest idea of what God is apart from the Lord Jesus Christ. "In Him dwelleth all the fullness of the Godhead [Θεοτης] bodily." "God who commanded the light to shine out of darkness, hath shined in our hearts, to give the light of the knowledge of the glory of God, in the face of Jesus Christ."

Nothing can exceed the power and blessedness of all this. There is no darkness here, no uncertainty. "The darkness is past and the true light now shineth." Yes; it shineth in the face of Jesus Christ. We can gaze, by faith, on that blessed One; we can trace His marvelous path on the earth; see Him going about doing good, and healing all that were oppressed of the devil; mark His very looks, His words, His works, His ways; see Him healing the sick, cleansing the leper, opening the eyes of the blind, unstopping the ears of the deaf, causing the lame to walk, the maimed to be whole, raising the dead, drying the widow's tears, feeding the hungry, binding up broken hearts, meeting every form of human need, soothing human sorrow, hushing human fears; and doing all these things in such a style, with such touching grace and sweetness, as to make each one feel, in his very inmost soul, that it was the deep delight of that loving heart thus to minister to his need.

Now, in all this He was revealing God to man; so that if we want to know what God is, we have simply to look at Jesus. When Philip said, "Lord, shew us the Father, and it sufficeth us," the prompt reply was, "Have I been so long time with you, and yet hast thou not known Me, Philip? he that hath seen Me hath seen the Father; and how sayest thou then, 'Shew us the Father'? Believest thou not that I am in the Father, and the Father in Me? the words that I speak unto you I speak not of Myself; but the Father that dwelleth in Me, He doeth the works. Believe Me that I am in the Father, and the Father in Me: or else believe Me for the very works' sake."

Here is true rest for the heart. We know the true God, and Jesus Christ, whom He hath sent; and this is life eternal. We know Him as our own very God and Father, and Christ as our own personal, loving Lord and Saviour; we can delight in Him, walk with Him, lean on Him, trust in Him, cling to Him, draw from Him, find all our living springs in Him, rejoice in Him all the day long, find our meat and our drink in doing His blessed will, furthering His cause, and promoting His glory.

Do you know all this for yourself? Is it a living, divinely real thing in your own soul this moment? This is true Christianity, and you should not be satisfied with any thing less. You will perhaps tell us we have wandered far from the third chapter of Deuteronomy. But whither have we wandered? To the Son of God and to the soul of the reader. If this be wandering, be it so; it most assuredly is not wandering from the object for which we are penning these *Notes,* which is, to bring Christ and the soul together, or to bind them together, as the case may be. We would never, for one moment, lose sight of the fact that, both in writing and speaking, we have not merely to expound Scripture, but to seek the salvation and blessing of souls. Hence it is that we feel constrained, from time to time, to appeal to the heart and conscience of the reader, as to his practical state, and as to how far he has made his very own of these imperishable realities which pass in review before us. And we earnestly beseech the reader, whoever he may be, to seek a deeper acquaintance with God in Christ; and, as a sure consequence of this, a closer walk with Him and more thorough consecration of heart to Him.

This, we are thoroughly persuaded, is what is needed in this day of unrest and unreality in the world, and of lukewarmness and indifference in the professing church. We want a very much higher standard of personal devotedness, more real purpose of heart to cleave to the Lord and follow Him. There is much—very much—to discourage and hinder in the condition of things around us. The language of the men of Judah in the days of Nehemiah may, with some measure of appropriateness and force, be applied to our times—"The strength of the bearers of burdens is decayed, and there is much rubbish." But, thank God, the remedy now, as then, is to be found in this soul-stirring sentence, "Remember the Lord."

We now return to our chapter, in the remainder of which the lawgiver rehearses in the ears of the congregation the story of their dealings with the two kings of the Amorites, together with the facts connected with the inheritance of the two tribes and a half on the wilderness side of Jordan. And with regard to the latter subject, it is interesting to notice that he raises no question as to the right or the wrong of their choosing their possession short of the land of promise. Indeed, from the narrative given here, it could not be known that the two tribes and a half had expressed any wish in the matter. So far is our book from being a mere repetition of its predecessors.

Here are the words: "And this land, which we possessed at that time, from Aroer, which is by the river Arnon, and half Mount Gilead, and the cities thereof, *gave I unto the Reubenites and to the Gadites.* And the rest of Gilead, and all Bashan, being the kingdom of Og, *gave I unto the half tribe of*

*Manasseh;* all the region of Argob, with all Bashan, which was called the land of giants. . . . And *I gave* Gilead unto Machir. And unto the Reubenites and unto the Gadites *I gave* from Gilead even unto the river Arnon half the valley, and the border even unto the river Jabbok, which is the border of the children of Ammon. . . . And I commanded you at that time, saying, *The Lord your God hath given you this land to possess it": not* a word about their having asked it—"ye shall pass over armed before your brethren the children of Israel, all that are meet for the war. But your wives, and your little ones, and your cattle (for I know that ye have much cattle), shall abide in your cities *which I have given you;* until the Lord have given rest unto your brethren, as well as unto you, and until they also possess the land which the Lord your God hath given them beyond Jordan; and then shall ye return every man unto his possession, which I have given you."

In our studies on the book of Numbers, we have dwelt upon certain facts connected with the settlement of the two tribes and a half, proving that they were below the mark of the Israel of God in choosing their inheritance any where short of the other side of Jordan; but in the passage we have just quoted, there is no allusion at all to this side of the question, because the object of Moses is to set before the whole congregation the exceeding goodness, loving-kindness, and faithfulness of God, not only in bringing them through all the difficulties and dangers of the wilderness, but also in giving them, even already, such signal victories over the Amorites, and putting them in possession of regions so attractive and so suited to them. In all this, he is laying down the solid basis of Jehovah's claim upon their hearty obedience to His commandments; and we can at once see and appreciate the moral beauty of overlooking entirely, in such a rehearsal, the question as to whether Reuben, Gad, and the half tribe of Manasseh were wrong in stopping short of the land of promise. It is, to every devout Christian, a striking proof of the touching and exquisite grace of God, and also of the divine perfectness of Scripture.

No doubt, every true believer enters upon the study of Scripture with the full and deeply wrought conviction of its absolute perfectness in every part. He reverently believes that there is not, from the opening of Genesis to the close of Revelation, a single flaw, a single hitch, a single discrepancy—not one; all is as perfect as its divine Author.

But then the cordial belief of the divine perfectness of Scripture as a whole can never lessen our appreciation of the evidences which come out in detail; nay, it enhances it exceedingly. Thus, for example, in the passage now before us, is it not perfectly beautiful to mark the absence of all reference to the failure of the two tribes and a half in the matter of choosing their inheritance, seeing that any such reference would be entirely foreign to the object of the lawgiver and to the scope of the book? Is it not the joy of our hearts to trace such infinite perfections, such exquisite and inimitable touches? Assuredly it is; and not only so, but we are persuaded that the more the moral glories of the volume dawn upon our souls, and its living and exhaustless depths are unfolded to our hearts, the more we shall be convinced of the utter folly of infidel assaults upon it, and of the feebleness and gratuitousness of many well-meant efforts to prove that it does not contradict itself. Thank God, His Word stands in no need of human apologists. It speaks for itself, and carries with it its own powerful evidences; so that we can say of it what the apostle says of his gospel, that "if it be hid, it is hid to them that are lost; in whom the god of this world hath blinded the minds of them which believe not, lest the light of the glorious gospel of Christ, who is the image of God, should shine unto them." We are more and more convinced each day, that the most effective method of answering all infidel attacks upon the Bible is, to cherish a more profound faith in its divine power and authority, and to use it as those who are most thoroughly persuaded of its truth and preciousness. The Spirit of God alone can enable any one to believe in the plenary inspiration of the holy Scriptures. Human arguments may go for what they are worth; they may doubtless silence gainsayers, but they cannot reach the heart—they cannot bring the genial rays of divine revelation to bear down in living, saving power upon the soul. This is a work divine; and until it is done, all the evidences and arguments in the world must leave the soul in the moral darkness of unbelief; but when it is done, there is no need of human testimony in defense of the Bible. External evidences, however interesting and valuable (and they are both), cannot add a single jot or tittle to the glory of that peerless revelation, which bears on every page, every paragraph, every sentence, the clear impress of its divine Author. As with the sun in the heavens, its every ray tells of the Hand that made it, so of the Bible, its every sentence tells of the Heart that inspired it. But inasmuch as a blind man cannot see the sunlight, so neither can the unconverted soul see the force and beauty of holy Scripture. The eye must be anointed with heavenly eye-salve ere the infinite perfections of the divine volume can be discerned or appreciated.

Now, we must own that it is the deep and ever-deepening sense of all this that has led us to the determination not to occupy our time by reference to the attacks which have been made by rationalistic writers on that portion of the Word of God with which we are now engaged. We leave this to other and abler hands. What we desire for ourselves and our readers is, that we may feed in peace upon the green pastures which the Shepherd and Bishop of our souls has graciously thrown open to us; that we may help each other, as we pass along, to see more and more of the moral glory of that which lies before us, and thus to build each other up on our most holy faith. This will be far more grateful work to us, and we trust also to our readers, than replying to men who, in all their puny efforts to find out flaws in the holy volume, only prove, to those capable of judging, that they understand neither what they say nor whereof they affirm. If men *will* abide in the dark vaults and tunnels of a dreary infidelity, and there find fault with the sun, or deny that it shines at all, let it be ours to bask in the light, and help others to do the same.

We shall now dwell for a little on the remaining verses of our chapter, in which we shall find much to interest, instruct, and profit us.

And first, Moses rehearses in the ears of the people his charge to Joshua. "And I commanded Joshua at that time, saying, 'Thine eyes have seen all that the Lord our God hath done unto these two kings; so shall the Lord do unto all the kingdoms whither thou passest. Ye shall not fear them; for the Lord your God He shall fight for you" (ver. 21-22).

The remembrance of the Lord's dealings with us in the past should strengthen our confidence in going on. The One who had given His people such a victory over the Amorites, who had destroyed such a formidable foe as Og, king of Bashan, and given into their hands all the land of the giants, what could He not do for them? They could hardly expect to encounter in all the land of Canaan any enemy more powerful than Og, whose bedstead was of such enormous dimensions as to call for the special notice of Moses; but what was he in the presence of his almighty Creator? Dwarfs and giants are all alike to Him. The grand point is to keep God Himself ever before our eyes; then difficulties vanish. If He covers the eyes, we can see nothing else; and this is the true secret of peace, and the real power of progress. "Thine eyes have seen all that the Lord your God hath done." And *as* He has done, *so* He will do. He *hath* delivered, and He *doth* deliver, and He *will* deliver. Past, present, and future are all marked by divine deliverance.

Reader, art thou in any difficulty? Is there any pressure upon thee? Art thou anticipating, with nervous apprehension, some formidable evil? Is thine heart trembling at the very thought of it? It may be thou art like one who has come to the far end, like the apostle Paul in Asia—"Pressed out of measure, above strength, insomuch that we despaired even of life." If so, beloved friend, accept a word of encouragement. It is our deep and earnest desire to strengthen your hands in God, and to encourage your heart to trust Him for all that is before you. "Fear not:" only believe. He never fails a trusting heart—no, never. Make use of the resources which are treasured up for you in Him. Just put yourself, your surroundings, your fears, your anxieties, all into His hands, *and leave them there.*

Yes, leave them there. It is of little use your putting your difficulties, your necessities, into His hands and then, almost immediately, taking them into your own. We often do this. When in pressure, in need, in deep trial of some kind or other, we go to God in prayer, we cast our burden upon Him and seem to get relief; but, alas! no sooner have we risen from our knees than we begin again to look at the difficulty, ponder the trial, dwell upon all the sorrowful circumstances, until we are again at our very wits' end.

Now, this will never do. It sadly dishonors God, and, of course, leaves us unrelieved and unhappy. He would have our minds as free from care as the conscience is free from guilt. His word to us is, "Be careful for nothing; but in every thing by prayer and supplication with thanksgiving let your requests be made known unto God." And what then? "The peace of God, which passeth all understanding, shall keep (or garrison—Φρουρησει] your hearts and minds through Christ Jesus."

Thus it was that Moses, that beloved man of God and honored servant of Christ, sought to encourage his fellow-laborer and successor, Joshua, in reference to all that was before him. "Ye shall not fear them; for the Lord your God He shall fight for you." Thus, too, did the blessed apostle Paul encourage his beloved son and fellow-servant Timothy to trust in the living God; to be strong in the grace which is in Christ Jesus; to lean, with unshaken confidence, on God's sure foundation; to commit himself, with unquestioning assurance, to the authority, teaching, and guidance of the holy Scriptures; and thus armed and furnished, to give himself, with holy diligence and true spiritual courage, to that work to which he was called. And thus, too, the writer and the reader can encourage one another, in these days of increasing difficulty, to cling, in simple faith, to that Word which is settled forever in heaven; to have it hidden in the heart as a living power and authority in the soul—something that will sustain us, though heart and flesh should fail, and though we had not the countenance or support of a human being. "All flesh is as grass, and all the glory of man as the flower of grass. The grass withereth, and the flower thereof falleth away; but the Word of the Lord endureth forever. And this is the Word which by the gospel is preached unto you" (1 Pet. 1:24-25).

How precious is this! What comfort and consolation! What stability and rest! What real strength, victory, and moral elevation! It is not within the compass of human language to set forth the preciousness of the Word of God, or to define, in adequate terms, the comfort of knowing that the self-same Word which is settled forever in heaven, and which shall endure throughout the countless ages of eternity, is that which has reached our hearts in the glad tidings of the gospel, imparting to us eternal life, and giving us peace and rest in the finished work of Christ, and a perfectly satisfying object in His adorable Person. Truly, as we think of all this, we cannot but own that every breath should be a halleluiah. Thus it shall be by and by, and that forever, all homage to His peerless name!

The closing verses of our chapter present a peculiarly touching passage between Moses and his Lord, the record of which, as given here, is in lovely keeping, as we might expect, with the character of the entire book of Deuteronomy. "And I besought the Lord at that time, saying, 'O Lord God, Thou hast begun to show Thy servant Thy greatness, and Thy mighty hand; for what god is there in heaven or in earth that can do according to Thy works and according to Thy might? I pray Thee, let me go over, and see the good land that is beyond Jordan, that goodly mountain, and Lebanon.' But the Lord was wroth with me for your sakes, and would not hear me: and the Lord said unto me, 'Let it suffice thee; speak no more unto Me of this matter. Get thee up into the top of

Pisgah, and lift up thine eyes westward, and northward, and southward, and eastward, and behold it with thine eyes: for thou shalt not go over this Jordan. But charge Joshua, and encourage him, and strengthen him; for he shall go over before this people, and he shall cause them to inherit the land which thou shalt see' " (ver. 23-28).

It is very affecting to find this eminent servant of God urging a request which could not be granted. He longed to see that good land beyond Jordan. The portion chosen by the two tribes and a half could not satisfy his heart; he desired to plant his foot upon the proper inheritance of the Israel of God. But it was not to be. He had spoken unadvisedly with his lips at the waters of Meribah; and, by the solemn and irreversible enactment of the divine government, he was prohibited from crossing the Jordan.

All this, the beloved servant of Christ most meekly rehearses in the ears of the people. He does not hide from them the fact that the Lord had refused to grant his request. True, he had to remind them that it was on their account—that was morally needful for them to hear; still he tells them, in the most unreserved manner, that Jehovah was wroth with him, and that He refused to hear him—refused to allow him to cross the Jordan, and called upon him to resign his office and appoint his successor.

Now, it is most edifying to hear all this from the lips of Moses himself. It teaches us a fine lesson, if only we are willing to learn it. Some of us find it very hard indeed to confess that we have done or said any thing wrong—very hard to own before our brethren that we have entirely missed the Lord's mind in any particular case. We are careful of our reputation; we are touchy and tenacious. And yet, with strange inconsistency, we admit, or seem to admit, in general terms, that we are poor, feeble, erring creatures; and that, if left to ourselves, there is nothing too bad for us to say or to do. But it is one thing to make a most humiliating general confession, and another thing altogether to own that, in some given case, we have made a gross mistake. This latter is a confession which very few have grace to make. Some can hardly ever admit that they have done wrong.

Not so that honored servant whose words we have just quoted. He, notwithstanding his elevated position as the called, trusted, and beloved servant of Jehovah—the leader of the congregation, whose rod had made the land of Egypt to tremble, was not ashamed to stand before the whole assembly of his brethren and confess his mistake—own that he had said what he ought not, and that he had earnestly urged a request which Jehovah could not grant.

Does this lower Moses in our estimation? The very reverse: it raises him immensely. It is morally lovely to hear his confession, to see how meekly he bows his head to the governmental dealings of God, to mark the unselfishness of his acting toward the man who was to succeed him in his high office. There was not a trace of jealousy or envy; no exhibition of mortified pride. With beautiful self-emptiness he steps down from his elevated position, throws his mantle over the shoulders of his successor, and encourages him to discharge, with holy fidelity, the duties of that high office which he himself had to resign.

"He that humbleth himself shall be exalted." How true was this in Moses' case! He humbled himself under the mighty hand of God. He accepted the holy discipline imposed upon him by the divine government. He uttered not a murmuring word at the refusal of his request; he bows to it all, and hence he was exalted in due time. If government kept him out of Canaan, grace conducted him to Pisgah's top, from whence, in company with his Lord, he was permitted to see that good land, in all its fair proportions—see it, not as inherited by Israel, but as given of God.

The reader will do well to ponder deeply the subject of grace and government. It is indeed a very weighty and practical theme, and one largely illustrated in Scripture, though but little understood amongst us. It may seem wonderful to us, hard to be understood, that one so beloved as Moses should be refused an entrance into the promised land; but in this we see the solemn action of the divine government, and we have to bow our heads and worship. It was not merely that Moses, in his official capacity, or as representing the legal system, could not bring Israel into the land. This is true; but it is not all. Moses spake unadvisedly with his lips. He and Aaron his brother failed to glorify God, in the presence of the congregation, and for this cause "the Lord spake unto Moses and Aaron, 'Because ye believed Me not, to sanctify Me in the eyes of the children of Israel, therefore ye shall not bring this congregation into the land which I have given them.' " And again, we read, "The Lord spake unto Moses and Aaron in Mount Hor, by the coast of the land of Edom, saying, 'Aaron shall be gathered unto his people; for he shall not enter into the land which I have given unto the children of Israel, because ye rebelled against My word at the water of Meribah. Take Aaron and Eleazar his son, and bring them up unto Mount Hor; and strip Aaron of his garments, and put them upon Eleazar his son; and Aaron shall be gathered unto his people, and shall die there.' "

All this is most solemn. Here we have the two leading men in the congregation, the very men whom God had used to bring His people out of the land of Egypt, with mighty signs and wonders—"that Moses and Aaron"—men highly honored of God, and yet refused entrance into Canaan. And for what? Let us mark the reason. *"Because ye rebelled against My word."*

Let these words sink down into our hearts. It is a terrible thing to rebel against the Word of God; and the more elevated the position of those who so rebel, the more serious it is in every way, and the more solemn and speedy must be the divine judgment. "For rebellion is as the sin of witchcraft, and stubbornness is as iniquity and idolatry."

These are weighty words, and we ought to ponder them deeply. They were uttered in the ears of Saul, when he had failed to obey the word of the Lord; and thus we have before us examples of a prophet, a priest, and a king, all judged, under the government of God, for an act of disobedience. The prophet and the priest were refused entrance into the land of Canaan, and the king was deprived of his throne, simply because they disobeyed the word of the Lord.

Let us remember this. We, in our fancied wisdom, might deem all this very severe. Are we competent judges? This is a grand question in all such matters. Let us beware how we presume to sit in judgment on the enactments of divine government. Adam was driven out of paradise, Aaron was stripped of his priestly robes, Moses was sternly refused entrance into Canaan, and Saul was deprived of his kingdom—and for what? Was it for what men would call a grave moral offense—some scandalous sin? No; it was, in each case, for neglecting the word of the Lord. This is the serious thing for us to keep before us, in this day of human willfulness, in which men undertake to set up their own opinions, to think for themselves, and judge for themselves, and act for themselves. Men proudly put the question, "Has not every man a right to think for himself?" We reply, Most certainly not; we have a right to obey. To obey what? Not the commandments of men, not the authority of the so-called church, not the decrees of general councils—in a word, not any merely human authority, call it what you please, but simply the Word of the living God—the testimony of the Holy Ghost—the voice of holy Scripture. This it is that justly claims our implicit, unhesitating, unquestioning obedience. To this we are to bow down our whole moral being. We are not to reason, we are not to speculate, we are not to weigh consequences, we have nothing to do with results, we are not to say "Why?" or "Wherefore?" It is ours to obey, and leave all the rest in the hands of our Master. What has a servant to do with consequences? what business has he to reason as to results? It is of the very essence of a servant to do what he is told, regardless of all other considerations. Had Adam remembered this, he would not have been turned out of Eden; had Moses and Aaron remembered it, they might have crossed the Jordan; had Saul remembered it, he would not have been deprived of his throne. And so, as we pass down along the stream of human history, we see this weighty principle illustrated over and over again; and we may rest assured, it is a principle of abiding and universal importance.

And be it remembered, we are not to attempt to weaken this great principle by any reasonings grounded upon God's foreknowledge of all that was to happen, and all that man would do, in the course of time. Men do reason in this way, but it is a fatal mistake. What has God's foreknowledge to do with man's responsibility? Is man responsible, or not? This is the question. If, as we most surely believe, he is, then nothing must be allowed to interfere with this responsibility. Man is called to obey the plain word of God; he is in no wise responsible to know aught about God's secret purposes and counsels. Man's responsibility rests upon what is revealed, not upon what is secret. What, for example, did Adam know about God's eternal plans and purposes when he was set in the garden of Eden and forbidden to eat of the tree of the knowledge of good and evil? Was his transgression in any wise modified by the stupendous fact that God took occasion from that very transgression to display, in the view of all created intelligences, His glorious scheme of redemption through the blood of the Lamb? Clearly not. He received a plain commandment, and by that commandment his conduct should have been absolutely governed. He disobeyed, and was driven out of paradise into a world which has, for well-nigh six thousand years, exhibited the terrible consequences of one single act of disobedience—the act of taking the forbidden fruit.

True it is, blessed be God, that grace has come into this poor sin-stricken world and there reaped a harvest which could never have been reaped in the fields of an unfallen creation. But man was judged for his transgression; he was driven out by the hand of God in government, and by an enactment of that government, he has been compelled to eat bread in the sweat of his brow. "Whatsoever *a man* [no matter who] soweth, that shall he also reap."

Here we have the condensed statement of the principle which runs all through the Word, and is illustrated on every page of the history of God's government. It demands our very gravest consideration. It is, alas! but little understood. We allow our minds to get under the influence of one-sided and therefore false ideas of grace, the effect of which is most pernicious. Grace is one thing, and government is another: they must never be confounded. We would earnestly impress upon the heart of the reader the weighty fact that the most magnificent display of God's sovereign grace can never interfere with the solemn enactments of His government.

## *CHAPTER 4*

"NOW therefore *hearken,* O Israel, unto the statutes and unto the judgments which I teach you, for to *do* them, that ye may *live,* and go in and *possess* the land which the Lord God of your fathers giveth you."

Here we have very prominently before us the special characteristic of the entire book of Deuteronomy. "Hearken" and "do," that ye may "live" and "possess." This is a universal and abiding principle. It was true for Israel, and it is true for us. The pathway of life and the true secret of possession is simple obedience to the holy commandments of God. We see this all through the inspired volume, from cover to cover. God has given us His Word, not to speculate upon it or discuss it, but that we may obey it. And it is as we, through grace, yield a hearty and happy obedience to our Father's statutes and judgments, that we tread the bright pathway of life, and enter into the reality of all that God has treasured up for us in Christ. "He that hath My commandments, and keepeth them, he it is that loveth Me; and he that loveth Me shall be loved of My Father, and I will love him, and will manifest Myself to him."

How precious is this! Indeed, it is unspeakable. It is something quite peculiar. It would be a very serious mistake to suppose that the privilege here spoken of is enjoyed by all believers. It is not. It is only enjoyed by such as yield a loving obedience to the commandments of our Lord Jesus Christ. It lies within the reach of all, but all do not enjoy it, because all are not obedient. It is one thing to be a child, and quite another to be an obedient child; it is one thing to be saved, and quite another thing to love the Saviour, and delight in all His most precious precepts.

We may see this continually illustrated in our family circles. There, for example, are two sons, and one of them only thinks of pleasing himself, doing his will, gratifying his own desires. He takes no pleasure in his father's society, does not take any pains to carry out his father's wishes, knows hardly any thing of his mind, and what he does know he utterly neglects or despises. He is ready enough to avail himself of all the benefits which accrue to him from the relationship in which he stands to his father—ready enough to accept clothes, books, money—all, in short, that the father gives; but he never seeks to gratify the father's heart by a loving attention to his will, even in the smallest matters. The other son is the direct opposite to all this. He delights in being with his father; he loves his society, loves his ways, loves his words; he is constantly taking occasion to carry out his father's wishes, to get him something that he knows will be agreeable to him. He loves his father, not for his gifts, but for himself; and he finds his richest enjoyment in being in his father's company and in doing his will.

Now, can we have any difficulty in seeing how very differently the father will feel towards those two sons? True, they are both his sons, and he loves them both, with a love grounded upon the relationship in which they stand to him; but beside the love of relationship common to both, there is the love of complacency peculiar to the obedient child. It is impossible that a father can find pleasure in the society of a willful, self-indulgent, careless son. Such a son may occupy much of his thoughts, he may spend many a sleepless night thinking about him and praying for him, he would gladly spend and be spent for him; but he is not agreeable to him, does not possess his confidence, cannot be the depositary of his thoughts.

All this demands the serious consideration of those who really desire to be acceptable or agreeable to the heart of our heavenly Father and our Lord Jesus Christ. We may rest assured of this, that obedience is grateful to God; and "His commandments are not grievous"—nay, they are the sweet and precious expression of His love, and the fruit and evidence of the relationship in which He stands to us. And not only so, but He graciously rewards our obedience by a fuller manifestation of Himself to our souls, and His dwelling with us. This comes out in great fullness and beauty in our Lord's reply to Judas, not Iscariot, for whose question we may be thankful—" 'Lord, how is it that Thou wilt manifest Thyself unto us, and not unto the world?' Jesus answered and said unto him, 'If a man love Me, he will keep My words; and My Father will love him, and We will come unto him, and make Our abode with him' " (John 14).

Here we are taught that it is not a question of the difference between "the world" and "us," inasmuch as the world knows nothing either of relationship or obedience, and is therefore in no wise contemplated in our Lord's words. The world hates Christ, because it does not know Him. Its language is, "Depart from us; for we desire not the knowledge of Thy ways." "We will not have this Man to reign over us."

Such is the world, even when polished by civilization, and gilded with the profession of Christianity. There is, underneath all the gilding, all the polish, a deep-seated hatred of the Person and authority of Christ. His sacred, peerless name is tacked on to the world's religion, at least throughout baptized christendom; but behind the drapery of religious profession, there lurks a heart at enmity with God and His Christ.

But our Lord is not speaking of the world in John 14. He is shut in with "His own," and it is of them He is speaking. Were He to manifest Himself to the world, it could only be for judgment and eternal destruction. But, blessed be His name, He does manifest

Himself to His own obedient children, to those who have His commandments and keep them, to those who love Him and keep His words.

And, let the reader thoroughly understand that when our Lord speaks of His commandments, His words, and His sayings, He does not mean the ten commandments, or law of Moses. No doubt, those ten commandments form a part of the whole canon of Scripture —the inspired Word of God; but to confound the law of Moses with the commandments of Christ would be simply turning things upside down, it would be to confound Judaism with Christianity—law and grace. The two things are as distinct as any two things can be, and must be so maintained by all who would be found in the current of the mind of God.

We are sometimes led astray by the mere sound of words; and hence, when we meet with the word "commandments," we instantly conclude that it must needs refer to the law of Moses. But this is a very great and mischievous mistake. If the reader is not clear and established as to this, let him close this volume and turn to the first eight chapters of the Epistle to the Romans, and the whole of the Epistle to the Galatians, and read them calmly and prayerfully, as in the very presence of God, with a mind freed from all theological bias and the influence of all previous religious training. There he will learn, in the fullest and clearest manner, that the Christian is not under law in any way, or for any object whatsoever, either for life, for righteousness, for holiness, for walk, or for any thing else. In short, the teaching of the entire New Testament goes to establish, beyond all question, that the Christian is not under law, not of the world, not in the flesh, not in his sins. The solid ground of all this is the accomplished redemption which we have in Christ Jesus, in virtue of which we are sealed by the Holy Ghost, and thus indissolubly united to, and inseparably identified with a risen and glorified Christ; so that the apostle John can say of all believers, all God's dear children, "*As* He [Christ] *is, so are we* in this world." This settles the whole question, for all who are content to be governed by holy Scripture. And as to all beside, discussion is worse than useless.

We have digressed from our immediate subject, in order to meet any difficulty arising from a misunderstanding of the word "commandments." The reader cannot too carefully guard against the tendency to confound the commandments spoken of in John 14 with the commandments of Moses, given in Exodus 20. And yet we reverently believe that Exodus 20 is as truly inspired as John 14.

And now, ere we finally turn from the subject which has been engaging us, we would ask the reader to refer, for a few moments, to a piece of inspired history which illustrates, in a very striking way, the difference between an obedient and disobedient child of God. He will find it in Genesis 18—19. It is a profoundly interesting study, presenting a contrast instructive, suggestive, and practical beyond expression. We are not going to dwell upon it, having in some measure done so in our *Notes on the Book of Genesis;* but we would merely remind the reader that he has before him, in these two chapters, the history of two saints of God. Lot was just as much a child of God as Abraham. We have no more doubt that Lot is amongst "the spirits of just men made perfect" than that Abraham is there. This, we think, cannot be called in question, inasmuch as the inspired apostle Peter tells us that Lot's "righteous soul was vexed with the filthy conversation of the wicked."

But mark the grave difference between the two men. The Lord Himself visited Abraham, sat with him, and partook readily of his hospitality. This was a high honor indeed, a rare privilege—a privilege which Lot never knew, an honor to which he never attained. The Lord never visited him in Sodom; He merely sent His angels, His ministers of power, the agents of His government. And even they, at first, sternly refused to enter Lot's house or to partake of his proffered hospitality. Their withering reply was, "Nay, but we will abide in the street all night." And when they did enter his house, it was only to protect him from the lawless violence with which he was surrounded, and to drag him out of the wretched circumstances into which for worldly gain and position, he had plunged himself. Could contrast be more vivid?

But further, the Lord delighted in Abraham, manifested Himself to him, opened His mind to him, told him of His plans and purposes—what He was about to do with Sodom. "Shall I," said He, "hide from Abraham that thing which I do; seeing that Abraham shall surely become a great and mighty nation, and all the nations of the earth shall be blessed in him? For *I know him, that he will command his children and his household after him, and they shall keep the way of the Lord, to do justice and judgment,* that the Lord may bring upon Abraham that which He hath spoken of him."

We could hardly have a more telling illustration of John 14:21,23, although the scene occurred two thousand years before the words were uttered. Have we aught like this in the history of Lot? Alas! no. It could not be. He had no nearness to God, no knowledge of His mind, no insight into His plans and purposes. How could he? Sunk, as he was, in the low moral depths of Sodom, how could he know the mind of God? Blinded by the murky atmosphere which inwrapped the guilty cities of the plain, how could he see into the future? Utterly impossible. If a man is mixed up with the world, he can only see things from the world's stand-point; he can only measure things by the world's standard, and think of them with the world's thoughts. Hence it is that the Church, in its Sardis condition, is *threatened* with the coming of the Lord as a thief, instead of being *cheered* with the hope of His coming as the bright and morning star. If the professing church has sunk to the world's level—as, alas! she has—she can only contemplate the future from the world's point of view. This accounts for the feeling of dread with which the great majority of professing Christians look at the subject of the Lord's coming. They are looking for Him as a thief, instead of the blessed Bridegroom of their hearts. How few there are, comparatively, who *love His appearing!* The great majority of professors (we grieve to have to pen the words) find their type in Lot rather than in Abraham. The Church has departed from her proper ground; she has gone down from her true moral elevation, and mingled herself with that world which hates and despises her absent Lord.

Still, thank God, there are "a few names, even in Sardis, which have not defiled their garments"—a few living stones, amid the smouldering ashes of lifeless profession—a few lights twinkling amid the moral gloom of cold, nominal, heartless, worldly Christianity. And not only so, but in the Laodicean phase of the Church's history, which presents a still lower and more hopeless condition of things, when the whole professing body is about to be spued out of the mouth of "the faithful and true witness"—even at this advanced stage of failure and departure, those gracious words fall, with soul-stirring power, on the attentive ear, "Behold, I stand at the door, and knock: if *any man* hear My voice, and open the door, I will come in *to him,* and will sup with him, and he with Me."*

Thus, in the days of professing Christianity, as in the days of the patriarchs—in the times of the New Testament, as in those of the Old, we see the same value and impor-

*To apply the solemn address of Christ to the church of Laodicea, as we sometimes find it done in modern evangelical preaching, to the case of the sinner, is a great mistake. No doubt, what the preacher means is right enough, but it is not presented here. It is not Christ knocking at the door of a sinner's heart, but knocking at the door of the professing church. What a fact is this! How full of deep and awful solemnity as regards the church! What an end to come to!—Christ outside! But what grace, as regards Christ, for He is knocking! He wants to come in; He is still lingering, in patient grace and changeless love, ready to come in to any faithful individual heart that will only open to Him. "If any man"—even one! In Sardis, He could speak *positively* of *"a few;"* in Laodicea, He can only speak *doubtfully* as to finding *one.* But should there be even one, He will come in to him, and sup with him. Precious Saviour! Faithful Lover of our souls! "Jesus Christ, the same yesterday, to-day, and forever."

Need we wonder that the enemy should seek to mutilate and misapply the solemn and searching address to the church of Laodicea—the professing body in the last dreary stage of its history? We have no hesitation in saying that to apply it *merely* to the case of an unconverted soul is to deprive the professing church of one of the most pertinent, pungent, and powerful appeals within the covers of the New Testament.

tance attached to a hearing ear and an obedient heart. Abraham, in the plains of Mamre, the pilgrim and the stranger, the faithful and obedient child of God, tasted the rare privilege of entertaining the Lord of glory—a privilege which could not be known by one who had chosen his place and his portion in a sphere doomed to destruction. So, also, in the days of Laodicean indifference and boastful pretension, the truly obedient heart is cheered with the sweet promise of sitting down to sup with Him who is "the Amen, the faithful and true witness, the beginning of the creation of God." In a word, let the condition of things be what it may, there is no limit to the blessing of the individual soul who will only hearken to the voice of Christ, and keep His commandments.

Let us remember this. Let it sink down into the very deepest depths of our moral being. Nothing can rob us of the blessings and privileges flowing from obedience. The truth of this shines out before our eyes in every section and on every page of the volume of God. At all times, in all places, and under all circumstances, the obedient soul was happy in God, and God was happy in him. It always holds good, whatever be the character of the dispensation, that, "To this man will I look, even to him who is of a contrite spirit, and trembles at My word." Nothing can ever alter or touch this. It meets us in the fourth chapter of our blessed book of Deuteronomy, in the words with which this section opens—"Now therefore *hearken,* O Israel, unto *the statutes* and unto *the judgments which I teach you,* for *to do,* that ye may live, and go in and possess the land which the Lord God of your fathers giveth you." It meets us in those precious words of our Lord, in John 14, on which we have been dwelling—"He that hath *My commandments* and keepeth them, he it is that loveth Me," etc. And again, "If a man love Me, *he will keep My sayings.*"* It shines with peculiar brightness in the words of the inspired apostle John—"Beloved, if our heart condemn us not, then have we confidence toward God. And whatsoever we ask, we receive of Him, *because we keep His commandments,* and *do those things that are pleasing in His sight.* And this is His commandment, that we should believe on the name of His Son Jesus Christ, and love one another, as He gave us commandment. And he that keepeth His commandments dwelleth in Him, and He in him" (1 John 3:21-24).

Passages might easily be multiplied, but there is no need. Those which we have quoted set before us, in the clearest and fullest way possible, the very highest motive for obedience, namely, its being agreeable to the heart of our Lord Jesus Christ—well-pleasing to God. True, we owe a hearty obedience on every ground. "We are not our own; we are bought with a price." We owe our life, our peace, our righteousness, our salvation, our everlasting felicity and glory, all to Him; so that nothing can exceed the moral weight of His claims upon us for a life of whole-hearted obedience. But above and beyond His moral claims stands the marvelous fact that His heart is gratified, His spirit refreshed, by our keeping His commandments and doing those things that are pleasing in His sight.

Can any thing exceed the moral power of such a motive as this? Only think of our being privileged to give pleasure to the heart of our beloved Lord! What sweetness, what interest, what preciousness, what holy dig-

---

*There is an interesting difference between the Lord's "commandments" and "sayings." The former set forth, distinctly and definitely, what we ought to do; the latter are the expression of His mind. If I give my child a command, it is the statement of his duty; and if he loves me, he will delight to do it. But if he has heard me *say* I like to see such a thing done, although I have not actually told him to do it, it will touch my heart much more deeply to see him go and do that thing in order to gratify me, than if I had given him a positive command. Now, ought we not to try and please the heart of Christ? Should we not "labor to be agreeable to Him"? He has made us accepted; surely we ought to seek, in every possible way, to be acceptable to Him. He delights in a loving obedience; it was what He Himself rendered to the Father. "I delight to do Thy will; yea, *Thy law* is within *My heart.*" "If ye keep My commandments, ye shall abide in My love; even as I have kept My Father's commandments, and abide in His love." Oh, that we may drink more deeply into the spirit of Jesus, walk in His blessed footsteps, and render Him a more loving, devoted, and whole-hearted obedience in all things! Let us earnestly seek after these things, that His heart may be gratified, and His name glorified in us, and in our entire practical career from day to day.

nity, it imparts to every little act of obedience to know that it is grateful to the heart of our Father! How far beyond the legal system is this! It is a most perfect contrast, in its every phase and every feature. The difference between the legal system and Christianity is the difference between death and life, bondage and liberty, condemnation and righteousness, distance and nearness, doubt and certainty. How monstrous the attempt to amalgamate these two things—to work them up into one system, as though they were but two branches from the one stem! What hopeless confusion must be the result of any such effort! How terrible the effect of seeking to place souls under the influence of the two things! As well might we attempt to combine the sun's meridian beams with the profound darkness of midnight. Looked at from a divine and heavenly stand-point, judged in the light of the New Testament, measured by the standard of the heart of God, the mind of Christ, there could not be a more hideous anomaly than that which presents itself to our view in christendom's effort to combine law and grace. And as to the dishonor done to God, the wound inflicted on the heart of Christ, the grief and despite offered to the Holy Ghost, the damage done to the truth of God, the grievous wrong perpetrated upon the beloved lambs and sheep of the flock of Christ, the terrible stumbling-block thrown in the way of both Jew and Gentile, and, in short, the serious injury done to the entire testimony of God during the last eighteen centuries, the judgment-seat of Christ can alone declare it; and oh, what an awful declaration that will be! It is too tremendous to contemplate.

But there are many pious souls throughout the length and breath of the professing church who conscientiously believe that the only possible way to produce obedience, to attain to practical holiness, to secure a godly walk, to keep our evil nature in order, is to put people under the law. They seem to fear that if souls are taken from under the school-master, with his rod and rudiments, there is an end to all moral order. In the absence of the authority of law, they look for nothing but hopeless confusion. To take away the ten commandments as a rule of life, is, in their judgment, to remove those grand moral embankments which the hand of God has erected to stem the tide of human lawlessness.

We can fully understand their difficulty. Most of us have had to encounter it, in one shape or another. But we must seek to meet it in God's way. It is of no possible use to cling, with fond tenacity, to our own notions, in the face of the plainest and most direct teaching of holy Scripture. We must, sooner or later, give up all such notions. Nothing will, nothing can, stand but the Word of our God—the voice of the Holy Ghost—the authority of Scripture—the imperishable teachings of that peerless revelation which our Father has, in His infinite grace, put into our hands. To that we must listen, with profound and reverent attention; to it we must bow down, with unquestioning and unqualified obedience. We must not presume to hold a single opinion of our own: God's opinion must be ours. We must clear out all the rubbish, which, by the influence of mere human teaching, has accumulated in our minds, and have every chamber thoroughly cleansed by the action of the Word and Spirit of God, and thoroughly ventilated by the pure and bracing air of the new creation.

Furthermore, we must learn to confide implicitly in every word that proceedeth out of the mouth of God. We must not reason, we must not judge, we must not discuss: we must simply believe. If man speaks, if it be a mere question of human authority, then indeed we must judge, because man has no right to command. We must judge what he says, not by our own opinions, or by any human standard, creed, or confession of faith, but by the Word of God. But when Scripture speaks, all discussion is closed.

This is an unspeakable consolation. It is not within the compass of human language to set forth adequately the value or the moral importance of this great fact. It delivers the soul completely from the blinding power of self-will on the one hand, and of mere subjection to human authority on the other. It brings us into direct, personal, living contact with the authority of God; and this is life, peace, liberty, moral power, true elevation, divine certainty, and holy stability. It puts an end to doubts and fears, to all the fluctuations of mere human opinion, so perplexing to the mind, so torturing to the heart. We are no longer tossed about with every wind of doctrine, every wave of human thought. *God has spoken.* This is quite enough. Here the heart finds its deep and settled repose. It has made its escape from the stormy ocean of theological controversy, and cast anchor in the blessed haven of divine revelation.

Hence, therefore, we would say to the pious reader of these lines, if you would know the mind of God on the subject before us—if you would know the ground, character, and object of Christian obedience, you must simply listen to the voice of holy Scripture. And what does it say? Does it send us back to Moses, to teach us how to live? Does it send us back "to the palpable mount," in order to secure holy living? Does it put us under the law, to keep the flesh in order? Hear what it says. Yes; hearken and ponder. Take the following words from Romans 6—words of emancipating, holy power: "For sin shall not have dominion over you; for *ye are not under law,* but under grace."

Now, we most earnestly entreat the reader to let these words enter into the very depths of his soul. The Holy Ghost declares, in the simplest and most emphatic manner, that Christians are not under law. If we were under law, sin would have dominion over us. Indeed, we invariably find, in Scripture, that "sin," "law," and "flesh" are linked together. A soul under law cannot possibly enjoy full deliverance from the dominion of sin; and in this we can see at a glance the fallacy of the whole legal system, and the utter delusion of seeking to produce holy living by putting souls under the law. It is simply putting them into the very place where sin can lord it over them, and rule them with absolute sway. How is it possible, then, to produce holiness by law? It is absolutely hopeless.

But let us turn, for a moment, to Romans 7: "Wherefore, my brethren, ye also"—and all true believers, all God's people—"are become *dead to the law* by the body of Christ; that ye should be married to another, even to Him who is raised from the dead, that we should bring forth fruit unto God." Now, it is perfectly plain that we cannot be "dead to the law" and "under the law" at the same time. It may perhaps be argued that the expression, "dead to the law" is merely a figure. Well, supposing it be so, we ask, A figure of what? Surely it cannot be a figure of persons under law. Nay, it is a figure of the very opposite.

And let us mark particularly, the apostle does not say the law is dead. Nothing of the kind. The law is not dead, but we are dead to it. We have passed, by the death of Christ, out of the sphere to which the law belongs. Christ took our place; He was made under the law; and, on the cross, He was made sin for us. But He died for us, and we died in Him; and He has thus taken us clean out of the position in which we were under the dominion of sin, and under law, and introduced us into an entirely new position, in living association and union with Himself, so that it can be said, "*As* He is, *so* are we in this world." Is He under law? Assuredly not. Well, neither are we. Has sin any claim upon Him? None whatever. Neither has it any upon us. We are, as to our standing, as He is in the presence of God; and therefore to put us back under law would be a complete overturning of the entire Christian position, and a most positive and flagrant contradiction of the very plainest statements of holy Scripture.

Now, we would, in all simplicity and godly sincerity, ask, How could holy living be promoted by removing the very foundation of Christianity? How could indwelling sin be subdued by putting us under the very system that gave sin power over us? How could true Christian obedience ever be produced by flying in the face of holy Scripture? We confess we cannot conceive any thing more thoroughly preposterous. Surely a divine end can only be gained by pursuing a divine way. Now, God's way of giving us deliverance from the dominion of sin is by delivering us from under law; and hence all those who teach that Christians are under law are plainly at issue with God. Tremendous consideration for all who desire to be teachers of the law!

But let us hear further words from the seventh chapter of Romans. The apostle goes on to say, "For *when we were in the flesh,* the motions of sins, which were by the law, did work in our members to bring forth fruit unto *death.* But now *we are delivered from the law,* being dead [or, having died] to that wherein we were held: *that we should serve* in newness of spirit, and not in the oldness of the letter."*

Here, again, all is as clear as a sunbeam. What means the expression, "When we *were* in the flesh"? Does it—can it mean that we *are* still in that condition? Clearly not. If I were to say, When I *was* in London, would any one understand that I am in London still? The thought is absurd.

But what does the apostle mean by the expression, "When we were in the flesh"? He simply refers to a thing of the past—to a condition that no longer obtains. Are believers, then, not in the flesh? So Scripture emphatically declares. But does this mean that they are not in the body? Assuredly not. They are in the body as to the fact of their existence, but not in the flesh as to the ground of their standing before God.

In chapter 8 we have the most distinct statement of this point. "So then they that are in the flesh cannot please God. *But ye are not in the flesh,* but in the Spirit, if so be that the Spirit of God dwell in you." Here we have the statement of a most solemn fact, and the setting forth of a most precious, glorious privilege. "They that are in the flesh *cannot please God.*" They may be very moral, very amiable, very religious, very benevolent; but they cannot please God. Their entire position is false. The source whence all the streams flow is corrupt; the root and stem whence all the branches emanate are rotten—hopelessly bad. They cannot produce a single atom of good fruit—fruit that God can accept. "They cannot please God." They must get into an entirely new position; they must have a new life, new motives, new objects—in a word, they must be a new creation. How solemn is all this! Let us weigh it thoroughly, and see if we understand the apostle's words.

But on the other hand, mark the glorious privilege of all true believers. *"Ye are not in the flesh."* Believers are no longer in a position in which they cannot please God. They have a new nature—a new life, every movement, every outflow, of which is agreeable to God. The very feeblest breathing of the divine life is precious to God. Of this life, the Holy Ghost is the power, Christ the object, glory the goal, heaven the home. All is divine, and therefore perfect. True, the believer is liable to err, prone in himself to wander, capable of sinning. In him (that is, in his flesh,) dwelleth no good thing. But his *standing* is based on the eternal stability of the grace of God, and his *state* is met by the divine provision which that grace has made for him in the precious atonement and all-prevailing advocacy of our Lord Jesus Christ. Thus he is forever delivered from that terrible system in which the prominent figures are, "Flesh," "Law," "Sin," "Death"—melancholy group, most surely!—and he is brought into that glorious scene in which the prominent figures are, "Life," "Liberty," "Grace," "Peace," "Righteousness," "Holiness," "Glory," "Christ." "For *ye are not come* to the mount that might be touched" —that is, the palpable mount—"and that burned with fire, nor unto blackness, and darkness, and tempest, and the sound of a trumpet, and the voice of words; which voice they that heard, entreated that the word should not be spoken to them any more: (For they could not endure that which was commanded, 'And if so much as a beast touch the mountain, it shall be stoned,

*The rendering of Romans 7:6 in our authorized version is manifestly erroneous, inasmuch as it teaches that the law is dead, which is not true. "The law is good, if a man use it lawfully" (1 Tim. 1). And again, "The law is holy" (Rom. 7). Scripture never teaches that the law is dead, but it teaches that the believer is dead to the law—a totally different thing.

But further, ἀποθανοντες cannot possibly apply to the law, as any well-taught school-boy can see at a glance; it applies to us—believers. Were it the law, the word would be ἀποθανοντος.

or thrust through with a dart:' and so terrible was the sight, that Moses said, 'I exceedingly fear and quake:') but *ye are come* unto Mount Sion, and unto the city of the living God, the heavenly Jerusalem, and to an innumerable company of angels, the general assembly, the church of the first-born [ones] which are written in heaven, and to God the Judge of all, and to the spirits of just men made perfect, and to Jesus the Mediator of the new covenant, and to the blood of sprinkling, that speaketh better things than Abel" (Heb. 12).

Thus we have endeavored to meet the difficulty of any conscientious reader who up to the moment in which he opened this volume had cherished the conviction that it is only by putting believers under the law that practical holiness and true obedience can be attained. We trust he has followed us through the line of Scripture evidence which we have laid before him. If so, he will see that to place believers in such a position is to do away with the very foundations of Christianity—to abandon grace—to give up Christ —to go back to the flesh, in which we cannot please God, and to place ourselves under the curse. In short, the legal system of men is diametrically opposed to the teaching of the entire New Testament. It was against this system and its upholders that the blessed apostle Paul, during his whole life, ever testified. He absolutely abhorred it, and continually denounced it. The law-teachers were ever seeking to sap and undermine his blessed labors, and subvert the souls of his beloved children in the faith. It is impossible to read his burning sentences in the Epistle to the Galatians, his withering references in his Epistle to the Philippians, or his solemn warnings in the Epistle to the Hebrews, and not see how intense was his abhorrence of the whole legal system of the law-teachers, and how bitterly he wept over the ruins of the testimony so dear to his large, loving, devoted heart.

But it is possible that after all we have written, and notwithstanding the full tide of Scripture evidence to which we have called the reader's attention, he may still feel disposed to ask, Is there not a danger of unholy laxity and levity if the restraining power of the law be removed? To this we reply, God is wiser than we are. He knows best how to cure laxity and levity, and how to produce the right sort of obedience. He tried the law, and what did it do? It worked wrath; it caused the offense to abound; it developed "the motions of sins"; it brought in death; it was the strength of sin; it deprived the sinner of all power; it slew him; it was condemnation; it cursed all who had to do with it—"As many as are of the works of the law are under the curse"; and all this, not because of any defect in the law, but because of man's total inability to keep it.

Is it not plain that neither life nor righteousness nor holiness nor true Christian obedience could ever be attained under law? Is it possible, after all that has passed in review before us, that he can have a single question, a single doubt, a single difficulty? We trust not. No one who is willing to bow down to the teaching and authority of the New Testament can adhere to the legal system for one hour.

However, ere we turn from this weighty and all-important subject, we shall place before the reader a passage or two of Scripture in which the moral glories of Christianity shine forth with peculiar lustre, in vivid contrast to the entire Mosaic economy.

First of all, let us take that familiar passage at the opening of the eighth of Romans, "There is therefore now *no condemnation* to them which are *in Christ Jesus.* For the law of the spirit of life in Christ Jesus *hath made me free* from the law of sin and death. For what the law could not do, in that it was weak through the flesh, God sending His own Son *in the likeness* of sinful flesh, and for sin, condemned sin in the flesh; that the righteousness [δικαιωμα] of the law might be fulfilled in us, who walk not after the flesh, but after the Spirit" (ver. 1-4).

Now, we must bear in mind that verse 1 sets forth the *standing* of every Christian—his *position* before God. He is "in Christ Jesus." This settles every thing. He is not in the flesh; he is not under law; he is absolutely and eternally "in Christ Jesus." Hence there is, there can be, no condemnation. The apostle is not speaking of or referring to our *walk* or our *state*. If he were, he could not possibly speak of "no condemnation." The most perfect Christian walk that ever was exhibited, the most perfect Christian state that ever was attained, would afford some ground for judgment and condemnation. There is not a Christian on the face of the earth who has not daily to judge his state and his walk—his moral condition and his practical ways. How, then, could "no condemnation" ever stand connected with, or be based upon, Christian walk? Utterly impossible. In order to be free from all condemnation, we must have what is divinely perfect, and no Christian walk is or ever was that. Even a Paul had to withdraw his words (Acts 23:5). He repented of having written a letter (2 Cor. 7:8). A perfect walk and a perfect state were only found in One. In all beside—even the holiest and best, failure is found.

Hence, therefore, the second clause of Romans 8:1 must be rejected: it is not Scripture. This, we think, would be seen by any one really taught of God, apart from all question of mere criticism. Any spiritual mind would detect the incongruity between the words "no condemnation" and "walk." The two things cannot be made to harmonize. And here, we doubt not, is just where thousands of pious souls have been plunged into difficulty as to this really magnificent and emancipating passage. The joyful sound, "No condemnation," has been robbed of its deep, full, and blessed significance by a clause introduced by some scribe or copyist whose feeble vision was doubtless dazzled by the brightness of that free, absolute, sovereign grace which shines in the opening statement of the chapter. How often have we heard such words as these: "Oh, yes; I know there is no condemnation to them that are in Christ Jesus; but that is if they walk not after the flesh, but after the Spirit. Now, I cannot say that I walk thus. I long to do so, and I mourn over my failure. I would give worlds to be able to walk more perfectly; but, alas! I have to judge myself—my state, my walk, my ways—each day, each hour. This being so, I dare not apply to myself the precious words, 'no condemnation.' I hope to be able to do so some day, when I have made more progress in personal holiness; but in my present state, I should deem it the very height of presumption to appropriate to myself the precious truth contained in the first clause of Romans 8."

Such thoughts as these have passed through the minds of most of us, if they have not been clothed in words. But the simple and conclusive answer to all such legal reasonings is found in the fact that the second clause of Romans 8:1 is not Scripture at all, but a very misleading interpolation, foreign to the spirit and genius of Christianity, opposed to the whole line of argument in the context where it occurs, and utterly subversive of the solid peace of the Christian. It is a fact well known to all who are conversant with Biblical criticism, that all the leading authorities are agreed in rejecting the second clause of Romans 8:1.* And in this, it is simply a matter of criticism confirming, as all sound criticism must do, the conclusion at which a really spiritual mind would arrive without any knowledge of criticism at all.

But in addition to all that has been advanced in reference to this question, we can-

*It may be that the reader feels a little jealous of any interference with our excellent English Bible. He may, like many others, feel disposed to say, "How is an uneducated man to know what is Scripture and what is not? Must he depend upon scholars and critics to give him certainty on so grave and important a question? If so, is it not the same old story of looking to human authority to confirm the Word of God?" By no means. It is a totally different thing. We all know that all copies and translations must be, in some points, imperfect, as being human; but we believe that the same grace which gave the Word in the original Hebrew and Greek languages, has most marvelously watched over our English translation, so that a poor man, at the back of a mountain, may rest assured that he possesses in his common English Bible the revelation of the mind of God. It is wonderful, after all the labors of scholars and critics, how few passages, comparatively, have had to be touched; and not one affecting any foundation-doctrine of Christianity. God, who graciously gave us the holy Scriptures at the first, has watched over them and preserved them to His Church in a most wonderful manner. Moreover, He has seen fit to make use of the labors of scholars and critics, from age to age, to clear the sacred text of errors which, through the infirmity attaching to all human agency, had crept into it. Should these corrections shake our confidence in the integrity of Scripture as a whole? or lead us to doubt that we possess, in very deed, the Word of God? Nay, rather should they lead us to bless God for His goodness in watching over His Word in order to preserve it in its integrity for His Church.

not but think that the occurrence of the clause, "who walk not after the flesh, but after the Spirit," in verse 4, affords abundant evidence of its misplacement in verse 1. We cannot, for a moment, admit the thought of redundancy in holy Scripture. Now, in verse 4 it *is* a question of walk—a question of our fulfilling "the righteousness [mark the word—*δικαιωμα*] of the law," and hence the clause is in its right, because divinely fitted, place. A person who walks in the Spirit—as every Christian ought—fulfills the righteousness of the law. Love is the fulfilling of the law; and love will lead us to do what the ten commandments could never effect, namely, to love our enemies. No lover of holiness, no advocate of practical righteousness, need ever be the least afraid of losing aught by abandoning the legal ground, and taking his place on the elevated platform of true Christianity—by turning from Mount Sinai to Mount Zion—by passing from Moses to Christ. No; he only reaches a higher source, a deeper spring, a wider sphere of holiness, righteousness, and practical obedience.

And then, if any one should feel disposed to ask, Does not the line of argument which we have been pursuing tend to rob the law of its characteristic glory? We reply, Most assuredly not. So far from this, the law was never so magnified, never so vindicated, never so established, never so glorified, as by that precious work which forms the imperishable foundation of all the privileges, the blessings, the dignities, and the glories of Christianity. The blessed apostle anticipates and answers this very question in the earlier part of his Epistle to the Romans. "Do we then," he says, "make void the law through faith? Far be the thought; yea, we establish the law." How could the law be more gloriously vindicated, honored, and magnified than in the life and death of the Lord Jesus Christ? Will any one seek, for a moment, to maintain the extravagant notion that it is magnifying the law to put Christians under it? We fondly trust the reader will not. Ah! no; all this line of things must be completely abandoned by those whose privilege it is to walk in the light of the new creation; who know Christ as their life and Christ as their righteousness, Christ their sanctification, Christ their great exemplar, Christ their model, Christ their all and in all; who find their motive for obedience, not in the fear of the curses of a broken law, but in the love of Christ, according to those exquisitely beautiful words, "The love of Christ"—not the law of Moses—"constraineth us; because we thus judge, that if one died for all, then were all dead. And He died for all, that they which live should not henceforth live unto themselves, but unto Him which died for them and rose again" (2 Cor. 5).

Could the law ever produce aught like this? Impossible. But, blessed forever be the God of all grace, "what the law could not do," not because it was not holy, just, and good, but "in that it was weak through the flesh"—the workman was all right, but the material was rotten, and nothing could be made of it; but "God sending His own Son in the likeness of sinful flesh, and for sin, condemned sin in the flesh, that the righteousness of the law might be fulfilled in us, who," as risen with Christ, linked with Him by the Holy Ghost, in the power of a new and everlasting life, "walk not after the flesh, but after the Spirit."

This, and only this, is true, practical Christianity; and if the reader will turn to the second of Galatians, he will find another of those fine, glowing utterances of the blessed apostle, setting forth, with divine force and fullness, the special glory of Christian life and walk. It is in connection with his faithful rebuke of the apostle Peter at Antioch, when that beloved and honored servant of Christ, through his characteristic weakness, had been led to step down, for a moment, from the elevated moral ground on which the gospel of the grace of God places the soul. We cannot do better than quote the entire paragraph: every sentence of it is pregnant with spiritual power.

"But when Peter was come to Antioch, I withstood him *to the face.*" He did not go behind his back, to disparage and depreciate him in the view of others, even though "he was to be blamed. For before that certain came from James, he did eat with the Gentiles; but when they were come, he withdrew and separated himself, fearing them which were of the circumcision. And the other Jews dissembled likewise with him, insomuch that Barnabas also was carried away with their dissimulation. But when I saw that they walked not uprightly according to the truth of the gospel, I said unto Peter before them all, If thou, being a Jew, livest after the manner of Gentiles, and not as do the Jews, why compellest thou the Gentiles to live as do the Jews? We who are Jews by nature, and not sinners of the Gentiles, knowing that a man is not justified by works of law, but by the faith of Jesus Christ, even we have believed in Jesus Christ, that we might be justified by the faith of Christ, and not by works of law; for by works of law shall no flesh be justified. But if, while we seek to be justified by Christ, we ourselves also are found sinners, is therefore Christ the minister of sin? God forbid [or, Far be the thought—*μη γενοιτο*.]. For if I build again the things which I destroyed, I make myself a transgressor." For if the things were right, why destroy them? and if they were wrong, why build them again? "For I, through law, am *dead to law,* that I might live unto God. I am crucified with Christ: nevertheless I live; yet not I, but Christ liveth in me; and the life which I now live in the flesh, I live [not by the law, as a rule of life, but] by the faith of the Son of God, *who loved me,* and gave *Himself for me.* I do not frustrate the grace of God; for if righteousness come by law, then Christ is dead in vain [or, has died for nothing—*δωρεαν*.]" (Gal. 2:11-21).

Here, then, we have one of the very finest statements of the truth as to practical Christianity any where to be found. But what specially claims our attention just now is, the very marked and beautiful way in which the gospel of God opens up the path of the true believer between the two fatal errors of legality on the one side and carnal laxity on the other. Verse 19, in the passage just quoted, contains the divine remedy for both these deadly evils. To all—whoever or wherever they are—who would seek to put the Christian under the law, in any shape or for any object whatsoever, our apostle exclaims, in the ears of dissembling Jews, with Peter at their head, and as an answer to all the law-teachers of every age, *"I am dead to law."*

What can the law have to say to a dead man? Nothing. The law applies to a living man, to curse him and kill him because he has not kept it. It is a very grave mistake indeed to teach that the law is dead or abolished. It is nothing of the sort. It is alive in all its force, in all its stringency, in all its majesty, in all its unbending dignity. It would be a very serious mistake to say that the law of England against murder is dead; but if a man is dead, the law no longer applies to him, inasmuch as he has passed entirely out of its range.

But how is the believer dead to law? The apostle replies, "I through law am dead to law." The law had brought the sentence of death into his conscience, as we read in Romans 7, "I was alive without the law once; but when the commandment came, sin revived and I died. And the commandment, which was ordained to life, I found to be unto death. For sin, taking occasion by the commandment, deceived me, and by it slew me."

But there is more than this. The apostle goes on to say, "I am crucified with Christ: nevertheless I live; yet not I, but Christ liveth in me." And here is the triumphant answer of the Christian to those who say that inasmuch as the Mosaic law is abrogated, there is no longer any demand for the legal restraint under which the Jews were called to live. To all who would seek liberty for self-indulgence, the answer is, "I am dead to law, [not that I might give a loose rein to the flesh, but] that I might live unto God."

Thus nothing can be more complete, nothing more morally beautiful, than the answer of true Christianity to legality on the one hand and licentiousness on the other. Self crucified; sin condemned; new life in Christ; a life to be lived to God; a life of faith in the Son of God; the motive-spring of that life, the constraining love of Christ—what can exceed this? Will any one, in view of the moral glories of Christianity, contend for putting believers under the law, putting them back into the flesh—back into the old creation—back to the sentence of death in the conscience—back to bondage, darkness, distance, fear of death, condemnation?

Is it possible that any one who has ever tasted, even in the very feeblest measure, the heavenly sweetness of God's most blessed gospel, can accept the wretched mongrel system, composed of half law and half grace, which christendom offers to the soul? How terrible to find the children of God—members of the body of Christ—temples of the Holy Ghost—robbed of their glorious privileges, and burdened with a heavy yoke, which, as Peter says, "neither our fathers nor we were able to bear." We earnestly entreat the Christian reader to consider what has been placed before him. Search the Scriptures; and if you find these things to be so, then fling aside forever the grave-clothes in which christendom inwraps its deluded votaries, and walk in the liberty wherewith Christ makes His people free; tear off the bandage with which it covers the eyes of men, and gaze on the moral glories which shine with such heavenly brilliancy in the gospel of the grace of God.

And then let us prove, by a holy, happy, gracious walk and conversation, that grace can do what law never could. Let our practical ways from day to day, in the midst of the scenes, circumstances, relationships, and associations in which we are called to live, be the most convincing reply to all who contend for the law as a rule of life.

Finally, let it be our earnest, loving desire and aim to seek, insofar as in us lies, to lead all the dear children of God into a clearer knowledge of their standing and privileges in a risen and glorified Christ. May the Lord send out His light and His truth, in the power of the Holy Ghost, and gather His beloved people around Himself, to walk in the joy of His salvation, in the purity and light of His presence, and to wait for His coming.

We do not attempt to offer any apology for what may perhaps appear to some of our readers to be a very lengthened digression from the fourth chapter of Deuteronomy. The fact is, we have been led into what we judge to be a very needed line of practical truth by the very first verse of the chapter, as quoted at the opening of this section. We felt it absolutely necessary, in speaking of the weighty question of obedience, to seek to place it on its true basis. If Israel was called to "hearken and do," how much more are we, who are so richly blessed—yea, "blessed with *all* spiritual blessings in the heavenlies in Christ Jesus." We are called to obedience, even to the obedience of Jesus Christ, as we have it in 1 Peter 1, "Elect according to the foreknowledge of God the Father, through sanctification of the Spirit, unto obedience and sprinkling of the blood of Jesus Christ." We are called to the very same character of obedience as that which marked the life of our blessed Lord Jesus Christ Himself. Of course, in Him there was no hindering influence as, alas! there is in us; but as to the character of the obedience, it is the same.

This is an immense privilege. We are called to walk in the footsteps of Jesus. "He that saith he abideth in Him ought himself also so to walk even as He walked." Now, in pondering the path of our Lord, in considering His marvelous life, there is one point which demands our profound and reverent attention—a point which connects itself, in a very special manner, with the book of Deuteronomy—and that is, the way in which He ever used the Word of God—the place which He ever gave to the holy Scriptures. This we consider to be a subject of the last possible importance at the present moment. It holds a prominent place throughout the lovely book with which we are at present engaged. Indeed, as we have already remarked, it characterizes the book, and marks it off from the three books which precede it in the divine canon. We shall find proofs and illustrations of this in abundance as we pass along. Every where, the Word of God gets its own paramount place, as the only rule, the only standard, the only authority, for man. It meets him in every position, in every relationship, in every sphere of action, and in every stage of his moral and spiritual history. It tells him what he ought to do, and what he ought not. It furnishes him with ample guidance in every difficulty. It descends, as we shall see, to the most minute details—such details, indeed, as fill us with amazement to think that the High and Mighty One that inhabiteth eternity could occupy Himself with them—to think that the Omnipotent Creator and Sustainer of the vast universe could stoop to legislate about a bird's nest (chap. 22:6).

Such is the Word of God—that peerless revelation—that perfect and inimitable volume which stands alone in the history of literature. And we may say that one special charm of the book of Deuteronomy—one peculiar feature of interest is, the way in which it exalts the Word of God, and enforces upon us the holy and happy duty of unqualified and unhesitating obedience.

Yes; we repeat and would fervently emphasize the words—unqualified and unhesitating obedience. We would have these wholesome words sounded in the ears of Christian professors throughout the length and breadth of the earth. We live in a day specially marked by the setting up of man's reason, man's judgment, man's will; in short, we live in what the inspired apostle calls "man's day." On all hands we are encountered by lofty and boastful words about human reason, and the right of every man to judge and reason and think for himself. The thought of being absolutely and completely governed by the authority of holy Scripture is treated with sovereign contempt by thousands of men who are the religious guides and teachers of the professing church. For any one to assert his reverent belief in the plenary inspiration, the all-sufficiency, and the absolute authority of Scripture, is quite sufficient to stamp him as an ignorant, narrow-minded man, if not a semi-lunatic, in the judgment of some who occupy the very highest position in the professing church. In our universities, our colleges, and our schools, the moral glory of the divine volume is fast fading away, and instead thereof our young people are led and taught to walk in the light of science—the light of human reason. The Word of God itself is impiously placed at the bar of man's judgment, and reduced to the level of the human understanding. Every thing is rejected which soars beyond man's feeble vision.

Thus the Word of God is virtually set aside. For, clearly, if Scripture is to be submitted to human judgment, it ceases to be the Word of God. It is the very height of folly to think of submitting a divine and therefore perfect revelation to any tribunal whatsoever. Either God has given us a revelation or He has not. If He has, that revelation must be paramount, supreme, above and beyond all question, absolutely unquestionable, unerring, divine. To its authority all must bow down, without a single question. To suppose for a moment that man is competent to judge the Word of God, able to pronounce upon what is or what is not worthy of God to say or to write, is simply to put man in God's place. And this is precisely what the devil is aiming at, although many of his instruments are not aware that they are helping on his designs.

But the question is continually cropping up before us, "How can we be sure that we have, in our English Bible, the *bona-fide* revelation of God?" We reply, God can make us sure of it. If He does not, no one can; if He does, no one need. This is our ground, and we deem it unassailable. We should like to ask all those who start this infidel question (for such we must honestly call it), Supposing that God cannot give us the absolute certainty that, in our common English Bible, we do actually possess His own most precious, priceless revelation, then whither are we to turn? Of course, in such a weighty matter, on which momentous and eternal consequences hang, a single doubt is torture and misery. If I am not sure of possessing a revelation from God, I am left without a single ray of light for my path; I am plunged in darkness, gloom, and mental misery. What am I to do? Can man help me by his learning, his wisdom, or his reason? Can he satisfy my soul by his decision? Can he solve my difficulty, answer my question, remove my doubt, dissipate my fear? Is man better able than God to give me the assurance that God has spoken?

The idea is absolutely monstrous—monstrous in the very highest degree. The plain fact is this: If God cannot give us the certainty that He has spoken, we are left without His Word altogether. If we must turn to human authority, call it what you please, in order to guarantee the Word of God to our souls, then that authority is higher and greater, safer and more trustworthy, than the Word which it guarantees. Blessed be God, it is not so. He has spoken to our hearts. He has given us His Word, and that Word carries its own credentials with it. It stands in no need of letters of commendation from a human hand. What! turn to man to accredit the Word of the living God! —apply to a worm to give us the assurance that our God has spoken to us in His Word! Away forever with the blasphemous notion, and let our whole moral being—all our ransomed powers adore the matchless grace, the sovereign mercy, that has not left us to grope in the darkness of our own minds, or to be bewildered by the conflicting opinions of men; but has given us His own perfect and most precious revelation, the divine light of His Word, to guide our feet into the path of certainty and peace, to enlighten our understandings and comfort our hearts, to preserve us from every form of doctrinal error and moral pravity, and finally, to conduct us into the rest, blessedness, and glory of His own heavenly kingdom. All praise to His name throughout the everlasting ages!

But we must bear in mind that the marvelous privilege of which we have spoken—and truly it is most marvelous—is the basis of a most solemn responsibility. If it be true that God has, in His infinite goodness, given us a perfect revelation of His mind, then what should be our attitude in reference to it? Are we to sit in judgment upon it? Are we to discuss, argue, or reason? Alas! for all who do so. They will find themselves on terribly dangerous ground. The only true, the only proper, the only safe attitude for man in the presence of God's revelation is, obedience—simple, unqualified, hearty obedience. This is the only right thing for us, and this is the thing which is pleasing to God. The path of obedience is the path of sweetest privilege, rest, and blessing. This path can be trodden by the merest babe in Christ, as well as by the "young men" and the "fathers." There is the one straight and blessed path for all. Narrow it is, no doubt; but, oh! it is safe, bright, and elevated. The light of our Father's approving countenance ever shines upon it; and in this blessed light the obedient soul finds the most triumphant answer to all the reproaches of those who talk, in high-sounding words, about breadth of mind, liberality of thought, freedom of opinion, progress, development, and such like. The obedient child of God can afford to put up with all this, because he feels and knows, he believes and is sure, that he is treading a path indicated for him by the precious Word of God. He is not careful to explain or apologize, feeling assured that those who object, oppose, and reproach are utterly incapable of understanding or appreciating his explanation. And, moreover, he feels that it is no part of his duty to explain or defend. He has but to obey; and as for objectors and opposers, he has but to refer them to his Master.

This makes it all so simple, so plain, so certain. It delivers the heart from a thousand difficulties and perplexities. If we were to set about replying to all who undertake to raise questions or start difficulties, our whole life would be spent in the profitless task. We may rest assured the best possible answer to all infidel objectors is, the steady, earnest, onward path of unqualified obedience. Let us leave infidels, skeptics, and rationalists to their own worthless theories, while we, with unswerving purpose and firm step, pursue that blessed path of childlike obedience which, like the shining light, shineth more and more unto the perfect day. Thus shall our minds be kept tranquil, for the peace of God, which passeth all understanding, shall garrison our hearts and minds through Christ Jesus. When the Word of God, which is settled forever in heaven, is hidden deep down in our hearts, there will be a calm certainty, a holy stability, and a marked progress in our Christian career, which will afford the best possible answer to the gainsayer, the most effectual testimony to the truth of God, and the most convincing evidence and solid confirmation to every wavering heart.

The chapter before us abounds in the

most solemn exhortation to Israel, grounded upon the fact of their having heard the word of God. Thus in the second verse we have a sentence or two which should be deeply engraved on the tablets of every Christian's heart. "Ye shall not add unto the word which I command you, neither shall ye diminish aught from it."

These words involve two grand facts with regard to the Word of God. It is not to be added to, for the simplest of all reasons, because there is nothing lacking; it is not to be diminished, because there is nothing superfluous. Every thing we want is there, and nothing that is there can be done without. "Add thou not unto His words, lest He reprove thee, and thou be found a liar." To suppose that aught can be added to God's Word is, upon the very face of it, to deny that it is God's Word; and, on the other hand, if we admit that it is the Word of God, then it follows of necessity (blessed necessity!) that we could not afford to do without a single sentence of it. There would be a blank in the volume which no human hand could fill up, if a single clause were dropped from its place in the canon. We have all we want, and hence we must not add: we want it all, and hence we must not diminish.

How deeply important is all this, in this day of human tampering with the Word of God! How blessed to know that we have in our possession a book so divinely perfect that not a sentence, not a clause, not a word, can be added to it. We speak not, of course, of translations or versions, but of the Scriptures as originally given of God—His own perfect revelation. To this, not a touch can be given. As well might a human finger have dared to touch the creation of God, on the morning when all the sons of God sang together, as to add a jot or a tittle to the inspired Word of God. And on the other hand, to take away a jot or a tittle from it, is to say that the Holy Ghost has penned what was unnecessary. Thus the holy volume is divinely guarded at both ends. It is securely fenced round about, so that no rude hand should touch its sacred contents.

What! it may be said in reply, do you mean to say that every sentence, from the opening lines of Genesis to the close of Revelation, is divinely inspired? Yes; that is precisely the ground we take. We claim for every line between the covers of the volume a divine origin. To question that is to attack the very pillars of the Christian faith. A single flaw in the canon would be sufficient to prove it not of God. To touch a single stone in the arch is to bring down the whole fabric in ruins around us. "All Scripture is divinely inspired, and" being so, must be "profitable for doctrine, for reproof, for correction, for instruction in righteousness; that the man of God may be perfect [*αρτιος*], throughly furnished unto all good works" (2 Tim. 3).

This stronghold must on no account be surrendered; nay, it must be tenaciously held, in the face of every infidel assault. If it be given up, all is hopelessly lost—we have nothing to lean upon. Either the Word of God is perfect, or we are left without any divine foundation for our faith. If there be a word too much or a word too little in the revelation which God has given us, then verily we are left, like a ship without compass, rudder, or chart, to be drifted about on the wild, tumultuous ocean of infidel thought; in short, if we have not an absolutely perfect revelation, we are of all men most miserable.

But we may still be challenged with such a question as this: Do you believe that the long string of names in the opening chapters of 1 Chronicles—those genealogical tables—are divinely inspired? were they written for our learning? and if so, what are we to learn from them? We unhesitatingly declare our reverent belief in the divine inspiration of all these; and we have no doubt whatever but that their value, interest, and importance will be fully proved by and by in the history of that people to whom they specially apply.

And then, as to what we are to learn from those genealogical records, we believe they teach us a most precious lesson as to Jehovah's faithful care of His people Israel, and His loving interest in them and in all that concerns them. He watches over them from generation to generation, even though they are scattered and lost to human view. He knows all about "the twelve tribes," and He will manifest them in due time, and plant them in their destined inheritance, in the land of Canaan, according to His promise to Abraham, Isaac, and Jacob.

Now, is not all this full of blessed instruction for us? Is it not full of comfort for our souls? Is it not most confirmatory of our faith to mark the gracious pains-taking of our God, His minute care and vigilance in reference to His earthly people? Most assuredly it is. And ought not our hearts to be interested in all that interests the heart of our Father? Are we not to take an interest in any thing save what directly concerns ourselves? Where is there a loving child who would not take an interest in all his father's concerns, and delight to read every line that drops from his father's pen?

Let us not be misunderstood. We do not, by any means, attempt to imply that all portions of the Word of God are of like interest and importance to us. We do not presume to assert that we are to hang with equal interest over the first chapter of 1 Chronicles and the seventeenth chapter of John or the eighth chapter of Romans. It seems hardly necessary to make such a statement, inasmuch as no such question is raised. But what we assert is that each of the above Scriptures is divinely inspired, one just as much as another; and not only so, but we further assert that 1 Chronicles 1 and such like passages fill a niche which John 17 cannot fill, and do a work which Romans 8 cannot do.

And finally, above and beyond all, we must remember that we are not competent to judge what is and what is not worthy of a place in the inspired canon. We are ignorant and short-sighted; and the very portion which we might deem beneath the dignity of inspiration may have some very important bearing upon the history of God's ways with the world at large or with His people in particular.

In short, it simply resolves itself into this with every truly pious soul—every really spiritual mind: We reverently believe in the divine inspiration of every line of our precious Bible, from beginning to end; and we believe this not on the ground of any human authority whatsoever. To believe in holy Scripture because it comes to us accredited by any authority upon earth, would be to set that authority above holy Scripture, inasmuch as that which guarantees has more weight—more value than the thing guaranteed. Hence, we should no more think of looking to human authority to confirm the Word of God than we should of bringing out a rush-light to prove that the sun was shining.

No; we must be clear and decided as to this. It must be, in the judgment of our souls, a great cardinal truth which we hold dearer than life itself—the plenary inspiration of holy Scripture. Thus shall we have wherewithal to answer the cool audacity of modern skepticism, rationalism, and infidelity. We do not mean to say that we shall be able to convince infidels. God will deal with them in His own way, and convince them with His own unanswerable arguments in His own time. It is labor and time lost to argue with such men. But we feel persuaded that the most dignified and effective answer to infidelity, in its every phase, will be found in the calm repose of the heart that rests in the blessed assurance that "all Scripture is given by inspiration of God"; and again, "Whatsoever things were written aforetime were written for our learning; that we through patience and comfort of the Scriptures might have hope." The former of these precious quotations proves that Scripture has come from God; the latter, that it has come to us. Both together go to prove that we must neither add to nor take from the Word of God. There is nothing lacking, and nothing superfluous. The Lord be praised for this solid foundation-truth, and for all the comfort and consolation that flows from it to every true believer!

We shall now proceed to quote a few of the passages in this fourth chapter of Deuteronomy which so emphatically set forth the value, importance, and authority of the Word of God. In them, as in the whole of this book, we shall see that it is not so much a question of any particular ordinance, rite, or ceremony, but of the weight, solemnity, and dignity of the Word of God itself, whatever that Word may set before us.

"Behold, I have taught you statutes and judgments, even as the Lord my God commanded me, that ye should do so in the land whither ye go to possess it." Their conduct was to be ruled and formed, in all things, by the divine commandments. Immense principle for them, for us, for all! "Keep, therefore, and *do* them; for *this is your wisdom* and *your understanding* in the sight of the nations, which shall hear all these statutes, and say, Surely this great nation is a wise and understanding people."

Let us specially weigh these words. Their wisdom and their understanding were to consist in their simply keeping and doing the divine statutes and judgments. It was not by learned discussion or arguments that their wisdom was to be displayed, but by childlike, unquestioning obedience. All the wisdom was in the statutes and judgments, not in their thoughts and reasonings respecting them. The profound and marvelous wisdom of God was seen in His Word, and this was what the nations were to see and admire. The light of the divine judgments shining in the conduct and character of the people of God was to draw forth the admiring testimony of the nations around.

Alas! how differently it turned out! How little did the nations of the earth learn, from the actings of Israel, about God and His Word! Yea, His name was blasphemed continually through their ways. Instead of occupying the high and holy and happy ground of loving obedience to the divine commandments, they descended to the level of the nations around them—adopted their habits, worshiped their gods, and walked in their ways; so that those nations, instead of seeing the lofty wisdom, purity, and moral glory of the divine statutes, saw only the weakness, folly, and moral degradation of a people who made their boast in being the depositary of those oracles which condemned themselves (Rom. 2—3).

Still, blessed be God, His Word must stand forever, however His people may fail to carry it out. His standard is perfect, and therefore must never be lowered; and if the power of His Word be not seen in the ways of His people, it will shine in the condemnation of those ways, and ever abide for the guidance, comfort, strength, and blessing of any who desire, however feebly or falteringly, to tread the path of obedience.

However, in the chapter with which we are at present occupied, the lawgiver seeks to set the divine standard faithfully before the people, in all its dignity and moral glory. He fails not to unfold to them the true effect of obedience, while he solemnly warns them against the danger of turning away from the holy commandments of God. Hear his powerful pleadings with their hearts. "What nation is there so great," he says, "who hath God so nigh unto them, as the Lord our God is in all things that we call upon Him for? And what nation is there so great, that hath statutes and judgments so righteous as all this law, which I set before you this day?"

Here is true moral greatness, at all times and in all places, for a nation, for a people, for a household, or for an individual. To have the living God nigh unto us; to have the sweet privilege of calling upon Him, in all things; to have His power and His mercy ever exercised toward us; to have the light of His blessed countenance shining approvingly upon us, in all our ways; to have the moral effect of His righteous statutes and holy commandments seen in our practical career, from day to day; to have Him manifesting Himself to us, and making His abode with us.

What human language can adequately set forth the deep blessedness of such privileges as these? and yet they are placed, by infinite grace, within the reach of every child of God on the face of the earth. We do not mean to assert that every child of God enjoys them. Far from it. They are reserved, as we have already seen, for those who, through grace, are enabled to render a loving, hearty, reverent obedience to the divine word. Here lies the precious secret of the whole matter. It was true for Israel of old, and it is true for the Church now—it was true for the individual soul then, and it is true for the individual soul now, that divine complacency is the priceless reward of human obedience. And we may further add that obedience is the bounden duty and high privilege of all God's people, and of each in particular. Come what may, implicit obedience is our privilege and our duty, divine complacency our present sweet reward.

But the poor human heart is prone to wander, and manifold influences are at work around us to draw us off from the narrow path of obedience. We need not marvel, therefore, at the solemn and oft-repeated admonitions addressed by Moses to the hearts and consciences of his hearers. He pours his large, loving heart out to the congregation so dear to him, in glowing, earnest, soul-stirring accents. "Only take heed to thyself," he says, "and keep thy soul diligently, lest thou forget the things which thine eyes have seen, and lest they depart from thy heart all the days of thy life; but teach them thy sons, and thy sons' sons."

These are weighty words for all of us. They set before us two things of unspeakable importance, namely, individual and domestic responsibility—personal and household testimony. God's people of old were responsible to keep the heart with all diligence, lest it should let slip the precious Word of God. And not only so, but they were solemnly responsible to instruct their children and their grandchildren in the same. Are we, with all our light and privilege, less responsible than Israel of old? Surely not. We are imperatively called upon to give ourselves to the careful study of the Word of God—to apply our hearts to it. It is not enough that we hurry over a few verses or a chapter, as a piece of daily religious routine. This will not meet the case at all. We want to make the Bible our supreme and absorbing study—that in which we delight—in which we find our refreshment and recreation.

It is to be feared that some of us read the Bible as a matter of duty, while we find our delight and refreshment in the newspaper and light literature. Need we wonder at our shallow knowledge of Scripture? How could we know aught of the living depths or the moral glories of a volume which we merely take up as a cold matter of duty, and read a few verses with a yawning indifference, while, at the same time, the newspaper or the sensational novel is literally devoured?

It will perhaps be said, in reply, We cannot be always reading the Bible. Would those who thus speak say, We cannot be always reading the newspaper or the novel? And, we would further inquire, what must be the actual state of a person who can say, "We cannot be always reading the Bible"? Can he be in a healthy condition of soul? Can he really love the Word of God? Can he have any just sense of its preciousness, its excellence, its moral glories? Impossible.

What mean the following words to Israel: "Therefore shall ye lay up these My words *in your heart* and *in your soul,* and bind them for a sign upon *your hand,* that they may be as frontlets between *your eyes*"? The "heart," and "soul," the "hand," the "eyes" —all engaged about the precious Word of God. This was real work. It was to be no empty formality, no barren routine. The whole man was to be given up, in holy devotion, to the statutes and judgments of God.

"And ye shall teach them your children, speaking of them when thou sittest in thine house, and when thou walkest by the way, when thou liest down, and when thou risest up. And thou shalt write them upon the door-posts of thine house, and upon thy gates." Do we, Christians, enter into such words as these? Has the Word of God such a place in our hearts, in our homes, and in our habits? Do those who enter our houses, or come in contact with us in daily life, see that the Word of God is paramount with us? Do those with whom we do business see that we are governed by the precepts of holy Scripture? Do our servants and our children see that we live in the very atmosphere of Scripture, and that our whole character is formed and our conduct governed by it?

These are searching questions for our hearts, beloved Christian reader. Let us not put them away from us. We may rest assured there is no more correct indicator of our moral and spiritual condition than that afforded by our treatment of the Word of God. If we do not love it—love to study it—thirst after it—delight in it—long for the quiet hour in the which we can hang over its sacred page and drink in its most precious teaching—meditate upon it, in the closet, in the family, in the street; in short, if we do not breathe its holy atmosphere—if we could ever give utterance to such a sentiment as that given above, that "we cannot be always reading the Bible," then, verily, we have urgent need to look well to our spiritual state, for we are sadly out of health. The new nature loves the Word of God—earnestly desires it, as we read in 1 Peter 2, "As new-born babes, desire the sincere milk of the Word, that ye may grow thereby."

This is the true idea. If the sincere milk of the Word be not sought after, diligently used and eagerly fed upon, we must be in a low, unhealthy, dangerous condition of soul. There may not be any thing outwardly wrong in our conduct, we may not be publicly dishonoring the Lord in our ways, but we are grieving His loving heart by our gross neglect of His Word, which is but another term for the neglect of Himself. It is the very height of folly to talk of loving Christ if we do not love and live upon His Word. It is a delusion to imagine that the new life can be in a healthy, prosperous condition where the Word of God is habitually neglected in the closet and the family.

We do not, of course, mean that no other book but the Bible should be read, or we should not pen these *Notes,* but nothing demands greater watchfulness than the matter of reading. All things are to be done in the name of Jesus, and to the glory of God, and this is amongst the "all things." We should read no book that we cannot read to the glory of God, and on which we cannot ask God's blessing.

We feel that this entire subject demands the most serious consideration of all God's people, and we trust that the Spirit of God may use our meditation on the chapter before us to stir up our hearts and consciences in reference to what is due to the Word of God, both in our hearts and in our houses.

No doubt, if it has its right place in the heart, it will have its right place also in the house; but if there be no acknowledgment of the Word of God in the bosom of the family, it is hard to believe that it has its right place in the heart. Heads of houses should ponder this matter seriously. We are most fully persuaded that there ought to be, in every Christian household, a daily acknowledgment of God and His Word. Some may perhaps look upon it as bondage, as legality, as religious routine, to have regular family worship. We would ask such objectors, Is it bondage for the family to assemble at meals? Are the family reunions around the social board ever regarded as a wearisome duty—a piece of dull routine? Certainly not, if the family be a well-ordered and happy one. Why, then, should it be regarded as a burdensome thing for the head of a Christian household to gather his children and his servants around him and read a few verses of the precious Word of God, and breathe a few words of prayer before the throne of grace? We believe it to be a habit in perfect accordance with the teaching of both the Old and the New Testaments—a habit grateful to the heart of God—a holy, blessed, edifying habit.

What should we think of a professing Christian who never prayed, never read the Word of God, in private? Could we possibly regard him as a happy, healthy, true Christian? Assuredly not. Indeed we should seriously question the existence of divine life in such a soul. Prayer and the Word of God are absolutely essential to healthy, vigorous Christian life; so that a man who habitually neglects these must be in an utterly dead state.

Now, if it be thus in reference to an individual, how can a family be regarded as in a right state where there is no family reading, no family prayer, no family acknowledgment of God or His Word? Can we conceive a God-fearing household going on from Lord's day morning to Saturday night without any collective recognition of the One to whom they owe every thing? Day after day rolls on, domestic duties are attended to, the family assemble regularly at meals, but there is no thought of summoning the household around the Word of God, or around the mercy-seat. We ask, Where is the difference between such a family and any poor heathen household? Is it not most sad—most deplorable to find those who make the very highest profession, and who take their places at the Lord's table, yet living in the gross neglect of family reading—family worship?

Are you the head of a household? If so, what are your thoughts on the subject? and what is your line of action? Have you family reading and family prayer, daily in your house? If not (bear with us when we ask you), why not? Search and see what is the real root of the matter. Has your heart declined from God, from His Word and His ways? Do you read and pray in private? Do you love the Word and prayer? Do you find delight in them? If so, how is it you neglect them in your household? Perhaps you seek to excuse yourself on the ground of nervousness and timidity; if so, look to the Lord to enable you to overcome the weakness. Just cast yourself on His unfailing grace, and gather your household around you at a certain hour each day, read a few verses of Scripture and breathe half a dozen words of prayer; or, if you cannot do this at first, just let the family kneel for a few moments in silence before the throne.

Any thing, in short, like a family acknowledgment, a family testimony: any thing but a godless, careless, prayerless life in your household. Do, dear friend, suffer the word of exhortation in this matter. Let us entreat you to begin at once, looking to God to help you, as He most assuredly will, for He never fails a really trusting, dependent heart. Do not any longer go on neglecting God and His Word in your family circle. It is really terrible. Let no arguments about bondage, legality, or formalism weigh with you for a moment. We almost feel disposed to exclaim, Blessed bondage! If indeed it be bondage to read the Word, we cordially welcome it, and fearlessly glory in it.

But, no; we cannot for a moment regard it in any such light. We believe it to be a most delightful privilege for every one whom God has set at the head of a household to gather all the members of that household around him and read a portion of the blessed book, and pour out his heart in prayer to God. We believe it is *specially* the duty of the head so to do. It is by no means necessary to make it a long, wearisome service. As a rule, both in our houses and in our public assemblies, short, fresh, fervent exercises are by far the most edifying.

But this, of course, is an open question, as to which we merely give our judgment, which must go for what it is worth. The length and character of the service must, in every case, be left to the person who conducts it. But we do most earnestly trust that if these lines should be scanned by any one who is the head of a household, and if he has hitherto neglected the holy privilege of family worship—family reading, he will, henceforth, do so no more. May he be enabled to say, with Joshua, "Let others do as they will, as for me and my house, we will serve the Lord."

It is not, surely, that we would lead any to imagine that the mere act of family reading takes in all that is comprehended in that weighty sentence, "We will serve the Lord." Far from it. That blessed service takes in every thing belonging to our private and domestic history: it takes in the most minute details of practical daily life. All this is most true and invaluable. But we are most thoroughly persuaded that nothing can go right in any household in which family reading and family prayer are habitually neglected.

It may be said that there are many families who seem very particular about their morning and evening reading and prayer, and yet their whole domestic history, from morning till night, is a flagrant contradiction of their so-called religious service. It may be that the head of the house, instead of shedding sunlight upon the family circle, is morose in his temper, rude and coarse in his manners, rough and contradictory to his wife, arbitrary and severe to his children, unreasonable and exacting to his servants, finding fault with what is laid on the table, after having asked God's blessing upon it; and, in short, in every way giving the lie to his reading and his prayer in the family. So also as to the wife and the mother, and the children and the servants. The whole domestic economy is out of order. There is disorder and confusion; meals are unpunctual; there is a want of kindly consideration one of another; the children are rude, selfish, and willful; the servants are thoughtless, wasteful, and disobedient, if not much worse; the tone, atmosphere, and style of the entire establishment are unchristian, ungodly, utterly unbecoming.

And then, when you travel outside the domestic circle, and mark the conduct of the heads and members of the family toward those outside—mark their business, if they be in business, hear the testimony of those who deal with them, as to the quality of their goods, the style and character of their work; the spirit and temper in which they carry on their business; such grasping and griping, such covetousness, such commercial trickery; nothing of God, nothing of Christ, nothing to distinguish them from the most thorough worldlings around; yea, the conduct of those very worldlings, of those who would never think of such a thing as family worship, would put them to shame.

Under such painful and humiliating circumstances, what of the family worship—the family reading—the family altar? Alas! it is an empty formality—a powerless, worthless, unseemly proceeding; in place of being a morning and evening sacrifice, it is a morning and evening lie—a solemn mockery—an insult to God.

All this is sadly true. There is a terrible lack of household testimony—of common, practical righteousness in our families and in the entire economy of our houses. There is but little of the white raiment—the fine linen, which is the righteousness of saints. We seem to forget those weighty words of the inspired apostle in Romans 14: "The kingdom of God is not meat and drink; but *righteousness,* and peace, and joy in the Holy Ghost." Some of us seem to think that whenever we meet with the word "righteousness," it must needs mean the righteousness of God in which we stand, or righteousness imputed to us. This is a very great mistake indeed. We must remember there is a practical and human side of this question; there is the subjective as well as the objective—the walk as well as the standing—the condition as well as the position.

These things must never be separated. It is of little use to set up or seek to maintain a family altar amid the ruins of family testimony. It is nothing short of a hideous caricature to begin and end with so-called family worship a day characterized throughout by ungodliness and unrighteousness, levity, folly, and vanity. Can aught be more unsightly or more miserably inconsistent than an evening spent in song-singing, charades, and other light games, closed up with a contemptible bit of religion in the shape of reading and prayer?

All this line of things is most deplorable. It ought not to be found in connection with the holy name of Christ, with His assembly, or the holy exercises of His table. We must measure every thing in our private life, in our domestic economy, in our daily history, in all our intercourse, and in all our business transactions, with that one standard, namely, the glory of Christ. Our one grand question, in reference to every thing that comes before us or solicits our attention, must be, Is this worthy of the holy name which is called upon me? If not, let us not touch it; yea, let us turn our back upon it with stern decision, and flee from it with holy energy. Let us not listen for a moment to the contemptible question, "What harm is there in it?" Nothing but harm if Christ be not in it. No truly devoted heart would ever entertain, much less put, such a question. Whenever you hear any one speaking thus, you may at once conclude that Christ is not the governing object of the heart.

We trust the reader is not weary of all this homely, practical truth. We believe it is loudly called for in this day of high profession. We have all of us much need to consider our ways, to look well to the real state of our hearts as to Christ; for here lies the true secret of the whole matter. If the heart be not true to Him, nothing can be right—nothing in the private life, nothing in the family, nothing in the business, nothing in the assembly, nothing any where; but if the heart be true to Him, *all* will be—must be right.

No marvel, therefore, if the blessed apostle, when he reaches the close of that wonderful Epistle to the Corinthians, sums all up with this solemn declaration: "If any man love not the Lord Jesus Christ, let him be Anathema Maran-atha." In the course of his letter, he deals with various forms of doctrinal error and moral pravity; but when he comes to the close, instead of pronouncing his solemn sentence upon any particular error or evil, he hurls it with holy indignation against any one, no matter who or what, who does not love the Lord Jesus Christ. Love to Christ is the grand safeguard against every form of error and evil. A heart filled with Christ has no room for aught beside; but if there be no love to Him, there is no security against the wildest error or the worst form of moral evil.

We must now return to our chapter.

The attention of the people is specially called to the solemn scenes at Mount Horeb—scenes which should surely have deeply and abidingly impressed their hearts. "Specially the day that thou stoodest before the Lord thy God in Horeb, when the Lord said unto me, Gather Me the people together, and *I will make them hear My words.*" The grand and all-important point for Israel of old, for the Church now, for each, for all, at all times and in all places, is, to be brought into direct, living contact with the eternal Word of the living God, to the end "that they may learn to fear Me all the days that they shall live upon the earth, and *that they may teach their children.*"

It is very beautiful to note the intimate connection between hearing God's Word and fearing His name. It is one of those great root-principles which never change, never lose their power or their intrinsic value. The Word and the name go together; and the heart that loves the one will reverence the other, and bow down to its holy authority in all things. "He that loveth Me not keepeth not My sayings." "He that saith, I know Him, and keepeth not His commandments, is a liar, and the truth is not in him. But whoso keepeth His word, in him verily is the love of God perfected" (John 14; 1 John 2). Every true lover of God will treasure up His Word in the heart, and where the Word is thus lovingly treasured in the heart, its hallowed influence will be seen in the whole life, character, and conduct. God's object in giving His Word is that it may govern our conduct, form our character, and shape our ways; and if His Word has not this practical effect upon us, it is utterly vain for us to speak of loving Him—yea, it is nothing short of positive mockery, which He must sooner or later resent.

And let us note particularly the solemn responsibility of Israel as to their children. They were not only to "hear" and "learn" for themselves, but they were also to teach their children. This is a universal and abiding duty, which cannot be neglected with impunity. God attaches very great importance to this matter. We hear Him saying as to Abraham, "I know him, that he will *command his children and his household* after him, and they shall keep the way of the Lord, to do justice and judgment; that the Lord may bring upon Abraham that which He hath spoken of him" (Gen. 18).

These words are most important, as setting before us the divine estimate of domestic training and family piety. In all ages, and under all dispensations, God has been pleased to give expression to His approbation of the proper education of the children of His people—their faithful training according to His holy Word. We find no such thing sanctioned in Scripture as children being allowed to grow up in ignorance and carelessness and willfulness. Some professing Christians, under the baneful influence of a certain school of theology, seem to think that it is, in some way, an interference with the sovereignty of God, with His purposes and counsels, to instruct their children in the truth of the gospel and the letter of holy Scripture. They consider that the children ought to be left to the action of the Holy Ghost, which they are sure to experience in God's own time if indeed they are of God's elect, and if not, all human effort is perfectly useless.

Now, we must, in all faithfulness to the truth of God and to the souls of our readers, bear the clearest and strongest testimony against this one-sided view of the great practical subject before us. There is nothing more mischievous, nothing more pernicious in its effect upon the conscience, the heart, the life, the whole practical career and moral character, than one-sided theology. It does not matter what side you take, so long as you only take one. It is sure to produce what we must term a spiritual malformation. We feel we cannot too strongly and earnestly warn the reader against this sore evil. It can only lead to the most disastrous results; and as to its effect in reference to the training of our children and the management of our households—the subject now before us—it is mischievous in the extreme. Indeed we have seen the most deplorable consequences follow the carrying out of this line of thought. We have known the children of Christian parents to grow up in utter ignorance of divine things, in carelessness, recklessness, and open infidelity; and if a word of admonition were offered, it has been met by arguments based upon the dogmas of a one-sided divinity—and the one side turned the wrong way. It has been said, "We cannot make Christians of our children, and we must not make them formalists or hypocrites. It must be a divine work or nothing. When God's time comes, He will effectually call them, if indeed they are among the number of His elect; if not, all our efforts are perfectly useless."

To all this we reply, that this line of argument, if carried to its fullest extent, would prevent the farmer from plowing his ground or sowing his seed. It is very plain that he cannot make the seed to germinate or fructify. He could no more cause a solitary grain of wheat to grow than he could create the universe. Does this prevent his plowing and sowing? does it cause him to fold his arms and say, I can do nothing. I cannot, by any effort of mine, make corn grow. It is a divine operation, and therefore I must wait God's time? Does any farmer reason and act like this? Surely not, unless he be a lunatic. Every sound-minded person knows that plowing and sowing must go before the reaping; and if the former be neglected, it is the height of extravagant folly to look for the latter.

Nor is it otherwise in the matter of training our children. We know God is sovereign; we believe in His eternal counsels and purposes; we fully recognize the grand doctrines of election and predestination—yea, we are as thoroughly persuaded of them as of the truth that God is, or that Christ died and rose again. Moreover, we believe that the new birth must take place in every instance—in the case of our children as of all beside; we are convinced that this new birth is entirely a divine operation, effected by the Holy Ghost, through the Word, as we are distinctly taught in our Lord's discourse with Nicodemus in John 3, and also in James 1:18 and 1 Peter 1:23.

But does all this touch, in the most remote way, the solemn responsibility of Christian parents to teach and train their children, diligently and faithfully, from their earliest moments? Most certainly not. Woe be to the parents who, on any plea or on any ground whatsoever, be it one-sided theology, misapplied Scripture, or aught else, deny their responsibility, or neglect their plain, bounden duty, in this holy business. True, we cannot make our children Christians, and we ought not to make them formalists or hypocrites; but we are not called to *make* them any thing. We are simply called to do our duty by them, and leave results to God. We are instructed and commanded to bring up our children "in the nurture and admonition of the Lord." When is this "bringing up" to commence? when are we to begin the sacred work of training our little ones? Surely, at the beginning. The very moment we enter upon a relationship, we enter also upon the responsibility which that relationship entails. We cannot deny this; we cannot shake it off. We may neglect it, and have to reap the sad consequences of our neglect, in various ways. It is a very serious thing to stand in the sacred relationship of a parent—very interesting and very delightful, no doubt; but most serious, because of the responsibility involved. True it is, blessed be God, His grace is sufficient for us in this as in all beside, and "if any man lack wisdom, let him ask of God, who giveth to all liberally, and upbraideth not; and it shall be given him." "We are not sufficient of ourselves," in this weighty matter, to think or to do any thing as ourselves, but our sufficiency is of God, and He will meet our every need. We have simply to draw upon Him, for exigence of every hour.

But we must do our duty. Some do not like the homely word "duty." They think it has a legal ring about it. We trust the reader does not think so, for it is a very great mistake indeed. We look upon the word as a very sound and morally wholesome one, and we believe that every true Christian loves it. One thing is certain, it is only in the path of duty we can count on God. To talk of trusting God, when out of the path of duty, is a miserable conceit, and a delusion; and in the matter of our relationship as parents, to neglect our duty is to bring down upon us the most disastrous consequences.

We believe the whole business of Christian education is summed up in two brief sentences, namely, Count on God for your children, and, Train your children for God. To take the first without the second is antinomianism; to take the second without the first is legality; to take both together is sound, practical Christianity—true religion in the sight of God and man.

It is the sweet privilege of every Christian parent to count, with all possible confidence, upon God for his children. But then we must remember that there is, in the government of God, an inseparable link connecting this privilege with the most solemn responsibility as to training. For a Christian parent to speak of counting on God for the salvation of his children, and for the moral integrity of their future career in this world, while the duty of training is neglected, is simply a miserable delusion.

We press this most solemnly upon all Christian parents, but especially upon those who have just entered upon the relationship. There is great danger of shirking our duty to our children, of shifting it over upon others, or neglecting it altogether. We do not like the trouble of it; we shrink from the constant worry as it seems to us. But we shall find that the trouble and the worry and the sorrow and the heart-scalding arising from the neglect of our duty will be a thousand times worse than all that can be involved in the discharge of it. To every true lover of God there is deep delight in treading the path of duty. Every step taken in that path strengthens our confidence to go on. And then we can always count upon the infinite resources that we have in God when we are keeping His commandments. We have simply to betake ourselves, morning by morning, yea, hour by hour, to our Father's exhaustless treasury, and there get all we want, in the way of grace and wisdom and moral power, to enable us to discharge aright the holy functions of our relationship. "He giveth more grace." This always holds good. But if we, instead of seeking grace to discharge our duty, seek ease in neglecting it, we are simply laying up a store of sorrow which will accumulate rapidly and fall upon us heavily at a future day. "Be not deceived; God is not mocked; for whatsoever a man soweth, that shall he also reap. For he that soweth to his flesh, shall of the flesh reap corruption; but he that soweth to the Spirit, shall of the Spirit reap life everlasting" (Gal. 6).

This is the condensed statement of a great principle of God's moral government—a principle of universal application, and one which applies, with singular force, to the subject before us. *As* we sow, in the matter of the education of our children, *so* we shall, most assuredly, reap. There is no getting out of this.

But let not any dear Christian parent, whose eye may scan these lines, be at all discouraged or faint-hearted. There is no reason whatever for this, but, on the contrary, every reason for the most joyful confidence in God. "The name of the Lord is a strong tower; the righteous runneth into it, and is safe." Let us tread, with firm step, the path of duty; and then we can count, with unwavering confidence, upon our ever-faithful and gracious God for the need of each day as it rolls along. And in due time we shall reap the precious fruit of our labor, according to the appointment of God, and in pursuance of the enactments of His moral government.

We do not attempt to lay down any rules

or regulations for the training. We do not believe in such. Children cannot be trained by dry rules. Who could attempt to embody in rules all that is wrapped up in that one sentence, "Bring them up in the nurture and admonition of the Lord"?

Here we have, indeed, a golden rule which takes in every thing from the cradle to matured manhood. Yes, we repeat, "from the cradle," for we are most fully persuaded that all true Christian training begins at the very beginning. Some of us have little idea of how soon and how sharply children begin to observe, and how much they take in as they gaze at us through their dear expressive eyes.

And then how marvelously susceptible they are of the moral atmosphere which surrounds them! Yes; and it is this very moral atmosphere that constitutes the grand secret of training our families. Our children should be permitted to breathe, from day to day, the atmosphere of love and peace, purity, holiness, and true practical righteousness. This has an amazing effect in forming the character. It is a great thing for our children to see their parents walking in love, in harmony, in tender care one for the other, in kind consideration for the servants, in love and sympathy for the poor. Who can measure the moral effect upon a child of the very first angry look, or unkind word, between father and mother? And in cases where the daily history is one of unsightly strife and contention—the father contradicting the mother, and the mother disparaging the father—how are children to grow in such an atmosphere as this?

The fact is, it is not within the compass of human language to set forth all that is involved in the moral tone of the entire family circle—the spirit, style, and atmosphere of the whole household, the drawing-room, the dining-room, the nursery, the kitchen; where circumstances admit of such distinctions, or where the family have to confine themselves to two rooms. It is not a question of rank, position, or wealth, but of the beauteous grace of God shining out in all. There may be the stalled ox or the dinner of herbs—these are not, at present, in question. But what we press on all fathers and mothers—all heads of households, high and low, rich and poor, learned and ignorant, is the necessity of training their children in an atmosphere of love and peace, truth and holiness, purity and kindness. Thus will our households be the practical exhibition of the character of God; and all who come in contact with them will, at least, have before their eyes a practical witness to the truth of Christianity.

But, ere we turn from the subject of domestic government, there is one special point to which we desire to call the attention of Christian parents—a point of the utmost possible moment, yet too much neglected amongst us, and that is, the need of inculcating upon our children the duty of implicit obedience. This cannot be too strongly insisted upon, inasmuch as it not only affects the order and comfort of our households, but, what is infinitely more important, it concerns the glory of God and the practical carrying out of His truth. "Children, obey your parents in the Lord; for this is right." And again, "Children, obey your parents *in all things;* for this is well pleasing unto the Lord" (Eph. 6; Col. 3).

This is absolutely essential, and must be firmly insisted upon from the very outset. The child must be taught to obey from his earliest moments. He must be trained to submit himself to divinely appointed authority, and that, as the apostle puts it, "in all things." If this be not attended to from the very first, it will be found almost impossible to attend to it afterwards. If the will be allowed to act, it grows, with terrible rapidity, and each day's growth increases the difficulty of bringing it under control. Hence, the parent should begin at once to establish his authority on a basis of moral strength and firmness; and when this is done, he may be as gentle and tender as the most loving heart could desire. We do not believe in sternness, harshness, or severity. They are by no means necessary, and are generally the accompaniments of bad training and the proofs of bad temper. God has put into the parent's hand the reins of government and the rod of authority, but it is not needful—if we may so express it—to be continually chucking the reins and brandishing the rod, which are the sure proofs of moral weakness. Whenever you hear a man continually talking about his authority, you may be sure his authority is not properly established. There is a quiet dignity about true moral power which is perfectly unmistakable.

Furthermore, we judge it to be a mistake for a parent to be perpetually crossing a child's will in matters of no moment. Such a line of action tends to break the child's spirit, whereas the object of all sound training is to break the will. The child should ever be impressed with the idea that the parent seeks *only* his real good, and that if he has to refuse or prohibit any thing, it is not for the purpose of curtailing the child's enjoyment, but simply for the promotion of his true interests.

One grand object of domestic government is to protect each member of the household in the enjoyment of his privileges, and in the proper discharge of his relative duties. Now, inasmuch as it is the divinely appointed duty of a child to obey, the parent is responsible to see this duty discharged, for if it be neglected, some other members of the domestic circle must suffer.

There can be no greater nuisance in a house than a naughty, willful child; and, as a general rule, wherever you find such, it is to be traced to bad training. We are aware, of course, that children differ in temper and disposition—that some children have peculiarly strong wills and sturdy tempers, and are therefore specially hard to manage.

All this we quite understand; but it leaves wholly untouched the question of the parent's responsibility to insist upon implicit obedience. He can always count on God for the needed grace and power to carry out this point. Even in the case of a widowed mother, we believe, most assuredly, she can look to God to enable her to command her children and her household. In no case, therefore, should parental authority be surrendered for a moment.

It sometimes happens that, through injudicious fondness, the parent is tempted to pamper the will of the child; but it is sowing to the flesh, and must yield corruption. It is not true love at all to indulge a child's will, neither can it possibly minister to his true happiness or legitimate enjoyment. An over-indulged, self-willed child is miserable himself and a grievous infliction on all who have to do with him. Children should be taught to think of others, and to seek to promote their comfort and happiness in every way. How very unseemly it is, for example, for a child to enter the house and ascend the stairs whistling, singing, and shouting, in total disregard of other members of the household who may be seriously disturbed and annoyed by such conduct! No properly trained child would think of acting in such a way; and where such unsubdued, unruly, inconsiderate conduct is allowed, there is a serious defect in the domestic government.

It is essential to family peace, harmony, and comfort, that all the members should "consider one another." We are responsible to seek the good and the happiness of those around us, and not our own. If all would but remember this, what different households we should have! and what a different tale would families have to tell! Every Christian household should be the reflection of the divine character. The atmosphere should just be the very atmosphere of heaven. How is this to be? Simply by each one—parent, child, master, and servant—seeking to walk in the footsteps of Jesus, and manifest His spirit. He never pleased Himself, never sought His own interest in any thing; He did always the thing that pleased the Father; He came to serve and to give; He went about doing good, and healing all that were oppressed of the devil. Thus it was ever with that most blessed One—the gracious, loving, sympathizing Friend of all the sons and daughters of want, weakness, and sorrow; and if only the various members of each Christian family were formed on this perfect model, we should, at least, realize something of the power and efficacy of personal and domestic Christianity, which, blessed be God, can ever be maintained and exhibited notwithstanding the hopeless ruin of the professing church. "Thou and thy house" suggests a great golden principle which runs through the volume of God, from beginning to end. In every age, under every dispensation, in the days of the patriarchs, in the days of the law, and in the days of Christianity, we find, to our exceeding comfort and encouragement, that personal and domestic godliness has its place as something grateful to the heart of God and to the glory of His holy name.

This we consider to be most consolatory at all times, but more particularly at a time like the present, when the professing church seems so rapidly sinking into gross worldliness and open infidelity; and not this only, but when those who most earnestly desire to walk in obedience to the Word of God, and to act on the grand foundation-truth of the unity of the body, find it so difficult to maintain a corporate testimony. In view of all this, we may well bless God, with overflowing hearts, that personal and family piety can always be maintained, and that from the heart and the home of every Christian a constant stream of praise may ascend to the throne of God, and a stream of active benevolence flow out to a needy, sorrowful, sin-stricken world. May it be so more and more, through the mighty ministry of God the Holy Ghost, that God, in all things, may be glorified in the hearts and homes of His beloved people.

We have now to consider the very solemn warning addressed to the congregation of Israel against the terrible sin of idolatry—a sin to which, alas! the poor human heart is ever prone, in one way or another. It is quite possible to be guilty of the sin of idolatry without bowing down before a graven image; wherefore it behooves us to weigh well the words of warning which fell from the lips of Israel's venerable lawgiver. They are most assuredly written for our learning.

"And ye came near and stood under the mountain; and the mountain burned with fire unto the midst of heaven, with darkness, clouds, and thick darkness." Solemn and suited accompaniments of the occasion! "And the Lord spake unto you out of the midst of the fire." Oh, how differently He speaks in the gospel of His grace! "Ye heard the voice of the words, but saw no similitude." Important fact for them to ponder! *"Only a voice."* And "faith cometh by hearing, and hearing by the Word of God." "And He declared unto you His covenant, which He commanded you to perform—ten commandments; and He wrote them upon two tables of stone. And the Lord commanded me at that time to teach you statutes and judgments," not that they might discuss them, sit in judgment upon them, or argue about them, but "that *ye might do them*"—the grand old story, the Deuteronomic theme of *obedience,* most precious! whether out of or "in the land whither ye go over to possess it."

Here lies the solid ground of the appeal against idolatry. They *saw* nothing. God did not show Himself to them. He did not assume any bodily shape, of which they might form an image. He gave them His word—His holy commandments, so plain that a child could understand them, and the wayfaring men though fools need not err therein. There was no need for them, therefore, to set about imagining what God was like; nay, this was *the* very sin against which they were so faithfully warned. They were called to hear God's voice, not to see His shape—to obey His commandment, not to make an image of Him. Superstition vainly seeks to do honor to God by forming and worshiping an image; Faith, on the contrary, lovingly receives and reverently obeys His holy commandments. "If a man love Me," says our blessed Lord, "he will"—what? make an image of Me, and worship it? Nay, but "he will keep My words." This makes it so simple, so safe, so certain. We are not called to work up our minds to form any conception of God; we have simply to hear His word and keep His commandments. We can have no idea whatever of God but as He has been pleased to reveal Himself. "No man hath seen God at any time; the only begotten Son, which is in the bosom of the Father, He hath declared Him" "God, who commanded the light to shine out of darkness, hath shined in our hearts, to give the light of the knowledge of the glory of God in the face of Jesus Christ."

Jesus is declared to be the brightness of God's glory and the exact impression of His substance. He could say, "He that hath seen Me hath seen the Father." Thus the Son reveals the Father; and it is by the Word, through the power of the Holy Ghost, that we know any thing of the Son; and therefore for any one to attempt, by any efforts of his mind or workings of his imagination, to conceive an image of God, or of Christ, is simply idolatry. To endeavor to arrive at any knowledge of God or of Christ save by Scripture, is simply mysticism and confusion; nay, more, it is to put ourselves directly into the hands of the devil, to be led by him into the wildest, darkest, and deadliest delusion.

Hence, therefore, as Israel, at Mount Horeb, was shut up to the *"voice"* of God and warned against any similitude, so we are shut up to holy Scripture and warned against every thing which would draw us away, the breadth of a hair, from that holy and all-sufficient standard. We must not listen to the suggestions of our own minds, nor to those of any other human mind: we must absolutely and sternly refuse to listen to any thing but the voice of God—the voice of holy Scripture. Here is true security, true rest; here we have absolute certainty, so that we can say, "I know *whom*"—not merely *what*—"I have believed; and am persuaded that *He,*" etc.

"Take ye therefore good heed unto yourselves, (for ye saw no manner of similitude on the day that the Lord spake unto you in Horeb out of the midst of the fire,) lest ye corrupt yourselves, and make you a graven image, the similitude of any figure, the likeness of male or female, the likeness of any beast that is on the earth, the likeness of any winged fowl that flieth in the air, the likeness of any thing that creepeth on the ground, the likeness of any fish that is in the waters beneath the earth; and lest thou lift up thine eyes unto heaven, and when thou seest the sun, and the moon, and the stars, even all the host of heaven, shouldest be driven to worship them, and serve them, which the Lord thy God hath divided unto all nations under the whole heaven. But the Lord hath taken you, and brought you forth out of the iron furnace, even out of Egypt, to be unto Him a people of inheritance, as ye are this day."

There is a very weighty truth set before us here. The people are expressly taught that in making any image and bowing down thereto, they, in reality, lowered and corrupted themselves. Hence, when they made the golden calf, the Lord said unto Moses, "Go, get thee down; for thy people, which thou broughtest out of the land of Egypt, have corrupted themselves." It could not be otherwise. The worshiper must be inferior to the object of his worship; and therefore, in worshiping a calf, they actually put themselves below the level of the beasts that perish. Well, therefore, might He say, They "have corrupted themselves; they have turned aside quickly out of the way which I commanded them; they have made them a molten calf, and have worshiped it, and have sacrificed thereunto, and said, 'These be thy gods, O Israel, which have brought thee up out of the land of Egypt.' "

What a spectacle! A whole congregation, led by Aaron the high-priest, bowing in worship before a thing formed by a graving tool out of the earrings which had just been taken from the ears of their wives and daughters! Only conceive a number of intelligent beings—people endowed with reason, understanding, and conscience—saying of a molten calf, "These be thy gods, O Israel, which have brought thee up out of the land of Egypt"! They actually displaced Jehovah by an image graven by art and man's device! And these were the people who had seen the mighty works of Jehovah in the land of Egypt. They had seen plague after plague falling upon Egypt and its obdurate king; they had seen the land, as it were, shaken to its very centre by the successive strokes of Jehovah's governmental rod; they had seen Egypt's first-born laid in death by the sword of the destroying angel; they had seen the Red Sea divided by one stroke of Jehovah's rod, and they had passed through upon dry ground between those crystal walls which afterwards fell, in crushing power, upon their enemies—all these things had passed before their eyes, and yet they could so soon forget all and say of a molten calf, "These be thy gods, O Israel, which have brought thee up out of the land of Egypt." Did they really believe that a molten image had made the land of Egypt to tremble, humbled its proud monarch, and brought them forth victoriously? Had a calf divided the sea for them, and led them majestically through its depths? So, at least, they said; for what will people not say when the eye and the heart are turned away from God and His Word?

But we may perhaps be asked, Has all this a voice for us? Are Christians to learn any thing from Israel's molten calf? and do the warnings addressed to Israel against idolatry convey any voice to the ear of the Church? Are we in danger of bowing down to a graven image? Is it possible that we, whose high privilege it is to walk in the full-orbed light of New Testament Christianity, could ever worship a molten calf?

To all this we reply, first of all, in the language of Romans 15:4, "*Whatsoever things* were written aforetime"—Exodus 32 and Deuteronomy 4 included—"were written for our learning, that we through patience and comfort of the Scriptures might have hope." This brief passage contains our chartered right to range through the wide field of Old Testament Scripture and gather up and appropriate its golden lessons, to feed upon its "exceeding great and precious promises," to drink in its deep and varied consolation, and to profit by its solemn warnings and wholesome admonitions.

And then, as to our being capable of or liable to the gross sin of idolatry, we have a striking answer in 1 Corinthians 10, where the inspired apostle uses the very scene at Mount Horeb as a warning to the Church of God. We cannot do better than quote the entire passage for the reader. There is nothing like the Word of God; may we love, prize, and reverence it more and more each day.

"Moreover, brethren, I would not that ye should be ignorant, how that *all* our fathers were under the cloud"—those whose carcasses fell in the wilderness, as well as those who reached the land of promise—"and all passed through the sea; and were all baptized unto Moses in the cloud and in the sea; and did all eat the same spiritual meat; and did all drink the same spiritual drink: for they drank of that spiritual Rock that followed them; and that Rock was Christ." How strong, how solemn, and how searching is this for all professors! "But with many of them God was not well pleased; for they were overthrown in the wilderness. Now these things were *our examples*" (let us carefully mark this), "to the intent we should not lust after *evil things*"—things in any way contrary to the mind of Christ, "as they also lusted. Neither *be ye idolaters*" (so that professing Christians may be idolaters) "as were some of them; as it is written, 'The people sat down to eat and drink, and rose up to play.' Neither let us commit fornication, as some of them committed, and fell in one day three and twenty thousand. Neither let us tempt Christ, as some of them also tempted, and were destroyed of serpents. Neither murmur ye, as some of them also murmured, and were destroyed of the destroyer. Now *all these things* happened unto them for examples; and *they are written for our admonition,* upon whom the ends of the ages are come. Wherefore let him that thinketh he standeth take heed lest he fall."

Here we learn, in the plainest manner, that there is no depth of sin and folly, no form of moral pravity, into which we are not capable of plunging, at any moment, if not kept by the mighty power of God. There is no security for us save in the moral shelter of the divine presence. We know that the Spirit of God does not warn us against things to which we are not liable. He would not say to us, "Neither be ye idolaters," if we were not capable of being such. Idolatry takes various shapes. It is not, therefore, a question of the shape of the thing, but the thing itself—not the outward form, but the root or principle of the thing. We read that "covetousness is idolatry," and that a covetous man is an idolater; that is, a man desiring to possess himself of more than God has given him is an idolater—is actually guilty of the sin of Israel when they made the golden calf and worshiped it. Well might the blessed apostle say to the Corinthians—say to us, "Wherefore, my dearly beloved, flee from idolatry." Why be warned to *flee* from a thing to which we are not liable? Are there any idle words in the volume of God? What mean those closing words of the first Epistle of John—"Little children, keep yourselves from idols"? Do they not tell us that we are in danger of worshiping idols? Assuredly they do. Our treacherous hearts are capable of departing from the living God, and setting up some other object beside Him; and what is this but idolatry? Whatever commands the heart is the heart's idol, be it what it may—money, pleasure, power, or aught else—so that we may well see the urgent need for the many warnings given us by the Holy Ghost against the sin of idolatry.

But we have in the fourth chapter of Galatians a very remarkable passage, and one which speaks in most impressive accents to the professing church. The Galatians had, like all other Gentiles, worshiped idols; but, on the reception of the gospel, had turned from idols to serve the living and true God. The Judaizing teachers, however, had come among them and taught them that unless they were circumcised and kept the law, they could not be saved.

Now this, the blessed apostle unhesitatingly pronounces to be idolatry—a going back to the grossness and moral degradation of their former days, and all this after having professed to receive the glorious gospel of Christ. Hence the moral force of the apostle's inquiry, "Howbeit then, when ye knew not God, ye did service unto them which by nature are no gods. *But now,* after that ye have known God, or rather are known of God, how *turn ye again* to the weak and beggarly elements, whereunto ye desire *again* to be in bondage? Ye observe days, and months, and times, and years. I am afraid of you, lest I have bestowed upon you labor in vain."

This is peculiarly striking. The Galatians were not outwardly going back to the worship of idols. It is not improbable that they would have indignantly repudiated any such idea. But, for all that, the inspired apostle asks them, "How turn ye again?" What does this inquiry mean if they were not going back to idolatry? and what are we now to learn from the whole passage? Simply this, that circumcision, and getting under the law, and observing days, and months, and times, and years—that all this, though apparently so different, was nothing more or less than going back to their old idolatry. The observance of days and the worship of false gods were both a turning away from the living and true God, from His Son Jesus Christ, from the Holy Ghost, from the brilliant cluster of dignities and glories which belong to Christianity.

All this is peculiarly solemn for professing Christians. We question if the full import of Galatians 4:8-10 is really apprehended by the great majority of those who profess to believe the Bible. We solemnly press this whole subject upon the attention of all whom it may concern. We pray God to use it for the purpose of stirring up the hearts and consciences of His people every where to consider their position, their habits, ways, and associations; and to inquire how far they are really following the example of the assemblies of Galatia, in the observance of saints' days and such like, which can only lead away from Christ and His glorious salvation. There is a day coming which will open the eyes of thousands to the reality of these things, and then they will see what they now refuse to see, that the very darkest and grossest forms of paganism may be reproduced under the name of Christianity, and in connection with the very highest truths that ever shone on the human understanding.

But however slow we may be to admit our tendency to fall into the sin of idolatry, it is very plain, in Israel's case, that Moses, as taught and inspired of God, felt the deep need of warning them against it, in the most solemn and affecting terms. He appeals to them on every possible ground, and reiterates his counsels and admonitions in a manner so impressive as to leave them, assuredly, without any excuse. They never could say that they fell into idolatry from the want of warning, or of the most gracious and affectionate entreaty. Take such words as the following: "But the Lord hath taken you, and brought you forth out of the iron furnace, even out of Egypt, to be unto Him a people of inheritance, as ye are this day" (ver. 20).

Could any thing be more affecting than this? Jehovah, in His rich and sovereign grace, and by His mighty hand, brought them forth from the land of death and darkness, a redeemed and delivered people. He had brought them to Himself, that they might be to Him a peculiar treasure, above all the people upon earth. How, then, could they turn away from Him, from His holy covenant, and from His precious commandments?

Alas! they could and did. "They *made* a calf, and said, 'These be thy gods, O Israel, which have brought thee up out of the land of Egypt.' " Think of this! A calf, made by their own hands—an image, graven by art and man's device, had brought them up out of Egypt! A thing made out of the women's earrings had redeemed and delivered them! And this has been written for our admonition. But why should it be written for us if we are not capable of and liable to the very same sin? We must either admit that God the Holy Ghost has penned an unnecessary sentence, or admit our need of an admonition against the sin of idolatry; and assuredly, our needing the admonition proves our tendency to the sin.

Are we better than Israel? In no wise. We have brighter light and higher privileges, but, so far as we are concerned, we are made of the same material, have the same capabilities and the same tendencies, as they. Our idolatry may take a different shape from theirs; but idolatry is idolatry, be the shape what it may; and the higher our privileges, the greater our sin. We may perhaps feel disposed to wonder how a rational people could be guilty of such egregious folly as to make a calf and bow down to it, and this, too, after having had such a display of the majesty, power, and glory of God. Let us remember that their folly is recorded for our admonition; and that we, with all our light, all our knowledge, all our privileges, are warned to "flee from idolatry."

Let us deeply ponder all this and seek to profit by it. May every chamber of our hearts be filled with Christ, and then we shall have no room for idols. This is our only safeguard. If we slip away the breadth of a hair from our precious Saviour and Shepherd, we are capable of plunging into the darkest forms of error and moral evil. Light, knowledge, spiritual privileges, church position, sacramental benefits, are no security for the soul. They are very good in their right place and if rightly used, but in themselves they only increase our moral danger.

Nothing can keep us safe, right, and happy but having Christ dwelling in our hearts by faith. Abiding in Him and He in us, that wicked one toucheth us not. But if personal communion be not diligently maintained, the higher our position, the greater our danger and the more disastrous our fall. There was not a nation beneath the canopy of heaven more favored and exalted than Israel when they gathered around Mount Horeb to hear the word of God: there was not a nation on the face of the earth more degraded or more guilty than they when they bowed before the golden calf—an image of their own formation.

We must now give our attention to a fact of very deep interest, presented at verse 21 of our chapter, and that is, that Moses, for the third time, reminds the congregation of God's judicial dealing with himself. He had spoken of it, as we have seen, in chapter 1:37, and again at chapter 3:26, and here, again, he says to them, "Furthermore *the Lord was angry with me for your sakes,* and sware that I should not go over Jordan, and that I should not go in unto that good land which the Lord thy God giveth thee for an inheritance; but I must die in this land, I must not go over Jordan; but ye shall go over and possess that good land."

Now, we may ask, Why this threefold reference to the same fact? and why the special mention, in each instance, of the circumstance that Jehovah was angry with him on their account? One thing is certain, it was not for the purpose of throwing the blame over upon the people, or of exculpating himself. No one but an infidel could think this. We believe the simple object was, to give increased moral force to his appeal, more solemnity to his warning voice. If Jehovah was angry with such an one as Moses—if he, for his unadvised speaking at the waters of Meribah, was forbidden to enter the promised land (much as he desired it), how needful for them to take heed! It is a serious thing to have to do with God—blessed, no doubt, beyond all human expression or thought, but most serious, as the lawgiver himself was called to prove in his own person.

That this is the correct view of this interesting question seems evident from the following words: *"Take heed unto yourselves,* lest ye forget the covenant of the Lord your God, which He made with you, and make you a graven image, or the likeness of any thing which the Lord thy God hath forbidden thee. For the Lord thy God is a consuming fire, even a jealous God."

This is peculiarly solemn. We must allow this statement to have its full, moral weight with our souls. We must not attempt to turn aside its sharp edge by any false notions about grace. We sometimes hear it said that "God is a consuming fire to the world." By and by He will be so, no doubt; but now He is dealing in grace, patience, and long-suffering mercy with the world. He is not dealing in judgment with the world now; but, as the apostle Peter tells us, "the time is come that judgment must begin at the house of God; and if it first begin at us, what shall the end be of them that obey not the gospel of God?" So also, in Hebrews 12, we read, "For *our* God *is* a consuming fire." He is not speaking of what God will be to the world, but of what He is to us. Neither is it, as some put it, "God is a consuming fire out of Christ." We know nothing of God out of Christ. He could not be "*our* God" out of Christ.

No; Scripture does not need such twistings and turnings: it must be taken as it stands. It is clear and distinct, and all we have to do is to hearken and obey. "Our God is a consuming fire," "a jealous God," not to consume us, blessed be His holy name, but to consume the evil in us and in our ways. He is intolerant of every thing in us that is contrary to Himself—contrary to His holiness, and therefore contrary to our true happiness, our real, solid blessing. As the "Holy Father," He keeps us in a way worthy of Himself, and He chastens us in order to make us partakers of His holiness. He allows the world to go on its way for the present, not interfering publicly with it; but He judges His house, and He chastens His children, in order that they may more fully answer to His mind and be the expression of His moral image.

And is not this an immense privilege? Yes, verily; it is a privilege of the very highest order—a privilege flowing from the infinite grace of our God, who condescends to interest Himself in us, and occupy Himself even with our infirmities, our failures, and our sins, in order to deliver us from them, and make us partakers of His holiness.

There is a very fine passage bearing upon this subject in the opening of Hebrews 12, which, because of its immense practical importance, we must quote: "My son, despise not thou the chastening of the Lord, nor faint when thou art rebuked of Him; for *whom the Lord loveth He chasteneth,* and *scourgeth every son* whom He receiveth. If ye endure chastening, God dealeth with you as with sons; for *what son* is he whom the Father chasteneth not? But if ye be *without chastisement,* whereof all are partakers, then are ye *bastards* and *not sons.* Furthermore, we have had fathers of our flesh which corrected us, and we gave them reverence; shall we not much rather be in subjection unto the Father of spirits, and live? For they verily for a few days chastened us after their own pleasure; *but He for our profit, that we might be partakers of His holiness.* Now no chastening for the present *seemeth* to be joyous, but grievous; nevertheless afterward it yieldeth the peaceable fruit of righteousness unto them which are exercised thereby. Wherefore lift up the hands which hang down, and the feeble knees."

There are three ways of meeting divine chastening: We may *"despise"* it, as something common-place—something that may happen to any one; we do not see *the hand of God* in it. Again, we may *"faint"* under it, as something too heavy for us to bear—

something entirely beyond endurance; we do not see *the Father's heart* in it, or recognize His gracious object in it, namely, to make us partakers of His holiness. Lastly, we may be *"exercised"* by it. This is the way to reap "the peaceable fruit of righteousness afterward." We dare not *"despise"* a thing in which we trace the hand of God: we need not *"faint"* under a trial in which we plainly discern the heart of a loving Father, who will not suffer us to be tried above what we are able, but will with the trial make an issue, that we may be able to bear it, and who also graciously explains to us His object in the discipline, and assures us that every stroke of His rod is a proof of His love, and a direct response to the prayer of Christ in John 17:11, wherein He commends us to the care of the "Holy Father," to be kept according to that name and all that name involves.

Furthermore, there are three distinct attitudes of heart in reference to divine chastening, namely, subjection, acquiescence, and rejoicing. When the will is broken, there is subjection; when the understanding is enlightened as to the object of the chastening, there is calm acquiescence; and when the affections are engaged with the Father's heart, there is rejoicing, and we can go forth with glad hearts to reap a golden harvest of the peaceable fruit of righteousness, to the praise of Him who, in His painstaking love, undertakes to care for us and to deal with us in holy government, and concentrate His care upon each one as though there were but that one to attend to.

How wonderful is all this! and how the thought of it should help us in all our trials and exercises! We are in the hands of One whose love is infinite, whose wisdom is unerring, whose power is omnipotent, whose resources are inexhaustible. Why, then, should we ever be cast down? If He chastens us, it is because He loves us and seeks our real good. We may think the chastening grievous—we may feel disposed to wonder, at times, how love can inflict pain and sickness upon us; but we must remember that divine love is wise and faithful, and only inflicts the pain, the sickness, or the sorrow for our profit and blessing. We must not always judge of love by the form in which it clothes itself. Look at that fond and tender mother applying a blister to her child whom she loves as her own soul. She knows full well that the blister will cause her child real pain and suffering, and yet she unhesitatingly applies it, though her heart feels keenly at having to do it. But she knows it is absolutely necessary; she believes that, humanly and medically speaking, the child's life depends upon it; she feels that a few moments' pain may, with the blessing of God, restore the health of her precious child. Thus, while the child is only occupied with the transient suffering, the mother is thinking of the permanent good; and if the child could but think with the mother, the blister would not seem so hard to bear.

Now, it is just thus in the matter of our Father's disciplinary dealings with us; and the remembrance of this would greatly help us to endure whatever His chastening hand may lay upon us. It may perhaps be said that there is a very wide difference between a blister laid on for a few minutes, and years of intense bodily suffering. No doubt there is; but there is also a very wide difference between the result reached in each case. It is only with the principle of the thing we have to do. When we see a beloved child of God, or servant of Christ, called to pass through years of intense suffering, we may feel disposed to wonder why it is; and perhaps the beloved sufferer may also feel disposed to wonder, and at times be ready to faint under the weight of his long-protracted affliction. He may feel led to cry out, Why am I thus? Can this be love? can this be the expression of a Father's tender care? "Yes, verily," is Faith's bright and decided reply. "It is all love—all divinely right. I would not have it otherwise for worlds. I know this transient suffering is working out eternal blessing. I know my loving Father has put me into this furnace to purge away my dross and bring out in me the expression of His own image. I know that divine love will always do the very best for its object, and therefore this intense suffering is the very best thing for me. Of course, I feel it, for I am not a stick or a stone. My Father means me to feel it, just as the mother means the blister to rise, for it would do no good otherwise. But I bless Him, with my whole heart, for the grace that shines in the wondrous fact of His occupying Himself with me, in this way, to correct what He sees to be wrong in me. I praise Him for putting me into the furnace; and how can I but praise Him, when I see Himself, in infinite grace and patience, sitting over the furnace to watch the process, and lift me out the moment the work is done?"

This, beloved Christian reader, is the true way, and this the right spirit in which to pass through chastening of any kind, be it bodily affliction, sore bereavement, loss of property, or pressure of circumstances. We have to trace the hand of God, to read a Father's heart, to recognize the divine object in it all. This will enable us to vindicate, justify, and glorify God in the furnace of affliction. It will correct every murmuring thought, and hush every fretful utterance; it will fill our hearts with sweetest peace and our mouths with praise.

We must now turn, for a few moments, to the remaining verses of our chapter, in which we shall find some most touching and powerful appeals to the heart and conscience of the congregation. The lawgiver, in the deep, true, and fervent love of his heart, makes use of the most solemn warnings, the most earnest admonition, and the most tender entreaties, in order to move the people to the one grand and all-important point of obedience. If he speaks to them of the iron furnace of Egypt, out of which Jehovah, in His sovereign grace, had delivered them; if he dwells upon the mighty signs and wonders wrought on their behalf; if he holds up to their view the glories of that land on which they were about to plant their foot; or if he recounts the marvelous dealings of God with them in the wilderness, it is all for the purpose of strengthening the moral basis of Jehovah's claim upon their loving and reverent obedience. The past, the present, and the future are all brought to bear upon them—all made to furnish powerful arguments in favor of their whole-hearted consecration of themselves to the service of their gracious and almighty Deliverer. In short, there was every reason why they should obey, and no possible excuse for disobedience. All the facts of their history, from first to last, were eminently calculated to give moral force to the exhortation and warning of the following passage:

"Take heed unto yourselves, lest ye forget the covenant of the Lord your God, which He made with you, and make you a graven image, or the likeness of any thing, which the Lord thy God hath forbidden thee. For the Lord thy God is a consuming fire, even a jealous God. When thou shalt beget children, and children's children, and ye shall have remained long in the land, and shall corrupt yourselves, and make a graven image, or the likeness of any thing, and shall do evil in the sight of the Lord thy God, to provoke Him to anger; I call heaven and earth to witness against you this day, that ye shall soon utterly perish from off the land whereunto ye go over Jordan to possess it; ye shall not prolong your days upon it, but shall utterly be destroyed. And the Lord shall scatter you among the nations, and ye shall be left few in number among the heathen, whither the Lord shall lead you. And there ye shall serve gods, the work of men's hands, wood and stone, which neither see, nor hear, nor eat, nor smell."

How solemn is all this! What faithful warnings are here! Heaven and earth are summoned to witness. Alas! how soon and how completely all this was forgotten! and how literally all those heavy denunciations have been fulfilled in the history of the nation!

But, thank God, there is a bright side of the picture—there is mercy as well as judgment, and our God (blessed forever be His holy name) is something more than "a consuming fire and a jealous God." True, He is a consuming fire, because He is holy; He is intolerant of evil, and must consume our dross. Moreover, He is jealous, because He cannot suffer any rival to have a place in the hearts of those He loves. He must have the whole heart, because He alone is worthy of it, as He alone can fill and satisfy it forever.

And if His people turn away from Him and go after idols of their own making, they must be left to reap the bitter fruit of their own doings, and to prove, by sad and terrible experience, the truth of these words: "Their sorrows shall be multiplied that hasten after another."

But mark how touchingly Moses presents to the people the bright side of things—a brightness springing from the eternal stability of the grace of God, and the perfect provision which that grace has made for all His people's need, from first to last. *"But,"* he says—and O, how lovely are some of the "buts" of holy Scripture!—"if from thence thou shalt seek the Lord thy God, thou shalt find Him, if thou seek Him with all thy heart and with all thy soul." Exquisite grace! "When thou art in tribulation"—that is the time to find what our God is,—"and all these things are come upon thee, even in the latter days, if thou turn to the Lord thy God, and shalt be obedient unto His voice;"—what then? "A consuming fire"? Nay; but "the Lord *thy God* is a merciful God; He will not forsake thee, neither destroy thee, nor forget the covenant of thy fathers which He sware unto them."

Here we have a remarkable onlook into Israel's future, their departure from God and consequent dispersion among the nations, the complete breaking up of their polity, and the passing away of their national glory. But, blessed forever be the God of all grace, there is something beyond all this failure and sin and ruin and judgment. When we get to the far end of Israel's melancholy history—a history which may truly be summed up in that one brief but comprehensive sentence, "O Israel, thou hast destroyed thyself," we are met by the magnificent display of the grace, mercy, and faithfulness of Jehovah, the God of their fathers, whose heart of love tells itself out in that added sentence, "In Me is thy help." Yes; the whole matter is wrapped up in these two vigorous sentences, "Thou hast destroyed thyself," "But in Me is thy help." In the former, we have the sharp arrow for Israel's conscience; in the latter, the soothing balm for Israel's broken heart.

In thinking of the nation of Israel, there are two pages which we have to study, namely, the historic and the prophetic. The page of history records, with unerring faithfulness, their utter ruin: the page of prophecy unfolds, in accents of matchless grace, God's remedy. Israel's past has been dark and gloomy: Israel's future will be bright and glorious. In the former, we see the miserable actings of man; in the latter, the blessed ways of God. That gives the forcible illustration of what man is; this, the bright display of what God is. We must look at both if we would understand aright the history of this remarkable people—"a people terrible from their beginning hitherto," and, we may truly add, a people wonderful to the end of time.

We do not, of course, attempt to adduce, in this place, proofs of our statement as to Israel's past and Israel's future. To do so would, we may say, without any exaggeration, demand a volume, inasmuch as it would simply be to quote a very large portion of the historical books of the Bible on the one hand, and of the prophetic books on the other. This, we need hardly say, is out of the question; but we feel bound to press upon the reader's attention the precious teaching contained in the quotation given above. It embodies, in its brief compass, the whole truth as to Israel's past, present, and future. Mark how their past is vividly portrayed in these few words: "When thou shalt beget children, and children's children, and ye shall have remained long in the land, and shall corrupt yourselves, and make a graven image, or the likeness of any thing, and shall do evil in the sight of the Lord thy God, to provoke Him to anger."

Is not this precisely what they have done? Is it not here, as it were, in a nutshell? They have done evil in the sight of Jehovah their God, to provoke Him to anger. That one word, *"evil"* takes all in, from the calf at Horeb to the cross at Calvary. Such is Israel's past.

And now, what of their present? Are they not a standing monument of the imperishable truth of God? Has a single jot or tittle failed of all that God has spoken? Hearken to these glowing words: "I call heaven and earth to witness against you this day, that ye shall soon utterly perish from off the land whereunto ye go over Jordan to possess it; ye shall not prolong your days upon it, but shall utterly be destroyed. And the Lord shall scatter you among the nations, and ye shall be left few in number among the heathen, whither the Lord shall lead you."

Has not all this been fulfilled to the letter? Who can question it? Israel's past and Israel's present alike attest the truth of God's Word. And are we not justified in declaring that inasmuch as the past and the present are a literal accomplishment of the truth of God, so shall the future? Assuredly. The page of history and the page of prophecy were both indited by the same Spirit, and therefore they are both alike true; and as the history records Israel's sin and Israel's dispersion, so doth the prophecy predict Israel's repentance and Israel's restoration. The one is as true to faith as the other. As surely as Israel sinned in the past and are scattered at the present, so surely shall they repent and be restored in the future.

This, we conceive, is beyond all question; and we rejoice to think of it. There is not one of the prophets, from Isaiah to Malachi, that does not most distinctly set forth, in accents of sweetest grace and most tender mercy, the future blessings, pre-eminence, and glory of the seed of Abraham.* It would be simply delightful to quote some of the sublime passages bearing upon this most interesting subject; but we must leave the reader to search them out for himself, especially commending to his notice the precious passages contained in the closing chapters of Isaiah, in which he will find a perfect feast, as well as the fullest confirmation of the apostle's statement that "all Israel shall be saved." All the prophets, "from Samuel and those that follow after," agree as to this. The teachings of the New Testament harmonize with the voices of the prophets, and hence to call in question the truth of Israel's restoration to their own land, and final blessing there, under the rule of their own Messiah, is simply to ignore or deny the testimony of prophets and apostles, speaking and writing by the direct inspiration of God the Holy Ghost; it is to set aside a body of Scripture evidence perfectly overwhelming.

It seems passing strange that any true lover of Christ should seek to do this; yet so it is, and so it has been, through religious prejudice, theological bias, and various other causes. But, notwithstanding all this, the glorious truth of Israel's restoration and pre-eminence in the earth shines with undimmed lustre on the prophetic page, and all who seek to set it aside, or interfere with it in any way, are not only flying in the face of holy Scripture—contradicting the unanimous voice of apostles and prophets, but also seeking to tamper (ignorantly and unwittingly, no doubt) with the counsel, purpose, and promise of the Lord God of Israel, and to nullify His covenant with Abraham, Isaac, and Jacob.

This is serious work for any one to engage in, and we believe many are doing it without being aware of it; for we must understand that any one who applies the promises made to the Old Testament fathers to the New Testament Church is, in reality, doing the serious work of which we speak. We maintain that no one has the slightest warrant to alienate the promises made to the fathers. We may learn from those promises, delight in them, draw comfort and encouragement from their eternal stability and direct literal application—all this is blessedly true; but it is another thing altogether for men, under the influence of a system of interpretation falsely called spiritual, to apply to the Church, or to believers of the New Testament times, prophecies which, as simply and plainly as words can indicate, apply to Israel—to the literal seed of Abraham.

This is what we consider so very serious. We believe we have very little idea of how thoroughly opposed all this is to the mind and heart of God. He loves Israel—loves them for the fathers' sake, and we may rest assured He will not sanction our interference with their place, their portion, or their pros-

*Jonah, of course, is an exception; his mission was to Nineveh. He is the only prophet whose commission had exclusive reference to the Gentiles.

pect. We are all familiar with the words of the inspired apostle in Romans 11, however we may have missed or forgotten their true import and moral force.

Speaking of Israel, in connection with the olive-tree of promise, he says, "And they also, if they abide not still in unbelief, shall be graffed in; for" the most simple, solid, and blessed of all reasons—"*God is able,*" as He is most surely willing, "to graff them in again. For if thou wert cut out of the olive-tree which is wild by nature, and wert graffed contrary to nature into a good olive-tree; how much more shall these, which be the natural branches, be graffed into their own olive-tree? For I would not, brethren, that ye should be ignorant of this mystery, lest ye should be wise in your own conceits; that blindness *in part* is happened to Israel, until the fullness of the Gentiles be come in.* And so all Israel shall be saved: as it is written, 'There shall come out of Sion the Deliverer, and shall turn away ungodliness from Jacob: *for this is My covenant unto them,* when I shall take away their sins.' As concerning the gospel, they are enemies for your sakes; but as touching the election, they are beloved for the fathers' sake. For the gifts and calling of God are without repentance. For as ye in times past have not believed God, yet have now obtained mercy through their unbelief; even so have these also now not believed in your mercy [or, mercy to you. *See Greek.*] that they also may obtain mercy." That is, that instead of coming in on the ground of law, or fleshly descent, they should come in simply on the ground of sovereign mercy, just as the Gentiles. "For God hath concluded them all in unbelief, that He might have *mercy upon all.*"

Here ends the section bearing upon our immediate subject, but we cannot refrain from quoting the splendid doxology which bursts forth from the overflowing heart of the inspired apostle as he closes the grand dispensational division of his Epistle—"O the depth of the riches both of the wisdom and knowledge of God! how unsearchable are His judgments, and His ways past finding out! For who hath known the mind of the Lord? or who hath been His counselor? or who hath first given to Him, and it shall be recompensed unto him again? For *of* Him," as the source, "and *through* Him," as the channel, "and *to* Him," as the object, "are all things: to whom be glory forever. Amen."

The foregoing splendid passage, as indeed all Scripture, is in perfect keeping with the teaching of the fourth chapter of our book. Israel's present condition is the fruit of their dark unbelief: Israel's future glory will be the fruit of God's rich sovereign mercy. "The Lord thy God is a merciful God, He will not forsake thee, neither destroy thee, nor forget the covenant of thy fathers which He sware unto them. For ask now of the days that are past, which were before thee, since the day that God created man upon the earth, and ask from the one side of heaven unto the other"—the utmost bounds of time and space were to be appealed to, to see—"whether there hath been any such thing as this great thing is, or hath been heard like it? Did ever people hear the voice of God speaking out of the midst of the fire, as thou hast heard, and live? Or hath God assayed to go and take Him a nation from the midst of another nation, by temptations, by signs, and by wonders, and by war, and by a mighty hand, and by a stretched-out arm, and by great terrors, according to all that the Lord your God did for you in Egypt before your eyes? Unto thee it was showed, that thou mightest know that the Lord He is God; there is none else beside Him. Out of heaven He made thee to hear His voice, that He might instruct thee, and upon earth He showed thee His great fire; and thou heardest His words out of the midst of the fire."

Here we have set forth, with singular moral power, the grand object of all the divine actings on Israel's behalf. It was that

*The reader must seize the difference between "the fullness of the Gentiles" in Romans 11, and "the times of the Gentiles" in Luke 21. The former refers to those who are now being gathered into the Church: the latter, on the contrary, refers to the times of Gentile supremacy which began with Nebuchadnezzar, and runs on to the time when "the stone cut out without hands" shall fall, in crushing power, upon the great image of Daniel 2.

they might know that Jehovah was the one true and living God, and that there was and could be none beside Him. In a word, it was the purpose of God that Israel should be a witness for Him on the earth; and so they most assuredly shall, though hitherto they have signally failed and caused His great and holy name to be blasphemed among the nations. Nothing can hinder the purpose of God. His covenant shall stand forever. Israel shall yet be a blessed and effective witness for God on the earth, and a channel of rich and everlasting blessing to all nations. Jehovah has pledged His word as to this, and not all the powers of earth and hell—men and devils combined—can hinder the full accomplishment of all that He has spoken. His glory is involved in Israel's future, and if a single jot or tittle of His Word were to fail, it would be a dishonor cast upon His great name, and an occasion for the enemy, which is utterly impossible. Israel's future blessing and Jehovah's glory are bound together by a link which can never be snapped. If this be not clearly seen, we can neither understand Israel's past nor Israel's future. Nay, more; we may assert, with all possible confidence, that unless this blessed fact be fully grasped, our system of prophetic interpretation must be utterly false.

But there is another truth set forth in our chapter—a truth of peculiar interest and preciousness. It is not merely that the glory of Jehovah is involved in Israel's future restoration and blessedness; the love of His heart is also engaged. This comes out with touching sweetness in the following words: "And because He loved thy fathers, therefore He chose their seed after them, and brought thee out in His sight with His mighty power out of Egypt; to drive out nations from before thee greater and mightier than thou art, to bring thee in, to give thee their land for an inheritance, as it is this day."

Thus the truth of God's word, the glory of His great name, and the love of His heart are all involved in His dealings with the seed of Abraham His friend; and albeit they have broken the law, dishonored His name, despised His mercy, rejected His prophets, crucified His Son, and resisted His Spirit—although they have done all this, and, in consequence thereof, are scattered and peeled and broken, and shall yet pass through unexampled tribulation, yet will the God of Abraham, Isaac, and Jacob glorify His name, make good His word, and manifest the changeless love of His heart in the future history of His earthly people. "Nothing changeth God's affection." Whom He loves and as He loves He loves unto the end.

If we deny this in reference to Israel, we have not so much as a single inch of solid standing-ground for ourselves: if we touch the truth of God in one department, we have no security as to any thing. "Scripture cannot be broken." "All the promises of God in Him are yea, and in Him Amen, unto the glory of God." God has pledged Himself to the seed of Abraham; He has promised to give them the land of Canaan, *forever.* "His gifts and calling are without repentance." He never repents of His gift or His call; and therefore for any one to attempt to alienate His promises and His gifts, or to interfere in any way with their application to their true and proper object, must be a grievous offense to Him. It mars the integrity of divine truth, deprives us of all certainty in the interpretation of holy Scripture, and plunges the soul in darkness, doubt, and perplexity.

The teaching of Scripture is clear, definite, and distinct. The Holy Ghost, who indited the sacred volume, means what He says and says what He means. If He speaks of Israel, He means Israel—of Zion, He means Zion—of Jerusalem, He means Jerusalem. To apply any one of these names to the New Testament Church is to confound things that differ, and introduce a method of interpreting Scripture which, from its vagueness and looseness, can only lead to the most disastrous consequences. If we handle the Word of God in such a loose and careless manner, it is utterly impossible to realize its divine authority over our conscience, or exhibit its formative power in our course, conduct, and character.

We must now look, for a moment, at the powerful appeal with which Moses sums up his address in our chapter: it demands our profound and reverent attention: "Know *therefore* this day, and *consider it in thine heart,* that the Lord He is God in heaven above, and upon the earth beneath; there is none else. Thou shalt keep *therefore* His statutes, and His commandments, which I command thee this day, that it may go well with thee, and with thy children after thee, and that thou mayest prolong thy days upon the earth, which the Lord thy God giveth thee, forever" (ver. 39-40).

Here we see that the moral claim upon their hearty obedience is grounded upon the revealed character of God, and His marvelous actings on their behalf. In a word, they were bound to obey—bound by every argument that could possibly act on the heart, the conscience, and the understanding. The One who had brought them out of the land of Egypt, with a mighty hand and outstretched arm; who had made that land to tremble to its very centre, by stroke after stroke of His judicial rod; who had opened up a pathway for them through the sea; who had sent them bread from heaven, and brought forth water for them out of the flinty rock; and all this for the glory of His great name, and because He loved their fathers—surely He was entitled to their whole-hearted obedience.

This is the grand argument, so eminently characteristic of this blessed book of Deuteronomy. And surely this is full of instruction for Christians now. If Israel were morally bound to obey, how much more are we! If their motives and objects were powerful, how much more so are ours! Do we feel their power? do we consider them in our hearts? Do we ponder the claims of Christ upon us? Do we remember that we are not our own, but bought with a price, even the infinitely precious price of the blood of Christ? Do we realize this? Are we seeking to live for Him? Is His glory our ruling object?—His love our constraining motive? or are we living for ourselves? Are we seeking to get on in the world—that world that crucified our blessed Lord and Saviour? Are we seeking to make money? do we love it in our hearts, either for its own sake or for the sake of what it can procure? does money *govern* us? Are we seeking a place in the world, either for ourselves or for our children? Let us honestly challenge our hearts, as in the divine presence, in the light of God's truth, what is our object—our real, governing, cherished, heart-sought object?

These are searching questions. Let us not put them aside: let us really weigh them in the very light of the judgment-seat of Christ. We believe they are wholesome, much-needed questions. We live in very solemn times. There is a fearful amount of sham on every side, and in nothing is this sham so awfully apparent as in so-called religion.

The very days in which our lot is cast have been sketched by a pen that never colors—never exaggerates, but always presents men and things precisely as they are. "This know also, that in *the last days"*—quite distinct from *"the latter times"* of 1 Timothy 4—far in advance, more pronounced, more closely defined, more strongly marked, these last days in which "perilous [or difficult] times shall come. For men shall be *lovers of their own selves,* covetous, *boasters,* proud, blasphemers, *disobedient to parents,* unthankful, unholy, *without natural affection,* truce-breakers, *false accusers,* incontinent, fierce, despisers of those that are good, traitors, heady, high-minded, *lovers of pleasures more* [or rather] *than lovers of God."* And then mark the crown which the inspired apostle puts upon this appalling superstructure!—"Having a form of godliness, but denying the power thereof" (2 Tim. 3:1-5).

What a terrible picture! We have here, in a few glowing, weighty sentences, *infidel* christendom, just as in 1 Timothy 4 we have *superstitious* christendom. In the latter, we see popery; in the former, infidelity. Both elements are at work around us, but the latter will yet rise into prominence—indeed, even now it is advancing with rapid strides. The very leaders and teachers of christendom are not ashamed or afraid to attack the foundations of Christianity. A so-called Christian bishop is not ashamed or afraid to call in question the integrity of the five books of Moses, and, with them, of the whole Bible; for, most assuredly, if Moses was not the inspired writer of the Pentateuch, the entire edifice of holy Scripture is swept from beneath our feet. The writings of Moses are so intimately bound up with all the other grand divisions of the divine volume, that if they are touched, all is gone. We boldly affirm that if the Holy Ghost did not inspire Moses, the servant of God, to write the first five books of our English Bible, we have not an inch of solid ground to stand upon; we are positively left without a single atom of divine authority on which to rest our souls; the very pillars of our glorious Christianity are swept away, and we are left to grope our way, in hopeless perplexity, amid the conflicting opinions and theories of infidel doctors, without so much as a single ray from Inspiration's heavenly lamp.

Does this appear too strong for the reader? Does he believe that we can listen, for a moment, to the infidel denier of Moses, and yet believe in the inspiration of the psalms, the prophets, and the New Testament? If he does, let him be well assured he is under the power of a fatal delusion. Let him take such passages as the following, and ask himself, What do they mean, and what is wrapped up in them? Our Lord, in speaking to the Jews—who, by the way, would not have agreed with a Christian bishop in denying the authenticity of Moses—says, "Do not think that I will accuse you to the Father; there is one that accuseth you, even Moses, in whom ye trust. For had ye believed Moses, ye would have believed Me; for he wrote of Me. But if ye believe not his writings, how shall ye believe My words?" (John 5:45-47)

Think of this: The man that does not believe in the writings of Moses—does not receive every line of his as divinely inspired, does not believe in Christ's words, and therefore cannot have any divinely wrought faith in Christ Himself—cannot be a Christian at all. This makes it a very serious matter for any one to deny the divine inspiration of the Pentateuch, and equally serious for any one to listen to him or sympathize with him. It is all very well to talk of Christian charity and liberality of spirit; but we have yet to learn that it is charity or liberality to sanction, in any way, a man who has the audacity to sweep from beneath our feet the very foundations of our faith. To speak of him as a Christian bishop, or a Christian minister of any kind, is only to make the matter a thousand times worse. We can understand a Voltaire or a Paine attacking the Bible—we do not look for any thing else from them; but when those who assume to be the recognized and ordained ministers of religion, and the guardians of the faith of God's elect—those who consider themselves alone entitled to teach and preach Jesus Christ, and feed and tend the Church of God—when they actually call in question the inspiration of the five books of Moses, may we not well ask, Where are we? What has the professing church come to?

But let us take another passage. It is the powerful appeal of the risen Saviour to the two bewildered disciples on their way to Emmaus: " 'O fools, and slow of heart to believe all that the prophets have spoken; ought not Christ to have suffered these things, and to enter into His glory?' And *beginning at Moses* and all the prophets, He expounded unto them in all the Scriptures the things concerning Himself." And again, to the eleven and others with them, He says, "These are the words which I spake unto you, while I was yet with you, that all things must be fulfilled, which were written *in the law of Moses,* and in the prophets, and in the psalms, concerning Me" (Luke 24:25-27,44).

Here we find that our Lord, in the most distinct and positive manner, recognizes the law of Moses as an integral part of the canon of inspiration, and binds it up with all the other grand divisions of the divine volume in such a way that it is utterly impossible to touch one without destroying the integrity of the whole. If Moses is not to be trusted, neither are the prophets, nor the psalms. They stand or fall together. And not only so, but we must either admit the divine authenticity of the Pentateuch or draw the blasphemous inference that our adorable Lord and Saviour gave the sanction of His authority to a set of spurious documents, by quoting as the writings of Moses what Moses never wrote at all! There is positively not a single inch of consistent standing-ground between these two conclusions.

Again, take the following most weighty and important passage at the close of the parable of the rich man and Lazarus: "Abraham saith unto him, 'They have *Moses and the prophets; let them hear them.'* And he said, 'Nay, father Abraham; but if one went unto them from the dead, they will repent.' And he said unto him, 'If they hear not Moses and the prophets, neither will they be persuaded though one rose from the dead" (Luke 16:29-31).

Finally, if we add to all this the fact that our Lord, in His conflict with Satan in the wilderness, quotes only from the writings of Moses, we have a body of evidence quite sufficient, not only to establish, beyond all question, the divine inspiration of Moses, but also to prove that the man who calls in question the authenticity of the first five books of the Bible, can really have no Bible, no divine revelation, no authority, no solid foundation for his faith. He may call himself, or be called by others, a Christian bishop or a Christian minister; but, in solemn fact, he is a skeptic, and should be treated as such by all who believe and know the truth. We cannot understand how any one with a spark of divine life in his soul could be guilty of the awful sin of denying the inspiration of a large portion of the Word of God, or asserting that our Lord Christ could quote from spurious documents.

We may be deemed severe in thus writing. It seems the fashion nowadays to own as Christians those who deny the very foundations of Christianity. It is a very popular notion that, provided people are moral, amiable, benevolent, charitable, and philanthropic, it is of very small consequence what they believe. Life is better than creed or dogma, we are told. All this sounds very plausible: but the reader may rest assured that the direct tendency of all this manner of speech and line of argument is to get rid of the Bible—rid of the Holy Ghost—rid of Christ—rid of God—rid of all that the Bible reveals to our souls. Let him bear this in mind, and seek to keep close to the precious Word of God; let him treasure that Word in his heart, and give himself more and more to the prayerful study of it. Thus he will be preserved from the withering influence of skepticism and infidelity, in every shape and form; his soul will be fed and nourished by the sincere milk of the Word, and his whole moral being be kept in the shelter of the divine presence continually. This is what is needed: nothing else will do.

We must now close our meditations on this marvelous chapter which has been engaging our attention; but ere doing so, we would glance for a moment at the remarkable notice of the three cities of refuge. It might, to a cursory reader, seem abrupt; but, so far from that, it is, as we might expect, in perfect and beautiful moral order. Scripture is always divinely perfect, and if we do not see and appreciate its beauties and moral glories, it is simply owing to our blindness and insensibility.

"Then Moses severed three cities on this side Jordan toward the sunrising; that the slayer might flee thither, which should kill his neighbor unawares, and hated him not in times past; and that fleeing unto one of those cities he might live; namely, Bezer in the wilderness, in the plain country, of the Reubenites; and Ramoth in Gilead, of the Gadites; and Golan in Bashan, of the Manassites."

Here we have a lovely display of the grace of God rising, as it ever does, above human weakness and failure. The two tribes and a half, in choosing their inheritance on this side Jordan, were manifestly stopping short of the proper portion of the Israel of God, which lay on the other side of the river of death; but, notwithstanding this failure, God, in His abounding grace, would not leave the poor slayer without a refuge in the day of his distress. If man cannot come up to the height of God's thoughts, God can come down to the depths of man's need; and so blessedly does He do so in this case, that the two tribes and a half were to have as many cities of refuge on this side Jordan as the nine tribes and a half had in the land of Canaan.

This, truly, was grace abounding. How unlike the manner of man! How far above mere law or legal righteousness! It might, in a legal way, have been said to the two tribes and a half, If you are going to choose your inheritance short of the divine mark—if you are content with less than Canaan, the land of promise, you must not expect to enjoy the privileges and blessings of that land. The institutions of Canaan must be confined to Canaan, and hence your manslayer must try and make his way across the Jordan and find refuge there.

Law might speak thus, but Grace spoke differently. God's thoughts are not ours, nor His ways as ours. We might deem it marvelous grace to provide even one city for the two and a half tribes; but our God does exceeding abundantly above all that we ask or think, and hence the comparatively small district on this side Jordan was furnished with as full a provision of grace as the entire land of Canaan.

Does this prove that the two and a half tribes were right? Nay; but it proves that God was good, and that He must ever act like Himself, spite of all our weakness and folly. Could He leave a poor slayer without a place of refuge in the land of Gilead, though Gilead was not Canaan? Surely not. This would not be worthy of the One who says, "*I bring near* My righteousness." He took care to bring the city of refuge "near" to the slayer. He would cause His rich and precious grace to flow over and meet the needy one just where he was. Such is the way of our God, blessed be His holy name for evermore!

"And this is the law which Moses set before the children of Israel: these are the testimonies, and the statutes, and the judgments, which Moses spake unto the children of Israel, after they came forth out of Egypt, on this side Jordan, in the valley over against Beth-peor, in the land of Sihon king of the Amorites, who dwelt at Heshbon, whom Moses and the children of Israel smote, after they were come forth out of Egypt: and they possessed his land, and the land of Og king of Bashan, two kings of the Amorites, which were on this side Jordan toward the sunrising; from Aroer, which is by the bank of the river Arnon, even unto Mount Sion, which is Hermon, and all the plain on this side Jordan eastward, even unto the sea of the plain, under the springs of Pisgah."

Here closes this marvelous discourse. The Spirit of God delights to trace the boundaries of the people, and dwell on the most minute details connected with their history. He takes a lively and loving interest in all that concerns them—their conflicts, their victories, their possessions, all their landmarks; every thing about them is dwelt upon with a minuteness which, by its touching grace and condescension, fills the heart with wonder, love, and praise. Man, in his contemptible self-importance, thinks it beneath his dignity to enter upon minute details; but *our* God counts the hairs of our heads, puts our tears into His bottle, takes knowledge of our every care, our every sorrow, our every need. There is nothing too small for His love, as there is nothing too great for His power. He concentrates His loving care upon each one of His people as though He had only that one to attend to; and there is not a single circumstance in our private history, from day to day, however trivial, in which He does not take a loving interest.

Let us ever remember this, for our comfort; and may we learn to trust Him better, and use, with a more artless faith, His fatherly love and care. He tells us to cast *all* our care upon Him, in the assurance that He careth for us. He would have our hearts as free from care as our conscience is free from guilt. "Be careful for *nothing;* but in every thing by prayer and supplication with thanksgiving let your requests be made known unto God. And the peace of God, which passeth *all* understanding, shall keep your hearts and minds through Christ Jesus" (Phil. 4:6-7).

It is to be feared that the great majority of us know but little of the real depth, meaning, and power of such words as these. We read them and hear them, but we do not take them in and make our own of them—we do not digest them and reduce them to practice. How little do we really enter into the blessed truth that our Father is interested in all our little cares and sorrows, and that we may go to Him with all our little wants and difficulties. We imagine that such things are beneath the notice of the high and mighty One who inhabiteth eternity and sitteth upon the circle of the earth. This is a serious mistake, and one that robs us of incalculable blessing in our daily history. We should ever remember that there is nothing great or small with our God: all things are alike to Him who sustains the vast universe by the word of His power, and takes notice of a falling sparrow. It is quite as easy to Him to create a world as to provide a breakfast for some poor widow. The greatness of His power, the moral grandeur of His government, and the minuteness of His tender care, do all alike command the wonder and the worship of our hearts.

Christian reader, see that you make your own of all these things. Seek to live nearer to God in your daily walk. Lean more upon Him. Use Him more. Go to Him in all your need, and you will never have to tell your need to a poor fellow-mortal. "My God shall supply *all* your need, according to His riches in glory by Christ Jesus." What a source—"God"! What a standard—"His riches in glory"! What a channel—"Christ Jesus"! It is your sweet privilege to place all *your need* over against *His riches,* and lose sight of the former in the presence of the latter. His exhaustless treasury is thrown open to you, in all the love of His heart; go and draw upon it, in the artless simplicity of faith, and you will never have occasion to look to a creature-stream or lean on a creature-prop.

---

## *CHAPTER 5*

"AND Moses called all Israel, and said unto them, 'Hear O Israel, the statutes and judgments which I speak in your ears this day, that ye may learn them, and keep and do them.' "

Let us carefully note these four words, so specially characteristic of the book of Deuteronomy, and so seasonable for the Lord's people at all times and in all places: *"Hear," "Learn," "Keep," "Do."* These are words of unspeakable preciousness to every truly pious soul—to every one who honestly desires to walk in that narrow path of practical righteousness so pleasing to God, and so safe and so happy for us.

The first of these words places the soul in the most blessed attitude in which any one can be found, namely, that of *hearing.* "Faith cometh by *hearing,* and hearing by the Word of God." "I will *hear* what God the Lord will speak." *"Hear,* and your soul shall live." The hearing ear lies at the very foundation of all true, practical Christian life. It places the soul in the only true and proper attitude for the creature. It is the real secret of all peace and blessedness.

It can scarcely be needful to remind the reader that when we speak of the soul in the attitude of hearing, it is assumed that what is heard is simply the Word of God. Israel had to hearken to "the statutes and judgments" of Jehovah, and to nothing else. It was not to the commandments, traditions, and doctrines of men they were to give ear, but to the very words of the living God, who had redeemed and delivered them from the land of Egypt—the place of bondage, darkness, and death.

It is well to bear this in mind. It will preserve the soul from many a snare, many a difficulty. We hear a good deal, in certain quarters, about obedience, and about the moral fitness of surrendering our own will and submitting ourselves to authority. All this sounds very well, and has great weight with a large class of very religious and morally excellent people; but when men speak to us about obedience, we must ask the question, obedience to what? when they speak to us about surrendering our own will, we must inquire of them, To whom are we to surrender it? when they speak to us about submitting to authority, we must insist upon their telling us the source or foundation of the authority.

This is of the deepest possible moment to every member of the household of faith. There are many very sincere and very earnest people who deem it very delightful to be saved the trouble of thinking for themselves, and to have their sphere of action and line of service laid out for them by wiser heads than their own. It seems a very restful and very pleasing thing to have each day's work laid out for us by some master-hand. It relieves the heart of a great load of responsibility, and it looks like humility and self-distrust to submit ourselves to some authority.

But we are bound, before God, to look well to the basis of the authority to which we surrender ourselves, else we may find ourselves in an utterly false position. Take, for example, a monk, or a nun, or a member of a sisterhood. A monk obeys his abbot, a nun obeys her mother-abbess, "a sister" obeys her "lady-superior"; but the position and relationship of each is utterly false. There is not a shadow of authority in the New Testament for monasteries, convents, or sisterhoods; on the contrary, the teaching of holy Scripture, as well as the voice of nature, is utterly opposed to every one of them, inasmuch as they take men and women out of the place and out of the relationship in which God has set them, and in which they are designed and fitted to move, and form them into societies which are utterly destructive of natural affection, and subversive of all true Christian obedience.

We feel it right to call the attention of the Christian reader to this subject just now, seeing that the enemy is making a vigorous effort to revive the monastic system in our midst under various forms. Indeed some have had the temerity to tell us that monastic life is the only true form of Christianity. Surely, when such monstrous statements are made and listened to, it becomes us to look at the whole subject in the light of Scripture, and to call upon the advocates and adherents of monasticism to show us the foundations of the system in the Word of God. Where, within the covers of the New Testament, is there any thing, in the most remote degree, like a monastery, a convent, or a sisterhood? Where can we find an authority for any such office as that of an abbot, an abbess, or a lady-superior? There is absolutely no such thing, nor the shadow of it; and hence we have no hesitation in pronouncing the whole system, from foundation to top-stone, a fabric of superstition, alike opposed to the voice of nature and the voice of God: nor can we understand how any one, in his sober senses, could presume to tell us that a monk or a nun is the only true exponent of Christian life. Yet there are those who thus speak, and there are those who listen to them, and that, too, in this day when the full, clear light of our glorious Christianity is shining upon us from the pages of the New Testament.*

But, blessed be God, we are called to obedience. We are called to "hear"—called to bow down, in holy and reverent submission, to authority. And here we join issue with infidelity and its lofty pretensions. The path of the devout and lowly Christian is alike removed from superstition on the one hand and from infidelity on the other. Peter's noble reply to the council, in Acts 5, embodies, in its brief compass, a complete answer to both. "We ought to obey God rather than men." We meet infidelity, in all its phases, in all its stages, and in its very deepest roots, with this one weighty sentence, "We ought to *obey*"; and we meet superstition, in every garb in which it clothes itself, with the all-important clause, "We ought to *obey God.*"

Here we have set forth, in the most simple form, the duty of every true Christian. He is to obey God. The infidel may smile contemptuously at a monk or a nun, and marvel how any rational being can so completely surrender his reason and his understanding to the authority of a fellow-mortal, or submit himself to rules and practices so absurd, so degrading, and so contrary to nature. The infidel glories in his fancied intellectual free-

*We must accurately distinguish between *"nature"* and *"flesh."* The former is recognized in Scripture; the latter is condemned and set aside. "Doth not even nature itself teach you?" says the apostle (1 Cor. 11:14). Jesus beholding the young ruler in Mark 10, "loved him" although there was nothing but nature. To be without natural affection is one of the marks of the apostasy. Scripture teaches that we are dead to sin, not to nature, else what becomes of our natural relationships?

dom, and imagines that his own reason is quite a sufficient guide for him. He does not see that he is further from God than the poor monk or nun whom he so despises. He does not know that, while priding himself in his self-will, he is really led captive by Satan—the prince and god of this world. Man is formed to obey—formed to look up to some one above him. The Christian is sanctified unto the obedience of Jesus Christ, that is, to the very same character of obedience as that which was rendered by our adorable Lord and Saviour Himself.

This is of the deepest possible moment to every one who really desires to know what true Christian obedience is. To understand this is the real secret of deliverance from the self-will of the infidel and the false obedience of superstition. It can never be right to do our own will: it may be quite wrong to do the will of our fellow: it must always be right to do the will of God. This was what Jesus came to do, and what He always did. "Lo, I come to do Thy will, O God." "I delight to do Thy will, O My God; yea, Thy law is within My heart."

Now, we are called and set apart to the blessed character of obedience, as we learn from the inspired apostle Peter, in the opening of his first Epistle, where he speaks of believers as "elect according to the foreknowledge of God the Father, through sanctification of the Spirit, unto obedience and sprinkling of the blood of Jesus Christ."

This is an immense privilege, and at the same time a most holy and solemn responsibility. We must never forget for a moment that God has elected us, and the Holy Spirit has set us apart, not only to the sprinkling of the blood of Jesus Christ, but also to His obedience. Such is the obvious meaning and moral force of the words just quoted—words of unspeakable preciousness to every lover of holiness—words which effectually deliver us from self-will, from legality, and from superstition. Blessed deliverance!

But it may be that the pious reader feels disposed to call our attention to the exhortation in Hebrews 13—"Obey them that have the rule over you, and submit yourselves; for they watch for your souls, as they that must give account; that they may do it with joy and not with grief; for that is unprofitable for you."

A deeply important word, most surely, with which we should also connect a passage in 1 Thessalonians—"And we beseech you, brethren, to know them that labor among you, and are over you in the Lord, and admonish you, and to esteem them very highly in love for their work's sake" (chap. 5:12-13). And again, in 1 Corinthians 16:15-16—"I beseech you, brethren, (ye know the house of Stephanas, that it is the first-fruits of Achaia, and that they have addicted themselves to the ministry [or service] of the saints,) that ye submit yourselves unto such, and to every one that helpeth with us and laboreth." To all these we must add another very lovely passage from the first Epistle of Peter—"The elders which are among you I exhort, who am also an elder, and a witness of the sufferings of Christ, and also a partaker of the glory that shall be revealed: feed the flock of God which is among you, taking the oversight thereof, not by constraint, but willingly; not for filthy lucre, but of a ready mind; neither as being lords over God's heritage, but being ensamples to the flock. And when the chief Shepherd shall appear, ye shall receive a crown of glory that fadeth not away" (chap. 5:1-4).

We may be asked, Do not the above passages set forth the principle of obedience to certain men? and if so, why object to human authority? The answer is very simple. Wherever Christ imparts a spiritual gift, whether it be the gift of teaching, the gift of rule, or the gift of pastorship, it is the bounden duty and privilege of Christians to recognize and appreciate such gifts. Not to do so would be to forsake our own mercies. But then we must bear in mind that in all such cases the gift must be a reality—a plain, palpable, *bona-fide,* divinely given thing. It is not a man assuming a certain office or position, or being appointed by his fellow to any so-called ministry. All this is perfectly worthless, and worse than worthless; it is a daring intrusion upon a sacred domain which must bring down the judgment of God.

All true ministry is of God, and based upon the possession of a positive gift from the Head of the Church; so that we may truly say, no gift, no ministry. In all the passages quoted above, we see positive gift possessed, and actual work done. Moreover, we see a true heart for the lambs and sheep of the flock of Christ; we see divine grace and power. The word in Hebrews 13 is, "Obey them that guide you [ἡγουμενοις]." Now, it is essential to a true guide that he should go before you in the way. It would be the height of folly for any one to assume the title of guide if he were ignorant of the way, and neither able nor willing to go in it. Who would think of obeying such?

So also when the apostle exhorts the Thessalonians to "know" and "esteem" certain persons, on what does he found his exhortation? Is it upon the mere assumption of a title, an office, or a position? Nothing of the kind. He grounds his appeal upon the actual, well-known fact that these persons were "over them, *in the Lord,*" and that they admonished them. And why were they to "esteem them very highly in love"? Was it for their office or their title? No; but "for their work's sake." And why were the Corinthians exhorted to submit themselves to the household of Stephanas? Was it because of an empty title or assumed office? By no means; but because "they addicted themselves to the ministry of the saints." They were actually in the work. They had received gift and grace from Christ, and they had a heart for His people. They were not boasting of their office or insisting upon their title, but giving themselves devotedly to the service of Christ, in the persons of His dear people.

Now this is the true principle of ministry. It is not human authority at all, but divine gift and spiritual power communicated by Christ to His servants, exercised by them, in responsibility to Him, and thankfully recognized by His saints. A man may set up to be a teacher or a pastor, or he may be appointed by his fellows to the office or title of a pastor; but unless he possesses a positive gift from the Head of the Church, it is all the merest sham, a hollow assumption, an empty conceit; and his voice will be the voice of a stranger, which the true sheep of Christ do not know and ought not to recognize.*

But, on the other hand, where there is the divinely gifted teacher, the true, loving, wise, faithful, laborious pastor, watching for souls, weeping over them, waiting upon them, like a gentle, tender nurse, able to say to them, "Now we live, if ye stand fast in the Lord" —where these things are found, there will not be much difficulty in recognizing and appreciating them. How do we know a good dentist? Is it by seeing his name on a brass plate? No; but by his work. A man may call himself a dentist ten thousand times over, but if he be only an unskillful operator, who would think of employing him?

Thus it is in all human affairs, and thus it is in the matter of ministry. If a man has a gift, he is a minister; if he has not, all the appointment, authority, and ordination in the world could not make him a minister of Christ. It may make him a minister of religion; but a minister of religion and a minister of Christ—a minister in christendom and a minister in the Church of God, are two

*The reader will do well to ponder the fact that there is no such thing in the New Testament as human appointment to preach the gospel, teach in the assembly of God, or feed the flock of Christ. Elders and deacons were ordained by the apostles or their delegates, Timothy and Titus; but evangelists, pastors, and teachers were never so ordained. We must distinguish between gift and local charge. Elders and deacons might possess a special gift or not; it had nothing to do with their local charge. If the reader would understand the subject of ministry, let him study 1 Corinthians 12–14, and Ephesians 4:8-13. In the former we have, first, the *basis* of all true ministry in the Church of God, namely, *divine appointment*—"God hath set the members," etc.; secondly, *the motive-spring*—"love"; thirdly, *the object*—"that the Church may receive edifying." In Ephesians 4, we have the *source* of all ministry—a risen and ascended Lord; the *design*—"to perfect the saints for the work of the ministry"; the *duration*—"till we all come unto a perfect man, unto the measure of the stature of the fullness of Christ."

In a word, ministry, in all its departments, is *entirely* a divine institution. It is not of man or by man, but of God. The Master must, in every case, fit, fill, and appoint the vessel. There is no authority in Scripture for the notion that every man has a right to minister in the Church of God. Liberty for men is radicalism and not Scripture. Liberty for the Holy Ghost to minister by whom He will is what we are taught in the New Testament. May we learn it.

totally different things. All true ministry has its source in God; it rests on divine authority, and its object is to bring the soul into His presence, and link it on to Him. False ministry, on the contrary, has its source in man; it rests on human authority, and its object is to link the soul on to itself. This marks the immense difference between the two. The former leads to God; the latter leads away from Him; that feeds, nourishes, and strengthens the new life; this hinders its progress, in every way, and plunges it in doubt and darkness. In a word, we may say, true ministry is of God, through Him, and to Him: false ministry is of man, through him, and to him. The former we prize more than we can say; the latter we reject with all the energy of our moral being.

We trust sufficient has been said to satisfy the mind of the reader in reference to the matter of obedience to those whom the Lord may see fit to call to the work of the ministry. We are bound, in every case, to judge by the Word of God, and to be assured that it is a divine reality and not a human sham—a positive gift from the Head of the Church, and not an empty title conferred by men. In all cases where there is real gift and grace, it is a sweet privilege to obey and submit ourselves, inasmuch as we discern Christ in the person and ministry of His beloved servants.

There is no difficulty, to a spiritual mind, in owning real grace and power. We can easily tell whether a man is seeking, in true love, to feed our souls with the bread of life, and lead us on in the ways of God, or whether he is seeking to exalt himself, and promote his own interests. Those who are living near the Lord can readily discern between true power and hollow assumption. Moreover, we never find Christ's true ministers parading their authority, or vaunting themselves of their office; they do the work and leave it to speak for itself. In the case of the blessed apostle Paul, we find him referring again and again to the plain proofs of his ministry—the unquestionable evidence afforded in the conversion and blessing of souls. He could say to the poor misguided Corinthians, when, under the influence of some self-exalting pretender, they foolishly called in question his apostleship, "Since ye seek a proof of Christ speaking in me . . . examine yourselves."

This was close, pointed dealing with them. They themselves were the living proofs of his ministry. If his ministry was not of God, what and when, were they? But it was of God, and this was his joy, his comfort, and his strength. He was "an apostle, not of men, neither by man, but by Jesus Christ, and God the Father, who raised Him from the dead." He gloried in the source of his ministry; and as to its character, he had but to appeal to a body of evidence quite sufficient to carry conviction to any right mind. In his case, it could be truly said, it was not the speech, but the power.

Thus it must be, in measure, in every case. We must look for the power: we must have reality. Mere titles are nothing. Men may undertake to confer titles and appoint to offices, but they have no more authority to do so than they have to appoint admirals in her majesty's fleet or generals in her army. If we were to see a man assuming the style and title of an admiral or a general, without her majesty's commission, we should pronounce him an idiot or a lunatic. This is but a feeble illustration to set forth the folly of men taking upon them the title of ministers of Christ without one atom of spiritual gift or divine authority.

Shall we be told, We must not judge? We are bound to judge. "Beware of false prophets." How can we beware if we are not to judge? But how are we to judge? "By their fruits ye shall know them." Can the Lord's people not tell the difference between a man who comes to them in the power of the Spirit, gifted by the Head of the Church, full of love to their souls, earnestly desiring their true blessing, seeking not theirs but them—a holy, gracious, humble, self-emptied servant of Christ; and a man who comes with a self-assumed or a humanly conferred title, without a single trace of any thing divine or heavenly either in his ministry or in his life? Of course they can; no one in his senses would think of calling in question a fact so obvious.

But further, we may ask, What mean those words of the venerable apostle John—"Beloved, believe not every spirit, but try the spirits whether they are of God; because many false prophets are gone out into the world"? How are we to try the spirits, or how are we to discern between the true and the false, if we are not to judge? Again, the same apostle, writing to "the elect lady," gives her the following most solemn admonition: "If there come any unto you, and bring not this doctrine, receive him not into your house, neither bid him Godspeed; for he that biddeth him Godspeed is partaker of his evil deeds." Was she not responsible to act on this admonition? Assuredly. But how could she if we are not to judge? And what had she to judge? Was it as to whether those who came to her house were ordained, authorized, or licensed by any man or body of men? Nothing of the kind. The one great and all-important question for her was as to the doctrine. If they brought the true, the divine doctrine of Christ—the doctrine of Jesus Christ come in the flesh, she was to receive them; if not, she was to shut her door, with a firm hand, against them, no matter who they were or where they came from. If they had all the credentials that man could bestow upon them, yet if they brought not *the truth,* she was to reject them with stern decision. This might seem very harsh, very narrow-minded, very bigoted; but with this she had nothing whatever to do. She had just to be as broad and as narrow as the truth. Her door and her heart were to be wide enough to admit all who brought Christ, and no wider. Was she to pay compliments at the expense of her Lord? was she to seek a name for largeness of heart or breadth of mind by receiving to her house and to her table the teachers of a false Christ? The very thought is absolutely horrible.

But finally, in the second chapter of Revelation, we find the church at Ephesus commended for having tried those who said they were apostles and were not. How could this be if we are not to judge? Is it not most evident to the reader that an utterly false use is made of our Lord's words in Matthew 7:1—"Judge not, that ye be not judged," and also of the apostle's words in 1 Corinthians 4:5—"Therefore judge nothing before the time"? It is impossible that Scripture can contradict itself; and hence, whatever be the true meaning of our Lord's "Judge not," or the apostle's "Judge nothing," it is perfectly certain that they do not, in the most remote way, interfere with the solemn responsibility of all Christians to judge the gift, the doctrine, and the life of all who take the place of preachers, teachers, and pastors in the Church of God.

And then, if we be asked as to the meaning of "Judge not" and "Judge nothing," we believe the words simply forbid our judging motives, or hidden springs of action. With these we have nothing whatever to do. We cannot penetrate below the surface, and, thanks be to God, we are not asked to do so—yea, we are positively forbidden. We cannot read the counsels of the heart; it is the province and prerogative of God alone to do this: but to say that we are not to judge the doctrine, the gift, or the manner of life of those who take the place of preachers, teachers, and pastors in the Church of God, is simply to fly in the face of holy Scripture, and to ignore the very instincts of the divine nature implanted in us by the Holy Ghost.

Hence, therefore, we can return, with increased clearness and decision, to our thesis of Christian obedience. It seems perfectly plain that the fullest recognition of all true ministry in the Church, and the most gracious submission of ourselves to all those whom our Lord Christ may see fit to raise up as pastors, teachers, and guides in our midst, can never, in the smallest degree, interfere with the grand fundamental principle set forth in Peter's magnificent reply to the council—"We ought to obey God rather than men."

It will ever be the aim and object of all true ministers of Christ to lead those to whom they minister in the true path of obedience to the Word of God. The chapter which lies open before us, as indeed the entire book of Deuteronomy, shows us very plainly how Moses, that eminent servant of God, ever sought and diligently labored to press upon the congregation of Israel the urgent necessity of the most implicit obedience to all the statutes and judgments of God. He did not seek any place of authority for himself: he never lorded it over God's heritage. His one grand theme, from first to last, was obedience. This was the burden of all his discourses—obedience, not to him, but to his and their Lord. He rightly judged that this was the true secret of their happiness, their moral security, their dignity, and their strength. He knew that an obedient people must also, of necessity, be an invincible and invulnerable people. No weapon formed against them could prosper so long as they were governed by the word of God. In a word, he knew and believed that Israel's province was to obey Jehovah, as it was Jehovah's province to bless Israel. It was their one simple business to "hear," "learn," "keep," and "do" the revealed will of God; and so doing, they might count on Him, with all possible confidence, to be their shield, their strength, their safeguard, their refuge, their resource, their all in all. The only true and proper path for the Israel of God is that narrow path of obedience on which the light of God's approving countenance ever shines, and all who, through grace, tread that path will find Him "a guide, a glory, a defense, to save from every fear."

This, surely, is quite enough. We have nothing to do with consequences: these we may, in simple confidence, leave to Him whose we are and whom we are responsible to serve. "The name of the Lord is a strong tower; the righteous runneth into it and is safe." If we are doing His will, we shall ever find His name a strong tower; but, on the other hand, if we are not walking in a path of practical righteousness—if we are doing our own will—if we are living in the habitual neglect of the plain Word of God, then, verily, it is utterly vain for us to think that the name of the Lord will be a strong tower to us; rather would His name be reproof to us, leading us to judge our ways and to return to the path of righteousness from which we have wandered.

Blessed be His name, His grace will ever meet us, in all its precious fullness and freeness, in the place of self-judgment and confession, however we may have failed and wandered; but this is a totally different thing. We may have to say, with the Psalmist, "Out of the depths have I cried unto Thee, O Lord. Lord, hear my voice; let Thine ears be attentive to the voice of my supplications. If Thou, Lord, shouldest mark iniquities, O Lord, who shall stand? But there is forgiveness with Thee, that Thou mayest be feared." But then, a soul crying to God from the depths, and getting forgiveness, is one thing; and a soul looking to Him in the path of practical righteousness is quite another. We must carefully distinguish between these two things. Confessing our sins and finding pardon must never be confounded with walking uprightly and counting on God. Both are blessedly true, but they are not the same thing.

We shall now proceed with our chapter.

At the second verse, Moses reminds the people of their covenant-relationship with Jehovah. He says, "The Lord *our* God made a covenant with us in Horeb. The Lord made not this covenant with our fathers, but with us, even us, who are all of us here alive this day. The Lord talked with you face to face, in the mount, out of the midst of the fire, (I stood between the Lord and you at that time, to show you the word of the Lord; for ye were afraid by reason of the fire, and went not up into the mount) saying," etc.

The reader must distinguish and thoroughly understand the difference between the covenant made at Horeb and the covenant made with Abraham, Isaac, and Jacob. They are essentially different. The former was a covenant of works, in which the people undertook to do all that the Lord had spoken: the latter was a covenant of pure grace, in which God pledged Himself with an oath to do all which He promised.

Human language would utterly fail us to set forth the immense difference, in every respect, between these two covenants. In their basis, in their character, in their accompaniments, and in their practical result, they are as different as any two things could possibly be. The Horeb covenant rested upon human competency for the fulfillment of its terms, and this one fact is quite sufficient to account for the total failure of the whole thing. The Abrahamic covenant rested upon divine competency for the fulfillment of its terms, and hence the utter impossibility of its failure in a single jot or tittle.

Having in our *Notes on the Book of Exodus* gone somewhat fully into the subject of the law, and endeavored to set forth the divine object in giving it, and, further, the utter impossibility of any one getting life or righteousness by keeping it, we must refer the reader to what we have there advanced on this profoundly interesting subject.

It seems strange, to one taught exclusively by Scripture, that such confusion of thought should prevail amongst professing Christians in reference to a question so distinctly and definitively settled by the Holy Ghost. Were it merely a question of the divine authority of Exodus 20, or Deuteronomy 5, as inspired portions of the Bible, we should not have a word to say. We most fully believe that these chapters are as much inspired as the seventeenth of John or the eighth of Romans.

But this is not the point. All true Christians receive, with devout thankfulness, the precious statement that "all Scripture is given by inspiration of God"; and, further, they rejoice in the assurance that "whatsoever things were written aforetime were written for our learning; that we through patience and comfort of the Scriptures might have hope"; and, finally, they believe that the morality of the law is of abiding and universal application. Murder, adultery, theft, false witness, covetousness, are wrong —always wrong—every-where wrong: to honor our parents is right—always and everywhere right. We read, in the fourth chapter of Ephesians, "Let him that stole steal no more"; and again, in chapter 6 we read, "Honor thy father and mother; which is the first commandment with promise; that it may be well with thee, and thou mayest live long on the earth."

All this is so divinely plain and settled that discussion is definitively closed; but when we come to look at the law as a ground of relationship with God, we get into an entirely different region of thought. Scripture, in manifold places, and in the clearest possible manner, teaches us that, as Christians, as children of God, we are not on that ground at all. The Jew was on that ground, but he could not stand there with God. It was death and condemnation. "They could not endure that which was commanded, 'And if so much as a beast touch the mountain, it shall be stoned, or thrust through with a dart;' and so terrible was the sight, that Moses said, 'I exceedingly fear and quake.' " The Jew found the law to be a bed on which he could not stretch himself, and a covering in which he could not wrap himself.

As to the Gentile, he was never, by any one branch of the divine economy, placed under law. His condition is expressly declared, in the opening of the Epistle to the Romans, to be "without law [*ανομως*]." "For when the Gentiles, which have not the law," etc., and, "As many as have sinned without law shall perish without law; and as many as have sinned in the law shall be judged by the law."

Here the two classes are brought into sharp and vivid contrast, in the matter of their dispensational position. The Jew, under law; the Gentile, without law—nothing can be more distinct. The Gentile was placed under government, in the person of Noah; but never under law. Should any one feel disposed to call this in question, let him produce a single line of Scripture to prove that God ever placed the Gentiles under the law. Let him search and see. It is of no possible use to argue and reason and object,—it is utterly vain to say, "*We think*" this or that: the question is, "What saith the Scripture?" If it says that the Gentiles were put under the law, let the passage be produced. We solemnly declare it says nothing of the kind, but the very reverse. It describes the condition and the position of the Gentile as "without law"—"having not the law."

In Acts 10 we see God opening the kingdom of heaven to the Gentile; in Acts 14:27, we see Him opening "the door of faith" to the Gentile; in Acts 28:28, we see Him sending His salvation to the Gentile: but we search in vain, from cover to cover of the blessed Book, for a passage in which He places the Gentile under the law.

We would very earnestly entreat the Christian reader to give this deeply interesting and important question his calm attention. Let him lay aside all his preconceived thoughts, and examine the matter simply in the light of holy Scripture. We are quite aware that our statements on this subject will be regarded by thousands as novel, if not actually heretical; but this does not move us, in the smallest degree. It is our one grand desire to be taught absolutely and exclusively by Scripture. The opinions, commandments, and doctrines of men have no weight whatever with us. The dogmas of the various schools of divinity must just go for what they are worth. We demand Scripture. A single line of inspiration is amply sufficient to settle this question, and close all discussion, forever. Let us be shown from the Word of God that the Gentiles were ever put under the law, and we shall at once bow; but inasmuch as we cannot find it there, we reject the notion altogether, and we would have the reader to do the same. The invariable language of Scripture, in describing the position of the Jew, is, "under law;" and, in describing the position of the Gentile, is, "without law." This is so obvious that we cannot but marvel how any reader of the Bible can fail to see it.*

If the reader will turn, for a few moments, to the fifteenth chapter of the Acts of the Apostles, he will see how the first attempt to put Gentile converts under the law was met by the apostles and the whole church at Jerusalem. The question was raised at Antioch; and God, in His infinite goodness and wisdom, so ordered that it should not be settled there, but that Paul and Barnabas should go up to Jerusalem and have the matter fully and freely discussed, and definitively settled by the unanimous voice of the twelve apostles and the whole church.

How we can bless our God for this! We can at once see that the decision of a local assembly, such as Antioch, even though approved by Paul and Barnabas, would not carry the same weight as that of the twelve apostles assembled in council at Jerusalem. But the Lord, blessed be His name, took care that the enemy should be completely confounded, and that the law-teachers of that day, and of every other day, should be distinctly and authoritatively taught that it was not according to His mind that Christians should be put under law, for any object whatsoever.

The subject is so deeply important that we cannot forbear quoting a few passages. We believe it will refresh both the reader and the writer to refer to the soul-stirring addresses delivered at the most remarkable and interesting council that ever sat.

"And certain men which came down from Judea taught the brethren, 'Except ye be circumcised after the manner of Moses, ye cannot be saved.' " How awful! How terribly chilling! What a death-knell to ring in the ears of those who had been converted under Paul's splendid address in the synagogue at Antioch: "Be it known unto you therefore, men and brethren, that *through this Man*"—without circumcision or works of law of any kind whatsoever—"is preached unto you the forgiveness of sins; and *by Him* all that believe"—irrespective altogether of circumcision—"*are* justified *from all things,* from which ye could not be justified by the law of Moses . . . And when the Jews were gone out of the synagogue, the Gentiles besought that these words might be preached to them the next Sabbath."

Such was the glorious message sent to the Gentiles by the lips of the apostle Paul—a message of free, full, immediate, and perfect salvation—full remission of sins and perfect justification, through faith in our Lord Jesus Christ. But according to the teaching of the

*The reader may perhaps feel disposed to inquire, On what ground will the Gentile be judged if he is not under the law? Romans 1:20 teaches us distinctly that the testimony of *creation* leaves him without excuse. Then, in chapter 2:15, he is taken up on the ground of *conscience.*—"For *when the Gentiles, which have not the law,* do by nature the things contained in the law, these, having not the law, are a law unto themselves; which show the work of the law written in their hearts, their conscience also bearing witness," etc. Finally, as regards those nations that have become professedly Christian, they will be judged on the ground of their profession.

"certain men which came down from Judea," all this was insufficient—Christ was not enough, without circumcision and the law of Moses. Poor Gentiles, who had never heard of circumcision or the law of Moses, must add to Christ and His glorious salvation the keeping of the whole law.

How must Paul's heart have burned within him to have the beloved Gentile converts brought under such monstrous teaching as this! He saw in it nothing short of the complete surrender of Christianity. If circumcision must be added to the cross of Christ—if the law of Moses must supplement the grace of God, then verily all was gone.

But, blessed forever be the God of all grace, He caused a noble stand to be made against such deadly teaching. When the enemy came in like a flood, the Spirit of the Lord raised up a standard against him. "When therefore Paul and Barnabas had no small dissension and disputation with them, they determined that Paul and Barnabas, and certain other of them, should go up to Jerusalem, unto the apostles and elders about this question. And being brought on their way by the church, they passed through Phenice and Samaria, declaring," not the circumcision, but "the conversion of the Gentiles; and they caused great joy unto all the brethren."

The brethren were in the current of the mind of Christ, and in sweet communion with the heart of God; and hence they rejoiced to hear of the conversion and salvation of the Gentiles. We may rest assured it would have afforded them no joy to hear of the heavy yoke of circumcision and the law of Moses being put upon the necks of those beloved disciples who had just been brought into the glorious liberty of the gospel. But to hear of their conversion to God, their salvation by Christ, their being sealed by the Holy Ghost, filled their hearts with a joy which was in lovely harmony with the mind of heaven.

"And when they were come to Jerusalem, they were received of the church, and of the apostles and elders, and they declared all things that God had done with them. But there rose up certain of the sect of the Pharisees which believed, saying that it was needful to circumcise them, and to command them to keep the law of Moses."

Who made it "needful"? Not God, surely; inasmuch as He had, in His infinite grace, opened the door of faith to them without circumcision or any command to keep the law of Moses. No; it was "certain men" who presumed to speak of such things as needful —men who have troubled the Church of God from that day to the present—men "desiring to be teachers of the law, knowing neither what they say nor whereof they affirm." Law-teachers never know what is involved in their dark and dismal teaching. They have not the most distant idea of how thoroughly hateful their teaching is to the God of all grace, the Father of mercies.

But, thanks be to God, the chapter from which we are now quoting affords the very clearest and most forcible evidence that could be given as to the divine mind on the subject. It proves, beyond all question, that it was not of God to put Gentile believers under the law.

"And the apostles and elders came together for to consider of this matter. And when there had been much disputing" (alas! how soon it began!) "Peter rose up and said unto them, Men and brethren, ye know how that a good while ago God made choice among us, that the Gentiles by my mouth should hear," not the law of Moses or circumcision, but "the word of the gospel, and believe. And God which knoweth the hearts, bare them witness, giving them the Holy Ghost, even as unto us. *And put no difference between us and them,* purifying their hearts by faith. Now therefore *why tempt ye God,* to put a yoke upon the neck of the disciples, which neither our fathers nor we were able to bear?"

Mark this: the law had proved an intolerable yoke to those who were under it, that is, the Jews; and, further, it was nothing short of tempting God to put that yoke upon the neck of Gentile Christians. Would that all the law-teachers throughout the length and breadth of christendom would but open their eyes to this grand fact! and not only so, but that all the Lord's beloved people every where were given to see that it is in positive opposition to the will of God that they should be put under the law for any object whatsoever. "But," adds the blessed apostle of the circumcision, "we believe that through the grace of the Lord Jesus Christ," and not by law in any shape or form, "*we shall be saved even as they.*"

This is uncommonly fine, coming from the lips of the apostle of the circumcision. He does not say, They shall be saved even as we; but, "We shall be saved even as they." The Jew is well content to come down from his lofty dispensational position, and be saved after the pattern of the poor uncircumcised Gentile. Surely, those noble utterances must have fallen in stunning force upon the ears of the law-party. They left them, as we say, not a leg to stand upon.

"Then all the multitude kept silence, and gave audience to Barnabas and Paul, declaring what miracles and wonders God had wrought among the Gentiles by them." The inspiring Spirit has not thought good to tell us what Paul and Barnabas said on this memorable occasion, and we can see His wisdom in this. It is evidently His object to give prominence to Peter and James, as men whose words would, of necessity, have more weight with the law-teachers than those of the apostle to the Gentiles and his companion.

"And after they had held their peace, James answered, saying, Men and brethren, hearken unto me: Simeon hath declared how God at the first did visit the Gentiles," not to convert them all, but "to take out of them a people for His name. And to this agree the words of the prophets;" (here he brings an overwhelming tide of evidence from the Old Testament to bear down upon the Judaizers,) "as it is written, After this I will return, and will build again the tabernacle of David, which is fallen down; and I will build again the ruins thereof, and I will set it up: that the residue of men might seek after the Lord, and *all the Gentiles,*" without the slightest reference to circumcision or the law of Moses, but "upon whom My name is called, saith the Lord, who doeth all these things. Known unto God are all His works from the beginning of the world. Wherefore my sentence is, that we trouble not them, which from among the Gentiles are turned to God."

Here, then, we have this great question definitively settled by the Holy Ghost, the twelve apostles, and the whole Church; and we cannot but be struck with the fact that, at this most important council, none spoke more emphatically, more distinctly, or more decidedly than Peter and James; the former, the apostle of the circumcision, and the latter, the one who specially addressed the twelve tribes, and whose position and ministry were calculated to give great weight to his words, in the judgment of all who were still, in any measure, occupying Jewish or legal ground. Both these eminent apostles were clear and decided in their judgment that the Gentile converts were not to be "troubled" or burdened with the law. They proved, in their powerful addresses, that to place the Gentile Christians under the law was directly contrary to the Word, the will, and the ways of God.

Who can fail to see the marvelous wisdom of God in this? The words of Paul and Barnabas are not recorded. We are simply told that they rehearsed what things God had wrought among the Gentiles. That they should be utterly opposed to putting the Gentiles under the law was only what might be expected; but to find Peter and James so decided would carry great weight with all parties.

But if the reader would have a clear view of Paul's thoughts on the question of the law, he should study the Epistle to the Galatians. There this blessed apostle, under the direct inspiration of the Holy Ghost, pours out his heart to the Gentile converts in words of glowing earnestness and commanding power. It is perfectly amazing how any one can read this wonderful Epistle and yet maintain that Christians are under the law, in any way or for any purpose. Hardly has the apostle got through his brief opening address when he plunges, with his characteristic energy, into the subject with which his large, loving, though grieved and troubled heart is full to overflowing. "I marvel," he says—and well he might—"that ye are so soon removed from Him that called you into"—what? The law of Moses? Nay, but "the grace of Christ into a different gospel which is not another [*έ'τερον εὐαγγέλιον ὸ οὐκ ἐ'στιν ἀλλο*]; but there be some that trouble you, and would pervert the gospel of Christ. But though we or an angel from heaven preach any other gospel unto you than that which we have preached unto you, let him be accursed. As we said before, so say I now again, If any man preach any other gospel unto you than that ye have received, let him be accursed."

Let all law-teachers ponder these burning words. Do they seem strong and severe? Let us remember that they are the very words of God the Holy Ghost. Yes, reader, God the Holy Ghost hurls His awful anathema at any one who presumes to add the law of Moses to the gospel of Christ—any one who attempts to place Christians under the law. How is it that men are not afraid, in the face of such words, to contend for the law? Are they not afraid of coming under the solemn curse of God the Holy Ghost?

Some, however, seek to meet this question by telling us that they do not take the law for justification, but as a rule of life; but this is neither reasonable nor intelligent, inasmuch as we may very lawfully inquire, Who gave us authority to decide as to the use we are to make of the law? We are either under the law or we are not. If we are under it at all, it is not a question of how we take it, but how it takes us.

This makes all the difference. The law knows no such distinctions as those which some theologians contend for. If we are under it for any object whatsoever, we are under the curse; for it is written, "Cursed is every one that continueth not in *all* things which are written in the book of the law to do them." To say that I am born again, I am a Christian, will not meet the case at all; for what has the law to do with the question of new birth, or of Christianity? Nothing whatever. The law is addressed to man, as a responsible being. It demands perfect obedience, and pronounces its curse upon every one who fails to render it.

Moreover, it will not do to say that though we have failed to keep the law, yet Christ has fulfilled it in our room and stead. The law knows nothing of obedience by proxy. Its language is, "The man that doeth them shall live in them."

Nor is it merely on the man who fails to keep the law that the curse is pronounced, but, as if to put the principle in the clearest possible light before us, we read that "as many as are of works of law are under the curse" (see Greek). That is, as many as take their stand on legal ground—as many as are on that principle—in a word, as many as have to do with works of law, are, of necessity, under the curse. Hence we may see at a glance the terrible inconsistency of a Christian's maintaining the idea of being under the law as a rule of life and yet not being under the curse. It is simply flying in the face of the very plainest statements of holy Scripture. Blessed be the God of all grace, the Christian is not under the curse. But why? Is it because the law has lost its power, its majesty, its dignity, its holy stringency? By no means. To say so were to blaspheme the law. To say that any "man," call him what you please—Christian, Jew, or heathen—can be under the law, can stand on that ground, and yet not be under the curse, is to say that he perfectly fulfills the law or that the law is abrogated—it is to make it null and void. Who will dare to say this? Woe be to all who do so.

But how comes it to pass that the Christian is not under the curse? Because he is not under the law. And how has he passed from under the law? Is it by another having fulfilled it in his stead? Nay; we repeat the statement, there is no such idea throughout the entire legal economy as obedience by proxy. How is it, then? Here it is, in all its moral force, fullness, and beauty: *"I through law am dead to law, that I might live unto God."**

---

*The omission of the article adds immensely to the force, fullness, and clearness of the passage. It is *δια νομου νομω απέθανον*. A wonderful clause, surely. Would that it were better understood! It demolishes a vast mass of human theology. It leaves the law in its own proper sphere; but takes the believer completely from under its power, and out of its range, by

Now, if it be true, and the apostle says it is, that we are *dead to law,* how can the law, by any possibility, be a rule of life to us? It proved *only* a rule of death, curse, and condemnation to those who were under it—those who had received it by the disposition of angels. Can it prove to be aught else to us? Did the law ever produce a single cluster of living fruit, or of the fruits of righteousness, in the history of any son or daughter of Adam? Hear the apostle's reply —"When we were in the flesh," that is, when we were viewed as men in our fallen nature, "the motions of sins, which were by the law, did work in our members to bring forth fruit unto death."

It is very important for the reader to understand the real force of the expression, "in the flesh." It does not, in this passage, mean "in the body." It simply sets forth the condition of unconverted men and women responsible to keep the law. Now, in this condition, all that was or ever could be produced was "fruit unto death"—"motions of sins." No life, no righteousness, no holiness, nothing for God, nothing right at all.*

But where are we now, as Christians? Hear the reply—"I through law am dead to law, that I might live unto God. I am crucified with Christ: nevertheless I live; yet not I, but Christ liveth in me; and the life which I now live in the flesh" (here it means in the body) "I live"—how? By the law, as a rule of life? Not a hint at such a thing, but "by the faith of the Son of God, who loved me, and gave Himself for me."

This, and nothing else, is Christianity. Do we understand it? do we enter into it? are we in the power of it? There are two distinct evils from which we are completely delivered by the precious death of Christ, namely, legality on the one hand and licentiousness on the other. Instead of those terrible evils, it introduces us into the holy liberty of grace—liberty to serve God—liberty to "mortify our members which are upon the earth"—liberty to deny "ungodliness and worldly lusts"—liberty to "live soberly, righteously, and godly"—liberty to "keep under the body and bring it into subjection."

Yes, let us remember this; let us deeply ponder the words, "I am crucified with Christ: nevertheless I live; yet not I, but Christ liveth in me." The old "I" dead—crucified, buried: the new "I" alive in Christ. Let us not mistake this. We know of nothing more awful, nothing more dangerous, than for the old "I" to assume the new ground; or, in other words, the glorious doctrines of Christianity taken up in the flesh—unconverted people talking of being free from the law, and turning the grace of God into lasciviousness. We must confess we would rather, a thousand times, have legality than licentiousness. It is this latter that many of us have to watch against with all possible earnestness. It is growing around us with appalling rapidity, and paving the way for that dark and desolating tide of infidelity which shall, ere long, roll over the length and breadth of christendom.

To talk of being free from the law in any way save by being dead to it, and alive to God, is not Christianity at all, but licentiousness, from which every pious soul must shrink with holy horror. If we are dead to the law, we are dead to sin also; and hence we are not to do our own will, which is only another name for sin; but the will of God,

death. "Wherefore, my brethren, ye also are become dead to the law by the body of Christ; that ye should be married to another, even to Him who is raised from the dead, that we should bring forth fruit unto God" (which we never could do if under the law). "For when we were in the flesh"—a correlative term with being under the law—"the motions of sins, which were by the law, did work in our members to bring forth fruit unto death." Mark the melancholy combination—"under the law"—"in the flesh"—"motions of sins"—"fruit unto death"! Can any thing be more strongly marked? But there is another side, thank God, to this question—His own bright and blessed side. Here it is: "But now *we are delivered from the law.*" How? Is it by another's having fulfilled it for us? Nay; but, *"Having died to that* [αποθανοντες εν ω] wherein we were held; that we should serve in newness of spirit, and not in the oldness of the letter." How perfect and how lovely is the harmony of Romans 7 and Galatians 2! "I through law am dead to law, that I might live unto God."

*It is needful to bear in mind that although the Gentile was never, by the dispensational dealings of God, put under the law, yet, in point of fact, all baptized professors take that ground. Hence there is a vast difference between christendom and the heathen in reference to the question of the law. Thousands of unconverted people, every week, ask God to incline their hearts to keep the law. Surely, such persons stand on very different ground from the heathen who never heard of the law, and never heard of the Bible.

which is true practical holiness.

Further, let us ever bear in mind that if we are dead to the law, we are dead to this present evil world also, and linked with a risen, ascended, and glorified Christ. Hence, we are not of the world, even as Christ is not of the world. To contend for position in the world is to deny that we are dead to the law; for we cannot be alive to the one and dead to the other. The death of Christ has delivered us from the law, from the power of sin, from this present evil world, and from the fear of death. But then all these things hang together, and we cannot be delivered from one without being delivered from all. To assert our freedom from the law, while pursuing a course of carnality, self-indulgence, and worldliness, is one of the darkest and deadliest evils of the last days.

The Christian is called to prove, in his daily life, that grace can produce results that law could never reach. It is one of the moral glories of Christianity to enable a man to surrender self and live for others. Law never could do this. It occupied a man with himself. Under its rule, every man had to do the best he could for himself. If he tried to love his neighbor, it was to work out a righteousness for himself. Under grace, all is blessedly and gloriously reversed—self is set aside as a thing crucified, dead, and buried; the old "I" is gone, and the new "I" is before God in all the acceptability and preciousness of Christ; He is our life, our righteousness, our holiness, our object, our model, our all; He is in us and we are in Him, and our daily practical life is to be simply Christ reproduced in us by the power of the Holy Ghost. Hence, we are not only called to love our neighbor, but our enemy; and this, not to work out a righteousness, for we have become the righteousness of God in Christ: it is simply the outflow of the life which we possess—which is in us, and this life is Christ. A Christian is a man who should live Christ. He is neither a Jew "under law" nor a Gentile "without law," but "a man in Christ," standing in grace, called to the same character of obedience as that which was rendered by the Lord Jesus Himself.

We shall not pursue this subject further here, but we earnestly entreat the Christian reader to study attentively the fifteenth chapter of Acts and the Epistle to the Galatians. Let him drink in the blessed teaching of these Scriptures, and we feel assured he will arrive at a clear understanding of the great question of the law. He will see that the Christian is not under the law for any purpose whatsoever; that his life, his righteousness, his holiness, are on a different ground or principle altogether; that to place the Christian under law in any way is to deny the very foundations of Christianity and contradict the plainest statements of the Word. He will learn, from the third chapter of Galatians, that to put ourselves under the law is to give up Christ, to give up the Holy Ghost, to give up faith, to give up the promises.

Tremendous consequences! But there they are, plainly set forth before our eyes; and truly, when we contemplate the state of the professing church, we cannot but see how terribly those consequences are being realized.

May God the Holy Ghost open the eyes of all Christians to the truth of these things. May He lead them to study the Scriptures, and to submit themselves to their holy authority in all things. This is the special need of this our day. We do not study Scripture sufficiently; we are not governed by it; we do not see the absolute necessity of testing every thing by the light of Scripture, and rejecting all that will not stand the test; we go on with a quantity of things that have no foundation whatever in the Word—yea, that are positively opposed to it.

What must be the end of all this? We tremble to think of it. We know, blessed be God, that our Lord Jesus Christ will soon come and take His own beloved and blood-bought people home to the prepared place in the Father's house, to be forever with Himself, in the ineffable blessedness of that bright home; but what of those who shall be left behind? what of that vast mass of baptized worldly profession? These are solemn questions, which must be weighed in the immediate presence of God, in order to have the true, the divine answer. Let the reader ponder them there, in all tenderness of heart and teachableness of spirit, and the Holy Ghost will lead him to the true answer.

Having sought to set forth, from various parts of Scripture, the glorious truth that believers are not under law, but under grace, we may now pursue our study of this fifth chapter of Deuteronomy. In it we have the ten commandments, but not exactly as we have them in the twentieth chapter of Exodus. There are some characteristic touches which demand the reader's attention.

In Exodus 20 we have history; in Deuteronomy 5 we have not only history, but commentary. In the latter, the lawgiver presents moral motives, and makes appeals which would be wholly out of place in the former. In the one, we have naked facts; in the other, facts and comments—facts and their practical application. In a word, there is not the slightest ground for imagining that Deuteronomy 5 is intended to be a literal repetition of Exodus 20; and hence the miserable arguments which infidels ground upon their apparent divergence just crumble into dust beneath our feet. They are simply baseless, and utterly contemptible.

Let us, for instance, compare the two Scriptures in reference to the subject of the Sabbath. In Exodus 20 we read, "Remember the Sabbath day, to keep it holy. Six days shalt thou labor, and do all thy work; but the seventh day is the Sabbath of the Lord thy God; in it thou shalt not do any work, thou, nor thy son, nor thy daughter, thy man-servant, nor thy maid-servant, nor thy cattle, nor thy stranger that is within thy gates: *for in six days the Lord made heaven and earth, the sea, and all that in them is,* and rested the seventh day; wherefore the Lord blessed the Sabbath day, and hallowed it."

In Deuteronomy 5 we read, "Keep the Sabbath day to sanctify it, *as the Lord thy God hath commanded thee.* Six days thou shalt labor, and do all thy work; but the seventh day is the Sabbath of the Lord thy God; in it thou shalt not do any work, thou, nor thy son, nor thy daughter, nor thy man-servant, nor thy maid-servant, *nor thine ox, nor thine ass,* nor any of thy cattle, nor thy stranger that is within thy gates; that thy man-servant and thy maid-servant may rest as well as thou. *And remember that thou wast a servant in the land of Egypt, and that the Lord thy God brought thee out thence, through a mighty hand and by a stretched-out arm; therefore the Lord thy God commanded thee to keep the Sabbath day*" (ver. 12-15).

Now, the reader can see at a glance the difference between the two passages. In Exodus 20 the command to keep the Sabbath is grounded on *creation;* in Deuteronomy 5 it is grounded on *redemption,* without any allusion to creation at all. In short, the points of difference arise out of the distinct character of each book, and are perfectly plain to every spiritual mind.

With regard to the institution of the Sabbath, we must remember that it rests wholly upon the direct authority of the word of God. Other commandments set forth plain moral duties. Every man knows it to be morally wrong to kill or steal; but as to the observance of the Sabbath, no one could possibly recognize it as a duty had it not been distinctly appointed by divine authority. Hence its immense importance and interest. Both in our chapter and in Exodus 20 it stands side by side with all those great moral duties which are universally recognized by the human conscience.

And not only so, but we find, in various other Scriptures, that the Sabbath is singled out and presented, with special prominence, as a precious link between Jehovah and Israel, a seal of His covenant with them, and a powerful test of their devotedness to Him. Every one could recognize the moral wrong of theft and murder; only those who loved Jehovah and His word would love and honor His Sabbath.

Thus, in the sixteenth chapter of Exodus, in connection with the giving of the manna, we read, "And it came to pass, that on the sixth day they gathered twice as much bread, two omers for one man; and all the rulers of the congregation came and told Moses. And he said unto them, 'This is that which the Lord hath said, To-morrow is *the rest of the holy Sabbath unto the Lord:* bake that which ye will bake to-day, and seethe that ye will seethe; and that which remaineth over lay up for you, to be kept until the morning.' . . . And Moses said, 'Eat that to-day; for to-day is *a Sabbath unto the Lord;* to-day ye shall not find it in the field. Six days ye shall gather it; but on the seventh day, which is the Sabbath, in it there shall be none.' And it came to pass"—so little were they capable of appreciating the high and holy privilege of keeping Jehovah's Sabbath—"that there went out some of the people on the seventh day for to gather, and they found none. And the Lord said unto Moses, 'How long refuse ye to keep My commandments and My laws?' " Their neglect of the Sabbath proved their moral condition to be all wrong—proved them to be astray as to all the commandments and laws of God. The Sabbath was the great touchstone—the measure and gauge of the real state of their hearts toward Jehovah. "See, for that the Lord hath *given you* the Sabbath, therefore He giveth you on the sixth day the bread of two days; abide ye every man in his place; let no man go out of his place on the seventh day. So the people rested on the seventh day." They found rest and food on the holy Sabbath.

Again, at the close of chapter 31 we have a very remarkable passage in proof of the importance and interest attaching to the Sabbath in the mind of Jehovah. A full description of the tabernacle and its furniture had been given to Moses, and he was about to receive the tables of testimony from the hand of Jehovah; but, as if to prove the prominent place which the holy Sabbath held in the divine mind, we read, "And the Lord spake unto Moses, saying, 'Speak thou also unto the children of Israel, saying, Verily My Sabbaths ye shall keep: *for it is a sign between Me and you throughout your generations;* that ye may know that I am the Lord that doth sanctify you. Ye shall keep the Sabbath therefore; for it is holy unto you: every one that defileth it shall surely be put to death; for whosoever doeth any work therein, that soul shall be cut off from among his people. Six days may work be done; but in the seventh is the Sabbath of rest, holy to the Lord: whosoever doeth any work in the Sabbath day, he shall surely be put to death. Wherefore the children of Israel shall keep the Sabbath, to observe the Sabbath throughout their generations, *for a perpetual covenant. It is a sign between Me and the children of Israel forever:* for in six days the Lord made heaven and earth, and on the seventh day He rested, and was refreshed" (Exod. 31:12-17).

Now, this is a very important passage. It proves very distinctly the abiding character of the Sabbath. The terms in which it is spoken of are quite sufficient to show that it was no mere temporary institution. "A sign between Me and you throughout your generations." "A perpetual covenant." "A sign forever."

Let the reader carefully mark these words. They prove, beyond all question, first, that the Sabbath was for Israel; secondly, that the Sabbath is, in the mind of God, a permanent institution. It is needful to bear these things in mind in order to avoid all vagueness of thought and looseness of expression on this deeply interesting subject.

The Sabbath was distinctly and exclusively for the Jewish nation. It is spoken of emphatically as a sign between Jehovah and His people Israel. There is not the most remote hint of its being intended for the Gentiles. We shall see, further on, that it is a lovely type of the times of the restitution of all things, of which God has spoken by the mouth of all His holy prophets since the world began; but this in no wise touches the fact of its being an exclusively Jewish institution. There is not so much as a single sentence of Scripture to show that the Sabbath had any reference whatever to the Gentiles.

Some would teach us that inasmuch as we read of the Sabbath day in the second chapter of Genesis, it must, of necessity, have a wider range than the Jewish nation. But let us turn to the passage and see what it says. "And on the seventh day God ended His work which He had made; and He rested on the seventh day from all His work which He had made. And God blessed the seventh day, and sanctified it; because that in it He had rested from all His work which God created and made."

This is simple enough. There is no mention here of man at all. We are not told that man rested on the seventh day. Men may infer, conclude, or imagine that he did so; but the second of Genesis says nothing about it. And not only so, but we look in vain for any allusion to the Sabbath throughout the entire book of Genesis. The very first notice we have of the Sabbath in connection with man, is in the sixteenth of Exodus, a passage already quoted; and there we see, most distinctly, that it was given to Israel, as a people in recognized covenant-relationship with Jehovah. That they did not understand or appreciate it is perfectly plain; that they never entered into it is equally plain, according to Psalm 95 and Hebrews 4. But we are now speaking of what it was in the mind of God; and He tells us it was a sign between Him and His people Israel, and a powerful test of their moral condition and of the state of their heart as to Him. It was not only an integral part of the law, as given by Moses to the congregation of Israel, but it is specially referred to and singled out, again and again, as an institution holding a very peculiar place in the mind of God.

Thus, in the book of the prophet Isaiah, we read, "Blessed is the man that doeth this, and the son of man that layeth hold on it; that keepeth the Sabbath from polluting it, and keepeth his hand from doing any evil. Neither let the son of the stranger, that hath joined himself to the Lord, speak, saying, The Lord hath utterly separated me from His people; neither let the eunuch say, Behold I am a dry tree. For thus saith the Lord unto the eunuchs that keep My Sabbaths, and choose the things that please Me, and take hold of My covenant; even unto them will I give in Mine house, and within My walls, a place and a name better than of sons and of daughters: I will give them an everlasting name that shall not be cut off. Also the sons of the stranger" (here, of course, viewed in connection with Israel, as in Numbers 15 and other Scriptures) "that join themselves to the Lord, to serve Him, and to love the name of the Lord, to be His servants, every one that keepeth the Sabbath from polluting it, and taketh hold of My covenant; even them will I bring to My holy mountain, and make them joyful in My house of prayer: their burnt-offerings and their sacrifices shall be accepted upon Mine altar; for Mine house shall be called a house of prayer for all people."

Again, "If thou turn away thy foot from the Sabbath, from doing thy pleasure on My holy day; and call the Sabbath a delight, the holy of the Lord, honorable; and shalt honor Him, not doing thine own ways, nor finding thine own pleasure, nor speaking thine own words: then shalt thou delight thyself in the Lord; and I will cause thee to ride upon the high places of the earth, and feed thee with the heritage of Jacob thy father; for the mouth of the Lord hath spoken it" (Isaiah 58:13-14).

The foregoing quotations are amply sufficient to show the place which the Sabbath holds in the mind of God. It is needless to multiply passages, but there is just one to which we must refer the reader, in connection with our present subject, namely, Leviticus 23: "And the Lord spake unto Moses, saying, 'Speak unto the children of Israel, and say unto them, Concerning the feasts of the Lord, which ye shall proclaim to be holy convocations, even these are My feasts. Six days shall work be done; but the seventh day is the Sabbath of rest, a holy convocation, ye shall do no work therein: it is the Sabbath of the Lord in all your dwellings" (ver. 1-3).

Here it stands at the head of all the feasts given in this marvelous chapter, in which we have foreshadowed the entire history of God's dealings with His people Israel. The Sabbath is the expression of God's eternal rest, into which it is His purpose yet to bring His people, when all their toils and sorrows, their trials and tribulations, shall have passed away—that blessed "Sabbath-keeping [σαββατισμος]" which "remaineth for the people of God." In various ways He sought to keep this glorious rest before the hearts of His people; the seventh day, the seventh year, the year of jubilee—all these lovely sabbatic seasons were designed to set forth that blessed time when Israel shall be gathered back to their own beloved land, when the Sabbath shall be kept, in all its deep, divine blessedness, as it never has been kept yet.

And this leads us, naturally, to the second point in connection with the Sabbath, namely, its permanency. This is plainly proved by such expressions as, "perpetual," "a sign forever," "throughout your generations." Such words would never be applied to any merely temporary institution. True it is, alas! that Israel never really kept the Sabbath according to God; they never understood its meaning, never entered into its blessedness, never drank into its spirit. They made it a badge of their own righteousness; they boasted in it as a national institution, and used it for self-exaltation; but they never celebrated it in communion with God.

We speak of the nation as a whole. We doubt not there were precious souls who, in secret, enjoyed the Sabbath, and entered into the thoughts of God about it; but as a nation, Israel never kept the Sabbath according to God. Hear what Isaiah says, "Bring no more vain oblations; incense is an abomination unto Me; the new moons and *Sabbaths,* the calling of assemblies, I cannot away with; it is iniquity, even the solemn meeting" (chap. 1:13).

Here we see that the precious and beautiful institution of the Sabbath which God had given as a sign of His covenant with His people, had, in their hands, become a positive abomination, perfectly intolerable to Him. And when we open the pages of the New Testament, we find the leaders and heads of the Jewish people continually at issue with our Lord Jesus Christ in reference to the Sabbath. Look, for example, at the opening verses of Luke 6—"And it came to pass on the second Sabbath after the first, that He went through the corn-fields; and His disciples plucked the ears of corn, and did eat, rubbing them in their hands. And certain of the Pharisees said unto them, 'Why do ye that which is not lawful to do on the Sabbath days?' And Jesus answering them said, 'Have ye not read so much as this, what David did, when himself was a hungred, and they which were with him; how he went into the house of God, and did take and eat the show-bread, and gave also to them that were with him; which it is not lawful to eat, but for the priests alone?' And He said unto them that the Son of Man is Lord also of the Sabbath."

And again, we read, "It came to pass also on another Sabbath, that He entered into the synagogue and taught; and there was a man whose right hand was withered. And the scribes and Pharisees *watched Him,* whether He would heal on the Sabbath day, that they might find an accusation against Him." (Only conceive, an accusation for healing a poor, afflicted fellow-mortal!) "But He knew their thoughts"—yes, He read their hearts through to their very centre, "and said to the man which had the withered hand, 'Rise up, and stand forth in the midst.' And he arose and stood forth. Then said Jesus unto them, 'I will ask you one thing, Is it lawful on the Sabbath day to do good, or to do evil? to save life, or to destroy it?' And looking round about upon them all, He said unto the man, 'Stretch forth thine hand.' And he did so; and his hand was restored whole as the other. And they were filled with madness; and communed one with another what they might do to Jesus."

What an insight we have here into the hollowness and worthlessness of man's Sabbath-keeping! Those religious guides would rather let the disciples starve than have *their* Sabbath interfered with; they would allow the man to carry his withered hand to the grave rather than have him healed on *their* Sabbath. Alas! it was indeed their Sabbath, and not God's. His rest could never comport with hunger and withered hands. They had never read aright the record of David's act in eating the show-bread. They did not understand that legal institutions must give way in the presence of divine grace meeting human need. Grace rises, in its magnificence, above all legal barriers, and faith rejoices in its lustre; but mere religiousness is offended by the activities of grace and the boldness of faith. The Pharisees did not see that the man with the withered hand was a striking commentary upon the nation's moral condition, a living proof of the fact that they were far away from God. If they were as they ought to be, there would have been no withered hands to heal; but they were not, and hence their Sabbath was an empty formality—a powerless, worthless ordinance—a hideous anomaly, hateful to God, and utterly inconsistent with the condition of man.

Take another instance, in Luke 13: "And He was teaching in one of the synagogues on the Sabbath." (Assuredly, the Sabbath was no day of rest to Him.) "And, behold, there was a woman which had a spirit of infirmity eighteen years, and was bowed together, and could in no wise lift up herself. And when Jesus saw her, He called her to Him, and said unto her, 'Woman, thou art loosed from thine infirmity.' And He laid His hands on her, and *immediately she was made straight, and glorified God.*" Beautiful illustration of the work of grace in the soul, and the practical result, in every case. All on whom Christ lays His blessed hands are "immediately made straight," and enabled to glorify God.

But man's Sabbath was touched. "The ruler of the synagogue answered with indignation, because that Jesus had healed on the Sabbath day." He was indignant at the gracious work of healing, though quite indifferent as to the humiliating case of infirmity; and he "said unto the people, 'There are six days in which men ought to work: in them therefore come and be healed, and not on the Sabbath day." How little this poor hollow religionist knew that he was in the very presence of the Lord of the true Sabbath! How utterly insensible he was to the moral inconsistency of attempting to keep a Sabbath while man's condition called aloud for divine work! "The Lord then answered him, and said, 'Thou hypocrite, doth not each one of you on the Sabbath loose his ox or his ass from the stall, and lead him away to watering? And ought not this woman, being a daughter of Abraham, whom Satan hath bound, lo, these eighteen years, be loosed from this bond on the Sabbath day?' "

What a withering rebuke! What an opening up of the hollowness and utter wretchedness of their whole system of Judaism! Only think of the glaring incongruity of a Sabbath and a daughter of Abraham bound by the cruel hand of Satan for eighteen years! There is nothing in all this world so blinding to the mind, so hardening to the heart, so deadening to the conscience, so demoralizing to the whole being, as religion without Christ. Its deceiving and degrading power can only be thoroughly judged in the light of the divine presence. For aught that the ruler of the synagogue cared, that poor woman might have gone on to the end of her days bowed together and unable to lift up herself. He would have been well content to let her go on as a sad witness of the power of Satan, provided he could keep his Sabbath. His religious indignation was excited, not by the power of Satan as seen in the woman's condition, but by the power of Christ as seen in her complete deliverance.

But the Lord gave him his answer. "And when He had said these things, all His adversaries were ashamed" (as well they might); "and all the people rejoiced for all the glorious things that were done by Him." What a striking contrast! The advocates of a powerless, heartless, worthless religion unmasked and covered with shame and confusion on the one hand, and on the other, all the people rejoicing in the glorious actings of the Son of God, who had come into their midst to deliver them from the crushing power of Satan, and fill their hearts with the joy of God's salvation, and their mouths with His praise!

We must now ask the reader to turn to the Gospel of John for further illustration of our subject. We earnestly desire that this vexed question of the Sabbath should be thoroughly examined in the light of Scripture. We are convinced that there is very much more involved in it than many professing Christians are aware.

At the opening of John 5, we are introduced to a scene strikingly indicative of Israel's condition. We do not here attempt to go fully into the passage, we merely refer to it in connection with the subject before us.

The pool of Bethesda, or "house of mercy"—while it was undoubtedly the expression of the mercy of God toward His people —afforded abundant evidence of the miserable condition of man in general, and of Israel in particular. Its five porches were thronged with "a great multitude of impotent folk, of blind, halt, withered, waiting for the moving of the water." What a sample of the whole human family, and of the nation of Israel! What a striking illustration of their moral and spiritual condition as viewed from a divine stand-point. "Blind, halt, withered"—such is man's real state, if he only knew it.

But there was one man in the midst of this impotent throng so far gone—so feeble and helpless, that the pool of Bethesda could not meet his case. "A certain man was there, which had an infirmity thirty and eight years. When Jesus saw him lie, and knew that he had been now a long time in that case, He saith unto him, 'Wilt thou *be made* whole?' " What grace and power in this question! It went far beyond the utmost stretch of the impotent man's thoughts. He thought only of human help, or of his own ability to get into the pool. He knew not that the speaker was above and beyond the pool, with its occasional movement—beyond angelic ministry—beyond all human help and effort, the Possessor of all power in heaven and on earth. "The impotent man answered Him, 'Sir, I have no man, when the water is troubled, to put me into the pool; but while I am coming, another steppeth down before me.' " What a true picture of all those who are seeking salvation by ordinances! Each one doing the best he could for himself. No care for others. No thought of helping them. "Jesus saith unto him, 'Rise, take up thy bed, and walk.' And immediately the man was made whole, and took up his bed, and walked: *and on the same day was the Sabbath.*" Here we have man's Sabbath again. It certainly was not God's Sabbath. The miserable multitude gathered around the pool proved that God's full rest had not yet come—that His glorious antitype of the Sabbath had not yet dawned on this sin-stricken earth. When that bright day comes, there will be no blind, halt, and withered folk thronging the porches of the pool of Bethesda. God's Sabbath and human misery are wholly incompatible.

But it was man's Sabbath. It was no longer the seal of Jehovah's covenant with the seed of Abraham (as it was once, and will be again), but the badge of man's self-righteousness. "The Jews therefore said unto him that was cured, 'It is the Sabbath day; it is not lawful for thee to carry thy bed.' " It was no doubt lawful enough for him to lie on that bed, week after week, month after month, year after year, while they were going on with their empty, worthless, hollow attempt at Sabbath-keeping. If they had had one ray of spiritual light, they would have seen the flagrant inconsistency of attempting to maintain their traditionary notions respecting the Sabbath in the presence of human misery, disease, and degradation. But they were utterly blind, and hence when the glorious fruits of Christ's ministry were being displayed, they had the temerity to pronounce them unlawful.

Nor this only; but "therefore did the Jews persecute Jesus, and sought to slay Him, because He had done these things on the Sabbath day." What a spectacle! Religious people—yea, the leaders and teachers of religion—the guides of the professed people of God, seeking to slay the Lord of the Sabbath because He had made a man every whit whole on the Sabbath day!

But mark our Lord's reply: "My Father *worketh* hitherto, and I work." This brief but comprehensive statement gives us the root of the whole matter. It opens up to us the real condition of mankind in general, and of Israel in particular; and, in the most affecting manner, presents the grand secret of our Lord's life and ministry. Blessed be His name, He had not come into this world to rest. How could He rest? how could He keep a Sabbath in the midst of human need and misery? Ought not that impotent, blind, halt, and withered multitude which thronged the porches of the pool of Bethesda have taught "the Jews" the folly of their notions about the Sabbath? For what was that multitude but a sample of the condition of the nation of Israel, and of the whole human family? and how could divine love rest in the midst of such a condition of things? Utterly impossible. Love can only be a worker in a scene of sin and sorrow. From the moment of man's fall, the Father had been working; then the Son appeared to carry on the work; and now, the Holy Ghost is working. Work, and not rest, is the divine order in a world like this. "There remaineth therefore a rest to the people of God."

The blessed Lord Jesus went about doing good on the Sabbath day as well as on every other day; and finally, having accomplished the glorious work of redemption, He spent the Sabbath in the grave, and rose on the first day of the week, as the First-begotten from the dead, and Head of the new creation, in which all things are of God, and to which, we may surely add, the question of "days and months and times and years" can have no possible application. No one who thoroughly understands the meaning of death and resurrection could sanction for a moment the observance of days. The death of Christ put an end to all that order of things, and His resurrection introduces us into another sphere entirely, where it is our high privilege to walk in the light and power of those eternal realities which are ours in Christ, and which stand in vivid contrast with the superstitious observances of a carnal and worldly religiousness.

But here we approach a very interesting point in our subject, namely, the difference between the Sabbath and the Lord's day, or first day of the week. These two are often confounded. We frequently hear, from the lips of truly pious people, the phrase, "Christian Sabbath," an expression no where to be found in the New Testament. It may be that some who make use of it mean a right thing; but we should not only mean right, but also seek to express ourselves according to the teaching of holy Scripture.

We are persuaded that the enemy of God and of His Christ has had a great deal more to do with the conventionalisms of christendom than many of us are aware; and this it is which makes the matter so very serious. The reader may perhaps feel disposed to pronounce it mere hair-splitting to find any fault with the term "Christian Sabbath"; but he may rest assured it is nothing of the sort: on the contrary, if he will only calmly examine the matter in the light of the New Testament, he will find that it involves questions not only interesting, but also weighty and important. It is a common saying, "There is nothing in a name;" but in the matter now before us, there is much in a name.

We have already remarked that our Lord spent the Sabbath in the grave. Is not this a telling and deeply significant fact? We cannot doubt it. We read in it, at least, the setting aside of the old condition of things, and the utter impossibility of keeping a Sabbath in a world of sin and death. Love could not rest in a world like this; it could only labor and die. This is the inscription which we read on the tomb where the Lord of the Sabbath lay buried.

But what of the first day of the week? Is not it the Sabbath on a new footing—the Christian Sabbath? It is never so called in the New Testament. There is not so much as a hint of any thing of the kind. If we look through the Acts of the Apostles, we shall find the two days spoken of in the most distinct way. On the Sabbath, we find the Jews assembled in their synagogues for the reading of the law and the prophets: on the first day of the week, we find the Christians assembled to break bread. The two days were as distinct as Judaism and Christianity; nor is there so much as a shadow of Scripture foundation for the idea that the Sabbath was merged in the first day of the week. Where is the slightest authority for the assertion that the Sabbath is changed from the seventh day to the eighth, or first, day of the week? Surely, if there be any, nothing is easier than to produce it; but there is absolutely none.

And be it remembered that the Sabbath is not merely *a* seventh day, but *the* seventh day. It is well to note this, inasmuch as some entertain the idea that provided a seventh portion of time be given to rest and the public ordinances of religion, it is quite sufficient, and it does not matter what you call it; and thus different nations and different religious systems have their Sabbath day. But this can never satisfy any one who desires to be taught exclusively by Scripture. The Sabbath of Eden was *the* seventh day: the Sabbath for Israel was *the* seventh day. But the eighth day leads our thoughts onward into eternity; and, in the New Testament, it is called "the first day of the week," as indicating the beginning of that new order of things of which the cross is the imperishable foundation, and a risen Christ the glorious Head and Centre. To call this day the "Christian Sabbath" is simply to confound things earthly and heavenly; it is to bring the Christian down from his elevated position as associated with a risen and glorified Head in the heavens, and occupy him with the superstitious observance of days, the very thing which made the blessed apostle stand in doubt of the assemblies in Galatia.

In short, the more deeply we ponder the phrase "Christian Sabbath," the more we are convinced that its tendency is, like many other formularies of christendom, to rob the Christian of all those grand distinctive truths of the New Testament which mark off the Church of God from all that went before and all that is to follow after. The Church, though on the earth, is not of this world, even as Christ is not of this world. It is heavenly in its origin, heavenly in its character, heavenly in its principles, walk, and hope. It stands between the cross and the glory. The boundaries of its existence on earth are, the day of Pentecost, when the Holy Ghost came down to form it, and the coming of Christ to receive it to Himself.

Nothing can be more strongly marked than this; and hence, for any one to attempt to enjoin upon the Church of God the legal or superstitious observance of "days and months and times and years," is to falsify the entire Christian position, mar the integrity of divine revelation, and rob the Christian of the place and portion which belong to him through the infinite grace of God and the accomplished atonement of Christ.

Does the reader deem this statement unwarrantably strong? If so, let him ponder the following splendid passage from Paul's Epistle to the Colossians—a passage which ought to be written in letters of gold: "As ye have therefore received Christ Jesus the Lord, so walk ye in Him; rooted and built up in Him, and established in the faith, as ye have been taught, abounding therein with thanksgiving. Beware lest any man spoil [or make a prey of] you through *philosophy and vain deceit*"—mark the combination! not very flattering to philosophy—"after the tradition of men, after the rudiments of the world, and not after Christ. For in Him dwelleth *all the fullness of the Godhead* [Θεότης, deity] bodily. And ye are complete in Him, which is the head of all principality and power." What more can we possibly want? "In whom also ye are circumcised with the circumcision *made without hands,* in putting off the body of the sins of the flesh by the circumcision of Christ: buried with Him in baptism, wherein also ye are risen with Him through the faith of the operation of God, who hath raised Him from the dead. And you, being dead in your sins and the uncircumcision of your flesh, hath He quickened together with Him, *having forgiven you all trespasses;* blotting out the handwriting of ordinances that was against us, which was contrary to us, and took it out of the way, nailing it to His cross; and having spoiled principalities and powers, He made a show of them openly, triumphing over them in it."

Magnificent victory! A victory gained single-handed—gained for us! Universal and eternal homage to His peerless name! What remains? "Let no man *therefore* judge you in meat, or in drink, or in respect of a holy day, or of the new moon, or of the Sabbath: which are a shadow of things to come; but the body is of Christ."

What can one who is complete and accepted in a risen and glorified Christ have to do with meats, drinks or holy days? What can philosophy, tradition, or human religiousness do for him? What can passing shadows add to one who has grasped, by faith, the eternal substance? Surely nothing; and hence the blessed apostle proceeds—"Let no man beguile you of your reward, in a voluntary humility, and worshiping of angels, intruding into those things which he hath not seen, vainly puffed up by his fleshly mind, and *not holding the Head,* from which all the body by joints and bands having nourishment ministered, and knit together, increaseth with the increase of God. Wherefore *if ye be dead with Christ* from the rudiments of the world, why, *as though living in the world,* are ye subject to ordinances, [such as,] 'Touch not [this],' 'Taste not [that],' 'Handle not [the other]'; which all are to perish with the using; after the commandments and doctrines of men? Which things have indeed a show of wisdom in will-worship, and humility, and neglecting of the body; not in any honor to the satisfying of the flesh;" that is, not giving the measure of honor to the body which is due to it as God's vessel, but puffing up the flesh with religious pride, fed by a hollow and worthless sanctimoniousness (Col. 2:6-23).

It is not possible for any one to understand this marvelous passage and not have a complete settlement, not only of the Sabbath question, but also of that entire system of things with which this question stands connected. The Christian who understands his position, is done forever with all questions of meats and drinks, days and months and times and years. He knows nothing of holy seasons and holy places. He is dead with Christ from the rudiments of the world, and as such, is delivered from all the ordinances of a traditionary religion. He belongs to heaven, where new moons, holy days, and Sabbaths have no place. He is in the new creation, where all things are of God; and hence he can see no moral force in such words as "Touch not, taste not, handle not." They have no possible application to him. He lives in a region where the clouds, vapors, and mists of monasticism and asceticism are never seen. He has given up all the worthless forms of mere fleshly pietism, and got, in exchange, the solid realities of Christian life. His ear has been opened to hear, and his heart to understand, the powerful exhortation of the inspired apostle, "If ye then be risen with Christ, seek those things which are above, where Christ sitteth on the right hand of God. Set your affection on things above, not on things on the earth. For *ye are dead,* and your life is hid with Christ in God. When Christ, our life, shall appear, then shall ye also appear with Him in glory. Mortify therefore your members which are upon the earth."

Here we have unfolded before our eyes some of the glories of true, practical, vital Christianity, in striking contrast with all the barren and dreary forms of carnal and worldly religiousness. Christian life does not consist in the observance of certain rules, commandments, or traditions of men. It is a divine reality. It is Christ in the heart, and Christ reproduced in the daily life, by the power of the Holy Ghost. It is the new man, formed on the model of Christ Himself, and displaying itself in all the most minute details of our daily history—in the family, in the business, in all our intercourse with our fellow-men, in our temper, spirit, style, deportment, all. It is not a matter of mere profession, or of dogma, or of opinion, or of sentiment; it is an unmistakable, living reality. It is the kingdom of God, set up in the heart, asserting its blessed sway over the whole moral being, and shedding its genial influence upon the entire sphere in which we are called to move from day to day. It is the Christian walking in the blessed footsteps of Him who went about doing good; meeting, so far as in him lies, every form of human need; living not for himself, but for others; finding his delight in serving and giving; ready to soothe and sympathize wherever he finds a crushed spirit or a bereaved and desolate heart.

This is Christianity. And oh, how it differs from all the forms in which legality and superstition clothe themselves! How different from the unintelligent and unmeaning observance of days and months and times and years, abstaining from meats, forbidding to marry, and such like! How different from the vaporings of the mystic, the gloom of the ascetic, and the austerities of the monk! How totally different from all these! Yes, and we may add, how different from the unsightly union of high profession and low practice—lofty truths held in the intellect, professed, taught, and discussed, and worldliness, self-indulgence, and unsubduedness!

The Christianity of the New Testament differs alike from all these things. It is the divine, the heavenly, and the spiritual, displayed amid the human, the earthly, and the natural. May it be the holy purpose of the writer and the reader of these lines to be satisfied with nothing short of that morally glorious Christianity revealed in the pages of the New Testament.

It is needless, we trust, to add more on the question of the Sabbath. If the reader has at all seized the import of those Scriptures which have passed before us, he will have little difficulty in seeing the place which the Sabbath holds in the dispensational ways of God. He will see that it has direct reference to Israel and the earth—that it was a sign of the covenant between Jehovah and His earthly people, and a powerful test of their moral condition.

Furthermore, he will see that Israel never really kept the Sabbath, never understood its import, never appreciated its value. This was made manifest in the life, ministry, and death of our Lord Jesus Christ; who performed many of His works of healing on the Sabbath day, and, at the end, spent that day in the tomb.

Finally, he will clearly understand the difference between the Jewish Sabbath and the first day of the week, or the Lord's day; that the latter is never once called the Sabbath in the New Testament, but on the contrary, is constantly presented in its own proper distinctness: it is not the Sabbath changed or transferred, but a new day altogether, having its own special basis and its own peculiar range of thought, leaving the Sabbath wholly untouched, as a suspended institution, to be resumed by and by, when the seed of Abraham shall be restored to their own land (see Ezek. 46:1,12).

But we cannot happily turn from this interesting subject without a few words on the place assigned, in the New Testament, to the Lord's day, or first day of the week. Though it is not the Sabbath; and though it has nothing to do with holy days, or new moons, or "days and months and times and years"; yet it has its own unique place in Christianity, as is evident from manifold passages in the Scriptures of the New Testament.

Our Lord rose from the dead on that day; He met His disciples again and again on that day; the apostle and the brethren at Troas came together to break bread on that day (Acts 20:7); the apostle instructs the Corinthians, and all that in every place call on the name of our Lord Jesus Christ, to lay by their offerings on that day; thus teaching us, distinctly, that the first day of the week was *the* special day for the Lord's people to assemble for the Lord's supper, and the worship, communion, and ministry connected with that most precious institution. The blessed apostle John expressly tells us that he was in the Spirit on that day, and received that marvelous revelation which closes the divine volume.*

Thus, then, we have a body of Scripture evidence before us amply sufficient to prove to every pious mind that the Lord's day must not be reduced to the level of ordinary days. It is, to the true Christian, neither the Jewish Sabbath on the one hand, nor the Gentile Sunday on the other; but the Lord's day, on which His people gladly and thankfully assemble around His table, to keep that precious feast by which they show forth His death until He come.

Now, it is needless to say that there is not a shade of legal bondage or of superstition connected with the first day of the week. To

*Some are of opinion that the expression, "on the Lord's day" ought to be rendered, "on the day of the Lord," meaning that the apostle was in the spirit of that day when our Lord Christ shall take to Himself His great power and reign. But to this view there are two grave objections. In the first place, the words τη κυριακη ἡμερα, rendered, in Revelation 1:10, "The Lord's day," are quite distinct from η ημερα κυριου, in 1 Thessalonians 5:2; 2 Thessalonians 2:2; 2 Peter 3:10, properly rendered, "The day of the Lord."

This we consider a very weighty objection, and one quite sufficient to settle the question. But in addition to this, we have the argument based on the fact that by far the greater portion of the book of Revelation is occupied, not with "the day of the Lord," but with events prior thereto.

Hence, therefore, we feel persuaded that "the Lord's day" and "the first day of the week" are identical; and this we deem a very important fact, as proving that that day has a very special place in the Word of God—a place which every intelligent Christian will thankfully own.

say so, or to think so, would be to deny the entire circle of truths with which that day stands connected. We have no direct commandment respecting the observance of the day, but the passages already referred to are amply sufficient for every spiritual mind; and further, we may say that the instincts of the divine nature would lead every true Christian to honor and love the Lord's day, and to set it apart, in the most reverent manner, for the worship and service of God. The very thought of any one professing to love Christ engaging in business or unnecessary traveling on the Lord's day, would, in our judgment, be revolting to every pious feeling. We believe it to be a hallowed privilege to return, as much as possible, from all the distractions of natural things, and to devote the hours of the Lord's day to Himself and to His service.

It will perhaps be said that the Christian ought to devote every day to the Lord. Most surely; we are the Lord's, in the very fullest and highest sense. All we have and all we are belongs to Him; this we fully, gladly own. We are called to do every thing in His name and to His glory. It is our high privilege to buy and sell, eat and drink, yea, to carry on all our business, under His eye, and in the fear and love of His holy name. We should not put our hand to any thing, on any day in the week, on which we could not, with the fullest confidence, ask the Lord's blessing.

All this is most fully admitted. Every true Christian joyfully owns it. But, at the same time, we deem it impossible to read the New Testament and not see that the Lord's day gets a unique place; that it is marked off for us, in the most distinct way; that it has a significance and an importance which cannot, with justice, be claimed for any other day in the week. Indeed, so fully are we convinced of the truth of all this, that even though it were not the law of England that the Lord's day should be observed, we should deem it to be both our sacred duty and holy privilege to abstain from all business engagements, save such as were absolutely unavoidable.

Thanks be to God, it is the law of England that the Lord's day should be observed. This is a signal mercy to all who love the day for the Lord's sake. We cannot but own His great goodness in having wrested the day from the covetous grasp of the world, and bestowed it upon His people and His servants to be devoted to His worship and to His work.

What a boon is the Lord's day, with its profound retirement from worldly things! What should we do without it? What a blessed break in upon the week's toil! How refreshing its exercises to the spiritual mind! How precious the assembly around the Lord's table to remember Him, to show forth His death, and celebrate His praise! How delightful the varied services of the Lord's day, whether those of the evangelist, the pastor, the teacher, the Sunday-school worker, or the tract distributor! What human language can adequately set forth the value and interest of all these things? True it is that the Lord's day is any thing but a day of bodily rest to His servants; indeed, they are often more fatigued on that day than on any other day of the week. But oh! it is a blessed fatigue—a delightful fatigue—a fatigue which will meet its bright reward in the rest that remains for the people of God.

Once more, then, let us lift up our hearts in a note of praise to our God for the blessed boon of the Lord's day. May He continue it to His Church until He come. May He countervail, by His almighty power, every effort of the infidel and the atheist to remove the barriers which English law has erected around the Lord's day. Truly, it will be a sad day for England when those barriers are removed.

It may perhaps be said by some that the Jewish Sabbath is done away, and is therefore no longer binding. A large number of professing Christians have taken this ground, and pleaded for the opening of the parks and places of public recreation on the Sunday. Alas! it is easily seen where such people are drifting to, and what they are seeking. They would set aside the law, in order to procure a license for fleshly indulgence. They do not understand that the only way in which any one can be free from the law is by being dead to it; and if dead to the law, we are also, of blessed necessity, dead to sin and dead to the world.

This makes it a different matter altogether. The Christian is, thank God, free from the law; but if he is, it is not that he may amuse and indulge himself, on the Lord's day or any other day, but that he may live to God. "I through law am dead to law, that I might live unto God." This is Christian ground, and it can only be occupied by those who are truly born of God. The world cannot understand it; neither can they understand the holy privileges and spiritual exercises of the Lord's day.

All this is true; but, at the same time, we are thoroughly convinced that were England to remove the barriers which surround the Lord's day, it would afford a melancholy proof of her abandonment of that profession of religion which has so long characterized her as a nation, and of her drifting away in the direction of infidelity and atheism. We must not lose sight of the weighty fact that England has taken the ground of being a Christian nation—a nation professing to be governed by the Word of God. She is therefore much more responsible than those nations wrapped in the dark shades of heathenism. We believe that nations, like individuals, will be held responsible for the profession they make; and hence those nations which profess and call themselves Christian shall be judged, not merely by the light of creation, nor by the law of Moses, but by the full-orbed light of that Christianity which they profess—by all the truth contained within the covers of that blessed bookwhich they possess, and in which they make their boast. The heathen shall be judged on the ground of creation; the Jew, on the ground of the law; the nominal Christian, on the ground of the truth of Christianity.

Now this grave fact renders the position of England, and all other professing Christian nations, most serious. God will most assuredly deal with them on the ground of their profession. It is of no use to say they do not understand what they profess; for why profess what they do not understand and believe? The fact is, they profess to understand and believe; and by this fact they shall be judged. They make their boast in this familiar sentence, that "the Bible, and the Bible alone, is the religion of Protestants."

If this be so, how solemn is the thought of England judged by the standard of an open Bible! What will be her judgment?—what her end? Let all whom it may concern ponder the appalling answer.

We must now turn from the deeply interesting subject of the Sabbath and the Lord's day, and draw this section to a close by quoting the remarkable paragraph with which our chapter ends. It does not call for any lengthened comment, but we deem it profitable, in these *Notes on Deuteronomy,* to furnish the reader with very full quotations from the book itself, in order that he may have before him the very words of the Holy Ghost, without even the trouble of laying aside the volume which he holds in his hand.

Having laid before the people the ten commandments, the lawgiver proceeds to remind them of the solemn circumstances which accompanied the giving of the law, together with their own feelings and utterances on the occasion.

"These words the Lord spake unto all your assembly in the mount out of the midst of the fire, of the cloud, and of the thick darkness, with a great voice; and He added no more. And He wrote them in two tables of stone, and delivered them unto me. And it came to pass, when ye heard the voice out of the midst of the darkness, (for the mountain did burn with fire,) that ye came near unto me, even all the heads of your tribes, and your elders; and ye said, 'Behold, the Lord our God hath showed us His glory and His greatness, and we have heard His voice out of the midst of the fire: we have seen this day that God doth talk with man, and he liveth. Now therefore why should we die? for this great fire will consume us: if we hear the voice of the Lord our God any more, then we shall die. For who is there of all flesh, that hath heard the voice of the living God speaking out of the midst of the fire, as we have, and lived? Go thou near, and hear all that the Lord our God shall say; and speak thou unto us all that the Lord our God shall speak unto thee, and *we will hear it and do it.'* And the Lord heard the voice of your words, when ye spake unto me; and the Lord said unto me, 'I have heard the voice of the words of this people, which they have spoken unto thee: they have well said all that they have spoken. O that there were such a heart in them, that they would fear Me, and keep *all* My commandments *always,* that it might be well with them, and with their children forever! Go say to them, Get you into your tents again. But as for thee, stand thou here by Me, and I will speak unto thee all the commandments, and the statutes, and the judgments, which thou shalt teach them, that they may do them in the land which I give them to possess it.' Ye shall observe to do therefore as the Lord your God hath commanded you: ye shall not turn aside either to the right hand or to the left. Ye shall walk in *all the ways* which the Lord your God hath commanded you, that ye may live, and that it may be well with you, and that ye may prolong your days in the land which ye shall possess."

Here the grand principle of the book of Deuteronomy shines out with uncommon lustre. It is embodied in those touching and forcible words which form the very heart's core of the splendid passage just quoted. "O that there were *such a heart in them, that they would fear Me,* and keep all My commandments always, that it might be well with them, and with their children forever!"

Precious words! They set before us, most blessedly, the secret spring of that life which we, as Christians, are called to live from day to day—the life of simple, implicit, and unqualified obedience, namely, a heart fearing the Lord—fearing Him, not in a servile spirit, but with all that deep, true, adoring love which the Holy Ghost sheds abroad in our hearts. It is this that delights the heart of our loving Father. His word to us is, "My son, give Me thine heart." Where the heart is given, all follows, in lovely moral order. A loving heart finds its very deepest joy in obeying all God's commandments; and nothing is of any value to God but what springs from a loving heart. The heart is the source of all the issues of life; and hence, when it is governed by the love of God, there is a loving response to all His commandments. We love His commandments because we love Him. Every word of His is precious to the heart that loves Him. Every precept, every statute, every judgment—in a word, His whole law is loved, reverenced, and obeyed, because it has His name and His authority attached to it.

The reader will find in Psalm 119 an uncommonly fine illustration of the special point now before us—a most striking example of one who blessedly answered to the words quoted above—"O that there were *such a heart* in them, that they would fear Me, and keep *all* My commandments *always!"* It is the lovely breathing of a soul who found its deep, unfailing, constant delight in the law of God. There are no less than one hundred and seventy allusions to that precious law, under some one title or another. We find scattered along the surface of this marvelous psalm, in rich profusion, such gems as the following:

"Thy Word have I *hid* in mine *heart,* that I might not sin against Thee." "I have rejoiced in the way of Thy testimonies as much as in all riches." "I will meditate in Thy precepts, and have respect unto Thy ways." *"I will delight myself* in Thy statutes; I will not forget Thy Word." "My soul breaketh for the longing that it hath unto Thy judgments at all times." *"Thy testimonies* are also *my delight,* and my counselors." *"I have stuck* unto Thy testimonies." "Behold, *I have longed* after Thy precepts." *"I trust* in Thy Word." *"I have hoped* in Thy judgments." *"I seek* Thy precepts." *"I will delight myself* in Thy commandments, which *I have loved." "I remembered* Thy judgments." *"Thy statutes* have been *my songs* in the house of my pilgrimage." "I turned *my feet* unto *Thy testimonies." "I have believed* Thy commandments." *"The law of Thy mouth* is better unto me than thousands of gold and silver." *"I have hoped* in Thy Word." *"Thy law* is *my delight." "Mine eyes* fail for *Thy Word." "All* Thy commandments are faithful." "Forever, O Lord, Thy Word is settled in heaven." *"I will never forget* Thy precepts." *"I have sought* Thy precepts." *"I will consider* Thy testimonies." "Thy commandment is exceeding broad." "O how love I *Thy law!* it is *my meditation* all the day." "How sweet are *Thy words* unto *my taste!* yea, sweeter than honey to my mouth." *"Thy testimonies* have I taken as a *heritage forever;* for they are *the rejoicing of my heart."* "I will have respect unto Thy statutes *continually."* "I love Thy commandments above gold, yea, above fine gold." "I esteem *all* Thy precepts concerning *all* things to be *right."* "Thy testimonies are wonderful." "I opened my mouth and *panted,* for I *longed* for Thy commandments." "Upright are Thy judgments." "Thy testimonies . . . are righteous, and very faithful." "Thy Word is very pure." "Thy law is the truth." "The righteousness of Thy testimonies is everlasting." "All Thy commandments are truth." "Thy Word is *true from the beginning;* and every one of Thy righteous judgments *endureth forever."* *"My heart* standeth *in awe* of *Thy Word." "I rejoice* at Thy Word, as one that findeth great spoil." "Great peace have they that love Thy Law." *"My soul* hath kept *Thy testimonies;* and I love them exceedingly." "I have chosen Thy precepts." "Thy law is my delight."

Truly, it does the heart good, and refreshes the spirit, to transcribe such utterances as the foregoing, many of which are the suited utterances of our Lord Himself, in the days of His flesh. He ever lived upon the Word. It was the food of His soul, the authority of His path, the material of His ministry. By it He vanquished Satan; by it He silenced Sadducees, Pharisees, and Herodians; by it He taught His disciples; to it He commended His servants, as He was about to ascend into the heavens.

How important is all this for us! How intensely interesting! How deeply practical! What a place it gives the holy Scriptures! For we remember that it is, in very deed, the blessed volume of inspiration which is brought before us in all those golden sentences culled from Psalm 119. How strengthening, refreshing, and encouraging for us to mark the way in which our Lord uses the holy Scriptures at all times, the place He gives them, and the dignity He puts upon them! He appeals to them on all occasions as a divine authority from which there can be no appeal. He, though Himself as God over all, the Author of the volume, having taken His place as man on the earth, sets forth with all possible plainness what is man's bounden duty and high privilege, namely, to live by the Word of God, to bow down in reverent subjection to its divine authority.

And have we not here a very complete answer to the oft-raised question of infidelity, "How do we know that the Bible is the Word of God?" If indeed we believe in Christ—if we own Him to be the Son of God, God manifest in the flesh, very God and very man, we cannot fail to see the moral force of the fact that this divine Person constantly appeals to the Scriptures—to Moses, the prophets, and the psalms, as to a divine standard. Did He not know them to be the Word of God? Undoubtedly. As God, He had given them; as Man, He received them, lived by them, and owned their paramount authority, in all things.

What a weighty fact is here for the professing church! What a withering rebuke to all those so-called Christian doctors and writers who have presumed to tamper with the grand fundamental truth of the plenary inspiration of the holy Scriptures in general, and of the five books of Moses in particular! How terrible to think of the professed teachers of the Church of God daring to designate as spurious, writings which our Lord and Master received and owned as divine!

And yet we are told, and we are expected to believe that things are improving! Alas! it is a miserable delusion. The degrading absurdities of ritualism, and the blasphemous reasonings of infidelity, are rapidly increasing around us; and where these influences are not actually dominant, we observe, for the most part, a cold indifference, carnal ease, self-indulgence, and worldliness—any thing and every thing, in short, but the evidence of improvement. If people are not led away by infidelity on the one hand, or by ritualism on the other, it is, for the most part, owing to the fact that they are too much occupied with pleasure and gain to think of any thing else. And as to the religion of the day, if you subtract money and music, you will have a lamentably trifling balance.

Hence, therefore, it is impossible to shake off the conviction that the combined testimony of observation and experience is directly opposed to the notion that things are improving. Indeed, for any one, in the face of such an array of evidence to the contrary, to cling to such a theory, can only be regarded as the fruit of a most unaccountable credulity.

But perhaps some may feel disposed to say that we must not judge by the sight of our eyes; we must be hopeful. True, provided only we have a divine warrant for our hopefulness. If a single line of Scripture can be produced to prove that the present system of things is to be marked by gradual improvement, religiously, politically, morally, or socially, then, by all means, be hopeful. Yes; hope against hope. A single clause of inspiration is quite sufficient to form the basis of a hope which will lift the heart above the very darkest and most depressing surroundings.

But where is such a clause to be found? Simply no where. The testimony of the Bible, from cover to cover; the distinct teaching of holy Scripture, from beginning to end; the voices of prophets and apostles, in unbroken harmony—all, without a single divergent note, go to prove, with a force and clearness perfectly unanswerable, that the present condition of things, so far from gradually improving, will rapidly grow worse; that ere the bright beams of millennial glory can gladden this groaning earth, the sword of judgment must do its appalling work. To quote the passages in proof of our assertion would literally fill a volume; it would simply be to transcribe a large portion of the prophetic Scriptures of the Old and New Testament.

This, of course, we do not attempt. There is no need. The reader has his Bible before him; let him search it diligently. Let him lay aside all his preconceived ideas, all the conventionalisms of christendom, all the ordinary phraseology of the religious world, all the dogmas of the schools of divinity, and come, with the simplicity of a little child, to the pure fountain of holy Scripture, and drink in its heavenly teaching. If he will only do this, he will rise from the study with the clear and settled conviction that the world will, most assuredly, not be converted by the means now in operation—that it is not the gospel of peace, but the besom of destruction that shall prepare the earth for glory.

Is it, then, that we deny the good that is being done? Are we insensible to it? Far be the thought! We heartily bless God for every atom of it. We rejoice in every effort put forth to spread the precious gospel of the grace of God; we render thanks for every soul gathered within the blessed circle of God's salvation. We delight to think of eighty-five millions of Bibles scattered over the earth. What human mind can calculate the results of all these, yea, the results of a single copy? We earnestly wish Godspeed to every true-hearted missionary who goes forth with the glad tidings of salvation, whether into the lanes and court-yards of London, or to the most distant parts of the earth.

But, admitting all this, as we most heartily do, we nevertheless do not believe in the conversion of the world by the means now in operation. Scripture tells us that it is when the divine judgments are in the earth, the inhabitants of the world shall learn righteousness. This one clause of inspiration ought to be sufficient to prove that it is not by the gospel that the world is to be converted; and there are hundreds of clauses which speak the same language and teach the same truth. It is not by grace, but by judgment, that the inhabitants of the world shall learn righteousness.

What, then, is the object of the gospel? If it be not to convert the world, for what purpose is it preached? The apostle James, in his address at the memorable council at Jerusalem, gives an answer, direct and conclusive, to the question. He says, "Simeon hath declared how God at the first did visit the Gentiles." For what? To convert them all? The very reverse—"*To take out of them* a people for His name." Nothing can be more distinct than this. It sets before us that which ought to be the grand object of all missionary effort—that which every divinely sent and divinely taught missionary will keep before his mind in all his blessed labors. It is "to take out a people for His name."

How important to remember this! How needful to have ever before us a true object in all our work! Of what possible use can it be to work for a false object? Is it not much better to work with a direct view to what God is doing? Will it cripple the missionary's energies, or clip his wings, to keep before his eyes the divine purpose in his work? Surely not. Take the case of two missionaries going forth to some distant mission-field: the one has for his object the conversion of the world; the other, the gathering out of a people. Will the latter, by reason of his object, be less devoted, less energetic, less enthusiastic, than the former? We cannot believe it; on the contrary, the very fact of his being in the current of the divine mind will impart stability and consistency to his work, and, at the same time, encourage his heart in the face of the difficulties and hindrances which surround him.

But however this may be, it is perfectly plain that the apostles of our Lord and Saviour Jesus Christ had no such object, in going forth to their work, as the conversion of the world. "Go ye into all the world, and preach the gospel to every creature; he that believeth and is baptized shall be saved; but he that believeth not shall be damned."

This was to the twelve. The world was to be their sphere. The aspect of their message was, unto every creature; the application, to him that believeth. It was pre-eminently an individual thing. The conversion of the whole world was not to be their object; that will be effected by a different agency altogether, when God's present action by the gospel shall have resulted in the gathering out of a people for the heavens.* The Holy Ghost came down on the day of Pentecost, not to convert the world, but to *"convict [ἐλέγξει]"* it, or demonstrate its guilt in having rejected the Son of God.† The effect of His presence was to prove the world guilty; and as to the grand object of His mission, it was to form a body composed of believers from amongst both Jews and Gentiles. With this He has been occupied for the last eighteen hundred years. This is "the mystery" of which the apostle Paul was made a minister, and which he unfolds, so fully and blessedly, in his Epistle to the Ephesians. It is impossible for any one to understand the truth set forth in this marvelous document, and not see that the conversion of the world and the formation of the body of Christ are two totally different things, which could not possibly go on together.

Let the reader ponder the following beautiful passage: "For this cause I Paul, the prisoner of Jesus Christ for you Gentiles, if ye have heard of the dispensation of the grace of God which is given me to you-ward: how that by revelation He made known unto me the mystery; (as I wrote afore in few words, whereby, when ye read, ye may understand my knowledge in the mystery of Christ) which in other ages was not made known unto the sons of men"—not made known in the Scriptures of the Old Testament, nor revealed to the Old Testament saints or prophets—"as it is now revealed unto His holy apostles and prophets" (that is, to the New Testament prophets) "by the Spirit; that the Gentiles should be fellowheirs, and of the same body, and partakers of His promise in Christ by the gospel: whereof I was made a minister according to the gift of the grace of God given unto me by the effectual working of His power. Unto

*We would commend to the reader's attention Psalm 67. It is one of a large class of passages which prove that the blessing of the nations is consequent upon Israel's restoration. "God be merciful unto us [Israel], and bless us; and cause His face to shine upon us, that Thy way may be known upon earth, Thy saving health among *all nations*. . . . God shall bless us; and *all the ends of the earth* shall fear Him." There could not be a more lovely or forcible proof of the fact that it is Israel, and not the Church, that will be used for the blessing of the nations.

†The application of John 16:8-11 to the Spirit's work in the individual is, in our judgment, a serious mistake. It refers to the effect of His presence on earth, in reference to the world as a whole. His work in the soul is a precious truth, we need hardly say, but it is not the truth taught in this passage.

me, who am less than the least of all saints, is this grace given, that I should preach among the Gentiles the unsearchable riches of Christ; and to make all men see what is the dispensation [οἰκονομια] of the mystery, which *from the beginning of the world* hath been *hid in God,* who created all things by Jesus Christ: to the intent that now unto the principalities and powers in the heavenlies might be known by the Church the manifold wisdom of God" (Eph. 3:1-10).

Take another passage from the Epistle to the Colossians. "If ye continue in the faith grounded and settled, and be not moved away from the hope of the gospel, which ye have heard, and which was preached to every creature which is under heaven, whereof I Paul am made a minister, who now rejoice in my sufferings for you, and fill up that which is behind of the afflictions of Christ in my flesh for His body's sake, which is the Church: whereof I am made a minister, according to the dispensation of God which is given to me for you, to complete the Word of God; even the mystery which hath been hid from ages and from generations, but now is made manifest to His saints: to whom God would make known what is the riches of the glory of this mystery among the Gentiles; which is Christ in you, the hope of glory: whom we preach, warning every man, and teaching every man in all wisdom; that we may present every man perfect in Christ Jesus: whereunto I also labor, striving according to His working, which worketh in me mightily" (chap. 1:23-29).

From these and numerous other passages, the reader may see the special object of Paul's ministry. Assuredly he had no such thought in his mind as the conversion of the world. True, he preached the gospel, in all its depth, fullness, and power—preached it "from Jerusalem and round about unto Illyricum"—"preached among the Gentiles the unsearchable riches of Christ," but with no thought of converting the world. He knew better. He knew and taught that the world was ripening for judgment—yes, ripening rapidly; that "evil men and seducers shall wax worse and worse;" that "in *the latter times* some shall depart from the faith, giving heed to seducing spirits, and doctrines of devils; speaking lies in hypocrisy; having their conscience seared with a hot iron; forbidding to marry, and commanding to abstain from meats, which God had created to be received with thanksgiving of them which believe and know the truth."

And further still, this faithful and divinely inspired witness taught that "in *the last days*" far in advance of "the latter times" "perilous [or difficult] times shall come. For men shall be lovers of their own selves, covetous, boasters, proud, blasphemers, disobedient to parents, unthankful, unholy, without natural affection, truce-breakers, false accusers, incontinent, fierce, despisers of those that are good, traitors, heady, highminded, *lovers of pleasures rather than lovers of God;* having a form of godliness, but denying the power thereof" (compare 1 Tim. 4:1-3 with 2 Tim. 3:1-5).

What a picture! It brings us back to the close of the first of Romans, where the same inspired pen portrays for us the dark forms of heathenism; but with this terrible difference, that in 2 Timothy it is not heathenism, but nominal Christianity—"a form of godliness."

And is this to be the end of the present condition of things? Is this the converted world of which we hear so much? Alas! there are false prophets abroad; there are those who cry, Peace, peace, when there is no peace; there are those who attempt to daub the crumbling walls of christendom with untempered mortar.

But it will not do. Judgment is at the door. The professing church has utterly, shamefully failed; she has grievously departed from the Word of God, and revolted from the authority of her Lord. There is not a single ray of hope for christendom. It is the darkest moral blot in the wide universe of God, or on the page of history. The same blessed apostle from whose writings we have already so largely quoted, tells us that "the mystery of iniquity doth already work"; hence it has been working now for over eighteen centuries. "Only He that now hindereth will hinder until He be taken out of the way. And then shall that Wicked be revealed, whom the Lord shall consume with the spirit of His mouth, and shall destroy with the brightness of His coming: even him, whose coming is after the working of Satan with all power and signs and lying wonders, and with all deceivableness of unrighteousness in them that perish; because they received not the love of the truth, that they might be saved. And for this cause God shall send them strong delusion, that they should believe a lie: that they all might be damned who believed not the truth, but had pleasure in unrighteousness" (2 Thess. 2:7-12).

How awful is the doom of christendom! Strong delusion! Dark damnation! And all this in the face of the dreams of those false prophets who talk to the people about "the bright side of things." Thank God, there is a bright side for all those who belong to Christ. To them, the apostle can speak in bright and cheering accents. "We are bound to give thanks alway to God for you, brethren beloved of the Lord, because God hath from the beginning chosen you to salvation through sanctification of the Spirit and belief of the truth: whereunto He called you by our gospel, to the obtaining of the glory of our Lord Jesus Christ" (2 Thess. 2: 13-14).

Here we have, most surely, the bright side of things—the bright and blessed hope of the Church of God—the hope of seeing "the bright and morning Star." All rightly instructed Christians are on the look-out, not for an improved or a converted world, but for their coming Lord and Saviour, who has gone to prepare a place for them in the Father's house, and is coming again to receive them to Himself, that where He is, there they may be also. This is His own sweet promise, which may be fulfilled at any moment. He only waits, as Peter tells us, in long-suffering mercy, not willing that any should perish, but that all should come to repentance. But when the last member shall be incorporated, by the Holy Ghost, into the blessed body of Christ, then shall the voice of the archangel and the trump of God summon *all* the redeemed, from the beginning, to meet their descending Lord in the air, to be forever with Him.

This is the true and proper hope of the Church of God—a hope which He would have ever shining down into the hearts of all His beloved people, in its purifying and elevating power. Of this blessed hope the enemy has succeeded in robbing a large number of the Lord's people. Indeed, for centuries it was well-nigh blotted out from the Church's horizon; and it has only been partially recovered within the last fifty years. And, alas! how partially! Where do we hear of it, throughout the length and breadth of the professing church? Do the pulpits of christendom ring with the joyful sound, "Behold the Bridegroom cometh"? Far from it. Even the few beloved servants of Christ who are looking for His coming, hardly dare to preach it, because they fear it would be utterly rejected. And so it would. We are thoroughly persuaded that, in the vast majority of cases, men who should venture to preach the glorious truth that the Lord is coming for His Church, would speedily have to vacate their pulpits.

What a solemn and striking proof of Satan's blinding power! He has robbed the Church of her divinely given hope, and instead thereof, he has given her a delusion—a lie. Instead of looking out for "the bright and morning Star," he has set her looking for a converted world—a millennium without Christ. He has succeeded in casting such a haze over the future, that the Church has completely lost her bearings. She does not know where she is. She is like a vessel tossed on the stormy ocean, having neither compass nor rudder, seeing neither sun nor stars. All is darkness and confusion.

And how is this? Simply because the Church has lost sight of the pure and precious word of her Lord, and accepted instead those bewildering creeds and confessions of men which so mar and mutilate the truth of God that Christians seem utterly at sea as to their proper standing and their proper hope.

And yet they have the Bible in their hands. True; but so had the Jews, and yet they rejected that blessed One who is the great theme of the Bible from beginning to end. This was the moral inconsistency with which our Lord charged them in John 5: "Ye search the Scriptures; for in them ye think ye have eternal life; and they are they which testify of Me; and ye will not come to Me, that ye might have life."*

And why was this? Simply because their minds were blinded by religious prejudice. They were under the influence of the doctrines and commandments of men. Hence, although they had the Scriptures, and boasted of having them, they were as ignorant of them, and as little governed by them, as the poor dark heathen around them. It is one thing to have the Bible in our hands, in our homes, and in our assemblies, and quite another thing to have the truths of the Bible acting on our hearts and consciences, and shining in our lives.

Take, for instance, the great subject now before us, and which has led us into this very lengthened digression. Can any thing be more plainly taught in the New Testament than this, namely, that the end of the present condition of things will be terrible apostasy from the truth, and open rebellion against God and the Lamb? The Gospels, the Epistles, and the Revelation all agree in setting forth this most solemn truth, with such distinctness and simplicity that a babe in Christ may see it.

And yet how few, comparatively, believe it! The vast majority believe the very reverse. They believe that by means of the various agencies now in operation all nations shall be converted. In vain we call attention to our Lord's parables in Matthew 13:—the tares, the leaven, and the mustard-seed. How do these agree with the idea of a converted world? If the whole world is to be converted by a preached gospel, how is it that tares are found in the field at the end of the age? how is it that there are as many foolish virgins as wise ones when the Bridegroom comes? If the whole world is to be converted by the gospel, then on whom will "the day of the Lord so come as a thief in the night"? or what mean those awful words, "For when they shall say, Peace and safety; then sudden destruction cometh upon them, as travail upon a woman with child; and they shall not escape"? In view of a converted world, what would be the just application, what the moral force, of those most solemn words in the first of Revelation, "Behold, He cometh with clouds, and every eye shall see Him, and they also which pierced Him; and *all kindreds of the earth shall wail* because of Him"? Where are all those wailing kindreds to be found if the whole world is to be converted?

Is it not as clear as a sunbeam that the two things cannot stand for a moment together? Is it not perfectly plain that the theory of a world converted by the gospel is diametrically opposed to the teaching of the entire New Testament? How is it, then, that the vast majority of professing Christians persist in holding it? There can be but the one reply, and that is, they do not bow to the authority of Scripture. It is most sorrowful and solemn to have to say it; but it is, alas! too true. The Bible is read in christendom, but the truths of the Bible are not believed—nay, they are persistently rejected; and all this in view of the oft-repeated boast that "the Bible, and the Bible alone, is the religion of Protestants."

But we shall not pursue this subject further here, much as we feel its weight and importance. We trust the reader may be led by the Spirit of God to feel its deep solemnity. We believe the Lord's people every where need to be thoroughly roused to a sense of how entirely the professing church has departed from the authority of Scripture. Here, we may rest assured, lies the real cause of all the confusion, all the error, all the evil, in our midst. We have departed from the Word of the Lord, and from Himself. Until this is seen, felt, and owned, we cannot be right. The Lord looks for true repentance, real brokenness of spirit, in His

*The word ἐρευνατε may be either imperative or indicative; but the context, we judge, demands the latter. They had the Scriptures; they were read in their synagogues every Sabbath day; they professed to believe that in them they had eternal life; they testified of Him; and yet they would not come to Him. Here was the flagrant inconsistency. Now, if ἐρευνατε be taken as a command, the whole force of the passage is lost.

Need we remind the reader that there are plenty of arguments and inducements leading us to search the Scriptures, without appealing to what we believe to be an inaccurate rendering of John 5:39?

presence. "*To this man* will I look, even to him that is *poor,* and of a *contrite* spirit, and trembleth at My Word."

This always holds good. There is no limit to the blessing when the soul is in this truly blessed attitude. But it must be a reality. It will not do to talk of being "poor and contrite," we must be in the condition. It is an individual matter. "*To this man* will I look."

Oh may the Lord, in His infinite mercy, lead us, every one, into true self-judgment, under the action of His Word. May our ears be open to hear His voice. May there .be a real turning of our hearts to Himself and to His Word. May we turn our backs, in holy decision, once and forever, upon every thing that will not stand the test of Scripture. This, we are persuaded, is what our Lord Christ looks for on the part of all who belong to Him, amid the terrible and hopeless *debris* of christendom.

---

## *CHAPTER 6*

"NOW these are the commandments, the statutes, and the judgments, which the Lord your God commanded to teach you, that ye might do them in the land whither ye go to possess it: that thou mightest fear the Lord thy God, to keep all His statutes and His commandments, which I command thee, thou, and thy son, and thy son's son, all the days of thy life; and that thy days may be prolonged. Hear therefore, O Israel, and observe to do it; that it may be well with thee, and that ye may increase mightily, as the Lord God of thy fathers hath promised thee, in the land that floweth with milk and honey. Hear, O Israel: The Lord our God is one Lord."

We have here presented to us that great cardinal truth which the nation of Israel was specially responsible to hold fast and confess, namely, the unity of the Godhead. This truth lay at the very foundation of the Jewish economy. It was the grand centre around which the people were to rally. So long as they maintained this, they were a happy, prosperous, fruitful people; but when it was let go, all was gone. It was their great national bulwark, and that which was to mark them off from all the nations of the earth. They were called to confess this glorious truth in the face of an idolatrous world, with "its gods many, and lords many." It was Israel's high privilege and holy responsibility to bear a steady witness to the truth contained in that one weighty sentence, "The Lord our God is one Lord," in marked opposition to the false gods innumerable of the heathen around. Their father Abraham had been called out from the very midst of heathen idolatry, to be a witness to the one true and living God, to trust Him, to walk with Him, to lean on Him, and to obey Him.

If the reader will turn to the last chapter of Joshua, he will find a very striking allusion to this fact, and a very important use made of it, in his closing address to the people. "And Joshua gathered all the tribes of Israel to Shechem, and called for the elders of Israel, and for their heads, and for their judges, and for their officers; and they presented themselves before God. And Joshua said unto all the people, 'Thus saith the Lord God of Israel, Your fathers dwelt on the other side of the flood in old time, even Terah, the father of Abraham, and the father of Nachor; and *they served other gods.* And I took your father Abraham from the other side of the flood, and led him throughout all the land of Canaan, and multiplied his seed, and gave him Isaac.' "

Here Joshua reminds the people of the fact that their fathers had served other gods —a very solemn and weighty fact most surely, and one which they ought never to have forgotten, inasmuch as the remembrance of it would have taught them their deep need of watchfulness over themselves, lest by any means they should be drawn back into that gross and terrible evil out of which God, in His sovereign grace and electing love, had called their father Abraham. It would have been their wisdom to consider that the selfsame evil in which their fathers had lived, in the olden time, was just the one into which they themselves were likely to fall.

Having presented this fact to the people,

Joshua brings before them, with uncommon force and vividness, all the leading events of their history, from the birth of their father Isaac, down to the moment in which he was addressing them; and then sums up with the following telling appeal: "Now therefore fear the Lord, and serve Him in sincerity and in truth; and *put away the gods which your fathers served on the other side of the flood, and in Egypt;* and serve ye the Lord. And if it seem evil unto you to serve the Lord, choose you this day whom ye will serve; whether *the gods which your fathers served that were on the other side of the flood,* or the gods of the Amorites in whose land ye dwell; but as for me and my house, we will serve the Lord."

Mark the repeated allusion to the fact that their fathers had worshiped false gods; and further, that the land into which Jehovah had brought them had been polluted, from one end to the other, by the dark abominations of heathen idolatry.

Thus does this faithful servant of the Lord, evidently by the inspiration of the Holy Ghost, seek to set before the people their danger of giving up the grand central and foundation truth of the one true and living God, and falling back into the worship of idols. He urges upon them the absolute necessity of whole-hearted decision. "Choose you *this day* whom ye will serve." There is nothing like plain, out-and-out decision for God. It is due to Him always. He had proved Himself to be unmistakably for them in redeeming them from the bondage of Egypt, bringing them through the wilderness, and planting them in the land of Canaan; hence, therefore, that they should be wholly for Him was nothing more than their reasonable service.

How deeply Joshua felt all this for himself is evident from those very memorable words, "As for me and my house, we will serve the Lord." Lovely words! Precious decision! National religion might, and, alas! did, go to ruin; but personal and family religion could, by the grace of God, be maintained every where and at all times.

Thank God for this! May we never forget it. "Me and my house" is Faith's clear and delightful response to God's "Thou and thy house." Let the condition of the ostensible, professed people of God, at any given time, be what it may, it is the privilege of every true-hearted man of God to adopt and act upon this immortal decision: "As for me and my house, we will serve the Lord."

True, it is only by the grace of God, continually supplied, that this holy resolution can be carried out; but we may rest assured that where the bent of the heart is to follow the Lord fully, all needed grace will be ministered, day by day; for those encouraging words must ever hold good, "*My* grace is sufficient for *thee;* for My strength is made perfect in weakness."

Let us now look for a moment at the apparent effect of Joshua's soul-stirring appeal to the congregation. It seemed very promising. "The people answered and said, 'God forbid that we should forsake the Lord, to serve other gods; for the Lord our God, He it is that brought us up and our fathers out of the land of Egypt, from the house of bondage, and which did those great signs in our sight, and preserved us in all the way wherein we went, and among all the people through whom we passed: and the Lord drave out from before us all the people, even the Amorites which dwelt in the land; therefore will we also serve the Lord, for He is our God."

All this sounded very well, and looked very hopeful. They seemed to have a clear sense of the moral basis of Jehovah's claim upon them for implicit obedience. They could accurately recount all His mighty deeds on their behalf, and make very earnest and no doubt sincere protestations against idolatry, and promises of obedience to Jehovah, their God.

But it is very evident that Joshua was not particularly sanguine about all this profession, for he "said unto the people, 'Ye cannot serve the Lord: for He is a holy God; He is a jealous God; He will not forgive your transgressions nor your sins. If ye forsake the Lord, and serve strange gods, then He will turn and do you hurt, and consume you, after that He hath done you good.' And the people said unto Joshua, 'Nay; but we will serve the Lord.' And Joshua said unto the people, 'Ye are witnesses against yourselves that ye have chosen you the Lord, to serve Him.' And they said, 'We are witnesses.' 'Now therefore put away,' said he, *'the strange gods which are among you,* and *incline your heart unto the Lord God of Israel.'* And the people said unto Joshua, 'The Lord our God will we serve, and His voice will we obey.' "

We do not now stop to contemplate the aspect in which Joshua presents God to the congregation of Israel, inasmuch as our object in referring to the passage is to show the prominent place assigned, in Joshua's address, to the truth of the unity of the Godhead. This was the truth to which Israel was called to bear witness, in view of all the nations of the earth, and in which they were to find their moral safeguard against the ensnaring influences of idolatry.

But, alas! this very truth was *the* one as to which they most speedily and signally failed. The promises, vows, and resolutions made under the powerful influence of Joshua's appeal soon proved to be like the early dew and the morning cloud, that passeth away. "The people served the Lord all the days of Joshua, and all the days of the elders that outlived Joshua, who had seen all the great works of the Lord, that He did for Israel. And Joshua, the son of Nun, the servant of the Lord, died, being a hundred and ten years old. . . . And also all that generation were gathered unto their fathers; and there arose another generation after them, which knew not the Lord, nor yet the works which He had done for Israel. And the children of Israel did evil in the sight of the Lord, *and served Baalim;* and they forsook the Lord God of their fathers, which brought them out of the land of Egypt, *and followed* other gods, of the gods of the people that were round about them, *and bowed themselves unto them,* and provoked the Lord to anger. And they forsook the Lord, and served Baal and Ashtaroth" (Judges 2:7-13).

How admonitory is all this! how full of solemn warning to us all! The grand, all-important, special, and characteristic truth so soon abandoned! The one only true and living God given up for Baal and Ashtaroth! So long as Joshua and the elders lived, their presence and their influence kept Israel from open apostasy; but no sooner were those moral embankments removed than the dark tide of idolatry rolled in and swept away the very foundations of the national faith. Jehovah of Israel was displaced by Baal and Ashtaroth. Human influence is a poor prop, a feeble barrier. We must be sustained by the power of God, else we shall, sooner or later, give way. The faith that stands merely in the wisdom of men, and not in the power of God, must prove a poor, flimsy, worthless faith. It will not stand the day of trial; it will not bear the furnace; it will most assuredly break down.

It is well to remember this. Second-hand faith will never do. There must be a living link connecting the soul with God. We must have to do with God for ourselves individually, else we shall give way when the testing-time comes. Human example and human influence may be all very good in their place. It was all very well to look at Joshua and the elders, and see how they followed the Lord. It is quite true that "as iron sharpeneth iron, so doth the countenance of a man his friend." It is very encouraging to be surrounded by a number of truly devoted hearts—very delightful to be borne along upon the bosom of the tide of collective loyalty to Christ—to His Person and to His cause. But if this be all, if there be not the deep spring of personal faith and personal knowledge, if there be not the divinely formed and the divinely sustained link of individual relationship and communion, then when the human props are removed—when the tide of human influence ebbs—when general declension sets in—we shall be, in principle, like Israel following the Lord all the days of Joshua and the elders, and then giving up the confession of His name and returning to the follies and vanities of this present world—things no better, in reality, than Baal and Ashtaroth.

But, on the other hand, when the heart is thoroughly established in the truth and grace of God—when we can say—as it is the privilege of each true believer to say—"I know *whom* I have believed, and am persuaded that He is able to keep that which I have committed unto Him against that day," then, although all should turn aside from the public confession of Christ, although we should find ourselves left without the help of a human countenance or the support of a human arm, we shall find "the foundation of God" as sure as ever, and the path of obedience as plain before us as though thousands were treading it with holy decision and energy.

We must never lose sight of the fact that it is the divine purpose that the professing church of God should learn deep and holy lessons from the history of Israel. "Whatsoever things were written aforetime were written for our learning, that we through patience and comfort of the Scriptures might have hope." Nor is it by any means necessary, in order to our thus learning from the Old Testament Scriptures, that we should occupy ourselves in searching out fanciful analogies, curious theories, or far-fetched illustrations. Many, alas! have tried these things, and instead of finding "comfort" in the Scriptures, they have been led away into empty and foolish conceits, if not into deadly errors.

But our business is with the living facts recorded on the page of inspired history. These are to be our study; from these we are to draw our great practical lessons. Take, for example, the weighty and admonitory fact now before us—a fact standing out in characters deep and broad on the page of Israel's history from Joshua to Isaiah—the fact of Israel's lamentable departure from that very truth which they were specially called to hold and confess—the truth of the unity of the Godhead. The very first thing they did was to let go this grand and all-important truth, this key-stone of the arch, the foundation of the whole edifice, the very heart of their national existence, the living centre of their national polity. They gave it up, and turned back to the idolatry of their fathers on the other side of the flood, and of the heathen nations around them. They abandoned that most glorious and distinctive truth on the maintenance of which their very existence as a nation depended. Had they only held fast this truth, they would have been invincible; but in surrendering it, they surrendered all, and became much worse than the nations around them, inasmuch as they sinned against light and knowledge—sinned with their eyes open—sinned in the face of the most solemn warnings and earnest entreaties, and, we may add, in the face of the most vehement and oft-repeated promises and protestations of obedience.

Yes, Israel gave up the worship of the one true and living God, Jehovah-Elohim, their covenant-God; not only their Creator, but their Redeemer—the One who had brought them up out of the land of Egypt, conducted them through the Red Sea, led them through the wilderness, brought them across the Jordan, and planted them in triumph in the inheritance which He had promised to Abraham their father—"a land flowing with milk and honey, which is the glory of all lands." They turned their backs upon Him, and gave themselves up to the worship of false gods; "they provoked Him to anger with their high places, and moved Him to jealousy with their graven images."

It seems perfectly wonderful that a people who had seen and known so much of the goodness and loving-kindness of God—His mighty acts, His faithfulness, His majesty, His glory, could ever bring themselves to bow down to the stock of a tree; but so it was. Their whole history, from the days of the calf at the foot of Mount Sinai, to the day in which Nebuchadnezzar reduced Jerusalem to ruins, is marked by an unconquerable spirit of idolatry. In vain did Jehovah, in His long-suffering mercy and abounding goodness, raise up deliverers for them, to lift them from beneath the terrible consequences of their sin and folly. Again and again, in His inexhaustible mercy and patience, He saved them from the hand of their enemies. He raised up an Othniel, an Ehud, a Barak, a Gideon, a Jephthah, a Samson—those instruments of His mercy and power—those witnesses of His deep and tender love and compassion toward His poor infatuated people. No sooner had each judge passed off the scene than back the nation plunged into their besetting sin of idolatry.

So, also, in the days of the kings; it is the same melancholy, heart-rending story. True, there were bright spots here and there—some brilliant stars shining out through the deep gloom of the nation's history; we have a David, an Asa, a Jehoshaphat, a Hezekiah, a Josiah—refreshing and blessed exceptions to the dark and dismal rule. But even men like these failed to eradicate from the heart of the nation the pernicious root of idolatry. Even amid the unexampled splendors of Solomon's reign, that root sent forth its bitter shoots, in the monstrous form of high places to Ashtaroth, the goddess of the Zidonians; Milcom, the abomination of the Ammonites; and Chemosh, the abomination of Moab.

Think of this! Pause for a moment, and contemplate the astounding fact of the writer of the Canticles, Ecclesiastes, and Proverbs bowing at the shrine of Molech! Only conceive, the wisest, the wealthiest, and the most glorious of Israel's monarchs burning incense and offering sacrifices upon the altar of Chemosh!

Truly, there is something here for us to ponder. It was written for our learning. The reign of Solomon affords one of the most striking and impressive evidences of the fact which is just now engaging our attention, namely, Israel's complete and hopeless apostasy from the grand truth of the unity of the Godhead—their unconquerable spirit of idolatry. The truth which they were specially called out to hold and confess was the very truth which they first of all and most persistently abandoned.

We shall not pursue the dark line of evidence further, neither shall we dwell upon the appalling picture of the nation's judgment in consequence of their idolatry. They are now in the condition of which the prophet Hosea speaks—"The children of Israel shall abide many days without a king, and without a prince, and without a sacrifice, and without an image, and without an ephod, and without teraphim." "The unclean spirit of idolatry has gone out of them," during these "many days," to return, by and by, with "seven other spirits more wicked than himself"—the very perfection of spiritual wickedness. And then will come days of unparalleled tribulation upon that long misguided and deeply revolted people—"the time of Jacob's trouble."

But deliverance will come, blessed be God! Bright days are in store for the restored nation—"days of heaven upon earth"—as the same prophet Hosea tells us, "Afterward shall the children of Israel return, and seek the Lord their God, and David their king; and shall fear the Lord and His goodness in the latter days." All the promises of God to Abraham, Isaac, Jacob, and David shall be blessedly accomplished; all the brilliant predictions of the prophets, from Isaiah to Malachi, shall be gloriously fulfilled. Yes, both promises and prophecies shall be literally and gloriously made good to restored Israel, in the land of Canaan; for "the Scripture cannot be broken." The long, dark, dreary night shall be followed by the brightest day that has ever shone upon this earth; the daughter of Zion shall bask in the bright and blessed beams of "the Sun of Righteousness"; and "the earth shall be filled with the knowledge of the Lord as the waters cover the sea."

It would indeed be a most delightful exercise to reproduce upon the pages of this volume those glowing passages from the prophets which speak of Israel's future; but this we cannot attempt; it is not needful; and we have a duty to fulfill which, if not so pleasing to us or so refreshing to the reader, will, we earnestly hope, prove not less profitable.

The duty is this: to press upon the attention of the reader (and upon the attention of the whole Church of God) the practical application of that solemn fact in Israel's history on which we have dwelt at such length—the fact of their having so speedily and so completely given up the great truth set forth in Deuteronomy 6:4, "Hear, O Israel; the Lord our God is one Lord."

We may perhaps be asked, What bearing can this fact have upon the Church of God? We believe it has a most solemn bearing; and further, we believe we should be guilty of a very culpable shirking of our duty to Christ and to His Church if we failed to point it out. We know that all the great facts of Israel's history are full of instruction, full of admonition, full of warning, for us. It is our business, our bounden duty, to see that we profit by them—to take heed that we study them aright.

Now, in contemplating the history of the Church of God as a public witness for Christ on the earth, we find that hardly had it been set up, in all the fullness of blessing and privilege which marked the opening of its career, ere it began to slip away from those very truths which it was specially responsible to maintain and confess. Like Adam in the garden of Eden; like Noah in the restored earth; like Israel in Canaan; so the Church, as the responsible steward of the mysteries of God, was no sooner set in its place than it began to totter and fall. It almost immediately began to give up those grand truths which were characteristic of its very existence, and which were to mark off Christianity from all that had gone before. Even under the eyes of the apostles of our Lord and Saviour Jesus Christ, errors and evils had begun to work which sapped the very foundations of the Church's testimony.

Are we asked for proofs? Alas! we have them in melancholy abundance. Hear the words of that blessed apostle who shed more tears and heaved more sighs over the ruins of the Church than any man that ever lived. "I marvel," he says, and well he might, "that ye are *so soon* removed from Him that called you into the grace of Christ, unto another gospel: which is not another." "O foolish Galatians, who hath bewitched you, that ye should not obey the truth, before whose eyes Jesus Christ hath been evidently set forth, crucified among you?" "Howbeit then, when ye knew not God, ye did service to them which by nature are no gods. But now, after that ye have known God, or rather are known of God, how turn ye again to the weak and beggarly elements, whereunto ye desire again to be in bondage? Ye observe days and months and times and years;" Christian festivals, so called, very imposing and gratifying to religious nature; but, in the judgment of the apostle, the judgment of the Holy Ghost, it was simply giving up Christianity and going back to the worship of idols. "I am afraid of you"—and no wonder, when they could thus so speedily turn away from the grand characteristic truths of a heavenly Christianity, and occupy themselves with superstitious observances. "I am afraid of you, lest I have bestowed upon you labor in vain." "Ye did run well; who did hinder you, that ye should not obey the truth? This persuasion cometh not of Him that calleth you. A little leaven leaveneth the whole lump."

And all this in the apostle's own day. The departure was even more rapid than in Israel's case; for they served the Lord all the days of Joshua, and all the days of the elders that outlived Joshua; but in the Church's sad and humiliating history, the enemy succeeded almost immediately in introducing leaven into the meal, tares among the wheat. Ere the apostles themselves had left the scene, seed was sown which has been bearing its pernicious fruit ever since, and shall continue to bear till angelic reapers clear the field.

But we must give futher proof from Scripture. Let us hearken to the same inspired witness, near the close of his ministry, pouring out his heart to his beloved son Timothy, in accents at once pathetic and solemn. "This thou knowest, that all they which are in Asia be turned away from me." Again, "Preach the Word; be instant in season, out of season; reprove, rebuke, exhort with all long-suffering and doctrine. For the time will come when they will not endure sound doctrine; but after their own lusts shall they heap to themselves teachers, having itching ears; and *they shall turn away their ears from the truth,* and shall be turned unto fables."

Here is the testimony of the man who, as a wise master-builder, had laid the foundation of the Church. And what was his own personal experience? He was, like his blessed Master, left alone, deserted by those who had once gathered around him in the freshness, bloom, and ardor of early days. His large loving heart was broken by Judaizing teachers, who sought to overturn the very foundations of Christianity, and to overthrow the faith of God's elect. He wept over the ways of many who, while they made a profession, were nevertheless "the enemies of the cross of Christ."

In a word, the Apostle Paul, as he looked forth from his prison at Rome, saw the hopeless wreck and ruin of the professing body. He saw that it would happen to that body as it had happened to the ship in which he had made his last voyage—a voyage strikingly significant and illustrative of the Church's sad history in this world.

But here let us just remind the reader that we are dealing now only with the question of the Church as a responsible witness for Christ on the earth. This must be distinctly seen, else we shall greatly err in our thoughts on the subject. We must accurately distinguish between the Church as the body of Christ, and as His light-bearer or witness in the world. In the former character, failure is impossible; in the latter, the ruin is complete and hopeless.

The Church as the body of Christ, united to her living and glorified Head in the heavens, by the presence and indwelling of the Holy Ghost, can never, by any possibility, fail—never be smashed to pieces, like Paul's ship, by the storms and billows of this hostile world. It is as safe as Christ Himself. The Head and the body are one—indissolubly one. No power of earth or hell—men or devils can ever touch the feeblest and most obscure member of that blessed body. All stand before God, all are under His gracious eye, in the fullness, beauty, and acceptability of Christ Himself. As is the Head, so are the members—all the members together—each member in particular. All stand in the full eternal results of Christ's finished work on the cross. There is, there can be, no question of responsibility here. The Head made Himself responsible for the members. He perfectly met every claim, and discharged every liability. Nothing remains but love—love, deep as the heart of Christ, perfect as His work, unchanging as His throne. Every question that could possibly be raised against any one or all of the members of the Church of God was raised, gone into, and definitively settled, between God and His Christ, on the cross. All the sins, all the iniquities, all the transgressions, all the guilt, of each member in particular, and all the members together—yes, all, in the fullest and most absolute way, was laid on Christ and borne by Him. God, in His inflexible justice, in His infinite holiness, in His eternal righteousness, dealt with every thing that could ever, in any possible manner, stand in the way of the full salvation, perfect blessedness, and everlasting glory of every one of the members of the body of Christ—the assembly of God. Every member of the body is permeated by the life of the Head; every stone in the building is animated by the life of the Chief Corner-Stone. All are bound together in the power of a bond which can never—no, never be dissolved.

And furthermore, let it be distinctly understood that the unity of the body of Christ is absolutely indissoluble. This is a cardinal point which must be tenaciously held and faithfully confessed. But obviously it cannot be held and confessed unless it is understood and believed; and, judging from the expressions which one sometimes hears in speaking on the subject, it is very questionable indeed if people so expressing themselves have ever grasped in a divine way the glorious truth of the unity of the body of Christ—a unity maintained on earth by the indwelling of the Holy Ghost.

Thus, for example, we sometimes hear people speak of "rending the body of Christ." It is a complete mistake. Such a thing is utterly impossible. The Reformers were accused of rending the body of Christ when they turned their backs upon the Romish system. What a gross misconception! It simply amounted to the monstrous assumption that a vast mass of moral evil, doctrinal error, ecclesiastical corruption, and debasing superstition was to be owned as the body of Christ! How could any one with the New Testament in his hand regard the so-called church of Rome, with its numberless and nameless abominations, as the body of Christ? How could any one possessing the very faintest idea of the true Church of God ever think of bestowing that title upon the darkest mass of wickedness, the greatest masterpiece of Satan the world has ever beheld?

No; we must never confound the ecclesiastical systems of this world—ancient, medieval, or modern; Greek, Latin, Anglican; national or popular, established or dissenting—with the true Church of God, the body of Christ. There is not, beneath the canopy of heaven, this day, nor ever was, a religious system, call it what you please, possessing the very smallest claim to be called "the Church of God," or "the body of Christ." And, as a consequence, it can never be rightly or intelligently called schism, or rending the body of Christ, to separate from such systems; nay, on the contrary, it is the bounden duty of every one who would faithfully maintain and confess the truth of the unity of the body to separate, with the most unqualified decision, from every thing falsely calling itself a church. It can only be viewed as schism to separate from those who are unmistakably and unquestionably gathered on the ground of the assembly of God.

No body of Christians can now lay claim to the title of the body of Christ, or Church of God. The members of that body are scattered every where; they are to be found in all the various religious organizations of the day, save such as deny the deity of our Lord Jesus Christ. We cannot admit the idea that any true Christian could continue to frequent a place where his Lord is blasphemed. But although no body of Christians can lay claim to the title of the assembly of God, all Christians are responsible to be gathered on the ground of that assembly, and on no other.

And if we be asked, How are we to know—where are we to find this ground? We reply, "If thine eye be single, thy whole body shall be full of light." "If any man *will do* His will, he shall know of the doctrine." *"There is a path"* (thanks be to God for it!) though "no fowl knoweth, and the vulture's eye hath not seen it. The lion's whelps have not trodden it, nor the fierce lion passed by it." Nature's keenest vision cannot see this path, nor its greatest strength tread it. Where is it, then? Here it is: *"Unto man"*—to the reader and to the writer, to each, to all—"He said, 'Behold, *the fear of the Lord,* that is wisdom; and *to depart from evil* is understanding' " (Job 28).

But there is another expression which we not unfrequently hear from persons from whom we might expect more intelligence, namely, "Cutting off the members of the body of Christ."* This, too, blessed be God, is impossible. Not a single member of the body of Christ can ever be severed from the Head, or ever disturbed from the place into which he has been incorporated by the Holy Ghost, in pursuance of the eternal purpose of God, and in virtue of the accomplished atonement of our Lord Jesus Christ. The divine Three in One are pledged for the eternal security of the very feeblest member of the body, and for the maintenance of the indissoluble unity of the whole.

In a word, then, it is as true to-day as it was when the inspired apostle penned the fourth chapter of his Epistle to the Ephesians, that "there is one body," of which Christ is Head, of which the Holy Ghost is the formative power, and of which all true believers are members. This body has been on earth since the day of Pentecost, is on earth now, and shall continue on earth until that moment, so rapidly approaching, when Christ shall come and take it to His Father's house. It is the same body, with a continual succession of members, just as we speak of a certain regiment of her majesty's army having been at Waterloo, and now quartered at Aldershop, though not a man in the regiment of today appeared at the memorable battle of 1815.

Does the reader feel any difficulty as to all this? It may be that he finds it hard, in the present broken and scattered condition of the members, to believe and confess the unbroken unity of the whole. He may feel disposed, perhaps, to limit the application of

*The expression, "Cutting off the members of Christ's body" is generally applied in cases of discipline; but it is quite misapplication. The discipline of the assembly can never touch the unity of the body. A member of the body may so fail i morals or err in doctrine as to call for the action of the assembly in putting him away from the table, but that has nothing t do with his place in the body. The two things are perfectly distinct.

Ephesians 4:4 to the day in which the apostle penned the words, when Christians were manifestly one, and when there was no such thing thought of as being a member of this church or a member of that church, because all believers were members of *the* one Church.*

In reply, we must protest against the very idea of limiting the Word of God. What possible right have we to single out one clause from Ephesians 4:4-6, and say it only applied to the days of the apostles? If one clause is to be so limited, why not all? Are there not still "one Spirit, one Lord, one faith, one baptism, one God and Father of all"? Will any question this? Surely not. Well, then, it follows that there is as surely one body as there is one Spirit, one Lord, one God. All are intimately bound up together, and you cannot touch one without touching all. We have no more right to deny the existence of the one body than we have to deny the existence of God, inasmuch as the selfsame passage that declares to us the one declares to us the other also.

But some will doubtless inquire, Where is this one body to be seen? Is it not an absurdity to speak of such a thing, in the face of the almost numberless denominations of christendom? Our answer is this: We are not going to surrender the truth of God because man has so signally failed to carry it out. Did not Israel utterly fail to maintain, confess, and carry out the truth of the unity of the Godhead? and was that glorious truth, in the smallest degree, touched by their failure? Was it not as true that there was one God, though there were as many idolatrous altars as streets in Jerusalem, and every housetop sent up a cloud of incense to the queen of heaven, as when Moses sounded forth, in the ears of the whole congregation, those sublime words, "Hear, O Israel, the Lord our God is one Lord"? Blessed be God, His truth does not depend upon the faithless, foolish ways of men. It stands in its own divine integrity; it shines in its own heavenly, undimmed lustre, spite of the grossest human failure. Were it not so, what should we do? whither should we turn? or what would become of us? In fact, it comes to this: if we were only to believe the measure of truth which we see practically carried out in the ways of men, we might give up in despair, and be of all men most miserable.

But how is the truth of the one body to be practically carried out? By refusing to own any other principle of Christian fellowship—any other ground of meeting. All true believers should meet on the simple ground of membership of the body of Christ, and on no other. They should assemble, on the first day of the week, around the Lord's table, and break bread, as members of the one body, as we read in 1 Corinthians 10, "For we, being many, are one loaf, one body; for we are all partakers of that one loaf." This is as true and as practical to-day as it was when the apostle addressed the assembly at Corinth. True, there were divisions at Corinth as there are divisions in christendom; but that did not in any wise touch the truth of God. The apostle rebuked the divisions—pronounced them carnal. He had no sympathy with the poor, low idea which one sometimes hears advocated, that divisions

*The unity of the Church may be compared to a chain thrown across a river; we see it at each side, but it dips in the middle. But though it dips, it is not broken; though we do not *see* the union in the middle, we *believe* it is there all the same. The Church was seen in its unity on the day of Pentecost, and it will be seen in its unity in the glory; and although we do not see it now, we nevertheless believe it most surely.

And be it remembered that the unity of the body is a great practical, formative truth; and one very weighty practical deduction from it is that the state and walk of each member affect the whole body. "If one member suffer all the members suffer with it." A member of what? Some local assembly? Nay; but a member of the body. We must not make the body of Christ a matter of geography.

But, we may be asked, are we affected by what we do not see or know? Assuredly. Are we to limit the grand truth of the unity of the body, with all its practical consequences, to the measure of our personal knowledge and experience? Far be the thought. It is the presence of the Holy Ghost that unites the members of the body to the Head and to one another; and hence it is that the walk and ways of each affect all. Even in Israel's case, where it was not a corporate but a national unity, when Achan sinned, it was said, "Israel hath sinned"; and the whole congregation suffered a humiliating defeat on account of a sin of which they were ignorant.

It is perfectly marvelous how little the Lord's people seem to understand the glorious truth of the unity of the body, and the practical consequences flowing from it.

are good things, as superinducing emulation. He believed they were very bad things—the fruit of the flesh, the work of Satan.

Neither, we feel persuaded, would the apostle have accepted the popular illustration that divisions in the Church are like so many regiments, with different facings, all fighting under the same commander-in-chief. It would not hold good for a moment; indeed, it has no application whatever, but rather gives a flat contradiction to that distinct and emphatic statement, "There is one body."

This is a most glorious truth. Let us ponder it deeply. Let us look at christendom in the light of it. Let us judge our own position and ways by it. Are we acting on it? Do we give expression to it, at the Lord's table, every Lord's day? Be assured it is our sacred duty and high privilege so to do. Say not there are difficulties of all sorts, many stumbling-blocks in the way, much to dishearten us in the conduct of those who profess to meet on this very ground of which we speak.

All this is, alas! but too true. We must be quite prepared for it. The devil will leave no stone unturned to cast dust in our eyes, so that we may not see God's blessed way for His people. But we must not give heed to his suggestions or be snared by his devices. There always have been, and there always will be difficulties in the way of carrying out the precious truth of God; and perhaps one of the greatest difficulties is found in the inconsistent conduct of those who profess to act upon it.

But then we must ever distinguish between the truth and those who profess it—between the ground and the conduct of those who occupy it. Of course, they ought to harmonize, but they do not; and hence we are imperatively called to judge the conduct by the ground, not the ground by the conduct. If we saw a man farming on a principle which we knew to be thoroughly sound, but he was a bad farmer, what should we do? Of course, we should reject his mode of working, but hold the principle all the same.

Not otherwise is it in reference to the truth now before us. There were heresies at Corinth, schisms, errors, evils of all sorts. What then? Was the truth of God to be surrendered as a myth, as something wholly impracticable? was it all to be given up? Were the Corinthians to meet on some other principle? were they to organize themselves on some new ground? were they to gather around some fresh centre? No, thank God! His truth was not to be surrendered for a moment, although Corinth was split up into ten thousand sects, and its horizon darkened by ten thousand heresies. The body of Christ is one; and the apostle simply displays in their view the banner with this blessed inscription: "Ye are the body of Christ, and members in particular."

Now, these words were addressed, not merely "unto the church at Corinth," but also, "to all that in every place call upon the name of Jesus Christ our Lord, both theirs and ours." Hence, the truth of the one body is abiding and universal. Every true Christian is bound to recognize it and to act on it, and every assembly of Christians, wherever convened, should be the local expression of this grand and all-important truth.

Some might perhaps feel disposed to ask how it could be said to any one assembly, "Ye are the body of Christ." Were there not saints at Ephesus, Colosse, and Philippi? No doubt; and had the apostle been addressing them on the same subject, he could have said to them likewise, "Ye are the body of Christ," inasmuch as they were the local expression of the body; and not only so, but, in addressing them, he had before his mind all saints, to the end of the Church's earthly career.

But we must bear in mind that the apostle could not possibly address such words to any human organization, ancient or modern. No; nor if all such organizations, call them what you please, were amalgamated into one, could he speak of it as "the body of Christ." That body, let it be distinctly understood, consists of all true believers on the face of the earth. That they are not gathered on that only divine ground, is their serious loss and their Lord's dishonor. The precious truth holds good all the same—"There is one body," and this is the divine standard by which to measure every ecclesiastical association and every religious system under the sun.

We deem it needful to go somewhat fully into the divine side of the question of the church, in order to guard the truth of God from the results of misapprehension, and also that the reader may clearly understand that in speaking of the utter failure and ruin of the church, we are looking at the human side of the subject. To this latter we must return for a moment.

It is impossible to read the New Testament with a calm and unprejudiced mind and not see that the church as a responsible witness for Christ on the earth has most signally and shamefully failed. To quote all the passages in proof of this statement would literally fill a small volume; but let us glance at the second and third chapters of the book of Revelation, where the church is seen under judgment. We have, in these solemn chapters, what we may call a divine church-history. Seven assemblies are taken up, as illustrative of the various phases of the church's history, from the day in which it was set up, in responsibility, on the earth, until it shall be spued out of the Lord's mouth, as something utterly intolerable. If we do not see that these two chapters are prophetic, as well as historic, we shall deprive ourselves of a vast field of most valuable instruction. For ourselves, we can only assure the reader that no human language could adequately set forth what we have gathered from Revelation 2 and 3, in their prophetic aspect.

However, we are only referring to them now as the last of a series of Scripture proofs of our present thesis. Take the address to Ephesus, the self-same church to which the apostle Paul wrote his marvelous Epistle, opening up so blessedly the heavenly side of things, God's eternal purpose respecting the Church—the position and portion of the Church, as accepted in Christ and blessed with all spiritual blessings in the heavenlies in Him. No failure here; no thought of such a thing; no possibility of it. All is in God's hands here. The counsel is His; the work His. It is His grace, His glory, His mighty power, His good pleasure; and all founded upon the blood of Christ. There is no question of responsibility here. The Church was "dead in trespasses and sins"; but Christ died for her; He placed Himself judicially where she was morally; and God, in His sovereign grace, entered the scene and raised up Christ from the dead, and the Church in Him. Glorious fact! Here all is sure and settled. It is the Church in the heavenlies *in* Christ, not the church on earth *for* Christ; it is *the body "accepted,"* not *the candlestick judged.* If we do not see both sides of this great question, we have much to learn.

But there is the earthly side as well as the heavenly—the human as well as the divine—the candlestick as well as the body. Hence it is that in the judicial address in Revelation 2 we read such solemn words as these: *"I have against thee,* that thou hast left thy first love."

How very distinct! Nothing like this in Ephesians; nothing against the body, nothing against the bride; but there is something against the candlestick. The light had even already become dim. Hardly had it been lighted ere the snuffers were needed.

Thus, at the very outset, symptoms of decline showed themselves, unmistakably, to the penetrating eye of Him who walked amongst the seven golden candlesticks; and when we reach the close, and contemplate the last phase of the church's condition —the last stage of its earthly history, as illustrated by the assembly at Laodicea—there is not a single redeeming feature. The case is almost hopeless. The Lord is outside the door. "Behold, I stand at the door, and knock." It is not here as at Ephesus, "I have somewhat against thee." The whole condition is bad. The whole professing body is about to be given up. "I will spue thee out of My mouth." He still lingers, blessed be His name, for He is ever slow to leave the place of mercy, or enter the place of judgment. It reminds us of the departure of the glory, in the opening of Ezekiel. It moved with a slow and measured pace, loth to leave the house, the people, and the land. "Then the glory of the Lord went up from the cherub, and stood over the threshold of the house; and the house was filled with the cloud, and the court was full of the brightness of the Lord's glory." "Then the glory of the Lord departed from off the threshold of the house, and stood over the cherubim." And finally, "the glory of the Lord went up from the midst of the city, and stood upon the mountain which is on the east side of the city" (Ezek. 10:4,18; 11:23).

This is deeply affecting. How striking the contrast between this slow departure of the glory and its speedy entrance, in the day of Solomon's dedication of the house in 2 Chronicles 7:1. Jehovah was quick to enter His abode in the midst of His people; slow to leave it. He was, to speak after the manner of men, forced away by the sins and hopeless impenitence of His infatuated people.

So also with the Church. We see in the second of Acts His rapid entrance into His spiritual house. He came like a rushing mighty wind to fill the house with His glory. But in the third of Revelation, see His attitude: He is outside. Yes; but He is knocking. He lingers, not indeed with any hope of corporate restoration, but if haply *"any man* would hear His voice and open the door." The fact of His being outside shows what the church is. The fact of His knocking shows what He is.

Christian reader, see that you thoroughly understand this whole subject: it is of the very last importance that you should. We are surrounded on all sides with false notions as to the present condition and future destiny of the professing church. We must fling these all behind our backs, with holy decision, and listen, with circumcised ear and reverent mind, to the teaching of holy Scripture. That teaching is as clear as noonday. The professing church is a hopeless ruin, and judgment is at the door. Read the Epistle of Jude; read 2 Peter 2 and 3; read 2 Timothy. Just lay aside this volume and look closely into those solemn Scriptures, and we feel persuaded you will rise from the study with the deep and thorough conviction that there is nothing whatever before christendom but the unmitigated wrath of Almighty God. Its doom is set forth in that solemn sentence in Romans 11, "Thou also shalt be cut off."

Yes; such is the language of Scripture. "Cut off"—"spued out." The professing church has utterly failed as Christ's witness on the earth. As with Israel, so with the church, the very truth which she was responsible to maintain and confess, she had faithlessly surrendered. Hardly had the canon of New Testament Scripture closed, hardly had the first set of laborers left the field, ere gross darkness set in, and settled down upon the whole professing body. Turn where you will, range through the ponderous tomes of "the fathers," as they are called, and you will not find a trace of those grand characteristic truths of our glorious Christianity. All, all was shamefully abandoned. As Israel in Canaan abandoned Jehovah for Baal and Ashtaroth, so the church abandoned the pure and precious truth of God for puerile fables and deadly errors. The rapid departure is perfectly astounding; but it was just as the apostle Paul forewarned the elders of Ephesus. "Take heed therefore unto yourselves, and to all the flock, over the which the Holy Ghost hath made you overseers, to feed the Church of God, which He hath purchased with His own blood. For I know this, that after my departing shall grievous wolves enter in among you, not sparing the flock. Also from among your own selves shall men arise, speaking perverse things, to draw away disciples after them" (Acts 20).

How truly deplorable! The holy apostles of our Lord and Saviour Jesus Christ almost immediately succeeded by "grievous wolves" and teachers of perverse things; the whole church plunged into thick darkness; the lamp of divine revelation almost hidden from view; ecclesiastical corruption in every form; priestly domination with all its terrible accompaniments. In short, the history of the church—the history of christendom—is the most appalling record ever penned.

True it is, thanks be to God, He left not Himself without a witness. Here and there, from time to time, just as in Israel of old, He raised up one and another to speak for Him. Even amid the deepest gloom of the middle ages, an occasional star appears upon the horizon. The Waldenses and others were enabled, by the grace of God, to hold fast His Word and to confess the name of Jesus in the face of Rome's dark and terrible tyranny, and diabolical cruelty.

Then came that gracious season, in the sixteenth century, when God raised up Luther and his beloved and honored fellow-laborers to preach the great truth of justification by faith, and to give the precious volume of God to the people, in their own tongue wherein they were born. It is not within the compass of human language to set forth the blessing of that memorable time. Thousands heard the glad tidings of salvation—heard, believed, and were saved. Thousands, who had long groaned beneath the intolerable weight of Romish superstition, hailed, with profound thankfulness, the heavenly message. Thousands flocked, with intense delight, to draw water from those wells of inspiration which had been stopped for ages by papal ignorance and intolerance. The blessed lamp of divine revelation, so long hidden by the enemy's hand, was permitted to cast its rays athwart the gloom, and thousands rejoiced in its heavenly light.

But while we heartily bless God for all the glorious results of what is commonly called the reformation, in the sixteenth century, we should make a very grave mistake indeed were we to imagine that it was any thing approaching to a restoration of the Church to its original condition. Far, very far, from it. Luther and his companions, if we are to judge from their writings—precious writings, many of them—never grasped the divine idea of the Church as the body of Christ. They did not understand the unity of the body; the presence of the Holy Ghost in the assembly, as well as His indwelling in the individual believer; they never reached the grand truth of ministry in the Church, "its nature, source, power, and responsibility"; they never got beyond the idea of human authority as the basis of ministry; they were silent as to the specific hope of the Church, namely, the coming of Christ for His people—the bright and morning Star; they failed to seize the proper scope of prophecy, and proved themselves incompetent rightly to divide the Word of truth.

Let us not be misunderstood. We love the memory of the reformers. Their names are familiar household words amongst us. They were dear, devoted, earnest, blessed servants of Christ. Would that we had their like amongst us in this day of revived popery and rampant infidelity. We would yield to none in our love and esteem for Luther, Melanchthon, Farel, Latimer, and Knox. They were truly bright and shining lights in their day; and thousands, yea, millions, will thank God throughout eternity that they ever lived and preached and wrote. Not only so, but, looked at in their private life and public ministry, they put to shame many of those who have been favored with a range of truth for which we look in vain in the voluminous writings of the reformers.

But, admitting all this, as we most freely and gratefully do, we are nevertheless convinced that those beloved and honored servants of Christ failed to seize, and therefore failed to preach and teach, many of the special and characteristic truths of Christianity; at least, we have failed to find these truths in their writings. They preached the precious truth of justification by faith; they gave the holy Scriptures to the people; they trampled under foot much of the rubbish of Romish superstition.

All this they did, by the grace of God, and for all this we bow our heads in deep thankfulness and praise to the Father of mercies. But Protestantism is not Christianity; nor are the so-called churches of the reformation, whether national or dissenting, the Church of God. Far from it. We look back over the course of eighteen centuries, and spite of the occasional revivals, spite of the brilliant lights which at various times have shone upon the Church's horizon—lights which appeared all the brighter in contrast with the deep gloom that surrounded them—spite of the many gracious visitations of God's Spirit, both in Europe and America, during the past and present century—spite of all these things, for which we most heartily bless God, we return with decision to the statement already advanced, that the professing church is a hopeless wreck; that christendom is rapidly hastening down the inclined plane, to the blackness of darkness forever; that those highly favored lands, where much evangelical truth has been preached, where Bibles have been circulated in millions, and gospel tracts in billions, shall yet be covered with thick darkness—given over to strong delusion to believe a lie.

And then?—ah, what then? *A converted world?* Nay, but *a judged church.* The true saints of God, scattered throughout christendom—all the true members of the body of Christ, will be caught up to meet their coming Lord—the dead saints raised, the living changed, in a moment, and all taken up together to be forever with the Lord. Then the mystery will rise to a head in the person of the man of sin—the lawless one, the Antichrist. The Lord Jesus shall come, and all His saints with Him, to execute judgment on the beast, or revived Roman empire, and the false prophet, or Antichrist—the former in the west, the latter in the east.

This will be a summary act of direct warrior judgment, without any judicial process whatever, inasmuch as both the beast and false prophet shall be found in open rebellion and blasphemous opposition to God and the Lamb. Then comes the sessional judgment of the living nations, as recorded in Matthew 25:31-46.

Thus, all evil having been put down, Christ shall reign, in righteousness and peace, for a thousand years. A bright and blessed time! the true Sabbath for Israel and the whole earth—a period marked by the grand facts, Satan bound and Christ reigning. Glorious facts! The very reference to them causes the heart to overflow in praise and thanksgiving. What will the reality be?

But Satan shall be loosed from his thousand years' captivity, and allowed to make one more effort against God and His Christ. "And when the thousand years are expired, Satan shall be loosed out of his prison, and shall go out to deceive the nations which are in the four quarters of the earth, Gog and Magog, to gather them together to battle, the number of whom is as the sand of the sea.* And they went up on the breadth of the earth, and compassed the camp of the saints about, and the beloved city; and fire came down from God out of heaven, and devoured them. And the devil that deceived them was cast into the lake of fire and brimstone, where the beast and the false prophet are, and shall be tormented day and night forever and ever" (Rev. 20:7-10).

This will be Satan's last effort, issuing in his eternal perdition. Then we have the judgment of the dead, "small and great"—the sessional judgment of all those who shall have died in their sins, from the days of Cain down to the last apostate from millennial glory. Tremendous scene! No heart can conceive, no tongue—no pen set forth, its awful solemnity.

Finally, we have unfolded to the vision of our souls the everlasting state—the new heaven and the new earth wherein righteousness shall dwell, throughout the golden ages of eternity.

Such is the order of events as set forth, with all possible clearness, on the page of inspiration. We have given a brief summary of them in connection with the line of truth on which we have been dwelling—a line, as we are fully aware, by no means popular; but we dare not withhold it on that account. Our business is to declare the whole counsel of God, not to seek popularity. We do not expect the truth of God to be popular in christendom; so far from this, we have been seeking to prove that just as Israel abandoned the truth which they were responsible to maintain, so the professing church has let slip all those great truths which characterize the Christianity of the New Testament. And we may assure the reader that our one object in pursuing this line of argument is to arouse the hearts of all true Christians to a sense of the value of those truths, and of their responsibility, not only to receive them, but to seek a fuller realization and a bolder confession of them. We long to see a band of men raised up, in these closing hours of the Church's earthly history, who shall go forth, in true spiritual power, and proclaim, with unction and energy, the long-forgotten

*The reader must distinguish between the Gog and Magog of Revelation 20, and those of Ezekiel 38 and 39. The former are post-millennial; the latter, pre-millennial.

truths of the gospel of God. May God, in His great mercy to His people, raise up such and send them forth. May the Lord Jesus knock louder and louder at the door, so that many may hear and open to Him, according to the desire of His loving heart, and taste the blessedness of deep personal communion with Himself, while waiting for His coming.

Blessed be God, there is no limit whatever to the blessing of the individual soul who hears Christ's voice and opens the door; and what is true of one is true of hundreds or thousands. Only let us be real and simple and true, feeling and owning our utter feebleness and nothingness, laying aside all assumption and empty pretension, not seeking to be anything or to set up any thing, but holding fast Christ's word and not denying His name, finding our happy place at His feet, our satisfying portion in Himself, and our real delight in serving Him in any little way. Thus we shall get on harmoniously, lovingly, and happily together, finding our common centre in Christ, and our common object in seeking to further His cause and promote His glory. O that it were thus with all the Lord's beloved people in this our day! we should then have a very different tale to tell, and present a very different aspect to the world around. May the Lord revive His work.

It may perhaps seem to the reader that we have wandered a long way from the sixth chapter of Deuteronomy; but we must remind him, once for all, that it is not merely what each chapter *contains* that demands our attention, but also what it *suggests.* And further, we may add that, in sitting down to write, from time to time, it is our one desire to be led by God's Spirit into the very line of truth which may be suited to the need of all our readers. If only the beloved flock of Christ be fed, instructed, and comforted, we care not whether it be by well-connected notes or broken fragments.

We shall now proceed with our chapter.

Moses having laid down the grand foundation-truth contained in the fourth verse—"Hear, O Israel; the Lord our God is one Lord," proceeds to press upon the congregation their sacred duty in respect to this blessed One. It was not merely that there was *a* God, but He was *their* God. He had deigned to link Himself with them, in covenant-relationship. He had redeemed them, borne them on eagles' wings, and brought them unto Himself, in order that they might be to Him a people, and that He might be their God.

Blessed fact! Blessed relationship! But Israel had to be reminded of the conduct suited to such a relationship—conduct which could only flow from a loving heart. "Thou shalt love the Lord *thy* God with *all* thy *heart,* and with *all* thy soul, and with *all* thy might." Here lies the secret of all true practical religion. Without this, all is valueless to God. "My son, give me thine heart." Where the heart is given, all will be right. The heart may be compared to the regulator of a watch, which acts on the hair-spring, and the hair-spring acts on the main-spring, and the main-spring acts on the hands, as they move around the dial. If your watch goes wrong, it will not do merely to alter the hands, you must touch the regulator. God looks for real heart-work, blessed be His name! His word to us is, "My little children, let us not love in word, neither in tongue; but in deed and in truth."

How we ought to bless Him for such touching words! they do so reveal His own loving heart to us. Assuredly, He loved us in deed and in truth, and He cannot be satisfied with any thing else, whether in our ways with Him or our ways one with another: all must flow straight from the heart.

"And these words which I command thee this day, shall be *in thine heart*"—at the very source of all the issues of life. This is peculiarly precious. Whatever is in the heart comes out through the lips and in the life. How important, then, to have the heart full of the Word of God—so full, that we shall have no room for the vanities and follies of this present evil world. Thus shall our conversation be always with grace, seasoned with salt. "Out of the abundance of the heart the mouth speaketh." Hence we can judge of what is in the heart by what cometh out of the mouth. The tongue is the organ of the heart—the organ of the man. "A good man out of the good treasure of the heart bringeth forth good things; and an evil man out of the evil treasure bringeth forth evil things." When the heart is really governed by the Word of God, the whole character reveals the blessed result. It must be so, inasmuch as the heart is the main-spring of our entire moral condition; it lies at the centre of all those moral influences which govern our personal history and shape our practical career.

In every part of the divine volume, we see how much importance God attaches to the attitude and state of the heart, with respect to Him or to His Word, which is one and the same thing. When the heart is true to Him, all is sure to come right; but on the other hand, we shall find that where the heart grows cold and careless as to God and His truth, there will, sooner or later, be open departure from the path of truth and righteousness. There is, therefore, much force and value in the exhortation addressed by Barnabas to the converts at Antioch—"He exhorted them all, that with *purpose of heart* they would cleave unto the Lord."

How needful then, now, always! This "purpose of heart" is most precious to God. It is what we may venture to call the grand moral regulator. It imparts a lovely earnestness to the Christian character which is greatly to be coveted by all of us. It is a divine antidote against coldness, deadness, and formality, all of which are so hateful to God. The outward life may be very correct, and the creed may be very orthodox; but if the earnest purpose of heart be lacking—the affectionate cleaving of the whole moral being to God and His Christ, all is utterly worthless.

It is through the heart that the Holy Ghost instructs us. Hence, the apostle prayed for the saints at Ephesus, that "the eyes of their *heart* [καρδιας, not διανοιας] might be enlightened": and again, "That Christ may dwell in your *heart* by faith."

Thus we see how all Scripture is in perfect harmony with exhortation recorded in our chapter, "And these words which I command thee this day, shall be in thine heart." How near this would have kept them to their covenant-God! How safe, too, from all evil, and specially from the abominable evil of idolatry—their national sin, their terrible besetment! If Jehovah's precious words had only found their right place in the heart, there would have been little fear of Baal, Chemosh, or Ashtaroth. In a word, all the idols of the heathen would have found their right place, and been estimated at their true value, if only the word of Jehovah had been allowed to dwell in Israel's heart.

And be it specially noted here how beautifully characteristic all this is of the book of Deuteronomy. It is not so much a question of keeping up a certain order of religious observances, the offering of sacrifices, or attention to rites and ceremonies. All these things, no doubt, had their place, but they are by no means the prominent or paramount thing in Deuteronomy. *No; the Word* is the all-important matter here. It is *Jehovah's word* in *Israel's heart.*

The reader must seize this fact if he really desires to possess the key to the lovely book of Deuteronomy. It is not a book of ceremonial; it is a book of moral and affectionate obedience. It teaches, in almost every section, that invaluable lesson, that the heart that loves, prizes, and honors the Word of God is ready for every act of obedience, whether it be the offering of a sacrifice or the observance of a day. It might so happen that an Israelite would find himself in a place and under circumstances in which a rigid adherence to rites and ceremonies would be impossible; but he never could be in a place or in circumstances in which he could not love, reverence, and obey the Word of God. Let him go where he would—let him be carried, as a captive exile, to the ends of the earth, nothing could rob him of the high privilege of uttering and acting on those blessed words, "Thy Word have I hid in mine heart, that I might not sin against Thee."

Precious words! They contain, in their brief compass, the great principle of the book of Deuteronomy, and, we may add, the great principle of the divine life, at all times and in all places. It can never lose its moral force and value: it always holds good. It was true in the days of the patriarchs, true for Israel in the land, true for Israel scattered to the ends of the earth, true for the Church as a whole, true for each individual believer amid the Church's hopeless ruins. In a word, obedience is always the creature's holy duty and exalted privilege—simple, unhesitating, unqualified obedience to the Word of the Lord. This is an unspeakable mercy for which we may well praise our God, day and night. He has given us His Word, blessed be His name, and He exhorts us to let that Word dwell in us richly—dwell in our hearts, and assert its holy sway over our entire course and character.

"And these words, which I command thee this day, shall be in thine heart: and thou shalt teach them diligently unto thy children, and shalt talk of them when thou sittest in thine house, and when thou walkest by the way, and when thou liest down, and when thou risest up. And thou shalt bind them for a sign upon thine hand, and they shall be as frontlets between thine eyes. And thou shalt write them upon the posts of thy house, and on thy gates."

All this is perfectly beautiful. The Word of God hidden in the heart; flowing out in loving instruction to the children, and in holy conversation in the bosom of the family; shining out in all the activities of daily life, so that all who came inside the gates or entered the house might see that the Word of God was the standard for each, for all, and in every thing.

Thus it was to be with Israel of old, and surely thus it ought to be with Christians now. But is it so? Are our children thus taught? Is it our constant aim to present the Word of God, in all its heavenly attractiveness, to their young hearts? Do they see it shining out in our daily life? do they see its influence upon our habits, our temper, our family intercourse, our business transactions? This is what we understand by binding the Word as a sign upon the hands, having it as a frontlet between the eyes, writing it upon the door-posts and upon the gates.

Is it thus with us? It is of little use attempting to teach our children the Word of God if our lives are not governed by that Word. We do not believe in making the blessed Word of God a mere school-book for our children; to do so is to turn a delightful privilege into a wearisome drudgery. Our children should see that we live in the very atmosphere of Scripture; that it forms the material of our conversation when we sit in the bosom of the family, in our moments of relaxation.

Alas! how little is this the case! Have we not to be deeply humbled in the presence of God when we reflect upon the general character and tone of our conversation at table, and in the family circle? How little there is of Deuteronomy 6:7! How much of "foolish talking and jesting, which are not convenient"! How much evil-speaking of our brethren, our neighbors, our fellow-laborers! How much idle gossip! How much worthless small talk!

And from what does all this proceed? Simply from the state of the heart. The Word of God, the commandments and sayings of our Lord and Saviour Jesus Christ, are not dwelling in our hearts; and hence they are not welling up and flowing out in living streams of grace and edification.

Will any one say that Christians do not need to consider these things? If so, let him ponder the following wholesome words: "Let no corrupt communication proceed out of your mouth, but that which is good to the use of edifying, that it may minister grace unto the hearers." And again, "Be filled with the Spirit; speaking to yourselves in psalms and hymns and spiritual songs, singing and making melody in your heart to the Lord; giving thanks always for all things unto God and the Father in the name of our Lord Jesus Christ" (Eph. 4:29; 5:18-20).

These words were addressed to the saints at Ephesus; and, most assuredly, we should apply our hearts diligently to them. We are little aware, perhaps, of how deeply and constantly we fail in maintaining the habit of spiritual conversation. It is specially in the bosom of the family, and in our ordinary intercourse, that this failure is most manifest. Hence our need of those words of exhortation which we have just penned. It is evident the Holy Spirit foresaw the need, and graciously anticipated it. Hear what He says "to the saints and faithful brethren in Christ at Colosse": "Let the peace of Christ rule in your hearts, to the which also ye are called in one body; and be ye thankful. Let the word of Christ dwell in you richly in all wisdom; teaching and admonishing one another in psalms and hymns and spiritual songs, singing with grace in your hearts to the Lord" (Col. 3).

Lovely picture of ordinary Christian life! It is but a fuller and higher development of what we have in our chapter, where the Israelite is seen in the midst of his family, with the Word of God flowing forth from his heart in loving instruction to his children—seen in his daily life, in all his intercourse at home and abroad, under the hallowed influence of Jehovah's words.

Beloved Christian reader, do we not long to see more of all this in our midst? Is it not, at times, very sorrowful and very humbling to mark the style of conversation that obtains in the midst of our family circles? Should we not sometimes blush if we could see our conversation reproduced in print? What is the remedy? Here it is—a heart filled with the peace of Christ, the word of Christ, Christ Himself: nothing else will do. We must begin with the heart, and where that is thoroughly preoccupied with heavenly things, we shall make very short work with all attempts at evil-speaking, foolish talking, and jesting.

"And it shall be, when the Lord thy God shall have brought thee unto the land which He sware unto thy fathers, to Abraham, to Isaac, and to Jacob, to give thee great and goodly cities which thou buildedst not, and houses full of all good things which thou filledst not, and wells digged which thou diggedst not, and vineyards and olive-trees which thou plantedst not; when thou shalt have eaten and be full; then beware lest thou forget the Lord, which brought thee forth out of the land of Egypt, from the house of bondage" (ver. 10-12).

Amid all the blessings, the mercies, and the privileges of the land of Canaan, they were to remember that gracious and faithful One who had redeemed them out of the land of bondage. They were to remember, too, that all these things were His free gift. The land, with all that it contained, was bestowed upon them in virtue of His promises to Abraham, Isaac, and Jacob. Cities built and houses furnished, flowing wells, fruitful vineyards and oliveyards, all ready to their hand, the free gift of sovereign grace and covenant mercy. All they had to do was to take possession, in simple faith, and to keep ever in the remembrance of the thoughts of their hearts the bounteous Giver of it all. They were to think of Him, and find in His redeeming love the true motive-spring of a life of loving obedience. Wherever they turned their eyes, they beheld the tokens of His great goodness—the rich fruit of His marvelous love. Every city, every house, every well, every vine, olive and fig-tree, spoke to their hearts of Jehovah's abounding grace, and furnished a substantial proof of His infallible faithfulness to His promise.

"Thou shalt fear the Lord thy God, and serve Him, and shalt swear by His name. Ye shall not go after other gods, of the gods of the people which are round about you; (for the Lord thy God is a jealous God among you) lest the anger of the Lord thy God be kindled against thee, and destroy thee from off the face of the earth."

There are two great motives set before the congregation, in our chapter, namely, "love," in verse 5, and "fear," in verse 13. These are found all through Scripture; and their importance in guiding the life and forming the character cannot possibly be too highly estimated. "The fear of the Lord is the beginning of wisdom." We are exhorted to be "in the fear of the Lord all the day." It is a grand moral safeguard against all evil. "Unto man He said, 'Behold, the fear of the Lord, that is wisdom; and to depart from evil is understanding.' "

The blessed Book abounds in passages setting forth, in every possible form, the immense importance of the fear of God. "How," says Joseph, "can I do this great wickedness, and sin against God?" The man who walks habitually in the fear of God is preserved from every form of moral pravity. The abiding realization of the divine presence must prove an effectual shelter from every temptation. How often do we find the presence of some very holy and spiritual person a wholesome check upon levity and folly; and if such be the moral influence of a fellow-mortal, how much more powerful would be the realized presence of God!

Let us give our serious attention to this weighty matter. Let us seek to live in the consciousness that we are in the immediate presence of God. Thus shall we be preserved from a thousand forms of evil, to which we are exposed from day to day, and to which, alas! we are predisposed. The remembrance that the eye of God rests upon us would exert a far more powerful influence upon our life and conversation than the presence of all the saints upon earth and all the angels in heaven. We could not speak falsely, we could not utter with our lips what we do not feel in the heart, we could not talk folly, we could not speak evil of our brother or our neighbor, we could not speak unkindly of any one, if only we felt ourselves in the presence of God. In a word, the holy fear of the Lord, of which Scripture speaks so much, would act as a most blessed restraint upon evil thoughts, evil words, evil ways, evil in every shape and form.

Moreover, it would tend to make us very real and genuine in all our sayings and doings. There is a sad amount of sham and nonsense about us. We frequently say a great deal more than we feel. We are not honest; we do not speak, every man, truth with our neighbor; we give expressions to sentiments which are not the genuine utterance of the heart; we act the hypocrite one with another.

All these things afford melancholy proof of how little we live, move, and have our being in the presence of God. If we could only bear in mind that God hears us and sees us—hears our every word and sees our every thought, our every way, how differently we should carry ourselves! What holy watchfulness we should maintain over our thoughts, our tempers, and our tongues! What purity of heart and mind! What truth and uprightness in all our intercourse with our fellows! What reality and simplicity in our deportment! What happy freedom from all affectation, assumption, and pretension! What deliverance from every form of self-occupation! O, to live ever in the deep sense of the divine presence! to walk in the fear of the Lord all the day long!

And then to prove the "vast constraining influence" of His love! To be led out in all the holy activities which that love would ever suggest! To find our delight in doing good! To taste the spiritual luxury of making hearts glad! To be continually meditating plans of usefulness! To live close by the fountain of divine love, so that we must be streams of refreshing in the midst of this thirsty scene—rays of light amid the moral gloom around us! "The love of Christ," says the blessed apostle, "constraineth us; because we thus judge, that if one died for all, then were all dead; and that He died for all, that they which live should not henceforth live unto themselves, but unto Him which died for them, and rose again."

How morally lovely is all this! Would that it were more fully realized and faithfully exhibited amongst us! May the fear and love of God be continually in our hearts, in all their blessed power and formative influence, that thus our daily life may shine to His praise and the real profit, comfort, and blessing of all who come in contact with us, whether in private or in public. God, in His infinite mercy, grant it, for Christ's sake!

The sixteenth verse of our chapter demands our special attention: "Ye shall not tempt the Lord your God, as ye tempted Him in Massah." These words were quoted by our blessed Lord when tempted by Satan to cast Himself from the pinnacle of the temple. "Then the devil taketh Him up into the holy city, and setteth Him on a pinnacle of the temple, and saith unto Him, 'If Thou be the Son of God, cast Thyself down; for it is written, He shall give His angels charge concerning Thee; and in their hands they shall bear Thee up, lest at any time Thou dash Thy foot against a stone.' "

This is a very remarkable passage. It proves how Satan can quote Scripture when it suits his purpose. But he omits a most important clause—"To keep Thee in all Thy ways." Now, it formed no part of the ways of Christ to cast Himself from the pinnacle of the temple. It was not the path of duty. He had no command from God to do any such thing, and hence He refused to do it. He had no need to tempt God—to put Him to the test. He had, as a man, the most perfect confidence in God—the fullest assurance of His protection.

Moreover, He was not going to abandon the path of duty in order to prove God's care of Him; and herein He teaches us a most valuable lesson. We can always count on God's protecting hand when we are treading the path of duty; but if we are walking in a self-chosen path—if we are seeking our own pleasure or our own interest, our own ends or objects, then to talk of counting on God would be simply wicked presumption.

No doubt, our God is very merciful, very gracious, and His tender mercy is over us, even when we wander off the path of duty; but this is another thing altogether, and it leaves wholly untouched the statement that we can only count on divine protection when our feet are in the pathway of duty. If a Christian goes out boating for his amusement, or if he goes clambering over the Alps merely for sightseeing, has he any right to believe that God will take care of him? Let conscience give the answer. If God calls us to cross a stormy lake to preach the gospel, if He summons us to cross the Alps on some special service for Him, then, assuredly, we can commit ourselves to His mighty hand to protect us from all evil. The grand point for all of us is, to be found in the holy path of duty. It may be narrow, rough, and lonely; but it is a path overshadowed by the wings of the Almighty and illumined by the light of His approving countenance.

Ere turning from the subject suggested by verse 16, we would briefly notice the very interesting and instructive fact that our Lord, in His reply to Satan, takes no notice whatever of his misquotation of Psalm 91:11. Let us carefully note this fact and seek to bear it in mind. In place of saying to the enemy, You have left out a most important clause of the passage which you undertake to quote, He simply quotes another passage, as authority for His own conduct. Thus He vanquished the tempter, and thus He left us a blessed example.

It is worthy of our special notice that the Lord Jesus Christ did not overcome Satan in virtue of His divine power. Had He done so, it could not be an example for us. But when we see Him as a man using the Word as His only weapon, and thus gaining a glorious victory, our hearts are encouraged and comforted; and not only so, but we learn a most precious lesson as to how we, in our sphere and measure, are to stand in the conflict. The Man Christ Jesus overcame by simple dependence upon God and obedience to His Word.

Blessed fact! A fact full of comfort and consolation for us. Satan could do nothing with one who would only act by divine authority, and by the power of the Spirit. Jesus never did His own will, though, as we know (blessed be His holy name!), His will was absolutely perfect. He came down from heaven, as He Himself tells us, in John 6, not to do His own will, but the will of the Father that sent Him. He was a perfect servant, from first to last. His rule of action was the Word of God; His power of action, the Holy Ghost; His only motive for action, the will of God; hence the prince of this world had nothing in Him. Satan could not, by all his subtle wiles, draw Him out of the path of obedience, or out of the place of dependence.

Let us consider these things; let us deeply ponder them; let us remember that our blessed Lord and Master left us an example that we should follow His steps. Oh, may we follow them diligently during the little while that yet remains. May we, by the gracious ministry of the Holy Ghost, enter more fully into the great fact that we are called to walk even as Jesus walked. He is our great Exemplar in all things. Let us study Him more profoundly, so that we may reproduce Him more faithfully.

We shall now close this lengthened section by quoting the last paragraph of the chapter on which we have been dwelling; it is a passage of singular fullness, depth, and power, and strikingly characteristic of the entire book of Deuteronomy.

"Ye shall *diligently* keep the commandments of the Lord your God, and His testimonies, and His statutes, which He hath commanded thee. And thou shalt do that which is right and good in the sight of the Lord; that it may be well with thee, and that thou mayest go in and possess the good land which the Lord sware unto thy fathers; to cast out all thine enemies from before thee, as the Lord hath spoken. And when thy son asketh thee in time to come, saying, What mean the testimonies and the statutes and the judgments which the Lord our God hath commanded you? Then thou shalt say unto thy son, We were Pharaoh's bondmen in Egypt; and the Lord brought us out of Egypt with a mighty hand; and the Lord showed signs and wonders, great and sore, upon Egypt, upon Pharaoh, and upon all his household, before our eyes; and He brought us out from thence, that He might bring us in, to give us the land which He sware unto our fathers. And the Lord commanded us to do all these statutes, to fear the Lord our God, for our good always, that He might preserve us alive, as it is at this day. And it shall be our righteousness, if we observe to do all these commandments before the Lord our God, as He hath commanded us."

How prominently is the Word of God kept before the soul, in every page and every paragraph of this book! It is the one great subject on the heart and in all the discourses of the revered lawgiver. It is his one aim to exalt the Word of God, in all its aspects, whether in the form of testimonies, commandments, statutes, or judgments; and to set forth the moral importance, yea, the urgent necessity of whole-hearted, earnest, diligent obedience, on the part of the people. "Ye shall *diligently* keep the commandments of the Lord your God." And again, "Thou shalt do that which is *right* and *good* in the sight of the Lord."

All this is morally lovely. We have here unfolded before our eyes those eternal principles which no change of dispensation, no change of scene, place, or circumstances can ever touch. "That which is right and good" must ever be of universal and abiding application. It reminds us of the words of the apostle John to his beloved friend Gaius, "Beloved, follow not that which is evil, but that which is good." The assembly might be in a very low condition; there might be very much to try the heart and depress the spirit of Gaius; Diotrephes might be carrying himself most unbecomingly and unwarrantably toward the beloved and venerable apostle and others; all this might be true, and much more—yea, the whole professing body might go wrong. What then? What remained for Gaius to do? Simply to follow that which was right and good; to open his heart and his hand and his house to every one who brought *the truth;* to seek to help on the cause of Christ in every right way.

This was the business of Gaius in his day, and this is the business of every true lover of Christ at all times, in all places, and under all circumstances. We may not have many to join us; we may perhaps find ourselves, at times, almost alone; but we are still to follow what is good, cost what it may. We are to *depart* from iniquity—*purge* ourselves from dishonorable vessels—*flee* youthful lusts—*turn away* from powerless professors. And what then? "Follow righteousness, faith, love, peace." How? In isolation? Nay. I may find myself alone in any given place for a time, but there can be no such thing as isolation so long as the body of Christ is on earth, and that will be till He comes for us. Hence we never expect to see the day in which we cannot find a few that call on the Lord out of a pure heart; whoever they are and wherever they are, it is our bounden duty to find them, and, having found them, to walk with them in holy fellowship "until the end."

---

## CHAPTER 7

"WHEN the Lord thy God shall bring thee into the land whither thou goest to possess it, and hath cast out many nations before thee . . . seven nations greater and mightier than thou, and when the Lord thy God shall deliver them before thee, thou shalt smite them, and utterly destroy them; thou shalt make no covenant with them, nor show mercy unto them."

In reading the record of God's dealings with the nations, in connection with His people Israel, we are reminded of the opening words of Psalm 101—"I will sing of mercy and of judgment." We see the display of mercy to His people, in pursuance of His covenant with Abraham, Isaac, and Jacob; and we see also the execution of judgment upon the nations, in consequence of their evil ways. In the former, we see divine sovereignty; in the latter, divine justice; in both, divine glory shines out. All the ways of God, whether in mercy or in judgment, speak His praise, and shall call forth the homage of His people forever. "Great and marvelous are Thy works, Lord God Almighty; just and true are Thy ways, Thou King of nations.* Who shall not fear Thee, O Lord, and glorify Thy name? for Thou art holy; for all nations shall come and worship before Thee; for Thy judgments are made manifest" (Rev. 15:3-4).

This is the true spirit in which to contemplate the ways of God in government. Some persons, allowing themselves to be influenced by a morbid feeling and false sentimentality, rather than by an enlightened judgment, find difficulty in the directions given to Israel in reference to the Canaanites, in the opening of our chapter. It seems to them inconsistent with a benevolent Being to command His people to smite their fellow-creatures, and to show them no mercy. They cannot understand how a merciful God could commission His people to slay women and children with the edge of the sword.

It is very plain that such persons could not adopt the language of Revelation 15:3-4. They are not prepared to say, "Just and true are Thy ways, Thou King of nations." They cannot justify God in *all* His ways; nay, they are actually sitting in judgment upon Him. They presume to measure the actings of divine government by the standard of their own shallow thoughts—to scan the infinite by the finite; in short, they measure God by themselves.

This is a fatal mistake. We are not competent to form a judgment upon the ways of God, and hence it is the very height of presumption for poor, ignorant, shortsighted mortals to attempt to do so. We read in the seventh chapter of Luke that "Wisdom is justified of *all* her children." Let us remember this, and hush all our sinful reasonings. "Let God be true, but every man a liar; as it is written, 'That Thou mightest be justified in Thy sayings, and mightest overcome when Thou art judged.' "

Is the reader at all troubled with difficulties on this subject? If so, we should much like to quote a very fine passage which may help him. "O give thanks unto the Lord; for He is good; for His mercy endureth forever. . . . To Him *that smote Egypt in their first-born;* for His mercy endureth forever; and brought out Israel from among them; for His mercy endureth forever; with a strong hand, and with a stretched-out arm; for His mercy endureth forever. To Him which divided the Red Sea into parts; for His mercy endureth forever; and made Israel to pass through the midst of it; for His mercy endureth forever; but *overthrew Pharaoh and his host* in the Red Sea; for His mercy endureth forever. To Him which *smote great kings;* for His mercy endureth forever; and *slew famous kings;* for His mercy endureth forever; Sihon, king of the Amorites; for His mercy endureth forever; and Og, the king of Bashan; for His mercy endureth forever; and gave their land for a heritage; for His mercy endureth forever; even a heritage unto Israel His servant; for His mercy endureth forever" (Ps. 136).

Here we see that the smiting of Egypt's first-born and the deliverance of Israel, the passage through the Red Sea and the utter destruction of Pharaoh's host, the slaughter of the Canaanites and giving their lands to Israel—all alike illustrated the everlasting mercy of Jehovah.† Thus it was, thus it is, and thus it shall be. All must redound to the

---

*"Nations" is read by most editors: Christ is not called the "King of saints."

†"Very many Christians find considerable difficulty in intrepreting and applying the language of a large number of the

glory of God. Let us remember this, and fling to the winds all our silly reasonings and ignorant arguments. It is our privilege to justify God in all His ways, to bow our heads in holy worship, in view of His unsearchable judgments, and rest in the calm assurance that all God's ways are right. We do not understand them all; this would be impossible. The finite cannot grasp the infinite. This is where so many go wrong. They reason upon the actings of God's government, not considering that those actings lie as far beyond the range of human reason as the Creator is beyond the creature. What human mind can unravel the profound mysteries of divine providence? Can we account for the fact of a city full of human beings—men, women, and children, in one hour, plunged beneath a tide of burning lava? Utterly impossible; and yet this is but one fact of thousands that stand recorded on the page of human history, all lying far beyond the grasp of the most gigantic intellect. Go through the lanes, alleys, wynds, closes, and court-yards of our cities and towns; see the thousands of human beings that throng these places, living in squalid misery, poverty, wretchedness, and moral degradation. Can we account for all this? can we tell why God permits it? are we called upon to do so? Is it not perfectly plain to the reader that it is not part of our business to discuss such questions? and if we, in our ignorance and stupid folly, set about reasoning and speculating upon the inscrutable mysteries of the divine government, what can we expect but utter bewilderment, if not positive infidelity?

The foregoing line of thought will enable the reader to understand the opening lines of our chapter. The Canaanites were to receive no mercy at the hands of Israel. Their iniquities had reached the culminating point, and nothing remained but the stern execution of divine judgment. "Thou shalt smite them, and utterly destroy them; thou shalt make no covenant with them, nor show mercy unto them; neither shalt thou make marriages with them; thy daughter thou shalt not give unto his son, nor his daughter shalt thou take unto thy son. For they will turn away thy son from following Me, that they may serve other gods; so will the anger of the Lord be kindled against you, and destroy thee suddenly. But thus shall ye deal with them; ye shall destroy their altars, and break down their images, and cut down their groves, and burn their graven images with fire."

Such were the instructions given by Jehovah to His people. They were clear and explicit. No mercy for the Canaanites, no covenant with them, no union, no fellowship of any kind, unsparing judgment, intense separation.

We know, alas! how soon and how completely Israel failed to carry out these instructions. Hardly had they planted their foot upon the land of Canaan ere they made a covenant with the Gibeonites. Even Joshua himself fell into the snare. The tattered garments and mouldy bread of those wily people beguiled the princes of the congregation, and caused them to act in direct opposition to the plain commandment of God. Had they been governed by the authority of the

---

psalms which call for judgment upon the wicked. Such language would, of course, be quite unsuitable for Christians now, inasmuch as we are taught to love our enemies, to do good to them that hate us, and to pray for them that despitefully use us and persecute us.

But we must remember that what would be wholly out of place for the Church of God, a heavenly people, under grace, was, and will yet be, perfectly consistent for Israel, an earthly people, under government. No intelligent Christian could think for a moment of calling down vengeance upon his enemies or upon the wicked. It would be grossly inconsistent. We are called to be the living exponents of the grace of God to the world—to walk in the footsteps of the meek and lowly Jesus—to suffer for righteousness—not to resist evil. God is now dealing in long-suffering mercy with the world. "He maketh His sun to rise on the evil and on the good, and sendeth rain on the just and on the unjust." This is to be our model. We are, in this, to be "perfect, even as our Father which is in heaven is perfect." For a Christian to deal with the world on the principle of righteous judgment, would be to misrepresent his heavenly Father and falsify his profession.

But by and by, when the Church shall have left the scene, God will deal with the world in righteousness; He will judge the nations for their treatment of His people Israel.

We do not attempt to quote passages, but merely call the reader's attention to the principle, in order to enable him to understand the just application of the prophetic psalms.

Word, they would have been preserved from the grave error of making a league with people who ought to have been utterly destroyed; but they judged by the sight of their eyes, and had to reap the consequences.*

Implicit obedience is the grand moral safeguard against the wiles of the enemy. No doubt the story of the Gibeonites was very plausible, and their whole appearance gave a show of truth to their statements; but none of these things should have had the slightest moral weight with Joshua and the princes; nor would they, if they had but remembered the Word of the Lord. But they failed in this. They reasoned on what they saw, instead of obeying what they had heard. Reason is no guide for the people of God; we must be, absolutely and completely, guided and governed by the Word of God.

This is a privilege of the very highest order, and it lies within the reach of the simplest and most unlettered child of God. The Father's word, the Father's voice, the Father's eye, can guide the youngest, feeblest child in His family. All we need is the lowly and obedient heart. It does not demand great intellectual power or cleverness; if it did, what would become of the vast majority of Christians? If it were only the educated, the deep-thinking, and the far-seeing that were capable of meeting the wiles of the adversary, then verily most of us might give up in despair.

But, thanks be to God, it is not so; indeed, on the contrary, we find, in looking through the history of the people of God in all ages, that human wisdom, human learning, human cleverness, if not kept in their right place, have proved a positive snare, and rendered their possessors only the more efficient tools in the enemy's hand. By whom have most, if not all, of the heresies been introduced which have disturbed the Church of God from age to age? Not by the simple and the unlearned, but by the educated and the intellectual. And in the passage to which we have just referred, in the book of Joshua, who was it that made a covenant with the Gibeonites? The common people? Nay; but the princes of the congregation. No doubt all were involved in the mischief, but it was the princes that led the way. The heads and leaders of the assembly fell into the snare of the devil through neglect of the plain Word of God.

"Thou shalt make no covenant with them." Could aught be plainer than this? Could tattered garments, old shoes, and mouldy bread alter the meaning of the divine command, or do away with the urgent necessity for strict obedience on the part of the congregation? Assuredly not. Nothing can ever afford a warrant for lowering, the breadth of a hair, the standard of obedience to the Word of God. If there are difficulties in the way, if perplexing circumstances come before us, if things crop up for which we are not prepared, and as to which we are unable to form a judgment, what are we to do? Reason? Jump to conclusions? Act on our own or on any human judgment? Most certainly not. What then? Wait on God; wait patiently, humbly, believingly, and He will assuredly counsel and guide. "The meek will He guide in judgment; and the meek will He teach His way." Had Joshua and the princes acted thus, they never would have made a league with the Gibeonites; and if the reader acts thus, he will be delivered from every evil work and preserved unto the everlasting kingdom of our Lord and Saviour Jesus Christ.

In verse six of our chapter, Moses sets before the people the moral ground of the line of action which they were to adopt in reference to the Canaanites—the rigid separation and the unsparing judgment. "*For* thou art a *holy people unto the Lord thy God;* the Lord thy God hath chosen thee to be a

*It is at once instructive and admonitory to see that the garments, the mouldy bread, and the plausible words of the Gibeonites did what the walls of Jericho could not do. Satan's *wiles* are more to be dreaded than his *power.* "Put on the whole armor of God, that ye may be able to stand against the *wiles* of the devil." The more deeply we ponder the various parts of the whole armor of God, the more clearly we shall see that they are ranged under these two heads—obedience and dependence. The soul that is really governed by the authority of the Word, and wholly dependent upon the power of the Spirit, is fully equipped for the conflict. It was thus the Man Christ Jesus vanquished the enemy. The devil could do nothing with a man who was perfectly obedient and perfectly dependent. May we study, in this, as in all beside, our great Exemplar.

special people unto Himself, above all people that are upon the face of the earth."

The principle here laid down is of the very weightiest character. Why were the people to maintain the most marked separation from the Canaanites? Why were they to refuse, with firm decision, to make any covenant, or form any matrimonial alliance with them? Why were they to demolish their altars, break their images, and cut down their groves? Simply because they were a holy people. And who had constituted them a holy people? Jehovah. He had chosen them and set His love upon them; He had redeemed them, and separated them to Himself; and hence it was His province and prerogative to prescribe what they were to be, and how they were to act. "Be ye holy, for I am holy."

It was not by any means on the principle of "Stand by thyself, I am holier than thou." This is manifest from what follows. "The Lord did not set His love upon you, nor choose you, because ye were more in number than any people; for ye were the fewest of all people; but because the Lord loved you, and because He would keep the oath which He had sworn unto your fathers, hath the Lord brought you out with a mighty hand, and redeemed you out of the house of bondmen, from the hand of Pharaoh king of Egypt" (Ver. 7-8).

Seasonable words these for Israel!—most healthful and needful! They were to remember that they owed all their dignity, all their privileges, all their blessings, not to aught in themselves—their own goodness or their own greatness, but simply to the fact of Jehovah's having identified Himself with them, in His infinite goodness and sovereign grace, and in virtue of His covenant with their fathers—"a covenant ordered in all things and sure." This, while it furnished a divine antidote against self-complacency and self-confidence, formed the solid basis of their happiness and their moral security. All rested upon the eternal stability of the grace of God, and therefore human boasting was excluded. "My soul shall make her boast in the Lord; the humble shall hear thereof and be glad."

It is the settled purpose of God that "no flesh shall glory in His presence." All human pretension must be set aside. He will hide pride from man. Israel had to be taught to remember their origin and their true condition—"bondmen in Egypt"—"fewest of all people." No room for pride or boasting. They were in no wise better than the nations around them; and therefore, if called to account for their high elevation and moral greatness, they had simply to trace it all up to the free love of God and His faithfulness to His oath. "Not unto us, O Lord, not unto us, but unto Thy name give glory, for Thy mercy and for Thy truth's sake" (Ps. 115:1).

"Know therefore that the Lord thy God, He is God, the faithful God, which keepeth covenant and mercy with them that love Him and keep His commandments, to a thousand generations; and repayeth them that hate Him to their face, to destroy them: He will not be slack to him that hateth Him, He will repay him to his face" (ver. 9-10).

We have two weighty facts set before us here: one, full of rich consolation and comfort to every true lover of God; the other, fraught with deep solemnity to every hater of God. All who really love God and keep His commandments may count on His infallible faithfulness and tender mercy at all times and under all circumstances. "*All things* work *together* for good to them that love God, to them who are the called according to His purpose." If, through infinite grace, we have the love of God in our hearts, and His fear before our eyes, we may move on with good courage and joyful confidence, assured that all shall be well—must be well. "Beloved, if our heart condemn us not, then have we confidence toward God. And whatsoever we ask, we receive of Him, because we keep His commandments, and do those things that are pleasing in His sight."

This is a grand, eternal truth—a truth for Israel, a truth for the Church. Dispensations make no difference as to this. Whether we study the seventh of Deuteronomy or the third chapter of 1 John, we learn the same great practical truth, that God delights in those who fear Him and love Him and keep His commandments.

Is there aught of the legal element in this? Not a tinge. Love and legality having nothing in common; they are as far removed as the poles. "This is the love of God, that we keep His commandments; and His commandments are not grievous." The spirit and genius, the ground and character of our obedience all go to prove it the very reverse of legality. It is our deep and settled conviction that those persons who are ever ready to cry out, "Legal! Legal!" whenever obedience is pressed upon them, are sadly and grossly mistaken. If indeed it were taught that we must earn by our obedience the high position and relationship of children of God, then verily the solemn charge of legality might justly be urged; but to bestow such an epithet on Christian obedience, is, we repeat, a serious moral mistake. Obedience could never precede sonship, but sonship should ever be followed by obedience.

And while we are on this subject, we must call the attention of the reader to a passage or two of New Testament Scripture as to which there is a want of clearness in many minds. In the fifth chapter of Matthew, we read, "Ye have heard that it hath been said, 'Thou shalt love thy neighbor and hate thine enemy;' but *I* say unto you, Love your enemies, bless them that curse you, do good to them that hate you, and pray for them which despitefully use you and persecute you; that ye may be the sons [*υιοι*] of your Father which is in heaven; for He maketh His sun to rise on the evil and on the good, and sendeth rain on the just and on the unjust. . . . Be ye therefore perfect, even as your Father which is in heaven is perfect" (ver. 43-48).

This passage might, in the judgment of some, seem to teach that the relationship of children can be attained by a certain line of action; but it is not so. It is a question of moral conformity or suitability to the character and ways of our Father. We sometimes hear, in every-day life, the saying, "You would not be your father's son if you were to act in such a way." It is as though our Lord had said, If you want to be the sons of your heavenly Father, you must act in grace to all; for that is what He is doing.

Again, in 2 Corinthians 6 we read, "Wherefore come out from among them, and be ye separate, saith the Lord, and touch not the unclean; and I will receive you, and will be a Father unto you, and ye shall be My sons and daughters, saith the Lord Almighty." Here, it is not a question of the secret relationship of children, formed by a divine operation, but the public acknowledgment of the position of *sons* [*υιους*] as the result of our separation from evil.*

It will be well for the reader to seize this important distinction; it is of great practical value. We do not become children by separation from the world, "for ye are all the children of God by faith in Christ Jesus." "As many as received Him, to them gave He power [or authority, *εξουσιαν*] to become children [*τεκνα*] of God, to them that believe on His name; which were born, not of blood, nor of the will of the flesh, nor of the will of man, but of God" (Gal. 3:26; John 1:12-13). "Of His own will begat He us by the word of truth" (James 1:18). We become children by new birth, which, thanks be to God, is a divine operation from first to last. What had we to do with our natural birth? Nothing. And what have we to do with our spiritual birth? Clearly nothing.

But then we must remember that God can only identify Himself with, and publicly acknowledge those who, through grace, seek to walk in a way worthy of Him—a way befitting the sons and daughters of the Lord Almighty. If our ways are unlike Him, if we are mixed up with all sorts of wrong things, if we are unequally yoked together with unbelievers, how can we expect God to own us as His sons? We read, in Hebrews 11, of those who "confessed that they were strangers and pilgrims on the earth," and who "declared plainly that they sought a country;" and of them we are told that "*God was not ashamed* to be called their God." He

*Speaking in a general way, the word *τεκνον*, child, is a term of endearment; *υιος*, son, of moral dignity. *παις* is either a child or a servant; *νηπιος*, a babe.

could publicly identify Himself with them, and acknowledge them; He could own them as His.

Let us seriously apply our hearts to the consideration of this great practical question. Let us look, seriously and honestly, to our ways. Let us, in truthfulness and uprightness of heart, inquire whether we are "unequally yoked together with unbelievers," on any ground, or for any object whatsoever. If so, let us give earnest heed to the words, "Come out from among them, and be ye separate, and touch not the unclean thing." It may be that the carrying out of this holy commandment will expose us to the charge of bigotry, narrowness, and intolerance; it may wear the aspect of pharisaic pride and self-complacency. We may be told, we are not to judge, or set ourselves up to be holier or better than other people.

To all this line of argument we have the one simple, conclusive answer, namely, God's plain command. He tells us to be separate, to come out, to touch not the unclean; and all this in order to His receiving us, and acknowledging us as His sons and daughters. This ought to be quite sufficient for us. Let people think or say what they will of us; let them call us what they please; God will settle the matter with them, sooner or later; our duty is to separate ourselves from unbelievers, if we would be received and owned of God. If believers are mixed up with unbelievers, how are they to be known or distinguished as the sons and daughters of the Lord Almighty?

But we may perhaps be asked, How are we to know who are unbelievers? All profess to be Christians—all take the ground of belonging to Christ: we are not surrounded by ignorant heathen, or unbelieving Jews; how then are we to judge? It was plain enough in the early days of Christianity, when the apostle wrote his Epistle to the assembly at Corinth—then the line of demarkation was as clear as a sunbeam; there were the three distinct classes—"the Jew, the Gentile, and the Church of God;" but now all is changed: we live in a Christian land, under a Christian government, we are surrounded on all hands by Christians, and therefore 2 Corinthians 6 cannot apply to us; it was all very well when the Church was in its infancy, having just emerged from Judaism on the one hand and heathenism on the other, but to think of applying such a principle at this advanced stage of the Church's history, is wholly out of the question.

To all who take this ground, we would put a very plain question: Is it true that the Church has reached a stage of her history in which the New Testament is no longer her guide and authority? Have we got beyond the range of holy Scripture? If so, what are we to do? whither are we to turn for guidance? If we admit for a moment that 2 Corinthians 6 does not apply to Christians now, what warrant have we for appropriating to ourselves any portion of the New Testament?

The fact is, Scripture is designed for the Church of God as a whole, and for each member of that Church in particular; and hence, as long as the Church is on earth, so long will the Scripture apply. To question this is to offer a flat contradiction to the words of the inspired apostle when he tells us that the holy Scriptures are able to make us *"wise unto salvation"*—that is, "wise" right onward to the day of glory, for such is the blessed force of the word "salvation" in 2 Timothy 3:15.

We want no new light—no fresh revelation; we have *"all truth"* within the covers of our precious Bible. Thank God for it! We do not want science or philosophy to make us wise. All true science and all sound philosophy will leave untouched the testimony of holy Scripture; they cannot add to it, but they will not contradict it. When infidels talk to us about "progress," "development," "the light of science," we fall back, in holy confidence and tranquility, upon those precious words, "all truth," "wise unto salvation." It is blessedly impossible to get beyond these. What can be added to "all truth"? What more do we or can we want than to be made wise right onward to the coming of our Lord Jesus Christ?

And further, let us remember that there is no change whatever in the relative position of the Church and the world. It is as true to-day as it was eighteen hundred and fifty years ago, when our Lord uttered the words, that His people are not of the world, even as He Himself is not of the world (John 17). The world is the world still. It may, in some places, have changed its dress, but not its true character, spirit, and principles. Hence, therefore, it is as wrong to-day for Christians to be "unequally yoked together with unbelievers" as it was when Paul penned his Epistle to the Church at Corinth. We cannot get over this; we cannot set aside our responsibility in this matter. It will not, by any means, meet the case to say, "We must not judge." We are bound to judge. If we refuse to judge, we refuse to obey, and what is this but positive rebellion? God says, "Come out from among them and be ye separate"; if we reply, We cannot judge, where are we? The fact is, we are absolutely commanded to judge. "Do not ye judge them that are *within?* but them that are *without* God judgeth" (1 Cor. 5:12-13).

But we shall not pursue this line of argument any further. We trust the reader is one who fully owns the direct application to himself of the passage which we have just quoted. It is as plain as it is pointed; it calls upon all God's people to come out and be separate, and touch not the unclean thing. This is what God requires of His people, in order to His owning them as His; and surely it ought to be the deep and earnest desire of our hearts to respond to His gracious will in this matter, utterly regardless of the world's thoughts respecting us. Some of us are very much afraid of being thought narrow and bigoted; but, oh, how little it imports to a truly devoted heart what men think of us! Human thoughts perish in an hour. When we are manifested before the judgment-seat of Christ, when we stand in the full blaze of the glory, what will it matter to us whether men considered us narrow or broad, bigoted or liberal? and what should it matter to us now? Not the weight of a feather. Our one grand object should be, so to act—so to carry ourselves as to be "acceptable" to Him who has made us "accepted." May it be so with the writer and the reader, and with every member of the body of Christ.

Let us now turn, for a moment, to the weighty and very solemn truth presented to us in verse 10 of our chapter. "He will not be slack to him that hateth Him, He will repay him to his face." If the lovers of God are comforted in verse 9, and most blessedly encouraged to keep His commandments, the haters of God are called to hearken to a warning note in verse 10.

There is a time coming when God will deal personally, face to face, with His enemies. How awful the thought that any one should be *a hater of God*—a hater of that One who is said to be and who is "Light" and "Love"; the very fountain of goodness, the Author and Giver of every good and perfect gift, the Father of lights; the One whose liberal hand supplies the need of every living thing, who hears the cry of the young ravens, and quenches the thirst of the wild ass; the infinitely good, the only wise, the perfectly holy God, the Lord of all power and might, the creator of the ends of the earth, and the One who has power to destroy both soul and body in hell!

Only think of any one being a hater of such a One as God; and we know that all who are not lovers must be haters. People may not see this; very few would be disposed to own themselves to be absolute haters of God, but there is no neutral ground in this great question; we must either be for or against; and in point of fact, people are not slow in showing their colors. It often happens that the heart's deep-seated enmity to God comes out in hatred to His people, to His Word, His worship, His service. How frequently do we hear such expressions as, "I hate religious people," "I hate all cant," "I hate preachers"! The truth is, it is God Himself that is hated. "The carnal mind is enmity against God; it is not subject to the law of God, neither indeed can be;" and this enmity comes out in reference to every one and every thing connected with God. There lies deep down in every unconverted heart the most positive enmity to God. Every man in his natural state hates God.

Now, God declares, in Deuteronomy 7:10, that "He will not be slack to him that hateth Him; He will repay him to his face."

This is a most solemn truth, and one which ought to be more pressed upon the attention of all whom it may concern. Men do not like to hear it; many affect and profess not to believe it. They would fain persuade themselves and persuade others also that God is too good, too kind, too merciful, too benevolent, to deal in stern judgment with His creatures. They forget that God's ways in government are as perfect as His ways in grace. They imagine that the government of God will pass over or deal lightly with evil and evil-doers.

This is a most miserable and fatal mistake, and men will find it to be so to their heavy and eternal cost. True it is, blessed be God, He can, in His rich sovereign grace and mercy, forgive us our sins, blot out our transgressions, cancel our guilt, justify us perfectly, and fill our hearts with the spirit of adoption; but this is another thing altogether. This is grace reigning through righteousness unto eternal life by Jesus Christ our Lord. It is God, in His wondrous love, providing righteousness for the poor, guilty, hell-deserving sinner who knows and feels and owns that he has no righteousness of his own, and never could have it. God, in the marvelous love of His heart, has provided a means whereby He can be just and the justifier of every poor broken-hearted, bankrupt sinner that simply believes in Jesus.

But how, we may ask, was all this done? Was it by passing over sin, as though it were nothing? was it by relaxing the claims of the divine government, lowering the standard of divine holiness, or touching, in the most remote way, the dignity, stringency, and majesty of law? No; thanks and praise to redeeming love, it was the very reverse. Never was there or could there be a more terrible expression of God's eternal hatred of sin, or of His unflinching purpose to condemn it utterly and punish it eternally; never was there or could there be a more glorious vindication of the divine government, a more perfect maintenance of the standard of divine holiness, truth, and righteousness; never was the law more gloriously vindicated or more thoroughly established than by that most glorious scheme of redemption, planned, executed, and revealed by the Eternal Three in One—planned by the Father, executed by the Son, and revealed by the Holy Ghost.

If we would have a just sense of the awful reality of the government of God, His wrath against sin, and the true character of His holiness, we must gaze at the cross; we must hearken to that bitter cry that issued from the heart of the Son of God and broke through the dark shadows of Calvary, "My God, My God, why hast Thou forsaken Me?" Never had such a question been asked before, never has such a question been asked since, and never shall—never can such a question be asked again. Whether we consider the One who asked it, the One of whom it was asked, or the answer, we must see that the question stands absolutely alone in the annals of eternity. The cross is the measure of God's hatred of sin, as it is the measure of His love to the sinner. It is the imperishable foundation of the throne of grace, the divinely righteous ground on which God can pardon our sins and constitute us perfectly righteous in a risen and glorified Christ.

But then if men despise all this, and persist in their hatred of God, and yet talk of His being too good and too kind to punish evil-doers, how will it be with them? "He that obeyeth not [απειθων] the Son shall not see life, but the wrath of God abideth upon him" (John 3:36).* Can it be possible —can we believe for a moment that a just God should exercise judgment upon His only

*John 3:36 is a passage of immense weight and importance. It not only sets forth the great truth that all who believe in the Son of God are the privileged possessors of eternal life, but it also cuts up by the roots two leading heresies of the day, namely, universalism and annihilationism. The universalist professes to believe that, ultimately, all shall be restored and blessed. Not so, says our passage; for those who obey not the Son "shall not see life."

The annihilationist professes to believe that all who are out of Christ shall perish like the beasts. Not so, for "the wrath of God *abideth*" upon the disobedient. Abiding wrath and annihilation are wholly incompatible. It is utterly impossible to reconcile them.

It is interesting and instructive to notice the difference between the words ο πιστευων—"he that believeth"—and ο απειθων—"he that obeyeth not." They give us the two sides of the subject of faith.

begotten Son, His well-beloved, His eternal delight, because He was bearing our sins in His own body on the tree, and yet allow impenitent sinners to escape? Had Jesus, the spotless, holy, perfect Man—the only perfect Man that ever trod this earth—had He to suffer for sins, the just for the unjust, and shall evil-doers, unbelievers, and haters of God be saved and blessed and taken to heaven? and all this, forsooth, because God is too kind and too good to punish sinners in hell forever! Did it cost God the giving up, the forsaking, and the bruising of His beloved Son in order to save His people *from their sins,* and shall ungodly sinners, despisers, and rebels be saved *in their sins?* Did the Lord Jesus Christ die for nothing? did Jehovah put Him to grief and hide His face from Him when there was no necessity? Why the awful horrors of Calvary? why the three hours' darkness? why that bitter cry, "My God, My God, why hast Thou forsaken Me?"—why all this if sinners can get to heaven without it? Why all this inconceivable sorrow and suffering for our blessed Lord if God is too kind and too gracious and too tender to send sinners to hell?

What egregious folly! What will not men believe, provided it be not the truth of God? The poor dark human mind will affect to believe the most monstrous absurdity in order to get a plea for rejecting the plain teaching of holy Scripture. The very thing which men would never think of attributing to a good human government they do not hesitate to attribute to the government of the only wise, the only true, the only just God. What should we think of a government that could not or would not punish evildoers? Would we like to live under it? What should we think of the government of England if, because her majesty is so kind, so gracious, so tender-hearted, she could not allow criminals to be punished as the law directs? Who would care to live in England?

Do you not see how that one verse which is now before us demolishes completely all the theories and arguments which men, in their folly and ignorance, have advanced on the subject of the divine government? "The Lord thy God, He is God, the faithful God, which . . . repayeth them that hate Him to their face, to destroy them; He will not be slack to him that hateth Him, He will repay him to his face."

Oh that men would hearken to the Word of God! that they would be warned by its clear, emphatic, and solemn statements as to coming wrath, judgment, and eternal punishment! that, instead of seeking to persuade themselves and others that there is no hell, no deathless worm and unquenchable fire, no eternal torment, they would listen to the warning voice, and, ere it be too late, flee for refuge to the hope set before them in the gospel! Truly this would be their wisdom. God declares that He will repay those that hate Him. How awful the thought of this repayment! Who can meet it? The government of God is perfect, and because it is so, it is utterly impossible that it can allow evil to pass unjudged. Nothing can be plainer than this. All Scripture, from Genesis to Revelation, sets it forth in terms so clear and forcible as to render it the very height of folly for men to argue against it. How much better and wiser and safer to flee from the wrath to come than to deny that it is coming, and that when it does come, it will be eternal in its duration. It is utterly vain for any one to attempt to reason in opposition to the truth of God. Every word of God shall stand forever. We see the actings of His government in reference to His people Israel, and in reference to Christians now. Did He pass over evil in His people of old? Nay; on the contrary, He visited them continually with His chastening rod, and this, too, just because they were His people, as He said to them by His prophet Amos—"Hear this word which the Lord hath spoken against you, O children of Israel, against the whole family which I brought up from the land of Egypt, saying, 'You only have I known of all the families of the earth; therefore I will punish you for all your iniquities' " (Amos 3:1-2).

We have the same weighty principle set forth in the first Epistle of Peter, in its application to Christians now. "For the time is come that *judgment must begin* at the house of God; and if it first begin at us, what shall the end be of them that obey not the gospel of God? And if the righteous scarcely be saved, where shall the ungodly and the sinner appear?" (chap. 4:17-18)

God chastens His own just because they are His own, and that they may not be condemned with the world (1 Cor. 11). The children of this world are allowed to go on their way; but their day is coming—a dark and heavy day—a day of judgment and unmitigated wrath. Men may question and argue and reason, but Scripture is distinct and emphatic. "God hath appointed a day in which He will judge the world in righteousness, by that Man whom He hath ordained." The great day of reckoning is at hand, when God will repay every man to his face.

It is truly edifying to mark the way in which Moses, that beloved and honored servant of God, led assuredly by the Spirit of God, pressed the grand and solemn realities of the divine government upon the conscience of the congregation. Hear how he pleads and exhorts: "Thou shalt *therefore* keep the commandments, and the statutes, and the judgments, which I command thee this day, *to do them.* Wherefore it shall come to pass, if ye *hearken* to these judgments, and *keep* and *do* them, that the Lord thy God shall keep unto thee the covenant and the mercy which He sware unto thy fathers. And He will *love* thee, and *bless* thee, and *multiply* thee; He will also bless the fruit of thy womb, and the fruit of thy land, thy corn, and thy wine, and thine oil, the increase of thy kine, and the flocks of thy sheep, in the land which He sware unto thy fathers to give thee. Thou shalt be blessed above all people; there shall not be male nor female barren among you or among your cattle. And the Lord will take away from thee all sickness, and will put none of the evil diseases of Egypt, which thou knowest, upon thee; but will lay them upon all them that hate thee. And thou shalt consume all the people which the Lord thy God shall deliver thee; thine eye shall have no pity upon them; neither shalt thou serve their gods; for that will be a snare unto thee" (ver. 11-16).

What a powerful appeal! how affecting! Mark the two groups of words. Israel was to "hearken," "keep," and "do." Jehovah was to "love," "bless," and "multiply." Alas! Israel failed—sadly, shamefully failed, under law and under government; and hence, instead of the love and the blessing and the multiplying, there has been judgment, curse, barrenness, dispersion, desolation.

But, blessed be the God of Abraham, Isaac, and Jacob, the God and Father of our Lord Jesus Christ, if Israel has failed under *law* and *government,* He has not failed in His rich and precious sovereign *grace* and *mercy.* He will keep the covenant and the mercy which He sware unto their fathers. Not one jot or tittle of His covenant-promise shall ever fail. He will make all good by and by. He will fulfill, to the very letter, all His gracious promises. Though He cannot do this on the ground of Israel's obedience, He can and will do it through the blood of the everlasting covenant, the precious blood of Jesus, His eternal Son—all homage to His peerless name!

The God of Israel cannot suffer one of His precious promises to fall to the ground. What would become of us if He could? What security, what rest, what peace could we have, if Jehovah's covenant with Abraham were to fail in any single point? True it is that Israel has forfeited all claim. If it be a question of fleshly descent, Ishmael and Esau have a prior claim: if it be a question of legal obedience, the golden calf and the broken tables tell their melancholy tale: if it be a question of government on the ground of the Moab covenant, they have not a single plea to urge.

But God will be God, spite of Israel's lamentable unfaithfulness. "The gifts and calling of God are without repentance," and hence "all Israel shall be saved." God will most assuredly make good His oath to Abraham, spite of all the wreck and ruin of Abraham's seed. We must steadfastly hold to this, in the face of every opposing thought, feeling, or opinion. Israel shall be restored and blessed and multiplied in their own beloved and holy land. They shall take down their harps from the willows and, beneath the peaceful shade of their own vines and fig-trees, chant the high praises of their loving Saviour and God, throughout that bright millennial Sabbath which lies before them. Such is the unvarying testimony of Scripture, from beginning to end, which must be maintained in its integrity, and made good in every particular, to the glory of God, and on the ground of His everlasting covenant.

But we must return to our chapter, the closing verses of which demand our special attention. It is very touching and beautiful to mark the way in which Moses seeks to encourage the heart of the people in reference to the dreaded nations of Canaan. He enters into and anticipates their very inmost thoughts and feelings.

"If thou shalt say *in thine heart,* These nations are more than I; how can I dispossess them? Thou shalt not be afraid of them; but shalt *well remember* what the Lord thy God did unto Pharaoh, and unto all Egypt; the great temptations which thine eyes saw, and the signs, and the wonders, and the mighty hand, and the stretched-out arm, whereby the Lord thy God brought thee out: *so* shall the Lord thy God do unto all the people of whom thou art afraid. Moreover, the Lord thy God will send the hornet among them, until they that are left, and hide themselves from thee, be destroyed. Thou shalt not be affrighted at them; for *the Lord thy God is among you, a mighty God and terrible.* And the Lord thy God will put out those nations before thee by little and little; thou mayest not consume them at once, lest the beasts of the field increase upon thee. But the Lord thy God shall deliver them unto thee, and shall destroy them with a mighty destruction, until they be destroyed. And He shall deliver their kings into thine hand, and thou shalt destroy their name from under heaven; there shall no man be able to stand before thee, until thou have destroyed them. The graven images of their gods shall ye burn with fire; thou shalt not desire the silver or gold that is on them, nor take it unto thee, lest thou be snared therein; for it is an abomination to the Lord thy God. Neither shalt thou bring *an abomination into thine house, lest thou be a cursed thing like it;* but thou shalt utterly detest it . . . shalt utterly abhor it, for it is a cursed thing" (ver. 17-26).

The grand remedy for all unbelieving fears is simply to fix the eye upon the living God; thus the heart is raised above the difficulties, whatever they may be. It is of no possible use to deny that there are difficulties and opposing influences of all sorts. This will not minister comfort and encouragement to the sinking heart. Some people affect a certain style of speaking of trials and difficulties which just goes to prove, not their practical knowledge of God, but their profound ignorance of the stern realities of life. They would fain persuade us that we ought not to feel the trials, sorrows, and difficulties of the way. They might as well tell us that we ought not to have a head on our shoulders or a heart in our bosom. Such persons know not how to comfort those that are cast down. They are mere visionary theorists, wholly unfit to deal with souls passing through conflict or grappling with the actual facts of our daily history.

How did Moses seek to encourage the hearts of his brethren? "Be not affrighted," he says; but why? Was it that there were no enemies, no difficulties, no dangers? No; but "the Lord thy God is among you, a mighty God and terrible." Here is the true comfort and encouragement. The enemies were there, but God is the sure resource. Thus it was that Jehoshaphat, in his time of trial and pressure, sought to encourage himself and his brethren. "O our God, wilt Thou not judge them? For we have no might against this great company that cometh against us, neither know we what to do; but *our eyes are upon Thee.*"

Here lies the precious secret. The eyes are upon God. His power is brought in, and this settles every thing. "If God be for us, who can be against us?" Moses meets, by his precious ministry, the rising fears in the heart of Israel—"These nations are more than I." Yes, but they are not more than the "mighty and terrible God." What nations could stand before Him? He had a solemn controversy with those nations because of their terrible sins; their iniquity was full; the reckoning-time had come, and the God of Israel was going to drive them out before His people.

Hence, therefore, Israel had no need to fear the *power* of the enemy. Jehovah would see to that. But there was something far more to be dreaded than the enemy's power, and that was, the insnaring influence of their idolatry. "The graven images of their gods shall ye burn with fire." What! the heart might say, are we to destroy the gold and silver that adorn these images? Might not that be turned to some good account? Is it not a pity to destroy what is so very valuable in itself? It is all right to burn the images, but why not spare the gold and silver?

Ah, it is just thus the poor heart is prone to reason; thus ofttimes we deceive ourselves when called to judge and abandon what is evil. We persuade ourselves of the rightness of making some reserve; we imagine we can pick and choose and make some distinction. We are prepared to give up some of the evil, but not all. We are ready to burn the wood of the idol, but spare the gold and silver.

Fatal delusion! "Thou shalt not desire the silver or gold that is on them, nor take it unto thee, *lest thou be snared therein;* for it is an abomination to the Lord thy God." All must be given up, all destroyed. To retain an atom of the accursed thing is to fall into the snare of the devil, and link ourselves with that which, however highly esteemed among men, is an abomination in the sight of God.

And let us mark and ponder the closing verses of our chapter. To bring an abomination into the house is to become like it! How very solemn! Do we fully understand it? The man who brought an abomination into his house became a cursed thing like it!

May the Lord keep our hearts separated from all evil, and true and loyal to Himself.

---

## *CHAPTER 8*

"ALL the commandments which I command thee this day shall ye observe to do, that ye may live, and multiply, and go in and possess the land which the Lord sware unto your fathers. And thou shalt remember *all the way* which the Lord thy God led thee these forty years in the wilderness, to humble thee, and to prove thee, to know what was in thine heart, whether thou wouldest keep His commandments or no" (ver. 1-2).

It is at once refreshing, edifying, and encouraging to look back over the whole course along which the faithful hand of our God has conducted us; to trace His wise and gracious dealings with us; to call to mind His many marvelous interpositions on our behalf; how He delivered us out of this strait and that difficulty; how, ofttimes, when we were at our wits' end, He appeared for our help, and opened the way before us, rebuking our fears and filling our hearts with songs of praise and thanksgiving.

We must not, by any means, confound this delightful exercise with the miserable habit of looking back at *our* ways, our attainments, our progress, our service, what we have been able to do, even though we are ready to admit, in a general way, that it was only by the grace of God that we were enabled to do any little work for Him. All this only ministers to self-complacency, which is destructive of all true spirituality of mind. Self-retrospection, if we may be allowed to use such a term, is quite as injurious in its moral effect as self-introspection. In short, self-occupation, in any of its multiplied phases, is most pernicious; it is, insofar as it is allowed to operate, the death-blow to fellowship. Any thing that tends to bring self before the mind must be judged and refused, with stern decision; it brings in barrenness, darkness, and feebleness. For a person to sit down to look back at his attainments or his doings, is about as wretched an occupation as any one could engage in. We may be sure it was not to any such thing as this that Moses exhorted the people when he charged them to "remember all the way by which the Lord their God had led them."

We may here recur, for a moment, to the memorable words of the apostle in Philippians 3—"Brethren, I count not myself to have apprehended; but this one thing I do, *forgetting those things which are behind,* and reaching forth unto those things which are before, I press toward the mark for the prize of the high calling of God in Christ Jesus."

Now, the question is, what were the "things" of which the blessed apostle speaks? Did he forget the precious dealings of God with his soul throughout the whole of his wilderness-journey? Impossible!—indeed we have the very fullest and clearest evidence to the contrary. Hear his touching words before Agrippa—"Having therefore obtained help of God, I continue unto this day, witnessing both to small and great." So also, in writing to his beloved son and fellow-laborer, Timothy, he reviews the past, and speaks of the persecutions and afflictions which he had endured; "but," he adds, "out of them all the Lord delivered me." And again, "At my first answer no man stood with me, but all forsook me; I pray God that it may not be laid to their charge. Notwithstanding, the Lord stood with me, and strengthened me; that by me the preaching might be fully known, and that all the Gentiles might hear; and I was delivered out of the mouth of the lion."

To what then does the apostle refer when he speaks of "forgetting those things which are behind?" We believe he refers to all those things which had no connection with Christ—things in which the heart might rest, and nature might glory—things which might act as weights and hindrances,—all these were to be forgotten in the ardent pursuit of those grand and glorious realities which lay before him. We do not believe that Paul, or any other child of God or servant of Christ, could ever desire to forget a single scene or circumstance in his whole earthly career in any way illustrative of the goodness, the loving-kindness, the tender mercy, the faithfulness of God. On the contrary, we believe it will ever be one of our very sweetest exercises to dwell upon the blessed memory of all our Father's ways with us while passing across the desert, home to our everlasting rest.

> There with what joy reviewing
> Past conflicts, dangers, fears,
> Thy hand our foes subduing,
> And drying all our tears.
> Our hearts with rapture burning,
> The path we shall retrace,
> Where now our souls are learning
> The riches of Thy grace.

But let us not be misunderstood. We do not, by any means, wish to give countenance to the habit of dwelling merely upon our own experience. This is often very poor work, and resolves itself into self-occupation. We have to guard against this as one of the many things which tend to lower our spiritual tone and draw our hearts away from Christ. But we need never be afraid of the result of dwelling upon the record of the Lord's dealings and ways with us. This is a blessed habit, tending ever to lift us out of ourselves, and fill us with praise and thanksgiving.

Why, we may ask, were Israel charged to "remember *all* the way" by which the Lord their God had led them? Assuredly, to draw out their hearts in praise for the past, and to strengthen their confidence in God for the future. Thus it must ever be.

> We'll praise Him for all that is past,
> And trust Him for all that's to come.

May we do so more and more. May we just move on, day by day, praising and trusting, trusting and praising. These are the two things which redound to the glory of God, and to our peace and joy in Him. When the eye rests on the "Ebenezers" which lie all along the way, the heart must give forth its sweet "halleluiahs" to Him who has helped us hitherto, and will help us right on to the end. He *hath* delivered, and He *doth* deliver, and He *will* deliver. Blessed chain! Its every link is divine deliverance.

Nor is it merely upon the signal mercies and gracious deliverances of our Father's hand that we are to dwell, with devout thankfulness, but also upon the "humblings" and the "provings" of His wise, faithful, and holy love. All these things are full of richest blessing to our souls. They are not, as people sometimes call them, "mercies in disguise," but plain, palpable, unmistakable mercies, for which we shall have to praise our God throughout the golden ages of that bright eternity which lies before us.

"Thou shalt remember *all* the way"—every stage of the journey, every scene of wilderness-life, all the dealings of God, from first to last, with the special object thereof, "to humble thee, and to prove thee, *to know what was in thine heart.*"

How wonderful to think of God's patient grace and painstaking love with His people in the wilderness! What precious instruction for us! With what intense interest and spiritual delight we can hang over the record of the divine dealings with Israel in all their desert-wanderings! How much we can learn from the marvelous history! We, too, have to be humbled and proved, and made to know what is in our hearts. It is very profitable and morally wholesome.

On our first setting out to follow the Lord, we know but little of the depths of evil and folly in our hearts. Indeed, we are superficial in every thing. It is as we get on in our practical career that we begin to prove the reality of things; we find out the depths of evil in ourselves, the utter hollowness and worthlessness of all that is in the world, and the urgent need of the most complete dependence upon the grace of God every moment. All this is very good; it makes us humble and self-distrusting; it delivers us from pride and self-sufficiency, and leads us to cling, in childlike simplicity, to the One who alone is able to keep us from falling. Thus, as we grow in self-knowledge, we get a deeper sense of grace, a more profound acquaintance with the wondrous love of the heart of God, His tenderness toward us, His marvelous patience in bearing with all our infirmities and failings, His rich mercy in having taken us up at all, His loving ministry to all our varied need, His numberless interpositions on our behalf, the exercises through which He has seen fit to lead us for our souls' deep and permanent profit.

The practical effect of all this is invaluable; it imparts depth, solidity, and mellowness to the character; it cures us of all our crude notions and vain theories; it delivers us from one-sidedness and wild extremes; it makes us tender, thoughtful, patient, and considerate toward others; it corrects our harsh judgments and gives a gracious desire to put the best possible construction upon the actions of others, and a readiness to attribute the best motives in cases which may seem to us equivocal. These are precious fruits of wilderness-experience which we may all earnestly covet.

"And He humbled thee, and suffered thee to hunger, and fed thee with manna, which thou knewest not, neither did thy fathers know, that He might make thee know that man doth not live by bread only, but by every word which proceedeth out of the mouth of the Lord doth man live" (ver. 3).

This passage derives special interest and importance from the fact that it is the first of our Lord's quotations from the book of Deuteronomy in His conflict with the adversary in the wilderness. Let us ponder this deeply; it demands our earnest attention. Why did our Lord quote from Deuteronomy? Because that was the book which, above all others, specially applied to the condition of Israel at the moment. Israel had utterly failed, and this weighty fact is assumed in the book of Deuteronomy from beginning to end. But notwithstanding the failure of the nation, the path of obedience lay open to every faithful Israelite. It was the privilege and duty of every one who loved God to abide by His Word under all circumstances and in all places.

Now, our blessed Lord was divinely true to the position of the Israel of God. Israel after the flesh had failed and forfeited every thing; He was there, in the wilderness, as the true Israel of God, to meet the enemy by the simple authority of the Word of God. "And Jesus, being full of the Holy Ghost, returned from Jordan, and was led by the Spirit into the wilderness, being forty days tempted of the devil. And in those days He did eat nothing; and when they were ended, He afterward hungered. And the devil said unto Him, 'If Thou be the Son of God, command this stone that it be made bread.' And Jesus answered Him, saying, '*It is written,* that man shall not live by bread alone, but by every word of God'" (Luke 4).

Here, then, is something for us to ponder. The perfect Man, the true Israel, in the wilderness, surrounded by the wild beasts, fasting for forty days, in the presence of the great adversary of God, of man, of Israel. There was not a single feature in the scene to speak for God. It was not with the second Man as it was with the first; He was not surrounded with all the delights of Eden, but with all the dreariness and desolation of a desert—there in loneliness and hunger, but there for God!

Yes, blessed be His name, and there for man,—there to show man how to meet the enemy in all his varied temptations, there to show man how to live. We must not suppose for a moment that our adorable Lord met the adversary as God over all. True, He was God, but if it were only as such that He stood in the conflict, it could not afford any example for us. Besides, it would be needless to tell us that God was able to vanquish and put to flight a creature which His own hand had formed. But to see One who was, in every respect, a man, and in all the circumstances of humanity, sin excepted—to see Him there in weakness, in hunger, standing amid the consequences of man's fall, and to find Him triumphing completely over the terrible foe, it is this which is so full of comfort, consolation, strength, and encouragement for us.

And how did He triumph? This is the grand and all-important question for us, a question demanding the most profound attention of every member of the Church of God—a question the magnitude and importance of which it would be utterly impossible to overstate. How, then, did the Man Christ Jesus vanquish Satan in the wilderness? Simply by the Word of God. He overcame, not as the almighty God, but as the humble, dependent, self-emptied, and obedient Man. We have before us the magnificent spectacle of a Man standing in the presence of the devil and utterly confounding him with no other weapon whatsoever save the Word of God. It was not by the display of divine power, for that could be no model for us; it was simply with the Word of God, in His heart and in His mouth, that the Second Man confounded the terrible enemy of God and man.

And let us carefully note that our blessed Lord does not reason with Satan. He does not appeal to any facts connected with Himself—facts with which the enemy was well acquainted. He does not say, I know I am the Son of God; the opened heavens, the descending Spirit, the Father's voice, have all borne witness to the fact of My being the Son of God. No; this would not do; it would not and could not be an example for us. *The* one special point for us to seize and learn from is, that our great Exemplar, when meeting all the temptations of the enemy, used only the weapon which we have in our possession, namely, the simple, precious, written, Word of God.

We say, "all the temptations," because in all the three instances our Lord's unvarying reply is, *"It is written."* He does not say, "I know"—"I think"—"I feel"—"I believe" this, that, or the other; He simply appeals to the written Word of God—the book of Deuteronomy in particular, that very book which infidels have dared to insult, but which is pre-eminently the book for every obedient man, in the face of total, universal, hopeless, wreck and ruin.

This is of unspeakable moment for us. It is as though our Lord Christ had said to the adversary, Whether I am the Son of God or not is not now the question, but how *man* is to live, and the answer to this question is only to be found in holy Scripture; and it is to be found there as clear as a sunbeam, quite irrespective of all questions respecting Me. Whoever I am, the Scripture is the same: "man doth not live by bread only, but by every word that proceedeth out of the mouth of the Lord."

Here we have the only true, the only safe, the only happy attitude for man, namely, hanging in earnest dependence upon "every word that proceedeth out of the mouth of the Lord." Blessed attitude! We may well say there is nothing like it in all this world. It brings the soul into direct, living, personal contact with the Lord Himself, by means of His Word. It makes the Word so absolutely essential to us, in every thing; we cannot do without it. As the natural life is sustained by bread, so the spiritual life is sustained by the Word of God. It is not merely going to the Bible to find doctrines there, or to have our opinions or views confirmed; it is very much more than this; it is going to the Bible for the staple commodity of life—the life of the new man; it is going there for food, for light, for guidance, for comfort, for authority, for strength—for all, in short, that the soul can possibly need, from first to last.

And let us specially note the force and value of the expression, "*every* word." How fully it shows that we cannot afford to dispense with a single word that has proceeded out of the mouth of the Lord. We want it all. We cannot tell the moment in which some exigence may present itself for which Scripture has already provided. We may not perhaps have specially noticed the Scripture before, but when the difficulty arises, if we are in a right condition of soul—the true posture of heart, the Spirit of God will furnish us with the needed Scripture, and we shall see a force, beauty, depth, and moral adaptation in the passage which we had never seen before. Scripture is a divine and therefore exhaustless treasury, in which God has made ample provision for all the need of His people, and for each believer in particular, right on to the end. Hence we should study it all, ponder it, dig deeply into it, and have it treasured up in our hearts, ready for use when the demand arises.

There is not a single crisis occurring in the entire history of the Church of God, not a single difficulty in the entire path of any individual believer, from beginning to end, which has not been perfectly provided for in the Bible. We have all we want in that blessed volume, and hence we should be ever seeking to make ourselves more and more acquainted with what that volume contains, so as to be "thoroughly furnished" for whatever may arise, whether it be temptation of the devil, an allurement of the world, or a lust of the flesh; or, on the other hand, for equipment for that path of good works which God has afore prepared that we should walk in it.

And we should, further, give special attention to the expression, "*Out of the mouth of the Lord.*" This is unspeakably precious. It brings the Lord so very near to us, and gives us such a sense of the reality of feeding upon His every word-yea, of hanging upon it as something absolutely essential and indispensable. It sets forth the blessed fact that our souls can no more exist without the Word than our bodies could without the food. In a word, we are taught by this passage that *man's* true position, his proper attitude, his only place of strength, safety, rest, and blessing, is to be found in habitual dependence upon the Word of God.

This is the life of faith which we are called to live—the life of dependence—the life of obedience—the life that Jesus lived perfectly. That blessed One would not move a step, utter a word, or do a single thing save by the authority of the Word of God. No doubt He could have turned stone into bread, but He had no command from God to do that; and inasmuch as He had no command, He had no motive for action. Hence Satan's temptations were perfectly powerless. He could do nothing with a man who would only act on the authority of the Word of God.

And we may also note, with very much interest and profit, that our blessed Lord does not quote Scripture for the purpose of silencing the adversary, but simply as authority for His position and conduct. Here is where we are so apt to fail; we do not sufficiently use the precious Word of God in this way; we quote it, at times, more for victory over the enemy than for power and authority for our own souls. Thus it loses its power in our hearts. We want to use the Word as a hungry man uses bread, or as a mariner uses his chart and his compass; it is that on which we live, and by which we move and act and think and speak. Such it really is, and the more fully we prove it to be all this to us, the more we shall know of its infinite preciousness. Who is it that knows most of the real value of bread? Is it a chemist? No; but a hungry man. A chemist may analyze it, and discuss its component parts, but a hungry man proves its worth. Who knows most of the real value of a chart; is it the teacher of navigation? No; but the mariner as he sails along an unknown and dangerous coast.

These are but feeble figures to illustrate what the Word of God is to the true Christian. He cannot do without it. It is absolutely indispensable in every relationship of life and in every sphere of action. His hidden life is fed and sustained by it; his practical life is guided by it. In all the scenes and circumstances of his personal and domestic history, in the privacy of his closet, in the bosom of his family, in the management of his affairs, he is cast upon the Word of God for guidance and counsel.

And it never fails those who simply cleave to it and confide in it. We may trust Scripture without a single shade of misgiving. Go to it when we will, we shall always find what we want. Are we in sorrow? is the poor heart bereaved, crushed, and desolate? What can soothe and comfort us like the balmy words which the Holy Spirit has penned for us? One sentence of Holy Scripture can do more, in the way of comfort and consolation, than all the letters of condolence that ever were penned by human hand. Are we discouraged, faint-hearted, and cast down? The Word of God meets us with its bright and soul-stirring assurances. Are we pressed by pinching poverty? The Holy Ghost brings home to our hearts some golden promise from the page of inspiration, recalling us to Him who is "the Possessor of heaven and earth," and who, in His infinite grace, has pledged Himself to "supply all *our need* according to *His riches* in glory by Christ Jesus." Are we perplexed and harassed by the conflicting opinions of men, by the dogmas of conflicting schools of divinity, by religious and theological difficulties? A few sentences of holy Scripture will pour in a flood of divine light upon the heart and conscience, and set us at perfect rest, answering every question, solving every difficulty, removing every doubt, chasing away every cloud, giving us to know the mind of God, putting an end to conflicting opinions by the one divinely competent authority.

What a boon, therefore, is holy Scripture! What a precious treasure we possess in the Word of God! How we should bless His holy name for having given it to us! Yes? and bless Him, too, for every thing that tends to make us more fully acquainted with the depth, fullness, and power of those words of our chapter, "Man shall not live by bread only, but by every word that proceedeth out of the mouth of the Lord doth man live."

Truly precious are these words to the heart of the believer! And hardly less so are those that follow, in which the beloved and revered lawgiver refers, with touching sweetness, to Jehovah's tender care throughout the whole of Israel's desert-wanderings. "Thy raiment," he says, "waxed not old upon thee, neither did thy foot swell, these forty years."

What marvelous grace shines out in these words! Only think of Jehovah looking after His people in such a manner, to see that their garments should not wax old or their foot swell! He not only fed them, but clothed them and cared for them in every way. He even stooped to look after their feet, that the sand of the desert might not injure them. Thus, for forty years, did He watch over them, with all the exquisite tenderness of a father's heart. What will not love undertake to do for its object? Jehovah had set His love upon His people, and this one blessed fact secured every thing for them, had they only understood it. There was not a single thing within the range of Israel's necessities, from Egypt to Canaan, which was not secured to them and included in the fact that Jehovah had undertaken to do for them. With infinite love and almighty power on their side, what could be lacking?

But then, as we know, love clothes itself in various forms. It has something more to do than to provide food and raiment for its objects. It has not only to take account of their physical but also of their moral and spiritual wants. Of this the lawgiver does not fail to remind the people. "Thou shalt also consider," he says, *"in thine heart"*—the only true and effective way to consider—"that, as a man chasteneth his son, so the Lord thy God chasteneth thee."

Now, we do not like chastening; it is not joyous, but grievous. It is all very well for a son to receive food and raiment from a father's hand, and to have all his comforts provided by a father's thoughtful love, but he does not like to see him taking down the rod. And yet that dreaded rod may be the very best thing for the son; it may do for him what no material benefits or earthly blessings could effect; it may correct some bad habit, or deliver him from some wrong tendency, or save him from some evil influence, and thus prove a great moral and spiritual blessing for which he shall have to be forever thankful. The grand point for the son is, to see a father's love and care in the discipline and chastening just as distinctly as in the various material benefits which strew his path from day to day.

Here is precisely where we so signally fail in reference to the dealings of our father. We rejoice in His benefits and blessings; we are filled with praise and thankfulness as we receive, day by day, from His liberal hand, the rich supply of all our need; we delight to dwell upon His marvelous interposition on our behalf in times of pressure and difficulty; it is a most precious exercise to look back over the path by which His good hand has led us, and mark those "Ebenezers" which tell of gracious help supplied all along the road.

All this is very good and very right and very precious, but then there is a great danger of our resting in the mercies, the blessings, and the benefits which flow, in such rich profusion, from our Father's loving heart and liberal hand. We are apt to rest in these things, and say with the Psalmist, "In *my prosperity* I said, 'I shall never be moved. Lord, by Thy favor Thou hast made *my mountain* to stand strong.' " True, it is "by Thy favor," but yet we are prone to be occupied with *our* mountain and *our* prosperity; we allow these things to come in between our hearts and the Lord, and thus they become a snare to us. Hence the need of chastening. Our Father, in His faithful love and care, is watching over us; He sees the danger and He sends trial, in one shape or another. Perhaps a telegram comes announcing the death of a beloved child, or the crash of a bank involving the loss of our earthly all; or, it may be, we are laid on a bed of pain and sickness, or called to watch by the sick bed of a beloved relative.

In a word, we are called to wade through deep waters which seem, to our poor, feeble, coward hearts, absolutely overwhelming. The enemy suggests the question. Is this love? Faith replies, without hesitation and without reserve, Yea; it is all love—perfect love; the death of the child, the loss of the property, the long, heavy, painful illness, all the sorrow, all the pressure, all the exercise, the deep waters and dark shadows—all, all is love—perfect love and unerring wisdom. I feel assured of it, even now; I do not wait to know it by and by, when I shall look back on the path from amid the full light of the glory; I know it now, and delight to own it to the praise of that infinite grace which has taken me up from the depth of my ruin, and charged itself with all that concerns me, and which deigns to occupy itself with my very failures, follies, and sins, in order to deliver me from them, and to make me a partaker of divine holiness, and conform me to the image of that blessed One who "loved Me and gave Himself for me."

Christian reader, this is the way to answer Satan, and to hush the dark reasonings which may spring up in our hearts. We must always justify God. We must look at all His disciplinary dealings in the light of His love. "Thou shalt also consider in thine heart that, *as a man chasteneth his son,* so the Lord thy God chasteneth thee." Most surely we should not like to be without the blessed pledge and proof of sonship. "*My son,* despise not thou the chastening of the Lord, nor faint when thou art rebuked of Him; for *whom the Lord loveth He chasteneth,* and scourgeth *every son* whom He receiveth. If ye endure chastening, God dealeth with you as with sons; for what son is he whom the father chasteneth not? But if ye be without chastisement, whereof all are partakers, then are ye bastards, and not sons. Furthermore, we have had fathers of our flesh which corrected us, and we gave them reverence; shall we not much rather be in subjection to the Father of spirits, and live? For they verily for a few days chastened us after their own pleasure; but He for our profit, that we might be partakers of His holiness. Now, no chastening for the present seemeth to be joyous, but grievous; nevertheless, afterward it yieldeth the peaceable fruit of righteousness unto them which are exercised thereby. Wherefore lift up the hands which hang down, and the feeble knees; and make straight paths for your feet, lest that which is lame be turned out of the way; but let it rather be healed" (Heb. 12:5-13).

It is at once interesting and profitable to mark the way in which Moses presses upon the congregation the varied motives of obedience arising from the past, the present, and the future. Every thing is brought to bear upon them to quicken and deepen their sense of Jehovah's claims upon them. They were to "remember" the past, they were to "consider" the present, and they were to anticipate the future; and all this was to act on their hearts, and lead them forth in holy obedience arising from the past, the present, and they were to anticipate the future; and all this was to act on their hearts, and lead them forth in holy obedience to that blessed and gracious One who had done, who was doing, and who would do such great things for them.

The thoughtful reader can hardly fail to observe in this constant presentation of moral motives a marked feature of this lovely book of Deuteronomy, and a striking proof that it is no mere attempt at a repetition of what we have in Exodus; but, on the contrary, that our book has a province, a range, a scope, and design entirely its own. To speak of mere repetition is absurd; to speak of contradiction is impious.

"Therefore thou shalt keep the commandments of the Lord thy God, to walk in His ways, and to fear Him." The word "therefore" had a retrospective and prospective force. It was designed to lead the heart back over the past dealings of Jehovah, and forward into the future. They were to think of the marvelous history of those forty years in the desert—the teaching, the humbling, the proving, the watchful care, the gracious ministry, the full supply of all their need, the manna from heaven, the stream from the smitten rock, the care of their garments, and of their very feet, the wholesome discipline for their moral good. What powerful moral motives were here for Israel's obedience!

But this was not all: they were to look forward into the future; they were to anticipate the bright prospect which lay before them; they were to find in the future, as well as in the past and the present, the solid basis of Jehovah's claims upon their reverent and whole-hearted obedience.

"For the Lord thy God bringeth thee into a good land, a land of brooks of water, of fountains and depths that spring out of valleys and hills; a land of wheat, and barley, and vines, and fig-trees, and pomegranates, a land of oil olive, and honey; a land wherein thou shalt eat bread without scarceness, thou shalt not lack any thing in it; a land whose stones are iron, and out of whose hills thou mayest dig brass."

How fair was the prospect! how bright the vision! How marked the contrast to the Egypt behind them and the wilderness through which they had passed! The Lord's land lay before them in all its beauty and verdure, its vine-clad hills and honeyed plains, its gushing fountains and flowing streams. How refreshing the thought of the vine, the fig-tree, the pomegranate, and the olive! How different from the leeks, onions, and garlic of Egypt! Yes, all so different! It was the Lord's own land: this was enough. It produced and contained all they could possibly want. Above its surface, rich profusion; below, untold wealth—exhaustless treasure.

What a prospect! How the faithful Israelite would long to enter upon it!—long to exchange the sand of the desert for that bright inheritance! True, the desert had its deep and blessed experiences, its holy lessons, its precious memories; there they had known Jehovah in a way they could not know Him even in Canaan; all this was quite true, and we can fully understand it; but still the wilderness was not Canaan, and every true Israelite would long to set his foot on the land of promise, and truly we may say that Moses presents the land, in the passage just quoted, in a way eminently calculated to attract the heart. "A land," he says, "wherein thou shalt eat bread without scarceness, *thou shalt not lack any thing in it.*" What more could be said? Here was the grand fact in reference to that good land into which the hand of covenant-love was about to introduce them. All their wants would be divinely met. Hunger and thirst should never be known there. Health and plenty, joy and gladness, peace and blessing, were to be the assured portion of the Israel of God in the fair inheritance upon which they were about to enter. Every enemy was to be subdued; every obstacle swept away; "the pleasant land" was to pour forth its treasures for their use; watered continually by heaven's rain, and warmed by its sunlight, it was to bring forth, in rich abundance, all that the heart could desire.

What a land! what an inheritance! what a home! Of course, we are looking at it now from a divine stand-point—looking at it according to what it was in the mind of God, and what it shall most assuredly be to Israel during that bright millennial age which lies before them. We should have but a very poor idea indeed of the Lord's land were we to think of it merely as possessed by Israel in the past, even in the very brightest days of its history, as it appeared amid the splendors of Solomon's reign. We must look onward to "the times of the restitution of all things," in order to have any thing like a true idea of what the land of Canaan will yet be to the Israel of God.

Now, Moses speaks of the land according to the divine idea of it. He presents it as given by God, and not as possessed by Israel. This makes all the difference. According to his charming description, there was neither enemy nor evil occurrent: nothing but fruitfulness and blessing from end to end. That is what it would have been, that is what it should have been, and that is what it shall be, by and by, to the seed of Abraham, in pursuance of the covenant made with their fathers—the new, the everlasting covenant, founded on the sovereign grace of God and ratified by the blood of the cross. No power of earth or hell can hinder the purpose or the promise of God. "Hath He said, and shall He not do it?" God will make good, to the letter, every word, spite of all the enemy's opposition and the lamentable failure of His people. Though Abraham's seed have utterly failed under law and under government, yet Abraham's God will give grace and glory, for His gifts and calling are without repentance.

Moses fully understood all this. He knew how it would turn out with those who stood before him, and with their children after them, for many generations; and he looked forward into that bright future in which a covenant-God would display, in the view of all created intelligences, the triumphs of His grace in His dealings with the seed of Abraham His friend.

Meanwhile, however, the faithful servant of Jehovah, true to the object before his mind, in all those marvelous discourses on which they were about to plant their foot. As he had spoken of the past and of the present, so would he make use of the future; he would turn all to account in his holy effort to urge upon the people their obvious, bounden duty to that blessed One who had so graciously and tenderly cared for them all their journey through, and who was about to bring them in and plant them in the mountain of His inheritance. Let us hearken to his touching and powerful exhortations.

"When thou hast eaten and art full, then thou shalt bless the Lord thy God for the good land which He has given thee." How simple! how lovely! how morally suitable! Filled with the fruit of Jehovah's goodness, they were to bless and praise His holy name. He delights to surround Himself with hearts filled to overflowing with the sweet sense of His goodness, and pouring forth songs of praise and thanksgiving. He inhabits the praises of His people. He says, "Whoso offereth praise glorifieth Me." The feeblest note of praise from a grateful heart ascends as fragrant incense to the throne and to the heart of God.

Let us remember this. It is as true for us, most surely, as it was for Israel, that praise is comely. Our grand primary business is to praise the Lord. Our every breath should be a halleluiah. It is to this blessed and most sacred exercise the Holy Ghost exhorts us, in manifold places. "By Him therefore let us offer the sacrifice of praise to God continually, that is, the fruit of our lips giving thanks to His name." We should ever remember that nothing so gratifies the heart and glorifies the name of our God as a thankful, worshiping spirit on the part of His people. It is well to do good and communicate—God is well pleased with such sacrifices; it is our high privilege, while we have opportunity, to do good unto all men, and especially unto them who are of the household of faith; we are called to be channels of blessing between the loving heart of our Father and every form of human need that comes before us in our daily path; all this is most blessedly true, but we must never forget that the very highest place is assigned to praise. It is this which shall employ our ransomed powers throughout the golden ages of eternity, when the sacrifices of active benevolence shall no longer be needed.

But the faithful lawgiver knew but too well the sad proneness of the human heart to forget all this—to lose sight of the gracious Giver, and rest in His gifts; hence he addresses the following admonitory words to the congregation—wholesome words, truly, for them and for us. May we bend our ears and our hearts to them, in holy reverence and teachableness of spirit.

"Beware that thou forget not the Lord thy God, in not keeping His commandments, and His judgments, and His statutes, which I command thee this day. Lest *when thou hast eaten and art full,* and hast built goodly houses, and dwelt therein; and when thy herds and thy flocks multiply, and thy silver and thy gold is multiplied, and all that thou hast is multiplied; then thine heart be lifted up, and thou forget the Lord thy God, which brought thee forth out of the land of Egypt, from the house of bondage; who led thee through that great and terrible wilderness, wherein were fiery serpents, and scorpions, and drought, where there was no water; who brought thee forth water out of the rock of flint; who fed thee in the wilderness with manna, which thy fathers knew not, that He might humble thee, and that He might prove thee, *to do thee good at thy latter end;* and thou say in thine heart, My power and the might of mine hand hath gotten me this wealth. But thou shalt remember the Lord thy God; for it is He that giveth thee power to get wealth, that He may establish His covenant which He sware unto thy fathers, as it is this day. And it shall be, if thou do at all forget the Lord thy God, and walk after other gods and serve them, and worship them, I testify against you this day that ye shall surely perish. As the nations which the Lord destroyeth before your face, so shall ye perish, *because ye would not be obedient unto the voice of the Lord your God"* (ver. 11-20).

Here is something for us to ponder deeply. It has most assuredly a voice for us, as it had for Israel. We may perhaps feel disposed to marvel at the frequent reiteration of the note of warning and admonition, the constant appeals to the heart and conscience of the people as to their bounden duty to obey in all things the Word of God, the recurrence again and again to those grand soul-stirring facts connected with their deliverance out of Egypt and their journey through the wilderness.

But wherefore should we marvel? In the first place, do we not deeply feel and fully admit our own urgent need of warning, admonition, and exhortation? Do we not need line upon line, precept upon precept, and that continually? Are we not prone to forget the Lord our God—to rest in His gifts instead of Himself: Alas! we cannot deny it. We rest in the stream, instead of getting up to the Fountain; we turn the very mercies, blessings, and benefits which strew our path in rich profusion into an occasion of self-complacency and gratulation, instead of finding in them the blessed ground of continual praise and thanksgiving.

As to those great facts of which Moses so continually reminds the people, could they ever lose their moral weight, power, or preciousness? Surely not. Isreal might forget and fail to appreciate those facts, but the facts remained the same. The terrible plagues of Egypt, the night of the passover, their deliverance from the land of darkness, bondage, and degradation, their marvelous passage through the Red Sea, the descent of that mysterious food from heaven morning by morning, the refreshing stream gushing forth from the flinty rock,—how could such facts as these ever lose their power over a heart possessing a spark of genuine love to God? and why should we wonder to find Moses again and again appealing to them and using them as a most powerful lever wherewith to move the hearts of the people? Moses felt the mighty moral influence of these things himself, and he would fain lead others to feel it also. To him, they were precious beyond expression, and he longed to make his brethren feel their preciousness as well as himself. It was his one object to set before them, in every possible way, the powerful claims of Jehovah upon their hearty and unreserved obedience.

This will account for what might, to an unspiritual, unintelligent, cursory reader, seem the too frequent recurrence to the scenes of the past in those wonderful discourses of Moses. We are reminded, as we read them, of the lovely words of Peter, in his second Epistle: "Wherefore I will not be negligent to put you *always in remembrance of these things,* though ye know them, and be established in the present truth. Yea, I think it meet, as long as I am in this tabernacle, *to stir you up, by putting you in remembrance;* knowing that shortly I must put off this my tabernacle, even as our Lord Jesus Christ hath showed me. Moreover, I will endeavor that ye may be able, after my decease, to have *these things always in remembrance"* (chap. 1:12-15).

How striking the unity of spirit and purpose in these two beloved and venerable servants of God! Both the one and the other felt the supreme importance and infinite value of the things of which they spoke; hence their earnest desire to keep them continually before the hearts and abidingly in the remembrance of the Lord's beloved people. Unbelieving, restless nature might say to Moses, or to Peter, Have you nothing new to tell us? Why are you perpetually dwelling on the same old themes? We know all you have got to say; we have heard it again and again. Why not strike out into some new field of thought? Would it not be well to try and keep abreast of the science of the day? If we keep perpetually moping over those antiquated themes, we shall be left stranded on the bank, while the stream of civilization rushes on. Pray give us something new.

Thus might the poor unbelieving mind—the worldly heart reason, but faith knows the answer to all such miserable suggestions. We can well believe that both Moses and Peter would have made short work with all such reasonings. And so should we. We know whence they emanate, whither they tend, and what they are worth; and we should have, if not on our lips, at least deep down in our hearts, a ready answer—an answer perfectly safisfactory to us, however contemptible it may seem to the men of this world. Could a true Israelite ever tire of hearing of what the Lord had done for him, in Egypt, in the Red Sea, and in the wilderness? Never! Such themes would be ever fresh, ever welcome to his heart. And just so with the Christian. Can he ever tire of the cross and all the grand and glorious realities that cluster around it? can he ever tire of Christ, His peerless glories and unsearchable riches, His Person, His work, His offices? Never! No, never, throughout the bright ages of eternity. Does he crave any thing new? Can science improve upon Christ? can human learning add aught to the great mystery of godliness, which has for its foundation God manifest in the flesh, and for its topstone a Man glorified in heaven? can we ever get beyond this? No, we could not if we would, and we would not if we could.

And even were we, for a moment, to take a lower range, and look at the works of God in creation; do we ever tire of the sun? He is not new; he has been pouring his beams upon this world for well-nigh six thousand years, and yet those beams are as fresh and as welcome to-day as they were when first created. Do we ever tire of the sea? It is not new; its tide has been ebbing and flowing for nearly six thousand years, but its waves are as fresh and as welcome on our shores as ever. True, the sun is often too dazzling to man's feeble vision, and the sea often swallows up, in a moment, man's boasted works; but yet the sun and the sea never lose their power, their freshness, their charm. Do we ever tire of the dew-drops that fall in refreshing virtue upon our gardens and fields? do we ever tire of the perfume that emanates from our hedge-rows? do we ever tire of the notes of the nightingale and the thrush? And what are all these when compared with the glories which cluster around the Person and the cross of Christ? what are they when put in contrast with the grand realities of that eternity which is before us?

Let us beware how we listen to such suggestions, whether they come from without or spring from the depths of our own evil hearts, lest we be found, like Israel after the flesh, loathing the heavenly manna and despising the pleasant land; or like Demas, who forsook the blessed apostle, having loved this present age; or like those of whom we read in the sixth of John, who, offended by our Lord's close and pointed teaching, "went back, and walked no more with Him." May the Lord keep our hearts true to Himself, and fresh and fervent in His blessed cause, till He come.

---

## *CHAPTER 9*

"HEAR, O Israel: Thou art to pass over Jordan this day, to go in to possess nations greater and mightier than thyself, cities great and fenced up to heaven, a people great and tall, the children of the Anakims, whom thou knowest, and of whom thou hast heard say, 'Who can stand before the children of Anak!' " (ver. 1-2)

This chapter opens with the same grand Deuteronomic sentence, *"Hear,* O Israel." This, we may say, is the key-note of this most blessed book, and especially of those opening discourses which have been engaging our attention. But the chapter which now lies open before us presents subjects of immense weight and importance. In the first place, the lawgiver sets before the congregation, in terms of deep solemnity, that which lay before them in their entrance upon the land. He does not hide from them the fact that there were serious difficulties and formidable enemies to be encountered. This he does, we need hardly say, not to discourage their hearts, but that they might be forewarned, forearmed, and prepared. What that preparation was we shall see presently; but the faithful servant of God felt the rightness, yea, the urgent need of putting the true state of the case before his brethren.

There are two ways of looking at difficulties; we may look at them from a human stand-point, or from a divine one; we may look at them in a spirit of unbelief, or we may look at them in the calmness and quietness of confidence in the living God. We have an instance of the former in the report of the unbelieving spies in Numbers 13; we have an instance of the latter in the opening of our present chapter.

It is not the province, nor the path, of faith to deny that there are difficulties to be encountered by the people of God; it would be the height of folly to do so, inasmuch as there are difficulties, and it would be but fool-hardiness, fanaticism, or fleshly enthusiasm to deny it. It is always well for people to know what they are about, and not to rush blindly into a path for which they are not prepared. An unbelieving sluggard may say, There is a lion in the way; a blind enthusiast may say, There is no such thing; the true man of faith will say, Though there were a thousand lions in the way, God can soon dispose of them.

But, as a great practical principle of general application, it is very important for all the Lord's people to consider deeply and calmly, what they are about, ere they enter upon any particular path of service or line of action. If this were more attended to, we should not witness so many moral and spiritual wrecks around us. What mean those most solemn, searching, and testing words addressed by our blessed Lord to the multitudes that thronged around Him in Luke 14? "He turned and said to them, 'If any man *come to Me,* and hate not his father and mother, his wife and children, and brethren and sisters, yea, and his own life also, he cannot be My disciple. And whosoever doth not bear his cross, and come after Me, cannot be My disciple. For which of you, intending to build a tower, sitteth not down first, and counteth the cost, whether he have sufficient to finish it? lest haply, after he hath laid the foundation, and is not able to finish, all that behold it begin to mock him, saying,

This man began to build, and was not able to finish' " (ver. 26-30).

These are solemn and seasonable words for the heart. How many unfinished buildings meet our view as we look forth over the wide field of Christian profession, giving sad occasion to the beholders for mockery! How many set out upon a path of discipleship under sudden impulse, or under the pressure of mere human influence, without a proper understanding, or a due consideration of all that is involved; and then when difficulties arise, when trials come, when the path is found to be narrow, rough, lonely, unpopular, they give it up, thus proving that they had never really counted the cost, never taken the path in communion with God, never understood what they were doing.

Now, such cases are very sorrowful; they bring great reproach on the cause of Christ, give occasion to the adversary to blaspheme, and greatly dishearten those who care for the glory of God and the good of souls. Better far not to take the ground at all than, having taken it, to abandon it in dark unbelief and worldly-mindedness.

Hence, therefore, we can perceive the wisdom and faithfulness of the opening words of our chapter. Moses tells the people plainly what was before them; not, surely, to discourage them, but to preserve them from self-confidence, which is sure to give way in the moment of trial, and to cast them upon the living God, who never fails a trusting heart.

"Understand therefore this day, that the Lord thy God, is He which goeth over before thee; as a consuming fire He shall destroy them, and He shall bring them down before thy face: so shalt thou drive them out, and destroy them quickly, as the Lord hath said unto thee."

Here, then, is the divine answer to all difficulties, be they ever so formidable. What were mighty nations, great cities, fenced walls, in the presence of Jehovah? Simply as chaff before the whirlwind. "If God be for us, who can be against us?" The very things which scare and stumble the coward heart afford an occasion for the display of God's power, and the magnificent triumphs of faith. Faith says, Grant me but this, that God is before me and with me, and I can go any where. Thus the only thing in all this world that really glorifies God is the faith that can trust Him and use Him and praise Him; and inasmuch as faith is the only thing that glorifies God, so is it the only thing that gives man his proper place, even the place of complete dependence upon God, and this insures victory and inspires unceasing praise.

But we must never forget that there is moral danger in the very moment of victory —danger arising out of what we are in ourselves. There is the danger of self-gratulation —a terrible snare to us poor mortals. In the hour of conflict we feel our weakness, our nothingness, our need. This is good and morally safe. It is well to be brought down to the very bottom of self and all that pertains to it, for there we find God, in all the fullness and blessedness of what He is, and this is sure and certain victory and consequent praise.

But our treacherous and deceitful hearts are prone to forget whence the strength and victory come; hence the moral force, value, and seasonableness of the following admonitory words addressed by the faithful minister of God to the hearts and consciences of his brethren: "Speak not thou *in thine heart*"—here is where the mischief always begins—"after that the Lord hath cast them out from before thee, saying, for my righteousness the Lord hath brought me in to possess this land; but for the wickedness of these nations the Lord doth drive them out from before thee."

Alas! what materials there are in us! what ignorance of our own hearts! what a shallow sense of the real character of our ways! How terrible to think that we are capable of saying in our hearts such words as, "For my righteousness"! Yes, we are verily capable of such egregious folly; for as Israel was capable of it, so are we, inasmuch as we are made of the very same material; and that they were capable of it is evident from the fact of their being warned against it; for, most assuredly, the Spirit of God does not warn against phantom dangers or imaginary temptations. We are verily capable of turning the actings of God on our behalf into an occasion of self-complacency; instead of seeing in those gracious actings a ground for heartfelt praise to God, we use them as a ground for self-exaltation.

Hence, therefore, we would do well to ponder the words of faithful admonition addressed by Moses to the hearts and consciences of the people; they furnish a very wholesome antidote for the self-righteousness so natural to us as well as to Israel. "Not for thy righteousness, or for the uprightness of thine heart, dost thou go to possess their land; but for the wickedness of those nations the Lord thy God doth drive them out from before thee, and that He may perform the word which the Lord sware unto thy fathers, Abraham, Isaac, and Jacob. Understand, therefore, that the Lord giveth thee not this good land to possess it for thy righteousness; for thou art a stiff-necked people. Remember, and forget not, how thou provokedst the Lord thy God to wrath in the wilderness; from the day that thou didst depart out of the land of Egypt, until ye came unto this place, ye have been rebellious against the Lord" (ver. 5-7).

This paragraph sets forth two great principles, which, if fully laid hold of, must put the heart into a right moral attitude. In the first place, the people were reminded that their possession of the land of Canaan was simply in pursuance of God's promise to their fathers. This was placing the matter on the most solid basis—a basis which nothing could ever disturb.

As to the seven nations which were to be dispossessed, it was on the ground of their wickedness that God, in the exercise of His righteous government, was about to drive them out. Every landlord has a perfect right to eject bad tenants; and the nations of Canaan had not only failed to pay their rent, as we say, but they had injured and defiled the property to such an extent that God could no longer endure them, and therefore He was going to drive them out, irrespective altogether of the incoming tenants. Whoever was going to get possession of the property, these dreadful tenants must be evicted. The iniquity of the Amorites had reached its highest point, and nothing remained but that judgment should take its course. Men might argue and reason as to the moral fitness and consistency of a benevolent Being unroofing the houses of thousands of families and putting the occupants to the sword, but we may depend upon it the government of God will make very short work with all such arguments. God, blessed forever be His holy name, knows how to manage His own affairs, and that, too, without asking man's opinion. He had borne with the wickedness of the seven nations to such a degree that it had become absolutely insufferable; the very land itself could not bear it. Any further exercise of forbearance would have been a sanction of the most terrible abominations; and this, of course, was a moral impossibility. The glory of God absolutely demanded the expulsion of the Canaanites.

Yes; and we may add, the glory of God demanded the introduction of the seed of Abraham into possession of the property, to hold as tenants forever under the Lord God Almighty—the Most High God, Possessor of heaven and earth. Thus the matter stood for Israel, had they but seen it. Their possession of the land of promise and the maintenance of the divine glory were so bound up together that one could not be touched without touching the other. God had promised to give the land of Canaan to the seed of Abraham as an everlasting possession. Had He not a right to do so? Will infidels question God's right to do as He will with His own? Will they refuse to the Creator and Governor of the universe a right which they claim for themselves? The land was Jehovah's, and He gave it to Abraham His friend forever; and although this was true, yet were not the Canaanites disturbed in their tenure of the property until their wickedness had become positively unbearable.

Thus we see that in the matter both of the outgoing and incoming tenants the glory of God was involved. That glory demanded that the Canaanites should be expelled, because of their ways; and that glory demanded that Israel should be put in possession, because of the promise to Abraham, Isaac, and Jacob.

But, in the second place, Israel had no

ground for self-complacency, as Moses most plainly and faithfully instructs them. He rehearses in their ears, in the most touching and impressive manner, all the leading scenes of their history from Horeb to Kadesh-barnea; he refers to the golden calf, to the broken tables of the covenant, to Taberah and Massah, and Kibroth-hattaavah; and sums all up, at verse 24, with these pungent, humbling words, "Ye have been rebellious against the Lord from the day that I knew you."

This was plain dealing with heart and conscience. The solemn review of their whole career was eminently calculated to correct all false notions about themselves; every scene and circumstance in their entire history, if viewed from a proper stand-point, only brought to light the humbling fact of what they were, and how near they had been, again and again, to utter destruction. With what stunning force must the following words have fallen upon their ears!—"And the Lord said unto me, 'Arise, get thee down quickly from hence, for *thy* people which *thou* hast brought forth out of Egypt have corrupted themselves; they are quickly turned aside out of the way which I commanded them; they have made them a molten image.' Furthermore, the Lord spake unto me, saying, 'I have seen this people, and behold, it is a stiff-necked people; *let Me alone, that I may destroy* them, and blot out their name from under heaven; and I will make of thee a nation mightier and greater than they' " (ver. 12-14).

How withering was all this to their natural vanity, pride, and self-righteousness! How should their hearts have been moved to their very deepest depths by those tremendous words, "Let Me alone, that I may destroy them"! How solemn to reflect upon the fact which these words revealed—their appalling nearness to national ruin and destruction! How ignorant they had been of all that passed between Jehovah and Moses on the top of Mount Horeb! They had been on the very brink of an awful precipice. Another moment might have dashed them over. The intercession of Moses had saved them, the very man whom they had accused of taking too much upon him. Alas! how they had mistaken and misjudged him! How utterly astray they had been in all their thoughts! Why, the very man whom they had accused of self-seeking and desiring to make himself altogether a prince over them, had actually refused a divinely given opportunity of becoming the head of a greater and mightier nation than they! Yes, and this same man had earnestly requested that if they were not to be forgiven and brought into the land, his name might be blotted out of the book.

How wonderful was all this! What a turning of the tables upon them! How exceedingly small they must have felt, in view of all these wonderful facts! Surely, as they reviewed all these things, they might well see the utter folly of the words, "For my righteousness the Lord hath brought me in to possess this land." How could the makers of a molten image use such language! Ought they not rather to see and feel and own themselves to be no better than the nations that were about to be driven out from before them? For what had made them to differ? The sovereign mercy and electing love of their covenant-God. And to what did they owe their deliverance out of Egypt, their sustenance in the wilderness, and their entrance into the land? Simply to the eternal stability of the covenant made with their fathers, "a covenant ordered in all things and sure," a covenant ratified and established by the blood of the Lamb, in virtue of which all Israel shall yet be saved and blessed in their own land.

But we must now quote the splendid paragraph with which our chapter closes—a paragraph eminently fitted to open Israel's eyes to the utter folly of all their thoughts respecting Moses, their thoughts respecting themselves, and their thoughts respecting that blessed One who had so marvelously borne with all their dark unbelief and daring rebellion.

"Thus I fell down before the Lord forty days and forty nights, as I fell down at the first; because the Lord had said He would destroy you. I prayed therefore unto the Lord, and said, 'O Lord God, destroy not *Thy people* and *Thine inheritance*, which

Thou hast redeemed through Thy greatness, which Thou hast brought forth out of Egypt with a mighty hand. Remember Thy servants, Abraham, Isaac, and Jacob; *look not unto the stubbornness of this people, nor to their wickedness, nor to their sin;* lest the land whence Thou broughtest us out say, Because the Lord was not able to bring them into the land which He promised them, and because He hated them, He hath brought them out to slay them in the wilderness. *Yet they are Thy people, and Thine inheritance,* which Thou broughtest out by Thy mighty power, and by Thy stretched-out arm.' "

What marvelous words are these to be addressed by a human being to the living God! What powerful pleadings for Israel! what self-renunciation! Moses refuses the offered dignity of being the founder of a greater and mightier nation than Israel. He only desires that Jehovah should be glorified, and Israel pardoned, blessed, and brought into the promised land. He could not endure the thought of any reproach being brought upon that glorious Name so dear to his heart, neither could he bear to witness Israel's destruction. These were the two things he dreaded; and as to his own exaltation, it was just the thing about which he cared nothing at all. This beloved and honored servant cared *only* for the glory of God and the salvation of His people; and as to himself, his hopes, his interests, his all, he could rest, with perfect composure, in the assurance that his individual blessing and the divine glory were bound together by a link which could never be snapped.

Oh, how grateful must all this have been to the heart of God! How refreshing to His spirit were those earnest, loving pleadings of His servant! How much more in harmony with His mind than the intercession of Elias against Israel hundreds of years afterward! How they remind us of the blessed ministry of our great High-Priest, who ever liveth to make intercession for His people, and whose active intervention on our behalf never ceases for a single moment!

Then how very touching and beautiful to mark the way in which Moses insists upon the fact that the people were Jehovah's inheritance, and that He had brought them up out of Egypt. The Lord had said, "*Thy* people which *thou* hast brought forth out of Egypt"; but Moses says, "They are *Thy* people, and *Thine* inheritance, which *Thou* broughtest out." This is perfectly exquisite. Indeed this whole scene is full of profound interest.

---

## *CHAPTER 10*

"AT that time the Lord said unto me, 'Hew thee two tables of stone like unto the first, and come up unto Me into the mount, and make thee an ark of wood; and I will write on the tables the words that were in the first tables which thou brakest, and thou shalt put them in the ark.' And I made an ark of shittim wood, and hewed two tables of stone like unto the first, and went up into the mount, having the two tables in mine hand. And He wrote on the tables, according to the first writing, the ten commandments, which the Lord spake unto you in the mount out of the midst of the fire, in the day of the assembly; and the Lord gave them unto me. And I turned myself and came down from the mount, and put the tables in the ark which I had made; and there they be, as the Lord commanded me" (ver. 1-5).

The beloved and revered servant of God seemed never to weary of rehearsing in the ears of the people the interesting, momentous, and significant sentences of the past. To him they were ever fresh, ever precious. His heart delighted in them. They could never lose their charm in his eyes; he found in them an exhaustless treasury for his own heart, and a mighty moral lever wherewith to move the heart of Israel.

We are constantly reminded, in these powerful and deeply affecting addresses, of the inspired apostle's words to his beloved Philippians—"To write the same things to you, to me is not grievous, but for you it is safe." The poor, restless, fickle, vagrant heart might long for some new theme; but the faithful apostle found his deep and unfailing delight in unfolding and dwelling upon those precious subjects which clustered, in rich luxuriance, around the Person and the cross of his adorable Lord and Saviour Jesus Christ. He had found in Christ all he needed for time and eternity. The glory of His Person had completely eclipsed all the glories of earth and of nature. He could say, "What things were *gain to me,* those I counted *loss for Christ.* Yea, doubtless, and I count all things but loss, for the excellency of the knowledge of Christ Jesus my Lord; for whom I have suffered the loss of all things, and do count them but dung, that I may win Christ" (Phil. 3:7-8).

This is the language of a true Christian, of one who had found a perfectly absorbing and commanding object in Christ. What could the world offer to such an one? what could it do for him? Did he want its riches, its honors, its distinctions, its pleasures? He counted them all as dung. How was this? Because he had found Christ; he had seen an object in Him which so riveted his heart that to win Him and know more of Him and be found in Him was the one ruling desire of his soul. If any one had talked to Paul about something new, what would have been his answer? If any one had suggested to him the thought of getting on in the world or of seeking to make money, what would have been his reply? Simply this: I have found my *all* in Christ; I want no more. I have found in Him *"unsearchable* riches"—*"durable* riches and righteousness." In Him are hid *all* the treasures of wisdom and knowledge. What do I want of this world's riches, its wisdom, or its learning? These things all pass away like the vapors of the morning; and even while they last, are wholly inadequate to satisfy the desires and aspirations of an immortal spirit. Christ is an eternal object, heaven's centre, the delight of the heart of God; He shall satisfy me throughout the countless ages of that bright eternity which is before me; and surely, if He can satisfy me forever, He can satisfy me now. Shall I turn to the wretched rubbish of this world—its pursuits, its pleasures, its amusements, its theatres, its concerts, its riches, or its honors to supplement my portion in Christ? God forbid! All such things would be simply an intolerable nuisance to me. Christ is my all and in all, now and forever.

Such, we may well believe, would have been the distinctly pronounced reply of the blessed apostle; such was the distinct reply of his whole life; and such should be ours also. How truly deplorable, how deeply humbling, to find a Christian turning to the world for enjoyment, recreation, or pastime! It simply proves that he has not found a satisfying portion in Christ. We may set it down as a fixed principle that the heart which is filled with Christ has no room for aught beside. It is not a question of the right or the wrong of things; the heart does not want them, would not have them; it has found its present and everlasting portion and rest in that blessed One that fills the heart of God, and will fill the vast universe with the beams of His glory throughout the everlasting ages.

We have been led into the foregoing line of thought in connection with the interesting fact of Moses' unwearied rehearsal of all the grand events in Israel's marvelous history from Egypt to the borders of the promised land. To him they furnished a perpetual feast; and he not only found his own deep, personal delight in dwelling upon them, but he also felt the immense importance of unfolding them before the whole congregation. To him, most surely, it was not grievous, but for them it was safe. How delightful for him, and how good and needful for them, to dwell upon the facts connected with the two sets of tables—the first set smashed to atoms, at the foot of the mountain, and the second set inclosed in the ark.

What human language could possibly unfold the deep significance and moral weight of such facts as these? Those broken tables! how impressive! how pregnant with wholesome instruction for the people! how powerfully suggestive! Will any one presume to say that we have here a mere barren repetition of the facts recorded in Exodus? Certainly no one who reverently believes in the divine inspiration of the Pentateuch.

No, the tenth of Deuteronomy fills a niche and does a work entirely its own. In it the lawgiver holds up to the hearts of the people past scenes and circumstances in such a way as to rivet them upon the very tablets of the soul. He allows them to hear the conversation between Jehovah and himself; he tells them what took place during those mysterious forty days upon that cloud-capped mountain; he lets them hear Jehovah's reference to the broken tables—the apt and forcible expression of the utter worthlessness of man's covenant. For why were those tables broken? Because they had shamefully failed. Those shattered fragments told the humiliating tale of their hopeless ruin on the ground of the law. All was gone. Such was the obvious meaning of the fact. It was striking, impressive, unmistakable. Like a broken pillar over a grave, which tells at a glance that the prop and stay of the family lies mouldering beneath. There is no need of any inscription, for no human language could speak with such eloquence to the heart as that most expressive emblem. So the broken tables were calculated to convey to the heart of Israel the tremendous fact that, so far as their covenant was concerned, they were utterly ruined—hopelessly undone; they were complete bankrupts on the score of righteousness.

But then that second set of tables! What of them? Thank God, they tell a different tale altogether. They were not broken. God took care of them. "I turned myself and came down from the mount, and put the tables in the ark which I had made; and *there they be,* as the Lord commanded me."

Blessed fact! "There they be." Yes, covered up in that ark which spoke of Christ, that blessed One who magnified the law and made it honorable, who established every jot and tittle of it, to the glory of God and the everlasting blessing of His people. Thus, while the broken fragments of the first tables told the sad and humbling tale of Israel's utter failure and ruin, the second tables, shut up intact in the ark, set forth the glorious truth that Christ is the end of the law for righteousness to every one that believeth.

We do not, of course, mean to say that Israel understood the deep meaning and far-reaching application of those wonderful facts which Moses rehearsed in their ears. As a nation, they certainly did not then, though, through the sovereign mercy of God, they will by and by. Individuals may, and doubtless did, enter into somewhat of their significance. This is not now the question. It is for us to see and make our own of the precious truth set forth in those two sets of tables, namely, the failure of every thing in the hands of man, and the eternal stability of God's covenant of grace, ratified by the blood of Christ, and to be displayed in all its glorious results, in the kingdom, by and by, when the Son of David shall reign from sea to sea, and from the river to the ends of the earth; when the seed of Abraham shall possess, according to the divine gift, the land of promise; and when all the nations of the earth shall rejoice under the beneficent reign of the Prince of peace.

Bright and glorious prospect for the now desolate land of Israel, and this groaning earth of ours! The King of righteousness and peace will then have it all His own way. All evil will be put down with a powerful hand. There will be no weakness in that government; no rebel tongue will be permitted to prate, in accents of insolent sedition, against the decrees and enactments thereof; no rude and senseless demagogue will be allowed to disturb the peace of the people, or to insult the majesty of the throne. Every abuse will be put down, every disturbing element will be neutralized, every stumbling-block will be removed, and every root of bitterness eradicated. The poor and the needy shall be well looked after, yea, all shall be divinely attended to; toil, sorrow, poverty, and desolation shall be unknown; the wilderness and the solitary place shall be glad, and the desert shall rejoice and blossom as the rose. "Behold a king shall reign in righteousness, and princes shall rule in judgment. And a man shall be as a hiding-place from the wind, and a covert from the tempest; as rivers of water in a dry place, as the shadow of a great rock in a weary land."

What glorious scenes are yet to be enacted

in this poor sin-stricken, Satan-enslaved, sorrowful world of ours! How refreshing to think of them! What a relief to the heart amid all the mental misery, the moral degradation, and physical wretchedness exhibited around us on every side! Thank God, the day is rapidly approaching when the prince of this world shall be hurled from his throne and consigned to the bottomless pit, and the Prince of heaven, the glorious Emmanuel shall stretch forth His blessed sceptre over the wide universe of God, and heaven and earth shall bask in the sunlight of His royal countenance. Well may we cry out, O Lord, hasten the time!

"And the children of Israel took their journey from Beeroth of the children of Jaakan to Mosera; there Aaron died, and there he was buried; and Eleazar his son ministered in the priest's office in his stead. From thence they journeyed unto Gudgodah; and from Gudgodah to Jotbath, a land of rivers of waters. At that time the Lord separated the tribe of Levi, to bear the ark of the covenant of the Lord, to stand before the Lord to minister unto Him, and to bless in His name, unto this day. Wherefore Levi hath no part nor inheritance with his brethren; the Lord is His inheritance, according as the Lord thy God promised him."

The reader must not allow his mind to be disturbed by any question of historical sequence in the foregoing passage. It is simply a parenthesis in which the lawgiver groups together, in a very striking and forcible manner, circumstances culled, with holy skill, from the history of the people, illustrative at once of the government and grace of God. The death of Aaron exhibits the former; the election and elevation of Levi presents the latter. Both are placed together, not with a view to chronology, but for the grand moral end which was ever present to the mind of the lawgiver—an end which lies far away beyond the range of infidel reason, but which commends itself to the heart and understanding of the devout student of Scripture.

How utterly contemptible are the quibbles of the infidel when looked at in the brilliant light of divine inspiration! How miserable the condition of a mind which can occupy itself with chronological hair-splittings in order, if possible, to find a flaw in the divine volume, instead of grasping the real aim and object of the inspired writer!

But why does Moses bring in, in this parenthetical and apparently abrupt manner, those two special events in Israel's history? Simply to move the heart of the people toward the one grand point of obedience. To this end he culls and groups according to the wisdom given unto him. Do we expect to find in this divinely taught servant of God the petty preciseness of a mere copyist? Infidels may affect to do so, but the true Christians know better. A mere scribe could copy events in their chronological order; a true prophet will bring those events to bear, in a moral way, upon the heart and conscience. Thus, while the poor deluded infidel is groping amid the shadows of his own creation, the pious student delights himself in the moral glories of that peerless volume which stands like a rock, against which the waves of infidel thought dash themselves with contemptible impotency.

We do not attempt to dwell upon the circumstances referred to in the above parenthesis; they have been gone into elsewhere, and therefore we only feel it needful, in this place, to point out to the reader what we may venture to call the Deuteronomic bearing of the facts—the use which the lawgiver makes of them to strengthen the foundation of his final appeal to the heart and conscience of the people, to give pungency and power to his exhortation, as he urged upon them the absolute necessity of unqualified obedience to the statutes and judgments of their covenant-God. Such was his reason for referring to the solemn fact of the death of Aaron. They were to remember that notwithstanding Aaron's high position as the high-priest of Israel, yet he was stripped of his robes and deprived of his life for disobedience to the word of Jehovah. How important, then, that they should take heed to themselves! The government of God was not to be trifled with, and the very fact of Aaron's elevation only rendered it all the more needful that his sin should be dealt with, in order that others might fear.

And then they were to remember the Lord's dealings with Levi, in which grace shines with such marvelous lustre. The fierce, cruel, self-willed Levi was taken up from the depths of his moral ruin and brought nigh to God, "to bear the ark of the covenant of the Lord, to stand before the Lord, to minister unto Him, and to bless in His name."

But why should this account of Levi be coupled with the death of Aaron? Simply to set forth the blessed consequences of obedience. If the death of Aaron displayed the awful result of disobedience, the elevation of Levi illustrates the precious fruit of obedience. Hear what the prophet Malachi says on this point. "And ye shall know that I have sent this *commandment* unto you, that My covenant might be with Levi, saith the Lord of hosts. My covenant was with him of life and peace; and *I gave them to him for the fear wherewith he feared Me, and was afraid before My name.* The law of truth was in his mouth, and iniquity was not found in his lips; he walked with Me in peace and equity, and did turn many away from iniquity" (chap. 2:4-6).

This is a very remarkable passage, and throws much light upon the subject now before us. It tells us distinctly that Jehovah gave His covenant of life and peace to Levi "for the fear wherewith he feared" Him on the terrible occasion of the golden calf which Aaron (himself a Levite of the very highest order) made. Why was Aaron judged? Because of his rebellion at the waters of Meribah (Num. 20:24). Why was Levi blessed? Because of his reverent obedience at the foot of Mount Horeb (Exod. 32). Why are both grouped together in Deuteronomy 10? In order to impress upon the heart and conscience of the congregation the urgent necessity of implicit obedience to the commandments of their covenant-God. How perfect is Scripture in all its parts! how beautifully it hangs together! and how plain it is to the devout reader that the lovely book of Deuteronomy has its own divine niche to fill, its own distinctive work to do, its own appointed sphere, scope, and object! How manifest it is that the fifth division of the Pentateuch is neither a contradiction nor a repetition, but a divine application of its divinely inspired predecessors! And, finally, we cannot help adding, how convincing the evidence that infidel writers know neither what they say nor whereof they affirm, when they dare to insult the oracles of God —yea, that they greatly err, not knowing the Scriptures, nor the power of God!*

At verse 10 of our chapter, Moses returns to the subject of his discourse. "And I stayed in the mount, according to the first time, forty days and forty nights; and the Lord hearkened unto me at that time also, and the Lord would not destroy thee. And the Lord said unto me, 'Arise, take thy journey before the people, that they may go in and possess the land which I sware unto their fathers to give unto them.' "

Jehovah would accomplish His promise to the fathers spite of every hindrance. He would put Israel in full possession of the land concerning which He had sworn to Abraham, Isaac, and Jacob, to give it to their seed for an everlasting inheritance.

"And now, Israel, what doth the Lord *thy* God require of thee, but to fear the Lord thy God, to walk in *all His ways,* and to love Him, and to serve the Lord *thy* God with all thy heart and with all thy soul. To keep the commandments of the Lord, and His statutes, which I command thee this day, *for thy good.*" It was all for their real good—their deep, full blessing to walk in the way of the divine commandments. The path of

---

*We have, in human writings, numerous examples of the same thing that infidels object to in Deuteronomy 10:6-9. Suppose a man is anxious to call the attention of the English nation to some great principle of political economy, or some matter of national importance; he does not hesitate to select facts however widely separated on the page of history, and group them together in order to illustrate his subject. Do infidels object to this? No; not when found in the writings of men. It is only when it occurs in Scripture, because they hate the Word of God, and cannot bear the idea that He should give to His creatures a book-revelation of His mind. Blessed be His name, He has given it notwithstanding, and we have it in all its infinite preciousness and divine authority, for the comfort of our hearts and the guidance of our path amid all the darkness and confusion of this scene through which we are passing home to glory.

whole-hearted obedience is the only path of true happiness; and, blessed be God, this path can always be trodden by those who love the Lord.

This is an unspeakable comfort, at all times. God has given us His precious Word, the perfect revelation of His mind; and He has given us what Israel had not, even His Holy Spirit to dwell in us, whereby we can understand and appreciate His Word. Hence our obligations are vastly higher than were Israel's. We are bound to a life of obedience by every argument that could be brought to bear on the heart and understanding.

And surely it is for our good to be obedient. There is indeed "great reward" in keeping the commandments of our loving Father. Every thought of Him and of His gracious ways, every reference to His marvelous dealings with us—His loving ministry, His tender care, His thoughtful love—all should bend our hearts in affectionate devotion to Him, and quicken our steps in treading the path of loving obedience to Him. Wherever we turn our eyes we are met by the most powerful evidences of His claim upon our heart's affections and upon all the energies of our ransomed being; and, blessed be His name, the more fully we are enabled, by His grace, to respond to His most precious claims, the brighter and happier our path must be. There is nothing in all this world more deeply blessed than the path and portion of an obedient soul. "Great peace have they that love Thy law, and nothing shall offend them." The lowly disciple who finds his meat and his drink in doing the will of his beloved Lord and Master, possesses a peace which the world can neither give nor take away. True, he may be misunderstood and misinterpreted; he may be dubbed narrow and bigoted, and such like; but none of these things move him. One approving smile from his Lord is more than ample recompense for all the reproach that men can heap upon him. He knows how to estimate at their proper worth the thoughts of men; they are to him as the chaff which the wind driveth away. The deep utterance of his heart, as he moves steadily along the sacred path of obedience, is—

> Let me my feebleness recline
> On that eternal love of Thine,
> And human thoughts forget;
> Childlike attend what Thou wilt say,
> Go forth and serve Thee while 'tis day,
> Nor leave Thy sweet retreat.

In the closing verses of our chapter, the lawgiver seems to rise higher and higher in his presentation of moral motives for obedience, and to come closer and closer to the hearts of the people. "Behold," he says, "the heaven and the heaven of heavens is the Lord's thy God, the earth also, with all that therein is. Only the Lord had a delight in thy fathers to love them, and He chose their seed after them, even you above all people, as it is this day." What a marvelous privilege to be chosen and loved by the Possessor of heaven and earth! what an honor to be called to serve and obey Him! Surely nothing in all this world could be higher or better. To be identified and associated with the Most High God, to have His name called upon them, to be His peculiar people, His special possession, the people of His choice, to be set apart from all the nations of the earth to be the servants of Jehovah and His witnesses. What, we may ask, could exceed this, except it be that to which the Church of God and the individual believer are called?

Assuredly, our privileges are higher, inasmuch as we know God in a higher, deeper, nearer, more intimate manner than the nation of Israel ever did. We know Him as the God and Father of the Lord Jesus Christ, and as our God and Father. We have the Holy Ghost dwelling in us, shedding abroad the love of God in our hearts, and leading us to cry, Abba, Father. All this is far beyond any thing that God's earthly people ever knew or could know; and, inasmuch as our privileges are higher, His claims upon our hearty and unreserved obedience are also higher. Every appeal to the heart of Israel should come home with augmented force to our hearts, beloved Christian reader; every exhortation addressed to them should speak far more powerfully to us. We occupy the very highest ground on which any creature could stand. Neither the seed of Abraham on earth nor the angels of God in heaven could say what we can say or know what we know. We are linked and eternally associated with the risen and glorified Son of God. We can adopt as our own the wondrous language of 1 John 4:17, and say, "As He is, so are we in this world." What can exceed this, as to privilege and dignity? Surely nothing, save to be, in body, soul, and spirit, conformed to His adorable image, as we shall be ere long, through the abounding grace of God.

Well then, let us ever bear in mind—yea, let us have it deep, deep down in our hearts, that according to our privileges are our obligations. Let us not refuse the wholesome word "obligation," as though it had a legal ring about it. Far from it! it would be utterly impossible to conceive any thing further removed from all thought of legality than the obligations which flow out of the Christian's position. It is a very serious mistake to be continually raising the cry of "Legal! legal!" whenever the holy responsibilities of our position are pressed upon us. We believe that every truly pious Christian will delight in all the appeals and exhortations which the Holy Ghost addresses to us as to our obligations, seeing they are all grounded upon privileges conferred upon us by the sovereign grace of God, through the precious blood of Christ, and made good to us by the mighty ministry of the Holy Ghost.

But let us hearken still further to the stirring appeals of Moses. They are truly profitable for us, with all our higher light, knowledge, and privilege.

"Circumcise therefore *the foreskin of your heart,* and be no more stiff-necked. For the Lord your God is God of gods, and Lord of lords, a great God, a mighty, and a terrible, which regardeth not persons, nor taketh reward. He doth execute the judgment of the fatherless and widow, and loveth the stranger, in giving him food and raiment."

Here, Moses speaks not merely of God's doings and dealings and ways, but of Himself, of what He is. He is high over all, the great, the mighty, and the terrible. But He has a heart for the widow and the fatherless—those helpless objects deprived of all earthly and natural props, the poor bereaved and broken-hearted widow, and the desolate orphan. God thinks of and cares for such in a very special way; they have a claim upon His loving heart and mighty hand. "A father of the fatherless, and a Judge of the widow is God in His holy habitation." "She that is a widow indeed and desolate trusteth in God, and continueth in supplications and prayers night and day." "Leave thy fatherless children, I will preserve them alive; and let thy widows trust in Me."

What a rich provision is here for widows and orphans! How wondrous God's care of such! How many widows are much better off than when they had their husbands! how many orphans are better cared and provided for than when they had their parents! God looks after them! This is enough. Thousands of husbands and thousands of parents are worse, by far, than none; but God never fails those who are cast upon Him. He is ever true to His own name, whatever relationship He takes. Let all widows and orphans remember this for their comfort and encouragement.

And then the poor stranger! He is not forgotten. "He loveth the stranger, in giving him food and raiment." How precious is this! Our God cares for all those who are bereft of earthly props, human hopes, and creature-confidences. All such have a special claim upon Him, to which He will most surely respond according to all the love of His heart. The widow, the fatherless, and the stranger are the special objects of His tender care, and all such have but to look to Him, and draw upon His exhaustless resources in all their varied need.

But then He must be known in order to be trusted. "They that know Thy name will put their trust in Thee; for Thou, Lord, hast not forsaken them that seek Thee." Those who do not know God would vastly prefer an insurance policy or a government annuity to His promise; but the true believer finds in that promise the unfailing stay of his heart, because he knows and trusts and loves the Promiser. He delights in the thought of being absolutely shut up to God—wholly dependent upon Him. He would not, for worlds, be in any other position. The very thing which would almost drive an unbeliever out of his senses is to the Christian—the man of faith—the very deepest joy of his heart. The language of such an one will ever be, "My soul, wait thou *only* upon God; for my expectation is from Him. He *only* is my rock." Blessed position! precious portion! May the reader know it as a divine reality, a living power, in his heart, by the mighty ministry of the Holy Ghost. Then will he be able to sit loose to earthly things. He will be able to tell the world that he is independent of it, having found all he wants, for time and eternity, in the living God and His Christ.

Thou, O Christ, art all I want;
More than all in Thee I find.

But let us specially note the provision which God makes for the stranger. It is very simple—"food and raiment." This is enough for a true stranger, as the blessed apostle says to his son Timothy, "We brought nothing into this world, and it is certain we can carry nothing out. And having food and raiment, let us be therewith content."

Let us ponder this. What a cure for restless ambition is here! what an antidote against covetousness! What a blessed deliverance from the feverish excitement of commercial life, the grasping spirit of the age in which our lot is cast! If we were only content with the divinely appointed provision for the stranger, what a different tale we should have to tell! how calm and even would be the current of our daily life! how simple our habits and tastes! how unworldly our spirit and style! what moral elevation above the self-indulgence and luxury so prevalent amongst professing Christians! We should simply eat and drink to the glory of God, and to keep the body in proper working order. To go beyond this, either in eating or drinking, is to indulge in "fleshly lusts, which war against the soul."

Alas! how much of this there is, specially in reference to drink! It is perfectly appalling to think of the consumption of intoxicating drink amongst professing Christians. It is our thorough conviction that the devil has succeeded in ruining the testimony of hundreds, and in causing them to make shipwreck of faith and a good conscience, by the use of stimulants. Thousands ruin their fortunes, ruin their families, ruin their health, ruin their souls, through the senseless, vile, and cursed desire for stimulants.

We are not going to preach a crusade against stimulants or narcotics. The wrong is not in the things themselves, but in our inordinate and sinful use of them. It not unfrequently happens that persons who fall under the horrible dominion of drink seek to lay the blame on their medical adviser, but surely no proper medical man would ever advise his patient to *indulge* in the use of stimulants. He may prescribe the use of "a *little* wine, for the stomach's sake and frequent infirmities," and he has the very highest authority for so doing; but why should this lead any one to become a drunkard? Each one is responsible to walk in the fear of God in reference to both eating and drinking. If a doctor prescribes a little nourishing food for his patient, is he to be blamed if that patient becomes a glutton? Surely not. The evil is not in the doctor's prescription, or in the stimulant or in the nourishment, but in the wretched lust of the heart.

Here, we are persuaded, lies the root of the evil; and the remedy is found in that precious grace of God which, while it bringeth salvation unto all men, teacheth those who are saved "to live *soberly,* righteously, and godly in this present world." And be it remembered that "to live soberly" means a great deal more than temperance in eating and drinking; it means this, most surely, but it takes in also the whole range of inward self-government—the government of the thoughts, the government of the temper, the government of the tongue. The grace that saves us not only *tells* us how to live, but *teaches* how to do it, and if we follow its teachings, we shall be well content with God's provision for the stranger.

It is at once interesting and edifying to notice the way in which Moses sets the divine example before the people as their model. Jehovah "loveth the stranger, in giving him food and raiment. Love ye therefore the stranger; for ye were strangers in the land of Egypt." This is very touching. They were not only to keep before their eyes the divine model, but also to remember their own past history and experience, in order that their hearts might be drawn out in sympathy and compassion toward the poor homeless stranger. It was the bounden duty and high privilege of the Israel of God to place themselves in the circumstances and enter into the feelings of others. They were to be the moral representatives of that blessed One whose people they were, and whose name was called upon them. They were to imitate Him in meeting the wants and gladdening the hearts of the fatherless, the widow, and the stranger. And if God's earthly people were called to this lovely course of action, how much more are we who are "blessed with all spiritual blessings in the heavenlies in Christ Jesus." May we abide more in His presence, and drink more into His spirit, that so we may more faithfully reflect His moral glories upon all with whom we come in contact.

The closing lines of our chapter give us a very fine summing up of the practical teaching which has been engaging our attention. "Thou shalt fear the Lord thy God; Him shalt thou serve, and to Him shalt thou cleave, and swear by His name. He is thy praise, and He is thy God, that hath done for thee these great and terrible things, which thine eyes have seen. Thy fathers went down into Egypt with threescore and ten persons, and now the Lord hath made thee as the stars of heaven for multitude" (ver. 20-22).

How thoroughly bracing is all this to the moral being! This binding of the heart to the Lord Himself by means of all that He is, and all His wondrous actings and gracious ways, is unspeakably precious. It is, we may truly say, the secret spring of all true devotedness. God grant that the writer and the reader may abidingly realize its motive power.

---

## *CHAPTER 11*

"THEREFORE thou shalt love the Lord thy God, and keep His charge, and His statutes, and His judgments, and His commandments, *alway.* And know ye this day; for I speak not with your children which have not known, and which have not seen the chastisements of the Lord your God, His greatness, His mighty hand, and His stretched-out arm, and His miracles, and His acts, which He did in the midst of Egypt unto Pharaoh the king of Egypt, and unto all his land; and what He did unto the army of Egypt, unto their horses, and to their chariots; how He made the water of the Red Sea to overflow them as they pursued after you, and how the Lord hath destroyed them unto this day; and what He did unto you in the wilderness, until ye came into this place; and what He did unto Dathan and Abiram, the sons of Eliab, the son of Reuben; how the earth opened her mouth, and swallowed them up, and their households, and their tents, and all the substance that was in their possession, in the midst of all Israel; but your eyes have seen all the great acts of the Lord which He did."

Moses felt it to be of the very highest importance that all the mighty acts of Jehovah should be kept prominently before the hearts of the people, and deeply engraved on the tablets of their memory. The poor human mind is vagrant, and the heart volatile, and notwithstanding all that Israel had seen of the solemn judgments of God upon Egypt and upon Pharaoh, they were in danger of forgetting them, and losing the impression which they were designed and eminently fitted to make upon them.

It may be we feel disposed to wonder how Israel could ever forget the impressive scenes of their history in Egypt from first to last—the descent of their fathers thither as a mere handful, their steady growth and progress as a people, spite of formidable difficulties and hindrances, so that from the insignificant few, they had become, by the good hand of their God upon them, as the stars of heaven for multitude.

And then those ten plagues upon the land of Egypt! How full of awful solemnity! how pre-eminently calculated to impress the heart with a sense of the mighty power of God, the utter impotency and insignificance of man, in all his boasted wisdom, strength, and glory, and the egregious folly of his attempting to set himself up against the almighty God! What was all the power of Pharaoh and of Egypt in the presence of the Lord God of Israel? In one hour all was plunged into hopeless ruin and destruction. All the chariots of Egypt, all the pomp and glory, the valor and might, of that ancient and far-famed nation—all was overwhelmed in the depths of the sea.

And why? Because they had presumed to meddle with the Israel of God; they had dared to set themselves in opposition to the eternal purpose and counsel of the Most High. They sought to crush those on whom He had set His love. He had sworn to bless the seed of Abraham, and no power of earth or hell could possibly annul His oath. Pharaoh, in his pride and hardness of heart, attempted to countervail the divine actings, but he only meddled to his own destruction. His land was shaken to its very centre, and himself and his mighty army overthrown in the Red Sea, a solemn example to all who should ever attempt to stand in the way of Jehovah's purpose to bless the seed of Abraham His friend.

Nor was it merely what Jehovah had done to Egypt and to Pharaoh that the people were called to remember, but also what He had done amongst themselves. How soul-subduing the judgment upon Dathan and Abiram and their households! How awful the thought of the earth opening her mouth and swallowing them up! And for what? For their rebellion against the divine appointment. In the history given in Numbers, Korah, the Levite, is the prominent character; but here, he is omitted, and the two Reubenites are named—two members of the congregation, because Moses is seeking to act on the whole body of the people by setting before them the terrible consequence of self-will in two of their number—two ordinary members, as we should say, and not merely a privileged Levite.

In a word, then, whether the attention was called to the divine actings without or within, abroad or at home, it was all for the purpose of impressing their hearts and minds with a deep sense of the moral importance of obedience. This was the one grand aim of all the rehearsals, all the comments, all the exhortations, of the faithful servant of God who was so soon to be removed from their midst. For this, he ranges over their history for centuries, culling, grouping, commenting, taking up this fact and omitting that, as guided by the Spirit of God. The journey down to Egypt, the sojourn there, the heavy judgments upon the self-willed Pharaoh, the exodus, the passage through the sea, the scenes in the wilderness, and specially the awful fate of the two rebellious Reubenites—all is brought to bear, with marvelous force and clearness, upon the conscience of the people, in order to strengthen the basis of Jehovah's claim upon their unqualified obedience to His holy commandments.

"Therefore shall ye *keep all the commandments* which I command you this day, *that ye may be strong,* and go in and possess the land, whither ye go to possess it; and that ye may prolong your days in the land, which the Lord sware unto your fathers to give unto them and to their seed, a land that floweth with milk and honey."

Let the reader note the beautiful moral link between those two clauses—"keep *all* the commandments"—"that ye may be strong." There is great strength gained by unreserved obedience to the Word of God. It will not do to pick and choose. We are prone to this—prone to take up certain commandments and precepts which suit ourselves; but this is really self-will. What right have we to select such and such precepts from the Word, and neglect others? None whatever. To do so is, in principle, simply self-will and rebellion. What business has a servant to decide as to which of his master's commands he will obey? Surely none whatever; each commandment stands clothed with the master's authority, and therefore claims the servant's attention; and, we may add, the more implicitly the servant obeys, the more he bends his respectful attention to every one of his master's commands, be it ever so trivial, the more does he strengthen himself in his position and grow in his master's confidence and esteem. Every master loves and values an obedient, faithful, devoted servant. We all know what a comfort it is to have a servant whom we can trust—one who finds his delight in carrying out our every wish, and who does not require perpetual looking after, but knows his duty and attends to it.

Now, ought we not to seek to refresh the heart of our blessed Master, by a loving obedience to all His commandments? Only think what a privilege it is to be allowed to give joy to the heart of that blessed One who loved us and gave Himself for us. It is something wonderful that poor creatures such as we can in any way refresh the heart of Jesus; yet so it is, blessed be His name. He delights in our keeping His commandments; and assuredly the thought of this should stir our whole moral being, and lead us to study His Word, in order to find out, more and more, what His commandments are, so that we may do them.

We are forcibly reminded, by those words of Moses which we have just quoted, of the apostle's prayer for "the saints and faithful brethren in Christ at Colosse." "For this cause we also, since the day we heard it, do not cease to pray for you, and to desire that ye might be filled with the knowledge of His will in all wisdom and spiritual understanding; that ye might walk worthy of the Lord *unto all pleasing,* being fruitful in every good work, and *increasing in the knowledge of God; strengthened with all might,* according to His glorious power, unto all patience and long-suffering with joyfulness; giving thanks unto the Father, which hath made us meet to be partakers of the inheritance of the saints in light; who hath delivered us from the power of darkness, and hath translated us into the kingdom of the Son of His love; in whom we have redemption through His blood, the forgiveness of sins" (Col. 1:9-14).

Making allowance for the difference between the earthly and the heavenly—between Israel and the Church, there is a striking similarity between the words of the lawgiver and the words of the apostle. Both together are eminently fitted to set forth the beauty and preciousness of a willing-hearted, loving obedience. It is precious to the Father, precious to Christ, precious to the Holy Ghost; and this surely ought to be enough to create and strengthen in our hearts the desire to be filled with the knowledge of His will, that so we might walk worthy of Him to all pleasing, being fruitful *in every good work,* and increasing in the knowledge of God. It should lead us to a more diligent study of the Word of God, so that we might be ever finding out more and more of our Lord's mind and will, learning what is well-pleasing to Him, and looking to Him for grace to do it. Thus should our hearts be kept near to Him, and we should find an ever-deepening interest in searching the Scriptures, not merely to grow in the knowledge of truth, but in the knowledge of God, the knowledge of Christ—the deep, personal, experimental knowledge of all that is treasured up in that blessed One who is the fullness of the Godhead bodily. Oh, may the Spirit of God, by His most precious and powerful ministry, awaken in us a more intense desire to know and to do the will of our blessed Lord and Saviour Jesus Christ, that thus we may refresh His loving heart and be well-pleasing to Him in all things.

We must now turn, for a moment, to the lovely picture of the promised land which Moses holds up before the eyes of the people. "For the land whither thou goest in to possess it, is not as the land of Egypt, from whence ye came out, where thou sowedst thy seed, and wateredst it with thy foot, as a garden of herbs; but the land whither ye go to possess it, is a land of hills and valleys, and drinketh water of the rain of heaven; a land which the Lord thy God careth for; the eyes of the Lord thy God are always upon it, for the beginning of the year even unto the end of the year" (ver. 10-12).

What a vivid contrast between Egypt and Canaan! Egypt had no rain from heaven; it was all human effort there. Not so in the Lord's land; the human foot could do nothing there, nor was there any need, for the blessed rain from heaven dropped upon it; Jehovah Himself cared for it and watered it with the early and latter rain. The land of Egypt was dependent upon its own resources; the land of Canaan was wholly dependent upon God—upon what came down from heaven. "My river is mine own," was the language of Egypt; "the river of God" was the hope of Canaan. The habit in Egypt was to water with the foot; the habit in Canaan was to look up to heaven.

We have in the sixty-fifth psalm a lovely statement of the condition of things in the Lord's land, as viewed by the eye of faith. "Thou visitest the earth, and waterest it; Thou greatly enrichest it with the river of God, which is full of water; Thou preparest them corn, when Thou hast so provided for it. Thou waterest the ridges thereof abundantly; Thou settlest the furrows thereof; Thou makest it soft with showers; Thou blessest the springing thereof. Thou crownest the year with Thy goodness, and Thy paths drop fatness. They drop upon the pastures of the wilderness; and the little hills rejoice on every side. The pastures are clothed with flocks; the valleys also are covered over with corn; they shout for joy, they also sing" (ver. 9-13).

How perfectly beautiful! Only think of God watering the ridges and settling the furrows! think of His stooping down to do the work of a husbandman for His people! Yes, and delighting to do it! It was the joy of His heart to pour His sunbeams and His refreshing showers upon the "hills and valleys" of His beloved people. It was refreshing to His spirit, as it was to the praise of His name, to see the vine, the fig-tree, and the olive flourishing, the valleys covered with the golden grain, and the rich pastures covered with flocks of sheep.

Thus it should ever have been, and thus it would have been, had Israel only walked in simple obedience to the holy law of God. "It shall come to pass, if ye shall hearken diligently unto My commandments which I command you this day, *to love the Lord your God, and to serve Him with all your heart and with all your soul,* that I will give you the rain of your land in his due season, the first rain and the latter rain, that thou mayest gather in thy corn, and thy wine, and thine oil. And I will send grass in thy fields for thy cattle, that thou mayest eat and be full" (ver. 13-15).

Thus the matter stood between the God of Israel and the Israel of God. Nothing could be simpler, nothing more blessed. It was Israel's high and holy privilege to love and serve Jehovah; it was Jehovah's prerogative to bless and prosper Israel. Happiness and fruitfulness were to be the sure accompaniments of obedience. The people and their land were wholly dependent upon God. All their supplies were to come down from heaven; and hence, so long as they walked in loving obedience, the copious showers dropped upon their fields and vineyards, the heavens dropped down the dew, and the earth responded in fruitfulness and blessing.

But, on the other hand, when Israel forgot the Lord, and forsook His precious commandments, the heaven became brass and the earth iron; barrenness, desolation, famine, and misery were the melancholy accompaniments of disobedience. How could it be otherwise? "If ye be willing and obedient, ye shall eat the good of the land; but if ye refuse and rebel, ye shall be devoured with the sword; for the mouth of the Lord hath spoken it."

Now, in all this there is deep, practical instruction for the Church of God. Although we are not under law, we are called to obedience; and as we are enabled, through grace, to yield a loving, hearty obedience, we are blessed in our own spiritual state, our souls are watered, refreshed, and strengthened, and we bring forth the fruits of righteousness which are by Jesus Christ to the glory and praise of God.

The reader may refer with much profit, in connection with this great practical subject, to the opening of John 15—a most precious Scripture, and one demanding the earnest attention of every true-hearted child of God. "I am the true vine, and My Father is the Husbandman. Every branch in Me that beareth not fruit He taketh away; and every branch that beareth fruit, He purgeth it, *that it may bring forth more fruit.* Now ye are clean through the word which I have spoken unto you. Abide in Me, and I in you. As the branch cannot bear fruit of itself, except it abide in the vine; no more can ye, except ye abide in Me. I am the vine, ye are the branches: he that abideth in Me, and I in him, the same bringeth forth much fruit; for without [or apart from] Me ye can do nothing. If a man abide not in Me, he is cast forth as a branch, and is withered; and men gather them, and cast them into the fire, and they are burned. If ye abide in Me, and My words abide in you, ye shall ask what ye will, and it shall be done unto you. Herein is My Father glorified that ye bear much fruit; so shall ye be My disciples. As the Father hath loved Me, so have I loved you; continue ye in My love. *If ye keep My commandments, ye shall abide in My love;* even as I have kept My Father's commandments, and abide in His love" (ver. 1-10).

This weighty passage of Scripture has suffered immensely through theological controversy and religious strife. It is as plain as it is practical, and only needs to be taken as it stands, in its own divine simplicity. If we seek to import into it what does not belong to it, we mar its integrity and miss its true application. In it we have Christ, the true vine, taking the place of Israel, who had become to Jehovah the degenerate plant of a strange vine. The scene of the parable is obviously earth, and not heaven; we do not think of a vine and a husbandman (γεωργος) in heaven. Besides, our Lord says, "I *am* the true vine." The figure is very distinct. It is not the head and the members, but a tree and its branches. Moreover, the subject of the parable is as distinct as the parable itself; it is not eternal life, but fruit-bearing. If this were borne in mind, it would greatly help to an understanding of this much-misunderstood passage of Scripture.

In a word, then, we learn from the figure of the vine and its branches that the true secret of fruitbearing is, to abide in Christ, and the way to abide in Christ is, to keep His precious commandments. "If ye keep My commandments, ye shall abide in My love; even as I have kept My Father's commandments, and abide in His love." This makes it all so simple. The way to bear fruit in season is, to abide in the love of Christ, and this abiding is proved by our treasuring up His commandments in our hearts and yielding a loving obedience to every one of them. It is not running hither and thither in the mere energy of nature; it is not the excitement of mere fleshly zeal displaying itself in spasmodic efforts after devotedness. No; it is something quite different from all this; it is the calm and holy obedience of the heart—a loving obedience to our own beloved Lord, which refreshes His heart and glorifies His name.

> How blest are they who still abide
> Close sheltered by Thy watchful side;
> Who life and strength from Thee receive,
> And with Thee move and in Thee live.

May we apply our hearts diligently to this great subject of fruit-bearing. May we better understand what it is. We are apt to make great mistakes about it. It is to be feared that much—very much of what passes for fruit would not be accredited in the divine presence. God cannot own any thing as fruit which is not the direct result of abiding in Christ. We may earn a great name among our fellows for zeal, energy, and devotedness; we may be abundant in labors, in every department of the work; we may acquit ourselves as great travelers, great preachers, earnest workers in the vineyard, great philanthropists and moral reformers; we may spend a princely fortune in promoting all the great objects of Christian benevolence, and all the while not produce a single cluster of fruit acceptable to the Father's heart.

On the other hand, it may be our lot to pass the time of our sojourn here in obscurity and retirement from human gaze; we may be little accounted of by the world and the professing church; we may seem to leave but little mark on the sands of time; but if only we abide in Christ, abide in His love, treasure up His precious words in our hearts, and yield ourselves up to a holy and loving obedience to His commandments, then shall our fruit be in season, and our Father will be glorified, and we shall grow in the experimental knowledge of our Lord and Saviour Jesus Christ.

We shall now look for a moment at the remainder of our chapter, in which Moses, in words of intense earnestness, presses upon the congregation the urgent need of watchfulness and diligence in reference to all the statutes and judgments of the Lord their God. The beloved and faithful servant of God, and true lover of the people, was unwearied in his efforts to brace them up to that whole-hearted obedience which he knew to be at once the spring of their happiness and their fruitfulness; and just as our blessed Lord warns His disciples by setting before them the solemn judgment of the unfruitful branch, so does Moses warn the people as to the sure and terrible consequences of disobedience.

"Take heed to yourselves, that *your heart be not deceived*, and ye turn aside, and serve other gods, and worship them." Sad progress downward: The heart deceived. This is the beginning of all declension. "And ye turn aside." The feet are sure to follow the heart. Hence the deep need of keeping the heart with all diligence; it is the citadel of the whole moral being, and so long as it is kept for the Lord, the enemy can gain no advantage; but when once it is surrendered, all is really gone—there is the turning aside; the secret departure of the heart is proved by the practical ways—"other gods" are served and worshiped. The descent down along the inclined plane is terribly rapid.

"And then"—mark the sure and solemn consequences—"the Lord's wrath be kindled against you, and He *shut up the heaven,* that there be no rain, and that the land yield not her fruit; and ye perish quickly from off the good land which the Lord giveth you." What barrenness and desolation there must be when heaven is shut up! No refreshing showers coming down, no dew-drops falling, no communication between the heaven and the earth. Alas! how often had Israel tasted the awful reality of this! "He turneth rivers into a wilderness, and the water-springs into dry ground; a fruitful land into barrenness, for the wickedness of them that dwell therein."

And may we not see in the barren land and the desolate wilderness an apt and striking illustration of a soul out of communion through disobedience to the precious commandments of Christ? Such an one has no refreshing communications with heaven—no showers coming down—no unfoldings of the preciousness of Christ to the heart—no sweet ministrations of an ungrieved Spirit to the soul; the Bible seems a sealed book; all is dark, dreary, and desolate. Oh, there cannot be any thing more miserable in all this world than a soul in this condition. May the writer and the reader never experience it. May we bend our ears to the fervent exhortations addressed by Moses to the congregation of Israel. They are most seasonable, most healthful, most needful, in this day of cold indifferentism and positive willfulness. They set before us the divine antidote against the special evils to which the Church of God is exposed at this very hour—an hour critical and solemn beyond all human conception.

"Therefore shall ye lay up these *my words* in *your heart* and in *your soul*, and bind them for a sign upon your hand, that they may be as frontlets between your eyes. And ye shall teach them your children, speaking of them when thou sittest in thine house, and when thou walkest by the way, when thou liest down, and when thou risest up; and thou shalt write them upon the doorposts of thine house, and upon thy gates, that your days may be multiplied, and the days of your children, in the land which the Lord sware unto your fathers to give them, as the days of heaven upon the earth."

Blessed days! Oh, how ardently the large, loving heart of Moses longed that the people might enjoy many such days! And how simple the condition! Truly nothing could be simpler, nothing more precious. It was not a heavy yoke laid upon them, but the sweet privilege of treasuring up the precious commandments of the Lord their God in their hearts, and breathing the very atmosphere of His holy Word. All was to hinge upon this. All the blessings of the land of Canaan—that goodly, highly favored land, a land flowing with milk and honey, a land on which Jehovah's eyes ever rested in loving interest and tender care—all its precious fruits, all its rare privileges, were to be theirs in perpetuity, on the one simple condition of loving obedience to the word of their covenant-God.

"For if ye shall *diligently keep all* these commandments which I command you, to do them, *to love the Lord your God, to walk in all His ways*, and *to cleave unto* Him; then will the Lord drive out all these nations from before you, and ye shall possess greater nations and mightier than yourselves." In a word, sure and certain victory was before them, a most complete overthrow of all enemies and obstacles, a triumphal march into the promised inheritance—all secured to them on the blessed ground of affectionate and reverential obedience to the most precious statutes and judgments that had ever been addressed to the human heart—statutes and judgments every one of which was but the very voice of their most gracious Deliverer.

"Every place whereon the soles of your feet shall tread shall be yours; from the wilderness and Lebanon, from the river, the river Euphrates, even unto the uttermost sea, shall your coast be. There shall no man be able to stand before you; for the Lord your God shall lay the fear of you and the dread of you upon all the land that ye shall tread upon, as He hath said unto you."

Here was the divine side of the question. The whole land, in its length, breadth, and fullness, lay before them; they had but to take possession of it, as the free gift of God; it was for them simply to plant the foot, in artless, appropriating faith, upon that fair inheritance which sovereign grace had bestowed upon them. All this we see made good in the book of Joshua, as we read in chapter 11. "So Joshua took *the whole land*, according to all that the Lord said unto Moses; and Joshua gave it for an inheritance unto Israel, according to their divisions by their tribes. And the land rested from war" (ver. 23).*

But alas! there was the human side of the question as well as the divine. Canaan as promised by Jehovah and made good by the faith of Joshua was one thing, and Canaan as possessed by Israel was quite another. Hence the vast difference between Joshua and Judges. In Joshua, we see the infallible faithfulness of God to His promise; in Judges, we see Israel's miserable failure from the very outset. God pledged His immutable word that not a man should be able to stand before them, and the sword of Joshua—type of the great Captain of our salvation—made good this pledge in its every jot and tittle; but the book of Judges records the melancholy fact that Israel failed to drive out the enemy—failed to take possession of the divine grant in all its royal magnificence.

What then? Is the promise of God made of none effect? Nay, verily; but the utter failure of man is made apparent. At "Gilgal," the banner of victory floated over the twelve tribes, with their invincible captain at their head; at "Bochim," the weepers had to mourn over Israel's lamentable defeat.

Have we any difficulty in understanding the difference? None whatever. We see the two things running all through the divine volume. Man fails to rise to the height of the divine revelation—fails to take possession of what grace bestows. This is as true in the history of the Church as it was in the history of Israel; in the New Testament, as well as in the Old, we have Judges as well as Joshua.

Yes, and in the history of each individual member of the Church we see the same thing. Where is the Christian, beneath the canopy of heaven, that lives up to the height of his spiritual privileges? Where is the child of God who has not to mourn over his humiliating failure in grasping and making good practically the high and holy privileges of his calling of God? But does this make the truth of God of none effect? No; blessed forever be His holy name. His Word holds good in all its divine integrity and eternal stability. Just as in Israel's case, the land of promise lay before them in all its fair proportions and divinely given attractions; and not only so, but they could count on the faithfulness and almighty power of God to bring them in and put them in full possession; so with us, we are blessed with all spiritual blessings in the heavenlies in Christ. There is absolutely no limit to the privileges connected with our standing, and as to our actual enjoyment, it is only a question of faith taking possession of all that God's sovereign grace has made ours in Christ.

We must never forget that it is the privilege of the Christian to live at the very height of the divine revelation. There is no excuse for a shallow experience or a low walk. We have no right whatever to say that we cannot realize the fullness of our portion in Christ, that the standard is too high, the privileges are too vast, that we cannot expect

*No doubt it was in faith that Joshua took—and could take nothing less than—the whole land; but as to actual possession, chapter 13:1 shows there was "yet much land to be possessed."

to enjoy such marvelous blessings and dignities in our present imperfect state.

All this is downright unbelief, and should be so treated by every true Christian. The question is, Has the grace of God bestowed the privileges upon us? has the death of Christ made good our title to them? and has the Holy Ghost declared them to be the proper portion of the very feeblest member of the body of Christ? If so—and Scripture declares it is so—why should we not enjoy them? There is no hindrance on the divine side. It is the desire of the heart of God that we should enter into the fullness of our portion in Christ. Hear the earnest breathing of the inspired apostle on behalf of the saints at Ephesus and of all saints. "Wherefore I also, after I heard of your faith in the Lord Jesus, and love unto all the saints, cease not to give thanks for you, making mention of you in my prayers; that the God of our Lord Jesus Christ, the Father of glory, may give unto you the spirit of wisdom and revelation in the knowledge of Him: the eyes of your understanding being enlightened; that ye may know what is the hope of His calling, and what the riches of the glory of His inheritance in the saints, and what the exceeding greatness of His power to usward who believe, according to the working of His mighty power, which He wrought in Christ, when He raised Him from the dead, and set Him at His own right hand in the heavenlies, far above all principality, and power, and might, and dominion, and every name that is named, not only in this world, but also in that which is to come: and hath put all things under His feet, and gave Him to be the head over all things to the Church, which is His body, the fullness of Him that filleth all in all" (Eph. 1:15-23).

From this marvelous prayer we may learn how earnestly the Spirit of God desires that we should apprehend and enjoy the glorious privileges of the true Christian position. He would ever, by His precious and powerful ministry, keep our hearts up to the mark; but, alas! like Israel, we grieve Him by our sinful unbelief, and rob our own souls of incalculable blessing.

But, all praise to the God of all grace, the Father of glory, the God and Father of our Lord Jesus Christ, He will yet make good every jot and tittle of His most precious truth, both as to His earthly and heavenly people. Israel shall yet enjoy to the full all the blessings secured to them by the everlasting covenant; and the Church shall yet enter upon the perfect fruition of all that which eternal love and divine counsels have laid up for her in Christ; and not only so, but the blessed Comforter is able and willing to lead the individual believer into the present enjoyment of the hope of God's glorious calling, and the practical power of that hope, in detaching the heart from present things and separating it to God in true holiness and living devotedness.

May our hearts long more ardently after the full realization of all this, that thus we may live more as those who are finding their portion and their rest in a risen and glorified Christ. God, in His infinite goodness, grant it, for Jesus Christ's name and glory's sake.

The remaining verses of our chapter close the first division of the book of Deuteronomy, which, as the reader will notice, consists of a series of discourses addressed by Moses to the congregation of Israel—memorable discourses, most surely, in whatever way we view them. The closing sentences are, we need hardly say, in perfect keeping with the whole, and breathe the same deep-toned earnestness in reference to the subject of obedience—a subject which, as we have seen, formed the special burden on the heart of the beloved speaker in his affecting farewell addresses to the people.

"Behold, I set before you this day a blessing and a curse." How pointed and solemn is this!—"a blessing, if ye obey the commandments of the Lord your God, which I command you this day; and a curse, if ye will not obey the commandments of the Lord your God, but turn aside out of the way which I command you this day, to go after other gods, which ye have not known. And it shall come to pass, when the Lord thy God hath brought thee in unto the land whither thou goest to possess it, that thou shalt put the blessing upon Mount Gerizim, and the curse upon Mount Ebal. Are they not on the other side Jordan, by the way where the sun goeth down, in the land of the Canaanites, which dwell in the champaign over against Gilgal, beside the plains of Moreh? For ye shall pass over Jordan, to go in to possess the land which the Lord your God giveth you, and ye shall possess it, and dwell therein. *And ye shall observe to do all the statutes and judgments which I set before you this day*" (ver. 26-32).

Here we have the summing up of the whole matter. The blessing is linked on to obedience; the curse, to disobedience. Mount Gerizim stands over against Mount Ebal—fruitfulness and barrenness. We shall see, when we come to chapter 27, that Mount Gerizim and its blessings are entirely passed over. The curses of Mount Ebal fall, with awful distinctness, on Israel's ear, while terrible silence reigns on Mount Gerizim. "As many as are of the works of the law, are under the curse." The blessing of Abraham can only come on those who are on the ground of faith. But more of this by and by.

---

## *CHAPTER 12*

WE now enter upon a new section of our marvelous book. The discourses contained in the first eleven chapters having established the all-important principle of obedience, we now come to the practical application of the principle to the habits and ways of the people when settled in possession of the land. "These are the statutes and judgments which ye shall observe to do in the land which the Lord God of thy fathers giveth thee to possess it all the days that ye live upon the earth."

It is of the utmost moral importance that the heart and conscience should be brought into their true attitude in reference to divine authority, irrespective altogether of any question as to details. These will find their due place when once the heart is taught to bow down, in complete and absolute submission, to the supreme authority of the Word of God.

Now, as we have seen in our studies on the first eleven chapters, the lawgiver labors, most earnestly and faithfully, to lead the heart of Israel into this all-essential condition. He felt, to speak after the manner of men, it was of no use entering upon practical details until the grand foundation-principle of all morality was fully established in the very deepest depths of the soul. The principle is this (let us Christians apply our hearts to it): It is man's bounden duty to bow implicitly to the authority of the Word of God. It matters not, in the smallest degree, what that Word may enjoin, or whether we can see the reason of this, that, or the other institution. The one grand, all-important, and conclusive point is this: Has God spoken? If He has, that is quite enough. There is no room, no need, for any further question.

Until this point is fully established, or rather until the heart is brought directly under its full moral force, we are not in a condition to enter upon details. If self-will be allowed to operate, if blind reason be permitted to speak, the heart will send up its endless questionings; as each divine institution is laid before us, some fresh difficulty will present itself as a stumbling-block in the path of simple obedience.

What! it may be said, are we not to use our reason? If not, to what end was it given? To this we have a twofold reply. In the first place, our reason is not as it was when God gave it. We have to remember that sin has come in; man is a fallen creature; his reason, his judgment, his understanding—his whole moral being is a complete wreck; and moreover, it was the neglect of the Word of God that caused all this wreck and ruin.

And then, in the second place, we must bear in mind that if reason were in a sound condition, it would prove its soundness by bowing to the Word of God. But it is not sound; it is blind, and utterly perverted; it is not to be trusted for a moment in things spiritual, divine, or heavenly.

If this simple fact were thoroughly understood, it would settle a thousand questions and remove a thousand difficulties. It is reason that makes all the infidels. The devil whispers into man's ear, "You are endowed with reason; why not use it? It was given to be used—used in every thing; you ought not to give your assent to any thing which your reason cannot grasp. It is your chartered right as a man to submit every thing to the test of your reason; it is only for a fool or an idiot to receive, in blind credulity, all that is set before him."

What is our answer to such wily and dangerous suggestions? A very simple and conclusive one; namely, this: The Word of God is above and beyond reason altogether; it is as far above reason as God is above the creature, or heaven above earth. Hence, when God speaks, all reasonings must be cast down. If it be merely man's word, man's opinion, man's judgment, then verily reason may exert its powers; or rather, to speak more correctly, we must judge what is said by the only perfect standard—the Word of God. But if reason be set to work on the Word of God, the soul must inevitably be plunged in the thick darkness of infidelity, from which the descent to the awful blackness of atheism is but too easy.

In a word, then, we have to remember—yea, to cherish in the very deepest depths of our moral being, that the only safe ground for the soul is, divinely wrought faith in the paramount authority, divine majesty, and all-sufficiency of the Word of God. This was the ground which Moses occupied in dealing with the heart and conscience of Israel. His one grand object was, to lead the people into the attitude of profound, unqualified subjection to divine authority. Without this, all was useless. If every statute, every judgment, every precept, every institution, were to be submitted to the action of human reason, then farewell to divine authority, farewell to Scripture, farewell to certainty, farewell to peace; but, on the other hand, when the soul is led by God's Spirit into the delightful attitude of absolute and unquestioning submission to the authority of God's Word, then every one of His judgments, every one of His commandments, every sentence of His blessed book, is received as coming direct from Himself, and the most simple ordinance or institution stands invested with all the importance which His authority is fitted to impart. We may not be able to understand the full meaning or exact bearing of each statute and judgment—that is not the question; it is sufficient for us to know that it comes from God. He has spoken; this is conclusive. Till this great principle is grasped, or rather till it takes full possession of the soul, nothing is done; but when it is fully understood and submitted to, the solid foundation is laid for all true morality.

The foregoing line of thought will enable the reader to seize the connection between the chapter which now lies open before us and the preceding section of this book; and not only will it do this, but we trust it will also help him to understand the special place and bearing of the opening verses of chapter 12.

"Ye shall utterly destroy all the places wherein the nations which ye shall possess served their gods, upon the high mountains, and upon the hills, and under every green tree. And ye shall overthrow their altars, and break their pillars, and burn their groves with fire; and ye shall hew down the graven images of their gods, and destroy the names of them out of that place" (ver. 2-3).

The land was Jehovah's; they were to hold as tenants under Him, and therefore their very first duty on entering upon possession was, to demolish every trace of the old idolatry. This was absolutely indispensable. It might, according to human reason, seem to be very intolerant to act in this way toward other people's religion. We reply, without any hesitation, Yes, it was intolerant; for how could the one only true and living God be otherwise than intolerant of all false gods and false worship? To suppose for a moment that He could permit the worship of idols in His land would be to suppose that He could deny Himself, which were simply blasphemy.

Let us not be misunderstood. It is not that God does not bear with the world, in His long-suffering mercy. It seems hardly needful to state this, with the history of well-nigh six thousand years of divine forbearance before our eyes. Blessed forever be His holy name, He has borne with the world most marvelously from the days of Noah, and He still bears with it, though stained with the guilt of crucifying His beloved Son.

All this is plain, but it leaves wholly untouched the great principle laid down in our chapter. Israel had to learn that they were about to take possession of the Lord's land, and that, as His tenants, their first and indispensable duty was, to obliterate every trace of idolatry. To them there was to be but "the one God." His name was called upon them. They were His people, and He could not permit them to have fellowship with demons. "Thou shalt worship the Lord thy God; and Him *only* shalt thou serve."

This might, in the judgment of the uncircumcised nations around, seem very intolerant, very narrow, very bigoted. They indeed might boast of their freedom, and glory in the broad platform of their worship which admitted "gods many and lords many." It might, according to their thinking, argue greater breadth of mind to let every one think for himself in matters of religion, and choose his own object of worship, and his own mode of worshiping also; or, still further, it might give evidence of a more advanced condition of civilization, greater polish and refinement, to erect, as in Rome, a Pantheon, in which all the gods of heathendom might find a place. "What did it matter about the form of a man's religion, or the object of his worship, provided he himself were sincere? All would be sure to come right in the end; the great point for all was, to attend to material progress, to help on national prosperity as the surest means of securing individual interests. Of course, it is all right for every man to have some religion, but as to the form of that religion, it is immaterial. The great question is, what you are yourself, not what your religion is."

All this, we can well conceive, would admirably suit the carnal mind, and be very popular amongst the uncircumcised nations; but as for Israel, they had to remember that one commanding sentence, "The Lord thy God is one God"; and again, "Thou shalt have none other gods before Me." This was to be their religion; the platform of their worship was to be as wide and as narrow as the one true and living God, their Creator and Redeemer. That, assuredly, was broad enough for every true worshiper—every member of the circumcised assembly—all whose high and holy privilege it was to belong to the Israel of God. They were not to concern themselves with the opinions or observations of the uncircumcised nations around. What were they worth? Not the weight of a feather. What could they know about the claims of the God of Israel upon His circumcised people? Just nothing. Were they competent to decide as to the proper breadth of Israel's platform? Clearly not; they were wholly ignorant of the subject. Hence their thoughts, reasonings, arguments, and objections were perfectly worthless, not to be listened to for a moment. It was Israel's one, simple, bounden duty to bow down to the supreme and absolute authority of the word of God; and that word insisted upon the complete abolition of every trace of idolatry from the goodly land which they were privileged to hold as tenants under Him.

But not only was it incumbent upon Israel to abolish all the places in which the heathen had worshiped their gods—this they were solemnly bound to do, most surely; but there was more than this. The heart might readily conceive the thought of doing away with idolatry in the various places, and setting up the altar of the true God instead—this might seem to be the right course to adopt; but God thought differently. "Ye shall not do so unto the Lord your God. But unto the place which the Lord your God shall choose out of all your tribes, to put His name there, even *unto His habitations* shall ye seek, and thither thou shalt come; and thither ye shall bring your burnt-offerings, and your sacrifices, and your tithes, and heave-offerings of your hand, and your vows, and your free-will offerings, and the firstlings of your herds and of your flocks; and *there ye shall eat before the Lord your God*; and ye shall rejoice in all that ye put your hand unto, ye and your households, wherein the Lord thy God hath blessed thee."

Here a great cardinal truth is unfolded to the congregation of Israel. They were to have one place of worship—a place chosen of God, and not of man. His habitation—the place of His presence—was to be Israel's grand centre; thither they were to come with their sacrifices and their offerings, and there they were to offer their worship, and find their common joy.

Does this seem exclusive? Of course it was exclusive; how else could it be? If God was pleased to select a spot in which He would take up His abode in the midst of His redeemed people, surely they were, of necessity, shut up to that spot as their place of worship. This was divine exclusiveness, and every pious soul would delight in it. Every true lover of Jehovah would say, with all his heart, "Lord, I have loved *the habitation of Thy house*, and the place where Thine honor dwelleth"; and again, "How amiable are Thy tabernacles, O Lord of hosts! My soul longeth, yea, even fainteth for the courts of the Lord; my heart and my flesh crieth out for the living God. . . . Blessed are they that dwell *in Thy house;* they will be still praising Thee. . . . A day *in Thy courts* is better than a thousand. I had rather be a door-keeper *in the house of My God,* than to dwell in the tents of wickedness" (Ps. 26;84).

Here was *the* one grand and all-important point. It was the dwelling-place of Jehovah which was dear to the heart of every true Israelite. Restless self-will might desire to run hither and thither, the poor vagrant heart might long for some change, but, for the heart that loved God, any change from the place of His presence, the place where He had recorded His blessed name, could only be a change for the worse. The truly devout worshiper could find satisfaction and delight, blessing and rest, only in the place of the divine presence; and this, on the double ground—the authority of His precious Word and the powerful attractions of His presence. Such an one could never think of going anywhere else. Whither could he go? There was but one altar, one habitation, one God—that was the place for every right-minded, every true-hearted Israelite. To think of any other place of worship would be not only a departure from the word of Jehovah, but from His holy habitation.

This great principle is largely insisted upon throughout the whole of our chapter. Moses reminds the people that from the moment they entered Jehovah's land there was to be an end to all the irregularity and self-will that had characterized them in the plains of Moab, or in the wilderness. "Ye shall not do after all the things that we do here this day, *every man whatsoever is right in his own eyes.* For ye are not as yet come to the rest and to the inheritance, which the Lord your God giveth you. *But when ye go over Jordan*, and dwell in the land which the Lord your God giveth you to inherit, and *when He giveth you rest from all your enemies round about, so that ye dwell in safety*; then there shall be a place *which the Lord your God shall choose*, to cause His name to dwell *there; thither* shall ye bring all that I command you. . . .Take heed to thyself that thou offer not thy burnt-offerings *in every place that thou seest*; but *in the place which the Lord shall choose* in one of thy tribes, there thou shalt offer thy burnt-offerings, and there thou shalt do all that I command thee" (ver. 4-14).

Thus, not only in the object, but also in the place and mode of Israel's worship, they were absolutely shut up to the commandment of Jehovah. Self-pleasing—self-choosing—self-will was to have an end, in reference to the worship of God, the moment they crossed the river of death and, as a redeemed people, planted their foot on their divinely given inheritance. Once there, in the enjoyment of Jehovah's land, and the rest which the land afforded, obedience to His word was to be their reasonable, their intelligent service. Things might be allowed to pass in the wilderness which could not be tolerated in Canaan. The higher the range of privilege, the higher the responsibility and the standard of action.

Now, it may be that our broad thinkers, and those who contend for freedom of will and freedom of action, for the right of private judgment in matters of religion, for liberality of mind and catholicity of spirit, will be ready to pronounce all this which has been engaging our attention extremely narrow, and wholly unsuited to our enlightened age, and to men of intelligence and education.

What is our answer to all who adopt this form of speech? A very simple and conclusive one; it is this: Has not God a right to prescribe the mode in which His people should worship Him? Had He not a perfect right to fix the place where He would meet His people Israel? Surely we must either deny His existence, or admit His absolute and unquestionable right to set forth His will as to how, when, and where His people should approach Him. Will any one, however educated and enlightened, deny this? Is it a proof of high culture, refinement, breadth of mind, or catholicity of spirit to deny God His rights?

If then God has a right to command, is it narrowness or bigotry for His people to obey? This is just the point. It is, in our judgment, as simple as any thing can be. We are thoroughly convinced that the only true breadth of mind, largeness of heart, and catholicity of spirit is, to obey the commandments of God. Hence, when Israel were commanded to go to one place and there offer their sacrifices, it most assuredly was neither bigotry nor narrowness on their part to go thither, and to refuse, with holy decision, to go any where else. Uncircumcised Gentiles might go where they pleased; the Israel of God were to go *only* to the place of His appointment.

Oh, what an unspeakable privilege for all who loved God and loved one another to assemble themselves at the place where He recorded His name! and what touching grace shines in the fact of His desiring to gather His people around Himself from time to time! Did that fact infringe their personal rights and domestic privileges? Nay, it enhanced them immensely. God, in His infinite goodness, took care of this. It was His delight to minister the joy and blessing of His people, privately, socially, and publicly. Hence we read, "When the Lord thy God shall enlarge thy border, as He hath promised thee, and thou shalt say, I will eat flesh, because thy soul longeth to eat flesh, thou mayest eat flesh, whatsoever thy soul lusteth after. If the place which the Lord thy God hath chosen to put His name there be too far from thee, then thou shalt kill of thy herd and of thy flock, *which the Lord hath given thee*, as I have commanded thee, and thou shalt eat in thy gates whatsoever thy soul lusteth after. Even as the roebuck and the hart is eaten, so thou shalt eat them; the unclean and the clean shall eat of them alike."

Here we have, most surely, a broad margin afforded by the goodness and tender mercy of God for the fullest range of personal and family enjoyment. The only restriction was in reference to the blood. "Only be sure that thou eat not the blood; *for the blood is the life,* and thou mayest not eat the life with the flesh. Thou shalt not eat it; thou shalt pour it upon the earth as water. Thou shalt not eat it; that it may go well with thee, and with thy children after thee, when thou shalt do that which is right in the sight of the Lord."

This was a great cardinal principle under the law, to which reference has been made in our *Notes on Leviticus.* How far Israel understood it is not the question; they were to obey, that it might go well with them and with their children after them. They were to own, in this matter, the solemn rights of God.

Having made this exception in reference to personal and family habits, the lawgiver returns to the all-important subject of their public worship. "Only thy holy things which thou hast, and thy vows, thou shalt take, *and go unto the place which the Lord shall choose*; and thou shalt offer thy burnt-offerings, *the flesh and the blood*, upon the altar of the Lord thy God; and the blood of the sacrifices shall be poured out upon the altar of the Lord thy God, and thou shalt eat the flesh" (ver. 26-27).

If reason, or self-will, were permitted to speak, it might say, Why must we all go to this one place? Can we not have an altar at home? or, at least, an altar in each principal town, or in the centre of each tribe? The conclusive answer is, God has commanded otherwise; this is enough for every true Israelite. Even though we may not be able, by reason of our ignorance, to see the why or the wherefore, simple obedience is our obvious and bounden duty. It may be, moreover, that, as we cheerfully tread the path of obedience, light will break in upon our souls as to the reason, and we shall find abundant blessing in doing that which is well-pleasing to the Lord our God.

Yes, this is the proper method of answering all the reasonings and questionings of the carnal mind, which is not subject to the law of God, neither indeed can be. Light is sure to break in upon our souls as we tread, with a lowly mind, the sacred path of obedience; and not only so, but untold blessing will flow into the heart in that conscious nearness to God which is only known to those who lovingly keep His most precious commandments. Are we called upon to explain to carnal objectors and infidels our reasons for doing this or that? Most certainly not; that is no part of our business: it would be time and labor lost, inasmuch as objectors and reasoners are wholly incapable of understanding or appreciating our reasons.

For example, in the matter now under our consideration, could a carnal mind—an unbeliever—a mere child of nature understand why Israel's twelve tribes were commanded to worship at one altar, to gather in one place, to cluster around one centre? Not in the smallest degree. The grand moral reason of such a lovely institution lies far away beyond his ken.

But to the spiritual mind, all is as plain as it is beautiful. Jehovah would gather His beloved people around Himself, from time to time, that they might rejoice together before Him, and that He might have His own peculiar joy in them. Was not this something most precious? Assuredly it was, to all who really loved the Lord.

No doubt, if the heart were cold and careless toward God, it would matter little about the place of worship—all places would be alike; but we may set it down as a fixed principle that every loyal, loving heart, from Dan to Beersheba, would rejoice to flock to the place where Jehovah had recorded His name, and where He had appointed to meet His people. "I was glad when they said unto me, Let us go unto the house of the Lord. Our feet shall stand within thy gates, O Jerusalem [God's centre for Israel]. Jerusalem is builded as a city that is *compact together;* whither the tribes go up, the tribes of the Lord, *unto the testimony of Israel,* to give thanks unto the name of the Lord. For *there*"—and no where else—"are set thrones of judgment, the thrones of the house of David. Pray for the peace of Jerusalem: they shall prosper that love thee. Peace be within thy walls, and prosperity within thy palaces. *For my brethren and companions' sakes,* I will now say, Peace be within thee. Because of the house of the Lord our God I will seek thy good" (Ps. 122).

Here we have the lovely breathings of a heart that loved the habitation of the God of Israel—His blessed centre—the gathering-place of Israel's twelve tribes—that hallowed spot which was associated, in the mind of every true Israelite, with all that was bright and joyous in connection with the worship of Jehovah and the communion of His people.

We shall have occasion to refer to this most delightful theme again when we come to study the sixteenth chapter of our book, and shall draw this section to a close by quoting for the reader the last paragraph of the chapter before us.

"When the Lord thy God shall cut off the nations from before thee, whither thou goest to possess them, and thou succeedest them, and dwellest in their land; take heed to thyself, that thou be not snared by following them, after that they be destroyed from before thee; and that thou inquire not after their gods, saying, How did these nations serve their gods? even so will I do likewise. Thou shalt not do so unto the Lord thy God: for every abomination to the Lord, which He hateth, have they done unto their gods; for even their sons and their daughters they have burnt in the fire to their gods. *What thing soever I command you, observe to do it: thou shalt not add thereto, nor diminish from it*" (ver. 29-32).

The precious Word of God was to form a sacred inclosure round about His people, within which they might enjoy His presence, and delight themselves in the abundance of His mercy and loving-kindness, and wherein they were to be entirely apart from all that was offensive to Him whose presence was to be, at once, their glory, their joy, and their grand moral safeguard from every snare and every abomination.

Alas! they did not abide within that inclosure; they speedily broke down the walls thereof, and wandered away from the holy commandment of God. They did the very things they were told not to do, and they have had to reap the terrible consequences. But more of this and of their future by and by.

---

## *CHAPTER 13*

THIS chapter abounds in most weighty principles. It consists of three distinct sections, each one of which claims our deep attention. We must not attempt to weaken the admonitory force of such a Scripture, or turn aside its keen edge, by saying that it does not apply to Christians—that it is wholly Jewish in its scope and application. No doubt, primarily, it was addressed to Israel; this is so obvious as not to admit of a question. But let us not forget that it was "written for our learning," and not only so, but the more closely we study it, the more we shall see that its teaching is of universal importance.

"If there arise among you a prophet, or a dreamer of dreams, and giveth thee a sign or a wonder, and the sign or the wonder come to pass, whereof he spake unto thee, saying, Let us go after other gods, which thou hast not known, and let us serve them: thou shalt not hearken unto the words of that prophet, or that dreamer of dreams; for the Lord your God proveth you, to know whether ye love the Lord your God with all your heart and with all your soul. Ye shall walk after the Lord your God, and fear Him, and keep His commandments, and obey His voice, and ye shall serve Him, and cleave unto Him. And that prophet, or that dreamer of dreams, shall be put to death; because he hath spoken to turn you away from the Lord your God, which brought you out of the land of Egypt, and redeemed you out of the house of bondage, to thrust thee out of the way which the Lord thy God commanded thee to walk in. So shalt thou put the evil away from the midst of thee" (ver. 1-5).

Here we have divine provision made for all cases of false teaching and false religious influence. We all know how easily the poor human heart is led astray by any thing in the shape of a sign or a wonder, and especially when such things stand connected with religion. This is not confined to the nation of Israel; we see it every where and at all times. Any thing supernatural, any thing involving an infringement of what are called the ordinary laws of nature, is almost sure to act powerfully on the human mind. A prophet rising up in the midst of the people and confirming his teaching by miracles, signs, and wonders, would be almost sure to get a hearing and obtain an influence.

In this way, Satan has worked in all ages, and he will work yet more powerfully, at the end of this present age, in order to deceive and lead to their everlasting destruction those who will not hearken to the precious truth of the gospel. "The mystery of iniquity," which has been working in the professing church for eighteen centuries, will be headed up in the person of "*that Wicked* whom the Lord shall consume with the spirit of His mouth, and shall destroy with the brightness of His coming; even him, whose coming is after the working of Satan, with all *power* and *signs* and lying *wonders,* and with all deceivableness of righteousness in them that perish; because they received not *the love of the truth,* that they might be saved. And for this cause God shall send them strong delusion, that they should believe a lie; that they all might be damned *who believed not the truth,* but had pleasure in unrighteousness" (2 Thess. 2:8-12).

So also in the twenty-fourth chapter of Matthew, our Lord warns His disciples against the same kind of influence. "Then if any man shall say unto you, Lo, here is

Christ, or there; believe it not. For there shall arise false Christs, and false prophets, and *shall show great signs and wonders;* insomuch that, if it were possible, they shall deceive the very elect. Behold, *I have told you before"* (ver. 23-25).

Again, in Revelation 13, we read of the second beast, coming up out of the earth, the great false prophet, the antichrist, doing great wonders, "so that he maketh fire come down from heaven on the earth in the sight of men, and deceiveth them that dwell on the earth by means of those miracles which he had power to do in the sight of the beast; saying to them that dwell on the earth that they should make an image to the beast, which had the wound by a sword, and did live" (ver. 13-14).

Now, each of the above three passages of holy Scripture refers to scenes which shall be enacted after the Church has been taken away out of this world; but on this we do not dwell, inasmuch as our object in quoting them for the reader is, to let him see how far the devil can go in the way of signs and wonders, to lead people away from the truth; and also to set before him the one divine and therefore perfect safeguard against all the delusive power of the enemy.

The human heart has no ability whatever to resist the influence of "great signs and wonders," put forth in favor of the most deadly error. There is but the one thing which can fortify the soul, and enable it to resist the devil and his deadly delusions, and that is, the Word of God. To have the precious truth of God treasured up in the heart is the divine secret of preservation from all error, even though backed up by the most astounding miracles.

Hence, in the first of the above quotations, we see that the reason why people will be deceived by the signs and lying wonders of "that wicked" one is, "because they received not the love of the truth, that they might be saved." It is the love of the truth that preserves from error, be it ever so persuasive, ever so fascinating, ever so strongly supported by the powerful evidence of "great signs and wonders." It is not cleverness, intellectual power, mental grasp, extensive learning—all these things are perfectly powerless in the presence of Satan's wiles and machinations. The most gigantic human intellect must fall an easy prey to the wiles of the serpent.

But, blessed be God, the craft, the subtilty, the signs and lying wonders, all the resources of Satan, all the machinery of hell, are perfectly powerless with a heart that is governed by the love of the truth. A little child who knows and believes and loves the truth is blessedly shielded, sheltered, and divinely preserved from the blinding and deceiving power of the wicked one. If ten thousand false prophets were to arise and perform the most extraordinary miracles that were ever presented to the human gaze, in order to prove that the Bible is not the inspired Word of God, or that our Lord Jesus Christ is not God over all, blessed forever, or in order to set aside the glorious truth that the blood of Jesus Christ, God's Son, cleanseth from all sin, or any other precious truth revealed in holy Scripture, it could have no effect whatever on the very simplest babe in Christ whose heart is governed by the Word of God. Yea, if an angel from heaven were to come down and preach any thing contrary to what we are taught in the Word of God, we have a divine warrant to pronounce him anathema, without any discussion or argument whatever.

This is an unspeakable mercy. It puts the simplehearted, unlettered child of God into the most blessed position—a position, not only of moral security, but of sweetest repose. We are not called upon to analyze the false doctrine, or to weigh the evidence advanced in favor of it; we reject, with stern decision, both the one and the other, simply because we have the certainty of the truth and the love of it in our hearts. "Thou shalt not hearken unto the words of that prophet, or that dreamer of dreams"—although the sign or the wonder had come to pass—"for the Lord your God proveth you, to know whether ye love the Lord your God with all your heart and with all your soul."

Here was the all-important point for Israel, and it is the same for us. Then, now, and always, the true moral security is in having the heart fortified with the love of the truth, which is only another way of expressing the love of God. The faithful Israelite who loved Jehovah, with all his heart and with all his soul, would have a ready and conclusive answer for all the false prophets and dreamers who might arise—a thoroughly effectual method of dealing with them. *"Thou shalt not hearken."* If the enemy does not get the ear, he is not likely to reach the heart. The sheep follow the Shepherd; "for they know His voice. And a stranger" —even though showing signs and wonders— "will they not follow, but will *flee from him.*" Why? Is it because they are able to discuss and argue and analyze? No, thanks and praise to God; but because "they know not the voice of strangers." The simple fact of not knowing the voice is a sufficient reason for not following the speaker.

All this is full of comfort and consolation for the beloved lambs and sheep of the flock of Christ. They can hear the voice of their loving, faithful Shepherd; they can gather around Him, and find in His presence true rest and perfect safety. He makes them to lie down in green pastures, and leads them by the still waters of His love. This is enough. They may be very weak—yea, perfect weakness in themselves—but this is no hindrance to their rest and blessing; quite the contrary, it only casts them more upon His almighty power. We need never be afraid of weakness; it is fancied strength we have to dread, vain confidence in our own wisdom, our own intelligence, our scriptural knowledge, our spiritual attainments—these are the things we have to fear; but as for our weakness, the more deeply we feel it the better, for our Shepherd's strength is made perfect in weakness, and His precious grace is amply sufficient for all the need of His beloved and blood-bought flock as a whole, and for each member in particular. Only let us keep near to Him in the abiding sense of our own perfect helplessness and nothingness; let us treasure up His precious Word in our hearts; let us feed upon it, as the very sustenance of our souls, day by day, the staple article of our lives, the living bread for the strengthening of the inward man. Thus shall we be safe from every strange voice, every false prophet, every snare of the devil, every influence which might tend to draw us away from the path of obedience, and the practical confession of the name of Christ.

We must now quote the second paragraph of our chapter, in which the Lord's people are warned against another snare of the devil. Oh, how many and varied are his snares and wiles! how manifold are the dangers of the people of God! but, blessed be His holy name, there is full provision in His Word for all.

"If thy brother, *the son of thy mother"*— nearer, dearer, and more tender than the son of the father—"or thy son, or thy daughter, or the wife of thy bosom, or thy friend which is as thine own soul, entice thee secretly, saying, Let us go and serve other gods, *which thou hast not known,* thou, nor thy fathers, namely, of the gods of the people which are round about you, nigh unto thee, or far off from thee, from the one end of the earth even unto the other end of the earth; thou shalt not consent unto him, nor hearken unto him; neither shall thine eye pity him, neither shalt thou spare, neither shalt thou conceal him; but thou shalt surely kill him; thine hand shall be first upon him to put him to death, and afterwards the hand of all the people. And thou shalt stone him with stones that he die; because he hath sought to thrust thee away from the Lord thy God, which brought thee out of the land of Egypt, from the house of bondage. And all Israel shall hear, and fear, and shall do no more any such wickedness as this is among you" (ver. 6-11).

Here, then, we have something quite different from the false prophet or the dreamer of dreams. Thousands might be proof against the influence of these, and yet fall before the insnaring and seductive power of natural affection. It is very hard to resist the action of this latter. It demands deep-toned devotedness, great singleness of eye, firm purpose of heart, to deal faithfully with those who live deep down in our hearts' tender affections. The trial to some of withstanding and rejecting a prophet or a dreamer with whom there was no personal relationship, no tender link of fond affection, would be as nothing compared with having to treat with stern and severe decision the wife of the bosom, the beloved brother or sister, the devoted and tenderly loved friend.

But where the claims of God, of Christ, of truth are at stake, there must be no hesitation. If any should seek to make use of the ties of affection in order to draw us aside from our allegiance to Christ, we must resist them with unqualified decision. "If any man come to Me, and hate not his father, and mother, and wife, and children, and brethren, and sisters, yea, and his own life also, he cannot be My disciple" (Luke 10:26).

Let us see that we thoroughly understand this aspect of the truth, and also that we give it its proper place. If poor blind reason be listened to, it will be sure to present to the mind the most hideous perversion of this great practical subject. Reason, whenever it attempts to exercise its powers in the things of God, is sure to prove itself the active and efficient agent of the devil in opposition to the truth. In things human and earthly, reason may go for what it is worth; but in things divine and heavenly, it is not only worthless, but positively mischievous.

What then, we may ask, is the true moral force of Luke 14:26 and Deuteronomy 13:8-10? Most assuredly, they do not mean that we are to be "without natural affection," which is one of the special marks of the apostasy of the last days. This is perfectly clear. God Himself has established our natural relationships, and each of these relationships has its characteristic affections, the exercise and display of which are in lovely harmony with the mind of God. Christianity does not interfere with our relationships in nature, but it introduces a power whereby the responsibilities which attach to those relationships can be duly fulfilled to the glory of God. And not only so, but in the various Epistles, the Holy Ghost has given the most ample instructions to husbands and wives, parents and children, masters and servants, thus proving, in the very fullest and most blessed manner, the divine sanction of those relationships and the affections which belong to them.

All this is perfectly plain; but still we have to inquire how it fits in with Luke 14 and Deuteronomy 13. The answer is simply this: The harmony is divinely perfect. Those Scriptures apply only to cases in which our natural relationships and affections interfere with the claims of God and of Christ. When they operate in this way, they must be denied and mortified. If they dare to intrude upon a domain which is wholly divine, the sentence of death must be written upon them.

In contemplating the life of the only perfect man that ever trod this earth of ours, we can see how beautifully He adjusted the various claims which, as a man and a servant, He had to meet. He could say to His mother, "Woman, what have I to do with thee?" and yet, at the fitting moment, He could, with exquisite tenderness, commend that mother to the care of the disciple whom He loved. He could say to His parents, "Wist ye not that I must be about My Father's business?" and, at the same time, go home with them and be sweetly subject to parental authority. Thus the written teachings of holy Scripture, and the perfect ways of the living Christ, do both combine to teach us how to discharge aright the claims of nature and the claims of God.

But it may be that the reader feels considerable difficulty in reference to the line of action enjoined in Deuteronomy 13:9-10. He may find it hard to reconcile it with a God of love, and with the grace, gentleness, and tenderness inculcated in the New Testament Scriptures. Here again we must keep a vigilant eye upon reason. It always affects to find ample scope for its powers in the stern enactments of the divine government; but, in reality, it only displays its blindness and folly. Still though we would make very short work with infidel reason, we earnestly desire to help any honest soul who may not be able to see his way through this question.

We have had occasion, in our studies on the earlier chapters of this book, to refer to the very weighty subject of God's governmental dealings both with Israel and the nations; but, in addition to what has already come under our notice, we have to bear in mind the very important difference between the two economies of law and grace. If this be not clearly apprehended, we shall find very considerable difficulty in such passages as Deuteronomy 13:9-10. The great characteristic principle of the Jewish economy was *righteousness;* the characteristic principle of Christianity is *grace*—pure, unqualified grace.

If this fact be fully grasped, all difficulty vanishes. It was perfectly right, perfectly consistent, and in perfect harmony with the mind of God for Israel to slay their enemies. God commanded them to do so. And, in like manner, it was right and consistent for them to execute righteous judgment, even unto death, upon any member of the congregation who should seek to draw them aside after false gods, as in the passage before us. To do so was in full moral harmony with the grand ruling principles of government and law, under which they were placed, in accordance with the dispensational wisdom of God. All this is perfectly plain. It runs through the entire canon of Old Testament Scripture. God's government in Israel, and His government of the world in connection with Israel, was on the strict principle of righteousness. And as it was in the past, so shall it be in the future: "A king shall reign in righteousness, and princes shall rule in judgment."

But in Christianity, we see something quite different. The moment we open the pages of the New Testament, and hearken to the teachings and mark the actings of the Son of God, we find ourselves on entirely new ground, and in a new atmosphere; in a word, we are in the atmosphere and on the ground of pure, unqualified grace.

Thus, as a sample of the teaching, take a passage or two from what is called The Sermon on the Mount—that marvelous and precious compendium of the principles of the kingdom of heaven. "Ye have heard that it hath been said, 'An eye for an eye, and a tooth for a tooth'; *but I say unto you,* that ye resist not evil; but whosoever shall smite thee on the one cheek, turn to him the other also. And if any man will sue thee at the law, and take away thy coat, let him have thy cloke also. And whosoever shall compel thee to go a mile, go with him twain." Again, "Ye have heard that it hath been said, 'Thou shalt love thy neighbor and hate thine enemy'; *but I say unto you,* Love your enemies, bless them that curse you, do good to them that hate you, and pray for them which despitefully use you, and persecute you; that ye may be the *sons* [υιοι] of your Father which is in heaven; *for* He maketh His sun to rise on the evil and on the good, and sendeth rain on the just and on the unjust. . . . Be ye therefore perfect [τελειοι], even as your Father which is in heaven is perfect" (Matt. 5:38-48).

We cannot now dwell upon those blessed sentences; we merely quote them for the reader in order to let him see the immense difference between the Jewish and Christian economy. What was perfectly right and consistent for a Jew, might be quite wrong and inconsistent for a Christian.

This is so plain that a child may see it; and yet, strange to say, many of the Lord's beloved people seem to be clouded on the subject. They judge it to be perfectly right for Christians to deal in righteousness, and go to war, and to exercise worldly power. Well, then, if it be right for Christians to act thus, we would simply ask, Where is it taught in the New Testament? where have we a single sentence from the lips of our Lord Jesus Christ, or from the pen of the Holy Ghost, to warrant or sanction such a thing? As we have said, in reference to other questions that have come before us in our studies on this book, it is of no possible use for us to say, *"We think* so and so." Our thoughts are simply worth nothing. The one grand question, in all matters of Christian faith and morals, is, "What saith the New Testament?" What did our Lord and Master teach, and what did He do? He taught that His people now are not to act as His people of old acted. *Righteousness* was the principle of the old economy; *grace* is the principle of the new.

This was what Christ taught, as may be seen in numberless passages of Scripture. And how did He act? Did He deal in righteousness with people? did He assert His rights? did He exercise worldly power? did

He go to law? did He vindicate Himself, or retaliate? When His poor disciples, in utter ignorance of the heavenly principles which He taught, and in total forgetfulness of His whole course of action, said to Him, on one occasion in the which a certain village of the Samaritans refused to receive Him, "Lord, wilt Thou that we command fire to come down from heaven and consume them, even as Elias did?" what was His answer? "He turned and rebuked them, and said, 'Ye know not what manner of spirit ye are of; for the Son of Man is not come to destroy men's lives, but to save.' And they went to another village." It was perfectly consistent with the spirit, principle, and genius of the dispensation of which Elias was the exponent and representative, to call down fire from heaven to consume the men sent by a godless king to arrest him; but the blessed Lord was the perfect Exponent and divine Representative of another dispensation altogether. His was a life of perfect self-surrender, from first to last. He never asserted His rights. He came to serve and to give; He came to represent God—to be the perfect expression of the Father in every way. The Father's character shone out in His every look, His every word, His every act, His every movement.

Such was the Lord Christ when He was down here among men, and such was His teaching. He did what He taught, and He taught what He did. His words expressed what He was, and His ways illustrated His words. He came to serve and to give, and His whole life was marked by those two things, from the manger to the cross. We may truly say, time would fail us to quote the passages in proof and illustration of this; nor is there any need, inasmuch as the truth of it will hardly be called in question.

Well, then, is not He our great Exemplar in all things? is it not by His teaching and ways that our course and character as Christians are to be formed? How are we to know how we ought to walk, save by hearkening to His blessed words and gazing on His perfect ways? If we as Christians are to be guided and governed by the principles and precepts of the Mosaic economy, then, assuredly, it would be right for us to go to law, to contend for our rights, to engage in war, to destroy our enemies; but then what becomes of the teaching and example of our adorable Lord and Saviour? what of the teachings of the Holy Ghost? what of the New Testament? Is it not as plain as a sunbeam to the reader that for a Christian to do these things is to act in flagrant opposition to the teaching and example of his Lord?

Here, however, we may be met by the old and oft-repeated inquiry, "What would become of the world, what would become of its institutions, what would become of society, if such principles were to be universally dominant?" The infidel historian, in speaking of the early Christians, and their refusal to join the Roman army, sneeringly inquires, "What would have become of the empire, surrounded as it was on all sides by barbarians, if every one had indulged in such pusillanimous ideas as these?"

We reply at once, If those spiritual and heavenly principles were universally dominant, there would be no wars—no fighting, and hence there would be no need of soldiers, no need of standing armies or navies, no need of constabulary or police; there would be no wrong-doings, no strife about property, and hence no need of courts of law, judges, or magistrates; in short, the world as it now is would have an end; the kingdoms of this world would have become the kingdoms of our Lord and of His Christ.

But the plain fact is, those heavenly principles of which we speak are not intended for the world at all, inasmuch as the world could not adopt them, or act upon them for a single hour; to do so would involve the immediate and complete break-up of the present system of things, the dissolution of the entire framework of society as at present constituted.

Hence, the objection of the infidel crumbles into dust beneath our feet, like all other infidel objections, and the questions and the difficulties which are based upon them. They are deprived of every atom of moral force. Heavenly principles are not designed for "this present evil world" at all; they are designed for the Church, which is not of the world, even as Jesus is not of the world. "If," said our Lord to Pilate, "My kingdom were of this world, then would My servants fight, that I should not be delivered to the Jews; but *now* is My kingdom not from hence."

Mark the word "now." By and by, the kingdoms of this world will become the kingdom of our Lord; but now, He is rejected, and all who belong to Him—His Church—His people—are called to share His rejection, to follow Him into the outside place, and walk as pilgrims and strangers here below, waiting for the moment when He shall come to receive them to Himself, that where He is, there they may be also.

Now, it is the attempt to mix the world and the Church together that produces such terrible confusion. It is one of Satan's special wiles, and it has done more to mar the testimony of the Church of God and hinder its progress than most of us are aware. It involves a complete turning of things upside down, a confounding of things that differ essentially, an utter denial of the Church's true character, her position, her walk, and her hope. We sometimes hear the expression, "Christian world:" what does it mean? It is simply an attempt to combine two things which in their source, nature, and character are as diverse as light and darkness. It is an effort to tack a new piece upon an old garment, which, as our Lord tells us, only makes the rent worse.

It is not God's object to Christianize the world, but to call His people out of the world, to be a heavenly people, governed by heavenly principles, formed by a heavenly object, and cheered by a heavenly hope. If this be not clearly seen; if the truth as to the Church's true calling and course be not realized as a living power in the soul, we shall be sure to make the most grievous mistakes in our work, walk, and service. We shall make an entirely wrong use of the Old Testament Scriptures, not only on prophetic subjects, but in reference to the whole range of practical life; indeed, it would be utterly impossible to calculate the loss which must result from not seeing the distinctive calling, position, and hope of the Church of God, her association and identification—her living union with a rejected, risen, and glorified Christ.

We cannot attempt to enlarge upon this most precious and interesting theme; but we should just like to point out to the reader an instance or two illustrative of the Spirit's method of quoting and applying Old Testament Scripture. Take, for example, the following passage from that lovely thirty-fourth psalm, "The face of the Lord is against them that do evil, to cut off the remembrance of them from the earth." Now, mark the way in which the Holy Spirit quotes this passage in the first Epistle of Peter. "The face of the Lord is against them that do evil" (chap. 3:12). Not a word about cutting off. Why is this? Because the Lord is not now acting upon the principle of cutting off. He acted upon it under the law, and He will act upon it in the kingdom by and by; but just now, He is acting in grace and long-suffering mercy. His face is quite as much and quite as decidedly against all evil-doers as ever it was or ever it will be, but not now to cut off the remembrance of them from the earth. The most striking illustration of this marvelous grace and forbearance, and of the difference between the two principles on which we have been dwelling, is seen in the fact that the very men who with wicked hands crucified His only begotten and well-beloved Son—evil-doers, surely, of the most pronounced type—instead of being cut off from the earth, were the very first to hear the message of full and free pardon through the blood of the cross.

Now, it may appear to some that we are making too much of the mere omission of a single clause of Old Testament Scripture. Let not the reader think so. Even had we but this one instance, it would be a serious mistake to treat it with any thing like indifference. But the fact is, there are scores of passages of the same character as the one just quoted, all illustrative of the contrast between the Jewish and Christian economies, and also between Christianity and the coming kingdom.

God is now dealing in grace with the world, and so should His people, if they want to be like Him, and such they are called to be. "Be ye therefore perfect, even as your Father which is in heaven is perfect." And again, "Be ye therefore imitators of God, as dear children; and walk in love, as Christ also hath loved us, and hath given Himself for us, an offering and a sacrifice to God for a sweet-smelling savor" (Eph. 5:1).

This is our model. We are called to copy our Father's example—to imitate Him. He is not going to law with the world; He is not enforcing His rights with the strong hand of power. By and by He will; but just now, in this day of grace, He showers His blessings and benefits in rich profusion upon those whose life is one of enmity and rebellion against Him.

All this is perfectly marvelous, but this it is; and we, as Christians, are called to act on this morally glorious principle. It may be said by some, How could we ever get on in the world—how could we conduct our business on such a principle as this? We should be robbed and ruined; designing people would take advantage of us if they knew that we would not go to law with them; they would take our goods, or borrow our money, or occupy our houses, and refuse to pay us. In short, we could never get on in a world like this if we did not assert our rights and establish our claims by the strong hand of power. What is the law for but to make people behave themselves? Are not the powers that be ordained of God for the very purpose of maintaining peace and good order in our midst? What would become of society if we had not soldiers, policemen, magistrates, and judges? And if God has ordained that such things should be, why should not His people avail themselves of them? and not only so, but who so fit to occupy places of authority and power, or to wield the sword of justice, as the people of God?

There is, no doubt, very great apparent force in all this line of argument. The powers that be are ordained of God. The king, the governor, the judge, the magistrate, are, each in his place, the expression of the power of God. It is God who invests each with the power which he wields; it is He who has put the sword into his hand, for the punishment of evil-doers, and the praise of them that do well. We bless God with all our hearts for the constituted authorities of the country. Day and night, in private and in public, we pray for them. It is our bounden duty to obey and submit ourselves to them in all things, provided always that they do not call upon us to disobey God, or do violence to conscience. If they do this, we must—what? Resist? Nay, but suffer.

All this is perfectly plain. The world as it now is could not go on for a single day if men were not kept in order by the strong hand of power. We could not live, or at least life would be perfectly intolerable, were it not that evil-doers are kept in terror of the glittering sword of justice. Even as it is, through lack of moral power on the part of those who bear the sword, lawless demagogues are allowed to stir up the evil passions of men to resist the law of the land and disturb the peace and threaten the lives and property of well-disposed and harmless subjects of the government.

But admitting all this, in the fullest possible manner, as every intelligent Christian, every one taught by Scripture, most assuredly will, it leaves wholly untouched the question of the Christian's path in this world. Christianity fully recognizes all the governmental institutions of the country. It forms no part of the Christian's business to interfere, in any one way, with such institutions. Wherever he is, whatever be the principle or character of the government of the country in which his lot is cast, it is his duty to recognize its municipal and political arrangements, to pay taxes, pray for the government, honor governors in their official capacity, wish well to the legislature and the executive, pray for the peace of the country, live in peace with all, so far as in him lies.

We see all this in the blessed Master Himself in perfection, blessed be His holy name for evermore! In His memorable reply to the crafty Herodians, He recognizes the principle of subjection to the powers that be—"Render to Caesar the things that be Caesar's, and to God the things that be God's." And not only so, but we find Him also paying tribute, although personally free. They had no right to demand it of Him, as He plainly shows to Peter; and it might be said, Why did He not appeal? Appeal! Nay; He shows us something quite different. Hear His exquisite reply to His mistaken apostle—"Not withstanding, *lest we should offend them,* go thou to the sea, and cast a hook, and take up the fish that first cometh up; and when thou hast opened his mouth, thou shalt find a piece of money; that take and give unto them *for Me and thee*"* (Matt. 17).

And here we get back, with increased moral force, to our thesis, namely, the Christian's path in this world. What is it? He is to follow his Master—to imitate Him in all things. Did He assert His rights? did He go to law? did He try to regulate the world? did He meddle with municipal or political matters? was He a politician? did He wield the sword? did He consent to be a judge or a divider, even when appealed to, as we say, to arbitrate about property? was not His whole life one of complete self-surrender, from first to last? was He not continually giving up, until, at the cross, He gave up His precious life as a ransom for many?

We shall leave these questions to find their answer deep down in the heart of the Christian reader, and to produce their practical effect in his life. We trust that the foregoing line of truth will enable him to interpret aright such passages as Deuteronomy 13: 9-10. Our opposition to idolatry and our separation from evil, in every shape and form, while not less intense and decided, most surely, than that of Israel of old, is not to be displayed in the same way. The Church is imperatively called upon to put away evil and evil-doers, but not after the same fashion as Israel. It is no part of her duty to stone idolaters and blasphemers, or burn witches. The church of Rome has acted upon this principle, and even Protestants (to the shame of Protestantism) have followed her example.† The Church is not called—nay, she is positively and peremptorily forbidden to use the temporal sword. It is a flat denial of her calling, character, and mission to do so. When Peter, in ignorant zeal and carnal haste, drew the sword in defense of his blessed Master, he was at once corrected by his Master's faithful word, and instructed by his Master's gracious act: "Put up thy sword into the sheath; for all they that take the sword shall perish by the sword." And having thus reproved the act of His mistaken though well-meaning servant, He undid the mischief by His gracious touch. "The weapons of our warfare," says the inspired apostle, "are not carnal, but mighty through God to the pulling down of strongholds, casting down imaginations, and every high thing that exalteth itself against the knowledge of God, and bringing into captivity every thought to the obedience of Christ" (2 Cor. 10:4-5).

The professing church has gone all astray as to this great and most important question. She has joined herself with the world, and sought to further the cause of Christ by carnal and worldly agency. She had ignorantly attempted to maintain the Christian faith by the most shameful denial of Christian practice. The burning of heretics stands as a most fearful moral blot upon the page of the church's history. We can form no adequate idea of the terrible consequences resulting from the notion that the Church was called to take Israel's place and act on Israel's principles.‡ It completely falsified her testi-

*The fact that the tribute-money may have been for the temple does not touch the principle set forth in the text.

†The burning of Servetus, in 1553, for his theological opinions, is a frightful blot upon the Reformation, and upon the man who sanctioned such an unchristian proceeding. True, the opinions of Servetus were fatally and fundamentally false—he held the Arian heresy, which is simply blasphemy against the Son of God; but to burn him, or anyone else, for false doctrine, was a flagrant sin against the spirit, genius, and principle of the gospel, the deplorable fruit of ignorance as to the essential difference between Judaism and Christianity.

‡It is one thing for the Church to learn from the history of Israel, and another thing altogether to take Israel's place, act on Israel's principles, and appropriate Israel's promises. The former is the Church's duty and privilege; the latter has been the Church's fatal mistake.

mony, robbed her of her entirely spiritual and heavenly character, and led her upon a path which ends in Revelation 17 and 18. Let him that readeth understand.

But we must not pursue this line of things further here. We trust that what has passed before us will lead all whom it may concern to consider the whole subject in the light of the New Testament, and thus be the means, through the infinite goodness of God, of leading them to see the path of entire separation which we as Christians are called to tread; *in* the world, but not *of* it, even as our Lord Christ is not of it. This will solve a thousand difficulties, and furnish a grand general principle which can be practically applied to a thousand details.

We shall now conclude our study of Deuteronomy 13 by a glance at its closing paragraph.

"If thou shalt hear say in one of thy cities, which the Lord thy God hath given thee to dwell there, saying, Certain men, the children of Belial, are gone out from among you, and have withdrawn the inhabitants of their city, saying, Let us go and serve other gods, which ye have not known; *then shalt thou inquire, and make search, and ask diligently;* and, behold, *if it be truth, and the thing certain,* that such abomination is *wrought among you,* thou shalt surely smite the inhabitants of that city with the edge of the sword, destroying it utterly, and all that is therein, and the cattle thereof, with the edge of the sword. And thou shalt gather all the spoil of it into the midst of the street thereof, and shalt burn with fire the city, and all the spoil thereof every whit, *for the Lord thy God;* and it shall be a heap forever; it shall not be built again. And there shall cleave naught of the cursed thing to thine hand; that the Lord may turn from the fierceness of His anger, and show thee mercy, and have compassion upon thee, and multiply thee, as He hath sworn unto thy fathers; when thou shalt hearken to the voice of the Lord thy God, to keep all His commandments which I command thee this day, to do that which is right in the eyes of the Lord thy God" (ver. 12-18).

Here we have instruction of the most solemn and weighty character. But the reader must bear in mind that, solemn and weighty as it most surely is, it is based upon a truth of unspeakable value, and that is, Israel's national unity. If we do not see this, we shall miss the real force and meaning of the foregoing quotation. A case is supposed of grave error in some one of the cities of Israel, and the question might naturally arise, Are all the cities involved in the evil of one?*

Assuredly, inasmuch as the nation was one. The cities and tribes were not independent; they were bound up together by a sacred bond of national unity—a unity which had its centre in the place of the divine presence. Israel's twelve tribes were indissolubly bound together. The twelve loaves on the golden table in the sanctuary formed the beauteous type of this unity, and every true Israelite owned and rejoiced in this unity. The twelve stones in Jordan's bed, the twelve stones on Jordan's bank, Elijah's twelve stones on Mount Carmel—all set forth the same grand truth—the indissoluble unity of Israel's twelve tribes. The good king Hezekiah recognized this truth when he commanded that the burnt-offering and the sin-offering should be made for *all Israel* (2 Chron. 29:24). The faithful Josiah owned it and acted upon it when he carried his reformatory operations into all the countries that pertained to the children of Israel (2 Chron. 34:33). Paul, in his magnificent address before king Agrippa, bears witness to the same truth when he says, "Unto which promise *our twelve tribes,* instantly serving God day and night, hope to come"† (Acts 26:7). And when we look forward into the bright future, the same glorious truth shines,

*It is, of course, needful to bear in mind that the evil referred to in the text was of the very gravest character. It was an attempt to draw the people away from the one living and true God. It touched the very foundation of Israel's national existence. It was not merely a local or municipal question, but a national one.

†It may interest the reader to know that the word rendered in the above passage, "twelve tribes," is singular—*το δωδεκαθυλον.* It certainly gives very full and vivid expression to the grand idea of indissoluble unity which is so precious to God, and therefore so precious to faith.

with heavenly lustre, in the seventh chapter of Revelation, where we see the twelve tribes sealed and secured for blessing, rest, and glory, in connection with a countless multitude of the Gentiles. And finally, in Revelation 21, we see the names of the twelve tribes engraved on the gates of the holy Jerusalem, the seat and centre of the glory of God and the Lamb.

Thus, from the golden table in the sanctuary to the golden city descending out of heaven from God, we have a marvelous chain of evidence in proof of the grand truth of the indissoluble unity of Israel's twelve tribes.

Then, if the question be asked, Where is this unity to be seen? or how did Elijah or Hezekiah or Josiah or Paul see it? The answer is a very simple one—They saw it by faith; they looked within the sanctuary of God, and there, on the golden table, they beheld the twelve loaves, setting forth the perfect distinctness and yet the perfect oneness of the twelve tribes. Nothing can be more beautiful. The truth of God must stand forever. Israel's unity was seen in the past, and it will be seen in the future; and though, like the higher unity of the Church, it is unseen in the present, faith believes it all the same, holds it and confesses it in the face of ten thousand hostile influences.

Now let us look for a moment at the practical application of this most glorious truth, as presented in the closing paragraph of Deuteronomy 13. A report reaches a city in the far north of the land of Israel of serious error taught in a certain city in the extreme south—deadly error, tending to draw the inhabitants away from the true God.

What is to be done? The law is as plain as possible; the path of duty is laid down with such distinctness that it only needs a single eye to see it, and a devoted heart to tread it. "Then shalt thou inquire, and make search, and ask diligently." This surely is simple enough.

But some of the citizens might say, "What have we in the north to do with error taught in the south? Thank God, there is no error taught amongst us; it is entirely a local question; each city is responsible for the maintenance of the truth within its own walls. How could we be expected to examine into every case of error which may spring up here and there all over the land? our whole time would be taken up, so that we could not attend to our fields, our vineyards, our oliveyards, our flocks, and our herds. It is quite as much as we can do to keep our own borders all right. We certainly condemn the error, and if any one holding or teaching it were to come here, and that we knew of it, we should most decidedly shut our gates against him. Beyond this, we do not feel ourselves responsible to go.

Now, what, we may ask, would be the reply of the faithful Israelite to all this line of argument which, in the judgment of mere nature, seems so exceedingly plausible? A very simple and very conclusive one, we may be sure. He would say it was simply a denial of Israel's unity. If every city and every tribe were to take independent ground, then verily the high-priest might take the twelve loaves off the golden table before the Lord and scatter them here and there and every where; our unity is gone; we are all broken up into independent atoms, having no national ground of action.

Besides, the commandment is most distinct and explicit—"Thou shalt inquire, and make search, and ask diligently." We are bound, therefore, on the double ground of the nation's unity and the plain command of our covenant-God. It is of no possible use to say there is no error taught amongst *us,* unless we want to separate ourselves from the nation; if we belong to Israel, then verily the error is taught amongst us, as the Word says, "Such abomination is wrought *among you.*" How far does the "you" extend? As far as the national boundaries. Error taught at Dan affects those dwelling at Beersheba. How is this? Because Israel is one.

And then the Word is so plain, so distinct, so emphatic. We are bound to search into it. We cannot fold our arms and sit down in cold indifference and culpable neutrality, else we shall be involved in the awful consequences of this evil; yea, we *are* involved until we clear ourselves of it by judging it, with unflinching decision and unsparing severity.

Such would be the language of every loyal Israelite, and such his mode of acting in reference to error and evil wherever found. To speak or act otherwise would simply be indifference as to the truth and glory of God, and independency as regards Israel. For any to say that they were not responsible to act according to the instructions given in Deuteronomy 13:12-18, would be a complete surrender of the truth of God and of Israel's unity. All were bound to act, or else be involved in the judgment of the guilty city.

And surely if all this was true in Israel of old, it is not less true in the Church of God now. We may rest assured that any thing like indifference where Christ is concerned is most hateful to God. It is the eternal purpose and counsel of God to glorify His Son; that every knee should bow to Him, and every tongue confess that He is Lord to the glory of God the Father; "that all should honor the Son even as they honor the Father."

Hence, if Christ be dishonored, if doctrines be taught derogatory to the glory of His Person, the efficacy of His work, or the virtue of His offices, we are bound, by every motive which could possibly act on our hearts, to reject, with stern decision, such doctrines. Indifference or neutrality where the Son of God is concerned is high treason in the judgment of the high court of Heaven. We would not be indifferent if it were a question of our own reputation, our personal character, or our personal or family property; we should be thoroughly alive to any thing affecting ourselves or those dear to us. How much more deeply ought we to feel in reference to what concerns the glory and honor, the name and cause, of the One to whom we owe our present and everlasting all—the One who laid aside His glory, came down into this wretched world, and died a shameful death upon the cross, in order to save us from the everlasting flames of hell. Could we be indifferent to Him? neutral where He is concerned? God, in His great mercy, forbid!

No, it must not be. The honor and glory of Christ must be more to us than all beside. Reputation, property, family, friends—all must stand aside if the claims of Christ are involved. Does not the Christian reader own this, with all the energy of his ransomed soul? We feel persuaded he does, even now; and oh, how shall we feel when we see Him face to face, and stand in the full light of His moral glory? with what feelings shall we then contemplate the idea of indifference or neutrality with respect to Him!

And are we not justified in declaring that next to the glory of the Head stands the great truth of the unity of His body—the Church? Unquestionably. If the nation of Israel was one, how much more is the body of Christ one! and if independency was wrong in Israel, how much more wrong in the Church of God! The plain fact is this: the idea of independency cannot be maintained for a moment in the light of the New Testament. As well might we say that the hand is independent of the foot, or the eye of the ear, as assert that the members of the body of Christ are independent one of another. "For as the body is one, and hath many members, and all the members of that one body, being many, are one body; *so also is Christ*"—a very remarkable statement, setting forth the intimate union of Christ and the Church. "*For by one Spirit are we all baptized into one body,* whether we be Jews or Gentiles, whether bond or free; and have been all made to drink into one Spirit. For the body is not one member, but many. If the foot shall say, Because I am not the hand, I am not of the body; is it therefore not of the body? And if the the ear shall say, Because I am not the eye, I am not of the body; is it therefore not of the body? If the whole body were an eye, where were the hearing? If the whole were hearing, where were the smelling? But now hath God set the members every one of them in the body, as it hath pleased Him. And if they were all one member, where were the body? But now are they many members, yet but one body. And the eye cannot say unto the hand, I have no need of thee; nor again, the head to the feet, I have no need of you. Nay, much more, those members of the body which seem to be more feeble, are necessary; and those members of the body which we think to be less honorable, upon these we bestow more abundant honor; and our uncomely parts have more abundant comeliness; for our comely parts have no need; but God hath tempered the body together, having given more abundant honor to that part which lacked: *that there should be no schism in the body;* but that the members should have the same care one for another. And whether one member suffer, all the members suffer with it; or one member be honored, all the members rejoice with it. *Now ye are the body of Christ, and members in particular*" (1 Cor. 12:12-27).

We do not attempt to dwell upon this truly marvelous Scripture; but we earnestly desire to call the attention of the Christian reader to the special truth which it so forcibly sets before us—a truth which intimately concerns every true believer on the face of the earth, namely, *that he is a member of the body of Christ.* This is a great practical truth, involving, at once, the very highest privileges and the very weightiest responsibilities. It is not merely a true doctrine, a sound principle, or an orthodox opinion; it is a living fact, designed to be a divine power in the soul. The Christian can no longer view himself as an independent person, having no association, no vital link, with others. He is livingly bound up with all the children of God—all true believers—all the members of Christ's body upon the face of the earth.

"By one Spirit are we all baptized into one body." The Church of God is not a mere club, or a society, an association, or a brotherhood; it is a body united by the Holy Ghost to the Head in heaven; and all its members on earth are indissolubly bound together. This being so, it follows, of necessity, that all the members of the body are affected by the state and walk of each. "If one member suffer, all the members suffer with it"—that is, all the members of the body. If there is any thing wrong with the foot, the hand feels it. How? Through the head. So in the Church of God, if any thing goes wrong with an individual member, all feel it through the Head with whom all are livingly connected by the Holy Ghost.

Some find it very hard to grasp this great truth; but there it stands plainly revealed on the inspired page, not to be reasoned about, or submitted in any way to the human judgment, but simply to be believed. It is a divine revelation. No human mind could ever have conceived such a thought; but God reveals it, faith believes it, and walks in the blessed power of it.

It may be the reader feels disposed to ask, How is it possible for the state of one believer to affect those who know nothing about it? The answer is, "If one member suffer, all the members suffer with it." All the members of what? Is it of any mere local assembly or company who may happen to know or be locally connected with the person concerned? Nay, but the members of the body wherever they are. Even in the case of Israel, where it was only a national unity, we have seen that if there was evil in any one of their cities, all were concerned, all involved, all affected. Hence, when Achan sinned, although there were myriads of people totally ignorant of the fact, the Lord said, "*Israel* hath sinned," and the whole assembly suffered a humiliating defeat.

Can reason grasp this weighty truth? No; but faith can. If we listen to reason, we shall believe nothing; but, by the grace of God, we shall not listen to reason, but believe what God says because He says it.

And oh, what an immense truth is this unity of the body! What practical consequences flow out of it! How eminently calculated it is to minister to holiness of walk and life! How watchful it would make us over ourselves—our habits, our ways, our whole moral condition! How careful it would make us not to dishonor the Head *to* whom we are united, or grieve the Spirit *by* whom we are united, or injure the members *with* whom we are united!

But we must close this chapter, much as we should like to linger over one of the very grandest, most profound, and most powerful formative truths that can possibly engage our attention. May the Spirit of God make it a living power in the soul of every true believer on the face of the earth.

---

## *CHAPTER 14*

"YE are the children of the Lord your God; ye shall not cut yourselves, nor make any baldness between your eyes for the dead; for thou art a holy people unto the Lord thy God, and the Lord hath chosen thee to be a peculiar people unto Himself, above all the nations that are upon the earth" (ver. 1-2).

The opening clause of this chapter sets before us the basis of all the privileges and responsibilities of the Israel of God. It is a familiar thought amongst us that we must be in a relationship before we can know the affections or discharge the duties which belong to it. This is a plain and undeniable truth. If a man were not a father, no amount of argument or explanation could make him understand the feelings or affections of a father's heart; but the very moment he enters upon the relationship, he knows all about them.

Thus it is as to every relationship and position, and thus it is in the things of God. We cannot understand the affections or the duties of a child of God until we are on the ground. We must be Christians before we can perform Christian duties. Even when we are Christians, it is only by the gracious aid of the Holy Ghost that we can walk as such; but clearly, if we are not on Christian ground, we can know nothing of Christian affections or Christian duties. This is so obvious that argument is needless.

Now, most evidently, it is God's prerogative to declare how His children ought to conduct themselves, and it is their high privilege and holy responsibility to seek, in all things, to meet His gracious approval. "Ye *are* the children of the Lord your God: ye shall not cut yourselves." They were not their own; they belonged to Him, and therefore they had no right to cut themselves or disfigure their faces for the dead. Nature, in its pride and self will, might say, Why may we not do like other people? What harm can there be in cutting ourselves, or making a baldness between our eyes? It is only an expression of grief, an affectionate tribute to our loved departed ones. Surely there can be nothing morally wrong in such a suited expression of sorrow.

To all this there was one simple but conclusive answer—"Ye are the children of the Lord your God." This fact altered every thing. The poor ignorant and uncircumcised Gentiles around them might cut and disfigure themselves, inasmuch as they knew not God, and were not in relationship to Him; but as for Israel, they were on the high and holy ground of nearness to God, and this one fact was to give tone and character to all their habits. They were not called upon to adopt or refrain from any particular habit or custom *in order to be* the children of God. This would be, as we say, beginning at the wrong end; but *being* His children, they were to act as such.

"Thou *art* a holy people unto the Lord thy God." He does not say, Ye *ought to be* a holy people. How could they ever make themselves a holy people, or a peculiar people, unto Jehovah? Utterly impossible. If they were not His people, no efforts of theirs could ever make them such. But God, in His sovereign grace, in pursuance of His covenant with their fathers, had *made* them His children, *made* them a peculiar people above all the nations that were upon the earth. Here was the solid foundation of Israel's moral edifice. All their habits and customs, all their doings and ways, their food and their clothing, what they did and what they did not do—all was to flow out of the one grand fact, with which they had no more to do than with their natural birth, namely, that they actually were the children of God, the people of His choice, the people of His own special possession.

Now, we cannot but acknowledge it to be a privilege of the very highest order to have the Lord so near to us, and so interested in all our habits and ways. To mere nature, no doubt—to one who does not know the Lord—is not in relationship to Him, the very idea of His holy presence, or of nearness to Him, would be simply intolerable: but to every true believer—every one who really loves God, it is a most delightful thought to have Him near us, and to know that He interests Himself in all the most minute details of our personal history and most private life; that He takes cognizance of what we eat and what we wear; that He looks after us by day and by night, sleeping and waking, at home and abroad; in short, that His interest in and care for us go far beyond those of the most tender, loving mother for her babe.

All this is perfectly wonderful; and surely, if we only realized it more fully, we should live a very different sort of life, and have a very different tale to tell. What a holy privilege—what a precious reality, to know that our loving Lord is about our path day by day, and about our bed by night; that His eye rests upon us when we are dressing in the morning, when we sit down to our meals, when we go about our business, and in all our intercourse from morning till night! May the sense of this be a living and abiding power in the heart of every child of God on the face of the earth.

From verse 3 to 20, we have the law as to clean and unclean beasts, fishes, and fowls. The leading principles as to all these have already come under our notice in the eleventh chapter of Leviticus;* but there is a very important difference between the two Scriptures. The instructions in Leviticus are given primarily to Moses and Aaron; in Deuteronomy, they are given directly to the people. This is perfectly characteristic of the two books. Leviticus may be specially termed, The priest's guide-book. In Deuteronomy, the priests are almost entirely in the back-ground, and the people are prominent. This is strikingly apparent all through the book, so that there is not the slightest foundation for the idea that Deuteronomy merely repeats Leviticus. Nothing can be further from the truth. Each book has its own peculiar province, its own design, its own work. The devout student sees and owns this with deep delight. Infidels are willfully blind, and can see nothing.

In verse 21 of our chapter, the marked distinction between the Israel of God and the stranger is strikingly presented. "Ye shall not eat of any thing that dieth of itself; *thou shalt give it unto the stranger* that is in thy gates, that *he may eat it;* or thou mayest sell it unto an alien; for thou art a holy people unto the Lord thy God." The grand fact of Israel's relationship to Jehovah marked them off from all the nations under the sun. It was not that they were, in themselves, a whit better or holier than others; but Jehovah was holy, and they were His people. "Be ye holy, for I am holy."

Worldly people often think that Christians are very pharisaic in separating themselves from other people, and refusing to take part in the pleasures and amusements of the world; but they do not really understand the question. The fact is, for a Christian to participate in the vanities and follies of a sinful world would be, to use a typical phrase, like an Israelite eating that which had died of itself. The Christian, thank God, has gotten something better to feed upon than the poor dead things of the world. He has the Living Bread that came down from heaven—the true Manna; and not only so, but he eats of "the old corn of the land of Canaan," type of the risen and glorified Man in the heavens. Of these most precious things the poor unconverted worldling knows absolutely nothing, and hence he must feed upon what the world has to offer him. It is not a question of the right or the wrong of things looked at in themselves. No one could possibly have known aught about the wrong of eating of any thing that had died of itself if God's Word had not settled it.

This is the all-important point for us. We cannot expect the world to see or feel with us as to matters of right and wrong. It is our business to look at things from a divine stand-point. Many things may be quite consistent for a worldly man to do which a Christian could not touch at all, simply because he is a Christian. The question which the true believer has to ask as to every thing which comes before him is simply, Can I do

*As we have given in our *Notes on the Book of Leviticus,* chapter 11, what we believe to be the scriptural import of verses 4-20 of our chapter, we must refer the reader to what is there advanced.

this to the glory of God? can I connect the name of Christ with it? If not, he must not touch it.

In a word, the Christian's standard and test for every thing is Christ. This makes it all so simple. Instead of asking, Is such a thing consistent with *our* profession, *our* principles, *our* character, or *our* reputation? we have to ask, Is it consistent with Christ? This makes all the difference. Whatever is unworthy of Christ is unworthy of a Christian. If this be thoroughly understood and laid hold of, it will furnish a great practical rule which may be applied to a thousand details. If the heart be true to Christ, if we walk according to the instincts of the divine nature, as strengthened by the ministry of the Holy Ghost, and guided by the authority of holy Scripture, we shall not be much troubled with questions of right or wrong in our daily life.

Before proceeding to quote the lovely paragraph which closes our chapter, we would very briefly call attention to the last clause of verse 21: "Thou shalt not seethe a kid in his mother's milk." The fact that this commandment is given three times, in various connections, is sufficient to mark it as one of special interest and practical importance. The question is, what does it mean? what are we to learn from it? We believe it teaches very plainly that the Lord's people must carefully avoid every thing contrary to nature. Now, it was manifestly contrary to nature that what was intended for a creature's nourishment should be used to seethe it.

We find, all through the Word of God, great prominence given to what is according to nature—what is comely. "Does not even nature itself teach you?" says the inspired apostle to the assembly at Corinth. There are certain feelings and instincts implanted in nature by the Creator which must never be outraged. We may set it down as a fixed principle, an axiom in Christian ethics, that no action can possibly be of God that offers violence to the sensibilities proper to nature. The Spirit of God may, and often does, lead us beyond and above nature, but never against it.

We shall now turn to the closing verses of our chapter, in which we shall find some uncommonly fine practical instruction. "Thou shalt truly tithe all the increase of thy seed, that the field bringeth forth year by year. And thou shalt eat before the Lord thy God, in the place which He shall choose to place His name there, the tithe of thy corn, of thy wine, and of thine oil, and the firstlings of thy herds and of thy flocks; that thou mayest learn to fear the Lord thy God always. And if the way be too long for thee, so that thou art not able to carry it; or if the place be too far from thee, which the Lord thy God shall choose to set His name there, when the Lord thy God hath blessed thee; then shalt thou turn it into money, and bind up the money in thine hand, and shalt go unto the place which the Lord thy God shall choose; and thou shalt bestow that money for whatsoever thy soul lusteth after—for oxen, or for sheep, or for wine, or for strong drink, or for whatsoever thy soul desireth; and thou shalt eat there before the Lord thy God, and thou shalt rejoice, thou, and thine household, and the Levite that is within thy gates; thou shalt not forsake him, for he hath no part nor inheritance with thee. At the end of three years thou shalt bring forth all the tithe of thine increase the same year, and shalt lay it up within thy gates. And the Levite (because he hath no part nor inheritance with thee), and the stranger, and the fatherless, and the widow, which are within thy gates, shall come, and shall eat and be satisfied, that the Lord thy God may bless thee in all the work of thine hand which thou doest" (ver. 22-29).

This is a deeply interesting and most important passage, setting before us, with special simplicity, the *basis,* the *centre,* and *practical features* of Israel's national and domestic religion. The grand foundation of Israel's worship was laid in the fact that both they themselves and their land belonged to Jehovah. The land was His, and they held as tenants under Him. To this precious truth they were called, periodically, to bear testimony by faithfully tithing their land. "Thou shalt *truly* tithe all the increase of thy seed that thy field bringeth forth year by year."

They were to own, in this practical way, the proprietorship of Jehovah, and never lose sight of it: they were to own no other landlord but the Lord their God. All they were and all they had belonged to Him. This was the solid ground-work of their national worship—their national religion.

And then as to the centre, it is set forth with equal clearness. They were to gather to the place where Jehovah recorded His name. Precious privilege for all who truly loved that glorious name! We see in this passage, as also in many other portions of the Word of God, what importance He attached to the periodical gatherings of His people around Himself. Blessed be His name, He delighted to see His beloved people assembled in His presence, happy in Him and in one another; rejoicing together in their common portion, and feeding in sweet and loving fellowship on the fruit of Jehovah's land. "Thou shalt eat before the Lord thy God, *in the place which He shall choose,* to place His name there, the tithe of thy corn . . . *that thou mayest learn to fear the Lord thy God always.*"

There was, there could be, no other place like that, in the judgment of every faithful Israelite, every true lover of Jehovah. All such would delight to flock to the hallowed spot where that beloved and revered name was recorded. It might seem strange and unaccountable to those who knew not the God of Israel, and cared nothing about Him, to see the people traveling—many of them—a long distance from their homes, and carrying their tithes to one particular spot. They might feel disposed to call in question the needs-be for such a custom. Why not eat at home? they might say. But the simple fact is, such persons knew nothing whatever about the matter, and were wholly incapable of entering into the preciousness of it. To the Israel of God, there was the one grand moral reason for journeying to the appointed place, and that reason was found in the glorious motto, *Jehovah Shammah*—"The Lord is there." If an Israelite had willfully determined to stay at home, or to go to some place of his own choosing, he would neither have met Jehovah there nor his brethren, and hence he would have eaten alone. Such a course would have incurred the judgment of God; it would have been an abomination. There was but one centre, and that was not of man's choosing, but of God's. The godless Jeroboam, for his own selfish, political ends, presumed to interfere with the divine order, and set up his calves at Bethel and Dan; but the worship offered there was offered to demons and not to God. It was a daring act of wickedness, which brought down upon him and upon his house the righteous judgment of God; and we see, in Israel's after history, that "Jeroboam the son of Nebat" is used as the terrible model of iniquity for all the wicked kings.

But all the faithful in Israel were sure to be found at the one divine centre, and no where else. You would not find such making all sorts of excuses for staying at home; neither would you find them running hither and thither to places of their own or other people's choosing; no, you would find them gathered to Jehovah Shammah, and there alone. Was this narrowness and bigotry? Nay; it was the fear and love of God. If Jehovah had appointed a place where He would meet His people, assuredly His people should meet Him there.

And not only had He appointed a place, but, in His abounding goodness, He devised a means of making that place as convenient as possible for His worshiping people. Thus we read, "And if the way be too long for thee, so that thou art not able to carry it; or if *the place* be too far from thee *which the Lord thy God shall choose to set His name there,* when the Lord thy God hath blessed thee; then thou shalt turn it into money, and bind up the money in thine hand, and shalt go unto the place which the Lord thy God shall choose . . . and *thou shalt eat there before the Lord thy God,* and thou shalt rejoice, thou and thy household."

This is perfectly beautiful. The Lord, in His tender care and considerate love, took account of every thing. He would not leave a single difficulty in the way of His beloved people, in the matter of their assembling around Himself. He had His own special joy in seeing His redeemed people happy in His presence, and all who loved His name would delight to meet the loving desire of His heart by being found at the divinely appointed centre.

If any Israelite were found neglecting the blessed occasion of assembling with his brethren at the divinely chosen place and time, it would have simply proved that he had no heart for God or for His people, or, what was worse, that he was willfully absent. He might reason as he pleased about his being happy at home, happy elsewhere; it was a false happiness, inasmuch as it was happiness found in the path of disobedience, the path of willful neglect of the divine appointment.

All this is full of most valuable instruction for the Church of God now. It is the will of God now, no less than of old, that His people should assemble in His presence, on divinely appointed ground, and to a divinely appointed centre. This, we presume, will hardly be called in question by any one having a spark of divine light in his soul. The instincts of the divine nature, the leadings of the Holy Ghost, and the teachings of holy Scripture do all most unquestionably lead the Lord's people to assemble themselves together for worship, communion, and edification. However dispensations may differ, there are certain great principles and leading characteristics which always hold good, and the assembling of ourselves together is most assuredly one of these. Whether under the old economy or under the new, the assembling of the Lord's people is a divine institution.

Now, this being so, it is not a question of *our* happiness, one way or the other; though we may be perfectly sure that all true Christians will be happy in being found in their divinely appointed place. There is ever deep joy and blessing in the assembly of God's people. It is impossible for us to find ourselves together in the Lord's presence and not be truly happy. It is simply heaven upon earth for the Lord's dear people—those who love His name, love His person, love one another, to be together around His table, around Himself. What can exceed the blessedness of being allowed to break bread together in remembrance of our beloved and adorable Lord, to show forth His death until He come; to raise, in holy concert, our anthems of praise to God and the Lamb; to edify, exhort, and comfort one another, according to the gift and grace bestowed upon us by the risen and glorified Head of the Church; to pour out our hearts, in sweet fellowship, in prayer, supplication, intercession, and giving of thanks for all men, for kings and all in authority, for the whole household of faith—the Church of God—the body of Christ, for the Lord's work and workmen all over the earth?

Where, we would ask with all possible confidence, is there a true Christian, in a right state of soul, who would not delight in all this, and say, from the very depths of his heart, that there is nothing this side the glory to be compared with it?

But, we repeat, our happiness is not the question; it is less than secondary. We are to be ruled, in this as in all beside, by the will of God as revealed in His holy Word. The question for us is simply this: Is it according to the mind of God that His people should assemble themselves together for worship and mutual edification? If this be so, woe be to all who willfully refuse, or indolently neglect to do so, on any ground whatsoever; they not only suffer serious loss in their own souls, but they are offering dishonor to God, grieving His Spirit, and doing injury to the assembly of His people.

These are very weighty consequences, and they demand the serious attention of all the Lord's people. It must be obvious to the reader that it is according to the revealed will of God that His people should assemble themselves together, in His presence. The inspired apostle exhorts us, in the tenth chapter of his Epistle to the Hebrews, not to forsake the assembling of ourselves together. There is special value, interest, and importance attaching to the assembly. The truth as to this begins to dawn upon us in the opening pages of the New Testament. Thus, in Matthew 18:20, we read the words of our blessed Lord—"Where *two or three are gathered together* in My name, *there am I* in the midst of them." Here we have the divine centre. *"My name."* This answers to "The place which the Lord thy God shall choose to place His name there," so constantly named and so strongly insisted upon in the book of Deuteronomy. It was absolutely essential that Israel should gather at that one place. It was not a matter as to which people might choose for themselves. Human choice was absolutely and rigidly excluded. It was "*The* place which the Lord thy God shall choose," and no other. This we have seen distinctly. It is so plain that we have only to say, "How readest thou?"

Nor is it otherwise with the Church of God. It is not human choice, or human judgment, or human opinion, or human reason, or human any thing. It is absolutely and entirely divine. The *ground* of our gathering is divine, for it is accomplished redemption; the *centre* around which we are gathered is divine, for it is the Name of Jesus; the *power* by which we are gathered is divine, for it is the Holy Ghost; and the *authority* for our gathering is divine, for it is the Word of God.

All this is as clear as it is precious, and all we need is the simplicity of faith to take it in and act upon it. If we begin to reason about it, we shall be sure to get into darkness; and if we listen to human opinions, we shall be plunged in hopeless perplexity between the conflicting claims of christendom's sects and parties. Our only refuge, our only resource, our only strength, our only comfort, our only authority, is the precious Word of God. Take away that, and we have absolutely nothing; give us that, and we want no more.

This is what makes it all so real and so solid for our souls. Yes, and so consolatory and tranquilizing too. The truth as to our assembly is as clear and as simple and as unquestionable as the truth in reference to our salvation. It is the privilege of all Christians to be as sure that they are gathered on God's ground, around God's centre, by God's power, and on God's authority, as that they are within the blessed circle of God's salvation.

And then, if we be asked, How can we be certain of being around God's centre? we reply, Simply by the Word of God. How could Israel of old be sure as to God's chosen place for their assembly? By His express commandment. Were they at any loss for guidance? Surely not. His word was as clear and as distinct as to their place of worship as it was in reference to every thing else. It left not the slightest ground for uncertainty. It was so plainly set before them that for any one to raise a question could only be regarded as willful ignorance or positive disobedience.

Now, the question is, Are Christians worse off than Israel in reference to the great subject of their place of worship, the centre and ground of their assembly? Are they left in doubt and uncertainty? Is it an open question? Is it a matter as to which every man is left to do what is right in his own eyes? Has God given us no positive, definite instruction on a question so intensely interesting and so vitally important? Could we imagine for a moment that the One who graciously condescended to instruct His people of old in matters which we, in our fancied wisdom, would deem unworthy of notice, would leave His Church now without any definite guidance as to the ground, centre, and characteristic features of our worship? Utterly impossible! Every spiritual mind must reject, with decision and energy, any such idea.

No, it would not be like our gracious God to deal thus with His heavenly people. True, there is no such thing now as a particular place to which all Christians are to betake themselves periodically for worship. There *was* such a place for God's earthly people, and there *will be* such a place for restored Israel and for all nations by and by. "It shall come to pass in the last days, that the mountain of the Lord's house shall be established in the top of the mountains, and shall be exalted above the hills; and *all nations* shall flow unto it. And many people shall go and say, Come ye, and let us go up to the mountain of the Lord, to the house of the God of Jacob; and He will teach us of His ways, and we will walk in His paths; for *out of Zion* shall go forth the law, and the word of the Lord from Jerusalem" (Isa. 2). And again, "It shall come to pass, that every one that is left of all the nations which came against Jerusalem shall even go up from year to year to worship the King, the Lord of Hosts, and to keep the feast of tabernacles. And it shall be that whoso will not come up of *all the families of the earth unto Jerusalem* to worship the King, the Lord of Hosts, even upon them shall be no rain" (Zech. 14:16-17).

Here are two passages culled, one from the first, and the other from the last but one of the divinely inspired prophets, both pointing forward to the glorious time when Jerusalem shall be God's centre for Israel and for all nations. And we may assert, with all possible confidence, that the reader will find all the prophets, with one consent, in full harmony with Isaiah and Zechariah on this profoundly interesting subject. To apply such passages to the Church, or to heaven, is to do violence to the clearest and grandest utterances that ever fell on human ears; it is to confound things heavenly and earthly, and to give a flat contradiction to the divinely harmonious voices of prophets and apostles.

It is needless to multiply quotations. All Scripture goes to prove that Jerusalem was, and will yet be, God's earthly centre for His people, and for all nations; but *just now*—that is to say, from the day of Pentecost, when God the Holy Ghost came down to form the Church of God, the body of Christ, until the moment when our Lord Jesus Christ shall come to take His people away out of this world—there is no place, no city, no sacred locality, no earthly centre, for the Lord's people. To talk to Christians about holy places, or consecrated ground, is as thoroughly foreign to them (at least, it ought to be) as it would have been to talk to a Jew about having his place of worship in heaven. The idea is wholly out of place, wholly out of character.

If the reader will turn for a moment to the fourth chapter of John, he will find, in our Lord's marvelous discourse with the woman of Sychar, the most blessed teaching on this subject. "The woman saith unto Him, 'Sir, I perceive that Thou art a prophet. Our fathers worshiped in this mountain, and ye say that in Jerusalem is the place where men ought to worship.' Jesus saith unto her, 'Woman, believe Me; the hour cometh, when ye shall neither in this mountain nor yet at Jerusalem worship the Father. Ye worship ye know not what; we know what we worship, for salvation is of the Jews. But the hour cometh, and now is, when the true worshipers shall worship the Father in spirit and in truth, for the Father *seeketh* such to worship Him. God is a spirit, and they that worship Him *must* worship Him in spirit and in truth' " (ver. 19-24).

This passage entirely sets aside the thought of any special place of worship now. There really is no such thing. *"The Most High dwelleth not in temples made with hands;* as saith the prophet, 'Heaven is My throne, and earth is My footstool: what house will ye build Me?' saith the Lord, 'or what is the place of My rest? Hath not My hand made all these things?' " (Acts 7: 48-50) And again, "God that made the world, and all things therein, seeing that He is Lord of heaven and earth, *dwelleth not in temples made with hands; neither is worshiped with men's hands,* as though He needed any thing, seeing He giveth to all life and breath and all things" (Acts 17:24-25).

The teaching of the New Testament, from beginning to end, is clear and decided as to the subject of worship; and the Christian reader is solemnly bound to give heed to that teaching, and to seek to understand, and submit his whole moral being to its authority. There has ever been, from the very earliest ages of the Church's history, a strong and fatal tendency to return to Judaism, not only on the subject of righteousness, but also on that of worship. Christians have not only been put under the law for life and righteousness, but also under the Levitical ritual for the order and character of their worship. We have dealt with the former of these in chapters 4 and 5 of these *Notes,* but the latter is hardly less serious in its effect upon the whole tone and character of Christian life and conduct.

We have to bear in mind that Satan's great object is, to cast the Church of God down from her excellency, in reference to her standing, her walk, and her worship. No sooner was the Church set up on the day of Pentecost than he commenced his corrupting and undermining process, and for eighteen long centuries he has carried it on with diabolical persistency. In the face of these plain passages quoted above, in reference to the character of worship which the Father is now seeking, and as to the fact that God does not dwell in temples made with hands, we have seen, in all ages, the strong tendency to return to the condition of things under the Mosaic economy. Hence the desire for great buildings, imposing rituals, sacerdotal orders, choral services, all of which are in direct opposition to the mind of Christ and to the plainest teachings of the New Testament. The professing church has entirely departed from the spirit and authority of the Lord in all these things; and yet, strange and sad to say, these very things are continually appealed to as proofs of the wonderful progress of Christianity. We are told by some of our public teachers and guides that the blessed apostle Paul had little idea of the grandeur to which the Church was to attain; but if he could only see one of our venerable cathedrals, with its lofty aisles and painted windows, and listen to the peals of the organ and the voices of the choristers, he would see what an advance had been made upon the upper room at Jerusalem!

Ah! be assured, it is all a most thorough delusion. It is true indeed, the Church has made progress, but it is in the wrong direction; it is not upward, but downward. It is away from Christ, away from the Father, away from the Spirit, away from the Word.

We should like to ask the reader this one question: If the apostle Paul were to come to London for next Lord's day, where could he find what he found in Troas eighteen hundred years ago, as recorded in Acts 20:7? Where could he find a company of disciples gathered simply by the Holy Ghost, to the Name of Jesus, to break bread in remembrance of Him, and to show forth His death till He come? Such was the divine order then, and such must be the divine order now. We cannot for a moment believe that the apostle would accept any thing else. He would look for the divine thing; he would have that or nothing. Now, where could he find it? where could he go and find the table of his Lord, as appointed by Himself the same night in which He was betrayed?

Mark, we are bound to believe that the apostle Paul would insist upon having the table and the supper of his Lord as he had received them direct from Himself in the glory, and given them by the Spirit in the tenth and eleventh chapters of his Epistle to the Corinthians—an Epistle addressed to "all that in every place call on the name of our Lord Jesus Christ, both theirs and ours." We cannot believe that he would teach God's order in the first century and accept man's disorder in the nineteenth. Man has no right to tamper with a divine institution. He has no more authority to alter a single jot or tittle connected with the Lord's supper than Israel had to interfere with the order of the passover.

Now, we repeat the question, and earnestly entreat the reader to ponder and answer it in the divine presence and in the light of Scripture: Where could the apostle find this in London, or any where else in christendom, on next Lord's day? Where could he go and take his seat at the table of his Lord, in the midst of a company of disciples gathered simply on the *ground* of the one body, to the one *centre*—the Name of Jesus, by the *power* of the Holy Ghost, and on the *authority* of the Word of God? Where could he find a sphere in which he could exercise his gifts without human authority, appointment, or ordination? We ask these questions in order to exercise the heart and conscience of the reader. We are fully convinced that there are places here and there where Paul could find these things carried out, though in weakness and failure, and we believe the Christian reader is solemnly responsible to find them out. Alas! they are few and far between, compared with the mass of Christians meeting otherwise.

We may perhaps be told that if people knew that it was the apostle Paul, they would willingly allow him to minister. But then he would neither seek nor accept their permission, inasmuch as he tells us plainly, in the first chapter of Galatians, that his ministry was "not of men, neither by man, but by Jesus Christ, and God the Father, who raised Him from the dead."

Not only so, but we may rest assured that the blessed apostle would insist upon having the Lord's table spread upon the divine ground of the one body, and he could only consent to eat the Lord's supper according to its divine order as laid down in the New Testament. He could not accept for a moment any thing but the divine reality. He would say, Either that or nothing. He could not admit any human interference with a divine institution; neither could he accept any new ground of gathering, or any new principle of organization. He would repeat his own inspired statements—"There is *one body* and one Spirit," and, "We being many, are one bread—*one body,* for we are all partakers of that one bread." These words apply to "all that in every place call on the name of Jesus Christ our Lord," and they hold good in all ages of the Church's existence on earth.

The reader must be very clear and distinct as to this. God's principle of gathering and unity must on no account be surrendered. The moment men begin to organize—to form societies, churches, or associations, they act in direct opposition to the Word of God, the mind of Christ, and the present action of the Holy Ghost. Man might as well set about to form a world as to form a church. It is entirely a divine work. The Holy Ghost came down on the day of Pentecost to form *the* Church of God—*the* body of Christ, and this is the only Church—the only body that Scripture recognizes; all else is contrary to God, even though it may be sanctioned and defended by thousands of true Christians.

Let not the reader misunderstand us. We are not speaking of salvation, of eternal life, or of divine righteousness, but of the true ground of gathering, the divine principle on which the Lord's table should be spread and the Lord's supper celebrated. Thousands of the Lord's beloved people have lived and died in the communion of the church of Rome; but the church of Rome is not the Church of God, but a horrible apostasy; and the sacrifice of the mass is not the Lord's supper, but a marred, mutilated, and miserable invention of the devil. If the question in the mind of the reader be merely what amount of error he can sanction without forfeiting his soul's salvation, it is useless to proceed with the grand important subject before us.

But where is the heart that loves Christ that could be content to take such miserably low ground as this? What would have been thought of an Israelite of old who could content himself with being a child of Abraham, and could enjoy his vine and his fig-tree, his flocks and his herds, but never think of going to worship at the place where Jehovah had recorded His name? Where was the faithful Jew who did not love that sacred spot? "Lord, I have loved the habitation of Thine house, and the place where Thine honor dwelleth."

When, by reason of Israel's sin, the national polity was broken up, and the people were in captivity, we hear the true-hearted exiles amongst them pouring forth their lament in the following touching and eloquent strain, "By the rivers of Babylon, there we sat down; yea, *we wept when we remembered Zion.* We hanged our harps upon the willows in the midst thereof. For there they that carried us away captive required of us a song, and they that wasted us required of us mirth, saying, 'Sing us one of the songs of Zion.' How shall we sing the Lord's song in a strange land? If I forget thee, O Jerusalem [God's centre for His earthly people], let my right hand forget her cunning. If I do not remember thee, let my tongue cleave to the roof of my mouth; if I prefer not Jerusalem above my chief joy" (Ps. 137).

Again, in the sixth chapter of Daniel, we find that beloved exile opening his window three times a day, and praying toward Jerusalem, although he knew that the lions' den was the penalty. But why insist upon praying toward Jerusalem? Was it a piece of Jewish superstition? Nay, it was a magnificent display of divine principle; it was an unfurling of the divine standard amid the depressing and humiliating consequences of Israel's folly and sin. True, Jerusalem was in ruins; but God's thoughts respecting Jerusalem were not in ruins. It was His centre for His earthly people. "Jerusalem is builded as a city that is compact together, whither the tribes go up, the tribes of the Lord, unto the testimony of Israel, to give thanks unto the name of the Lord. For there are set thrones of judgment, the thrones of the house of David. Pray for the peace of Jerusalem; they shall prosper that love thee. Peace be within thy walls, and prosperity within thy palaces. *For my brethren and companions' sakes,* I will now say, Peace be within thee. *Because of the house of the Lord our God* I will seek thy good" (Ps. 122).

Jerusalem was the centre for Israel's twelve tribes in days gone by, and it will be so in the future. To apply the above and similar passages to the Church of God here or hereafter—on earth or in heaven, is simply turning things upside down, confounding things essentially different, and thus doing an incalculable amount of damage both to Scripture and the souls of men. We must not allow ourselves to take such unwarrantable liberties with the Word of God.

Jerusalem was and will be God's earthly centre; but now, the Church of God should own no centre but the glorious and infinitely precious Name of Jesus. "Where two or three are gathered together in My name, there am I in the midst of them." Precious centre! To this alone the New Testament points, to this alone the Holy Ghost gathers. It matters not where we are gathered—in Jerusalem or Rome, London, Paris, or Canton. It is not *where*, but *how.*

But be it remembered, it must be a divinely real thing. It is of no possible use to profess to be gathered in, or to, the blessed Name of Jesus, if we are not really so. The apostle's word as to faith may apply with equal force to the question of our centre of gathering. "What doth it profit, my brethren, though a man *say*" he is gathered to the Name of Jesus? God deals in moral realities; and while it is perfectly clear that a man who desires to be true to Christ cannot possibly consent to own any other centre or any other ground of gathering but His Name, yet it is quite possible—alas! how very possible—for people to profess to be on that blessed and holy ground, while their spirit and conduct, their habits and ways, their whole course and character, go to prove that they are not in the power of their profession.

The apostle said to the Corinthians that he would "know, not the speech, but the power." A weighty word, most surely, and much needed at all times, but specially needed in reference to the important subject now before us. We would lovingly, yet most solemnly, press upon the conscience of the Christian reader his responsibility to consider this matter in the holy retirement of the Lord's presence, and in the light of the New Testament. Let him not set it aside on the plea of its not being essential. It is in the very highest degree essential, inasmuch as it concerns the Lord's glory and the maintenance of His truth. This is the only standard by which to decide what is essential and what is not. Was it essential for Israel to gather at the divinely appointed centre? Was it left an open question? Might every man choose a centre for himself? Let the answer be weighed in the light of Deuteronomy 14. It was absolutely essential that the Israel of God should assemble around the centre of the God of Israel. This is unquestionable. Woe be to the man who presumed to turn his back on the place where Jehovah had set His Name. He would very speedily have been taught his mistake. And if this was true for God's earthly people, is it not equally true for the Church and the individual Christian? Assuredly it is. We are bound, by the very highest and most sacred obligations, to refuse every *ground* of gathering but the one body, every *centre* of gathering but the Name of Jesus, every *power* of gathering but the Holy Ghost, every *authority* of gathering but the Word of God. May all the Lord's beloved people every where be led to consider these things, in the fear and love of His holy name.

We shall now close this section by quoting the last paragraph of our chapter, in which we shall find some valuable practical teaching.

"At the end of three years, thou shalt bring forth all the tithe of thine increase the same year, and shalt lay it up within thy gates; and the Levite, (because he hath no part nor inheritance with thee,) and the stranger, and the fatherless, and the widow, which are within thy gates, *shall come,* and *shall eat* and *be satisfied;* that the Lord thy God may bless thee in all the work of thine hand which thou doest."

Here we have a lovely home-scene, a most touching display of the divine character, a beautiful outshining of the grace and kindness of the God of Israel. It does the heart good to breathe the fragrant air of such a passage as this. It stands in vivid and striking contrast with the cold selfishness of the scene around us. God would teach His people to think of and care for all who were in need. The tithe belonged to Him, but He would give them the rare and exquisite privilege of devoting it to the blessed object of making hearts glad.

There is peculiar sweetness in the words, "shall come"—"shall eat"—"and be satisfied." So like our own ever-gracious God! He delights to meet the need of all. He opens His hand, and satisfies the desire of every living thing. And not only so, but it is His joy to make His people the channel through which the grace, the kindness, and the sympathy of His heart may flow forth to all. How precious is this! What a privilege to be God's almoners—the dispensers of His bounty—the exponents of His goodness! Would that we entered more fully into the deep blessedness of all this! May we breathe more the atmosphere of the divine presence, and then we shall more faithfully reflect the divine character.

As the deeply interesting and practical subject presented in verses 28 and 29 will come before us in another connection in our study of chapter 26, we shall not dwell further upon it here.

---

## *CHAPTER 15*

"AT the end of every seven years thou shalt make a release. And this is the manner of the release: Every creditor that lendeth aught unto his neighbor shall release it; he shall not exact it of his neighbor, or of his brother, *because it is called the Lord's release.* Of a foreigner thou mayest exact it again; but that which is thine with thy brother thine hand shall release, save when there shall be no poor among you; for the Lord shall greatly bless thee in the land which the Lord thy God giveth thee for an inheritance to possess it; only if thou carefully hearken unto the voice of the Lord thy God, to observe to do all these commandments which I command thee this day. For the Lord thy God blesseth thee, as He promised thee; and thou shalt lend unto many nations, but thou shalt not borrow; and thou shalt reign over many nations, but they shall not reign over thee" (ver. 1-6).

It is truly edifying to mark the way in which the God of Israel was ever seeking to draw the hearts of His people to Himself by means of the various sacrifices, solemnities, and institutions of the Levitical ceremonial. There was the morning and evening lamb every *day,* there was the holy Sabbath every *week,* there was the new moon every *month,* there was the passover every *year,* there was the tithing every *three years,* there was the release every *seven years,* and there was the jubilee every *fifty years.*

All this is full of deepest interest. It tells its own sweet tale, and teaches its own precious lesson to the heart. The morning and evening lamb, as we know, pointed ever to "the Lamb of God, which taketh away the sin of the world"; the Sabbath was the lovely type of the rest that remaineth to the people of God; the new moon beautifully prefigured the time when restored Israel shall reflect back the beams of the Sun of Righteousness upon the nations; the passover was the standing memorial of the nation's deliverance from Egyptian bondage; the year of tithing set forth the fact of Jehovah's proprietorship of the land, as also the lovely way in which His rents were to be expended in meeting the need of His workmen and of His poor; the sabbatic year gave promise of a bright time when all debts would be canceled, all loans disposed of, all burdens removed; and finally, the jubilee was the magnificent type of the times of the restitution of all things, when the captive shall be set free, when the exile shall return to his long-lost home and inheritance, and when the land of Israel and the whole earth shall rejoice beneath the beneficent government of the Son of David.

Now, in all these lovely institutions we notice two prominent characteristic features, namely, glory to God, and blessing to man. These two things are linked together by a divine and everlasting bond. God has so ordained that His full glory and the creature's full blessing should be indissolubly bound up together. This is deep joy to the heart, and it helps us to understand more fully the force and beauty of that familiar sentence—"We rejoice in hope of the glory of God." When that glory shines forth in its full lustre, then, assuredly, human blessedness, rest, and felicity shall reach their full and eternal consummation.

We see a lovely pledge and foreshadowing of all this in the seventh year. It was "the Lord's release," and therefore its blessed influence was to be felt by every poor debtor from Dan to Beersheba. Jehovah would grant unto His people the high and holy privilege of having fellowship with Him in causing the debtor's heart to sing for joy. He would teach them, if they would only learn, the deep blessedness of frankly forgiving all. This is what He Himself delights in, blessed forever be His great and glorious name.

But, alas! the poor human heart is not up to this lovely mark. It is not fully prepared to tread this heavenly road. It is sadly cramped and hindered, by a low and miserable selfishness, in grasping and carrying out the divine principle of grace. It is not quite at home in this heavenly atmosphere; it is but ill-prepared for being the vessel and channel of that royal grace which shines so brightly in all the ways of God. This will only too fully account for the cautionary clauses of the following passage. "If there be among you a poor man of one of thy brethren within any of thy gates, in thy land, which the Lord thy God giveth thee, *thou shalt not harden thine heart, nor shut thine hand* from thy poor brother; but thou shalt *open thine hand wide* unto him, and surely lend him sufficient for his need, in that which he wanteth. Beware that there be not a thought *in thy wicked heart,* saying, The seventh year, the year of release, is at hand; and *thine eye be evil* against thy poor brother, and thou *givest* him naught; and he cry unto the Lord against thee, and it be sin unto thee. *Thou shalt surely give him,* and thine heart shall not be grieved when thou givest unto him; because that for this thing the Lord thy God shall bless thee in all thy works, and in all that thou puttest thine hand unto. For the poor shall never cease out of thy land; therefore I command thee, saying, *Thou shalt open thine hand wide* unto thy brother, to thy poor, and to thy needy, in thy land" (ver. 7-11).

Here the deep springs of the poor selfish heart are discovered and judged. There is nothing like grace for making manifest the hidden roots of evil in human nature. Man must be renewed in the very deepest springs of his moral being ere he can be the vehicle of divine love; and even those who are thus through grace renewed, have to watch continually against the hideous forms of selfishness in which our fallen nature clothes itself. Nothing but grace can keep the heart open wide to every form of human need. We must abide hard by the fountain of heavenly love if we would be channels of blessing in the midst of a scene of misery and desolation like that in which our lot is cast.

How lovely are those words, "Thou shalt open thine hand wide"! They breathe the very air of heaven. An open heart and a wide hand are like God. "The Lord loveth a cheerful giver," because that is precisely what He is Himself. "He giveth to all liberally, and upbraideth not." And He would grant unto us the rare and most exquisite privilege of being imitators of Him. Marvelous grace! The very thought of it fills the heart with wonder, love, and praise. We are not only saved by grace, but we stand in grace, live under the blessed reign of grace, breathe the very atmosphere of grace, and are called to be the living exponents of grace, not only to our brethren, but to the whole human family. "As we therefore have opportunity, let us do good unto all, especially unto them which are of the household of faith."

Let us diligently apply our hearts to all this divine instruction. It is most precious; but its real preciousness can only be tasted in the practical carrying out of it. We are surrounded by ten thousand forms of human misery, human sorrow, human need. There are broken hearts, crushed spirits, desolate homes, around us on every side. The widow, the orphan, and the stranger meet us daily in our walks. How do we carry ourselves in reference to all these? Are we hardening our hearts and closing our hands against them? or are we seeking to act in the lovely spirit of "the Lord's release"? We must bear in mind that we are called to be reflectors of the divine nature and character—to be direct channels of communication between our Father's loving heart and every form of human need. We are not to live for ourselves; to do so is a most miserable denial of every feature and principle of that morally glorious Christianity which we profess. It is our high and holy privilege, yea, it is our special mission, to shed around us the blessed light of that heaven to which we belong. Wherever we are—in the family, in the field, in the mart or the manufactory, in the shop or in the counting-house, all who come in contact with us should see the grace of Jesus shining out in our ways, our words, our very looks. And then, if any object of need come before us, if we can do nothing more, we should drop a soothing word into the ear, or shed a tear or heave a sigh of genuine, heart-felt sympathy.

Is it thus with us? Are we so living near the fountain of divine love, and so breathing the very air of heaven, that the blessed fragrance of these things shall be diffused around us? or are we displaying the odious selfishness of nature, the unholy tempers and dispositions of our fallen and corrupt humanity? What an unsightly object is a selfish Christian! He is a standing contradiction, a living, moving lie. The Christianity which he professes throws into dark and terrible relief the unholy selfishness which governs his heart and comes out in his life.

The Lord grant that all who profess and call themselves Christians may so carry themselves, in daily life, as to be an unblotted epistle of Christ, known and read of all men. In this way, infidelity will, at least, be deprived of one of its weightiest arguments, its gravest objections. Nothing affords a stronger plea to the infidel than the inconsistent lives of professing Christians.

Not that such a plea will stand for a moment, or even be urged, before the judgment-seat of Christ, inasmuch as each one who has within his reach a copy of the holy Scriptures will be judged by the light of those Scriptures, even though there were not a single consistent Christian on the face of the earth. Nevertheless, Christians are solemnly responsible to let their light so shine before men that they may see their good works and glorify our Father in heaven. We are solemnly bound to exhibit and illustrate in daily life the heavenly principles unfolded in the Word of God. We should leave the infidel without a shred of a plea or an argument; we are responsible so to do.

May we lay these things to heart, and then we shall have occasion to bless God for our meditation on the delightful institution of "the Lord's release."

We shall now quote for the reader the touching and beautiful institution in reference to the Hebrew servant. We increasingly feel the importance of giving the veritable language of the Holy Ghost; for albeit it may be said that the reader has his Bible to refer to, yet we know, as a fact, that when passages of Scripture are referred to, there is, in many cases, a reluctance to lay down the volume which we hold in our hand in order to read the reference. And beside, there is nothing like the Word of God; and as to any remarks which we may offer, their object is simply to help the beloved Christian reader to understand and appreciate the Scriptures which we quote.

"If thy brother, a Hebrew man, or a Hebrew woman, be sold unto thee, and serve thee six years, then in the seventh year thou shalt let him go free from thee. And when thou sendest him out free from thee, thou shalt not let him go away empty; *thou shalt furnish him liberally* out of thy flock, and out of thy floor, and out of thy wine-press; of that wherewith the Lord thy God hath blessed thee thou shalt give unto him."

How perfectly beautiful! how like our own ever-gracious God is all this! He would not have the brother go away empty. Liberty and poverty would not be in moral harmony. The brother was to be sent on his way free and full, emancipated and endowed, not only with his liberty, but with a liberal fortune to start with.

Truly, this is divine. We do not want to be told the school where such exquisite ethics are taught. They have the very ring of heaven about them; they emit the fragrant odor of the very paradise of God. Is it not in this way that our God has dealt with us? All praise to His glorious name! He has not only given us life and liberty, but He has furnished us liberally with all we can possibly want for time and eternity. He has opened the exhaustless treasury of heaven for us; yea, He has given the Son of His bosom for us and to us—*for* us, to *save; to* us, to *satisfy.* He has given us all things that pertain to life and godliness; all that pertains to the life that now is, and to that which is to come, is fully and perfectly secured by our Father's liberal hand.

And is it not deeply affecting to mark how the heart of God expresses itself in the style in which the Hebrew servant was to be treated? "Thou shalt furnish him *liberally.*" Not grudgingly, or of necessity. It was to be done in a manner worthy of God. The actings of His people are to be the reflection of Himself. We are called to the high and holy dignity of being His moral representatives. It is marvelous; but thus it is, through His infinite grace. He has not only delivered us from the flames of an everlasting hell, but He calls us to act for Him, and to be like Him, in the midst of a world that crucified His Son. And not only has He conferred this lofty dignity upon us, but He has endowed us with a princely fortune to support it. The inexhaustible resources of heaven are at our disposal. "All things are ours," through His infinite grace. Oh that we may more fully realize our privileges, and thus more faithfully discharge our holy responsibilities!

At verse 15 of our chapter, we have a very touching motive presented to the heart of the people, one eminently calculated to stir their affections and sympathies. "And thou shalt remember that thou wast a bondman in the land of Egypt, and the Lord thy God redeemed thee; *therefore* I command thee this thing to-day." The remembrance of Jehovah's grace in redeeming them out of Egypt was to be the ever-abiding and all-powerful motive-spring of their actings toward the poor brother. This is a never-failing principle, and nothing lower than this will ever stand. If we look for our motive-springs any where but in God Himself, and in His dealings with us, we shall soon break down in our practical career. It is only as we keep before our hearts the marvelous grace of God displayed toward us in the redemption which is in Christ Jesus that we shall be able to pursue a course of true, active benevolence, whether toward our brethren or those outside. Mere kindly feelings, bubbling up in our own hearts, or drawn out by the sorrows and distresses and necessities of others, will prove evanescent. It is only in the living God Himself we can find perennial springs.

At verse 16, a case is contemplated in which a servant might prefer remaining with his master. "And it shall be, if he say unto thee, I will not go away from thee, because he loveth thee and thine house, because he is well with thee, then thou shalt take an awl, and thrust it through his ear unto the door, and he shall be thy servant forever."

In comparing this passage with Exodus 21:1-6, we observe a marked difference arising, as we might expect, from the distinctive character of each book. In Exodus, the *typical* feature is prominent; in Deuteronomy, the *moral.* Hence, in the latter, the inspired writer omits all about the wife and the children, as foreign to his purpose here, though so essential to the beauty and perfectness of the type in Exodus 21. We merely notice this as one of the many striking proofs that Deuteronomy is very far indeed from being a barren repetition of its predecessors. There is neither repetition on the one hand, nor contradiction on the other, but lovely variety in perfect accordance with the divine object and scope of each book. So much for the contemptible shallowness and ignorance of those infidel writers who have had the impious temerity to level their shafts at this magnificent portion of the oracles of God.

In our chapter, then, we have the moral aspect of this interesting institution. The servant loved his master, and was happy with him. He preferred perpetual slavery and the mark thereof with a master whom he loved, to liberty and a liberal portion away from him. This, of course, would argue well for both parties. It is ever a good sign for both master and servant when the connection is of long standing. Perpetual changing may, as a general rule, be taken as a proof of moral wrong somewhere. No doubt there are exceptions; and not only so, but in the relation of master and servant, as in every thing else, there are two sides to be considered. For instance, we have to consider whether the master is perpetually changing his servants, or the servant perpetually changing his masters. In the former case, appearances would tell against the master; in the latter, against the servant.

The fact is, we have all to judge ourselves in this matter. Those of us who are masters have to consider how far we really seek the comfort, happiness, and solid profit of our servants. We should bear in mind that we have very much more to think of, in reference to our servants, than the amount of work we can get out of them. Even upon the low-level principle of "live and let live," we are bound to seek, in every possible way, to make our servants happy and comfortable; to make them feel that they have a home under our roof; that we are not content merely with the labor of their hands, but that we want the love of their hearts. We remember once asking the head of a very large establishment, "How many *hearts* do you employ?" He shook his head, and owned, with real sorrow, how little heart there is in the relation of master and servant. Hence the common, heartless phrase of "employing *hands.*"

But the Christian master is called to stand upon a higher level altogether; he is privileged to be an imitator of his Master—Christ. The remembrance of this will regulate all his actings toward the servant; it will lead him to study, with ever-deepening interest and solid profit, his divine model, in order to reproduce Him in all the practical details of daily life.

So also in reference to the Christian servant, in his position and line of action. He, as well as the master, has to study the great example set before him in the path and ministry of the only true Servant that ever trod this earth. He is called to walk in His blessed footsteps, to drink into His spirit, to study His Word. It is not a little remarkable that the Holy Ghost has devoted more attention to the instruction of servants than to all the other relationships put together. This the reader can see at a glance, in the Epistles to the Ephesians, Colossians, and Titus. The Christian servant can adorn the doctrine of God our Saviour by not purloining and not answering again. He can serve the Lord Christ in the most common-place duties of domestic life just as effectually as the man who is called to address thousands on the grand realities of eternity.

Thus, when both master and servant are mutually governed by heavenly principles, both seeking to serve and glorify the one Lord, they will get on happily together. The master will not be severe, arbitrary, and exacting; and the servant will not be self-seeking, heady, and high-minded; each will contribute, by the faithful discharge of their relative duties, to the comfort and happiness of the other, and to the peace and happiness of the whole domestic circle. Would that it were more after this heavenly fashion in every Christian household on the face of the earth! Then indeed would the truth of God be vindicated, His Word honored, and His name glorified in our domestic relations and practical ways.

In verse 18, we have an admonitory word which reveals to us, very faithfully, but with great delicacy, a moral root in the poor human heart. "It shall not seem hard unto thee when thou sendest him away free from thee, for he has been worth a double hired servant to thee in serving thee six years, and the Lord thy God shall bless thee in all that thou doest."

This is very affecting. Only think of the most high God condescending to stand before the human heart—the heart of a master, to plead the cause of a poor servant, and set forth his claims! It is as if He were asking a favor for Himself. He leaves nothing unsaid in order to strengthen the case; He reminds the master of the value of six years' service, and encourages him by the promise of enlarged blessing as a reward for his generous acting. It is perfectly beautiful. The Lord would not only have the generous thing done, but done in such a way as to gladden the heart of the one to whom it was done; He thinks not only of the *substance* of an action, but also of the *style.* We may, at times, brace ourselves up to the business of doing a kindness; we do it as a matter of duty, and all the while it may *"seem hard"* that we should have to do it; thus the act will be robbed of all its charms. It is the generous heart that adorns the generous act. We should so do a kindness as to assure the recipient that our own heart is made glad by the act. This is the divine way: "When they had nothing to pay, he *frankly* forgave them both." "It is meet that *we* should make merry, and be glad." "There is joy in heaven over one sinner that repenteth." Oh, to be a brighter reflection of the precious grace of our Father's heart!

Ere closing our remarks on this deeply interesting chapter, we shall quote for the reader its last paragraph. "All the firstling males that come of thy herd and of thy flock thou shalt sanctify unto the Lord thy God; thou shalt do no work with the firstling of thy bullock, nor shear the firstling of thy sheep; thou shalt eat it before the Lord thy God year by year *in the place which the Lord shall choose,* thou and thy household. And if there be any blemish therein, as if it be lame, or blind, or have any ill blemish, thou shalt not sacrifice it unto the Lord thy God. Thou shalt eat it within thy gates, the unclean and the clean person shall eat it alike, as the roebuck, and as the hart. Only thou shalt not eat the blood thereof; thou shalt pour it upon the ground as water" (ver. 19-23).

Only that which was perfect was to be offered to God. The first-born, unblemished male, the apt figure of the spotless Lamb of God, offered upon the cross for us, the imperishable foundation of our peace, and the precious food of our souls, in the presence of God. This was the divine thing, the assembly gathered together around the divine centre, feasting in the presence of God on that which was the appointed type of Christ, who is at once our sacrifice, our centre, and our feast. Eternal and universal homage to His most precious and glorious Name!

## *CHAPTER 16*

We now approach one of the most profound and comprehensive sections of the book of Deuteronomy, in which the inspired writer presents to our view what we may call the three great cardinal feasts of the Jewish year, namely, the passover, Pentecost, and tabernacles; or, redemption, the Holy Ghost, and the glory. We have here a more condensed view of those lovely institutions than that given in Leviticus 23, where we have, if we count the Sabbath, eight feasts; but if we view the Sabbath as distinct, and having its own special place as the type of God's own eternal rest, then there are seven feasts, namely, the passover, the feast of unleavened bread, the feast of first-fruits, Pentecost, trumpets, the day of atonement, and tabernacles.

Such is the order of feasts in the book of Leviticus, which, as we have ventured to remark in our studies on that most marvelous book, may be called *"The priest's* guide-book." But in Deuteronomy, which is preeminently *the people's* book, we have less of ceremonial detail, and the lawgiver confines himself to those great moral and national landmarks which, in the very simplest manner, as adapted to the people, present the past, the present, and the future.

"Observe the month of Abib, and keep the passover unto the Lord thy God; for in the month of Abib the Lord thy God brought thee forth out of Egypt by night. Thou shalt therefore sacrifice the passover unto the Lord thy God, of the flock and the herd, *in the place which the Lord shall choose to place His name there.* Thou shalt eat no leavened bread with it; seven days shalt thou eat unleavened bread therewith, even *the bread of affliction;* for thou camest forth out of the land of Egypt in haste: that thou mayest remember the day when thou camest forth out of the land of Egypt all the days of thy life. And there shall be no leavened bread seen with thee in all thy coasts seven days; neither shall there any thing of the flesh, which whou sacrificedst the first day at even, remain all night until the morning. Thou mayest not sacrifice the passover within any of thy gates which the Lord thy God giveth thee"—as if it were a matter of no importance where, provided the feast were kept—*"but at the place which the Lord thy God shall choose to place His name in, there* [and no where else] thou shalt sacrifice the passover at even, at the going down of the sun, at the season that thou camest forth out of Egypt. And thou shalt roast and eat it *in the place which the Lord thy God shall choose;* and thou shalt turn in the morning, and go unto thy tents. Six days thou shalt eat unleavened bread; and on the seventh day shall be a solemn assembly to the Lord thy God: thou shalt do no work therein" (ver. 1-8).

Having, in our *Notes on Exodus,* gone somewhat fully into the great leading principles of this foundation-feast, we must refer the reader to that volume if he desires to study the subject. But there are certain features peculiar to Deuteronomy to which we feel it our duty to call his special attention; and, in the first place, we have to notice the remarkable emphasis laid upon "the place" where the feast was to be kept. This is full of interest and practical moment. The people were not to choose for themselves. It might, according to human thinking, appear a very small matter how or where the feast was kept, provided it was kept at all. But, be it carefully noted and deeply pondered by the reader, human thinking had nothing whatever to do in the matter; it was divine thinking and divine authority altogether. God had a right to prescribe and definitively settle where He would meet His people; and this He does in the most distinct and emphatic manner, in the above passage, where, three times over, He inserts the weighty clause, "In the place which the Lord thy God shall choose."

Is this vain repetition? Let no one dare to think, much less to assert it. It is most necessary emphasis. Why most necessary? Because of our ignorance, our indifference, and our willfulness. God, in His infinite goodness, takes special pains to impress upon the heart, the conscience, and the understanding of His people that He would have one place in particular where the memorable and most significant feast of the passover was to be kept.

And be it remarked that it is only in Deuteronomy that the *place* of celebration is insisted upon. We have nothing about it in Exodus, because there it was kept *in Egypt;* we having nothing about it in Numbers, because there it was kept *in the wilderness;* but in Deuteronomy it is authoritatively and definitively settled, because there we have the instructions for *the land.* Another striking proof that Deuteronomy is very far indeed from being a barren repetition of its predecessors.

The all-important point in reference to "the place," so prominently and so peremptorily insisted upon in all the three great solemnities recorded in our chapter, is this: God would gather His beloved people around Himself, that they might feast together in His presence, that He might rejoice in them and they in Him and in one another. All this could only be in the one special place of divine appointment. All who desired to meet Jehovah and to meet His people—all who desired worship and communion according to God, would thankfully betake themselves to the divinely appointed centre. Self-will might say, Can we not keep the feast in the bosom of our families? What need is there of a long journey? Surely if the heart is right, it cannot matter much as to the place. To all this we reply that the clearest, finest, and best proof of the heart being right would be found in the simple, earnest desire to do the will of God. It was quite sufficient for every one who loved and feared God that He had appointed a place where He would meet His people; there they would be found, and no where else. His presence it was that could alone impart joy, comfort, strength, and blessing to all their great national reunions. It was not the mere fact of a large number of people gathering together, three times a year, to feast and rejoice together; this might minister to human pride, self-complacency, and excitement. But to flock together to meet Jehovah, to assemble in His blessed presence, to own the place where He had recorded His Name, this would be the deep joy of every truly loyal heart throughout the twelve tribes of Israel. For any one *willfully* to abide at home, or to go any where else than to the one divinely appointed place, would not only be to neglect and insult Jehovah, but actually to rebel against His supreme authority.

Now, having briefly spoken of the *place,* we may, for a moment, glance at the *mode* of celebration. This, too, is, as we might expect, quite characteristic of our book. The leading feature here is "the unleavened bread." But the reader will specially note the interesting fact that this bread is styled *"The bread of affliction."* Now, what is the meaning of this? We all understand that unleavened bread is the type of that holiness of heart and life so absolutely essential to the enjoyment of true communion with God. We are not saved *by* personal holiness, but, thank God, we are saved *to* it. It is not the ground of our salvation, but it is an essential element in our communion. *Allowed leaven is the death-blow to communion and worship.*

We must never, for one moment, lose sight of this great cardinal principle in that life of personal holiness and practical godliness which, as redeemed by the blood of the Lamb, we are called, bound, and privileged to live from day to day, in the midst of the scenes and circumstances through which we are journeying home to our eternal rest in the heavens. To speak of communion and worship while living in known sin is the melancholy proof that we know nothing of either the one or the other. In order to enjoy communion with God or the communion of saints, and in order to worship God in spirit and in truth, we must be living a life of personal holiness, a life of separation from all known evil. To take our place in the assembly of God's people, and appear to take part in the holy fellowship and worship pertaining thereto, while living in secret sin, or allowing evil in others, is to defile the assembly, grieve the Holy Ghost, sin against Christ, and bring down upon us the judgment of God, who is *now* judging His house and chastening His children in order that they may not ultimately be condemned with the world.

All this is most solemn, and calls for the earnest attention of all who really desire to walk with God and serve Him with reverence and godly fear. It is one thing to have the doctrine of the type in the region of our understanding, and another thing altogether to have its greal moral lesson engraved on the heart and worked out in the life. May all who profess to have the blood of the Lamb sprinkled on their conscience seek to keep the feast of unleavened bread. "Know ye not that a little leaven leaveneth the whole lump? Purge out therefore the old leaven, that ye may be a new lump, as ye are unleavened. For even Christ our passover is sacrificed for us; therefore let us keep the feast, not with old leaven, neither with the leaven of malice and wickedness, but with the unleavened bread of sincerity and truth" (1 Cor. 5:6-8).

But what are we to understand by "the bread of affliction"? Should we not rather look for joy, praise, and triumph in connection with a feast in memory of deliverance from Egyptian bondage and misery? No doubt there is very deep and real joy, thankfulness, and praise in realizing the blessed truth of our full deliverance from our former condition, with all its accompaniments and all its consequences; but it is very plain that these were not the prominent features of the paschal feast–indeed, they are not even named. We have "the bread of affliction," but not a word about joy, praise, or triumph.

Now, why is this? what great moral lesson is conveyed to our hearts by the bread of affliction? We believe it sets before us those deep exercises of heart which the Holy Ghost produces by bringing powerfully before us what it cost our adorable Lord and Saviour to deliver us from our sins and from the judgment which those sins deserved. Those exercises are also typified by the "bitter herbs" of Exodus 12, and they are illustrated again and again in the history of God's people of old, who were led, under the powerful action of the Word and Spirit of God, to chasten themselves and "afflict their souls" in the divine presence.

And be it remembered that there is not a tinge of the legal element or of unbelief in these holy exercises—far from it. When an Israelite partook of the bread of affliction, with the roasted flesh of the passover, did it express a doubt or a fear as to his full deliverance? Impossible! How could it? He was in the land; he was gathered to God's own centre—His own very presence. How could he, then, doubt his full and final deliverance from the land of Egypt? The thought is simply absurd.

But although he had no doubts or fears as to his deliverance, yet had he to eat the bread of affliction; it was an essential element in his paschal feast, "For thou camest forth out of the land of Egypt *in haste,* that thou mayest remember the day when thou camest forth out of the land of Egypt *all the days of thy life.*"

This was very deep and real work. They were never to forget their exodus out of Egypt, but to keep up the remembrance of it, in the promised land, throughout all generations. They were to commemorate their deliverance by a feast emblematical of those holy exercises which ever characterize true, practical, Christian piety.

We would very earnestly commend to the serious attention of the Christian reader the whole line of truth indicated by "the bread of affliction." We believe it is much needed by those who profess great familiarity with what are called the doctrines of grace. There is very great danger, especially to young professors, while seeking to avoid legality and bondage, of running into the opposite extreme of levity—a most terrible snare. Aged and experienced Christians are not so liable to fall into this sad evil; it is the young amongst us who so need to be most solemnly warned against it. They hear, it may be, a great deal about salvation by grace, justification by faith, deliverance from the law, and all the peculiar privileges of the Christian position.

Now, we need hardly say that all these are of cardinal importance; and it would be utterly impossible for any one to hear too much about them. Would they were more spoken about, written about, and preached about! Thousands of the Lord's beloved people spend all their days in darkness, doubt, and legal bondage, through ignorance of those great foundation-truths.

But while all this is perfectly true, there are, on the other hand, many—alas! too many—who have a merely intellectual familiarity with the principles of grace, but (if we are to judge from their habits and manners, their style and deportment—the only way we have of judging) who know but little of the sanctifying power of those great principles—their power in the heart and in the life.

Now, to speak according to the teaching of the paschal feast, it would not have been according to the mind of God for any one to attempt to keep that feast without the unleavened bread, even the bread of affliction. Such a thing would not have been tolerated in Israel of old. It was an absolutely essential ingredient. And so, we may rest assured, it is an integral part of that feast which we, as Christians, are exhorted to keep, to cultivate personal holiness and that condition of soul which is so aptly expressed by the "bitter herbs" of Exodus 12, or the Deuteronomic ingredient—"the bread of affliction," which latter would seem to be the permanent figure for the land.

In a word, then, we believe there is a deep and urgent need amongst us of those spiritual feelings and affections, those profound exercises of soul, which the Holy Ghost would produce by unfolding to our hearts the sufferings of Christ—what it cost Him to put our sins away—what He endured for us when passing under the billows and waves of God's righteous wrath against our sins. We are sadly lacking—if one may be permitted to speak for others—in that deep contrition of heart which flows from spiritual occupation with the sufferings and death of our precious Saviour. It is one thing to have the blood of Christ sprinkled on the conscience, and another thing to have the death of Christ brought home, in a spiritual way, to the heart, and the cross of Christ applied, in a practical way, to our whole course and character.

How is it that we can so lightly commit sin, in thought, word, and deed? how is it that there is so much levity, so much unsubduedness, so much self-indulgence, so much carnal ease, so much that is merely frothy and superficial? Is it not because that ingredient typified by "the bread of affliction" is lacking in our feast? We cannot doubt it. We fear there is a very deplorable lack of depth and seriousness in our Christianity. There is too much flippant discussion of the profound mysteries of the Christian faith, too much head-knowledge without the inward power.

All this demands the serious attention of the reader. We cannot shake off the impression that not a little of this melancholy condition of things is but too justly traceable to a certain style of preaching the gospel, adapted, no doubt, with the very best intentions, but none the less pernicious in its moral effects. It is all right to preach a simple gospel. It cannot, by any possibility, be put more simply than God the Holy Ghost has given it to us in Scripture.

All this is fully admitted; but, at the same time, we are persuaded there is a very serious defect in the preaching of which we speak. There is a want of spiritual depth, a lack of holy seriousness. In the effort to counteract legality, there is that which tends to levity. Now, while legality is a great evil, levity is much greater. We must guard against both. We believe grace is the remedy for the former, truth for the latter; but spiritual wisdom is needed to enable us rightly to adjust and apply these two. If we find a soul deeply exercised under the powerful action of truth, thoroughly plowed up by the mighty ministry of the Holy Ghost, we should pour in the deep consolation of the pure and precious grace of God, as set forth in the divinely efficacious sacrifice of Christ. This is the divine remedy for a broken heart, a contrite spirit, a convicted conscience. When the deep furrow has been made by the spiritual plowshare, we have only to cast in the incorruptible seed of the gospel of God, in the assurance that it will take root, and bring forth fruit in due season.

But, on the other hand, if we find a person going on in a light, airy, unbroken condition, using very high-flown language about grace, talking loudly against legality, and seeking, in a merely human way, to set forth an easy way of being saved, we consider this to be a case calling for a very solemn application of *truth* to the heart and conscience.

Now, we greatly fear there is a vast amount of this last named element abroad in the professing church. To speak according to the language of our type, there is a tendency to separate the passover from the feast of unleavened bread—to rest in the fact of being delivered from judgment and forget the *roasted* lamb, the bread of *holiness,* and the bread of *affliction.* In reality, they never can be separated, inasmuch as God has bound them together; and hence we do not believe that any soul can be really in the enjoyment of the precious truth that "Christ our passover is sacrificed for us," who is not seeking to "keep the feast." When the Holy Spirit unfolds to our hearts something of the deep blessedness, preciousness, and efficacy of the death of our Lord Jesus Christ, He leads us to meditate upon the soul-subduing mystery of His sufferings—to ponder in our hearts all that He passed through for us, all that it cost Him to save us from the eternal consequences of that which we, alas! so often lightly commit.

Now, this is very deep and holy work, and leads the soul into those exercises which correspond with "the bread of affliction" in the feast of unleavened bread. There is a wide difference between the feelings produced by dwelling upon our sins and those which flow from dwelling upon the sufferings of Christ to put those sins away.

True, we can never forget our sins, never forget the hole of the pit from whence we were digged; but it is one thing to dwell upon the pit, and another and a deeper thing altogether to dwell upon the grace that digged us out of it, and what it cost our precious Saviour to do it. It is this latter we so much need to keep continually in the remembrance of the thoughts of our hearts. We are so terribly volatile, so ready to forget.

We need to look very earnestly to God to enable us to enter more deeply and practically into the sufferings of Christ, and into the application of the cross to all that in us which is contrary to Him. This will impart depth of tone, tenderness of spirit, an intense breathing after holiness of heart and life, practical separation from the world, in its every phase, a holy subduedness, jealous watchfulness over ourselves, our thoughts, our words, our ways, our whole deportment in daily life. In a word, it would lead to a totally different type of Christianity from what we see around us, and what, alas! we exhibit in our own personal history. May the Spirit of God graciously unfold to our hearts, by His own direct and powerful ministry, more and more of what is meant by "the *roasted* lamb," the *"unleavened* bread," and "the bread of *affliction.*" *

We shall now briefly consider the feast of Pentecost, which stands next in order to the passover. "Seven weeks shalt thou number unto thee; begin to number the seven weeks from such time as thou beginnest to put the sickle to the corn. And thou shalt keep the feast of weeks unto the Lord thy God with a tribute of a free-will offering of thine hand, which thou shalt give unto the Lord thy God; according as the Lord thy God hath blessed thee; and thou shalt rejoice before the Lord thy God, thou, and thy son, and thy daughter, and thy man-servant, and thy maid-servant, and the Levite that is within thy gates, and the stranger, and the fatherless, and the widow, that are among you, *in the place which the Lord thy God hath chosen to place His name there.* And thou shalt remember that thou wast a bondman in Egypt; and thou shalt observe and do these statutes" (ver. 9-12).

Here we have the well-known and beautiful type of the day of Pentecost. The passover sets forth the death of Christ; the sheaf of first-fruits is the striking figure of a risen

---

*For further remarks on the passover and the feast of unleavened bread, the reader is referred to Exodus 12 and Numbers 9. Specially in the latter—the connection between the passover and the Lord's supper. This is a point of deepest interest and immense practical importance. The passover looked forward to the death of Christ; the Lord's supper looks back to it. What the former was to a faithful Israelite, the latter is to the Church. If this were more fully seen, it would greatly tend to meet the prevailing laxity, indifference, and error as to the table and supper of the Lord.

To any one who lives habitually in the holy atmosphere of Scripture, it must seem strange indeed to mark the confusion of thought and the diversity of practice in reference to a subject so very important, and one so simply and clearly presented in the Word of God.

It can hardly be called in question, by any one who bows to Scripture, that the apostles and the early Church assembled on the first day of the week to break bread. There is not a shadow of warrant in the New Testament for confining that most precious ordinance to once a month, once a quarter, or once in six months. This can only be viewed as a human interference with a divine institution. We are aware that much is sought to be made of the words, "As oft as ye do it;" but we do not see how any argument based on this clause can stand for a moment in the face of apostolic precedent in Acts 20:7. The first day of the week is unquestionably the day for the Church to celebrate the Lord's supper.

Does the Christian reader admit this? If so, does he act upon it? It is a serious thing to neglect a special ordinance of Christ, and one appointed by Him the same night in which He was betrayed, under circumstances so deeply affecting. Surely, all who love the Lord Jesus Christ in sincerity would desire to remember Him in this special way, according to His own word—"This do in remembrance of Me." Can we understand any true lover of Christ living in the habitual neglect of this precious memorial? If an Israelite of old neglected the passover, he would have been "cut off." But this was law, and we are under grace. True; but is that a reason for neglecting our Lord's commandment?

We would commend this subject to the reader's careful attention. There is much more involved in it than most of us are aware. We believe the entire history of the Lord's supper for the last eighteen centuries is full of interest and instruction. We may see in the way in which the Lord's table has been treated a striking moral index of the Church's real condition. In proportion as the Church departed from Christ and His Word did she neglect and pervert the precious institution of the Lord's supper; and on the other hand, just as the Spirit of God wrought, at any time, with special power in the Church, the Lord's supper has found its true place in the hearts of His people.

Christ; and in the feast of weeks, we have prefigured before us the descent of the Holy Ghost, fifty days after the resurrection.

We speak, of course, of what these feasts convey to us, according to the mind of God, irrespective altogether of the question of Israel's apprehension of their meaning. It is our privilege to look at all these typical institutions in the light of the New Testament; and when we so view them, we are filled with wonder and delight at the divine perfectness, beauty, and order of all those marvelous types.

And not only so, but—what is of immense value to us—we see how the Scriptures of the New Testament dovetail, as it were, into those of the Old; we see the lovely unity of the divine volume, and how manifestly it is one Spirit that breathes through the whole from beginning to end. In this way we are inwardly strengthened in our apprehension of the precious truth of the divine inspiration of the holy Scriptures, and our hearts are fortified against all the blasphemous attacks of infidel writers. Our souls are conducted to the top of the mountain where the moral glories of the Word shine upon us in all their heavenly lustre, and from whence we can look down and see the clouds and chilling mists of infidel thought rolling beneath us. These clouds and mists cannot affect us, inasmuch as they are far away below the level on which, through infinite grace, we stand. Infidel writers know absolutely nothing of the moral glories of Scripture; but one thing is awfully certain, namely, that one moment in eternity will completely revolutionize the thoughts of all the infidels and atheists that have ever raved or written against the Bible and its Author.

Now, in looking at the deeply interesting feast of weeks, or Pentecost, we are at once struck with the difference between it and the feast of unleavened bread. In the first place, we read of "a free-will offering." Here we have a figure of the Church, formed by the Holy Ghost and presented to God as "a kind of first-fruits of His creatures."

We have dwelt upon this feature of the type in the *Notes on Leviticus,* chapter 23, and shall not therefore enter upon it here, but confine ourselves to what is purely Deuteronomic. The people were to present a tribute of a free-will offering of their hand, according as the Lord their God had blessed them. There was nothing like this at the passover, because that sets forth Christ offering Himself for us, as a sacrifice, and not our offering any thing. We remember our deliverance from sin and Satan, and what the deliverance cost; we meditate upon the deep and varied sufferings of our precious Saviour as prefigured by the roasted lamb; we remember that it was our sins that were laid upon Him. He was bruised for our iniquities—judged in our stead, and this leads to deep and heavy contrition, or, what we may call true Christian repentance. For we must never forget that repentance is not a mere transient emotion of a sinner when his eyes are first opened, but an abiding moral condition of the Christian, in view of the cross and passion of our Lord Jesus Christ. If this were better understood and more fully entered into, it would impart a depth and solidity to the Christian life and character in which the great majority of us are lamentably deficient.

But in the feast of Pentecost, we have before us the power of the Holy Ghost, and the varied effects of His blessed presence in us and with us. He enables us to present our bodies and all that we have as a free-will offering unto our God, according as He hath blessed us. This, we need hardly say, can only be done by the power of the Holy Ghost; and hence the striking type of it is presented, not in the passover, which prefigures the death of Christ; not in the feast of unleavened bread, which sets forth the moral effect of that death upon us, in repentance, self-judgment, and practical holiness; but in Pentecost, which is the acknowledged type of the precious gift of the Holy Ghost.

Now, it is the Spirit who enables us to enter into the claims of God upon us—claims which are to be measured only by the extent of the divine blessing. He gives us to see and understand that all we are and all we have belong to God. He gives us to delight in consecrating ourselves—spirit, soul, and body—to God. It is truly "a free-will offering." It is not of constraint, but willingly. There is not an atom of bondage, for "where the Spirit of the Lord is, there is liberty."

In short, we have here the lovely spirit and moral character of the entire Christian life and service. A soul under law cannot understand the force and beauty of this. Souls under the law never received the Spirit. The two things are wholly incompatible. Thus the apostle says to the poor misguided assemblies of Galatia, "This only would I learn of you, Received ye the Spirit by works of law, or by the hearing of faith? . . . He therefore that ministereth to you the Spirit, and worketh miracles among you, doeth He it by works of law, or by the hearing of faith?" The precious gift of the Spirit is consequent upon the death, resurrection, ascension, and glorification of our adorable Lord and Saviour Jesus Christ, and consequently can have nothing whatever to do with "works of law" in any shape or form. The presence of the Holy Ghost on earth, His dwelling with and in all true believers, is a grand characteristic truth of Christianity. It was not, and could not be, known in Old Testament times. It was not even known by the disciples in our Lord's lifetime. He Himself said to them, on the eve of His departure, "Nevertheless, I tell you the truth; it is expedient [or profitable—συμφέρει] for you that I go away; for if I go not away, the Comforter will not come unto you; but if I depart, I will send Him unto you" (John 16:7).

This proves, in the most conclusive manner, that even the very men who enjoyed the high and precious privilege of personal companionship with the Lord Himself were to be put in an advanced position by His going away and the coming of the Comforter. Again, we read, "If ye love Me, keep My commandments; and I will pray the Father, and He shall give you another Comforter, that He may abide with you forever; even the Spirit of truth; whom the world cannot receive, because it seeth Him not, neither knoweth Him; but ye know Him, for He dwelleth with you and shall be in you."

We cannot, however, attempt to go elaborately into this immense subject here; our space does not admit of it, much as we should delight in it. We must confine ourselves to one or two points suggested by the feast of weeks, as presented in our chapter.

We have referred to the very interesting fact that the Spirit of God is the living spring and power of the life of personal devotedness and consecration beautifully prefigured by "the tribute of a free-will offering." The sacrifice of Christ is the ground, the presence of the Holy Ghost is the power, of the Christian's dedication of himself—spirit, soul, and body—to God. "I beseech you therefore, brethren, by the mercies of God, that ye present your bodies a living sacrifice, holy, acceptable unto God, which is your reasonable service" (Rom. 12:1).

But there is another point of deepest interest presented in verse 11 of our chapter, "And thou shalt *rejoice* before the Lord thy God." We have no such word in the paschal feast, or in the feast of unleavened bread. It would not be in moral keeping with either of these solemnities. True it is, the passover lies at the very foundation of all the joy we can or ever shall realize here or hereafter; but we must ever think of the death of Christ, His sufferings, His sorrows—all that He passed through when the waves and billows of God's righteous wrath passed over His soul. It is upon these profound mysteries that our hearts are, or ought to be, mainly fixed when we surround the Lord's table and keep the feast by which we show the Lord's death until He come.

Now, it is plain to the spiritual and thoughtful reader that the feelings proper to such a holy and solemn institution are not of a jubilant character. We certainly can and do rejoice that the sorrows and sufferings of our blessed Lord are over, and over forever—that those terrible hours are passed, never to return; but what we recall in the feast is not simply their being over, but their being gone through, and that for us. "Ye do show the Lord's death;" and we know that whatever may accrue to us from that precious death, yet when we are called to meditate upon it, our joy is chastened by those profound exercises of soul which the Holy Spirit produces by unfolding to us the sorrows, the sufferings, the cross, and passion of our blessed Saviour. Our Lord's words are, "This do in remembrance of *Me*;" but what we especially *remember* in the supper is, Christ suffering and dying for us; what we *show*, is His death; and with these solemn realities before our souls, in the power of the Holy Ghost, there will, there must be, holy subduedness and seriousness.

We speak, of course, of what becomes the immediate occasion of the celebration of the supper—the suited feelings and affections of such a moment. But these must be produced by the powerful ministry of the Holy Ghost. It can be of no possible use to seek, by any pious efforts of our own, to work ourselves up to a suitable state of mind. This would be ascending by steps to the altar, a thing most offensive to God. It is only by the Holy Spirit's ministry that we can worthily celebrate the holy supper of the Lord. He alone can enable us to put away all levity, all formality, all mere routine, all wandering thoughts, and to discern the body and blood of the Lord in those memorials which, by His own appointment, are laid on His table.

But in the feast of Pentecost, rejoicing was a prominent feature. We hear nothing of "bitter herbs" or "bread of affliction" on this occasion, because it is the type of the coming of the other Comforter—the descent of the Holy Ghost, proceeding from the Father, and sent down by the risen, ascended, and glorified Head in the heavens, to fill the hearts of His people with praise, thanksgiving, and triumphant joy—yea, to lead them into full and blessed fellowship with their glorified Head, in His triumph over sin, death, hell, Satan, and all the powers of darkness. The Spirit's presence is connected with liberty, light, power, and joy. Thus we read, "The disciples were filled with joy and with the Holy Ghost." Doubts, fears, and legal bondage flee away before the precious ministry of the Holy Ghost.

But we must distinguish between His work and His indwelling—His quickening and His sealing. The very first dawn of conviction in the soul is the fruit of the Spirit's work. It is His blessed operation that leads to all true repentance, and this is not joyful work. It is very good, very needful, absolutely essential; but it is not joy—nay, it is deep sorrow. But when, through grace, we are enabled to believe in a risen and glorified Saviour, then the Holy Ghost comes and takes up His abode in us, as the seal of our acceptance and earnest of our inheritance.

Now, this fills us with joy unspeakable and full of glory; and being thus filled ourselves, we become channels of blessing to others. "He that believeth on Me, as the Scripture hath said, out of his belly shall flow rivers of living water. But this spake He of the Spirit, which they that believe on Him should receive; for the Holy Ghost was not yet, because that Jesus was not yet glorified." The Spirit is the spring of power and joy in the heart of the believer. He fits, fills, and uses us as His vessels in ministering to poor thirsty, needy souls around us. He links us with the Man in the glory, maintains us in living communion with Him, and enables us to be, in our feeble measure, the expression of what He is. Every movement of the Christian should be redolent with the fragrance of Christ. For one who professes to be a Christian to exhibit unholy tempers, selfish ways, a grasping, covetous, worldly spirit, envy and jealousy, pride and ambition, is to belie his profession, dishonor the holy name of Christ, and bring reproach upon that glorious Christianity which he professes, and of which we have the lovely type in the feast of weeks—a feast pre-eminently characterized by a joy which had its source in the goodness of God, and which flowed out far and wide, and embraced in its hallowed circle every object of need. "Thou shalt rejoice before the Lord thy God, thou, and thy son, and thy daughter, and thy man-servant, and thy maid-servant, and *the Levite* that is within thy gates, and *the stranger*, and *the fatherless*, and *the widow*, that are among you."

How lovely! how perfectly beautiful! Oh that its antitype were more faithfully exhibited amongst us! Where are those streams of refreshing which ought to flow from the Church of God? where those unblotted epistles of Christ known and read of all men? where can we see a practical exhibition of Christ in the ways of His people—something to which we could point and say, There is true Christianity? Oh, may the Spirit of God stir up our hearts to a more intense desire after conformity to the image of Christ, in all things! May He clothe with His own mighty power the Word of God, which we have in our hands and in our homes, that it may speak to our hearts and consciences, and lead us to judge ourselves, our ways, and our associations by its heavenly light, so that there may be a thoroughly devoted band of witnesses gathered out to His name, to wait for His appearing. Will the reader join us in asking for this?

We shall now turn for a moment to the lovely institution of the feast of tabernacles, which gives such remarkable completeness to the range of truth presented in our chapter.

"Thou shalt observe the feast of tabernacles seven days, after that thou hast gathered in thy corn and thy wine; and thou shalt rejoice in thy feast, thou, and thy son, and thy daughter, and thy man-servant, and thy maid-servant, and the Levite, the stranger, and the fatherless, and the widow, that are within thy gates. Seven days shalt thou keep a solemn feast unto the Lord thy God *in the place which the Lord* shall choose; because the Lord thy God shall bless thee in all thine increase, and in all the works of thine hands, therefore thou shalt surely rejoice. Three times in a year shall all thy males appear before the Lord thy God *in the place which He shall choose*; in the feast of unleavened bread, and in the feast of weeks, and in the feast of tabernacles; and they shall not appear before the Lord empty; every man shall give as he is able, according to the blessing of the Lord thy God which He hath given thee" (ver. 13-17).

Here, then, we have the striking and beautiful type of Israel's future. The feast of tabernacles has not yet had its antitype. The passover and Pentecost have had their fulfillment in the precious death of Christ and the descent of the Holy Ghost, but the third great solemnity points forward to the times of the restitution of all things, which God has spoken of by the mouth of all His holy prophets which have been since the world began.

And note particularly the time of the celebration of this feast. It was to be "after thou hast gathered in thy corn and thy wine;" in other words, it was after the harvest and the vintage. Now, there is a very marked distinction between these two things. The one speaks of grace, the other of judgment. At the end of the age, God will gather His wheat into His garner, and then will come the treading of the wine-press, in awful judgment.

We have in the fourteenth chapter of the book of Revelation a very solemn passage bearing upon the subject now before us. "And I looked, and behold a white cloud, and upon the cloud one sat like unto the Son of Man, having on his head a golden crown, and in his hand a sharp sickle. And another angel came out of the temple, crying with a loud voice to him that sat on the cloud, 'Thrust in thy sickle, and reap; for the time is come for thee to reap; for the harvest of the earth is ripe.' And he that sat on the cloud thrust in his sickle on the earth, and the earth was reaped."

Here we have the harvest; and then "another angel came out of the temple which is in heaven, he also having a sharp sickle. And another angel came out from the altar, which had power over fire"—the emblem of judgment—"and cried with a loud cry to him that had the sharp sickle, saying, 'Thrust in thy sharp sickle, and gather the clusters of the vine of the earth, for her grapes are fully ripe.' And the angel thrust in his sickle into the earth, and gathered the vine of the earth, and cast it into the great wine-press of the wrath of God. And the wine-press was trodden without the city, and blood came out of the wine-press, even unto the horse-bridles, by the space of a thousand and six hundred furlongs"—equal to the whole length of the land of Palestine!

Now, these apocalyptic figures set before us, in their own characteristic way, scenes which must be enacted previous to the celebration of the feast of tabernacles. Christ will gather His wheat into His heavenly garner, and after that He will come in crushing judgment upon christendom. Thus, every section of the volume of inspiration—Moses, the Psalms, the Prophets, the Gospels (or the acts of Christ), the Acts of the Holy Ghost, the Epistles, and Apocalypse—all go to establish, unanswerably, the fact that the world will not be converted by the gospel, that things are not improving, and will not improve, but grow worse and worse. That glorious time prefigured by the feast of tabernacles *must* be preceded by the vintage, the treading of the wine-press of the wrath of almighty God.

Why, then, we may well ask, in the face of such an overwhelming body of divine evidence, furnished by every section of the inspired canon, will men persist in cherishing the delusive hope of a world converted by the gospel? What mean "gathered wheat and a trodden wine-press"? Assuredly, they do not and cannot mean a converted world.

We shall perhaps be told that we cannot build any thing upon Mosaic types and apocalyptic symbols. Perhaps not, if we had but types and symbols; but when the accumulated rays of Inspiration's heavenly lamp converge upon these types and symbols and unfold their deep meaning to our souls, we find them in perfect harmony with the voices of prophets and apostles, and the living teachings of our Lord Himself. In a word, all speak the same language, all teach the same lesson, all bear the same unequivocal testimony to the solemn truth that at the end of this age, instead of a converted world, prepared for a spiritual millennium, there will be a vine covered and borne down with terrible clusters, fully ripe for the wine-press of the wrath of almighty God.

Oh, may the men and women of christendom, and the teachers thereof, apply their hearts to these solemn realities! May these things sink down into their ears, and into the very depths of their souls, so that they may fling to the winds their fondly cherished delusion, and accept instead the plainly revealed and clearly established truth of God!

But we must draw this section to a close; and ere doing so, we would remind the Christian reader that we are called to exhibit in our daily life the blessed influence of all those great truths presented to us in three interesting types on which we have been meditating. Christianity is characterized by those three great formative facts—redemption, the presence of the Holy Ghost, and the hope of glory. The Christian is redeemed by the precious blood of Christ, sealed by the Holy Ghost, and he is looking for the Saviour.

Yes, these are solid facts, divine realities, great formative truths. They are not mere principles or opinions, but they are designed to be a living power in our souls, and to shine in our lives. See how thoroughly practical were these solemnities on which we have been dwelling; mark what a tide of praise and thanksgiving and joy and blessing and active benevolence flowed from the assembly of Israel when gathered around Jehovah in the place which He had chosen. Praise and thanksgiving ascended to God, and the blessed streams of a large-hearted benevolence flowed forth to every object of need. "Three times in a year shall all thy males appear before the Lord thy God. . . . *And they shall not appear before the Lord empty; every man shall give as he is able, according to the blessing of the Lord thy God which He hath given thee.*"

Lovely words! They were not to come empty into the Lord's presence; they were to come with the heart full of praise, and the hands full of the fruits of divine goodness to gladden the hearts of the Lord's workmen and the Lord's poor. All this was perfectly beautiful. Jehovah would gather His people around Himself, to fill them to overflowing with joy and praise, and to make them His channels of blessing to others. They were not to remain under their vine and under their fig-tree, and there congratulate themselves upon the rich and varied mercies which surrounded them. This might be all right and good in its place, but it would not have fully met the mind and heart of God. No; three times in the year they had to arise and betake themselves to the divinely appointed meeting-place, and there raise their halleluiahs to the Lord their God, and there, too, to minister liberally of that which He had bestowed upon them to every form of human need. God would confer upon His people the rich privilege of rejoicing the heart of the Levite, the stranger, the widow, and the fatherless. This is the work in which He Himself delights—blessed forever be His name—and He would share His delight with His people. He would have it to be known, seen, and felt that the place where He met His people was a sphere of joy and praise, and a centre from whence streams of blessing were to flow forth in all directions.

Has not all this a voice and a lesson for the Church of God? Does it not speak home to the writer and the reader of these lines? Assuredly it does. May we listen to it; may it tell upon our hearts. May the marvelous grace of God so act upon us that our hearts may be full of praise to Him, and our hands full of good works. If the mere types and shadows of our blessings were connected with so much thanksgiving and active benevolence, how much more powerful should be the effect of the blessings themselves!

But ah! the question is, Are we realizing the blessings? are we making our own of them? are we grasping them in the power of an artless faith? Here lies the secret of the whole matter. Where do we find professing Christians in the full and settled enjoyment of what the passover prefigured, namely, full deliverance from judgment and this present evil world? Where do we find them in the full and settled enjoyment of their Pentecost, even the indwelling of the Holy Ghost—the seal, the earnest, the unction, and the witness? Ask the vast majority of professors the plain question, "Have you received the Holy Ghost?" and see what answer you will get. What answer can the reader give? Can he say, Yes, thank God, *I know* I am washed in the precious blood of Christ, and sealed with the Holy Ghost? It is greatly to be feared that comparatively few of the vast multitudes of professors around us know anything of these precious things, which nevertheless are the chartered privileges of the very simplest member of the body of Christ.

So also as to the feast of tabernacles, how few understand its meaning! True, it has not yet been fulfilled; but the Christian is called to live in the present power of that which it sets forth. "Faith is the substance of things hoped for, the evidence of things not seen." Our life is to be governed and our character formed by the combined influence of the "grace" in which we stand and the "glory" for which we wait.

But if souls are not established in grace—if they do not even know that their sins are forgiven—if they are taught that it is presumption to be sure of salvation, and that it is humility and piety to live in perpetual doubt and fear, and that no one can be sure of their salvation until they stand before the judgment-seat of Christ, how can they possibly take Christian ground, manifest the fruits of Christian life, or cherish proper Christian hope? If an Israelite of old was in doubt as to whether he was a child of Abraham, a member of the congregation of the Lord, and in the land, how could he keep the feast of unleavened bread, Pentecost, or tabernacles? There would have been no sense, meaning, or value in such a thing; indeed, we may safely affirm that no Israelite would have thought for a moment of any thing so utterly absurd.

How is it, then, that professing Christians—many of them, we cannot doubt, real children of God—never seem to be able to enter upon proper Christian ground? They spend their days in doubt and fear, darkness and uncertainty. Their religious exercises and services, instead of being the outcome of life possessed and enjoyed, are entered upon and gone through more as a matter of legal duty, and as a moral preparation for the life to come. Many truly pious souls are kept in this state all their days; and as to "the blessed hope" which grace has set before us, to cheer our hearts and detach us from present things, they do not enter into it or understand it. It is looked upon as a mere speculation, indulged in by a few visionary enthusiasts here and there. They are looking forward to the day of judgment, instead of looking out for "the bright and morning Star"; they are praying for the forgiveness of their sins, and asking God to give them His Holy Spirit, when they ought to be rejoicing in the assured possession of eternal life, divine righteousness, and the Spirit of adoption.

All this is directly opposed to the simplest

and clearest teaching of the New Testament; it is utterly foreign to the very genius of Christianity, subversive of the Christian's peace and liberty, and destructive of all true and intelligent Christian worship, service, and testimony. It is plainly impossible that people can appear before the Lord with their hearts full of praise for privileges which they do not enjoy, or their hands full of the blessing which they have never realized.

We call the earnest attention of all the Lord's people, throughout the length and breadth of the professing church, to this weighty subject. We entreat them to search the Scriptures, and see if they afford any warrant for keeping souls in darkness, doubt, and bondage all their days. That there are solemn warnings, searching appeals, weighty admonitions, is most true, and we bless God for them—we need them, and should diligently apply our hearts to them; but let the reader distinctly understand that it is the sweet privilege of the very babes in Christ to know that their sins are all forgiven, that they are accepted in a risen Christ, sealed by the Holy Ghost, and heirs of eternal glory. Such, through infinite and sovereign grace, are their clearly established and assured blessings—blessings to which the love of God makes them welcome, for which the blood of Christ makes them fit, and as to which the testimony of the Holy Ghost makes them sure.

May the great Shepherd and Bishop of souls lead all His beloved people—the lambs and sheep of His blood-bought flock—to know, by the teaching of His Holy Spirit, the things that are freely given to them of God; and may those who do know them, in measure, know them more fully, and exhibit the precious fruits of them in a life of genuine devotedness to Christ and His service.

It is greatly to be feared that many of us who profess to be acquainted with the very highest truths of the Christian faith are not answering to our profession; we are not acting up to the principle set forth in verse 17 of our beautiful chapter, *Every man* shall give *as he is able*, according to the blessing of the Lord thy God which He hath given thee." We seem to forget that although we have nothing to do and nothing to give for salvation, we have much that we can do for the Saviour, and much that we can give to His workmen and to His poor. There is very great danger of pushing the do-nothing and give-nothing principle too far. If in the days of our ignorance and legal bondage we worked and gave upon a false principle and with a false object, we surely ought not to do less and give less now that we profess to know that we are not only saved, but blessed with all spiritual blessings in a risen and glorified Christ. We have need to take care that we are not resting in the mere intellectual perception and verbal profession of these great and glorious truths, while the heart and conscience have never felt their sacred action, nor the conduct and character been brought under their powerful and holy influence.

We venture, in all tenderness and love, just to offer these practical suggestions to the reader for his prayerful consideration. We would not wound, offend, or discourage the very feeblest lamb in all the flock of Christ; and further, we can assure the reader that we are not casting a stone at any one, but simply writing as in the immediate presence of God, and sounding in the ears of the Church a note of warning as to that which we deeply feel to be our common danger. We believe there is an urgent call, on all sides, to consider our ways, to humble ourselves before the Lord on account of our manifold failures, shortcomings, and inconsistencies, and to seek grace from Him to be more real, more thoroughly devoted, more pronounced in our testimony for Him, in this dark and evil day.

---

## *CHAPTER 17*

WE must remember that the division of Scripture into chapters and verses is entirely a human arrangement, often very convenient, no doubt, for reference; but not unfrequently it is quite unwarrantable, and interferes with the connection. Thus we can see at a glance that the closing verses of chapter 16 are much more connected with what follows than with what goes before.

"Judges and officers shalt thou make thee in all thy gates, which the Lord thy God giveth thee, throughout thy tribes; and they shall judge the people with just judgment. Thou shalt not wrest judgment; thou shalt not respect persons, neither take a gift; for a gift doth blind the eyes of the wise, and pervert the words of the righteous. That which is altogether just shalt thou follow, that thou mayest live and inherit the land which the Lord thy God giveth thee."

These words teach us a twofold lesson; in the first place, they set forth the even-handed justice and perfect truth which ever characterize the government of God. Every case is dealt with according to its own merits and on the ground of its own facts. The judgment is so plain that there is not a shadow of ground for a question; all dissension is absolutely closed; and if any murmur is raised, the murmurer is at once silenced by "Friend, I do thee no wrong." This holds good every where, and at all times, in the holy government of God, and it makes us long for the time when that government shall be established from sea to sea, and from the river to the ends of the earth.

But on the other hand, we learn, from the lines just quoted, what man's judgment is worth if left to himself. It cannot be trusted for a moment. Man is capable of "*wresting* judgment," of "respecting persons," of "taking a gift," of attaching importance to a person because of his position and wealth. That he is capable of all this is evident from the fact of his being told not to do it. We must ever remember this. If God commands man not to steal, it is plain that man has theft in his nature.

Hence, therefore, human judgment and human government are liable to the grossest corruption. Judges and governors, if left to themselves, if not under the direct sway of divine principle, are capable of perverting justice for filthy lucre's sake—of favoring a wicked man because he is rich, and of condemning a righteous man because he is poor—of giving a judgment in flagrant opposition to the plainest facts because of some advantage to be gained, whether in the shape of money or influence or popularity or power.

To prove this, it is not necessary to point to such men as Pilate and Herod and Felix and Festus; we have no need to go beyond the passage just quoted, in order to see what *man* is, even when clothed in the robes of official dignity, seated on the throne of government, or on the bench of justice.

Some, as they read these lines, may feel disposed to say, in the language of Hazael, "Is thy servant a dog, that he should do this thing?" But let such reflect for a moment on the fact that the human heart is the seed-plot of every sin, and of every vile and abominable and contemptible wickedness that ever was committed in this world; and the unanswerable proof of this is found in the enactments, commandments, and prohibitions which appear on the sacred page of inspiration.

And herein we have an uncommonly fine reply to the oft-repeated question, "What have we to do with many of the laws and institutions set forth in the Mosaic economy? Why are such things set down in the Bible? Can they possibly be inspired?" Yes, they are inspired, and they appear on the page of inspiration in order that we may see, as reflected in a divinely perfect mirror, the moral material of which we ourselves are made—the thoughts we are capable of thinking, the words we are capable of speaking, and the deeds we are capable of doing.

Is not this something? Is it not good and wholesome to find, for example, in some of the passages of this most profound and beautiful book of Deuteronomy, that human nature is capable, and hence *we* are capable, of doing things that put us morally below the level of a beast? Assuredly it is; and well would it be for many a one who walks in pharisaic pride and self-complacency—puffed up with false notions of his own dignity and high-toned morality, to learn this deeply humbling lesson.

But how morally lovely, how pure, how refined and elevated, were the divine enactments for Israel! They were not to wrest judgment, but allow it to flow in its own straight and even channel, irrespective altogether of persons. The poor man in vile raiment was to have the same impartial justice as the man with a gold ring and gay clothing. The decision of the judgment-seat was not to be warped by partiality or prejudice, or the robe of justice to be defiled by the stain of bribery.

Oh, what will it be for this oppressed and groaning earth to be governed by the admirable laws which are recorded in the inspired pages of the Pentateuch, when a king shall reign in righteousness, and princes shall decree justice! "Give the king Thy judgments, O God, and Thy righteousness unto the king's son. He shall judge Thy people with righteousness, and *Thy poor* with judgment"—no wresting, no bribery, no partial judgments then. "The mountains [or higher dignities] shall bring peace to the people, and the little hills [or lesser dignities], by righteousness. He shall judge [or defend] *the poor* of the people, he shall save the children of *the needy*, and shall break in pieces the oppressor. They shall fear Thee as long as the sun and moon endure, throughout all generations. He shall come down like rain upon the mown grass; as showers that water the earth. In His days shall the righteous flourish, and abundance of peace so long as the moon endureth. He shall have dominion also from sea to sea, and from the river unto the ends of the earth. . . . He shall deliver *the needy* when he crieth, *the poor* also, and *him that hath no helper.* He shall spare *the poor and needy*, and shall save *the souls of the needy.* He shall redeem their souls from deceit and violence, and precious shall their blood be in His sight" (Ps. 72).

Well may the heart long for the time—the bright and blessed time when all this shall be made good, when the earth shall be full of the knowledge of the Lord as the waters cover the sea, when the Lord Jesus shall take to Himself His great power and reign, when the Church in the heavens shall reflect the beams of His glory upon the earth, when Israel's twelve tribes shall repose beneath the vine and fig-tree in their own promised land, and all the nations of the earth shall rejoice beneath the peaceful and beneficent rule of the Son of David. Thanks and praise be to our God, thus it shall be, ere long, as sure as His throne is in the heavens. A little while and all shall be made good, according to the eternal counsels and immutable promise of God. Till then, beloved Christian reader, be it ours to live in the constant, earnest, believing anticipation of this bright and blessed time, and to pass through this ungodly scene as thorough strangers and pilgrims, having no place or portion down here, but ever breathing forth the prayer, "Come, Lord Jesus!"

In the closing lines of chapter 16, Israel is warned against the most distant approach to the religious customs of the nations around. "Thou shalt not plant thee a grove of any trees near unto the altar of the Lord thy God, which thou shalt make thee. Neither shalt thou set thee up any image which the Lord thy God hateth." They were carefully to avoid every thing which might lead them in the direction of the dark and abominable idolatries of the heathen nations around. The altar of God was to stand out in distinct and unmistakable separation from those groves and shady places where false gods were worshiped, and things were done which are not to be named.* In a word, every thing was to be most carefully avoided which might in any way draw the heart away from the one living and true God.

Nor this only; it was not enough to maintain a correct outward form; images and groves might be abolished, and the nation might profess the dogma of the unity of the Godhead, and all the while there might be an utter want of heart and genuine devotedness

*It may interest the reader to know that the Holy Ghost, in speaking of the altar of God in the New Testament, does not apply to it the word used to express a heathen altar, but has a comparatively new word—a word unknown in the world's classics. The heathen altar is βωμον (Acts 17:23): the altar of God is θυσιαστηριων. The former occurs but once; the latter, twenty-three times. So jealously is the worship of the only true God guarded and preserved from the defiling touch of heathen idolatry. Men may feel disposed to inquire why this should be, or how could the altar of God be affected by a name? We reply, The Holy Ghost is wiser than we are; and although the heathen word was before Him—a short and convenient word, too—He refuses to apply it to the altar of the one true and living God.

See Trench's *Synonyms of the New Testament,* p.242. New edition revised.

in the worship rendered. Hence we read, "Thou shalt not sacrifice unto the Lord thy God any bullock or sheep wherein is blemish, or any ill-favoredness, for that is an abomination unto the Lord."

That which was absolutely perfect could alone suit the altar and answer to the heart of God. To offer a blemished thing to Him was simply to prove the absence of all true sense of what became Him, and of all real heart for Him. To attempt to offer an imperfect sacrifice was tantamount to the horrible blasphemy of saying that any thing was good enough for Him.

Let us hearken to the indignant pleadings of the Spirit of God, by the mouth of the prophet Malachi. "Ye offer polluted bread upon Mine altar; and ye say, 'Wherein have we polluted Thee?' In that ye say, 'The table of the Lord is contemptible.' And if ye offer the blind for sacrifice, is it not evil? and if ye offer the lame and sick, is it not evil? offer it now unto thy governor; will he be pleased with thee, or accept thy person? saith the Lord of Hosts. And now, I pray you, beseech God that He will be gracious unto us; this hath been by your means; will He regard your persons? saith the Lord of Hosts. Who is there even among you that would shut the doors for naught? neither do ye kindle fire on Mine altar for naught. I have no pleasure in you, saith the Lord of Hosts, neither will I accept an offering at your hand. For from the rising of the sun unto the going down of the same, My name shall be great among the Gentiles; and in every place incense shall be offered unto My name, and a pure offering; for My name shall be great among the heathen, saith the Lord of Hosts. But ye have profaned it, in that ye say, 'The table of the Lord is polluted, and the fruit thereof, even His meat is contemptible.' Ye said also, 'Behold, what a weariness is it!' and ye have snuffed at it, saith the Lord of Hosts; and ye brought that which was torn, and the lame, and the sick; thus ye brought an offering: should I accept this of your hand? saith the Lord. But cursed be the deceiver, which hath in his flock a male, and voweth and sacrificeth unto the Lord a corrupt thing; for I am a great King, saith the Lord of Hosts, and My name is dreadful among the heathen (Mal. 1:7-14).

Has all this no voice for the professing church? has it no voice for the writer and the reader of these lines? Assuredly it has. Is there not in our private and public worship a deplorable lack of *heart*, of real devotedness, deep-toned earnestness, holy energy, and integrity of purpose? Is there not much that answers to the offering of the lame and the sick, the blemished and the ill-favored? Is there not a deplorable amount of cold formality and dead routine in our seasons of worship, both in the closet and in the assembly? Have we not to judge ourselves for barrenness, distraction, and wandering, even at the very table of our Lord? How often are our bodies at the table while our vagrant hearts and volatile minds are at the ends of the earth! how often do our lips utter words which are not the true expression of our whole moral being! We express far more than we feel; we sing beyond our experience.

And then, when we are favored with the blessed opportunity of dropping our offerings in our Lord's treasury, what heartless formality! what an absence of loving, earnest, hearty devotedness! what little reference to the apostolic rule—"as God hath prospered us"! what detestable niggardliness! how little of the whole-heartedness of the poor widow who having but two mites in the world, and having the option of at least keeping one for her living, willingly cast in both—cast in her all! Pounds may be spent on ourselves, perhaps on superfluities, during the week, but when the claims of the Lord's work, His poor, and His cause in general are brought before us, how meagre is the response!

Let us consider these things; let us look at the whole subject of worship and devotedness in the divine presence, and in the presence of the grace that has saved us from everlasting burnings; let us calmly reflect upon the precious and powerful claims of Christ upon us. We are not our own; we are bought with a price. It is not merely our *best*, but our *all*, we owe to that blessed One who gave Himself for us. Do we not fully own it? do not our hearts own it? Then may our lives express it! May we more distinctly declare whose we are and whom we serve. May the heart, the head, the hands, the feet—the whole man be dedicated, in unreserved devotedness, to Him, in the power of the Holy Ghost, and according to the direct teaching of holy Scripture. God grant it may be so, with us and with all His beloved people!

A very weighty and practical subject now claims our attention. We feel it right to adhere as much as possible to the custom of quoting at full length the passages for the reader; we believe it to be profitable to give the very Word of God itself; and moreover, it is convenient to the great majority of readers to be saved the trouble of laying aside the volume and turning to the Bible in order to find the passages for themselves.

"If there be found among you, within any of thy gates which the Lord thy God giveth thee, man or woman that hath wrought wickedness in the sight of the Lord thy God, in transgressing His covenant, and hath gone and served other gods, and worshiped them, either the sun or moon, or any of the hosts of heaven, which I have not commanded; and it be told thee, and thou hast heard of it, and *inquired diligently*, and, behold, it be *true*, and the thing *certain*, that such abomination is *wrought in Israel*"—something affecting the whole nation—"then shalt thou bring forth that man or that woman, which have committed that wicked thing, unto thy gates, even that man or that woman, and shalt stone them with stones till they die. At the mouth of two witnesses, or three witnesses, shall he that is worthy of death be put to death; but at the mouth of one witness he shall not be put to death. The hands of the witnesses shall be first upon him to put him to death, and afterward the hands of all the people. So thou shalt put the evil away from among you" (ver. 2-7).

We have already had occasion to refer to the great principle laid down in the foregoing passage. It is one of immense importance, namely, the absolute necessity of having competent testimony ere forming a judgment in any case. It meets us constantly in Scripture; indeed, it is the invariable rule in the divine government, and therefore it claims our earnest attention. We may be sure it is a safe and wholesome rule, the neglect of which must always lead us astray. We should never allow ourselves to form, much less to express and act upon, a judgment without the testimony of two or three witnesses. However trustworthy and morally reliable any one witness may be, it is not a sufficient basis for a conclusion. We may feel convinced in our minds that the thing is true because affirmed by one in whom we have confidence; but God is wiser than we. It may be that the one witness is thoroughly upright and truthful, that he would not for worlds tell an untruth or bear false witness against any one—all this may be true, but we must adhere to the divine rule—"In the mouth of two or three witnesses shall every word be established."

Would that this were more diligently attended to in the Church of God! Its value in all cases of discipline, and in all cases affecting the character or reputation of any one, is simply incalculable. Ere ever an assembly reaches a conclusion or acts on a judgment in any given case, it should insist on adequate evidence. If this be not forthcoming, let all wait on God—wait patiently and confidingly, and He will surely supply what is needed.

For instance, if there be moral evil or doctrinal error in an assembly of Christians, but it is only known to one; that one is perfectly certain—deeply and thoroughly convinced of the fact. What is to be done? Wait on God for further witness. To act without this, is to infringe a divine principle laid down with all possible clearness again and again in the Word of God. Is the one witness to feel himself aggrieved or insulted because his testimony is not acted upon? Assuredly not; indeed he ought not to expect such a thing, yea, he ought not to come forward as a witness until he can corroborate his testimony by the evidence of one or two more. Is the assembly to be deemed indifferent or supine because it refuses to act on the testimony of a solitary witness? Nay, it would be flying in the face of a divine command were it to do so.

And be it remembered that this great practical principle is not confined in its application to cases of discipline, or questions connected with an assembly of the Lord's people; it is of universal application. We should never allow ourselves to form a judgment or come to a conclusion without the divinely appointed measure of evidence; if that be not forthcoming, it is our plain duty to wait, and if it be needful for us to judge in the case, God will, in due time, furnish the needed evidence. We have known a case in which a man was falsely accused because the accuser based his charge upon the evidence of one of his senses; had he taken the trouble of getting the evidence of one or two more of his senses, he would not have made the charge.

Thus the entire subject of evidence claims the serious attention of the reader, let his position be what it may. We are all prone to rush to hasty conclusions, to take up impressions, to give place to baseless surmisings, and allow our minds to be warped and carried away by prejudice. All these have to be most carefully guarded against. We need more calmness, seriousness, and cool deliberation in forming and expressing our judgment about men and things; but especially about men, inasmuch as we may inflict a grievous wrong upon a friend, a brother, or a neighbor by giving utterance to a false impression or a baseless charge. We may allow ourselves to be the vehicle of an utterly groundless accusation, whereby the character of another may be seriously damaged. This is very sinful in the sight of God, and should be most jealously watched against in ourselves, and sternly rebuked in others, whenever it comes before us. Whenever any one brings a charge against another behind his back, we should insist upon his proving or withdrawing his statement. Were this plan adopted, we should be delivered from a vast amount of evil-speaking, which is not only most unprofitable, but positively wicked, and not to be tolerated.

Before turning from the subject of evidence, we may just remark that inspired history supplies us with more than one instance in which a righteous man has been condemned with an appearance of attention to Deuteronomy 17:6-7. Witness the case of Naboth, in 1 Kings 21; and the case of Stephen, in Acts 6 and 7; and above all, the case of the only perfect Man that ever trod this earth. Alas! men can, at times, put on the appearance of wonderful attention to the letter of Scripture when it suits their own ungodly ends; they can quote its sacred words in defense of the most flagrant unrighteousness and shocking immorality. Two witnesses accused Naboth of blaspheming God and the king, and that faithful Israelite was deprived of his inheritance and of his life on the testimony of two liars, hired by the direction of a godless, cruel woman. Stephen, a man full of the Holy Ghost, was stoned to death for blasphemy, on the testimony of false witnesses received and acted upon by the great religious leaders of the day, who could doubtless quote Deuteronomy 17 as their authority.

But all this, while it so sadly and forcibly illustrates what man is, and what mere human religiousness without conscience is, leaves wholly untouched the fine moral rule laid down for our guidance in the opening lines of our chapter. Religion without conscience or the fear of God is the most degrading, demoralizing, hardening thing beneath the canopy of heaven; and one of its most terrible features is seen in this, that men under its influence are not ashamed or afraid to make use of the letter of holy Scripture as a cloak wherewith to cover the most horrible wickedness.

But thanks and praise to our God, His Word stands forth before the vision of our souls in all its heavenly purity, divine virtue, and holy morality, and flings back in the face of the enemy his every attempt to draw from its sacred pages a plea for aught that is not true, venerable, just, pure, lovely, and of good report.

We quote the second paragraph of our chapter, in which we shall find instruction of great moral value, and much needed in this day of self-will and independence.

"If there arise a matter too hard for thee in judgment, between blood and blood, between plea and plea, and between stroke and stroke, being matters of controversy within thy gates; then shalt thou arise and get thee up *into the place which the Lord thy God shall choose;* and thou shalt come unto the priests the Levites, and unto the judges that shall be in those days, and inquire; and they shall show thee the sentence of judgment: and thou shalt do according to the sentence which they of *that place which the Lord shall choose* shall show thee; and thou shalt observe to do according to all that they inform thee; according to the sentence of the law which they shall teach thee, and according to the judgment which they shall tell thee, thou shalt do: thou shalt not decline from the sentence which they shall show thee, to the right hand, nor to the left, and the man that will do presumptuously, and will not hearken unto the priest that standeth to minister there before the Lord thy God, or unto the judge, even that man shall die; and thou shalt put away the evil from Israel. And all the people shall *hear* and *fear* and *do no more presumptuously*" (ver. 8-13).

Here we have divine provision made for the perfect settlement of all questions which might arise throughout the congregation of Israel. They were to be settled in the divine presence, at the divinely appointed centre, by the divinely appointed authority. Thus self-will and presumption were effectually guarded against. All matters of controversy were to be definitively settled by the judgment of God as expressed by the priest or the judge appointed by God for the purpose.

In a word, it was absolutely and entirely a matter of divine authority. It was not for one man to set himself up in self-will and presumption against another. This would never do in the assembly of God. Each one had to submit his cause to a divine tribunal, and bow implicitly to its decision. There was to be no appeal, inasmuch as there was no higher court. The divinely appointed priest or judge spoke as the oracle of God, and both plaintiff and defendant had to bow, without a demur, to the decision.

Now, it must be very evident that no member of the congregation of Israel would ever have thought of bringing his case before a Gentile tribunal for judgment. This, we may feel assured, would have been utterly foreign to the thoughts and feelings of every true Israelite. It would have involved a positive insult to Jehovah Himself, who was in their midst to give judgment in every case which might arise. Surely He was sufficient. He knew the ins and outs, the *pros* and *cons,* the roots and issues, of every controversy, however involved or difficult. All were to look to Him, and to bring their causes to the place which He had chosen, and no where else. The idea of two members of the assembly of God appearing before a tribunal of the uncircumcised for judgment would not have been tolerated for a moment. It would be as much as to say that there was a defect in the divine arrangement for the congregation.

Has this any voice for us? How are Christians to have their questions and their controversies settled? Are they to betake themselves to the world for judgment? Is there no provision in the assembly of God for the proper settlement of cases which may arise? Hear what the inspired apostle says on the point to the assembly at Corinth, and "to all that in every place call on the name of our Lord Jesus Christ, both theirs and ours," and therefore to all true Christians now.

"Dare any of you, having a matter against another, go to law before the unjust, and not before the saints? Do ye not know that the saints shall judge the world? and if the world shall be judged by you, are ye unworthy to judge the smallest matters? Know ye not that we shall judge angels? how much more things that pertain to this life! If then ye have judgments of things pertaining to this life, set them to judge who are least esteemed in the Church. I speak to your shame. Is it so, that there is not a wise man among you? no, not one that shall be able to judge between his brethren? But brother goeth to law with brother, and that before the unbelievers. Now therefore there is utterly a fault among you, because ye go to law one with another. Why do ye not rather take wrong? why do ye not rather be defrauded? Nay, ye do wrong, and defraud, and that your brethren. Know ye not that the unrighteous shall not inherit the kingdom of God? *Be not deceived"* (1 Cor. 6:1-9).

Here, then, we have divine instruction for the Church of God in all ages. We must never, for a moment, lose sight of the fact that the Bible is *the* book for every stage of the Church's earthly career. True it is, alas! the Church is not as it was when the above lines were penned by the inspired apostle; a vast change has taken place in the Church's practical condition. There was no difficulty in early days in distinguishing between the Church and the world—between "the saints" and "unbelievers"—between "those within" and "those without." The line of demarkation was broad, distinct, and unmistakable in those days. Any one who looked at the face of society in a religious point of view would see three things, namely, Paganism, Judaism, and Christianity—the Gentile, the Jew, and the Church of God—the heathen temple, the synagogue, and the assembly of God. There was no confounding these things. The Christian assembly stood out in vivid contrast with all beside. Christianity was strongly and clearly pronounced in those primitive times. It was neither a national, provincial, nor parochial affair, but a personal, practical, living reality. It was not a mere nominal, national, professional creed, but a divinely wrought faith, a living power in the heart flowing out in the life.

But now, things are totally changed. The Church and the world are so mixed up, that the vast majority of professors could hardly understand the real force and proper application of the passage which we have just quoted. Were we to speak to them about "the saints" going to law "before the unbelievers," it would seem like a foreign tongue. Indeed, the term "saint" is hardly heard in the professing church, save when used with a sneer, or as applied to such as have been canonized by a superstitious reverence.

But has any change come over the Word of God, or over the grand truths which that Word unfolds to our souls? Has any change come over the thoughts of God in reference to what His Church is, or what the world is, or as to the proper relation of the one to the other? Does He not know who are "saints" and who are "unbelievers"? Has it ceased to be "a fault" for "brother to go to law with brother, and that before the unbelievers"? In a word, has holy Scripture lost its power, its point, its divine application? Is it no longer our guide, our authority, our one perfect rule and unerring standard? Has the marked change that has come over the Church's moral condition deprived the Word of God of all power of application to *us*—"to all that in every place call on the name of our Lord Jesus Christ"? Has our Father's most precious revelation become, in any one particular, a dead letter—a piece of obsolete writing—a document pertaining to days long gone by? Has our altered condition robbed the Word of God of a single one of its moral glories?

What answer does your heart return to these questions? Let us most earnestly entreat of you to weigh them honestly, humbly, and prayerfully in the presence of your Lord. We believe your answer will be a wonderfully correct index of your real position and moral state. Do you not clearly see and fully admit that Scripture can never lose its power? Can the principles of 1 Corinthians 6 ever cease to be binding on the Church of God? It is fully admitted—for who can deny that things are sadly changed?—but "Scripture cannot be broken," and therefore what was "a fault" in the first century cannot be right in the nineteenth; there may be more difficulty in carrying out divine principles, but we must never consent to surrender them, or to act on any lower ground. If once we admit the idea that because the whole professing church has gone wrong it is impossible for us to do right, the whole principle of Christian obedience is surrendered. It is as wrong for "brother to go to law with brother before the unbelievers" to-day as when the apostle wrote his Epistle to the assembly at Corinth.* True, the Church's *visible* unity is gone; she is shorn of many

*It is well for us to bear in mind that wherever there are "two or three" gathered to the Name of the Lord Jesus, in ever such weakness, there will be found, if only they are truly humble and dependent, spiritual ability to judge in any case that may arise between brethren. They can count on divine wisdom being supplied for the settlement of any question, plea, or

gifts, she has departed from her normal condition; but the principles of the Word of God can no more lose their power than the blood of Christ can lose its virtue or His priesthood lose its efficacy.

Further, we must bear in mind that there are resources of wisdom, grace, power, and spiritual gift treasured up for the Church in Christ her Head, ever available for those who have faith to use them. We are not straitened in our blessed and adorable Head. We need never expect to see the body restored to its normal condition on the earth, but for all that, it is our privilege to see what the true ground of the body is, and it is our duty to occupy that ground and no other.

Now, it is perfectly wonderful the change that takes place in our whole condition—in our view of things, in our thoughts of ourselves and our surroundings—the moment we plant our foot on the true ground of the Church of God. Every thing seems changed; the Bible seems a new book; we see every thing in a new light; portions of Scripture which we have been reading for years without interest or profit now sparkle with divine light, and fill us with wonder, love, and praise. We see everything from a new standpoint; our whole range of vision is changed; we have made our escape from the murky atmosphere which inwraps the whole professing church, and can now look around and see things clearly in the heavenly light of Scripture. In fact, it seems like a new conversion; and we find we can now read Scripture intelligently, because we have the divine key. We see Christ to be the centre and object of all the thoughts, purposes, and counsels of God from everlasting to everlasting, and hence we are conducted into that marvelous sphere of grace and glory which the Holy Ghost delights to unfold in the precious Word of God.

May the reader be led into the thorough understanding of all this, by the direct and powerful ministry of the Holy Spirit. May he be enabled to give himself to the study of Scripture, and to surrender himself, unreservedly, to its teaching and authority. Let him not confer with flesh and blood, but cast himself, like a little child, on the Lord, and seek to be led on in spiritual intelligence and practical conformity to the mind of Christ.

We must now look for a moment at the closing verses of our chapter, in which we have a remarkable onlook into Israel's future, anticipating the moment in which they should seek to set a king over them.

"When thou art come unto the land which the Lord thy God giveth thee, and shalt possess it, and shalt dwell therein, and shalt say, I will set a king over me, like as all the nations that are about me; thou shalt in any wise set him king over thee whom the Lord thy God shall choose; one from among thy brethren shalt thou set king over thee; thou mayest not set a stranger over thee, which is not thy brother. But he shall not multiply horses to himself, nor cause the people to return to Egypt, to the end that he should multiply horses; forasmuch as the Lord hath

controversy, so that there need not be any reference to a worldly tribunal.

No doubt worldly men would smile at such an idea; but we must adhere, with holy decision, to the guidance of Scripture. Brother must not go to law with brother before the unbelievers. This is distinct and emphatic. There are resources available for the assembly in Christ, the Head and Lord, for the settlement of every possible question.

Let the Lord's people seriously apply their hearts to the consideration of this subject. Let them see that they are gathered on the true ground of the Church of God; and then, though ever conscious that things are not as they once were in the Church—though sensible of the greatest weakness, failure, and shortcoming, they will nevertheless find the grace of Christ ever sufficient for them, and the Word of God full of all needed instruction and authority, so that they need never betake themselves to the world for help, counsel, or judgment. "Where two or three are gathered together in My name, there am I in the midst of them."

This surely is enough for every exigence. Is there any question that our Lord Christ cannot settle? Do we want natural cleverness, worldly wisdom, long-headedness, great learning, keen sagacity, if we have Him? Surely not; indeed all such things can only prove like Saul's armor to David. All we want is, simply to use the resources which we have in Christ. We shall assuredly find, "in the place where His name is recorded," priestly wisdom to judge in every case which may arise between brethren.

And further, let the Lord's dear people remember, in all cases of local difficulty which may arise, that there is no need whatever for them to look for extraneous aid, to write to other places to get some wise man to come and help them. No doubt, if the Lord sends any of His beloved servants at the moment, their sympathy, fellowship, counsel, and help will be highly prized. We are not encouraging independence one of the other, but absolute and complete dependence upon Christ, our Head and Lord.

said unto you, 'Ye shall henceforth return no more that way.' Neither shall he multiply wives to himself, that his heart turn not away; neither shall he greatly multiply to himself silver and gold."

How very remarkable that the three things which the king was not to do were just *the* very things which were done—and extensively done by the greatest and wisest of Israel's monarchs. "King Solomon made a navy of ships in Ezion-geber, which is beside Eloth, on the shore of the Red Sea, in the land of Edom. And Hiram sent in the navy his servants, shipmen that had knowledge of the sea, with the servants of Solomon. And they came to Ophir, and fetched from thence *gold*, four hundred and twenty talents [over two millions], and brought it to king Solomon." "And Hiram sent to the king sixscore talents of gold." "And the weight of gold that came to Solomon in one year was six hundred threescore and six talents of gold [nearly three and a half millions], beside that he had of the merchantmen, and of the traffic of the spice merchants, and of all the kings of Arabia, and of the governors of the country." Again, we read, "And the king made *silver* to be in Jerusalem as stones. . . . And Solomon had *horses brought out of Egypt*. . . . But king Solomon loved many strange women. . . . And he had seven hundred wives, princesses, and three hundred concubines; and his wives turned away his heart" (1 Kings 9—11).

What a tale this tells! what a commentary it furnishes upon man in his very best and highest estate! Here was a man endowed with wisdom beyond all others, surrounded by unexampled blessings, dignities, honors, and privileges; his earthly cup was full to the brim; there was nothing lacking which this world could supply to minister to human happiness. And not only so, but his remarkable prayer at the dedication of the temple might well lead us to cherish the brightest hopes respecting him, both personally and officially.

But sad to say, he broke down most deplorably in every one of the particulars as to which the law of his God had spoken so definitely and so clearly. He was told not to multiply silver and gold, and yet he multiplied them; he was told not to return to Egypt to multiply horses, and yet to Egypt he went for horses; he was told not to multiply wives, and yet he had a thousand of them, and they turned away his heart. Such is man! Oh, how little is he to be counted upon! "All flesh is as grass, and all the glory of man as the flower of grass. The grass withereth, and the flower thereof falleth away." "Cease ye from man whose breath is in his nostrils, for wherein is he to be accounted of?"

But we may ask, How are we to account for Solomon's signal, sorrowful, and humiliating failure? what was the real secret of it? To answer this, we must quote for the reader the closing verses of our chapter.

"And it shall be, when he sitteth upon the throne of his kingdom, that he shall write him a copy of this law in a book out of that which is before the priests the Levites; *and it shall be with him,* and *he shall read therein all the days of his life;* that he may learn to fear the Lord his God, to keep all the words of this law and these statutes, to do them; that his heart be not lifted up above his brethren, and that he turn not aside from the commandment, to the right hand or to the left; to the end that he may prolong his days in his kingdom, he and his children, in the midst of Israel" (ver. 18-20).

Had Solomon attended to these most precious and weighty words, his historian would have had a very different task to perform; but he did not. We hear nothing of his having made a copy of the law; and most assuredly, if he did make a copy of it, he did not attend to it—yea, he turned his back upon it, and did the very things which he was told not to do. In a word, the cause of all the wreck and ruin that so rapidly followed the splendor of Solomon's reign, was the neglect of the plain Word of God.

It is this which makes it all so solemn for us, in this our own day, and which leads us to call the earnest attention of the reader to it. We deeply feel the need of seeking to rouse the attention of the whole Church of God to this great subject. Neglect of the Word of God is the source of all the failure, all the sin, all the error, all the mischief and confusion, the heresies, sects, and schisms that have ever been or are now in this world. And we may add, with equal confidence, that the only real, sovereign remedy for our present lamentable condition will be found in returning, *every one for himself and herself,* to the simple but sadly neglected authority of the Word of God. Let each one see his own departure, and that of the whole professing body, from the plain and positive teaching of the New Testament—the commandments of our blessed Lord and Saviour Jesus Christ. Let us humble ourselves under the mighty hand of our God, because of our common sin, and let us turn to Him in true self-judgment, and He will graciously restore and heal and bless us, and lead us in that most blessed path of obedience which lies open before every truly humble soul.

May God the Holy Ghost, in His own resistless power, bring home to the heart and conscience of every member of the body of Christ on the face of the earth, the urgent need of an immediate and unreserved surrender to the authority of the Word of God.

---

## *CHAPTER 18*

THE opening paragraph of this chapter suggests a deeply interesting and practical line of truth. "The priests the Levites, and all the tribe of Levi, shall have no part nor inheritance with Israel; they shall eat the offerings of the Lord made by fire, and His inheritance. Therefore shall they have no inheritance among their brethren: the Lord is their inheritance, as He hath said unto them. And this shall be the priest's due from the people, from them that offer a sacrifice, whether it be ox or sheep; and they shall give unto the priest the shoulder, and the two cheeks, and the maw. The first-fruits also of thy corn, of thy wine, and of thine oil, and the first of the fleece of thy sheep shalt thou give him. For the Lord thy God hath chosen him out of all thy tribes, to stand to minister in the name of the Lord, him and his sons forever. And if a Levite come from any of thy gates out of all Israel, where he sojourned, and *come with all the desire of his mind unto the place which the Lord shall choose;* then he shall minister in the name of the Lord his God, as all his brethren the Levites do, which stand there before the Lord. They shall have like portions to eat, beside that which cometh out of the sale of his patrimony" (ver. 1-8).

Here, as in every part of the book of Deuteronomy, the priests are classed with the Levites in a very marked way. We have called the reader's attention to this as a special characteristic feature of our book, and shall not dwell upon it now, but merely, in passing, remind the reader of it, as something claiming his attention. Let him weigh the opening words of our chapter, "The priests the Levites," and compare them with the way in which the priests the sons of Aaron are spoken of in Exodus, Leviticus, and Numbers; and if he should be disposed to ask the reason of this distinction, we believe it to be this, that in Deuteronomy the divine object is, to bring the whole assembly of Israel more into prominence, and hence it is that the priests in their official capacity come rarely before us. The grand Deuteronomic idea is, *Israel in immediate relationship with Jehovah.*

Now, in the passage just quoted, we have the priests and the Levites linked together, and presented as the Lord's servants, wholly dependent upon Him, and intimately identified with His altar and His service. This is full of interest, and opens up a very important field of practical truth, to which the Church of God would do well to attend.

In looking through the history of Israel, we observe that when things were in any thing like a healthful condition, the altar of God was well attended to, and, as a consequence, the priests and the Levites were well supplied. If Jehovah had His portion, His servants were sure to have theirs; if He was neglected, so were they. They were bound up together. The people were to bring their offerings to God, and He shared them with His servants. The priests the Levites were not to exact or demand of the people, but the people were privileged to bring their gifts to the altar of God, and He permitted His servants to feed upon the fruit of His people's devotedness to Him.

Such was the true, the divine idea as to the Lord's servants of old. They were to live upon the voluntary offerings presented to God by the whole congregation. True it is that in the dark and evil days of the sons of Eli we find something sadly different from this lovely moral order. Then, "the priest's custom with the people was, that when any one offered sacrifice, the priest's servant came, while the flesh was in seething, with a flesh-hook of three teeth in his hand; and he struck it into the pan, or kettle, or caldron, or pot; all that the flesh-hook brought up, the priest took for himself. So they did in Shiloh unto all the Israelites that came thither. Also before they burnt the fat [God's special portion], the priest's servant came, and said to the man that sacrificed, 'Give flesh to roast for the priest; for he will not have sodden flesh of thee, but raw.' And if any man said unto him, Let them not fail to burn the fat presently, and then take as much as thy soul desireth; then he would answer him, 'Nay; but thou shalt give it me now; and if not, *I will take it by force.*' Wherefore the sin of the young men was very great before the Lord; for men abhorred the offering of the Lord" (1 Sam. 2:13-17).

All this was truly deplorable, and ended in the solemn judgment of God upon the house of Eli. It could not be otherwise. If those who ministered at the altar could be guilty of such terrible iniquity and impiety, judgment must take its course.

But the normal condition of things, as presented in our chapter, was in vivid contrast with all this frightful iniquity. Jehovah would surround Himself with the willing offerings of His people, and from these offerings He would feed His servants who ministered at His altar. Hence, therefore, when the altar of God was diligently, fervently, and devotedly attended to, the priests the Levites had a rich portion—an abundant supply; and on the other hand, when Jehovah and His altar were treated with cold neglect, or merely waited upon in a barren routine or heartless formalism, the Lord's servants were correspondingly neglected. In a word, they stood intimately identified with the worship and service of the God of Israel.

Thus, for example, in the bright days of the good king Hezekiah, when things were fresh and hearts happy and true, we read, "And Hezekiah appointed the courses of the priests and the Levites after their courses, every man according to his service, the priests and Levites for burnt-offerings and for peace-offerings, to minister, and to give thanks, and to praise in the gates of the tents of the Lord. He appointed also the king's portion of his substance for the burnt-offerings, to wit, for the morning and evening burnt-offerings, and the burnt-offerings for the Sabbaths, and for the new moons, and for the set feasts, *as it is written in the law of the Lord.* Moreover, he commanded the people that dwelt in Jerusalem *to give the portion of the priests and the Levites, that they might be encouraged in the law of the Lord.* And as soon as the commandment came abroad, the children of Israel brought *in abundance* the first-fruits of corn, wine, and oil, and honey, and of all the increase of the field; and the tithe of *all things* brought they in *abundantly.* And concerning the children of Israel and Judah, that dwelt in the cities of Judah, they also brought in the tithe of oxen and sheep, and the tithe of holy things which were consecrated unto the Lord their God, *and laid them by heaps.* In the third month they began to lay the foundation of the heaps, and finished them in the seventh month. And when Hezekiah and the princes came and saw the heaps, they blessed the Lord and His people Israel. Then Hezekiah questioned with the priests and the Levites concerning the heaps. And Azariah the chief priest of the house of Zadok answered him, and said, *'Since the people began to bring the offerings into the house of the Lord, we have had enough to eat, and have left plenty; for the Lord hath blessed His people; and that which is left is this great store*" (2 Chron. 31:2-10).

How truly refreshing is all this! and how encouraging! The deep, full, silvery tide of devotedness flowed around the altar of God, bearing upon its bosom an ample supply to meet all the need of the Lord's servants, and "heaps" beside. This, we may feel assured, was grateful to the heart of the God of Israel, as it was to the hearts of those who had given themselves, at His call and by His appointment, to the service of His altar and His sanctuary.

And let the reader specially note those precious words, *"As it is written in the law of the Lord."* Here was Hezekiah's authority, the solid basis of this whole line of conduct from first to last. True, the nation's visible unity was gone; the condition of things when he began his blessed work was most discouraging; but the word of the Lord was as true, as real, and as direct in its application in Hezekiah's day as it was in the days of David or Joshua. Hezekiah rightly felt that Deuteronomy 18:1-8 applied to his day and to his conscience, and that he and the people were responsible to act upon it, according to their ability. Were the priests and the Levites to starve because Israel's national unity was gone? Surely not. They were to stand or fall with the Word, the worship, and the work of God. Circumstances might vary, and the Israelite might find himself in a position in which it would be impossible to carry out in detail all the ordinances of the Levitical ceremonial, but he never could find himself in circumstances in which it was not his high privilege to give full expression to his heart's devotedness to the service, the altar, and the law of Jehovah.

Thus, then, we see, throughout the entire history of Israel, that when things were at all bright and healthy, the Lord's worship, His work, and His workmen were blessedly attended to; but on the other hand, when things were low, when hearts were cold, when self and its interests had the uppermost place, then all these great objects were treated with heartless neglect. Look, for example, at Nehemiah 13. When that beloved and faithful servant returned to Jerusalem, after an absence of certain days, he found, to his deep sorrow, that, even in that short time, various things had gone sadly astray; amongst the rest, the poor Levites had been left without any thing to eat. "And I perceived that the portions of the Levites had not been given them; for the Levites and the singers that did the work were fled every one to his field." There were no "heaps" of first-fruits in those dismal days, and surely it was hard for men to work and sing when they had nothing to eat. This was not according to the law of Jehovah, nor according to His loving heart. It was a sad reproach upon the people that the Lord's servants were obliged, through their gross neglect, to abandon His worship and His work in order to keep themselves from starving.

This, truly, was a deplorable condition of things. Nehemiah felt it keenly, as we read, "Then contended I with the rulers, and said, *'Why is the house of God forsaken?'* And I gathered them together, and set them in their place. Then brought all Judah the tithe of the corn, and the new wine, and the oil, unto the treasuries. And I made treasurers over the treasuries . . . for they were counted faithful"—they were entitled to the confidence of their brethren—"and their office was to distribute unto their brethren." It needed a number of tried and faithful men to occupy the high position of distributing to their brethren the precious fruit of the people's devotedness; they could take counsel together, and see that the Lord's treasury was faithfully managed, according to His Word, and the need of His true and *bona-fide* workmen fully met, without prejudice or partiality.

Such was the lovely order of the God of Israel—an order to which every true Israelite such as Nehemiah and Hezekiah would delight to attend. The rich tide of blessing flowed forth from Jehovah to His people, and back from His people to Him, and from that flowing tide His servants were to draw a full supply for all their need. It was a dishonor to Him to have the Levites obliged to return to their fields; it proved that His house was forsaken, and that there was no sustenance for His servants.

Now, the question may here be asked, What has all this to say to us? what has the Church of God to learn from Deuteronomy

18:1-8? In order to answer this question, we must turn to 1 Corinthians 9, where the inspired apostle deals with the very important subject of the support of the Christian ministry—a subject so little understood by the great mass of professing Christians. As to *the law of the case,* it is as distinct as possible. "Who goeth a warfare at any time at his own charges? who planteth a vineyard, and eateth not of the fruit thereof? or who feedeth a flock, and eateth not of the milk of the flock? Say I these things as a man? or saith not the law the same also? For it is written in the law of Moses, 'Thou shalt not muzzle the mouth of the ox that treadeth out the corn. Doth God take care for oxen? or saith He it altogether for our sakes? For our sakes, no doubt, this is written; that he that ploweth should plow in hope, and that he that thresheth in hope should be partaker of his hope. If we have sown unto you spiritual things, is it a great thing if we shall reap your carnal things? If others be partakers of this power over you, are not we rather? Nevertheless"—here grace shines out, in all its heavenly lustre—"we have not used this power; but suffer all things lest we should hinder the gospel of Christ. Do ye not know that they which minister about holy things live of the things of the temple? and they which wait at the altar are partakers with the altar? Even so hath the Lord ordained that they which preach the gospel should live of the gospel. But"—here again grace asserts its holy dignity—"I have used none of these things; neither have I written these things that it should be so done unto me; for it were better for me to die than that any man should make my glorying void. For though I preach the gospel, I have nothing to glory of; for necessity is laid upon me; yea, woe is unto me if I preach not the gospel! For if I do this thing willingly, I have a reward; but if against my will, a dispensation of the gospel is committed unto me. What is my reward, then? Verily that when I preach the gospel, I may make the gospel of Christ without charge, that I abuse not my power in the gospel" (ver. 7-18).

Here we have this interesting and weighty subject presented in all its bearings. The inspired apostle lays down, with all possible decision and clearness, the divine law on the point. There is no mistaking it. "The Lord hath ordained that they that preach the gospel should live of the gospel;" that just as the priests and the Levites of old lived on the offerings presented by the people, so now, those who are really called of God, gifted by Christ, and fitted by the Holy Ghost to preach the gospel, and who are giving themselves constantly and diligently to that glorious work, are morally entitled to temporal support. It is not that they should look to those to whom they preach for a certain stipulated sum. There is no such idea as this in the New Testament. The workman must look to his Master, and to Him alone, for support. Woe be to him if he looks to the church, or to men in any way. The priests and Levites had their portion in and from Jehovah. He was the lot of their inheritance. True, He expected the people to minister to Him in the persons of His servants. He told them what to give, and blessed them in giving: it was their high privilege, as well as their bounden duty, to give; had they refused or neglected, it would have brought drought and barrenness upon their fields and vineyards (Hag. 1:5-11).

But the priests the Levites had to look *only* to Jehovah. If the people failed in their offerings, the Levites had to fly to their fields and work for their living. They could not go to law with any one for tithes and offerings; their only appeal was to the God of Israel, who had ordained them to the work and given them the work to do.

So also with the Lord's workmen now—they must look *only* to Him. They must be well assured that He has fitted them for the work, and called them to it, ere they attempt to push out (if we may so express it) from the shore of circumstances, and give themselves wholly to the work of preaching. They must take their eyes completely off from men—from all creature-streams and human props, and lean exclusively upon the living God. We have seen the most disastrous consequences resulting from acting under a mistaken impulse in this most solemn matter; men not called of God, or fitted for the work, giving up their occupations, and coming forth, as they said, to live by faith and give themselves to the work. Deplorable shipwreck was the result in every instance. Some, when they began to look the stern realities of the path straight in the face, became so alarmed that they actually lost their mental balance, lost their reason for a time; some lost their peace, and some went right back into the world again.

In short, it is our deep and thorough conviction, after forty years' observation, that the cases are few and far between in which it is morally safe and good for one to abandon his bread-winning calling in order to preach the gospel. It must be so distinct and unquestionable to the man himself, that he has only to say, with Luther, at the Diet of Worms, "Here I am; I can do no otherwise: God help me! Amen." Then he may be perfectly sure that God will sustain him in the work to which He has called him, and meet all his need "according to His riches in glory by Christ Jesus." And as to men and their thoughts respecting him and his course, he has simply to refer them to his Master. He is not responsible to them, nor has he ever asked them for any thing. If they were compelled to support him, reason would that they might complain or raise questions; but as they are not, they must just leave him, remembering that to his own Master he standeth or falleth.

But when we look at the splendid passage just quoted from 1 Corinthians 9, we find that the blessed apostle, after having established, beyond all question, his right to be supported, relinquishes it completely. "Nevertheless, I have used none of these things." He worked with his hands; he wrought with labor and travail night and day, in order not to be chargeable or burdensome to any. "These hands," he says, "have ministered to my necessities, and those that were with me." He coveted no man's silver or gold or apparel. He traveled, he preached, he visited from house to house, he was the laborious apostle, the earnest evangelist, the diligent pastor, he had the care of all the churches. Was not he entitled to support? Assuredly he was. It ought to have been the joy of the Church of God to minister to his every need. But he never enforced his claim—nay, he surrendered it. He supported himself and his companions by the labor of his hands; and all this as an example, as he says to the elders of Ephesus, "I have showed you all things, how that so laboring ye ought to support the weak, and to remember the words of the Lord Jesus, how He said, 'It is more blessed to give than to receive.' "

Now, it is perfectly wonderful to think of this beloved and revered servant of Christ, with his extensive travels from Jerusalem and round about to Illyricum, his gigantic labors as an evangelist, a pastor, and a teacher, and yet finding time to support himself and others by the work of his hands. Truly he occupied high moral ground. His case is a standing testimony against hirelingism, in every shape and form. The infidel's sneering references to well-paid ministers could have no application whatever to him. He certainly did not preach for hire.

And yet he thankfully received help from those who knew how to give it. Again and again the beloved assembly at Philippi ministered to the necessities of their revered and beloved father in Christ. How well for them that they did so! It will never be forgotten. Millions have read the sweet record of their devotedness, and been refreshed by the odor of their sacrifice; it is recorded in heaven, where nothing of the kind is ever forgotten—yea, it is engraved on the very tablets of the heart of Christ. Hear how the blessed apostle pours out his grateful heart to his much-loved children. "I rejoiced in the Lord greatly, that now at the last your care of me hath flourished again; wherein ye were also careful, but ye lacked opportunity. Not that I speak in respect of want"—blessed, self-denying servant!—"for I have learned, in whatsoever state I am, to be content. I know both how to be abased, and I know how to abound; every where and in all things I am instructed both to be full and to be hungry, both to abound and to suffer need. I can do all things through Christ, which strengtheneth me. Notwithstanding, ye have well done that ye did communicate with my affliction. Now ye Philippians know also, that in the beginning of the gospel, when I departed from Macedonia, no church communicated with me as concerning giving and receiving, but ye only. For even in Thessalonica ye sent once and again unto my necessity. Not because I desire a gift; but I desire fruit that may abound to your account. But I have all, and abound; I am full, having received from Epaphroditus the things which were sent from you, an odor of a sweet smell, a sacrifice acceptable, well-pleasing to God. But my God shall supply all your need according to His riches in glory by Christ Jesus" (Phil. 4:10-19).

What a rare privilege to be allowed to comfort the heart of such an honored servant of Christ, at the close of his career, and in the solitude of his prison at Rome! How seasonable, how right, how lovely, was their ministry! What joy to receive the apostle's grateful acknowledgments! and then how precious the assurance that their service had gone up, as an odor of sweet smell, to the very throne and heart of God! Who would not rather be a Philippian ministering to the apostle's need, than a Corinthian calling his ministry in question, or a Galatian breaking his heart? How vast the difference! The apostle could not take any thing from the assembly at Corinth; their state did not admit of it. Individuals in that assembly did minister to him, and their service is recorded on the page of inspiration, remembered above, and it will be abundantly rewarded in the kingdom by and by. "I am glad of the coming of Stephanas and Fortunatus and Achaicus; for *that which was lacking on your part they have supplied.* For they have refreshed my spirit and yours, therefore acknowledge ye them that are such" (1 Cor. 16:17-18).

Thus, then, from all that has passed before us, we learn most distinctly that both under the law and under the gospel it is according to the revealed will, and according to the heart of God, that those who are really called of Him to the work, and who devote themselves earnestly, diligently, and faithfully to it, should have the hearty sympathy and practical help of His people. All who love Christ will count it their deepest joy to minister to Him in the persons of His servants. When He Himself was here upon earth, He graciously accepted help from the hands of those who loved Him, and had reaped the fruit of His most precious ministry—"certain women, which had been healed of evil spirits and infirmities, Mary, called Magdalene, out of whom went seven devils, and Joanna the wife of Chuza, Herod's steward, and Susanna, and many others, which ministered unto Him of their substance" (Luke 8:2-3).

Happy, highly privileged women! What joy to be allowed to minister to the Lord of glory, in the days of His human need and humiliation! There stand their honored names, on the divine page, written down by God the Holy Ghost, to be read by untold millions, to be borne along the stream of time right onward into eternity. How well it was for those women that they did not waste their substance in self-indulgence, or hoard it up to be rust on their souls, or a positive curse, as money must ever be if not used for God!

But on the other hand, we learn the urgent need, on the part of all who take the place of workers, whether in or out of the assembly, of keeping themselves perfectly free from all human influence, all looking to men, in any shape or form. They must have to do with God in the secret of their own souls, or they will assuredly break down, sooner or later. They must look to Him alone for the supply of their need. If the church neglect them, the church will be the serious loser here and hereafter. If they can support themselves by the labor of their hands, without curtailing their direct service to Christ, so much the better; it is unquestionably the more excellent way. We are as persuaded of this as of the truth of any proposition that could be submitted to us. There is nothing more spiritually and morally noble than a truly gifted servant of Christ supporting himself and his family by the sweat of his brow or the sweat of his brain, and, at the same time, giving himself diligently to the Lord's work, whether as an evangelist, a pastor, or a teacher. The moral antipodes of this is presented to our view in the person of a man who, without gift or grace or spiritual life, enters what is called the ministry, as a mere profession or means of living. The position of such a man is morally dangerous and miserable in the extreme. We shall not dwell upon it, inasmuch as it does not come within the range of the subject which has been engaging our attention, and we are only too thankful to leave it and proceed with our chapter.

"When thou art come into the land which the Lord thy God giveth thee, thou shalt not learn to do after the abominations of those nations. There shall not be found among you any one that maketh his son or his daughter to pass through the fire, or that useth divination, or an observer of times, or an enchanter, or a witch, or a charmer, or a consulter with familiar spirits, or a wizard, or a necromancer; for *all that do these things are an abomination unto the Lord,* and because of these abominations the Lord thy God doth drive them out from before thee. Thou shalt be perfect with the Lord thy God. For these nations, which thou shalt possess, hearkened unto observers of times, and unto diviners; *but as for thee, the Lord thy God hath not suffered thee so to do*" (ver. 9-14).

Now, it may be that, on reading the foregoing quotation, the reader feels disposed to ask what possible application it can have to professing Christians. We ask, in reply, are there any professing Christians who are in the habit of going to witness the performances of wizards, magicians, and necromancers? are there any who take part in table-turning, spirit-rapping, mesmerism, or *clairvoyance?** If so, the passage which we have just quoted bears very pointedly and solemnly upon all such. We most surely believe that all these things which we have named are of the devil. This may sound harsh and severe, but we cannot help that. We are thoroughly persuaded that when people lend themselves to the awful business of bringing up, in any way, the spirits of the departed, they are simply putting themselves into the hands of the devil, to be deceived and deluded by his lies. What, we may ask, do those who hold in their hands a perfect revelation from God want of table-turning and spirit-rapping? Surely nothing. And if, not content with that precious Word, they turn to the spirits of departed friends or others, what can they expect but that God will judicially give them over to be blinded and deceived by wicked spirits, who come up and personate the departed, and tell all manner of lies?

We cannot attempt to go fully into this subject here; we have no time, nor space, nor inclination, for any thing of the sort. We merely feel it to be our solemn duty to warn the reader against having any thing whatever to do with consulting departed spirits. We believe it to be *most dangerous* work. We do not enter upon the question as to whether souls can come back to this world; no doubt God could permit them to come if He saw fit, but this we leave. The great point for us to keep ever before our hearts is, the perfect sufficiency of divine revelation. What do we want of departed spirits? The rich man imagined that if Lazarus were to go back to earth and speak to his five brethren, it would have a great effect. "'I pray thee therefore, father, that thou wouldest send him to my father's house; for I have five brethren; that he may testify unto them, lest they also come into this place of torment.' Abraham saith unto him, 'They have *Moses and the prophets; let them hear them.*' And he said, 'Nay, father Abraham; but if one went unto them from the dead, they will repent.' And he said unto him, 'If they hear not *Moses and the prophets,* neither will they be persuaded though one rose from the dead' " (Luke 16:27-31).

Here we have a thorough settlement of this question. If people will not hear the Word of God, if they will not believe its clear and solemn statements as to themselves, their present condition, and their fu-

*Some of our readers may object to our classing mesmerism with spirit-rapping and table-turning. It may be they would regard it in the same light, and use it in the same way, as ether or chloroform, in medical practice. We do not attempt to dogmatize on the point. We can only say that we could have nothing whatever to do with it. We consider it a most solemn thing for any one to allow himself to be placed by another in a state of utter unconsciousness, for any purpose whatsoever. And as to the idea of listening to, or being guided by, the ravings of a person in that state, we can only regard it as absolutely absurd, if not positively sinful.

ture destiny, neither will they be persuaded though a thousand departed souls were to come back and tell them what they saw and heard and felt in heaven above or in hell beneath; it would produce no saving or permanent effect upon them. It might cause great excitement—great sensation, furnish great material for talk, and fill the newspapers far and wide; but there it would end. People would go on all the same with their traffic and gain, their folly and vanity, their pleasure-hunting and self-indulgence. "If they hear not Moses and the prophets, [and, we may add, Christ and His holy apostles,] neither will they be persuaded though one rose from the dead." The heart that will not bow to Scripture will not be convinced by any thing; and as to the true believer, he has in Scripture all he can possibly want, and therefore he has no need to have recourse to table-turning, spirit-rapping, or magic. "And when they shall say unto you, Seek unto them that have familiar spirits, and unto wizards that peep, and that mutter; should not a people seek unto their God? for the living to the dead? *To the law and to the testimony;* if they speak not according to this word, it is because there is no light in them" (Isa. 8:19-20).

Here is the divine resource of the Lord's people, at all times and in all places; and to this it is that Moses refers the congregation in the splendid paragraph which closes our chapter. He shows them very distinctly that they had no need to apply to familiar spirits, enchanters, wizards, or witches, which were all an abomination to the Lord. "The Lord thy God," he says, "will raise up unto thee a Prophet from the midst of thee, of thy brethren, like unto me; *unto him ye shall hearken;* according to all that thou desiredst of the Lord thy God in Horeb in the day of the assembly, saying, 'Let me not hear again the voice of the Lord my God, neither let me see this great fire any more, that I die not.' And the Lord said unto me, 'They have well spoken that which they have spoken. I will raise them up a Prophet from among their brethren, like unto thee, and will put My words into his mouth; and he shall speak unto them all that I shall command him. And it shall come to pass that whosoever will not hearken unto My words which he shall speak in My name, I will require it of him. But the prophet which shall presume to speak a word in My name which I have not commanded him to speak, or that shall speak in the name of other gods, even that prophet shall die. And if thou say in thine heart, How shall we know the word which the Lord hath not spoken? When a prophet speaketh in the name of the Lord, if the thing follow not, nor come to pass, that is the thing which the Lord hath not spoken, but the prophet hath spoken it presumptuously: thou shalt not be afraid of him" (ver. 15-22).

We can be at no loss to know who this Prophet is, namely, our adorable Lord and Saviour Jesus Christ. In the third chapter of Acts, Peter so applies the words of Moses. "He shall send Jesus Christ, which before was preached unto you; whom the heaven must receive until the times of restitution of all things, which God hath spoken by the mouth of all His holy prophets since the world began. For Moses truly said unto the fathers, 'A Prophet shall the Lord your God raise up unto you of your brethren, like unto me; him shall ye hear in all things whatsoever he shall say unto you. And it shall come to pass that every soul which will not hear that Prophet shall be destroyed from among the people' " (ver. 20-23).

How precious the privilege of hearing the voice of such a Prophet! It is the voice of God speaking through the lips of the Man Christ Jesus—speaking, not in thunder, not with flaming fire, nor the lightning's flash, but in that still small voice of love and mercy which falls in soothing power on the broken heart and contrite spirit, which distills like the gentle dew of heaven upon the thirsty ground. This voice we have in the holy Scriptures—that precious revelation which comes so constantly and so powerfully before us in our studies on this blessed book of Deuteronomy. We must never forget this. The voice of Scripture is the voice of Christ, and the voice of Christ is the voice of God.

We want no more. If any one presumes to

come with a fresh revelation, with some new truth not contained in the divine volume, we must judge him and his communication by the standard of Scripture and reject them utterly. "Thou shalt not be afraid of him." False prophets come with great pretensions, high-sounding words, and sanctimonious bearing. Moreover, they seek to surround themselves with a sort of dignity, weight, and impressiveness which are apt to impose on the ignorant. But they cannot stand the searching power of the Word of God. Some simple clause of holy Scripture will strip them of all their imposing surroundings, and cut up by the roots their wonderful revelations. Those who know the voice of the true Prophet will not listen to any other: those who have heard the voice of the good Shepherd will not listen to the voice of a stranger.

Reader, see that you listen *only* to the voice of Jesus.

---

## *CHAPTER 19*

"WHEN the Lord thy God hath cut off the nations whose land the Lord thy God giveth thee, and thou succeedest them, and dwellest in their cities, and in their houses; thou shalt separate three cities for thee *in the midst of thy land,* which the Lord thy God giveth thee to possess it. *Thou shalt prepare thee a way,* and divide the coasts of thy land, which the Lord thy God giveth thee to inherit, into three parts, *that every slayer may flee thither*" (ver. 1-3).

What a very striking combination of "goodness and severity" we observe in these few lines! We have the "cutting off" of the nations of Canaan because of their consummated wickedness, which had become positively unbearable; and on the other hand, we have a most touching display of divine goodness in the provision made for the poor manslayer in the day of his deep distress, when flying for his life from the avenger of blood. The government and the goodness of God are, we need hardly say, both divinely perfect. There are cases in which goodness would be nothing but a toleration of sheer wickedness and open rebellion, which is utterly impossible under the government of God. If men imagine that because God is good they may go on and sin with a high hand, they will sooner or later find out their woeful mistake.

"Behold," says the inspired apostle, "the goodness and severity of God!"* God will most assuredly cut off evil-doers who despise His goodness and long-suffering mercy. He is slow to anger, blessed be His holy name! and of great kindness. For hundreds of years He bore with the seven nations of Canaan, until their wickedness rose up to the very heavens, and the land itself could bear them no longer. He bore with the enormous wickedness of the guilty cities of the plain; and if He had found even ten righteous people in Sodom, He would have spared it for their sakes. But the day of terrible vengeance came, and they were "cut off."

And so will it be ere long with guilty christendom. "Thou also shalt be cut off." The reckoning-time will come, and oh, what a reckoning-time it will be! The heart trembles at the thought of it, while the eye scans and the pen traces the soul-subduing words.

But mark how divine "goodness" shines out in the opening lines of our chapter. See the gracious painstaking of our God to make the city of refuge as available as possible for the slayer. The three cities were to be "*in the midst of thy land.*" It would not do to have them in remote corners, or in places difficult of access. And not only so, but "*thou shalt prepare thee a way*;" and again, "Thou shalt divide the coasts of thy land. . . *into three parts.*" Everything was to be done to facilitate the slayer's escape. The gracious Lord thought of the feelings of the distressed one "flying for refuge to lay hold on the hope set before him." The city of refuge was to be "brought near," just as the righteousness of God" is brought near to the poor broken-hearted helpless sinner—so near, that it is "to him that *worketh not*, but believeth on Him that justifieth the ungodly."

*The word rendered "severity" is ἀποτομια, which literally means "cutting off."

There is peculiar sweetness in the expression, "*Thou shalt prepare thee a way.*" How like our own ever-gracious God—"the God and Father of our Lord Jesus Christ"! and yet it was the same God that cut off the nations of Canaan in righteous judgment who thus made such gracious provision for the man-slayer. "Behold, the goodness and severity of God."

"And this is the case of the slayer, which shall flee thither, *that he may live*: Whoso killeth his neighbor ignorantly, whom he hated not in time past; as when a man goeth into the wood with his neighbor to hew wood, and his hand fetcheth a stroke with the axe to cut down the tree, and the head slippeth from the helve, and lighteth upon his neighbor, that he die; he shall flee unto one of those cities and live; lest the avenger of the blood pursue the slayer, while his heart is hot, and overtake him, *because the way is long*"—most touching and exquisite grace!—"and slay him; whereas he was not worthy of death, inasmuch as he hated him not in time past. Wherefore I command thee, saying, 'Thou shalt separate three cities for thee' " (ver. 4-7).

Here we have a most minute description of the man for whom the city of refuge was provided. If he did not answer to this, the city was not for him; but if he did, he might feel the most perfect assurance that a gracious God had thought of him, and found a refuge for him, where he might be as safe as the hand of God could make him. Once the slayer found himself within the precincts of the city of refuge, he might breathe freely, and enjoy calm and sweet repose. No avenging sword could reach him there, not a hair of his head could be touched there.

He was safe—yes, perfectly safe; and not only perfectly safe, but perfectly *certain.* He was not hoping to be saved, he was sure of it. He was in the city, and that was enough. Before he got in, he might have many a struggle deep down in his poor terrified heart, many doubts and fears and painful exercises. He was flying for his life, and this was a serious and an all-absorbing matter for him—a matter that would make all beside seem light and trifling. We could not imagine the flying slayer stopping to gather flowers by the roadside. Flowers! he would say, What have I to do with flowers just now? My life is at stake. I am flying for my life. What if the avenger should come and find me gathering flowers? No; the city is my one grand and all-engrossing object; nothing else has the smallest interest or charm for me. I want to be saved; that is my exclusive business now.

But the moment he found himself within the blessed gates, he was safe, *and he knew it.* How did he know it? By his feelings? by his evidences? by experience? Nay; but simply by the Word of God. No doubt he had the feeling, the evidence, and the experience, and most precious they would be to him after his tremendous struggle and conflict to get in; but these things were by no means the ground of his certainty or the basis of his peace. He knew he was safe because God told him so. The *grace* of God had made him *safe*, and the *Word* of God made him *sure*.

We cannot conceive a man-slayer within the walls of the city of refuge expressing himself as many of the Lord's dear people do in reference to the question of safety and certainty. He would not deem it presumption to be sure he was safe. If any one had asked him, Are you sure you are safe? Sure! he would say, How can I be otherwise than sure? Was I not a slayer? have I not fled to this city of refuge? has not Jehovah, our covenant-God, pledged His Word for it? has He not said that "fleeing thither he may live"? Yes, thank God, I am perfectly sure. I had a terrible run for it—a fearful struggle. At times, I almost felt as if the avenger had me in his dreaded grasp. I gave myself up for lost; but then, God, in His infinite mercy, made the way so plain, and made the city so easy of access to me, that, spite of all my doubts and fears, here I am, safe and certain. The struggle is all over, the conflict past and gone. I can breathe freely now, and walk up and down in the perfect security of this blessed place, praising our gracious covenant-God for His great goodness in having provided such a sweet retreat for a poor slayer like me.

Can the reader speak thus as to his safety

in Christ? Is he saved, and does he know it? If not, may the Spirit of God apply to his heart the simple illustration of the man-slayer within the walls of the city of refuge. May he know that "strong consolation" which is the sure, because divinely appointed, portion of all those who have "fled for refuge to lay hold on the hope set before them" (Heb. 6:18).

We must now proceed with our chapter; and in so doing, we shall find that there was more to be thought of in the cities of refuge than the question of the slayer's safety. That was provided for perfectly, as we have seen; but the glory of God, the purity of His land, and the integrity of His government had to be duly maintained. If these things were touched, there could be no safety for any one. This great principle shines on every page of the history of God's ways with man. Man's true blessing and God's glory are indissolubly bound together, and both the one and the other rest on the same imperishable foundation, namely, Christ and His precious work.

"And if the Lord thy God enlarge thy coasts, as He hath sworn unto thy fathers, and give thee all the land which He promised to give unto thy fathers; if thou shalt keep all these commandments to do them, which I command thee this day, to love the Lord thy God, and to walk ever in His ways; then shalt thou add three cities more for thee, beside these three; *that innocent blood be not shed in thy land*, which the Lord thy God giveth thee for an inheritance, and so blood be upon thee. But if any man hate his neighbor, and lie in wait for him, and rise up against him, and smite him mortally that he die, and fleeth into one of these cities; then the elders of his city shall send and fetch him thence, and deliver him into the hand of the avenger of blood, that he may die. Thine eye shall not pity him, *but thou shalt put away the guilt of innocent blood from Israel*, that it may go well with thee" (ver. 8-13).

Thus, whether it was *grace* for the slayer, or *judgment* for the murderer, the glory of God and the claims of His government had to be duly maintained. The unwitting man-slayer was met by the provision of mercy; the guilty murderer fell beneath the stern sentence of inflexible justice. We must never forget the solemn reality of divine government. It meets us every where; and if it were more fully recognized, it would effectually deliver us from one-sided views of the divine character. Take such words as these—"Thine eye shall not pity him." Who uttered them? Jehovah. Who penned them? God the Holy Ghost. What do they mean? Solemn judgment upon wickedness. Let men beware how they trifle with these weighty matters. Let the Lord's people beware how they give place to foolish reasonings in reference to things wholly beyond their range. Let them remember that a false sentimentality may constantly be found in league with an audacious infidelity in calling in question the solemn enactments of divine government. This is a very serious consideration. Evil doers must look out for the sure judgment of a sin-hating God. If a willful murderer presumed to avail himself of God's provision for the ignorant man-slayer, the hand of justice laid hold of him and put him to death, without mercy. Such was the government of God in Israel of old, and such will it be in a day that is rapidly approaching. Just now, God is dealing in long-suffering mercy with the world; this is the day of salvation—the acceptable time. The day of vengeance is at hand. Oh that man, instead of reasoning about the justice of God's dealings with evildoers, would flee for refuge to that precious Saviour who died on the cross to save us from the flames of an everlasting hell!*

Before quoting the closing paragraph of our chapter, we would just call attention to verse 14, in which we have a very beautiful proof of God's tender care for His people, and His most gracious interest in every thing which directly or indirectly concerned them. "Thou shalt not remove thy neighbor's landmark, which they of old time have set in thine inheritance, which thou shalt inherit in the land that the Lord thy God giveth thee to possess it."

*For other points presented in the cities of refuge we must refer the reader to *Notes on the Book of Numbers*, chapter 35.

This passage, taken in its plain import and primary application, is full of sweetness, as presenting the loving heart of our God, and showing us how marvelously He entered into all the circumstances of His beloved people. The landmarks were not to be meddled with. Each one's portion was to be left intact, according to the boundary-lines set up by those of old time. Jehovah had given the land to Israel, and not only so, but He had assigned to each tribe and to each family their proper portion, marked off with perfect precision, and indicated by landmarks so plain that there could be no confusion, no clashing of interests, no interference one with another, no ground for lawsuit or controversy about property. There stood the ancient landmarks, marking off each one's portion in such a manner as to remove all possible ground of dispute. Each one held as a tenant under the God of Israel, who knew all about his little holding, as we say, and every tenant had the comfort of knowing that the eye of the gracious and almighty Landlord was upon his bit of land, and His hand over it to protect it from every intruder. Thus he could abide in peace under his vine and under his fig-tree, enjoying the portion assigned him by the God of Abraham, Isaac, and Jacob.

Thus much as to the obvious sense of this beautiful clause of our chapter; but surely it has a deep spiritual meaning also. Are there not spiritual landmarks for the Church of God, and for each individual member thereof, marking off, with divine accuracy, the boundaries of our heavenly inheritance—those landmarks which they of old time, even the apostles of our Lord and Saviour Jesus Christ, have set up. Assuredly there are, and God has His eye upon them, and He will not permit them to be removed with impunity. Woe be to the man that attempts to touch them; he will have to give account to God for so doing. It is a serious thing for any one to interfere, in any way, with the place, portion, and prospect of the Church of God; and it is to be feared that many are doing it without being aware of it.

We do not attempt to go into the question of what these landmarks are; we have sought to do this earlier in our *Notes on Deuteronomy*, as well as in the other four books of the Pentateuch; but we feel it to be our duty to warn, in the most solemn manner, all whom it may concern against doing that which, in the Church of God, answers to the removal of the landmarks in Israel. If any one had come forward in the land of Israel to suggest some new arrangements in the inheritance of the tribes, to adjust the property of each upon some new principle, to set up some new boundary-lines, what would have been the reply of the faithful Israelite? A very simple one, we may be sure. He would have replied in the language of Deuteronomy 19:14. He would have said, We want no novelties here; we are perfectly content with those sacred and time-honored landmarks which they of old time have set in our inheritance. We are determined, by the grace of God, to keep to them, and to resist, with firm purpose, any modern innovation.

Such, we believe, would have been the prompt reply of every true member of the congregation of Israel; and surely the Christian ought not to be less prompt or less decided in his answer to all those who, under the plea of progress and development, would remove the landmarks of the Church of God and, instead of the precious teaching of Christ and His apostles, offer us the so-called light of science and the resources of philosophy. Thank God, we want them not. We have Christ and His Word; what can be added to these? What do we want of human progress or development, when we have "that which was *from the beginning*"? What can science or philosophy do for those who possess "*all truth*"? No doubt, we want—yea, long to make progress in the knowledge of Christ; long for a fuller, clearer development of the life of Christ in our daily history; but science and philosophy cannot help us in these; nay, they could only prove a most serious hindrance.

Let us seek to keep close to Christ, close to His Word. This is our only security in this dark and evil day. Apart from Him, we are nothing, have nothing, can do nothing; in Him, we have all. He is the portion of our cup and the lot of our inheritance. May we know what it is not only to be safe *in* Him, but separated *to* Him, and satisfied *with* Him, till that bright day when we shall see Him as He is, and be like Him and with Him forever.

We shall now do little more than quote the few remaining verses of our chapter. They need no exposition. They set forth wholesome truth, to which professing Christians, with all their light and knowledge, may well give attention.

"One witness shall not rise up against a man for any iniquity, or for any sin, in any sin that he sinneth; at the mouth of two witnesses, or at the mouth of three witnesses, shall the matter be established" (ver. 15).

This subject has already come before us. It cannot be too strongly insisted upon. We may judge of its importance from the fact that not only does Moses again and again press it upon Israel's attention, but our Lord Jesus Christ Himself, and the Holy Ghost in the apostle Paul, in two of his Epistles, insists upon the principle of "two or three witnesses," in every case. One witness, be he ever so trustworthy, is not sufficient to decide a case. If this plain fact were more carefully weighed and duly attended to, it would put an end to a vast amount of strife and contention. We, in our fancied wisdom, might imagine that one thoroughly reliable witness ought to be sufficient to settle any question. Let us remember that God is wiser than we are, and that it is ever our truest wisdom, as well as our greatest moral security, to hold fast by His unerring Word.

"If a false witness rise up against any man, to testify against him that which is wrong; then both the men, between whom the controversy is, shall stand before the Lord, before the priests and the judges which shall be in those days; and *the judges shall make diligent inquisition*: and, behold, if the witness be a false witness, and have testified falsely against his brother; then shall ye do unto him as he had thought to have done unto his brother: so shalt thou put the evil away from among you. And those which remain shall hear and fear, and shall henceforth commit no more any such evil among you. And thine eye shall not pity; but life shall go for life, eye for eye, tooth for tooth, hand for hand, foot for foot" (ver. 16-21).

We may here see how God hates false witness; and further, we have to bear in mind that though we are not under law, but under grace, false witness is not less hateful to God; and surely the more fully we enter into the grace in which we stand, the more intensely we shall abhor false witness, slander, and evil-speaking, in every shape and form. The good Lord preserve us from all such.

---

## *CHAPTER 20*

"WHEN thou goest out to battle against thine enemies, and seest horses and chariots, and a people more than thou, be not afraid of them; for the Lord thy God is with thee, which brought thee up out of the land of Egypt. And it shall be, when ye are come nigh unto the battle, that the priest shall approach and speak unto the people, and shall say unto them, Hear, O Israel! ye approach this day unto battle against your enemies; let not your hearts faint; fear not, and do not tremble, neither be ye terrified because of them; for the Lord your God is He that goeth with you to fight for you against your enemies, to save you" (ver. 1-4).

How wonderful to think of the Lord as a Man of war! Think of His fighting against people! Some find it very hard to take in the idea—hard to understand how a benevolent Being could act in such a character. But the difficulty arises mainly from not distinguishing between the different dispensations. It was just as consistent with the character of the God of Abraham, Isaac, and Jacob to fight against His enemies, as it is with the character of the God and Father of our Lord Jesus Christ to forgive them. And inasmuch as it is the revealed character of God that furnishes the model on which His people are to be formed—the standard by which they are to act, it was quite as consistent for Israel to cut their enemies in pieces as it is for us to love them, pray for them, and do them good.

If this very simple principle were borne in mind, it would remove a quantity of misunderstanding, and save a vast amount of unintelligent discussion. No doubt it is thoroughly wrong for the Church of God to go to war. No one can read the New Testament with a mind free from bias and not see this. We are positively commanded to love our enemies, to do good to them that hate us, and to pray for them that despitefully use us. "Put up again thy sword into his place, for all they that take the sword shall perish with the sword." And again, in another gospel, "Then said Jesus unto Peter, 'Put up thy sword into the sheath: the cup which My Father hath given Me, shall I not drink it?' " Again, our Lord says to Pilate, "My kingdom is not of this world: if My kingdom were of this world, *then would My servants fight*"—it would be perfectly consistent for them so to do—"but *now* is My kingdom not from hence"—and therefore it would be wholly out of character, utterly inconsistent, thoroughly wrong, for them to fight.

All this is so plain that we need only say, "How readest thou?" Our blessed Lord did not fight; He meekly and patiently submitted to all manner of abuse and ill-treatment, and in so doing, He left us an example, that we should follow His steps. If we only honestly ask ourselves the question, What would Jesus do? it would close all discussion on this point, as well as upon a thousand other points besides. There is really no use in reasoning—no need of it. If the words and ways of our blessed Lord, and the distinct teaching of His Spirit by His holy apostles, be not sufficient for our guidance, all discussion is utterly vain.

If we be asked, What does the Holy Ghost teach on this great practical point? hear His precious, clear, and pointed words: "Dearly beloved, avenge not yourselves; but rather give place unto wrath; for it is written, 'Vengeance is Mine; *I will repay*, saith the Lord.' Therefore, if thine enemy hunger, feed him; if he thirst, give him drink; for in so doing, thou shalt heap coals of fire on his head. Be not overcome of evil, but overcome evil with good" (Rom. 12).

These are the lovely ethics of the Church of God, the principles of that heavenly kingdom to which all true Christians belong. Would they have suited Israel of old? Certainly not. Only conceive Joshua acting toward the Canaanites on the principles of Romans 12! It would have been as flagrant an inconsistency as for us to act on the principle of Deuteronomy 20. How is this? Simply because in Joshua's day God was executing judgment in righteousness, whereas now He is dealing in unqualified grace. This makes all the difference. The principle of divine action is the grand moral regulator for God's people in all ages. If this be seen, all difficulty is removed, all discussion definitively closed.

But then, if any feel disposed to ask, What about the world? how could it get on upon the principle of grace? Could it act on the doctrine of Romans 12:20? Not for a moment. The idea is simply absurd. To attempt to amalgamate the principles of grace with the law of nations, or to infuse the spirit of the New Testament into the frame-work of political economy, would instantly plunge civilized society into hopeless confusion. And here is just where many most excellent and well-meaning people are astray. They want to press the nations of the world into the adoption of a principle which would be destructive of their national existence. The time is not come yet for nations to beat their swords into plowshares, and their spears into pruning-hooks, and learn war no more. That blessed time will come, thank God, when this groaning earth shall be filled with the knowledge of the Lord as the waters cover the sea; but to seek to get nations *now* to act upon peace principles is simply to ask them to cease to be—in a word, it is thoroughly hopeless, unintelligent labor. It cannot be. We are not called upon to regulate the world, but to pass through it as pilgrims and strangers. Jesus did not come to set the world right. He came to seek and to save that which was lost; and as to the world, He testified of it that its deeds were evil. He will, ere long, come to set things right; He will take to Himself His great power and reign. The kingdoms of this world shall most assuredly become the kingdoms of our Lord and of His Christ. He will gather out of His kingdom all things that offend, and them that do iniquity. All this is most blessedly true, but we must wait His time. It can be of no possible use for us, by our ignorant efforts, to seek to bring about a condition of things which all Scripture goes to prove can *only* be introduced by the personal presence and rule of our beloved and adorable Lord and Saviour Jesus Christ.

Israel were called to fight the Lord's battles. The moment they put their foot upon the land of Canaan it was war to the knife with the doomed inhabitants. "Of the cities of these people which the Lord thy God doth give thee for an inheritance, thou shalt save alive nothing that breatheth." This was distinct and emphatic. The seed of Abraham were not only to possess the land of Canaan, but they were to be God's instruments in executing His just judgment upon the guilty inhabitants, whose sins had risen up to heaven, and become absolutely intolerable.

Does any one feel called upon to apologize for the divine actings toward the seven nations of Canaan? If so, let him be well assured of this, that his labor is perfectly gratuitous, entirely uncalled for. What folly for any poor worm of the earth to think of entering upon such work! and what folly, too, for any one to require an apology or an explanation! It was a high honor put upon Israel to exterminate those guilty nations—an honor of which they proved themselves utterly unworthy, inasmuch as they failed to do as they were commanded. They left alive many of those who ought to have been utterly destroyed; they spared them to be the wretched instruments of their own ultimate ruin, by leading them into the self-same sins which had called for divine judgment.

But let us look for a moment at the qualifications which were necessary for those who would fight the Lord's battles. We shall find the opening paragraph of our chapter full of most precious instruction for ourselves in the spiritual warfare which we are called to wage.

The reader will observe that the people, on approaching to the battle, were to be addressed, first, by the priest, and secondly, by the officers. This order is very beautiful. The priests came forward to unfold to the people their high *privileges*; the officers came to remind them of their holy *responsibilities*. Such is the divine order here. Privilege comes first, and then responsibility. "The priest shall approach and speak unto the people, and shall say unto them, Hear, O Israel! ye approach this day unto battle against your enemies; let not your hearts faint, fear not, and do not tremble, neither be ye terrified because of them; for the Lord your God is He that goeth with you, to fight for you against your enemies, to save you.

What blessed words are these! how full of comfort and encouragement! how eminently calculated to banish all fear and depression, and to infuse courage and confidence into the most sinking, fainting heart! The priest was the very expression of the grace of God—his ministry a stream of most precious consolation flowing from the loving heart of the God of Israel to each individual warrior. His loving words were designed and fitted to gird up the loins of the mind, and nerve the feeblest arm for fight. He assures them of the divine presence with them. There is no question, no condition, no "if," no "but." It is an unqualified statement. Jehovah Elohim was with them. This surely was enough. It mattered not, in the smallest degree, how many, how powerful, or how formidable were their enemies, they would all prove to be as chaff before the whirlwind in the presence of the Lord of Hosts, the God of the armies of Israel.

But then the *officer* had to be heard as well as the *priest.* "And the officers shall speak unto the people, saying, What man is there that hath built a new house and hath not dedicated it? let him go and return to his house, lest he die in the battle, and another man dedicate it. And what man is he that hath planted a vineyard and hath not yet eaten of it? let him also go and return unto his house, lest he die in the battle, and another man eat of it. And what man is there that hath betrothed a wife and hath not taken her? let him go and return unto his house, lest he die in the battle, and another man take her. And the officers shall speak further unto the people, and they shall say, What man is there that is fearful and fainthearted? let him go and return unto his house, lest his brethren's heart faint as well as his heart. And it shall be that when the officers have made an end of speaking unto the people, that they shall make captains of the armies to lead the people" (ver. 5-9).

Thus we learn that there were two things absolutely essential to all who would fight the Lord's battles, namely, a heart thoroughly disentangled from the things of nature and of earth, and a bold unclouded confidence in God. "No man that warreth entangleth himself with the affairs of this life, that he may please him who hath chosen him to be a soldier." There is a very material difference between being *engaged* in the affairs of this life and being *entangled* by them. A man might have had a house, a vineyard, and a wife and yet have been fit for the battle. These things were not, in themselves, a hindrance; but it was having them under such conditions as rendered them an entanglement that unfitted a man for the conflict.

It is well to bear this in mind. We, as Christians, are called to carry on a constant spiritual warfare. We have to fight for every inch of heavenly ground. What the Canaanites were to Israel, the wicked spirits in the heavenlies are to us. We are not called to fight for eternal life; we have gotten that as God's free gift before we begin. We are not called to fight for salvation; we are saved before we enter upon the conflict. It is most needful to know what it is that we have to fight for, and whom we are to fight with. The object for which we fight is, to make good, maintain, and carry out practically our heavenly position and character in the midst of the scenes and circumstances of ordinary human life from day to day. And then as to our spiritual foes, they are wicked spirits, who, during this present time, are permitted to occupy the heavenlies. "We wrestle not against flesh and blood, [as Israel had to do in Canaan,] but against principalities, against powers, against the world-rulers [κοσμοκρατορας] of this darkness, against wicked spirits in the heavenlies."

Now, the question is, what do we want in carrying on such a conflict as this? Must we abandon our lawful earthly callings? must we detach ourselves from those relationships founded on nature and sanctioned of God? Is it needful to become an ascetic, a mystic, or a monk in order to carry on the spiritual warfare to which we are called? By no means; indeed, for a Christian to do any one of these things would, in itself, be a proof that he had completely mistaken his calling, or that he had, at the very outset, fallen in the battle. We are imperatively called upon to work with our hands the thing which is good, that we may have to give to him that needeth. And not only so, but we have the most ample guidance, in the pages of the New Testament, as to how we are to carry ourselves in the varied natural relationships which God Himself has established, and to which He has affixed the seal of His approval. Hence it is perfectly plain that earthly callings and natural relationships are, in themselves, no hindrance to our waging a successful spiritual warfare.

What, then, is needed by the Christian warrior? A heart thoroughly *disentangled* from things earthly and natural, and an unclouded confidence in God. But how are these things to be maintained? Hear the divine reply: "Wherefore take unto you the whole armor of God, that ye may be able to withstand in *the evil day*"—that is, the whole time from the cross to the coming of Christ —"and having done all, to stand. Stand, therefore; having your loins girt about with *truth*, and having on the breastplate of *righteousness*, and your feet shod with the preparation of the gospel of *peace*; above all, taking the shield of *faith*, wherewith ye shall be able to quench all the fiery darts of the wicked. And take the helmet of salvation, and the sword of the Spirit, which is the Word of God. Praying always with all prayer and supplication in the Spirit, and watching thereunto with all perseverance and supplication for all saints" (Eph. 6).

Mark the qualification of a Christian warrior as here set forth by the Holy Ghost. It is not the question of a house, a vineyard, or a wife, but of having the inward man governed by "truth," the outward conduct characterized by real practical "righteousness," the moral habits and ways marked by the sweet "peace" of the gospel, the whole man covered by the impenetrable shield of "faith," the seat of the understanding guarded by the full assurance of "salvation," and the heart continually sustained and strengthened by persevering prayer and supplication, and led forth in earnest intercession for all saints, and specially for the Lord's beloved workmen and their blessed work. This is the way in which the spiritual Israel of God are to be furnished for the warfare which they are called to wage with wicked spirits in the heavenlies. May the Lord, in His infinite goodness, make all these things very real in our souls' experience, and in our practical career from day to day.

The close of our chapter contains the principles which were to govern Israel in their warfare. They were most carefully to discriminate between the cities which were very far off from them and those that pertained to the seven judged nations. To the former, they were, in the first place, to make overtures of peace; with the latter, on the contrary, they were to make no terms whatever. "When thou comest nigh unto a city *to fight against it*, then *proclaim peace* unto it"—a marvelous method of fighting!—"And it shall be, if it make thee answer of peace, and open unto thee, then it shall be that all the people that is found therein shall be tributaries unto thee, and they shall serve thee. And if it will make no peace with thee, but will make war against thee, then thou shalt besiege it; and when the Lord thy God hath delivered it into thine hands, thou shalt smite every male thereof"—as expressing the positive energy of evil—"with the edge of the sword. But the women, and the little ones, and the cattle, and all that is in the city, even all the spoil thereof"—all that was capable of being turned to account in the service of God and of His people—"thou shalt take unto thyself; and thou shalt eat the spoil of thine enemies, which the Lord thy God hath given thee. Thus shalt thou do unto all the cities which are very far off from thee, which are not of the cities of these nations."

Indiscriminate slaughter and wholesale destruction formed no part of Israel's business. If any cities were disposed to accept the proffered terms of peace, they were to have the privilege of becoming tributaries to the people of God; and in reference to those cities which would make no peace, all within their walls which could be made use of was to be reserved.

There are things in nature and things of earth which are capable of being used for God—they are sanctified by the Word of God and prayer. We are told to make to ourselves friends of the mammon of unrighteousness, that when we fail, they may receive us into everlasting habitations; which simply means that if this world's riches come into the Christian's hands, he should diligently and faithfully use them in the service of Christ; he should freely distribute them to the poor, and to all the Lord's needy workmen; in short, he should make them available, in every right and prudent way, for the furtherance of the Lord's work in every department. In this way, the very riches which else might crumble into dust in their hands, or prove to be as rust on their souls, shall produce precious fruit that shall serve to minister an abundant entrance into the everlasting kingdom of our Lord and Saviour Jesus Christ.

Many seem to find considerable difficulty in Luke 16:9, but its teaching is as clear and forcible as it is practically important. We find very similar instruction in 1 Timothy 6: "Charge them that are rich in this world, that they be not high-minded, nor trust in uncertain riches, but in the living God, who giveth us richly all things to enjoy; that they do good, that they be rich in good works, *ready to distribute*, willing to communicate, laying up in store for themselves a good foundation against the time to come, that they may lay hold on eternal life."* There is

*It may interest the reader to know that the four leading authorities agree in reading ὀντως instead of *αιωνιου* in 1 Timothy 6:19. Thus the passage would be, "That they may lay hold on life in earnest," or in reality. The only real life is, to not a fraction which we spend directly and simply for Christ which will not be before us by and by. The thought of this, though it should not by any means be a motive-spring, may well encourage us to devote all we have and all we are to the service of our blessed Lord and Saviour Jesus Christ.

Such is the plain teaching of Luke 16 and 1 Timothy 6; let us see that we understand it. The expression, "That they may receive you into everlasting habitations" simply means that what is spent for Christ will be rewarded in the day that is coming. Even a cup of cold water given in His precious name shall have its sure reward in His everlasting kingdom. Oh, to spend and be spent for Him!

But we must close this section by quoting the few last lines of our chapter, in which we have a very beautiful illustration of the way in which our God looks after the smallest matters, and His gracious care that nothing should be lost or injured. "When thou shalt besiege a city a long time, in making war against it to take it, thou shalt not destroy the trees thereof, by forcing an ax against them; for thou mayest eat of them, and thou shalt not cut them down (for the tree of the field is man's life) to employ them in the siege; only the trees which thou knowest that they be not trees for meat, thou shalt destroy and cut them down; and thou shalt build bulwarks against the city that maketh war with thee, until it be subdued" (ver. 19-20).

"Let nothing be lost," is the Master's own word to us—a word which should ever be kept in remembrance. "Every creature of God is good, and nothing to be refused." We should carefully guard against all reckless waste of aught that can be made available for human use. Those who occupy the place of domestic servants should give their special attention to this matter. It is painful, at times, to witness the sinful waste of human food. Many a thing is flung out as offal which might supply a welcome meal for a needy family. If a Christian servant should read these lines, we would earnestly entreat him or her to weigh this subject in the divine presence, and never to practice or sanction the waste of the smallest atom that is capable of being turned to account for human use. We may depend upon it that to waste any creature of God is displeasing in His sight. Let us remember that His eye is upon us; and may it be our earnest desire to be agreeable to Him in all our ways.

---

## *CHAPTER 21*

"IF one be found slain in the land which the Lord thy God giveth thee to possess it, lying in the field, and it be not known who hath slain him; then thy *elders* and thy *judges*"—the guardians of the claims of truth and righteousness—"shall come forth, and they shall measure unto the cities that are round about him that is slain; and it shall be, that the city which is next unto the slain man, even the elders of that city shall take a heifer, which hath not been wrought with, and hath not drawn in the yoke; and the elders of that city shall bring down the heifer unto *a rough valley* which is neither eared nor sown, and shall strike off the heifer's neck there in the valley. And *the priests the sons of Levi*"—exponents of grace and mercy—"shall come near; for them the Lord thy God hath chosen *to minister* unto Him, and *to bless* in the name of the Lord, and by their word shall every controversy and every stroke be tried"—blessed, comforting fact!—"and all the elders of that city, that are next unto the slain man shall wash their hands over the heifer that is beheaded in the valley; and they shall answer and say, Our hands have not shed this blood, neither have our eyes seen it. Be merciful, O Lord, unto Thy people Israel, whom Thou hast redeemed, and lay not innocent blood to Thy people of Israel's charge. And the blood shall be forgiven them. So shalt thou put away the guilt of innocent blood from among you, when

live for Christ—to live in the light of eternity—to use all we possess for the promotion of God's glory and with an eye to the everlasting mansions. This, and only this, is life in earnest.

thou shalt do that which is right in the sight of the Lord" (ver. 1-9).

A very suggestive and interesting passage of holy Scripture now lies open before us, and claims our attention. A sin is committed—a man is found slain in the land, but no one knows aught about it; no one can tell whether it is murder or manslaughter, or who committed the deed. It lies entirely beyond the range of human knowledge; and yet there it is—an undeniable fact. Sin has been committed, and it lies as a stain on the Lord's land, and man is wholly incompetent to deal with it.

What, then, is to be done? The glory of God and the purity of His land must be maintained. He knows all about it, and He alone can deal with it; and truly His mode of dealing with it is full of most precious teaching.

First of all, the elders and judges appear on the scene. The claims of truth and righteousness must be duly attended to; justice and judgment must be perfectly maintained. This is a great cardinal truth, running all through the Word of God. *Sin* must be judged ere *sins* can be forgiven or the sinner justified. Ere mercy's heavenly voice can be heard, justice must be perfectly satisfied, the throne of God vindicated, and His name glorified. Grace must reign through righteousness. Blessed be God that it is so! What a glorious truth for all who have taken their true place as sinners! God has been glorified as to the question of sin, and therefore He can, in perfect righteousness, pardon and justify the sinner.

But we must confine ourselves simply to the interpretation of the passage before us, and in so doing, we shall find in it a very wonderful onlook into Israel's future. True, the great foundation-truth of atonement is presented, but it is with special reference to Israel. The death of Christ is here seen in its two grand aspects, namely, as the expression of man's guilt, and the display of God's grace. The former, we have in the man found slain in the field; the latter, in the heifer slain in the rough valley. The elders and the judges find out the city nearest to the slain man, and nothing can avail for that city save the blood of a spotless victim—the blood of the One who was slain at the guilty city of Jerusalem.

The reader will note with much interest that the moment the claims of justice were met by the death of the victim, a new element is introduced into the scene. "The priests the sons of Levi shall come near." This is grace acting on the blessed ground of righteousness. The priests are the channels of grace, as the judges are the guardians of righteousness. How perfect, how beautiful, is Scripture, in every page, every paragraph, every sentence! It was not until the blood was shed that the ministers of grace could present themselves. The heifer beheaded in the valley changed the aspect of things completely. "The priests the sons of Levi shall come near; for them the Lord thy God hath chosen to minister unto Him, and to bless in the name of the Lord; and *by their word*"—blessed fact for Israel! blessed fact for every true believer!—"shall *every controversy* and *every stroke be tried.*" All is to be settled on the glorious and eternal principle of grace reigning through righteousness.

Thus it is that God will deal with Israel by and by. We must not attempt to interfere with the primary application of all those striking institutions which come under our notice in this profound and marvelous book of Deuteronomy. No doubt there are lessons for us—precious lessons, but we may rest perfectly assured that the true way in which to understand and appreciate those lessons is to see their true and proper bearing. For instance, how precious, how full of consolation, the fact that it is by the word of the minister of grace that every controversy and every stroke is to be tried for repentant Israel by and by, and for every repentant soul now! Do we lose aught of the deep blessedness of this by seeing and owning the proper application of the Scripture? Assuredly not. So far from this, the true secret of profiting by any special passage of the Word of God is to understand its true scope and bearing.

"And all the elders of that city that are next unto the slain man shall wash their hands over the heifer that is beheaded in the valley."* "I will wash my hands in innocency, and so will I compass Thine altar." The true place to wash the hands is where the blood of atonement has forever expiated our guilt. "And they shall answer and say, Our hands have not shed this blood, neither have our eyes seen it. Be merciful, O Lord, unto Thy people Israel, whom Thou hast redeemed, and lay not innocent blood unto Thy people of Israel's charge. And the blood shall be forgiven them."

"Father, forgive them, for they know not what they do." "Unto you first, God having raised up His Son Jesus, sent Him to bless you, by turning away every one of you from his iniquities." Thus all Israel shall be saved and blessed by and by, according to the eternal counsels of God, and in pursuance of His promise and oath to Abraham, ratified and eternally established by the precious blood of Christ, to whom be all homage and praise, world without end!

Verses 10-17 bear in a very special way upon Israel's relationship to Jehovah. We shall not dwell upon it here. The reader will find numerous references to this subject throughout the pages of the prophets, in which the Holy Ghost makes the most touching appeals to the conscience of the nation—appeals grounded on the marvelous fact of the relationship into which He had brought them to Himself, but in which they had so signally and grievously failed. Israel has proved an unfaithful wife, and, in consequence thereof, has been set aside; but the time will come when this long-rejected but never-forgotten people shall not only be reinstated, but brought into a condition of blessedness, privilege, and glory beyond any thing ever known in the past.

This must never, for a moment, be lost sight of or interfered with. It runs like a brilliant golden line through the prophetic Scriptures, from Isaiah to Malachi, and the lovely theme is resumed and carried on in the New Testament. Take the following glowing passage, which is only one of a hundred: "For Zion's sake will I not hold my peace, and for Jerusalem's sake I will not rest, until the righteousness thereof go forth as brightness, and the salvation thereof as a lamp that burneth. And the Gentiles shall see thy righteousness, and all kings thy glory; and thou shalt be called by a new name, which the mouth of the Lord shall name. Thou shalt also be a crown of glory in the hand of the Lord, and a royal diadem in the hand of thy God. Thou shalt no more be termed Forsaken, neither shall thy land any more be termed Desolate; but thou shalt be called Hephzi-bah [My delight is in her], and thy land Beulah [married]; for the Lord delighteth in thee, and thy land shall be married. For as a young man marrieth a virgin, so shall thy sons marry thee; and as the bridegroom rejoiceth over the bride, so shall thy God rejoice over thee. I have set watchmen upon thy walls, O Jerusalem, which shall never hold their peace day nor night: ye that make mention of the Lord, keep not silence, and give Him no rest, till He establish, and till He make Jerusalem a praise in the earth. The Lord hath sworn by His right hand, and by the arm of His strength"—let men beware how they meddle with this!—"Surely I will no more give thy corn to be meat for thine enemies; and the sons of the stranger shall not drink thy wine, for the which thou hast labored; but they that have gathered it shall eat it and praise the Lord, and they that have brought it together shall drink it in the courts of My holiness. . . . Behold, the Lord hath proclaimed unto the end of the world, 'Say ye to the daughter of Zion, Behold, thy salvation cometh; behold, His reward is with Him, and His work before Him. And they shall call them, The holy people, The redeemed of the Lord; and thou shalt be

*How full of suggestive power is the figure of "the *rough valley*"! How aptly it sets forth what this world at large, and the land of Israel in particular, was to our blessed Lord and Saviour! Truly it was a rough place to Him, a place of humiliation, a dry and thirsty land, a place that had never been eared or sown. But, all homage to His Name! by His death in this rough valley, He has procured for this earth and for the land of Israel a rich harvest of blessing, which shall be reaped throughout the millennial age, to the full praise of redeeming love. And even now, He, from the throne of heaven's majesty, and we, in spirit with Him, can look back to that rough valley as the place where the blessed work was done which forms the imperishable foundation of God's glory, the Church's blessing, Israel's full restoration, the joy of countless nations, and the glorious deliverance of this groaning creation.

called, Sought out, A city not forsaken' " (Isa. 62).

To attempt to alienate this sublime and glorious passage from its proper object, and apply it to the Christian Church, either on earth or in heaven, is to do positive violence to the Word of God, and introduce a system of interpretation utterly destructive of the integrity of holy Scripture. The passage which we have just transcribed, with intense spiritual delight, applies only to the literal Zion, the literal Jerusalem, the literal land of Israel. Let the reader see that he thoroughly seizes and faithfully holds fast this fact.

As to the Church, her position on earth is that of an espoused virgin, not of a married wife. Her marriage will take place in heaven (Rev. 19:7-8). To apply to her such passages as the above is to falsify her position entirely, and deny the plainest statements of Scripture as to her calling, her portion, and her hope, which are purely heavenly.

Verses 18-21 of our chapter record the case of "a stubborn and rebellious son." Here again we have Israel viewed from another stand-point. It is the apostate generation, for which there is no forgiveness. "If a man have a stubborn and rebellious son, which will not obey the voice of his father, or the voice of his mother, and that when they have chastened him will not hearken unto them; then shall his father and his mother lay hold on him and bring him out unto the elders of his city, and unto the gate of his place; and they shall say unto the elders of his city, This our son is stubborn and rebellious; he will not obey our voice; he is a glutton and a drunkard. And all the men of his city shall stone him with stones, that he die; so shalt thou put evil away from among you; and all Israel shall hear and fear."

The reader may with much interest contrast the solemn action of law and government in the case of the rebellious son, with the lovely and familiar parable of the prodigal son in Luke 15. Our space does not admit of our dwelling upon it here, much as we should delight to do so. It is marvelous to think that it is the same God who speaks and acts in Deuteronomy 21 and in Luke 15; but oh, how different the action! how different the style! Under the law, the father is called upon to lay hold of his son and bring him forth to be stoned; under grace, the father runs to meet the returning son, falls on his neck and kisses him; clothes him in the best robe, puts a ring on his hand, and shoes on his feet, has the fatted calf killed for him, seats him at the table with himself, and makes the house ring with the joy that fills his own heart at getting back the poor wandering spendthrift.

Striking contrast! In Deuteronomy 21 we see *the hand of God,* in righteous government, executing judgment upon the rebellious; in Luke 15 we see *the heart of God* pouring itself out, in soul-subduing tenderness, upon the poor repentant one, giving him the sweet assurance that it is His own deep joy to get back His lost one. The persistent rebel meets the stone of judgment; the returning penitent meets the kiss of love.

But we must close this section by calling the reader's attention to the last verse of our chapter. It is referred to in a very remarkable way by the inspired apostle in the third chapter of Galatians. "Christ hath redeemed us from the curse of the law, being made a curse for us; for it is written, 'Cursed is every one that hangeth on a tree.' "

This reference is full of interest and value, not only because it presents to us the precious grace of our Lord and Saviour Jesus Christ, in making Himself a curse for us, in order that the blessing of Abraham might come on us poor sinners of the Gentiles, but also because it furnishes a very striking illustration of the way in which the Holy Spirit puts His seal upon the writings of Moses in general, and upon Deuteronomy 21 in particular. All Scripture hangs together so perfectly that if one part be touched, you mar the integrity of the whole. The same Spirit breathes in the writings of Moses, in the pages of the prophets, in the four evangelists, in the Acts, in the apostolic Epistles, general and particular, and in that most profound and precious section which closes the divine volume. We deem it our sacred duty—as it is most assuredly our high privilege—to press this weighty fact upon all with whom we come in contact; and we would very earnestly entreat the reader to give it his earnest attention, to hold it fast, and bear a steady testimony to it, in this day of carnal laxity, cold indifference, and positive hostility.

---

## *CHAPTERS 22–25*

THE portion of our book on which we now enter, though not calling for elaborate exposition, yet teaches us two very important practical lessons. In the first place, many of the institutions and ordinances here set forth prove and illustrate, in a most striking way, the terrible depravity of the human heart. They show us, with unmistakable distinctness, what man is capable of doing if left to himself. We must ever remember, as we read some of the paragraphs of this section of Deuteronomy, that God the Holy Ghost has indited them. We, in our fancied wisdom, may feel disposed to ask why such passages were ever penned. Can it be possible that they are actually inspired by the Holy Ghost? and of what possible value can they be to us? If they were written for our learning, then what are we to learn from them?

Our reply to all these questions is at once simple and direct; and it is this: The very passages which we might least expect to find on the page of inspiration teach us, in their own peculiar way, the moral material of which we are made, and the moral depths into which we are capable of plunging. And is not this of great moment? Is it not well to have a faithful mirror held up before our eyes, in which we may see every moral trait, feature, and lineament perfectly reflected? Unquestionably. We hear a great deal about the dignity of human nature, and very many find it exceedingly hard to admit that they are really capable of committing some of the sins prohibited in the section before us, and in other portions of the divine volume; but we may rest assured that when God commands us not to commit this or that particular sin, we are verily capable of committing it. This is beyond all question. Divine wisdom would never erect a dam if there was not a current to be resisted. There would be no necessity to tell an angel not to steal; but man has theft in his nature, and hence the command applies to him. And just so in reference to every other prohibited thing; the prohibition proves the tendency—proves it beyond all question. We must either admit this or imply the positive blasphemy that God has spoken in vain.

But then, it may be said, and is said by many, that while some very terrible samples of fallen humanity are capable of committing some of the abominable sins prohibited in Scripture, yet all are not so. This is a most thorough mistake. Hear what the Holy Ghost says in the seventeenth chapter of the prophet Jeremiah. "*The heart* is deceitful above all things, and desperately wicked." Whose heart is he speaking of? Is it the heart of some atrocious criminal, or of some untutored savage? Nay; it is the human heart—the heart of the writer and of the reader of these lines.

Hear also what our Lord Jesus Christ says on this subject. "Out of *the heart* proceed evil thoughts, murders, adulteries, fornications, thefts, false witness, blasphemies." Out of what heart? Is it the heart of some hideously depraved and abominable wretch, wholly unfit to appear in decent society? Nay; it is out of the human heart—the heart of the writer and of the reader of these lines.

Let us never forget this; it is a wholesome truth for every one of us. We all need to bear in mind that if God were to withdraw His sustaining grace for one moment, there is no depth of iniquity into which we are not capable of plunging; indeed, we may add—and we do it with deep thankfulness—it is His own gracious hand that preserves us, each moment, from becoming a complete wreck in every way—physically, mentally, morally, spiritually, and in our circumstances. May we keep this ever in the remembrance of the thoughts of our hearts, so that we may walk humbly and watchfully, and lean upon that arm which alone can sustain and preserve us.

But we have said there is another valuable lesson furnished by this section of our book which now lies open before us. It teaches us, in a manner peculiar to itself, the marvelous way in which God provided for every thing connected with His people. Nothing escaped His gracious notice; nothing was too trivial for His tender care. No mother could be more careful of the habits and manners of her little child than the almighty Creator and moral Governor of the universe was of the most minute details connected with the daily history of His people. By day and by night, waking and sleeping, at home and abroad, He looked after them. Their clothing, their food, their manners and ways toward one another, how they were to build their houses, how they were to plow and sow their ground, how they were to carry themselves in the deepest privacy of their personal life,—all was attended to and provided for in a manner that fills us with wonder, love, and praise. We may here see, in a most striking way, that there is nothing too small for our God to take notice of when His people are concerned. He takes a loving, tender, fatherly interest in their most minute concerns. We are amazed to find the Most High God, the Creator of the ends of the earth, the Sustainer of the vast universe, condescending to legislate about the matter of a bird's nest; and yet why should we be amazed when we know that it is just the same to Him to provide for a sparrow as to feed a thousand millions of people daily?

But there was one grand fact which was ever to be kept prominently before each member of the congregation of Israel, namely, the divine presence in their midst. This fact was to govern their most private habits, and give character to all their ways. "The Lord thy God walketh in the midst of thy camp, to deliver thee, and to give up thine enemies before thee; *therefore shall thy camp be holy;* that He see no unclean thing in thee, and turn away from thee" (chap. 23:14).

What a precious privilege to have Jehovah walking in their midst! what a motive for purity of conduct, and refined delicacy in their personal and domestic habits! If He was in their midst to secure victory over their enemies, He was also there to demand holiness of life. They were never for one moment to forget the august Person who walked up and down in their midst. Would the thought of this prove irksome to any? Only to such as did not love holiness, purity, and moral order. Every true Israelite would delight in the thought of having One dwelling in their midst who could not endure aught that was unholy, unseemly, or impure.

The Christian reader will be at no loss to seize the moral force and application of this holy principle. It is our privilege to have God the Spirit dwelling in us, individually and collectively. Thus we read, in 1 Corinthians 6:19, "What! know ye not that *your body* is the temple of the Holy Ghost, which is in you, which ye have of God, and ye are not your own?" This is individual. Each believer is a temple of the Holy Ghost, and this most glorious and precious truth is the ground of the exhortation given in Ephesians 4:30—"*Grieve* not the holy Spirit of God, whereby ye are sealed unto the day of redemption."

How very important to keep this ever in the remembrance of the thoughts of our hearts! what a mighty moral motive for the diligent cultivation of purity of heart and holiness of life! When tempted to indulge in any wrong current of thought or feeling, any unworthy manner of speech, any unseemly line of conduct, what a powerful corrective would be found in the realization of the blessed fact that the Holy Spirit dwells in our body as in His temple! If only we could keep this ever before us, it would preserve us from many a wandering thought, many an unguarded and foolish utterance, many an unbecoming act.

But not only does the Holy Spirit dwell in each individual believer, He also dwells in the Church collectively. "Know ye not that *ye are the temple of God,* and that the Spirit of God dwelleth *in you?*" (1 Cor. 3:16) It is upon this fact that the apostle grounds his exhortation in 1 Thessalonians 5:19—"*Quench* not the Spirit." How divinely perfect is Scripture! how blessedly it hangs together! The Holy Ghost dwells in us individually, hence we are not to *grieve* Him; He dwells in the assembly, hence we are not to *quench* Him, but give Him His right place, and allow full scope for His blessed operations. May these great practical truths find a deep place in our hearts, and exert a more powerful influence over our ways, both in private life and in the public assembly.

We shall now proceed to quote a few passages from the section of our book which now lies open before us strikingly illustrative of the wisdom, goodness, tenderness, holiness, and righteousness which marked all the dealings of God with His people of old. Take, for example, the very opening paragraph. "Thou shalt not see thy brother's ox or his sheep go astray, and *hide thyself from them;* thou shalt in any case bring them again unto thy brother. And if thy brother be not nigh unto thee, or if thou know him not, then thou shalt bring it unto thine own house, and it shall be with thee until thy brother seek after it, and thou shalt restore it to him again. In like manner shalt thou do with his ass; and so shalt thou do with his raiment; and with all lost things of thy brother's which he hath lost, and thou hast found, shalt thou do likewise; *thou mayest not hide thyself.* Thou shalt not see thy brother's ass or his ox fall down by the way, *and hide thyself from them;* thou shalt surely help him to lift them up again" (chap. 22:1-4).

Here the two lessons of which we have spoken are very distinctly presented. What a deeply humbling picture of the human heart have we in that one sentence, "Thou mayest not hide thyself"! We are capable of the base and detestable selfishness of hiding ourselves from our brother's claims upon our sympathy and succor—of shirking the holy duty of looking after his interests—of pretending not to see his real need of our aid. Such is man!—such is the writer!

But oh, how blessedly the character of our God shines out in this passage! The brother's ox, or his sheep, or his ass, was not (to use a modern phrase) to be thrust into pound for trespass; it was to be brought home, cared for, and restored, safe and sound, to the owner, without charge for damage. And so with the raiment. How lovely is all this! how it breathes upon us the very air of the divine presence, the fragrant atmosphere of divine goodness, tenderness, and thoughtful love! What a high and holy privilege for any people to have their conduct governed and their character formed by such exquisite statutes and judgments!

Again, take the following passage, so beautifully illustrative of divine thoughtfulness: "When thou buildest a new house, then thou shalt make a battlement for thy roof, that thou bring not blood upon thine house, if any man fall from thence." The Lord would have His people thoughtful and considerate of others; and hence, in building their houses, they were not merely to think of themselves and their convenience, but also of others and their safety.

Cannot Christians learn something from this? How prone we are to think only of ourselves, our own interests, our own comfort and convenience! How rarely it happens that in the building or furnishing of our houses we bestow a thought upon other people! We build and furnish for ourselves. Alas! self is too much our object and motive-spring in all our undertakings; nor can it be otherwise unless the heart be kept under the governing power of those motives and objects which belong to Christianity. We must live in the pure and heavenly atmosphere of the new creation in order to get above and beyond the base selfishness which characterizes fallen humanity. Every unconverted man, woman, and child on the face of the earth is governed simply by self in some shape or another. Self is the centre, the object, the motive-spring, of every action.

True, some are more amiable, more affectionate, more benevolent, more unselfish, more disinterested, more agreeable, than others; but it is utterly impossible that "the natural man" can be governed by spiritual motives, or an earthly man be animated by heavenly objects. Alas! we have to confess, with shame and sorrow, that we who profess to be heavenly and spiritual are so prone to live for ourselves, to seek our own things, to maintain our own interests, to consult our own ease and convenience. We are all alive and on the alert when *self* is concerned.

All this is most sad and deeply humbling. It really ought not to be, and it would not be if we were looking more simply and earnestly to Christ as our great Exemplar and model in all things. Earnest and constant occupation of heart with Christ is the true secret of all practical Christianity. It is not rules and regulations that will ever make us Christ-like in our spirit, manner, and ways. We must drink into His spirit, walk in His footsteps, dwell more profoundly upon His moral glories, and then we shall, of blessed necessity, be conformed to His image. "We all with open face beholding as in a glass [or mirroring—*κατοπτριζομενοι*] the glory, are changed into the same image, from glory to glory even as by the Spirit of the Lord" (2 Cor. 3).

We must now ask the reader to turn for a moment to the following very important practical instructions—full of suggestive power for all Christian workers: "Thou shalt not sow thy vineyard with *divers seeds,* lest the fruit of thy seed which thou hast sown and the fruit of thy vineyard be defiled" (chap. 22:9).

What a weighty principle is here! Do we really understand it? do we see its true spiritual application? It is to be feared there is a terrible amount of "mingled seed" used in the so-called spiritual husbandry of the present day. How much of "philosophy and vain deceit," how much of "science falsely so called," how much of "the rudiments of the world," do we find mixed up in the teaching and preaching throughout the length and breadth of the professing church! How little of the pure, unadulterated seed of the Word of God, the "incorruptible seed" of the precious gospel of Christ, is scattered broad-cast over the field of christendom in this our day! How few, comparatively, are content to confine themselves within the covers of the Bible for the material of their ministry! Those who are, by the grace of God, faithful enough to do so, are looked upon as men of one idea, men of the old school, narrow, and behind the times.

Well, we can only say, with a full and glowing heart, God bless the men of one idea—men of the precious old school of apostolic preaching! Most heartily do we congratulate them on their blessed narrowness, and their being behind these dark and infidel times. We are fully aware of what we expose ourselves to in thus writing, but this does not move us. We are persuaded that every true servant of Christ must be a man of one idea, and that idea is Christ; he must belong to the very oldest school—the school of Christ; he must be as narrow as the truth of God; and he must, with stern decision, refuse to move one hair's breadth in the direction of this infidel age. We cannot shake off the conviction that the effort on the part of the preachers and teachers of christendom to keep abreast of the literature of the day must, to a very large extent, account for the rapid advance of rationalism and infidelity. They have got away from the holy Scriptures, and sought to adorn their ministry by the resources of philosophy, science, and literature. They have catered more for the intellect than for the heart and conscience. The pure and precious doctrines of holy Scripture, the sincere milk of the Word, the gospel of the grace of God and of the glory of Christ, were found insufficient to attract and keep together large congregations. As Israel of old despised the manna, got tired of it, and pronounced it light food, so the professing church grew weary of the pure doctrines of that glorious Christianity unfolded in the pages of the New Testament, and sighed for something to gratify the intellect and feed the imagination. The doctrines of the cross, in which the blessed apostle gloried, have lost their charm for the professing church, and any who would be faithful enough to adhere and confine themselves in their ministry to those doctrines might abandon all thought of popularity.

But let all the true and faithful ministers of Christ, all true workers in His vineyard, apply their hearts to the spiritual principle set forth in Deuteronomy 22:9; let them, with unflinching decision, refuse to make use of "divers seeds" in their spiritual husbandry; let them confine themselves, in their ministry, to "the form of sound words," and ever seek "rightly to divide the word of truth," that so they may not be ashamed of their work, but receive a full reward in that day when every man's work shall be tried of what sort it is. We may depend upon it, the Word of God—the pure seed—is the only proper material for the spiritual workman to use. We do not despise learning; far from it; we consider it most valuable in its right place. The *facts* of science, too, and the resources of sound philosophy, may all be turned to profitable account in unfolding and illustrating the truth of holy Scripture. We find the blessed Master Himself and His inspired apostles making use of the facts of history and of nature in their public teaching; and who, in his sober senses, would think of calling into question the value and importance of a competent knowledge of the original languages of Hebrew and Greek in the private study and public exposition of the Word of God?

But admitting all this, as we most fully do, it leaves wholly untouched the great practical principle before us—a principle to which all the Lord's people and His servants are bound to adhere, namely, that the Holy Ghost is the only power, and holy Scripture the only material, for all true ministry in the gospel and the Church of God. If this were more fully understood and faithfully acted upon, we should witness a very different condition of things throughout the length and breadth of the vineyard of Christ.

Here, however, we must close this section. We have elsewhere sought to handle the subject of "The Unequal Yoke," and shall not therefore dwell upon it here.* The Israelite was not to plow with an ox and an ass together; neither was he to wear a garment of divers sorts, as of woolen and linen. The spiritual application of both these things is as simple as it is important. The Christian is not to link himself with an unbeliever for any object whatsoever, be it domestic, religious, philanthrophic, or commercial; neither must he allow himself to be governed by mixed principles. His character must be formed and his conduct ruled by the pure and lofty principles of the Word of God. Thus may it be with all who profess and call themselves Christians.

*See "The Unequal Yoke," in the author's *Miscellaneous Writings*, vol.2.

## CHAPTER 26

"AND it shall be, *when thou art come* in unto the land which the Lord thy God giveth thee for an inheritance, and *possessest it,* and *dwellest* therein; that thou shalt take of the first of all the fruit of the earth, which thou shalt bring of thy land that the Lord thy God giveth thee, and shalt put it in a basket, and shalt go unto *the place which the Lord thy God shall choose to place His name there"*— not to a place of their own or others' choosing. "And thou shalt go unto the priest that shall be in those days, and say unto him, I profess this day unto the Lord thy God that *I am come* unto the country which the Lord sware unto our fathers for to give us. And the priest shall take the basket out of thine hand, and set it down before the altar of the Lord thy God" (ver. 1-4).

The chapter on which we now enter contains the lovely ordinance of the basket of first-fruits, in which we shall find some principles of the deepest interest and practical importance. It was when the hand of Jehovah had conducted His people into the land of promise that the fruits of that land could be presented. It was obviously necessary to be in Canaan ere Canaan's fruits could be offered in worship. The worshiper was able to say, "I profess this day unto the Lord thy God that I am come unto the country which the Lord sware unto our fathers for to give us."

Here lay the root of the matter. *"I am come."* He does not say, I am coming, hoping to come, or longing to come. No; but, "I am come." Thus it must ever be. We must know ourselves saved ere we can offer the fruits of a known salvation. We may be most sincere in our desires after salvation, most earnest in our efforts to obtain it; but then we cannot but see that efforts to be saved, and the fruits of a known and enjoyed salvation, are wholly different. The Israelite did not offer the basket of first-fruits in order to get into the land, but because he was actually in it. "I profess this day . . . that I am come." There is no mistake about it—no question, no doubt, not even a hope. I am actually in the land, and here is the fruit of it.

"And thou shalt speak, and say before the Lord thy God, A Syrian ready to perish was my father; and he went down into Egypt, and sojourned there with a few, and became there a nation, great, mighty, and populous; and the Egyptians evil entreated us, and afflicted us, and laid upon us hard bondage; and when we cried unto the Lord God of our fathers, the Lord heard our voice, and looked on our affliction and our labor and our oppression; and the Lord brought us forth out of Egypt with a mighty hand, and with an outstretched arm, and with great terribleness, and with signs, and with wonders; and He hath brought us into this place, and hath given us this land, even a land that floweth with milk and honey. And now, behold, I have brought the first-fruits of the land, which Thou, O Lord, hast given me. And thou shalt set it before the Lord thy God, and worship before the Lord thy God; and thou shalt rejoice in every good thing which the Lord thy God hath given unto thee, and unto thine house, thou, and the Levite, and the stranger that is among you."

This is a very beautiful illustration of worship.

"A Syrian ready to perish." Such was the origin. There is nothing to boast of, so far as nature is concerned. And as to the condition in which grace had found them, what of it? Hard bondage in the land of Egypt; toiling amid the brick-kilns, beneath the cruel lash of Pharaoh's taskmasters. But then, "We cried unto Jehovah." Here was their sure and blessed resource. It was all they could do, but it was enough. That cry of helplessness went directly up to the throne and to the heart of God, and brought Him down into the very midst of the brick-kilns of Egypt. Hear Jehovah's gracious words to Moses—"I have surely seen the affliction of My people which are in Egypt, and have heard their cry, by reason of their taskmasters; for *I know their sorrows;* and I am come down to deliver them out of the hand of the Egyptians, and to bring them up out of that land unto a good land and a large, unto a land flowing with milk and honey . . . . Now therefore, behold, the cry of the children of Israel is come unto Me; and I have also seen the oppression wherewith the Egyptians oppress them" (Exod. 3:7-9).

Such was the immediate response of Jehovah to the cry of His people. "I am come down to deliver them." Yes, blessed be His name, He came down, in the exercise of His own free and sovereign grace, to deliver His people; and no power of men or devils—earth or hell could hold them for a moment beyond the appointed time. Hence, in our chapter, we have the grand result as set forth in the language of the worshiper and in the contents of his basket. "I am come unto the country which the Lord sware unto our fathers for to give us. . . . And now, behold, I have brought the first-fruits of the land, which Thou, O Lord, hast given me." The Lord had accomplished all, according to the love of His heart and the faithfulness of His word. Not one jot or tittle had failed. "I am come" and "I have brought the fruit." The fruit of what? of Egypt? Nay; but "of the land, which Thou, O Lord, hast given me." The worshiper's lips proclaimed the completeness of Jehovah's work; the worshiper's basket contained the fruit of Jehovah's land. Nothing could be simpler, nothing more real. There was no room for a doubt, no ground for a question. He had simply to declare Jehovah's work and show the fruit. It was all of God from first to last. He had brought them out of Egypt, and He had brought them into Canaan. He had filled their baskets with the mellow fruits of His land, and their hearts with His praise.

And now, let us just ask you, do you think it was presumption on the part of the Israelite to speak as he did? Was it right, was it modest, was it humble, of him to say, *"I am come"?* Would it have been more becoming in him merely to give expression to the faint hope that at some future period he might come? would doubt and hesitation as to his position and his portion have been more honoring and gratifying to the God of Israel? What say you? It may be that, anticipating our argument, you are ready to say, There is no analogy. Why not? If an Israelite could say, "I am come unto the country which the Lord sware unto our Fathers for to give us," why cannot the believer now say, I am come unto Jesus? True, in the one case, it was sight; in the other, it is faith. But is the latter less real than the former? Does not the inspired apostle say to the Hebrews, "Ye *are come* unto Mount Zion"? and again, "We *receiving* a kingdom which cannot be moved, let us have grace whereby we may serve God with reverence and godly fear." If we are in doubt as to whether we have "come" or not, and as to whether we have "received the kingdom" or not, it is impossible to worship in truth or serve with acceptance. It is when we are in intelligent and peaceful possession of the place and portion in Christ that true worship can ascend to the throne above, and effective service be rendered in the vineyard below.

For what, let us ask, is true worship? It is simply telling out, in the presence of God, what He is, and what He has done. It is the heart occupied with and delighting in God and in all His marvelous actings and ways. Now, if we have no knowledge of God, and no faith in what He has done, how can we worship Him? "He that cometh to God must believe that He is, and that He is a rewarder of them that diligently seek Him." But then to know God is eternal life. I cannot worship God if I do not know Him, and I cannot know Him without having eternal life. The Athenians had erected an altar "to the unknown God," and Paul told them that they were worshiping in ignorance, and proceeded to declare unto them the true God as revealed in the Person and work of the Man Christ Jesus.

It is deeply important to be clear as to this. I must know God ere I can worship Him. I may "feel after Him, if haply I may find Him;" but feeling after One whom I have not found, and worshiping and delighting in One whom I have found, are two totally different things. God has revealed Himself, blessed be His name! He has given us the light of the knowledge of His glory in the face of Jesus Christ. He has come near to us in the Person of that blessed One, so that we may know Him, love Him, trust in Him, delight in Him, and use Him, in all our weakness and in all our need. We have no longer to grope for Him amid the darkness of nature, nor yet among the clouds and mists of spurious religion, in its ten thousand forms. No; our God has made Himself known by a revelation so plain that the wayfaring man, though a fool in all beside, may not err therein. The Christian can say, "*I know* whom I have believed." This is the basis of all true worship. There may be a vast amount of fleshly pietism, mechanical religion, and ceremonial routine without a single atom of true spiritual worship. This latter can only flow from the knowledge of God.

But our object is not to write a treatise on worship, but simply to unfold the instructive and beautiful ordinance of the basket of first-fruits. And having shown that worship was the first thing with an Israelite who found himself in possession of the land—and further, that we now must know our place and privilege in Christ before we can truthfully and intelligently worship the Father—we shall proceed to point out another very important practical result illustrated in our chapter, namely, *active benevolence.*

"When thou hast made an end of tithing all the tithes of thine increase the third year, which is the year of tithing, and hast given it unto the Levite, the stranger, the fatherless, and the widow, that they may eat within thy gates, and be filled; then thou shalt say before the Lord thy God, I have brought away the hallowed things out of mine house, and also have given them unto the Levite, and unto the stranger, to the fatherless, and to the widow, according to all Thy commandments, which Thou hast commanded me; I have not transgressed Thy commandments, neither have I forgotten them" (ver. 12-13).

Nothing can be more beautiful than the moral order of these things. It is precisely similar to what we have in Hebrews 13. "By Him therefore let us offer the sacrifice of praise to God continually, that is, *the fruit* of our lips giving thanks to His name." Here is the worship. "But to do good and to communicate forget not; for with such sacrifices God is well pleased." Here is the active benevolence. Putting both together, we have what we may call the upper and the nether side of the Christian's character—praising God and doing good to men. Precious characteristics! May we exhibit them more faithfully. One thing is certain, they will always go together. Show us a man whose heart is full of praise to God, and we will show you one whose heart is open to every form of human need. He may not be rich in the world's goods; he may be obliged to say, like one of old who was not ashamed to say it, "Silver and gold have I none;" but he will have the tear of sympathy, the kindly look, the soothing word, and these things tell far more powerfully upon a sensitive heart than the opening of the purse-strings, and the jingling of silver and gold. Our adorable Lord and Master, our great Exemplar, "went about doing good;" but we never read of His giving money to any one; indeed, we are warranted in believing that the blessed One never possessed a penny. When He wanted to answer the Herodians on the subject of paying tribute to Caesar, He had to ask them to show Him a penny; and when asked to pay tribute, He sent Peter to the sea to get it. He never carried money, and most assuredly money is not named in the category of gifts bestowed by Him upon His servants. Still He went about doing good, and we are to do the same, in our little measure; it is at once our high privilege and our bounden duty to do so.

Mark the divine order laid down in Hebrews 13, and illustrated in Deuteronomy 26. Worship gets the first, the highest place. Let us never forget this. We, in our wisdom or our sentimentality, might imagine that doing good to men, usefulness, philanthropy, is the highest thing; but it is not so. "Whoso offereth *praise* glorifieth Me." God inhabits the praises of His people. He delights to surround Himself with hearts filled to overflowing with a sense of His goodness, His greatness, and His glory. Hence, we are to offer the sacrifice of praise to God "continually." So also the Psalmist says, "I will bless the Lord at all times; His praise shall continually be in my mouth." It is not merely now and then, or when all is bright and cheery round us, when every thing goes on smoothly and prosperously; no, but *"at all times"*—*"continually."* The stream of thanksgiving is to flow uninterruptedly. There is no interval for murmuring or complaining, fretfulness or dissatisfaction, gloom or despondency. Praise and thanksgiving are to be our continual occupation. We are ever to cultivate the spirit of worship. Every breath, as it were, ought to be a halleluiah. Thus it shall be by and by. Praise will be our happy and holy service while eternity rolls along its course of golden ages. When we shall have no further call to "communicate," no demand on our resources or our sympathies, when we shall have bid an eternal adieu to this scene of sorrow and need, death and desolation, then shall we praise our God for evermore, without let or interruption, in the sanctuary of His own blessed presence above.

"But to do good and to communicate *forget not.*" There is singular interest attaching to the mode in which this is put. He does not say, But to offer the sacrifice of praise forget not. No; but lest, in the full and happy enjoyment of our own place and portion in Christ, we should "forget" that we are passing through a scene of want and misery, trial and pressure, the apostle adds the salutary and much-needed admonition as to doing good and communicating. The spiritual Israelite is not only to rejoice in every good thing which the Lord his God has bestowed upon him, but he is also to remember the Levite, the stranger, the fatherless, and the widow—that is, the one who has no earthly portion, and is thoroughly devoted to the Lord's work, and the one who has no home, the one who has no natural protector, and the one who has no earthly stay. It must ever be thus. The rich tide of grace rolls down from the bosom of God, fills our hearts to overflowing, and in its overflow, refreshes and gladdens our whole sphere of action. If we were only living in the enjoyment of what is ours in God, our every moment, our every act, our every word, yea, our every look, would do good. The Christian, according to the divine idea, is one who stands with one hand lifted up to God in the presentation of the sacrifice of praise, and the other hand filled with the fragrant fruits of genuine benevolence to meet every form of human need.

Let us deeply ponder these things; let us really apply our whole hearts to the earnest consideration of them; let us seek a fuller realization and a truer expression of these two great branches of practical Christianity, and not be satisfied with any thing less.

We shall now briefly glance at the third point in the precious chapter before us. We shall do little more than quote the passage. The Israelite, having presented his basket and distributed his tithes, was further instructed to say, "I have not eaten thereof in my *mourning,* neither have I taken away aught thereof for any *unclean* use, nor given aught thereof for *the dead;* but I have hearkened to the voice of the Lord my God, and have done according to all that Thou hast commanded me. Look down from Thy holy habitation, from heaven, and bless Thy people Israel, and the land which Thou hast given us, as Thou swarest unto our fathers, a land that floweth with milk and honey. This day the Lord thy God hath commanded thee to do these statutes and judgments; thou shalt therefore *keep* and *do* them, *with all thine heart* and *with all thy soul.* Thou hast avouched the Lord this day to be thy God, and to *walk in His ways,* and to keep His statutes and His commandments and His judgments, and to hearken unto His voice: and the Lord hath avouched thee this day to be His peculiar people"—that is, a people of His own special possession—"as He hath promised thee, and that thou shouldest keep *all* His commandments; and to make thee high above all nations which He hath made, in praise and in name and in honor; and that thou mayest be *a holy people* unto the Lord thy God, as He hath spoken" (ver. 14-19).

Here we have personal holiness, practical sanctification, entire separation from every thing inconsistent with the holy place and relationship into which they had been introduced, in the sovereign grace and mercy of God. There must be no mourning, no uncleanness, no dead works. We have no room, no time, for any such things as these; they do not belong to that blessed sphere in which we are privileged to live and move and have our being. We have just three things to do: We look up to God, and offer the sacrifice of praise; we look around at a needy world, and do good; we look in upon the circle of our own being—our inner life, and seek, by grace, to keep ourselves unspotted. "Pure religion and undefiled before God and the Father is this: To visit the fatherless and widows in their affliction, and to keep himself unspotted from the world" (Jas. 1:27).

Thus, whether we hearken to Moses in Deuteronomy 26, or to Paul in Hebrews 13, or to James in his most wholesome, needed, practical Epistle, it is the same Spirit that speaks to us, and the same grand lessons that are impressed upon us—lessons of unspeakable value and moral importance—lessons loudly called for in this day of easy-going profession, in the which the doctrines of grace are taken up and held in a merely intellectual way, and connected with all sorts of worldliness and self-indulgence.

Truly, there is an urgent need of a more powerful, practical ministry amongst us. There is a deplorable lack of the prophetic and pastoral element in our ministrations. By the prophetic element, we mean that character of ministry that deals with the conscience, and brings it into the immediate presence of God. This is *greatly* needed. There is a good deal of ministry which addresses itself to the intelligence, but sadly too little for the heart and the conscience. The teacher speaks to the understanding; the prophet speaks to the conscience;* the pastor speaks to the heart. We speak, of course, generally. It may so happen that the three elements are found in the ministry of one man; but they are distinct; and we cannot but feel that where the prophetic and pastoral gifts are lacking in any assembly, the teachers should very earnestly wait upon the

*Very many seem to entertain the idea that a prophet is one who foretells future events, but it would be a mistake thus to confine the term. 1 Corinthians 14:28-32 lets us into the meaning of the words "prophet" and "prophesying." The teacher and the prophet are closely and beautifully connected. The teacher unfolds truth from the Word of God; the prophet applies it to the conscience; and, we may add, the pastor sees how the ministry of both the one and other is acting on the heart and in the life.

Lord for spiritual power to deal with the hearts and consciences of His beloved people. Blessed be His name, He has all needed gift, grace, and power for His servants. All we need is, to wait on Him in real earnestness and sincerity of heart, and He will most assuredly supply us with all suited grace and moral fitness for whatever service we may be called to render in His Church.

Oh, that all the Lord's servants may be stirred up to a more deep-toned earnestness, in every department of His blessed work! May we be "instant in season, out of season," and in no wise discouraged by the condition of things around us, but rather find in that very condition an urgent reason for more intense devotedness.

---

## *CHAPTER 27*

"AND Moses, with the elders of Israel, commanded the people, saying, 'Keep all the commandments which I command you this day. And it shall be on the day when ye shall pass over Jordan unto the land which the Lord thy God giveth thee, that thou shalt set thee up great stones, and plaster them with plaster; and thou shalt write upon them all the words of this law, when thou art passed over, that thou mayest go in unto the land which the Lord thy God giveth thee, a land that floweth with milk and honey; as the Lord God of thy fathers hath promised thee. Therefore it shall be when ye be gone over Jordan, that ye shall set up these stones, which I command you this day, in Mount Ebal, and thou shalt plaster them with plaster. And there shalt thou build an altar unto the Lord thy God, an altar of stones: thou shalt not lift up any iron tool upon them. Thou shalt build the altar of the Lord thy God of whole stones; and thou shalt offer burnt-offerings thereon unto the Lord thy God; and thou shalt offer peace-offerings, and shalt eat there, and rejoice before the Lord thy God. And thou shalt write upon the stones all the words of this law very plainly.' And Moses and the priests the Levites spake unto all Israel, saying, 'Take heed, and hearken, O Israel; *this day thou art become the people of the Lord thy God.* Thou shalt *therefore* obey the voice of the Lord thy God, and do His commandments and His statutes, which I command thee this day.' And Moses charged the people the same day, saying, 'These shall stand upon Mount Gerizim to bless the people, when ye are come over Jordan: Simeon and Levi and Judah and Issachar and Joseph and Benjamin. And these shall stand upon Mount Ebal to curse: Reuben, Gad, and Asher and Zebulun, Dan, and Naphtali" (ver. 1-13).

There could not be a more striking contrast than that which is presented in the opening and close of this chapter. In the paragraph which we have just penned, we see Israel entering upon the land of promise—that fair and fruitful land flowing with milk and honey, and there erecting an altar in Mount Ebal, for burnt-offerings and peace-offerings. We read nothing about sin-offerings or trespass-offerings here. The law, in all its fullness, was to be "written very plainly" upon the plastered stones, and the people, in full, recognized, covenant-relationship, were to offer on the altar those special offerings of sweet savor so blessedly expressive of worship and holy communion. The subject here is not the trespasser *in act* or the sinner *in nature* approaching the brazen altar with a trespass-offering or a sin-offering; but rather a people fully delivered, accepted, and blessed—a people in the actual enjoyment of their relationship and their inheritance.

True, they were trespassers and sinners, and as such, needed the precious provision of the brazen altar; this, of course, is obvious, and fully understood and admitted by every one taught of God; but it manifestly is not the subject of Deuteronomy 27:1-13, and the spiritual reader will at once perceive the reason. When we see the Israel of God, in full covenant-relationship, entering into possession of their inheritance, having the revealed will of their covenant-God, Jehovah, plainly and fully written before them, and the milk and honey flowing around them, we must conclude that all question as to trespasses and sins is definitively settled, and that nothing remains for a people so highly privileged and so richly blessed but to surround the altar of their covenant-God and present those sweet-savor offerings which were acceptable to Him and suited to them.

In short, the whole scene unfolded to our view in the first half of our chapter is perfectly beautiful. Israel having avouched Jehovah to be their God, and Jehovah having avouched Israel to be His peculiar people, to make them high above all nations which He had made, in praise and in name and in honor, and a holy people unto the Lord their God, as He had spoken; Israel thus privileged, blessed, and exalted, in full possession of the goodly land, and having all the precious commandments of God before their eyes, what remained but to present the sacrifices of praise and thanksgiving, in holy worship and happy fellowship?

But in the latter half of our chapter, we find something quite different. Moses appoints six tribes to stand upon Mount Gerizim to bless the people, and six on Mount Ebal to curse; but alas! when we come to the actual history—the positive facts of the case, there is not a single syllable of blessing, nothing but twelve awful curses, each confirmed by a solemn "amen" from the whole congregation.

What a sad change! what a striking contrast! It reminds us of what passed before us in our study of Exodus 19. There could not be a more impressive commentary on the words of the inspired apostle in Galatians 3:10. "For as many as are of the works of the law"—as many as are on that ground—"are under the curse; for it is written,"—and here he quotes Deuteronomy 27—"Cursed is every one that continueth not in all things which are written in the book of the law to do them."

Here we have the real solution of the question. Israel, as to their actual moral condition, were on the ground of law; and hence, although the opening of our chapter presents a lovely picture of God's thoughts respecting Israel, yet the close of it sets forth the sad and humiliating result of Israel's real state before God. There is not a sound from Mount Gerizim, not one word of benediction; but, instead thereof, curse upon curse falls on the ears of the people.

Nor could it possibly be otherwise. Let people contend for it as they will, nothing but a curse can come upon "as many as are of the works of the law." It does not merely say, As many as fail to keep the law, though that is true; but, as if to set the truth in the very clearest and most forcible manner before us, the Holy Ghost declares that for *all*, no matter who—Jew, Gentile, or nominal Christian—all who are on the ground or principle of works of law, there is and can be nothing but a curse.

Thus, then, the reader will be able intelligently to account for the profound silence that reigned on Mount Gerizim in the day of Deuteronomy 27. The simple fact is, if one solitary benediction had been heard, it would have been a contradiction to the entire teaching of holy Scripture on the question of law.

We have so fully gone into the weighty subject of the law in the earlier pages of these *Notes* that we do not feel called upon to dwell upon it here. We can only say that the more we study Scripture, and the more we ponder the law question in the light of the New Testament, the more amazed we are at the manner in which some persist in contending for the opinion that Christians are under the law, whether for life, for righteousness, for holiness, or for any object whatsoever. How can such an opinion stand for a moment in the face of that magnificent and conclusive statement in Romans 6—"*Ye are not under law, but under grace*"?

---

## *CHAPTER 28*

IN approaching the study of this remarkable section of our book, the reader must bear in mind that it is by no means to be confounded with chapter 27. Some expositors, in seeking to account for the absence of the blessings in the latter, have sought for them here; but it is a grand mistake—a mistake absolutely fatal to the proper understanding of either chapter. The obvious fact is, the two chapters are wholly distinct, in basis, scope, and practical application. Chapter 27 is (to put it as pointedly and briefly as possible) *moral* and *personal;* chapter 28 is *dispensational* and *national.* That deals with the great root-principle of man's moral condition as a sinner, utterly ruined and wholly incapable of meeting God on the ground of law; this, on the other hand, takes up the question of Israel as a nation, under the government of God. In short, a careful comparison of two chapters will enable the reader to see their entire distinctness. For instance, what connection can we trace between the six blessings of our chapter and the twelve curses of chapter 27? None whatever. It is not possible to establish the slightest relationship. But a child can see the moral link between the blessings and curses of chapter 28.

Let us quote a passage or two in proof. "And it shall come to pass, if thou shalt *hearken diligently unto the voice of the Lord thy God*"—the grand old Deuteronomic motto, the key-note of the book—"to observe and to do all His commandments which I command thee this day, that the Lord thy God will set thee on high above all nations of the earth; and all these blessings shall come on thee, and overtake thee, *if thou shalt hearken unto the voice of the Lord thy God*"—the only safeguard, the true secret of happiness, security, victory, and strength. "Blessed shalt thou be in the city, and blessed shalt thou be in the field. Blessed shall be the fruit of thy body, and the fruit of thy ground, and the fruit of thy cattle, the increase of thy kine, and the flocks of thy sheep. Blessed shall be thy basket and thy store. Blessed shalt thou be when thou comest in, and blessed shalt thou be when thou goest out."

Is it not perfectly plain to the reader that these are not the blessings pronounced by the six tribes on Mount Gerizim? What is here presented to us is Israel's national dignity, prosperity, and glory, founded upon their diligent attention to all the commandments set before them in this book. It was the eternal purpose of God that Israel should be pre-eminent on the earth, high above all the nations. This purpose shall assuredly be made good, although Israel, in the past, have shamefully failed to render that perfect obedience which was to form the basis of their national pre-eminence and glory.

We must never forget or surrender this great truth. Some expositors have adopted a system of interpretation by which the covenant-blessings of Israel are spiritualized and made over to the Church of God. This is a most fatal mistake. Indeed, it is hardly possible to set forth in language, or even to conceive, the pernicious effects of such a method of handling the precious Word of God. Nothing is more certain than that it is diametrically opposed to the mind and will of God. He will not and cannot sanction such tampering with His truth, or such an unwarrantable alienation of the blessings and privileges of His people Israel.

True, we read, in Galatians 3, "That the blessing of Abraham might come on the Gentiles through Jesus Christ, that we might receive"—what? Blessings in the city and in the field? blessings in our basket and store? Nay; but "the promise of the Spirit through faith." So also we learn from the same Epistle, in chapter 4, that restored Israel will be permitted to reckon amongst her children all those who are born of the Spirit during the Christian period. "But Jerusalem which is above is free, which is the mother of us all. For it is written, 'Rejoice, thou barren, that bearest not; break forth and cry, thou that travailest not; for the desolate hath many more children than she which hath a husband.' "

All this is blessedly true, but it affords no warrant whatever for transferring the promises made to Israel to New Testament believers. God has pledged Himself by an oath to bless the seed of Abraham His friend—to bless them with all earthly blessings, in the land of Canaan. This promise holds good, and is absolutely inalienable. Woe be to all who attempt to interfere with its literal fulfillment in God's own time. We have referred to this in our studies on the earlier part of this book, and must now rest content with warning the reader most solemnly against every system of interpretation which involves such serious consequences as to the Word and ways of God. We must ever remember that Israel's blessings are earthly; the Church's blessings are heavenly. "Blessed be the God and Father of our Lord Jesus Christ, who hath blessed us with *all spiritual blessings in the heavenlies in Christ.*"

Thus, both the nature and the sphere of the Church's blessings are wholly different from those of Israel, and must never be confounded. But the system of interpretation above referred to does confound them, to the marring of the integrity of holy Scripture, and the serious damage of souls. To attempt to apply the promises made to Israel to the Church of God, either now or hereafter, on earth or in heaven, is to turn things completely upside down, and to produce the most hopeless confusion in the exposition and application of Scripture. We feel called upon, in simple faithfulness to the Word of God and to the soul of the reader, to press this matter upon his earnest attention. He may rest assured it is by no means an unimportant question; so far from this, we are persuaded that it is utterly impossible for any one who confounds Israel and the Church—the earthly and the heavenly, to be a sound or accurate interpreter of the Word of God.

However, we cannot pursue this subject further here. We only trust that the Spirit of God will arouse the heart of the reader to feel its interest and importance, and give him to see the necessity of rightly dividing the Word of truth. If this be so, our object will be fully gained.

With regard to this twenty-eighth of Deuteronomy, if the reader only seizes the fact of its entire distinctness from its predecessor, he will be able to read it with spiritual intelligence and real profit. There is no need whatever for elaborate exposition. It divides itself naturally and obviously into two parts. In the first, we have a full and most blessed statement of the results of obedience (see verses 1-15); in the second, we have a deeply solemn and affecting statement of the awful consequences of disobedience (see verses 16-68). And we cannot but be struck with the fact that the section containing the curses is more than three times the length of the one containing the blessings. That consists of fifteen verses; this, of fifty-three. The whole chapter furnishes an impressive commentary on the government of God, and a most forcible illustration of the fact that "our God is a consuming fire." All the nations of the earth may learn from Israel's marvelous history that God must punish disobedience, and that, too, first of all, in His own. And if He has not spared His own people, what shall be the end of those who know Him not? "The wicked shall be turned into hell, and all the nations that forget God." "It is a fearful thing to fall into the hands of the living God." It is the very height of extravagant folly for any one to attempt to evade the full force of such passages, or to explain them away. It cannot be done. Let any one read the chapter before us and compare it with the actual history of Israel, and he will see that as sure as there is a God on the throne of the majesty in the heavens, so surely will He punish evil-doers, both here and hereafter. It cannot be otherwise. The government that could or would allow evil to go unjudged, uncondemned, unpunished, would not be a perfect government—would not be the government of God. It is vain to found arguments upon one-sided views of the goodness, kindness, and mercy of God. Blessed be His name, He is kind and good and merciful and gracious, long-suffering and full of compassion; but He is holy and just, righteous and true, and "He hath appointed a day, in the which He will judge the world [the habitable earth—*οικουμενην*] in righteousness by that Man whom He hath ordained; whereof He hath given assurance [given proof—*πιστιν*] unto all, in that He hath raised Him from the dead" (Acts 17).

However, we must draw this section to a close, but ere doing so, we feel it to be our duty to call the reader's attention to a very interesting point in connection with verse 13 of our chapter. "The Lord shall make thee the head, and not the tail; and thou shalt be above only, and thou shalt not be beneath; if that thou hearken unto the commandments of the Lord thy God, which I command thee this day, to observe and to do them."

This, no doubt, refers to Israel as a nation. They are destined to be the head of all the nations of the earth. Such is the sure and settled purpose and counsel of God respecting them. Low as they are now sunk, scattered and lost amongst the nations, suffering the terrible consequences of their persistent disobedience, sleeping, as we read in Daniel 12, in the dust of the earth, yet they shall, *as a nation* arise and shine in far brighter glory than that of Solomon.

All this is blessedly true, and established beyond all question in manifold passages in Moses, the Psalms, the prophets, and the New Testament; but in looking through the history of Israel, we find some very striking instances of individuals who were permitted and enabled, through infinite grace, to make their own of the precious promise contained in verse 13, and that, too, in very dark and depressing periods of the national history, when Israel, as a nation, was the tail and not the head. We shall just give the reader an instance or two, not only to illustrate our point, but also to set before him a principle of immense practical importance and universal application.

Let us turn for a moment to that charming little book of Esther—a book so little understood or appreciated—a book which, we may truly say, fills a niche and teaches a lesson which no other book does. It belongs to a period when most assuredly Israel was not the head, but the tail; but, notwithstanding, it presents to our view the very edifying and encouraging picture of an individual son of Abraham so carrying himself as to reach the very highest position, and gaining a splendid victory over Israel's bitterest foe.

As to Israel's condition in the days of Esther, it was such that God could not publicly own them. Hence it is that His name is not found in this book, from beginning to end. The Gentile was the head and Israel the tail. The relationship between Jehovah and Israel could no longer be publicly owned; but the heart of Jehovah could never forget His people, and, we may add, the heart of a faithful Israelite could never forget Jehovah or His holy law; and these are just the two facts that specially characterize this most interesting little book. God was acting for Israel behind the scenes, and Mordecai was acting for God before the scenes. It is worthy of remark that neither Israel's best Friend nor their worst enemy is once named in the book of Esther, and yet the whole book is full of the actings of both. The finger of God is stamped on every link in the marvelous chain of providence; and on the other hand, the bitter enmity of Amalek comes out in the cruel plot of the haughty Agagite.

All this is intensely interesting. Indeed, in rising from the study of this book, we may well say, "Oh, scenes surpassing fable and yet true." No romance could possibly exceed in interest this simple but most blessed history. But we must not expatiate, much as we should like to do so. Time and space forbid. We merely refer to it now in order to point out to the reader the unspeakable value and importance of individual faithfulness at a moment when the national glory was faded and gone. Mordecai stood like a rock for the truth of God. He refused, with stern decision, to own Amalek. He would save the life of Ahasuerus, and bow to his authority as the expression of the power of God; but he would not bow to Haman. His conduct in this matter was governed simply by the Word of God. The authority for his course was to be found in this blessed book of Deuteronomy. "*Remember* what Amalek did unto thee by the way, when ye were come forth out of Egypt; how he met thee by the way, and smote the hindmost of thee, even all that were feeble behind thee, when thou wast faint and weary: and *he feared not God*"—here was the true secret of the whole matter—"therefore it shall be, when the Lord thy God hath given thee rest from all thine enemies round about, in the land which the Lord thy God giveth for an inheritance to possess it, that thou shalt blot out the remembrance of Amalek from under heaven; *thou shalt not forget it*" (chap. 25: 17-19).

This was distinct enough for every circumcised ear, every obedient heart, every upright conscience. Equally distinct is the language of Exodus 17—"And the Lord said unto Moses, 'Write this for a memorial in a book, and rehearse it in the ears of Joshua; for I will utterly put out the remembrance of Amalek from under heaven.' And Moses built an altar, and called the name of it *Jehovah*-nissi [the Lord my banner] ; for he said, 'Because the Lord hath sworn that the Lord will have war with Amalek from generation to generation" (ver. 14-16).

Here, then, was Mordecai's authority for refusing a single nod of his head to the Agagite. How could a faithful member of the house of Israel bow to a member of a house with which Jehovah was at war? Impossible. He could clothe himself in sackcloth, fast and weep for his people, but he could not, he would not, he dare not, bow to an Amalekite. He might be charged with presumption, blind obstinacy, stupid bigotry, and contemptible narrow-mindedness; but with that he had nothing whatever to do. It might seem the most unaccountable folly to withhold the common mark of respect from the highest noble in the kingdom; but that noble was an Amalekite, and that was enough for Mordecai. The apparent folly was simple obedience.

It is this which makes the case so interesting and important for us. Nothing can ever do away with our responsibility to obey the Word of God. It might be said to Mordecai that the commandment as to Amalek was a by-gone thing, having reference to Israel's palmy days. It was quite right for Joshua to fight with Amalek; Saul, too, ought to have obeyed the word of Jehovah instead of sparing Agag; but now, all was changed; the glory was departed from Israel, and it was perfectly useless to attempt to act on Exodus 17 or Deuteronomy 25.

All such arguments, we feel assured, would have no weight whatever with Mordecai. It was enough for him that Jehovah had said, *"Remember* what Amalek did. . . . *Thou shalt not forget it."* How long was this to hold good? "From generation to generation." Jehovah's war with Amalek was never to cease until his very name and remembrance were blotted out from under heaven. And why? Because of his cruel and heartless treatment of Israel. Such was the kindness of God toward His people! How, then, could a faithful Israelite ever bow to an Amalekite? Impossible. Could Joshua bow to Amalek? Nay. Did Samuel? Nay; "he hewed Agag in pieces before the Lord in Gilgal." How, then, could Mordecai bow to him? He could not do it, cost what it might. It mattered not to him that the gallows was erected for him. He could be hanged, but he could never do homage to Amalek.

And what was the result? A magnificent triumph! There stood the proud Amalekite near the throne, basking in the sunshine of royal favor, boasting himself in his riches, his greatness, his glory, and about to crush beneath his foot the seed of Abraham. There, on the other hand, lay poor Mordecai in sackcloth and ashes and tears. What could he do? He could obey. He had neither sword nor spear; but he had the Word of God, and by simply obeying that Word, he gained a victory over Amalek quite as decisive and splendid in its way as that gained by Joshua in Exodus 17—a victory which Saul failed to gain, though surrounded by a host of warriors selected from the twelve tribes of Israel. Amalek sought to get Mordecai hanged; but instead of that, he was obliged to act as his footman, and conduct him, in all but regal pomp and splendor, through the street of the city. "And Haman answered the king, 'For the man whom the king delighteth to honor, let the royal apparel be brought which the king useth to wear, and the horse that the king rideth upon, and the crown royal which is set upon his head; and let this apparel and horse be delivered to the hand of one of the king's most noble princes, that they may array the man withal whom the king delighteth to honor, and bring him on horseback through the street of the city, and proclaim before him, Thus shall it be done to the man whom the king delighteth to honor.' Then the king said to Haman, 'Make haste, and take the apparel and the horse, as thou hast said, and do even so to Mordecai the Jew, that sitteth at the king's gate: let nothing fail of all that thou hast spoken.'

Then took Haman the apparel and the horse, and arrayed Mordecai, and brought him on horseback through the street of the city, and proclaimed before him, 'Thus shall it be done unto the man whom the king delighteth to honor.' And Mordecai came again to the king's gate; but Haman hasted to his house mourning, and having his head covered."

Here, assuredly, Israel was the head and Amalek the tail—Israel, not nationally, but individually. But this was only the beginning of Amalek's defeat and of Israel's glory. Haman was hanged on the very gallows he had erected for Mordecai, "and Mordecai went out from the presence of the king in royal apparel of blue and white, and with a great crown of gold, and with a garment of fine linen and purple; and the city of Shushan rejoiced and was glad."

Nor was this all. The effect of Mordecai's marvelous victory was felt far and wide over the hundred and twenty-seven provinces of the empire. "In every province, and in every city whithersoever the king's commandment and his decree came, the Jews had joy and gladness, a feast and a good day. And many people of the land became Jews, for the fear of the Jews fell upon them." And, to crown all, we read that "Mordecai the Jew was next unto king Ahaseurus, and great among the Jews, and accepted of the multitude of his brethren, seeking the wealth of his people, and speaking peace to all his seed."

Does not all this prove to us, in the most striking manner, the immense importance of individual faithfulness? Is it not eminently calculated to encourage us to stand for the truth of God, cost what it may? Only see what marvelous results followed from the actings of one man! Many might have condemned Mordecai's conduct. It might have seemed like unaccountable obstinacy to refuse a simple mark of respect to the highest noble in the empire; but it was not so. It was simple obedience; it was decision for God, and it led to a most magnificent victory, the spoils of which were reaped by his brethren at the very ends of the earth.

For further illustration of the subject suggested by Deuteronomy 28:13, we must refer to Daniel 3 and 6. There we will see what morally glorious results can be reached by individual faithfulness to the true God, at a moment when Israel's national glory was gone—their city and temple in ruins. The three worthies refused to worship the golden image. They dared to face the wrath of the king, to withstand the universal voice of the empire, yea, to meet the fiery furnace itself, rather than disobey. They could surrender life, but they could not surrender the truth of God.

And what was the result? A splendid victory! They walked through the furnace with the Son of God, and were called forth from the furnace as witnesses and servants of the Most High God. Glorious privilege! wondrous dignity! and all the simple result of obedience. Had they gone with the crowd, and bowed the head in worship to the national god, in order to escape the dreadful furnace, see what they would have lost! But, blessed be God, they were enabled to stand fast in the confession of the grand foundation-truth of the unity of the Godhead—that truth which had been trampled underfoot amid the splendors of Solomon's reign; and the record of their faithfulness has been penned for us by the Holy Spirit in order to encourage us to tread, with firm step, the path of individual devotedness, in the face of a God-hating, Christ-rejecting world, and in the face of a truth-neglecting christendom. It is impossible to read the narrative and not have our whole renewed being stirred up and drawn out in earnest desire for more deep-toned personal devotedness to Christ and His precious cause.

Similar must be the effect produced by the study of Daniel 6. We cannot allow ourselves to quote or expatiate; we can only commend the soul-stirring record to the attention of the reader. It is uncommonly fine, and it furnishes a splendid lesson for this day of soft, self-indulgent, easy-going profession, in which it costs people nothing to give a nominal assent to the truths of Christianity; but in which, notwithstanding, there is so little desire or readiness to follow, with whole-hearted decision, a rejected Lord, or to yield an unqualified and unhesitating obedience to His commandments.

How refreshing, in the face of so much heartless indifference, to read of the faithfulness of Daniel! He, with unflinching decision, persisted in his holy habit of praying three times a day, with his window open toward Jerusalem, although he knew that the den of lions was the penalty of his act. He might have closed his window and drawn his curtains and retired into the privacy of his chamber to pray, or he might have waited for the midnight hour, when no human eye could see or human ear hear him. But no; this beloved servant of God would not hide his light under a bed or a bushel. There was a great principle at stake. It was not merely that he would pray to the one living and true God, but he would pray with "*his windows open toward Jerusalem.*" And why "toward Jerusalem"? Because it was God's centre. But it was in ruins. True, for the present, and as looked at from a human stand-point; but to faith, and from a divine stand-point, Jerusalem was God's centre for His earthly people. It was, and it shall be, beyond all question. And not only so, but its dust is precious to Jehovah; and hence Daniel was in full communion with the mind of God when he opened his windows toward Jerusalem and prayed. He had Scripture for what he did, as the reader may see by referring to 2 Chronicles 6. "If they return to thee with all their heart and with all their soul in the land of their captivity, whither they have carried them captives, and pray *toward their land*, which Thou gavest unto their fathers, and *toward the city* which Thou hast chosen, and *toward the house* which I have built for Thy name."

Here was Daniel's warrant. This was what he did, utterly regardless of human opinions, and utterly regardless, too, of pains and penalties. He would rather be thrown into the den of lions than surrender the truth of God; he would rather go to heaven with a good conscience than remain on earth with a bad one.

And what was the result? Another splendid triumph! "Daniel was taken up out of the den, and no manner of hurt was found upon him, *because he believed in his God.*"

Blessed servant! noble witness! Assuredly he was the head on this occasion, and his enemies the tail. And how? Simply by obedience to the Word of God. This is what we deem to be of such vast moral importance for this our day. It is to illustrate and enforce this that we refer to those brilliant examples of individual faithfulness at a time when Israel's national glory was in the dust, their unity gone, and their polity broken up. We cannot but regard it as a fact full of interest, full of encouragement, full of suggestive power, that in the darkest days of Israel's history as a nation we have the brightest and noblest examples of personal faith and devotedness. We earnestly press this upon the attention of the Christian reader. We consider it eminently calculated to strengthen and cheer up our hearts in standing for the truth of God at a moment like the present, when there is so much to discourage us in the general condition of the professing church. It is not that we are to look for such speedy, striking, and splendid results as were realized in those cases to which we have referred. This is by no means the question. What we have to keep before our hearts is the fact that, no matter what may be the condition of the ostensible people of God at any given time, it is the privilege of the individual man of God to tread the narrow path and reap the precious fruits of simple obedience to the Word of God and the precious commandments of our Lord and Saviour Jesus Christ.

This, we feel persuaded, is a truth for the day. May we all feel its holy power. We are in imminent danger of lowering the standard of personal devotedness because of the general condition. This is a fatal mistake, yea, it is the positive suggestion of the enemy of Christ and His cause. If Mordecai, Shadrach, Meshach, Abednego, and Daniel had acted thus, what would have been the result?

Ah, no; we have ever to bear in mind that our one great business is, to obey, and leave results with God. It may please Him to permit His servants to see striking results, or He may see fit to allow them to wait for that great day that is coming, when there will be no danger of our being puffed up by seeing any little fruit of our testimony. Be this as it may, it is our plain and bounden duty to tread that bright and blessed path indicated for us by the commandments of our precious and adorable Lord and Saviour Jesus Christ. May God enable us, by the grace of His Holy Spirit, so to do. May we cleave to the truth of God with purpose of heart, utterly regardless of the opinions of our fellow-men who may charge us with narrowness, bigotry, intolerance, and such like. *We have just to go on with the Lord!*

---

## *CHAPTER 29*

THIS chapter closes the second grand division of our book. In it we have a most solemn appeal to the conscience of the congregation. It is what we may term the summing up and practical application of all that has gone before in this most profound, practical, and hortatory section of the five books of Moses.

"These are the words of the covenant, which the Lord commanded Moses to make with the children of Israel *in the land of Moab, beside the covenant which He made with them in Horeb.*" Allusion has already been made to this passage as one of the many proofs of the entire distinctness of the book of Deuteronomy from the preceding section of the Pentateuch; but it claims the reader's attention on another ground. It speaks of a special covenant made with the children of Israel in the land of Moab, in virtue of which they were to be brought into the land. This covenant was as distinct from the covenant made at Sinai as it was from the covenant made with Abraham, Isaac, and Jacob. In a word, it was neither pure *law* on the one hand, nor pure *grace* on the other, but *government* exercised in sovereign mercy.

It is perfectly clear that Israel *could* not enter the land on the ground of the Sinai or Horeb-covenant, inasmuch as they had completely failed under it, by making a golden calf. They forfeited all right and title to the land, and were only saved from instant destruction by sovereign mercy exercised toward them through the mediation and earnest intercession of Moses. It is equally plain that they *did* not enter the land on the ground of the Abrahamic covenant of grace, for had they done so, they would not have been turned out of it. Neither the extent nor the duration of their tenure answered to the terms of the covenant made with their fathers. It was by the terms of the Moab-covenant that they entered upon the limited and temporary possession of the land of Canaan; and inasmuch as they have as signally failed under the Moab-covenant as under that of Horeb—failed under government as completely as under law, they are expelled from the land and scattered over the face of the earth, under the governmental dealings of God.

But not forever. Blessed be the God of all grace, the seed of Abraham His friend shall yet possess the land of Canaan according to the magnificent terms of the original grant. "The gifts and calling of God are without repentance." Gifts and calling must not be confounded with law and government. Mount Zion can never be classed with Horeb and Moab. The new and everlasting covenant of grace, ratified by the precious blood of the Lamb of God, shall be gloriously fulfilled to the letter, spite of all the powers of earth and hell—men and devils combined. " 'Behold, the days come, saith the Lord, when I will make a new covenant with the house of Israel and with the house of Judah; not according to the covenant that I made with their fathers in the day when I took them by the hand to lead them out of the land of Egypt; because they continued not in My covenant, and I regarded them not, saith the Lord. For this is the covenant that I will make with the house of Israel after those days, saith the Lord: I will put My laws into their mind, and write them in their hearts; and I will be to them a God, and they shall be to Me a people; and they shall not teach every man his neighbor, and every man his brother, saying, Know the Lord; for all shall know Me, from the least to the greatest. For I will be merciful to their unrighteousness, and their sins and their iniquities will I remember no more.' In that He saith, 'A new covenant,' He hath made the first old. Now that which decayeth and waxeth old is ready to vanish away" (Heb. 8:8-13).

Now, the reader must carefully guard against a system of interpretation that would apply this precious and beautiful passage to the Church. It involves a threefold wrong, namely, a wrong to the truth of God, a wrong to the Church, and a wrong to Israel. We have raised a warning note on this subject again and again in the course of our studies on the Pentateuch, because we feel its immense importance. It is our deep and thorough conviction that no one can understand, much less expound, the Word of God who confounds Israel with the Church. The two things are as distinct as heaven and earth; and hence, when God speaks of Israel, Jerusalem, and Zion, if we presume to apply those names to the New Testament Church, it can only issue in utter confusion. We believe it to be a simple impossibility to set forth the mischievous consequences of such a method of handling the Word of God. It puts an end to all accuracy of interpretation, and to all that holy precision and divine certainty which Scripture is designed and fitted to impart; it mars the integrity of truth, damages the souls of God's people, and hinders their progress in divine life and spiritual intelligence. In short, we cannot too strongly urge upon every one who reads these lines the absolute necessity of guarding against this fatally false system of handling holy Scripture.

We must beware of meddling with the scope of prophecy, or the true application of the promises of God. We have no warrant whatever to interfere with the divinely appointed sphere of the covenants. The inspired apostle tells us distinctly, in the ninth of Romans, that they pertain to Israel; and if we attempt to alienate them from the Old Testament fathers and transfer them to the Church of God—the body of Christ, we may depend upon it, we are doing what Jehovah-Elohim will never sanction. The Church forms no part of the ways of God with Israel and the earth. Her place, her portion, her privileges, her prospect, are all heavenly. She is called into existence in this time of Christ's rejection, to be associated with Him where He is now hidden in the heavens, and to share His glory in the coming day. If the reader fully grasps this grand and glorious truth, it will go far toward helping him to put things into their right places and leave them there.

We must now turn our attention to the very solemn, practical application of all that has passed before us to the conscience of every member of the congregation.

"And Moses called unto all Israel, and said unto them, 'Ye have seen all that the Lord did before your eyes in the land of Egypt unto Pharaoh, and unto all his servants, and unto all his land; the great temptations which thine eyes have seen, the signs, and those great miracles; yet the Lord hath not given you a heart to perceive, and eyes to see, and ears to hear, unto this day.' "

This is peculiarly solemn. The most astounding miracles and signs may pass before us, and leave *the heart* untouched. These things may produce a transient effect upon the mind and upon the natural feelings, but unless the conscience is brought into the light of the divine presence, and the heart brought under the immediate action of the truth by the power of the Spirit of God, there is no permanent result reached. Nicodemus inferred from the miracles of Christ that He was a teacher come from God; but this was not enough. He had to learn the deep and wondrous meaning of that mighty sentence, "Ye must be born again." A faith founded on miracles may leave people unsaved, unblessed, unconverted—awfully responsible, no doubt, but wholly unconverted. We read, at the close of the second chapter of John's Gospel, of many who professed to believe on Christ when they saw His miracles; but He did not commit Himself unto them. There was no divine work, nothing to be trusted. There must be a new life—a new nature, and miracles and signs cannot impart this. We must be born again—born of the Word and Spirit of God. The new life is communicated by the incorruptible seed of the gospel of God, lodged in the heart by the power of the Holy Ghost. It is not a head-belief founded on miracles, but a heart-belief in the Son of God. It is something which could never be known under law or government. "The *gift* of God is eternal life, through Jesus Christ our Lord." Precious gift! glorious source! blessed channel! Universal and everlasting praise to the Eternal Trinity!

"And I have led you forty years in the wilderness; your clothes are not waxen old upon you, and thy shoe is not waxen old upon thy foot." Wonderful clothes! wonderful shoes! God took care of them and made them last, blessed forever be His great and holy name! "Ye have not eaten bread, neither have ye drunk wine or strong drink; that ye might know that I am the Lord your God." They were fed and clothed by God's own gracious hand. "Man did eat angels' food." They had no need of wine or strong drink—no need of stimulants. "They drank of that spiritual rock that followed them, and that rock was Christ." That pure stream refreshed them in the dreary desert, and the heavenly manna sustained them day by day. All they wanted was the capacity to enjoy the divine provision.

Here, alas! like ourselves, they failed; they got tired of the heavenly food, and lusted for other things. How sad that we should be so like them! how very humbling that we should so fail to appreciate that precious One whom God has given to be our life, our portion, our object, our all in all! How terrible to find our hearts craving the wretched vanities and follies of this poor passing world—its riches, its honors, its distinctions, its pleasures, which all perish in the using, and which, even if they were lasting, are not for a moment to be compared with "the unsearchable riches of Christ"! May God, in His infinite goodness, "grant us, according to the riches of His glory, to be strengthened with might by His Spirit in the inner man; that Christ may dwell in our hearts by faith; that we, being rooted and grounded in love, may be able to comprehend with all saints what is the breadth and length and depth and height; and *to know the love of Christ,* which passeth knowledge, that we may be filled with *all the fullness of God.*" Oh, that this most blessed prayer may be answered in the deep and abiding experience of the reader and the writer!

"And when ye came unto this place, Sihon the king of Heshbon, and Og the king of Bashan"—formidable and much-dreaded foes!—"came out against us unto battle, and we smote them." And had they been ten thousand times as great and as formidable, they would have proved to be as chaff before the presence of the God of the armies of Israel. "And we took their land, and gave it for an inheritance unto the Reubenites, and to the Gadites, and to the half tribe of Manasseh." Will any one dare to compare this with what human history records respecting the invasion of South America by the Spaniards? Woe be to those who do so! they will find themselves terribly mistaken. There is this grand and all-important difference, that Israel had the direct authority of God for what they did to Sihon and Og; the Spaniards could show no such authority for what they did to the poor ignorant savages of South America. This alters the case completely. The introduction of God and His authority is the one perfect answer to every question, the divine solution of every difficulty. May we ever keep this weighty fact in the remembrance of the thoughts of our hearts, as a divine antidote against every infidel suggestion!

"Keep therefore the words of this [the Moab] covenant, and do them, *that ye may prosper in all that ye do.*" Simple obedience to the Word of God ever has been, is now, and ever shall be the deep and real secret of all true prosperity. To the Christian, of course, the prosperity is not in earthly or material things, but in heavenly and spiritual; and we must never forget that it is the very height of folly to think of prospering or making progress in the divine life if we are not yielding an implicit obedience to all the commandments of our blessed and adorable Lord and Saviour Jesus Christ. "If ye abide in Me, and My words abide in you, ye shall ask what ye will, and it shall be done unto you. Herein is My Father glorified, that ye bear much fruit; so shall ye be My disciples.

As the Father hath loved Me, so have I loved you; continue ye in My love. *If ye keep My commandments,* ye shall abide in My love; even as I have kept My Father's commandments, and abide in His love." Here is true Christian prosperity. May we earnestly long after it, and diligently pursue the proper method of attaining it.

"Ye stand this day, *all of you,* before the Lord your God; your captains of your tribes, your elders, and your officers, with all the men of Israel, *your little ones*"—touching and interesting fact!—"your wives, and *thy stranger* that is in thy camp." How exquisite, how deeply affecting, the expression, "*thy* stranger"! What a powerful appeal to Israel's heart on behalf of the stranger! "From the hewer of thy wood unto the drawer of thy water; that thou shouldest enter into covenant with the Lord thy God, and into His oath, which the Lord thy God maketh with thee this day; that He may establish thee to-day for a people unto Himself, and that He may be unto thee a God, as He hath said unto thee, and as He hath sworn unto thy fathers, to Abraham, to Isaac, and to Jacob. Neither with you only do I make this covenant and this oath, but with him that standeth here with us this day before the Lord our God, and also with him that is not here with us this day; for ye know how we have dwelt in the land of Egypt, and how we came through the nations which ye passed by; and ye have seen their abominations [that is, the objects of their worship—their false gods] and their idols, wood and stone, silver and gold, which were among them" (ver. 10-17).

This earnest appeal is not only general, but also intensely individual. This is very important. We are ever prone to generalize, and thus miss the application of truth to our individual conscience. This is a grave mistake, and a most serious loss to our souls. We are every one of us responsible to yield an implicit obedience to the precious commandments of our Lord. It is thus we enter into the real enjoyment of our relationship, as Moses says to the people, "that He may establish thee for a people unto Himself, and that He may be unto thee a God."

Nothing can be more precious. And then it is so very simple. There is no vagueness, obscurity, or mysticism about it. It is simply having His most precious commandments treasured up in our hearts, acting upon the conscience, and carried out in the life. This is the true secret of habitually realizing our relationship with our Father and with our Lord and Saviour Jesus Christ.

For any one to imagine that he can enjoy the blessed sense of intimate relationship while living in the habitual neglect of our Lord's commandments is a miserable and mischievous delusion. "If ye keep My commandments, ye shall abide in My love." This is *the* grand point; let us deeply ponder it. "If ye love Me, keep My commandments." "Not every one that saith unto Me, Lord, Lord, shall enter into the kingdom of heaven; but he that doeth the will of My Father which is in heaven." "For whosoever shall do the will of My Father which is in heaven, the same is My brother, and sister, and mother." "Circumcision is nothing, and uncircumcision is nothing, but the keeping of the commandments of God."

These are seasonable words for this day of easy-going, self-indulgent, worldly profession. May they sink down into our ears and into our hearts. May they take full possession of our whole moral being, and bring forth fruit in our individual history. We feel persuaded of the need of this practical side of things. We are in imminent danger, while seeking to keep clear of every thing like legality, of running into the opposite evil of carnal laxity. The passages of holy Scripture which we have just quoted—and they are but a few of many—supply the divine safeguard against both these pernicious and deadly errors. It is blessedly true that we are brought into the holy relationship of children by the sovereign grace of God, through the power of His Word and Spirit. This one fact cuts up by the roots the noxious weed of legality.

But then, surely the relationship has its suited affections, its duties, and its responsibilities, the due recognition of which furnishes the true remedy for the terrible evil of carnal laxity so prevalent on all hands. If we are delivered from *law-works*—as, thank

God, we are, if we are true Christians—it is not that we should be good-for-nothing self-pleasers, but that *life-works* might be produced in us, to the glory of Him whose name we bear, whose we are, and whom we are bound, by every argument, to love, obey, and serve.

May we earnestly seek to apply our hearts to this practical line of things. We are imperatively called upon to do so, and we may fully count upon the abundant grace of our Lord Jesus Christ to enable us to respond to the call, spite of the ten thousand difficulties and hindrances that lie in our way. Oh, for a deeper work of grace in our souls, a closer walk with God, a more pronounced discipleship! Let us give ourselves to the earnest pursuit of these things!

We must now proceed with the lawgiver's solemn appeal. He warns the people to take heed, "lest there should be among you man or woman or family or tribe whose heart turneth away this day from the Lord our God, to go and serve the gods of these nations; lest there should be among you *a root* that beareth gall and wormwood."

These searching words are referred to by the inspired apostle in his Epistle to the Hebrews in a very emphatic manner. *"Looking diligently,"* he says, "lest any man fail of the grace of God; lest any root of bitterness springing up trouble you, and thereby many be defiled."

What weighty words are these! how full of wholesome admonition and warning! They set forth the solemn responsibility of all Christians. We are all called upon to exercise a holy, jealous, godly care over each other, which, alas! is but little understood or recognized. We are not all called to be pastors or teachers. The passage just quoted does not refer particularly to such; it refers to all Christians, and we are bound to attend to it. We hear great complaints on all sides, of the sad lack of pastoral care. No doubt there is a great lack of true pastors in the Church of God, as there is of every other gift. This is only what we might expect. How could it be otherwise? How could we expect a profusion of spiritual gifts in our present miserable condition? The Spirit is grieved and quenched by our lamentable divisions, our worldliness, our gross unfaithfulness. Need we, then, marvel at our deplorable poverty?

But our blessed Lord is full of deep and tender compassion toward us in the midst of our ruin and spiritual desolation, and if we only humbled ourselves under His mighty hand, He would graciously lift us up, and enable us, in many ways, to meet the deficiency of pastoral gift amongst us. We might, through His precious grace, look more diligently and lovingly after one another, and seek each other's spiritual progress and prosperity in a thousand ways.

Let not the reader imagine for a moment that we mean to give the smallest countenance to prying officiousness or unwarrantable espionage on the part of Christians. Far away be the thought! We look upon such things as perfectly insufferable in the Church of God. They stand at the very moral antipodes of that loving, holy, tender, diligent pastoral care of which we speak and for which we long.

But does it not strike the reader that, while giving the widest possible berth to these most contemptible evils to which we have just referred, we might cultivate and exercise a loving, prayerful interest in one another, and a holy watchfulness and care, which might prevent many a root of bitterness from springing up? We cannot doubt it. It is quite true we are not all called to be pastors, and it is equally true that there is a grievous dearth of pastors in the Church of God. We mean, of course, true pastors—pastors given by the Head of the Church—men with a pastor's heart, and real pastoral gift and power. All this is undeniable, and for this very reason it ought to stir the hearts of the Lord's beloved people every where to seek of Him grace to enable them to exercise a tender, loving, brotherly care over one another, which might go a great way toward supplying the need of pastors amongst us. One thing is clear, that in the passage just quoted from Hebrews 12, there is nothing said about pastors. It is simply a most stirring exhortation to all Christians to exercise a mutual care, and to watch against the springing up of any root of bitterness.

And oh, how needful this is! How terrible are those roots! How bitter they are! How widely spread are their pernicious tendrils at times! What irreparable mischief they do! How many are defiled by them! How many precious links of friendship are snapped, and how many hearts broken by them! Yes, reader, and how often we have felt persuaded that a little judicious pastoral or even brotherly care, a little loving, godly counsel, might have nipped the evil in the bud, and thus hindered an incalculable amount of mischief and sorrow. May we all lay these things to heart, and earnestly seek grace to do what we can to prevent roots of bitterness springing up and spreading abroad their defiling influence.

But we must hearken to further weighty and searching words from the beloved and venerable lawgiver. He draws a most solemn picture of the end of the one who caused the root of bitterness to spring up.

"And it come to pass, when he heareth the words of this curse, *that he bless himself in his heart,* saying, I shall have peace, though I walk in the imagination of mine heart, to add drunkenness to thirst." Fatal delusion! Crying, Peace, peace! when there is no peace, but imminent wrath and judgment. "The Lord will not spare him, but then the anger of the Lord and His jealousy shall smoke against that man, and"—instead of the "peace" which he vainly promised himself—"all the curses that are written in this book shall lie upon him, and the Lord shall blot out his name from under heaven." Awful warning to all who act as roots of bitterness in the midst of the people of God, and to all who countenance them!

"And the Lord shall separate him unto evil out of all the tribes of Israel, according to all the curses of the covenant that are written in this book of the law; so that the generation to come of your children, that shall rise up after you, and the stranger that shall come from a far land, shall say, when they see the plagues of that land, and the sicknesses which the Lord hath laid upon it; and that the whole land thereof is brimstone and salt and burning, that it is not sown, nor beareth, nor any grass groweth therein, like the overthrow of Sodom and Gomorrah, Admah and Zeboim, which the Lord overthrew in His anger and in His wrath"—Soul-subduing examples of the governmental dealings of the living God, which ought to speak with a voice of thunder in the ears of all those who are turning the grace of our God into lasciviousness, and denying the Lord that bought them—"even all nations shall say, Wherefore hath the Lord done thus unto this land? What meaneth the heat of this great anger? Then men shall say, Because they have forsaken the covenant of the Lord God of their fathers, which He made with them when He brought them forth out of the land of Egypt; for they went and served other gods, and worshiped them, gods whom they knew not, and whom He had not given unto them; and the anger of the Lord was kindled against this land, to bring upon it all the curses that are written in this book; and the Lord rooted them out of their land in anger, and in wrath, and in great indignation, and cast them into another land, as it is this day" (ver. 19-28).

How peculiarly solemn is all this! What a powerful illustration of the apostle's words, "It is a fearful thing to fall into the hands of the living God"! and again, "Our God is a consuming fire"! How important that the professing church should give heed to such warning notes! Most assuredly, she is called to learn much from the history of God's dealings with His people Israel; Romans 11 is perfectly clear and conclusive as to this. The apostle, in speaking of the divine judgment upon the unbelieving branches of the olive-tree, thus appeals to christendom: "If some of the branches be broken off, and thou, being a wild olive-tree, wert graffed in among them, and with them partakest of the root and fatness of the olive-tree; boast not against the branches. But if thou boast, thou bearest not the root, but the root thee. Thou wilt say then, The branches were broken off that I might be graffed in. Well; because of unbelief they were broken off; and thou standest by faith. *Be not high-minded, but fear;* for if God spared not the natural branches, take heed lest He also spare not thee. Behold therefore the goodness and severity of God; on them which fell severity; but toward thee, goodness, *if thou continue in His goodness;* otherwise *thou also shalt be cut off.*"

Alas! the professing church has not continued in the goodness of God. It is utterly impossible to read her history in the light of Scripture and not see this. She has grievously departed, and there is nothing before her save the unmingled wrath of Almighty God. The beloved members of the body of Christ who, sad to say, are mingled with the terrible mass of corrupt profession, will be gathered out of it and taken to the place prepared in the Father's house in heaven. Then, if not before, they will see how wrong it was to have remained in connection with what was so flagrantly opposed to the mind of Christ as revealed, with divine clearness and simplicity, in the holy Scriptures.

But as to the great thing known as christendom, it will be "spued out" and "cut off." It will be given over to strong delusion, to believe a lie, "that they all might be damned who believed not the truth, but *had pleasure in unrighteousness.*"

Tremendous words! May they ring in the ears and sink down into the hearts of thousands who are going on from day to day, week to week, and year to year, content with a mere name to live, a form of godliness, but denying the power, *"lovers of pleasure rather than lovers of God."* What an awfully graphic picture of so-called Christian England! How appalling the condition and the destiny of the pleasure-hunting thousands who are rushing blindly, heedlessly, and madly down the inclined plane that leads to hopeless and everlasting misery! May God, in His infinite goodness, by the power of His Spirit and by the mighty action of His Word, rouse the hearts of His people every where to a more profound and influential sense of these things.

We must now, ere closing this section, briefly direct attention to the last verse of our chapter. It is one of those passages of Scripture sadly misunderstood and misapplied. "The secret things belong unto the Lord our God; but those things which are revealed belong unto us, and to our children forever, that we may do all the words of this law." This verse is constantly used to hinder the progress of souls in the knowledge of "the deep things of God," but its simple meaning is this: The things "revealed" are what we have had before us in the preceding chapter of this book; the things "secret," on the other hand, refer to those resources of grace which God had in store, to be unfolded when the people should have utterly failed to "do all the words of this law." The revealed things are what Israel ought to have done, but did not do; the secret things are what God would do, spite of Israel's sad and shameful failure, and they are most blessedly presented in the following chapters—the counsels of divine grace, the provisions of sovereign mercy to be displayed when Israel shall have thoroughly learnt the lesson of their utter failure under both the Moab and the Horeb-covenants.

Thus this passage, when rightly understood, so far from affording any warrant for the use so constantly made of it, encourages the heart to search into these things which, though "secret" to Israel in the plains of Moab, are fully and clearly "revealed" to us for our profit, comfort, and edification.* The Holy Spirit came down, on the day of Pentecost, to lead the disciples into *all truth.* The canon of Scripture is complete; all the purposes and counsels of God are fully revealed. The mystery of the Church com-

*1 Corinthians 2:9 is another of the misunderstood and misapplied passages. "But, as it is written, 'Eye hath not seen, nor ear heard, neither have entered into the heart of man, the things which God hath prepared for them that love Him.' " Here, people are sure to stop, and hence conclude that we cannot possibly know aught of the precious things which God has in store for us; but the very next verse proves the gross absurdity of any such conclusion. "But God *hath revealed* them unto us by His Spirit; for the Spirit searcheth all things, yea, the deep things of God. For what man knoweth the things, yea, the deep things of God. For what man knoweth the things of a man, save the spirit of man which is in him? even so the things of God knoweth no man, but the Spirit of God. Now we [that is, all the Lord's people] have received, not the spirit of the world, but the spirit which is of God; *that we might know the things that are freely given to us of God.*" Thus this passage, like Deuteronomy 19:29, teaches the very opposite of what is so constantly deduced from it. How important to examine and weigh the context of the passages which are quoted!

pletes the entire circle of divine truth. The apostle John could say to all God's children, "Ye have an unction from the Holy One, and know *all things.*"

Thus the entire New Testament abounds with evidence to prove the mistaken use that is so constantly made of Deuteronomy 29:29. We have dwelt upon it because we are aware that the Lord's beloved people are sadly hindered by it in their progress in divine knowledge. The enemy would ever seek to keep them in the dark, when they ought to be walking in the sunlight of divine revelation—to keep them as babes feeding upon milk, when they ought, as those "of full age," to be feeding upon the "strong meat" so freely provided for the Church of God. We have but little idea of how the Spirit of God is grieved and Christ dishonored by the low tone of things amongst us. How few really "know the things that are freely given to us of God"! Where are the proper privileges of the Christian understood, believed, and realized? How meagre is our apprehension of divine things! How stunted our growth! How feeble our practical exposition of the truth of God! What a blotted epistle of Christ we present!

Let us seriously ponder these things in the divine presence. Let us honestly search out the root of all this lamentable failure, and have it judged and put away, that so we may more faithfully and unmistakably declare whose we are and whom we serve. May it be more thoroughly manifest that Christ is our one absorbing object.

---

## *CHAPTER 30*

THIS chapter is one of very deep interest and importance. It is prophetic, and presents to us some of "the secret things" referred to at the close of the preceding chapter. It unfolds some of those most precious resources of grace treasured up in the heart of God, to be unfolded when Israel, having utterly failed to keep the law, should be scattered to the ends of the earth.

"And it shall come to pass, when all these things are come upon thee, the blessing and the curse, which I have set before thee, and *thou shalt call them to mind* among all the nations, whither the Lord thy God hath driven thee, and *shalt return unto the Lord thy God,* and shalt obey His voice according to all that I command thee this day, *thou and thy children, with all thine heart and with all thy soul;* that then the Lord thy God will turn thy captivity, and *have compassion upon thee,* and will return and gather thee from all the nations, whither the Lord thy God hath scattered thee."

How touching, how perfectly beautiful, is all this! It is no question of law-keeping, but something far deeper, far more precious; it is the turning of the heart—the whole heart—the whole soul to Jehovah, at a time when a literal obedience to the law is utterly impossible. It is a broken and contrite heart turning to God, and God, in deep and tender compassion, meeting that heart. This is true blessedness, at all times and in all places. It is something above and beyond all dispensational dealings and arrangements. It is God Himself, in all the fullness and ineffable blessedness of what He is, meeting a repentant soul; and we may truly say that when these two meet, all is divinely and eternally settled.

It must be perfectly clear that what we have now before us is something as far removed from law-keeping and human righteousness as heaven is above earth. The first verse of our chapter proves in the clearest possible manner that the people are viewed as in a condition in which the carrying out of the ordinances of the law is a simple impossibility. But blessed be God, there is not a spot on the face of the earth, be it ever so remote, from which the heart cannot turn to God. The *hands* might not be able to present a victim for the altar, the *feet* might not be able to travel to the appointed place of worship, but the *heart* could travel to God. Yes; the poor crushed, broken, contrite heart could go directly to God, and God, in the depth of His compassion and tender mercy, could meet that heart, bind it up, and fill it to overflowing with the rich comfort and consolation of His love, and the full joy of His salvation.

But let us hearken yet further to those "secret things" which "belong to God"—things precious beyond all human thought. "If any of thine be driven out unto *the utmost parts of heaven*"— as far as they could go—"from thence will the Lord thy God *gather thee,* and from thence will He *fetch thee;* and the Lord thy God will bring thee into the land which thy fathers possessed, and thou shalt possess it; and *He will do thee good,* and multiply thee above thy fathers."

How precious is all this! But there is something far better still. Not only will He gather them, fetch them, and multiply them —not only will He act in power *for* them, but He will do a mighty work of grace *in* them of far more value than any outward prosperity however desirable. "And the Lord thy God will *circumcise thine heart*"—the very centre of the whole moral being, the source of all those influences which go to form the character—"and the heart of thy seed, to love the Lord thy God with all thine heart"—the grand moral regulator of the entire life—"and with all thy soul, that thou mayest live. And the Lord thy God will put all these curses upon thine enemies, and on them that hate thee, which persecuted thee"—a solemn word for all those nations who have ever sought to oppress the Jews!— "And thou shalt return, and obey the voice of the Lord, and do all His commandments, which I command thee this day."

Nothing can be more morally lovely than all this. The people gathered, fetched, multiplied, blessed, circumcised in heart, thoroughly devoted to Jehovah, and yielding a whole-hearted, loving obedience to all His precious commandments! What can exceed this in blessedness for a people on the earth?

"And the Lord thy God will make thee plenteous on every work of thine hand, in the fruit of thy body, and in the fruit of thy cattle, and in the fruit of thy land, for good; for the Lord will again rejoice over thee for good, as He rejoiced over thy fathers: if thou shalt hearken unto the voice of the Lord thy God, to keep His commandments and His statutes which are written in this book of the law, and if thou turn unto the Lord thy God, with all thine heart and with all thy soul. For this commandment which I command thee this day, it is not hidden from thee, neither is it far off. It is not in heaven, that thou shouldest say, Who shall go up for us to heaven, and bring it unto us, that we may hear it and do it? Neither is it beyond the sea, that thou shouldest say, Who shall go over the sea for us, and bring it unto us, that we may hear it and do it? But the Word is *very nigh unto thee,* in thy *mouth,* and in thy *heart,* that thou mayest do it" (ver. 10-14).

This is a singularly interesting passage. It furnishes a key to "the secret things" already referred to, and sets forth the great principles of divine righteousness, in vivid and beautiful contrast to legal righteousness in every possible aspect. According to the truth here unfolded, it matters not in the least where a soul may be—here, there, or any where; "the Word is nigh thee." It could not possibly be nigher. What could be nigher than "in thy mouth, and in thy heart"? We need not, as we say, move a muscle to get it. If it were above us or beyond us, reason would that we might complain of our utter inability to reach it; but no, there is no need of either *hands* or *feet* in this most blessed and all-important matter. The *heart* and the *mouth* are here called into exercise.

There is a very beautiful allusion to the above passage in the tenth chapter of the Epistle to the Romans, to which the reader may refer with much interest and profit. Indeed, it is so full of evangelic sweetness, that we must quote it.

"Brethren, my heart's desire and prayer to God for Israel is, that they might be saved. For I bear them record, that they have a zeal of God, but not according to knowledge. For they, being *ignorant of God's righteousness,* and *going about* to establish their own righteousness, *have not submitted themselves* unto the righteousness of God. For Christ is the end of the law for righteousness to *every one that believeth*"—not to every one who *says* he believes, as in James 2:14. "For Moses describeth the righteousness which is of the law, that the man who doeth those things shall live by them. But the righteousness which is of faith speaketh on this wise: Say not in thine heart, Who shall ascend into heaven? (that is, to bring Christ down)"—Striking parenthesis! Marvelous instance of the Spirit's use of Old Testament Scripture! It bears the distinct stamp of His master-hand, "or, Who shall descend into the deep? (that is, to bring up Christ again from the dead.) But what saith it? The Word is nigh thee, even in thy mouth, and in thy heart; that is, *the word of faith, which we preach;"*—How perfectly beautiful the addition! Who but the Spirit could have supplied it?—"that if thou shalt *confess with thy mouth* the Lord Jesus, and shalt *believe in thine heart* that God hath raised Him from the dead, thou shalt be saved. For with the heart man believeth unto righteousness, and with the mouth confession is made unto salvation. For the Scripture saith, 'Whosoever believeth on Him shall not be ashamed.' "

Mark this beautiful word—"whosoever." It most assuredly takes in the Jew. It meets him wherever he may be, a poor exile at the very ends of the earth, under circumstances where obedience to the law as such is simply impossible, but where the rich and precious grace of God and His most glorious salvation could meet him in the depth of his need. There, though he could not keep the law, he could confess with his mouth the Lord Jesus, and believe in his heart that God had raised Him from the dead; and this is salvation.

But then, if it be "whosoever," it cannot possibly be confined to the Jew; nay, it cannot be confined at all; and hence the apostle goes on to say, "There *is* no difference between the Jew and the Greek." There *was* the greatest possible difference under the law. There could not be a broader or more distinct line of demarkation than that which the lawgiver had drawn between the Jew and the Greek; but that line is obliterated, for a double reason: first, because "all have sinned and come short of the glory of God" (chap. 3:23); and secondly, because "the same Lord over all is rich unto all that call upon Him; for whosoever shall call upon the name of the Lord shall be saved."

How blessedly simple! "Calling"—"believing"—"confessing"! Nothing can exceed the transcendent grace that shines in these words. No doubt it is assumed that the soul is really in earnest—that the *heart* is engaged. God deals in moral realities. It is not a nominal, notional head-belief; but divine faith wrought in the heart by the Holy Ghost—a living faith, which connects the soul, in a divine way and by an everlasting link, to Christ.

And then there is the confessing with the mouth the Lord Jesus. This is of cardinal importance. A man may say, I believe in my heart, but I am not one for parading my religious belief. I am not a talker. I keep my religion to myself. It is entirely a matter between my soul and God; I do not believe in that perpetual intruding our religious impressions upon other people. Many who talk loudly and largely about their religion in public, make but a sorry figure in private, and I certainly do not want to be identified with such. I utterly abhor all cant. Deeds, not words, for me.

All this sounds very plausible, but it cannot stand for a moment in the light of Romans 10:9. There must be the confession with the mouth. Many would like to be saved by Christ, but they shrink from the reproach of confessing His precious Name. They would like to get to heaven when they die, but they do not want to be identified with a rejected Christ. Now God does not own such. He looks for the full, bold, clear confession of Christ, in the face of a hostile world. Our Lord Christ, too, looks for this confession. He declares that whoso confesses Him before men, He will confess before the angels of God; but whoso denies Him before men, He will deny before the angels of God. The thief on the cross exhibited the two great branches of true saving faith. He believed with his heart, and confessed with his mouth. Yes, he gave a flat contradiction to the whole world on the most vital question that ever was or ever could be raised, and that question was Christ. He was a thoroughly pronounced disciple of Christ. Oh, that there were more such! There is a terrible amount of indefiniteness and cold half-heartedness in the professing church, grievous to the Holy Ghost, offensive to Christ, hateful to God. We long for bold decision, out-and-out, unmistakable testimony to the Lord Jesus. May God the Holy Spirit stir up all our hearts, and lead us forth, in more thorough consecration of heart, to that blessed One who freely gave His life to save us from everlasting burnings!

We shall close this section by quoting for the reader the last few verses of our chapter, in which Moses makes a peculiarly solemn appeal to the hearts and consciences of the people. It is a most powerful word of exhortation.

"See, I have set before thee this day *life and good* and *death and evil.*" Thus it is ever in the government of God. The two things are inseparably linked together. Let no man dare to snap the link. God "will render to every man according to his deeds; to them who, by patient continuance in well-doing, seek for glory and honor and immortality, eternal life; but unto them that are contentious, and do not obey the truth, but obey unrighteousness, indignation and wrath, tribulation and anguish, upon *every soul of man that doeth evil,* of the Jew first, and also of the Gentile; but glory, honor, and peace to *every man that worketh good,* to the Jew first, and also to the Gentile: *for there is no respect of persons with God*" (Rom. 2: 6-11).

The apostle does not, in this great practical passage, go into the question of power; he simply states the broad fact—a fact applicable at all times and under all dispensations—government, law, and Christianity; it ever holds good that "God will render to every man according to his deeds." This is of the very last possible importance. May we ever bear it in mind. It may perhaps be said, Are not Christians under grace? Yes, thank God; but does this weaken, in the smallest degree, the grand governmental principle stated above? Nay, it strengthens and confirms it immensely.

But again, some may feel disposed to say, Can any unconverted person do good? We reply, This question is not raised in the Scripture just quoted. Every one taught of God knows and feels and owns that not one atom of "good" has ever been done in this world but by the grace of God; that man left to himself will do evil only—evil continually. "Every good gift and every perfect gift is from above, and cometh down from the Father of lights." All this is most blessedly true, and thankfully owned by every pious soul, but it leaves wholly untouched the fact, set forth in Deuteronomy 30 and confirmed by Romans 2, that *life and good, death and evil,* are bound together by an inseparable link. May we never forget it. May it ever abide in the remembrance of the thoughts of our hearts.

"See, I have set before thee this day life and good, and death and evil; in that I command thee this day to love the Lord thy God, to walk in His ways, and to keep His commandments and His statutes and His judgments, that thou mayest live and multiply; and the Lord thy God shall bless thee in the land whither thou goest to possess it. But if *thine heart turn away,* so that *thou wilt not hear,* but shalt be drawn away, and worship other gods, and serve them; I denounce unto you this day, that ye shall surely perish, and that ye shall not prolong your days upon the land, whither thou passest over Jordan to go to possess it. I call heaven and earth to record this day against you, that I have set before you life and death, blessing and cursing; therefore choose life, that both thou and thy seed may live; that thou mayest love the Lord thy God, and that thou mayest obey His voice, and that thou mayest *cleave unto Him*"—the all-important, essential thing for each, for all, the very spring and power of all true religion, in every age, in every place—"*for He is thy life,* and *the length of thy days*"—How close! how vital! how real! how very precious!—"that thou mayest dwell in the land which the Lord sware unto thy fathers, to Abraham, to Isaac, and to Jacob, to give them" (ver. 15-20).

Nothing can be more solemn than this closing appeal to the congregation; it is in full keeping with the tone and character of the entire book of Deuteronomy—a book marked throughout by the most powerful exhortations that ever fell on mortal ears. We have no such soul-stirring appeals in any of the preceding sections of the Pentateuch. Each book, we need not say, has its own specific niche to fill, its own distinct object and character; but the great burden of Deuteronomy, from beginning to end, is exhortation; its thesis, the Word of God; its object, obedience—whole-hearted, earnest, loving obedience, grounded on a known relationship and enjoyed privileges.

---

## *CHAPTER 31*

THE heart of Moses still lingers, with deep tenderness and affectionate solicitude, over the congregation. It seems as though he could never weary of pouring into their ears his earnest exhortations. He felt their need, he foresaw their danger, and, like a true and faithful shepherd, he sought, with all the deep and tender affection of His large, loving heart, to prepare them for what was before them. No one can read his closing words without being struck with their peculiarly solemn tone. They remind us of Paul's touching farewell to the elders of Ephesus. Both these beloved and honored servants realized, in a very vivid manner, the seriousness of their own position and that of the persons they were addressing. They felt the uncommon gravity of the interests at stake, and the urgent need of the most faithful dealing with the heart and conscience. This will account for what we may term the awful solemnity of their appeals. All who really enter into the situation and destiny of the people of God in a world like this *must* be serious. The true sense of these things, the apprehension of them in the divine presence, must, of necessity, impart a holy gravity to the character, and a special pungency and power to the testimony.

"And Moses went and spake these words unto all Israel. And he said unto them, 'I am a hundred and twenty years old this day; I can no more go out and come in; also the Lord hath said unto me, Thou shalt not go over this Jordan.' " How very touching this allusion to his great age, and this fresh and final reference to the solemn governmental dealing of God with himself personally! The direct and manifest object of both was, to give effect to his appeal to the hearts and consciences of the people, to strengthen the moral lever by which this beloved and honored servant of God sought to move them in the direction of simple obedience. If he points to his gray hairs, or to the holy discipline exercised toward him, it most assuredly is not for the purpose of bringing himself, his circumstances, or his feelings before them, but simply to touch the deepest springs of their moral being by every possible means.

"The Lord thy God, He will go over before thee, and He will destroy these nations from before thee, and thou shalt possess them; and Joshua, he shall go over before thee, as the Lord hath said. And the Lord shall do unto them as He did to Sihon and to Og, kings of the Amorites, and unto the land of them whom He destroyed. And the Lord shall give them up before your face, that ye may do unto them according unto all the commandments which I have commanded you." Not a word of murmuring or repining as to himself, not the faintest tinge of envy or jealousy in his reference to the one who was to take his place, not the most distant approach to aught of the kind; every selfish consideration is swallowed up in the one grand object of encouraging the hearts of the people to tread, with firm step, the pathway of obedience, which was then, is now, and ever must be the path of victory, the path of blessing, the path of peace.

"Be strong and of a good courage, fear not, nor be afraid of them; for the Lord thy God, He it is that doth go with thee; He will not fail thee nor forsake thee." What precious, soul-sustaining words are these! How eminently calculated to lift the heart above every discouraging influence! The blessed consciousness of the Lord's presence with us, and the remembrance of His gracious ways with us, in days gone by, must ever prove the true secret of strength in moving onward. The same mighty hand which had subdued before them Sihon and Og, could subdue all the kings of Canaan. The Amorites were quite as formidable as the Canaanites; Jehovah was more than a match for all. "We have heard with our ears, O God, our fathers have told us, what work Thou didst in their days, in the times of old. How Thou didst drive out the heathen with Thy hand, and plantedst them; how Thou didst afflict the people, and cast them out."

Only think of God driving out people with His own hand! What an answer to all the arguments and difficulties of a morbid sentimentality! How very shallow and erroneous are the thoughts of some in reference to the governmental ways of God! How miserably one-sided their notions of His character and actings! How perfectly absurd the attempt to measure God by the standard of human judgment and feeling! It is very evident that Moses had not the smallest particle of sympathy with such sentiments when he addressed to the congregation of Israel the magnificent exhortation quoted above. He knew something of the gravity and solemnity of the government of God, something, too, of the blessedness of having Him as a shield in the day of battle, a refuge and a resource in every hour of peril and need.

Let us hearken to his encouraging words addressed to the man who was to succeed him. "And Moses called unto Joshua, and said unto him in the sight of all Israel, *'Be strong and of a good courage;* for thou must go with this people unto the land which the Lord hath sworn unto their fathers to give them; and thou shalt cause them to inherit it. And the Lord, He it is that doth go before thee; He will be with thee; He will not fail thee, neither forsake thee; fear not, neither be dismayed.' "

Joshua needed a special word for himself, as one called to occupy a prominent and very distinguished place in the congregation. But the word to him embodies the same precious truth as that addressed to the whole assembly. He is assured of the divine presence and power with him. This is enough for each, for all; for Joshua as for the most obscure member of the assembly. Yes, reader, and enough for thee, whoever thou art, or whatever be thy sphere of action. It matters not in the least what difficulties or dangers may lie before us, our God is amply sufficient for all. If only we have the sense of the Lord's presence with us, and the authority of His Word for the work in which we are engaged, we may move on with joyful confidence, spite of ten thousand difficulties and hostile influences.

"And Moses wrote this law, and delivered it unto the priests the sons of Levi, which bear the ark of the covenant of the Lord, and unto all the elders of Israel. And Moses commanded them, saying, 'At the end of every seven years, in the solemnity of the year of release, in the feast of tabernacles, when *all Israel* is come to appear before the Lord thy God in the place which He shall choose, thou shalt read this law before all Israel, in their hearing. Gather the people together, *men* and *women* and *children,* and *thy stranger* that is within thy gates, that they may *hear,* and that they may *learn,* and *fear* the Lord your God, and *observe to do all the words* of this law; and that *their children, which have not known any thing, may hear, and learn to fear the Lord your God,* as long as ye live in the land whither ye go over Jordan to possess it" (ver. 9-35).

Two things in the foregoing passage claim our special attention; first, the fact that Jehovah attached the most solemn importance to the public assembly of His people for the purpose of hearing His Word. "All Israel"—"men, women, and children"—with the stranger who had cast in his lot amongst them, were commanded to assemble themselves together to hear the reading of the book of the law of God, that all might learn His holy will and their duty. Each member of the assembly, from the eldest to the youngest, was to be brought into direct personal contact with the revealed will of Jehovah, that each one might know his solemn responsibility.

And secondly, we have to weigh the fact that the children were to be gathered before the Lord to hearken to His Word. Both these facts are full of weighty instruction for all the members of the Church of God—instruction urgently called for on all sides. There is a most deplorable amount of failure as to these two points. We sadly neglect the assembling of ourselves together for the simple reading of the holy Scriptures. There does not seem to be sufficient attraction in the Word of God itself to bring us together. There is an unhealthy craving for other things; human oratory, music, religious excitement of some kind or other seems needful to bring people together—any thing and every thing but the precious Word of God.

It will perhaps be said that people have the Word of God in their houses, that it is quite different now from what it was with Israel; every one can read the Scriptures at home, and there is not the same necessity for the public reading. Such a plea will not stand the test of truth for a moment. We may rest assured, if the Word of God were loved and prized and studied in private and in the family, it would be loved and prized and studied in public. We should delight to gather together around the fountain of holy Scripture, to drink, in happy fellowship, of the living water, for our common refreshment and blessing.

But it is not so. The Word of God is not loved and studied, either privately or publicly. Trashy literature is devoured in private, and music, ritualistic services, and imposing ceremonies are eagerly sought after in public. Thousands will flock to hear music, and pay for admission, but how few care for a meeting to read the holy Scriptures! These are facts, and facts are powerful arguments. We cannot get over them. There is a growing thirst for religious excitement, and a growing distaste for the calm study of holy Scripture and the spiritual exercises of the Christian assembly. It is perfectly useless to deny it. We cannot shut our eyes to it. The evidence of it meets us on every hand.

Thank God, there are a few, here and there, who really love the Word of God, and delight to meet, in holy fellowship, for the study of its precious truths. May the Lord increase the number of such, and bless them abundantly. May our lot be cast with them, "till traveling days are done." They are but an obscure and feeble remnant every where; but they love Christ and cleave to His Word, and their richest enjoyment is, to get together and think and speak and sing of Him. May God bless them and keep them. May He deepen His precious work in their souls, and bind them more closely to Himself and one another, and thus prepare them, in the state of their affections, for the appearing of "the Bright and Morning Star."

We must now turn for a few moments to the closing verses of our chapter, in which Jehovah speaks to His beloved and honored servant, in tones of deep and touching solemnity, as to his own death, and as to Israel's dark and gloomy future.

"And the Lord said unto Moses, 'Behold, thy days approach that thou must die: call Joshua, and present yourselves in the tabernacle of the congregation, that I may give him a charge.' And Moses and Joshua went and presented themselves in the tabernacle of the congregation. And the Lord appeared in the tabernacle in a pillar of a cloud; and the pillar of the cloud stood over the door of the tabernacle. And the Lord said unto Moses, 'Behold, thou shalt sleep with thy fathers; and this people will rise up and go a whoring after the gods of the strangers of the land, whither they go to be among them, and will forsake Me, and break My covenant which I have made with them. Then My anger shall be kindled against them in that day, and I will forsake them, and I will hide My face from them, and they shall be devoured, and many evils and troubles shall befall them; so that they will say in that day, *Are not these evils come upon us because our God is not among us?* And I will surely hide My face in that day, for all the evils which they shall have wrought, in that they are turned unto other gods.' "

"Their sorrows shall be multiplied that hasten after another god." So says the Spirit of Christ in Psalm 16. Israel has proved, is proving, and shall yet more fully prove the solemn truth of these words. Their history in the past, their present dispersion and desolation, and, beyond all, that "great tribulation" through which they have yet to pass, at "the time of the end"—all go to confirm and illustrate the truth that the sure and certain way to multiply our sorrows is, to turn away from the Lord and look to any creature-resource. This is one of the many and varied practical lessons which we have to gather from the marvelous history of the seed of Abraham. May we learn it effectually. May we learn to cleave to the Lord with purpose of heart, and turn away, with holy decision, from every other object. This, we feel persuaded, is the only path of true happiness and peace. May we ever be found in it.

"Now therefore write ye this song for you, and teach it the children of Israel; put it in their mouths, *that this song may be a witness for Me against the children of Israel.* For when I shall have brought them into the land which I sware unto their fathers, that floweth with milk and honey; and they shall have eaten and filled themselves and waxen fat; then will they turn unto other gods, and serve them, and provoke Me, and break My covenant. And it shall come to pass, when many evils and troubles are befallen them, that this song shall testify against them as a witness; for it shall not be forgotten out of the mouths of their seed; for I know their imaginations which they go about, even now, before I have brought them into the land which I sware."

How deeply affecting, how peculiarly solemn, is all this! Instead of Israel being a witness for Jehovah before all nations, the song of Moses was to be a witness for Jehovah against the children of Israel. They were called to be His witnesses; they were responsible to declare His name and to show forth His praise in that land into which, in His faithfulness and sovereign mercy, He conducted them; but alas! they utterly and shamefully failed, and hence, in view of this sad and most humiliating failure, a song was to be written which, in the first place, as we shall see, sets forth, in most magnificent strains, the glory of God; and secondly, records, in accents of inflexible faithfulness, Israel's deplorable failure, in every stage of their history.

"Moses therefore wrote this song the same day, and taught it the children of Israel. And he gave Joshua the son of Nun a charge, and said, *'Be strong, and of a good courage;* for thou shalt bring the children of Israel into the land which I sware unto them; and *I will be with thee."* Joshua was not to be discouraged or faint-hearted because of the predicted unfaithfulness of the people. He was, like his great progenitor, to be strong in faith giving glory to God. He was to move forward with joyful confidence, leaning on the arm and confiding in the word of Jehovah, the covenant-God of Israel, in nothing terrified by his adversaries, but resting in the precious, soul-sustaining assurance that, however the seed of Abraham might fail to obey, and, as a consequence, bring down judgment on themselves, yet the God of Abraham would infallibly maintain and make good His promise, and glorify His name in the final restoration and everlasting blessing of His chosen people.

All this comes out with uncommon vividness and power in the song of Moses, and Joshua was called to serve in the faith of it. He was to fix his eye, not upon Israel's ways, but upon the eternal stability of the divine covenant with Abraham. He was to conduct Israel across the Jordan and plant them in that fair inheritance designed for them in the purpose of God. Had Joshua occupied his mind with Israel, he must have flung down his sword and given up in despair; but no, he had to encourage himself in the Lord his God, and serve in the energy of a faith that endures as seeing Him who is invisible.

Precious, soul-sustaining, God-honoring faith! May the reader, whatever be his line of life or sphere of action, know, in the profoundest depths of his soul, the moral power of this divine principle. May every beloved child of God and every servant of Christ know it. It is the only thing which will enable us to grapple with the difficulties, hindrances, and hostile influences which surround us in the scene through which we are passing, and to finish our course with joy.

"And it came to pass when Moses had made an end of writing the words of this law in a book, until they were finished, that Moses commanded the Levites, which bare the ark of the covenant of the Lord, saying, 'Take this book of the law, and put it in the side of the ark of the covenant of the Lord your God, *that it may be there for a witness against thee.* For I know thy rebellion, and thy stiff neck; behold, while I am yet alive with you this day, ye have been rebellious against the Lord; and how much more after my death? Gather unto me all the elders of your tribes, and your officers, that I may speak these words in their ears, and call heaven and earth to record against them. For I know that after my death ye will utterly corrupt yourselves, and turn aside from the way which I have commanded you; and evil will befall you in the latter days; because ye will do evil in the sight of the Lord, to provoke Him to anger through the work of your hands.' "

How forcibly we are here reminded of Paul's farewell address to the elders of Ephesus! "For I know this, that after my departing shall grievous wolves enter in among you, not sparing the flock. Also from among your own selves shall men arise, speaking perverse things, to draw away disciples after them. Therefore *watch, and remember,* that by the space of three years I ceased not to warn every one night and day with tears. And now, brethren, I commend you to God, and to the word of His grace, which is able to build you up, and to give you an inheritance among all them which are sanctified" (Act 20:29-32).

Man is the same always and every where. His history is a blotted one from beginning to end. But oh, it is such a relief and solace to the heart to know and remember that God is ever the same, and His Word abides and is "settled forever in heaven." It was hid in the side of the ark of the covenant and there preserved intact, spite of all the grievous sin and folly of the people. This gives sweet rest to the heart at all times, in the face of human failure, and the wreck and ruin of every thing committed to man's hand. "The Word of our God shall stand forever;" and while it bears a true and solemn testimony against man and his ways, it also conveys home to the heart the most precious and tranquilizing assurance that God is above all man's sin and folly, that His resources are absolutely inexhaustible, and that ere long His glory shall shine out and fill the whole scene. The Lord be praised for the deep consolation of all this!

---

## CHAPTER 32

"AND Moses spake in the ears of all the congregation of Israel the words of this song, until they were ended." It is not too much to say that one of the very grandest and most comprehensive sections in the divine volume now lies open before us and claims our prayerful attention. It takes in the whole range of God's dealings with Israel from first to last, and presents a most solemn record of their grievous sin and of divine wrath and judgment. But, blessed be God, it begins and ends with Him; and this is full of deepest and richest blessing for the soul. If it were not so, if we had only the melancholy story of man's ways, we should be completely overwhelmed; but in this magnificent song, as indeed in the entire volume, we begin with God and we end with God. This tranquilizes the spirit most blessedly, and enables us, in calm and holy confidence, to pursue the history of man, to see every thing going to pieces in his hands, and to mark the actings of the enemy in opposition to the counsels and purposes of God. We can afford to see the complete failure and ruin of the creature, in every shape and form, because we know and are assured that God will be God in spite of every thing. He will have the upper hand in the end, and then all will be—must be right. God shall be all in all, and there shall be neither enemy nor evil occurrent throughout that vast universe of bliss of which our adorable Lord Christ shall be the central sun forever.

But we must turn to the song.

"Give ear, O ye heavens, and I will speak; and hear, O earth, the words of my mouth." Heaven and earth are summoned to hearken to this magnificent outpouring. Its range is commensurate with its vast moral importance. "My doctrine shall drop as the rain, my speech shall distill as the dew, as the small rain upon the tender herb, and as the showers upon the grass; because I will publish the name of the Lord; ascribe ye greatness unto our God."

Here lies the solid, the imperishable foundation of every thing. Come what may, the name of our God shall stand forever. No power of earth or hell can possibly countervail the divine purpose, or hinder the outshining of the divine glory. What sweet rest this gives the heart in the midst of this dark, sorrowful, sin-stricken world, and in the face of the apparently successful schemes of the enemy! Our refuge, our resource, our sweet relief and solace, are found in the name of the Lord our God, the God and Father of our Lord Jesus Christ. Truly the publication of that blessed name must ever be as the refreshing dew and tender rain falling upon the heart. This is, of a truth, the divine and heavenly doctrine on which the soul can feed, and by which it is sustained, at all times, and under all circumstances.

"He is *the* Rock"—not merely *a* rock. There is, there can be, no other Rock but Himself. Eternal and universal homage to His glorious name!—"His work is perfect"—not a single flaw in aught that comes from His blessed hand; all bears the stamp of absolute perfection. This will be made manifest to all created intelligences by and by. It is manifest to faith now, and is a spring of divine consolation to all true believers. The very thought of it distills as the dew upon the thirsty soul. "For *all* His ways are judgment; a God of truth, and without iniquity; just and right is He." Infidels may cavil and sneer; they may, in their fancied wisdom, try to pick holes in the divine actings; but their folly shall be manifest to all. "Let God be true, but every man a liar; as it is written, 'That Thou mightest be justified in Thy sayings, and mightest overcome when Thou art judged.' " God must have the upper hand in the end. Let men beware how they presume to call in question the sayings and doings of the only true, the only wise, and the almighty God.

There is something uncommonly fine in the opening notes of this song. It gives the sweetest rest to the heart to know that however man, and even the people of God, may fail and come to ruin, yet we have to do with One who abideth faithful and cannot deny Himself, whose ways are absolutely perfect, and who, when the enemy has done his very utmost, and brought all his malignant designs to a head, shall glorify Himself, and bring in universal and everlasting blessedness.

True, He has to execute judgment upon man's ways. He is constrained to take down the rod of discipline and use it, at times, with terrible severity upon His own people. He is perfectly intolerant of evil in those who bear His holy name. All this comes out, with special solemnity in the song before us. Israel's ways are exposed and dealt with unsparingly; nothing is allowed to pass; all is set forth with holy precision and faithfulness. Thus we read, "They have corrupted themselves; their spot is not the spot of His children; they are a perverse and crooked generation. Do ye thus requite the Lord, O foolish people and unwise? is not He thy Father that hath bought thee? Hath He not made thee, and established thee?"

Here we have the first note of reproof in this song, but no sooner has it fallen on the ear than it is followed by a most precious outpouring of testimony to the goodness, loving-kindness, faithfulness, and tender mercy of Jehovah, the Elohim of Israel, and the Most High, or Elion of all the earth. "Remember the days of old, consider the years of many generations; ask thy father, and he will show thee; thy elders, and they will tell thee; when the Most High [God's millennial title] divided to the nations their inheritance, when He separated the sons of Adam, He set the bounds of the people according to the number of the children of Israel."

What a glorious fact is here unfolded to our view! a fact but little understood or taken account of by the nations of the earth. How little do men consider that, in the original settlement of the great national boundaries, the Most High had direct reference to "the children of Israel"! Yet thus it was, and the reader should seek to grasp this grand and intensely interesting fact. When we look at geography and history from a divine stand-point, we find that Canaan and the seed of Jacob are God's centre. Yes; Canaan, a little strip of land lying along the eastern coast of the Mediterranean, with an area of eleven thousand square miles, (about a third of the extent of Ireland,) is the centre of God's geography, and the twelve tribes of Israel are the central object of God's history. How little have geographers and historians thought of this! They have described countries, and written the history of nations, which, in geographical extent and political importance, far outstrip Palestine and its people, according to human thinking, but which, in God's account, are as nothing compared with that little strip of land which He deigns to call His own, and which it is His fixed purpose to inherit through the seed of Abraham His friend.*

We cannot attempt to dwell upon this most important and suggestive fact, but we would ask the reader to give it his serious consideration. He will find it fully developed and strikingly illustrated in the prophetic Scriptures of the Old and New Testaments. "The Lord's portion is His people; Jacob is the lot of His inheritance. He found him in a desert land, and in the waste howling wilderness; He led him about, He instructed him, He kept him *as the apple of His eye*"—the most sensitive, delicate part of the human body. "As an eagle stirreth up her nest, fluttereth over her young, spreadeth abroad her wings, taketh them, beareth them upon her wings"—to teach them to fly and to keep them from falling—"so the Lord alone did lead him, and there was no strange god with him. He made him ride on the high places of the earth, that he might eat the increase of the fields; and He made him to suck honey out of the rock, and oil out of the flinty rock; butter of kine, and milk of sheep, with fat of lambs, and rams of the breed of Bashan, and goats, with the fat of kidneys of wheat; and thou didst drink the pure blood of the grape."

Need we say that the primary application of all this is to Israel? No doubt the Church may learn from it and profit by it, but to apply it to the Church would involve a double mistake, a mistake of the most serious nature; it would involve nothing less than the reducing of the Church from a heavenly to an earthly level, and the most unwarrantable interference with Israel's divinely appointed place and portion. What, we may lawfully inquire, had the Church of God, the body of Christ, to do with the settlement of the nations of the earth? Nothing whatever. The Church, *according to the mind of God,* is a stranger on the earth. Her portion, her hope, her home, her inheritance, her all, is heavenly. It would make no difference in the current of this world's history if the Church had never been heard of. Her calling, her walk, her destiny, her whole character and course, her principles and morals, are or ought to be heavenly. The Church has nothing to do with the politics of this world. Her citizenship is in heaven, from whence she looks for the Saviour. She proves false to her Lord, false to her calling, false to her principles, insofar as she meddles with the affairs of nations. It is her high and holy privilege to be linked and morally identified with a

*How true it is that God's thoughts are not man's thoughts, or His ways as man's ways! Man attaches importance to extensive territories, material strength, pecuniary resources, well-disciplined armies, powerful fleets; God, on the contrary, takes no account of such things; they are to Him as the small dust of the balance. "Have ye not known? have ye not heard? hath it not been told you from the beginning? have ye not understood from the foundations of the earth? It is He that sitteth upon the circle of the earth, and the inhabitants thereof are as grasshoppers; that stretcheth out the heavens as a curtain, and spreadeth them out as a tent to dwell in; that bringeth the princes to nothing; He maketh the judges of the earth as vanity." Hence we may see the moral reason why, in selecting a country to be the centre of His earthly plans and counsels, Jehovah did not select one of vast extent, but a very small and insignificant strip of land, of little account in the thoughts of men. But oh, what importance attaches to that little spot! what principles have been unfolded there! what events have taken place there! what deeds have been done there! what plans and purposes are yet to be wrought out there! There is not a spot on the face of the earth so interesting to the heart of God as the land of Canaan and the city of Jerusalem. Scripture teems with evidence as to this: we could fill a small volume with proofs. The time is rapidly approaching when living facts will do what the fullest and clearest testimony of Scripture fails to do, namely, convince men that the land of Israel was, is, and ever shall be God's earthly centre. All other nations owe their importance, their interest, their place in the pages of inspiration, simply to the fact of their being, in some way or other, connected with the land and people of Israel. How little do historians know or think of this! But surely every one who loves God ought to know it and ponder it.

rejected, crucified, risen, and glorified Christ. She has no more to do with the present system of things, or with the current of this world's history, than her glorified Head in the heavens. "They," says our Lord Christ, speaking of His people, "are not of the world, even as I am not of the world."

This is conclusive. It fixes our position and our path in the most precise and definite way possible. "As He is, so are we in this world." This involves a double truth, namely, our perfect acceptance with God and our complete separation from the world. We are *in* the world, but not *of* it. We have to pass through it as pilgrims and strangers, looking out for the coming of our Lord, the appearing of the Bright and Morning Star. It is not part of our business to interfere with municipal or political matters. We are called and exhorted to obey the powers that be, to pray for all in authority, to pay tribute, and owe no man any thing; "to be blameless and harmless, the sons of God without rebuke in the midst of a crooked and perverse nation," among whom we are to "shine as lights in the world, holding forth the word of life."

From all this we may gather something of the immense practical importance of "rightly dividing the word of truth." We have but little idea of the injury done, both to the truth of God and to the souls of His people, by confounding Israel with the Church—the earthly and the heavenly. It hinders all progress in the knowledge of Scripture, and mars the integrity of Christian walk and testimony. This may seem a strong statement, but we have seen the truth of it painfully illustrated times without number; and we feel that we cannot too urgently call the attention of the reader to the subject. We have more than once referred to it in the progress of our studies on the Pentateuch, and therefore we shall not further pursue it here, but proceed with our chapter.

At verse 15, we reach a very different note in the song of Moses. Up to this point, we have had before us God and His actings, His purposes, His counsels, His thoughts, His loving interest in His people Israel, His tender, gracious dealings with them. All this is full of deepest, richest blessing. There is, there can be, no drawback here. When we have God and His ways before us, there is no hindrance to the heart's enjoyment. All is perfection—absolute, divine perfection, and as we dwell upon it, we are filled with wonder, love, and praise.

But there is the human side, and here, alas! all is failure and disappointment. Thus at the fifteenth verse of our chapter we read, "But Jeshurun waxed fat and kicked"—what a very full and suggestive statement! How vividly it presents, in its brief compass, the moral history of Israel!—"thou art waxen fat, thou art grown thick, thou art covered with fatness; then he forsook God which made him, and lightly esteemed the Rock of his salvation. They provoked Him to jealousy with strange gods, with abominations provoked they Him to anger. They sacrificed unto devils, not to God; to gods whom they knew not, to new gods that came newly up, whom your fathers feared not. Of the Rock that begat thee thou art unmindful, and hast forgotten God that formed thee."

There is a solemn voice in all this for the writer and the reader. We are each of us in danger of treading the moral path indicated by the words just quoted. Surrounded on all hands by the rich and varied mercies of God, we are apt to make use of them to nourish a spirit of self-complacency. We make use of the gifts to shut out the Giver. In a word, we, too, like Israel, wax fat and kick—we forget God. We lose the sweet and precious sense of His presence and of His perfect sufficiency, and turn to other objects, as Israel did to false gods. How often do we forget the Rock that begat us, the God that formed us, the Lord that redeemed us! And all this is so much the more inexcusable in us, inasmuch as our privileges are so much higher than theirs. We are brought into a relationship and a position of which Israel knew absolutely nothing; our privileges and blessings are of the very highest order; it is our privilege to have fellowship with the Father and with His Son Jesus Christ; we are the objects of that perfect love which stopped not short of introducing us into a position in which it can be said of us, "As He [Christ] is, so are we in this world."

Nothing could exceed the blessedness of this; even divine love itself could go no further than this. It is not merely that the love of God has been manifested to us in the gift and the death of His only begotten and well-beloved Son, and in giving us His Spirit, but it has been made perfect with us by placing us in the very same position as that blessed One on the throne of God.

All this is perfectly marvelous. It passeth knowledge. And yet how prone we are to forget the blessed One who has so loved us and wrought for us and blessed us! How often we slip away from Him in the spirit of our minds and the affections of our hearts! It is not merely a question of what the professing church, as a whole, has done, but the very much deeper, closer, more pointed question of what our own wretched hearts are constantly prone to do. We are apt to forget God, and to turn to other objects, to our serious loss and His dishonor.

Would we know how the heart of God feels as to all this? would we form any thing like a correct idea of how he resents it? Let us hearken to the burning words addressed to His erring people Israel, the overwhelming strains of the song of Moses. May we have grace to hear them aright, and deeply profit by them.

"And when the Lord saw it, He abhorred them, *because of the provoking of His sons and of His daughters.* And He said, 'I will hide My face from them, I will see what their end shall be;' "—alas! a truly deplorable end—" 'for they are a very froward generation, children in whom is no faith. They have moved Me to jealousy with that which is not God; they have provoked Me to anger with their vanities; and I will move them to jealousy with those which are not a people; I will provoke them to anger with a foolish nation. For a fire is kindled in Mine anger, and shall burn unto the lowest hell, and shall consume the earth with her increase, and shall set on fire the foundations of the mountains. I will heap mischiefs upon them; I will spend Mine arrows upon them. They shall be burnt with hunger, and devoured with burning heat and with bitter destruction; I will also send the teeth of beasts upon them, with the poison of serpents of the dust. The sword without and terror within shall destroy both the young man and the virgin, the suckling also with the man of gray hairs' " (ver. 19-26).

Here we have a most solemn record of God's governmental dealings with His people—a record eminently calculated to set forth the awful truth of Hebrews 10:31—"It is a fearful thing to fall into the hands of the living God." The history of Israel in the past, their condition at present, and what they are yet to pass through in the future—all goes to prove, in the most impressive manner, that "our God is a consuming fire." No nation on the face of the earth has ever been called to pass through such severe discipline as the nation of Israel. As the Lord reminds them in those deeply solemn words, "You only have I known of all the families of the earth, therefore will I punish you for your iniquities." No other nation was ever called to occupy the highly privileged place of actual relationship with Jehovah. This dignity was reserved for one nation; but the very dignity was the basis of a most solemn responsibility. If they were called to be His people, they were responsible to conduct themselves in a way worthy of such a wondrous position, or else have to undergo the heaviest chastenings ever endured by any nation under the sun. Men may reason about all this; they may raise all manner of questions as to the moral consistency of a benevolent Being acting according to the terms set forth in verses 22-25 of our chapter. But all such questions and reasonings must sooner or later be discovered to be utter folly. It is perfectly useless for men to argue against the solemn actings of divine government, or the terrible severity of the discipline exercised toward the chosen people of God. How much wiser and better and safer to be warned by the facts of Israel's history to flee from the wrath to come, and lay hold upon eternal life and full salvation revealed in the precious gospel of God!

And then, with regard to the use which Christians should make of the record of His dealings with His earthly people, we are bound to turn it to most profitable account by learning from it the urgent need of walking humbly, watchfully, and faithfully in our high and holy position. True, we are the possessors of eternal life, the privileged subjects of that magnificent grace which reigns through righteousness unto eternal life by Jesus Christ our Lord; we are members of the body of Christ, temples of the Holy Ghost, and heirs of eternal glory; but does all this afford any warrant for neglecting the warning voice which Israel's history utters in our ears? Are we, because of our incomparably higher privileges, to walk carelessly and despise the wholesome admonitions which Israel's history supplies? God forbid! Nay, we are bound to give earnest heed to the things which the Holy Ghost has written for our learning. The higher our privileges, the richer our blessings, the nearer our relationship, the more does it become us, the more solemnly are we bound, to be faithful, and to seek in all things to carry ourselves in such a way as to be well-pleasing to Him who has called us into the very highest and most blessed place that even His perfect love could bestow. The Lord, in His great goodness, grant that we may, in true purpose of heart, ponder these things in His holy presence, and earnestly seek to serve Him with reverence and godly fear.

But we must proceed with our chapter.

At verse 26, we have a point of deepest interest in connection with the history of the divine dealings with Israel. "I said I would scatter them into corners, *I would make the remembrance of them to cease from among men.*" And why did He not? The answer to this question presents a truth of infinite value and importance to Israel—a truth which lies at the very foundation of all their future blessing. No doubt, so far as they are concerned, they deserved to have their remembrance blotted out from among men; but God has His own thoughts and counsels and purposes respecting them; and not only so, but He takes account of the thoughts and actings of the nations in reference to His people. This comes out with singular force and beauty at verse 27. He condescends to give us His reasons for not obliterating every trace of the sinful and rebellious people—and oh, what a touching reason it is—"*Were it not that I feared the wrath of the enemy,* lest their adversaries should behave themselves strangely, and lest they should say, Our hand is high, and the Lord hath not done all this."

Can aught be more affecting than the grace that breathes in these words? God will not permit the nations to behave themselves strangely toward His poor erring people. He will use them as His rod of discipline, but the moment they attempt, in the indulgence of their own bitter animosity, to exceed their appointed limit, He will break the rod in pieces, and make it manifest to all that He Himself is dealing with His beloved though erring people, for their ultimate blessing and His glory.

This is a truth of unspeakable preciousness. It is the fixed purpose of Jehovah to teach all the nations of the earth that Israel has a special place in His heart, and a destined place of pre-eminence on the earth. This is beyond all question. The pages of the prophets furnish a body of evidence perfectly unanswerable on the point. If nations forget or oppose, so much the worse for them. It is utterly vain for them to attempt to countervail the divine purpose, for they may rest assured that the God of Abraham, Isaac, and Jacob will confound every scheme formed against the people of His choice. Men may think, in their pride and folly, that their hand is high, but they will have to learn that God's hand is higher still.

But our space does not admit of our dwelling upon this deeply interesting subject; we must allow the reader to pursue it for himself, in the light of holy Scripture. He will find it a most profitable and refreshing study. Most gladly would we accompany him through the precious pages of the prophetic Scriptures, but we must just now confine ourselves to the magnificent song which is in itself a remarkable epitome of the entire teaching on the point—a brief but comprehensive and impressive history of God's ways with Israel and Israel's ways with God, from first to last—a history strikingly illustrative of the great principles of grace, law, government, and glory.

At verse 29, we have a very touching appeal. "O that they were wise, that they understood this, that they would *consider their latter end!* How should one chase a thousand, and two put ten thousand to flight, except their Rock had sold them, and the Lord had shut them up? For their rock is not as our Rock, even our enemies themselves being judges."—There is, there can be, but the one Rock, blessed throughout all ages be His glorious name—"For their vine is of the vine of Sodom, and of the fields of Gomorrah; their grapes are grapes of gall, their clusters are bitter; their wine is the poison of dragons, and the cruel venom of asps."

Terrible picture of a people's moral condition drawn by a master-hand! Such is the divine estimate of the real state of all those whose rock was not as the Rock of Israel. But a day of vengeance will come. It is delayed in long-suffering mercy, but it *will* come as sure as there is a God on the throne of heaven. A day is coming when all those nations which have dealt proudly with Israel shall have to answer at the bar of the Son of Man for their conduct, hear His solemn sentence, and meet His unsparing wrath.

"Is not this laid up in store with Me, and *sealed up among My treasures?* To Me belongeth vengeance and recompense; their foot shall slide in due time; for the day of their calamity is at hand, and the things that shall come upon them make haste. For the Lord shall judge [vindicate, defend, or avenge] His people, and *repent Himself for His servants,* when He seeth that their power is gone, and there is none shut up or left." Precious grace for Israel by and by—for each, for all, *now,* who feel and own their need.

"And He shall say, Where are their gods, their rock in whom they trusted; which did eat the fat of their sacrifices, and drank the wine of their drink-offerings? let them rise up and help you and be your protection. See now that I, even I, am He, and there is no god with Me; I kill, and I make alive; I wound, and I heal"—wound in governmental wrath, and heal in pardoning grace; all homage to His great and holy name, throughout the everlasting ages!—"neither is there any that can deliver out of My hand. For I lift up My hand to heaven, and say, 'I live forever.' " Glory be to God in the highest! Let all created intelligences adore His matchless name!—"If I whet My glittering sword, and Mine hand take hold on judgment"—as it most assuredly will—"I will render vengeance to Mine enemies, and will reward them that hate Me"—whoever and wherever they are. Tremendous sentence for all whom it may concern, for all haters of God—all lovers of pleasure rather than lovers of God!—"I will make Mine arrows drunk with blood, and My sword shall devour flesh; and that with the blood of the slain and of the captives, *from the beginning of revenges upon the enemy.*"

Here we reach the end of the heavy record of judgment, wrath, and vengeance so briefly presented in this song of Moses, but so largely unfolded throughout the prophetic Scriptures. The reader can refer, with much interest and profit, to Ezekiel 38 and 39 where we have the judgment of Gog and Magog, the great northern foe who is to come up, at the end, against the land of Israel, and there meet his ignominious fall and utter destruction.

He may also turn to Joel 3 which opens with words of balm and consolation for the Israel of the future. "For behold, in those days, and in that time, when I shall bring again the captivity of Judah and Jerusalem, I will also gather all nations, and will bring them down into the valley of Jehoshaphat, and will plead with them there for My people and for My heritage Israel, whom they have scattered among the nations, and parted My land." Thus he will see how perfectly the voices of the prophets harmonize with the song of Moses, and how fully, how clearly, and how unanswerably, in both the one and the other, does the Holy Ghost set forth and establish the grand truth of Israel's future restoration, supremacy, and glory.

And then, how truly delightful is the closing note of our song! how magnificently it places the topstone upon the whole superstructure! All the hostile nations are judged, under whatever style or title they appear upon the scene, whether it be Gog and

Magog, the Assyrian, or the king of the north—all the foes of Israel shall be confounded and consigned to everlasting perdition, and then this sweet note falls upon the ear—"*Rejoice, O ye nations, with His people; for He will avenge the blood of His servants, and will render vengeance to His adversaries, and will be merciful unto His land and to His people.*"

Here ends this marvelous song, one of the very finest, fullest, and most forcible utterances in the whole volume of God. It begins and ends with God, and takes in, in its comprehensive range, the history of His earthly people Israel—past, present, and future. It shows us the ordering of the nations in direct reference to the divine purpose as to the seed of Abraham. It unfolds the final judgment of all those nations that have acted or shall yet act in opposition to the chosen seed; and then, when Israel is fully restored and blessed, according to the covenant made with their fathers, the saved nations are summoned to rejoice with them.

How glorious is all this! What a splendid circle of truth is presented to the vision of our souls in the thirty-second chapter of Deuteronomy! Well may it be said, "God is *the* Rock, His work is perfect." Here the heart can rest, in holy tranquility, come what may. Every thing may go to pieces in man's hand, all that is merely human may and must issue in hopeless wreck and ruin, but "the Rock" shall stand forever, and every "work" of the divine Hand shall shine in everlasting perfection to the glory of God and the perfect blessing of His people.

Such, then, is the song of Moses; such its scope, range, and application. The intelligent reader does not need to be told that the Church of God, the body of Christ, the mystery of which the blessed apostle Paul was made the minister, finds no place in this song. When Moses wrote this song, the mystery of the Church lay hid in the bosom of God. If we do not see this, we are wholly incompetent to interpret, or even to understand, the holy Scriptures. To a simple mind, taught exclusively by Scripture, it is as clear as a sunbeam that the song of Moses has for its thesis the government of God, in connection with Israel and the nations; for its sphere, the earth; and for its centre, the land of Canaan.

"And Moses came and spake all the words of this song in the ears of the people, he, and Hoshea the son of Nun. And Moses made an end of speaking all these words to all Israel; and he said unto them, '*Set your hearts unto all the words* which I testify among you this day, which *ye shall command your children to observe to do, all the words of this law.* For it is not a vain thing for you, because *it is your life;* and through this thing ye shall prolong your days in the land, whither ye go over Jordan to possess it' " (ver. 44-47).

Thus, from first to last, through every section of this precious book of Deuteronomy, we find Moses, that beloved and most honored servant of God, urging upon the people the solemn duty of implicit, unqualified, hearty obedience to the Word of God. In this lay the precious secret of life, peace, progress, prosperity—all. They had nothing else to do but *obey*. Blessed business! happy, holy duty! May it be ours in this day of conflict and confusion, in the which man's will is so fearfully dominant. The world and the so-called church are rushing on together, with appalling rapidity, along the dark pathway of self-will—a pathway which must end in the blackness of darkness forever. Let us bear this in mind, and earnestly seek to tread the narrow path of simple obedience to all the precious commandments of our Lord and Saviour Jesus Christ. Thus shall our hearts be kept in sweet peace; and although we may seem, to the men of this world, and even to professing Christians, to be odd and narrow-minded, let us not be moved the breadth of a hair from the path indicated by the Word of God. May the word of Christ dwell in us richly, and the peace of Christ rule in our hearts, *until the end.*

It is very remarkable, and indeed eminently impressive, to find our chapter closing with another reference to Jehovah's governmental dealing with His beloved servant Moses. "And the Lord spake unto Moses *that self-same day*"—the very day in which he uttered his song in the ears of the people—

"saying, 'Get thee up into this mountain Abarim, unto Mount Nebo, which is in the land of Moab, that is over against Jericho; and behold the land of Canaan, which I give unto the children of Israel for a possession; and die in the mount whither thou goest up, and be gathered unto thy people; as Aaron thy brother died in Mount Hor, and was gathered unto his people; because ye trespassed against Me among the children of Israel at the waters of Meribah-Kadesh, in the wilderness of Zin, because ye sanctified Me not in the midst of the children of Israel. Yet thou shalt see the land before thee; *but thou shalt not go thither unto the land which I give the children of Israel'* " (ver. 48-52).

How solemn and soul-subduing is the government of God! Surely it ought to make the heart tremble at the very thought of disobedience. If such an eminent servant as Moses was judged for speaking unadvisedly with his lips, what will be the end of those who live from day to day, week to week, month to month, and year to year in deliberate and habitual neglect of the plainest commandments of God, and positive self-willed rejection of His authority?

Oh, for a lowly mind, a broken and contrite heart! This is what God looks for and delights in; it is with such He can make His blessed abode. "To this man will I look, even to him who is poor and of a contrite spirit, and trembleth at My word." God, in His infinite goodness, grant much of this sweet spirit to each of His beloved children, for Jesus Christ's sake.

---

## *CHAPTER 33*

"AND this is the blessing wherewith Moses, the man of God, blessed the children of Israel before his death."

It is full of interest and comfort to find that the last words of the lawgiver were words of unmingled blessing. We have dwelt upon his various discourses—those solemn, searching, and deeply affecting homilies addressed to the congregation of Israel; we have meditated upon that marvelous song, with its mingled notes of grace and government: but we are now called to hearken to words of most precious benediction, words of sweetest comfort and consolation, words flowing from the very heart of the God of Israel and giving His own loving thoughts respecting them, and His onlook into their glorious future.

The reader will doubtless notice a marked difference between the last words of Moses as recorded in Deuteronomy 33 and the last words of Jacob as given in Genesis 49. It is needless to say that both are given by the same pen—both divinely inspired, and hence, although they differ, they do not and cannot clash; there is, there can be, no discrepancy between two sections of the volume of God. This is a cardinal truth, a vital and fundamental principle with every devout Christian, every true believer—a truth to be tenaciously grasped and faithfully confessed, in the face of all the ignorant and insolent assaults of infidelity.

We are not, of course, going to enter upon an elaborate comparison of the two chapters. But there is one grand point of difference, which can be seized at a glance. Jacob gives the history of the actings of his sons—some of them, alas! most sad and humiliating: Moses, on the contrary, presents the actings of divine grace, whether in them or toward them. This will at once account for the difference. The evil actings of Reuben, of Simeon, and of Levi are recorded by Jacob, but entirely omitted by Moses. Is this discrepancy? Nay, but divine harmony. Jacob views his sons in their personal history; Moses views them in their covenant-relationship with Jehovah. Jacob gives us human failure, infirmity, and sin: Moses gives us divine faithfulness, goodness, and loving-kindness. Jacob gives us human actings, and judgment thereon: Moses gives us divine counsels, and unmingled blessing flowing out of them. Thanks and praise to our God, His counsels and His blessings and His glory are above and beyond all human failure, sin, and folly. He will ultimately have it all His own way, and that forever;

then, Israel and the nations shall be fully blessed, and shall rejoice together in the abundant goodness of God, and celebrate His praise from shore to shore, and from the river to the ends of the earth.

We shall now do little more than quote the various blessings of the tribes. They are full of most precious instruction, and do not call for much in the way of exposition.

"And he said, 'The Lord came from Sinai, and rose up from Seir unto them; He shined forth from Mount Paran, and He came with ten thousands of saints [holy ones]; from His right hand went a fiery law for them. Yea, *He loved the people"*—precious, unfailing source of all their future blessing—*"all His saints are in Thy hand;"*—true secret of their perfect security—"and they sat down *at Thy feet"*—the only safe and proper attitude for them, for us, for each, for all!—"every one shall receive of Thy words." Blessed boon! precious treasure! Every word that proceedeth out of the mouth of the Lord is more precious, by far, than thousands of gold and silver; sweeter also than honey and the honey-comb. "Moses commanded us a law, even the inheritance of the congregation of Jacob. And he was king in Jeshurun, when the heads of the people and the tribes of Israel were gathered together. Let Reuben live and not die, and let not his men be few.' "

We have nothing here about Reuben's instability, nothing about his sin. Grace is in the ascendant; blessings are flowing in rich abundance from the loving heart of the One who delights to bless and to surround Himself with hearts filled to overflowing with the sense of His goodness.

"And this is the blessing of Judah; and he said, 'Hear, Lord, the voice of Judah, and bring him unto his people; let his hands be sufficient for him; and be Thou a help to him from his enemies.' " Judah is the royal line. "Our Lord sprang out of Judah," thus illustrating, in a truly marvelous manner, how divine grace rises, in its majesty, above human sin, and triumphs gloriously over circumstances which reveal man's utter weakness. "Judas begat Phares and Zara of Thamar"! Who but the Holy Spirit could have penned these words? How plainly they declare that God's thoughts are not as our thoughts! What human hand would have introduced Thamar into the genealogical line of our adorable Lord and Saviour Jesus Christ? Not one. The stamp of divinity is strikingly impressed on Matthew 1:3, as it is upon every clause of the holy volume from beginning to end. The Lord be praised that it is so!

"Judah, thou art he whom thy brethren shall praise; thy hand shall be in the neck of thine enemies; thy father's children shall bow down before thee. Judah is a lion's whelp; from the prey, my son, thou art gone up; he stooped down, he couched as a lion, and as an old lion; who shall rouse him up? The sceptre shall not depart from Judah, nor a lawgiver from between his feet, until Shiloh come; and unto him shall the gathering of the people be. Binding his foal unto the vine, and his ass's colt unto the choice vine; he washed his garments in wine, and his clothes in the blood of grapes; his eyes shall be red with wine, and his teeth white with milk" (Gen. 49:8-12).

"And I saw in the right hand of Him that sat on the throne a book written within and on the backside, sealed with seven seals. And I saw a strong angel proclaiming with a loud voice, 'Who is worthy to open the book, and to loose the seals thereof?' And no man in heaven, nor in earth, neither under the earth, was able to open the book, neither to look thereon. And I wept much, because no man was found worthy to open and to read the book, neither to look thereon. And one of the elders saith unto me, 'Weep not: behold, *the Lion of the tribe of Juda,* the Root of David, hath prevailed to open the book and to loose the seven seals thereof.' And I beheld, and lo, in the midst of the throne and of the four living creatures, and in the midst of the elders, stood *a Lamb,* as it had been *slain,* having seven horns and seven eyes, which are the seven spirits of God sent forth into all the earth."

How highly favored is the tribe of Judah! Surely, to be in the genealogical line from which our Lord sprang is a high honor, and yet we know—for our Lord Himself has told us—that it is far higher, far more blessed, to hear the Word of God and keep it. To do the will of God, to treasure up in our hearts His precious commandments, brings us morally nearer to Christ than even the fact of being of His kindred according to the flesh (Matt. 12:46-50).

"And of Levi he said, Let Thy Thummim and Thy Urim [lights and perfections] be with Thy holy one, whom Thou didst prove at Massah, and with whom Thou didst strive at the waters of Meribah; *who said unto his father and to his mother, I have not seen him; neither did he acknowledge his brethren, nor knew* his own children; *for they have observed Thy word and kept Thy covenant.* They shall teach Jacob Thy judgments, and Israel Thy law; they shall put incense before Thee, and whole burnt-sacrifice upon Thine altar. Bless, Lord, his substance, and accept the work of his hands; smite through the loins of them that rise against him, and of them that hate him, that they rise not again" (ver. 8-11).

The reader will notice the fact that Simeon is left out here, though so intimately associated with Levi in Genesis 49. "Simeon and Levi are brethren; instruments of cruelty are in their habitations. O my soul, come not thou into their secret; unto their assembly, mine honor, be not thou united; for *in their anger they slew a man,* and *in their self-will* they digged down a wall. Cursed be their anger, for it was fierce; and their wrath, for it was cruel: I will divide them in Jacob, and scatter them in Israel."

Now, when we compare Genesis 49 with Deuteronomy 33, we observe two things, namely, human responsibility on the one hand, and divine sovereignty on the other. Moreover, we see nature and its actings; grace and its fruits. Jacob looks at Simeon and Levi linked together in nature, and displaying nature's tempers and ways. So far as they were concerned, they both alike deserved the curse; but in Levi, we see the glorious triumphs of sovereign grace. It was grace which enabled Levi, in the days of the golden calf, to gird on the sword and stand for the glory of the God of Israel. "Then Moses stood in the gate of the camp, and said, 'Who is on the Lord's side? let him come unto me.' And all the sons of Levi gathered themselves together unto him. And he said unto them, 'Thus saith the Lord God of Israel, Put every man his sword by his side, and go in and out from gate to gate throughout the camp, and slay every man his brother, and every man his companion, and every man his neighbor.' And the children of Levi did according to the word of Moses; and there fell of the people that day about three thousand men. For Moses had said, 'Consecrate yourselves to-day to the Lord, even every man upon his son, and upon his brother; that he may bestow upon you a blessing this day' " (Exod. 32:26-29).

Where was Simeon on this occasion? He was with Levi in the day of nature's self-will, fierce anger, and cruel wrath; why not in the day of bold decision for Jehovah? He was ready to go with his brother to avenge a family insult, why not to vindicate the honor of God, insulted as it was by the idolatrous act of the whole congregation? Will any one say he was not responsible? Let such an one beware how he raises such a question. The call of Moses was addressed to the whole congregation; Levi alone responded, and he got the blessing. He stood for God in a dark and evil day, and for this he was honored with the priesthood—the very highest dignity that could be conferred upon him. The call was addressed to Simeon as well as to Levi, but Simeon did not respond. Is there any difficulty here? To a mere theologian there may be, but to a devout Christian there is none. God is sovereign. He does as He pleases, and gives none account of any of His matters. If any one feels disposed to ask, Why is Simeon omitted in Deuteronomy 33? The simple and conclusive answer is, "O man, who art thou that repliest against God?" In Simeon, we see nature's actings judged; in Levi, we see the fruits of grace rewarded; in both, we see God's truth vindicated and His name glorified. Thus it ever has been, thus it is, and thus it shall be. Man is responsible: God is sovereign. Are we called upon to reconcile these two propositions? Nay; we are called to believe them. They are reconciled already, inasmuch as they appear side by side on the page of inspiration. This is enough for every pious mind; and as for cavilers, they will get their definitive answer by and by.*

"And of Benjamin ["the son of my right hand"] he said, 'The beloved of the Lord shall dwell in safety by Him; and the Lord shall cover him all the day long, and he shall dwell between His shoulders.' "

Blessed place for Benjamin! blessed place for each beloved child of God! How precious is the thought of dwelling in safety in the divine presence, in conscious nearness to the true and faithful Shepherd and Bishop of our souls, day and night abiding under the covert of His sheltering wings!

> How blest are they who still abide,
> Close sheltered by Thy watchful side!
> Who life and strength from Thee receive,
> And with Thee move and in Thee live.

Seek to know more and more the reality and blessedness of Benjamin's place and portion. Be not satisfied with any thing short of the enjoyed presence of Christ, the abiding sense of relationship and nearness to Him. Be assured of it, it is your happy privilege. Let nothing rob you of it. Keep ever near the Shepherd's side, reposing in His love, lying down in the green pastures and beside the still waters. The Lord grant that the writer and the reader may prove the deep blessedness of this, in this day of hollow profession and empty talk. May we know the unspeakable preciousness of deep, personal intimacy with Himself. This is the special need of the day in which our lot is cast—a day of so much intellectual traffic in truth, but of so little heart-knowledge and true appreciation of Christ.

"And of Joseph he said, 'Blessed of the Lord be his land, for the precious things of heaven, for the dew, and for the deep that coucheth beneath, and for the precious fruits brought forth by the sun, and for the precious things put forth by the moon, and for the chief things of the ancient mountains, and for the precious things of the lasting hills, and for the precious things of the earth and fullness thereof, and for the good-will of Him that dwelt in the bush; let the blessing come upon the head of Joseph, and upon the top of the head of him that was separated from his brethren. His glory is like the firstling of his bullock, and his horns are like the horns of unicorns; with them he shall push the people together to the ends of the earth; and they are the ten thousands of Ephraim, and they are the thousands of Manasseh.' "

Joseph is a very remarkable type of Christ. We have dwelt upon his history in our studies on the book of Genesis. The reader will notice the emphatic way in which Moses speaks of the fact of his having been separated from his brethren. He was rejected and cast into the pit. He passed, in figure, through the deep waters of death, and thus reached the place of dignity and glory. He was raised from the dungeon to be ruler over the land of Egypt, and the preserver and sustainer of his brethren. The iron entered into his soul, and he was made to taste the bitterness of the place of death ere he entered the sphere of glory. Striking type of Him who hung upon the cross, lay in the grave, and is now on the throne of the Majesty of heaven.

We cannot but be struck with the fullness of the blessing pronounced upon Joseph both by Moses in Deuteronomy 33 and by Jacob in Genesis 49. Jacob's utterance is uncommonly fine. "Joseph is a fruitful bough, even a fruitful bough by a well" —exquisitely beautiful figure—"whose branches run over the wall. The archers have sorely grieved him, and shot at him, and hated him; but his bow abode in strength, and the arms of his hands were made strong by the hands of the mighty God of Jacob; *(from thence is the Shepherd, the Stone of Israel:)* even by the God of thy father, who shall help thee; and by the Almighty, who shall bless thee with blessings of heaven above, blessings of the deep that lieth under, blessings of the breasts and of the womb: the blessings of thy father have prevailed

*For further remarks on the tribe of Levi, the reader is referred to *Notes on the Book of Exodus,* chapter 32; *Notes on the Book of Numbers,* chapters 3, 4, and 8; also a pamphlet, first published in the year 1846, entitled, "The History of the Tribe of Levi Considered," in the author's *Miscellaneous Writings,* vol. 4.

above the blessings of my progenitors unto the utmost bound of the everlasting hills: they shall be on the head of Joseph, and on the crown of the head of him that was separate from his brethren."

Magnificent range of blessing! And all this flowing from and based upon his sufferings. It is needless to say that all these blessings will be made good in the experience of Israel by and by. The sufferings of the true Joseph will form the imperishable foundation of the future blessedness of His brethren in the land of Canaan; and not only so, but the tide of blessing, deep and full, shall flow forth from that highly favored though now desolate land, in refreshing virtue into all the earth. "And it shall be in that day, that living waters shall go out from Jerusalem; half of them toward the former sea, and half of them toward the hinder sea; in summer and in winter shall it be." Bright and blessed prospect for Jerusalem, for the land of Israel, and for the whole earth! What a sad mistake to apply such Scriptures to the gospel dispensation or to the Church of God! How contrary to the testimony of holy Scripture, to the heart of God, and to the mind of Christ!

"And of Zebulun he said, 'Rejoice, Zebulun, in thy going out; and, Issachar, in thy tents. They shall call the people unto the mountain; there they shall offer sacrifices of righteousness: for they shall suck of the abundance of the seas, and of the treasures hid in the sand.' "

Zebulun is to rejoice in his going forth, and Issachar in abiding in his tents. It will be joy at home and abroad; and there will be power to act on others also—calling the people unto the mountain to offer the sacrifices of righteousness. All this grounded upon the fact that they themselves shall suck of the abundance of the seas and of hidden treasures. Thus it is always, in principle. It is our privilege to rejoice in the Lord, come what may, and to draw from those eternal springs and hidden treasures that are to be found in Himself. Then shall we be in a condition of soul to call others to taste and see that the Lord is good; and not only so, but to present to God those sacrifices of righteousness so acceptable to Him.

"And of Gad he said, 'Blessed be he that enlargeth Gad: he dwelleth as a lion, and teareth the arm with the crown of the head. And he provided the first part for himself, because there, in a portion of the lawgiver, was he seated; and he came with the heads of the people, he executed the justice of the Lord, and His judgments with Israel.' And of Dan he said, 'Dan is a lion's whelp; he shall leap from Bashan.' And of Naphtali he said, 'O Naphtali, satisfied with favor, and full with the blessing of the Lord: possess thou the west and the south.' And of Asher he said, 'Let Asher be blessed with children; let him be acceptable to his brethren, and let him dip his foot in oil. Thy shoes shall be iron and brass; and as thy days thy strength. There is none like unto the God of Jeshurun, who rideth upon the heaven in thy help, and in His excellency on the sky. The eternal God is thy refuge, and underneath are the everlasting arms: and He shall thrust out the enemy from before thee; and shall say, Destroy them. Israel then shall dwell in safety alone: the fountain of Jacob shall be upon a land of corn and wine; also his heavens shall drop down dew. Happy art thou, O Israel: who is like unto thee, O people saved by the Lord, the shield of thy help, and who is the sword of thy excellency! and thine enemies shall be found liars unto thee; and thou shalt tread upon their high places' " (ver. 20-29).

Truly we may say human comment is uncalled for here. Nothing can exceed the preciousness of the grace that breathes in the closing lines of our book. The blessings of this chapter, like the song of chapter 32, begin and end with God and His marvelous ways with Israel. It is refreshing and comforting beyond expression, at the close of all the appeals, all the exhortations, all the solemn warnings, all the faithful declarations, all the prophetic records as to failure and sin, judgment and governmental wrath—after all these, to listen to such accents as those which we have just penned. It is indeed a most magnificent termination to this blessed book of Deuteronomy. Grace and glory shine out with uncommon lustre. God will yet be glorified in Israel, and Israel fully and forever blessed in God. Nothing can hinder this. The gifts and calling of God are without repentance. He will make good every jot and tittle of His precious Word to Israel. The last words of the lawgiver bear the clearest and fullest testimony to all this. Had we nothing but the last four verses of the precious chapter on which we have been dwelling, they would be amply sufficient to prove, beyond all question, the future restoration, blessing, pre-eminence, and glory of the twelve tribes of Israel in their own land.

True it is—blessedly true—that the Lord's people now can draw instruction, comfort, and refreshment from the blessings pronounced upon Israel. Blessed be God, we can know what it is to be "satisfied with favor, and full of the blessing of the Lord;" we may take comfort from the assurance that "as our days so shall our strength be." We too can say, "The eternal God is our refuge, and underneath are the everlasting arms"—we can say all this, and much more. We can say what Israel never could and never can say. The Church's blessings and privileges are all heavenly and spiritual, but that does not hinder our taking comfort from the promises made to Israel. The grand mistake of professing Christians is in applying to the Church exclusively what most manifestly applies to God's earthly people. We must once more earnestly entreat the Christian reader to watch against this serious error. He need not be in the least afraid of losing aught of his own special blessing by leaving to the seed of Abraham the place and the portion assigned them by the counsels and promises of God; on the contrary, it is only when these are clearly understood and fully acknowledged that we can make an intelligent use of the entire canon of Old Testament Scripture. We may lay it down as a great root-principle that no one can possibly understand or interpret Scripture who does not clearly recognize the grand distinction between Israel and the Church of God.

---

## *CHAPTER 34*

THIS brief chapter forms an inspired postscript to the book of Deuteronomy. We are not told who was employed as the instrument in the hand of the inspiring Spirit, but this is a matter of no moment to the devout student of holy Scripture. We are fully persuaded that the postscript is as truly inspired as the book, and the book as the Pentateuch, and the Pentateuch as the whole volume of God.

"And Moses went up from the plains of Moab unto the mountain of Nebo, to the top of Pisgah, that is over against Jericho. And the Lord showed him all the land of Gilead, unto Dan, and all Naphtali, and the land of Ephraim and Manasseh, and all the land of Judah, unto the utmost sea, and the south, and the plain of the valley of Jericho, the city of palm-trees, unto Zoar. And the Lord said unto him, 'This is the land which I sware unto Abraham, unto Isaac, and unto Jacob, saying, I will give it unto thy seed; I have caused thee to see it with thine eyes, but thou shalt not go over thither.' So Moses the servant of the Lord died there in the land of Moab, according to the word of the Lord. And He buried him in a valley in the land of Moab, over against Beth-peor; but no man knoweth of his sepulchre unto this day."

In our studies on the books of Numbers and Deuteronomy, we have had occasion to dwell upon the very solemn and, we may truly add, soul-subduing fact recorded in the above quotation. It will not therefore be needful to add many words in this our closing section. We would merely remind the reader that if he would have a full understanding of the whole subject, he must look at Moses in a twofold aspect, namely, officially and personally.

Now, looking at this beloved and honored man in his official capacity, it is very plain that it lay not in his province to conduct the congregation of Israel into the promised land. The wilderness was his sphere of action; it pertained not to him to lead the people across the river of death into their destined inheritance. His ministry was connected with man's responsibility under law and the government of God, and hence it never could lead the people into the enjoyment of the promise: it was reserved for his successor to do this. Joshua, a type of the risen Saviour, was God's appointed instrument to lead His people across the Jordan, and plant them in their divinely given inheritance.

All this is plain, and deeply interesting; but we must look at Moses personally, as well as officially; and here too we must view him in a twofold aspect—as the subject of government, and the object of grace. We must never lose sight of this most important distinction: it runs all through Scripture, and is strikingly illustrated in the history of many of the Lord's beloved people and of His most eminent servants. The subject of grace and government demands the reader's most profound attention. We have dwelt upon it again and again in the course of our studies, but no words of ours could adequately set forth its moral importance and immense practical value. We consider it one of the weightiest and most seasonable subjects that could possibly engage the attention of the Lord's people.

It was the government of God which, with stern decision, forbad the entrance of Moses into the promised land, much as he longed to do so. He spoke unadvisedly with his lips—he failed to glorify God in the eyes of the congregation at the waters of Meribah, and for this he was forbidden to cross the Jordan and plant his foot on the promised land.

Let us deeply ponder this. Let us see that we fully apprehend its moral force and practical application. It is surely with the greatest tenderness and delicacy that we would refer to the failure of one of the most beloved and illustrious of the Lord's servants, but it has been recorded for our learning and solemn admonition, and therefore we are bound to give earnest heed to it. We should ever remember that we too, though under grace, are also the subjects of divine government. We are here on this earth, in the place of solemn responsibility, under a government which cannot be trifled with. True, we are children of the Father, loved with an infinite and everlasting love—loved even as Jesus is loved; we are members of the body of Christ, loved, cherished, and nourished according to all the perfect love of His heart. There is no question of responsibility here, no possibility of failure; all is divinely settled, divinely sure: but we are the subjects of divine government also. Let us never for a moment lose sight of this. Let us beware of one-sided and pernicious notions of grace. The very fact of our being objects of divine favor and love, children of God, members of Christ, should lead us to yield all the more reverent attention to the divine government.

To use an illustration drawn from human affairs, her majesty's children should, above all others, just because they are her children, respect her government; and were they in any way to transgress her laws, the dignity of government would be strikingly illustrated by their being made to pay the penalty. If they, because of being the queen's children, were to be allowed to transgress with impunity the enactments of her majesty's government, it would be simply exposing the government to public contempt, and affording a warrant to all her subjects to do the same. And if it be thus in the case of a human government, how much more in the government of God! "You only have I known of all the families of the earth, *therefore* will I punish you for your iniquities." "The time is come that judgment must *begin at the house of God;* and if it first begin at us, what shall the end be of them that obey not the gospel of God? And if the righteous scarcely be saved, where shall the ungodly and the sinner appear?" Solemn fact! solemn inquiry! May we ponder them deeply.

But, as we have said, Moses was the subject of grace, as well as of government; and truly that grace shines with special lustre on the top of Pisgah. There the venerable servant of God was permitted to stand in his Master's presence, and, with undimmed eye, survey the land of promise, in all its fair proportions. He was permitted to see it from a divine stand-point—see it, not merely as possessed by Israel, but as given by God.

And what then? He fell asleep and was gathered to his people. He died, not as a withered and feeble old man, but in all the freshness and vigor of matured manhood. "And Moses was a hundred and twenty years old when he died: his eye was not dim, nor his natural force abated." Striking testimony! Rare fact in the annals of our fallen race! The life of Moses was divided into three important and strongly marked periods of forty years each. He spent forty years in the house of Pharaoh, forty years "at the backside of the desert," and forty years in the wilderness. Marvelous life! eventful history! How instructive! how suggestive! how rich in its lessons from first to last! How profoundly interesting the study of such a life!—to trace him from the river's brink, where he lay a helpless babe, up to the top of Pisgah, where he stood, in company with his Lord, to gaze with undimmed vision upon the fair inheritance of the Israel of God; and to see him again on the Mount of Transfiguration, in company with his honored fellow-servant Elias, "talking with Jesus" on the grandest theme that could possibly engage the attention of men or angels. Highly favored man! blessed servant! marvelous vessel!

And then let us hearken to the divine testimony to this most beloved man of God. "And there arose not a prophet since in Israel like unto Moses, whom the Lord knew face to face, in all the signs and the wonders which the Lord sent him to do in the land of Egypt to Pharaoh, and to all his servants, and to all his land, and in all that mighty hand, and in all the great terror which Moses showed in the sight of all Israel."

May the Lord, in His infinite goodness, bless our study of the book of Deuteronomy. May its precious lessons be engraved upon the tablets of our hearts with the eternal pen of the Holy Ghost, and produce their proper result in forming our character, governing our conduct, and shaping our way through this world. May we earnestly seek to tread, with a humble spirit and firm step, the narrow path of obedience, till traveling days are done.